CONTRACTS:
CASES AND MATERIALS

CONTRACTS: CASES AND MATERIALS

SEVENTH EDITION

JOHN EDWARD MURRAY, JR.
Chancellor
Professor of Law
Duquesne University

ISBN 978-0-7698-9805-6
Looseleaf ISBN: 978-0-7698-9806-3
eBook ISBN: 978-0-7698-9807-0

Library of Congress Cataloging-in-Publication Data

Murray, John E., Jr. (John Edward), 1932- author.
  Contracts : cases and materials / John Edward Murray, Jr., Chancellor, Professor of Law, Duquesne University. --
Seventh edition.
    pages cm.
  Includes index.
  ISBN 978-0-7698-9805-6 (hardbound) -- ISBN 978-0-7698-9806-3 (looseleaf)
  1. Contracts--United States--Cases. I. Title.
   KF801.A7M8 2014
   346.7302'2--dc23
   2015009200

Library of Congress Cataloging-in-Publication Data

Murray, John E., Jr. (John Edward), 1932- author.
  Contracts : cases and materials / John Edward Murray, Jr., Chancellor, Professor of Law, Duquesne University. --
Seventh edition.
    1 online resource.
  Includes index.
  Description based on print version record and CIP data provided by publisher; resource not viewed.
  ISBN 978-0-7698-9807-0 (epub) -- ISBN 978-0-7698-9805-6 (hardbound)
  1. Contracts--United States--Cases. I. Title.
   KF801.A7
   346.7302'2--dc23
   2015009541

NOTE TO USERS
To ensure that you are using the latest materials available in this area, please be sure to periodically check the LexisNexis Law School web site for downloadable updates and supplements at www.lexisnexis.com/lawschool.

Editorial Offices
630 Central Ave., New Providence, NJ 07974 (908) 464-6800
201 Mission St., San Francisco, CA 94105-1831 (415) 908-3200
www.lexisnexis.com

MATTHEW◆BENDER

(2015–Pub.3022)

In Memoriam

John Edward Murray, Jr.
(1932-2015)

Preface

The essential purpose of a contracts casebook is to provide a vehicle that will facilitate a clear understanding of contract law for success in the lifetime practice of law. One of the principal benefits of such a book in its seventh edition is the fact that the success level of each section of the book can be and has been measured in each edition. If the experience with a given section has proven highly successful in terms of student reactions and outcomes, the changes in that section will be limited in any subsequent edition. Where the success of a section has been moderate, it becomes a candidate for modification or even replacement. The Seventh Edition has clearly benefitted from this approach.

The Seventh Edition continues the tradition of providing cutting edge coverage of new and developing concepts in contract law. Additional material in this edition was essential to reflect important new dimensions — changes reflecting dire warnings such as those suggesting that even the "chronology of contract-making has become unsettled." *Schnabel v. Trilegiant Corp.*, 697 F.3d 110, 121 (2d Cir. 2012). Indeed, a new theory currently being pursued in contract law "may be as controversial an idea as exists today in the staid world of contract law." *Howard v. Ferrellgas Partners, L.P.*, 748 F.3d 975, 982 (10th Cir. 2014). An entire sequences of cases and related material must now be pursued dealing with "terms later" and the "rolling contract" theory.

Still other major developments include the favored status of arbitration as the United States Supreme Court continues to emphasize unqualified support for its all-encompassing presence pursuant to the Federal Arbitration Act. The enforcement of arbitration clauses that include terms allegedly favorable to the party with superior bargaining power continues to present courts with difficult issues, but this dilemma may be seen as part of the perennial challenges surrounding standardized "boilerplate" provisions and their operative effects which have yet to find a solid conceptual footing. There is the attendant concern that the apotheosis of arbitration as an adjudicative process providing no precedent or necessary rationale for its awards constitutes an underlying danger to the social institution of contract.

Beyond these additions to the casebook, the continued development of the contract law of the Uniform Commercial Code must be addressed as well as the more recent contract law of the United Nations Convention on Contracts for the International Sale of Goods (CISG). Simultaneously, the common law of contracts continues its ineluctable journey toward a more effective reaction to the felt needs of society.

All of these developments must be considered in an era of curricular change that may lessen the classroom time available for the teaching of contract law. Thus, a casebook must be effective regardless of the hours available for its perusal in a given law school. As in past editions, this edition includes all of these important dimensions and allows the professor teaching the course to make the necessary selective judgments.

John E. Murray, Jr.
Pittsburgh, PA
2015

Table of Contents

Table of Contents

Table of Contents

Table of Contents

Table of Contents

Table of Contents

Table of Contents

Table of Contents

Table of Contents

Table of Contents

xvii

Table of Contents

Table of Contents

Table of Contents

Table of Contents

Table of Contents

Chapter 1

INTRODUCTION

A. THE CONCEPT OF "CONTRACT"

Historically and philosophically, the most fundamental concept of contract is that promises ought to be kept — *pacta sunt servanda*.[1] The concept is at least as old as the covenant between Jehovah and the people of Israel. The failure of the people to adhere to the covenant was a sin, but it was also a breach of contract.[2] Political philosophers who differ markedly in other respects recognize a social contract theory, or government by the mutual consent of the governed.[3]

The concept of social contract forms the basis of our constitutional philosophy,[4] and more recent elaborations of the same view maintain the concept of social contract as the indispensable element of a just society.[5] Early American judicial thinking is clearly the product of a natural law tradition that regarded contract rights as emanating from immutable principles that preceded human law.[6] In the

---

[1] "It is, therefore, a most sacred precept of natural law, and one that governs the grace, manner and reasonableness of all human life, *That every man keep his given word*, that is, carry out his promises and agreements." S. PUFENDORF, DE JURE NATURAE ET GENTIUM, Bk. III, ch. IV, § 2. In the same section, Pufendorf quotes ARISTOTLE, RHETORIC, Bk. I, ch. XV[22]: "If contracts are invalidated, the intercourse of men is abolished."

[2] "When the people of Israel in the wilderness worshiped at the feet of the golden calf, they were guilty of sin, but even worse — as my beloved friend and master, Edwin Patterson would have said — they were guilty of material breach of contract discharging Jehovah from performance of his side of the holy bargain." Jones, *The Jurisprudence of Contracts*, 44 U. CINN. L. REV. 43, 45 (1975).

[3] *See, e.g.*, T. HOBBES, LEVIATHAN XIV; J.J. ROUSSEAU, THE SOCIAL CONTRACT; J. LOCKE, THE SECOND TREATISE OF GOVERNMENT CH. VIII; I. KANT, THE FOUNDATIONS OF THE METAPHYSICS OF MORALS.

[4] J. LOCKE, THE SECOND TREATISE OF GOVERNMENT CH. VIII, *Of the Beginning of Political Societies*.

[5] "My aim is to present a concept of justice which generalizes and carries to a higher level of abstraction the familiar theory of the social contract as found, say, in Locke, Rousseau, and Kant. In order to do this we are not to think of the original contract as one to enter a particular society or to set up a particular form of government. Rather, the guiding idea is that the principles of justice of the basic structure of society are the object of the original agreement. They are the principles that free and rational persons concerned to further their own interests would accept in an initial position of equality as defining the fundamental terms of their association. These principles are to regulate all further agreements; they specify the kinds of social cooperation that can be entered into and the forms of government that can be established. This way of regarding the principles of justice I shall call justice as fairness." J. RAWLS, A THEORY OF JUSTICE 11 (1971).

[6] "If, on tracing the right to contract, and the obligations created by contract, to their source, we find them to exist anterior to, and independent of society, we may reasonably conclude, that those original and pre-existing principles are, like many other natural rights, brought with man into society; and, *although they may be controlled, are not given by human legislation*." Ogden v. Saunders, 25 U.S. 213, 344 (1827) (Marshall, Chief Justice) (emphasis added).

late nineteenth century, Sir Henry Maine wrote, "The movement of the progressive societies has hitherto been a movement *from status to contract.*"[7] In these "progressive" societies, the determination of the legal rights and duties of any member of that society no longer depends upon the status into which one was born. The development described by Maine was inevitable because the status society did not reflect the felt needs and desires of its members. Human beings wish to make choices — they seek freedom to elect among alternatives. They have free will. Human beings are also aware of the future, and they are capable of projecting into the future. They wish to plan and to design their futures. They are capable of bringing the future plan into the present and contemplating that plan. They are capable of recognizing the geometric benefits available through reciprocal planning with others.[8]

The basic challenge of society has been described as that of "establishing, maintaining and perfecting the conditions necessary for community life to perform its role in the complete development of man."[9] If man cannot project his realistic needs, desires, and aspirations into the future and be assured that they will be fulfilled, there is a major deficiency in society that can only be remedied by the social institution of contract.

B.   MEANING OF THE WORD "CONTRACT"

"Contracts" pervade our society. Every person working for another has a contract with an employer. The self-employed worker makes contracts with suppliers and customers. Every student has a contract with a school system, college or university. The purchase and sale of land, buildings, raw materials, products and services by individuals, corporations or governments are based on contracts. The supply of electricity or natural gas energy that we use is activated through contracts with utility companies. The use of telephones, access to computer data bases and cable television begin with a contract for such services. When we write checks or use credit cards, their acceptance as payment is based upon our contract with a bank that has promised to pay the amount we have decided to spend. Marriage is a contract and divorce settlements are contracts. There are contracts between parents, physicians and hospitals to assist our birth, and final contracts with those who will deal with our remains.

Since contracts are so pervasive in our society, the definition of "contract" may appear obvious until we attempt to articulate that definition. The concept of contract suggests "agreement." We make agreements every day. An ordinary dictionary definition of agreement suggests harmonization of thought — coming to one mind on a particular subject or topic. A moment's reflection, however, quickly reveals that

---

[7] H. MAINE, ANCIENT LAW 141 (NEW UNIVERSAL LIBRARY ED. 1905).

[8] Professor Ian Macneil identifies the "primal roots" of contract as society, specialization of labor and exchange, choice, and awareness of the future. I. MACNEIL, THE NEW SOCIAL CONTRACT 1–4 (1980).

[9] Snee, *Leviathan at the Bar of Justice,* in GOVERNMENT UNDER LAW (essays prepared for discussion at a conference on the occasion of the two hundredth anniversary of the birth of John Marshall, at the Harvard Law School, September 22–24 (1955)) 47, 52, *as cited in* H. HART, JR. & A. SACKS, THE LEGAL PROCESS: BASIC PROBLEMS IN THE MAKING AND APPLICATION OF LAW (10TH ED. 1958).

"agreement" is much broader than the concept of "contract." We can agree on innumerable issues such as the correct spelling of a word, the date of an historical event such as "Lincoln was assassinated in 1865" or when certain family members were born or married. Such agreements are not contracts. "Contract" suggests a future plan, commitments to do or not do something in the future. Ames writes a letter to a builder, Barnes, which states, "I will pay you, builder, $400,000 for the new house you have constructed on lot 23 in the Marbury development of the City of Lawnview in exchange for your promise to sell the house to me." If Barnes responds with a letter agreeing to this proposal, i.e., if he accepts Ames' offer, a contract is formed. The parties are committed to buy and sell the house and the law will enforce that contract.

Contrast that contract with other agreements to do or not to do something in the future such as an agreement to go to dinner next Friday or play golf on Saturday. If one of the parties fails to appear for dinner or golf, absent some reasonable excuse for not appearing, he or she may suffer social consequences of not being invited again or otherwise injuring a relationship with a friend. Should breaching a social agreement, however, have legal consequences? Can you be sued for not appearing for dinner or golf? You could be sued, but a court will quickly dismiss the case as frivolous since such agreements are deemed not to be binding at law. They are "agreements," but they are not "contracts." Why is this so?

The essential reason is that parties do not contemplate legal consequences when they make social or family agreements. They do not feel legally bound to perform them though, again, they may feel compelled to keep such promises for reasons beyond the law, such as not disappointing friends. If such agreements were deemed to be legally enforceable, courts would also face practical difficulties in any attempt to measure the losses in money (damages) caused by the breach. How would a court place a price tag on the disappointment felt by a party whose friend failed to appear for a social event? On the other hand, if builder Barnes refused to perform his promise to sell the house to Ames, Ames would have legal right to enforce the contract and the damages caused by the breach would be measurable. A court would recognize this agreement as a contract because reasonable parties typically contemplate legal consequences from such an agreement. They intend to be bound by it and the court would have a reasonable basis for providing a remedy if either party breaches the contract. Ames was entitled to have a house of certain description in exchange for a payment of $400,000. If Ames had to pay another builder $500,000 for the same house, she has been damaged to the extent of the difference between what she expected to pay ($400,000) and the price she was forced to pay to achieve the same result ($500,000). Ames may recover $100,000 for the loss caused by Barnes' breach of contract.

At this point, we may say that "contract" requires an agreement by two or more parties to pursue future action of a kind that reasonable parties would view as legally binding and which allow courts to measure the loss suffered with reasonable certainty to provide an adequate remedy. What other characteristics can be unearthed to help define "contract"?

Promise. It is important to consider how parties make legally binding agreements for future action — the anatomy of agreement. An agreement designed to regulate future action between two or more parties requires commitment, a *promise* to do or not to do something in the future. Contracts may, therefore, be viewed as legally binding promises or, as one authoritative source puts it, contract is "*a promise or set of promises for the breach of which the law gives a remedy, or the performance of which the law in some way recognizes as a duty.*"[10]

While the ideal may be expressed in the Roman notion of *pacta sunt servanda* (all promises must be kept), the definition of contract clearly indicates that not all promises will be enforced which raises a central question in the study of contract law: *How does our law distinguish enforceable from unenforceable promises?* Again, a promise to participate in a social engagement is not enforceable essentially because the members of society do not expect to be bound by such promises and the law should reflect the reasonable expectations of the society it represents. If we only had to distinguish social promises from other types of promises, contract law would be simple. Over the centuries, however, our contract law has developed a sophisticated analysis to determine which promises ought to be enforced.

We have no difficulty in finding the promise to sell an automobile for $25,000 to be a contract. Both promises are legally enforceable, i.e., the law will provide a remedy if one of the promises is breached. Suppose, however, that Albert promises to *give* a $25,000 automobile to his friend, Martha and Martha promises to accept it. Is this promise legally enforceable? What is the essential difference in the two examples? The first example involves an *exchange* of something of value from each of the parties, the auto for the $25,000, while the second (a promise to give the auto) involves no such exchange. Albert promises to provide something of value to Martha, but he receives nothing in exchange for his promise. As we will see, such a "gift" or "donative" promise is typically unenforceable because there is no exchange. The exchange of something of value is called "consideration" which is one of the principal topics of contract law.

The exchange of value in one sense "validates" the promise and makes it enforceable. Thus, the chapter dealing with consideration is called the "validation process." While consideration is, by far, the principal validation device, we will also see other validation devices that can make a promise enforceable.

To this point, therefore, three critical elements are essential in thinking about "contract":

> (1) *promise* — an undertaking or commitment that something shall or shall not be done in the future;

> (2) *exchange* — something that the law recognizes as "value" is exchanged between the parties (consideration — the validation process); and

> (3) *enforcement* — the law sanctions such promissory exchanges by putting its coercive machinery behind them.

Unfortunately, the use of the term "contract" as just described is not consistently adhered to. Lawyers as well as laypersons frequently use it to express other and

---

[10] RESTATEMENT (SECOND) OF CONTRACTS § 1 (emphasis supplied). The Restatement of Contracts and other sources of contract law will be analyzed later in this chapter.

quite different thoughts. This may not be terribly harmful if the connotation of the word in the particular situation is observed, but the student must be aware of careful distinctions in the use of the word. To prevent needless confusion in the sections that follow, it is important to consider other senses in which the word is commonly, though imprecisely, employed.

Frequently the word "contract" is used to refer to the written memorial.[11] (the signed writing) or other utterance that evidences a legally enforceable promise or group of promises. The writing is not *the* contract. We will see that certain types of contracts are required to be *evidenced* by a writing, but other contracts that are evidenced by spoken words or actions (conduct) that manifest the intention of the parties to be bound need no written evidence to be enforceable. Many contracts are now evidenced by electronic records instead of traditional paper documents. The electronic file is not *the* contract anymore than the writings or spoken words the parties use if they contract orally. The conduct or customs of the parties that manifest their intention to be bound to an agreement are not *the* contract. All of these manifestations are mere *evidence* of the contract. Where is the contract? One cannot touch, hear, smell, or feel the contract. The *evidence* of the contract is subject to sensory perception, but the contract is an abstract legal relationship between the parties.

The contractual relationship is composed of enforceable rights and correlative enforceable duties. The evidence of the contract typically takes the form of words communicated orally or in writing. A contract, however, can be made without words.

The cart filled with groceries moves to the supermarket checkout counter where the shopper places the items on the conveyor. The cashier computes the total price and the shopper pays. Nary a word is spoken except, perhaps, for some pleasant-ries, but there is a contract whereby the shopper agreed to buy the selected items and the store agreed to sell them to the shopper for a price. You hail a taxi and only state the address of your destination. With or without any further conversation with the driver, you arrive at the destination, four miles away. The driver would be shocked to hear you say "Thank you very much" without paying for the service. The passenger should have understood that the service was not provided as a gift. Similarly, you would be shocked to hear the driver inform you that the price of the service is $5,000. Without any words concerning the agreement, the driver expected to be paid for the service and you expected to pay only a reasonable price for a four mile taxi ride rather than an exorbitant price. The law will enforce a contract in accordance with these reasonable expectations.

So would court enforce cont. w/ unreasonable consideration

Sometimes the word "contract" is used to designate a transaction involving the exchange of goods or land for money. When money is exchanged for goods, this constitutes a *sale*. When money is exchanged for land, this constitutes a *conveyance*. Sales and conveyances are typically the result of a previous contract, i.e., they are the *performance* of the contract, but they are not contracts in themselves. There is no undertaking or commitment to do or refrain from doing anything in the future. This indispensable element of contract is missing. If *A* and *B* make a contract for

---

[11] *See* Simpson v. Dyer, 268 Mich. 328, 256 N.W. 341 (1934); Southern R.R. v. Huntsville Lumber Co., 191 Ala. 333, 67 So. 695 (1914).

the purchase and sale of a car, they have committed themselves to this exchange in the future. When *A* delivers the automobile to *B* and is paid a price in exchange for the car, it is incorrect to suggest that a "contract" results from this sale.[12] There is a present transfer of property rights leaving nothing to be done in the future. The legal rights that are created by a sale of goods or conveyance of land are rights *in rem*[13] or rights in the property itself. There are no special rights *in personam* between the parties to the transaction. If *A* should deprive *B* of the automobile after selling and delivering it to him, *B* could not maintain an action for breach of contract but would be relegated to an action in tort for wrongful conversion of the auto. If a total stranger to the transaction, *C*, should deprive *B* of the auto, *B* would have the same right against *C* in tort. The legal relations created by the sale are relations *in rem* affecting not only the two parties involved in the transaction but all other members of society. When *A promised* to sell and deliver the auto to *B* in return for *B'* s promise[14] to pay the agreed price, the legal relations created would be *in personam* rights and correlative duties between only *A* and *B*. If either party refused to perform his promise, the other would have the exclusive *in personam* right to bring an action in contract for breach, but neither party would have any rights against any third party.

C. SOURCES OF THE LAW OF CONTRACT

The principles of contract law evolved from innumerable judicial decisions resolving countless disputes as part of the common law of England.[15] Contract law is, therefore, case law which continuously evolves and sometimes modifies the principles of contract law which trace their roots to the sixteenth century.[16] The most significant statutory modifications of the common law principles are found in Article 2 of the *Uniform Commercial Code* (UCC) which we analyze in the next section.

---

[12] *But see* W.F. Boardman Co. v. Petch, 186 Cal. 476, 482, 199 P. 1047, 1050 (1921); White v. Treat, 100 F. 290, 291 (2d Cir. 1900). Sometimes such a transaction is referred to as an executed contract. *See* 2 Blackstone's Commentaries 443 (1941); Mettel v. Gales, 12 S.D. 632, 639, 82 N.W. 181 (1900).

[13] 1 Corbin On Contracts § 4 (1963).

[14] *See* Douglass v. W.L. Williams Art Co., 143 Ga. 846, 85 S.E. 993 (1915); Lords Buller & Kenyon in Cooke v. Oxley, 3 Term. Rep. 653, 1 R.R. 783 (1790).

[15] For an extensive treatment of this history, see A. W. B. Simpson, A History Of The Common Law Of Contract (1987). "Roman concepts of contract were known in England in the twelfth and thirteenth centuries. But although they inspired the comparable evolution of a general theory of contract in the civil law systems of the Continent, they exercised no significant influence on the common law. The common law was thus able to chart its own peculiar course in the direction of a general basis of the enforcement of promises." *See* Farnsworth, *The Past of Promise: An Historical Introduction to Contract*, 60 Colum. L. Rev. 576, 591 (1969).

[16] English courts adjudicated private contract disputes long before the 16th century, but it was in the 16th century that what is sometimes called the modern English law of contracts developed around the common law writ called "assumpsit" which is often defined simply as stating that a person "undertook" to do something. While agreeing that "assumpsit" may be viewed as an "undertaking," legal historian A. W. B. Simpson suggests a "wider range of overtones" surround that terms as used in the 15th and 16th centuries. *See* Simpson, A History Of The Common Law 215–18.

A system of law based on evolving judicial decisions presents a challenge of certainty, stability and uniformity. While state courts within the United States each inherited the basic common law principles of contract law, the decisions of the courts in one state are not binding on the decisions of courts in other states. To enhance uniformity in the application of common law principles, the American Law Institute, formed in 1923, sponsored the publication of *restatements* of the law in various fields of law. The original RESTATEMENT, the RESTATEMENT OF CONTRACTS, was published in 1932 by the Institute for the guidance of the bench and bar.

Since the Institute is a private organization, RESTATEMENTS do not have the force of law. However, the Chief Reporter for the original RESTATEMENT OF CONTRACTS was Professor Samuel Williston, generally regarded as the leading contracts scholar in America at that time. With the assistance of other luminaries, particularly Professor Arthur Linton Corbin, Professor Williston directed the effort to analyze the existing judicial decisions and to distill therefrom sound principles of contract law. The effect was more than substantial. Courts and lawyers have relied heavily on the RESTATEMENT to furnish guidance in the analysis of contracts questions, and the citations to the RESTATEMENT as sound authority in contracts cases are legion. With the enactment of the UCC throughout the country and with new conflicts among jurisdictions developing in various contracts cases, the American Law Institute undertook the compilation of a new RESTATEMENT OF CONTRACTS, the RESTATEMENT (SECOND) OF CONTRACTS. The RESTATEMENT 2d was published in 1981 and incorporated most of the major changes in contract law effected by the Code. Beyond this effort, the RESTATEMENT 2d performs the more traditional task of promoting sound resolutions of conflicting judicial decisions in contracts cases that have emerged since the publication of the FIRST RESTATEMENT.

In addition to the RESTATEMENT 2d, the development of a scholarly contracts analysis has been aided by the production of two monumental, multi-volume treatises. The Williston treatise (first published in 1920)[17] was almost exclusively relied upon by courts and lawyers seeking a discourse on any topic in the field. The later treatise of Professor Corbin (first published in 1950)[18] tends to be regarded as the principal comprehensive work on the subject. It is difficult to overestimate the contribution of these two giants of contract law. There is, however, a substantial difference in perspective between them.

The Williston view tends to be more rigid and rule-oriented than the Corbin view. Often characterized as a positivist view, the Williston analysis suggests a system of rules or compartments into which any fact situation can be fit (or to use the terminology of certain critics, "squeezed"). The Williston position has undergone considerable criticism to the effect that it is mechanical and monistic.[19] On the other hand, Professor Corbin enjoyed wide approval during the last four decades of the twentieth century. In the American "Legal Realist" tradition, the Corbin approach is much more flexible in that it incorporates economic, social, moral, and ethical

---

[17] WILLISTON, CONTRACTS (1920) [hereinafter cited as WILLISTON]. Subsequently revised in 1936. The third edition, begun in 1957, was completed in 1979.

[18] These volumes have been revised and the treatise is also supplemented twice each year.

[19] *See* F. KESSLER & G. GILMORE, CONTRACT AS A PRINCIPLE OF ORDER, CONTRACTS, CASES AND MATERIALS (2D ED. 1970).

considerations. It recognizes the frailty of human institutions in judicial decision making. It suggests that rules of law should be pliable and workable. It is willing to sacrifice some of the values of certainty and predictability in exchange for what Professor Corbin would hope are more relevant rationales and just results. The traditional criticism of the Corbin approach is its lack of certainty and predictability and its incorporation of extra-legal concepts into the "science" of law. The RESTATEMENT (SECOND) OF CONTRACTS manifests a strong Corbin influence that is destined to prevail for a considerable time. Notwithstanding the current dominance of the Corbin approach, there are other perspectives that suggest alternative, significant analyses of contract law.[20] Their ultimate course of development is a matter of speculation.

D. THE UNIFORM COMMERCIAL CODE — UNITED NATIONS CONVENTION

The UCC. The Uniform Commercial Code (UCC) is the product of two distinguished organizations: The National Conference of Commissioners on Uniform State Laws[21] (NCCUSL) which promotes uniformity in state laws, and the American Law Institute (ALI).[22] A large number of practicing and academic lawyers as well as businessmen (merchants) were involved in the production of the UCC in the 1940s under the leadership of Professor Karl N. Llewellyn, one of the great legal scholars of the twentieth century. From an original design to revise the Uniform Sales Act, which governed the law of Sales in most of the United States, the design was more than substantially augmented to provide uniformity in all of commercial law. The keystone of the UCC is Article 2, drafted by Professor Llewellyn.[23] Article 2 deals with the sale of goods which may be defined essentially

---

[20] The contract theory of the Uniform Commercial Code and Restatement (Second) is often called "neoclassical," i.e., it is a more realistic and flexible approach than the contract theory of the common law or first Restatement and is the dominant contract theory at present. The economic analysis of contract law has seen wide development among contracts scholars. *See* R. POSNER, ECONOMIC ANALYSIS OF LAW, CH. 4 (3D ED. 1986). *See also* Goetz & Scott, *Enforcing Promises: An Examination of the Basis of contract*, 89 YALE L.J. 1261 (1980). Another development may be called the "relational" school which is critical of traditional contract theory because of its focus on discrete or static transactions since contract transactions range from the isolated sale of a product to long term relationships that change over time. *See* I. MACNEIL, THE NEW SOCIAL CONTRACT (1980). A view that can only be described as hostile to contract theory is that of the *critical legal scholars* ("crits") who see modern contract theory as "preaching equality in distrust" which is "hostile to personal authority as a source of order." Unger, *The Critical Legal Studies Movement*, 96 HARV. L. REV. 563, 624 (1983). The attending effort of the movement has been to deconstruct traditional contract doctrine.

[21] The Commission is composed of Commissioners from each of the states as well as the District of Columbia and Puerto Rico.

[22] The Institute is a voluntary organization composed of some 1500 judges, law professors and leading practitioners.

[23] The two sponsoring organizations, ALI and NCCUSL, considered major revisions in Article 2 throughout the 1990s. A 1999 revision was approved by the ALI but it was not approved by NCCUSL. The compromise led to the production of *Proposed Amendments to Article 2* (2003). Though the amendments have not been enacted in any jurisdiction at the time of his writing, they are considered at appropriate places throughout this book.

as tangible, moveable property.[24] Thus, any contract dealing with everything from autos to zithers are covered by Article 2. Raw materials that will be made into other goods are still goods. The bricks and mortar that become buildings are goods before they are permanently incorporated into the building at which time they become part of the real (as contrasted with personal) property and are no longer goods. Service contracts including employment contracts are not contracts for the sale of goods. Nonetheless, the contract law concepts of Article 2 are found in cases dealing with these and other types of contracts to which Article 2 technically does not apply. Courts apply Article 2 concepts by analogy to other types of contracts. Moreover, the influential RESTATEMENT (SECOND) OF CONTRACTS on which courts rely generally incorporated the concepts of Article 2 for all contracts.

UCC Article 2A deals with leases of goods. Leases are not sales since the ownership of the good remains in the lessor. If you lease a snowblower from an equipment lessor, you have the right to use it according to the terms of the lease which is a contract. Other UCC Articles deal with negotiable instruments such as checks, and promissory notes (Article 3), bank deposits and collections (Article 4), another relatively recent addition, wire transfers (Article 4A), letters of credit (Article 5), bulk transfers (Article 6), documents of title (Article 7), investment securities (Article 8) and secured transactions (Article 9). Since the first enactment of the Code in Pennsylvania in 1953,[25] all other states have enacted the UCC, though Louisiana has enacted only certain articles.[26]

The United Nations Convention (CISG). The United Nations Convention on Contracts for the International Sale of Goods (CISG) is a uniform law for international sale-of-goods contracts. The Vienna Convention became effective in the United States as of January 1, 1988. At the time of this writing, eighty-one nations have adopted the Convention which contains 101 articles dealing with all aspects of contracts for the sale of goods where the Convention applies. While CISG suggests some similarities to the domestic contract law of the United States, there is a strong continental law influence which differs significantly from the common law concept of contracts as well as the UCC. Students must be attuned to CISG since it is United States law that preempts our general contract law and the contract law of the UCC. It is an official treaty of the United States government. Thus, in a contract for the sale of goods between an American corporation and a corporation in any of more than 80 other nations including Canada, Mexico, France, Germany, China, Russia and other major trading nations as well as developing nations, neither the common law principles or Article 2 provisions of contract law govern. CISG displaces such domestic law in contracts between parties with their principal places of business in CISG countries. This book will refer to CISG, particularly with respect to those areas of contract law which are materially different under CISG.

---

[24] The official definition is found in UCC Section 2-105: "Goods means all things (including specially manufactured goods) which are movable at the time of identification to the contract for sale" ["identification" occurs when the goods have been marked or designated for a particular buyer — § 2-501].

[25] The enactment became effective in 1954.

[26] The Louisiana legal system is based on the French Napoleonic Code system. Louisiana has not enacted Article 2 of the Code dealing with contracts for the sale of goods.

E. ELECTRONIC CONTRACTS — COMPUTER INFORMATION TRANSACTIONS

Technological developments invariably require effective legal reactions. As recently as 1996 only 3 million people throughout the world used the Internet. Today, the number of people using the internet is approaching three billion. The existing law in certain countries including the United States requires certain types of contracts such as contracts for the sale of land or the sale of goods to be evidenced by a "writing." While some courts have expanded the definition of "writing" to include electronic records, courts are not legislatures. They may not issue abstract judgments about the law. A case or controversy must be presented to a court before it could rule that a term such as "writing" would include electronic records. Both the Congress of the United States and state legislatures recognized an immediate need to create new statutes that would place electronic records on a par with traditional paper writings evidencing contracts.

The National Conference of Commissioners on Uniform State Laws (NCCUSL) published the *Uniform Electronic Transactions Act* (UETA) in 1999 to foster the enactment of a uniform law that would facilitate electronic commerce by removing barriers to the recognition of electronic records. At the time of this writing, all but a few states have enacted UETA. While Congress is normally content to leave commercial law matters to state legislatures, the sudden impact of electronic commerce induced the enactment of the *Electronic Signatures in Global and National Commerce Act* (popularly known as "E-Sign") that became effective on October 1, 2000. E-Sign has the same limited objective as UETA to facilitate electronic commerce. Enactment of UETA in a given state will automatically satisfy the Federal E-Sign statute. These statutes and related materials dealing with electronic contracts are analyzed in the portions of Chapter 4 of this volume dealing with the requirement that certain types of contracts must be evidenced by a writing.

There were other concerns in the 1990s that Article 2 of the Uniform Commercial Code, designed to deal with contracts for the sale of goods, was not adequate to deal with computer information transactions which are not sales since computer information is typically licensed rather than sold. Neither are they transactions in "goods" which are tangible and movable things, while "information" is an intangible good that maybe protected by the Federal Copyright statute. Court had nonetheless applied Article 2 concepts analogously to the licensing of software and other computer information transactions. NCCUSL presented the *Uniform Computer Information Transactions Act* (UCITA) designed exclusively for such transactions. While computers now commonly appear in goods such as automobiles, appliances, industrial equipment, and the like, UCITA was not designed to apply to such "smart" goods simply because their operations are governed by computer chip. Article 2 would continue to apply to transactions in such tangible goods. Though confined to intangible computer information, UCITA proved highly controversial and after enactment in only two states, Maryland and Virginia, it failed to garner additional support. Four states have enacted anti-UCITA ("bomb shelter") statutes to preclude the enforceability of choice-of-law provisions in contracts that would require contract interpretations according the law of any state governed by UCITA: Iowa Code § 554D.125 (2013); N. C. Gen. Stat. § 66-329 (2013); Vt. 0 V. S. A. § 2463a

(2013); W. Va. Code § 55-8-15 (2014).

F.　TO BEGIN THE STUDY OF CONTRACT LAW

It is logical to begin the study of contract law by exploring the myriad questions dealing with the "agreement process," how a court determines whether a contract was formed and how it was formed. There are, however, other desirable points of departure. One of the most important inquiries that must be pursued is, what will the legal system do for an aggrieved party where the other party has breached a contract, i.e., what legal *remedies* are available for a breach of contract and how do courts apply them? Still another desirable starting point could pursue the critical question, among the billions of agreements that are made every day, how does a court decide which of these agreements are legally binding, i.e., which agreements are contracts? This basic question requires an analysis of the concept called *consideration* and other "validation devices" that make promises legally enforceable.

The next chapter of this book begins our exploration of the agreement process. The reason it is the second chapter instead of this (first) chapter is because the cases chosen to illustrate contract formation may refer to contract remedies as well as consideration or another validation device — concepts which the student has not had an opportunity to understand. To avoid confusion concerning these important perspectives, the remainder of this chapter *introduces* them by providing brief explorations of contract remedies and the validation process. While each of these topics will be explored later in depth, the following introductions will not only avoid confusion in the exploration of subsequent cases, but will highlight the importance of these issues in all cases. The introduction to these concepts will also allow the student to explore them with more confidence and understanding when they appear in later chapters.

G.　AN INTRODUCTION TO CONTRACT REMEDIES

ATACS CORP. v. TRANS WORLD COMMUNICATIONS, INC.
United States Court of Appeals, Third Circuit
155 F.3d 659 (1998)

Theories of Contract Enforcement by an Award of Damages

In general, contract law espouses three distinct, yet equally important, theories of damages to remedy a breach of contract: "expectation" damages, "reliance" damages, and "restitution" damages. *See* RESTATEMENT (SECOND) CONTRACTS § 344. The preferred basis of contract damages seeks to protect an injured party's "expectation interest" — that is, the interest in having the benefit of the bargain — and accordingly awards damages designed to place the aggrieved in as good a position as would have occurred had the contract been performed.

While the traditional law of contract remedies implements the policy that goods and services should be consumed by the person who values them most highly, and hence the preference for expectation damages, other theories of damages provide alternative avenues for contract enforcement. This is especially so where an injured party is entitled to recover for breach of contract, but recovery based on traditional notions of expectation damages is clouded because of the uncertainty in measuring the loss in value to the aggrieved contracting party. Thus, where a court cannot measure lost profits with certainty, contract law protects an injured parties reliance interest by seeking to achieve the position that it would have obtained had the contract never been made, usually through the recovery of expenditures actually made in performance or in anticipation of performance.

Finally, damages under a theory of restitution provides an appropriate form of relief in many contract cases. The objective is not the enforcement of contracts through the protection of an injured party's expectation or reliance interests, but is instead rooted in common notions of equity through the protection of the injured's restitution interest to prevent the unjust enrichment of the party who has received benefits at the expense of another.

[1]   The Expectation Interest

The typical interest protected in contract law is what the court called the "preferred" *expectation interest*. In *MCA Television Ltd. v. Public Interest Corp.*, 171 F.3d 1265, 1271 (11th Cir. 1999), a television station in Lakeland, Florida contracted to obtain a license to televise shows from MCA which owned the rights to such shows. When the station claimed that it was not obligated to perform the contract, MCA sued. The court found that the station had breached the contract and proceeded to determine the remedy to which MCA was entitled. The court stated the typical purpose of contract law:

> Contract law is designed to protect the expectations of the contracting parties. *See* Murray On Contracts, § 117, at 67[27] (describing the purpose of contract law as "the fulfillment of those expectations which have been induced by the making of a promise"). When a contract is breached, an injured party can look to the legal system for help in achieving the position he or she would have occupied upon the performance of the promise — that is, for his or her "expectation interest," otherwise known as "the benefit of the bargain."

The station had been showing the MCA programs for some time before claiming it was not bound to the contract. The court found that MCA was entitled to the unpaid contract price which placed MCA in the position it would have been had the contract been performed, protecting MCA's expectation interest.

---

[27] The court is referring to an earlier edition of Murray On Contracts (the treatise) which is now in its 5th edition (2011). References to earlier edition of this treatise by courts in the cases will often be to earlier editions where the section numbers may be different. Section numbers in the current (5th 2011) edition are typically one number ahead of the similar sections in earlier editions. References to the treatise in notes or other text will be to the current 5th edition.

PROBLEM

Karl signed a contract to purchase a new car from Power Auto Sales at a price of $25,000. Power breached the contract by refusing to deliver the car. Karl can sign a contract to purchase the same car (model, year and equipment) at another dealership for $28,000, which appears to be the price at other dealerships as well. Before signing this contract, Karl seeks your advice. Since this is a contract for the sale of goods, you know that the Uniform Commercial Code applies to this situation. UCC Section 1-106(1) states: "The remedies provided by this Act shall be liberally administered to the end that the aggrieved party may be in as good a position as if the other party had fully performed." More specifically, you find UCC Section 2-712, known as the buyer's "cover" remedy. Before advising Karl, consider the following case.

HUNTINGTON BEACH SCHOOL DISTRICT v. CONTINENTAL INFORMATION SYSTEMS CORP

United States Court of Appeals, Ninth Circuit
621 F.2d 353 (1980)

Choy, J.

The district court found that Continental Information Systems Corp. (CIS) breached its contract to deliver a computer to the Huntington Beach Union High School District (School District), and awarded damages. The School District, intending to purchase a computer, sent out a Notice Inviting Bids. CIS, a computer broker, responded with what the district court held was an offer to deliver a satisfactory computer by the end of July, and the School District formally accepted. CIS failed to acquire a satisfactory computer by July, and therefore failed to deliver. The School District had allowed the other bidders' offers to expire on July 12, so it had to rebid the contract. The winning bid in the second contest was almost $60,000 higher than CIS's contract price.

A. General Damages

The defeated bidders' offers to sell the School District a computer remained open, by their required terms, until July 12. On that date, the School District knew that CIS had not yet formally refused to perform and in fact was actively negotiating to obtain a computer from a third party. Rather than declare CIS in breach on July 12 and accept the second-best bidder's offer (thus running the risk of winding up with two computers or being held liable to CIS for breach), the School District chose to let the other offers lapse and to hope that CIS could obtain and deliver a satisfactory computer by July 31.

The district court found as facts that this was a "reasonable" course of action and that the School District acted "in good faith," and the court's conclusion of law was that the School District "acted reasonably." Nonetheless, since the court believed that it would have been "more reasonable" to accept the second-best offer on July 12, it limited the School District's general damages to $12,403.06, the difference between CIS' offer and the offer of the second-best bidder.

This was clear error. A buyer can cover through "any reasonable purchase," Cal. Commercial Code § 2712(1), and failure to mitigate reduces recoverable damages only when the course of action chosen is affirmatively unreasonable or in bad faith. "The test of proper cover is whether at the time and place the buyer acted in good faith and in a reasonable manner, and it is immaterial that hindsight may later prove that the method of cover used was not the cheapest or most effective." UCC § 2-712, Official Comment 2.

As a California court has said, "The reasonableness of the efforts of the injured party must be judged in the light of the situation confronting him at the time the loss was threatened and not by the judgment of hindsight. [Citations.] The fact that reasonable measures other than the one taken would have avoided damage is not, in and of itself, proof of the fact that the one taken, though unsuccessful, was unreasonable. [Citation.] If a choice of two reasonable courses presents itself, the person whose wrong forced the choice cannot complain that one rather than the other is chosen. [Citation.] The standard by which the reasonableness of the injured party's efforts is to be measured is not as high as the standard required in other areas of law. [Citations.] It is sufficient if he acts reasonably and with due diligence, in good faith. [Citations.] *Green v. Smith*, 261 Cal. App. 2d 392, 396–97, 67 Cal. Rptr. 796, 800 (1968).

Applying the facts as found by the district court to the applicable law, we hold that the School District was entitled as a matter of law to recover as general damages the difference between the contract price and its actual cover price: $59,424.66.

B. Consequential Damages

The district court awarded the School District consequential damages of $9,782.10. This sum covered, among other things, three months' rental of peripheral equipment, which the School District had ordered for the new computer. As to the peripherals, which sit idle because of CIS's nonperformance, the district court might have based its award on the School District's "reliance" on CIS's representation. If so, the court erred, because the peripherals were ordered before CIS made its bid.

Nonetheless, the award of consequential damages was correct. Under Cal. Commercial Code § 2715(2)(a), "Consequential damages resulting from the seller's breach include . . . any loss resulting from general or particular requirements and needs of which the seller at the time of contracting had reason to know and which could not reasonably be prevented by cover or otherwise." See also UCC § 2-715, Official Comment 3 (seller need not consciously accept liability). The Notice Inviting Bids stated that the School District had ordered the peripherals, thus giving CIS reason to know that fact. No more is needed to establish the School District's right to consequential damages at law.

We will affirm a district court's decision if it is correct, regardless whether the district court relied upon a wrong ground or gave a wrong reason. Since CIS does not contest the amount of the alleged damages in regard to the peripherals, we affirm the district court's award of consequential damages.

The district court's award of general damages is *Reversed* and remanded with instruction to award the School District general damages of $59,424.66, plus prejudgment interest from July 20, 1977, until June 22, 1978, and postjudgment interest thereafter until paid. In all other respects, the judgment of the district court is *Affirmed.*

NOTES

(1) *Protecting the Expectation Interest.* Since this case was governed by the Uniform Commercial Code, consider whether the court was faithful to the UCC principle in Section 1-106: "The remedies provided by this Act shall be liberally administered to the end that the aggrieved party may be put in as good a position as if the other party had fully performed."

(2) *The Foreseeability Limitation.* The court awarded $59,424.66 in *general* damages that conforms to UCC § 2-712 (2): "the difference between the cost of cover and the contract price . . ." In addition to such general damages, the same section of the UCC states that the buyer may recover "*consequential* damages as hereinafter defined in § 2-715(2)." Section 2-715(2)(a) defines consequential damages as "any loss resulting from general or particular requirements *which the seller at the time of contract had reason to know* . . . ." The court found that CIS "had reason to know" about the peripherals which became useless because of its breach. The "reason to know" requirement is not a UCC invention. As Comment 2 to § 2-715 indicates, this is an "older" common law rule. It is, indeed, an older rule, emanating from what may be the most famous case in contract law literature, *Hadley v. Baxendale*, 9 Ex. 341, 156 Eng. Rep. 145 (1854). We will carefully consider that case in the later chapter on contract remedies. The basic rule spawned by the case is that the breaching party may not be liable for damages unless those damages were foreseeable at the time the contract was formed. If CIS was unaware of the peripherals at the time it made the contract with the School District, CIS would not be liable for these damages. It is important to see why this is so. When parties make a contract, they are each assuming certain risks, but a party cannot assume a risk of which she doesn't know or have reason to know. When the contract is later breached, one of the limitations on the recovery of damages will be based on what risks were foreseeable by the breaching party. Why should the law worry about being fair to the contract breaker?

Consider Karl's contract for the automobile that Power Auto Sales breached. Karl had to pay $28,000 for a substitute car. Assuming that was a reasonable "cover" purchase, Karl's damages appear to be $3,000 — the difference between the contract price and the cover price. Upon receipt of those damages from Power, Karl ends up with the car he should have had at a net price ($25,000) that he expected to pay. He is in the position he should have been in had the contract been performed with respect to the cost of the car. Suppose, however, that Karl claimed additional damages for Power's breach: (1) because Karl could not procure the substitute car for a week, he lost a job opportunity that would have paid him $20,000 more annually than his current salary; multiplied by 40 years of work based upon Karl's young age, Karl claims additional damages of $800,000; (2) Karl was so distressed over Power's breach that he was irritable which led to an argument with his fiance who left Karl causing him to require psychological treatments likely to continue for three years at a total cost of $30,000; (3) Karl claimed that Power *knowingly and wilfully* breached the contract for which he claimed another million dollars in punitive damages. Thus, instead of seeking $3,000 from Power, Karl sues for $1,833,000. Absent additional facts, Karl will not recover the $800,000 for loss of a job opportunity that was unforeseeable by Power. The psychological needs of Karl were unforeseeable by Power at the time the contract was formed, so Karl does not recover the $30,000. Later, we will see that, with only rare exceptions, contract damages do not include damages for mental pain and suffering. As to the $1 million claimed for Power's wilful breach, Karl is seeking "punitive" damages that are generally not recoverable for breach of contract. Again, the purpose of contract law is not to punish contract breakers, it is to compensate the injured party by placing that party in the position he or she would have been in had the contract been performed.

(3) *Other UCC Remedies.* The "cover" remedy is one of the buyer's remedies. It is a popular remedy since the buyer typically needs the goods ordered from the breaching seller and when that seller does not perform the contract, the buyer makes a substitute purchase from another supplier, i.e., the buyer "covers" through the substitute purchase. The cover remedy protects the buyer's expectation interest. The buyer, however, is not limited to the cover remedy. It is one of several remedies which the buyer may choose as listed in UCC Section 2-711. Similarly, where the buyer breaches a contract for the sale of goods, the seller may choose a remedy from those listed in Section 2-703. These and other remedies will be analyzed in Chapter 8.

[2] The Expectation Interest in Construction and Employment Contracts

PROBLEMS

(1) Cox, a building contractor, agreed to construct a building for Davis at a price of $500,000. Assume that, when the building was half completed,

(a) without justification, Cox refused to complete the building and Davis was forced to hire another contractor to complete it. Advise Davis.

(b) without justification, Davis refused to permit Cox to complete the building and hired another contractor to complete it. How should a court fulfill the reasonable expectations of Cox?

(2) Edwards, an engineer, signed a one year contract to work for the Fortran Company at an annual salary of $100,000. Edwards worked effectively for six months and received $50,000 in salary from Fortran. Assume that, at the end of the six months, either (a) without justification, Edwards quit and took a position with another engineering company at a salary of $120,000 per year, or (b) without justification, Fortran fired Edwards, who was unable to find a job as an engineer for the remaining six months of his contract. How should a court fulfill the reasonable expectations of Fortran and Edwards?

(3)   Suppose that after Edwards was fired without cause, he could have worked as an engineer doing the same type of work in his local area for the second six months of the year at a salary of $50,000 for another employer but chose not to do so. What should Edwards recover as a result of Fortran's breach?

[3]   Damages Must Be Reasonably Certain

FREUND v. WASHINGTON SQUARE PRESS, INC.
New York Court of Appeals
314 N.E.2d 419 (1974)

RABIN, J.

In this action for breach of a publishing contract, we must decide what damages are recoverable for defendant's failure to publish plaintiff's manuscript. In 1965, plaintiff, an author and a college teacher, and defendant, Washington Square Press, Inc., entered into a written agreement which, in relevant part, provided as follows. Plaintiff ("author") granted defendant ("publisher") exclusive rights to publish and sell in book form plaintiff's work on modern drama. Upon plaintiff's delivery of the manuscript, defendant agreed to complete payment of a nonreturnable $2,000 "advance." Thereafter, if defendant deemed the manuscript not "suitable for publication," it had the right to terminate the agreement by written notice within 60 days of delivery. Unless so terminated, defendant agreed to publish the work in hardbound edition within 18 months and afterwards in paperbound edition. The contract further provided that defendant would pay royalties to plaintiff, based upon specified percentages of sales. (For example, plaintiff was to receive 10% of the retail price of the first 10,000 copies sold in the continental United States.) If defendant failed to publish within 18 months, the contract provided that "this agreement shall terminate and the rights herein granted to the Publisher shall revert to the Author. In such event all payments theretofore made to the Author shall belong to the Author without prejudice to any other remedies which the Author may have."

Plaintiff performed by delivering his manuscript to defendant and was paid his $2,000 advance. Defendant thereafter merged with another publisher and ceased publishing in hardbound. Although defendant did not exercise its 60-day right to terminate, it has refused to publish the manuscript in any form. At trial, plaintiff sought to prove: (1) delay of his academic promotion; (2) loss of royalties which would have been earned; and (3) the cost of publication if plaintiff had made his own arrangements to publish. The trial court found that plaintiff had been promoted despite defendant's failure to publish, and that there was no evidence that the breach had caused any delay. Recovery of lost royalties was denied without discussion. The court found, however, that the cost of hardcover publication to plaintiff was the natural and probable consequence of the breach and, based upon expert testimony, awarded $10,000 to cover this cost. It denied recovery of the expenses of paperbound publication on the ground that plaintiff's proof was conjectural.

The Appellate Division (3 to 2) affirmed, finding that the cost of publication was the proper measure of damages. In support of its conclusion, the majority analogized to the construction contract situation where the cost of completion may be the proper measure of damages for a builder's failure to complete a house or for use of wrong materials. The dissent concluded that the cost of publication is not an appropriate measure of damages and consequently, that plaintiff may recover nominal damages only. We agree with the dissent. In so concluding, we look to the basic purpose of damage recovery and the nature and effect of the parties' contract.

It is axiomatic that, except where punitive damages are allowable, the law awards damages for breach of contract to compensate for injury caused by the breach — injury which was foreseeable, i.e., reasonably within the contemplation of the parties, at the time the contract was entered into. Money damages are substitutional relief designed in theory "to put the injured party in as good a position as he would have been put by full performance of the contract, at the least cost to the defendant and without charging him with harms that he had no sufficient reason to foresee when he made the contract." (5 CORBIN, CONTRACTS, § 1002, pp. 31–32; 11 WILLISTON, CONTRACTS [3D ED.], § 1338, p. 198.) In other words, so far as possible, the law attempts to secure to the injured party the benefit of his bargain, subject to the limitations that the injury — whether it be losses suffered or gains prevented — was foreseeable, and that the amount of damages claimed be measurable with a reasonable degree of certainty and, of course, adequately proven. But it is equally fundamental that the injured party should not recover more from the breach than he would have gained had the contract been fully performed.

Measurement of damages in this case according to the cost of publication to the plaintiff would confer greater advantage than performance of the contract would have entailed to plaintiff and would place him in a far better position than he would have occupied had the defendant fully performed. Such measurement bears no relation to compensation for plaintiff's actual loss or anticipated profit. Far beyond compensating plaintiff for the interests he had in the defendant's performance of the contract — whether restitution, reliance or expectation (see Fuller & Perdue, *Reliance Interest in Contract Damages*, 46 YALE L.J. 52, 53–56), an award of the cost of publication would enrich plaintiff at defendant's expense.

Pursuant to the contract, plaintiff delivered his manuscript to the defendant. In doing so, he conferred a value on the defendant which, upon defendant's breach, was required to be restored to him. Special Term, in addition to ordering a trial on the issue of damages, ordered defendant to return the manuscript to plaintiff and plaintiff's restitution interest in the contract was thereby protected.

At the trial on the issue of damages, plaintiff alleged no reliance losses suffered in performing the contract or in making necessary preparations to perform. Had such losses, if foreseeable and ascertainable, been incurred, plaintiff would have been entitled to compensation for them.

As for plaintiff's expectation interest in the contract, it was basically two-fold — the "advance" and the royalties. (To be sure, plaintiff may have expected to enjoy whatever notoriety, prestige or other benefits that might have attended publication, but even if these expectations were compensable, plaintiff did not attempt at trial to place a monetary value on them.) There is no dispute that plaintiff's expectancy in the "advance" was fulfilled — he has received his $2,000. His expectancy interest in the royalties — the profit he stood to gain from sale of the published book — while theoretically compensable, was speculative. Although this work is not plaintiff's first, at trial he provided no stable foundation for a reasonable estimate of royalties he would have earned had defendant not breached its promise to publish. In these circumstances, his claim for royalties falls for uncertainty.

Since the damages which would have compensated plaintiff for anticipated royalties were not proved with the required certainty, we agree with the dissent in the Appellate Division that nominal damages alone are recoverable. Though these are damages in name only and not at all compensatory, they are nevertheless awarded as a formal vindication of plaintiff's legal right to compensation which has not been given a sufficiently certain monetary valuation.

In our view, the analogy by the majority in the Appellate Division to the construction contract situation was inapposite. In the typical construction contract, the owner agrees to pay money or other consideration to a builder and expects, under the contract, to receive a completed building in return. The value of the promised performance to the owner is the properly constructed building. In this case, unlike the typical construction contract, the value to plaintiff of the promised performance — publication — was a percentage of sales of the books published and not the books themselves. Had the plaintiff contracted for the printing, binding and delivery of a number of hardbound copies of his manuscript, to be sold or disposed of as he wished, then perhaps the construction analogy, and measurement of damages by the cost of replacement or completion, would have some application.

Here, however, the specific value to plaintiff of the promised publication was the royalties he stood to receive from defendant's sales of the published book. Essentially, publication represented what it would have cost the defendant to confer that value upon the plaintiff, and, by its breach, defendant saved that cost. The error by the courts below was in measuring damages not by the value to plaintiff of the promised performance but by the cost of that performance to defendant. Damages are not measured, however, by what the defaulting party saved by the breach, but by the natural and probable consequences of the breach *to the plaintiff.* In this case, the consequence to plaintiff of defendant's failure to publish is that he is prevented from realizing the gains promised by the contract — the royalties. But, as we have stated, the amount of royalties plaintiff would have realized was not ascertained with adequate certainty and, as a consequence, plaintiff may recover nominal damages only.

Accordingly, the order of the Appellate Division should be modified to the extent of reducing the damage award of $10,000 for the cost of publication to six cents, but with costs and disbursements to the plaintiff.

NOTES

(1) Suppose Professor Freund had authored three previous books, each of which has sold more than 500,000 copies, establishing him as one of the leading non-fiction writers of his time. Would that experience have any impact in recovering damages?

(2)   If the basic purpose of contract law is to place the injured party in the position he would have been in had the contract been performed, precisely why was the court powerless to achieve that result for Professor Freund? If Professor Freund had asked you, his lawyer, to review his contract with the publisher before he signed it, should you have recognized the possibility that the publisher would fail to publish the manuscript and leave your client in the position of being unable to prove his damages with reasonable certainty? If you should have and did recognize this possibility, what advice should you have provided to your client?

(3)   When confronted with this situation, a lawyer should consider what is known as a *liquidated damages clause*. Contracting parties are free to include a clause stating that they have agreed upon specific damages that will be payable in the event of a breach. Such a clause is found in various types of contracts where it is foreseeable that damages will be difficult to measure in the event of a breach. The other party (here, the publisher) would have to agree to such a clause, but it is precisely the type of clause that could have afforded Professor Freund a remedy. The clause must be carefully drafted to assure that it is an honest and reasonable forecast of damages that are likely to ensue in the event of a breach such as the one in this case. The royalties that Professor Freund could have reasonably expected to earn had the contract been performed are highly speculative, but reasonable estimates of the prospective royalties on an academic book such as the one in question could be made. If the clause included an excessive amount the court would refuse to enforce it because it was not a reasonable forecast. Rather, it would be a penalty clause that will not be enforced since the object of contract damages is not to penalize (punish), but to compensate the injured party. Among other types of contracts, liquidated damages clauses are popular in highway construction contracts where a contractor's failure or delay in completing a project may cause expenses to a State highway department that are uncertain at the time the contract is made.

[4]   Damages Must Be "Foreseeable"

In the *Freund* case, the court states that the damages the plaintiff seeks must be "foreseeable" as well as reasonably certain. As we have seen, the principle of forseeability is based on *Hadley v. Baxendale*. It appears in modern form in § 351(1) of the RESTATEMENT (SECOND) OF CONTRACTS: "Damages are not recoverable for loss that a party in breach did not have reason to foresee as a probable result of the breach when the contract was made." The same concept in § 2-715(2) of the Uniform Commercial Code that allows the buyer to recover for losses "which the seller at the time of contracting had reason to know." The damages to Professor Freund by the defendant's failure to publish the manuscript were clearly foreseeable (the loss of royalties), but Professor Freund could not prove them with reasonable certainty. Thus, Professor Freund could meet one of the limitations on contract damages (foreseeability) but not the other (reasonable certainty).

[5]   "Efficient Breach"

Since the focus of contract remedies is to compensate the injured party for loss of bargain and not to punish the contract breaker, suppose a contract can be breached without any harm to the other party. Is such a breach justifiable? Consider the following.

Assume that you, as Professor Freund's lawyer, had reviewed the contract before he signed it. You recommended a liquidated damages clause requiring the publisher to pay your client $50,000 if the manuscript was not published. The publisher agreed to this clause that was added to the contract before the parties signed. A week later, however, the publisher discovered that a better known, though not nearly as skilled writer, Zack Barnes, had just finished a manuscript dealing with the same subject as Professor Freund's manuscript. Because Barnes had achieved a certain notoriety on television talk shows and in various controversies, it is clear that his book of inferior quality would nonetheless sell in much greater volume than Professor Freund's book. It would be counterproductive for the publisher to publish both books and the publisher would earn at least $200,000 more on the Barnes book after paying Barnes his royalties *and* paying Professor Freund $50,000 in damages. From an economist's perspective, it would be *efficient* for the publisher to breach his contract with Freund to create what is called a "Pareto superior" outcome that occurs where one party ends up better off and no party ends up worse off. Freund receives his $50,000 that he expected to receive as a reasonable forecast of damages, and the publisher is $200,000 better off, even after paying the $50,000 to Freund and paying Barnes the royalties earned from the sale of Barnes' book. The efficient breach concept, however, has been criticized on several fronts. The notion of efficient breach is devoid of any moral obligation to keep one's promises. It is concerned exclusively with efficiency. While he receives $50,000, the primary result Professor Freund may have desired was the publication of his manuscript. The $50,000 is compensation for the failure of performance, but may not be as desirable to Professor Freund as having his book published. In our illustration, the profit that Freund expected was made sufficiently certain by the amount in the liquidated damages clause. Anticipated profits, however, are not always calculated easily in other cases without such clauses. Finally, if Professor Freund had to sue for his $50,000, additional "transaction costs" would reduce his compensation since in our system, even the winning party must pay his own attorney's fees.

[6]   Inadequate Damages — Specific Performance

While the normal remedy for breach of contract will be money (damages), there may be situations where that remedy will be inadequate. In *Hoffmann v. Sprinchorn*, 1997 U.S. DIST. LEXIS 3130 (W.D.N.Y. 1997),[28] Hoffmann formed a contract to purchase a 1933 Duesenberg J. Murphy Convertible Coupe automobile for $375,000. Sprinchorn refused to deliver the car. There were no substitutes for this extremely rare automobile. Thus, an award of damages would be inadequate. Since no amount of damages will provide the buyer with its expectation interest in

---

[28] This opinion is published only electronically.

this kind of situation, an aggrieved party will seek extraordinary relief just as parties sought such relief centuries ago when courts of law were unable to provide effective remedies for their meritorious claims. They called upon the "Chancellor," the keeper of the King's conscience, to provide special relief. The Chancellor, in his discretion, could provide "equitable" relief — *ex aequo et bono* (in equity and good conscience). Courts of equity, separate from courts of law, were empowered to grant such relief if overriding considerations of justice and fairness were present and no adequate remedy at law were available. While separate equity courts no longer exist, courts of law that normally award only damages may "sit" as courts of equity and grant equitable relief when the remedy at law (damages) would be inadequate. Where damages will not place the aggrieved party in the position she would have occupied had the contract been performed, a court of equity may *order* the defendant to perform the contract — the remedy of *specific performance*.

Hoffmann sought such relief in this case. The opinion of the court reads in pertinent part: "Inasmuch as there is no doubt that the Duesenberg is unique, Hoffmann is entitled to specific performance." *Id.* at *14. It then issued its decree:

> Sprinchorn shall, no later than thirty days from the date of this Order, make available and deliver to Hoffmann or to Hoffman's duly appointed agent, in Jamestown, N. Y., the unencumbered title to and possession of the 1933 Duesenberg J Murphy Convertible Coupe at issue, vehicle identification number 2435 and "J" number J413 and that Hoffmann shall, simultaneously with the delivery to him (or to his agent) of such automobile and title, deliver to Sprinchorn \$375,000 in cash or a certified check in such amount, that the parties shall communicate with each other forthwith to facilitate and make reasonable arrangements for such exchange and that this case shall be closed.

Id. at *17–18, This remedy is the literal fulfillment of Hoffman's expectation interest.

NOTES

(1) *Unique Property.* In cases where the subject matter of the contract is unique, such as the Duesenberg, the remedy of specific performance is obvious. Money (damages) will be inadequate since the same property cannot be purchased elsewhere with any amount of money. This is true of any objectively unique item such as a Picasso painting. An item may be subjectively unique and particularly valuable to a given individual though it would have little or no market value. An old and inexpensive pocket watch or other heirloom that had belonged to a grandfather may be worth a considerable sum to a grandchild. A court would grant specific performance of a promise to sell that watch to the grandchild. If the subject matter of the contract is a tract of land, it is necessarily unique since, at least in terms of location, there is no other like it in the world. Section 2-716(1) of the Uniform Commercial Code has enlarged the possibility of specific performance by allowing that remedy where "the goods are unique or in other proper circumstances." The most obvious illustration of "other proper circumstances" would occur where the goods, though generally available elsewhere and, therefore, not unique, would become in effect unique at a given time through scarcity. Thus, if ordinary

commercial steel or other generally available products became scarce because of a national emergency, a court could decree specific performance of such a contract.

(2)   *Personal Service Contracts.* If a nurse, office or factory worker or other worker breaches an employment contract, should a court accede to the demand of an employer that the employee be ordered to perform or risk being held in contempt of court and possibly land in jail? The general reaction of courts is well stated in *Woolley v. Embassy Suites*, 227 Cal. App. 3d 1520, 1533, 278 Cal. Rptr. 719, 726–27 (1991):

> There are a variety of reasons why courts are loathe to order specific performance of personal service contracts. Such an order would impose upon the court the prodigious if not impossible task of passing judgment on the quality of performance. It would also run counter to the Thirteenth Amendment's prohibition against involuntary servitude. Courts wish to avoid the friction and social costs when the parties are reunited in a relationship that has already failed; especially where the services involve mutual confidence and the exercise of discretionary authority. Finally, it is impractical to require judicial oversight of a contract which calls for special knowledge, skill or ability.

Unlike workers in ordinary occupations, however, parties with unique talents may be subject to other remedies. When the famous golfer Tiger Woods agrees to appear in a tournament, the sponsors are assured of greater revenues through larger attendances and television audiences. Suppose Tiger agreed to participate in a given tournament but breached that agreement to appear in a competing tournament scheduled on the same days. The sponsors of the first tournament could not force Tiger to perform for the reasons already stated. They could bring an action for damages if they could provide reasonably certain proof of such damages which may be quite possible in light of prior differences in revenue between tournaments with and without Tiger. They may also seek an equitable remedy, but not specific performance for the reasons given by the court. They could seek an injunction against Tiger's performance at the second tournament. Where a noted professional baseball player breached his contract to play for another team, the court found his talents sufficiently unique to allow for an injunction against his playing for the other team. The court found he had special talents without which the team would be injured and revenues from attendance would suffer. The court concluded, "He may not be the sun in the baseball firmament, but he is certainly a bright and particular star." *Philadelphia Ball Club v. Lajoie*, 202 Pa. 210, 217, 51 A. 973, 974 (1902). The seminal case is *Luinley v. Wagner*, 1 DeG. M. & G., 604, 42 Eng. Rep. 687 (Ch. 1852), where a Prussian opera singer breached her contract to sing exclusively for Her Majesty's Theatre in London to perform in another theater. The Chancellor granted an injunction against her performing elsewhere.

[7]   The Reliance and Restitution Interests

PROBLEMS

(1)   The Computerex Corporation announced the development of a revolutionary personal computer — the XT-6000 — with power "approaching a supercomputer." To display the XT-6000 in all of its grandeur, it was necessary to use a special modem to be supplied by Redstone Electronics, Inc. Redstone agreed to produce the modem and to deliver it to the site of the 17th Annual Computer Exhibition, the critical exhibition for manufacturers of new computers, to be held in New York City on October 9, 10 and 11. Redstone told Computerex that the modem would be "delivered and installed at least 48 hours prior to the opening of the exhibition on October 9. Computerex leased exhibition space and sent five members of its staff to exhibit the XT-6000. The costs of the leased space plus food, lodging and transportation amounted to $14,000. Redstone failed to deliver the modem until the late afternoon of October 11, when virtually all potential customers for the XT-6000 had left the exhibition. It was impossible to demonstrate the XT-6000's significant capabilities without the modem. Redstone explained that there was a "mix up" in arrangements to deliver the special modem. Other modems available in New York were unsuitable. If you represent Computerex, what do you advise concerning any claim against Redstone? For a similar case, see *Security Stove & Mfg. Co. v. American Ry. Express Co.*, 227 Mo. App. 175, 51 S.W.2d 572 (1932).

(2)   John Smiley was despondent. Two friends were visiting when John left the room. Moments later, the friends heard a shotgun blast and rushed back to find Smiley unconscious, suffering from a severe, self-inflicted wound. They called the Smiley family physician who brought Smiley to the hospital, where he was attended by Dr. Matheson. Notwithstanding Matheson's efforts, Smiley died. Is Dr. Matheson entitled to recover a fee for his services from Smiley's estate? What is the basis for this recovery? Was there a contract between Matheson and Smiley? If Matheson should recover, what is the amount of his recovery? *See Matheson v. Smiley*, [1932] 2 D.L.R. 787 (Manitoba).

(3)   CBS negotiated a contract with the famous producer, David Merrick, to produce a television movie based on the novel, "Blood and Money," since Merrick owned the rights to produce such a film from the book. In reliance on this contract, CBS agreed to pay a director $500,000 and a screenwriter $250,000, both chosen by Merrick, for work on the film. The contracts stated that the director and screen writer would be paid regardless of whether the film was ever produced. (Do you see why?) CBS also paid Merrick over $833,000 in advance under the contract. Merrick breached the contract and the film was never produced. Advise CBS. The problem is based on CBS, Inc. v. Merrick, 716 F.2d 1292 (1983).

NOTE

Relatively simple distinctions between the three interests protected in contract law may be understood as follows: While the expectation interest seeks to place a party in the position it would have been in had the contract been performed, the reliance interest is concerned only with the actual loss — the out-of-pocket — loss suffered by the aggrieved party — a *minus* quantity caused by the wrongful act of another. The *restitution* interest is concerned with the *prevention of unjust enrichment.* It involves both a *minus and plus* quantity. Notice that the *reliance* interest is measured by the amount of the loss — the out-of-pocket loss, while the *restitution* interest is measured by the *benefit* or gain to the unjustly enriched party. Moreover, both the reliance and restitution interests simply return the aggrieved party to the position it occupied *before* the contract was made — *status quo ante.* The *expectation* interest, however, places the aggrieved party in the position it would have occupied had the contract been performed — the *future* position. Thus, again, the expectation interest is the normal interest protected in contract law.

H.   AN INTRODUCTION TO THE VALIDATION PROCESS

One of the key differences between human beings and other forms of life is that humans can make promises. The collective number of promises made every day taxes the imagination. A number in the billions would be an extremely conservative estimate. Among all of these promises, which promises should be legally enforced? While the virtuous person may wish to live by the ideal, *pacta sunt servanda* ("promises must be kept"), even the virtuous person will not feel compelled to keep all promises. As we saw earlier, a promise to go to dinner with a friend or other social promises do not contemplate enforcement in a court of law. A promise to make a gift of a considerable sum or an expensive item may be made in a moment of affection for a loved one. Contrast such a gift (donative) promise with promises by two business firms to buy and sell goods or services. A promise to make a gift seeks nothing in return. The businesses, however, are not promising to make gifts. They are not motivated by affection or altruism. One firm needs the goods or services to operate, while the other firm needs the money that will be earned by delivering the goods or services. If these promises were not enforceable at law, neither party could be assured that their needs will be satisfied. The entire economic system depends upon the enforceability of such promises which the social institution of contract guarantees. Moreover, since both parties are aware that their failure to perform will invoke legal consequences, they have another incentive to keep their promises. The gift promise involves no exchange, while the only reason for the promise by either business is to receive the desired exchange that the other party has promised. The exchange of valuable items has a wealth-redistribution effect, while the enforcement of a gift promise would have only trivial effect on wealth redistribution.[29] There is, therefore, no compelling economic reason to enforce gift promises except in one situation. If a promise is made in exchange for nothing in return, it may still have the effect of inducing the promisee to suffer a detriment in reliance on that promise. If the promisor should have reasonably expected her promise to induce such reliance, justice may require the enforcement of that promise.

To distinguish enforceable from unenforceable promises, modern contract law recognizes these fundamental concepts by requiring either (a) evidence of a bargained-for-exchange between parties to make their mutual promises enforceable

---

[29] *See* Melvin Eisenberg, *Donative Promises*, 47 U. CHI. L. REV. 1 (1979).

(*consideration*), or (b) in the absence of any bargained-for-exchange, evidence of a promise which the promisor should reasonably expect to induce reliance by the promisee and which does, in fact, induce such reliance in such a fashion that justice requires its enforcement (*promissory estoppel*). While there are historical antecedents for both doctrines, early common lawyers did not think in these terms.

The oldest validation device to make a promise enforceable was the *seal*. No inquiry was necessary to determine whether anything of value was promised in exchange or whether the promise induced reliance. A promise made under seal was enforceable *simply because it contained the seal* — originally a wax impression containing the distinctive symbol of the promisor. This *formality* provided a simple evidentiary test to determine whether the promise was enforceable. It was either "sealed" or "not sealed." Thus, enforceability of a promise was a matter of *form* while the modern validation devices of consideration and promissory estoppel require factual evidence of bargained-for-exchange or induced reliance. The bother of heating wax and impressing it with one's distinctive symbol eventually led to the substitute use of the words, as *locus sigilli* ("the place of the seal"), the initials, *l.s.*, or simply the word "seal." The term "seal" began to appear on preprinted forms and courts worried over whether the party signing the instrument intended the import of that word to make the promise enforceable. In many jurisdictions the seal lost all or most of its legal effect. The Uniform Commercial Code, § 2-203, made the seal inoperative in contracts for the sale of goods. As we will see in Chapter 3, dealing with a complete analysis of the validation process, however, the seal is still effective with respect to certain contracts in some jurisdictions. Moreover with the demise of the seal, statutes were enacted to make certain promises enforceable without either of the two principal validation devices, consideration or promissory estoppel.

It is important to mention one other possible validation device, often called *"moral obligation,"* that is recognized generally only with respect to two isolated types of promises. While there are other rare exceptions recognized in only a few jurisdictions, the general rule is that "moral obligation" will not make a promise enforceable since, in one sense, every promise imports a moral obligation to perform it and that would make all promises legally enforceable — a result that courts have never accepted. The most important validation devices are consideration and promissory estoppel.

[1] Consideration

RESTATEMENT (SECOND) OF CONTRACTS § 71:

> (1) To constitute consideration, a performance or a return promise must be bargained for.
>
> (2) A performance or return promise is bargained for if it is sought by the promisor in exchange for his promise and is given by the promisee in exchange for that promise.
>
> (3) The performance may consist of (a) an act other than a promise, or (b) a forbearance, or (c) the creation, modification or destruction of a legal relation.

(4) The performance or return promise may be given to the promisor or to some other person. It may be given by the promisee or some other person.

This formulation is often stated in the cases as requiring two basic elements: (i) a benefit to the promisor *or* a detriment to the promisee *and* (ii) a bargained-for-exchange.

PROBLEMS

(1)   Ames promised to sell his two-year-old automobile to Barnes for $15,000 and Barnes promised to buy the car for $15,000. Describe the benefits to the promisors and detriments to the promisees and demonstrate how there is a bargained-for-exchange in this agreement. In a typical contract to purchase and sell any property — goods, real estate or any other property — the contract is clearly supported by consideration. Do you see why?

(2)   Ames promised to employ Barnes for one year at a monthly salary of $3,000 and Barnes promised to perform certain duties for Ames. Where is the consideration in this agreement?

(3)   Los Angeles police were engaged in an intense search for a serial killer. One unit was led by Seargent Ernesto Hernandez who had been twice decorated for heroism. Two weeks into the intense search, Hernandez read a story in the Los Angeles Times in which the wealthy father of one of the victims offered $50,000 for the arrest and conviction of the serial killer. Two days later, Hernandez, alone, arrested a suspect who was later tried and convicted for the serial killings. Hernandez was the toast of Los Angeles and received another commendation from the Chief of Police. He seeks the $50,000 reward which the father now refuses to pay. Analyze.

(4)   Ames owned 100 acres of land and desired to sell 100 separate one-acre lots at the highest prices he could obtain. He placed an advertisement in local newspapers stating that any person over 18 years of age who came to an auction of these lots would be entitled to a chance to win a new Taurus automobile manufactured by the Ford Motor Company. Among many others, Sylvia Porter attended the auction and entered the contest though she did not purchase one of the auctioned lots. Sylvia was declared the winner of the contest. Ames, however, refused to deliver the Ford. Was Ames' promise supported by consideration? *See Maughs v. Porter*, 157 Va. 415, 161 S.E. 242 (1931).

(5)   George Adams saw a homeless person, Harry Billings, shivering in the cold in downtown Chicago. Adams owned a clothing store located five blocks away. He handed Billings a business card on which he wrote, "Come to my store and I will give you an overcoat of your choice . . . (Signed) George Adams." Billings walked to the store and went to the overcoat section from which he selected an expensive cashmere coat. He presented the coat and the card to the cashier who called Adams' office in the store. At the end of her call, she said, "I'm sorry. You'll have to pay for the coat." An irate Billings grabbed the card signed by Adams and left the store. The next day, he found the local Neighborhood Legal Services office where he told his story to a young attorney. You are the NLS attorney. Advise Billings. (This problem is a paraphrase of the famous "tramp" illustration by Professor Williston

which is mentioned in several cases, including the *Maughs* case cited in Problem 4). In a famous opinion by Justice O. W. Holmes, Jr., he writes:

> No matter what the actual motive may have been, by the express or implied terms of the supposed contract, the promise and the consideration must purport to be the motive each for the other, in whole or at least in part. *It is not enough that the promise induces the detriment or that the detriment induces the promise, if the other half is wanting.*

Wisconsin & Mich. Ry. v. Powers, 191 U.S. 379, 386 (1903) (emphasis supplied).

HARRIS v. TIME, INC.
California Court of Appeal
237 Cal. Rptr. 584 (1987)

KING, J.

It all began one day when Joshua Gnaizda, the three-year-old son of a prominent Bay Area public interest attorney, received what he (or his mother) thought was a tantalizing offer in the mail from Time. The front of the envelope contained two see-through windows partially revealing the envelope's contents. One window showed Joshua's name and address. The other revealed the following statement: "JOSHUA A. GNAIZDA, I'LL GIVE YOU THIS VERSATILE NEW CALCULA-TOR WATCH FREE Just for Opening this Envelope Before Feb. 15, 1985." Beneath the offer was a picture of the calculator watch itself. Joshua's mother opened the envelope and apparently realized she had been deceived by a ploy to get her to open a piece of junk mail. The see-through window had not revealed the full text of Time's offer. Printed below the picture of the calculator watch, and not viewable through the see-through window, were the following additional words: "AND MAILING THIS CERTIFICATE TODAY!" The certificate itself clearly required that Joshua purchase a subscription to Fortune magazine in order to receive the free calculator watch.

The action was prosecuted by Joshua, through his father, and by Mark Harris and Richard Baker, who had also received the same mailer. We are not informed of the ages of Harris and Baker.

The complaint sought the following relief: (1) a declaration that all recipients of the mailer were entitled to receive the promised item or to rescind subscriptions they had purchased, (2) an injunction against future similar mailings, (3) compensatory damages in an amount equal to the value of the item, and (4) $15 million punitive damages to be awarded to a consumer fund "to be used for education and advocacy on behalf of consumer protection and enforcement of laws against unfair business practices."

The complaint also alleged that before commencing litigation, Joshua's father demanded that Time give Joshua a calculator watch without requiring a subscription. Time not only refused to give a watch, it did not even give Joshua or his father the time of day. There was no allegation that Harris or Baker made such a demand on Time.

In sustaining [Time's] demurrer as to the cause of action for breach of contract, the court stated no specific grounds for its ruling. Time had argued the complaint did not allege adequate consideration, and did not allege notice of performance by the plaintiffs. Time argues that there was no contract because the mere act of opening the envelope was valueless and therefore did not constitute adequate consideration. Technically, this is incorrect. It is basic modern contract law that any bargained-for act or forbearance will constitute adequate consideration for a unilateral contract. Courts will not require equivalence in the values exchanged or otherwise question the adequacy of the consideration.

Moreover, the act at issue here — the opening of the envelope, with consequent exposure to Time's sales pitch — may have been relatively insignificant to the plaintiffs, but it was of great value to Time. At a time when our homes are bombarded daily by direct mail advertisements and solicitations, the name of the game for the advertiser or solicitor is to get the recipient to open the envelope. Some advertisers, like Time in the present case, will resort to ruse or trick to achieve this goal. From Time's perspective, the opening of the envelope was "valuable consideration" in every sense of that phrase.

As a final argument, Time claims the judgment of dismissal was correct based on the legal maxim "de minimis non curat lex," or "the law disregards trifles." (Civ. Code, § 3533.) In this age of the consumer class action this maxim usually has little value. However, the present action is "de minimus" in the extreme. This lawsuit is an absurd waste of the resources of this court, the superior court, the public interest law firm handling the case and the citizens of California whose taxes fund our judicial system. It is not a use for which our legal system is designed.

As a practical matter, plaintiffs' real complaint is that they were tricked into opening a piece of junk mail, not that they were misled into buying anything or expending more than the effort necessary to open an envelope. For many, an unpleasant aspect of contemporary American life is returning to the sanctity of one's home each day and emptying the mailbox, only to be inundated with advertisements and solicitations. Some days, among all of the junk mail, one is fortunate to be able to locate a bill, let alone a letter from a friend or loved one. Insult is added to injury when one realizes that individual citizens must pay first class postage rates to send their mail, while junk mail, for reasons apparent only to Congress and the United States Postal Service, is sent at less than one-half of that rate.

As much as one might decry this intrusion into our lives and our homes and sympathize with Joshua's plight, eliminating it lies with Congress, not the courts. The courts cannot solve every complaint or right every technical wrong, particularly one which causes no actual damage beyond the loss of the few seconds it takes to open an envelope and examine its contents. Our courts are too heavily overburdened to be used as a vehicle to punish by one whose only real damage is feeling foolish for having opened what obviously was junk mail. Only in circumstances of actual detriment should a court intrude upon the exercise of what the senders of junk mail might call commercial free speech and the recipients might call intrusive harassment. We therefore affirm the judgment.

NOTES

(1) *"Adequacy" of Consideration.* The opinion states, "Courts will not require equivalence in the values exchanged or otherwise question the adequacy of consideration." Do you see why? Consider the problems that courts would confront if they countenanced arguments that what was received in exchange for a promise was not as valuable as that which was promised. Should courts determine the worth or value of land, commodities or services in our society? Parties to a contract have different views of the value each is receiving in exchange for what they are surrendering. In addition to an incredible augmentation of litigation in an already litigious society, if courts did inquire into the "adequacy" of consideration, i.e., if they began to compare the values exchanged, what effect would such inquires have on our economic structure?

(2) *"Sufficient" Consideration.* There is a tendency by some courts to use the phrase, "sufficient consideration." If "sufficient" is used to mean "adequate," we have just seen that courts do not inquire into "adequacy." "Sufficient consideration" may be used to mean that the consideration did not fail, i.e., both parties performed their promises. This usage, therefore, would suggest that consideration that fails (one of the parties fails to perform) is "insufficient" consideration. This usage confuses "sufficient" or "insufficient" consideration with performance of the contract. The contract was either performed or not. If *failure* of performance occurs, the contract has been breached. The adjective "sufficient," therefore, is not only useless; it is counterproductive. If a promise is supported by consideration, it is an enforceable promise. There are no degrees of consideration. Thus, consideration either exists or it doesn't. If it exists, it is necessarily "sufficient" and it has nothing to do with whether performance has or has not occurred in accordance with the promises of the parties. In such a case, consideration has "failed." It is not and never was "insufficient." In general, see MURRAY ON CONTRACTS at § 60 (5th ed. 2011).

[2] Promissory Estoppel

A modern statement of the doctrine usually called promissory estoppel is found in RESTATEMENT (SECOND) OF CONTRACTS § 90:

> A promise which the promisor should reasonably expect to induce action or forbearance on the part of the promisee or a third person and which does induce such action or forbearance is binding if injustice can be avoided only by enforcement of the promise. The remedy granted for breach may be limited as justice requires.

MILES HOMES DIVISION v. FIRST STATE
BANK OF JOPLIN
Missouri Court of Appeals
782 S.W.2d 798 (1990)

MAUS, J.

The designation of the parties involved is as follows: Gerald J. Ames and Magdalyn Ames, his wife — Buyers. Plaintiff Miles Homes Division of Insilco Corporation — Seller. Defendant First State Bank of Joplin — Bank.

On February 17, 1982, the Seller entered into a retail installment sales contract to sell the Buyers materials and plans for the construction of a kit house. The price was $41,151.12, payable in monthly installments of $359.59 for twenty-two months, with a balloon payment of $33,240.00. The contract provided the Buyers would secure the purchase price by a first deed of trust lien upon the real estate upon which the house was to be built. Paragraph 4 of the contract provided the Seller "may refuse to ship any materials until it has received all required security instruments."

On February 18, 1982, the Buyers purchased three acres from Lee Edwards for $8,500.00. To partially finance that purchase, the Buyers borrowed $6,800.00 from the Bank and secured repayment of the same by a mortgage[30] on that three acres. On February 19, 1982, the Seller, upon the basis of information supplied by the Buyers, directed an initial credit inquiry to the Bank, attention of Wayne Martin. The letter contained a number of blanks to be completed concerning the Buyers and the purchase of the land upon which the home was to be built. The blanks were completed, the form signed by Wayne Martin and returned to the Seller.

Thereafter, the Seller advised Buyers their credit had been approved. The Seller sent to the Buyers, for their execution, a mortgage to secure the purchase price. Seller then sent to the Bank a letter dated March 23, 1982. That letter forms the basis for this action.

The letter advised the Bank that Seller had taken a second mortgage on the three acres and understood that the Bank held the first mortgage on the three acres. It continued by saying that the Seller planned to furnish materials to the Buyers to improve the three acres with a new house. It then asked if the Bank would notify the Seller if the Buyers became seriously delinquent in their monthly payments on the first mortgage and notify the Seller prior to the commencement of any foreclosure proceedings so that the Seller "may take the necessary steps to protect our position."

The second page of the letter consisted of a form to be completed by the Bank concerning the purchase price for the three acres. It contained the following

---

[30] [Ed. Note: Throughout the opinion, the court uses "deed of trust" and "mortgage" to identify the security interests in real estate of the seller and the bank. While there is a distinction between "deed of trust" and "mortgage," they are both intended as devices to secure the repayment of the loan through an interest in the real property. To avoid confusion, we use the term "mortgage" throughout.]

commitment: "We will notify you of serious delinquencies and provide you the opportunity to make payment before a mortgage foreclosure is started." It was signed on behalf of the Bank by Wayne Martin.

The Buyers executed the document which granted the Seller a second mortgage on the three acres to secure the purchase price for the materials. After receiving that mortgage and the commitment of the Bank, the Seller shipped the materials for the house to the Buyers.

The Buyers partially completed construction of the house, but apparently abandoned the project. By November 1983, the Buyers had become seriously delinquent in payment of the note held by the Bank.

Lee Edwards, who had developed the subdivision in which the three acre tract was located, believed the uncompleted house detracted from the appearance of the subdivision. On November 6, 1985, he bought the note secured by the first deed of trust on the three acres from the bank for $5,125.00, the unpaid balance. On January 3, 1986, Edwards purchased the three acres at the sale foreclosing the first mortgage for $6,000.00. In February 1986, Edwards sold the three acres for $27,500.00.

The Bank did not give the Seller notice the Buyers were delinquent in payment of the Bank's note nor of the foreclosure of the mortgage securing that note. The Seller had no notice of such delinquency or foreclosure sale. If it had been given such notice, it would have protected its second mortgage by buying the note held by the Bank.

The trial court found the Bank's commitment to notify the Seller was supported by consideration. It also found:

> The Court finds that the bank did violate its contractual obligation to Miles by failing to notify Miles of the serious delinquencies and by assigning the note and mortgage to Edwards, thus permitting him to foreclose and buy the property at a fraction of its real value, thereby cutting off Miles' security for its note.

> By deducting the unpaid balance of the Bank's note of $5,125.00 from the February sale price of $27,500.00, the trial court determined Seller's damage to be $22,375.00 and entered judgment for that amount.

The Bank first contends the trial court erred because there was no consideration to support a contractual duty on behalf of the Bank to give the Seller any notice. The Bank points out that the Seller was not obligated to pay the Bank's note or render any other performance to the Bank. It asserts "[T]he agreement was unilateral and lacked consideration for want of mutuality."

The Seller counters with the proposition that consideration may be found in a detriment suffered by a promisee. It points out that the promisee Seller suffered a detriment by shipping the materials to the Buyers. The Seller cites cases holding that detriment may constitute consideration.

However, in relying upon such cases, the Seller overlooks the following fundamental concept of consideration:

> The classic doctrine is that "the promise and the consideration must purport to be the motive each for the other, in whole or at least in part; it is not enough that the promise induces the detriment or that the detriment induces the promise if the other half is wanting."

> Or, to put it another way, to constitute consideration in the classic sense, a promisee must suffer a detriment at the request of the promisor. 1 WILLISTON ON CONTRACTS (3d ed.) § 113. Here, the Bank did not bargain for the Seller to suffer a detriment by shipping the materials. Recovery by the Seller may not be sustained by a determination that such detriment was, in the classic sense, consideration for the Bank's commitment.

> However, that does not mandate reversal. "[T]he judgment must be affirmed if it is sustainable on any theory set forth in the pleadings or supported by the evidence." *Oldham's Farm Sausage Co. v. Salco, Inc.*, 633 S.W.2d 177, 180 (Mo. App. 1982).

> This state has long recognized the doctrine of promissory estoppel. The following is an early expression of that doctrine couched in the terms of consideration.

> The question, then, is, can these notes be enforced, as valid contracts, notwithstanding Sheidley received no benefit therefrom, and intended them as purely gratuitous donations? If so, there must have been a legal consideration moving from the district to him. To constitute such consideration, it is not essential that Sheidley should have derived some benefit from the promise. The consideration will be sufficient to support the promise if the district expended money and incurred enforceable liabilities in reliance thereon.

School Dist. of City of Kansas City v. Sheidley, 138 Mo. 672, 684, 40 S.W. 656, 658 (en banc 1897).

The Supreme Court applied that doctrine in *In re Jamison's Estate*, 202 S.W.2d 879 (Mo. 1947) in which it cited, with approval, Section 90 of the Restatement of Contracts:

> Section 90 of the Restatement of the Law of Contracts states that: "A promise which the promisor should reasonably expect to induce action or forbearance of a definite and substantial character on the part of the promisee and which does induce such action or forbearance is binding if injustice can be avoided only by enforcement of the promise." This doctrine has been described as that of "promissory estoppel." *Feinberg v. Pfeiffer Company*, 322 S.W.2d 163, 167–168 (Mo. App. 1959).

> The Bank had to know the Seller's letter of March 23, 1982, was sent to the Bank for a purpose. The letter stated the Seller had taken a second mortgage on the three acres. It said "We plan to furnish building materials." It requested notice so that "we may take the necessary steps to protect our position." It was obvious the Seller wanted a commitment from the Bank to give the specified notice for that purpose. Since the letter

advised the Bank that the Seller merely "planned" to provide the materials, the Bank should have reasonably known the Seller would carry out that plan only in reliance upon the Bank's commitment to give such notice. Injustice can be avoided only by enforcing the commitment of the Bank.

The Bank argues the Seller suffered no detriment in shipping the materials because it was legally obligated to do so. That argument fails because it ignores paragraph 4 of the contract which provides the Seller could refuse to ship any materials until it received "all required security instruments."

PROBLEM

After his brother died, George was worried about his sister-in-law, Ann and her children, who lived some sixty miles away in a drug-infested neighborhood. George wrote a letter to Ann promising to allow her to live in one of the houses on his estate and encouraging her to give up her small home. The home had little value because of the neighborhood. Ann abandoned her home and moved the sixty miles to live in one of George's comfortable houses with her family during that year. For no apparent reason, George then told her to move to a much smaller and less comfortable house. She remained there for another two years and then was told by George that she would have to vacate the premises and fend for herself and her children. Again, there was no apparent reason for George's change of heart since he had increased his wealth substantially after Ann's arrival, though none of that increase was due to Ann or her family. Was there consideration for George's promise? Can Ann enforce George's promise? For a classic case upon which this problem is based, though it long antedates the modern doctrine of promissory estoppel, see *Kirksey v. Kirksey*, 8 Ala. 131 (1845).

[3] Moral Obligation

If a promise is made in appreciation for a past benefit conferred, is that promise supported by consideration? Suppose a family member promises to pay $50,000 to a relative because of the love and affection shown by that relative over many years, or suppose an employer promises to pay a loyal employee a certain sum after that employee retires for past services. Are either of these promises supported by consideration?

HARRINGTON v. TAYLOR
North Carolina Supreme Court
36 S.E.2d 227 (1945)

Per Curiam.

The plaintiff in this case sought to recover of the defendant upon a promise made by him under the following peculiar circumstances:

> The defendant had assaulted his wife, who took refuge in plaintiff's house. The next day the defendant gained access to the house and began another assault upon his wife. The defendant's wife knocked him down with an axe,

and was on the point of cutting his head open or decapitating him while he was laying on the floor, and the plaintiff intervened, caught the axe as it was descending, and the blow intended for defendant fell upon her hand, mutilating it badly, but saving defendant's life.

Subsequently, defendant orally promised to pay the plaintiff her damages; but, after paying a small sum, failed to pay anything more. So, substantially, states the complaint. The defendant demurred to the complaint as not stating a cause of action, and the demurrer was sustained. Plaintiff appealed.

The question presented is whether there was a consideration recognized by our law as sufficient to support the promise. The Court is of the opinion that however much the defendant should be impelled by common gratitude to alleviate the plaintiff's misfortune, a humanitarian act of this kind, voluntarily performed, is not such consideration as would entitle her to recover at law.

The judgment sustaining the demurrer is *Affirmed.*

NOTES

(1) *"Past Consideration."* When the defendant promised to pay the plaintiff for her injuries, he had already received the benefit of her action and the plaintiff had already suffered the detriment of injury to save the life of the defendant. Thus, the promise did not induce the detriment and the detriment did not induce the promise. There was no "bargained-for-exchange" and, therefore, there was no consideration. Any "consideration" was "past," i.e., already received, and "past" consideration is, therefore, no consideration. Nor is the alternate validation device of promissory estoppel available since the promise of the defendant did not induce the detriment suffered by the plaintiff. Since the promise was not made under *seal*, assuming the continuing effectiveness of the seal in this jurisdiction at the time the promise was made, none of these three validation devices will support the enforcement of the defendant's promise.

When a plaintiff had served a corporation as its president for 12 years, he was told that he would be replaced but would receive a severance payment for his years of service. When the payment was not made, the plaintiff sued, the court stated that past service is not consideration for a promise to make a severance payment. *Rubenstein v. S1 Corporation*, 2005 U.S. Dist. LEXIS 5388 (S.D.N.Y. 2005).

There are historical precedents for enforcing promises made after the promisor had received the benefit. *See, e.g., Riggs v. Bullingham*, Cro. Eliz. 715, 78 Eng. Rep. 949 [1599], but they were based on the evolution of the common law writ of assumpsit before the modern concept of consideration developed. With only isolated exceptions that will be discussed in Chapter 3, a promise for a past benefit received will not be enforceable.

(2) *Moral Obligation.* In the principal case, the court recognizes the "common gratitude" that must be induced by any "humanitarian act" such as that performed by the plaintiff. Though no modern validation device is available to make the

defendant's promise enforceable, why not enforce such promises by recognizing that they are supported by common gratitude or "moral obligation"?

One of the greatest names in the history of Anglo-American law is Lord Mansfield, Chief Justice of King's Bench in England from 1756 to 1788. Trained in the civil law, he imported certain civil law concepts into the developing common law. In *Hawkes v. Saunders*, 1 Cowper 289, 290, 98 Eng. Rep. 1091 [1782], he wrote, "Where a man is under a moral obligation which no Court of Law or Equity can enforce, and promises, the honesty and rectitude of the thing is a consideration." This view survived for some time after Mansfield's death. It was, however, repudiated in England in *Eastwood v. Kenyon*, 11 A. & E. 438 [1840].

With only isolated exceptions that will be reviewed in Chapter 3, the current view of "moral obligation" as a validation device is found in *Manwill v. Oyler*, 11 Utah 2d 433, 361 P.2d 177, 178 (1961):

> "The difficulty we see with the doctrine is that if a mere moral, as distinguished from a legal, obligation were recognized as a valid consideration for a contract, that would practically erode to the vanishing point the necessity for finding a consideration. This is so, first because in nearly all circumstances where a promise is made there is some moral aspect of the situation which provides the motivation for making the promise even if it is to make an outright gift. And second, if we are dealing with the moral concepts, the making of a promise itself creates a moral obligation to perform it. It seems obvious that if a contract to be legally enforceable need be anything other than a naked promise, something more than mere moral consideration is necessary. The principle that in order for a contract to be valid and binding, each party must be bound to give some legal consideration to the other by conferring a benefit upon him or suffering a legal detriment at his request is firmly implanted in the roots of our law."

(3) *Promises to Pay Past Debts Barred by the Statute of Limitations or Discharged in Bankruptcy.* To prevent injustice against stale claims, actions must be commenced within the period allowed by the relevant statute of limitations. As one court rather colorfully suggests, "The purpose of the statute of limitations is to prevent people from sleeping on their rights until evidence is lost or witnesses have forgotten." *Ferris v. Veco, Inc.*, 896 F. Supp. 966, 967 (D. Alaska 1995). In a personal injury tort action, the statute may be only two years from the time of the injury. Statutes of limitations in contract action are longer. In relation to contracts for the sale of goods, the UCC statute of limitations is four years from the time of breach, regardless of the aggrieved party's lack of knowledge of the breach — Section 2-725.

Where an action for breach of contract is "time-barred" by the relevant statute of limitations but the breaching promisor has made a new promise to perform the contract by, for example, paying an amount that is due under the contract, courts will generally enforce such promises on the basis of moral obligation. This rare exception to the general view that moral obligation will not make promises enforceable is based on the fact that the underlying obligation had been precluded by the technical bar of the statute of limitations. The new promise to perform raises the bar of the limitations statute. The uncertainty attending other moral obligations is removed in this situation since the original promise was enforceable at law, typically supported by consideration.

A similar moral obligation rationale had been applied to new promises to pay debts discharged under the Federal Bankruptcy Code (11 U.S.C.). Under the 1978 Bankruptcy Reform Act and 1984 amendments thereto, however, such new promises must now meet several conditions to avoid undue pressure on debtors discharged in bankruptcy. The effect of these changes has substantially diminished the possibility of making such promises enforceable.

Chapter 2

THE AGREEMENT PROCESS

A. INTENTION TO BE LEGALLY BOUND

"A contract has, strictly speaking, nothing to do with the personal, or individual, intent of the parties. A contract is an obligation attached by the mere force of law to certain acts of the parties, usually words, which ordinarily accompany and represent a known intent. If, however, it were proved by twenty bishops that either party, when he used the words, intended something else than the usual meaning which the law imposes upon them, he would still be held, unless there were some mutual mistake, or something else of the sort. Of course, if it appear by other words, or acts, of the parties, that they attribute a peculiar meaning to such words as they use in the contract, that meaning will prevail, but only by virtue of the other words, and not because of their unexpressed intent." Judge L. Hand in *Hotchkiss v. National City Bank*, 200 F. 287, 293 (S.D.N.Y. 1911).

[1] The Objective Theory

LUCY v. ZEHMER
North Carolina Supreme Court
84 S.E.2d 516 (1954)

BUCHANAN. J.,

This suit was instituted by W. O. Lucy and J. C. Lucy, complainants, against A. H. Zehmer and Ida S. Zehmer, his wife, defendants, to have specific performance of a contract by which it was alleged the Zehmers had sold to W. O. Lucy a tract of land owned by A. H. Zehmer in Dinwiddie county containing 471.6 acres, more or less, known as the Ferguson farm, for $50,000. J. C. Lucy, the other complainant, is a brother of W. O. Lucy, to whom W. O. Lucy transferred a half interest in his alleged purchase.

The instrument sought to be enforced was written by A. H. Zehmer on December 20, 1952, in these words: "We hereby agree to sell to W. O. Lucy the Ferguson Farm complete for $50,000.00, title satisfactory to buyer," and signed by the defendants, A. H. Zehmer and Ida S. Zehmer.

The answer of A. H. Zehmer admitted that at the time mentioned W. O. Lucy offered him $50,000 cash for the farm, but that he, Zehmer, considered that the offer was made in jest; that so thinking, and both he and Lucy having had several drinks, he wrote out "the memorandum" quoted above and induced his wife to sign it; that

39

he did not deliver the memorandum to Lucy, but that Lucy picked it up, read it, put it in his pocket, attempted to offer Zehmer $5 to bind the bargain, which Zehmer refused to accept, and realizing for the first time that Lucy was serious, Zehmer assured him that he had no intention of selling the farm and that the whole matter was a joke. Lucy left the premises insisting that he had purchased the farm.

Depositions were taken and the decree appealed from was entered holding that the complainants had failed to establish their right to specific performance, and dismissing their bill. The assignment of error is to this action of the court.

The defendants insist that the evidence was ample to support their contention that the writing sought to be enforced was prepared as a bluff or dare to force Lucy to admit that he did not have $50,000; that the whole matter was a joke; that the writing was not delivered to Lucy and no binding contract was ever made between the parties.

It is an unusual, if not bizarre, defense. When made to the writing admittedly prepared by one of the defendants and signed by both, clear evidence is required to sustain it.

In his testimony Zehmer claimed that he "was high as a Georgia pine," and that the transaction "was just a bunch of two doggoned drunks bluffing to see who could talk the biggest and say the most." That claim is inconsistent with his attempt to testify in great detail as to what was said and what was done. It is contradicted by other evidence as to the condition of both parties, and rendered of no weight by the testimony of his wife that when Lucy left the restaurant she suggested that Zehmer drive him home. The record is convincing that Zehmer was not intoxicated to the extent of being unable to comprehend the nature and consequences of the instrument he executed, and hence that instrument is not to be invalidated on that ground. It was in fact conceded by defendants' counsel in oral argument that under the evidence Zehmer was not too drunk to make a valid contract.

The evidence is convincing also that Zehmer wrote two agreements, the first one beginning "I hereby agree to sell." Zehmer first said he could not remember about that, then that "I don't think I wrote but one out." Mrs. Zehmer said that what he wrote was "I hereby agree," but that the "I" was changed to "We" after that night. The agreement that was written and signed is in the record and indicates no such change. Neither are the mistakes in spelling that Zehmer sought to point out readily apparent.

The appearance of the contract, the fact that it was under discussion for forty minutes or more before it was signed; Lucy's objection to the first draft because it was written in the singular, and he wanted Mrs. Zehmer to sign it also; the rewriting to meet that objection and the signing by Mrs. Zehmer; the discussion of what was to be included in the sale, the provision for the examination of the title, the completeness of the instrument that was executed, the taking possession of it by Lucy with no request or suggestion by either of the defendants that he give it back, are facts which furnish persuasive evidence that the execution of the contract was a serious business transaction rather than a casual, jesting matter as defendants now contend.

If it be assumed, contrary to what we think the evidence shows, that Zehmer was

jesting about selling his farm to Lucy and that the transaction was intended by him
to be a joke, nevertheless the evidence shows that Lucy did not so understand it but
considered it to be a serious business transaction and the contract to be binding on
the Zehmers as well as on himself. The very next day he arranged with his brother
to put up half the money and take a half interest in the land. The day after that he
employed an attorney to examine the title. The next night, Tuesday, he was back at
Zehmer's place and there Zehmer told him for the first time, Lucy said, that he
wasn't going to sell and he told Zehmer, "You know you sold that place fair and
square." After receiving the report from his attorney that the title was good he
wrote to Zehmer that he was ready to close the deal.

[handwritten margin note: everything Lucy did show that he thought it was serious]

Not only did Lucy actually believe, but the evidence shows he was warranted in
believing, that the contract represented a serious business transaction and a good
faith sale and purchase of the farm.

In the field of contracts, as generally elsewhere, "We must look to the outward
expression of a person as manifesting his intention rather than to his secret and
unexpressed intention. 'The law imputes to a person an intention corresponding to
the reasonable meaning of his words and acts.' " *First Nat. Bank v. Roanoke Oil Co.*,
169 Va. 99, 114, 192 S.E. 764, 770.

At no time prior to the execution of the contract had Zehmer indicated to Lucy
by word or act that he was not in earnest about selling the farm. They had argued
about it and discussed its terms, as Zehmer admitted, for a long time. Lucy testified
that if there was any jesting it was about paying $50,000 that night. The contract
and the evidence show that he was not expected to pay the money that night.
Zehmer said that after the writing was signed he laid it down on the counter in front
of Lucy. Lucy said Zehmer handed it to him. In any event there had been what
appeared to be a good faith offer and a good faith acceptance, followed by the
execution and apparent delivery of a written contract. Both said that Lucy put the
writing in his pocket and then offered Zehmer $5 to seal the bargain. Not until then,
even under the defendants' evidence, was anything said or done to indicate that the
matter was a joke. Both of the Zehmers testified that when Zehmer asked his wife
to sign he whispered that it was a joke so Lucy wouldn't hear and that it was not
intended that he should hear.

The mental assent of the parties is not requisite for the formation of a contract.
If the words or other acts of one of the parties have but one reasonable meaning, his
undisclosed intention is immaterial except when an unreasonable meaning which he
attaches to his manifestations is known to the other party. RESTATEMENT OF THE LAW
OF CONTRACTS, VOL. I, § 71, p. 74.

An agreement or mutual assent is of course essential to a valid contract but the
law imputes to a person an intention corresponding to the reasonable meaning of his
words and acts. If his words and acts, judged by a reasonable standard, manifest an
intention to agree, it is immaterial what may be the real but unexpressed state of
his mind. So a person cannot set up that he was merely jesting when his conduct and
words would warrant a reasonable person in believing that he intended a real
agreement.

[handwritten margin note: reasonable standard]

Whether the writing signed by the defendants and now sought to be enforced by the complainants was the result of a serious offer by Lucy and a serious acceptance by the defendants, or was a serious offer by Lucy and an acceptance in secret jest by the defendants, in either event it constituted a binding contract of sale between the parties.

The complainants are entitled to have specific performance of the contracts sued on. The decree appealed from is therefore reversed and the cause is remanded for the entry of a proper decree requiring the defendants to perform the contract in accordance with the prayer of the bill. Reversed and remanded.

NOTES

(1) In their article, *When Money Grew on Trees: Lucy v. Zehmer and Contracting in a Boom Market*, 61 Duke L. J. 1511 (2012) , Barak Richman and Dennis Schmeizer state that Lucy was one of many middlemen seeking valuable timberland for the pulp and paper industry. Lucy sold the land and natural resources for approximately 142,000 which, the authors suggest, casts some doubt on the court's view that 50,000 was a reasonable price.

(2) *Leonard v. Pepsico*, 88 F. Supp. 2d 116 (S.D.N.Y. 1999) arose out of a promotional campaign conducted by Pepsico entitled "Pepsi Stuff" that encouraged consumers to collect "Pepsi Points" from specially marked packages of Pepsi or Diet Pepsi and redeem these points for merchandise featuring the Pepsi logo. To test market the campaign, a television commercial was created and shown in the Pacific Northwest. The commercial opens on a suburban house where a well-coifed teenager prepares to leave for school. The sound of a military drum introduces the subtitle, "MONDAY 7:58 AM." While the teenager confidently preens, the military drumroll again sounds as the subtitle "T-SHIRT 75 PEPSI POINTS" scrolls across the screen. Bursting from his room, the teenager strides down the hallway wearing a leather jacket. The drumroll sounds again, as the subtitle "LEATHER JACKET 1450 PEPSI POINTS" appears. The teenager opens the door of his house and, unfazed by the glare of the early morning sunshine, puts on a pair of sunglasses. The drumroll then accompanies the subtitle "SHADES 175 PEPSI POINTS." A voiceover then intones, "Introducing the new Pepsi Stuff catalog," as the camera focuses on the cover of the catalog. The scene then shifts to three young boys sitting in front of a high school building. The boy in the middle is intent on his Pepsi Stuff Catalog, while the boys on either side are each drinking Pepsi. The three boys gaze in awe at an object rushing overhead, as the military march builds to a crescendo. The observer senses the presence of a mighty plane as the extreme winds generated by its flight create a paper maelstrom in a classroom. Finally, the Harrier Jet swings into view and lands by the side of the school building, next to a bicycle rack. Several students run for cover, and the velocity of the wind strips one hapless faculty member down to his underwear. The teenager opens the cockpit of the fighter and can be seen, helmetless, holding a Pepsi. "Looking very pleased with himself," the teenager exclaims, "Sure beats the bus," and chortles. The military drumroll sounds a final time, as the following words appear: "HARRIER FIGHTER 7,000,000 PEPSI POINTS." A few seconds later, the following appears in more stylized script: "Drink Pepsi — Get Stuff." The commercial ends. [A video of the commercial may be found on youtube by searching under "Leonard v.

Pepsico"] "Pepsi points" could be purchased for 10 cents each. The plaintiff accumulated over 700,000 and demanded a HarrierJet though the Jet did not appear in the Pepsi catalogue merchandise. The court concluded that the plaintiff's understanding of the commercial as an offer must be rejected because the no objective person could reasonably have concluded that the commercial actually offered consumers a Harrier Jet. It recognized that the court must not consider defendant's subjective intent in making the commercial, or plaintiff's subjective view of what the commercial offered, but what an objective, reasonable person would have understood the commercial to convey. *See Kay-R Elec. Corp. v. Stone & Webster Constr. Co.*, 23 F.3d 55, 57 (2d Cir. 1994) ("We are not concerned with what was going through the heads of the parties at the time [of the alleged contract]. Rather, we are talking about the objective principles of contract law."); *Mesaros*, 845 F.2d at 1581 ("A basic rule of contracts holds that whether an offer has been made depends on the objective reasonableness of the alleged offeree's belief that the advertisement or solicitation was intended as an offer."). If it is clear that an offer was not serious, then no offer has been made. What kind of act creates a power of acceptance and is therefore an offer? It must be an expression of will or intention. It must be an act that leads the offeree reasonably to conclude that a power to create a contract is conferred. This applies to the content of the power as well as to the fact of its existence. It is on this ground that we must exclude acts evidently done in jest or without intent to create legal relations. An obvious joke, of course, would not give rise to a contract. On the other hand, if there is no indication that the offer is "evidently in jest," and that an objective, reasonable person would find that the offer was serious, then there may be a valid offer. *See Barnes v. Treece*, 549 P.2d 1152, 1155 ("If the jest is not apparent and a reasonable hearer would believe that an offer was being made, then the speaker risks the formation of a contract which was not intended.").

(3) In *Barnes v. Treece*, 15 Wash. App. 437, 549 P.2d 1152 (1976), the defendant Treece was the Vice-President and half-owner of a company distributing punch-boards, i.e., boards containing small, tightly wrapped pieces of paper, each with a number, which a contestant (for a fee) would "punch" through the board to obtain the paper. The number on the paper may represent the cash amount "won," or it could refer to a chart with prizes. Treece appeared before the Washington State Gambling Commission in support of the legitimacy of punchboards and made the statement, "I'll put a hundred thousand dollars to anyone to find a crooked board. If they find it, I'll pay it." The statement brought laughter from the audience. The next day, Barnes watched a television news report of the proceedings and heard Treece's 100,000 statement. Barnes found two fraudulent punchboards and phoned Treece with this information, asking Treece whether his 100,000 statement had been made seriously. Treece informed Barnes that the statement was serious, that it was firm, and that 100,000 was held safely in escrow. Barnes then produced one of the fraudulent boards for inspection as directed by Treece, and produced the other before another meeting of the Washington Commission. Upon refusal by Treece or his Company to pay Barnes, Barnes brought this action. The court found an objective manifestation of mutual assent because Treece's subsequent statements (after the original statement which drew laughter) would have been understood by a reasonable person in the position of Barnes as serious manifestations of assent to a particular transaction.

(4) "It is a basic legal principle that mutual assent is necessary for the formation of a contract. A significant doctrinal struggle in the development of contract law revolved around whether it was a party's actual or apparent assent that was necessary. This was a struggle between subjective and objective theorists. The subjectivist looked to actual assent. Both parties had to actually assent to an agreement for there to be a contract. External acts were merely necessary evidence to prove or disprove the requisite state of mind. The familiar cliche was that a contract required a 'meeting of the minds' of the parties. The objectivists, on the other looked to apparent assent. The expression of mutual assent, and not the assent itself, was the essential element in the formation of a contract." *Newman v. Schiff*, 778 F.2d 460 (8th Cir. 1985).

[2]   Interpreting Statements to Determine Legal Consequences

We have just seen how courts address arguments that one of the parties to an apparent agreement did not intend legal consequences because he or she was joking or bragging and should not, therefore, have been reasonably understood as intending legal consequences. The objective standard applied in the interpretation of the manifestations of the parties provides the basis for a cogent analysis of these questions.

We now ask, should a party who makes statements that appear to be serious always be understood as intending legal consequences?

BALFOUR v. BALFOUR
King's Bench
2 K.B. 571 (1919)

The plaintiff sued the defendant (her husband) for money which she claimed to be due in respect of an agreed allowance of 30£ a month. The alleged agreement was entered into under the following circumstances. The parties were married in August, 1900. The husband, a civil engineer, had a post under the Government of Ceylon as Director of Irrigation, and after the marriage he and his wife went to Ceylon, and lived there together until the year 1915, except that in 1906 they paid a short visit to this country, and in 1908 the wife came to England in order to undergo an operation, after which she returned to Ceylon. In November, 1915, she came to this country with her husband, who was on leave. They remained in England until August, 1916, when the husband's leave was up and he had to return. The wife however on the doctor's advice remained in England. On August 8, 1916, the husband being about to sail, the alleged parole agreement sued upon was made. The plaintiff, as appeared from the judge's note, gave the following evidence of what took place: "In August, 1916, defendant's leave was up. I was suffering from rheumatic arthritis. The doctor advised my staying in England for some months, not to go out till November 4. On August 8 my husband sailed. He gave me a cheque from 8th to 31st for 24£, and promised to give me 30£ per month till I returned." Later on she said: "My husband and I wrote the figures together on August 8; 34£ shown. Afterwards he said 30£" In cross-examination she said that they had not agreed to live apart until subsequent differences arose between them, and that the agreement of August, 1916, was one which might be made by a couple in amity. Her husband in consultation with her assessed her needs, and said he would send 30£ per month for her maintenance. She further said that she then understood that the defendant would be returning to England in a few months, but that he afterwards wrote to her suggesting that they had better remain apart. In March, 1918, she commenced proceedings for restitution of conjugal rights, and on July 30 she obtained a decree nisi. On December 16, 1918, she obtained an order for alimony.

SARGANT J. held that the husband was under an obligation to support his wife, and the parties had contracted that the extent of that obligation should be defined in terms of so much a month. The consent of the wife to that arrangement was a sufficient consideration to constitute a contract which could be sued upon. He accordingly gave judgment for the plaintiff. The husband appealed.

ATKIN L.J.

The defence to this action on the alleged contract is that the defendant, the husband, entered into no contract with his wife, and for the determination of that it is necessary to remember that there are agreements between parties which do not result in contracts within the meaning of that term in our law. The ordinary example is where two parties agree to take a walk together, or where there is an offer and an acceptance of hospitality. Nobody would suggest in ordinary circumstances that those agreements result in what we know as a contract, and one of the most usual forms of agreement which does not constitute a contract appears to me to be the arrangements which are made between husband and wife. It is quite common, and it is the natural and inevitable result of the relationship of husband and wife, that the two spouses should make arrangements between themselves — agreements such as are in dispute in this action — agreements for allowances, by which the husband agrees that he will pay to his wife a certain sum of money, per week, or per month, or per year, to cover either her own expenses or the necessary expenses of the household and of the children of the marriage, and in which the wife promises either expressly or impliedly to apply the allowance for the purpose for which it is given. To my mind those agreements, or many of them, do not result in contracts at all, and they do not result in contracts even though there may be what as between other parties would constitute consideration for the agreement. The consideration, as we know, may consist either in some right, interest, profit or benefit accruing to one party, or some forbearance, detriment, loss or responsibility given, suffered or undertaken by the other. That is a well-known definition, and it constantly happens, I think, that such arrangements made between husband and wife are arrangements in which there are mutual promises, or in which there is consideration in form within the definition that I have mentioned. Nevertheless they are not contracts, and they are not contracts because the parties did not intend that they should be attended by legal consequences. To my mind it would be of the worst possible example to hold that agreements such as this resulted in legal obligations which could be enforced in the Courts. It would mean this, that when the husband makes his wife a promise to give her an allowance of *30s.* or 2£ a week, whatever he can afford to give her, for the maintenance of the household and children, and she promises so to apply it, not only could she sue him for his failure in any week to supply the allowance, but he could sue her for non-performance of the obligation, express or implied, which she had undertaken upon her part. All I can say is that the small Courts of this country would have to be multiplied one hundredfold if these arrangements were held to result in legal obligations. They are not sued upon, not because the parties are reluctant to enforce their legal rights when the agreement is broken, but because the parties, in the inception of the arrangement, never intended that they should be sued upon. Agreements such as these are outside the realm of contracts altogether.

NOTES

(1) While social and domestic agreements are typically viewed as unenforceable because parties do not contemplate legal consequences arising from such agreements, if family members enter into a business relationship, their agreements are contracts. The line between enforceable and unenforceable domestic agreements may be difficult to draw. In *Shetney v. Shetney*, 49 Wis. 2d 26, 181 N.W.2d 516 (1970), the wife brought an action on an antenuptial contract alleging that she agreed to assist her husband to secure his Ph.D. in exchange for his agreement to assist her in securing hers. The court did not deal with the question of intention of legal consequences since it found the agreement too indefinite to enforce.

(2) An agreement between friends to go duck hunting is not a contract, *Mitzel v. Hauck*, 78 S.D. 543, 105 N.W.2d 378 (1960). If, however, an invitation to an expert at duck hunting were extended with the promise of compensation, a contract results. Similarly, if friends agree to go to dinner, there is no contract, but if an individual is invited to greet or entertain guests for fee, a contract to pay the fee may be found. RESTATEMENT (SECOND) OF CONTRACTS § 21, illustration 5.

GAULT v. SIDEMAN
Illinois Appellate Court
191 N.E.2d 436 (1963)

MCCORMICK, JUSTICE.

The plaintiff, Theodore Gault, filed a suit in the Circuit Court of Cook County against Dr. Sidney Sideman, Dr. Frank Glassman, and Dr. Irving Wolin. [T]he complaint alleged "that in the course of said treatment, the said Defendants advised the Plaintiff that his said condition could be cured by a surgical operation on the spine, and recommended to the Plaintiff that he submit himself to such an operation for the cure of his said condition, and the said Plaintiff relying upon the Defendants' representations that they could alleviate and cure his said condition consented to subjecting himself to the said operation by the said Defendants." . . .

The plaintiff in this court strongly contends that this was an express contract by virtue of which the defendants agreed that they would "cure" the plaintiff by an operation. We are aware that it has been held in other jurisdictions that a physician may make a contract with a patient by an express agreement with the patient to cure, and if such contract is breached an action will lie . . . . However, the courts which lay down such a rule insist that the complaint set out the contract and definitely show the plaintiff's reliance on such contract and on the breach thereof.

Proof of the existence of the contract must be clear. In *Hawkins v. McGee*, 84 N.H. 114, 146 A. 641, an action was brought against a surgeon for the breach of an alleged warranty of the success of an operation. In that case there was testimony that the defendant, in answer to a question as to the length of time the patient would be in the hospital, replied: "Three or four days, not over four; then the boy can go home and it will be just a few days when he will go back to work with a good hand." The court said:

> Clearly this and other testimony to the same effect would not justify a finding that the doctor contracted to complete the hospital treatment in three or four days or that the plaintiff would be able to go back to work within a few days thereafter. The above statements could only be construed as expressions of opinion or predictions as to the probable duration of the treatment and plaintiff's resulting disability, and the fact that these estimates were exceeded would impose no contractual liability upon the defendant.

Under the peculiar facts in that case the court held that a guaranty on the part of the physician to make the hand a "hundred per cent good hand" should be submitted to the jury.

We have been unable to find any case in Illinois which holds that a doctor may be held liable for an agreement made by him with the patient that an operation would cure the condition from which the plaintiff was then suffering. The courts which have held that such a contract is valid and not opposed to public policy have qualified that holding by the imposition of many conditions. *Safian v. Aetna Life Ins. Co.*, 260 App. Div. 765, 24 N.Y.S.2d 92, which held that where a doctor made a contract to effect a cure and fails to do so he is liable for the breach of the contract even though he uses the highest possible professional skill, nevertheless holds that the physician is not covered for such contractual liability by an insurance contract covering claims arising out of "malpractice, error or mistake," and the court said:

> Insurance of such a contract could protect only medical charlatans. The honorable member of the medical profession is more keenly conscious than the rest of us that medicine is not an exact science, and he undertakes only to give his best judgment and skill. He knows he cannot warrant a cure.

In *Stewart v. Rudner*, 349 Mich. 459, 84 N.W.2d 816, the court, after laying down the rule that the physician and patient could contract that the physician would cure, said:

> It is proper to note, with respect to the contracts of physicians, that certain qualitative differences should be observed, since the doctor's therapeutic reassurance that his patient will be all right, not to worry, must not be converted into a binding promise by the disappointed or quarrelsome.

See also the discussion in *Johnston v. Rodis*, D.C., 151 F. Supp. 345, and in 251 F.2d 917, 102 U.S. App. D.C. 209. In the latter case the court said: "Doubtless a physician's statement that he would cure a disease could seldom if ever be regarded as a warranty . . . ."

The application of the ordinary rules dealing with mercantile contracts to a contract entered into between a physician and a patient in our opinion is not justified. The relationship is a peculiar relationship inasmuch as the physician cannot, and should not, so terrify the patient by pointing out to him the manifold dangers which are present at any time the slightest surgical operation is performed. To do so might produce a psychic reaction which would seriously retard the success of the physician's treatment. All of the cases which we have read have this problem in mind, and even in the jurisdictions where it is held that a specific contract of a physician to cure the plaintiff is enforceable, nevertheless the courts have insisted that the contract be clear and specific. Attention has been called by courts to the fact that a promise to cure is not made by a competent and honorable physician and that such a physician knows that he cannot warrant a cure. *Safian v. Aetna Life Ins. Co.*, *supra.* As was said in *Zostautas v. St. Anthony De Padua Hospital*, 23 Ill. 2d 326, 178 N.E.2d 303: "These questions involve not only an interpretation of legal history, but a balance of the legal policies of protecting the public in its dealings with the medical practitioner, and of protecting the practitioner in the pursuit of this highly essential profession from the fraudulent minded."

The plaintiff here contends that the *Zostautas* case supports his position. As a matter of fact it does not. The question involved in that case was as to whether the trial court properly dismissed a certain count of the complaint. In that count it was alleged that the defendant-surgeon entered into an express contract with the plaintiffs to perform a tonsillectomy upon their son "with the degree of care which physicians and surgeons of ordinary skill, care and diligence would exercise under the circumstances, and plaintiffs agreed to pay defendant the reasonable value of his professional services"; that the defendant breached his contract; and that as a result of such breach the son of the plaintiffs died. The court first determined that that count sounded in contract. The count was not a specific agreement to cure, but merely to use ordinary skill in treating the patient, and the court further held that actions of this character may either sound in tort or in contract, and that if a suit was brought under the said contract count by a surviving patient the pleading would have been proper. However, it further holds that because of the provisions of the Wrongful Death Act a common law contract action is not sustainable and the court affirmed the judgment order of the trial court in dismissing the count.

Under the pleadings and evidence in this case the trial court properly directed a verdict for the defendants, and the judgment of the Circuit Court of Cook County in favor of the defendants is *affirmed.*

NOTE

The main case refers to the well-known case of *Hawkins v. McGee*, a 1929 case from the New Hampshire Supreme Court which came to be known as the "hairy hand" case. A family physician was eager to operate on George Hawkins, who, at age eleven, had sustained a burn on his right hand leaving a scar. For three years, Dr. McGee tried to convince George's parents to allow him to operate but they refused. When George turned eighteen, he consented to the operation which Dr. McGee described as simple, effective and quick. As the main case indicates, Dr. McGee also stated that George would be in the hospital for three of four days and within a few days thereafter, he could return to work "with a good hand." The operation failed, worsening the scar and densely covering it with hair. The jury awarded George damages of 3,000. The case was settled for 1,400 plus lawyer's fees. More than six decades later, the same court had occasion to revisit *Hawkins v. McGee*, which it distinguished in *Anglin v. Kleeman*, 140 N.H. 257, 260, 665 A.2d 747, 750 (1995), as the following excerpt indicates.

Whether a contract or warranty of medical services existed is initially a question of law for the trial court to decide. Statements of opinion regarding the result of a medical procedure will not impose contractual liability even if they ultimately prove incorrect. In this case, the plaintiff testified he was told that the "operation could give me a knee that was stronger than . . . before," and that following surgery "if [he] was committed, [he] would be able to play ball again." The language quoted by the plaintiff does not rise to the level required under *Hawkins v. McGee* to allow a finding of a contract or warranty to cure by a physician. Additionally, unlike the doctor in *Hawkins v. McGee*, [the physician in this case,] Dr. Kleeman, did not solicit or request that he be allowed to perform the plaintiff's surgery. In fact, the plaintiff testified that Dr. Kleeman had informed him that he could have another surgeon perform the surgery, and the plaintiff did consult another surgeon prior to agreeing to surgery. The statements attributed to Dr. Kleeman "could only be construed as expressions of opinion or predictions as to the probable duration of the treatment and plaintiffs resulting disability[;] . . . the fact that these estimates were exceeded . . . impose[s] no contractual liability upon the defendant."

[3] Express Statements Concerning Legal Consequences — Letters of Intent

If the parties expressly state that they intend legal consequences to attach to their agreement, should courts always follow this expressed intention? Suppose the parties enter into a wagering agreement or an agreement exclusively for meretricious services with an express provision that they intend to be legally bound? Suppose there is a similar provision in an agreement that has been induced by fraud or duress? What about an agreement between husband and wife living together amicably that would normally be viewed as legally unenforceable but which states that the parties intend legal consequences to attach? While agreements expressly stating that legal consequences attach are rare, agreements expressly stating that legal consequences should not attach (often called "not legally binding" clauses) are not uncommon. The classic exposition of the principle that courts will recognize the parties' intention that the agreement is not legally binding, but binding only "in honor" (a "gentleman's agreement") is *Rose & Frank Co. v. J. B. Crompton Bros.*, [1923] 2 K.B. 251 (C.A.), *rev'd on other grounds*, [1925] A.C. 445, where the agreement provided:

> This agreement is not entered into, nor is this memorandum written, as a formal or legal agreement, and shall not be subject to legal jurisdiction in the Law Court of the United States or England, but it is only a definite expression and record of the purpose and intention of the three parties concerned to which they each honorably pledge themselves with the fullest confidence, based on past business with each other, that it will be carried through by each of the three parties with mutual loyalty and friendly

cooperation. Parties to major transactions such as mergers, acquisitions and long-term contracts find it useful to maintain a record of their negotiations which are often complex. In effect, a record will facilitate the negotiations by recording matters of agreement, avoiding misunderstandings and duplication of effort as parties evolve their tentative agreements toward a final contract. At some point, this record may result in the execution of a "letter of intent" in which both parties agree on certain items of their future agreement. Such a document may manifest a great deal of agreement on many specific terms. The typical letter of intent, however, will merely express the intention of the parties in a continuing negotiation. It will not constitute a binding contract. It will ordinarily include a statement to the effect that neither party is legally bound to the other, e.g., "no liability or obligation of whatsoever nature is intended to be created" by the document. *See Dunhill Securities Corp. v. Microthermal Applications, Inc.*, 308 F. Supp. 195 (1969). Notwithstanding their normal pre-contractual nature, some letters of intent may include certain binding obligations. Moreover, the fact that parties have signed a document captioned, "letter of intent," will not preclude the finding of a contract between them if they manifest their intention to be bound to such a contract.

VENTURE ASSOCIATES CORP. v. ZENITH DATA SYSTEMS CORP.
United States Court of Appeals, Seventh Circuit
96 F.3d 275 (1996)

POSNER, CHIEF JUDGE.

One of the most difficult areas of contract law concerns the enforceability of letters of intent and other preliminary agreements, and in particular the subset of such agreements that consists of agreements to negotiate toward a final contract. When if ever are such agreements enforceable as contracts? If they are enforceable, how is a breach to be determined? Is "breach" even the right word? Or is the proper rubric "bad faith"? Could the duty of good faith negotiation that a letter of intent creates be a tort duty rather than a contract duty, even though created by a contract? And can the victim of bad faith ever get more than his reliance damages? These questions lurk on or just beneath the surface of the principal appeal, which is from a judgment by the district court, after a bench trial, finding that the defendant had not acted in bad faith and was not liable for any damages to the plaintiff. Federal jurisdiction is based on diversity of citizenship, and the substantive issues are governed by Illinois law.

The defendant, Zenith Data Systems Corporation (ZDS), owned Heath Company, the manufacturer of "Heathkits" — do-it-yourself kits for building stereos, computers, and other electronic systems. Heath was losing money, and in 1990 ZDS decided to sell it together with a related subsidiary, Prokit, but we shall generally use "Heath" to denote both Heath and Prokit. ZDS hired an investment banker to find someone who would buy Heath at a price, then estimated at 11 million, at which ZDS would lose no more than 6 million on the sale, the loss being calculated with reference to the net asset value shown for Heath on the books of ZDS. One of the prospects that the investment banker found was the plaintiff, Venture Associates Corporation. Apparently the investment banker did not conduct a credit check of Venture. Instead he relied on a representation by Venture that its most recent acquisitions had been of companies with revenues of 55 and 97 million.

On May 31, 1991, Venture sent a letter to the investment banker, for forwarding to ZDS, proposing to form a new company to acquire Heath for 5 million in cash, a 4 million promissory note, and 2 million in preferred stock of the new company — a total of 11 million, the price ZDS was seeking. The letter stated that it was "merely a letter of intent subject to the execution by Seller and Buyer of a definitive Purchase Agreement (except for the following paragraph of this letter, which shall be binding . . .) [and] does not constitute a binding obligation on either of us." The following paragraph stated that "this letter is intended to evidence the preliminary understandings which we have reached regarding the proposed transaction and our mutual intent to negotiate in good faith to enter into a definitive Purchase Agreement, and [ZDS] hereby agrees that, pending execution of a definitive Purchase Agreement and as long as the parties thereto continue to negotiate in good faith," ZDS shall not "solicit, entertain, or encourage" other offers for Heath or "engage in any transaction not in the ordinary course of business which adversely affects" Heath's value.

The letter invited ZDS to sign it. ZDS refused, but did write Venture on June 11 stating that "we are willing to begin negotiations with Venture Associates for the acquisition of the Heath Business based in principle on the terms and conditions outlined in" Venture's May 31 letter. The next day, Venture wrote ZDS accepting the proposal in the June 11 letter.

Let us pause here and ask what if any enforceable obligations were created by this correspondence. The use of the words "in principle" showed that ZDS had not agreed to any of the terms in Venture's offer. This is the usual force of "in principle" and is the meaning we gave the term in *Skycom Corp. v. Telstar Corp.*, 813 F.2d 810, 814 (7th Cir. 1987). That construal is reinforced by Venture's statement in its letter that the only binding obligation that ZDS's signing the letter would create would be an obligation of both parties to negotiate in good faith and, on ZDS's part, a further obligation not to entertain other offers or strip Heath of its assets — obligations that might be thought in any event entailed by the concept of good faith but which Venture thought useful to spell out. When last this case was before us, on appeal from an earlier decision (812 F. Supp. 788 (N.D. Ill. 1992)) by a different district judge dismissing Venture's suit, we held that the exchange of letters had established a binding agreement to negotiate in good faith toward the formation of a contract of sale.

We therefore have no occasion to revisit the determination on this appeal, though we are mindful of the powerful argument that the parties' undertakings were too vague to be judicially enforceable — since courts are not well equipped to determine whether people are negotiating with each other in good faith. This is the approach taken in some states. But interpreting Illinois law, we have held that agreements to negotiate toward the formation of a contract are themselves enforceable as contracts if the parties intended to be legally bound.

The process of negotiating multimillion dollar transactions, like the performance of a complex commercial contract, often is costly and time-consuming. The parties may want assurance that their investments in time and money and effort will not be wiped out by the other party's footdragging or change of heart or taking advantage of a vulnerable position created by the negotiation. Suppose the prospective buyer spends 100,000 on research, planning, and consultants during the negotiation, money that will have bought nothing of value if the negotiation falls through, while the seller has spent nothing and at the end of the negotiation demands an extra 50,000, threatening to cancel the deal unless the buyer consents. This would be an extortionate demand, and, as it is profoundly unclear whether it would be independently tortious, the parties to a negotiation would want a contractual remedy. But they might prefer to create one in the form of a deposit or drop fee (what in publishing is called a "kill fee") rather than rely on a vague duty to bargain in good faith. That is one reason why the notion of a legally enforceable duty to negotiate in good faith toward the formation of a contract rests on somewhat shaky foundations, though some contracts do create such a duty.

In the prior round of appeals Venture's principal argument, which this court rejected, was that the parties' exchange of nonidentical contract drafts during the negotiation period had created a binding contract on the terms, specifically the 11 million sale price, in Venture's letter of May 31. The argument failed because of the "mirror image" rule;[1] neither party had accepted the terms in the other party's offer. Venture continues to insist that it should be awarded damages equal to the difference between the 11 million price in the letter of May 31 and the current value of Heath (which was sold in 1995 to another purchaser, though we have not discovered at what price). Does this mean that Venture is treating the letter of intent as the contract of sale? It does not. Damages for breach of an agreement to negotiate may be, although they are unlikely to be, the same as the damages for breach of the final contract that the parties would have signed had it not been for the defendant's bad faith. If, quite apart from any bad faith, the negotiations would have broken down, the party led on by the other party's bad faith to persist in futile negotiations can recover only his reliance damages — the expenses he incurred by being misled, in violation of the parties' agreement to negotiate in good faith, into continuing to negotiate futilely. But if the plaintiff can prove that had it not been for the defendant's bad faith the parties would have made a final contract, then the loss of the benefit of the contract is a consequence of the defendant's bad faith, and, provided that it is a foreseeable consequence, the defendant is liable for that loss — liable, that is, for the plaintiff's consequential damages. The difficulty, which may well be insuperable, is that since by hypothesis the parties had not agreed on any of the terms of their contract, it may be impossible to determine what those terms would have been and hence what profit the victim of bad faith would have had. But this goes to the practicality of the remedy, not the principle of it. Bad faith is deliberate misconduct, whereas many breaches of "final" contracts are involuntary — liability for breach of contract being, in general, strict liability. It would be a paradox to place a lower ceiling on damages for bad faith than on damages for a

---

[1] [Ed. Note: The "mirror image" rule is the common law concept that an acceptance of an offer must exactly match the terms of the offer. Otherwise, it is not an acceptance but a counter offer. Later in this chapter, we will see how the "matching acceptance" or "mirror image" rule has been eroded.]

perfectly innocent breach, though a paradox that the practicalities of roof may require the courts in many or even all cases to accept.

After Venture's confirmatory letter of June 12, the parties negotiated for six months. At the end of that time, with no sale contract signed, ZDS broke off the negotiations on the ground that Venture was refusing to furnish third-party guaranties of its post-closing financial obligations (namely to pay the 4 million promissory note and to honor the terms of the preferred stock) and agree to certain post-closing price adjustments. Venture argues that since the letter of intent — its May 31 letter, which ZDS accepted in principle — made no reference to third-party guaranties or contract-price adjustments, ZDS exhibited bad faith by insisting on these terms to the point of impasse. This argument overlooks the difference between an agreement to negotiate a contract and the contract to be thrashed out in those negotiations. The agreement to negotiate does not contain the terms of the final agreement. Otherwise it would be the final agreement. A preliminary agreement might contain closed terms (terms as to which a final agreement had been reached) as well as open terms, and thus be preliminary solely by virtue of having some open terms. The parties would be bound by the closed terms. There were no such terms here.

Venture has another argument — that ZDS decided to pull out after the negotiations began because Heath's fortunes began to improve, and to this end imposed new conditions that it knew Venture would not accept. Since ZDS had not agreed on the sale price, it remained free to demand a higher price in order to reflect the market value of the company at the time of actual sale. Self-interest is not bad faith. Not having locked itself into the 11 million price, ZDS was free to demand as high a price as it thought the market would bear, provided that it was not trying to scuttle the deal or to take advantage of costs sunk by Venture in the negotiating process. The qualification is vital. If the market value of Heath rose, say, to 25 million, ZDS would not be acting in bad faith to demand that amount from Venture even if it knew that Venture would not go so high. ZDS would be acting in bad faith only if its purpose in charging more than Venture would pay was to induce Venture to back out of the deal.

As Venture's financial responsibility was in question, and was an important consideration because this was not a cash purchase, ZDS did not exhibit bad faith in insisting on the protection that a guaranty by a financially responsible third party would provide. Indeed, the investment banker testified that he had raised the question of a guaranty with Venture before the letter agreement. Venture argues that since ZDS did not demand a guaranty in its "in principle" letter, it agreed to do without one. But this argument, if accepted, would turn the agreement to negotiate into an agreement with some closed terms (such as, no guaranties) and some open ones. It would no longer be a simple agreement to negotiate; it would be an agreement to the closed terms plus an agreement to negotiate toward a resolution of the open ones.

A finding of good faith, like a finding of negligence or possession, is treated as a finding of fact, and is therefore reviewed under the deferential "clear error" standard. Venture has made little effort to show clear error. *Affirmed.*

NOTES

(1)   Other cases are in agreement in holding that though a letter of intent may not evidence the ultimate contract toward which the parties have been negotiating, it may evidence a contract to negotiate in good faith. *See Channel Home Centers v. Grossman*, 795 F.2d 291 (3d Cir. 1986); *Teachers Insurance & Annuity Assn. Of America v. Butler*, 626 F. Supp. 1229 (S.D.N.Y. 1986), *appeal dismissed*, 816 F.2d 670 (2d Cir. 1987). An obligation to negotiate in good faith, however, can only arise from a contract albeit, as in the principal case, a contract found in a letter of intent. Absent a contractual obligation, there is no duty to negotiate in good faith since there is no duty to negotiate at all. *See Racine & Laramie, Ltd. v. Department of Parks and Recreation*, 11 Cal. App. 4th 1026, 14 Cal. Rptr. 2d 335 (1992).

(2)   RESTATEMENT (SECOND) OF CONTRACTS § 21, comment b, suggests that parties are free to include "not legally binding" clauses in their agreements, and such clauses are normally enforced. The Comment further suggests, however, that such clauses may raise difficult questions of interpretation, misrepresentation, mistake, or overreaching, i.e., unconscionability, a concept discussed later in the course.

[4]   Contemplation of Final Writing

ARNOLD PALMER GOLF CO. v. FUQUA INDUSTRIES
United States Court of Appeals, Sixth Circuit
541 F.2d 584 (1976)

McCREE, CIRCUIT JUDGE.

Arnold Palmer Golf Company (Palmer) was incorporated under Ohio law in 1961, and has been primarily engaged in designing and marketing various lines of golf clubs, balls, bags, gloves, and other golf accessories. Palmer did none of its own manufacturing, but engaged other companies to produce its products. In the late 1960's, Palmer's management concluded that it was essential for future growth and profitability to acquire manufacturing facilities.

To that end, in January, 1969, Mark McCormack, Palmer's Executive Vice-President, and E.D. Kenna, Fuqua's President, met in New York City to consider a possible business relationship between the two corporations. The parties' interest in establishing a business relationship continued and they held several more meetings and discussions where the general outline of the proposed relationship was defined. In November 1969, Fuqua, with Palmer's assistance and approval, acquired Fernquest and Johnson, a California manufacturer of golf clubs. The minutes of the Fuqua Board of Directors meeting on November 3, 1969, reveal that Fuqua:

> proposed that this Corporation participate in the golf equipment industry in association with Arnold Palmer Golf Co. and Arnold Palmer Enterprises, Inc. The business would be conducted in two parts. One part would be composed of a corporation engaged in the manufacture and sale of golf clubs and equipment directly related to the playing of the game of golf. This Corporation would be owned to the extent of 25% by Fuqua and 75% by the

Arnold Palmer interests. Fuqua would transfer the Fernquest & Johnson business to the new corporation as Fuqua's contribution.

In November and December of 1969 further discussions and negotiations occurred and revised drafts of a memorandum of intent were distributed.

The culmination of the discussions was a six page document denominated as a Memorandum of Intent. It provided in the first paragraph that:

> This memorandum will serve to confirm the general understanding which has been reached regarding the acquisition of 25% of the stock of Arnold Palmer Golf Company ("Palmer") by Fuqua Industries, Inc. ("Fuqua") in exchange for all of the outstanding stock of Fernquest and Johnson Golf Company, Inc. ("F & J"), a wholly-owned California subsidiary of Fuqua, and money in the amount of 700,000; and for the rendition of management services by Fuqua.

The Memorandum of Intent contained detailed statements concerning, *inter alia*, the form of the combination, the manner in which the business would be conducted, the loans that Fuqua agreed to make to Palmer, and the warranties and covenants to be contained in the definitive agreement.

Paragraph 10 of the Memorandum of Intent stated:

> (10) Preparation of Definitive Agreement. Counsel for Palmer and counsel for Fuqua will proceed as promptly as possible to prepare an agreement acceptable to Palmer and Fuqua for the proposed combination of businesses. Such agreement will contain the representations, warranties, covenants and conditions, as generally outlined in the example submitted by Fuqua to Palmer . . . .

In the last paragraph of the Memorandum of Intent, the parties indicated that:

> (11) Conditions. The obligations of Palmer and Fuqua shall be subject to fulfillment of the following conditions:
>
> > (i) preparation of the definitive agreement for the proposed combination in form and content satisfactory to both parties and their respective counsel;
> >
> > (ii) approval of such definitive agreement by the Board of Directors of Fuqua; . . . .

The Memorandum of Intent was signed by Palmer and by the President of Fuqua. Fuqua had earlier released a statement to the press upon Palmer's signing that "Fuqua Industries, Inc., and The Arnold Palmer Golf Co. have agreed to cooperate in an enterprise that will serve the golfing industry, from the golfer to the greens keeper."

In February, 1970, the Chairman of Fuqua's Board of Directors, J.B. Fuqua, told Douglas Kenna, Fuqua's President, that he did not want to go through with the Palmer deal. Shortly thereafter Kenna informed one of Palmer's corporate officers that the transaction was terminated.

Palmer filed the complaint in this case on July 24, 1970. Nearly three and one-half years later, on January 14, 1974, the defendant filed a motion for summary judgment. More than one year after the briefs had been filed by the parties, on May 30, 1975, the district court granted defendant's motion.

The district court determined that:

> The parties were not to be subject to any obligations until a definitive agreement satisfactory to the parties and their counsel had been prepared. The fact that this agreement had to be "satisfactory" implies necessarily that such an agreement might be unsatisfactory . . . . The parties by the terms they used elected not to be bound by this memorandum and the Court finds that they were not bound.

issue

The primary issue in this case is whether the parties intended to enter into a binding agreement when they signed the Memorandum of Intent, and the primary issue in this appeal is whether the district court erred in determining this question on a motion for summary judgment. The substantive law of Ohio applies.

holding

We agree with the district court that both parties must have a clear understanding of the terms of an agreement and an intention to be bound by its terms before an enforceable contract is created. As Professor Corbin has observed:

intent

> The courts are quite agreed upon general principles. The parties have power to contract as they please. They can bind themselves orally or by informal letters or telegrams if they like. On the other hand, they can maintain complete immunity from all obligation, even though they have expressed agreement orally or informally upon every detail of a complex transaction. The matter is merely one of expressed intention. If their expressions convince the court that they intended to be bound without a formal document, their contract is consummated, and the expected formal document will be nothing more than a memorial of that contract. 1 CORBIN ON CONTRACTS § 30.

Section 26 of the Restatement of Contracts states the general rule that Ohio follows:

> Mutual manifestations of assent that are in themselves sufficient to make a contract will not be prevented from so operating by the mere fact that the parties also manifest an intention to prepare and adopt a written memorial thereof; but other facts may show that the manifestations are merely preliminary expressions as stated in Section 25.

Comment to Section 26 of the Restatement explains the considerations that enter into a determination whether a binding contract exists:

reasoning

> Parties who plan to make a final written instrument as the expression of their contract, necessarily discuss the proposed terms of the contract before they enter into it and often, before the final writing is made, agree upon all the terms which they plan to incorporate therein. This they may do orally or by exchange of several writings. It is possible thus to make a contract to execute subsequently a final writing which shall contain certain provisions. If parties have definitely agreed that they will do so, and that the final writing shall contain these provisions and no others, they have

then fulfilled all the requisites for the formation of a contract. On the other hand, if the preliminary agreement is incomplete, it being apparent that the determination of certain details is deferred until the writing is made out; or if an intention is manifested in any way that legal obligations between the parties shall be deferred until the writing is made, the preliminary negotiations and agreements do not constitute a contract.

The decision whether the parties intended to enter a contract must be based upon an evaluation of the circumstances surrounding the parties' discussions. The greatest latitude should be given in developing the surrounding situations and conditions attending the negotiations for the consummation of a contract, and the language employed in a contract should be construed in the light of circumstances surrounding the contracting parties at the time. Circumstantial evidence is as competent to prove a contract as it is to prove a crime.

At bottom, the question whether the parties intended a contract is a factual one, not a legal one, and, except in the clearest cases, the question is for the finder of fact to resolve.

In a Third Circuit opinion, *Melo-Sonics Corp. v. Cropp*, 342 F.2d 856 (1965), the court reversed a district court's judgment in favor of defendants on a motion to dismiss a complaint. The plaintiffs contended that they had a contract with defendants which the latter had breached. Plaintiffs relied on a telegram they sent to defendants, and defendants' subsequent acceptance, as constituting a contractual agreement. The telegram provided in pertinent part:

> My three clients are willing to sell their capital stock in said corporations for the total price of one million five hundred thousand (1,500,000) dollars subject to formalizing a preliminary agreement along lines previously discussed. Will be in your office at 10:00 AM on February 15, 1960 with my clients for purpose of formalizing such an agreement. 342 F.2d at 858.

The defendants eventually notified plaintiffs that they would not sign the agreement, whereupon plaintiffs filed suit.

The reviewing court pointed out that it would be permissible for the district court to make a finding of fact that no contract existed after it had conducted a full hearing, but that where no trial had been conducted and no findings of fact had been made it was improper to grant the defendants' motion to dismiss because plaintiff's claim, if proved, entitled him to recovery.

Considering this appeal in the light of these authorities, we determine that our proper course is to remand this case to the district court for trial because we believe that the issue of the parties' intention to be bound is a proper one for resolution by the trier of fact. Upon first blush it may appear that the Memorandum of Intent is no more than preliminary negotiation between the parties. A cursory reading of the conditions contained in paragraph 11, by themselves, may suggest that the parties did not intend to be bound by the Memorandum of Intent.

Nevertheless, the memorandum recited that a "general understanding [had] been reached." [T]he entire document and relevant circumstances surrounding its adoption must be considered in making a determination of the parties' intention.[2] In this case we find an extensive document that appears to reflect all essential terms concerning the transfer of Arnold Palmer stock to Fuqua in exchange for all outstanding stock in Fernquist and Johnson. The form of combination, the location of the principal office of Palmer, the license rights, employment contracts of Palmer personnel and the financial obligations of Fuqua are a few of the many areas covered in the Memorandum of Intent, and they are all described in unqualified terms. The Memorandum states, for instance, that "Fuqua *will* transfer all of the . . . stock," that the "principal office of Palmer *will* be moved to Atlanta," that "Palmer . . . *shall* possess an exclusive license," and that "Fuqua *agrees* to advance to Palmer up to an aggregate of 700,000 . . . ." [Emphasis added.]

Paragraph 10 of the Memorandum states, also in unqualified language, that counsel for the parties "will proceed as promptly as possible to prepare an agreement acceptable to [the parties] . . . ." We believe that this paragraph may be read merely to impose an obligation upon the parties to memorialize their agreement. We do not mean to suggest that this is the correct interpretation. The provision is also susceptible to an interpretation that the parties did not intend to be bound.

[I]t is permissible to refer to extrinsic evidence to determine whether the parties intended to be bound by the Memorandum of Intent. In this regard, we observe that Fuqua circulated a press release in January 1970 that would tend to sustain Palmer's claim that the two parties intended to be bound by the Memorandum of Intent. Fuqua's statement said that the two companies "have agreed to cooperate in an enterprise that will serve the golfing industry."

Upon a review of the evidence submitted in connection with the motion for summary judgment, we believe that there is presented a factual issue whether the parties contractually obligated themselves to prepare a definitive agreement in accordance with the understanding of the parties contained in the Memorandum of Intent. [W]e believe that the parties may properly "disagree about the inferences to be drawn from [the basic facts that are not in dispute or] what the intention of the parties was as shown by the facts." 315 F.2d at 237. Because the facts and the inferences from the facts in this case indicate that the parties may have intended to be bound by the Memorandum of Intent, we hold that the district court erred in determining that no contract existed as a matter of law.

We reject appellee's argument that summary judgment was appropriate because the obligations of the parties were subject to an express condition that was not met. We believe a question of fact is presented whether the parties intended the conditions in paragraph 11 to operate only if the definitive agreement was not in conformity with the general understanding contained in the Memorandum of Intent. The parties may well have intended that there should be no binding obligation until the definitive agreement was signed, but we regard this question as one for the fact finder to determine after a consideration of the relevant evidence.

---

[2] [3] Parties may orally or by informal memoranda, or by both, agree upon all essential terms of the contract and effectively bind themselves, if that is their intention, even though they contemplate the execution, at a later time, of a formal document to memorialize their undertaking. Comerata v. Chaumont, Inc., 145 A.2d 471 (Super. Ct. App. Div. N.J. 1958).

Accordingly, the judgment of the district court is reversed and the case is remanded for proceedings not inconsistent with this opinion.

NOTES

(1)   The question of intention to be legally bound arose in the much publicized dispute between the Texaco Corporation and the Pennzoil Company. Pennzoil made several attempts to take control of the Getty Oil Co. Its final attempt resulted in an "agreement in principle" for the merger of Getty Oil and a new entity to be owned jointly by Pennzoil and Gordon B. Getty as trustee of a family trust and a charitable trust. While lawyers worked on the implementation of that plan, Getty's representatives were negotiating another arrangement with Texaco Corporation. Shortly thereafter, it was announced that Getty would be acquired by Texaco. After unsuccessful attempts to enjoin this merger, Pennzoil brought an action in a Texas court on a theory of tortious interference with Pennzoil's contract rights under its contract with Getty. The critical question was whether the "agreement in principle" was intended to be a binding agreement before all of the implementing details were effectuated. The jury found that the "agreement in principle" was intended to be binding and awarded Pennzoil what has been called the largest civil judgment in history, 11,120,976,110.83, including 3 billion in punitive damages and prejudgment interest. On appeal, the court affirmed the trial court judgment but remitted 2 billion of the punitive damages award. *Texaco, Inc. v. Pennzoil Co.*, 729 S.W.2d 768 (1987). A subsequent attack on the constitutionality of the Texas proceedings failed. *See Pennzoil v. Texaco*, 481 U.S. 1, 107 S. Ct. 1519, 95 L. Ed. 2d 1 (1987).

(2)   In *Lambert Corp. v. Evans*, 575 F.2d 132 (7th Cir. 1978), the parties exchanged correspondence concerning the acquisition of a particular line of products owned by the plaintiff. The defendant's vice president visited plaintiff for an entire day, discussing the proposed acquisition. This was followed by further correspondence and, later, by a telephone conversation in which the parties congratulated each other on having reached an agreement though they contemplated the later execution of a formal document. Defendant argued that the parties were not bound by the telephone agreement since a more extensive review of the product line and related matters by engineers, accountants and lawyers would be appropriate in such an acquisition. The court rejected this argument on the footing that a sensible businessman would not engage in such a costly review for an acquisition valued at only 20,000. Moreover, the defendant had not followed such procedures in prior small acquisitions. Contrast this analysis with the analysis in the principal case.

(3)   Courts generally agree that the issue of whether parties are bound prior to the execution of a formal document that would serve as evidence of a prior contract, or whether they are not bound until such a final document is executed, is a question of intention. *See Courtin v. Sharp*, 280 F.2d 345 (5th Cir. 1960). Moreover, as one court suggests in following the views of the contract giants, Professors Williston and Corbin, "The emphasis of these two eminent writers is, it seems to us, inclined toward finding the formation of a contract prior to the signing of the document unless the parties pretty clearly show that such signing is a condition precedent to legal obligation." *Smith v. Onyx Oil & Chem. Corp.*, 218 F.2d 104, 108 (3d Cir. 1955).

See MURRAY ON CONTRACTS, *supra* Chapter 1, note 1, at § 33 (5th ed. 2011).

[5] "Agreements to Agree" — Missing Terms

If negotiating parties agree that they will later agree upon certain terms, particularly important (material) terms, the traditional view was that such an "agreement to agree" amounted to nothing in the eyes of the law for the pragmatic reason that courts would not be able to determine what the negotiations would have produced and, therefore, would be unable to determine what damages, if any, were attributable to a breach by one of the parties. *See Shepard v. Carpenter*, 54 Minn. 153, 55 N.W. 906 (1893). Indeed, for many years, a so-called "agreement to agree" was viewed as a contradiction in terms. *Ridgway v. Wharton*, 6 Clark's H.L. Cases 238, 306 (1857). This strict position has been substantially modified in modern contract law.

ARBITRON, INC. v. TRALYN BROADCASTING, INC.
United States Court of Appeals, Second Circuit
400 F.3d 130 (2005)

CALABRESI, J.

Arbitron licenses its copyrighted listener data to regional AM and FM stations, which then use the demographic profiles of station listeners to attract advertisers. In 1997, Arbitron entered into one such license with defendant Tralyn Broadcasting, Inc., a Mississippi corporation. The License Agreement permitted Tralyn's only radio station [WLNF-FM] to use Arbitron listening data reports. Over its five-year term, the License Agreement charged Tralyn a monthly rate of 1,729.57 for the use of Arbitron's listening data reports by this single station.

Pursuant to [an] "escalation clause," Arbitron was given the right to increase the license fee as Tralyn purchased additional stations (or as entities owning additional stations purchased Tralyn). Thus, the escalation clause assumed that, as Tralyn acquired additional regional stations, it would share listener data among each of these stations, and, by allowing Arbitron to increase Tralyn's fees, the clause provided Arbitron with a mechanism to reflect this additional use.

On October 31, 1999, Tralyn was purchased by defendant JMD, Inc. [which] controlled at least four other stations in the Gulfport, Mississippi market. The purchase agreement between JMD and Tralyn assigned to IMD the License Agreement; JMD thereby assumed responsibility for paying Arbitron, and implicitly, for notifying Arbitron of the additional radio stations now operated by Tralyn's successor. But in violation of Paragraph 11 of the License Agreement, neither JMD nor Tralyn provided Arbitron with notice of a change in ownership of WLNF-FM. Instead, from November 1999 until June 2002, JIMD simply paid the original single-station monthly license fee (1,729.57) directly to Arbitron. In return, Arbitron provided WLNF-FM with updated listening data.

In June 2000, Arbitron discovered that JMD had purchased Tralyn and that the terms of the License Agreement had been breached. Arbitron notified JMD by letter that it was exercising its right to increase the monthly licensing fee under the escalation clause of the License Agreement. Arbitron determined JMD's new annual license fee by multiplying the single-station license fee (1,779.57) by five (8,897.85) to reflect the five JMD stations that could now share Arbitron's listener data. It then reduced that figure by 35% to reflect the typical volume discount for licenses covering five or more stations. The result was a revised monthly charge of 5,784.93. Based on this new licensing fee, which Arbitron claimed should have been paid since the October 1999 purchase, Arbitron sent JMD an invoice for "incomplete" payments made between October 1999 and June 2000. JMD never paid these invoices, and subsequently refused to pay anything — even the 1,779.57 due each month under the original one-station License Agreement. Arbitron therefore stopped sending JMD its listening data reports, as it was permitted to do under the License Agreement upon the licensee's nonpayment of the monthly licensing fee.

Arbitron filed the instant suit against Tralyn and JMD on November 1, 2001. Its complaint for breach of contract sought 172,394.22, representing all moneys due under the Licensing Agreement (plus interest) from June 1999 to the end of the contract's five-year term. The district court concluded that because "neither the escalation clause nor any other section of the Agreement, contains any basis for determining the new rate to be paid Arbitron in the event changes in ownership occur," the License Agreement's escalation clause was unenforceably vague under New York law and therefore awarded summary judgment to JMD. Arbitron challenges the district court's decision.

We conclude that the License Agreement's escalation clause is indeed enforceable under the common law of New York. The escalation clause . . . does not require the parties to reach an "agreement" on price at some point in the future. That is, the escalation clause is not an "agreement to agree." Instead . . . it is a mechanism for objectively setting material terms in the future without further negotiations between both parties.

The intent of the parties is manifest in the language of the agreement. Both Arbitron and Tralyn explicitly agreed that Arbitron was authorized to adjust the license fee in the event that Tralyn or its successors began to operate additional stations. This fact makes the instant case very different from those disputes in which courts are faced with "no objective evidence" of a shared intent to permit one party to set prices in the future. And it in no way leads a court enforcing the contract to "impose its own conception of what the parties should or might have undertaken." Accordingly, we conclude that the district court erred in holding the License Agreement's escalation clause "impenetrably vague" under New York law.

In reaching this conclusion, we note that [u]nder New York's implementation of the Uniform Commercial Code, there is a strong presumption that agreements are enforceable even if their price terms are not definite. N.Y. U.C.C. § 2-305 provides that:

> (1) The parties *if they so intend* can conclude a contract for sale even though the price is not settled. In such a case the price is a reasonable price at the time for delivery if (a) nothing is said as to price; or (b) the price is left to be agreed by the parties and they fail to agree; or (c) the price is to be fixed in terms of some agreed market or other standard as set or recorded by a third person or agency and it is not so set or recorded.

(2) *A price to be fixed by the seller or by the buyer means a price for him to fix in good faith.* (Emphases added.)

The commentary to this section of New York's commercial code makes clear that "this Article rejects in these instances the formula that 'an agreement to agree is unenforceable' . . . and rejects also defeating such agreements on the ground of 'indefiniteness.' Instead this Article recognizes the dominant intention of the parties to have the deal continue to be binding upon both." *See also* U.C.C. § 2-204(3) ("Even though one or more terms are left open a contract for sale [of goods] does not fail for indefiniteness if the parties have intended to make a contract and there is a reasonably certain basis for giving an appropriate remedy.").

It is not clear whether, under New York law, a license agreement of the sort at issue in this case constitutes a contract for the sale of goods, or is otherwise governed by the U.C.C. We note, however, that were this section of New York's commercial code applied to the License Agreement, the escalation clause would undoubtedly be a valid contract term under New York law; it would simply establish "[a] price to be fixed by the seller," and would be enforceable so long as that price was fixed "in good faith." N.Y. U.C.C. § 2-305. But the applicability of the U.C.C. to the license agreement before is not something we need to decide today.

We conclude that the district court erred in granting summary judgment to JMD. We therefore vacate the district court's order and remand the case for further proceedings On remand, the district court may wish to consider whether Arbitron has exercised its authority under the escalation clause in "good faith" within the meaning of N.Y. U.C.C. § 2-305 (which, as we have previously noted, may or may not apply to a "license" of this sort), or more generally, in a manner consistent with Arbitron's implied duty of fair dealing under New York law.

NOTES

(1) *Gap Fillers.* The court quotes § 2-204(3) of the Uniform Commercial Code, which is the general formation section that liberalized contract formation concepts of the common law. Section 2-204(1) allows a contract for the sale of goods to be made "in any reasonable manner sufficient to show agreement." Section 2-204(2) addresses the issue of whether a contract maybe recognized even though the precise moment of its making is not determinable. Section 2-204(3) provides a general rule that a contract does not fail for indefiniteness because one or more terms are left open if there is a manifested intention to make a contract and there is a reasonably certain basis for a court to afford a remedy. There are several specific UCC sections elaborating this general principle that are often referred to as "gap filling" terms. Thus, in addition to Section 2-305, discussed in the principal case, that allows the parties to make a contract even though the price term is missing, where there is no specification in the agreement as to whether goods should be delivered in a single shipment or in installment shipments, Section 2-307 fills this gap by directing that a single delivery is required unless circumstances indicate the contrary. Section 2-308 provides the place of delivery where the agreement is silent on that term. The general rule is that place of delivery will be the seller's place of business from which the seller would normally ship the goods via an independent carrier. If the goods are in another place at the time of contracting,

the place of delivery would be the location of the goods. Section 2-309 fills the gap where the party have not specified the time for delivery of the goods — a reasonable time. If the time for payment is not specified in the agreement, Section 2-310 provides the presumption that payment is due at the time and place the buyer is to receive the goods. Often, the contract will allow a certain time for payment, but in the absence of such a provision, again, the buyer must pay for the goods upon their delivery to the buyer. Each of these "gap-fillers" recognizes that parties do not always express themselves comprehensively when they make a contract. If, however, they intend to be bound and a court can discover a reasonable basis for affording a remedy, their agreement should be recognized as a contract.

(2)   Where a buyer of a truck paid a 120 deposit and signed a "work sheet" describing the truck as a new green or yellow 1974, 3/4 ton, 4-wheel drive vehicle with a radio, V-8 engine and an automatic transmission at a price of 3,650, the seller claimed that the failure of the writing to state the specific shade of green or yellow or to specify other items such as the specific engine size, the box size and style made the agreement fatally indefinite. Relying on UCC Section 2-204, the court stated: "That some terms are undetermined does not defeat the existence of a contract provided that the parties intended to make a contract and there is a reasonably certain basis for a remedy." The court found a contract and remanded the case to the trial court to determine any omitted items in the original written agreement. *Paloukos v. Intermountain Chevrolet Co.*, 99 Idaho 740, 743, 588 P.2d 939, 942 (1978).

(3)   Spartan's contract with producers of chickens and eggs required the buyers to use only Spartan feed in exchange for Spartan's promise to purchase all eggs they produced and arrange for them to be hatched. The contract did not specify a price. Under UCC Section 2-305, the price had to be a reasonable price. The producers claimed that Spartan's price was unreasonable based on evidence that other feed suppliers' prices were lower. The other feed suppliers, however, did not promise to take all of the producers' eggs for hatching. While one other supplier did provide a program similar to Spartan's program, the producers failed to present evidence of that supplier's prices. The court held that Spartan's prices were not unreasonable. *Spartan Grain & Mill Co. v. Ayers*, 517 F.2d 214 (5th Cir. 1975).

PROBLEM

Brattrud contracted to purchase specific quantities of different brands of petroleum products from Willhelm: 5,000 gallons of Worthmore Motor Oil, 3,000 gallons of Beterlube Motor Oil and 2,000 gallons of Costal Motor Oil. The contract specified that each of these brands could be purchased in any viscosity (weight) from SAE 10 to SAB 70. The price would depend upon the weight the buyer chose. When Willhelm asked Brattrud to choose the viscosities of each brand so that shipment could proceed, Brattrud declined to specify the SAB number and informed Willhelm that the contract was cancelled. The problem is based on *Willhelm Lubrication v. Brattrud*, 197 Minn. 626, 634 (1936), decided decades before the Uniform Commercial Code was enacted in any jurisdiction. Consider the effect of the UCC on the same case today. Specifically, consider UCC § 2-311.

B. THE ANATOMY OF AGREEMENTS — OFFER AND ACCEPTANCE

[1] Preliminary Negotiations Versus Offers

SOUTHWORTH v. OLIVER
Oregon Supreme Court
587 P.2d 994 (1978)

TONGUE, JUSTICE.

This is a suit in equity for a declaratory judgment that defendants "are obligated to sell" to plaintiff 2,933 acres of ranch lands in Grant County. Defendants appeal from a decree of specific performance in favor of plaintiff. We affirm.

Defendants contend on this appeal that a certain "writing" mailed by them to plaintiff was not an offer to sell such lands; that if it was an offer there was no proper acceptance of that offer and that any such offer and acceptance did not constitute a binding contract, at least so as to be specifically enforceable. Defendants also filed a demurrer in this court upon the ground that it appears from the face of plaintiff's complaint that the alleged agreement to sell such lands was void as in violation of the statute of frauds.

The parties and the property.

Defendants are ranchers in Grant County and owned ranches in both the Bear Valley area and also in the John Day valley. In 1976 defendants came to the conclusion that they should "cut the operation down" and sell some of the Bear Valley property, as well as some of their Forest Service grazing permits. Defendant Joseph Oliver discussed this matter with his wife, defendant Arlene Oliver, and also with his son, and the three of them "jointly arrived" at a decision to sell a portion of the Bear Valley property. Joseph Oliver also conferred with his accountant and attorney and, as a result, it was decided that the sale "had to be on terms" rather than cash, for income tax reasons. Defendant Joseph Oliver then had "a discussion with Mr. Southworth [the plaintiff] about the possibility of . . . selling this Bear Valley property." Plaintiff Southworth was also a cattle rancher in Bear Valley. The land which defendants had decided to sell was adjacent to land owned by him and was property that he had always wanted.

The initial meeting between the parties on May 20, 1976.

According to plaintiff, defendant Joseph Oliver stopped by his ranch on May 20, 1976, and said that he [Oliver] was interested in "selling the ranch" and asked "would I be interested in buying it, and I said 'yes'." Mr. Southworth also testified that "he thought I would be interested in the land and that Clyde [Holliday, also a neighbor] would be interested in the permits" and that "I told him that I was very interested in the land . . . ."

Plaintiff Southworth also testified that at that time defendant Oliver showed him a map, showing land that he "understood them to offer for sale"; that there was no discussion at that time of price or terms of sale, or whether the sale of the land was contingent on sale of any of the permits, but that the conversation terminated with the understanding:

> "That he would develop and determine value and price and I would make an investigation to determine whether or not I could find the money and get everything arranged for a purchase. In other words, he was going to do A and then I would B."

According to plaintiff Southworth, defendant Oliver said that when he determined the value of the property he would send that information to Southworth so as to give him "notice" of "what he wanted for the land," but did not say that he was also going to give that same information to Mr. Holliday, although he did say that "he planned to talk to Clyde [Holliday] about permits," with the result that plaintiff knew that Oliver "might very well be . . . talking to Clyde about the same thing he talked to you [plaintiff] about" and "give that information to Clyde Holliday as well as yourself."

According to defendant Joseph Oliver, the substance of that initial conversation with plaintiff was as follows:

> I told him we were going to condense our ranch down and sell some property and that we were in the process of trying to get some figures from the Assessor on it to determine what we wanted to sell and what we might want to do. Whenever we got this information together we were going to send it to him and some of my neighbors and give them first chance at it.

Mr. Oliver also testified that plaintiff said that "he was interested"; that he had a map with him; that he mentioned to plaintiff that he "was going to sell some permits," but that there was no discussion "about the permits going with the land at that time" and that he [Oliver] "talked along the lines that Clyde [Holliday] would probably be interested in those permits." On cross-examination Mr. Oliver also answered in the affirmative a question to the effect that the property which he and Mr. Southworth "delineated on the map" during that conversation "was the property" that he "finally decided to sell and made the general offering to the four neighbors."

Plaintiff also testified that on May 26, 1976, he called Clyde Holliday to ask if he was interested in buying the land and Mr. Holliday said "no," that he was interested only in the permits, but would be interested in trading some other land for some of the land plaintiff was buying from defendants.

The telephone call of June 13, 1976.

Plaintiff testified that on June 13, 1976, he called defendant Oliver by telephone to "ask him if his plans for selling . . . continued to be in force, and he said 'yes,'" that "he was progressing and there had been some delay in acquiring information from the Assessor, but they expected soon to have the information needed to establish the value on the land." Defendant Oliver's testimony was to the same effect, but he also recalled that at that time Mr. Southworth "said everything was in order and that I didn't have to worry, he had the money available and that everything was ready to go."

The letters of June 17, June 21, and June 24, 1976.

Several days later plaintiff received from defendants a letter dated June 17, 1976, as follows:

> "Enclosed please find the information about the ranch sales that I had discussed with you previously. These prices are the market value according to the records of the Grant County Assessor. Please contact me if there are any questions."

There were two enclosures with that letter. The first was as follows:

JOSEPH C. and ARLENE G. OLIVER
200 Ford Road
John Day, OR 97845

Selling approximately 2933 Acres in Grant County in T. 16 S., R. 31 E., W.M. near Seneca, Oregon at the assessed market value of:

LAND 306,409
IMPROVEMENTS 18,010
Total 324,419

Terms available — 29% down — balance over 5 years at 8% interest. Negotiate sale date for December 1, 1976 or January 1, 1977. Available after hay is harvested and arrangements made for removal of hay, equipment and supplies.

ALSO: Selling

Little Bear Creek allotment permit — 1000 head at 225
"Big Bear Creek allotment permit — 200 head at 250

The second enclosure related to "selling approximately 6365 acres" in Grant County near John Day — another ranch owned by the Oliver family.

Defendant Joseph Oliver testified that this letter and enclosures were "drafted" by his wife, defendant Arlene Oliver; that he then read and signed it; that he sent it not only to plaintiff, but also to Clyde Holliday and two other neighbors; that it was sent because "I told them I would send them all this information and we would go from there," that it was not made as an offer, and that it was his intention that the "property" and "permits" be transferred "together."

Upon receiving that letter and enclosures, plaintiff immediately responded by letter addressed to both defendants, dated June 21, 1976, as follows:

> "Re the land in Bear Valley near Seneca, Oregon, that you have offered to sell; I accept your offer."

Plaintiff testified that on June 23, 1976, Clyde Holliday called and said he needed to acquire a portion of the land "that I had agreed to buy from Joe [Oliver], and I said I have bought the land," and that we would "work out an exchange in accord with what we have previously mentioned," but that "[h]e said he needed more land."

Defendant Joseph Oliver testified that after receiving plaintiff's letter dated June 21, 1976, Clyde Holliday told him that "they [Holliday and plaintiff] were having a little difficulty getting this thing worked out," apparently referring to the "exchange" previously discussed between plaintiff and Holliday, and that he (Oliver) then told plaintiff that:

> "[T]here seemed to be some discrepancies between what I was getting the two parties and that I didn't exactly want to be an arbitrator or say you are right or you are wrong with my neighbors. I wished they would straighten the thing out, and if they didn't, I really didn't have to sell it, that I would pull it off the market, because I didn't want to get in trouble. I would have to live with my neighbors."

Finally, on June 24, 1976, defendants mailed the following letter to plaintiff:

> "We received your letter of June 21, 1976. You have misconstrued our prior negotiations and written summaries of the lands which we and J.C. wish to sell. That was not made as or intended to be a firm offer of sale, and especially was not an offer of sale of any portion of the lands and permits described to any one person separately from the rest of the lands and permits described.

> "The memorandum of ours was for informational purposes only and as a starting point for further negotiation between us and you and the others also interested in the properties.

> "It is also impossible to tell from the attachment to our letter of June 17, 1976, as to the legal description of the lands to be sold, and would not in any event constitute an enforceable contract.

> "We are open to further negotiation with you and other interested parties, but do not consider that we at this point have any binding enforceable contract with you."

This lawsuit then followed.

Defendants' letter of June 17, 1976, was an "offer to sell" the ranch lands.

Defendants first contend that defendants' letter of June 17, 1976, to plaintiff was "not an offer, both as a matter of law and under the facts of this case." In support of that contention defendants say that their testimony that the letter was not intended as an offer was uncontradicted and that similar writings have been held not to constitute offers. Defendants also say that there is "authority for the proposition that all the evidence of surrounding circumstances may be taken into consideration in making that determination" and that the circumstances in this case were such as to require the conclusion that defendants did not intend the letter as an offer and that plaintiff knew or reasonably should have known that it was not intended as an offer because:

> "1. Defendants obviously did not intend it as an offer.

"2. The wording of the 'offer' made it clear that this was 'information' that plaintiff had previously expressed an interest in receiving.

"3. It did not use the term offer, but only formally advised plaintiff that defendants are selling certain lands and permits and set forth generally the terms upon which they would consider selling.

"4. The plaintiff knew of the custom of transferring permits with land and had no knowledge from the writing or previous talk that defendants were selling any cattle.

"5. Plaintiff knew and expected this same information to go to others."

Defendants conclude that, "Considering the factors determined important by the authorities cited, these factors preponderate heavily that this was not an offer to sell the land only, or to sell at all, and should not reasonably have been so construed by the plaintiff."

In *Kitzke v. Turnidge*, 209 Ore. 563, 573, 307 P.2d 522 (1957), this court quoted with approval the following rule as stated in 1 WILLISTON ON CONTRACTS 49–50, § 22A (1957):

> " 'In the early law of assumpsit stress was laid on the necessity of a promise in terms, but the modern law rightly construes both acts and words as having the meaning which a reasonable person present would put upon them in view of the surrounding circumstances. Even where words are used, 'a contract includes not only what the parties said, but also what is necessarily to be implied from what they said.' And it may be said broadly that any conduct of one party, from which the other may reasonably draw the inference of a promise, is effective in law as such.' "

To the same effect, see *Kabil Developments Corp. v. Mignot*, 279 Ore. 151, 158, 566 P2d 505 (1977); *Klimek v. Perisich*, 231 Ore. 71, 78, 371 P2d 956 (1962); RESTATEMENT OF CONTRACTS 2d § 24 (1973); and MURRAY ON CONTRACTS 36, § 22 (1974).

As also stated in 1 RESTATEMENT OF CONTRACTS § 25, Comment (a) (1932), as quoted by this court with approval in *Metropolitan Life Ins. Co. v. Kimball*, 163 Ore. 31, 58, 94 P2d 1101 (1939): "It is often difficult to draw an exact line between offers and negotiations preliminary thereto. It is common for one who wishes to make a bargain to try to induce the other party to the intended transaction to make the definite offer, he himself suggesting with more or less definiteness the nature of the contract he is willing to enter into. Besides any direct language indicating an intent to defer the formation of a contract, the definiteness or indefiniteness of the words used in opening the negotiation must be considered, as well as the usages of business, and indeed all accompanying circumstances."

The difficulty in determining whether an offer has been made is particularly acute in cases involving price quotations, as in this case. It is recognized that although a price quotation, standing alone, is not an offer,[3] there may be circumstances under which a price quotation, when considered together with facts and circumstances, may constitute an offer which, if accepted, will result in a binding contract.[4] It is also recognized that such an offer may be made to more than one person.[5] Thus, the fact that a price quotation is sent to more than one person does not, of itself, require a holding that such a price quotation is not an offer.

We agree with the analysis of this problem as stated in Murray on Contracts 37–40, § 24 (1974),[6] as follows:

> "If A says to B, 'I am going to sell my car for 500,' and B replies, 'All right, here is 500, I will take it,' no contract results, assuming that A's statement is taken at its face value. A's statement does not involve any promise, commitment or undertaking; it is at most a statement of A's present intention. . . . However, a price quotation or advertisement may contain sufficient indication of willingness to enter a bargain so that the party to whom it is addressed would be justified in believing that his assent would conclude the bargain. . . . The basic problem is found in the expressions of the parties. People very seldom express themselves either accurately or in complete detail. Thus, difficulty is encountered in determining the correct interpretation of the expression in question. Over the years, some more or less trustworthy guides to interpretation have been developed."

The first and strongest guide is that the particular expression is to be judged on the basis of what a reasonable man in the position of the offeree has been led to believe. This requires an analysis of what the offeree should have understood under all of the surrounding circumstances, with all of his opportunities for comprehending the intention of the offeror, rather than what the offeror, in fact, intended. This guide may be regarded as simply another manifestation of the objective test. Beyond this universally accepted guide to interpretation, there are other guides which are found in the case law involving factors that tend to recur. The most important of the remaining guides is the language used. If there are no words of promise, undertaking or commitment, the tendency is to construe the expression to be an invitation for an offer or mere preliminary negotiations in the absence of strong, countervailing circumstances. Another guide which has been widely accepted is the determination of the party or parties to whom the purported offer has been addressed. If the expression definitely names a party or parties, it is more likely to be construed as an offer. If the addressee is an indefinite group, it is less likely to be an offer. The fact that this is simply a guide rather than a definite rule is illustrated by the exceptional cases which must be noted. The guide operates effectively in relation to such expressions as advertisements or circular letters. The addressee is indefinite and, therefore, the expression is probably not an offer. However, in reward cases, the addressee is equally indefinite and, yet, the

---

[3] See 1 Corbin on Contracts 77–78, § 26 (1963).

[4] See 1 Williston on Contracts 65, § 221 (1957); Murray on Contracts 37–40, § 24 (1974), and Calimari and Perillo, Contracts 39, § 2-10 (1977).

[5] Restatement of Contracts 36, § 28 (1932).

[6] [Ed. note: The analysis currently appears in the 5th edition (2011) of the treatise at § 35.]

expression is an offer. Finally, the definiteness of the proposal itself may have a bearing on whether it constitutes an offer. In general, the more definite the proposal, the more reasonable it is to treat the proposal as involving a commitment. . . ." (Footnotes omitted)

Upon application of these tests to the facts of this case we are of the opinion that defendants' letter to plaintiff dated June 17, 1976, was an offer to sell the ranch lands. We believe that the "surrounding circumstances" under which this letter was prepared by defendants and sent by them to plaintiff were such as to have led a reasonable person to believe that defendants were making an offer to sell to plaintiff the lands described in the letter's enclosure and upon the terms as there stated.

That letter did not come to plaintiff "out of the blue," as in some of the cases involving advertisements or price quotations. Neither was this a price quotation resulting from an inquiry by plaintiff. According to what we believe to be the most credible testimony, defendants decided to sell the lands in question and defendant Joseph Oliver then sought out the plaintiff who owned adjacent lands. Defendant Oliver told plaintiff that defendants were interested in selling that land, inquired whether plaintiff was interested, and was told by plaintiff that he was "very interested in the land," after which they discussed the particular lands to be sold. That conversation was terminated with the understanding that Mr. Oliver would "determine" the value and price of that land, i.e., "what he wanted for the land," and that plaintiff would undertake to arrange financing for the purchase of that land. In addition to that initial conversation, there was a further telephone conversation in which plaintiff called Mr. Oliver "to ask him if his plans for selling * * * continued to be in force" and was told "yes"; that there had been some delay in getting information from the assessor, as needed to establish the value of the land; and that plaintiff then told Mr. Oliver that "everything was in order" and that "he had the money available and everything was ready to go."

Under these facts and circumstances, we agree with the finding and conclusion by the trial court, in its written opinion, that when plaintiff received the letter of June 17th, with enclosures, which stated a price of 324,419 for the 2,933 acres in T 16 S, R 31 E., W.M., as previously identified by the parties with reference to a map, and stating "terms" of 29 percent down — balance over five years at eight percent interest — with a "sale date" of either December 1, 1976, or January 1, 1977, a reasonable person in the position of the plaintiff would have believed that defendants were making an offer to sell those lands to him.

This conclusion is further strengthened by "the definiteness of the proposal," not only with respect to price, but terms, and by the fact that "the addressee was not an indefinite group." *See* MURRAY, *supra*, at 40.

As previously noted, defendants contend that they "obviously did not intend [the letter] as an offer." While it may be proper to consider evidence of defendants' subjective intent under the "objective test" to which this court is committed, it is the manifestation of a previous intention that is controlling, rather than a "person's actual intent." We do not agree with defendants' contention that it was "obvious" to a reasonable person, under the facts and circumstances of this case that the letter of January 17th was not intended to be an offer to sell the ranch lands to plaintiff.

We recognize, as contended by defendants, that the failure to use the word "offer," the fact that the letter included the "information" previously discussed between the parties, and the fact that plaintiff knew that the same information was to be sent to others, were important facts to be considered in deciding whether plaintiff, as a reasonable person, would have been led to believe that this letter was an "offer." *See also* MURRAY, *supra*, at 40. We disagree, however, with defendants' contention that these and other factors relied upon by defendants "preponderate" so as to require a holding that the letter of January 17th was not an offer.

The failure to add the word "offer" and the use of the word "information" are also not controlling, and, as previously noted, an offer may be made to more than one person. The question is whether, under all of the facts and circumstances existing at the time that this letter was received, a reasonable person in the position of the plaintiff would have understood the letter to be an offer by defendants to sell the land to him.

Defendants also contend that "plaintiff knew of the custom of transferring [Forest Service grazing] permits with the land and had no knowledge from the writing or previous talk that defendants were selling any cattle" (so as to provide such a basis for a transfer of the permits). Plaintiff testified, however, that at the time of the initial conversation, Mr. Oliver told plaintiff that he thought plaintiff "would be interested in the land and that Clyde would be interested in the permits." In addition, defendant Joseph Oliver, in response to questions by the trial judge, although denying that at that time he told plaintiff that he was "going to offer the permits to Mr. Holliday," admitted that he "knew Mr. Holliday was interested in the permits" and "could have" told plaintiff that he was "going to talk to Mr. Holliday about him purchasing the permits."

On this record we believe that plaintiff's knowledge of the facts noted by defendants relating to the transfer of such permits did not require a holding that, as a reasonable man, he did not understand or should not have understood that defendants' letter of June 17th was an offer to sell the ranch lands to him.

Plaintiff's letter of June 21, 1976, was an acceptance of defendants' offer to sell the ranch lands.

NOTES

(1) *Lonergan v. Scolnick*, 129 Cal. App. 2d 179, 276 P.2d 8 (1954). In March, defendant placed an ad in a Los Angeles newspaper reading, "Joshua Tree vic. 40 acres . . . need cash, will sacrifice." The plaintiff made certain inquiries concerning this ad to which defendant responded on March 26 with a brief description of the property, directions, a statement that the rock-bottom price was 2,500 cash, and finally added, "This is a form letter." On April 7, plaintiff wrote to defendant saying that he was not sure he had found the property, asking for its legal description and whether the land was level or included a certain jutting rock, and suggesting a certain bank as escrow agent "should I desire to purchase the land." On April 8, defendant responded saying, "From your description you have found the property"; that this bank "is O.K. for escrow agent"; that the land was fairly level; giving the legal description; and then saying, "If you are really interested, you will have to

decide fast as I expect to have a buyer in the next day or so." On April 12, defendant sold the land to another buyer for 2,500. Plaintiff received defendant's April 8 letter on April 14. On April 15, plaintiff wrote a letter thanking the defendant for the April 8 letter "confirming that I was on the right land," stating that he would immediately proceed to have the escrow opened and would deposit 2,500 therein "in conformity with your offer," and asking the defendant to forward a deed with his instructions to the escrow agent. On April 17, plaintiff started the escrow account. Upon learning of the sale to another, the plaintiff brought this suit for specific performance, or damages if specific performance was impossible. The trial court found that the April 8 letter constituted an offer but was not accepted in a timely fashion. The appellate court affirmed the judgment, but found that all of plaintiff's communications, including the April 8 letter, were preliminary negotiations. Since plaintiff never made an offer, defendant had no power of acceptance to form a contract.

(2) In *Moulton v. Kershaw*, 59 Wis. 316, 18 N.W. 172 (1884), plaintiff received the following letter from defendant: "Dear Sir: In consequence of a rupture in the salt trade, we are authorized to offer Michigan fine salt, in full carload lots of 80 to 95 barrels, delivered at your city, at 85 cents per barrel, to be shipped per C. & N.W.R.R. Co. only. At this price it is a bargain, as the price in general remains unchanged. Shall be pleased to receive your order." Plaintiff wired an order for 2,000 barrels of salt and contends that, as a salt dealer who dealt in large quantities (a fact known to defendant), plaintiff often ordered such sizeable amounts. Plaintiff contends that it had accepted defendant's offer. Held: defendant's letter was a mere invitation to deal.

(3) An offer is the manifestation of willingness to enter into a bargain, so made as to justify another person in understanding that his assent to that bargain is invited and will conclude it. RESTATEMENT (SECOND) OF CONTRACTS § 24.

COMMENT: EFFECT OF OFFER

Why is it important to determine whether a particular communication is an offer rather than a mere preliminary negotiation? What is the legal effect of a preliminary negotiation? What is the legal effect of an offer? Professor Corbin suggests that an offer creates a legal power of acceptance in the offeree: "An acceptance is a voluntary act of the offeree whereby he exercises the power conferred upon him by the offer, and thereby creates the set of legal relations called a contract. What acts are sufficient to serve this purpose? We must look first to the terms in which the offer was expressed, either by words or by conduct. The offeror is the creator of the power and at the time of its creation he has full control over both the fact of its existence and its terms. The offeror has, in the beginning, full power to determine the acts that are to constitute acceptance. After he has once created the power, he may lose his control over it, and may become disabled to change or revoke it; but the fact that, in the beginning, the offeror has full control of the immediately succeeding relation called a power, is the characteristic that distinguishes contractual relations from noncontractual ones. After the offeror has created the power, the legal consequences thereof are out of his hands, and he may be brought into numerous consequential relations of which he did not dream, and to which he might not have consented. These later relations are nevertheless called contractual." Corbin, *Offer and Acceptance, and Some of the Resulting Legal Relations*, 26 YALE L.J. 169, 199–200 (1917).

PROBLEMS

(1)   A buyer wrote a letter to the seller which read in relevant part, "Please advise us the lowest price you can make us on our order for ten car loads of Mason green jars, complete, with caps, packed one dozen in a case." The seller replied by return mail, "We quote you Mason fruit jars, complete, on one-dozen boxes, delivered: Pints 4.50, quarts 5.00, half gallons, 6.50, per gross, for immediate acceptance, and shipment not later than May 15." The next day, the buyer replied by telegram, "Enter order ten car loads as per your quotation." Is there a contract? *See Fairmount Glassworks v. Crunden-Martin Wodden Ware Co.*, 106 Ky. 659, 51 S.W. 196 (1899). Also see UCC § 2-311.

(2)   Defendant was aboard a train journeying to Porus. Plaintiff sent a telegram to defendant on the train: "Will you sell us Bumper Hall Pen? Telegraph lowest cash price — answer paid." Bumper Hall Pen was the name of property owned by defendant. Defendant wired back: "Lowest price for Bumper Hall Pen £ 900." To this wire, plaintiff replied immediately with the following wire: "We agree to buy Bumper Hall Pen for the sum of £ 900 asked by you." Plaintiff claimed there was a contract while the defendant asserted that his telegram from the train was a mere price quotation. What result? *See Harvey v. Facey*, [1893] A.C. 552.

(3)   As agent for the Federal Deposit Insurance Corporation (FDIC) authorized to manage and sell property acquired by the FDIC, the defendant sent an email to the plaintiff describing certain property formerly owned by a bank that had been taken in receivership by the FDIC. While such property would normally be sold through the solicitation of sealed bids, the e-mail stated that, after talking with the plaintiff and learning of its interest in the property, "we would like to offer this to you before the sealed bid. We will set an asking price of 905,000. Please review that price and let me know an offer you would like to make on the property." The plaintiff replied that it "accepts your offer to purchase the property at 6601 South Dixie Highway for the full price of 905,000." When the defendant and FDIC refused to perform, the plaintiff brought this action. The defendant moved to dismiss the complaint on the ground that the defendant's e-mail did not constitute an offer for the sale of the property. Analyze. *See Romacorp v. Prescient, Inc.*, 2011 U.S. Dist. LEXIS 40611 (S.D. Fla. 2011).

ZANAKIS-PICO v. CUTTER DODGE, INC.
Hawaii Supreme Court
47 P.3d 1222 (2002)

LEVINSON, J.

This dispute involves an advertisement by Cutter appearing in the September 12, 1997 editions of both of the Honolulu daily newspapers of general circulation — the Advertiser and the Star-Bulletin. In large print at the top, the advertisement announced a "13,000,000 INVENTORY REDUCTION" and claimed, "We're #1

For a Reason! Volume = Low Prices[.] Come on Down and find out why!! 0 cash Down!*" At the bottom were five lines of text, including two asterisks, in a much smaller type-face. The first asterisk was followed by the qualification: "0 Cash Down on all Gold Key Plus pymnt. vehicles."

The main body of the advertisement, between the introductory text and the fine print, included pictorial depictions of and specific terms for fourteen different model vehicles. In each instance, the advertisement stated the number of vehicles of the particular model available at the stated terms or price and listed what appear to be their inventory identification numbers. Five of the models were listed with a cash price, while nine were simply advertised for "0 Cash Down," subject to varying monthly payments over various periods of time. The first and most prominently displayed vehicle was a "NEW '97 GRAND CHEROKEE LAREDO," priced at "229 Month* 24 Mos. 0 Cash Down or 20,988." A second asterisk in the fine print at the bottom of the advertisement read: "Rebate and APR on select models, not combinable, prices incl. 400 Recent College Grad, 750–1000 Loyalty Rebate on Grand Cherokees & Loyalty Rebate on Caravans & Grand Caravans on paymnts & prices & all other applicable rebates. On approved credit. All paymnts/prices plus tax, lic. & 195 doc fee."

The Picos advised Cutter that they were ready, willing and able to purchase the vehicle, whereupon the sales agent informed them that they would have to make a down payment of 1,400. The Picos protested, pointing out that according to the advertisement, the vehicle could be purchased for no cash down, but the sales agent explained that the "0 cash down/229 per month" offer was only available to recent college graduates who were entitled to a "loyalty rebate." On October 16, 1997, the Picos filed a complaint in the first circuit court, based on the advertisement. [The circuit court held that there was no contract between the parties. The Picos appealed.]

There is substantial agreement among the courts that have addressed the question that advertisements by merchants listing goods for sale at a particular price are generally invitations to deal, rather than binding contractual offers that consumers may freely accept. *See, e.g., Georgian Co. v. Bloom*, 27 Ga. App. 468, 108 S.E. 813, 814 (Ga. Ct. App. 1921) (holding that newspaper advertisements, " 'stating that the advertiser has a certain quantity of goods which he [or she] wants to dispose of at certain prices, are not offers which become contracts as soon as any person to whose notice they might come signifies his [or her] acceptance by notifying the [seller] that he [or she] will take a certain quantity of them[ ]' "); *Steinberg v. Chicago Med. Sch.*, 69 Ill. 2d 320, 371 N.E.2d 634, 639, 13 Ill. Dec. 699 (Ill. 1977) (noting that advertisements for sale of goods at a fixed price are invitations to deal rather than binding offers); *Osage Homestead, Inc. v. Sutphin*, 657 S.W.2d 346, 351–52 (Mo. Ct. App. 1983) (holding that an advertisement offering a rig for sale at a specified price was not a contractual offer); *Ehrlich v. Willis Music Co.*, 93 Ohio App. 246, 51 Ohio Op. 8, 113 N.E.2d 252 (Ohio Ct. App. 1952) (noting that an advertisement for sale of a television at a specified price "was no more than an invitation to patronize the store"). *See also* 1 WILLISTON, A TREATISE ON THE LAW OF CONTRACTS § 4.7 at 286–87 (4th ed. 1990) ("if goods are advertised for sale at a certain price, it is generally not an offer, and no contract is formed because of the statement of an intending purchaser that he will take a specified quantity of goods at that price"); RESTATEMENT (SECOND) OF CONTRACTS § 26 at 75 (1981) ("[a] manifestation of willingness to enter into a bargain is not an offer if the person to whom it is addressed knows or has reason to know that the person making it does not intend to conclude a bargain until he has made a further manifestation of assent"). Rather than make an offer, advertisements invite offers by prospective purchasers. "Only when the merchant takes the money is there an acceptance of the offer to purchase." *Steinberg*, 371 N.E.2d at 639; *see also Osage*, 657 S.W.2d at 351–52 (holding that a contract for sale of an advertised item was not complete until the seller accepted the buyer's offer to purchase based on the advertisement).

There is a very narrow, yet well-established, exception to this rule, which arises when an advertisement is "clear, definite, and explicit, and leaves nothing open for negotiation." *Lefkowitz v. Great Minneapolis Surplus Store*, 251 Minn. 188, 86 N.W.2d 689, 691 (Minn. 1957); *see also R.E. Crummer & Co. v. Nuveen*, 147 F.2d 3, 5 (7th Cir. 1945) (holding that advertisement inviting specific bond-holders to send their bonds to a designated bank for surrender pursuant to clearly specified terms constituted a binding contractual offer); *Leonard v. Pepsico, Inc.*, 88 F. Supp. 2d 116, 124 (S.D.N.Y. 1999) (holding that "the absence of any words of limitation[,] such as 'first come, first served,' [rendered] the alleged offer [for a fighter jet in exchange for 'Pepsi-points'] sufficiently indefinite that no contract could be formed[ ]"); *Donovan v. RRL Corp.*, 26 Cal. 4th 261, 109 Cal. Rptr. 2d 807, 27 P.3d 702, 711 (Cal. 2001) (holding that a licensed automobile dealer's advertisement regarding a particular vehicle at a specific price constituted an offer in light of the California Vehicle Code, which rendered illegal the failure to sell the vehicle at the advertised price to any person while it remained unsold); *Izadi v. Machado (Gus) Ford, Inc.*, 550 So. 2d 1135, 1139 (Fla. Dist. Ct. App. 1989) (holding that car dealer's advertisement offering a minimum 3,000 "allowance" for any vehicle that a consumer traded in, regardless of its actual value, constituted a binding contractual offer); *Oliver v. Henley*, 21 S.W.2d 576, 578–79 (Tex. Civ. App. 1929) (holding that an advertisement, offering to "ship sacks of 3 bushels each, freight prepaid, to any point in Texas for 4 per sack, said sack tagged according to our state seed laws," constituted a binding contractual offer); *Chang v. First Colonial Sav. Bank*, 242 Va. 388, 410 S.E.2d 928, 930 (Va. 1991) (holding that bank's advertisement promising two free gifts and 20,136.12 upon maturing in 3 1/2 years in exchange for a 14,000 deposit constituted an offer that was accepted when 14,000 was deposited). In such advertisements, "there must ordinarilybe some language of commitment or some invitation to take action without further communication." RESTATEMENT (SECOND) OF CONTRACTS § 26 at 76 (1981); *see also* 1 CORBIN ON CONTRACTS § 2.4 at 116–122(1993) (noting that advertisements are not presumed to be offers unless they contain unusually clear words to the contrary).

We agree with the foregoing well-established principles. Accordingly, we hold that advertisements are generally not binding contractual offers, unless they invite acceptance without further negotiations in clear, definite, express, and unconditional language. The provisions of Cutter's advertisement upon which the Picos rely do not constitute a binding contractual offer.

NOTE

The common law view that advertisement do not generally constitute offers is often based on two factors: they are addressed to the public at large and, since the offerees are not identified, there is no offer; (2) the number of offerees is uncertain, thereby creating an inordinate risk for the shopkeeper who may not have a sufficient supply of an advertised product to meet the requirements of an indefinite number of contracts formed if shopper could treat the advertisement as an offer which they accept by tendering the announced price.

The first factor is not persuasive since there are illustrations of advertisements that constitute offers since the offerees are identifiable albeit not identified at the time the contract is formed. The court refers to the well-known case of *Lefkowitz v. Great Minneapolis Suplus Store*, 251 Minn. 188, 86 N.W.2d 689 (1957), as an exception to the general rule that advertisements do not constitute offers. The Store published a newspaper advertisement stating: "Saturday, 9 A.M. sharp, 3 brand new fur coats worth to 100.00 — First Come, First Served — 1 Each." The following week, the Store published another ad stating: "Saturday, 9 A.M. — 12 Brand New Pastel Mink 3-Skin Scarfs Selling for 89.50 — Out they go Saturday: Each . . . 1.00 — 1 Black Lapin Stole, Beautiful, worth 139.50 . . . 1.00 — First Come, First Served." On each of the Saturdays, the plaintiff was the first to present himself at the appropriate counter in the defendant's store demanding the advertised coat for 1.00 and the following week demanding the stole. On both occasions, the defendant refused to sell the goods to the plaintiff. The appellate court upheld the trial court's disallowance of the claim made for the fur coat since the ad stated that they were "worth to 100," how much less being speculative and uncertain. As to the scarfs, however, the trial court held and the appellate court agreed that the value of the stole at 139.50 was established and the plaintiff was entitled to the stole or its equivalent in damages in exchange for 1 since the advertisement was an offer. The court found the ad to be an offer because it was "clear, definite and explicit." There are, however, innumerable advertisements for the sale of goods or service that are clear, definite and explicit, leaving nothing open for negotiation, which courts find to be mere preliminary negotiations called nothing more than what some of the older English cases referred to as "invitations to treat" rather than offers. The advertisement was an offer, but the "clear, definite and explicit" rationale limps. Exactly why was this advertisement an offer while other ads would not be offers? Consider the definition of "promise" in the Restatement (Second) of Contracts § 2(1): ". . . the manifestation of intention to act or refrain from acting in a specified way, so made as to justify a promisee in understanding that a commitment has been made." Also reconsider the definition of "offer" at § 24: "a manifestation of willingness to enter into a bargain, so made as to justify another person in understanding that his assent to that bargain is invited and will conclude it."

Even where the advertisement does not limit acceptance to a specific number of identifiable offerees, if the advertisement is construed to be an offer, the offerees will be the buyers who seek to accept it. The second concern of the shopkeeper's risk of a limited supply could be met by the shopkeeper demonstrating that it had a "reasonable" supply of the advertised item. It is not uncommon for current advertisements to include the phrase, "supplies limited."

A better rationale for the common law view that advertisements are not offers is simply the generally accepted guide to distinguish any preliminary negotiation from an offer by recognizing that a statement of present intention such as, "I intend to sell my car for 10,000," is not a statement creating a power of acceptance. By itself, it cannot be reasonably interpreted to mean, "I promise to sell my car to you for 10,000." It is simply an announcement of a present intention to sell that invites any interested party to offer to purchase the item at the suggested price.

PROBLEM

An English statute provided, "Any person who manufactures, sells or hires or offers for sale or hire, or lends or gives to any other person any knife which has a blade which opens automatically by hand pressure applied to a button, spring or other device in or attached to the handle of the knife, sometimes known as a 'flick knife' shall be guilty of an offense." A constable noticed that a retail shop in Bristol displayed one of these "flick knives" in the store window with a sign next to the knife that read, "Ejector knife§ 4s." The constable reported the store for a violation of the statute. The retailer argued that there was no violation. What result? *See Fisher v. Bell*, [Q. B. 1960] 3 All B. R. 731.

MARYLAND SUPREME CORP. v. BLAKE CO.
Maryland Court of Appeals
369 A.2d 1017 (1977)

ORTH, JUDGE.

We are called upon to decide whether there was a contract for sale of goods between Supreme and Blake, and if there was, the extent to which it was enforceable.

The controversy stemmed from the construction of the Western Heights Middle School. In such a building project there are basically three parties involved: the letting party, who calls for bids on its job; the general contractor, who makes a bid on the whole project; and the subcontractors, who bid only on that portion of the whole job which involves the field of its specialty. The usual procedure is that when a project is announced, a subcontractor, on his own initiative or at the general contractor's request, prepares an estimate and submits a bid to one or more of the general contractors interested in the project. The general contractor evaluates the bids made by the subcontractors in each field and uses them to compute its total bid to the letting party. After receiving bids from general contractors, the letting party ordinarily awards the contract to the lowest reputable bidder.[7]

From the evidence adduced, it is manifest that the usual method of operation in the construction industry was followed in the construction of the Western Heights Middle School. The letting party, the Board of Education, advertised for bids for the construction of the School. Blake was one of the general contractors who responded.

---

[7] [1] This analysis of the construction industry's method of operation is taken from *The "Firm Offer" Problem in Construction Bids and the Need for Promissory Estoppel*, 10 WM. & MARY L. REV. 212 (1968).

Supreme, a manufacturer of ready mixed concrete, learned through a trade journal what general contractors had bid on the job. After examining the specifications relating to concrete for the project, Supreme, as a subcontractor, wrote the interested general contractors with reference to supplying the concrete required. Its letter to Blake, dated 11 March 1975, read:

> The Blake Company
> P. O. Box 47
> Hagerstown, Maryland 21740
> Attention: Mr. Vernon Tetlow
>
> Re: Western Heights Middle School
>
> Dear Sirs:
>
> We are pleased to submit a quotation on ready mix for the above mentioned project.
>
> Please take note that the price will be guaranteed to hold throughout the job.
>
> 3,000 p.s.i. concrete 21.00 per yard, net.
>
> Hope that you are successful in your bid and that we may be favored with your valued order.
>
> Yours very truly,
>
> Maryland Supreme Corporation
> /s/ Ben Wicklein, Sales Representative

Blake was the successful bidder. About 24 May 1975, fifty-nine days after the bids were opened, it was informed that it had been awarded the job as the general contractor. There was no written notification by Blake to Supreme that Supreme would supply the concrete. Vernon L. Tetlow, Blake's Engineering Manager, testified that he notified subcontractors "as soon as we get a contract that they are going to get one." He verbally notified Benjamin F. Wicklein, Supreme's salesman, that Supreme was to furnish the concrete for the job. "'Ben' always asked me 'Are we good on that job? Are we going to furnish that job?' I said, 'Yes, give me a mix design.' Like we always do." That was the way he had notified Supreme on other jobs for which Supreme was to supply the concrete.

Supreme began delivering concrete to the job on 11 July 1975, and it is obvious that the procedure outlined by Wilson and Wicklein was followed. As shown by Supreme's ledger sheets listing invoices to Blake, deliveries were made a number of times a day on various days to supply the concrete to be poured from time to time.[8] Supreme billed Blake at the rate of 21 per yard in accordance with its letter of 11 March 1975, and the parties were apparently content.

Trouble brewed in late October. On 24 October 1975 Supreme wrote Blake: "Due to numerous increases in the cost of cement and other raw materials absorbed by

---

[8] [2] Through 29 October 1975 some 132 deliveries of various amounts of concrete were made covering about 13 days. Each delivery was represented by a separate invoice.

our company since our last increase, we are forced to raise our ready mix prices effective November 1, 1975 . . . . We regret we are unable to give any protection on jobs in progress." The price of the kind of concrete required for the School was increased to 27 per yard. The letter was signed for Supreme by its Sales Manager, and he testified that it was a form letter sent to all of Supreme's customers. Blake responded. Under date of 12 November 1975, its Engineering Manager wrote Supreme:

> I have received your form letter dated October 24, 1975. I assumed then and will continue to assume that this was meant for projects that you have not made a commitment and not, therefore, Western Heights Middle School for which the concrete price is guaranteed for the project duration.

> If this is incorrect, correspond directly by letter to our office that you intend to default your contract.

As a result of the letter of 12 November, Russell R. Reed, Jr., President of Supreme, called on M. William Dutton, Jr., President of Blake "to further amplify the fact that we were forced to raise our prices and to indicate to him that we would be most delighted to deliver concrete to the . . . School at the price of 27.00." Dutton testified that Reed explained to him the necessity for the increase in price, intimating that otherwise Supreme might have to discontinue business. Dutton told Reed that Blake could not accept the increase "because we had bid the job on firm prices." . . .

As of 1 November 1975, Supreme charged Blake 27 a yard for concrete delivered to the job. Supreme's last delivery was on 13 November. Blake purchased concrete thereafter from two other firms. [Supreme argues that it made no offer].

It is manifest that what was involved here was a sale of goods within the contemplation of the Maryland Uniform Commercial Code — Sales (hereinafter cited as UCC) Maryland Code (1975), Commercial Law, Title 2. "Offer," however, is not defined in the UCC, and with respect to it we look to the common law and the law merchant. UCC § 1-103.

"An essential feature of every contract is the parties' mutual assent . . . ." *Peer v. First Fed. S. & L. Ass'n*, 273 Md. 610, 614, 331 A.2d 299, 301 (1975). Thus, it is usually necessary for one of the parties to propose to the other a promise which he will make for a certain consideration, or to state the consideration which he will give for a certain promise. The promise is an offer. "An offer necessarily looks to the future. It is an expression by the offeror of his agreement that something over which he at least assumes to have control shall be done or happen or shall not be done or happen if the conditions stated in the offer are complied with. Unless the statement gives to the person to whom it is addressed an assurance that, on some contingency at least, he shall have something, the statement is not an offer." WILLISTON ON CONTRACTS, § 24A (3rd ed. Jaeger 1957) (hereinafter cited as WILLISTON). So, an offer is always a conditional promise and it may become a contract. It is distinguished from other conditional promises "only because the performance of the condition in an offer is requested as the agreed exchange or return for the promise or its performance, thereby giving the offeree a power, by complying with the request, to turn the promise in the offer into a contract or sale." WILLISTON, § 25.

An offer must be definite and certain. To be capable of being converted into a contract of sale by an acceptance, it must be made under circumstances evidencing an express or implied intention that its acceptance shall constitute a binding contract. Accordingly, a mere expression of intention to do an act is not an offer to do it, and a general willingness to do something on the happening of a particular event or in return for something to be received does not amount to an offer. Thus, a mere quotation or a statement of a price or prices and an invitation to enter into negotiations, are not offers which may be turned into binding contracts upon acceptance. Such proposals may be merely suggestions to induce offers by others.

From the nature of the subject, the question whether certain acts of conduct constitute a definite proposal upon which a binding contract may be predicated without any further action on the part of the person from whom it proceeds, or a mere preliminary step which is not susceptible, without further action by such party, of being converted into a binding contract, depends upon the nature of the particular acts or conduct in question and the circumstances attending the transaction. It is impossible to formulate a general principle or criterion for its determination.

Therefore, in its final determination, the question of whether an offer was made seems to be one dependent on the intention of the parties, and, being such, it depends on the facts and circumstances of the particular case. The UCC changes none of these principles of law.

Supreme's proposal was evidenced by its letter of 11 March 1975 to Blake. Supreme would now have it be merely a price quotation, and claims that did not contain many of the essential terms of an offer "such as the quality and quantity of the product to be supplied, the number and dates of the deliveries, the terms of payment, the costs of shipment and the time for performance." We do not agree. Considered in light of the facts and circumstances, the trial court could have found, as it obviously did, that the letter of 11 March 1975 constituted a definite and certain offer with the intent that, if accepted, it would result in a contract. By the letter, Supreme proposed to furnish Blake with ready mix 3000 p.s.i. concrete at 21 per yard, net, in such quantity as Blake required for the Western Heights Middle School project. The language in the letter stating the quotation was "on ready mix for *the above mentioned project* [Western Heights Middle School]," and asserting that "the price will be guaranteed to hold *throughout the job*" (emphasis supplied) may be considered as measuring the quantity of the concrete by the requirements of the buyer, as recognized in UCC § 2-306(1). The contingency was that Blake be the successful bidder. If Blake were awarded the general contract for the construction of the School and accepted Supreme's offer, there would be a binding contract. When viewed with reference to the method of operation of the construction industry and the prior course of dealings between Supreme and Blake, it is manifest that Supreme's letter was no mere price quotation or invitation to negotiate. It gave Blake the assurance that if Blake were the general contractor on the School project Blake could obtain from Supreme the concrete necessary for the job at 21 per yard. Thus, it was an offer, and the trial court did not err in so considering it.

QUESTIONS

Are "quotations" always preliminary negotiations rather than offers? Would it be preferable to use a term other than "quotation" or "quote" if an offer is intended?

INTERSTATE INDUSTRIES v. BARCLAY INDUSTRIES
United States Court of Appeals, Seventh Circuit
540 F.2d 868 (1976)

Over a five year period, Interstate was involved in numerous business transactions with Barclay in which goods manufactured by Barclay were delivered in Interstate's facility in Michigan City, Indiana. Barclay sent a letter from its offices in Lodi, New Jersey advising Interstate that it would be able to manufacture fiberglass panels in accordance with certain specified standards.[9] In response, Interstate mailed two purchase orders with "F.O.B. Delvd." notations in the upper right hand corner. [Barclay notified Interstate that Barclay would be unable to provide the panels requested in the purchase order. Interstate filed a complaint against Barclay for breach of contract. In determining whether Barclay's letter of August 23 was an offer, the court relied upon several authorities including the following:]

> [I]f goods are advertised for sale at a certain price, it is not an offer, and no contract is formed by the statement of an intending purchaser that he

---

[9] [3] The letter essentially provides:

August 23, 1973

Mr. Bob Koelling
Interstate Industries, Inc.
Thomas & Fairfield Avenues
Michigan City, Indiana 46360

Dear Mr. Koelling:

In connection with the G.S.A. Contract Solicitation # 10054 dated August 14, 1973, we are pleased to advise you that we can meet the specifications called for the plastic panels as specified on Page 10 as amended by Amendment # 1.

Barclite Fire Retardant Reinforced Fiberglass Panels-Flame Spread not exceeding 25 and not exceeding 150 for Smoke Development-G.S.A. special color Green smooth two sides in the following sizes.

No quantity Specified

Federal Stock No.	Size	Sq. Ft. Per Piece	Price Per Sq. Ft.	Price Per Piece
7195-647-2115	26 ¾" X 15 ¾"	2.926	.44	1.287
7195-647-2116	26 ¾" X 33 ¾"	6.270	.44	2.759
7195-647-2117	26 ¾" X 57 ¾"	10.728	.44	4.720
7195-647-2118	26 ¾" X 65 2/3"	12.199	.44	5.368

This price quotation is based on orders of 75,000 sq. ft. or more (truckload quantities) freight prepaid. Orders less than 75,000 sq. ft. add.01/eq. ft., F.O.B. Lodi.

Very truly yours,

BARCLAY INDUSTRIES, INC.
/s/ Jules R. Raye
Sales Manager

will take a specified quantity of the goods at that price. The construction is rather favored that such an advertisement is a mere invitation to enter into a bargain rather than an offer. *So a published price list is not an offer to sell the goods listed at the published prices. Even where the parties are dealing exclusively with one another by private letters or telegrams, or by oral conversation, the same question may arise; and language that at first sight may seem an offer may be found merely preliminary in its character.* [Court's emphasis.] 1 WILLISTON, CONTRACTS § 27, p. 62 (3d ed. 1957).

[I]n RESTATEMENT OF CONTRACTS § 25 (1932):

> If from a promise, or manifestation of intention, or from the circumstances existing at the time, the person to whom the promise or manifestation is addressed knows or has reason to know that the person making it does not intend it as an expression of his fixed purpose until he has given a further expression of assent, he has not made an offer.

> It is often difficult to draw an exact line between offers and negotiations preliminary thereto. It is common for one who wishes to make a bargain to try to induce the other party to the intended transaction to make the definite offer, he himself suggesting with more or less definiteness the nature of the contract he is willing to enter into. Besides any direct language indicating an intent to defer the formation of a contract, the definiteness or indefiniteness of the words used in opening the negotiation must be considered, as well as the usages of business, and indeed all accompanying circumstances. (Comment a.)

> *A* writes to *B*, "I can quote you flour at 5 a barrel in carload lots." This is not an offer. The word "quote" and the incompleteness of the terms indicate that the writer is simply naming a current price which he is demanding. (Illustration 2.)

It is clear that an offer must be "sufficiently certain to enable a court to understand what is asked for, and what consideration is to mature the promise." *Oedekerk v. Muncie Gear Works*, 179 F.2d 821, 824 (7th Cir. 1950).

With these principles in mind, we turn to Barclay's letter containing the price quotations. It is not disputed that the letter: (1) advised Interstate of the availability; (2) specifically referred to its contents as a "price quotation"; (3) contained no language which indicated that an offer was being made; and (4) failed to mention the quantity, the time of delivery or payment terms. Under these circumstances, we are compelled to find that Barclay's letter did not constitute an offer. Consequently, [no contract was formed.]

NOTE — THE PURCHASE ORDER

A purchase order is the standard printed form used by businesses to order goods as it was in the *Interstate v. Barclay* case. It is typically filled with clauses in fine print ("boilerplate") which usually go unread by either buyer or seller. Both parties normally focus only on the word processed or typewritten terms that fill the blanks on the purchase order. These are the important terms, terms that were consciously considered and negotiated. Professor Karl Llwellyn aptly called these terms "dickered" terms — the description of the goods, quantity, price and delivery terms. Courts typically view the submission of a purchase order by a prospective buyer as an offer because, on its face, it appears to be an offer. The first document in such a transaction, however, will often be an "RFP," a request for proposal sent by the prospective buyer to the seller. This is not an offer since it is inviting a proposal. The response to this RFP will normally be a document captioned, "quotation." The quotation may be a mere statement of prices and descriptions of the goods, i.e., the seller is saying in effect, "We have these goods for sale at this price. Such a quotation is nothing more than an advertisement or trade circular. It is an announcement of goods and prices, such as the letter sent by Barclay to Interstate and is not, therefore, an offer. A quotation or other response to an RFP may, however, constitute an offer."

In *Earl M. Jorgensen Co. v. Mark Constr., Inc.*, 540 P.2d 978 (Haw. 1975), Mark sought a quotation from Jorgensen for certain materials on a construction bid which Mark intended to submit. Jorgensen sent the quotation and it was the lowest quote received by Mark. The quotation contained a clause limiting Jorgensen's liability. Mark used the quote in its bid and was awarded the contract. Mark then sent its purchase order that did not contain a clause concerning the limitation of liability. Jorgensen shipped the materials which Mark later claimed did not conform to contract specifications. Jorgensen relied upon the clause in its quotation limiting liability. Mark claimed that the clause was not part of the contract, on the assumption that the quotation was a preliminary negotiation with no legal effect, the offer was Mark's purchase order and the acceptance was Jorgensen's shipment of the goods. Jorgensen claimed that its quotation was, itself, an offer which Mark accepted (including the limitation of liability clause) by submitting its purchase order. The court agreed with Jorgensen on the basis that the parties treated the quotation as an offer and the purchase order as an acceptance. The limitation of liability clause, therefore, was a term of the contract, and that clause protected Jorgensen.

There are numerous other instances of courts treating purchase orders as acceptances. In the *Interstate* case, Interstate argued that its purchase order was an acceptance of Barclay's letter of August 23. If that letter had been an offer, the purchase order could have been viewed as an acceptance. Since the August 23 letter was not an offer, there was no power of acceptance in Interstate — there was nothing to accept. Its purchase order, therefore, was an offer. *It is important to understand that the characterization of a single document or other fact will depend on its use and relation to other documents or facts. The total transaction must be considered in context.* How, therefore, should the following questions be answered: (1) Is a purchase order an offer? (2) Is a quotation an offer or a mere preliminary document inviting offers?

We have already explored cases suggesting the fundamental warning that the heading or caption atop the writing cannot be trusted. *See* MURRAY at § 36 (5th ed. 2011). Purchase orders are used in chameleonic fashion by purchasing agents. Where a purchasing agent decides to order goods with no prior discussion with the supplier, e.g., simply ordering something from a catalogue or trade circular, the purchase order is an offer. If there has been a prior discussion with the supplier, that discussion may have resulted in a contract — an oral contract made by telephone or in person. The submission of a purchase order after such a deal is made is standard procedure. In this situation, however, the buyer's agent is attempting to use the purchase order not as an offer, but as a confirmation of an existing (oral) contract. If, as in the *Jorgensen* case, the purchase order is sent in response to a quotation, the purchase order will be an acceptance *if* the quotation is an offer. If, however, the quotation is a mere preliminary invitation describing the goods and stating the price, the purchase order will be an offer.

There are still other situations where purchase orders are used. A buyer and seller of goods may have a basic contract which covers all of the goods to be shipped by the supplier to the purchaser within a given period of time, e.g., a seller may agree to supply the buyer with all of its requirements for certain goods for a period of one year. Shipments will be made as directed by the purchaser because there may be uncertainty as to when the goods will be required. A given buyer may use the standard purchase order in this situation simply to direct a shipment of a certain quantity of the goods. In this situation, the purchase order is neither an offer nor an acceptance. Neither is it a confirmation. It is being used as a delivery order and its terms cannot affect the basic terms of the "blanket" contract which the parties had earlier formed. Typically, purchasing agents are unaware of the specific legal effect of a purchase order since that effect will change depending upon its use in a given situation. Purchase orders also tend to be used in the above situations for authentication and identification purposes. The purchase order contains a purchase order number which sellers often seek as the basic authorization to ship as well as the basic identification of the goods that are shipped.

The nuances of offer and acceptance in contract law are generally ignored by the agents of the buyer and seller. The printed forms they use (buyer's purchase orders and seller's quotations and acknowledgment forms) are drafted by lawyers who attempt to protect their clients by the insertion of various clauses (the boilerplate) which are rarely read and even more rarely understood by those using the forms. This can result in unintended legal effects because the forms often contain conflicting boilerplate provisions. The "battle of the forms" situation is one of the more difficult and controversial areas of contract law to which the Uniform Commercial Code applies. This troublesome situation will be explored later in this chapter.

[2] Identifying the Offeror and Offeree

BC TIRE CORP. v. GTE DIRECTORIES CORP.
Washington Court of Appeals
730 P.2d 726 (1986)

PEKELIS, J.

Appellant BC Tire Corporation (BC Tire) brought this action against GTE Directories Corporation (GTE) for breach of contract and negligence due to GTE's failure to publish a certain advertisement in the yellow pages of the Everett telephone directory. The trial court granted GTE's motion for summary judgment and dismissed the action. On appeal, BC Tire argues that an exclusionary clause contained in the application for advertising is unconscionable, and that even if the exclusionary clause is effective, GTE is nonetheless liable for negligence. We affirm.

BC Tire, of which Hobert Carl is the president and sole shareholder, owns and operates a retail tire store in Everett, Washington. GTE solicits and prints advertising in the yellow pages of the Everett telephone directory.

On February 10, 1982, Carl met with Mr. Balzarini, a GTE salesman, and signed a form entitled "APPLICATION FOR DIRECTORY ADVERTISING." At the bottom of the front side of the application, below the description of the advertising requested, the following paragraph appears:

IN ACCORDANCE WITH THE TERMS ON THE REVERSE SIDE OF THIS APPLICATION THE ABOVE APPLICANT requests the GTE DIRECTORIES CORPORATION to insert and/or make the changes shown in the above advertising items in the FORTHCOMING AND SUBSEQUENT issues of the Telephone Directory and agrees to pay the TOTAL AMOUNT PER MONTH as shown above EACH MONTH IN ADVANCE on publication of said advertising items.

The reverse side of the application is entitled "TERMS OF APPLICATION FOR DIRECTORY ADVERTISING." Below the title are seven numbered paragraphs, each of which begins with an introductory word or phrase in boldface print. Among these are the following:

1. ACCEPTANCE OF APPLICATION. It is mutually understood and agreed that the publication of the advertising requested in the Telephone Directory shall constitute an acceptance of this application by the Telephone Company and the GTE DIRECTORIES CORPORATION. Otherwise, this application is not binding on either of the parties.

3. ERRORS AND OMISSIONS. Neither the Telephone Company nor GTE DIRECTORIES CORPORATION shall be liable to the applicant for damages resulting from failure to include in the directory any item of advertising specified in this application or from errors in the advertising printed in the directory in excess of the amount paid by the applicant for said item of advertising for the issue in which the error or omission occurs.

Although Carl admits to having signed many directory advertising applications, some of which contained terms identical to those set out above, he contends that he was unaware of the provisions on the reverse side of the application. He also contends that the exclusionary clause[10] was never pointed out to him by a directory advertising salesman. Paragraph 3 on the reverse side of the application restricts the remedies available to the applicant, and is thus an exclusionary clause.

BC Tire's advertisement was omitted from the August, 1982 Everett telephone

---

[10] [1] We note that there is a distinction between disclaimers and exclusionary clauses: A disclaimer clause is a device used to exclude or limit the seller's warranties; it attempts to control the seller's liability by reducing the number of situations in which the seller can be in breach. An exclusionary clause, on the other hand, restricts the remedies available to one or both parties once a breach is established.

directory. Subsequently, Carl met with Balzarini and his supervisor, and, according to Carl, was told that Balzarini had "screwed up." Carl was not billed for the advertisement.

BC Tire brought suit, alleging that the omission of the advertisement was both a breach of contract and negligence on the part of GTE. BC Tire sought to recover damages for lost profits in an amount to be proven at trial.

GTE moved for summary judgment, on the grounds that (1) there was no contract between GTE and BC Tire, (2) GTE's liability was effectively limited by the exclusionary clause, and (3) BC Tire's negligence claim was simply a restatement of its contract claim. The trial court granted GTE's motion and dismissed the complaint. After the court denied its motion for reconsideration, BC Tire brought this appeal.

BC Tire has devoted by far the greater part of its argument to the proposition that its damages for breach of contract are not limited by the exclusionary clause on the reverse side of the application. However, before we consider the effect of the exclusionary clause, we must determine whether a contract in fact existed between BC Tire and GTE.

Paragraph 1 on the reverse side of the application states that "the publication of the advertising requested . . . shall constitute an acceptance of this application" by GTE. "Otherwise," it continues, "this application is not binding on either of the parties."

The application by its terms is an offer of a unilateral contract; that is, "an offer to enter into a contract upon the doing of a bargained for act by the offeree." *Knight v. Seattle-First Nat'l Bank*, 22 Wn. App. 493, 496, 589 P.2d 1279 (1979). "The performance by the [offeree] constitutes an acceptance of the offer and the contract then becomes executed." *Knight*, at 496 (quoting *Cook v. Johnson*, 37 Wn. 2d 19, 23, 221 P.2d 525 (1950)). In this case, BC Tire, the offeror, has offered to make certain monthly payments upon the publication of the requested advertisement by GTE. There is no acceptance of the offer, and hence no contract, until performance of the bargained for act; that is, until publication of the advertisement by GTE. Because the advertisement was never published, there was no acceptance, no contract, and, thus, no breach.

Because no contract existed between BC Tire and GTE, we need not consider whether the exclusionary clause is effective or whether, as BC Tire argues, it is unconscionable. In either case, BC Tire's claim for breach of contract was properly dismissed. [As to BC Tire's negligence claim], [t]his court will not review a claimed error unless it is (1) included in an assignment of error or clearly disclosed in the associated issue pertaining thereto, and (2) supported by argument and citation to legal authority. BC Tire's assertion fails on both accounts; hence, we will not consider it. *Affirmed.*

SYNNEX CORPORATION v. ADT
SECURITY SERVICES, INC.

Superior Court of New Jersey, Appellate Division

928 A.2d 37 (2007)

SKILLMAN, P.J.A.D.

In 2002, Synnex leased a large warehouse in Edison to use as a distribution center for computers and computer-related equipment. Synnex asked ADT to design and install a burglar alarm system for the building. After the parties reached an agreement concerning the burglar alarm system and purchase price, the ADT sales representative submitted a form ADT contract to the Synnex regional operations director, which they both signed on July 11, 2001. The agreed purchase price was 7,154 plus an annual service charge of 1,142 for a five-year term. A broad exculpatory clause in the contract limited ADT's liability to 10% or the annual service charge or 1000, whichever is greater.

The form ADT contract contained a clause, which stated: "This Agreement is not binding unless approved in writing by an authorized Representative of ADT." Although the contract was signed by an authorized representative of Synnex and the ADT sales representative, it was not signed by an "authorized Representative of ADT."

Approximately six months after installation of this system, someone broke into the warehouse and stole a substantial quantity of computers and computer equipment. A post-crime investigation revealed that the intruders disabled or destroyed parts of the alarm system, including the cellular backup. The company that insured the contents of the warehouse, Mitsui Sumitomo Insurance Group, paid Synnex 7.1 million in settlement of its claim for the merchandise and equipment lost as a result of the burglary and then brought this subrogation action in Synnex's name. The complaint alleged that ADT had been negligent both in designing the burglar alarm system and in communicating with Synnex after it received alarm signals on the night of the burglary.

The trial court ruled that the absence of the signature of an "authorized Representative of ADT" on the original contract precluded ADT from relying upon the exculpatory clause. The case was tried before a jury. The jury returned a verdict finding Synnex and ADT each 50% negligent and determining that the total losses sustained by Synnex as a result of the burglary were 7,645,580. The court molded the verdict and entered a judgment for 3,822,740 plus prejudgment interest in Synnex's favor.

ADT appeals from the judgment in Synnex's favor, arguing that the exculpatory clause was part of its contract for the sale of a burglar alarm system to Synnex, even though the contract was not signed by a person designated as an "authorized Representative of ADT".

There is no doubt a party may condition its acceptance of a contract upon the approval of the "home office" or a higher level company official, and in the absence of such approval, there is no binding contract. As we explained in *Iacono v. Toll*

Brothers, 217 N.J. Super. 475, 478, 526 A.2d 256 (App.Div.1987) (quoting 1 *Corbin on Contracts* § 61 (2 ed. 1963)):

> [I]f one who initiates a transaction or one who solicits offers expressly provides that he will not be bound by a contract until "approval at the home office" or until the expression of approval by an attorney or engineer, there will be no contract until that approval takes place, unless there are subsequent expressions of agreement to be bound without it.

If the party who has reserved the right to home office approval of a proposed contract indicates its unqualified acceptance in some other manner, such as by performance in accordance with the contract, the parties will be bound by the contract. *Corbin* contains an explanation of this alternative form of acceptance of a proposed contract with a home office approval provision:

> [W]here a manufacturer through a sales representative successfully solicits an order, the solicitation may result in the customer signing an order form prepared by the manufacturer. Usually this order form casts the customer in the role of the offeror. The form may specify that the manufacturer will be bound only by the signed acceptance at the home office. Such forms should be interpreted realistically and such maxims as "the offeror is master of the offer" should be applied warily in this context. *If the offeree authored the form and the clauses providing for the means of acceptance, it should have the power to waive such clauses, unless the offeror has relied on the terms of the offer.*

[1 *Corbin on Contracts* § 3.34 (Perillo rev. ed.1993) (emphasis added).]

The most unequivocal form of waiver of a provision of a contract reserving the right to home office approval is full performance by the party who has reserved that right. Indeed, even part performance is generally considered to be a sufficient expression of an intent to be bound by the contract without the formality of home office approval.

The rationale of these cases is that a seller includes a home office approval provision in its form contract solely for its own protection, to give its upper level officials an opportunity to review and approve the contract before it will be bound. Consequently, the seller can waive the requirement of such approval by an alternative form of acceptance, such as shipment of the goods or other performance in accordance with the terms of the contract.

Under this authority, ADT's shipment and installation of the security system at the Synnex warehouse and subsequent monitoring constituted an unequivocal acceptance of the contract. Moreover, Synnex's receipt and payment for these goods and services reflected its understanding that it had contracted with ADT in accordance with the terms of the ADT form contract. Once the security system was delivered and installed, Synnex had no interest in whether an authorized representative of ADT had signed the contract. Synnex's sole interest was in obtaining the goods and services it had contracted to buy. In fact, Synnex apparently did not become aware an authorized representative of ADT had not signed the contract until ADT's copy of the contract was produced in discovery.

The language of the home office approval provision of the ADT form contract reinforces the conclusion that it was only intended to be operative before ADT had undertaken performance. The second sentence states that "[i]n the event of failure of such [home office] approval, the only liability of ADT shall be to return to the Customer the amount, if any, paid to ADT upon signing of this Agreement." This is obviously a remedy that would be feasible only before ADT's delivery and installation of the burglar alarm system and the buyer's payment of the balance of the purchase price. Therefore, we conclude that ADT's performance of the contract by delivery and installation of the security system constituted acceptance without formal home office approval, thus binding both parties to the terms of that contract, including the exculpatory clause.

[The court noted that the] essential rationale of cases upholding the validity of such exculpatory clauses is that a property owner generally will maintain insurance coverage on its property, especially if it is valuable, and that the property owner "is in a far better position than the alarm system seller to know the property's value and to bargain with an insurance company for appropriate coverage and an appropriate premium." *Leon's Bakery, supra,* 990 F.2d at 49. Thus, the practical effect of an exculpatory clause in a contract for the sale of an alarm system is to foreclose an insurance company that has paid the owner for the loss from maintaining a subrogation action against the seller of the alarm system. The ADT form contract expressly recognizes this purpose of the exculpatory clause, by providing that "[c]ustomer agrees to look exclusively to customer's insurer to recover for injuries or damage in the event of any loss or injury and releases and waives all right of recovery against ADT arising by way of subrogation."

[T]he judgment in favor of Synnex is reversed and the case dismissed.

PROBLEM

In August, 1996,Troy Blackford had been issued a "trespass ban" by the Prairie Meadows Racetrack & Casino because he had struck a slot machine and broken its glass. The trespass ban stated, "ON THIS DATE YOU HAVE BEEN ADVISED THAT YOU HAVE BEEN PERMANENTLY DENIED ENTRANCE OR ACCESS TO THE FACILITY OF PRAIRIE MEADOWS RACETRACK AND CASINO." In 2006, Troy returned to the Casino and, over a period of several hours, won 9,387. Because of the high amount of his winnings, the Casino was required to hand pay the prize money and issue Blackford a W-2 form for tax purposes. Upon learning Troy's identity, the Casino refused to pay because the trespass ban was permanent. Troy sued for conversion of the 9,387. Analyze. The problem is based on Blackford v. Prairie Meadows Racetrack & Casino, 778 N.W.2d 184 (Iowa 2010).

[3] Duration of Offers

<h2 style="text-align:center">STARLITE LIMITED PARTNERSHIP v. LANDRY'S
RESTAURANTS, INC.</h2>

780 N.W.2d 396 (Minn. App. 2010)

LANSING, J.

Landry's Seafood House-Minnesota Inc. (Seafood House) extended a written, signed offer to Starlite Limited Partnership on April 30, 1998 to lease Starlite's property in Ramsey County. In addition to the terms of acceptance, the written offer set out the general lease terms over its twenty-year duration. One of the terms of the offer specifically stated that

> If [Starlite] has not executed multiple copies of this [l]ease and returned at least one (1) fully executed copy to [Seafood House] within six (6) days after the date of execution hereof by [Seafood House], [Seafood House's] offer to lease as provided for herein shall be deemed withdrawn, and this [l]ease shall be null, void[,] and of no force and effect.

Contemporaneously, Seafood House's parent corporation, Landry's Restaurants Inc. (Landry's) executed a written guaranty of Seafood House's April 30 lease agreement that presumed Starlite's acceptance. Starlite signed and returned the lease agreement on May 11, 1998, five days after the offer's May 6 deadline. Seafood House occupied the property and built a restaurant on the premises. Seafood House paid rent and property taxes through May 2007 when it vacated the property. Seafood House stopped paying rent in June 2007.

Starlite sued Landry's for payment under the guaranty and moved for summary judgment. Landry's argued, among other things, that the lease was void because Seafood House's offer had expired before it was accepted and, therefore, Landry's was not liable under the guaranty. Starlite argued that Seafood House waived the deadline in its offer through its performance. The district court granted summary judgment to Starlite, concluding that Seafood House waived its deadline for acceptance by occupying the property and paying the amounts owed. The district court ordered Landry's to pay Starlite damages for taxes, interest, past rent, late fees, and attorneys' fees. Landry's appeals arguing that summary judgment is not available on this theory because a term of acceptance cannot be waived by performance.

A fundamental purpose of contract law is to protect the reasonable expectations of the parties who enter into the bargain, which, in turn, promotes and facilitates business agreements. Enforcement of a contract's legal obligations in a way that is consistent with the parties' stated expectations provides certainty and predictability in contractual relationships.

The district court determined that Seafood House's conduct in occupying the property and paying rent and taxes for nine years waived the deadline in Seafood House's offer. Landry's agrees that a party to a contract can waive a term of performance through conduct but argues that this principle does not apply to contract formation and that a defect in the acceptance cannot be waived. Based on our reading of Minnesota case law, we agree.

The law governing contract formation is distinct from that of contract performance. The Minnesota Supreme Court has recognized that distinction in stating that "[b]ecause of strict rules governing offer and acceptance, which require that an acceptance be in terms of the offer, we are reluctant to follow by analogy rules laid down with respect to contracts already formed. In passing upon questions of offer and acceptance, courts may wisely require greater exactitude than when they are trying to salvage an existing contract."

States differ in whether they recognize waiver of a term for acceptance. Minnesota case law recognizes that when an offer specifies a deadline for acceptance and that time passes, the offeree's power to accept lapses and an offeree's late acceptance cannot create a contract. [The cases] establish that an offer expires on the date it specifies and cannot be accepted after that deadline. Consequently, an offeror cannot waive a term of the offer and create a valid agreement because there was no longer an offer that the offeree could accept.

This view is consistent with federal law on contract formation and traditional principles of contract law. *See Kurio v. United States*, 429 F. Supp. 42, 64 (S.D. Tex. 1970) (stating that "[when] an offer has terminated by lapse of time, an attempt to accept is ineffectual to create a contract"); *Restatement (Second) of Contracts § 41* (1981) (stating that offeree's power of acceptance is terminated at time specified in offer); 1 Samuel Williston, *A Treatise on the Law of Contracts § 5:5* (1990) (offeror can specify time for acceptance after which power of acceptance necessarily expires); 1 Corbin, *supra*, § 2.14 (stating that offer may specify time within which acceptance must occur; if so, power of acceptance is limited accordingly).

The waiver theory advanced by Starlite would inject uncertainty into contract formation. Under this theory the offeree is or may be bound by the contract from the time it accepted the offer but the offeror is free to choose whether or not a valid contract was formed and may make this choice "without communication to the offeree, and perhaps without any limitation of time." 2 Williston, *supra* § 6:55. The offeree does not know if it is bound and there are no clear limits to this uncertainty. *See Kurio*, 429 F. Supp. at 64 (stating that "[t]he [g]overnment's argument that the offeror may waive untimeliness does violence to the conceptual basis for contractual law") Also, because the lease offer contained a clear deadline for acceptance, Starlite was in an equally good position as Seafood House to determine the consequence of its late acceptance. *See Restatement (Second) of Contracts § 70* (1981) (discussing effect of late or otherwise defective acceptance).

We decline Landry's request to grant it summary judgment. Landry's argues that a tenancy at will was created when the offer lapsed and Seafood House occupied the property. But Starlite, on appeal, has raised the alternative theory that its late acceptance served as a counteroffer for which it can demonstrate acceptance. Because Starlite did not raise this argument in the district court, we do not consider it on appeal. We note, however, that this theory would comport with the general principles of contract law. *See Restatement (Second) of Contracts § 70* (stating late acceptance may be effective as offer to original offeror); 2 Williston, *supra*, § 6.56 (same); 1 Corbin, *supra*, § 3:20 (same). We do not resolve this question but remand the case for further proceedings.

When a provision in a proposed contract expressly limits the time for acceptance of the offer and states that the proposed contract becomes null and void, that provision operates as a termination if the offer is not accepted within the stated time period. The waiver doctrine does not apply to cure a defect in acceptance and to bind the other party to the contract. We recognize that other doctrines that result in enforcement may apply, and we therefore decline to grant summary judgment for Landry's and reverse and remand for further proceedings. Reversed and remanded.

NOTE

As the master of the offer, the offeror may require acceptance by a stated time. The offer expires at the end of that period. An attempt to exercise a power of acceptance after the stated time expired, therefore, is a nullity. As the principal case indicates, both the Williston and Cotrin treatises as well as § 70 of the Restatement (Second) of Contracts suggest that the late acceptance may be treated as an expression of a new offer by the former offeree to the original offeror. Silence in relation to such a new offer, however, will constitute acceptance only if the silence falls into one of the categories that treats such silence as an acceptance under § 69 which is discussed later in this volume. The notion that a late acceptance may be a *counter* offer is ineffective since there is no offer to counter after the time expires. Some courts suggest that the offeror has "waived" (voluntarily surrendered) the right to assume that the offer expired when it was stated to expire by proceeding to perform as if the offer had been accepted on time. That analysis, however, assumes the offeror and offeree both view all of the original terms of the expired offer as the terms of their new contract created by their conduct. The lesser assumption that the ineffective late acceptance creates a new offer is preferable.

VASKIE v. WEST AMERICAN INSURANCE CO.
Pennsylvania Superior Court
556 A.2d 436 (1989)

Beck, J.

On January 1, 1985, Ms. Vaskie was involved in an automobile accident with a vehicle owned and operated by persons who were insured by West American. Ms. Vaskie retained Harold Murnane, Esquire, to represent her. [P]rior to December 1986 Mr. Murnane and West American began negotiations aimed at settling Ms. Vaskie's claim. As of November 1986, West American had offered 25,000. On December 1, 1986 West American addressed a letter to Mr. Murnane which concluded by stating that West American had carefully reviewed Ms. Vaskie's claim and that West American's "offer will remain 25,000." This letter did not specify a date on which the offer would terminate. On January 9, 1987, Mr. Murnane sent a mailgram to West American in which he, on behalf of Ms. Vaskie, unconditionally accepted West American's 25,000 offer.

West American refused to pay, arguing that there was no contract between the parties because the statute of limitations on Ms. Vaskie's personal injury claim had run on January 1, 1987, eight days before she accepted West American's offer. Ms. Vaskie then instituted this suit for breach of the alleged settlement agreement. The trial court granted Ms. Vaskie's motion for summary judgment, awarding her 25,000, and denied West American's motion. West American appealed.

West American argues that no agreement was formed by Ms. Vaskie's acceptance because the offer had lapsed as a matter of law when the statute of limitations on personal injury claims, i.e. two years, had expired. Where an offer does not specify an expiration date or otherwise limit the allowable time for acceptance, it is both hornbook law and well established in Pennsylvania that the offer is deemed to be outstanding for a reasonable period of time. MURRAY, MURRAY ON CONTRACTS 60–1 (2d ed. 1974); RESTATEMENT (SECOND) CONTRACTS § 41 (1981). What is a reasonable time is ordinarily a question of fact to be decided by the jury and is dependent upon the numerous circumstances surrounding the transaction. MURRAY ON CONTRACTS, at 61; RESTATEMENT, § 41 comment b. Such circumstances as the nature of the contract, the relationship or situation of the parties and their course of dealing, and usages of the particular business are all relevant. *Id.*

The trial court in the instant matter decided that this was a case where the issue of reasonableness could be decided as a matter of law and found that Ms. Vaskie's acceptance on January 9, 1988 was tendered within a reasonable time. We reject West American's contention that its offer of December 1, 1986 lapsed as a matter of law two years after Ms. Vaskie suffered her injuries. However, we do agree with West American insofar as it argues that the trial court erred in deciding as a matter of law that Ms. Vaskie's acceptance was tendered within a reasonable time. We find that under the circumstances of this case, the question of reasonableness is a disputed material issue of fact that should not have been resolved as a matter of law on summary judgment.

There is no merit in the argument that offers of settlement of personal injury claims automatically terminate two years after the injuries were sustained. The argument is based on the incorrect assumption that in every personal injury case the statute of limitations will run precisely two years from the date of the accident. In fact, the statute may be tolled due to the inability of the plaintiff to discover his or her injuries or their cause or due to fraud or concealment of material information by the defendant. Thus, in each particular case the date on which the statute would be deemed to have run may vary. Given this variation, we cannot fashion a rule that creates an implied-in-law termination date, fixed on the expiration of the statute of limitations, in all settlement offers. To do so would leave the plaintiff-offeree in the untenable position of having to predict and, for purposes of settlement negotiations, accept the defendant-offeror's view of when the statute should be deemed to have run.

Moreover, to hold that every such offer contains an implied-in-law termination date would be to dictate a term of such offers which the parties themselves can and should decide upon. If an offering defendant wishes to limit the duration of his offer to a certain time, whether a date two years from the accident or otherwise, he need only so state in the offer itself. He is the master of his offer. There is no need for us to provide such a term where, as here, the defendant has not done so.

This is not to say, however, that the passing of the statute of limitations is irrelevant to a determination of whether an offer of settlement of a personal injury claim has been accepted within a reasonable time. The reasonableness of the time an offeree takes to accept an offer is measured from the perspective of the offeree. As the explanatory comment to the pertinent section of the RESTATEMENT (SECOND) OF CONTRACTS states: In general, the question is what time would be thought satisfactory to the offeror by a reasonable man in the position of the offeree . . . . RESTATEMENT (SECOND) OF CONTRACTS, § 41 comment b (1981).

The fact that the statute of limitations may already have run by the time Ms. Vaskie accepted is unquestionably relevant to a determination of the reasonableness of her conduct in waiting until January 9, 1987 to accept. Further, this is only one of many circumstances surrounding the parties' negotiations and the status of Ms. Vaskie's claim that may be relevant to a determination of reasonableness. The course and nature of settlement negotiations varies greatly from case to case. This is very unlike the situation of a merchant who offers goods for sale on a daily basis at a price that changes daily, where it is clear beyond cavil that an offer made at one day's price is not intended to continue to the next day. In settlement negotiations the reasonable duration of an offer is not fixed at a particular time because of clear and uniform courses of dealing and usages of the trade that invariably arise from the very nature of the transaction.

We conclude that the trial court erred in holding that Ms. Vaskie's January 9th acceptance was tendered within a time that was reasonable as a matter of law. Therefore, the entry of summary judgment in Ms. Vaskie's favor was in error on this ground. The judgment is reversed.

NOTES

(1)   In a similar case, the court held that the offer expired when the statute of limitations expired. The court noted that, a "reasonable time" is ordinarily a question of fact and where the offeree knew or should have known of the offeror's purpose, there is no power of acceptance if that purpose cannot be attained. *Brzezinek v. Covenant Ins. Co.*, 810 A.2d 306 (Conn. App. Ct. 2002).

(2)   Draft an offer to avoid any dispute over when the offer expired.

(3)   UCC § 2-309. *Absence of Specific Time Provisions; Notice of Termination.*

(1) The time for shipment or delivery or any other action under a contract if not provided in this Article or agreed upon shall be a reasonable time.

(2) Where the contract provides for successive performances but is indefinite in duration it is valid for a reasonable time but unless otherwise agreed may be terminated at any time by either party . . . .

(4)   *Speculative Transactions.* When the subject matter of the contract is property which is subject to rapid fluctuation in value, the "reasonable time" is relatively short. This is because the offeror does not assume the risk of such rapid fluctuations for an extended period and also because he does not intend to permit the offeree to speculate at the offeror's expense. Securities are the most obvious example of property subject to rapid fluctuation. Normally, the offeror expects an

immediate reply to his offer and, therefore, the "reasonable time" of such power of acceptance is very short.

Quaere: Suppose an offeree receives an offer by mail to buy, at a fixed price, corporate stock not listed on an exchange. The offeree waits for two days before sending his telegraphic acceptance, and, after learning of a significant increase in the price, bid over-the-counter. According to RESTATEMENT (SECOND) OF CONTRACTS § 41(1973), illustration 8, "The acceptance may be too late even though it arrives before a prompt acceptance by mail would have arrived." In comment *f* to this section, the Restatement (Second) suggests that, "If the offeree makes use for speculative purposes of time allowed for communication, there may be a lack of good faith, and an acceptance may not be timely even though it arrives within the time contemplated by the offeror." This is in keeping with UCC § 1-203: "Every contract or duty within this Act imposes an obligation of good faith in its performance or enforcement."

CALDWELL v. CLINE
West Virginia Supreme Court of Appeals
156 S.E. 55 (1930)

LIVELY, J.

In this chancery suit for the specific performance of a contract for the sale and exchange of real estate, the chancellor sustained a demurrer to plaintiff's bill of complaint and dismissed the bill. Plaintiff appeals.

According to the allegations contained in the bill, W. D. Cline, residing at Valls Creek, McDowell county, W. Va., owner of a tract of land on Indian Creek, McDowell county, addressed a letter, dated January 29, 1929, to W. H. Caldwell, at Peterstown, Monroe county, W. Va., in which Cline proposed to pay to Caldwell the sum of 6,000 cash and to deed to Caldwell his land on Indian Creek in exchange for Caldwell's land known as the McKinsey farm. The letter further provided that Cline "will give you (Caldwell) eight days in which" to accept or reject the offer. Caldwell received the letter at Peterstown on February 2, 1929. On February 8, 1929, the offeree wired Cline as follows: "Land deal is made. Prepare deed to me. See letter." The telegram reached Cline on February 9, 1929. Upon Cline's refusal to carry out the terms of the alleged agreement, plaintiff instituted this suit for specific performance; the titles to the farms remaining unchanged.

The first ground relied upon by defendant to sustain his demurrer to the bill is that the offer and acceptance are too vague and uncertain. These qualities can certainly not be attributed to defendant's offer. The uncertainty in the offer, if any, relates to the question as to when an offer becomes completed, and not to the duration of the offer. The letter provides for acceptance within eight days, which is indeed a mathematical certainty. If there is vagueness in the acceptance telegram, it is as to the intendment of the offeree in the use of the words "See letter," for it is not clear whether the words refer to defendant's offering letter, or to one confirming offeree's telegraphic acceptance. A letter purporting to accept an offer, which, in reality, varied the terms thereof, would constitute a defense; but, in the instant case, the record contains only the bill and demurrer, and the bill relates to but one letter, which is the offering letter of defendant. Without more, the telegram of acceptance appears sufficient to constitute an unconditional acceptance.

Defendant's main contention is that the offer was not accepted within the time limit specified in the offer, and counsel for defendant, in his brief, states the law to be as "the time for acceptance runs from the date of the offer and not from the date of its delivery." The subject of contract by mail began with the English case of *Kennedy v. Lee*, 3 Meriv. and was followed a few years later by *Adams v. Lindsell*, 1 B. & Ald. 681 (1818), and courts have had no hesitation in recognizing the validity of simple contracts thus made. PAGE, LAW OF CONTRACTS, § 198; *Campbell v. Beard*, 57 W. Va. 501, 50 S.E. 747; *Cobb v. Dunlevie*, 63 W. Va. 398, 60 S.E. 384. *Adams v. Lindsell, supra*, was an action for nondelivery of a lot of wool. On September 2, 1817, the defendant wrote from St. Ives to the plaintiffs, living in Bromsgrove, making an offer of a lot of wool on stated terms, one of which was contained in this phrase, "receiving your answer in due course of post." The letter was misdirected, and, in consequence, was not delivered to plaintiffs until September 5th, when an acceptance was sent by return of post and reached defendants on the 9th. Meanwhile, on the 8th, the wool had been sold to other parties. The court, adjudging that a contract had been made upon the posting of the acceptance, stated "that defendants must be considered in law as making, during every instant of the time their letter was traveling, the same identical offer to the plaintiffs." Taken literally, it would follow that an offer was made at the instant the letter is mailed. That the quoted statement from *Adams v. Lindsell* lends difficulty is recognized and criticized by an eminent writer, who finds "the truth of the matter" stated thus in *Bennett v. Cosgriff*, 38 L.T. Rep. (N.S.) 177: "A letter is a continuing offer or order, or statement by the sender which takes effect in the place where the person to whom it is sent receives it." WILLISTON, CONTRACTS, vol. 1, p. 50. And other courts and text-writers have followed the rule that, where a person uses the post to make an offer, the offer is not made when it is posted, but when it is received. *Hartley Silk Manufacturing Co. v. Berg*, 48 Pa. Super. Ct. 419. *See also* RESTATEMENT OF LAW OF CONTRACTS, Amer. Law Inst., § 23; PAGE, LAW OF CONTRACTS, § 198; 13 C.J. 300; *O'Donohoe v. Wiley*, 43 U.C.Q.B. 350. The reason for such a rule is clear. When contracting parties are present, words spoken by one party must strike the ear of the other before there can be mutual assent. So *inter absentes*, letters, which perform the office of words, must come to the knowledge of the party to whom they are addressed before they are accorded legal existence.

The distinction between contracts inter presentes and those inter absentes has no metaphysical existence, for even inter presentes some appreciable time must elapse between the offer on the one hand and the acceptance on the other. As the parties withdraw from each other this time increases, and when they are so far apart that they are obliged to resort to writing to communicate their thoughts to each other, it is none the less true of the communications made by this medium, than of those made by means of spoken words, that in law they are allowed no existence until they reach the intelligence of the person to whom they are addressed. 7 Amer. Law Rev. 434, 456.

As in other contracts, to consummate a contract for the sale of land, there must be mutual assent (27 R.C.L. 323), and, where the proposal to sell stipulates a limited time for acceptance, it is essential, to constitute a valid contract, that the acceptance be communicated to the proposer within the time limited. *Dyer v. Duffy*, 39 W. Va. 148, 19 S.E. 540, 24 L.R.A. 339.

The letter, proposing that Cline "will give you eight days" to accept or reject the offer, is, without more, conclusive of the offeror's intention; and, the unconditional acceptance having been received by Cline within the specified time limit, the result was a concurrence of the minds of the contracting parties upon the subject-matter of their negotiations, in other words, a consummated contract (*Iron Works v. Construction Co.*, 86 W. Va. 173, 102 S.E. 860), and one which equity may enforce (*Hastings v. Montgomery*, 95 W. Va. 734, 122 S.E. 155).

The contention of defendant, relied upon as a third ground in his demurrer, that acceptance could be made only by letter is without merit, since the offer did not provide the means of communication. *Lucas v. Telegraph Co.*, 131 Iowa 669, 108 N.W. 191, 6 L.R.A. (N.S.) 1016.

Being of the opinion that the allegations contained in the bill were sufficient, we reverse the decree of the lower court and reinstate plaintiff's bill of complaint. Decree reversed; bill reinstated; cause remanded.

NOTE

CISG. Article 20(1) of the Vienna Convention (contracts for the international sale of goods), reads as follows: "A period of time for acceptance fixed by the offeror in a telegram of a letter begins to run from the moment the telegram is handed in for dispatch or from the date shown on the letter, or, if no such date is shown, from the date shown on the envelope. A period of time fixed by the offeror by telephone, telex or other means of instantaneous communication, begins to run from the moment that the offer reaches the offeree."

Article 20(2) states that official holidays or non-business days are included in calculating the period except where, because of such holiday or non-business day, the acceptance cannot be delivered. In that situation, the period is extended until the first business day which follows.

Would the application of CISG change the result in the principal case?

C. TERMINATION OF POWER OF ACCEPTANCE

[1] Rejection

CHAPLIN v. CONSOLIDATED EDISON CO. OF NEW YORK
United States District Court, Southern District of New York
537 F. Supp. 1224 (1982)

LASKER, DISTRICT JUDGE.

The Epilepsy Foundation of America and Phyllis Chaplin, individually and as a representative of a proposed class, brought this action against Consolidated Edison Company of New York, Inc. ("Con Ed") and certain of its officials and physicians alleging that Con Ed discriminated against epileptics in violation of Sections 503 and 504 of the Rehabilitation Act of 1973, 29 U.S.C. §§ 793, 794. In 1979, Con Ed moved to dismiss the action on the grounds that Section 503 did not provide a private cause of action. The motion was denied on January 18, 1980, 482 F. Supp. 1165.

In August, 1981, Con Ed's counsel sent to plaintiff's attorney a copy of a settlement proposal which had been approved by Con Ed. Plaintiffs' counsel wrote to defendants' attorney, stating that plaintiffs had "a series of objections to the proposed settlement." In reply, defendants' counsel stated in a letter of September 16, 1981:

> We are still willing to finalize the agreement as it presently stands, thereby resolving this matter. Any further negotiation is an impossibility; and if this agreement is not satisfactory to your client in its present form, then I must withdraw all offers of settlement . . . .

Plaintiffs' attorney answered in a letter of September 17, 1981, which said:

> Based on my previous communications with my clients, I believed that I could convince them to accept the [proffered] terms. Unfortunately, that was not the case. After careful consideration they presented objections which have substantial merit.

> The settlement climate changed abruptly that day when the Second Circuit announced its decision in *Davis v. United Air Lines*, 662 F.2d 120, holding that Section 503 of the Rehabilitation Act did *not* create a private cause of action.

> On September 30th, plaintiffs' attorney informed defendants' counsel by letter that plaintiffs had had "a change of heart" and decided to accept the offer.

> Plaintiffs move to enjoin Con Ed to execute the Consent Agreement and, if the agreement is approved by the Court, to abide by it. They contend that the letter of September 16th constituted an offer, which they accepted by the "change of heart" letter of September 30th. In essence, plaintiffs argue

that Con Ed entered into a contract to settle the case, and that the Court should grant specific performance.

In answer, Con Ed focuses on plaintiffs' counsel's letter of September 17th, which, it argues, was a rejection of Con Ed's offer. It follows, according to Con Ed, that there was no offer remaining to be accepted at the time of plaintiffs' letter of September 30th.

Plaintiffs reply that their attorney's letter of September 17th was not a rejection, but only a statement that no agreement had yet been reached.

The inquiry turns upon a careful reading of the letters of September 16th and 17th. In her letter of September 16th, Con Ed's lawyer stated that the offer was still open. However, she emphatically limited the offer: "if this agreement is not satisfactory to your client in its present form, then I must withdraw all offers of settlement." Con Ed's position was explicit: take it or leave it. Plaintiffs' counsel wrote in reply that he could not convince his clients "to accept the proffered terms." While it is true that the letter does not reject the possibility of arriving at *some* settlement, it does reject the settlement proposed by Con Ed. The offer, as noted above, had been limited to the precise terms proffered and a rejection of those terms could only be a rejection of the offer. Reading the two letters together, we can only conclude that the September 17th letter was a rejection of Con Ed's offer.

An offer is extinguished upon rejection . . . . Thus, at the time of plaintiffs' purported acceptance, no offer existed. Accordingly, the motion to enjoin defendants to execute the Consent Agreement is denied.

QUESTIONS

(1) Suppose an offer states that the offeree has 90 days in which to accept regardless of any statement of rejection by the offeree during that time. Assume that the offeree rejects on the 45th day and, absent any further communication, attempts to accept on the 89th day. Is the acceptance effective?

(2) Assume that a reasonable time for accepting an offer is 50 days. On the 25th day, the offeree sends a letter to the offeror stating, "I reject the offer for the time being, but I will reconsider it later." Absent any further communication, the offeree attempts to accept on the 40th day. Is the acceptance effective?

[2] Revocations, Acceptances and the "Mailbox" Rule

FARLEY v. CHAMPS FINE FOODS, INC.
North Dakota Supreme Court
404 N.W.2d 493 (1987)

GIERKE, J.

During 1979 Champs hired Farley to manage four of its franchised "Kentucky Fried Chicken" restaurants in North Dakota and Minnesota. Pursuant to the employment agreement, Farley had an option to purchase up to 50 percent of Champs' common stock from its parent corporation, Champs Food Systems, Ltd. (Champs, Ltd.), if he met minimum operating profit quotas. Champs, Ltd., rejected Farley's attempt to exercise the option on the ground that Farley failed to meet the quotas. Farley and Champs, Ltd., then began negotiations outside of the terms and conditions of the option agreement. The parties disagree on whether the negotiations concerned a purchase of the stock or the assets of Champs.

On June 3, 1983, Farley submitted to Oscar Grubert, chairman of the board of Champs, Ltd., and president of Champs, a detailed purchase agreement to buy Champs for 548,174. The purchase agreement required Champs, Ltd., to finance the entire sale. This proposal was rejected by Grubert. In a letter to Grubert dated August 2, 1983, Farley proposed the same price terms but modified the financing terms so that only 148,174 of the purchase price would be financed by Champs, Ltd. Grubert also rejected this proposal.

On September 12, 1983, Grubert sent Farley the following letter:

> "Further to our telephone conversation, this is to confirm that our Company is not in a position to take a second position security wise on any monies owing to us if we were to sell the Kentucky Fried Chicken U.S. group to you. We would be prepared to take 450,000 plus the balance as a first charge on the said property and premises [sic]. If this is not possible, we would expect the full sum of 550,000 plus money expended on the drive-through or any other changes, in cash.

> "Unfortunately this matter has dragged out over too long a period of time, and we now feel that we must reach a conclusion by October 1, 1983 as to whether you are in a position to purchase said business. If by October 1, 1983 we have not entered into an agreement, it would be our intention to change the management of our American Kentucky Fried Chicken units by October 15, 1983."

On September 28, 1983, Farley telephoned Grubert. During that conversation Grubert told Farley that he was not going to enter into any agreement with him. A letter from Farley to Grubert was also dated and mailed September 28, 1983, in which Farley stated that "I am prepared to accept your offer to sell for 550,000 plus monies expended on the Drive-Thru, in cash at the time of closing." The parties dispute whether this letter was mailed before or after their telephone conversation. Champs refused to accept the terms of Farley's letter, and Farley commenced this specific performance action.

Following a bench trial, the court found that negotiations between the parties were for a sale of the stock of Champs, rather than the assets; that Farley's September 28, 1983, acceptance letter was mailed after his telephone conversation with Grubert; and that Farley conditioned his acceptance letter on terms outlined in his June 3, 1983, proposed purchase agreement which was rejected by Grubert. The trial court dismissed Farley's action, concluding, among other things, that the terms of Grubert's September 12, 1983, letter were orally withdrawn by Grubert before Farley purported to accept; that the September 12 letter did not constitute an offer but was part of "the preliminary negotiations of price terms"; and that

Farley's September 28 letter was not an acceptance of the terms of Grubert's September 12 letter sufficient to form a specifically enforceable contract.

We believe the dispositive issue is whether the trial court correctly determined that the terms contained in Grubert's September 12 letter were orally withdrawn by Grubert before Farley accepted.

A proposal may be revoked at any time before its acceptance is communicated to the proposer, but not afterwards. § 9-03-22, N.D.C.C. Even though a definite time in which acceptance may be made is named in a proposal, the proposer may revoke his proposal within that period unless it was given for consideration. Section 9-03-19, N.D.C.C., provides:

> 9-03-19. When consent communicated. — Consent is deemed to be communicated fully between the parties as soon as the party accepting a proposal has put his acceptance in the course of transmission to the proposer in conformity to section 9-03-18.

These statutes are a codification of the general rule concerning mailing as an effective mode of acceptance:

> " '. . . the acceptance of an offer is binding from the moment an offeree deposits a properly addressed letter of acceptance in the mailbox, but only if there is an express or implied authorization that the mails are to be used. Such an implied authorization would arise when the offer is communicated by mail.' " *Mansfield v. Smith*, 88 Wis. 2d 575, 277 N.W.2d 740, 746 (1979) [*quoting E.M. Boerke, Inc. v. Williams*, 28 Wis. 2d 627, 137 N.W.2d 489, 493–494 (1965)].

The trial court found as a fact that Farley mailed the acceptance letter after the telephone conversation in which Grubert informed him that the terms contained in the September 12 letter were withdrawn. We will not disturb a trial court's finding of fact unless it is clearly erroneous.

Farley testified that he mailed the letter from Grand Forks and then traveled to one of his restaurants in Grafton where he called Grubert in Winnipeg "to let him know that I've accepted and a copy of that acceptance is in the mail to him." According to Farley, Grubert told him " '[y]ou waited too long. We're not going to accept.' " Grubert testified that during the telephone call Farley asked him "how we were doing on the offer that he'd proposed," but recollected little else about the conversation. Grubert did testify, however, that Farley did not tell him that an acceptance letter had been mailed to him.

Farley asserts that the trial court's finding is clearly erroneous because his testimony that he mailed the letter prior to the telephone conversation is "positive and unimpeached," and is uncontradicted by Grubert's testimony. In *Fleck v. State*, 71 N.W.2d 636, 640 (N.D. 1955), we quoted with approval from *Crilly v. Morris*, 70 S.D. 584, 19 N.W.2d 836, 840 (1945):

> " 'The rule is well settled that where an unimpeached witness testifies distinctly and positively to a fact and is uncontradicted, but the statements of the witness are grossly improbable or he has an interest in the question

at issue, Courts are not bound to blindly adopt the statements of such witness.' "

In this case Farley is an interested party. Moreover, Grubert's testimony that Farley did not tell him that the letter had been sent, which the trial court was entitled to believe, permits a reasonable inference that Farley did not mail the acceptance letter prior to the telephone conversation. We conclude that the trial court's finding that Farley mailed the acceptance letter after the telephone conversation is not clearly erroneous.

Because Grubert withdrew his proposal before Farley's purported acceptance, no enforceable contract was formed and, therefore, the trial court correctly dismissed the action seeking specific performance.

NOTES

(1) *Offers, Revocations, Rejections and Acceptances.* Offers must be received to be effective. Since an offer creates a power of acceptance, the typical offer is revocable, but the revocation must be received by the offeree. Similarly, an offeree can reject an offer, but the rejection does not become effective until it reaches the offeror. A typical counteroffer rejects the original offer and creates a new power of acceptance in the former offeror. While offers, revocations and rejections are not effective until they are received, the principal case states the generally accepted common law rule that acceptances are effective upon mailing (dispatch). It is important to consider why this is so. There have been suggestions that the dispatch rule is predicated on the offeree's loss of control of the acceptance once it is placed in the mail. Postal regulations, however, have traditionally allowed a party to reclaim a mailed letter[11] and the acceptance is not affected by retrieving the letter. Neither is it affected by sending a revocation of acceptance by a faster medium that is received by the offeror before the letter of acceptance. As § 63, comment c of the RESTATEMENT (SECOND) OF CONTRACTS states, "[T]he offeree is not permitted to speculate at the offeror's expense during the time required for the letter to arrive."

As the master of the offer, an offeror can specify the particular manner (promise or performance) or medium (mail, fax, etc.) of acceptance. If the offer does not so specify, it may be accepted in any reasonable manner and by any reasonable medium.[12] If the offer is by mail, the offeree may respond by mail or some other generally accepted reasonable medium such as one of the other widely used mail services, fax or another reasonable medium.[13] Regardless of the reasonable medium used, there is a *risk of transmission.* Suppose the offeree can prove that a letter of acceptance was mailed, but the offeror can prove that it never arrived. Not hearing from the offeree, the offeror proceeded to make the same type of contract with another party. If there were a rule that an offeror had to notify the offeree that the acceptance had arrived, how would the offeror know that its notice of arrival had reached the offeree. Why not make the offeree notify the offeror that the notice of

---

[11] RESTATEMENT (SECOND) OF CONTRACTS § 63, cmt. c.

[12] RESTATEMENT (SECOND) OF CONTRACTS § 30; UCC § 2-206(1).

[13] RESTATEMENT (SECOND) OF CONTRACTS § 65.

the offeree's acceptance having arrived has been received? The impracticality of such repeated notices was suggested in the landmark case of *Adams v. Lindsell*, 1 B. & Ald. 681 (1818). The simple fact is that there is a risk of transmission that must be allocated to one of the parties, both of whom are innocent. Professor Corbin suggests that we simply need a definite rule. He preferred the disptach rule on the footing that it closes the deal more quickly (CORBIN ON CONTRACTS § 78). Another rationale supporting the mailbox rule is that the risk should be allocated to the offeror since only the offeror could have controlled that risk by insisting on receiving an acceptance. Having chosen not to control that risk, the offeror has impliedly assumed it by allowing an acceptance to be effective upon dispatch. *See* MURRAY ON CONTRACTS § 48 (5th ed. 2011). Still another rationale is provided by the RESTATEMENT (SECOND) OF CONTRACTS § 63(a), comment a: The offeree needs a dependable basis for her decision whether to accept an offer. In many legal systems, such a basis is provided because an offer is deemed to be irrevocable.[14] While the common law treats the typical offer as revocable, the common law provides a dependable basis by the rule that revocation is no longer possible once the acceptance is dispatched.

(2) *United Nations Convention on Contracts for the International Sale of Goods (CISG)*. The Civil Law tradition in Europe has always required acceptances to be received to be effective. Following that tradition, Article 18 of CISG rejects the dispatch rule and requires an acceptance to reach the offeror within the time fixed in the offer to be effective. Once an acceptance is dispatched, the offer cannot be revoked (Article 160), but, unlike the common law, Article 22 allows an acceptance to be withdrawn if it reaches the offeror before or at the same time as the acceptance would have become effective. In the previous case of *Caldwell v. Cline*, we saw the common law reaction to an offer providing the offeree with ten days in which to accept. Since the offer did not specify the date on which ten days began to run, the ten days would not begin until the offer reached the offeree. In that situation, however, Article 20(1) of CISG would begin counting the ten days from the date shown on the letter. If the letter itself was not dated, CISG would count the ten days from the date shown on the envelope.

(3) *Option Contracts.* Since offers are revocable under the common law, a party may desire to have time to consider an offer without assuming the risk that it may be revoked before he accepts it. The classic method to make an offer irrevocable is to create a separate option contract where the parties simply agree that, in exchange for consideration, the offer will not be revoked. Option contracts have only one purpose: to make an offer irrevocable. If an offeree has such an irrevocable power of acceptance, it is a firm and dependable basis for decision. Having surrendered the power of revocation of the offer, the offeror does not bear the risk of transmission. The mailbox rule does not apply to option contracts. This is particularly important in the typical case of an option with definite time limits. To be effective, the acceptance must be received within the time specified in the irrevocable offer. *See Romain v. A. Howard Wholesale Co.*, 506 N.E.2d 1124 (Ind. 1987). *See also* RESTATEMENT (SECOND) OF CONTRACTS § 63(b), cmt. f.

---

[14] CISG is heavily influenced by the Civil Law Tradition. Under Article 16(2)(a), if an offer merely states a fixed time for acceptance, the offer is irrevocable.

COMMENT: ELECTRONIC CONTRACTS AND
THE "MAILBOX" RULE

The RESTATEMENT (SECOND) OF CONTRACTS § 64 departs from the mailbox rule where the acceptance of an offer is by telephone or other "instantaneous two-way communication." The rationale for this suggested rule is that such communication is similar to parties being in the presence of each other where an "offeree can accept without being in doubt as to whether the offeror has attempted to revoke his offer or whether the offeree has received the acceptance" (comment a). This view, however, has not been adopted in the case law.

Telephone. In the leading case of *Linn v. Employers Reinsurance Corp.*, 392 Pa. 58, 139 A.2d 638 (1958), the court recognized this same analysis in the FIRST RESTATEMENT OF CONTRACTS (§ 65) as theoretically sound, but chose to follow the prevailing view in the reported cases where the issue is where the contract is made when the parties are in different jurisdictions. Thus, where the offer is made by telephone in Pennsylvania and the acceptance is spoken in New York, New York law would apply. Pennsylvania and North Carolina do not include contracts not performable within one year from the time they are made among contracts that must be evidenced by a writing (Statute of Frauds considered in Chapter 4). New York is among the jurisdictions that includes the one-year provision. If the oral contract was made in Pennsylvania, it would be enforceable. If made in New York it would be unenforceable. The court held that if sufficient facts were adduced to determine that the acceptance was spoken in New York, the contract was made where the acceptance was spoken.

Telegram. Courts have applied the "mailbox" rule in holding that a telegram acceptance is effective when the acceptance is deposited with the telegraph company. In *Weld & Co. v. Victory Mfg. Co.*, 205 F. 770 (E.D.N.C. 1913), the buyer made an offer by letter. The seller deposited a telegram at 10:15 A.M. on September 20 stating that the offer was accepted. That telegram did not reach the buyer until 12:35 P.M. On the same day, the buyer had deposited a telegram in the telegraph office at 9:55 A.M., stating that the offer was cancelled, that reached the seller at 10:40 A.M. The court held the contract was formed when the seller, prior to receiving the buyer's revocation, had accepted the offer by depositing the telegram of acceptance. The RESTATEMENT (SECOND) OF CONTRACTS § 63, comment a, would also apply the mailbox rule to telegram acceptances since it is not an "instantaneous" method of communication.

Fax and Telex. There is case law recognizing that the transmission of a fax acceptance is like mailing a letter under the mailbox rule making the acceptance effective upon dispatch. *See Osprey, L.L.C. v. Kelly-Moore Paint Co.*, 984 P.2d 194 (Ok. 1999); *Trinity Homes, L.L.C. v. Fang*, 2003 Va. Cir. LEXIS 349 (2003). In *Norse Petroleum A/S v. LVO International, Inc.*, 389 A.2d 771 (Del. Supr. Ct. 1978), relying on the *Linn* case, *supra*, the court recognized a telex acceptance sent from Norway as effective when sent, thereby employing Norwegian law. A different result occurred in an English case, *Entores Ltd. v. Miles Far East Corp.*, 2 Q.B. 327 (1955), which employed the rationale of parties being in the "presence" of each other resulting in the acceptance being effective when and where it was received.

E-Mail and Other Electronic Media. At the moment, there is no discernible case law as to whether the mailbox rule should apply to such communications. While the *Uniform Electronic Transactions Act* (UETA), which has been enacted in 48 jurisdictions, and its federal companion, the *Electronic Signatures in Global and National Commerce Act* ("E-Sign") share the same purpose of facilitating electronic commerce by validating electronic records and signatures as if they were traditional writings and traditional signatures, neither statute determines the time when an acceptance of an offer becomes effective. Comment 2 to UETA § 15 captioned, "Time and Place of Sending and Receipt," states: "The effect of sending and its import are determined by other law once it is determined that a sending has occurred."

The *Uniform Computer Information Transactions Act* (UCITA), however, adopts a time of receipt rule for an electronic acceptance (§ 203(4)(A) and comment 5). The limited scope of UCITA to computer information transactions and its current lack of support, having been enacted in only Maryland and Virginia, casts considerable doubt upon its significance in this respect or others.

[3]　Variations on the "Mailbox" (Dispatch) Theme

PROBLEMS

(1)　Ames in Pennsylvania mails an offer to sell his house for 500,000 to Barnes in Illinois. Barnes mails a letter of acceptance in reply to the offer. The same day, Ames changes his mind and, complying with U.S. Postal procedures, retrieves the letter of acceptance from the mail. Ames can prove these facts. Is there a contract?[15]

(2)　Ames mails the same offer to Barnes, who replies by mailing a letter of acceptance. The next day, Barnes changes his mind and sends an e-mail to Ames rejecting the offer, which is received by Ames three minutes after it was sent by Barnes. Ames relies on the e-mail and contracts to sell the house to Carr. The following day, Barnes' letter accepting Ames' offer is received by Ames. Barnes then informs Ames that he has, again, changed his mind and seeks to enforce the contract. What are the rights of the parties? Suppose Ames had not agreed to sell the house to Carr and, upon receiving Barnes' letter, Ames claims that he has a contract with Barnes. What are the rights of the parties?[16]

(3)　Ames mails the same offer to Barnes, who responds by mailing a letter rejecting Ames' offer. Two hours later, Barnes changes his mind and mails a letter accepting the offer. Consider: (a) the letter of acceptance was received by Barnes before the letter of rejection; (b) the letter of rejection was received by Barnes before the letter of acceptance; (c) both letters were received simultaneously. What are the rights of the parties?

(4)　Ames mails the same offer to Barnes, who responds by sending an e-mail to Ames accepting the offer. Sixty seconds before Ames receives Barnes' e-mail,

---

[15]　*See* RESTATEMENT (SECOND) OF CONTRACTS § 63, cmts. a, c.

[16]　*See* RESTATEMENT (SECOND) OF CONTRACTS § 63, cmt. c.

Barnes receives an e-mail from Ames revoking the offer. What are the rights of the parties?

(5) Ames mails the same offer to Barnes, who responds by telephoning Ames. Ames is not available and, pursuant to the general message on Ames' answering machine, Barnes leaves a message stating that he accepts Ames' offer. Ames had sent a revocation to Barnes that arrived after Barnes left the message. Ames claims that no enforceable contract exists. What are the rights of the parties?

(6) Ames and Barnes signed an agreement stating that, in exchange for a payment of 100, Barnes would have ten days in which to accept Ames' offer to sell the house to Barnes for 500,000. On the tenth day, Barnes mailed a letter of acceptance that Ames received two days later. Ames claims that there is no contract for the sale of the house. What are the rights of the parties?

(7) The Ames Corporation, with its principal place of business in Philadelphia, Pennsylvania, sent a letter dated October 5, 2005 offering to purchase a computerized lathe manufactured by the Barnes Corporation which has its principal place of business in Cologne, Germany. The letter, which arrived at Barnes Cologne plant on October 9, stated that Barnes had ten days in which to accept the offer. Barnes mailed an acceptance of the offer on October 13 which was received by the Ames Corporation on October 17. What are the rights of the panics?

(8) The Ames Corporation sent the same offer to Barnes in Cologne on October 5. Upon receiving the offer on October 9, Barnes immediately mailed an acceptance to Ames which arrived in Philadelphia on October 13. Suppose: (a) Ames had sent a revocation of its offer to Barnes which Barnes received on October 10, or (b) Barnes had sent a withdrawal of its acceptance to Ames which arrived at Ames' place of business simultaneously with Barnes' acceptance on October 13. What are the rights of the parties?

[4] Indirect Revocation

DICKINSON v. DODDS
Delaware Court of Chancery
2 Ch. D. 463 (1876)

On Wednesday, the 10th of June, 1874, the defendant John Dodds signed and delivered to the plaintiff, George Dickinson, a memorandum of which the material part was as follows: —

> "I hereby agree to sell to Mr. George Dickinson the whole of the dwelling-houses, garden ground, stabling, and outbuildings thereto belonging, situate at Croft, belonging to me, for the sum of 800 £. As witness my hand this tenth day of June, 1874.
>
> 800£. (Signed) John Dodds
>
> P.S. — This offer to be left over until Friday, 9 o'clock, A.M. J.D. (the twelfth), 12th June, 1874. (Signed) J. Dodds"

The bill alleged that Dodds understood and intended that the plaintiff should have until Friday, 9 A.M., within which to determine whether he would or would not purchase, and that he should absolutely have, until that time, the refusal of the property at the price of 800 £., and that the plaintiff in fact determined to accept the offer on the morning of Thursday, the 11th of June, but did not at once signify his acceptance to Dodds, believing that he had the power to accept it until 9 A.M. on the Friday.

In the afternoon of the Thursday the plaintiff was informed by a Mr. Berry that Dodds had been offering or agreeing to sell the property to Thomas Allan, the other defendant. Thereupon the plaintiff, at about half-past seven in the evening, went to the house of Mrs. Burgess, the mother-in-law of Dodds, where he was then staying, and left with her a formal acceptance, in writing, of the offer to sell the property. According to the evidence of Mrs. Burgess, this document never in fact reached Dodds, she having forgotten to give it to him.

On the following (Friday) morning, at about seven o'clock, Berry, who was acting as agent for Dickinson, found Dodds at the Darlington railway station, and handed to him a duplicate of the acceptance by Dickinson, and explained to Dodds its purport. He replied that it was too late, as he had sold the property. A few minutes later Dickinson himself found Dodds entering a railway carriage, and handed him another duplicate of the notice of acceptance, but Dodds declined to receive it, saying, "You are too late. I have sold the property."

It appeared that on the day before, Thursday, the 11th of June, Dodds had signed a formal contract for the sale of the property to the defendant Allan for 800 £., and had received from him a deposit of 40£.

The bill in this suit prayed that the defendant Dodds might be decreed specifically to perform the contract of the 10th of June, 1874; that he might be restrained from conveying the property to Allan; that Allan might be restrained from taking any such conveyance; that, if any such conveyance had been or should be made, Allan might be declared a trustee of the property for, and might be directed to convey the property to, the plaintiff; and for damages.

[BACON, V.C., decreed specific performance in favor of the plaintiff, on the ground that by the original offer or agreement with the plaintiff, and by relation back of the acceptance to the date of the offer, Dodds had lost the power to make a sale to Allan. From this decision the defendants appealed.]:

JAMES, L.J., after referring to the document of the 10th of June, 1874, continued: —

The document, though beginning "I hereby agree to sell," was nothing but an offer, and was only intended to be an offer, for the plaintiff himself tells us that he required time to consider whether he would enter into an agreement or not. Unless both parties had then agreed, there was no concluded agreement then made; it was in effect and substance only an offer to sell. The plaintiff, being minded not to complete the bargain at that time, added this memorandum: "This offer to be left over until Friday, 9 o'clock A.M., 12th June, 1874." That shows it was only an offer. There was no consideration given for the undertaking or promise, to whatever extent it may be considered binding, to keep the property unsold until 9 o'clock on

Friday morning; but apparently Dickinson was of opinion, and probably Dodds was of the same opinion, that he (Dodds) was bound by that promise, and could not in any way withdraw from it, or retract it, until 9 o'clock on Friday morning, and this probably explains a good deal of what afterwards took place. But it is clear settled law, on one of the clearest principles of law, that this promise, being a mere nudum pactum, was not binding, and that at any moment before a complete acceptance by Dickinson of the offer, Dodds was as free as Dickinson himself. Well, that being the state of things, it is said that the only mode in which Dodds could assert that freedom was by actually and distinctly saying to Dickinson, "Now I withdraw my offer." It appears to me that there is neither principle nor authority for the proposition that there must be an express and actual withdrawal of the offer, or what is called a retraction. It must, to constitute a contract, appear that the two minds were at one at the same moment of time; that is, that there was an offer continuing up to the time of the acceptance. If there was not such a continuing offer, then the acceptance comes to nothing. Of course, it may well be that the one man is bound in some way or other to let the other man know that his mind with regard to the offer has been changed; but in this case, beyond all question, the plaintiff knew that Dodds was no longer minded to sell the property to him as plainly and clearly as if Dodds had told him in so many words, "I withdraw the offer." This is evidence from the plaintiff's own statements in the bill.

The plaintiff says in effect that, having heard and knowing that Dodds was no longer minded to sell to him, and that he was selling or had sold to someone else, thinking that he could not, in point of law, withdraw his offer, meaning to fix him to it, and endeavoring to bind him.

I went to the house where he was lodging, and saw his mother-in-law, and left with her an acceptance of the offer, knowing all the while that he had entirely changed his mind. I got an agent to watch for him at 7 o'clock the next morning, and I went to the train just before 9 o'clock, in order that I might catch him and give him my notice of acceptance just before 9 o'clock, and when that occurred he told my agent, and he told me, you are too late, and he then threw back the paper.

It is to my mind quite clear that, before there was any attempt at acceptance by the plaintiff, he was perfectly well aware that Dodds had changed his mind, and that he had in fact agreed to sell the property to Allan. It is impossible, therefore, to say there was ever that existence of the same mind between the two parties which is essential in point of law to the making of an agreement. I am of opinion, therefore, that the plaintiff has failed to prove that there was any binding contract between Dodds and himself.

[The statement of facts has been rewritten and the concurring opinion of MELLISH, L.J., has been omitted.]

NOTES

(1) In *Hoover Motor Express Co. v. Clements Paper Co.*, 193 Tenn. 6, 241 S.W.2d 851 (1951), the defendant offered to sell certain land to the plaintiff on November 19, 1949. On January 13, 1950, a telephone conversation took place between the parties in which defendant indicated that it had not definitely decided to go through with the deal, that it might not go through with it, and, generally that it had other plans in mind. On January 20, 1950, the plaintiff sent its written acceptance of the offer to the defendant. The Supreme Court of Tennessee held that the telephone conversation of January 13 should have indicated to the offeree that the offeror-defendant had withdrawn the offer since, "It is sufficient to constitute a withdrawal that knowledge of acts by the offeror inconsistent with the continuance of the offer is brought home to the offeree." (55 Am. Jur. 488, quoted by the court.) Thus, even though the language used by the defendant was somewhat equivocal, the court held that it was effective to constitute a withdrawal.

(2) Suppose that *A*, after offering to sell his auto to *B* for 1,000, tells *B* that he is not sure that he wants to sell his car, or that the price is raised to 1,500. Is this enough to constitute a revocation?

(3) RESTATEMENT (SECOND) OF CONTRACTS § 43:

> *Indirect Communication of Revocation.* An offeree's power of acceptance is terminated when the offeror takes definite action inconsistent with an intention to enter the proposed contract and the offeree acquires reliable information to that effect.

(4) When the offeree learns of the offeror's intent to revoke through a third person, does it make any difference whether this person is the town banker or the village idiot? Suppose the town banker is inebriated?

[5] Counter Offers

ARDENTE v. HORAN
Rhode Island Supreme Court
366 A.2d 162 (1976)

DORIS, J.

In August 1975, certain residential property in the city of Newport was offered for sale by defendants. The plaintiff made a bid of 250,000 for the property which was communicated to defendants by their attorney. After defendants' attorney advised plaintiff that the bid was acceptable to defendants, he prepared a purchase and sale agreement at the direction of defendants and forwarded it to plaintiff's attorney for plaintiff's signature. After investigating certain title conditions, plaintiff executed the agreement. Thereafter plaintiff's attorney returned the document to defendants along with a check in the amount of 20,000 and a letter dated September 8, 1975, which read in relevant part as follows:

"My clients are concerned that the following items remain with the real estate: a) dining room set and tapestry wall covering in dining room; b) fireplace fixtures throughout; c) the sun parlor furniture. I would appreciate your confirming that these items are a part of the transaction, as they would be difficult to replace."

The defendants refused to agree to sell the enumerated items and did not sign the purchase and sale agreement. They directed their attorney to return the agreement and the deposit check to plaintiff and subsequently refused to sell the property to plaintiff. This action for specific performance followed. The plaintiff [contends] that the trial justice incorrectly applied the principles of contract law in deciding that the facts did not disclose a valid acceptance of defendants' offer. Again we cannot agree.

The trial justice proceeded on the theory that the delivery of the purchase and sale agreement to plaintiff constituted an offer by defendants to sell the property. Because we must view the evidence in the light most favorable to the party against whom summary judgment was entered, in this case plaintiff, we assume as the trial justice did that the delivery of the agreement was in fact an offer.

The question we must answer next is whether there was an acceptance of that offer. The general rule is that where, as here, there is an offer to form a bilateral contract, the offeree must communicate his acceptance to the offeror before any contractual obligation can come into being. A mere mental intent to accept the offer, no matter how carefully formed, is not sufficient. The acceptance must be transmitted to the offeror in some overt manner. A review of the record shows that the only expression of acceptance which was communicated to defendants was the delivery of the executed purchase and sale agreement accompanied by the letter of September 8. Therefore it is solely on the basis of the language used in these two documents that we must determine whether there was a valid acceptance. Whatever plaintiff's unexpressed intention may have been in sending the documents is irrelevant. We must be concerned only with the language actually used, not the language plaintiff thought he was using or intended to use.

There is no doubt that the execution and delivery of the purchase and sale agreement by plaintiff, without more, would have operated as an acceptance. The terms of the accompanying letter, however, apparently conditioned the acceptance upon the inclusion of various items of personalty. In assessing the effect of the terms of that letter we must keep in mind certain generally accepted rules. To be effective, an acceptance must be definite and unequivocal. "An offeror is entitled to know in clear terms whether the offeree accepts his proposal. It is not enough that the words of a reply justify a probable inference of assent." 1 Restatement Contracts § 58, comment a (1932). The acceptance may not impose additional conditions on the offer, nor may it add limitations. "An acceptance which is equivocal or upon condition or with a limitation is a counteroffer and requires acceptance by the original offeror before a contractual relationship can exist." *John Hancock Mut. Life Ins. Co. v. Dietlin*, 97 R.I. 515, 518, 199 A.2d 311, 313 (1964).

However, an acceptance may be valid despite conditional language if the acceptance is clearly independent of the condition. Many cases have so held. WILLISTON states the rule as follows:

Frequently an offeree, while making a positive acceptance of the offer, also makes a request or suggestion that some addition or modification be made. So long as it is clear that the meaning of the acceptance is positively and unequivocally to accept the offer whether such request is granted or not, a contract is formed.

1 WILLISTON, CONTRACTS § 79 at 261–62 (3d ed. 1957).

CORBIN is in agreement with the above view. 1 CORBIN, *supra* § 84 at 363–65. Thus our task is to decide whether plaintiff's letter is more reasonably interpreted as a qualified acceptance or as an absolute acceptance together with a mere inquiry concerning a collateral matter.

In making our decision we recognize that, as one text states, "The question whether a communication by an offeree is a conditional acceptance or counter-offer is not always easy to answer. It must be determined by the same common-sense process of interpretation that must be applied in so many other cases." 1 CORBIN, *supra* § 82 at 353. In our opinion, the language used in plaintiff's letter of September 8 is not consistent with an absolute acceptance accompanied by a request for a gratuitous benefit. We interpret the letter to impose a condition on plaintiff's acceptance of defendants' offer. The letter does not unequivocally state that even without the enumerated items plaintiff is willing to complete the contract. In fact, the letter seeks "confirmation" that the listed items "are a part of the transaction." Thus, far from being an independent, collateral request, the sale of the items in question is explicitly referred to as a part of the real estate transaction. Moreover, the letter goes on to stress the difficulty of finding replacements for these items. This is a further indication that plaintiff did not view the inclusion of the listed items as merely collateral or incidental to the real estate transaction. A review of the relevant case law discloses that those cases in which an acceptance was found valid despite an accompanying conditional term generally involved a more definite expression of acceptance than the one in the case at bar.

Accordingly, we hold that since the plaintiff's letter of acceptance dated September 8 was conditional, it operated as a rejection of the defendants' offer and no contractual obligation was created.

NOTES

(1)   At common law, a response that varies the terms of the offer cannot be an acceptance because of the "mirror image" or "matching acceptance" rule that requires the acceptance to match the offer. Later in this chapter we will explore a major modification of this common law prescription with respect to certain manifestations of offer and acceptance — the use of printed forms — under a radical change effected by the Uniform Commercial Code's chief architect, Professor Karl Llewellyn. For now, however, we remain with the "matching acceptance" rule which necessarily refuses recognize a response to an offer that deviates from the terms of the offer as an acceptance of that offer. If such a response is not an acceptance, it must be something else, and the only common law category remaining is the category of counter offer. It must be emphasized, however, than an unqualified acceptance accompanied by a *mere request* for additional terms is an

acceptance. Thus, in *Kodiak Island Borough v. Large*, 622 P.2d 440, 448 (Alaska 1981), the court states, "The fact that the assent was accompanied by a suggestion as to terms of payment, a detail not inconsistent with the offer, did not convert it into a counter offer." *See also Martindell v. Fiduciary Counsel, Inc.*, 131 N.J. Eq. 523, 26 A.2d 171, *aff'd*, 30 A.2d 281 (1943), and *Rucker v. Sanders*, 182 N.C. 607, 109 S.E. 857 (1921), both of which deal with a contract to purchase stock where the buyer *suggested* a method of payment.

(2) *Effect of Counter Offers.* The normal effect of a counter offer is to reject the original offer, i.e., it terminates the original power of acceptance in the offeree who is now a counter-offeror. RESTATEMENT 2d § 39. But a counter offer is different from a typical rejection in that it seeks to carry negotiations on rather than break them off, albeit on the offeree's new (counter offer) terms. Moreover, while the normal counter offer rejects the original offer, it need not do so. The offer itself may have expressly indicated its continuance notwithstanding one or more counter offers. *See* RESTATEMENT (SECOND) OF CONTRACTS § 39(2) and comment c. Thus, in response to Ames' offer to sell his car to Barnes for 10,000, Barnes could reply, "I would like to consider the offer for a few days. In the meantime, I will agree to purchase your car immediately for 9,000." This clear expression of intention that the counter offer is not designed to reject the original offer should have this effect. In general, see MURRAY ON CONTRACTS, *supra* Chapter 1, note 1, at § 43D (5th ed. 2011).

[6] Death or Incapacity

PROBLEM

A father named his two children as beneficiaries of a term life insurance policy in the face amount of $500,000. Though his monthly premium for June 2009 was fully paid through June 31, on June 18, he called a representative of the insurer requesting immediate cancellation of the policy. He was told that he would have to submit a signed and dated writing to cancel the policy which contained no cancellation clause. The father faxed a signed and dated writing on the same day. The father died on July 1. In a letter dated July 2, the insurer accepted the cancellation, but learned of the death only days later. The insurance policy included a grace period of 30 days after a failure to make a monthly payment. The insurer refused to pay the policy when claimed by the beneficiaries. Analyze. The problem is based on *Yosco v. Aviva Life & Annuity Co.*, 753 F. Supp. 2d 607 (E. D. Va. 2010).

BEALL v. BEALL
Maryland Court of Appeals
434 A.2d 1015 (1981)

COLE, JUDGE.

Calvin and Cecelia Beall were husband and wife, who in 1956 purchased as tenants by the entirety a 1/2 acre parcel of land, from John and Pearl Beall, Calvin's father and mother. In February of 1968, Carlton Beall, a second cousin to Calvin, obtained a written, three-year option to purchase Calvin and Cecelia's parcel for

28,000. This option recited consideration of 100.00 which was paid by check to Calvin. In February of 1971 the parties executed a new option for five years, on the same terms as the first, which again recited consideration of 100.00. Carlton never exercised either option, but in 1975 four lines were added to the bottom of the 1971 agreement which purported to extend it for three additional years. Calvin and Cecelia signed this addendum, which reads as follows:

> As of October 6, 1975, we, Calvin F. Beall and Cecelia M. Beall, agree to continue this option agreement three more years — February 1, 1976 to February 1, 1979.
>
> /s/ Calvin Beall
>
> /s/ Cecelia Beall

Calvin died in 1977. In May of 1978, Carlton advised Cecelia by letter that he was accepting the offer to sell and would be in a position to settle within thirty (30) days. Cecelia responded that she was unwilling to sell for 28,000. In September of 1978, Carlton again notified her of his intent to purchase and advised her of the settlement date. Again Cecelia refused and declined to attend the settlement.

[T]he purported extension of the option in 1975 was not a binding contract but merely an offer, which could be revoked at any time prior to acceptance.

Carlton argues that, . . . if the extension agreement was . . . a bare offer, he accepted this offer before it was withdrawn, thereby creating a binding contract between the parties which the court may enforce. Apparently what Carlton does not reckon with is the effect of Calvin's death in 1977 upon this offer, based upon the fact that Calvin and Cecelia owned the property in question as tenants by the entirety.

The general rule is that the death of an offeror revokes his offer or causes his offer to lapse. Death terminates the power of the deceased offeror to act. Therefore, after death, the formation of that "apparent state of mind of the parties which is embodied in an expression of mutual consent" is rendered impossible.

Cecelia asserts that the offer at issue was made by a single unit, tenants by the entirety, and, that when Calvin died the marriage of Calvin and Cecelia was terminated and operated as the legal death of the offeror, which, according to the long established rule, caused the offer to lapse. Carlton's rejoinder is that the offer to sell was signed by two individuals, each of whom had an interest in the whole, and that while the death of Calvin operated as a revocation of *his* offer to sell and terminated his interest, his death neither (1) terminated the offer made by Cecelia, an offer over which she retained, as an individual and as from the outset, the unrestricted power to revoke; (2) increased her interest; nor (3) destroyed her capacity to convey. In other words, Carlton suggests the effect of the death of Calvin was merely to free the estate from his participation. Such a view, however, flies in the face of common law principles regarding the nature of an offer and the attributes of an estate held by the entirety.

Viewing the offer of tenants by the entirety as being made by a team rather than the two individuals who make up this team provides a solution in the instant case. The continuation of an offer made in this fashion depends upon the continuous assent of both tenants, for neither can continue an offer to sell without the continued assent of the other. Here, in the absence of consideration to support an option, the vitality of the offer made by Calvin and Cecelia depended upon the continued assent of each; upon Calvin's death, his assent was no longer viable. Hence, the offer lapsed upon the death of Calvin Beall. After his death, one of two events was necessary to the formation of a contract in the instant case: (1) a renewal by Cecelia of the lapsed offer to sell, which offer was accepted by Carlton Beall, or (2) an offer to buy made by Carlton, which offer was accepted by Cecelia. Neither of the above sequences of events took place. We conclude that when Carlton sent his letter of acceptance in May of 1978 there was no viable offer for him to accept. Calvin's death had effectively caused the offer to lapse. We hold, therefore, that no enforceable contract was formed between the parties. [*Reversed.*]

NOTES

(1) It is important to emphasize the possible injustice of the traditional rule that death revokes an offer. An offeree may reasonably perform in response to an offer, thinking she has accepted the offer by such performance, only to discover that, prior to any performance, the offeror has died. There is no requirement that the fact of death be communicated to the offeree to constitute an effective revocation. The rule has been criticized by Professor Corbin in his article, *Offer and Acceptance and Some of the Resulting Legal Relations*, 26 YALE L.J. 169, 198 (1917) (while one cannot contract with a dead man, there is no obstacle in creating legal relations with the personal representative who will be responsible for paying the debts of the estate). Professor Williston, remarkably, failed to have the rule changed in the FIRST RESTATEMENT OF CONTRACTS, and the SECOND RESTATEMENT continues the rule but opines that it is "a relic of the obsolete view that a contract requires a 'meeting of the minds.' " RESTATEMENT 2D § 48, comment a. *See* ON CONTRACTS, *supra* Chapter 1, note 1, at § 43E (5th ed. 2011).

(2) The same rule applies to the incapacity of the offeror. Thus, in *Union Trust & Sav. Bank v. State Bank*, 188 N.W.2d 300 (Iowa 1971), an offer of guaranty (I will pay if he does not pay) was made and, before it was accepted, the offeror was deemed incapacitated and a conservator was appointed. The court held that the appointment of the conservator with plaintiff's knowledge served to revoke the then unaccepted offer.

D. MAKING OFFERS IRREVOCABLE

[1] Introduction

In our exploration of the several ways in which a power of acceptance may be terminated, we emphasized the common law view that offers are revocable. An offer creates a power of acceptance making the offeror susceptible to the exercise of that power in the offeree. The offeree, however, is subject to the termination of that power at any time prior to acceptance through direct or indirect communication of revocation or even the uncommunicated death of the offeror. It is not remarkable that an offeree may wish to avoid the offeror's power of revocation and retain the power of acceptance while deciding whether to accept the offer, or to avoid the risk of the offeror's revocation. It is important to consider carefully how offers may be made irrevocable.

[2] Option Contract — Rights of First Refusal

ORLOWSKI v. MOORE
Pennsylvania Superior Court
181 A.2d 692 (1962)

WOODSIDE, J.

This is an appeal from the final decree of the Court of Common Pleas of Armstrong County dismissing the appellant's complaint in equity.

Orlowski, the appellant here, filed the complaint against Mary H. Moore and W. Frank Moore, her husband, and the Apollo Trust Company for the specific performance of a contract for the sale of real estate.

During the year 1959, and prior thereto, the Moores were the owners of a property known as 212–214 First Avenue in Apollo. The Moores offered the property for sale at a price of 5500, and although there were several prospective purchasers, none was willing to pay that price. On September 1, 1959, the property was leased to Orlowski for a period of one year at a rental of 35 per month. The lease agreement was in writing and contained the following provision: "Lessee has the first chance to buy in case of sale of the property." Prior to the execution of the lease, Orlowski was notified that the Moores intended to sell the property upon securing a suitable buyer.

About the middle of January, 1960, the Apollo Trust Company advised the Moores that it would purchase the property for 5000. Immediately thereafter Orlowski was notified that the Moores had a purchaser for the price of 5000 to whom the property would be sold unless Orlowski exercised his right of first purchase. The rent for December and January was not paid on time, and at the time of the payment of the rental, in early February, Orlowski was again notified that the property would be sold to another person unless Orlowski arranged for the purchase. At this time, Orlowski notified the Moores that he had attempted to secure a loan from a bank and was unsuccessful, but that he would continue to try to secure the purchase money. On February 10, 1960, the Moores, believing that Orlowski could not secure the purchase price, gave an option for the purchase of the property for 5000 to the Apollo Trust Company for a period of 60 days. The trust company exercised the option, and a deed for the property was executed by the Moores and delivered to the trust company on March 9, 1960. After the option was given to the trust company by the Moores, but before they conveyed title, Orlowski notified the Moores that he had secured the purchase money and asked for the conveyance of the property to him.

The facts set forth above are not exactly in accord with the appellant's testimony, but are substantially those found by the chancellor and approved by the court. We have examined the record and have found the necessary evidence to support them.

Presiding Judge J. Frank Graff, in his opinion as chancellor, properly dealt with this case as follows:

> The sole question which arises in this case is whether a reasonable time was given to Orlowski to exercise his right of first purchase. It was unnecessary for the Moores to give Orlowski a written notice that they had secured a purchaser ready and willing to buy, and we are of the opinion that the verbal notice given in the middle of January 1960 was sufficient warning to the plaintiff that the property would be disposed of unless he exercised his right: *Wallach, Inc. v. Toll*, 381 Pa. 423 [113 A.2d 258].

Where no time is specified for the performance of an act, the law implies that it must be done within a reasonable time, and what is a reasonable time depends entirely upon the circumstances of each case: *Detwiler et al. v. Capone et ux.*, 357 Pa. 495 [55 A.2d 380]; *Barr v. Deiter*, 190 Pa. Super. Ct. 454 [154 A.2d 290].

For the reason that the Moores were losing money upon their property, the same had been offered for sale for more than a year prior to the execution of the deed to the Apollo Trust Company. This fact was known to the plaintiff when he became lessee under the lease dated September 1, 1959. It was known to him at the time of the execution of the lease that unless he purchased the property, it would be sold to another suitable person. In view of the fact Orlowski had difficulty in paying the small rental in the amount of 35.00 per month, and that he had on different occasions stated that he was either unable to secure the purchase money or was having difficulty in doing so, the Moores were reasonably led to believe that it would be impossible for him to exercise the right given to him in the lease. He was notified in January that unless he exercised this right, the property would be sold to another person. After this, the defendants Moore waited for a period of at least three weeks prior to giving the right of purchase to the Apollo Trust Company. A short time prior to the granting of the option to the Trust Company, the defendants Moore were reasonably led to believe that he could not secure the purchase money for the reason that he stated to them that he was unable to secure a loan from the bank and did not know what he could do.

It would be unfair to the Moores to prevent them from securing a purchaser by waiting for a longer period in which the plaintiff Orlowski might secure the necessary money. Under all of the circumstances, we believe that the notice given to Orlowski to purchase was for a reasonable time prior to the execution of the option to the Trust Company and, therefore, any right which he had under the lease was terminated . . . .

Decree affirmed at cost of appellant.

NOTES

(1) *The classical option contract is a separate contract with only one purpose*: to make an offer irrevocable. Thus, where Barnes is interested in an offer by Ames to sell Ames' property to Barnes for 100,000, but Barnes does not wish to make an immediate decision, he may offer Ames a certain sum (often nominal such as 10 or 100) to keep the offer open for a specified period of time (e.g., 30 days). If Ames agrees, an option contract has been formed and its only purpose is to keep the

100,000 offer open for 30 days. *See* RESTATEMENT (SECOND) OF CONTRACTS § 25.

(2) *Right of First Refusal Distinguished From Option Contracts.* Option contracts often arise in situations like the principal case where a lessee is provided a "right of first refusal" along with the leased premises in exchange for payment of the rent. The right of first refusal is not an option contract. It is a prelude to an option contract as a right to receive an offer. The typical situation involves a lease of real property where, for one consideration, the lessee receives the use of the premises *and* an offer to purchase the property at a price offered by a third party. A right of first refusal requires the occurrence of a condition precedent before it may be exercised, i.e., the owner must have received a bona fide offer from a third party which he or she is willing to accept. Upon receiving such an offer, the owner has a contractual duty under the lease to notify the lessee that the lessee has an irrevocable power of acceptance to purchase the property at the price offered by the third party. Thus, when this condition precedent occurs, the right of first refusal ripens into an option contract which provides the lessee with an irrevocable power of acceptance to purchase the property. See *Van Dam v. Spickler, 968 A. 2d 1040 (Me. 2009).*

(3) Courts are particularly strict in requiring adherence to the conditions of an option contract with respect to precise conformity to the terms of the main offer and timely exercise of the irrevocable power of acceptance. *See Westinghouse Broadcasting Co. v. New England Patriots Football Club, Inc.*, 10 Mass. App. 70, 406 N.E.2d 399 (1980).

(4) *Duty vs. Termination of Power.* At one time, the notion of the irrevocable offer was considered impossible. Thus, if the optionor revoked the offer, he was said to have merely breached his *duty* not to revoke, i.e., he breached the option contract for which he would be liable in damages. He had not surrendered his *power* to revoke. The practical effect of such an analysis was to undermine the very concept of the option contract, since damages for breach of the option contract would typically be too speculative and uncertain to be recoverable. This argument was put to rest long ago. *See* McGoveny, *Irrevocable Offers*, 27 HARV. L. REV. 644 (1914). *See also Solomon Mier Co. v. Hadden*, 148 Mich. 488, 111 N.W. 1040, 1043 (1907). Thus, an option contract is now said not only to create a duty in the optionor not to revoke, but also deprives him of the power to revoke the main offer.

(5) *Rejections and Counter Offers — Option Contract.* If an optionor has no power to revoke, any attempted revocation will be treated as inoperative, i.e., a nullity. Moreover, the death of the optionor will not revoke the offer. *See Crowley v. S.E. Bass*, 445 So. 2d 902 (Ala. 1984). Consider, however, a rejection or counter offer by the optionee. If the option holder notifies the optionor that the main offer is rejected, or if the optionee makes a counter offer, may he later, within the option period, still exercise his power of acceptance? If the optionor were to justifiably rely upon a rejection by the optionee, the option contract might be discharged. *See* RESTATEMENT (SECOND) OF CONTRACTS § 37, ill. 2. Absent such reliance, however, the general rule is that a rejection or counter offer will not discharge the option contract. Thus, the optionee could, within the option period, later exercise his irrevocable power of acceptance. RESTATEMENT (SECOND) OF CONTRACTS § 37. For an astute criticism of this majority view, see Cozzillio, *The Option Contract: Irrevo-*

cable Not Irrejectable, 39 CATH. U.L. REV. 491 (1990).

[3]   Irrevocability through Reliance — Firm Offers

PAVEL ENTERPRISES, INC. v. A. S. JOHNSON CO., INC.
Maryland Court of Appeals
674 A.2d 521 (1996)

KARWACKI, J.

The National Institutes of Health [hereinafter, "NIH"], solicited bids for a renovation project on Building 30 of its Bethesda, Maryland campus. The proposed work entailed some demolition work, but the major component of the job was mechanical, including heating, ventilation and air conditioning ["HVAC"]. Pavel Enterprises Incorporated [hereinafter, "PEI"], a general contractor, prepared a bid for the NIH work. In preparing its bid, PEI solicited sub-bids from various mechanical subcontractors. The A. S. Johnson Company [hereinafter, "Johnson"], a mechanical subcontractor, responded with a written scope of work proposal on July 27, 1993.[17] On the morning of August 5, 1993, the day NIH opened the general contractors' bids, Johnson verbally submitted a quote of 898,000 for the HVAC component. Neither party disputes that PEI used Johnson's sub-bid in computing its own bid. PEI submitted a bid of 1,585,000 for the entire project.

General contractors' bids were opened on the afternoon of August 5, 1993. PEI's bid was the second lowest bid. The government subsequently disqualified the apparent low bidder, however, and in mid-August, NIH notified PEI that its bid would be accepted.

With the knowledge that PEI was the lowest responsive bidder, Thomas F. Pavel, president of PEI, visited the offices of A. S. Johnson on August 26, 1993, and met with James Kick, Johnson's chief estimator, to discuss Johnson's proposed role in the work. Pavel testified at trial to the purpose of the meeting:

> "I wanted to go out and see where their facility was, see where they were located, and basically just sit down and talk to them. Because if we were going to use them on a project, I wanted to know who I was dealing with."

Pavel also asked if Johnson would object to PEI subcontracting directly with Powers for electric controls, rather than the arrangement originally envisioned in which Powers would be Johnson's subcontractor. Johnson did not object.

Following that meeting, PEI sent a fax to all of the mechanical subcontractors from whom it had received sub-bids on the NIH job. The text of that fax is reproduced:

> We herewith respectfully request that you review your bid on the above referenced project that was bid on 8/05/93. PEI has been notified that we

---

[17] [2] The scope of work proposal listed all work that Johnson proposed to perform, but omitted the price term. This is a standard practice in the construction industry. The subcontractor's bid price is then filled in immediately before the general contractor submits the general bid to the letting party.

will be awarded the project as [the original low bidder] has been found to be nonresponsive on the solicitation. We anticipate award on or around the first of September and therefor request that you supply the following information.

1. Please break out your cost for the "POWERS" supplied control work as we will be subcontracting directly to "POWERS".

2. Please resubmit your quote deleting the above referenced item.

We ask this in an effort to allow all prospective bidders to compete on an even playing field.

Should you have any questions, please call us immediately as time is of the essence.

On August 30, 1993, PEI informed NIH that Johnson was to be the mechanical subcontractor on the job. On September 1, 1993, PEI mailed and faxed a letter to Johnson formally accepting Johnson's bid.

Upon receipt of PEI's fax of September 1, James Kick called and informed PEI that Johnson's bid contained an error, and as a result the price was too low. According to Kick, Johnson had discovered the mistake earlier, but because Johnson believed that PEI had not been awarded the contract, they did not feel compelled to correct the error. Kick sought to withdraw Johnson's bid, both over the telephone and by a letter dated September 2, 1993. PEI responded expressing its refusal to permit Johnson to withdraw.

On September 28, 1993, NIH formally awarded the construction contract to PEI. PEI found a substitute subcontractor to do the mechanical work, but at a cost of 930,000. PEI brought suit against Johnson in the Circuit Court for Prince George's County to recover the 32,000 difference between Johnson's bid and the cost of the substitute mechanical subcontractor. The trial court made several findings of fact, which we summarize:

1. PEI relied upon Johnson's sub-bid in making its bid for the entire project;

2. The fact that PEI was not the low bidder, but was awarded the project only after the apparent low bidder was disqualified, takes this case out of the ordinary;

3. Prior to NIH awarding PEI the contract on September 28, Johnson, on September 2, withdrew its bid; and

4. PEI's letter to all potential mechanical subcontractors, dated August 26, 1993, indicates that there was no definite agreement between PEI and Johnson, and that PEI was not relying upon Johnson's bid.

PEI appealed to the Court of Special Appeals, raising both traditional offer and acceptance theory, and "promissory estoppel." Before our intermediate appellate court considered the case, we issued a writ of certiorari on our own motion.

The relationships involved in construction contracts have long posed a unique problem in the law of contracts. A brief overview of the mechanics of the construction bid process, as well as our legal system's attempts to regulate the process, is in order.

> In such a building project there are basically three parties involved: the letting party, who calls for bids on its job; the general contractor, who makes a bid on the whole project; and the subcontractors, who bid only on that portion of the whole job which involves the field of its specialty. The usual procedure is that when a project is announced, a subcontractor, on his own initiative or at the general contractor's request, prepares an estimate and submits a bid to one or more of the general contractors interested in the project. The general contractor evaluates the bids made by the subcontractors in each field and uses them to compute its total bid to the letting party. After receiving bids from general contractors, the letting party ordinarily awards the contract to the lowest reputable bidder.

[*Maryland Supreme Corp. v. Blake Co.*], 279 Md. 531, 533–34, 369 A.2d 1017, 1020–21 (1977).

The problem the construction bidding process poses is the determination of the precise points on the timeline that the various parties become bound to each other. The early landmark case was *James Baird Co. v. Gimbel Bros., Inc.*, 64 F.2d 344 (2d Cir. 1933). The plaintiff, James Baird Co., ["Baird"] was a general contractor from Washington, D.C., bidding to construct a government building in Harrisburg, Pennsylvania. Gimbel Bros., Inc., ["Gimbel"], the famous New York department store, sent its bid to supply linoleum to a number of bidding general contractors on December 24, and Baird received Gimbel's bid on December 28. Gimbel realized its bid was based on an incorrect computation and notified Baird of its withdrawal on December 28. The letting authority awarded Baird the job on December 30. Baird formally accepted the Gimbel bid on January 2. When Gimbel refused to perform, Baird sued for the additional cost of a substitute linoleum supplier. The Second Circuit Court of Appeals held that Gimbel's initial bid was an offer to contract and, under traditional contract law, remained open only until accepted or withdrawn. Because the offer was withdrawn before it was accepted there was no contract. Judge Learned Hand, speaking for the court, also rejected two alternative theories of the case: unilateral contract and promissory estoppel. He held that Gimbel's bid was not an offer of a unilateral contract that Baird could accept by performing, i.e., submitting the bid as part of the general bid; and second, he held that the theory of promissory estoppel was limited to cases involving charitable pledges.

JUDGE HAND'S opinion was widely criticized. The general contractor is bound to the price submitted to the letting party, but the subcontractors are not bound, and are free to withdraw.

As one commentator described it, "If the subcontractor revokes his bid before it is accepted by the general, any loss which results is a deduction from the general's profit and conceivably may transform overnight a profitable contract into a losing deal." Franklin M. Schultz, *The Firm Offer Puzzle: A Study of Business Practice in the Construction Industry*, 19 U. CHI. L. REV. 237, 239 (1952).

The unfairness of this regime to the general contractor was addressed in *Drennan v. Star Paving*, 51 Cal. 2d 409, 333 P.2d 757 (1958). Like *James Baird*, the

Drennan case arose in the context of a bid mistake. JUSTICE TRAYNOR, writing for the Supreme Court of California, relied upon § 90 of the Restatement (First) of Contracts:

> "A promise which the promisor should reasonably expect to induce action or forbearance of a definite and substantial character on the part of the promisee and which does induce such action or forbearance is binding if injustice can be avoided only by enforcement of the promise."

JUSTICE TRAYNOR reasoned that the subcontractor's bid contained an implied subsidiary promise not to revoke the bid. As the court stated:

> When plaintiff [, a General Contractor,] used defendant's offer in computing his own bid, he bound himself to perform in reliance on defendant's terms. Though defendant did not bargain for the use of its bid neither did defendant make it idly, indifferent to whether it would be used or not. On the contrary it is reasonable to suppose that defendant submitted its bid to obtain the subcontract. It was bound to realize the substantial possibility that its bid would be the lowest, and that it would be included by plaintiff in his bid. It was to its own interest that the contractor be awarded the general contract; the lower the subcontract bid, the lower the general contractor's bid was likely to be and the greater its chance of acceptance and hence the greater defendant's chance of getting the paving subcontract. Defendant had reason not only to expect plaintiff to rely on its bid but to want him to. Clearly defendant had a stake in plaintiff's reliance on its bid. Given this interest and the fact that plaintiff is bound by his own bid, it is only fair that plaintiff should have at least an opportunity to accept defendant's bid after the general contract has been awarded to him. 51 Cal. 2d at 415, 333 P.2d at 760.

The *Drennan* court however did not use "promissory estoppel" as a substitute for the entire contract, as is the doctrine's usual function. Instead, the Drennan court, applying the principle of § 90, interpreted the subcontractor's bid to be irrevocable. JUSTICE TRAYNOR'S analysis used promissory estoppel as consideration for an implied promise to keep the bid open for a reasonable time. Recovery was then predicated on traditional bilateral contract, with the sub-bid as the offer and promissory estoppel serving to replace acceptance.

The *Drennan* decision has been very influential. Many states have adopted the reasoning used by JUSTICE TRAYNOR. Despite the popularity of the *Drennan* reasoning, the case has subsequently come under some criticism. The criticism centers on the lack of symmetry of detrimental reliance in the bid process, in that subcontractors are bound to the general, but the general is not bound to the subcontractors The result is that the general is free to bid shop, bid chop, and to encourage bid peddling, to the detriment of the subcontractors. These problems have caused at least one court to reject promissory estoppel in the contractor-subcontractor relationship. *Home Elec. Co. v. Underdown Heating & Air Conditioning Co.*, 86 N.C. App. 540, 358 S.E.2d 539 (N.C. Ct. App. 1987). But other courts, while aware of the limitations of promissory estoppel, have adopted it nonetheless. *See, e.g., Alaska Bussell Elec. Co. v. Vern Hickel Constr. Co.*, 688 P.2d 576 (Alaska 1984).

The doctrine of detrimental reliance has evolved in the time since *Drennan* was decided in 1958. The American Law Institute, responding to *Drennan*, sought to make detrimental reliance more readily applicable to the construction bidding scenario by adding § 87. This new section was intended to make subcontractors' bids binding:

§ 87. Option Contract . . . .

(2) An offer which the offeror should reasonably expect to induce action or forbearance of a substantial character on the part of the offeree before acceptance and which does induce such action or forbearance is binding as an option contract to the extent necessary to avoid injustice.

Despite the drafter's intention that § 87 of the RESTATEMENT (SECOND) OF CONTRACTS (1979) should replace RESTATEMENT (FIRST) OF CONTRACTS § 90 (1932) in the construction bidding cases, few courts have availed themselves of the opportunity. *But see Arango Constr. Co. v. Success Roofing, Inc.*, 46 Wash. App. 314, 321–22, 730 P.2d 720, 725 (1986).

Courts and commentators have also suggested other solutions intended to bind the parties without the use of detrimental reliance theory. The most prevalent suggestion is the use of the firm offer provision of the Uniform Commercial Code,§ 2-205. That statute provides:

An offer by a merchant to buy or sell goods in a signed writing which by its terms gives assurance that it will be held open is not revocable, for lack of consideration, during the time stated or if no time is stated for a reasonable time, but in no event may such period of irrevocability exceed three months; but any such term of assurance on a form supplied by the offeree must be separately signed by the offeror.

In this manner, subcontractor's bids, made in writing and giving some assurance of an intent that the offer be held open, can be found to be irrevocable.[18]

The Supreme Judicial Court of Massachusetts has suggested three other traditional theories that might prove the existence of a contractual relationship between a general contractor and a sub: conditional bilateral contract analysis; unilateral contract analysis; and unrevoked offer analysis. *Loranger Constr. Corp. v. E. F. Hauserman Co.*, 376 Mass. 757, 384 N.E.2d 176 (1978). If the general contractor could prove that there was an exchange of promises binding the parties to each other, and that exchange of promises was made before bid opening, that would constitute a valid bilateral promise conditional upon the general being awarded the job. *Loranger*, 384 N.E.2d at 180, 376 Mass. at 762. This directly contrasts with JUDGE HAND's analysis in *James Baird*, that a general's use of a sub-bid constitutes acceptance conditional upon the award of the contract to the general. *James Baird*, 64 F.2d at 345–46.

---

[18] [22] We note that Johnson's sub-bid was made in the form of a signed writing, but without further evidence we are unable to determine if the offer "by its terms gives assurance that it will be held open" and if the sub-bid is for "goods" as that term is defined by Md. Code (1994 Repl. Vol.), § 2-105 (1) of the Commercial Law Article.

Alternatively, if the subcontractor intended its sub-bid as an offer to a unilateral contract, use of the sub-bid in the general's bid constitutes part performance, which renders the initial offer irrevocable under the Restatement (SECOND) OF CONTRACTS § 45 (1979). This resurrects a second theory dismissed by JUDGE LEARNED HAND in *James Baird*.

Finally, the *Loranger* court pointed out that a jury might choose to disbelieve that a subcontractor had withdrawn the winning bid, meaning that acceptance came before withdrawal, and a traditional bilateral contract was formed.

There is substantial evidence in the record to support the judge's conclusion that there was no meeting of the minds. PEI's letter of August 26, to all potential mechanical subcontractors, reproduced supra, indicates, as the trial judge found, that PEI and Johnson "did not have a definite, certain meeting of the minds on a certain price for a certain quantity of goods . . . ." Because this reason is itself sufficient to sustain the trial judge's finding that no contract was formed, we affirm.

Alternatively, we hold, that the evidence permitted the trial judge to find that Johnson revoked its offer prior to PEI's final acceptance. We review the relevant chronology. Johnson made its offer, in the form of a sub-bid, on August 5. On September 1, PEI accepted. Johnson withdrew its offer by letter dated September 2. On September 28, NIH awarded the contract to PEI. Thus, PEI's apparent acceptance came one day prior to Johnson's withdrawal.

PEI's alternative theory of the case is that PEI's detrimental reliance[19] binds Johnson to its bid. We are asked, as a threshold question, if detrimental reliance applies to the setting of construction bidding. Nothing in our previous cases suggests that the doctrine was intended to be limited to a specific factual setting.

This Court has decided cases based on detrimental reliance as early as 1854, and the general contours of the doctrine are well understood by Maryland courts. The historical development of promissory estoppel, or detrimental reliance, in Maryland has mirrored the development nationwide.

In a construction bidding case, where the general contractor seeks to bind the subcontractor to the sub-bid offered, the general must first prove that the subcontractor's sub-bid constituted an offer to perform a job at a given price. We do not express a judgment about how precise a bid must be to constitute an offer, or to what degree a general contractor may request to change the offered scope before an acceptance becomes a counter-offer. That fact-specific judgment is best reached on a case-by-case basis. In the instant case, the trial judge found that the sub-bid was sufficiently clear and definite to constitute an offer, and his finding was not clearly erroneous.

If the reliance is not "substantial and definite" justice will not compel enforcement. [T]he general must prove that the subcontractor reasonably expected that the general contractor would rely upon the offer. The subcontractor's expectation that the general contractor will rely upon the sub-bid may dissipate through time. In this case, the trial court correctly inquired into Johnson's belief that the bid

---

[19] [Ed. Note: The Court indicated its preference for the phrase "detrimental reliance" rather than "promissory estoppel" since the former more aptly describes the reason for enforcing the promise.]

remained open, and that consequently PEI was not relying on the Johnson bid. The judge found that due to the time lapse between bid opening and award, "it would be unreasonable for offers to continue." This is supported by the substantial evidence. James Kick testified that although he knew of his bid mistake, he did not bother to notify PEI because J J. Kirlin, Inc., and not PEI, was the apparent low bidder. The trial court's finding that Johnson's reasonable expectation had dissipated in the span of a month is not clearly erroneous.

[Promissory estoppel (detrimental reliance) also requires the] general contractor [to] prove that he actually and reasonably relied on the subcontractor's sub-bid. We decline to provide a checklist of potential methods of proving this reliance, but we will make several observations. First, a showing by the subcontractor, that the general contractor engaged in "bid shopping," or actively encouraged "bid chopping," or "bid peddling" is strong evidence that the general did not rely on the sub-bid. Second, prompt notice by the general contractor to the subcontractor that the general intends to use the sub on the job, is weighty evidence that the general did rely on the bid. Third, if a sub-bid is so low that a reasonably prudent general contractor would not rely upon it, the trier of fact may infer that the general contractor did not in fact rely upon the erroneous bid.

Finally the trial court, and not a jury, must determine that binding the subcontractor is necessary to prevent injustice. This element is to be enforced as required by common law equity courts-the general contractor must have "clean hands." This requirement includes, as did the previous element, that the general did not engage in bid shopping, chopping or peddling, but also requires the further determination that justice compels the result.

Because there was sufficient evidence in the record to support the trial judge's conclusion that PEI had not proven its case for detrimental reliance, we must, and hereby do, affirm the trial court's ruling.

NOTES

(1) *Limitations on Reliance Making Offers Irrevocable.* It is important to recognize the limitations of offers in transactions involving a bargained-for-exchange becoming irrevocable through reliance. It is unreasonable to rely on the irrevocability of a typical offer since offers are generally revocable. Suppose X receives an offer from Y which X considers to be very desirable. He then receives a similar offer from Z which is almost as desirable as Y's offer. Before accepting Y's offer, X decides to reject Z's offer only to have Y revoke its offer before X accepts. If Y had no reason to expect X to rely on Y's offer as irrevocable, that offer remains revocable and X's act of rejecting Z's offer would not constitute reasonable reliance. The subcontractor/general contractor situation is a rare exception in bargaining transactions because of the reasonable expectations of the parties. As Justice Traynor indicates in the famous *Drennan* opinion described in the principal case, a subcontractor not only expects but hopes that the general contractor will rely on the sub's offer by using that offer in the general's overall bid-offer which the general cannot revoke. Thus, when the general actually relies by using a particular subcontractor's bid, such reliance is reasonable and fully expected by the subcontractor.

(2) *Firm Offers.* Prior to the UCC, consideration validating an option contract was necessary to make an offer irrevocable. Commercial practice, however, suggested numerous instances of written offers assuring irrevocability. A reasonable merchant may have relied upon such statements. To react to such possibilities of reliance with respect to transactions involving sales of goods, § 2-205 of the Code, quoted in the principal case, makes such *written* offers *giving assurance that they will be held open* irrevocable. No actual reliance need be shown.

Caveat: It is particularly important to distinguish an offer which merely states a duration of acceptance from a *firm* offer. A statement in an offer placing a time limit on the power of acceptance (e.g., "eight days in which to accept") is not a firm offer. At the end of the period specified in the offer, the power of acceptance is terminated (the offer "lapses"). If the offeror chose to revoke that offer before it lapsed, she may do so because the offer is a typical revocable offer which states its duration. A *firm* offer, however, requires more than a mere statement of duration. It requires *assurance that it will be held open* during the time stated or, if no time is stated, for a reasonable time, in no event to exceed three months under § 2-205.

(3) *Firm Offers and Maximum Limitations.* Under UCC § 2-205, a written offer giving assurance that it will remain open will be irrevocable for the time stated in the offer or for a reasonable time. There is, however, a three month ceiling on the duration of such "firm offers." Thus, if an otherwise firm offer states a duration of four months, it become revocable at the end of three months. If it states no duration, the maximum period of irrevocability is three months.

A New York statute makes other written and signed offers irrevocable for the period of time stated in the offer or, absent such a stated duration, for a reasonable time. N.Y. Gen. Obl. Law § 5-1109. There is no maximum time limitation in the New York Statute. With respect to an offer to sell goods controlled by New York law, the Code provision, § 2-205, which is also New York law, would apply through a specific exception in § 5-1109.

(4) *Inadvertent Firm Offers.* Another part of UCC § 2-205 overcomes the possibility of an inadvertent "firm offer." As we have seen in prior cases, one party may supply a printed form to the other who may sign it without complete knowledge of its contents. The signing party may be unaware that he or she is merely making an offer. That same form may contain an assurance that the offer will remain open, i.e., a "firm offer." To avoid the possibility that a party may make a firm offer without knowing it, § 2-205 requires that "any such term of assurance [that the offer will remain open] on a form supplied by the offeree must be separately signed by the offeror." In general, see MURRAY ON CONTRACTS, *supra* Chapter 1, note 1, at § 44C (5th ed. 2011).

(5) *CISG and Firm Offers.* The Vienna Convention, which is the governing law in international sales of goods between parties in CISG countries, however, suggests a different analysis. While recognizing the general revocability of offers, Article 16(2) states:

> However, an offer cannot be revoked: (a) if it indicates by stating a fixed time for acceptance or otherwise, that it is irrevocable; or (b) if it was

reasonable to rely on the offer as being irrevocable and the offeree has acted in reliance on the offer.

Thus, the Convention would make an offer irrevocable if it merely states the duration of the power of acceptance under Article 16(2)(a). Subsection 2(b) then makes an offer irrevocable if the offeree has reasonably relied upon its irrevocability.

[4] Irrevocability through Part Performance — Section 45 of the Restatements

[a] Introduction — Unilateral Versus Bilateral Contracts

Traditional contract law classified contracts in several ways, including the distinction between unilateral and bilateral contracts. Neither the Uniform Commercial Code nor the RESTATEMENT (SECOND) OF CONTRACTS retains these labels. The concepts, however, are retained, and it is inevitable that the terminology will continue.

The basic distinction is quite simple. Citing *Murray on Contracts*, in *Stephan v. Waldron Elec. Heating & Cooling, LLC*, 100 A.3d 660 (Pa. Super. Ct. 2014), the court explained:

> Traditional contract law distinguishes between bilateral and unilateral contracts. Bilateral contracts involve two promises and are created when one party promises to do or forbear from doing something in exchange for a promise from the other party to do or forbear from doing something else. Unilateral contracts, in contrast, involve only one promise and are formed when one party makes a promise in exchange for the other party's act or performance. Significantly, a unilateral contract is not formed and is, thus, unenforceable until such time as the offeree completes performance . . .

Where parties exchange promises to form a contract, the contract is said to be "*bilateral*" insofar as there are two promisors and two promisees, with the formation of the contract occurring at the moment the promises are exchanged, assuming that other basic requirements are met. Where *A* promises to sell his car to *B* who promises to buy *A*'s car for the asking price of 5,000, the contract is formed upon the exchange of promises. At that moment, there are two promisors, two promisees, two rights and two duties. *A* has the right to *B*'s 5,000 and the duty to deliver the car to *B*. *B* has the right to *A*'s car and the duty to pay *A* 5,000.

A "*unilateral*" contract involves only one promisor and one promisee. *A* offers to pay 5,000 to *B* in exchange for *B*'s performance in painting *A's* house. Normally, *B* would simply promise to paint *A*'s house and a bilateral contract would be formed. If, however, *A*, the offeror, clearly; insists on *B*'s performance rather than a promise, *B* can accept *A*'s offer and form the contract in only one manner — by performance, i.e., painting the house. Recall that the offeror is master of the offer. Only when the house is completely painted is the contract formed, i.e., *A* offered to pay *B* 5,000 for the complete painting of the house and *B* has not accepted the offer until he completes that performance. At the moment of formation of the unilateral contract, there is only one right and one duty: *A* has one duty and *B* has one correlative right. *A* has a duty to pay *B* 5,000. *A* has no right since he has already received the bargained-for-exchange of *B*'s performance. *B* has a right but no duty because he has already performed and is entitled to enforce his right to collect 5,000 from *A*. It is sometimes suggested that a bilateral contract allows for a promissory acceptance whereas a unilateral contract requires a performance acceptance. As will be seen in the sections to follow, this is not a reliable distinction. Rather, the student should consider the number of rights and duties at the moment the contract is formed. If there are rights and duties on both sides at the moment of formation, the contract is "bilateral"; if there is only one right on one side and one duty on the other, the contract is "unilateral."

DAHL v. HEM PHARMACEUTICALS CORP.
United States Court of Appeals, Ninth Circuit
7 F.3d 1399 (1999)

KLEINFELD, J.

[Dahl and seventeen others suffering from chronic fatigue syndrome enrolled in an experimental program to test a new medication, Ampligen, made by the defendant. In this "double-blind" experiment designed to meet Food and Drug Administration (FDA) requirements, the intravenous solution given to some patients was Ampligen while the solution given to others was a placebo (saline solution). The patients also signed a consent form concerning possible side effects. The volunteers were free to withdraw at any time, but the defendant promised a full-year supply of Ampligen to any patient who completed the experiment, regardless of whether they actually received Ampligen or the placebo. Upon completion of the testing, the FDA concluded that the drug had not proven sufficiently safe for widespread use, but clinical testing on human beings could continue. HEM then refused to provide the patients who had completed the testing program with free Ampligen for a full year and the patients sought a mandatory injunction to ascertain the continuation of Ampligen. HEM argued that there was no contract.]

The patients submitted themselves to months of periodic injections with an experimental drug, or unbeknownst to them, mere saline solution, combined with intrusive and necessarily uncomfortable testing to determine their condition as the tests proceeded. HEM sought to have them participate in its study so that it could obtain FDA approval for its new drug. HEM argues that because petitioners participated voluntarily and were free to withdraw, they had no binding obligation and so gave no consideration. Somehow, the category of unilateral contracts appears to have escaped HEM's notice. The deal was, 'if you submit to our experiment, we will give you a year's supply of Ampligen at no charge."[20] HEM did not bargain for or seek a promise by the patients to submit to the double-blind testing. It sought

---

[20] [2] The form is also similar to the standard Brooklyn Bridge hypothetical case: Suppose A says to B, "I will give you 100 if you walk across the Brooklyn Bridge," and B walks — is there a contract? It is clear that A is not asking B for B's promise to walk across the Brooklyn Bridge. What A wants from B is the act of walking across the bridge. When B has walked across the bridge, there is a unilateral contract . . . . Wormser, *The True Conception of Unilateral Contracts*, 26 YALE L. J. 136 (1916).

and obtained their actual performance. Upon completion of the double-blind tests, there was a binding contract."

[b] The Part Performance Problem

In the *Dahl* case, *supra*, the court provides a footnote referring to the famous hypothetical case created by Professor Wormser of an offer to pay the offeree 100 if he will walk across the Brooklyn Bridge, i.e., the offeror is not seeking a promise, but the performance of the offeree. If the offeree completes the walk across the bridge, he thereby accepts the offer, precisely in accordance with the terms of the offer. Suppose, however, that the offeree *begins* to walk across the bridge and, when he is halfway across, the offeror shouts, "I revoke the offer." Since the offeror wanted the offeree to walk across the entire bridge, there can be no acceptance of that offer until the act is completed. The common law of contracts allows revocation of the offer prior to completion. Professor Wormser, himself, considered this situation and concluded that the offer could be revoked prior to the offeree's completion of the act requested in the offer. Wormser, *The True Conception of Unilateral Contracts*, 26 YALE L. J. 136 (1916). The manifest injustice that can result from allowing such a revocation, however, is illustrated by the more dramatic following example.

PROBLEM

Angela Darrington was a particularly courageous stunt person who had appeared in numerous films. Simon Saddam was a producer of films interested exclusively in box office receipts. Saddam wanted Angela to make a motorcycle jump over Snake River Canyon and promised to pay her 50,000 "if you make it." After much preparation, with rockets attached to her custom-made bike and a parachute for a soft landing, Angela was ready to make the jump. She was in contact with her assistants through a small microphone and speaker in her head gear. Angela managed to reach the precise speed on the jump ramp and proceeded to soar through the air. In the heart-stopping moments that followed, the jump appeared to be perfect. Just before she cleared the last portion of the Canyon on her way to a perfect landing, Saddam grabbed the assistant's microphone and shouted, "Offer revoked," which Angela heard. The "shot" of the action was perfect and later was used not only as part of the film but as the major advertisement inducing audiences to see the film. Saddam has refused to pay Angela. What theories may be pursued to enforce Saddam's promise?

In addition to the drama of this situation, there is the singular fact that, unlike other performances in response to offers requiring a performance acceptance, once begun, Angela could not stop her performance — a fact known to the offeror. Even where the offeree can stop the performance upon being notified of revocation, however, the injustice remains clear. If there is an ounce of justice in American contract law, there is no question that Angela should recover 50,000 from Saddam. In this situation, or in innumerable others that are much less dramatic, the primary question is not whether courts will allow a recovery, but only what theory or theories courts will develop to allow for a just result. Thus, the challenge was to create a cohesive theory to support holdings making an offer irrevocable through part performance.

THEORIES DESIGNED TO MAKE OFFERS IRREVOCABLE UPON PART PERFORMANCE

(1) *First Restatement of Contracts, Section 45.* "If an offer for a unilateral contract is made, and part of the consideration requested in the offer is given or tendered by the offeree in response thereto, the offeror is bound by a contract, the duty of immediate performance of which is conditioned on full consideration being given or tendered with the time stated in the offer, or, if not time is stated, within a reasonable time."

Comment b to this section reads: "The main offer includes as a subsidiary promise, necessarily implied, that if part of the requested performance is given, the offeror will not revoke his offer, and that if tender is made it will be accepted."

(2) *Restatement (Second) of Contracts, Section 45.* "(1) Where an offeror invites an offeree to accept by rendering a performance and does not invite a promissory acceptance, an option contract is created when the offeree begins the invited performance or tenders part of it. (2) The offeror's duty of performance under any option contract so created is conditioned on completion or tender of the invited performance in accordance with the terms of the offer."

(3) *The "Bilateral" Theory.* Upon the start of performance in response to an offer which can be accepted only by performance, the part performance will be viewed as a promise thereby enabling the contract to take on a "bilateral" character. Is this a desirable analysis? *See Los Angeles Traction Co. v. Wilshire*, 135 Cal. 654, 67 P. 1086 (1902), in which the court adopted this analysis. It was criticized by Professor Ashley in *Offers Calling for a Consideration Other than a Counter Promise*, 23 HARV. L. REV. 159 (1910). At page 164 of that article, Ashley states, "This is a remarkable instance of confusion of thought. By what magic the offer had been turned into a 'contract' does not appear."

There are many applications of both the first and second Restatement theories while the third theory has not seen extensive application. Which of the two Restatement theories is more sound? Consider Comment b to the First Restatement, § 45, quoted above. May that concept qualify as a theory unto itself? In general, see MURRAY ON CONTRACTS § 44D (5th ed. 2011).

PETTERSON v. PATTBERG
New York Court of Appeals
161 N.E. 428 (1928)

KELLOGG, J.

The evidence given upon the trial sanctions the following statement of facts: John Petterson, of whose last will and testament the plaintiff is the executrix, was the owner of a parcel of real estate in Brooklyn, known as 5301 Sixth avenue. The defendant was the owner of a bond executed by Petterson, which was secured by a third mortgage upon the parcel. On April 4, 1924, there remained unpaid upon the principal the sum of 5,450. This amount was payable in installments of 250 on April 25, 1924, and upon a like monthly date every three months thereafter. Thus the bond and mortgage had more than five years to run before the entire sum became due. Under date of the 4th of April, 1924, the defendant wrote Petterson as follows:

> I hereby agree to accept cash for the mortgage which I hold against premises 5301 6th Ave., Brooklyn, N. Y. It is understood and agreed as a consideration I will allow you 780 providing said mortgage is paid on or before May 31, 1924, and the regular quarterly payment due April 25, 1924, is paid when due.

On April 25, 1924, Petterson paid the defendant the installment of principal due on that date. Subsequently, on a day in the latter part of May, 1924, Petterson presented himself at the defendant's home, and knocked at the door. The defendant demanded the name of his caller. Petterson replied: "It is Mr. Petterson. I have come to pay off the mortgage." The defendant answered that he had sold the mortgage. Petterson stated that he would like to talk with the defendant, so the defendant partly opened the door. Thereupon Petterson exhibited the cash, and said he was ready to pay off the mortgage according to the agreement. The defendant refused to take the money. Prior to this conversation, Petterson had made a contract to sell the land to a third person free and clear of the mortgage to the defendant. Meanwhile, also, the defendant had sold the bond and mortgage to a third party. It therefore became necessary for Petterson to pay to such person the full amount of the bond and mortgage. It is claimed that he thereby sustained a loss of 780, the sum which the defendant agreed to allow upon the bond and mortgage, if payment in full of principal, less the sum, was made on or before May 31, 1924. The plaintiff has had a recovery for the sum thus claimed, with interest.

Clearly the defendant's letter proposed to Petterson the making of a unilateral contract, the gift of a promise in exchange for the performance of an act. The thing conditionally promised by the defendant was the reduction of the mortgage debt. The act requested to be done, in consideration of the offered promise, was payment in full of the reduced principal of the debt prior to the due date thereof. "If an act is requested, that very act, and no other, must be given." WILLISTON ON CONTRACTS, § 73. "In case of offers for a consideration, the performance of the consideration is always deemed a condition." LANGDELL'S SUMMARY OF THE LAW OF CONTRACTS, § 4. It is elementary that any offer to enter into a unilateral contract may be withdrawn before the act requested to be done has been performed. WILLISTON ON CONTRACTS, § 60; LANGDELL'S SUMMARY, § 4; *Offord v. Davies*, 12 C.B. (N.S.) 748. A bidder at a sheriff's sale may revoke his bid at any time before the property is struck down to him. *Fisher v. Seltzer*, 23 Pa. 308, 62 Am. Dec. 335. The offer of a reward in consideration of an act to be performed is revocable before the very act requested has been done. *Shuey v. United States*, 92 U.S. 73, 23 L. Ed. 697; *Biggers v. Owen*, 79 Ga. 658, 5 S.E. 193; *Fitch v. Snedaker*, 38 N.Y. 248, 97 Am. Dec. 791. So, also, an offer to pay a broker commissions, upon a sale of land for the offeror, is revocable at any time before the land is sold, although prior to revocation the broker performs services in an effort to effectuate a sale. *Stensgaard v. Smith*, 43 Minn. 11, 44 N.W. 669, 19 Am. St. Rep. 205; *Smith v. Cauthen*, 98 Miss. 746, 54 So. 844.

An interesting question arises when, as here, the offeree approaches offeror with the intention of proffering performance and, before actual tender is made, the offer is withdrawn. Of such a case WILLISTON says:

The offeror may see the approach of the offeree and know that an acceptance is contemplated. If the offeror can say "I revoke" before the offeree accepts, however brief the interval of time between the two acts, there is no escape from the conclusion that the offer is terminated. WILLISTON ON CONTRACTS, § 60b.

In this instance Petterson, standing at the door of the defendant's house, stated to the defendant that he had come to pay off the mortgage. Before a tender of the necessary moneys had been made the defendant informed Petterson that he had sold the mortgage. That was a definite notice to Petterson that the defendant could not perform his offered promise and that a tender to the defendant, who was no longer the creditor, would be ineffective to satisfy the debt.

"An offer to sell property may be withdrawn before acceptance without any formal notice to the person to whom the offer is made. It is sufficient if that person has actual knowledge that the person who made the offer has done some act inconsistent with the continuance of the offer, such as selling the property to a third person." *Dickinson v. Dodds*, 2 Ch. Div. 463, headnote. To the same effect is *Coleman v. Applegarth*, 68 Md. 21, 11 A. 284, 6 Am. St. Rep. 417. Thus it clearly appears that the defendant's offer was withdrawn before its acceptance had been tendered. It is unnecessary to determine, therefore what the legal situation might have been had tender been made before withdrawal. It is the individual view of the writer that the same result would follow. This would be so, for the act requested to be performed was the completed act of payment, a thing incapable of performance, unless assented to by the person to be paid. WILLISTON ON CONTRACTS, § 60b. Clearly an offering party has the right to name the precise act performance of which would convert his offer into a binding promise. Whatever the act may be until it is performed, the offer must be revocable. However, the supposed case is not before us for decision. We think that in this particular instance the offer of the defendant was withdrawn before it became a binding promise, and therefore that no contract was ever made for the breach of which the plaintiff may claim damages.

The judgment of the Appellate Division and that of the Trial Term should be reversed, and the complaint dismissed, with costs in all courts.

LEHMAN, J. (dissenting).

The defendant's letter to Petterson constituted a promise on his part to accept payment at a discount of the mortgage he held, provided the mortgage is paid on or before May 31, 1924. Doubtless, by the terms of the promise itself, the defendant made payment of the mortgage by the plaintiff, before the stipulated time, a condition precedent to performance by the defendant of his promise to accept payment at a discount. If the condition precedent has not been performed, it is because the defendant made performance impossible by refusing to accept payment, when the plaintiff came with an offer of immediate performance. "It is a principle of fundamental justice that if a promisor is himself the cause of the failure of performance either of an obligation due him or of a condition upon which his own liability depends, he cannot take advantage of the failure." WILLISTON ON CONTRACTS, § 677. The question in this case is not whether payment of the mortgage is a condition precedent to the performance of a promise made by the defendant but rather, whether, at the time the defendant refused the offer of payment, he had assumed any binding obligation, even though subject to condition.

The promise made by the defendant lacked consideration at the time it was made. Nevertheless, the promise was not made as a gift or mere gratuity to the plaintiff. It was made for the purpose of obtaining from the defendant something which the plaintiff desired. It constituted an offer which was to become binding whenever the plaintiff should give, in return for the defendant's promise, exactly the consideration which the defendant requested.

Here the defendant requested no counter promise from the plaintiff. The consideration requested by the defendant for his promise to accept payment was, I agree, some act to be performed by the plaintiff. Until the act requested was performed, the defendant might undoubtedly revoke his offer. Our problem is to determine from the words of the letter, read in the light of surrounding circumstances, what act the defendant requested as consideration for his promise.

The defendant undoubtedly made his offer as an inducement to the plaintiff to "pay" the mortgage before it was due. Therefore, it is said, that "the act requested to be performed was the completed act of payment, a thing incapable of performance, unless assented to by the person to be paid." In unmistakable terms the defendant agreed to accept payment, yet we are told that the defendant intended, and the plaintiff should have understood, that the act requested by the defendant, as consideration for his promise to accept payment, included performance by the defendant himself of the very promise for which the act was to be consideration [sic]. The defendant's promise was to become binding only when fully performed; and part of the consideration to be furnished by the plaintiff for the defendant's promise was to be the performance of that promise by the defendant. So construed, the defendant's promise or offer, though intended to induce action by the plaintiff, is but a snare and delusion. The plaintiff could not reasonably suppose that the defendant was asking him to procure the performance by the defendant of the very act which the defendant promised to do, yet we are told that, even after the plaintiff had done all else which the defendant requested, the defendant's promise was still not binding because the defendant chose not to perform.

I cannot believe that a result so extraordinary could have been intended when the defendant wrote the letter. "The thought behind the phrase proclaims itself misread when the outcome of the reading is injustice or absurdity." See opinion of CARDOZO, C.J., in *Surace v. Danna*, 248 N.Y. 18, 161 N.E. 315. If the defendant intended to induce payment by the plaintiff and yet reserve the right to refuse payment when offered he should have used a phrase better calculated to express his meaning than the words, "I agree to accept." A promise to accept payment, by its very terms, must necessarily become binding, if at all, not later than when a present offer to pay is made.

I recognize that in this case only an offer of payment, and not a formal tender of payment, was made before the defendant withdrew his offer to accept payment. Even the plaintiff's part in the act of payment was then not technically complete. Even so, under a fair construction of the words of the letter, I think the plaintiff had done the act which the defendant requested as consideration for his promise. The plaintiff offered to pay, with present intention and ability to make that payment. A formal tender is seldom made in business transactions, except to lay the foundation for subsequent assertion in a court of justice of rights which spring from refusal of the tender. If the defendant acted in good faith in making his offer to accept payment, he could not well have intended to draw a distinction in the act requested of the plaintiff in return, between an offer which, unless refused, would ripen into completed payment, and a formal tender. Certainly the defendant could not have expected or intended that the plaintiff would make a formal tender of payment without first stating that he had come to make payment. We should not read into the language of the defendant's offer a meaning which would prevent enforcement of the defendant's promise after it had been accepted by the plaintiff in the very way which the defendant must have intended it should be accepted, if he acted in good faith.

CARDOZO, C.J., and POUND, CRANE, and O'BRIEN, JJ., concur with KELLOGG, J. LEHMAN, J., dissents in opinion, in which ANDREWS, J., concurs. Judgments reversed, etc.

PROBLEM

Albert Sims was a house painter with an excellent reputation for his ability as a painter, but a poor reputation for reliability in completing any particular job on time. Albert enjoyed fishing and other relaxing activities. Knowing Albert's proclivities, Samantha (Sam) Miller informed Albert that she was about to leave for her one-month vacation in Hawaii and that she would pay Albert 1,000 if her house were painted its present color upon her return. Albert responded that he was not sure he could complete the job by the end of the month, since he was heavily "booked." However, he thought he could at least begin by the end of the month. Sam was also aware of Albert's reputation of completing a painting contract expeditiously once he had begun. Sam said, "O.K. If you have started the job upon my return, I will let you finish it. But please, do not promise anything because you are notorious for breaking your promises." Albert sighed and simply nodded. One day before Sam's return from Hawaii, Albert pursued the following activities. Consider each of the activities and decide whether Albert had begun performance:

(a) Albert rose at 5:30 a.m. and shaved. Albert never shaved if he intended to go fishing.

(b) After arising and shaving, Albert donned his painter's apparel and loaded four gallons of white (exterior) paint into his truck. The color was the color requested by Sam but it was a very popular color which Albert had used on numerous other houses.

(c) Albert drove the truck to a fork in the road. The West road would take him to Sam's house and the East road to the unpainted house of another potential customer who had made an offer to Albert very similar to Sam's offer. Albert turned West.

(d). Albert arrived at Sam's house and began to unload the ladders, drop cloths and other equipment.

(e) After Albert had unloaded most of the equipment, rain began, causing him to return his equipment to the truck. He then proceeded in the rain to one of his favorite afternoon haunts where he played darts for the remainder of the afternoon. The next morning, Sam returned from Hawaii. It was still raining. She immediately contracted with another painter to paint her house. Fifteen minutes later, Albert notified her that he would be there as soon as the rain stopped. He also informed Sam that he had attempted to start the previous day but was "rained out." Moreover, he told her that he had just refused another job in order to paint Sam's house and that he had made a volume purchase of the kind of paint which Sam required since he now had Sam's job, as well as one other, requiring a large amount of this paint. What are the rights of the parties?

E. THE NATURE OF ACCEPTANCE

[1] Knowledge and Motivation

SIMMONS v. UNITED STATES
United States Court of Appeals, Fourth Circuit
308 F.2d 160 (1962)

SOBELOFF, C. J.

Diamond Jim III, a rock fish, was one of millions of his species swimming in the Chesapeake Bay, but he was a very special fish, and he occasions some nice legal questions. Wearing a valuable identification tag, he was placed on June 19, 1958, in the waters of the Bay by employees of the American Brewery, Inc., with the cooperation of Maryland state game officials. According to the well-publicized rules governing the brewery-sponsored Third Annual American Beer Fishing Derby, anybody who caught Diamond Jim III and presented him to the company, together with the identification tag and an affidavit that he had been caught on hook and line, would be entitled to a cash prize of 25,000.00. The company also placed other tagged fish in the Chesapeake, carrying lesser prizes.

Fishing on the morning of August 6, 1958, William Simmons caught Diamond Jim III. At first, he took little notice of the tag, but upon re-examining it a half hour later, he realized that he had caught the 25,000.00 prize fish. After Simmons and his fishing companions appropriately marked the happy event, he hastened to comply with the conditions of the contest. Soon thereafter, in the course of a television appearance arranged by the brewery, he received the cash prize. The record shows that Simmons knew about the contest, but, as an experienced fisherman, he also knew that his chances of landing that fish were minuscule, and he did not have Diamond Jim III in mind when he set out that morning.

Thereupon, an alert District Director of the Internal Revenue Service came forward with the assertion that the cash prize was includable in Simmons' gross income and assessed a tax deficiency of 5,230.00. Promptly Simmons paid and filed a claim for refund. Simmons brought an action in the District Court on the theory that no part of the cash prize can be included in gross income. [Among other assertions, Simmons argued] that the prize falls within the exclusions of [Internal Revenue Code] section 102, pertaining to gifts.[21] On motion for summary judgment, the District Court held for the Government, and Simmons prosecutes this appeal.

The established fact is that there was no personal relationship between Simmons and the brewery to prompt it to render him financial assistance. Nor was it impelled by charitable impulses toward the community at large, for the prize was to be paid to whoever caught Diamond Jim III, regardless of need or affluence. Rather, the taxpayer has apparently rendered the company a valuable service, for, by catching the fish and receiving the award amid fanfare, he brought to the company the publicity the Fishing Derby was designed to generate.

Moreover, under accepted principles of contract law on which we may rely in the absence of pertinent Maryland cases, the company was legally obligated to award the prize once Simmons had caught the fish and complied with the remaining conditions precedent. The offer of a prize or reward for doing a specified act, like catching a criminal, is an offer for a unilateral contract. For the offer to be accepted and the contract to become binding, the desired act must be performed with knowledge of the offer. The evidence is clear that Simmons knew about the Fishing Derby the morning he caught Diamond Jim III. It is not fatal to his claim for refund that he did not go fishing for the express purpose of catching one of the prize fish. So long as the outstanding offer was known to him, a person may accept an offer for a unilateral contract by rendering performance, even if he does so primarily for reasons unrelated to the offer. Consequently, since Simmons could require the company to pay him the prize, the case is governed by *Robertson v. United States*, 343 U.S. 711, 713–714, 72 S. Ct. 994, 96 L. Ed. 1237 (1952). There, the Supreme Court held that, since the sponsor of a contest for the best symphonies submitted was legally obligated to award prizes in accordance with his offer, the payment made was not a gift to the recipient.

NOTES

(1) *Knowledge of Offer.* The Court suggests that one cannot accept an offer without knowledge of the offer. Consider a private 25,000 reward offer for information leading to the arrest and conviction of a murderer. Without knowledge of the reward offer, a public-spirited citizen provides the information. Absent knowledge of the offer before performing the act of acceptance, the citizen does not recover. On the other hand, a contract law analysis permits an individual who lacks even a scintilla of the duties of citizenship to recover if he provides the information with knowledge of the reward offer. *See Glover v. Jewish War Veterans of the United States*, 68 A.2d 233 (D.C. App. 1949).

As contrasted with private reward offers, governmental bodies may provide standing reward offers to create an atmosphere in which people do certain acts with the hope of earning unknown rewards. The performance of the required act without knowledge of the reward may, in such "public" reward cases, give rise to recovery

---

[21] [8] "§ 102. Gifts and inheritances. (a) General rule. — Gross income does not include the value of property acquired by gift, bequests, devise, or inheritance."

of the reward. *See State v. Malm*, 143 Conn. 462, 123 A.2d 276 (1956). *See* MURRAY ON CONTRACTS § 45B (5th ed. 2011).

(2) In *Anderson v. Douglas & Lomason Co.*, 540 N. W. 2d 277 (Iowa 1995), the court found that a statement in an employee handbook that the plaintiff, an employee-at-will, had not read, nonetheless constituted an offer that the employee accepted by continuing to work after receiving the book. The court was careful to note that its conclusion constituted a "narrow divergence" from the usual rule that it is impossible to become an offeree absent knowledge of the offer. It justified this narrow exception on the ground that employee handbooks distributed to all employees are standardized agreements between employers and a class of employees and the employer intends to treat all members of the class alike. The exception would also be limited to an offer to be accepted by performance (continuing working for the employer after receiving the handbook) — a unilateral contract — rather than a bilateral contract that would require a promissory acceptance. The full opinion appears in a later chapter of this volume.

(3) *Knowledge of Offer After Beginning Performance.* Suppose a private reward offer is made for information leading to the arrest and conviction of a murderer. A public-spirited citizen with no knowledge of the reward offer begins to provide appropriate authorities with this information. Before he provides all of the necessary information, he is interrupted by one of the policemen who says, "I don't know whether you know that there is a 25,000 reward for the kind of information you are now providing." The citizen proceeds to provide the remainder of the information. Is he entitled to the reward?

(4) *Motivation to Accept.* Must the offeree intend to accept the offer? An offeree's promise to accept is clear evidence of such intent. Performance, however, may be ambiguous. In the principal case, the court admits that William Simmons did not "go fishing" for the principal purpose of catching Diamond Jim III. Yet, the court finds that he accepted the offer. Is *motivation* relevant? Do multi-millionaire golfers such as Tiger Woods or Rory McIlroy appear in tournaments for the money? If a reward offer is known to a person who, through fear of arrest, informs the police of the whereabouts of a criminal, has he accepted the reward offer? *See Vitty v. Eley*, 51 A.D. 44, 64 N.Y.S. 397 (1900). How many motivations can one have to perform an act? Consider RESTATEMENT (SECOND) OF CONTRACTS § 53(3): "Where an offer . . . invites acceptance by performance . . . , the rendering of the invited performance does not constitute acceptance if before the offeror performs his promise, the offeree manifests *an intention not to accept*." (Emphasis added). In *"Industrial America", Inc. v. Fulton Indus.*, 285 A.2d 412, 416 (Del. 1971), the court states, "[T]he favored rule shifts the emphasis away from a manifestation of intent to accept to a manifestation of intent not to accept, thereby establishing, it would appear, a rebuttable presumption of acceptance arising from performance when the offer invites acceptance by performance." *See* MURRAY ON CONTRACTS § 45C (5th ed. 2011).

[2]   The Requirement of Volition

CARLILL v. CARBOLIC SMOKE BALL CO.
Queen's Bench
1 Q.B. 256 (1893)

[The defendants manufactured and sold a patent medicine known as "The Carbolic Smoke Ball." The following advertisement was inserted in several newspapers by the defendants:

> £ 100 reward will be paid by the Carbolic Smoke Ball Company to any person who contracts the increasing epidemic influenza, colds or any disease caused by taking cold, after having used the ball three times daily for two weeks according to the printed directions supplied with each ball. £ 1000 is deposited with the Alliance Bank, Regent Street, shewing our sincerity in the matter.

[After seeing this advertisement, the plaintiff purchased a ball and used it according to directions. However, she was attacked by influenza and brings this action to recover £ 100. She recovered in the lower court and the defendants appealed.]

We must first consider whether this was intended to be a promise to all, or whether it was a mere puff which meant nothing. Was it a mere puff? My answer to that question is "No," and I base my answer upon this passage: "£ 1000 is deposited with the Alliance Bank, shewing our sincerity in the matter." Now, for what was that money deposited or that statement made except to negative the suggestion that this was a mere puff and meant nothing at all? The deposit is called in aid by the advertiser as proof of his sincerity in the matter, that is, the sincerity of his promise to pay this £ 100 in the event which he has specified. I say this for the purpose of giving point to the observation that we are not inferring a promise; there is the promise, as plain as words can make it.

Then it is contended that it is not binding. In the first place, it is said that it is not made with anybody in particular. Now that point is common to the words of this advertisement and to the words of all other advertisements offering rewards. They are offers to anybody who performs the conditions named in the advertisement, and anybody who does perform the conditions accepts the offer. In point of law this advertisement is an offer to pay £ 100 to anybody who will perform these conditions, and the performance of the conditions, is the acceptance of the offer. That rests upon a string of authorities, the earliest of which is *Williams v. Carwardine*, 4 Barn. & Adol. 621, which has been followed by many other decisions upon advertisements offering rewards . . . .

We, therefore, find here all the elements which are necessary to form a binding contract enforceable in point of law, subject to two observations. First of all it is said that this advertisement is so vague that you can not really construe it as a promise — that the vagueness of the language shows that a legal promise was never intended or contemplated. The language is vague and uncertain in some respects, and particularly in this, that the £ 100 is to be paid to any person who contracts the increasing epidemic after having used the balls three times daily for two weeks

. . . . I do not think that business people or reasonable people would understand the words as meaning that if you took a smoke ball and used it three times daily for two weeks you were to be guaranteed against influenza for the rest of your life, and I think it would be pushing the language of the advertisement too far to construe it as meaning that. But if it does not mean that, what does it mean? It is for the defendants to shew what it does mean; and it strikes me that there are two, and possibly three, reasonable constructions to be put on this advertisement, any one of which will answer the purpose of the plaintiff. Possibly it may be limited to persons catching the "increasing epidemic" (that is, the then prevailing epidemic), or any colds or diseases caused by taking cold, during the prevalence of the increasing epidemic. That is one suggestion; but it does not commend itself to me. Another suggested meaning is that you are warranted free from catching the epidemic, or colds or other diseases caused by taking cold, whilst you are using this remedy after using it for two weeks. If that is the meaning, the plaintiff is right, for she used the remedy for two weeks and went on using it till she got the epidemic. Another meaning, and the one which I rather prefer, is that the reward is offered to any person who contracts the epidemic or other disease within a reasonable time after having used the smoke ball . . . .

Then it is asked, What is a reasonable time? It has been suggested that there is no standard of reasonableness; that it depends upon the reasonable time for a germ to develop! I do not feel pressed by that. It strikes me that a reasonable time may be ascertained in a business sense and in a sense satisfactory to a lawyer, in this way; find out from a chemist what the ingredients are; find out from a skilled physician how long the effect of such ingredients on the system could be reasonably expected to endure so as to protect a person from an epidemic or cold, and in that way you will get a standard to be laid before a jury, or a judge without a jury, by which they might exercise their judgment as to what a reasonable time would be. It strikes me, I confess, that the true construction of this advertisement is that £ 100 will be paid to anybody who uses this smoke ball three times daily for two weeks according to the printed directions, and who gets the influenza or cold or other diseases caused by taking cold within a reasonable time after so using it; and if that is the true construction, it is enough for the plaintiff . . . .

It appears to me, therefore, that the defendants must perform their promise, and, if they have been so unwary as to expose themselves to a great many actions, so much the worse for them.

BOWEN, L.J.

I am of the same opinion.

Then it was said that there was no notification of the acceptance of the contract. One cannot doubt that, as an ordinary rule of law, an acceptance of an offer made ought to be notified to the person who makes the offer, in order that the two minds may come together. Unless this is done the two minds may be apart, and there is not that consensus which is necessary according to the English law — I say nothing about the laws of other countries — to make a contract. But there is this clear gloss to be made upon that doctrine, that as notification of acceptance is required for the benefit of the person who makes the offer, the person who makes the offer may dispense with notice to himself if he thinks it desirable to do so, and I suppose there can be no doubt that where a person in an offer made by him to another person, expressly or impliedly intimates a particular mode of acceptance as sufficient to make the bargain binding, it is only necessary for the other person to whom such offer is made to follow the indicated method of acceptance; and if the person making the offer, expressly or impliedly intimates in his offer that it will be sufficient to act on the proposal without communicating acceptance of it to himself, performance of the condition is a sufficient acceptance without notification . . . .

Now, if that is the law, how are we to find out whether the person who makes the offer does intimate that notification of acceptance will not be necessary in order to constitute a binding bargain? In many cases you look to the offer itself. In many cases you extract from the character of the transaction that notification is not required, and in the advertisement cases it seems to me to follow as an inference to be drawn from the transaction itself that a person is not to notify his acceptance of the offer before he performs the condition, but that if he performs the condition notification is dispensed with. It seems to me that from the point of view of common sense no other idea could be entertained. If I advertise to the world that my dog is lost, and that anybody who brings the dog to a particular place will be paid some money, are all the police or other persons whose business it is to find lost dogs to be expected to sit down and write a note saying that they have accepted my proposal? Why, of course, they at once look after the dog, and as soon as they find the dog they have performed the condition. The essence of the transaction is that the dog should be found, and it is not necessary under such circumstances, as it seems to me, that in order to make the contract binding there should be any notification of acceptance. It follows from the nature of the thing that the performance of the condition is sufficient acceptance without the notification of it, and a person who makes an offer in an advertisement of that kind makes an offer which must be read by the light of that common sense reflection. He does, therefore, in his offer impliedly indicate that he does not require notification of the acceptance of the offer . . . .

Appeal dismissed.

NOTE

The storied Carbolic Smoke Ball was the size of a small ball. It contained carbolic acid and was inhaled to prevent a long list of illnesses including influenza, catarrh, asthma, bronchitis, whooping cough, neuralgia, colds in the head or chest, snoring, sore throat and sore eyes. The smoke ball was particularly popular during the 1889–1890 flu pandemic that killed a million people. The smoke ball advertisements contained testimonials from numerous Dukes, Earls, Lords, Bishops, the wife of the British Prime Minister, Catherine Gladstone, and a German Empress as well as prominent physicians and judges. The deposit was with the Alliance Bank of Regent Street, one of the main shopping streets in West London. The price of the smoke ball was ten shillings and it could be refilled for 5 shillings. There were only three £100 claims. The company continued. The plaintiff, Mrs. Louisa Elizabeth Carlill, died in 1942. She was 96. Carbolic acid was put on the British Poisons List in 1900.

F. MANNER OF ACCEPTANCE

[1] The Modern Analysis

EMPIRE MACHINERY CO. v. LITTON BUSINESS TELEPHONE SYSTEMS
Arizona Court of Appeals
566 P.2d 1044 (1977)

JACOBSON, J.

Empire is the dealer for Caterpillar Tractor Company in Arizona. In the summer of 1973, Empire became interested in acquiring an "interconnect" telephone system. An "interconnect" system is one in which the telephone customer owns the "in-house" switching equipment, telephones and wiring, as compared to this equipment being owned by the telephone company, in this case, Mountain Bell. Litton is a manufacturer and seller of interconnect systems and on April 2, 1973, Russell R. Murphy, National Accounts Manager for Litton wrote Empire a letter extolling the virtues of the Litton system and enclosing a card to be returned to Litton if Empire was interested in its system. Empire returned the card and on April 17, 1973 Murphy personally contacted Empire.

During this visit, Murphy explained that Litton was developing a "Superplex" switching system which would be available in approximately a year. Mr. Ronald E. Mathis, Jr., communications coordinator for Empire, expressed interest in Litton's system which embraced the "Superplex" switch.

On June 5, 1973, Litton, through Murphy, submitted a proposal to Empire which was rejected. Negotiations continued between Murphy and Mathis until July 30, 1973. On that date, Murphy submitted a letter to Empire which stated in pertinent part:

> To confirm our previous discussions, upon receipt of a signed order and deposit, Litton BTS will install a Common Control Crossbar Telephone System on your premises. This system will be replaced upon your request and in accordance with our normal delivery schedule with our computer-controlled electronic solid state TDM system ["Superplex"] at no further expense to your company.

Following receipt of this letter from Murphy, Mr. Jack W. Whitman, president of Empire, signed an "Equipment Sales Agreement" and delivered to Murphy a check in the sum of 8,546.00, as the down payment. Murphy, on the Equipment Sales Agreement, acknowledged receipt of this amount. This Equipment Sales Agreement contained on its face a clause which read:

> 6. This agreement shall become effective and binding upon the Purchaser and BTS [Litton] only upon approval, acceptance, and execution hereof by BTS and its home office.

At the right hand bottom of the front page, the following appeared:

"Approved and Accepted by Litton Business Telephone, Division of Litton Systems, Inc. (Seller)

"By: _____

(Signature) _____

(Type Name and Title) _____

(Date)"

It is acknowledged that Murphy did not sign this portion of the contract. It is also acknowledged that Empire's President, Mr. Whitman, read and understood paragraph 6 quoted above. The estimated date for installation of the Litton system was set at November 15, 1973.

On August 9, 1973, Mathis, on behalf of Empire, was requested by Murphy to send a form letter to Mountain Bell designating Litton as Empire's representative with authority to act in connection with the installation of the interconnect system. The form letter supplied by Litton contained the following lead paragraph:

> We have this date entered into a contractual agreement with LITTON BTS Division, Litton Systems, Inc. for the installation of an "interconnect telephone system."

On August 30, 1973, John Parlett, National Systems Representative for Litton, wrote Mountain Bell advising that company of the details of the installation of the interconnect system. The letter contained the following lead paragraph:

> We have this date entered into a contractual agreement with Empire Machinery Company for the installation of an "interconnect" telephone system.

Empire, at Litton's request, purchased approximately 12,000 worth of electrical equipment to facilitate Litton's equipment. On December 3, 1973, W. P. Scott, service manager of Litton, requested that Mountain Bell supply a new telephone number for Empire to be put in service as of December 21, 1973. Nothing further was done by either party in furtherance of the contract. Litton never shipped nor prepared the interconnect system.

Apparently Litton encountered difficulties in perfecting its "Superplex" system and on January 10, 1974, Mr. E. E. Bolles, then Mountain Area Manager for Litton, met with Murphy and Mathis and advised Mathis that Litton would be unable to supply Empire with a "Superplex" interconnect telephone system. At that time Bolles tendered back Empire's down payment. This oral tender was verified by a letter the following day. Subsequently, Empire purchased a Stromborg-Carlson [sic] interconnect telephone system in lieu of the Litton system . . . .

Empire first contends that the letter from Litton dated July 30, 1973, signed by Murphy which stated "upon receipt of a signed order and deposit, Litton BTS will install an ['interconnect system'] on your premises," constituted an offer to sell. They further argue that having complied with that offer by signing the Equipment Sales Agreement and giving Murphy a check in the sum of 8,546.00, they accepted that offer and a binding contract was created. The problem with this reasoning is that it ignores the express language of the Equipment Sales Agreement, stating that the agreement would become effective and binding "only upon approval, acceptance, and execution hereof by BTS and its home office." Because of this language, we believe the correct rule is that stated in 1 CORBIN, CONTRACTS § 88 (1963):

> When one party solicits and receives an order or other expression of agreement from another, clearly specifying that there is to be no contract until ratification or assent by some officer or representative of the solicitor, the solicitation is not itself an offer; it is a request for an offer. The order that is given upon such a request is an offer, not an acceptance.

We therefore hold that Murphy's letter of July 30, 1973 constituted a request for an offer from Empire, and that the Equipment Sales Agreement was in compliance with that request and therefore an offer which required Litton's acceptance.

This brings us to the second issue presented, that is, the offer having designated the manner in which it would be accepted, is this the exclusive means by which that acceptance can occur? Empire has argued in this matter that future discovery might disclose that in fact Litton did accept, approve and execute the Equipment Sales Agreement. The simple answer to this contention is that Litton moved for summary judgment on the basis that the agreement was not accepted, approved or executed by "BTS and its home office" . . . .

The crux of the problem is thus presented. Litton argues that because of clause 6 in the contract, Empire's offer was never accepted in the manner designated and therefore a binding contractual relationship never existed between the parties. Empire argues that clause number 6 can be waived by it and assented to by Litton and the conduct of Litton subsequent to the submission of the Equipment Sales Agreement shows such an assent or at least a fact issue which would preclude summary judgment. Litton counters this argument by contending that in any event, the conduct relied upon by Empire to show assent was performed by agents who had no authority to bind Litton.

As the ground floor for both Litton's and Empire's positions, both cite § 2-206, Uniform Commercial Code which provides in part:

> Unless otherwise unambiguously indicated by the language or circumstances:
>
> 1. An offer to make a contract shall be construed as inviting acceptance in any manner and by any medium reasonable in the circumstances.

Empire points to the language contained under paragraph 1 of this statute and contends the conduct of Litton constitutes, as a matter of law, an acceptance of its offer under the Equipment Sales Agreement. Litton, on the other hand, points to the lead paragraph of this statute and argues that paragraph 6 of the Equipment Sales Agreement, as a matter of law, "otherwise unambiguously indicated" that only home office acceptance shall constitute an acceptance of the contract. In our opinion, both arguments miss the mark.

As the official comment to § 2-206 of the Uniform Commercial Code makes clear, this section was an attempt to simplify the common law rule that an acceptance of a contract could only be made in the manner and medium of the offer, that is, a written offer could only be accepted by an acceptance in writing. Litton is correct that this statute did not intend to change the common law rule that if an offer by its terms indicated that acceptance would only be made in a particular manner, one must comply with the particular manner. Nor is such an acceptance clause contrary to the Uniform Commercial Code.

However, even under the common law, a contract containing a clause that acceptance can only be made by approval of officers at the home office could be accepted in a manner other than by such written approval. We have previously held that insofar as the Equipment Sales Agreement was concerned, Empire was the offeror and Litton the offeree. This is important for it is the offeror who creates the power of acceptance. While normally, in transactions such as this where the offer to purchase is made on forms supplied by the seller, the buyer may adopt the manner of acceptance suggested by the seller. However, it is clear under such circumstances that the offeror who has the power to control the manner of acceptance may waive that requirement. It is equally clear that the offeree can rely upon that manner of acceptance specified in the contract and the offeror's "waiver" of the manner of acceptance cannot create a contract without the assent of the offeree. This assent may be sufficiently expressed by the conduct of the soliciting offeree so as to bring into being a binding contract.

The conduct on the part of the offeree which will constitute assent under these circumstances must be directed towards fulfilling the contractual obligation (that is, beginning performance) and that conduct must be conveyed by the offeree to the offeror. Moreover, the conduct must be by persons who have at least apparent authority to bind the offeree.

The conduct of Litton contended by Empire to constitute assent is as follows: (1) Murphy's request to Empire that Empire inform Mountain Bell that Litton was Empire's representative to install the "interconnect" system and the existence of a contractual relationship between Litton and Empire. (2) Parlett's letter of August 30, 1973, on behalf of Litton to Mountain Bell advising Mountain Bell of the contractual relationship existing between Litton and Empire and advising of the details of the installation of the "interconnect" system. (3) The purchase by Empire of 12,000 worth of equipment in reliance upon the installation of the Litton "interconnect" system. (4) The cashing of Empire's down payment check and the retention of the proceeds of that check. (5) The request by Scott, Litton's Service Manager, to Mountain Bell for a new telephone number for Empire's business.

As to Murphy's request that Empire inform Mountain States that a contractual obligation existed between Litton and Empire, we would agree that such conduct could be considered by a trier of fact as constituting assent to the formation of a binding contractual relationship between the parties, if performed by an individual having authority to bind Litton. However, we also agree upon the record presented here that Murphy had no authority expressed or apparent to bind Litton. Here Empire was put on notice by paragraph 6 of the contract that Murphy had no authority to bind Litton by his actions. We therefore conclude upon the record presented here that Murphy had no apparent authority to bind Litton by his letter.

The same cannot be said of Parlett, National Systems Representative, and his letter of August 30, 1973, advising Mountain Bell of the contractual relationship existing between Litton and Empire. While Parlett may, in fact, have no actual authority to bind Litton, there is nothing in the record to indicate his buyer was aware of that defect. Moreover, we note that Parlett apparently represents a different division of Litton BTS than Murphy, his headquarters are in a different city than Murphy and on the face of his letter he appears to speak with the authority to bind Litton. In short, we are of the opinion that a question of fact exists as to whether Parlett's letter of August 30, 1973 constituted an assent by Litton to be bound by the Equipment Sales Agreement and whether Parlett had apparent authority to so bind Litton. The same can be said of Scott's letter to Mountain Bell concerning change of telephone numbers. In this regard, Empire's purchase of equipment in reliance on this authority, if this be the fact, can be considered by the trier of fact.

Likewise, in our opinion the cashing of Empire's down payment check raises an issue of fact as to whether Litton assented to the contract. We view this conduct not in the context of ratification of an agent's acts, but as evidence that Litton assented to the contractual relationship by converting the negotiable instrument. We agree with Litton that the mere acceptance of the check in accordance with the terms of the offer does not constitute any evidence of binding conduct on Litton's part. It is the cashing of that check and the retention of the proceeds over a period of several months that gives rise to the factual inferences as to Litton's intent to enter into a binding contractual relationship with Empire. Since the record is silent as to who in the Litton organization negotiated the instrument, that individual's authority to do so must abide the trial of this matter.

[I]f the offeree takes steps in furtherance of its contractual obligations which would lead a reasonable businessman to believe that the contract had been accepted, such conduct may, under the circumstances, constitute acceptance of the contract.

Judgment reversed and the matter remanded for proceedings consistent with this opinion.

NOTES

(1) *The Radical Change.* One of the often ignored but, nonetheless, radical changes effectuated by the Uniform Commercial Code is suggested by the statement by the court, "As the official comment to § 2-206 makes clear, this section was an attempt to simplify the *common law rule that an acceptance of a contract could only be made in a manner . . . of the offer . . .*" (emphasis supplied). Indeed, the first RESTATEMENT OF CONTRACTS, § 52 (1932), presumed that the *typical* offer requested a particular manner of acceptance, i.e., it requested either a return promise or an act (performance), and the offeree was limited to that particular manner of acceptance.[22]

---

[22] "Acceptance of an offer is an expression of assent to the terms thereof made by the offeree in a manner requested or authorized by the offeror. If anything except a promise is requested as consideration no contract exists until part of what is requested is performed or tendered. If a promise

In a well-known case, *Davis v. Jacoby*, 1 Cal. 2d 370, 34 P.2d 1026 (1934), a sickly uncle whose wife was ill wrote to his niece that if she and her husband would look after the uncle and his wife, the niece would inherit everything. The letter contained the phrase, "Will you let me hear from you as soon as possible." Upon receipt of this letter, the couple decided to leave their home in Canada to travel to California to look after the wife's aunt and uncle and sent a letter accepting the uncle's proposition on April 14. Before they arrived, however, the uncle committed suicide. The essential issue before the court was whether the uncle's offer could be accepted by promising or only by the act of beginning to take care of the elderly couple. If the only appropriate manner of acceptance was the act (performance), since the uncle died before the performance commenced, the offer would be revoked by the death of the offeror, thereby terminating the power of acceptance. If, however, the offer contemplated an acceptance by promise, the letter sent on April 14 would be an effective acceptance. Under the common law (FIRST RESTATEMENT) analysis, the court decided that the offer in this case was a relatively rare *ambiguous* offer giving rise to the application of § 31 of the FIRST RESTATEMENT OF CONTRACTS which stated that:

> In case of doubt, it is presumed than an offer invites the formation of a bilateral contract by an acceptance amounting in effect to a promise by the offeree to perform what the offer requests rather than the formation of one or more unilateral contract by actual performance on the part of the offeree.

Thus, the "doubtful" offer was the rare offer while the typical offer prescribed the manner of acceptance. In the event the offer required a promissory acceptance and the offeree failed to make such a promise but fully performed the act represented by the missing promise, the First Restatement had to make an exception since, after all, the offeror had received exactly what he requested in exchange for his promise.[23]

The radical change effected by Professor Llewellyn in creating UCC Section 2-206 is the recognition that the so-called "doubtful" offer is the *typical* offer, i.e., the offeror normally does not care how the offer is accepted, by promising or performing. Thus, as the court quotes the section, unless the offeror *unambiguously* insists upon a particular manner of acceptance, the offer may be accepted either by a promise or the performance which is the ultimate desire of the offeror.[24]

The RESTATEMENT (SECOND) OF CONTRACTS § 30(2) replicates the same concept in language that is virtually identical to UCC 2-206. A comment to Section 32 of the Second Restatement removes the last scintilla of doubt that a new assumption has replaces the old assumption: "[T]he usual offer invites an acceptance which either

---

is requested, no contract exists . . . until that promise is expressly or impliedly given."

[23] Section 63 of the RESTATEMENT (FIRST) OF CONTRACTS finds a contract in such a situation on the footing that the offeror had received something better that the promise requested, i.e., the very performance he sought.

[24] Comment 2 to UCC § 2-206 states, "Any reasonable manner of acceptance is intended to be regarded as available unless the offeror has made quite clear that it will not be acceptable." Comment 2 indicates that the purpose is to reject the "artificial theory" that only a single mode of acceptance is normally envisaged by an offer.

amounts to performance or constitutes a promise . . . . The offeror is often indifferent as to whether acceptance takes the form of words of promise or acts of performance . . . ."

Since *Davis v. Jacoby* was not a contract for the sale of goods, the application of the SECOND RESTATEMENT principle would have avoided the contest since the offer could have been accepted by a promise or performance. For more on the radical change, see Murray, *Contracts: A New Design for the Agreement Process*, 53 CORNELL L. REV. 785 (1968).

(2) *Master of the Offer.* Both the UCC and RESTATEMENT (SECOND) OF CONTRACTS emphasize the principle that the offeror is the "master" of the offer. Thus, the offeror may insist on a particular manner or medium (method of transmission) of acceptance. The UCC includes the term "unambiguously" to emphasize the clarity which must attend any such insistence.[25] An offer which insists on a particular manner or medium of acceptance is now viewed as the rare offer since, again, the normal or typical offer is indifferent as to the manner or medium of acceptance. Where, however, an offer is interpreted as requiring only one manner of acceptance (as in the principal case), a court may feel compelled to adhere to the offeror's command. It is important, therefore, to consider how the court in the principal case, while recognizing the requirement of UCC § 2-206, discovers an analysis that overcomes that requirement. *Quaere*, when Empire's president, Mr. Whitman, signed the form presented by BTS, is it reasonable to assume that he knew he was making an offer requiring a particular manner of acceptance? Indeed, is it reasonable to assume that he knew he was making an offer rather than signing a contract?

CORINTHIAN PHARMACEUTICAL SYSTEMS, INC. v. LEDERLE LABORATORIES
United States District Court, Southern District of Indiana
724 F. Supp. 605 (1989)

McKINNEY, J.

Defendant Lederle Laboratories is a pharmaceutical manufacturer and distributor that makes a number of drugs, including the DTP vaccine. Plaintiff Corinthian Pharmaceutical is a distributor of drugs that purchases supplies from manufacturers such as Lederle Labs and then resells the product to physicians and other providers. One of the products that Corinthian buys and distributes with some regularity is the DTP vaccine.

From 1985 through early 1986, Corinthian made a number of purchases of the vaccine from Lederle Labs. During this period of time, the largest single order ever placed by Corinthian with Lederle was for 100 vials. When Lederle Labs filled an order it sent an invoice to Corinthian. The one page, double-sided invoice contained the specifics of the transaction on the front, along with form statement at the

---

[25] The RESTATEMENT (SECOND) formulation does not use this term but this should not indicate any significant difference between the formulations.

bottom that the transaction "is governed by seller's standard terms and conditions of sale set forth on back hereof, notwithstanding any provisions submitted by buyer. "Acceptance of the order is expressly conditioned on buyer's assent to seller's terms and conditions."

[P]roduct liability lawsuits concerning DTP increased, and insurance became more difficult to procure. As a result, Lederle decided in early 1986 to self-insure against such risks. In order to cover the costs of self-insurance, Lederle concluded that a substantial increase in the price of the vaccine would be necessary.

In order to communicate the price change to its own sales people, Lederle's Price Manager prepared "PRICE LETTER NO. E-48." This document was dated May 19, 1986, and indicated that effective May 20, 1986, the price of the DTP vaccine would be raised from 51.00 to 171.00 per vial. Price letters such as these were routinely sent to Lederle's sales force, but did not go to customers. Corinthian Pharmaceutical did not know of the existence of this internal price letter until a Lederle representative presented it to Corinthian several weeks after May 20, 1986.

Additionally, Lederle Labs also wrote a letter dated May 20, 1986, to its customers announcing the price increase and explaining the liability and insurance problems that brought about the change. Corinthian somehow gained knowledge of this letter on May 19, 1986, the date before the price increase was to take effect. In response to the knowledge of the impending price increase, Corinthian immediately ordered 1000 vials of DTP vaccine from Lederle. Corinthian placed its order on May 19, 1986, by calling Lederle's "Telgo" system, a telephone computer ordering system that allows customers to place orders over the phone by communicating with a computer. After Corinthian placed its order with the Telgo system, the computer gave Corinthian a tracking number for its order. On the same date, Corinthian sent Lederle two written confirmations of its order. On each form Corinthian stated that this "order is to receive the 64.32 per vial price."

On June 3, 1986, Lederle sent invoice 1771 to Corinthian for 50 vials of DTP vaccine priced at 64.32 per vial. The invoice contained the standard Lederle conditions [including the condition that the price will be the price in effect at time of shipment]. The 50 vials were sent to Corinthian and were accepted. At the same time, Lederle sent its customers, including Corinthian, a letter regarding DTP vaccine pricing and orders. This letter stated that the "enclosed represents a partial shipment of the order for DTP vaccine, which you placed with Lederle on May 19, 1986." The letter stated that under Lederle's standard terms and conditions of sale the normal policy would be to invoice the order at the price when shipment was made. However, in light of the magnitude of the price increase, Lederle had decided to make an exception to its terms and conditions and ship a portion of the order at the lower price. The letter further stated that the balance would be priced at 171.00, and that shipment would be made during the week of June 16. The letter closed, "If for any reason you wish to cancel the balance of your order, please contact [us] . . . on or before June 13."

Based on these facts, plaintiff Corinthian Pharmaceutical brings this action seeking specific performance for the 950 vials of DTP vaccine that Lederle Labs chose not to deliver. In support of its summary judgment motion, Lederle urges a number of alternative grounds for disposing of this claim, including that no contract for the sale of 1000 vials was formed . . . .

[T]his is a straightforward sale of goods problem resembling those found in a contracts or sales casebook. The fundamental question is whether Lederle Labs agreed to sell Corinthian Pharmaceuticals 1,000 vials of DTP vaccine at 64.32 per vial. As shown below, the undisputed material facts mandate the conclusion as a matter of law that no such agreement was ever formed.

Initially, it should be noted that this is a sale of goods covered by the Uniform Commercial Code, and that both parties are merchants under the Code. . . . The starting point in this analysis is where did the first offer originate. An offer is "the manifestation of willingness to enter into a bargain, so made as to justify another person in understanding that his assent to that bargain is invited and will conclude it." H. Greenberg, Rights and Remedies Under U.C.C. Article 2 § 5.2 at 50 (1987) [hereinafter "Greenberg, U.C.C. Article 2"], (quoting 1 RESTATEMENT (SECOND), CONTRACTS § 4 (1981)). The only possible conclusion in this case is that Corinthian's "order" of May 19, 1986, for 1,000 vials at 64.32 was the first offer. Nothing that the seller had done prior to this point can be interpreted as an offer.

First, the price lists distributed by Lederle to its customers did not constitute offers. It is well settled that quotations are mere invitations to make an offer, Greenberg, U.C.C. Article 2 § 5.2 at 51; CORBIN ON CONTRACTS §§ 26, 28 (1982), particularly where, as here, the price lists specifically stated that prices were subject to change without notice and that all orders were subject to acceptance by Lederle. *Quaker State Mushroom v. Dominick's Finer Foods*, 635 F. Supp. 1281, 1284 (N.D. Ill. 1986) (No offer where price quotation is subject to change and orders are subject to seller's confirmation); *Interstate Industries, Inc. v. Barclay Industries, Inc.*, 540 F.2d 868, 873 (7th Cir. 1976) (price quotation not an offer).

Second, neither Lederle's internal price memorandum nor its letter to customers dated May 20, 1986, can be construed as an offer to sell 1,000 vials at the lower price. There is no evidence that Lederle intended Corinthian to receive the internal price memorandum, nor is there anything in the record to support the conclusion that the May 20, 1986, letter was an offer to sell 1,000 vials to Corinthian at the lower price. If anything, the evidence shows that Corinthian was not supposed to receive this letter until after the price increase had taken place. Moreover, the letter, just like the price lists, was a mere quotation (i.e., an invitation to submit an offer) sent to all customers. As such, it did not bestow on Corinthian nor other customers the power to form a binding contract for the sale of one thousand, or, for that matter, one million vials of vaccine.

Thus, as a matter of law, the first offer was made by Corinthian when it phoned in and subsequently confirmed its order for 1,000 vials at the lower price. The next question, then, is whether Lederle ever accepted that offer. Under § 2-206, an offer to make a contract shall be construed as inviting acceptance in any manner and by any medium reasonable in the circumstances. The first question regarding acceptance, therefore, is whether Lederle accepted the offer prior to sending the 50 vials of vaccine.

The record is clear that Lederle did not communicate or do any act prior to shipping the 50 vials that could support the finding of an acceptance. When

Corinthian placed its order, it merely received a tracking number from the Telgo computer. Such an automated, ministerial act cannot constitute an acceptance. *See, e.g., Foremost Pro Color, Inc. v. Eastman Kodak Co.*, 703 F.2d 534, 539 (9th Cir. 1983) (logging purchase orders as received did not manifest acceptance); *Southern Spindle & Flyer Co. v. Milliken & Co.*, 53 N.C. App. 785, 281 S.E.2d 734, 736 (1981) (seller's acknowledgment of receipt of purchase order did not constitute assent to its terms). Thus, there was no acceptance of Corinthian's offer prior to the deliver of 50 vials.

The next question, then, is what is to be made of the shipment of 50 vials and the accompanying letter. Section 2-206(b) of the Code speaks to this issue:

> An order or other offer to buy goods for prompt or current shipment shall be construed as inviting acceptance either by a prompt promise to ship or by the prompt or current shipment of conforming or non-conforming goods, but such a shipment of non-conforming goods does not constitute an acceptance if the seller seasonably notifies the buyer that the shipment is offered only as an accommodation to the buyer.

Thus, under the Code a seller accepts the offer by shipping goods, whether they are conforming or not, but if the seller ships non-conforming goods and seasonably notifies the buyer that the shipment is a mere accommodation, then the seller has not, in fact, accepted the buyer's offer.

In this case, the offer made by Corinthian was for 1,000 vials at 64.32. In response, Lederle Labs shipped only 50 vials at 64.32 per vial, and wrote Corinthian indicating that the balance of the order would be priced at 171.00 per vial and would be shipped during the week of June 16. The letter further indicated that the buyer could cancel its order by calling Lederle Labs. Clearly, Lederle's shipment was non-conforming, for it was for only 1/20th of the quantity desired by the buyer. *See* § 2-106(2) (goods or conduct are conforming when they are in accordance with the obligations under the contract); *Michiana Mack, Inc. v. Allendale Rural Fire Protection*, 428 N.E.2d 1367, 1370 (Ind. App. 1981) (non-conformity describes goods and conduct). The narrow issue, then, is whether Lederle's response to the offer was a shipment of non-conforming goods not constituting an acceptance because it was offered only as an accommodation under § 2-206.

An accommodation is an arrangement or engagement made as a favor to another. BLACK'S LAW DICTIONARY (5th ed. 1979). The term implies no consideration. *Id.* In this case, then, even taking all inferences favorably for the buyer, the only possible conclusion is that Lederle Labs' shipment of 50 vials was offered merely as an accommodation; that is to say, Lederle had no obligation to make the partial shipment, and did so only as a favor to the buyer. The accommodation letter, which Corinthian is sure it received, clearly stated that the 50 vials were being sent at the lower price as an exception to Lederle's general policy, and that the balance of the offer would be invoiced at the higher price. The letter further indicated that Lederle's proposal to ship the balance of the order at the higher price could be rejected by the buyer. Moreover, the standard terms of Lederle's invoice stated that acceptance of the order was expressly conditioned upon buyer's assent to the seller's terms.

Under these undisputed facts, § 2-206(1)(b) was satisfied. Where, as here, the notification is properly made, the shipment of nonconforming goods is treated as a counteroffer just as at common law, and the buyer may accept or reject the counteroffer under normal contract rules. 2 W. Hawkland, Uniform Commercial Code Series § 2-206:04 (1987).

Thus, the end result of this analysis is that Lederle Lab's price quotations were mere invitations to make an offer, that by placing its order Corinthian made an offer to buy 1,000 vials at the low price, that by shipping 50 vials at the low price Lederle's response was non-conforming, but the non-conforming response was a mere accommodation and thus constituted a counteroffer. Accordingly, there being no genuine issues of material fact on these issues and the law being in favor of the seller, summary judgment must be granted for Lederle Labs.

QUESTIONS

(1)   If Lederle had not notified Corinthian that its partial shipment was only an accommodation shipment, would there be a contract for the entire amount ordered at 64.32 each? Such a shipment would be "nonconforming" because the buyer is insisting upon a higher price for the remaining vials. Suppose, instead of a different price, the shipment was of a different drug? Again, absent a notice of accommodation, would such a nonconforming shipment form a contract? What are the terms of such a contract? Consider Comment 4 to § UCC 2-206: "Such a non-conforming shipment is normally to be understood to close the bargain, even though it proves to have been at the same time a breach." If a seller makes such a nonconforming shipment without a notice of accommodation, what is the remedy of the buyer for such a breach?

(2)   What is the effect of an accommodation notice? Section 2-206(1)(b) states that a non-conforming shipment "does not constitute an acceptance if the seller *seasonably* notifies the buyer that the shipment is offered only as an accommodation." (Emphasis supplied). What is the definition of "seasonably"? *See* UCC § 2-104. Must the accommodation notice arrive before the goods arrive?

HARRIS v. YELLOW TRANSPORTATION CO.
United States District Court, Northern District of Texas
2008 U.S. Dist. LEXIS 112143 (2008)

GODBEY, J.

Plaintiff Freeman Harris ("Harris"), a former employee of Yellow Transportation, brings a claim before this Court against Yellow Transportation for race discrimination, harassment, and retaliation pursuant to 42 U.S.C § 1981. Yellow Transportation moves to compel arbitration under the terms of the company's Dispute Resolution Process.[26] In 2004, Harris acknowledged in writing his receipt

---

[26] [Ed. note: Parties to a contract may agree that, in the event of any dispute concerning their contract, they will submit the dispute to arbitration instead of traditional litigation in a court of law. (See the Federal Arbitration Act. 9 U. S. C. §§ 1-14. There are various state arbitration acts) Arbitration is an

of Yellow Transportation's Policy Guide to Workplace Conduct ("Policy Guide"), which included the terms of the Dispute Resolution Process. By its terms, the Dispute Resolution Process applies to all applicants and nonunion employees, like Harris, and submitting to it is a condition of employment. Harris also received the Dispute Resolution Agreement ("Agreement") at that time, but he asserts that he never agreed to be bound to the arbitration process because he never signed, and in fact refused to sign, this Agreement. According to Harris, his shift supervisors accepted his refusal to sign, but told him to sign the employee log to indicate receipt of the Policy Guide. At that time, they allegedly advised him that he was not bound to go to arbitration in case of a dispute, and that he could choose whether or not to sign the Agreement later. After receiving the Policy Guide in 2004, Harris continued to work until sometime around April, 2007.

The Court first must decide whether the parties entered into a valid agreement to arbitrate. Contrary to Yellow Transportation's contention, there is no applicable "presumption of arbitrability" guiding the Court's decision. While Yellow Transportation points to the federal policy in support of broadly construing the scope of arbitration agreements, "the federal policy favoring arbitration does not apply to the determination of whether there is a valid agreement to arbitrate between the parties or to the determination of who is bound by the arbitration agreement." *Fleetwood Enters. Inc. v. Gaskamp*, 280 F.3d 1069, 1073–74 (5th Cir. 2002). Courts decide the antecedent question of whether there is a valid agreement to arbitrate on the basis of "ordinary state law principles that govern the formation of contracts." *Id.* (quoting *First Options of Chicago, Inc. v. Kaplan*, 514 U.S. 938, 944, 115 S. Ct. 1920, 131 L. Ed. 2d 985 (1995)).

Regardless of Harris's refusal to sign the Agreement, or any statements his shift supervisors may have made, the arbitration provision is enforceable against him. An employer may enforce an arbitration agreement entered into during an at-will employment relationship[27] if the employee received notice of the employer's arbitration policy and accepted it. Harris was an employee at-will. If he had notice of the Dispute Resolution process mandating arbitration, his decision to continuing working at Yellow Transportation constituted an acceptance of the terms of that process as a matter of law and irrespective of any express refusal to arbitrate or to sign the Agreement.

The question is whether Harris had notice. In order to prove notice in this case, Yellow Transportation must show that it unequivocally informed Harris about the arbitration provisions and that they applied to him. This Court finds the terms of

---

alternative method of adjudicating disputes. There are no judges or juries in the arbitration process. There may be one arbitrator or a panel of three arbitrators who decide the case. Their decision is final unless the arbitration process or the arbitration award can be shown to involve fraud, corruption, partiality, excessive use of power by arbitrators or other misbehavior that will be the basis for "vacatur," vacating the arbitration award. 9 U. S. C. § 10. In recent years, there has been considerable litigation over the basic issue of whether an employee has agreed to arbitrate when the employer has installed an arbitration process for any civil dispute between the employer and employees.]

[27] [Ed. note: An "at-will" employment relationship is the typical contractual relationship between an employee and employer whenever there is no duration in the contract of employment. The employee is free to leave the employment at any time and the employer is free to terminate the employment at any time. Further discussion of at-mill employment contracts appears later in this volume.]

the Dispute Resolution Process which Harris received to be plain and clear. Those terms indicate that acceptance of the Dispute Resolution Process was a condition of Harris's employment and that any questions about it should have been directed to a human resources manager or representative. Because Yellow Transportation's Policy Guide gave Harris unequivocal notice that the Dispute Resolution Process's applied to him, and clearly precluded reliance on his shift supervisors' alleged statements to the contrary, Harris's choice to continue working with the company constituted acceptance of the agreement to arbitrate.

[Another provision in the arbitration agreement required Harris to pay half of the costs of arbitration. The court found this part of the arbitration agreement to be unconscionable and severed it from the remainder of the clause, allowing allowed arbitration to proceed without the requirement that Harris pay half the costs. The unconscionability concept is explored in Chapter 5.]

QUESTIONS

When an employer presents an arbitration requirement to an "at-will" employee, may the employee accept by promising or only by performing? Harris claimed that he refused to sign the agreement that would govern any claim against the employer. Would such a refusal amount to a rejection of the offer? If it is a rejection, has the offer to Harris been extinguished., thereby precluding any acceptance of it thereafter by performance (continuing to work) or otherwise?

[2]   Silence as Acceptance

VOGT v. MADDEN
Idaho Court of Appeals
713 P.2d 442 (1985)

WALTERS, J.

Harold and Betty Vogt sued Bob and Neva Madden for damages allegedly resulting from the Maddens' breach, as landlords, of a sharecrop agreement. A jury returned a verdict in favor of the Vogts.

It was undisputed that Harold Vogt had an oral sharecrop agreement with Bob Madden to farm seventy acres of land owned by the Maddens, for the year 1979. It also was undisputed that the parties renewed the agreement for the year 1980. Under their agreement, certain expenses would be borne solely by Vogt, other expenses would be shared equally between Vogt and Madden, and the net profits derived from crops grown on the land would be divided equally between them. When the Vogts eventually filed suit contending a sharecrop agreement existed for the year 1981, Vogt also sought recovery from Madden of 2,000 for the Maddens' share of expenses incurred by Vogt in the years 1979 and 1980.

The dispositive issue in this appeal is whether Vogt and Madden had a sharecrop agreement that Vogt could continue to farm the seventy acres, during 1981. Vogt testified that because no profits had been realized from wheat crops grown on the

property in 1979 and 1980, he planned to raise beans on the land in 1981. He
testified that he met with Madden several times in August and September, after the
wheat crop had been harvested in 1980, concerning the expenses remaining for the
years 1979 and 1980. He testified:

> [W]e also discussed the 1981 crop, of what to do then. We had several
> discussions on this. I met with him two or three, four times — I'm not sure
> how many — and we both agreed it wasn't the best ground. It isn't number
> one soil out there, because of the steepness, but I had raised grain for two
> years, and I had left the straw and stubble on the ground. And I had raised
> a — let the volunteer grain grow, watered it and plowed it under the first
> year. And I anticipated plowing under the second year and at that point I
> told him I thought it would raise a fairly decent crop of pinto beans.

And at that time I told Bob [Madden] that I'd raised two years of grain, plowed
under this straw and stubble, and I thought it would raise a crop of pinto beans. And
at that time I had decided to do that. I was going to raise the pinto beans on there,
along with possibly a few acres of garden beans.

Q: And as a result of that conversation, it was your understanding that
            you were to farm that; is that correct?

A: Yes.

Q: And when you were discussing the fact of growing the bean crop
            with Mr. Madden, did he have any objection to that type of crop
            being grown on his ground?

A: No, not at all.

            On cross-examination, Vogt testified as follows:

Q: You talked about beans, then?

A: Yes, sir.

Q: But Mr. Madden never told you that he wanted to grow beans, did
            he?

A: No.

Q: He never expressly told you that he would enter into another
            agreement in the spring of '81?

A: Yes. What we done, we just — I told him I had raised this crop, the
            wheat and grain for two years, and the third year we could raise a
            crop of pintos, a crop of beans. And the price of beans at that time
            was good, and as far as I know that was the way the discussion
            ended.

Q: But Mr. Madden never agreed one way or another, right?

A: I would say I was under the impression that we had an agreement.

Q: But he never said anything to give you that indication?

A: Honestly, I don't think he said, "Yes, go ahead." No, he didn't say
            that.

Madden disputed that he and Vogt had agreed to a sharecrop arrangement for the year 1981. He testified that, following one of their discussions over the expense bills for 1979 and 1980,

And I said at that time, I told him, I said, "I just had it. I don't want you to farm it any more. I'll send you what I think is right. 'Harold,' " I said, "Life's too short to argue over these things, let's just — we're through."

In respect to that same discussion, Vogt denied on rebuttal that Madden had made any statement about Vogt not farming the Maddens' land the next year. In the late fall of 1980, Madden leased the property to another party for the 1981 crop year, thus preventing Vogt from pursuing his plan to raise beans on the land. This lawsuit for damages followed.

By its verdict in favor of Vogt for 18,540, the jury concluded that a sharecrop agreement existed between Vogt and Madden for the year 1981.[28] In order to reach such a conclusion the jury must have disbelieved Madden when he testified he informed Vogt that their relationship was "through," and that he, Madden, did not want Vogt to farm the property any longer. Otherwise, had the jury believed Madden, then clearly the parties would not have had a contract for 1981. If Madden were disbelieved, then the only evidence regarding the creation of a contract between Vogt and Madden for the year 1981 would be Vogt's testimony that he informed Madden of his intent to raise beans on the property in 1981, that Madden did not say "yes" to this proposal, but that Vogt nonetheless was left with the "impression" that a contract had been created.

The question whether silence or inaction may constitute acceptance of an offer was an issue in this case. Over Madden's objection, the jury was given an instruction concerning silence as an acceptance of an offer, creating a contract between the offeror, Vogt, and the offeree, Madden. The instruction was requested by Vogt, demonstrating that Vogt was pursuing a theory that the evidence showed the creation of a sharecrop agreement for 1981 arising because of silence on Madden's part.

The instruction stated:

Silence and inaction may constitute acceptance of an offer to contract, where a party is under a duty to speak or to reject the offer. Such a duty may arise under any one of the following circumstances.

1. Where because of previous dealings it is reasonable that the offeree should notify the offeror if the offeree does not intend to accept.

2. Where an offeree takes the benefit of offered services with reasonable opportunity to reject them and reason to believe the offeror thought the offer was accepted.

---

[28] [1] Vogt testified that, had he been allowed to farm the Maddens' property in 1981 under the same sharecrop arrangement as in 1979 and 1980, he would have realized a net profit of 16,540. That figure, when added to the 2,000 owed by Madden to Vogt for the 1979–80 expenses, totals 18,540, the amount of the verdict.

3. Where the offeror has stated or given the offeree reason to understand that assent may be manifested by silence or inaction, and the offeree in remaining silent and inactive intends to accept the offer.

This instruction was a slightly modified version of the RESTATEMENT (SECOND) OF CONTRACTS § 69 (1981).[29] The RESTATEMENT explains that silence by an offeree ordinarily does not operate as an acceptance of an offer. "The exceptional cases where silence is acceptance fall into two main classes: those where the offeree silently takes offered benefits, and those where one party relies on the other party's manifestation of intention that silence may operate as acceptance." *Id.* comment a, at 165.

Here, two of the exceptions stated in § 69, and in the court's instruction are patently inapplicable because they are wholly unsupported by the evidence. There was no evidence that Madden received "the benefit of offered services" for which Vogt expected to be compensated. ("when the recipient knows or has reason to know that services are being rendered with an expectation of compensation, and by a word could prevent the mistake, his privilege of inaction gives way; under Subsection (1)(a) he is held to an acceptance if he fails to speak."). Vogt did not, in fact, farm the property in 1981. Nor does the evidence show that Vogt stated or gave Madden reason to understand that assent to Vogt's expectation to farm the property might be manifested by silence or inaction, and the evidence does not show that Madden, by remaining silent and inactive intended to accept Vogt's offer.

Finally, the exception arising from "previous dealings" between the parties is inapposite. In their prior dealings, 1979 and 1980, the parties expressly reached oral agreements for sharecropping the farm. After completion of the contract for 1979, a new contract for 1980 did not automatically follow. It was preceded by discussions between Vogt and Madden resulting in an express understanding that Vogt could farm the property in 1980 on a sharecrop basis. We do not believe those previous transactions could give rise to a legitimate conclusion that Vogt's offer to farm the property in 1981 would be accepted in the absence of affirmative notification from Madden that the offer would not be accepted. To the contrary, the previous dealings always resulted in a contract only when both parties expressly agreed.

Absent the applicability of the exceptions stated in RESTATEMENT § 69, it is a general rule of law that silence and inaction, or mere silence or failure to reject an offer when it is made, does not constitute an acceptance of the offer. Because none of the exceptions is applicable in this case, we conclude as a matter of law that no contract to sharecrop the Maddens' property in 1981 was created by Madden's silence in response to Vogt's offer to farm the property. We therefore set aside that

---

[29] [2] (1) Where an offeree fails to reply to an offer, his silence and inaction operate as an acceptance in the following cases only:

   (a) Where an offeree takes the benefit of offered services with reasonable opportunity to reject them and reason to know that they were offered with the expectation of compensation.

   (b) Where the offeror has stated or given the offeree reason to understand that assent may be manifested by silence or inaction, and the offeree in remaining silent and inactive intends to accept the offer.

   (c) Where because of previous dealings or otherwise, it is reasonable that the offeree should notify the offeror if he does not intend to accept.

portion of the judgment awarding damages to the Vogts based on the alleged 1981 contract. We deem it unnecessary to discuss whether those damages were based on speculation or whether mitigation of damages was proved.

On appeal the Maddens do not question the award by the jury to the Vogts of 2,000 representing reimbursement of expenses for the years 1979 and 1980. We therefore affirm that portion of the judgment.

The judgment is reversed in respect to award of any damages for breach of the alleged 1981 contract. The case is remanded for entry of a modified judgment allowing recovery to the Vogts for 2,000 with interest from the date of the original judgment.

PROBLEMS

(1)   Because she once expressed admiration for your sports car, you offer to sell it to Nancy Miller, a friend, for 20,000. Your letter that states you will assume her acceptance if you do not hear from her within 10 days from her receipt of the letter. Nancy received the letter and you hear nothing from her for more than 10 days. You contact Nancy who tells you she is not interested in this arrangement. Do you have a contract with Nancy?

(2)   Assume that, after not hearing from Nancy for more than 10 days, an acquaintance, Rick Stafford, offers to buy the car from you for 28,000. You are in the midst of writing to Rick to accept his offer when Nancy notifies you that she has a cashier's check for 20,000 awaiting your delivery of the car. May Nancy enforce a contract for the car?

(3)   You and your neighbor have discussed the possibility of erecting a low brick wall between your two adjoining properties and sharing the cost. Though no final agreement was reached, one day you see your neighbor starting the construction of the wall and, without objection, you silently permit him to continue it to completion. Are you liable for half the reasonable cost of the wall? *See Day v. Caton*, 119 Mass. 513, 20 Am. Rep. 347 (1876).

(4)   You operate a store which buys supplies from a particular wholesaler. You have been giving orders to the wholesaler's salesperson for several years. Each time you order supplies, they are delivered within 10 days. The last order was placed with the wholesaler's representative, as usual. The order was not delivered within 10 days. Two weeks later when you inquire about the delay, the wholesaler informs you that it has rejected your offer. Do you have any legal basis for complaint? *See Ammons v. Wilson & Co.*, 176 Miss. 645, 170 So. 227 (1936).

[3] The Notice Requirement

PETERSEN v. THOMPSON
Oregon Supreme Court
506 P.2d 697 (1973)

McAllister, J.

The plaintiff Petersen brought this action to recover possession of a tractor which was in possession of the defendant Thompson who claimed to own it. Both men claimed ownership by purchase from J. I. Case Credit Corporation.

The court tried the case without a jury and when plaintiff rested granted defendant's motion for a nonsuit. Plaintiff appeals from the judgment of nonsuit.

This case arose out of the following facts. J. I. Case owned a repossessed tractor located in the woods near Morton, Washington. In the middle of February 1972, defendant Thompson telephoned Case's credit supervisor Henderson about buying the tractor. Henderson agreed to sell the tractor to Thompson for 1,000 "as is, where is." Thompson was to pick up the tractor in the woods and pay the purchase price in cash.

On March 1st Thompson picked up the tractor and brought it to Oregon. There is a dispute about when Thompson told Henderson that he had picked up the tractor. Thompson said it was about the middle of March, while Henderson testified that it was around the end of March. In any event, about March 10th or 12th plaintiff Petersen telephoned Henderson about buying the same tractor. Henderson testified that since he had heard nothing from Thompson he assumed that Thompson was no longer interested in the tractor and he therefore agreed to sell the tractor to Petersen. It is unnecessary to relate at this time the other evidence about what J. I. Case did when it discovered that it had sold the tractor to two different buyers.

Plaintiff states his assignment of error in language carefully chosen to avoid a decision of this case on its merits. His assignment of error alleges that "the trial court erred in holding that there was no evidence before it that would have supported a judgment for the plaintiff." In his statement of the question to be decided on appeal he contends that there was evidence from which the court could have found that the tractor belonged to plaintiff. In his brief defendant accepts plaintiff's "statement of the question to be decided."

Plaintiff's studied effort to limit the scope of review and defendant's acquiescence in the issue on appeal presents us with the same question we faced in *Karoblis v. Liebert*, 501 P.2d 315 (1972). That question was whether a motion for a nonsuit in an action tried by the court without a jury permits the court to decide only whether the plaintiff has proved a case sufficient to be submitted to the jury, if there had been a jury, or whether such a motion permits the court to decide the case on the merits. In *Karoblis* we adopted the equity procedure and held "that the defendant in a law action tried to the court without a jury may not test the legal sufficiency of plaintiff's evidence at the close of plaintiff's case. If he wishes to challenge the sufficiency of the evidence he must rest his case and submit the matter to the court on its merits."

501 P.2d at 320. Unfortunately this case was tried before *Karoblis* was decided.

It appears from the statement made from the bench by the trial judge when he ruled on the motion for a nonsuit that he thought he was deciding the case on its merits. He said:

> I hold that the contract was completed when he loaded the tractor upon his lowboy in the State of Washington and took delivery. There was nothing thereafter which would give Case and Company any right to rescind that contract. There was no showing of nonperformance on the part of the defendant. Therefore, the sale was completed. It was his property and he was entitled — he was the owner of it. He thereafter — what happened thereafter is the — is of no consequence.

Unfortunately, however, the trial judge spoke only of granting a nonsuit and entered only a judgment of nonsuit reading in pertinent part as follows:

> The Court was of the opinion that plaintiff failed to prove a cause *sufficient to be submitted to it for decision.*

Now, therefore, it is hereby ordered that a judgment of nonsuit be, and the same hereby is given against the plaintiff . . . . (Emphasis supplied.)

If the record contained any indication that plaintiff consented or acquiesced in a decision of the case on the merits, we would affirm; or, if we could hold, as a matter of law, that title to the tractor was vested in defendant, we would affirm. Although there is ample evidence to support a finding in defendant's favor, we cannot say as a matter of law that that was the only finding justified by the evidence. On the contrary, we agree with plaintiff that there was evidence from which the trial court could have found in favor of plaintiff, which evidence includes the following circumstances:

> Some time in February, between the 11th and the 20th, defendant telephoned Case's local credit officer, Henderson, about the possibility of purchasing the tractor. Henderson testified about this conversation:

> Q.   What transpired between you and Mr. Thompson concerning the equipment, if any?

> A.   Well, originally, I agreed to sell it to Mr. Thompson.

> Q.   Like under what terms and consideration?

> A.   Uh, same terms — same amount of money involved.

> Q.   Well, tell us a little more detail. What — what did you ask Mr. Thompson to do?

> A.   Well, we — we had the equipment in the woods near Morton, Washington. Mr. Thompson knew about it. He contacted me. I agreed to sell it to him for an amount as is, where is.

> Q.   Do you have any recollection as to what you told Thompson to do with regard to picking up this equipment and taking possession of it?

> A.   Other than picking it up and bringing it — taking it to wherever he wanted to take it, no.

Q.   And it was your understanding then that he was going to do that in — as a part of this agreement of sale, is that right?

A.   Yes, sir.

          Defendant testified about the same conversation:

Q.   Now what sort of an understanding did you have with Mr. Henderson, if any, about this purchase?

A.   I had —. I bought it with the understanding that I had it bought when I — when I — it hit the lowboy — when it got loaded on the lowboy, and he was suppose to come around and pick up the payment . . . they told me to go ahead and load it up then, which I did, on that call in February — make the repairs necessary to get it loaded on the loader.

ORS 72.4030(1) provides that "A purchaser of goods acquires all title which his transferor had or had power to transfer . . . ." Other sections of the statute provide for the power to transfer title under circumstances not present in this case. Under the general provision quoted above, plaintiff could acquire title from Case only if Case had title at the time of the purported sale to plaintiff. *See also Kelley v. Ness*, 182 Ore. 661, 189 P.2d 570 (1948), decided under the corresponding provision of the Uniform Sales Act. The precise issue, therefore, is whether there was any evidence from which the trial court could have found that title had not passed to defendant prior to the attempted sale to plaintiff.

From the testimony of defendant and of Henderson, quoted above, a trier of fact could infer that at the time of their telephone conversation in February their agreement was complete, and that they had agreed title was to pass when defendant picked up the tractor. ORS 72.4010(1) provides:

> . . . title to goods passes from the seller to the buyer in any manner and on any conditions explicitly agreed on by the parties.

Therefore, if the trier found that the agreement between Henderson and defendant was that suggested above, title was in defendant from the time he picked up the tractor, and the attempted sale to plaintiff was a nullity.

However, a trier of fact could also infer that during the telephone conversation Henderson had merely offered to sell the tractor to defendant, and that defendant could accept the offer by picking up the tractor at its Washington location. The nature of the agreement must be determined by inference, as both Henderson and defendant testified to what they understood the result of their conservation to be. Neither made any attempt to recount the conversation itself. Henderson's testimony that he "agreed to sell" to defendant, and defendant's testimony that his understanding was that he "had it bought" when he picked the tractor up, could reasonably be interpreted as resulting in an offer to sell which could be accepted by picking up the tractor.

If the contract of sale was not complete until defendant accepted by picking up the tractor, that acceptance did not bind the Case Corporation in the absence of proper notice. ORS 72.2060(2) provides:

Where the beginning of a requested performance is a reasonable mode of acceptance an offeror who is not notified of acceptance within a reasonable time may treat the offer as having lapsed before acceptance.[30]

ORS 71.2040(2) provides:

What is a reasonable time for taking any action depends on the nature, purpose and circumstances of such action.

Defendant did not inform Henderson that he had picked up the tractor until approximately two to four weeks after he had done so. Defendant's testimony and that of Henderson differ on when notice was given. Since we are not willing to hold that notice given four weeks after acceptance was, as a matter of law, given within a reasonable time, plaintiff's evidence was sufficient to make a case for a trier of fact. That is, the evidence would support a finding that Henderson's offer was not accepted until defendant picked up the tractor, and that defendant failed to give notice of his acceptance within a reasonable time, permitting Henderson to treat the offer as having lapsed under ORS 72.2060(2).

It follows that the judgment must be reversed and remanded with instruction to vacate the judgment, deny the motion for a nonsuit, require the defendant to put on his evidence or rest his case and to then decide the case on its merits. It is so ordered.

NOTE

In *Bishop v. Eaton*, 161 Mass. 496, 37 N.E. 665 (1894), [The] defendant wrote from Nova Scotia to plaintiff in Illinois, "If Harry [defendant's brother] needs more money, let him have it, or assist him to get it, and I will see that it is paid." Shortly thereafter plaintiff wrote to defendant telling him that he had signed a promissory note as surety for defendant's brother. The letter was properly addressed but never arrived. Plaintiff now seeks to collect from defendant after paying the brother's note. The court held for the plaintiff saying:

[T]his was not a proposition which was to become a contract only upon the giving of a promise for a promise, and it was not necessary that the plaintiff should accept it in words, or promise to do anything before acting upon it. It was an offer which was to become effective as a contract upon the doing of the act referred to. It was an offer to be bound in consideration of an act to be done, and in such a case the doing of the act constitutes the acceptance of the offer, and furnishes the consideration. Ordinarily, there is no occasion to notify the offeror of the acceptance of such an offer, for the doing of the act is a sufficient acceptance, and the promissor knows that he is bound when he sees that action has been taken on the faith of his offer. But, if the act is of such a kind that knowledge of it will not quickly come to the promisor, the promisee is bound to give him notice of his acceptance

---

[30] [1] Instead of this provision, plaintiff relies on ORS 72.6060 in support of his argument that acceptance must be communicated to the offeror. It appears that he has relied on the wrong statute, as ORS 72.6060 deals with the buyer's acceptance of the goods as being in conformance with the contract, and presupposes the existence of a valid contract of sale.

within a reasonable time after doing that which constitutes the acceptance
. . . [and] where the promise is in consideration of an act to be done, it
becomes binding upon the doing of the act so far that the promisee cannot
be affected by a subsequent withdrawal of it, if, within a reasonable time
afterwards, he notifies the promisor.

Id. at 499–500, 37 N.E. at 667.

PROBLEM

Eileen considered selling the house in which she had lived for many years. She
received a document captioned "letter of intent" which stated that the buyer
offered to purchase her house and she would later receive a real estate contract to
sign. She signed the letter of intent and received a check for $5000. She then
received a packet of documents including the real estate contract which she signed
before examining the remainder of the documents and crossing out two provisions.
She did not return the signed real estate contract. Nor did she deposit or negotiate
the check. She informed the buyers that she was not interested in selling her house
to them.The buyers claimed that she had formed a contract by signing the letter of
intent as well as the real estate document. Analyze. The problem is based on
Cochran v. Norkunas, 919 A.2d 700 (Md. 2007).

[4]   A Primer on the Concept of "Warranty"

The term "warranty" has been used in several distinct senses over the years.
More than forty years ago, the chief architect of the Uniform Commercial Code,
Karl Llewellyn, complained that, "To say 'warranty' is to say nothing definite as to
legal effect." K. LLEWELLYN, CASES AND MATERIALS ON THE LAW OF SALES 210 (1930).
Typically, the term is used in relation to contracts for the sale of goods and
connotes the seller's obligation as to the *quality* of the goods. There are three
distinct questions which may be posed: (1) Does the seller in a given sales
transaction, have any obligation as to the quality of the goods? While sellers
normally have some obligation as to quality, a sale of goods may occur on an "as is"
basis and the buyer is assuming all risks of quality. (2) If the seller does have
obligations as to quality, what kind of goods must he deliver in order to meet such
obligations? (3) Finally, if the seller fails to meet such obligations as to quality of
the goods, what are the buyer's remedies? While Llewellyn suggested many years
ago that "the sane course is to discard the word from one's thinking," the term is
used in the Uniform Commercial Code and its use therein must be analyzed. In
this section and the section to follow, the first two questions just posed will be
explored. The third question involving buyer's remedies for breach of warranty will
be explored in the discussion of the buyer's Code remedies in general in a
subsequent chapter.

A complete exploration of warranties under the UCC is beyond the scope of this
volume. However, since the UCC has so clearly transformed the law of sales of
goods from a property to a contracts orientation, the distinction between the
material traditionally dealt with in the law of sales or commercial transactions on
the one hand, and the law of contracts on the other, has become blurred. The
student of contract law must be aware of the fundamental concepts of warranties

as found in Article 2 of the Code just as she must be aware of other contracts concepts found in that Article. Therefore, the following summary of warranties under Article 2 is included at this point.

There are three types of warranties relating to the quality of the goods set forth in Article 2 of the Code. (UCC §§ 2-313, 2-314, 2-315.) The first is the *express warranty* which may be created by a promise or affirmation of *fact* by the seller relating to some quality or feature of the goods which are the subject matter of the contract of sale. (UCC § 2-313(1)(a).) Express warranties are also created by description, i.e., the goods must conform to their description as interpreted under the usual rules of interpretation. (UCC § 2-313(1)(b).) Trade usage, course of dealing or course of performance may affect the interpretation of the stated description of the goods. (UCC § 2-313, comment 5.) The buyer is entitled to receive goods as described since his reasonable expectation is that the quality of the goods will match the description. Express warranties may also be created by sample or model, (UCC § 2-313(1)(c)), i.e., an item may be drawn from a larger number of such items and shown to the buyer as the kinds of goods he will receive, or a miniature version of the actual product may be displayed as representative of the quality and features of the promises, description, sample and model. The buyer is entitled to receive goods complying with the quality expressed if the manifestations of quality become part of the *basis of the bargain.* (UCC § 2-313(1).) The "basis of the bargain" phrase used in the express warranty section of the Code has given rise to some consternation. The Code expressly indicates that the pre-Code requirement that the buyer actually rely on the manifestation of quality is no longer necessary to establish that manifestation as part of the "basis of the bargain." (UCC § 2-313, comment 7.) However, it is possible for a seller to negate a manifestation of quality as part of the basis of the bargain by clear, affirmative proof. (UCC § 2-313, comment 3.) There is no stated "test" to determine whether a manifestation of quality has become part of the "basis of the bargain." In effect, the Code would treat any manifestation of quality by the seller *prima facie* as part of the basis of the bargain, provided that the seller may rebut the *prima facie* showing with clear, affirmative proof to the contrary. Unless the seller can show that the alleged warranty was never made or that an effective disclaimer was part of the transaction, there would seem to be little possibility of "rebutting" the presumptive showing that the manifestation of quality was part of the basis of the bargain.

Another traditional difficulty in discovering whether an express warranty exists involves the necessary distinction between affirmations of fact and mere statements of opinion (or "puff") by the seller. (UCC § 2-313(2), comment 8.) While certain statements can easily be identified as statements of the seller's opinion as contrasted with statements of fact, the transaction may involve ambiguous statements which do not allow for easy classification. If an auto salesman states that "the car will get a minimum of 15 miles per gallon in the city and a minimum of 20 on the road," this is a statement of fact and will be regarded as an express warranty. On the other hand, if the salesman indicates that the car in question is "a great automobile," this is clearly a statement of opinion and does not give rise to any legally enforceable standard of quality. In an actual case, the car was described as being in "A-1 condition" and the court held that there was an express warranty created thereby. *See Wat Henry Pontiac Co. v. Bradley*, 202 Okla. 82, 210 P.2d 348 (1949). The decision could easily have gone the other way. *See Frederickson v. Hackney*, 159 Minn. 234, 198 N.W. 806 (1924). The question is one of interpretation and will be measured by the objective understanding of the reasonable man under all of the surrounding circumstances.

The most basic and important warranty in Article 2 is the *implied warranty of merchantability*. (UCC § 2-314.) The warranty of merchantability establishes the basic, legally-recognized quality of goods which the buyer is entitled to receive. If the warranty concept did not exist, it would not be difficult to arrive at the conclusion that a buyer is entitled to the quality of goods which a reasonable man in the position of the buyer expects to receive. Moreover, the reasonable expectations of the buyer could rather easily be established as goods of fair, average quality which are *fit for the ordinary purposes* of such goods. This is the essence of the implied warranty of merchantability under the Code. *See* UCC § 2-314(2)(c). The buyer is entitled to receive goods which may not reach the highest levels of perfection but which a reasonable buyer would normally expect to receive. If trade usage allows a certain margin of imperfection, e.g., five percent of certain kinds of fungible goods may be defective and yet the shipment would "pass without objection in the trade under the contract description," the goods are merchantable. *See, e.g., Agoos Kid Co. v. Blumenthal Import Co.*, 282 Mass. 1, 184 N.E. 279 (1932). Trade usage may also allow certain quality variations in each unit or among all units in a shipment. (UCC § 2-314(3).) Again, the goods would be merchantable within these accepted limitations. The implied warranty of merchantability also requires the goods to be adequately labeled and packaged, and the goods inside the container or package must conform to any affirmations on the label or container. (UCC § 2-314(3)(e).) While there are six statements of minimum quality in the Code section designed to describe the implied warranty of merchantability, it is generally agreed that they are all repetitions of the same basic thought which is best described in one of them: the goods must be at least such as "are fit for the ordinary purposes for which such goods are used." (UCC § 2-314(3)(c).) In order for this warranty to be operative, the seller must be "a merchant with respect to goods of that kind" as defined in the Code. While it is possible for this requirement to raise difficult questions in unusual fact situations, any merchant who sells goods of the kind in question on a regular basis (as contrasted with a seller making an isolated sale) fulfills the requirement. (UCC §§ 2-314(1), 2-104(1).) While the Code section clarifies and improves certain pre-Code difficulties relating to the warranty of merchantability, it is not a panacea. Whether particular goods are merchantable still requires a careful examination of reasonable standards of quality under all of the surrounding circumstances.

The third type of warranty of quality under the Code is the *implied warranty of fitness for a particular purpose*. (UCC § 2-315.) While the implied warranty of merchantability (just discussed) requires the goods to meet standards of *ordinary* fitness, there are occasions when a seller knows or has reason to know of a *particular* purpose which the buyer of goods expects the goods to fulfill. Moreover, the seller may also know or have reason to know that the buyer is relying on the seller's skill, expertise and judgment in selling the goods to the buyer for this particular purpose. If these two requirements are met and, if the buyer actually relies by purchasing and using the goods for that particular purpose, an implied warranty of fitness for a *particular* purpose is created. The goods in question may have been clearly merchantable, i.e., fit for ordinary purposes. However, when applied to the buyer's particular purpose, they are defective. If this higher or different standard has been established through the elements set forth, the buyer may reasonably expect the goods to meet that unusual standard. It should be noted, again, that to establish this warranty, the buyer must prove the reliance factor.

In general, see MURRAY ON CONTRACTS § 101 (5th ed. 2011).

[5] Self-Service Contracts

BARKER v. ALLIED SUPERMARKET
Oklahoma Supreme Court
596 P.2d 870 (1979)

WILLIAMS, JUSTICE.

Plaintiff alleges that he suffered personal injuries while he was shopping in the store of defendant, Allied Super Market, doing business as Arlan's Food Store in Midwest City, Oklahoma. He states that he picked up a carton of Dr. Pepper drinking soda from the self-service shelf and that while attempting to place it in a cart provided by Arlan's one of the bottles exploded and that a fractured piece of the glass bottle struck him in the right eye which resulted in ninety percent (90%) permanent loss of vision.

Plaintiff filed an action for damages for negligence and breach of implied warranty of merchantability against defendant Allied Super Market and defendant Dr. Pepper Bottling Co. of Oklahoma City on November 3, 1972, being 2 years and 1 day after he allegedly was so injured. The trial court sustained defendants' demurrers which averred that plaintiff's petition sounded in tort and that his alleged cause of action was barred by the supposedly applicable two year statute of limitation.

Plaintiff appealed. He argues that his second cause of action as to the alleged breach of implied warranty of merchantability arose pursuant to Oklahoma's Uniform Commercial Code and that the applicable period of limitations is five (5) years (12A O.S. 1961, § 2-725(1)).

The issue here is whether a buyer of goods who is invited by a merchant to take possession thereof from a self-service display and to defer payment to sometime subsequent to the taking of possession, has the protection of an implied warranty of merchantability. We hold he does.

Section 2-314(1) provides:

Unless excluded or modified (Section 2-316), a warranty that the goods shall be merchantable is implied *in a contract for their sale* if the seller is a merchant with respect to goods of that kind. Under this section the serving for value of food or drink to be consumed either on the premises or elsewhere is a sale. (Emphasis added.)

Plaintiff contends that taking possession of goods from a self-service display coupled with the intent to pay for them is sufficient to create a Section 2-314 "contract for their sale" which gives rise to the implied warranty of merchantability. We agree . . . .

The key to this case hinges upon the determination that a contract for sale exists as defined under the Uniform Commercial Code. Several relevant definitions are found in Section 2-106, including the following:

> (1) In this Article unless the context otherwise requires "contract" and "agreement" are limited to those relating to the present or future sale of goods. *"Contract for sale" includes both a present sale of goods and a contract to sell goods at a future time.* A "sale" consists in the passing of title from the seller to the buyer for a price (Section 2-401). A "present sale" means a sale which is accomplished by the making of the contract. (Emphasis added.)

A merchant who utilizes the self service shopping method thereby makes an open invitation to the public to enter his store and to inspect and take possession of any item so displayed. The merchant's act of stocking these self-service displays with goods thereby makes an offer to the shopper to enter a contract for their sale.

Section 2-206 reflects the Code's more flexible approach to contracting with respect to sales, and it provides that:

> (1) *Unless otherwise unambiguously indicated* by the language or circumstances
>
> > (a) an offer to make a contract shall be construed as inviting acceptance in any manner and by any medium reasonable in the circumstances;
>
> (2) Where the beginning of a requested performance is a reasonable mode of acceptance an offeror who is not notified of acceptance within a reasonable time may treat the offer as having lapsed before the acceptance. (Emphasis added.)

UCC Comment 1 suggests that:

> Any reasonable manner of acceptance is intended to be regarded as available unless the offeror has made quite clear that it will not be acceptable.

The Court of Special Appeals of Maryland has held, under a similar factual situation, that as to such an offer the manner by which acceptance was to be accomplished in the transaction . . . was not indicated by either language or circumstances. The seller did not make it clear that acceptance could not be accomplished by a promise rather than an act. Thus it is equally reasonable under the terms of this specific offer that acceptance could be accomplished in any of three ways: 1) by the act of delivering the goods to the check-out counter and paying for them; 2) by the promise to pay for the goods as evidenced by their physical delivery to the check-out counter; and 3) by the promise to deliver the goods to the check-out counter and to pay for them there as evidenced by taking physical possession of the goods by their removal from the shelf. (*Sheeskin v. Giant Food, Inc.*, 20 Md. App. 611, 318 A.2d 874, 882 (1974).)

The Court of Appeals of Georgia has also held these alternatives to be reasonable methods of acceptance and have applied them in a similar case. (*Fender v. Colonial Stores, Inc.*, 225 S.E.2d 691.) We agree, and adopt these alternative methods for the shopper's acceptance.

Further we recognize that the UCC provides a more flexible approach to contracting than more traditional approaches. Section 2-204 provides:

> (1) A contract for sale of goods may be made in any manner sufficient to show agreement, including conduct by both parties which recognizes the existence of such a contract.

> (2) An agreement sufficient to constitute a contract for sale may be found even though the moment of its making is undetermined.

> (3) Even though one or more terms are left open a contract for sale does not fail for indefiniteness if the parties have intended to make a contract and there is a reasonably certain basis for giving an appropriate remedy.

Allegedly it is common custom in grocery stores, defendant's included, for shoppers to change their minds and to return unwanted merchandise prior to paying for it. This custom of the trade does not in itself necessitate the conclusion that no contract for sale has arisen between the shopper and the merchant. Rather under the Commercial Code the contract for sale of the goods is merely "terminated"[31] pursuant to the parties' shopping agreement[32] made upon the shopper entering the store. Here the defendant-retailer allegedly permitted its shoppers to return goods and made no attempt to expressly modify this custom of the trade, and thereby such conduct became part of the shopping agreement.

In addition to the power of termination, a buyer or seller may have the power to "cancel" a contract for sale. " 'Cancellation' occurs when either party puts an end to the contract *for breach* by the other and its effect is the same as that of 'termination' except that the cancelling party also retains any remedy for breach of the whole contract or any unperformed balance." (Section 2-106(4).)

According to the allegations the bottle exploded after plaintiff-buyer picked up the beverage carton but before he made payment. Therefore, it would appear appropriate for the plaintiff-buyer to "cancel" the contract for sale, assuming that the evidence establishes a contract for sale and fails to establish that plaintiff in fact breached the contract himself.

---

[31] [2] UCC 2-106(3) provides: " '*Termination*' occurs when either party *pursuant to a power created by agreement or law puts an end to the contract otherwise than for breach*. On 'termination' all obligations which are still executory on both sides are discharged but *any right based on prior breach or performance survives*." (Emphasis added.)

[32] [3] UCC 1-201(3) provides: " 'Agreement' means the bargain of the parties in fact as found in their language or *by implication from other circumstances including course of dealing or usage of trade or course of performance* . . . ." (Emphasis added.)

The alleged contract for sale would include an implied warranty of merchantability arising by operation of Section 2-314(1). If the goods are found to not have been merchantable then the alleged contract for sale would have been breached on the seller's side which would have, in addition to giving the buyer cause for cancelling the contract for sale, giving rise to "consequential damages resulting from the seller's breach includ[ing] . . . (b) *injury to the person or property* proximately resulting from any breach of warranty." (UCC § 2-715; Emphasis added.)

For goods to be merchantable, Section 2-314(2) provides six minimum conditions[33] that such goods must satisfy. Uniform Commercial Code Comment 6 to that section states that:

> Subsection (2) does not purport to exhaust the meaning of "merchantable" nor to negate any of its attributes not specifically mentioned in the text of the statute, but arising by usage of trade or through case law. The language used is *"must be at least such as . . . ,"* and the *intention is to leave* open other possible attributes of merchantability. (Emphasis added.)

> It would appear as to the sale of beverages in glass bottles that subsections

> (c) goods . . . are fit for the ordinary purposes for which such goods are used, and

> (e) "goods . . . are adequately contained"

> would require that the bottles be of sufficient strength to withstand the ordinary pressures of the contents.

We conclude that the determination of whether there was a contract for sale of the Dr. Pepper and whether the involved bottle of Dr. Pepper failed to meet the minimum requirements of merchantability should be made by the trier of fact. So, assuming an applicable provision of the statute of limitations has not barred plaintiff's cause of action, the plaintiff is entitled to go to trial as against the grocery company. [*Reversed and remanded.*]

NOTES

(1) *Gentry v. Hershey Co.*, 687 F. Supp. 2d 711, 722 (M. D. Tenn. 2010). Kim Gentry often visited her local Petco store, accompanied by one of her dogs that would ride in her shopping cart. Kim would take a treat for the dog from the "treat island" and, as was her habit, she would take a York Peppermint Pattie from the

---

[33] [4] UCC 2-314(2) provides:

"Goods to be merchantable must be at least such as
(a)   pass without objection in the trade under the contract description; and
(b)   in the case of fungible goods, are of fair average quality within the description; and
(c)   are fit for the ordinary purposes of which such goods are used; and
(d)   run, within the variations permitted by the agreement, or even kind, quality and quantity within each unit and among all units involved; and
(e)   are adequately contained, packaged, and labeled as the agreement may require; and
(f)   conform to the promises or affirmations of fact made on the container or label if any."

candy island to enjoy her treat. It was her practice to pay for both treats as she exited the store. After biting into the candy, Kim noticed something crunchy and observed larvae and at least one wormlike creature. The discovery was traumatic to Kim who suffered illness and underwent extensive counselling. Her action included a count for breach of warranty. Petco argued that there was no "sale" of the candy. The court disagreed:

> Petco's suggestion that a "sale" only occurs when payment is received would eliminate any cause of action for breach of implied warranty of merchantability by restaurant patrons who discover foreign objects in their food prior to paying their bills. This is a result which the drafters of the statute undoubtedly did not contemplate. While the parties cite no Tennessee authority directly on point, the Court has located cases from other jurisdictions which have identical versions of the Uniform Commercial Code and which support this Court's conclusion that there was a sale for purposes of T.C.A. § 47-2-314 in this case. See, *Levondosky v. Marina Associates*, 731 F.Supp. 1210, 1212 (D.N.J. 1990) (sale occurred for purposes of Section 2-314 of the Uniform Commercial Code when casino cocktail waitress gave patron a drink since casino was "not offering these drinks out of any sense of hospitality or charity"); *Barker v. Allied Supermarket*, 1979 OK 79, 596 P.2d 870, 871 (Okla. 1979) ("taking possession of goods from a self-service display coupled with the intent to pay for them is sufficient to create a Section 2-314 'contract for their sale' which gives rise to the implied warranty of merchantability"); *Fender v. Colonial Stores, Inc.*, 138 Ga. App. 31, 225 S.E.2d 691, 693 (Ga. App. 1976) (placing goods on shelf of self-service food store for customer inspection and selection constituted offer to sell such goods at stated price, and customer's act of taking physical possession of goods with intent to pay for them constituted reasonable mode of acceptance, so that contract for sale of goods came into being at such time).

(2) In *Pharmaceutical Soc'y of Great Britain v. Boots Cash Chemists (Southern) Ltd.*, [1953] 1 Q.B. 401, the defendant operated a self-service drug store (chemists' shop). Certain of the shelves contained drugs which were listed in Part I of the Poisons List of the Pharmacy and Poisons Act of 1933 and such drugs had to be sold "under the supervision of a registered pharmacist" according to this Act of Parliament. A registered pharmacist was located at the check-out counter, but there was no pharmacist located at the shelves where the drugs on the Poisons List were located and taken therefrom by the customers for deposit in their shopping baskets. The Pharmaceutical Society of Great Britain claimed that, since the statute required a pharmacist to supervise the "sale" of the drugs on the Poisons List, the defendant's store had not complied with this requirement and, thereby, violated the law. The question before Queen's Bench was whether the contract was to be regarded as being completed when the article is "put into the receptacle" by the customer or when the customer offers to purchase the goods in his receptacle at the check-out counter and such offer is accepted (usually) by the storekeeper. The Court held that there was no contract until the store accepted the customer's offer to purchase at the counter. Thus, the customer makes the offer and the store has the power of acceptance. On this analysis, since a registered pharmacist was located at

the check-out counter, the "sale" was completed under his supervision and there was no violation of the Poisons Act. Compare this analysis with the analysis of the Court in the principal case.

[6]   Auction Contracts

MIAMI AVIATION SERVICE v. GREYHOUND LEASING & FINANCIAL CORP.

United States Court of Appeals, Eleventh Circuit
856 F.2d 166 (1988)

Per Curiam. This case arises from the auction of an aircraft and two aircraft engines. The auction was advertised by the secured lender (Greyhound) through public notice. At the auction, the auctioneer stated that sale would be to the highest bidder and that no minimum bid would be required. Appellant Miami Aviation bid one million dollars. Thereupon, Greyhound bid 3.3 million dollars and took the aircraft and engines. The only issue to be resolved is whether the sale was "without reserve" as that term is used within the Uniform Commercial Code (UCC).

Section 2-328 of the UCC deals with sales by auction. Sales by auction are held either "with reserve" or "without reserve." In an auction "with reserve," the auctioneer may withdraw the goods at any time until he announces completion of the sale. UCC § 2-328(3). In an auction "without reserve," after the auctioneer calls for bids on an item, that item cannot be withdrawn unless no bid is received within a reasonable time. UCC § 2-328(3). A bid by the owner of an item likely would be considered the equivalent of withdrawing it from sale. An auction sale is "with reserve, unless the goods are *in explicit terms* put up without reserve." UCC § 2-328(3) (emphasis added).

Appellant argues that the auctioneer's use of the words "no minimum bid" and sale to the "highest bidder" establish an auction "without reserve." After carefully reviewing the records and the briefs, we find nothing explicit about those terms that would create a sale "without reserve." A sale to the highest bidder has nothing to do with whether a sale is "without reserve" because every auction sale goes to the highest bidder. The only case appellant offers with respect to the term "no minimum bid" concerns the sale of realty, a sale not governed by the requirements of the UCC. Moreover, appellant's arguments that prior to the auction a Greyhound official stated that the auction would be "absolute" are irrelevant. The only statements that affect whether an auction is "with or without reserve" are those made at the time the item for sale is "put up" for auction. Appellee Greyhound made no explicit statement that the sale was "without reserve" at the time it "put up" the aircraft and engines for auction. Therefore, the sale was "with reserve," and Greyhound was entitled to bid on the aircraft and its engines. AFFIRMED.

CALLIMANOPULOS v. CHRISTIE'S INC.

United States District Court, Southern District of New York

621 F. Supp. 2d 127 (2009)

WILLIAM H. PAULEY III, J.

Plaintiff Gregory Callimanopulos ("Callimanopulos") brings this action against Defendant Christie's Inc. ("Christie's") seeking a declaratory judgment that he entered into a binding contract with Christie's for the purchase of the painting "Grey" by Sam Francis (the "Work") and that he holds title to the Work, subject to his payment to Christie's of 3 million and any applicable fees or charges. Callimanopulos also brings a claim for breach of contract and seeks performance of the contract by transfer of title and possession of the Work.

On May 15, 2009, this Court granted a temporary restraining order enjoining Christie's from (1) disposing, altering, or changing any audio and/or video recordings of Christie's May 13, 2009 Post-War and Contemporary Art Evening Sale Auction (the "Auction"); and (2) completing the sale of the Work or transfer of title to any putative purchaser. On May 27, 2009, this Court granted a request by the putative purchaser, Eli Broad, to intervene in this action. Callimanopulos now moves for a preliminary injunction. For the following reasons, the motion is denied.

Callimanopulos participated in the Auction by telephone. Valentina Casacchia ("Casacchia"), curator of Callimanopulos's collection, and Heidi Waumboldt ("Waumboldt"), Callimanopulos's assistant, attended the Auction in person. Callimanopulos was connected by telephone to April Richon Jacobs ("Jacobs"), Christie's Co-Head of Evening Sale, who conveyed his bids to the auctioneer, Christopher Burge ("Burge") who has been an auctioneer for over 34 years and has conducted more than 1,000 auctions. Joanne Heyler ("Heyler"), the Director/Chief Curator of the Broad Art Foundation, attended the Auction as Eli Broad's representative. Both Broad and Callimanopulos had determined prior to the Auction to bid on the Work.

At the auction, Heyler was seated in the front row, to the right of Burge. (Heyler Aff. P 3.) Heyler raised concerns about being seated in the front row because it can be a blind spot for the auctioneer. As a result, two Christie's employees — Brett Gorvey and Laura Paulson — paid attention to Heyler during the auction. Jacobs was seated at a bank of telephones located along the side wall, many rows back and to the left of Burge. Jacobs did not have a clear view of the first row of bidders. Gorvey and Paulson were standing on a raised platform facing the first row of seats to the right of Burge. Casacchia and Waumboldt sat in the front row.

Bidding on the Work commenced at 1.3 million and, through Jacobs, Callimanopulos entered at 2.9 million. After Callimanopulos bid 3 million, Burge surveyed the room for other bids, before stating: "Sold to the phone for three million dollars" and dropping the hammer. Jacobs told Callimanopulos that they had secured the Work. However, seconds later, Jacobs informed Callinmanopuls that Burge had re-opened the bidding and accepted a bid for 3.1 million. That bidder was Heyler. Callimanopulos protested the re-opening through Jacobs. After Burge rejected his challenge, Callimanopulos bid 3.15 million, with the intention of disputing the additional 150,000 later. However, after Heyler bid 3.2 million, Callimanopulos refused to bid further and Burge called the sale to Heyler.

According to Burge, at the same time that he called the sale to Callimanopulos, Christie's employees, including Gorvey, signaled to him that Heyler had raised her paddle prior to the fall of the hammer. Burge states that the use of spotters to signal to the auctioneer is common practice at auctions. Burge admits that he did not see Heyler's bid. Upon re-opening the bidding, Burge stated: "You all saw it, except for me." He also stated: "3,100,000 in time, with the hammer." Gorvey and Paulson confirm that Heyler had raised her paddle to bid prior to the fall of the hammer. The morning after the Auction, Jacobs conveyed to Callimanopulos that she believed he was the final bidder. However, she admits that from her vantage point she could not see whether or when Heyler placed her bid.

This Court has reviewed a video of the relevant portion of the Auction. In the video, a woman seated in the front row can be seen raising her paddle to chest-height as Burge calls "fair warning" and then raising it above her head as Burge is bringing down the hammer. Burge recognizes the woman's bid a few seconds after striking the hammer. The video also confirms that it would have been difficult for Jacobs to see bidding from the front row.

Christie's Conditions of Sale, included in the catalog for the Auction, provide that:

> The auctioneer has the right at his absolute and sole discretion . . . in the case of error or dispute, and whether during or after the sale, to determine the successful bidder, to continue the bidding, to cancel the sale or to reoffer and resell the item in dispute. If any dispute arises after the sale, our sale record is conclusive.

The terms "error" and "dispute" are not defined in the Conditions of Sale. The Conditions of Sale also provide that "[s]ubject to the auctioneer's discretion, the highest bidder accepted by the auctioneer will be the buyer and the striking of his hammer marks the acceptance of the highest bid and the conclusion of a contract for sale between the seller and the buyer."

The Uniform Commercial Code (UC.C.) which the parties agree governs this action, provides that:

> A sale by auction is complete when the auctioneer so announces by the fall of the hammer or in other customary manner. Where a bid is made while the hammer is falling in acceptance of a prior bid the auctioneer may in his discretion reopen the bidding or declare the goods sold under the bid on which the hammer was falling. N.Y. U.C.C. § 2-328.

Thus, under the U.C.C. it is clear that while the fall of the hammer concludes a sale, where a bid is made while the hammer is falling, the auctioneer has the discretion to recognize that bid even after the hammer has fallen. Christie's Conditions of Sale is consistent with the U.C.C.

Here, Burge exercised his discretion and re-opened the bidding, seconds after striking the hammer. The videotape and two Christie's employees confirm that Heyler raised her paddle as Burge said "fair warning" and then raised it even higher as he brought down the hammer. While Plaintiff argues that Burge could not exercise his discretion because he did not see Heyler's bid himself, nothing in the plain language of the U.C.C. or Christie's Conditions of Sale prevents an auctioneer from relying on Christie's employees in the exercise of his discretion. Moreover, as a highly experienced auctioneer, Burge represents that it is the custom of auctioneers to rely on spotters. Callimanopulos presents no evidence that this is not the custom. Accordingly, no contract was formed between Callimanopulos and Christie's. Because Callimanopulos fails to raise sufficiently serious questions going to the merits to make them a fair ground for litigation, let alone a likelihood of success, Callimanopulos's motion for a preliminary injunction is denied.

PROBLEM

Poole advertised certain goods which he owned to be auctioned at public sale on a given day. Freeman attended the sale and made a bid of 5,000. An agent of Poole, one Brigham, bid 5,100. Neither Freeman nor any member of the public attending the sale was aware that Brigham was really Poole's agent. The auctioneer closed the sale (by the fall of the hammer) indicating that the goods had been sold to Brigham. Later, Freeman discovered the real identity of Brigham and insisted that he (Freeman) was entitled to the goods for 5,000. What result? See UCC § 2-328(4).

G. THE DEVIANT ACCEPTANCE — THE "BATTLE OF THE FORMS"

DORTON v. COLLINS & AIKMAN CORP.
United States Court of Appeals, Sixth Circuit
453 F.2d 1161 (1972)

CELEBREEZE, J.

Under the common law, an acceptance or a confirmation which contained terms additional to or different from those of the offer or oral agreement constituted a rejection of the offer or agreement and thus became a counter-offer. The terms of the counter-offer were said to have been accepted by the original offeror when he proceeded to perform under the contract without objecting to the counter-offer. Thus, a buyer was deemed to have accepted the seller's counter-offer if he took receipt of the goods and paid for them without objection.

Under Section 2-207 the result is different. This section of the Code recognizes that in current commercial transactions, the terms of the offer and those of the acceptance will seldom be identical. Rather, under the current "battle of the forms," each party typically has a printed form drafted by his attorney and containing as many terms as could be envisioned to favor that party in his sales transactions. Whereas under common law the disparity between the fine print terms in the parties' forms would have prevented the consummation of a contract when these forms are exchanged, Section 2-207 recognizes that in many, but not all, cases the parties do not impart such significance to the terms on the printed forms. Subsection 2-207(1) therefore provides that "[a] definite and seasonable expression of acceptance or a written confinrnition . . . operates as an acceptance even though it states terms additional to or different from those offered or agreed upon, unless acceptance is expressly made conditional on assent to the additional or different terms." Thus, under Subsection (1), a contract is recognized notwithstanding the fact that an acceptance or confirmation contains terms additional to or different from those of the offer or prior agreement, provided that the offeree's intent to accept the offer is definitely expressed, *see* Sections 2-204 and 2-206, and provided that the offeree's acceptance is not expressly conditioned on the offeror's assent to the additional or different terms. When a contract is recognized under Subsection (1), the additional terms are treated as "proposals for addition to the contract" under Subsection (2), which contains special provisions under which such additional terms are deemed to have been accepted when the transaction is between merchants. Conversely, when no contract is recognized under Subsection 2-207(1) — either because no definite expression of acceptance exists or, more specifically, because the offeree's acceptance is expressly conditioned on the offeror's assent to the additional or different terms — the entire transaction aborts at this point. If, however, the subsequent conduct of the parties — particularly, performance by both parties under what they apparently believe to be a contract — recognizes the existence of a contract, under Subsection 2-207(3) such conduct by both parties is sufficient to establish a contract, notwithstanding the fact that no contract would have been recognized on the basis of their writings alone. Subsection 2-207(3) further provides how the terms of contracts recognized thereunder shall be determined.

COMMENT

The Common Law "Matching Acceptance" Rule. If an offeree attempts to accept an offer with different or additional terms, the common law treated such an attempted acceptance as a counter offer. If Ames offered to sell his car to Barnes for 10,000, Barnes could not accept that offer by promising to pay 9,000. If a corporation offered to buy 1,000 tons of aluminum and the offeree responded with a purported "acceptance" that promised to purchase 1,000 tons of steel or 2,000 tons of aluminum, neither response would constitute an acceptance because the acceptance must be the *"mirror image"* of the offer. Since the responses did not meet that *"matching acceptance"* rule, they are not grumbling acceptances or acceptances with mere suggestions of different terms. They are counter offers. The offeror did not assume the risk of being bound to a contract containing such different terms. The offer created a power of acceptance that could only be exercised by matching terms. Terms such as the price, identity of the subject matter and quantity are what Karl Llewellyn called "dickered" terms — terms that the parties consciously consider in making their bargain. Any change in such "dickered" terms will preclude the formation of a contract. This common law rule has not changed.

The situation typically arises because the response to an offer is found on a printed (standardized) form that a business ("merchant") uses for all of its transactions. Printed standardized forms are the written evidence in the overwhelming majority of contracts. They are used because they are efficient. Imagine the time that would be consumed if every one of the untold billions of contracts made on a regular basis had to be evidenced by carefully negotiated terms found in custom-tailored documents that each party analyzed. Unlike the consumer buyer, the merchant buyer has its own printed form — typically the purchase order. The seller responds with its printed "acknowledgment" form. Increasingly, such forms are found on computer screens rather than paper. Certain terms such as the description of the product, the price and the quantity term (the "dickered" terms) are word processed on each form. If there are differences in these dickered terms, the traditional "mirror image" rule controls. No contract is formed because the offeree's different or additional terms will convert a so-called "acceptance" with one or more different dickered terms into a counter offer. This common law analysis continues without difficulty.

The difficulty arises where the dickered terms that have been word processed into each forms are identical. Since the terms to which the parties pay attention match, they appear to form a contract but the forms contain other pre-printed boilerplate terms to which the parties (including businesses) pay little or no attention, ant these terms do not match. The non-matching additional or different terms will not deal with the subject matter, the price, or the quantity because changes in "dickered" terms will make the response to the offer a counteroffer. Typically, it is the "boilerplate" terms dealing with warranties, remedies and how any future disputes will be adjudicated that do not match.

The buyer can include clauses in its purchase order dealing with such terms, but the purchase order may not include them, i. e., it may be "silent" with respect to these terms on the assumption that the UCC implies warranties of merchantability and fitness for particular purposes as well as remedies in the event of a seller's breach. The UCC also contemplates that any contract dispute between will be adjudicated in a court of law rather than arbitration. The seller's acknowledgment, however, will often contain boilerplate clauses that disclaim implied warranties, reduce the UCC remedies and provide that any dispute will be subject to arbitration rather than a court of law. When these forms are exchanged, the parties intend to make a contract, but the different or additional boilerplate clauses in the seller's form violate the strict matching acceptance (mirror image) rule. At common law, even an additional or different boilerplate term would make the response a counter offer.

The "Battle of the Forms" and the Logical "Last Shot" Analysis at Common Law. Assume that a buyer sends a purchase order for 1,000 tons of commercial steel to a seller of such steel. The seller responds with its standard, prefabricated acknowledgment form in which the "dickered terms" (price, quantity description of the goods) are identical to the dickered terms of the purchase order. The seller's acknowledgment, however, contains the boilerplate disclaimer of warranties, limitation of remedies and an arbitration clause. Neither party devotes any time or attention to the other's boilerplate clauses. The steel is shipped and received by the buyer who begins to use the steel in manufacturing products but then discovers that the steel is unmerchantable because it does not meet commercial standards of fair, average quality. The buyer sues for breach of the implied warranty of merchantability and also seeks to recover lost profits (consequential damages) because it could not supply its customers with goods manufactured with the low-grade steel. The buyer lost the profits from those sales. The seller claims that it is not liable since the terms of its acknowledgment form disclaimed the implied warranty of merchantability and limited the buyer's remedy to the replacement of any defective steel but excluded such consequential damages as lost profits. The seller also insists that the arbitration clause in its form precludes any litigation in a court of law.

Under a strict application of the matching acceptance rule, a common law court would agree with the seller's logic. Since the seller's form contained terms that were additional to or different from the buyer's express or implied terms, the seller's acknowledgment did not match the offer. It was a counter offer. Having ignored the boilerplate clauses, neither the buyer or seller have consciously adverted to this legal analysis. They typically assumed they had a contract through their exchange of forms. Though no contract was formed through the exchange of the purchase order and acknowledgment forms, the seller shipped the steel and the buyer accepted the steel, thereby forming a contract. By accepting the steel after receiving the seller's counter offer, the buyer was said to have accepted the seller's boilerplate terms. The seller, therefore, won the "battle of the forms" simply because he fired the last shot in the battle. In creating Article 2 of the Uniform Commercial Code, Karl Llewellyn sought to overcome the manifest injustice created by the common law "last shot principle."

The Modification of the "Matching Acceptance" Rule.

§ 2-207. Additional Terms in Acceptance of Confirmation

(1) A definite and seasonable expression of acceptance or a written confirmation which is sent with a reasonable time operates as an acceptance even though it states terms additional to or different from those offered or agreed upon, unless acceptance is expressly made conditional on assent to the additional or different terms.

(2) The additional terms are to be construed as proposals for addition to the contract. Between merchants such terms become part of the contract unless:

(a) the offer expressly limits acceptance to the terms of the offer;

(b) they materially alter it; or

(c) notification of objection to them has already been given or is given with a reasonable time after notice of them is received.

(3) Conduct by both parties which recognizes the existence of a contract is sufficient to establish a contract for sale although the writings of the parties do not otherwise establish a contract. In such case, the terms of the particular contract consist of those terms on which the writings of the parties agree, together with any supplementary terms incorporated under any other provisions of this Act.

PROBLEM

The North Corporation sent a purchase order to the Barnes Corporation for a model X-47 computerized assembly device at a price of 285,000. Barnes responded with its acknowledgment form that promised to ship the model X-47 device at the price of 285,000. The Barnes form stated its "standard terms" which included a conspicuous disclaimer of the implied warranties of merchantability and fitness for a particular purpose, and a 90 day warranty under which Barnes promised to repair or replace any defective part in the device as the "sole and exclusive remedy" under the contract with a conspicuous exclusion of consequential damages. The Barnes terms also included a clause stating that, in the event of any dispute between the parties, the parties agree to resolve any dispute through arbitration under the rules of the American Arbitration Association. The X-47 was delivered and operated perfectly for four months, after which it ceased operating and could not be repaired.

(a) The Pre-Code Analysis

(1)   Assume that the North purchase order was "silent" concerning warranties, remedies or arbitration, i.e., there was nothing in the North purchase order dealing with these matters. Further assume that this case arose before the relevant jurisdiction enacted Article 2 of the Uniform Commercial Code. What are the terms of this contract? Describe how this contract was formed. Is this an illustration of the "last shot" principle?

(b) The Radical UCC Analysis — The Erosion of the "Mirror image" ("Matching Acceptance") Rule

(2)   Assume the same facts except that § 2-207 of the Uniform Commercial Code was enacted at the time the contract between North and Barnes was formed. Did a contract exist upon the exchange of forms? What is a "definite and seasonable expression ofacceptance" under § 2-207(1)?[34]

Suppose that Barnes' acknowledgment promised to ship a model X-52 device instead of the X-47? Suppose that Barnes' acknowledgment promised to ship an X-47 device at a price of 300,000?[35]

---

[34] For a recent illustration, see *Crossley Constr. Corp v. NCI Bldg. Sys., L.P.*, 2005 U.S. App. LEXIS 2702 (6th Cir. 2005), where a buyer sent a purchase order and the supplier responded that it only worked from its own contract rather than a customer's purchase order. The supplier then sent its contract form to the buyer who signed it but inserted a handwritten statement that the contract included the terms of the buyer's purchase order. The supplier notified the buyer that this was unacceptable and sent another copy of the supplier's own terms which the buyer signed without revision. The court found that the buyer's inclusion of the handwritten provision on the supplier's contract form was not a definite and seasonable expression of acceptance.

[35] Direct contradiction of prices in exchanged documents precluded contract formation in *Gage Prods. Co. v. Henkel Corp.*, 393 F. 3d 629 (6th Cir. 2004). In *Matrix International Textiles v. Jolie Intimates, Inc.*, 2005 N. Y. Misc. LEXIS 888 (Civ. Ct. 2005), the court states, "[I]f the return document diverges significantly as to a dickered term, it cannot be a 2-207(1) acceptance" (citing White & Summers, Uniform Commercial Code § 1-3 at 46(2000)). "The 'dickered' terms are those that are unique to each transaction such as price, quality, quantity or delivery terms as compared to the 'usual unbargained terms on the reverse side [of a form] concerning remedies, arbitration and the like.' "

Would either of these responses constitute a definite and seasonable expression of acceptance?

(c) "Material" or "Immaterial"

(3)   Unless the parties have otherwise agreed, the UCC assumes certain terms such as implied warranties and remedies. Implied warranties of merchantability and fitness for a particular purpose are viewed as the usual or "standard" warranties. The buyer's remedies include "cover," which allows the buyer to make a reasonable substitute purchase of goods from another supplier (§ 2-712). Alternately, the buyer may choose not to purchase a substitute but may recover the difference between the contract price and any higher market price of substitute goods (§ 2-713). In a proper case, the buyer may have the remedy of specific performance of the contract (§ 2-716). Moreover, buyers' remedies include consequential damages as defined in § 2-715. The UCC also assumes that any dispute between the parties will be adjudicated in a court of law rather than arbitration. Barnes' acknowledgment seeks to deprive the buyer of the buyer's normal implied warranties as well as the usual buyer's remedies under the UCC and subject North to arbitration rather than an adjudication in court.

If a contract existed when Barnes sent its acknowledgment promising to ship an X-47 device at 285,000, whether Barnes' terms become part of the contract is determined under § 2-207(2)(b). Between merchants, if an acceptance contains a term that is a material alteration, it does not become part of the contract. Is a disclaimer of an implied warranty a "material" alteration of the North offer? Is a limitation on North's normal remedies under the UCC and the exclusion of consequential damages to which North would normally be entitled a "material" alteration of North's offer? The UCC presumes that any litigation will be conducted in a court of law. Is the Barnes arbitration term a "material" alteration of North's offer?

To assist your analysis, Comment 4 to § 2-207 provides examples of typical clauses that would normally constitute "material alterations" because they result in "surprise or hardship" if incorporated without specific awareness by the other party. One example is "a clause negating such standard warranties as that of merchantability and fitness for a particular purpose." On the other hand, Comment 5 provides examples of clauses that result in no element or unreasonable surprise. They are "immaterial" alterations to be incorporated in the contract unless notice of objection is seasonably given. One of the examples of such immaterial clauses is a clause "limiting remedy in a reasonable manner." Neither list includes examples of arbitration clauses. While influential, the comments are not part of the enacted law and maybe disregarded by courts. Courts generally regard disclaimers of the implied warranties as "material" alterations.[36] They are much less uniform on

---

[36]   See, however, *All-Iowa Constr. Co. v. Linear Dynamics, Inc.*, 296 F. Supp. 2d 969 (N.D. Iowa 2003), where the court recognized that UCC Comment 4 includes warranty disclaimers among the type of clauses that normally are viewed as material alterations, but found that the party claiming such a material alteration had failed to create a genuine issue of material fact as to whether it was actually "surprised" by the warranty disclaimer. The court proceeded to hold that the disclaimer was not a material alteration and, therefore, became part of the contract.

whether an exclusion of consequential damages is a material alteration. Some courts find remedy limitations enforceable because of the language in Comment 5.[37] Arbitration clauses may or may not be viewed as material alterations depending upon the circumstances, particularly trade usage or course of dealing.[38] The burden of proving "materiality" falls on the party opposing inclusion of the variant term.[39]

(d) Eliminating the "Material" Issue

(4) Assume the facts of Problem 1, but assume that the North purchase order contained the following clause: "This offer expressly limits acceptance to the terms of this offer" (§ 2-207(2)(a)). What is the effect of such a clause?[40] Would such a clause preclude any variant term, whether it is material or immaterial such as a limitation of remedies and exclusion of consequential damages? Suppose the clause read, "Buyer hereby notifies seller of its objection to any terms other than those found in this purchase order" (§ 2-207(2)(c)). What is the effect of this clause?

(e) The § 2-207 Counter Offer

(5) Assume that Barnes' acknowledgment contained the following clause: "This acceptance is expressly conditioned on buyer's assent to any different or additional terms" (§ 2-207(1)). What is the effect of this clause? Is a contract formed by the exchange of these forms? If, after sending this acknowledgment, Barnes refused to ship the X-47, could North sue for breach of contract? If Barnes shipped the X-47 but North refused to accept it, could Barnes sue for breach of contract? If Barnes shipped the X-47 and the shipment was accepted by North is there a contract? *See* § 2-207(3).[41] When does § 2-207(3) apply? If there is a contract, what are its

---

[37] *See* S. Ill. Riverboat Casino Cruises, Inc. v. Triangle Insulation, 302 F.3d 667 (7th Cir. 2002).

[38] *See, e.g.*, Aceros Prefabricados, S. A. v. TradeArbed, Inc., 282 F.3d 92 (2d Cir. 2002) (insufficient proof of surprise or hardship to prove that an arbitration clause was a material alteration); Sibcoimtrex, Inc. v. Am. Foods Group, Inc., 241 F. Supp. 2d 104 (D. Mass. 2003) (focusing on the "materiality" issue which include, but are not limited to, surprise and hardship, the court found that the arbitration clause was a material alteration).

[39] *See Bayway Ref. Co. v. Oxygenated Mktg. & Trading Co.*, 215 F.3d 219, 223 (2d Cir. 2000), where the seller's additional term stated that the buyer was obligated to pay a federal tax on goods amounting to 464,035.12. On its face, this may appear to be a "material alteration." How should a court decide that issue?

[40] See *Great Am. Ins. Co. v. M/V Handy Laker*, 2003 U.S. Dist. LEXIS 26378 (S.D.N.Y. 2002), where the court held that the inclusion of a clause expressly limiting acceptance to the terms of the offer pursuant to § 2-207(2)(a) prevented added terms from becoming part of the contract, regardless of whether they were material or immaterial terms. In *Marion Mills, LLC v. Delta Mills Mktg. Co.*, 2000 U.S. Dist. LEXIS 21263 (W.D.N.C. 2000), the court held that such a clause in a purchase order precluded the inclusion of a term in a seller's form to recover attorney's fees.

[41] See *C. Itoh & Co. v. Jordan International Co.*, 552 F.2d 1228 (7th Cir. 1977), where the seller's acknowledgment contained such a clause along with an arbitration clause that was not mentioned in the buyer's purchase order. The issue was whether the arbitration clause became part of the contract. The court viewed the "expressly conditioned" clause tracking the statutory language of the last part of § 2-207(1) as necessarily creating a counter offer though the language was "ambiguous." The seller shipped the goods and the buyer accepted them. The court held that the seller's acknowledgment was a counter offer but the buyer did not accept the variant terms of the counter offer by accepting the goods since, to so hold, would be to revert to the evil which § 2-207 was designed to prevent — the "last shot" principle. The buyer's acceptance of the goods was insufficient to hold the buyer to the seller's variant

terms?[42] Suppose the clause in Barnes' form had read, "This agreement is subject to the terms and conditions in this form." Would the analysis change?[43]

(f) The Seller as Offeror

(6) Suppose that the terms of Barnes' acknowledgment (as described in Problem 1) were instead contained in Barnes' *offer* to sell the X-47 for 285,000. The North purchase order (as described in Problem 1) was sent in response to that offer and would be viewed as an acceptance — the seller is the offeror and the buyer is the offeree.[44] Is there a contract? If so, what are the terms of that contract?[45] Suppose that the North purchase order (as an acceptance) was as described in Problem 1, but also contained the clause in Problem 4: "This offer expressly limits acceptance to the terms of this offer." Would this clause convert the purchase order into a counter offer?[46]

(g) "Different" vs. "Additional" — The "Knockout" View

(7) To this point, we have assumed that the purchase order is "silent" with respect to variant terms in the seller's acknowledgment. As an offer, the buyer's purchase order contains implied terms such as implied warranties, UCC remedies (including consequential damages), and the presumption of adjudication in a court rather than arbitration. In Problem 1, the buyer's purchase order was silent on these terms. Quaere: are the seller's disclaimers of warranty, remedy limitations, exclusion of consequential damages and arbitration clauses *different* terms, or are they *additional* terms?

Curiously, § 2-207(1) refers to "additional" or "different" terms, but § 2-207(2)

---

terms. The buyer would be bound by such terms in a seller's counter offer only by expressly assenting to them. For a similar holding, see *PCS Nitrogen Fertilizer, L.P. v. Christy Refractories, L.L.C.*, 225 F. 3d 974 (7th Cir. 2000).

[42] See *Commerce & Indus. Ins. Co. v. Bayer Corp.*, 433 Mass. 388, 394, 742 N.E.2d 567, 572 (2001), where the court stated, "Where a contract is formed by the parties' conduct (as opposed to writings), the terms of the contract are determined exclusively by subsection (3) of 2-207." In *PCS Nitrogen Fertilizer, supra*, the court indicated that, where no contract is formed under § 2-207(1), there is no possibility of applying § 2-207(2). Though the exchange of forms did not form a contract, if the parties nonetheless proceed to manifest a contract by conduct, § 2-207(3) will apply.

[43] In *Dorton v. Collins & Aikman Corp.*, *supra*, 453 F.2d 1161, the court held that a seller's acknowledgment stating that its acceptance was "subject to all of the terms and conditions on the fact and reverse side" of its printed form was insufficient to convert the seller's acceptance into a counter offer because the language did not specify that the acceptance was "expressly conditional on the buyer's assent to the additional or different terms."

[44] For an illustration of a quotation/offer and a purchase order acceptance, see *Enidine, Inc. v. Dayton-Phoenix Group, Inc.*, 2003 U.S. Dist. LEXIS 18493 (W.D.N.Y. 2003).

[45] In *Wulf v. Adaptive Motion Control Sys.*, 2003 U.S. Dist. LEXIS 1085 (D. Neb. 2003), the court recognized that if the seller's quote was an offer and the buyer's purchase order constituted an acceptance containing terms that varied the seller's offer, the buyer's acceptance in the form of a purchase order may be deemed to contain additional terms that materially alter the offer and therefore do not become part of the contract.

[46] In *Polytop Corp. v. Chipsco, Inc.*, 826 A.2d 945 (R.I. 2003), the court held that a purchase order containing such a clause sent as an acceptance did not covert the acceptance into a purchase order, i.e., a purchase order expressly limiting acceptance to the terms of the order does not amount to a statement in an acceptance expressly conditioning such acceptance to its terms which would become a counter offer.

expressly deals only with "additional" terms. The question is, does § 2-207(2) nonetheless include "different" terms? Was this an inadvertent printer's error as has been suggested by sonic scholars? Comment 3 to § 2-207 states, "Whether or not additional or different terms will become part of the agreement depends upon the provisions of subsection (2)." This comment, therefore, would suggest that "different" terms are included in § 2-207(2), though "different" is not mentioned in the section language. The clearly prevailing view, however, is that § 2-207(2) does not include "different" terms and there is no other UCC language directing courts concerning such terms. Courts have been persuaded to adopt another rule in this situation called the "knockout" rule.

Suppose that the North purchase order expressly stated that it included the implied warranties of merchantability and fitness for a particular purpose as well as all UCC remedies, including consequential damages and a statement that any dispute between the parties will be decided by a court of law. Assume that the Barnes acknowledgment contains all of the express clauses that conflict with these provisions as stated in Problem 1. We now have expressly conflicting ("different") terms to which, under the overwhelming prevailing view, the "knockout" rule applies. What is the effect of applying the "knockout" rule to these expressly conflicting term?[47]

The further curiosity is that the "knockout" view applies only where the terms are expressly conflicting. Thus, where the purchase order is "silent" concerning these terms (as in Problem 1), the "knockout" view would not apply. Rather, even though the terms are just as conflicting or "different" when the terms in the purchase order are implied (silent) terms, the seller's different terms are treated as if they are "additional" rather than different terms. Consequently, where the terms do not expressly conflict with each other, § 2-207(2) applies. Unless the offer expressly limits acceptance to the terms of the offer (§ 2-207(2)(a)) or contains an objection to any variant terms in the acceptance (§ 2-207(2)(c)), whether a seller's variant terms in its acknowledgment become part of the contract will depend upon whether they materially alter the terms of the offer (§ 2-207(2)(b)).

Under the prevailing view, how would you draft a buyer's purchase order? In particular, recognizing that the purchasing managers who use the purchase order will not be aware of whether they are using the purchase order as an offer or (where the seller's quotation is an offer) using the purchase order as an acceptance, can you draft a purchase order that will protect the buyer in either situation? If you can draft a purchase order to protect the buyer from the seller's variant terms in either situation, what does that say about the current judicial construction of Section 2-207?

---

[47] See *Flender Corp. v. Tippins Int'l, Inc.*, 830 A.2d 1279 (Pa. Super. 2003), adopting the "knockout" view and reviewing case law throughout the country adopting that view. Where the conflicting terms are "knocked out," gaps are left and the gaps are filled with the "supplementary" terms of the UCC (implied warranties, remedies, court adjudication) which favor the buyer.

H.   CONFIRMATIONS

PACKGEN v. BERRY PLASTICS CORP.
United States District Court, District of Maine
973 F. Supp. 2d 48 (2013)

WOODCOCK, J.

Packgen manufactures intermediate bulk containers (IBCs), which are used by petroleum refineries for the transportation and storage of fresh and spent catalyst. Berry supplied Packgen with woven polypropylene fabric that was chemically bonded to a layer of aluminum foil. On September 25, 2007, Packgen sent Covalence Coated Products a purchase order for 61-inch laminated polypropylene foil. On November 26, 2007, Packgen sent a purchase order to Berry requesting 48-inch laminated polypropylene. The shipment of 61-inch laminated polypropylene was received by Packgen on December 27, 2007. On December 28, 2007, Berry sent Packgen an invoice for the 61-inch material by regular, first class U.S. Postal Service mail. The earliest date that Packgen would have received the invoice for the 61-inch laminated polypropylene by mail is January 2, 2008. The shipment of 48-inch laminated polypropylene was received by Packgen on January 21, 2008. On [the same day]Berry mailed Packgen an invoice for the 48-inch order by regular, first class Postal Service Mail. The earliest date that Packgen would have received the invoice for the 48-inch laminated polypropylene by mail is most likely January 24, 2008. [Berry's terms and conditions on the invoices included the following:]. "All remedies are intended to be cumulative and in addition to all other remedies available at law and in equity. To the extent it may apply, the limitation period in [UCC Section] 2-725 is reduced to one (1) year."

On December 9, 2011, Packgen filed suit against Berry claiming breach of contract, breach of express warranty, breach of implied warranty of fitness for a particular purpose, breach of implied warranty of merchantability. Berry moved for summary judgment, asserting that Packgen's claims were barred by the parties' contractual statute of limitations period. Packgen argued that the provision in both of Berry's invoices stating that a one-year statute of limitations applied to the contracts at issue does not render its claims untimely because the invoices never became part of the parties' contract. Packgen also argued that if the invoices are determined to be a confirmation of acceptance, the one-year limitation provisions are not part of the contracts because they are material alterations to the original agreement.

Berry argues that its additional terms constitute a written confirmation of its acceptance of Packgen's offer under section 2-207 and that the terms satisfy section 2-207(2)'s requirements. In response, Packgen contends that the parties did not form contracts under section 2-207(1) but instead under section 2-206, and that therefore section 2-207(2) does not apply. According to Packgen, the terms could only be added to the contracts pursuant to a section 2-209 modification because the "contract bell" rang before Packgen received Berry's additional terms.

A district court entertained similar legal arguments when Glyptal, Inc. (Glyptal) sued Engelhard Corp. (Engelhard) for breach of warranty claims on three contracts. 801 F. Supp. 887 (D. Mass. 1992). Engelhard supplied Glyptal with paint three times after receiving purchase orders from Glyptal. For each transaction, Engelhard shipped the paint before mailing Glyptal an acknowledgment form, which contained various terms and conditions of the sale printed on the back of the form. Ultimately, the paint Engelhard sent Glyptal did not meet Glyptal's specifications and Glyptal sued. In its motion for summary judgment, Engelhard argued that the remedy-limiting provisions in its terms and conditions attached to its acknowledgment form prevented Glyptal from obtaining consequential or incidental damages. Glyptal argued that the parties' contract was fully formed when Engelhard shipped the goods to Glyptal, and therefore the terms in its acknowledgment were mere proposals for additional terms that should not be incorporated into the parties' contracts under U.C.C. § 2-207.

The *Glyptal* Court agreed that Engelhard had accepted Glyptal's offers when it shipped the goods to Glyptal, pursuant to U.C.C. § 2-206(1)(b). The Court then — adopting the approach recommended by Professors James White and Robert Summers in their treatise on the UCC — treated the acknowledgment forms as proposals for additional terms to the contracts, "which either would be excluded from or incorporated into the parties' agreement depending upon the outcome of an analysis performed in accordance with section 2-207(2) of the Uniform Commercial Code." After analyzing whether the remedy-limiting provisions constituted a material alteration to the parties' agreement under section 2-207(2), the *Glyptal* Court concluded that the additional terms fell outside of the contract.

Applying the Court's analysis in *Glyptal*, this Court concludes that the parties here formed their contract when Berry accepted Packgen's offer by shipping the laminated polypropylene. Section 2-206(1) of the Maine Commercial Code states that a contract is formed through offer and acceptance when:

1) Unless otherwise unambiguously indicated by the language or circumstances

a) An offer to make a contract shall be construed as inviting acceptance in any manner and by any medium reasonable in the circumstances;

b) An order or other offer to buy goods for prompt or current shipment shall be construed as inviting acceptance either by a prompt promise to ship or by the prompt or current shipment of conforming or nonconforming goods . . . . 11 M.R.S. § 2-206.

The commentary to section 2-206 notes that "[a]ny reasonable manner of acceptance is intended to be regarded as available unless the offeror has made quite clear that it will not be acceptable." 11 M.R.S.A. § 2-206, cmt. 1. Further, the UCC's understanding of acceptance embraces [t]he common law idea that the offeror is the master of the offer. However, it reflects an underlying assumption that the offeror is often indifferent as to what words or non-verbal conduct will create an acceptance . . . [c]onsequently, a buyer's offer for the current shipment of goods may be accepted not only by shipment or promise to ship, but also by commencement of performance, as, for example, the preparation of the goods for shipment. CORBIN ON CONTRACTS § 3.8 (2013).

According to Packgen, Berry accepted its purchase order offers either when it began performance or when it shipped the goods to Packgen. Berry does not directly contest that point but argues that its invoices confirmed its acceptance of both purchase orders and therefore the invoices' terms may still form part of the contracts pursuant to sections 2-207(1)–(2). Packgen stated that "[f]ollowing its receipt of each purchase order, Berry informed Packgen that Berry was purchasing raw materials, beginning production, completing production, and shipping the goods to Packgen." The record establishes that the parties were in contact and were negotiating the details of their deals from around the time Packgen sent Berry its purchase orders until Berry shipped the polypropylene. Thus, given that Packgen did not expressly limit the manner in which Berry could accept its offers and section 2-206 confirms that Berry could accept Packgen's offer either through commencement of performance or shipment of the laminated polypropylene, the Court agrees with Packgen that Berry accepted Packgen's offers before it sent Packgen the relevant invoices. *See Glyptal*, 801 F. Supp. at 893 ("a seller's acknowledgment that arrives after the seller ships the goods would not constitute a counter-offer or even an acceptance because, pursuant to section 2-206(1)(b) of the Uniform Commercial Code, the shipment would constitute the seller's acceptance").

2. Section 2-207(1) and (2) Apply

a. Confirmation of Acceptance

Because the Court has determined that the parties formed a contract before Packgen's receipt of Berry's invoices, the Court must decide whether section 2-207(1) and (2) apply to Berry's proposed additional terms and conditions. Section 2-207 provides:

Additional Terms in Acceptance or Confirmation.

(1) A definite and seasonable expression of acceptance or a written confirmation which is sent within a reasonable time operates as an acceptance even though it states terms additional to or different from those offered or agreed upon, unless acceptance is expressly made conditional on assent to the additional or different terms.

(2) The additional terms are to be construed as proposals for addition to the contract. Between merchants such terms become part of the contract unless:

(a) the offer expressly limits acceptance to the terms of the offer;

(b) they materially alter it; or

(c) notification of objection to them has already been given or is given within a reasonable time after notice of them is received.

(3) Conduct by both parties which recognizes the existence of a contract is sufficient to establish a contract for sale although the writing of the

parties do not otherwise establish a contract. In such case the terms of the particular contract consist of those terms on which the writings of the parties agree, together with any supplementary terms incorporated under any other provisions of the Act. 11 M.R.S. § 2-207.

Packgen asserts that where the parties' contracts are not formed under section 2-207(1), section 2-207(2) does not apply because there is no "battle of the forms." Yet, there does not have to be a classic "battle of the forms" for section 2-207(1) and (2) to apply to a contractual dispute, as:

> Notwithstanding its popular characterization as the "battle of forms" section, the original section 2-207 was not limited to "battle of the forms" situations. Where, for example, an oral contract was followed by the issuance of one form containing terms that were not mentioned in the oral agreement, section 2-207 clearly applied. The "battle" in such cases was one between the terms in one form and the terms of the oral contract, but not between two forms. CORBIN ON CONTRACTS § 3.37A (2013); MURRAY ON CONTRACTS § 50[D] (2011) ("While the paradigm situation involves two forms, a purchase order and a seller's acknowledgment containing additional or different terms, a not uncommon situation involves only one form"); *see Continental Can Co. v. Poultry Processing, Inc.*, 649 F. Supp. 570, 574 (D. Me. 1986) (applying section 2-207(2) to an orally assigned contract where the parties' confirmation letters each included additional terms). Accordingly, "Section 2-207 applies to 'written confirmations of agreements already reached.'" *ICC Chem. Corp. v. Vitol.*, 425 F. App'x 57, 59 (2d Cir. 2011) (quoting *Aceros Prefabricados, S.A. v. TradeArbed, Inc.*, 282 F.3d 92, 98 (2d Cir. 2002)).

The same reasoning applied to oral contracts and confirmations applies to the contracts here and persuades the Court to conclude that Berry's invoices were confirmations of the parties' agreements. *See* MURRAY ON CONTRACTS § 51[G] ("A confirmation is necessarily subsequent to the formation of the oral contract . . . Section 2-207(1) treats a confirmation as *if it were an acceptance* so that any different or additional terms are subject to § 2-207(2) like any other definite expression of acceptance") (emphasis in original).

Notably, although section 2-207(3) references parties' conduct that evidences a contract even though the writings otherwise would not, that section only applies to situations where the parties exchange writings before performance and a parties' "response to the offer is a counter offer but the parties proceed to perform as if a contract had been formed." MURRAY ON CONTRACTS § 51[H][4]. Here, the parties' writings were not fully exchanged until Berry performed and accepted Packgen's offers by shipping the polypropylene. Thus, the Court rejects Packgen's section 2-207(3) argument. *cf. Ionics, Inc. v. Elmwood Sensors*, 110 F.3d 184, 185, 189 (1st Cir. 1997) (finding that because the seller's acknowledgment was received prior to shipment of the goods and contained terms that contradicted terms in the buyer's purchase order, the parties' contract fell out of section 2-207(1) and into 2-207(3)).

Moreover, a comment to section 2-207 that the *Glyptal* Court found persuasive when forming its decision states:

> Under this Article a proposed deal which in commercial understanding has
> in fact been closed is recognized as a contract. Therefore, any additional
> matter contained in the confirmation or in the acceptance falls within
> subsection (2) and must be regarded as a proposal for an added term unless
> the acceptance is made conditional on the acceptance of the additional or
> different terms. U.C.C. § 2-207, cmt. 2.

See Aceros Prefabricados, 282 F.3d at 98–99 (noting that whether writings are
treated as confirmations or acceptances of the parties' contracts, any additional
terms will be reviewed as proposals for additional terms and analyzed under section
2-207(2)); *Glyptal*, 801 F. Supp. at 893. Here, given Packgen's purchase order and
Berry's shipment of the goods, it is clear that the parties had a deal which in a
commercial understanding constituted a contract prior to Packgen's receipt of
Berry's invoices. *See* 11 M.R.S.A. § 2-207, cmt. 2. Thus, under section 2-207(1),
Berry's invoices were confirmations of its acceptance that contained proposals for
additional contractual terms. *See Aceros Prefabricados*, 282 F.3d at 98; *Glyptal*, 801
F. Supp. at 893.

b. Sent Within a Reasonable Time

Packgen asserts that it did not receive Berry's terms and conditions within a
reasonable time as required by section 2-207(1). *Pl.'s Opp'n* at 11; *see* M.R.S.
§ 2-207(1). Section 1-205 of the UCC states that "whether a time for taking an action
required by [the Uniform Commercial Code] is reasonable depends on the nature,
purpose, and circumstances of the action." U.C.C. § 1-205. Accordingly, "the
transactional context of the particular action" must be analyzed when assessing the
reasonableness of the timing when Packgen received Berry's invoices. *Id.* at cmt. 1.

Given the timeline in the record, the Court concludes that Berry sent Packgen
the invoices within a reasonable amount of time pursuant to section 2-207(1). The
record establishes that Packgen sent Berry a purchase order for the 61-inch
laminated polypropylene foil on September 25, 2007.The parties continued to
exchange e-mails while Berry secured final dates for delivery of materials,
production, and shipment. Berry shipped the polypropylene to Packgen on December 22, 2007, Packgen received the 61-inch polypropylene on December 27, 2007,
and Berry sent the relevant invoice to Packgen on December 28, 2007. The 48-inch
polypropylene shipment followed a similar time trajectory as Packgen sent a
purchase order on November 26, 2007, Berry shipped the polypropylene on January
18, 2008, Packgen received the 48-inch polypropylene on January 21, 2008, and
Packgen received the relevant invoice on or after January 24, 2008.

Although approximately three months passed between the time Packgen sent its
purchase orders and Berry sent its invoices, each invoice followed Packgen's receipt
of the polypropylene by only a few days and the parties appeared to be negotiating
and finalizing the details of their deals until the time Berry shipped each order.
Because the parties continued to negotiate the terms of the deals and the invoices
constituted confirmations of the parties' final agreements, the Court concludes that
a reasonable juror could find that the circumstances and transactional context of the
parties' dealings show that Berry sent Packgen the invoices within "a reasonable
time." *See* M.R.S. § 2-207(1); *Pl.'s Opp'n* at 11 (noting that after Packgen sent the

purchase orders "the parties had engaged in a number of communications concerning the purchase orders"); *Defs.' Reply* at 2 ("Indeed, Packgen's purchase order does not provide all of the terms of the agreement because negotiations between the parties continued through telephone calls and e-mails after Packgen sent the purchase orders to Berry").

c. Conditional Assent

Next, Packgen asserts that the terms and conditions contained in Berry's invoices fall within section 2-207(1)'s proviso because "they comprise a definite expression that Berry does not accept Packgen's purchase orders and rejects them." Thus, Packgen argues that Berry's "terms and conditions are a counteroffer and as such are expressly conditional on Packgen's assent." Section 2-207(1) states, "[a] definite and seasonable expression of acceptance or a written confirmation which is sent within a reasonable time operates as an acceptance even though it states terms additional to or different from those offered or agreed upon, unless acceptance is expressly made conditional on assent to the additional or different terms." 11 M.R.S. § 2-207(1). Packgen directs the Court to a portion of Berry's terms and conditions, which states, in part:

> *Notice . . . . No additional or different terms or attempted exclusions or modifications (by way of purchase order ("P.O."), acceptance, confirmation, communication, course of performance or otherwise, all of which may hereafter be referred to jointly and severally as "Reply") shall be effective against Berry in the absence of the express written consent of Berry, any attempt by Purchaser to add, exclude or modify terms shall be deemed to be material, is objected to and will be of no effect. Neither the submission of this document nor anything herein contained shall be construed to be an acceptance or confirmation of any prior or subsequent Reply; this document shall be a rejection and counter-offer with respect to any such Reply.*

At first glance, the language in Berry's "Notice" may appear to expressly condition the parties' agreement on Packgen's assent to its additional terms; however, Berry had already accepted Packgen's offer before Packgen's receipt of the invoices containing the conditional language. *See* Part III.C.1; *see also* CORBIN ON CONTRACTS § 3.37A (discussing the proviso and how it applies to "definite expression[s] of acceptance"). Accordingly, contrary to Packgen's position, the Court concludes that Berry's invoices were not "traditional counteroffer[s]" but rather constituted confirmations of the parties' prior agreements. Whether the additional terms and conditional language in the invoices become part of the parties' contracts depends on whether the proposed terms survive the Court's section 2-207(2) analysis.

D. The Terms of the Parties' Agreements

Applying section 2-207(2) to Berry's invoices, the central issue is whether the reduction of the default statute of limitations for breach of contract for a sale of goods from four years to one year would materially alter the parties' contract. *See* 11 M.R.S. § 2-725. Typically, "[a]n action for breach of any contract for sale must be commenced within 4 years after the cause of action has accrued." 11 M.R.S. § 2-725. The statute also allows parties to reduce the "period of limitation to not less than one year." *Id.* If the one-year statute of limitations in Berry's invoices applies, Packgen's lawsuit will be untimely and barred by the statute of limitations.

1. Section 2-207(2): Subsections (a) and (c) Do Not Bar Berry's Additional Term

Section 2-207(2) provides that in an acceptance or confirmation:

> 2) The additional terms are to be construed as proposals for addition to the contract. Between merchants such terms become part of the contract unless:
>
> a) The offer expressly limits acceptance to the terms of the offer;
>
> b) They materially alter it; or
>
> c) Notification of objection to them has already been given or is given within a reasonable time after notice of them is received.11 M.R.S. § 2-207(2).

Here, both parties are merchants within the meaning of the statute, so the "additional terms" in Berry's acceptances are to "become part of the contract unless" one of the three subsection-exceptions in Section 2-207(2).

Neither subsection (a) nor subsection (c) of Section 2-207(2) applies to Berry's one-year statute of limitations terms. Section 2-207(2)(a) does not apply because Packgen's purchase orders — the offers — did not "expressly limit" Berry's acceptances to the terms contained within Packgen's orders. *See* 61-inch Purchase Order; 48-inch Purchase Order. Also, Berry was not placed on "notice" that Packgen objected to its reduced statute of limitations terms under section 2-207(2)(c). *See* 61-inch Purchase Order, 48-inch Purchase Order. Packgen's purchase orders did not contain an express provision on the applicable statute of limitations, *id.*, and here, unlike in *Ionics, Inc. v. Elmwood Sensors*, there is no indication that the forms contained conflicting clauses. 110 F.3d at 189 (holding that "where the terms in two forms are contradictory," such terms do not "become part of the contract under [2-207(2)] because notification of objection has been given by the conflicting forms" under 2-207(2)(c)). Thus, subsections (a) and (c) of section 2-207(2) do not excise Berry's additional one-year statute of limitations term from the parties' contracts.

2. Subsection (b): Material Alteration

The Court turns to the key issue: Whether Berry's one-year statute of limitations terms "materially alter" the contracts between Packgen and Berry. Comment three to section 2-207 states:

> If [additional terms] are such as materially to alter the original bargain, they will not be included unless expressly agreed to by the other party. If, however, there are terms which would not so change the bargain they will be incorporated unless notice of objection to them has already been given or is given within a reasonable time. 11 M.R.S.A. § 2-207, cmt. 3.

The Maine Law Court has held that under section 2-207(2), "[a]n additional term materially alters the . . . agreement if it would result in unreasonable surprise or hardship to the buyer." "The test for materiality is objective." "Considerations relevant to the issue of surprise include 'the parties' prior course of dealing and the number of written confirmations that they exchanged, industry custom and the conspicuousness of the term.'" *Dermalogix Partners*, 2000 U.S. Dist. LEXIS 8009 (quoting *LTV Energy Products v. Northern States Contracting*, 162 B.R. 949, 957 (S.D.N.Y. 1994)). According to comment four of section 2-207:

> Examples of typical clauses which would "materially alter" the contract and so result in surprise or hardship if incorporated without express awareness by the other party [include] . . . a clause requiring that complaints be made in a time materially shorter than customary or reasonable. 11 M.R.S.A. § 2-207, cmt. 4.

Comment five of section 2-207 gives some examples of contractual clauses that "involve no element of unreasonable surprise" such as "a clause fixing a reasonable time for complaints within customary limits."

Although there is no First Circuit case on point, other federal courts have concluded that if a state adopts the UCC's statute of limitations provision authorizing parties to reduce their limitations term to one year, a one-year limitations period that is an "additional term" under section 2-207 is per se reasonable. In *Shur-Value*, the plaintiff claimed that the district court erred when it concluded that the limitations term became part of the parties' agreement under *Texas Business and Commercial Code*, section 2.207(b)(2), arguing that there were disputed factual issues for the jury regarding whether the term resulted in hardship or surprise to the plaintiff. *Id.* at 597–99. In response, the Eighth Circuit upheld the district court's decision and concluded that "[i]f a contractual provision stipulates a limitations period that falls within statutorily defined parameters . . . then presumably the provision is not only legal, but also reasonable, customary, acceptable and accepted." 50 F.3d at 598. Citing comments four and five to section 2-207, the Eighth Circuit recognized that "[c]onsiderations of surprise and hardship must remain part of the analysis," but determined that those considerations were already taken into account by the Texas Legislature when it adopted UCC section 2-725, thereby expressly allowing parties to include a one-year statute of limitations in contracts. *Id.* at 599. Accordingly, the Court declined to conduct a separate factual analysis of whether the reduced limitations term resulted in unreasonable surprise or hardship to the plaintiff because "the per se reasonableness of the POA's one-year time-bar" entitled the defendant to summary judgment. *Id.*

Other courts have arrived at the same conclusion under section 2-207(2) when determining the "reasonableness" of reduced statute of limitations terms [citing cases].

Packgen insists that to determine the materiality of the limitations term and whether it should be part of the parties' contractual agreement, the Court must assess whether the term unreasonably surprised or would impose hardship on Packgen according to the factors listed in *Dermalogix Partners*, 2000 U.S. Dist. LEXIS 8009. With respect to hardship, section "2-207 has been held to prevent a party from 'rely[ing] upon a boilerplate clause in a boilerplate form and a corresponding operation of law to shift substantial economic burdens from itself to a nonassenting party when it had every opportunity to negotiate such a term if it desired.' "

This Court concludes that there is a genuine dispute of material fact as to whether the one-year statute of limitations terms in this case "materially altered" the contract between Packgen and Berry. "Material alteration" under Maine law is an added term that would "result in unreasonable surprise or hardship to the buyer." The Maine Law Court supported this definition by citing comments four and five of section 2-207. Consequently, the Court must parse the language in comments four and five to determine whether the addition of the one-year statute of limitations " 'materially alter[s]' the contract and so result[s] in surprise or hardship . . . ." 11 M.R.S.A. § 2-207, cmt. 4.

"Unreasonable surprise or hardship" is assessed according to an objective standard. *A.E. Robinson Oil*, 2012 ME 29, ¶ 9, 40 A.3d 20 ("[t]he test for materiality is objective").

Comment four provides "[e]xamples of typical clauses which would normally 'materially alter' the contract," including "a clause requiring that complaints be made in a time materially shorter than customary *or* reasonable." *Id.* (emphasis added). Comment five provides "examples of clauses which involve no element of unreasonable surprise and are therefore to be incorporated in the contract unless notice of objection is seasonably given," including "a clause fixing a reasonable time for complaints within *customary* limits." 11 M.R.S.A. § 2-207, cmt. 5 (emphasis added). Although "customary" and "reasonable" may overlap in these examples, they remain separate parts of the material alteration inquiry; elsewise, the word "customary" would be surplusage. *Compare id.*, cmt. 4 ("customary or reasonable"), *with id.*, cmt. 5 ("reasonable time for complaints within customary limits").

Accordingly, a determination as to reasonableness alone is not sufficient to conclude whether there was no material alteration as a matter of law. A statute of limitations provision could be a "reasonable" modification, but still materially alter the contract, if the term is "materially shorter than customary" or otherwise results in "unreasonable surprise or hardship to the buyer." *See A.E. Robinson Oil*, 2012 ME 29, ¶ 9, 40 A.3d 20. This conclusion further supported by the First Circuit's observation that the examples in comments four and five are not comprehensive: "Comments 4 and 5 are illustrative only and the UCC provides no further elucidation of the terms 'surprise' or 'hardship.' " *JOM, Inc. v. Adell Plastics, Inc.*, 193 F.3d 47, 59 (1st Cir. 1999). Therefore, assuming without deciding that Berry's limitations terms are "per se reasonable" under Maine law, this reasoning would still not satisfy the larger material alteration

Based on the Maine Law Court's guidance, this Court interprets comments 4 and 5 of 11 M.R.S.A. section 2-207 to prevent this Court from treating "reasonableness" as the dispositive factor in the material alteration inquiry.

Viewing the record in the light most favorable to Packgen, a disputed issue of material fact remains as to whether Berry's one-year statute of limitations provisions resulted in "unreasonable surprise or hardship to the buyer." *See* 11 M.R.S.A. § 2-207, cmt. 4; *A.E. Robinson Oil*, 2012 ME 29, ¶ 9, 40 A.3d 20; *Phair*, 708

F. Supp. 2d at 61. Packgen has asserted that the limitations period was inconspicuous, vague, and that Packgen was neither informed of the proposed change nor aware of it. Packgen supports these assertions by describing how the limitations period was found within a one-page double-sided document that was stapled to Berry's invoice, "buried in the eighth sentence of a paragraph on the back side of the page" in small print.These facts make out an allegation of unreasonable surprise, consistent with the "[c]onsiderations relevant to the issue of surprise" set out in *Dermalogix Partners. See* 2000 U.S. Dist. LEXIS 8009 (listing factors to be considered as including "the parties' prior course of dealing and the number of written confirmations that they exchanged, industry custom and the conspicuousness of the term") (internal citations omitted). *See* 11 M.R.S.A. § 2-207, cmt. 4. Giving Packgen the benefit of all reasonable inferences in its favor, *Phair*, 708 F. Supp. 2d at 61, a reasonable person could conclude that the one-year statute of limitations provisions resulted in "unreasonable surprise" to Packgen, and thus materially altered the contracts at issue.

The Court concludes that there remains a genuine dispute of material fact as to whether Berry's one-year statute of limitations terms materially altered the two contracts between Packgen and Berry. The court denies Berry's Motion for Summary Judgment.

PROBLEM (cont'd)

(h) The Single Confirmation

(8) Suppose that North did not send a purchase order to buy the X-47 at 285,000. Rather, North placed its order with Barnes by telephone. There is a factual dispute as to whether Barnes accepted the offer during the call (an oral acceptance). Barnes sent an acknowledgment to North which contained the same terms as the Barnes acknowledgment in Problem 1. There was no discussion of these terms during the telephone order. The X-47 manifested the same defects as in Problem 1. Does current Section 2-207 apply to this situation?[48]

(9) Again, assume that North telephoned its order for the X-47. Barnes shipped the X-47 in a container. On the outside of the container, the standard terms of the Barnes acknowledgment in Problem 1 were printed with the following statement: "Opening this container indicates your acceptance of these terms. If you do not agree with them, promptly return the unopened container to Barnes, Inc. within 15 days and the contract will be cancelled." North opened the container and used the X-47 with the results stated in Problem 1. Is North bound to the terms printed on the outside of the box?[49]

---

[48] In *Dorton v. Collins & Aikman*, 453 F.2d 1161 (6th Cir. 1972), the court applied Section 2-207, treating the acknowledgment as a "confirmation" (Section 2-207(1) applies to a confirmation as well as an exchange of confirmations). Confirmations "operate" as acceptances for the purpose of Section 2-207.

[49] In *Step-Saver Data Systems, Inc. v. Wyse Technology*, 939 F.2d 91 (3d Cir. 1991), the court held that the terms printed on the outside of the box were not binding on the purchaser.

(i) "Terms Later" — "Rolling" ("Layered") Contracts

Under traditional contract theory, where a buyer has an opportunity to review a vendor's standardized terms before contracting and chooses to ignore them, absent fraud, duress, or unconscionability, the terms will be enforced under the proverbial "duty to read" rule.[50] Where the vendor's terms become available only after the purchase of the product ("terms later") and include additional terms that had not been previously negotiated or discussed, courts may choose treat such later terms as totally inoperative. In a contract for the sale of goods governed by the Uniform Commercial Code ("UCC"), additional terms in a post-purchase confirmation of the contract that materially alter the original terms are inoperative.

Under the rolling theory, however, where the terms are delivered for the first time with the goods inside the box, such additional, "later" terms are operative, and section 2-207 of the UCC is deemed "irrelevant" for reasons that contradict statutory language and precedent. The effect is to postpone the formation of the contract until the buyer has an opportunity to review the terms and decide whether such terms are acceptable.[51] If a buyer notices the boilerplate and objects to one or more of these additional terms, the sole and exclusive remedy is the return of the purchase price for the returned goods. There is no breach because no contract has been formed. If, however, the buyer does not object within the period specified in the seller's terms, the additional terms — material or immaterial — become part of the contract through the buyer's silence. This is the final "layer" in contract formation, regardless of any conscious assent to the later terms.

(10) The first case creating the new theory saw Matthew Zeindenberg entering a retail computer store and taking a box from the shelf called "SelectPhone" on which information from 3,000 telephone directories was complied at a cost of more than 10 million to its producer, ProCD. The same software was available to commercial buyers at a higher price, but Matthew's version was the retail version costing 150. The discs were accompanied by a "shrinkwrap" license (retail packages are covered in plastic or cellophane "shrinkwrap") that was inside the box. The license terms limited the use of the software to noncommercial purposes. If the user of the software did not agree with the license terms, the software could be returned and the purchase price would be repaid. No terms appeared on the outside of the box though there was a notice in small print that there were terms inside. Matthew took the box to the checkout counter and paid the retail price. Since information compiled from white pages of telephone books cannot be copyrighted, Matthew decided to ignore the license terms inside the box and recreate the software under his own commercial enterprise. He used his own source code since the SelectPhone source code was copyrighted. ProCD sought an injunction against Matthew's further dissemination of the data. The trial court held that the licenses were ineffectual because they did not appear on the outside of the box. The appellate court reversed. While recognizing that the package on the retail store shelf could be

---

[50] RESTATEMENT (SECOND) OF CONTRACTS § 23 cmt. b (1981). The failure to read terms to which a party apparently assents does not affect their operative effect. One is bound by the appearance of mutual assent, even if it was unintended.

[51] There is no requirement that the terms appear conspicuously.

viewed as an offer which the buyer accepted by paying the asking price and leaving the store, the court did not view this analysis as exclusive. The court relied upon Section 2-204(1) of the UCC that allows a contract to "be made in any manner sufficient to show agreement, including conduct by both parties which recognize the existence of a contract." Noting the impracticality of printing extensive terms on the outside of containers, the court stated, "Notice on the outside, terms on the inside, and a right to return the software for a refund if the terms are unacceptable may be a means of doing business valuable to buyers and sellers alike." In effect, the court found that the offer is not accepted by paying the price and leaving the store. Rather, the offer continues ("rolling") until the buyer has a reasonable opportunity to review the terms inside the box and decide whether to abide by them and retain the goods, or return them and receive the purchase price (the final "layer" of the contract). The court rejected any application of Section 2-207 as "irrelevant" *because there was only one form (inside the box) rather than two forms*. The court held that Matthew was bound by the license terms inside the box.[52]

Does Section 2-207 apply only where there are two forms? Consider, again, the analysis in Problem 9. Also consider the language of Section 2-207(1) referring to "a confirmation" as amplified in the *Packgen* case, above. Comment 1 recognizes that Section 2-207 is applicable where the parties have reached an oral agreement "followed by *one* or both of the parties sending formal memoranda embodying the terms so far as agreed and adding terms not discussed" (emphasis supplied). A clear consensus among scholars concludes that the court's view that Section 2-207 applies only where there are two forms is simply "wrong"?[53] Is the popular description of Section 2-207 — the "battle of the forms," which suggests that it applies to an exchange of two forms with different or additional terms — inaccurate? If Section 2-207 were applied to the *Zeidenberg* facts, what is the result? The lower court applied Section 2-207 and found that Matthew was not bound by the terms about which he learned only after taking the software and paying for it. If, however, Matthew was permitted to continue his business in competition with ProCD (for which Matthew paid 150), would a proper application of Section 2-207 result in ratifying what could be seen as unjustly using another's property? Six months later, the same court had an opportunity to revisit these issues.

---

[52] ProCD v. Zeidenberg, 76 F.3d 1447 (7th Cir. 1996).

[53] *See, e.g.*, Robert A Hillman, *Rolling Contracts*, 71 FORDHAM L. REV. 743, 753 (2002) ("[Judge] Easterbrook [who wrote the opinion for the court in the *ProCD* case] was plainly wrong about section 2-207's applicability. Nothing in the text of the section limits it to transaction involving more than one form."); James J. White, *Default Rules in Sales and the Myth of Contracting Out*, 48 LOY. L. REV. 53, 81(2002) ("When, Judge Easterbrook in *ProCD* states that Section 2-207 does not apply to transactions that involve only one document, he is wrong."); John E. Murray, Jr., *Contract Theories and the Rise of Neoformalism*, 71 FORDHAM L. REV. 869, 905, n.193 (2002) ("Even more troublesome is the superficial notion that U.C.C. § 2-207 applies only where there are two conflicting forms, which ignores the U.C.C's application where a single confirmation containing variant terms follows an oral contract for the sale of goods.").

HILL v. GATEWAY 2000, INC.
United States Court of Appeals, Seventh Circuit
105 F.3d 1147 (1997)

EASTERBROOK, J.

A customer picks up the phone, orders a computer, and gives a credit card number. Presently a box arrives, containing the computer and a list of terms, said to govern unless the customer returns the computer within 30 days. Are these terms effective as the parties' contract, or is the contract term-free because the order-taker did not read any terms over the phone and elicit the customers assent?

One of the terms in the box containing a Gateway 2000 system was an arbitration clause. Rich and Enza Hill, the customers, kept the computer more than 30 days before complaining about its components and performance. They filed suit in federal court. Gateway asked the district court to enforce the arbitration clause; the judge refused, writing that "the present record is insufficient to support a finding of a valid arbitration agreement between the parties or that the plaintiffs were given adequate notice of the arbitration clause." Gateway took an immediate appeal.

The Hills say that the arbitration clause did not stand out: they concede noticing the statement of terms but deny reading it closely enough to discover the agreement to arbitrate, and they ask us to conclude that they therefore may go to court. A contract need not be read to be effective; people who accept take the risk that the unread terms may in retrospect prove unwelcome. Terms inside Gateway's box stand or fall together. If they constitute the parties' contract because the Hills had an opportunity to return the computer after reading them, then all must be enforced.

ProCD, Inc. v. Zeidenberg, 86 F.3d 1447 (7th Cir. 1996), holds that terms inside a box of software bind consumers who use the software after an opportunity to read the terms and to reject them by returning the product. Likewise, *Carnival Cruise Lines, Inc. v. Shute*, 499 U.S. 585, 111 S. Ct. 1522, 113 L. Ed. 2d 622 (1991), enforces a forum-selection clause that was included among three pages of terms attached to a cruise ship ticket. *Pro CD* and *Carnival Cruise Lines* exemplify the many commercial transactions in which people pay for products with terms to follow; *ProCD* discusses others. The district court concluded in *ProCD* that the contract is formed when the consumer pays for the software; as a result, the court held, only terms known to the consumer at that moment are part of the contract, and provisos inside the box do not count. Although this is one way a contract could be formed, it is not the only way: "A vendor, as master of the offer, may invite acceptance by conduct, and may propose limitations on the kind of conduct that constitutes acceptance. A buyer may accept by performing the acts the vendor proposes to treat as acceptance." Gateway shipped computers with the same sort of accept-or-return offer *ProCD* made to users of its software. *ProCD* relied on the Uniform Commercial Code.

Plaintiffs ask us to limit *ProCD* to software, but where's the sense in that? *ProCD* is about the law of contract, not the law of software. Payment preceding the revelation of full terms is common for air transportation, insurance, and many other endeavors. Practical considerations support allowing vendors to enclose the full legal terms with their products. Cashiers cannot be expected to read legal documents to customers before ringing up sales. If the staff at the other end of the phone for direct-sales operations such as Gateway's had to read the four-page statement of terms before taking the buyer's credit card number, the droning voice would anesthetize rather than enlighten many potential buyers. Others would hang up in a rage over the waste of their time. And oral recitation would not avoid customers' assertions (whether true or feigned) that the clerk did not read term X to them, or that they did not remember or understand it. Writing provides benefits for both sides of commercial transactions. Customers as a group are better off when vendors skip costly and ineffectual steps such as telephonic recitation, and use instead a simple approve-or-return device. Competent adults are bound by such documents, read or unread.

For their second sally, the Hills contend that *ProCD* should be limited to executory contracts (to licenses in particular), and therefore does not apply because both parties' performance of this contract was complete when the box arrived at their home. This is legally and factually wrong: legally because the question at hand concerns the *formation* of the contract rather than its *performance*, and factually because both contracts were incompletely performed. *ProCD* did not depend on the fact that the seller characterized the transaction as a license rather than as a contract; we treated it as a contract for the sale of goods and reserved the question whether for other purposes a "license" characterization might be preferable. The transaction in *ProCD* was no more executory than the one here: Zeidenberg paid for the software and walked out of the store with a box under his arm, so if arrival of the box with the product ends the time for revelation of contractual terms, then the time ended in *ProCD* before Zeidenberg opened the box. But of course ProCD had not completed performance with delivery of the box, and neither had Gateway. One element of the transaction was the warranty, which obliges sellers to fix defects in their products. The Hills have invoked Gateway's warranty and are not satisfied with its response, so they are not well positioned to say that Gateway's obligations were fulfilled when the motor carrier unloaded the box. What is more, both ProCD and Gateway promised to help customers to use their products. Long-term service and information obligations are common in the computer business, on both hardware and software sides. Gateway offers "lifetime service" and has a round-the-clock telephone hotline to fulfil this promise. Some vendors spend more money helping customers use their products than on developing and manufacturing them. The document in Gateway's box includes promises of future performance that some consumers value highly; these promises bind Gateway just as the arbitration clause binds the Hills.

Next the Hills insist that *ProCD* is irrelevant because Zeidenberg was a "merchant" and they are not. Section 2-207(2) of the UCC, the infamous battle-of-the-forms section, states that "additional terms [following acceptance of an offer] are to be construed as proposals for addition to a contract. Between merchants such terms become part of the contract unless . . . ." Plaintiffs tell us that *ProCD* came out as it did only because Zeidenberg was a "merchant" and the terms inside ProCD's box were not excluded by the "unless" clause. This argument pays scant attention to the opinion in *ProCD*, which concluded that, when there is only one form, "§ 2-207 is irrelevant." The question in *ProCD* was not whether terms were added to a contract after its formation, but how and when the contract was formed — in particular, whether a vendor may propose that a contract of sale be formed, not in the store (or over the phone) with the payment of money or a general "send me the product," but after the customer has had a chance to inspect both the item and the terms. *ProCD* answers "yes," for merchants and consumers alike.

At oral argument the Hills propounded still another distinction: the box containing ProCD's software displayed a notice that additional terms were within, while the box containing Gateway's computer did not. The difference is functional, not legal. Consumers browsing the aisles of a store can look at the box, and if they are unwilling to deal with the prospect of additional terms can leave the box alone, avoiding the transactions costs of returning the package after reviewing its contents. Gateway's box, by contrast, is just a shipping carton; it is not on display anywhere. Its function is to protect the product during transit, and the information on its sides is for the use of handlers ("Fragile!" "This Side Up!") rather than would-be purchasers.

Perhaps the Hills would have had a better argument if they were first alerted to the bundling of hardware and legal-ware after opening the box and wanted to return the computer in order to avoid disagreeable terms, but were dissuaded by the expense of shipping. What the remedy would be in such a case — could it exceed the shipping charges? — is an interesting question, but one that need not detain us because the Hills knew before they ordered the computer that the carton would include some important terms, and they did not seek to discover these in advance. Gateway's ads state that their products come with limited warranties and lifetime support. How limited was the warranty — 30 days, with service contingent on shipping the computer back, or five years, with free onsite service? What sort of support was offered? Shoppers have three principal ways to discover these things. First, they can ask the vendor to send a copy before deciding whether to buy. Second, shoppers can consult public sources (computer magazines, the Web sites of vendors) that may contain this information. Third, they may inspect the documents after the product's delivery. Like Zeidenberg, the Hills took the third option. By keeping the computer beyond 30 days, the Hills accepted Gateway's offer, including the arbitration clause.

The decision of the district court is vacated, and this case is remanded with instructions to compel the Hills to submit their dispute to arbitration.

NOTES

(1) As seen earlier, merchants may sometimes avoid the use of a purchase order and enter an offer by telephone. Like the non-merchant Hills, if a merchant buyer receives terms inside the box in response to such an oral offer, the court states that its new theory is applicable to merchants and non-merchants alike. If, however, a buyer-merchant uses a purchase order and the seller sends its acknowledgment, the "rolling" theory would not apply since there are "two forms" requiring the application of Section 2-207. Apart from the erroneous notion that Section 2-207 only applies to transactions involving two forms, does it seem odd to make the application of Section 2-207 depend upon whether the buyer happens to use a form

to make its offer? Moreover, merchant-buyers have forms to use. Consumers do not. Thus, consumers appear to be the principal targets of the "rolling" theory. Is this desirable?

(2) The principal case suggests that Gateway is the offeror, but the Hills appear to be the offerors in placing their order for the computer. Gateway accepted their credit card promise as payment. It would appear that Gateway was the offeree that accepted the offer. Even if the Gateway telephone operator had not accepted the offer, Gateway certainly appeared to accept the offer when it shipped the computer, did it not? This analysis is clear under UCC Section 2-206(1)(b), which allows an acceptance either by a promise to ship or by "shipment." The court relies exclusively upon the more general UCC Section 2-204, allowing a contract to be formed in anyreasonable manner, but Section 2-206 is a more specific section which should control under normal statutory interpretation rules. Why doesn't the court mention Section 2-206? Again, why does the court, without explanation, insist on calling Gateway the offeror? Is this because, otherwise, its "rolling" theory would collapse like a house of cards?

(3) Suppose a buyer who made a telephone offer receives goods accompanied by warranty disclaimers, remedy exclusion and arbitration terms inside the box. The terms provide the buyer with 15 days to reject the terms and recover any purchase price that may have been paid. Assume that, within the 15 days, the buyer sends a message to the seller stating that the buyer is quite willing to pay the purchase price and retain the goods, but only if the other seller's terms inside the box are not part of the contract. The buyer's letter concludes with, "If I do not hear from you within 15 days, you will be deemed to have accepted the terms of this counter offer." Under the "rolling" theory, should the buyer be able to achieve such a result? Compare *Cook's Pest Control v. Rebar*, 852 So. 2d 730 (Ala. 2002), where Cook's sent the Rebars a form to renew pest control service for a one-year term at a certain price. The form contained an arbitration clause. The Rebars returned a check for the renewal price and the form with an addendum stating that they were not bound to arbitrate disputes. Cook's cashed the check. A subsequent dispute occurred and the Rebars sought to litigate in court. Cook's claimed the Rebars were bound by the arbitration clause. The court held that Cook's had accepted the Rebars' counter offer which eliminated arbitration.

(4) While the "rolling" or "layered" theory has not been tested in a large number of courts, there has been some tendency to suggest that most of the courts favor the theory. The case law progeny, however, reveals pervasive confusion and inconsistent results. See John E. Murray, Jr., *The Dubious Status of the Rolling Contract Formation Theory*, 50 Duq. L. Rev. 35, 58–71 (2012). Citing this article, the United States Court of Appeals for the Second Circuit notes that even "[t]he conventional chronology of contract making has become unsettled" due to "terms later" contracting. *Schnabel v. Trilegiant Corp.*, 697 F. 3d 110, 121 (2d Cir. 2012). Similarly, the Tenth Circuit cites the same article in stating that the "rolling contract formation theory may be about as controversial an idea as exists today in the staid world of contract law." *Howard v. Ferrellgas Partners, L. P.*, 748 F. 3d 975. 982 (10th Cir. 2014).

Chapter 3

THE VALIDATION PROCESS

A. INTRODUCTION

The validation process was introduced in Chapter 1 with brief descriptions of the four validation devices: the seal, consideration, promissory estoppel (detrimental reliance) and moral obligation. This chapter provides a comprehensive analysis of each of those devices. It is important to remember that the validation devices developed in common law fashion and, except for the seal (the writ of *covenant*), the other devices were not known at early common law, although there are antecedents of all of the devices in the early law. In the introduction of these concepts in Chapter 1, we indicated that the oldest device, the seal, has either been abolished in many jurisdictions or constitutes only presumptive evidence of enforceability in others. Where the seal is still effective, it is important to understand its application.

B. THE SEAL AND OTHER FORMALISTIC DEVICES

KNOTT v. RACICOT
Massachusetts Supreme Judicial Court
812 N.E.2d 1207 (2004)

MARSHALL, C.J.

For centuries under the Anglo-American common law, contracts executed under seal have conclusively been held to import consideration; the seal itself substitutes for the actual exchange of value between promisee and promisor. We are now asked to abolish the common-law presumption of consideration for option contracts[1] executed under seal. At issue is the validity of a right of first refusal[2] executed as a sealed contract between an owner of property and a tenant. The plaintiff, a potential buyer of the property, sought to invalidate the right of first refusal for lack of consideration. A judge found that consideration is not required for a sealed contract. The Appeals Court affirmed. We granted the plaintiff's application for further appellate review and conclude that no sound legal justification exists for

---

[1] [3] "An option is simply an irrevocable offer creating a power of acceptance in the optionee." Stapleton v. Macchi, 401 Mass. 725, 729 n.6, 519 N.E.2d 273 (1988).

[2] [4] "A right of first refusal provision is designed to afford the holder protection against a sale to others. That protection is only effective if, in the event the owner has elected to sell the property, the holder . . . has a realistic opportunity to meet the offer the owner has elected to accept." Roy v. George W. Greene, Inc., 404 Mass. 67, 71, 533 NE.2d 1323 (1989).

maintaining the common-law fiction that an option contract executed under seal conclusively imports consideration, and we adopt the position of the RESTATEMENT (SECOND) OF CONTRACTS § 87(1) (1981) concerning the validity of such contracts. However, for reasons we discuss below, our conclusion does not affect the judgment of the Probate Court, which we now affirm.

To understand the role of seals in the law, some background is useful. Seals have a venerable history in our law of contracts. In medieval England, a time when most adults were illiterate, unable even to sign their names, contracts routinely were executed "under seal." That is, each party impressed on the physical document a wax seal or other mark bearing his individual sign of identification. Under the common law, the seal became proof of the parties' identities and the document's authenticity, and loss or destruction of the sealed contract terminated the bargain. Moreover, the seal was said to import consideration, substituting for the actual giving of such. Over time, simply the words "under seal" or a similar phrase appearing in a mass-produced, form contract became sufficient to invest that document with the privileged status of a sealed instrument.

Despite its lengthy pedigree, however, the sealed contract doctrine has been under heavy assault at least since the days of the Industrial Revolution. In recent decades the majority of American jurisdictions have either abolished or significantly eliminated the distinction between sealed and unsealed contracts. See generally 1 S. Williston, Contracts, supra at § 2:17 (table of statutory provisions modifying or abolishing distinction between sealed and unsealed instruments); H.O. Hunter, Modern Law of Contracts § 7:2 (2003) ("More than one-half the states have abolished the distinction between sealed and unsealed instruments, and § 2-203 of the Uniform Commercial Code . . . abolishes the distinction for sales of goods"). Today the Commonwealth is one of the minority of American jurisdictions that have carried over significant elements of the sealed contract doctrine to the Twenty-first Century.

Nevertheless, the sealed contract doctrine has also "eroded considerably." Whatever the merits of upholding the common-law sealed contract doctrine may have been, they seem far less apparent today, when option contracts are often an important part of business, professional, employment, and investment transactions. Questions concerning the validity of option contracts are simply too important to our highly literate, highly mobile society to be decided by formalities that have lost all practical utility. As the Legislature has recognized, the written signature has replaced the wax impression as the natural formality authenticating a document. Thus we require no showing of injustice to conclude that the giving of consideration, a necessary element of ordinary (simple or informal) contracts, should be required for option contracts that happen either to be impressed with a seal or to recite a talismanic formula importing a seal.[3] We henceforth adopt the RESTATEMENT (SECOND) OF CONTRACTS § 87(1) (1981): "An offer is binding as an option contract if it (a) is in writing and signed by the offeror, recites a purported consideration for the making of the offer, and proposes an exchange on fair terms within a reasonable time; or (b) is made irrevocable by statute." See 3 A. CORBIN, CONTRACTS § 11.7 n.1

---

[3] [Ed. note. The recital was on a generic legal form stating that the right of first refusal was executed "under seal" and "for good and valuable consideration, the receipt of which is hereby acknowledged."]

(rev. ed. 1996) (under § 87[1], "the seal is not listed as a method of validating an option contract"). To the extent that prior cases are inconsistent with our ruling today, we overrule those cases.

The case for modifying the presumption of consideration for sealed option contracts might well apply to other types of contracts under seal. *See Kingston Hous. Auth. v. Sandonato & Bogue, Inc.*, 31 Mass. App. Ct. 270, 275 n.5, 577 N.E.2d 1 (1991) (noting "ceremony" of sealing as incompatible with "the high volume of documents in contemporary commerce"). *See also* 3 A. CORBIN, CONTRACTS § 10.18 at 439 (rev. ed. 1996) ("seals [have] ceased to function as form and should now be jettisoned"). Should the appropriate case present itself to us in the future, we would consider a request to substantially modify or abrogate the conclusive presumption of consideration for other types of sealed contracts, to the extent the Legislature has not directed otherwise.

We shall not, however, invalidate [the right of first refusal in this case] for lack of consideration. First, retroactivity generally is not appropriate where it would "alter rights in Massachusetts contract and property law where issues of reliance might impose hardship on unsuspecting parties." *MacCormack v. Boston Edison Co.*, 423 Mass. 652, 657, 672 N.E.2d 1 (1996). To disturb the contract rights and expectations of a potentially sizeable class of parties who have bound themselves under the previous law would potentially result in hardship. Second, the sealed right of first refusal in this case meets the criteria set out in the RESTATEMENT (SECOND) OF CONTRACTS § 87(1). The agreement is signed by the offeror, recites a "purported consideration for the making of the offer," and proposes a fair exchange of terms within a reasonable time frame. *Id.* The decedent's signature is the "natural formality" authenticating the agreement, *id.* at § 87 comment a, and "[a] recital in a written agreement that a stated consideration has been given is evidence of that fact as against a party to the agreement." *Id.* at § 87 comment c. We affirm the judgment.

NOTES

(1) *The Seal as a Validation Device.* The analysis of the abolishment or the decline of the seal manifests various legislative and judicial thrusts. As the court noted, Section 2-203 of the Uniform Commercial Code has made seals "inoperative" in contracts for the sale of goods. While it is popular to suggest that, otherwise, the seal has been abolished in more than half of the states, the accuracy of that statement is questioned in CORBIN ON CONTRACTS, § 10.18 for the following reasons:

> [I]n seven of the twenty-six jurisdictions purporting to abolish seals (Alaska, Michigan, Oregon, South Dakota, Utah, U.S. Virgin Islands, and Washington), it is questionable that their statutes completely abolish the common-law doctrine of seals. Second, twelve of the twenty-six jurisdictions (Arizona, California, Iowa, Kansas, Kentucky, Missouri, Montana, North Dakota, Oklahoma, South Dakota, Tennessee, and Texas) statutorily elevate written contracts to a presumption of consideration. Third, two of the twenty-six jurisdictions (Mississippi and possibly Texas) make written contracts the equivalent of sealed contracts. Fourth, New York has a series

of statutes that eliminate the necessity of consideration for particular types of promises if made in writing and signed.

(2) *Legislative Substitutes for the Seal.* The most significant legislative effort to replace the seal is the *Uniform Written Obligations Act* that allows a written promise to be enforceable if it states that the promisor intends to be legally bound. Enacted only in Pennsylvania and Utah, it was repealed in Utah and continues only in Pennsylvania (Pa. Stat. Ann., title 33, § 6). The absence of wide enactment has caused the title to be changed to the "Model" Written Obligations Act. Uniform Commercial Code § 2-209 allows good faith modifications of a contract to be enforceable without consideration, and § 2-205 allows "firm offers" by merchants (in a writing that gives assurance that it will be held open) to be irrevocable for the time stated in the offer or a reasonable time, but in no event to exceed three months. A similar New York statute (N. Y. Gen. Oblig. Law § 5-1109) achieves the same effect. Some state statutes require no consideration for a written release.

(3) *Statutes of Limitations.* In as many as twenty-seven jurisdictions, contracts or instruments under seal are included in the state's statute of limitations and may suggest substantial extensions. In some jurisdictions, the statute of limitations for a promise under seal may be as long as twenty years. For a list of statutes of limitations, see CORBIN ON CONTRACTS § 10.18.

(4) *Exception — Failure of Consideration.* It is important to distinguish a lack of consideration from a failure of consideration with respect to the seal. In a jurisdiction where the seal continues to be effective and an instrument under seal evidences a bargained-for-exchange, the failure of one party to perform as promised is a failure of consideration. Failure of consideration can be shown despite the seal. See *Joseph Gartner USA LP v. Consigli Constr. Co., Inc.*, 2011 U.S. Dist. LEXIS 62492 (D. Mass.). Where, for example, a writing under seal manifests an agreement for the sale of automobile at a certain price, failure of the seller to deliver the automobile will be a defense to the seller's action to collect the price, notwithstanding the seal.

C. CONSIDERATION

[1] The Elements of Consideration

In our introduction to "consideration" in Chapter 1, we recognized that consideration evolved from the common law forms of action. The modern concept of consideration is composed of two essential elements: (a) legal value, and (b) bargained-for-exchange. The classic description of the first element, legal value, is found in a nineteenth century case from the Court of Exchequer, *Currie v. Misa*:

> A valuable consideration, in the sense of the law, may consist either in some right, interest, profit or benefit accruing to the one party, or some forbearance, detriment, loss or responsibility, given, suffered or undertaken by another.[4]

---

[4] L.R. 10 Ex. 153, 162 [1875]. Modern versions of this statement can be found in a legion of cases,

Innumerable opinions reduce this formula to the simple statement that consideration requires either a benefit to the promisor or detriment to the promisee.[5] The legal value element (benefit or detriment) is, however, insufficient in itself to constitute consideration. The benefits and detriments must be *exchanged*, i.e., they must be *bargained-for.* Both of these elements are found in the RESTATEMENT (SECOND) OF CONTRACTS definition of consideration that was introduced in Chapter 1.[6]

It is important to recall that consideration is an historic accident. In Chapter 1, we recognized that early common law lawyers and judges would be unfamiliar with the concept of consideration. They were engulfed with common law writs, such as the writ of *covenant* used for actions to enforce promises made under seal. The writ called *debt* was used where the exchange between the parties was half completed and the party who had completed his part of the exchange sought to enforce the other's commitment. Since both of these writs were subject to *wager of law* which allowed the defendant to secure twelve persons who would swear that defendant told the truth, the need for a flexible writ or form of action to permit the enforcement of *informal* promises was clear.

That need began to be satisfied through the writ called *trespass on the case*, which was expanded to permit the development of an action in *special assumpsit* where a party undertook to perform an action and proceeded to perform it badly (*misfeasance*). The classic example was the blacksmith who undertook to shoe a horse and performed badly, injuring the horse. The undertaking, coupled with the *misfeasance*, allowed the action in special assumpsit. There was a *detriment* to the promisee (the owner of the horse). Thus, the origins of special assumption arose from an action in what modern lawyers would call tort (*ex delicto*) because the emphasis was on the *misfeasance*.

Suppose, however, that the party who failed to perform did not misfease, but simply failed to perform. He was guilty of *nonfeasance*. To allow for the precursor to the modern action for simple failure to perform a promise, the emphasis was placed on *deceit*, i.e., the failure to perform was viewed as deceitful. This marked the change in assumpsit from an action *ex delicto* to an action *ex contractu* where the emphasis was upon failure to perform the promise.

---

including very recent cases. *See, e.g.*, Cook v. Heck's, Inc., 342 S.E.2d 453 (W. Va. App. 1986); Artoe v. Cap, 140 Ill. App. 3d 980, 489 N.E.2d 420 (1986); Hyde v. Shapiro, 216 Neb. 785, 346 N.W.2d 241 (1984).

[5] *See, e.g.*, USLIFE Title Co. v. Gutkin, 152 Ariz. 349, 732 P.2d 579 (1986); Vogelhut v. Kandel, 308 Md. 183, 517 A.2d 1092 (1986); Chasan v. Village Dist. of Eastman, 128 N.H. 807, 523 A.2d 16 (1986); Nordwick v. Berg, 725 P.2d 1195 (Mont. 1986); Koehler Constr. Co. v. Medical Center of Blue Springs, 670 S.W.2d 558 (Mo. App. 1984); R & L Farms, Inc. v. Windle, 653 F.2d 328 (8th Cir. 1981).

[6] RESTATEMENT (SECOND) OF CONTRACTS § 71:

   (1) To constitute consideration, a performance or return promise must be bargained for.

   (2) A performance or return promise is bargained for if it is sought by the promisor in exchange for his promise and is given by the promisee in exchange for that promise.

   (3) The performance may consist of (a) an act other than a promise, or (b) a forbearance, or (c) the creation, modification or destruction of a legal relation.

   (4) The performance or return promise may be given to the promisor or some other person. It may be given by the promisee or by some other person.

The quantum leap in this development occurred in 1602. In *Slade's Case*, 4 Coke 92b [1602], the court no longer required a second promise that had been previously required to bring an action in *indebitatus assumpsit* (being indebted, he undertook). Thus, instead of the action in *debt* with its severe limitations, *assumpsit* became the popular remedy for breach of contract. The courts were now faced with the basic question: Would *assumpsit* lie for breach of *any* promise, or would there be limitations? The term "consideration" was used vaguely in early pleadings to suggest that there had to be some reason for enforcing the promise. To determine which promises should be enforced, the common lawyers turned to their familiar writs. They recognized that assumpsit was now being applied to actions that were formerly brought in *debt*, where a *benefit* had been conferred upon the promisor. They also recognized that assumpsit had been applied to the misfeasance situations where the promisee suffered a *detriment*. These concepts were joined with another, the requirement of a *quid pro quo*, a bargained-for-exchange. As suggested by Professor John Dawson in his work, GIFTS AND PROMISES 203 (1980), "[E]ach party had in fact desired some act of abstention of the other in return for which he had agreed to perform his own." The benefit to the promisor or detriment to the promisee with the promise inducing the detriment *and* the detriment inducing the promise evolved into what became clearly known as *consideration*.

[2]   The Legal Value Element — "Adequacy" or "Sufficiency" of Consideration"

The classic description of the legal value element of consideration is found in *Currie v. Misa*, L. R. 10 Ex. 153, 162 (1875), where the Court of Exchequer stated, "A valuable consideration, in the sense of the law, may consist either in some right, interest, profit of benefit accruing to the one party, or some forbearance, detriment, loss or responsibility, given, suffered or undertaken by the other." a modern formula for this element is stated in the alternative — benefit to the promisor or detriment to the promisee — the typical contract will manifest both benefits and detriments. Thus, in the simple, informal contract to buy and sell an automobile, the benefit to the buyer is the auto and the benefit to the seller is the price. The detriment to the buyer is the payment of the price, and the detriment to the seller is the surrender of the car. Our present challenge is to ascertain a comprehensive understanding of such benefits and detriments as they are legally recognized.

HAMER v. SIDWAY

New York Court of Appeals

27 N.E. 256 (1891)

PARKER, J.

The question which provoked the most discussion by counsel on this appeal, and which lies at the foundation of plaintiff's asserted right of recovery, is whether by virtue of a contract defendant's testator, William E. Story, became indebted to his nephew, William E. Story, 2d, on his twenty-first birthday in the sum of $5,000. The trial court found as a fact that "on the 20th day of March, 1869, . . . William E.

Story agreed to and with William E. Story, 2d, that if he would refrain from drinking liquor[,] using tobacco, swearing, and playing cards or billiards for money until [he] should become twenty-one years of age, then he, the said William E. Story, would at that time pay him, the said William E. Story, 2d, the sum of $5,000 for such refraining, to which the said William E. Story, 2d, agreed," and that he "in all things fully performed his part of said agreement." The defendant contends that the contract was without consideration to support it, and therefore invalid. He asserts that the promisee, by refraining from the use of liquor and tobacco, was not harmed, but benefitted; that which he did was best for him to do, independently of his uncle's promise, — and insists that it follows that, unless the promisor was benefitted, the contract was without consideration, — a contention which, if well founded, would seem to leave open for controversy in many cases whether that which the promisee did or omitted to do was in fact of such benefit to him as to leave no consideration to support the enforcement of the promisor's agreement. Such a rule could not be tolerated, and is without foundation in the law. The exchequer chamber in 1875 defined "consideration" as follows: "A valuable consideration, in the sense of the law, may consist either in some right, interest, profit, or benefit accruing to the one party, or some forbearance, detriment, loss, or responsibility given, suffered, or undertaken by the other." Courts "will not ask whether the thing which forms the consideration does in fact benefit the promisee or a third party, or is of any substantial value to anyone. It is enough that something is promised, done, forborne, or suffered by the party to whom the promise is made as consideration for the promise made to him." Anson. Cont. 63. "In general a waiver of any legal right at the request of another party is a sufficient consideration for a promise." Pars. Cont. *444. "Any damage, or suspension, or forbearance of a right will be sufficient to sustain a promise." 2 Kent, Comm. (12th Ed.) *465. Pollock in his work on Contracts, (page 166) after citing the definition given by the exchequer chamber, already quoted, says: "The second branch of this judicial description is really the most important one. 'Consideration' means not so much that one party is profiting as that the other abandons some legal right in the present, or limits his legal freedom of action in the future, as an inducement for the promise of the first." Now, applying this rule to the facts before us, the promisee used tobacco, occasionally drank liquor, and he had a legal right to do so. That right he abandoned for a period of years upon the strength of the promise of the testator that for such forbearance he would give him $5,000. We need not speculate on the effort which may have been required to give up the use of those stimulants. It is sufficient that he restricted his lawful freedom of action within certain prescribed limits upon the faith of his uncle's agreement, and now, having fully performed the conditions imposed, it is of no moment whether such performance actually proved a benefit to the promisor, and the court will not inquire into it; but, were it a proper subject of inquiry, we see nothing in this record that would permit a determination that the uncle was not benefitted in a legal sense. Few cases have been found which may be said to be precisely in point, but such as have been, support the position we have taken. In *Shadwell v. Shadwell*, 9 C.B. (N.S.) 159, an uncle wrote to his nephew as follows: "My dear Lancey: I am so glad to hear of your intended marriage with Ellen Nicholl, and, as I promised to assist you at starting, I am happy to tell you that I will pay you 150 pounds yearly during my life and until your annual income derived from your profession of a chancery barrister shall amount to 600 guineas, of which your own admission will be the only evidence that I shall receive or require. Your affectionate uncle, CHARLES SHADWELL." It was held that the promise was binding, and made upon good consideration. In *Lakota v. Newton,* (an unreported case in the superior court of Worcester, Mass.,) the complaint averred defendant's promise that "if you [meaning the plaintiff] will leave off drinking for a year I will give you $100," plaintiff's assent thereto, performance of the condition by him, and demanded judgment therefor. Defendant demurred, on the ground, among others, that the plaintiff's declaration did not allege a valid and sufficient consideration for the agreement of the defendant. The demurrer was overruled. In *Talbott v. Stemmons,* 12 S.W. Rep. 297, (a Kentucky case, not yet officially reported,) the step-grandmother of the plaintiff made with him the following agreement: "I do promise and bind myself to give my grandson Albert R. Talbott $500 at my death if he will never take another chew of tobacco or smoke another cigar during my life, from this date up to my death; and if he breaks this pledge he is to refund double the amount to his mother." The executor of Mrs. Stemmons demurred to the complaint on the ground that the agreement was not based on a sufficient consideration. The demurrer was sustained, and an appeal taken therefrom to the court of appeals, where the decision of the court below was reversed. In the opinion of the court it is said that "the right to use and enjoy the use of tobacco was a right that belonged to the plaintiff, and not forbidden by law. The abandonment of its use may have saved him money, or contributed to his health; nevertheless, the surrender of that right caused the promise, and, having the right to contract with reference to the subject-matter, the abandonment of the use was a sufficient consideration to uphold the promise." Abstinence from the use of intoxicating liquors was held to furnish a good consideration for a promissory note in *Lindell v. Rokes,* 60 Mo. 249. The cases cited by the defendant on this question are not in point. The order appealed from should be reversed, and the judgment of the special term affirmed, with costs payable out of the estate. All concur.

NOTES

(1)   Was there a benefit to the uncle-promisor or a detriment to the nephew-promisee, or both? Was there a benefit to the nephew-promisee? What kind of benefit? Was there a legal detriment to the nephew-promisee and a non-legal benefit to him?

(2)   Why is the formula always stated in terms of "benefit to the promisor or detriment to the promisee"? If the formula is reversed (benefit to promisee — detriment to the promisor) would there be consideration? Can you think of an example where the formula would be reversed?

(3)   In the typical contract, do we not usually have both a benefit to the promisor *and* a detriment to the promisee? Why do we insist on saying that the requirement is satisfied if we have either?

(4)   In situations like the principal case, it is possible to imagine various benefits to the promisor such as the satisfaction of helping a relative avoid harmful practices and preservation of the family name and reputation. If no specific benefit can be shown, however, the detriment to the promisee, if bargained-for, constitutes consideration. Such benefits, however, are speculative. Thus, even though the

formula is typically stated as requiring a bargained-for-exchange with a benefit to the promisor *or* detriment to the promisee, the emphasis is upon the detriment to the promisee.

While it is not necessary to discover any discernible benefit to the promisor to find consideration, it is essential to discover a detriment to the promisee. Attempts to imagine such cases where there is no detriment to the promisee suggest no consideration. Thus, if *A* says to *B*, I will pay you $100 tomorrow if you do not drive my car," assuming that *B* has no right to drive *A*'s car at any time, there is no detriment to *B* in forbearing from driving *A*'s car because he has surrendered no legally recognized right in such forbearance. There is also no benefit to *A* since *A* received nothing in exchange for his promise.

PROBLEMS

(1)   When Lee Hunter died, his estate was insufficient to pay his funeral expenses and other debts, including a note held by the bank secured by 50 shares of stock in Hunter's company that was worthless. His widow had no previous indebtedness to the bank, but exchanged her personal note for Lee's note which the bank surrendered. When the widow failed to pay her note, the bank brought an action to which the widow pleaded want of consideration. What result? This problem is based on the facts of *Newman & Snell's Bank v. Hunter*, 243 Mich. 331, 220 N.W. 665 (1928) where the court found no consideration. Do you agree?

(2)   The plaintiff attended his uncle's funeral and the widow, plaintiff's aunt, emphasized how important his presence was. At a subsequent family funeral, the aunt sought plaintiff's promise that, if he were alive and well, he would attend the aunt's funeral. The aunt was concerned that few if any family members would be available to attend her funeral. She told the plaintiff, "Ben, if you promise to attend my funeral, I promise to pay you $500 from my estate for attending." Ben then promised that he would attend absent death or serious illness. The aunt died. Ben was alive and well. He also knew of the aunt's death in time to attend the funeral but chose not to do so. The aunt's promise had been reduced to writing and was in the possession of her executor. The executor refused to pay the $500 to Ben. Ben brought an action for such payment. What result? This problem is based upon some of the facts in *Earle v. Angell*, 157 Mass. 294, 32 N.E. 164 (1892). If the aunt's promise is enforceable, would this be an illustration of a benefit to the promisor with no detriment to the promisee?

NOTE

It was not until the 16th century that actions on unsealed contracts containing mutual promises began to appear. At that time, such promises were enforced. In the late 19th and early 20th centuries, however, theoretical discussions concerning the enforcement of purely executory bilateral contracts occurred. The principal question was whether parties bargain for each other's promises (i.e., assurances), or whether they bargain for the performance of such promises. With respect to legal value, if the performance which has been promised would be of legal value absent the promise, the promise of such performance will be sufficient. However, where a promise is sought by a living person for a performance after his or her death, does the promisee seek the promise or the performance? Does it matter whether the promisee will be aware of the performance? Should courts engage in theological discussions of such awareness?

[3]   Exceptions to Refusals to Inquire Into Adequacy of Consideration

[a]   Inadequacy in Equity

McKINNON v. BENEDICT

Wisconsin Supreme Court

157 N.W.2d 665 (1968)

This is an appeal from a judgment of the county court of Vilas county for damages for a trespass on the property owned by Roderick W. McKinnon and Dorothy D. McKinnon, and from an injunction which restrained the defendants, Roy A. Benedict, Jr., and Evelyn M. Benedict, from operating a trailer park and campsite on certain resort property located in Vilas county. The Benedicts have appealed from this judgment.

The Benedict property is approximately an 80-acre tract located on the shores of Mamie Lake, one of the chain of Cisco Lakes, on the Michigan-Wisconsin border. It is operated as a resort known as Bent's Camp. The Benedict property is completely surrounded by the McKinnon tract of approximately 1,170 acres. The McKinnons have lived on Mamie Lake since 1925, although at the present time they reside there only during the summer months and during the Christmas holidays. During the remainder of the year, the McKinnons reside in Arizona, where Roderick McKinnon is an investment counselor. He is a member of the Wisconsin State Bar and at various times practiced law.

Until 1961, Bent's Camp was operated by a Mr. and Mrs. L. L. Dorsey. This property, although abutting Mamie Lake, is divided by county trunk *B*. The resort area is located near the lakeshore to the northeast of county trunk *B* and consists of 14 cabins and a main lodge. The area of Bent's Camp southwest of county trunk *B* is a small, undeveloped parcel of timberland. During 1960 the Dorseys were interested in selling the property. Their agent, one Handlos, located the Benedicts as prospective buyers. They, however, were in need of financial assistance to make the purchase, and they were referred to Roderick W. McKinnon, who agreed to loan the Benedicts the sum of $5,000 as a partial down payment. This loan was made on the basis of an understanding that the Benedicts would continue to operate Bent's Camp as an American Plan family resort. On August 31, 1960, McKinnon wrote a letter to the Benedicts incorporating the terms on which the advance was made:

Dear Roy:

It is my understanding that in consideration of my advancing you $5000, for use as a downpayment on Bent's Camp we agree between one another as follows:

(1) You and Mrs. Benedict will sign a non-interest bearing note for $5000, due January 1, 1961, and a first mortgage on your cottage in Gogebic County, Michigan. If you should sell this property or your property in Wheaton, Illinois prior to the time the note is paid, you will pay the note out of the proceeds.

(2) As soon as convenient after your acquisition of Bent's Camp, we will sign a recordable agreement providing that for a period of 25 years no trees will be cut between my land and Bent's Camp, nor between Bent's Camp and County Highway *B* nor will any improvements be constructed or placed closer to my property than the present buildings. This restriction will have no application to any of your land lying west of County Trunk *B* nor to your separate 40-acre "woodlot." If you wish, we will supply trees to be planted in this area at no cost to you.

(3) In the event you desire, we will from time to time designate certain trees or certain areas on our property where you may cut fire wood at no cost to you.

(4) I will help you try to reach a satisfactory solution concerning the lease held by Mrs. J. Stuart Vair. I will also try to generate business for your camp and to otherwise assist you in getting the operation well organized.

If the foregoing meets with your approval, will you and Mrs. Benedict please sign below and return one copy for my files.

The approval was signed by both of the Benedicts, and the letter was returned to McKinnon. Thereafter, the Benedicts executed a note in the sum of $5,000 and a mortgage on their cottage property in Michigan. The promised $5,000 was shortly thereafter transmitted and used as a down payment. The loan was paid in full in the spring of 1961. The Benedicts thus had the use of the $5,000 from early September, 1960, to April, 1961, a period of about seven months. The Benedicts purchased the property from the Dorseys on a land contract at a price of $60,000. That land contract provided that, while the Benedicts continued to be obligated to the Dorseys under the terms of the contract, they would replace all personal property so as to maintain it in substantially the same state as at the time of the agreement. They also agreed that no timber would be cut except for firewood without the written consent of the Dorseys and that the premises were to be operated substantially in the same manner as they had been operated by the Dorseys in the previous years.

At the time the land contract was executed, Bent's Camp consisted of 14 cottages, only five of which could be used for resort purposes. Between 1961 and 1964, the Benedicts invested $20,000 in cottages, installing bathrooms and kitchens so that all of the cabins were habitable. Roy Benedict testified that during the period between 1961 and 1964, the income from the operations of the American Plan resort substantially decreased and that it became increasingly difficult to make the land-contract payments.

One of the conditions of the letter of August 31, 1960, was that McKinnon would attempt to reach a satisfactory solution concerning the lease held by Mrs. J. Stuart

Vair. The record shows that Mrs. Vair held a fifty-year lease on one of the cabins at an annual rental of $5 per year. The record reveals only one attempt, and that unsuccessful, on the part of McKinnon to "reach a satisfactory solution." The agreement also provided that McKinnon would try to generate business for the camp and otherwise assist in getting the operation well organized. The record indicates no attempt whatsoever on the part of McKinnon to get the operation "well organized." There was evidence that at least one small group had spent a few days at Bent's Camp at the suggestion of McKinnon, but it is apparent that the amount of business generated by him was almost nil.

Because of financial pressures, the Benedicts, in the fall of 1964, decided to add to [sic] a trailer park and facilities for a tent camp. A trailer park was laid out just to the northeast of county trunk B. In the fall of 1964, Roy Benedict bulldozed the hills in that area and installed sewer, water, and electric facilities for 18 trailers at a cost of approximately $8,000. In the spring of 1965 work was commenced on a campsite on a hill located to the south of the cottages and across the bay from the McKinnon property. The Benedicts have invested to date approximately $1,200 on this campsite, most of which was expended for grading.

In June of 1965, McKinnon wrote to Benedict stating:

> I have heard indirectly that you are making some fairly major changes in the operation of Bent's Camp. Although I do not know the exact nature of the changes, I am confident that you and Ev will bear in mind our agreement of August 31, 1960. . . . I enclose a photostatic copy.

When the McKinnons returned to Wisconsin in June of 1965, they became aware of the nature of the work done by Benedict and immediately commenced suit to enjoin defendants "from the acts done or being done and uses to be made or being made" of the property. The McKinnons relied not only on the agreement of August 31, 1960, but also alleged the violation of county zoning and trailer ordinances and alleged a trespass across a point of land, wholly surrounded by the Benedict property, which was owned by McKinnon.

After a trial before the court, the trial judge found for the plaintiffs in accordance with the demands of the complaint enjoining the defendants from further bulldozing or hill leveling and from conducting on the premises a trailer park or a mobile home camp. The renting of any portion of the land for trailers or campers was prohibited by the judgment, and the Benedicts were restrained from using the premises for any other purpose than as an American Plan summer resort until August 31, 1985. It is from this judgment the defendants appeal.

HEFFERNAN, JUSTICE.

The judgment provided not only that the Benedicts be restrained from using the property as a site for a trailer park or campsite, but it also provided that the premises were to be used for no other purpose than as an American Plan summer resort until 1985. The judgment not only makes these restrictions applicable to the Benedicts but also provides, that these restrictions "be fully enforceable against any subsequent purchasers of said land, until August 31, 1985." Even the respondents do not contend that this portion of the judgment is valid, for they acknowledge in their brief that this is a simple contract action between the original parties and concede that the case does not involve the enforcement of the covenants against any subsequent grantees of the Benedicts. We, therefore, may dispose of that portion of the judgment that would bind all subsequent purchasers as being in error and, to that extent, even though we were to find that the agreement was otherwise enforceable, in equity we would be obliged to reverse.

The question posed, then, is whether the agreement was enforceable against the Benedicts. No action at law has been commenced for damages by virtue of the breach of the restrictions; and, in fact, the plaintiffs in their complaint claim that they have no adequate remedy at law. We are thus not confronted with the question of damages that may result from the breach of this contract and confine ourselves solely to the right of the plaintiffs to invoke the equitable remedy of specific performance, in this case the enjoining of the defendants from the breach of the contract.

28 Am. Jur., Injunctions, sec. 35, pages 528, 529, points out that:

> Courts of equity exercise discretionary power in the granting or withhold-
> ing of their extraordinary remedies, and this is particularly true in a case
> where injunctive relief is sought. . . . The relief is not given as a matter of
> course for any and every act done or threatened to the person or property
> of another; its granting rests in the sound discretion of the court to be
> exercised in accordance with well-settled equitable principles and in the
> light of all the facts and circumstances in the case.

In *Maitland v. Twin City Aviation Corp.* (1949), 254 Wis. 541, 549, 37 N.W.2d 74, 78, we stated that an injunction "should not be granted where the inconveniences and hardships caused outweigh the benefits." It is frequently stated that an injunction will not be granted where to do so shocks the "conscience" of the court. These rules are equally applicable whether the right which the plaintiff seeks to enforce arises out of a conveyance, a use of property (nuisance) which would be detrimental to the plaintiff's interests, or whether it arises out of a simple contract.

Restatement, Contracts, sec. 367, page 665, "Effect of Unfairness, Hardship, Mistake and Inequitable Conduct," cites three bases for a court of equity refusing specific performance of a contract. They are:

> (a) The consideration for it is grossly inadequate or its terms are otherwise
> unfair, or
>
> (b) its enforcement will cause unreasonable or disproportionate hardship or
> loss to the defendant or to third persons, or
>
> (c) it was induced by some sharp practice, misrepresentation, or mistake.

These, of course, are ancient principles of equity and date back at least to *Smith v. Wood* (1860), 12 Wis. 382. The court in *Mulligan v. Albertz* (1899), 103 Wis. 140, 143, 144, 78 N.W. 1093, 1094, summarized policies of the Wisconsin court in this regard, and we consider these principles applicable to this case:

> An action for the specific performance of a contract is an application to
> the sound discretion of the court. It does not come as a matter of course.

The jurisdiction to compel it is not compulsory. "A court of equity must be satisfied that the claim for a deed is fair and just and reasonable, and the contract equal in all its parts, and founded on an adequate consideration, before it will interpose with this extraordinary assistance." [Citing cases.]

Coupled with the general equitable principle that contracts that are oppressive will not be enforced in equity is the principle of public policy that restrictions on the use of land "are not favored in the law" (*Mueller v. Schier* (1926), 189 Wis. 70, 82, 205 N.W. 912, 916), and that restrictions and prohibitions as to the use of real estate should be resolved, if a doubt exists, in favor of the free use of the property. *Stein v. Endres Home Builders, Inc.* (1938), 228 Wis. 620, 629, 280 N.W. 316.

The bargain between the McKinnons and the Benedicts has proved to be a harsh one indeed. If the terms of the agreement of August 31, 1960, are to be enforced literally, the Benedicts have for a period of twenty-five years stripped themselves of the right to make an optimum and lawful use of their property. The agreement provides that no improvements can be constructed closer to the McKinnon property than those buildings and improvements that were in existence in 1960. This limits any possible expansion to the precise lakeshore area occupied by the buildings of Bent's Camp on that date. While the restriction does not apply to the area beyond the road to the west of county trunk *B*, that area is at the farthest point of the property from the lake and is the least desirable for any resort or camp purposes. McKinnon by this agreement sought the maintenance of the exact status quo for a period of twenty-five years. Even though additional cottages of the type presently existing were desired, they could not under this agreement have been erected except in the narrowly defined area.

There was clear testimony that Benedict found difficulty in meeting his land-contract obligations, and his efforts to construct a campsite and trailer camp were motivated by the desire to put the resort on a more stable financial basis. While it is understandable that McKinnon may object to the erection of a trailer park and a campsite on adjacent property, nevertheless, they are legal and proper uses, assuming that they conform with the ordinances and statutes and do not constitute a nuisance; and any contract that seeks to prohibit them on a neighbor's property must be supported by consideration that has some relationship to the detriment to be sustained by the property owner whose uses are thus curtailed.

The great hardship sought to be imposed upon the Benedicts is apparent. What was the consideration in exchange for this deprivation of use? The only monetary consideration was the granting of a $5,000 loan, interest free, for a period of seven months. The value of this money for that period of time, if taken at the same interest rate as the 5 percent used on the balance of the land contract, is approximately $145; and it should be noted that this was not an unsecured loan, since McKinnon took a mortgage on the cottage property of the Benedicts in Michigan. In addition, McKinnon stated that he would "help you try" to reach a solution of the problem posed by Mrs. Vair's occupancy of one of the cottages on a fifty-year lease at $5 per year. His one attempt, as stated above, was a failure; and McKinnon's promise to generate business resulted in an occupancy by only one group for less than a week. For this pittance and these feeble attempts to help with the operational problems of the camp, the Benedicts have sacrificed their right to make lawful and reasonable use of their property.

In oral argument it was pointed out that the value of the $5,000 loan could not be measured in terms of the interest value of the money, since, without this advance, Benedict would have been unable to purchase the camp at all. To our mind, this is evidence of the fact that Benedict was not able to deal at arm's length with McKinnon, for his need for these funds was obviously so great that he was willing to enter into a contract that results in gross inequities. Lord Chancellor Northington said "necessitous men are not, truly speaking, free men." *Vernon v. Bethell* (1762), 2 Eden 110, 113.

We find that the inadequacy of consideration is so gross as to be unconscionable and a bar to the plaintiffs' invocation of the extraordinary equitable powers of the court.

While there is no doubt that there are benefits from this agreement to McKinnon, they are more than outweighed by the oppressive terms that would be imposed upon the Benedicts. McKinnon testified that he and his wife spend only the summer months on their property. Undoubtedly, these are the months when it is most important that there be no disruption of the natural beauty or the quiet and pleasant enjoyment of the property, nevertheless, there was testimony that the trailer camp could not be seen from the McKinnon home, nor could the campsite be seen during the summer months of the year, when the leaves were on the trees. Thus, the detriment of which the McKinnons complain, that would be cognizable in an equity action, is minimal.[7]

Considering all the factors — the inadequacy of the consideration, the small benefit that would be accorded the McKinnons, and the oppressive conditions imposed upon the Benedicts — we conclude that this contract failed to meet the test of reasonableness that is the *sine qua non* of the enforcement of rights in an action in equity.

5A Corbin, Contracts, sec. 1164, p. 219, points out that, although a contract is harsh, oppressive, and unconscionable, it may nevertheless be enforceable at law; but, in the discretion of the court, equitable remedies will not be enforced against one who suffers from such harshness and oppression.

A fair reading of the transcript indicates no sharp practice, dishonesty, or overreaching on the part of McKinnon. However, there was a wide disparity between the business experience of the parties. McKinnon was a man of stature in the legal field, an investment counselor, a former officer of a major corporation, and had held posts of responsibility with the United States government, while, insofar as the record shows, Benedict was a retail jeweler and a man of limited financial ability. He no doubt overvalued the promises of McKinnon to assist in getting the operation "well organized" and to solve the lease problem and to "generate business." These factors, in view of Benedict's financial inability to enter into an

---

[7] [1] McKinnon testified that the value of his property had depreciated in the amount of $50,000. That testimony was properly admissible, but its probative value was slight, especially since plaintiffs' expert real estate witness stated that he was unable to testify to the amount of the depreciated value.

arms-length transaction, may be explanatory of the reason for the agreement, but the agreement viewed even as of the time of its execution was unfair and based upon inadequate consideration. We, therefore, have no hesitancy in denying the plaintiffs the equitable remedy of injunction.

Judgment affirmed in part, reversed in part, and the cause is remanded to the trial court for further proceedings not inconsistent with this opinion.

[b]   The Meaning of Legal "Value"

SCHNELL v. NELL

Indiana Supreme Court

79 Am. Dec. 453 (1861)

PERKINS, J.

Action by J. B. Nell against Zacharias Schnell, upon the following instrument:

This agreement, entered into this 13th day of February, 1856, between Zach. Schnell, of Indianapolis, Marion county, State of Indiana, as party of the first part, and J. B. Nell, of the same place, Wendelin Lorenz, of Stilesville, Hendricks county, State of Indiana, and Donata Lorenz, of Frickinger, Grand Duchy of Baden, Germany, as parties of the second part, witnesseth: The said Zacharias Schnell agrees as follows: whereas his wife, Theresa Schnell, now deceased, has made a last will and testament, in which, among other provisions, it was ordained that every one of the above named second parties, should receive the sum of $200; and whereas the said provisions of the will must remain a nullity, for the reason that no property, real or personal, was in the possession of the said Theresa Schnell, deceased, in her own name, at the time of her death, and all property held by Zacharias and Theresa Schnell jointly, therefore reverts to her husband; and whereas the said Theresa Schnell has also been a dutiful and loving wife to the said Zach. Schnell, and has materially aided him in the acquisition of all property, real and personal, now possessed by him; for, and in consideration of all this, and the love and respect he bears to his wife; and, furthermore, in consideration of one cent, received by him of the second parties, he, the said Zach. Schnell, agrees to pay the above named sums of money to the parties of the second part, to wit: $200 to the said J. B. Nell; $200 to the said Wendelin Lorenz; and $200 to the said Donata Lorenz, in the following installments, viz., $200 in one year from the date of these presents; $200 in two years, and $200 in three years; to be divided between the parties in equal portions of $66 2 3 each year, or as they may agree, till each one has received his full sum of $200.

And the said parties of the second part, for, and in consideration of this, agree to pay the above named sum of money [one cent], and to deliver up to said Schnell, and abstain from collecting any real or supposed claims upon him or his estate, arising from the said last will and testament of the said Theresa Schnell, deceased.

In witness whereof, the said parties have, on the 13th day of February, 1856, set hereunto their hands and seals.

Zacharias Schnell, [SEAL]
J. B. Nell, [SEAL]
Wen. Lorenz [SEAL]

The complaint contained no averment of a consideration for the instrument, outside of those expressed in it; and did not aver that the one cent agreed to be paid, had been paid or tendered.

The defendant answered, that the instrument sued on was given for no consideration whatever. He further answered, that it was given for no consideration because his said wife, Theresa, at the time she made the will mentioned, and at the time of her death, owned, neither separately, nor jointly with her husband, or any one else (except so far as the law gave her an interest in her husband's property), any property, real or personal &c.

The will is copied into the record, but need not be into this opinion.

The Court sustained a demurrer to these answers, evidently on the ground that they were regarded as contradicting the instrument sued on, which particularly set out the considerations upon which it was executed. But the instrument is latently ambiguous on this point. *See* Ind. Dig., p. 110.

The case turned below, and must turn here, upon the question whether the instrument sued on does express a consideration sufficient to give it legal obligation, as against Zacharias Schnell. It specifies three distinct considerations for his promise to pay $600:

1. A promise, on the part of the plaintiffs, to pay him one cent.

2. The love and affection he bore his deceased wife, and the fact that she had done her part, as his wife, in the acquisition of property.

3. The fact that she had expressed her desire, in the form of an inoperative will, that the persons named therein should have the sums of money specified.

The consideration of one cent will not support the promise of Schnell. It is true, that as a general proposition, inadequacy of consideration will not vitiate an agreement. *Baker v. Roberts*, 14 Ind. 552. But this doctrine does not apply to a mere exchange of sums of money, of coin, whose value is exactly fixed, but to the exchange of something of, in itself, indeterminate value, for money, or, perhaps, for some other thing of indeterminate value. In this case, had the one cent mentioned, been some particular one cent, a family piece, or ancient, remarkable coin, possessing an indeterminate value, extrinsic from its simple money value, a different view might be taken. As it is, the mere promise to pay six hundred dollars for one cent, even had the portion of that cent due from the plaintiff been tendered, is an unconscionable contract, void, at first blush, upon its face, if it be regarded as an earnest one. *Hardesty v. Smith*, 3 Ind. 39. The consideration of one cent is, plainly, in this case, merely nominal, and intended to be so. As the will and testament of Schnell's wife imposed no legal obligation upon him to discharge her bequests out of his property, and as she had none of her own, his promise to discharge them was not legally binding upon him, on that ground. A moral consideration, only, will not support a promise. Ind. Dig., p. 13. And for the same reason, a valid consideration for his promise can not be found in the fact of a compromise of a disputed claim; for where such claim is legally groundless, a promise upon a compromise of it, or of a suit upon it, is not legally binding. *Spahr v. Hollingshead*, 8 Blackf. 415. There was no mistake of law or fact in this case, as the agreement admits the will inoperative and void. The promise was simply one to make a gift. The past services of his wife, and the love and affection he had borne her, are objectionable as legal considerations for Schnell's promise on two grounds: 1. They are past considerations. Ind. Dig., p. 13. 2. The fact that Schnell loved his wife, and that she had been industrious, constituted no consideration for his promise to pay J. B. Nell, and the Lorenzes, a sum of money. Whether, if his wife, in her lifetime, had made a bargain with Schnell, that, in consideration of his promising to pay, after her death, to the persons named, a sum of money, she would be industrious, and worthy of his affection, such a promise would have been valid and consistent with public policy, we need not decide. Nor is the fact that Schnell now venerates the memory of his deceased wife, a legal consideration for a promise to pay any third person money.

The instrument sued on, interpreted in the light of the facts alleged in the second paragraph of the answer, will not support an action. The demurrer to the answer should have been overruled. *See Stevenson v. Druley*, 4 Ind. 519. *Per Curiam*. The judgment is reversed, with costs. Cause remanded.

NOTE

The case was supported by Section 76(c) of the First Restatement of Contracts which stated that consideration is not sufficient if it is "the transfer of money or fungible goods as consideration for a promise to transfer at the same time and place a larger amount of money or goods of the same quality." To construe this rule as an "exception" to the principle that courts of law will not inquire into the adequacy of consideration, however, has no redeeming analytical value. The court states that the promise to pay six hundred dollars in exchange for one cent — any cent, not a rare coin — is "an unconscionable contract, void at first blush." "Unconscionable" is a vague term defying precise definition as will be seen in a later chapter. A "void contract" is not a contract.

The court, however, then states, "The consideration of one cent is, plainly, in this case, merely nominal, and intended to be so." "Nominal" means "in name only." Thus, "nominal consideration" is not consideration. Again, however, the question is why not? Even one cent has "value." Section 79, comment d, to the RESTATEMENT (SECOND) OF CONTRACTS includes Illustration 5 which is based on the principal case. Comment d is captioned, "Pretended Exchange" and states that "Disparity in value . . . sometimes indicates that the purported consideration was not in fact bargained for but was a mere formality or pretense. Such 'sham' or nominal consideration does not satisfy the requirements of § 71 which describes the requirements for consideration. The first requirement is found in § 71(a): "To constitute consideration, a performance or a return promise must be bargained for."

Does this suggest that the determination of "legal value" has little or nothing to do with actual or objective value. Rather, the only question is whether the promisor in an alleged contract had a genuine desire (not necessarily the only desire) to receive whatever the other party was surrendering in exchange for the promise? In the principal case the alleged consideration of one cent had objective (market) value, but the court concluded that the promisor did not seek the one cent in *exchange* for his promise to pay $600. Is it, therefore, fair to say that the so-called element of "legal value" in defining consideration is unnecessary since the surrender of any money, property or right will be consideration if it is what the promisor seeks in exchange for her promise and, if she is not genuinely seeking it, what may be listed as "consideration" is a lie?

[4]   Nominal Consideration — Bargained-for-Exchange

THOMAS v. THOMAS
Queen's Bench
114 Eng. Rep. 330 (1842)

At the trial, before Coltman J., at the Glamorganshire Lent Assizes, 1841, it appeared that John Thomas, the deceased husband of the plaintiff, at the time of his death, in 1837, was possessed of a row of seven dwelling houses in Merthyr Tidvil, in one of which, being the dwelling house in question, he was himself residing; and that by his will he appointed his brother Samuel Thomas (since deceased) and the defendant executors thereof, to take possession of all his houses, &c., subject to certain payments in the will mentioned, among which were certain charges in money for the benefit of the plaintiff. In the evening before the day of his death, he expressed orally a wish to make some further provision for his wife; and on the following morning he declared orally, in the presence of two witnesses, that it was his will that his wife should have either the house in which he lived and all that it contained, or an additional sum of £ 100 instead thereof.

This declaration being shortly afterwards brought to the knowledge of Samuel Thomas and the defendant, the executors and residuary legatees, they consented to carry the intentions of the testator so expressed into effect; and, after the lapse of a few days, they and the plaintiff executed the agreement declared upon; which, after stating the parties, and briefly reciting the will, proceeded as follows.

"And, whereas the said testator, shortly before his death, declared, in the presence of several witnesses, that he was desirous his said wife should have and enjoy during her life, or so long as she should continue his widow, all and singular the dwelling house," &c., "or £ 100 out of his personal estate," in addition to the respective legacies and bequests given her in and by his said will; "but such declaration and desire was not reduced to writing in the lifetime of the said John Thomas and read over to him; but the said Samuel Thomas and Benjamin Thomas are fully convinced and satisfied that such was the desire of the said testator, and are willing and desirous that such intention should be carried into full effect: now these presents witness, and it is hereby agreed and declared by and between the parties, that, in consideration of such desire and of the premises," the executors would convey the dwelling house, &c. to the plaintiff and her assigns during her life, or for so long a time as she should continue a widow and unmarried: "provided nevertheless, and it is hereby further agreed and declared, that the said Eleanor Thomas, or her assigns, shall and will, at all times during which she shall have possession of the said dwelling house, &c., pay to the said Samuel Thomas and Benjamin Thomas, their executors, &c., the sum of £ 1 yearly towards the ground rent payable in respect of the said dwelling house and other premises thereto adjoining, and shall and will keep the said dwelling house and premises in good and tenantable repair:" with other provisions not affecting the questions in this case.

The plaintiff was left in possession of the dwelling house and premises for some time: but the defendant, after the death of his co-executor, refused to execute a conveyance tendered to him for execution pursuant to the agreement, and, shortly before the trial, brought an ejectment, under which he turned the plaintiff out of possession. It was objected for the defendant that, a part of the consideration proved being omitted in the declaration, there was a fatal variance. The learned Judge overruled the objection, reserving leave to move to enter a nonsuit. Ultimately a verdict was found for the plaintiff on all the issues; and, in Easter term last a rule nisi was obtained pursuant to the leave reserved.

LORD DENMAN C.J.

There is nothing in this case but a great deal of ingenuity, and a little wilful blindness to the actual terms of the instrument itself. There is nothing whatever to shew that the ground rent was payable to a superior landlord; and the stipulation for the payment of it is not a mere proviso, but an express agreement. (His Lordship here read the proviso.) This is in terms an express agreement, and shows a sufficient legal consideration quite independent of the moral feeling which disposed the executors to enter into such a contract. Mr. Williams's definition of consideration is too large: the word causa in the passage referred to means one which confers what the law considers a benefit on the party. Then the obligation to repair is one which might impose charges heavier than the value of the life estate.

PATTESON J.

It would be giving to causa too large a construction if we were to adopt the view urged for the defendant: it would be confounding consideration with motive. Motive is not the same thing with consideration. Consideration means something which is of some value in the eye of the law, moving from the plaintiff: it may be some benefit to the plaintiff, or some detriment to the defendant; but at all events it must be moving from the plaintiff. Now that which is suggested as the consideration here, a pious respect for the wishes of the testator, does not in any way move from the plaintiff; it moves from the testator; therefore, legally speaking, it forms no part of the consideration. Then it is said that, if that be so, there is no consideration at all, it is a mere voluntary gift: but when we look at the agreement we find that this is not a mere proviso that the donee shall take the gift with the burthens; but it is an express agreement to pay what seems to be a fresh apportionment of a ground rent, and which is made payable not to a superior landlord but to the executors. So that this rent is clearly not something incident to the assignment of the house; for in that case, instead of being payable to the executors, it would have been payable to the landlord. Then as to the repairs: these houses may very possibly be held under a lease containing covenants to repair; but we know nothing about it: for any thing that appears, the liability to repair is first created by this instrument. The proviso certainly struck me at first as Mr. Williams put it, that the rent and repairs were merely attached to the gift by the donors; and, had the instrument been executed by the donors only, there might have been some ground for that construction; but the fact is not so. Then it is suggested that this would be held to be a mere voluntary conveyance as against a subsequent purchaser for value: possibly that might be so: but suppose it would: the plaintiff contracts to take it, and does take it, whatever it is, for better for worse: perhaps a bona fide purchase for a valuable consideration might override it; but that cannot be helped.

COLERIDGE J.

The concessions made in the course of the argument have, in fact, disposed of the case. It is conceded that mere motive need not be stated: and we are not obliged to look for the legal consideration in any particular part of the instrument, merely because the consideration is usually stated in some particular part: *ut res magis valeat*, we may look to any part. In this instrument, in the part where it is usual to state the consideration, nothing certainly is expressed but a wish to fulfill the intentions of the testator: but in another part we find an express agreement to pay an annual sum for a particular purpose; and also a distinct agreement to repair. If these had occurred in the first part of the instrument, it could hardly have been argued that the declaration was not well drawn, and supported by the evidence. As to the suggestion of this being a voluntary conveyance, my impression is that this payment of £ 1 annually is more than a good consideration: it is a valuable consideration: it is clearly a thing newly created, and not part of the old ground rent. *Rule discharged.*

NOTE

RESTATEMENT (SECOND) OF CONTRACTS § 81 (1981):

(1) The fact that what is bargained for does not of itself induce the making of a promise does not prevent it from being consideration for the promise.

(2) The fact that a promise does not of itself induce a performance or return promise does not prevent the performance or return promise from being consideration for the promise.

Comment b. Immateriality of motive or cause. This Section makes explicit a limitation on the requirement that consideration be bargained for. Even in the typical commercial bargain, the promisor may have more than one motive, and the person furnishing the consideration need not inquire into the promisor's motives. Unless both parties know that the purported consideration is mere pretense, it is immaterial that the promisor's desire for the consideration is incidental to other objectives and even that the other party knows this to be so. . . . Subsection (2) states a similar rule with respect to the motives of the promisee.

RESTATEMENT (FIRST) OF CONTRACTS § 84, Illustration 1 (1932):

1. *A* wishes to make a binding promise to his son *B* to convey to *B* Blackacre, which is worth $5000. Being advised that a gratuitous promise is not binding, *A* writes to *B* an offer to sell Blackacre for $1. *B* accepts. *B*'s promise to pay $1 is sufficient consideration.

RESTATEMENT (SECOND) OF CONTRACTS § 71, Illustration 5 (1981):

5. *A* desires to make a binding promise to give $1000 to his son *B*. Being advised that a gratuitous promise is not binding, *A* offers to buy from *B* for $1000 a book worth less than $1. *B* accepts the offer knowing that the purchase of the book is a mere pretense. There is no consideration for *A*'s promise to pay $1000.

NOTE ON O.W. HOLMES AND "BARGAINED-FOR-EXCHANGE"

Justice Holmes is particularly well known for his insistence that the legal value element without the bargained-for-exchange element is insufficient to find consideration. In Chapter 1, we considered his memorable statement made in *Wisconsin & Mich. Ry. v. Powers*, 191 U.S. 379, 386 (1903):

> No matter what the actual motive may have been, by the express or implied terms of the supposed contract, the promise and the consideration must purport to be the motive each for the other, in whole or at least in part. It is not enough that the promise induces the detriment or that the detriment induces the promise, if the other half is wanting.

In his famous work, *The Common Law* (1881), Holmes had earlier stated his strong view that bargained-for-exchange is "reciprocal conventional inducement." *Id.* at 230. There is a view that Holmes created the bargain theory from whole cloth. G. GILMORE, THE DEATH OF CONTRACT, 17–21 (1974). The evidence, however, is compelling that, as early as the sixteenth century, English courts had discovered the central device for determining which promises were enforceable: "[E]ach party had in fact desired some act or abstention of the other in return for which he had agreed to perform his own." J. DAWSON, GIFTS AND PROMISES 203 (1980). Another scholar suggests that the concept of "bargain" is found in 14th and 15th century English cases. K. SUTTON, CONSIDERATION RECONSIDERED 6, 13–18 (1974). For a critical analysis of the Gilmore view, see Speidel, *An Essay on the Reported Death and Continued Vitality of Contract*, 27 STAN. L. REV. 1161 (1975).

PROBLEMS

(1) George and Alice Simon were happily married. One day, George phoned his wife to tell her that if she would meet him for lunch he would then take her to a nearby jewelry store and buy her a diamond necklace that she had admired for some time. Alice came to lunch but, afterward, the couple argued and George refused to purchase the necklace. Does Alice have a cause of action against George? Apply the Holmes formula.

(2)   Assume that George and Alice were estranged. George had moved away and all of his attempts to communicate with Alice failed. Alice had filed for divorce. George left a message on Alice's answering machine telling her that if she would meet him for lunch and talk with him, he would take her to the nearby jeweler's and purchase the diamond necklace she admired. Alice came to lunch and, in a civilized fashion, conversed with George for over an hour. George then refused to purchase the necklace. Does Alice have any cause of action against George? Apply the Holmes formula.

[5]   Promise of "Permanent" Employment — "Terminable at Will"

FISHER v. JACKSON
Connecticut Supreme Court
118 A.2d 316 (1955)

WYNNE, JUDGE.

The plaintiff instituted this action to recover damages for the breach of an oral agreement of employment. The defendant has appealed from the judgment rendered upon a plaintiff's verdict. The questions presented are whether the court was in error in denying the defendant's motion to set the verdict aside on the ground that it is not supported on the issue of liability, and in denying the defendant's motion for judgment notwithstanding the verdict.

The substituted complaint alleged that the defendant, through his authorized agent, induced the plaintiff to give up his employment with a firm of bakers, where he was making $50 per week, and to enter upon employment as a reporter, for $40 per week, under an oral contract that the employment would be for the life of the plaintiff or until he was physically disabled for work, with a yearly increase in salary of $5 per week. The defendant's contention is that there was no evidence that the parties had agreed upon such a contract. The defendant's claim is that the job under discussion was a permanent one rather than for a definite term and was terminable at will by either party.

In the absence of a consideration in addition to the rendering of services incident to the employment, an agreement for a permanent employment is no more than an indefinite general hiring, terminable at the will of either party without liability to the other.

The plaintiff was hired by the defendant's managing editor in January, 1944, and went to work as a reporter for the New Haven Register, a newspaper owned by the defendant. He was discharged on or about January 7, 1949. The contract between the parties began with a notice which was put in a trade magazine by the defendant, just prior to the admitted hiring of the plaintiff. That advertisement set forth that a "permanent position" as a reporter awaited an "all-around male newsman with experience on several beats and educational background that [would stand] up in a University city." The plaintiff wrote a letter in response to the advertisement and as a result was interviewed by the defendant's managing editor for about ten minutes and was thereafter hired. Whether or not the plaintiff was an "all-around newsman" with experience on several beats and with an educational background, however nebulous, that would stand up in a university city nowhere appears. The managing editor, who was the only other party to the interview was deceased at the time of the trial. The plaintiff, in his letter seeking an interview, had written that he was looking for a connection which, "in the event my services are satisfactory, will prove permanent." So it must be quite apparent that the significant thought expressed was in his mind during his brief interview with the defendant's managing editor. It seems clear to us that the negotiations amounted to nothing more than the hiring of a reporter for a job which was permanent in the sense that it was not a mere temporary place. The hiring was indefinite as to time and terminable by either party at his will.

There is no occasion to discuss at length the claim advanced by the plaintiff that special consideration moved to the defendant because the plaintiff gave up his job with the bakery firm. The plaintiff did no more than give up other activities and interests in order to enter into the service of the defendant. The mere giving up of a job by one who decides to accept a contract for alleged life employment is but an incident necessary on his part to place himself in a position to accept and perform the contract; it is not consideration for a contract of life employment . . . .

The plaintiff argues that he suffered a detriment by giving up his job. To constitute sufficient consideration for a promise, an act or promise not only must be a detriment to the promisee but must be bargained for and given in exchange for the promise . . . . In the present case, the plaintiff's giving up of his job at the bakery was not something for which the defendant bargained in exchange for his promise of permanent employment. Nowhere in the plaintiff's testimony does it appear that the defendant's agent even suggested that the plaintiff give up the job he had with the bakery firm, much less that the agent induced him to do so. It would thus appear that there was not even a semblance of a claim that the giving up of the plaintiff's job was consideration for any promise that may have been made by the defendant's agent.

There is error, the judgment is set aside and the case is remanded with direction to render judgment for the defendant notwithstanding the verdict.

QUESTIONS

When the plaintiff accepted the newspaper position, did he not rely to his detriment by giving up his job at the bakery? If so, why did this detriment not constitute consideration? Suppose the newspaper had specifically requested the plaintiff to quit the bakery job in order to join the newspaper?

When the plaintiff left the bakery to join the newspaper, was he not reasonable in assuming that the position would be "permanent" since this is what the newspaper advertisement stated? Why does the court construe such "permanent position" contracts to be terminable at will?

ANDERSON v. DOUGLAS & LOMASON CO.
Iowa Supreme Court
540 N.W.2d 277 (1995)

TERNUS, J.

Defendant, Douglas & Lomason Company (DLC), discharged plaintiff, Terry Anderson, for taking a box of pencils. Anderson responded with a breach-of-contract action claiming DLC failed to follow progressive discipline policies contained in the employee handbook. The district court granted DLC's motion for summary judgment, which argued, in part, that the handbook did not constitute a contract. Anderson appealed.

On Anderson's first day of work at DLC he attended a six hour orientation session for new employees. He was informed that DLC had a progressive discipline policy and he was given a fifty-three page employee handbook which included these policies. Anderson read only the first few pages of the handbook; he admits he never read the provisions on progressive discipline.

DLC fired Anderson after three years of employment. His termination was based on an incident which occurred as he was leaving the plant one day. Company personnel stopped his pickup and asked to search it. Anderson gave permission and the workers found a box of company pencils. As a result, they also asked to search his home and garage. Anderson consented and a subsequent search revealed no company property. However, that same day, DLC asked Anderson to resign. He refused and was immediately fired.

Anderson responded by filing this breach-of-contract action against DLC. He claims DLC did not follow the progressive discipline policies outlined in its handbook for unauthorized possession of company property. These progressive discipline policies require a written warning for the first offense, a three-day suspension without pay for the second offense, and discharge for the third offense. Because this was not Anderson's third offense, he claims DLC could not fire him.

DLC filed a motion for summary judgment claiming the handbook did not constitute a contract and therefore Anderson was employed at-will. First, DLC contended the handbook was never communicated to or accepted by Anderson because he did not read it. Second, DLC argued the handbook was not definite enough to constitute an offer. DLC cited two reasons for its vagueness claim: the handbook contains no written guarantees that discharge will occur only for cause or under certain conditions — the rules are mere guidance; and the manual contains a written disclaimer. The district court granted the employer's summary judgment motion without explanation in a calendar entry.

The central issue presented by this dispute is whether DLC's issuance of a handbook created an employment contract. This question arises because Iowa employment relationships are presumed to be at-will: In the absence of a valid employment contract either party may terminate the relationship without consequence. Indeed, the doctrine of employment at-will is merely a gap-filler, a judicially created presumption utilized when parties to an employment contract are silent as to duration. To understand our interpretation of employment contracts, particularly the nexus between the at-will doctrine and employee handbooks, we provide a brief overview.

The at-will presumption originated in English seasonal servant contract law. *See* Jay M. Feinman, *The Development of the Employment at Will Rule*, 20 AM. J. LEGAL HIST. 118, 118 (1976) (hereinafter "Feinman Article"). When parties remained silent as to the duration of service, the English courts filled the gap by presuming a certain duration and imposing a notice-of-termination requirement. 1 WILLIAM BLACKSTONE, COMMENTARIES ON THE LAWS OF ENGLAND 413 (U. Chi. Press 1979) ("If the hiring be general without any particular time limited, the law construes it to be a hiring for a year. . . . [Neither side can break the contract] without a quarter's warning.") (hereinafter "BLACKSTONE"). The judicially created doctrine complemented statutes imposing a ban on leaving one's position or firing a worker before the end of the term and reflected the judiciary's concern for fairness between masters and seasonal servants. Feinman Article, 20 AM. J. LEGAL HIST. at 120; see BLACKSTONE, at 413 (relationship continues "throughout all the revolutions of the respective seasons; as well as when there is work to be done, as when there is not").

The doctrine has never been static. As additional statutes were promulgated and the variety of employment situations far removed from the domestic environment increased, the English judiciary varied the amount of notice in accordance with the type of employment. Feinman Article, 20 AM. J. LEGAL HIST. at 121–22. "English law thus attempted to adapt to changing conditions and new situations. . . ." *Id.* at 121.

American courts relied heavily upon English precedent until the 1870s, when changing economic and social conditions prompted a dissolution of earlier law: the presumption of yearly hiring was seen as anachronistic and the concept of reasonable notice was disavowed. *Id.* at 125; cf. Richard J. Pratt, Comment, *Unilateral Modification of Employment Handbooks: Further Encroachments On the Employment-At-Will Doctrine*, 139 U. PA. L. REV. 197, 198–99 (1990) (hereinafter "Pratt Article"); Marla J. Weinstein, Comment, *The Limitations of Judicial Innovation: A Case Study of Wrongful Dismissal Litigation in Canada and the United States*, 14 COMP. LAB. L.J. 478 (1993) (comparing Canadian and American at-will jurisprudence; Canada retains the notice requirement). At this juncture, a new approach was suggested that changed the doctrine to a presumption of at-will employment:

> With us the rule is inflexible, that a general or indefinite hiring is prima facie a hiring at will, and if the servant seeks to make it out a yearly hiring, the burden is upon him to establish it by proof . . . . It is an indefinite hiring and is determinable at the will of either party, and in this respect there is no distinction between domestic and other servants. H.G. Wood, A Treatise on the Law of Master & Servant § 134, at 272 (1877). As the English presumption was a reflection of the economic and societal conditions in early Britain, Wood's rule was an outgrowth of prevailing American thought: ascendancy of freedom of contract, a reflection of the usual duration of employment contracts, and support for the development of advanced capitalism. Feinman Article, 20 AM. J. LEGAL HIST. at 130–31; *see*

also Pratt Article, 139 U. PA. L. REV. at 199–201.

Wood's version of employment at will quickly spread and was universally adopted. Despite the universal acceptance of the employment-at-will doctrine, legislatures and courts have restricted its application. For example, federal labor law gave rise to union contracts that include just cause discharge provisions. Michael J. Phillips, *Disclaimers of Wrongful Discharge Liability: Time for a Crackdown*, 70 WASH. U.L.Q. 1131, 1134 (1992). Similarly, public employees are protected from arbitrary dismissal under civil service statutes.

Reflecting the perceived need to protect employees from the harshness of the at-will doctrine, courts began to erode the doctrine with exceptions [that] generally fell within three categories: (1) discharges in violation of public policy, (2) discharges in violation of employee handbooks constituting a unilateral contract, and (3) discharges in violation of a covenant of good faith and fair dealing. Stephen F. Befort, *Employee Handbooks & the Legal Effect of Disclaimers*, 13 INDUS. REL. L.J. 326, 333–34 (1991/1992) (hereinafter "Befort Article"). However, Iowa's strong support of the at-will presumption is demonstrated by our reluctance to undermine the rule with exemptions. We have carved out only two narrow deviations: tort liability when a discharge is in clear violation of a "well-recognized and defined public policy of the State," *Springer v. Weeks & Leo Co.*, 429 N.W.2d 558, 560 (Iowa 1988), and employee handbooks that meet the requirements for a unilateral contract, *French v. Foods, Inc.*, 495 N.W.2d 768, 769–71 (Iowa 1993). We have consistently rejected recognition of a covenant of good faith and fair dealing. *E.g., id.* at 771; *Fogel*, 446 N.W.2d at 456–57.

Our prior handbook decisions concerned only "for-cause" provisions. However, we explicitly left room for future expansion: an employment handbook may guarantee an employee that discharge will occur "only for cause or under certain conditions." *French Foods*, 495 N.W.2d at 770; accord *Hunter*, 481 N.W.2d at 513; *Fogel*, 446 N.W.2d at 455. We now hold "or under certain conditions" to include progressive disciplinary procedures. Such provisions are enforceable if they are part of an employment contract. *Cf. Vaughn v. AG Processing, Inc.*, 459 N.W.2d 627, 639 (Iowa 1990) ("We have recognized that written personnel policies providing terms and procedures to be followed when discharging an employee would be considered part of an at-will employee's employment contract.") (emphasis added); *Hamilton v. First Baptist Elderly Hous. Found.*, 436 N.W.2d 336, 340–41 (Iowa 1989) (considering whether personnel policies are part of the employment contract). We must now determine whether Anderson's handbook constitutes an enforceable contract. If it does not, we presume the parties intended a contract at will.

When considering whether a handbook creates a contract we utilize unilateral contract theory. *McBride v. City of Sioux City*, 444 N.W.2d 85, 90–91 (Iowa 1989). A unilateral contract consists of an offeror making a promise and an offeree rendering some performance as acceptance. *See Hunter*, 481 N.W.2d at 503; *see also* 1 E. ALLAN FARNSWORTH, FARNSWORTH ON CONTRACTS § 3.4, at 165 (1990) (hereinafter "FARNSWORTH"). An employee handbook is a unilateral contract when three elements are present: (1) the handbook is sufficiently definite in its terms to create an offer; (2) the handbook is communicated to and accepted by the employee so as to constitute acceptance; and (3) the employee provides consideration. *McBride*, 444 N.W.2d at 91.

As with any contract, the party who seeks recovery on the basis of a unilateral contract has the burden to prove the existence of a contract. *Hawkeye Land Co. v. Iowa Power & Light Co.*, 497 N.W.2d 480, 486 (Iowa Ct. App. 1993). Therefore, Anderson has the burden to prove DLC's handbook created an enforceable contract.

[Here, the court notes that Anderson read only a few pages of the employee manual; he did not read the provisions on progressive discipline. Thus, DLC argued that there was no acceptance since a party must be aware of an offer to have a power of acceptance. Noting a very "narrow exception" to that general principle, the court held that Anderson's receipt of the handbook was sufficient communication to make him an offeree. The court also recognized the traditional view in unilateral contract that the offeree's performance must have been induced by the promise made. Where, however, a contract is based upon an employee handbook distributed to all employees, the court recognized that the contract is not an individually negotiated agreement; it is a standardized agreement between the employer and a class of employees. Moreover, "A standardized agreement 'is interpreted wherever reasonable as treating alike all those similarly situated, without regard to their knowledge or understanding of the standard terms of the writing.' " *Kinoshita v. Canadian P. Airlines, Ltd.*, 68 Haw. 594, 724 P.2d 110, 116–17 (Haw.1986) (*quoting* RESTATEMENT (SECOND) OF CONTRACTS § 211(2) (1981)). Thus, the court concluded,]

[We hold it unnecessary that the particular employee seeking to enforce a promise made in an employee manual have knowledge of the promise. Although this holding is a departure from traditional 'bargain-theory' contract analysis, we think it produces "the salutary result that all employees, those who read the handbook and those who did not, are treated alike." [The court found support for this view in other jurisdictions].

We now consider whether DLC's handbook constituted an offer to Anderson to utilize progressive disciplinary procedures. We believe this aspect of the analysis should be conducted according to traditional contract theory. All contracts must contain mutual assent; mode of assent is termed offer and acceptance. An offer is a "manifestation of willingness to enter into a bargain, so made as to justify another person in understanding that his assent to that bargain is invited and will conclude it." RESTATEMENT (SECOND) OF CONTRACTS § 24 (1981).

We look for the existence of an offer objectively — not subjectively. JUDGE LEARNED HAND explained this rule:

> A contract has, strictly speaking, nothing to do with the personal, or individual intent of the parties. A contract is an obligation attached by the mere force of law to certain acts of the parties, usually words, which ordinarily accompany and represent a known intent. If, however, it were proved by twenty bishops that either party, when he used the words, intended something else than the usual meaning which the law imposes upon them, he would still be held. . . . *Hotchkiss v. National City Bank*, 200 F. 287, 293 (S.D.N.Y. 1911).

When objectively examining the handbook to determine intent to create an offer, we look for terms with precise meaning that provide certainty of performance. This is a definiteness inquiry: if an offer is indefinite there is no intent to be bound. *See Architectural Metal Sys., Inc.*, 58 F.3d at 1229 ("A lack of essential detail would negate such a belief, since the sender could not reasonably be expected to empower the recipient to bind him to a contract of unknown terms . . . . The recipient of a hopelessly vague offer should know that it was not intended to be an offer that could be made legally enforceable by being accepted.").

DLC asserts the handbook was not definite enough to constitute an offer for two reasons: It claims there are no guarantees that the company will always follow the progressive discipline procedures, and the handbook includes a written disclaimer that expressly states there is no intent to create a contract. Therefore, DLC contends no offer existed for Anderson to accept.

When considering whether a handbook is objectively definite to create a contract we consider its language and context. Our analysis of case law reveals three factors to guide this highly fact-intensive inquiry: (1) Is the handbook in general and the progressive disciplinary procedures in particular mere guidelines or a statement of policy, or are they directives? (2) Is the language of the disciplinary procedures detailed and definite or general and vague? We ask these questions to determine whether an employee is reasonably justified in understanding a commitment has been made.

Here, the text of the disciplinary procedures contains language of command: "The following action is prohibited, and the penalties for violation of these Shop Rules shall be as follows [progressive discipline steps are then listed]." (Emphasis added.) However, the introduction to the section of the handbook containing the disciplinary procedures states twice that the rules "have been designed for the information and guidance of all employees." (Emphasis added.) Second, the procedures themselves are fairly specific. There are four categories that describe in detail the offenses included in each category. In addition, the discipline for each category is also specific: for unauthorized possession of company property, the first offense requires a written warning, the second offense a three day unpaid suspension and the third offense results in discharge. Finally, DLC retained the power to alter the procedures at will. We need not decide whether these factors alone result in a sufficiently definite offer, however, because we must also consider the effect of DLC's disclaimer.

A disclaimer can prevent the formation of a contract by clarifying the intent of the employer not to make an offer. For example, many jurisdictions require the disclaimer be "clear and conspicuous" to be enforceable and negate any contractual relationship between an employer and employee. While we have never considered whether a disclaimer in an employee handbook must be clear and conspicuous, our court of appeals has implicitly endorsed a conspicuous requirement by holding a disclaimer "prominently displayed in the first page" of a handbook prevented the formation of a contract. *Palmer v. Women's Christian Ass'n*, 485 N.W.2d 93, 95–96 (Iowa Ct. App. 1992).

The requirement that a disclaimer be conspicuous has given rise to much litigation [discussing cases suggesting considerable uncertainty as to whether a disclaimer in an employee handbook was conspicuous.] We think such uncertainty is unnecessary. A disclaimer should be considered in the same manner as any other language in the handbook to ascertain its impact on our search for the employer's intent. Therefore, we reject any special requirements for disclaimers; we simply examine the language and context of the disclaimer to decide whether a reasonable employee, reading the disclaimer, would understand it to mean that the employer has not assented to be bound by the handbook's provisions.

Similar to our consideration of handbook language in general, we believe two factors guide our inquiry. First, is the disclaimer clear in its terms: does the disclaimer state that the handbook does not create any rights, or does not alter the at-will employment status? Second, is the coverage of the disclaimer unambiguous: what is the scope of its applicability? Here the disclaimer appears on page fifty-three, the last page of the handbook, two inches below the preceding paragraph:

> This Employee Handbook is not intended to create any contractual rights in favor of you or the Company. The Company reserves the right to change the terms of this handbook at any time.

When examining the disclaimer we first consider the text employed. In no uncertain terms DLC's disclaimer states the handbook *"is not intended to create any contractual rights."* (Emphasis added.) We believe DLC's disclaimer is clear in its disavowal of any intent to create a contract.

Second, we examine the scope of the disclaimer. There is nothing about the location of DLC's disclaimer or the language used to suggest that the disclaimer does not apply to the progressive discipline policies. The disclaimer is found in the handbook itself and unequivocally applies to the entire employee handbook.

We think a reasonable person reading the handbook could not believe that DLC has assented to be bound to the provisions contained in the manual. Thus, we hold DLC's handbook is not sufficiently definite to constitute a valid offer. We hold as a matter of law no contract existed between Anderson and DLC. Anderson was employed at-will. Therefore, the trial court correctly granted summary judgment to DLC. *Affirmed.*

NOTES

(1)   In the last quarter of the 20th century, there was a startling growth in the case law concerning the question in the principal case, i.e., whether an employee handbook, manual or policy statement of the employer concerning employees becomes part of the employment contract, precluding discharge absent the due process set forth in such publication or absent "good cause" if that is set forth in the publication. While there is a split of authority in this area, most of the courts considering the question have taken a position similar or identical to the analyses set forth in the principal case, i.e., the unilateral contract and consideration analyses. *See Duldulao v. Saint Mary of Nazareth Hosp.*, 115 Ill. 2d 482, 505 N.E.2d 314 (1987); *Pine River State Bank v. Mettille*, 333 N.W.2d 622 (Minn. 1983).

(2)   There are numerous statutory and judicial restrictions protecting employees from arbitrary discharge or from discharge against public policy. The "public policy" restrictions are myriad. Of course, discharge for reasons of race, color, religion, sex or national origin is prohibited by federal statute (42 U.S.C. § 2000(e) — 2(a)(1)). Similarly, discharge because of age is prohibited by 29 U.S.C. § 623(a)(1). A discharge of an employee for responding to jury service is prohibited, *Reuther v. Fowler & Williams, Inc.*, 255 Pa. Super. 28, 386 A.2d 119 (1978), and an employee may not be discharged for refusing to take a polygraph examination in violation of a state statute, *Perks v. Firestone Tire & Rubber Co.*, 611 F.2d 1363 (3d Cir. 1979). Discharge because of union activities is prohibited by 29 U.S.C. § 158(a)(3). This is not an exhaustive list of the statutory and judicial bases for prohibiting discharge against public policy. The "terminable-at-will" policy in private employment, however, remains. "The legal protection of employee interests in job security is the exception, rather than the rule, in this state. In the absence of contractual agreements to the contrary, . . . and of unlawful reasons for discharge such as sex or race discrimination, private employees are terminable at the will of their employers." *State Employee's Ass'n v. Department of Mental Health*, 365 N. W. 2d 93, 96 (Mich. 1985).

(3)   In *Spriggs v. Diamond Auto Glass*, 165 F.3d 1015 (4th Cir. 1999), the plaintiff, an African-American, brought an action for "forced termination" of his employment-at-will for continuous racial harassment by his employer. The action was brought under 42 U.S.C. § 1981, based on the Civil Rights Acts of 1866 and 1870 that guarantee to all persons in the United States "the same right to make and enforce contracts as is enjoyed by white" persons. After the Supreme Court in 1989 provided a narrow construction of the phrase "make and enforce contracts," Section 1981 was amended in 1991 to provide a broad definition of the phrase to include the termination of contracts. Recognizing "at-will" contracts as real contracts without a duration, the court held that such relationships may serve as "contracts" within the meaning of Section 1981. The court concluded that the plaintiff "has alleged facts that, if true, indicate that he entered into an at-will employment contract with Diamond. He also alleges that purposeful, racially discriminatory actions by Diamond personnel were so severe that they caused a 'discriminatory and retaliatory forced termination' of his employment. Section 1981(b) specifically includes 'termination of contracts' as an aspect of making and enforcing contracts that is protected by § 1981(a). As a result, Spriggs states a § 1981 claim." *Id.* at 1020.

[6]   The Effect of Recitals

1464-EIGHT, LTD. v. JOPPICH
Texas Supreme Court
154 S.W.3d 101 (2004)

STEVEN WAYNE SMITH, J.

The question presented is whether section 87(1)(a) of the RESTATEMENT (SECOND) OF CONTRACTS should be incorporated into the common law of Texas.

In July 1997, Gail Ann Joppich entered into an earnest money contract with

1464-Eight, Ltd. and Millis Management Corporation (collectively "Millis") under which Joppich agreed to buy, and Millis agreed to convey, an undeveloped residential lot located in a subdivision being developed by Millis. The purchase price was $65,000. An addendum attached to the earnest money contract provided:

> All Lots being sold in Shiloh Lake Estates Subdivision are being sold pursuant to an Option Agreement to be executed by Buyer and Seller at closing that shall survive closing and provide Seller with an option to purchase the Property from the Buyer at a price equal to 90% of the sale price herein if Buyer fails to commence construction of a private residence on the Property within 18 months from the date of closing.

Grant of Option. In consideration of the sum of Ten and No/100 ($10.00) Dollars ("Option Fee") paid in cash by Developer, the receipt and sufficiency of which is hereby acknowledged and confessed, Purchaser hereby grants to Developer the exclusive right and option to purchase [the Property]. This Option may be exercised at any time from and after January 21, 1999.

In October 1999, Joppich filed suit against Millis, seeking a declaratory judgment that the Option Agreement was unenforceable. Joppich asserted that "although the Option Agreement states that a sum of Ten and No/100 dollars was given to Plaintiff in consideration for granting the option, this sum was not then nor has it ever been tendered to nor paid to Plaintiff," and she requested that "the Court declare that the Agreement granting the exclusive right and option to purchase [the Property] to the Developer is void and unenforceable for lack of consideration or alternatively, failure of consideration." Millis answered with a general denial. In September 2000, Millis filed a counterclaim seeking specific performance. In May 2001, the trial court rendered a final judgment declaring that the Option Agreement was enforceable, requiring Joppich to sell the property in compliance with the terms of the Option Agreement, and awarding attorney's fees to Millis. In December 2002, the court of appeals reversed and remanded, concluding that "summary judgment for [Millis] was improper."

In this Court, Millis asserts that "the court of appeals' holding that failure to deliver the nominal consideration recited in an option contract precludes its enforcement directly conflicts with the modern view reflected in the RESTATEMENT (SECOND) OF CONTRACTS." In response, Joppich argues that "the RESTATEMENT shows that its view is not the modern view but is in fact the minority view consisting of one and possibly two states." Joppich does not dispute Millis's contention, made in both its petition for review and its brief on the merits, that the Option Agreement satisfies section 87(1)(a) of the RESTATEMENT (SECOND) OF CONTRACTS, including its requirement that an offer propose an exchange on fair terms within a reasonable time.

"[A] promise to give an option is valid if supported by an independent consideration. For example, if a sum of money be paid for the option, the promisee may, at his election, enforce the contract." *Nat'l Oil & Pipe Line Co. v. Teel*, 95 Tex. 586, 68 S.W. 979, 980 (Tex. 1902); *see also* RESTATEMENT (SECOND) OF CONTRACTS § 25 (1981) ("An option contract is a promise which meets the requirements for the formation of a contract and limits the promisor's power to revoke an offer.").

In addition, under the RESTATEMENT (SECOND) OF CONTRACTS, certain promises that lack consideration are enforceable. *See* RESTATEMENT (SECOND) OF CONTRACTS § 82–94 (1981); *see also* 1 MURRAY, MURRAY ON CONTRACTS § 61(4th ed. 2001) ("The RESTATEMENT 2d expressly adopts the view that a clause reciting nominal consideration in either a guaranty or an option contract should operate as a formalistic validation device, supporting the promise in either type of contract, regardless of the fact that the recited amount was never paid."); 2 PERILLO & BENDER, CORBIN ON CONTRACTS § 5.17 (rev. ed. 1995) ("The RESTATEMENT (SECOND) has taken the position that in the commercially important situations of options and credit guaranties, a promise is made binding by a false recital of consideration.").

Section 87(1)(a) of the RESTATEMENT (SECOND) OF CONTRACTS provides: "An offer is binding as an option contract" if the offer "is in writing and signed by the offeror, recites a purported consideration for the making of the offer, and proposes an exchange on fair terms within a reasonable time." RESTATEMENT (SECOND) OF CONTRACTS § 87(1)(a) (1981). Similarly, section 88(a) provides: "A promise to be surety for the performance of a contractual obligation, made to the obligee, is binding" if the promise "is in writing and signed by the promisor and recites a purported consideration." *Id.* § 88(a).

Section 87(1) of the RESTATEMENT (SECOND) OF CONTRACTS provides:

(1) An offer is binding as an option contract if it

(a) is in writing and signed by the offeror, recites a purported consideration for the making of the offer, and proposes an exchange on fair terms within a reasonable time; or

(b) is made irrevocable by statute.

The official comment to section 87 states:

b. Nominal consideration. Offers made in consideration of one dollar paid or promised are often irrevocable under Subsection (1)(a). . . . A nominal consideration is regularly held sufficient to support a short-time option proposing an exchange on fair terms. The fact that the option is an appropriate preliminary step in the conclusion of a socially useful transaction provides a sufficient substantive basis for enforcement, and a signed writing taking a form appropriate to a bargain satisfies the desiderata of form. In the absence of statute, however, the bargaining form is essential: a payment of one dollar by each party to the other is so obviously not a bargaining transaction that it does not provide even the form of an exchange.

c. False recital of nominal consideration. A recital in a written agreement that a stated consideration has been given is evidence of that fact as against a party to the agreement, but such a recital may ordinarily be contradicted by evidence that no such consideration was given or expected. *See* § 218. In cases within Subsection (1)(a), however, the giving and recital of nominal consideration performs a formal function only. The signed writing has vital significance as a formality, while the ceremonial manual delivery of a dollar or a peppercorn is an inconsequential formality. In view of the dangers of permitting a solemn written agreement to be invalidated by oral testimony which is easily fabricated, therefore, the option agreement is not invalidated by proof that the recited consideration was not in fact given. A fictitious rationalization has sometimes been used for this rule: acceptance of delivery of the written instrument conclusively imports a promise to make good the recital, it is said, and that promise furnishes consideration. *Compare* § 218. But the sound basis for the rule is that stated above.

The illustration following comment c states:

3. A executes and delivers to B a written agreement "in consideration of one dollar in hand paid" giving B an option to buy described land belonging to A for $15,000, the option to expire at noon six days later. The fact that the dollar is not in fact paid does not prevent the offer from being irrevocable.

The authors of the national treatises on contracts have generally endorsed section 87(1)(a) of the RESTATEMENT (SECOND) OF CONTRACTS. For example, CORBIN ON CONTRACTS states:

But, even when the dollar was not paid, the option has been sustained. Some courts have estopped the promisor from denying that the dollar was paid. Others have sustained the option by virtue of an implied promise to pay the dollar. *See* FARNSWORTH, FARNSWORTH ON CONTRACTS § 3.23 (3d ed. 2004) ("The attempt is to make a recital of consideration as effective a formality as was the seal, where options are concerned."); 1 MURRAY, MURRAY ON CONTRACTS § 61 (4th ed. 2001) ("Notwithstanding the compelling view of the Restatement 2d, however, most courts hold that, upon proof that the recited amount has not been paid, the promise fails for want of consideration."); 3 WILLISTON & LORD, A TREATISE ON THE LAW OF CONTRACTS § 7:23 (4th ed. 1992) ("The drafters . . . have recognized that in the context of option contracts the formal recital of consideration, though false and nominal only, serves the useful purpose of facilitating the underlying bargain.").

In addition, the authors of law review commentary have agreed that the nonpayment of a recited nominal consideration should not preclude enforcement of a written option agreement.

The position taken by section 87(1)(a) of the RESTATEMENT (SECOND) OF CONTRACTS is admittedly the minority position among the limited number of state supreme courts that have addressed the question. *See, e.g., Lewis v. Fletcher*, 101 Idaho 530, 617 P.2d 834, 835 (Idaho 1980) (holding that a written option agreement that contains a fictional recital of a nominal consideration is unenforceable for lack of consideration); *Berryman v. Kmoch*, 221 Kan. 304, 559 P.2d 790, 793 (Kan. 1977) (same); *Am. Handkerchief v. Frannat Realty Co.*, 17 N.J. 12, 109 A.2d 793, 796–97 (N.J. 1954) (same); *Bard v. Kent*, 19 Cal. 2d 449, 122 P.2d 8, 10 (Cal. 1942) (same); *Kay v. Spencer*, 29 Wyo. 382, 213 P. 571, 574 (Wyo. 1923) (same); *Smith v. Wheeler*, 233 Ga. 166, 210 S.E.2d 702, 704 (Ga. 1974) (implying an obligation to pay the recited but unpaid nominal consideration); *Real Estate Co. v. Rudolph*, 301 Pa. 502, 153 A. 438, 439 (Pa. 1930) (employing an estoppel theory to prevent contradiction of a fictional recital of a nominal consideration).

Nevertheless, we are persuaded that the position of the RESTATEMENT (SECOND) OF CONTRACTS, which is supported by a well-articulated and sound rationale, represents the better approach. *See, e.g.*, RESTATEMENT (SECOND) OF CONTRACTS § 87 cmt. b (1981) ("The fact that the option is an appropriate preliminary step in the conclusion of a socially useful transaction provides a sufficient substantive basis for enforcement, and a signed writing taking a form appropriate to a bargain satisfies the desiderata of form."); Gordon, *Consideration and the Commercial-Gift Dichotomy*, 44 VAND. L. REV. 283, 293–94 (1991) ("Option contracts are related to economic exchanges — transactions based on self-interest, not altruism. Moreover, people expect that option contracts are serious and binding commitments.") Based on the foregoing analysis, we reverse the court of appeals's judgment and remand the case to the court of appeals for further proceedings.

[7] Absence of Detriment — "Mutuality of Obligation" — "Illusory Promises" — Requirements Contracts

CENTERVILLE BUILDERS, INC. v. WYNNE
Rhode Island Supreme Court
683 A.2d 1340 (1996)

PER CURIAM.

The buyer's claim for specific performance arises out of an alleged agreement with the seller for the sale and purchase of a tract of land (the property). [T]he buyer deposited $5,000 towards the purchase of the property for the sum of $565,000, with a total deposit of 5 percent of the sale price ($28,250) due upon signing of the purchase-and-sales agreement. There were nine numbered conditions outlined in the offer to purchase. The seller signed the document on September 7, 1993, after deleting the ninth condition, which read:

> "9. SUBJECT TO SELLER CEASING NEGOTIATIONS WITH ANY AND ALL OTHER PARTIES ON PURCHASE OF SUBJECT PROPERTY."

The agreement also contained a condition that provided:

> "6. SUBJECT TO SATISFACTORY PURCHASE & SALES AGREEMENT BETWEEN SELLER AND BUYER."

Subsequently, the seller sent the buyer an unsigned purchase-and-sale-agreement form. The buyer signed the agreement and returned it to the seller. The seller requested and received an extension of time to sign the agreement. On October 20, 1993, the date the extension expired, the seller notified the buyer that the seller wanted to "get more money" for the property and would therefore put the property back on the market.

The buyer filed this action for breach of contract in Superior Court, seeking specific performance of the purchase-and-sale agreement. The seller made a motion for judgment on the pleadings. The Superior Court granted the seller's motion. [The buyer] appealed to this court.

It is a fundamental principle of contract law that a bilateral contract requires mutuality of obligation. *B & D Appraisals v. Gaudette Machinery Movers, Inc.*, 733 F. Supp. 505, 507 (D.R.l. 1990) ("[a] bilateral contract involves mutual promises which simultaneously obligate the parties"). This mutuality is achieved when both parties are "legally bound through the making of reciprocal promises." However, when the promises of the parties depend on the occurrence of some future event within the unilateral control of the promisors, the promises are illusory and the agreement is nonbinding.

In the instant case, the buyer and the seller entered into a written offer-to-purchase agreement whereby the former would purchase the property, and the latter would sell it. However, their promises were illusory since each party reserved the unfettered discretion to thwart the purchase and sale by unilaterally invoking condition 6 of the offer-to-purchase agreement and rejecting any purchase-and-sale agreement as "unsatisfactory."

Although it is true that the seller displayed an intent to be bound by the offer-to-purchase agreement when he signed the document and agreed to sell the property subject to the conditions specified, the inclusion of condition 6 made this an illusory promise because its occurrence depended solely on the subjective will of either party.

The seller's deletion (with the buyer's consent) of the ninth condition further evidenced the lack of mutuality of obligation. Because the seller was allowed to negotiate with other prospective buyers, the offer to purchase amounted to little more than an agreement to see if the parties could agree on a purchase-and-sale agreement at some point in the future. As such, it was not an enforceable bilateral contract. Since no contract existed between the parties, the buyer would not be entitled to specific performance and the order appealed from is affirmed.

NOTES

(1) *Empty ("Illusory") Promises.* A promise to perform an act unless the promisor changes his mind promises nothing. There is no restraint on the promiser's future action. There is no binding commitment to do or refrain from doing anything. There is no benefit to the promisor and no detriment to the promisee. If Carl promises to sell his used car to Keri for $10,000 unless Carl changes his mind, and Keri promises to purchase the car for $10,000, Keri cannot be bound to her promise because she is receiving nothing for her promise. As a promisor, Keri is receiving no benefit from Carl because Carl is not bound by his promise. Carl, the promisee, is suffering no detriment in making a promise which he may choose not to keep. It is, therefore, obvious that where one or both promises are illusory, there is no consideration and no contract.

(2) *"Mutuality of Obligation."* The so-called "doctrine" of mutuality of obligation has caused considerable confusion. The court's use of that phrase in the principal case is unnecessary and confusing. The court properly found that the seller was not bound to perform since he could choose to sell the property to anyone. His liberty of action was not limited in any fashion. Thus, the buyer as promisor was receiving no benefit and there was no detriment to the seller as promisee. There was

no consideration to support either promise. To encumber this basic rationale with labels such as "mutuality of obligation" is unfortunate. The "doctrine" of "mutuality of obligation" is often defined through the shibboleth that either both parties are bound or neither is bound, traceable to a 17th century case, *Harrison v. Cage*, Mod. 411 [1698]. It is a tautology. "Mutuality of obligation" is simply a statement that bilateral contracts require consideration. *Riedman Corp. v. Jarosh*, 289 S.C. 191, 345 S.E.2d 732 (1986). *See also Zamore v. Whitten*, 395 A.2d 435, 443, n.3 (Me. 1978).

HAY v. FORTIER
Maine Supreme Judicial Court
102 A. 294 (1917)

KING, J.

The case made by the agreed statement is this: The defendant became a surety on a 15-day bond given by one Henry H. Sawyer to the plaintiff. The conditions of the bond were not complied with, and the defendant was notified of her liability under the bond and requested to make payment thereof. On February 4, 1915, the defendant's attorney wrote the attorney of the plaintiff as follows:

> have seen Mrs. Fortier, who says it will be a great hardship to pay this entire amount at the present time as the other signers are worthless. She suggests . . . that she will pay you $100 next week, if the papers are regular, and settle the balance by payments, the whole bill to be paid before your April term of court. . . .

To that the plaintiff, through his attorney, replied sending copies of the papers and saying:

> I am willing to accept $100 on account, providing you send same to me immediately and the balance on or before the first Tuesday of April . . . .

The defendant paid the $100 forthwith, but no more. The plaintiff waited till long after the first Tuesday of April, and on June 1, 1915, brought an action of debt on the bond against the principal and all the sureties. Mrs. Fortier answered to that action at the return term thereof, and at a subsequent term, on November 3, 1915, by agreement, that action was "discontinued without costs and without prejudice," the counsel of the respective parties signing the docket entry to that effect. Why that action was thus discontinued does not appear in this case. On the following day, November 4, 1915, this action was brought against Mrs. Fortier, based upon a breach of her alleged special promise to pay the balance due under the bond before the April term of court, as stated in the correspondence referred to. The declaration is not made a part of the case, but the parties stipulate that it "is in due form." The defense is that the alleged promise on which the action is based was without a legal consideration and is therefore nonenforceable.

We think the agreed statement justifies the conclusion, that the defendant promised to pay at once $100, and the balance due under the bond before the April term of court, provided the plaintiff would forbear action on the bond, and that the plaintiff on his part, in consideration of such part payment at once, and the promise to pay the balance on or before the time specified, agreed to forbear, and did in fact forbear, action on the bond until after the time specified. And a promise to forbear and give time for the payment of a debt followed by actual forbearance for the time specified or for a reasonable time when no definite time is named, is certainly a sufficient consideration for a promise to pay the debt. . . .

On the other hand, it is obvious that the defendant by her special promise did not agree to do anything that she was not then legally bound to do. Her liability under the bond was then due and payable. She might then have been required to pay it all forthwith. And it is a well-recognized principle that the payment, or promise of payment, of money which is then due and payable by virtue of an existing valid contract of the promisor, is not in contemplation of law a sufficient consideration for any new contract . . . . The defendant therefore contends that the plaintiff's promise to forbear action on the bond was without a legal consideration and not binding on him; in other words, that he could have brought action on the bond immediately after the part payment was made, in total disregard of his promise to wait until the April term of court. We think that contention is sound, and well supported by authorities. In *Warren v. Hodge*, 121 Mass. 106, the court said:

> It is too well settled to require discussion or reference to authorities that an agreement to forbear to sue upon a debt already due and payable, for no other consideration than a payment of a part of the debt, is without legal consideration, and cannot be availed of by the debtor, either by way of contract or of estoppel.

But it does not follow, as the defendant claims, that this action against her is not maintainable, simply because the plaintiff's promise to forbear action on the bond could not have been enforced against him during the specified period of forbearance.

If a contract, although not originally binding for want of mutuality, is nevertheless executed by the party not originally bound, so that the party asserting the invalidity of the contract has actually received the benefit contracted for, the latter will be estopped from refusing performance on his part on the ground that the contract was not originally binding on the other, who has performed. 6 R. C. L. 690.

Granting that the parties, through the correspondence referred to, entered into a bilateral contract, and that there was want of mutuality in that contract because the plaintiff was not bound to perform his part of it, nevertheless, he did fully perform the contract on his part, and the defendant received the full benefit contracted for. Having enjoyed the forbearance of the plaintiff from bringing action against her on the bond for the full period agreed upon, the defendant is now estopped from refusing performance on her part on the ground that the contract was not originally binding on the plaintiff, who did, nevertheless, perform it and she received the benefit thereof.

It is therefore the opinion of the court that this action is maintainable, and that the plaintiff is entitled to judgment against the defendant for $175.60 and costs, with interest from the date of the writ.

NOTE

Consider RESTATEMENT (SECOND) OF CONTRACTS § 75, Illustration 4:

> A promise to forbear suit against B in exchange for B's promise to pay a liquidated and undisputed debt to A. A's promise is not binding because B's promise is not consideration under § 73, but A's promise is nevertheless consideration for B's . . . . B's promise is conditional on A's forbearance and can be enforced only if the condition is met.

"Professor Murray is highly critical of the second RESTATEMENT position: 'The formulation of the RESTATEMENT 2d is devoid of any useful rationale and the unilateral analysis is highly preferable.' MURRAY ON CONTRACTS, § 65. He would hold that no executory bilateral contract was formed, but after A's forbearance a unilateral contract arose: 'It is submitted that A's promise is never consideration for B's promise. Rather [B's] promise becomes enforceable in exchange for [A's] act of forbearance.'" CORBIN ON CONTRACTS § 6.1, n.32.[8]

[8]   The Illusion of Illusory Promises

VANEGAS v. AMERICAN ENERGY SERVICES
Supreme Court of Texas
302 S.W.3d 299 (2009)

GREEN, J.

AES hired the petitioners in this case (collectively, the employees) that same year. The employees allege that, in an effort to provide an incentive for them to stay with the company, Carnett promised the employees, who were at-will and therefore free to leave the company at any time, that "in the event of sale or merger of AES, the original [eight] employees remaining with AES at that time would get 5% of the value of any sale or merger of AES." AES Acquisition, Inc. acquired AES in 2001. Seven of the eight original employees were still with AES at the time of the acquisition. Those remaining employees demanded their proceeds, and when the company refused to pay, the employees sued, claiming AES breached the oral agreement.

AES moved for summary judgment on two grounds: that the agreement was illusory and therefore not enforceable, and that it violated the statute of frauds. The employees responded that the promise represented a unilateral contract, and by remaining employed for the stated period, the employees performed, thereby making the promise enforceable. The trial court granted AES's motion for summary judgment, and the employees appealed. The court of appeals affirmed, holding that the alleged unilateral contract failed because it was not supported by at least one non-illusory promise.

---

[8] Though Professor Murray is the current author of supplements to CORBIN ON CONTRACTS and the reviser of Volume 9 of that treatise, this statement was written by another author prior to Professor Murray's contributions to the treatise.

AES argues, and the court of appeals held, that our holdings in *Light*, 224 S.W.3d at 553, and *Sheshunoff v. Johnson*, 209 S.W.3d 644 (Tex. 2006), dictate the result in this case. In *Light*, we stated:

> Consideration for a promise, by either the employee or the employer in an at-will employment, cannot be dependent on a period of continued employment. Such a promise would be illusory because it fails to bind the promisor who always retains the option of discontinuing employment in lieu of performance. When illusory promises are all that support a purported bilateral contract, there is no contract.

AES and the court of appeals also relied on two footnotes from that opinion to support their position. In footnote five, we stated that "[a]ny promise made by either employer or employee that depends on an additional period of employment is illusory because it is conditioned upon something that is exclusively within the control of the promisor." And in footnote six, we noted "[i]f only one promise is illusory, a unilateral contract can still be formed; the non-illusory promise can serve as an offer, which the promisor who made the illusory promise can accept by performance."

Citing our holdings in *Light* and *Sheshunoff*, the court of appeals stated that "[a] unilateral contract may be formed when one of the parties makes only an illusory promise but the other party makes a non-illusory promise. The non-illusory promise can serve as the offer for a unilateral contract, which the promisor who made the illusory promise can accept by performance." We agree with that statement, but the court of appeals erroneously applied those holdings to the current case.

The issue turns on the distinction between bilateral and unilateral contracts. "A bilateral contract is one in which there are mutual promises between two parties to the contract, each party being both a promisor and a promisee." *Hutchings v. Slemons*, 141 Tex. 448, 174 S.W.2d 487, 489 (Tex. 1943) (quoting RESTATEMENT (FIRST) OF CONTRACTS § 12). A unilateral contract, on the other hand, is "created by the promisor promising a benefit if the promisee performs. The contract becomes enforceable when the promisee performs." 1 RICHARD A. LORD, WILLISTON ON CONTRACTS § 1.17 (4th ed. 2007) ("A unilateral contract occurs when there is only one promisor and the other party accepts, not by mutual promise, but by actual performance or forbearance."). Both *Sheshunoff* and *Light* concerned *bilateral* contracts in which employers made promises in exchange for employees' promises not to compete with their companies after termination. *Sheshunoff*, 209 S.W.3d at 649 ("ASM promised to disclose confidential information and to provide specialized training under the Agreement, and Johnson promised not to disclose confidential information."); *Light*, 883 S.W.2d at 645 ("When illusory promises are all that support a purported *bilateral* contract, there is no contract.") (emphasis added). The court of appeals' explanation of these cases — describing an exchange of promises where one party makes an illusory promise and the other a non-illusory promise — describes the attempted formation of a *bilateral* contract, not a unilateral contract. 224 S.W.3d at 549. Our discussion in footnote six of *Light* was confined to situations where a non-illusory promise could salvage an otherwise ineffective bilateral contract by transforming it into a unilateral contract, enforceable upon performance. This was not a blanket pronouncement about unilateral contracts in general.

The court of appeals held that even if AES promised to pay the employees the five percent, that promise was illusory at the time it was made because the employees were at-will, and AES could have fired all of them prior to the acquisition. 224 S.W.3d at 549. But whether the promise was illusory at the time it was made is irrelevant; what matters is whether the promise became enforceable by the time of the breach. *See Sheshunoff*, 209 S.W.3d at 651 ("[A] unilateral contract formed when the employer performs a promise that was illusory when made can satisfy the requirements of the [Covenants Not to Compete] Act . . . . There is no sound reason why a unilateral contract made enforceable by performance should fail under the Act."); *see also* 2 Corbin on Contracts § 6.2 (1995) "[U]nilateral contract analysis is applicable to the employer's promise to pay a bonus or pension to an employee in case the latter continues to serve for a stated period."). Almost all unilateral contracts begin as illusory promises. Take, for instance, the classic textbook example of a unilateral contract: "I will pay you $ 50 if you paint my house." The offer to pay the individual to paint the house can be withdrawn at any point prior to performance. But once the individual accepts the offer by performing, the promise to pay the $ 50 becomes binding. The employees allege that AES made an offer to split five percent of the proceeds of the sale or merger of the company among any remaining original employees. Assuming that allegation is true, the seven remaining employees accepted this offer by remaining employed for the requested period of time. At that point, AES's promise became binding. AES then breached its agreement with the employees when it refused to pay the employees their five percent share.

Furthermore, the court of appeals' holding would potentially jeopardize all pension plans, vacation leave, and other forms of compensation made to at-will employees that are based on a particular term of service. *Corbin on Contracts* observed as much in discussing the court of appeals' opinion in this case:

> The court's analysis may attempt to prove too much. The argument that a promise to grant a raise to a terminable-at-will employee is necessarily illusory raises the question, why is an employer's original promise to pay a certain wage to an at-will employee enforceable when the employee performs? The court's analysis would suggest that the employer's promise was never enforceable. If an at-will employee is hired at a promised compensation and performs for some period, the court's analysis would suggest that the promised rate of compensation was never enforceable. 1 John E. Murray, Jr. & Timothy Murray, Corbin on Contracts § 1.17 (Supp. Fall 2009).

We agree that the court of appeals' opinion could have far-reaching adverse effects on well established forms of compensation. The fact that the employees were at-will and were already being compensated in the form of their salaries in exchange for remaining employed also does not make the promise to pay the bonus any less enforceable. AES allegedly promised to pay any remaining original employees five percent of the proceeds when AES was sold. Assuming AES did make such an offer, the seven remaining employees accepted the offer by staying with AES until the sale. Regardless of whether the promise was illusory at the time it was made, the promise became enforceable upon the employees' performance. The court of appeals erred in holding otherwise. Accordingly, we reverse the court of appeals' judgment and remand the case to the trial court for further proceedings consistent with this opinion.

PROBLEM

The parties agreed that the defendant would charter a commercial vessel to the plaintiff at specified rates if the defendant purchased the ship. The defendant then purchased the ship but chartered it to a third person. The defendant argued that there was no consideration for his promise since he did not promise to purchase the ship. Analyze. The problem is based on *Scott v. Moragues Lumber Co.*, 80 So. 394 (Ala. 1918).

[9] Requirement and Output Contracts

To assure a continuous supply of raw materials or other products used in their business, it is common for manufacturers to enter into requirements contracts which will provide their needs of such materials or products. Just as consumers require electricity and natural gas in their homes for which they contract with one supplier, businesses often make contracts with one supplier for all of the materials and parts that they use in their production of finished products. The exact quantity of such requirements is not available at the time the contract is formed since the requirements will depend upon market conditions and the competitive success of the business.[9] Though it is not identified at the time of contract formation, the quantity term is identifiable at the end of the contract period. The quantity may be a stated estimate or it may be based on the requirements of the buyer in prior years.

The output contract is the converse of the requirements contract under which a seller may agree to sell its entire production output to a single buyer for a certain period. Thus, a buyer needing certain parts or raw materials may agree to purchase a given seller's entire output. Again, the output will not be precisely identified at the time of formation, but, like the quantity in the requirements contract, it will be determined at the conclusion of the period.

The output contract provides the buyer with an assured source of supply and the output contract provides the seller with an assured market for its products. Since there is reasonable and good faith fluctuation in the quantities of such contracts, older cases sometimes reflected a concern that such contracts are not sufficient definite to enforce. Comment 2 to Section 2-306 of the Uniform Commercial Code states, "Under this article, a contract for output or requirements is not too indefinite since it is held to mean the actual output or requirements of the particular party."

Issues arise where a buyer increases its requirements to levels not contemplated by reasonable suppliers or lowers it requirements, perhaps to zero.

---

[9] The contracts may contain maximum or minimum quantity terms.

An output supplier may increase or decrease its output well beyond anticipated levels. Are these modifications made in good faith? If a requirements buyer has a long-term contract with a supplier that becomes particularly desirable for the buyer because the market price far exceeds the fixed price in the contract, the buyer may be tempted to disproportionately increase its demands beyond its genuine requirements to make a profit on resales of the commodity. A supplier may artificially restrict its output because it is either losing money on the production costs or determines that its profits are insufficient. A buyer may decide to reduce its requirements to very low levels or nothing from a given supplier because the market price for the product has decreased substantially. What are the "good faith" reasons that allow for major changes in requirements or outputs?

VULCAN MATERIALS COMPANY v. ATOFINA CHEMICALS, INC.
United States District Court, District of Kansas
355 F. Supp. 2d 1214 (2005)

J. THOMAS MARTEN, J.

[Plaintiff Vulcan operated chemical plants including one in Wichita, Kansas. The defendant, Atofina, is an affiliate of a French Corporation and also operated a chemical plant in Wichita where it made R-22, a chemical generally used as a refrigerant. One component of R-22 is chloroform that Vulcan supplied to Atofina at the Wichita plant. On September 1, 1999, the parties entered into an agreement under which Atofina promised to purchase its "entire requirements of chloroform" for the Wichita plant from Vulcan. Subsequently, Atofina stopped purchasing chloroform from Vulcan and closed the Wichita plant.]

Vulcan seeks by summary judgment a finding that defendant Atofina breached the 1999 Sales Agreement to purchase the chloroform requirements for its Wichita plant The parties agree that Kansas law governs Vulcan's breach of contract claim. The Kansas version of UCC § 2-306 provides:

> A term which measures the quantity by the output of the seller or the requirements of the buyer means such actual output or requirements as may occur in good faith, except that no quantity unreasonably disproportionate to any stated estimate or in the absence of a stated estimate to any normal or otherwise comparable prior output or requirements may be tendered or demanded.

The Kansas comments to this section state: "If in good faith a party has no actual output or requirements, it has no duty to perform under the contract." The UCC defines "good faith" generally as "honesty in fact in the conduct or transaction concerned." § 1-201(19). For merchants, the UCC defines "good faith" as "honesty in fact and the observance of reasonable commercial standards of fair dealing in the trade." § 2-103(1)(b).

The majority of courts addressing the subject have held that the "unreasonably disproportionate" language of 2-306(1) restricts the ability of the buyer to increase purchases, not to decrease them: the buyer can decrease its purchases, subject to the limitation not of reasonableness, but of good faith. *See MDC Corp. v. John H. Harland Co.*, 228 F. Supp. 2d 387, 396 (S.D.N.Y. 2002) ("most authorities [hold] a requirements buyer may decrease its orders as long as it does so in good faith").

The leading case on the issue of good faith in the modification of requirements contracts is *Empire Gas Corp. v. American Bakeries*, 840 F.2d 1333 (7th Cir. 1988). The bakery defendant contracted with Empire Gas to buy converters which would allow its fleet of delivery trucks to run on propane. Days after the contract was signed, the bakery decided not to convert its trucks. [T]he Seventh Circuit affirmed the decision for the plaintiff on the issue of bad faith, holding that it had met its burden by presenting evidence that the buyer kept its trucks and "the financial wherewithal to go through with the conversion process." 840 F.2d at 1341. The defendant failed to present any evidence of an independent business rationale for terminating its demand.

The court observed that the issue can present problems defining the scope of permissible conduct:

> The essential ingredient of good faith in the case of the buyer's reducing his estimated requirements is that he not merely have had second thoughts about the terms of the contract and want to get out of it. Whether the buyer has any greater obligation is unclear. The standard of good faith "requires at a minimum that the reduction of requirements not have been motivated solely by a reassessment of the balance of advantages and disadvantages under the contract to the buyer." *Id.* at 1341.

The Kansas comments to § 2-306 elaborate on the issue:

> In evaluating whether a reduction is made in good faith, courts distinguish between reductions "merely to curtail losses" (bad faith), . . . and reductions because of external events that threaten the viability of the entire undertaking (good faith).

The court has little difficulty, in light of the uncontroverted facts, in concluding that Atofina's decision to reduce its requirements for chloroform was not the product of good faith. The price of the chloroform under the 1999 Sales Agreement played an essential role in Atofina's decision. Alternative justifications used by Atofina to try and rationalize its actions were both relatively unimportant and were manifestly known to Atofina at the time it entered into the 1999 contract. Far from being prompted by business considerations which were not previously anticipated or independent of the underlying agreement, Atofina's decision was simply a reflection of its dissatisfaction with the terms of that agreement. Atofina did not get out of the R-22 business; it continues to sell roughly the same amount of product it did previously — except that it has freed itself of the consequences of its prior contract with Vulcan.

The evidentiary record is devoid of evidence demonstrating a downturn in R-22 demand. Orders for R-22 had not decreased. Atofina remains in the R-22 business; it has simply switched suppliers. "A buyer may go out of business altogether and hope to escape a burdensome requirements contract in this way. But if he only reorganizes the form of business, a court will surely see through this and hold him liable on the contract." J WHITE & R. SUMMERS, UNIFORM COMMERCIAL CODE § 3-9 at

155 (1995). The defendant acted in bad faith.

[10]   Exclusive Dealing — Implied Promises

WOOD v. LUCY, LADY DUFF-GORDON
Court of Appeals of New York
118 N.E. 214 (1917)

CARDOZO, J.

The defendant styles herself "a creator of fashions." Her favor helps a sale. Manufacturers of dresses, millinery and like articles are glad to pay for a certificate of her approval. The things which she designs, fabrics, parasols and what not, have a new value in the public mind when issued in her name. She employed the plaintiff to help her to turn this vogue into money. He was to have the exclusive right, subject always to her approval, to place her indorsements on the designs of others. He was also to have the exclusive right to place her own designs on sale, or to license others to market them. In return, she was to have one-half of "all profits and revenues" derived from any contracts he might make. The exclusive right was to last at least one year from April 1, 1915, and thereafter from year to year unless terminated by notice of ninety days. The plaintiff says that he kept the contract on his part, and that the defendant broke it. She placed her indorsement on fabrics, dresses and millinery without his knowledge, and withheld the profits. He sues her for the damages, and the case comes here on demurrer.

The agreement of employment is signed by both parties. It has a wealth of recitals. The defendant insists, however, that it lacks the elements of a contract. She says that the plaintiff does not bind himself to anything. It is true that he does not promise in so many words that he will use reasonable efforts to place the defendant's indorsements and market her designs. We think, however, that such a promise is fairly to be implied. The law has outgrown its primitive stage of formalism when the precise word was the sovereign talisman, and every slip was fatal. It takes a broader view to-day. A promise may be lacking, and yet the whole writing may be "instinct with an obligation," imperfectly expressed. If that is so, there is a contract.

The implication of a promise here finds support in many circumstances. The defendant gave an *exclusive* privilege. She was to have no right for at least a year to place her own indorsements or market her own designs except through the agency of the plaintiff. The acceptance of the exclusive agency was an assumption of its duties We are not to suppose that one party was to be placed at the mercy of the other Many other terms of the agreement point the same way. We are told at the outset by way of recital that "the said Otis F. Wood possesses a business organization adapted to the placing of such indorsements as the said Lucy, Lady Duff-Gordon has approved." The implication is that the plaintiff's business organization will be used for the purpose for which it is adapted. But the terms of the defendant's compensation are even more significant. Her sole compensation for the grant of an exclusive agency is to be one-half of all the profits resulting from the plaintiff's efforts. Unless he gave his efforts, she could never get anything. Without an implied promise, the transaction cannot have such business "efficacy as both parties must have intended that at all events it should have" But the contract does not stop there. The plaintiff goes on to promise that he will account monthly for all moneys received by him, and that he will take out all such patents and copyrights and trademarks as may in his judgment be necessary to protect the rights and articles affected by the agreement. It is true, of course, as the Appellate Division has said, that if he was under no duty to try to market designs or to place certificates of indorsement, his promise to account for profits or take out copyrights would be valueless. But in determining the intention of the parties, the promise *has* a value. It helps to enforce the conclusion that the plaintiff *had* some duties. His promise to pay the defendant one-half of the profits and revenues resulting from the exclusive agency and to render accounts monthly, was a promise to use reasonable efforts to bring profits and revenues into existence. For this conclusion, the authorities are ample.

The judgment of the Appellate Division should be reversed, and the order of the Special Term affirmed, with costs in the Appellate Division and in this court.

NOTES

(1) After her first marriage ended, Lucy Christiana Sutherland began working as a dressmaker at home to support herself and her child. In 1900, she married Scottish landowner Sir Cosmo Duff Gordon and would thereafter be known as Lady Duff Gordon. Opening London shops, she cultivated a wealthy clientele which included celebrities. The business expanded to New York, Paris and Chicago as Lucy became famous for her designs of lingerie, evening wear and tea gowns. She is often viewed as having trained the first professional fashion models as well as the runway for fashion shows. She is also well known as one of the survivors of the famous sinking of the *Titanic*. Her husband provided some crew members in a lifeboat with money to assist them since they had lost their employment. Media allegations suggested that he and Lucy had bribed the crew members not to assist other passengers for fear that their partially filled lifeboat would be swamped.

(2) In *B. Lewis Productions, Inc. v. Angelou*, 2005 U.S. Dist. LEXIS 9032 (S.D.N.Y. 2005), Lewis claimed a breach of contract by the renowned poet, Maya Angelou based on a letter agreement signed by both parties under which Angelou was to contribute certain literary work and Lewis would "exploit the rights for publishing of said Property in all media forms including, but not limtied to greeting cards, stationery and calendars, etc." Angelou claimed that the agreement was fatally indefinite in missing terms. Lewis had presented an arrangement under which Angelou's work would be published on Hallmark greeting cards, but Angelou rejected any contract with Lewis. She later singed a lucrative contract with Hallmark Noting a strong similarity between the case before it and the principal case which it described in considerable detail, the court denied Angelou's motion for summary judgment.

[11]   Voidable Promises and Consideration — Capacity to Contract

MILICIC v. THE BASKETBALL MARKETING CO., INC.
Pennsylvania Superior Court
857 A.2d 689 (2004)

McCaffery, J.

Appellant, The Basketball Marketing Company Inc., asks us to determine whether the trial court erred by issuing a preliminary injunction against it. The trial court summarized the pertinent facts and relevant procedural history as follows:

> Appellant is a Delaware Corporation with its principal place of business in Paoli, Pennsylvania. Appellant is in the business of the marketing, distribution and sale of basketball apparel and related products. Appellee, Darko Milicic, is an 18 year-old basketball player from Serbia, and was the 2003 second overall draft pick by the National Basketball Association's Detroit Pistons. The parties entered into an endorsement agreement ("the agreement") on June 15, 2002, when [Appellee] was just 16 years-old, whereby Appellant would pay [Appellee] certain monies and provide him with products in exchange for [Appellee's] endorsement. Although [Appellee] was virtually unknown in the United States at the time the agreement was executed, by April of this year his status had significantly changed and it was widely known he was likely to be a top five N.B.A. draft pick. As one would expect, [Appellee] was then in a position to sign a more lucrative endorsement deal. On June 20, 2003, four days after his 18th birthday, [Appellee] made a buy-out offer to Appellant, which was refused. About six days later, [Appellee] sent Appellant a letter disaffirming the agreement. He began returning all monies and products (or their equivalent value) he had received pursuant to the agreement. Appellant refused to accept [Appellee's] letter as a negation of the agreement. On July 11, 2003, Appellant wrote letters to Adidas America ("Adidas") and Reebok International Ltd. ("Reebok"), both of whom were believed to have offered endorsement contracts to [Appellee]. In the letters, Appellant informed the recipients that it was "involved in a contractual dispute" with [Appellee] and that the "agreement is valid and enforceable and will remain in force for several more years." Based upon Appellant's letter, Adidas ceased negotiations and a nearly finalized endorsement agreement was not executed. [Appellee] filed the underlying Complaint seeking a Temporary Restraining Order, a Preliminary Injunction and Declaratory Relief. The Court granted the TRO and after a hearing granted the Preliminary Injunction. This timely appeal followed.

Pennsylvania law recognizes, except as to necessities, the contract of a minor is voidable if the minor disaffirms it at any reasonable time after the minor attains majority. On July 1, 2003, just eleven days after his 18th birthday, [Appellee] sent Appellant a letter withdrawing from the agreement. This letter was sent within a reasonable time after [Appellee's] reaching the age of majority and stated his unequivocal revocation and voidance of the agreement. Injunctive relief was necessary to prevent immediate and irreparable harm that could not be adequately compensated by the awarding of monetary damages. Top N.B.A. draft picks generally solicit, negotiate and secure endorsement contracts within a short time after the draft to take advantage of the publicity, excitement and attendant marketability associated with the promotion. Appellant blocked [Appellee's] efforts to enter into such an endorsement agreement. After being contacted by Appellant, advanced negotiations between [Appellee] and Adidas were suspended. These business opportunity and market advantage losses may aptly be characterized as irreparable injury for purposes of equitable relief. The inability to obtain a principal endorsement contract may have the residual effect of impeding [Appellee's] ability to obtain other endorsement contracts. For this reason the injury cannot be precisely quantified nor adequately compensated by monetary damages.

Appellant['s] refusal to acknowledge [Appellee's] ability to disaffirm the contract is at odds with public policy. Because infants are not competent to contract, the ability to disaffirm protects them from their own immaturity and lack of discretion. By including a choice-of-law provision [Pennsylvania law], Appellee came under the protection of 23 Pa. C. S. § 5101 which provides that only individuals 18 years of age and older shall have the right to enter into contracts. Not only is harm to the petitioner considered, but harm to the public is an additional consideration in the issuance or denial of a preliminary injunction. The public policy consideration underlying the rule which allows a child to disaffirm a contract within a reasonable time after reaching the age of majority is that "minors should not be bound by mistakes resulting from their immaturity or the overbearance of unscrupulous adults."

[W]e affirm the trial court's order granting a preliminary injunction to the appellee.

NOTES

(1) A promise by a person who has not reached the age of majority, which is currently 18 in most jurisdictions, is provided with a power of avoidance ("disaffirmance"). The exercise of that power will avoid the contract. There is a contract supported by consideration when the contract is made, but the contract is avoidable for the public policy reasons announced in the principal case.

(2) Beyond minors (classically refened to as "infants"), a person suffering from mental illness also lacks capacity. "Mental illness" covers a wide range of mental illnesses including congenital deficiencies, brain damage caused by organic disease or accident, deterioriation caused by advanced age and other illnesses with symptoms such as hallucinations, delusions, confusion or depression. The traditional test is the *cognitive* test: *Did the party understand the nature and consequences of the transaction?* While the RESTATEMENT (SECOND) OF CONTRACTS, § 15, recognizes this test, it also recognizes that, though a party may have complete awareness of the transaction, she may lack the ability to control her acts in a reasonable manner because of mental illness. If the other party has reason to know of that illness, the contract is voidable. Where a person may have some understand-

ing of the transaction, the critical question is whether a reasonably competent person might have made such a contract. An intoxicated person incurs only voidable contractual duties if the other party has reason to know that the intoxicated person is unable to understand the nature and consequences of the transaction or is unable to act in a reasonable manner in relation to the transaction (RESTATEMENT (SECOND) OF CONTRACTS § 16). It is important to distinguish promises by persons under *guardianship* which is an adjudication with public notice that the ward has no control over the ward's property. Contracts with wards are not merely voidable, they are void.

(3) There are limitations on the exercise of the power of avoidance. As the court suggests, while a minor or mentally ill person may disaffirm the contract, he remains liable in quasi contract for the reasonable value of *necessaries*. While food, clothing and shelter are clear "necessaries," the particular quality of such benefits must be considered depending upon the status of the minor. If the minor has received goods under a contract which he disaffirms, he must return the goods received under the avoided contract as suggested in the principal case where the appellee returned the goods and money he had received.

On capacity to contract in general, see MURRAY ON CONTRACTS §§ 22–28 (5th ed. 2011).

[12] The Pre-Existing Duty Rule

SLATTERY v. WELLS FARGO ARMORED SERVICE CORP.
Florida Court of Appeal
366 So. 2d 157 (1979)

PER CURIAM.

Appellant/plaintiff, a licensed polygraph operator, appeals from an "order granting summary judgment and summary final judgment" rendered in favor of appellee/defendant Wells Fargo Armored Service Corp., in an action wherein appellant claimed and was denied the following reward offered by appellee:

$25,000 REWARD

Wells Fargo Armored Service Corporation of Florida announces a reward of up to $25,000 for information leading to the arrest and conviction of the person or persons participating in the shooting of a Wells Fargo agent, the subsequent robbery which occurred on Saturday, February 22, 1975 at Miami, Florida, and the recovery of valuables lost as a result of this occurrence.

Information should be directed to Wells Fargo Armored Service Corporation of Florida, P. O. Box 011028, Miami, Florida 33101, Telephone Number (305) 324-4900. The person or persons to whom the reward or any part thereof should be paid will be determined by the Board of Directors of Wells Fargo Armored Service Corporation of Florida.

Appellant contends that he was entitled to the reward by virtue of his questioning of the perpetrator of the crime during a polygraph examination on an unrelated matter. Such questioning, which occurred on two separate days, eventually resulted in a statement by the perpetrator that he had shot and killed the Wells Fargo guard, which ultimately led to his conviction and sentence for the crime. Appellant argues that, but for his expertise in interrogation and the operation of a polygraph, the authorities would not have linked the perpetrator to the crime. Thus, appellant contends, he is entitled to the reward offered by appellee.

The trial judge, rejecting appellant's argument, entered summary final judgment in favor of appellee on the ground that the offer of reward was never accepted by appellant in that the performance called for by the terms of the offer had not been completed. In particular, the trial judge referred to a stipulation entered into by the parties whereby it was agreed that the stolen property belonging to appellee had not been returned. In that both requirements of the unilateral offer of contract had not been performed (the arrest and conviction of the perpetrator *and* the return of the stolen property to Wells Fargo) the trial judge determined that appellant had not accepted the offer and thus, no contract had been established. Therefore, the trial judge entered summary final judgment in favor of appellee.

After carefully reviewing the record on appeal, it is our opinion that summary judgment was proper, but not for the reason relied upon by the trial judge. Initially, it must be kept in mind that a reward is contractual in nature, requiring the acceptance of an offer supported by consideration . . . .

. . . Firstly, while appellant was an independent contractor, during the polygraph interrogation he was employed by either the office of the State Attorney or the Dade County Public Safety Department and was paid for his services on an hourly rate. Further, while so employed, appellant was under a duty to provide his employers with any and all information ascertained by him through interrogation which might be of aid to the State Attorney or Public Safety Department in their capacity as law enforcement agencies.

Secondly, the record demonstrates that through the first day of interrogation, appellant was unaware of the offer of reward. Only on the second day of questioning did appellant have the knowledge that a reward had been offered by appellee. On that second day, the perpetrator of the crime confessed prior to the actual interrogation by appellant.

The law is well settled in this state that before a reward is entitled to be collected, the offeree must have knowledge of the existence of the offer of reward . . . . [A]ppellant had no knowledge of the reward until the second day of questioning, at which time the perpetrator confessed prior to any interrogation. On this basis alone, summary judgment would have been proper.

We, however, choose to uphold the summary judgment on the ground that appellant was under a pre-existing duty to furnish his employers with all useful information revealed to him through interrogation of the perpetrator. Thus, when appellant "accepted" the offer of reward by furnishing information to the authorities, he was doing no more than he was already bound to do as part of his employment. The performance of a pre-existing duty does not amount to the consideration necessary to support a contract . . . . As such, no contract was formed.

Further, as a corollary to the above and as a matter of public policy, it is our opinion that to allow appellant to recover a reward for the furnishing of information to the authorities, when he was under a duty to furnish such information as part of his employment, would be tantamount to undermining the integrity and the efforts of those involved in law enforcement. *Affirmed.*

NOTES

(1)   At a very early time it was said "that payment of a lesser sum on the day in satisfaction of a greater, cannot be any satisfaction for the whole, because it appears to the judges that by no possibility a lesser sum can be a satisfaction to the plaintiff for a greater sum." *Pinnel's Case,* 5 Coke 117a, 77 Eng. Rep. 237 (1600). It may be doubted whether this case intended to raise or decide a question of consideration although it has been so interpreted by later authorities.

In any event, ever since that time, it has been quite uniformly held that part payment of a liquidated debt which is due, is not consideration to discharge the whole debt, nor is part or full payment of a debt consideration for any other promise by the creditor. This is popularly referred to as the rule in *Foakes v. Beer,* 9 App. Cas. 605 (1884). *See* FERSON, *The Rule in Foakes v. Beer,* 31 YALE L.J. 15 (1921), SELECTED READINGS ON CONTRACTS 1205 (1931).

(2)   "Nowhere is the confusion between legal and moral ideas more manifest than in the law of contract. Among other things, here again the so called primary rights and duties are invested with a mystic significance beyond what can be assigned and explained. The duty to keep a contract at common law means a prediction that you must pay damages if you do not keep it, — and nothing else. If you commit a tort, you are liable to pay a compensatory sum. If you commit a contract, you are liable to pay a compensatory sum unless the promised event comes to pass, and that is all the difference. But such a mode of looking at the matter stinks in the nostrils of those who think it advantageous to get as much ethics into the law as they can." Holmes, *The Path of the Law,* 10 HARV. L. REV. 457, 462 (1897).

This is the classic exposition of the notion that one has the "right" to breach his contract and to pay damages for such breach. This is historically and analytically unsound. One has the *power* to do many things which he legally ought not to do. When a party breaches his contract, usually he cannot be compelled specifically to perform that which he promised to do. Thus, as a substitute for the performance promised by the breaching party, damages are awarded to the injured party. But, damages are not an alternative to performance; they are compensation to the injured party for the breach. The legal machinery is not adequate to compel any more satisfactory redress in the normal case.

(3)   RESTATEMENT (SECOND) OF CONTRACTS § 73 (1981) states:

Performance of a legal duty owed to a promisor which is neither doubtful nor the subject of honest dispute is not consideration; but a similar performance is consideration if it differs from what was required by the duty in a way which reflects more than a pretense of bargain.

(4) In *Rye v. Phillips*, 203 Minn. 567, 569–70, 282 N.W. 459, 460 (1938), JUSTICE STONE wrote an opinion for the court in which he stated, *inter alia:*

> The [pre-existing duty] doctrine is one of the relics of antique law which should have been discarded long ago. It is evidence of the former capacity of lawyers and judges to make the requirement of consideration an overworked shibboleth rather than a logical and just standard of actionability . . . . There is more than one ground of logic and good law upon which this old and indefensible rule may be discarded. There is no reason why a person should be prevented from making an executed gift of incorporeal as well as corporeal property. Why should a receipt in full for the entire debt not be taken in a proper case as sufficient evidence of an executed gift of the unpaid portion of the debt? Again, where there is proof, or on adequate evidence a finding, that a complete legal act such as waiver has set a matter at rest, why is it necessary to search for any consideration?

COMMENT: AVOIDING THE PRE-EXISTING DUTY RULE

In *Betterton v. First Interstate Bank of Arizona*, 800 F.2d 732 (8th Cir. 1986), Betterton purchased an over-the-road tractor and trailer which he financed through the defendant bank to use for transportation contracts procured through a "broker." Betterton fell behind in his payments and the bank had the right to repossess the vehicle. Betterton offered to have his broker send payments to the bank from the proceeds of the transportation contracts. The bank verified the broker's willingness to do so and the bank promised to forego repossession. Nonetheless, it repossessed the truck. Since Betterton had not promised to pay anything more than what he already owed, the bank claimed a lack of consideration in its promise not to repossess the vehicle. The court stated:

> A promise lacks consideration if the promisee is under a pre-existing duty to counter-perform. The rule is inapplicable, however, if the promisee undertakes any obligation not required by the pre-existing duty, even if the new obligation involves almost the same performance as the pre-existing duty. Further, Arizona's courts ordinarily do not inquire into the adequacy of consideration. Betterton was under no pre-existing duty to have his broker deduct funds from his paycheck and pay them to the bank on his behalf. Betterton's promise supplied the consideration necessary to make the [Bank's] promise binding. Id. at 734–35. In *Levine v. Blumenthal*, 117 N.J. L. 23, 186 A. 457 (1936), the court stated, "Yet, any consideration for the new undertaking, however insignificant, satisfies the rule."

DE CICCO v. SCHWEIZER
Court of Appeals New York
117 N.E. 807 (1917)

CARDOZO, J.

On January 16, 1902, "articles of agreement" were executed by the defendant Joseph Schweizer, his wife Ernestine, and Count Oberto Gulinelli. The agreement is in Italian. We quote from a translation the part essential to the decision of this controversy: "Whereas, Miss Blanche Josephine Schweizer, daughter of said Mr. Joseph Schweizer and of said Mrs. Ernestine Teresa Schweizer, is now affianced to and is to be married to the above said Count Oberto Giacomo Giovanni Francesco Maria Gulinelli, Now, in consideration of all that is herein set forth the said Mr. Joseph Schweizer promises and expressly agrees by the present contract to pay annually to his said daughter Blanche, during his own life and to send her, during her lifetime, the sum of Two Thousand Five Hundred dollars, or the equivalent of said sum in Francs, the first payment of said amount to be made on the 20th day of January, 1902." Later articles provide that "for the same reason heretofore set forth," Mr. Schweizer will not change the provision made in his will for the benefit of his daughter and her issue, if any. The yearly payments in the event of his death are to be continued by his wife.

On January 20, 1902, the marriage occurred. On the same day, the defendant made the first payment to his daughter. He continued the payments annually till 1912. This action is brought to recover the installment of that year. The plaintiff holds an assignment executed by the daughter, in which her husband joined. The question is whether there is any consideration for the promised annuity.

That marriage may be a sufficient consideration is not disputed. The argument for the defendant is, however, that Count Gulinelli was already affianced to Miss Schweizer, and that the marriage was merely the fulfilment of an existing legal duty. For this reason, it is insisted, consideration was lacking. The argument leads us to the discussion of a vexed problem of the law which has been debated by courts and writers with much subtlety of reasoning and little harmony of results. There is general acceptance of the proposition that where A is under a contract with B, a promise made by one to the other to induce performance is void. The trouble comes when the promise to induce performance is made by C, a stranger. Distinctions are then drawn between bilateral and unilateral contracts; between a promise by C in return for a new promise by A, and a promise by C in return for performance by A. Some jurists hold that there is consideration in both classes of cases. Others hold that there is consideration where the promise is made for a new promise, but not where it is made for performance (Others hold that there is no consideration in either class of cases)

The storm-centre about which this controversy has raged is the case of *Shadwell* v. *Shadwell* (9 C. B. [N. S.] 159; 99 E. C. L. 158) which arose out of a situation similar in many features to the one before us. Nearly everything that has been written on the subject has been a commentary on that decision. There an uncle promised to pay his nephew after marriage an annuity of £ 150. At the time of the promise the nephew was already engaged. The case was heard before Erle, Ch. J., and Keating and Byles, JJ. The first two judges held the promise to be enforcible. Byles, J., dissented. His view was that the nephew, being already affianced, had incurred no detriment upon the faith of the promise, and hence that consideration was lacking. Neither of the two opinions in *Shadwell* v. *Shadwell* can rule the case at bar. There are elements of difference in the two cases, which raise new problems. But the earlier case, with the literature which it has engendered, gives us a point of departure and a method of approach.

The courts of this state are committed to the view that a promise by A to B to induce him not to *break* his contract with C is void. If that is the true nature of this promise, there was no consideration. We have never held, however, that a like infirmity attaches to a promise by A, not merely to B, but to B and C jointly, to induce them not to *rescind* or *modify* a contract which they are free to abandon. To determine whether that is in substance the promise before us, there is need of closer analysis.

The defendant's contract, if it be one, is not bilateral. It is unilateral The consideration exacted is not a promise, but an act. The Count did not promise anything. In effect the defendant said to him: If you and my daughter marry, I will pay her an annuity for life. Until marriage occurred, the defendant was not bound. It would not have been enough that the Count remained willing to marry. The plain import of the contract is that his bride also should be willing, and that marriage should follow. The promise was intended to affect the conduct, not of one only, but of both. This becomes the more evident when we recall that though the promise ran to the Count, it was intended for the benefit of the daughter In doing so, she made herself a party to the contract. If the contract had been bilateral, her position might have been different. Since, however, it was unilateral, the consideration being performance, action on the faith of it put her in the same position as if she had been in form the promisee. That she learned of the promise before the marriage is a legitimate inference from the relation of the parties and from other attendant circumstances. The writing was signed by her parents; it was delivered to her intended husband; it was made four days before the marriage; it called for a payment on the day of the marriage; and on that day payment was made, and made to her. From all these circumstances, we may infer that at the time of the marriage the promise was known to the bride as well as the husband, and that both acted upon the faith of it.

The situation, therefore, is the same in substance as if the promise had run to husband and wife alike, and had been intended to induce performance by both. They were free by common consent to terminate their engagement or to postpone the marriage. If they forebore from exercising that right and assumed the responsibilities of marriage in reliance on the defendant's promise, he may not now retract it. The distinction between a promise by A to B to induce him not to break his contract with C, and a like promise to induce him not to join with C in a voluntary rescission, is not a new one. It has been suggested in cases where the new promise ran to B solely, and not to B and C jointly. The criticism has been made that in such circumstances there ought to be some evidence that C was ready to withdraw. Whether that is true of contracts to marry is not certain. Many elements foreign to the ordinary business contract enter into such engagements. It does not seem a far-fetched assumption in such cases that one will release where the other has repented. We shall assume, however, that the criticism is valid where the promise is intended as an inducement to only one of the two parties to the contract. It may then be sheer speculation to say that the other party could have been persuaded to rescind. But where the promise is held out as an inducement to both parties alike, there are new and different implications. One does not commonly apply pressure to coerce the will and action of those who are anxious to proceed. The attempt to sway their conduct by new inducements is an implied admission that both may waver; that one equally with the other must be strengthened and persuaded; and that rescission or at least delay is something to be averted, and something, therefore, within the range of not unreasonable expectation. If pressure, applied to both, and holding both to their course, is not the purpose of the promise, it is at least the natural tendency and the probable result.

The defendant knew that a man and a woman were assuming the responsibilities of wedlock in the belief that adequate provision had been made for the woman and for future offspring. He offered this inducement to both while they were free to retract or to delay. That they neither retracted nor delayed is certain. It is not to be expected that they should lay bare all the motives and promptings, some avowed and conscious, others perhaps half-conscious and inarticulate, which swayed their conduct. It is enough that the natural consequence of the defendant's promise was to induce them to put the thought of rescission or delay aside. From that moment, there was no longer a real alternative. There was no longer what philosophers call a "living" option. This in itself permits the inference of detriment. "If it is proved that the defendants with a view to induce the plaintiff to enter into a contract made a statement to the plaintiff of such a nature as would be likely to induce a person to enter into the contract, it is a fair inference of fact that he was induced to do so by the statement" (Blackburn, L. J., in *Smith* v. *Chadwick)*. The same inference follows, not so inevitably, but still legitimately, where the statement is made to induce the preservation of a contract. It will not do to divert the minds of others from a given line of conduct, and then to urge that because of the diversion the opportunity has gone by to say how their minds would otherwise have acted. If the tendency of the promise is to induce them to persevere, reliance and detriment may be inferred from the mere fact of performance. The springs of conduct are subtle and varied. One who meddles with them must not insist upon too nice a measure of proof that the spring which he released was effective to the exclusion of all others.

One other line of argument must be considered. The suggestion is made that the defendant's promise was not made *animo contrahendi*. It was not designed, we are told, to sway the conduct of any one; it was merely the offer of a gift which found its *motive* in the engagement of the daughter to the Count. "Nothing is consideration that is not regarded as such by both parties." But here the very formality of the agreement suggests a purpose to affect the legal relations of the signers. One does not commonly pledge one's self to generosity in the language of a covenant. That the parties believed there was a consideration is certain. The document recites the engagement and the coming marriage. It states that these are the "consideration" for the promise. The failure to marry would have made the promise ineffective. In these circumstances we cannot say that the promise was not intended to control the conduct of those whom it was designed to benefit. Certainly we cannot draw that inference as one of law. Both sides moved for the direction of a verdict, and the trial judge became by consent the trier of the facts. If conflicting inferences were possible, he chose those favorable to the plaintiff.

The conclusion to which we are thus led is reinforced by those considerations of public policy which cluster about contracts that touch the marriage relation. The law favors marriage settlements and seeks to uphold them. It puts them for many purposes in a class by themselves. It has enforced them at times where consideration, if present at all, has been dependent upon doubtful inference. It strains, if need be, to the uttermost the interpretation of equivocal words and conduct in the effort to hold men to the honorable fulfilment of engagements designed to influence in their deepest relations the lives of others. The judgment should be affirmed.

PROBLEMS

(1)   Nick Reed is a young golfer sponsored by the Rocket Golf Company that makes golf balls. Nick has contracted with Rocket to use his best efforts in winning golf tournaments that would promote the sale of Rocket balls. Nick uses Sterling golf clubs though he could use any brand of clubs since he is not sponsored by Sterling. Nick received a letter from Sterling stating, "If you win three PGA tournaments in this, your first year on the circuit, Sterling will pay you $100,000." Nick won three such tournaments, delighting Rocket whose sales of golf balls has soared . . . Sterling refuses to pay Nick. Is there consideration for Sterling's promise? See Restatement (Second) of Contracts, § 73, comment d.

(2)   If a Rhode Island policeman is vacationing in California where he provides information to California authorities leading to the arrest and conviction of a felon, is he entitled to a $50,000 reward in California of which he was aware before providing the information?

(3)   Jennifer Green was employed by the Martin Company under a one-year contract. Three months into the contract, Jennifer informed the president of Martin that she had an offer to work elsewhere at a higher salary. The president was pleased with Jennifer's work and agreed, in writing, to pay a higher salary to match the offer. Was there consideration for the president's promise to pay the higher salary? Suppose the parties agreed to rescind the original contract. The president tore the original contract document in half and handed it to Jennifer who tore it into quarters before tossing it into a nearby wastebasket. The parties then signed the new contract at the higher salary. Is there consideration for the higher salary? *See Schwartzreich v. Bauman-Basch*, 231 N.Y. 196, 131 N.E. 887 (1921).

[13] Modifications of the Pre-Existing Duty Rule

ANGEL v. MURRAY
Rhode Island Supreme Court
322 A.2d 630 (1974)

ROBERTS, C.J.

This is a civil action brought by Alfred L. Angel and others against John E. Murray, Jr., Director of Finance of the City of Newport, the City of Newport, and James L. Maher, alleging that Maher had illegally been paid the sum of $20,000 by the Director of Finance and praying that the defendant Maher be ordered to repay the city such sum. The case was heard by a justice of the Superior Court, sitting without a jury, who entered a judgment ordering Maher to repay the sum of $20,000 to the city of Newport. Maher is now before this court prosecuting an appeal.

The record discloses that Maher has provided the city of Newport with a refuse-collection service under a series of five-year contracts beginning in 1946. On March 12, 1964, Maher and the city entered into another such contract for a period of five years commencing on July 1, 1964, and terminating on June 30, 1969. The contract provided, among other things, that Maher would receive $137,000 per year in return for collecting and removing all combustible and noncombustible waste materials generated within the city.

In June of 1967 Maher requested an additional $10,000 per year from the city council because there had been a substantial increase in the cost of collection due to an unexpected and unanticipated increase of 400 new dwelling units. Maher's testimony, which is uncontradicted, indicates the 1964 contract had been predicated on the fact that since 1946 there had been an average increase of 20 to 25 new dwelling units per year. After a public meeting of the city council where Maher explained in detail the reasons for his request and was questioned by members of the city council, the city council agreed to pay him an additional $10,000 for the year ending on June 30, 1968. Maher made a similar request again in June of 1968 for the same reasons, and the city council again agreed to pay an additional $10,000 for the year ending on June 30, 1969.

The trial justice found that each such $10,000 payment was made in violation of law. . . . [H]e found that Maher was not entitled to extra compensation because the original contract already required him to collect all refuse generated within the city and, therefore, included the 400 additional units. The trial justice further found that these 400 additional units were within the contemplation of the parties when they entered into the contract. It appears that he based this portion of the decision upon the rule that Maher had a preexisting duty to collect the refuse generated by the 400 additional units, and thus there was no consideration for the two additional payments.

As previously stated, the city council made two $10,000 payments. The first was made in June of 1967 for the year beginning on July 1, 1967, and ending on June 30, 1968. Thus, by the time this action was commenced in October of 1968, the modification was completely executed. That is, the money had been paid by the city council, and Maher had collected all of the refuse. Since consideration is only a test of the enforceability of executory promises, the presence or absence of consideration for the first payment is unimportant because the city council's agreement to make the first payment was fully executed at the time of the commencement of this action . . . . However, since both payments were made under similar circumstances, our decision regarding the second payment (Part B, *infra*) is fully applicable to the first payment.

It is generally held that a modification of a contract is itself a contract, which is unenforceable unless supported by consideration. . . . The primary purpose of the preexisting duty rule is to prevent what has been referred to as the "hold-up game." *See* 1A CORBIN . . . § 171. A classic example of the "hold-up game" is found in *Alaska Packers' Ass'n v. Domenico*, 117 F. 99 (9th Cir. 1902). There 21 seamen entered into a written contract with Domenico to sail from San Francisco to Pyramid Harbor, Alaska. They were to work as sailors and fishermen out of Pyramid Harbor during the fishing season of 1900. The contract specified that each man would be paid $50 plus two cents for each red salmon he caught. Subsequent to their arrival at Pyramid Harbor, the men stopped work and demanded an additional $50. They threatened to return to San Francisco if Domenico did not agree to their demand. Since it was impossible for Domenico to find other men, he agreed to pay the men an additional $50. After they returned to San Francisco, Domenico refused to pay the men an additional $50. The court found that the subsequent agreement to pay the men an additional $50 was not supported by consideration because the men had a preexisting duty to work on the ship under the original contract, and thus the subsequent agreement was unenforceable.

Another example of the "hold-up game" is found in the area of construction contracts. Frequently, a contractor will refuse to complete work under an unprofitable contract unless he is awarded additional compensation. The courts have generally held that a subsequent agreement to award additional compensation is unenforceable if the contractor is only performing work which would have been required of him under the original contract.

These examples clearly illustrate that the courts will not enforce an agreement that has been procured by coercion or duress and will hold the parties to their original contract regardless of whether it is profitable or unprofitable. However, the courts have been reluctant to apply the preexisting duty rule when a party to a contract encounters unanticipated difficulties and the other party, not influenced by coercion or duress, voluntarily agrees to pay additional compensation for work already required to be performed under the contract. For example, the courts have found that the original contract was rescinded, *Linz v. Schuck*, 106 Md. 220, 67 A. 286 (1907); abandoned, *Connelly v. Devoe*, 37 Conn. 570 (1871), or waived, *Michaud v. McGregor*, 61 Minn. 198, 63 N.W. 479 (1895).

Although the preexisting duty rule has served a useful purpose insofar as it deters parties from using coercion and duress to obtain additional compensation, it has been widely criticized as a general rule of law. The modern trend appears to recognize the necessity that courts should enforce agreements modifying contracts when unexpected or unanticipated difficulties arise during the course of the performance of a contract, even though there is no consideration for the modification, as long as the parties agree voluntarily.

Under the Uniform Commercial Code, § 2-209(1), which has been adopted by 49 states, "[a]n agreement modifying a contract [for the sale of goods] needs no consideration to be binding." *See* G.L. 1956 (1969 Reenactment) § 6A-2-209(1). Although at first blush this section appears to validate modifications obtained by coercion and duress, the comments to this section indicate that a modification under this section must meet the test of good faith imposed by the Code, and a modification obtained by extortion without a legitimate commercial reason is unenforceable.

The modern trend away from a rigid application of the preexisting duty rule is reflected by [§ 89(a)] of the American Law Institute's RESTATEMENT, SECOND, LAW OF CONTRACTS. . . . We believe that [§ 89(a)] is the proper rule of law and find it applicable to the facts of this case.[10] It not only prohibits modifications obtained by coercion, duress, or extortion but also fulfills society's expectation that agreements entered into voluntarily will be enforced by the courts. *See generally* Horwitz, *The Historical Foundations of Modern Contract Law*, 87 HARV. L. REV. 917 (1974). Section [89(a)], of course, does not compel a modification of an unprofitable or unfair contract; it only enforces a modification if the parties voluntarily agree and if (1) the promise modifying the original contract was made before the contract was fully performed on either side, (2) the underlying circumstances which prompted the modification were unanticipated by the parties, and (3) the modification is fair and equitable.

The evidence, which is uncontradicted, reveals that in June of 1968 Maher requested the city council to pay him an additional $10,000 for the year beginning on July 1, 1968, and ending on June 30, 1969. This request was made at a public meeting of the city council, where Maher explained in detail his reasons for making the request. Thereafter, the city council voted to authorize the Mayor to sign an amendment to the 1954 contract which provided that Maher would receive an additional $10,000 per year for the duration of the contract. Under such circumstances we have no doubt that the city voluntarily agreed to modify the 1964 contract.

Having determined the voluntariness of this agreement, we turn our attention to the three criteria delineated above. First, the modification was made in June of 1968 at a time when the five-year contract which was made in 1964 had not been fully performed by either party. Second, although the 1964 contract provided that Maher collect all refuse generated within the city, it appears this contract was premised on Maher's past experience that the number of refuse-generating units would increase at a rate of 20 to 25 per year. Furthermore, the evidence is uncontradicted that the 1967–1968 increase of 400 units "went beyond any previous expectation." Clearly, the circumstances which prompted the city council to modify the 1964 contract were unanticipated.[11] Third, although the evidence does not indicate what proportion of

---

[10] [2] The fact that these additional payments were made by a municipal corporation rather than a private individual does not, in our opinion, affect the outcome of this case.

[11] The trial justice found that sec. 2(a) of the 1964 contract precluded Maher from recovering extra compensation for the 400 additional units. Section 2(a) provided: *"The Contractor, having made his*

the total this increase comprised, the evidence does indicate that it was a "substantial" increase. In light of this, we cannot say that the council's agreement to pay Maher the $10,000 increase was not fair and equitable in the circumstances.

The judgment appealed from is reversed, and the cause is remanded to the Superior Court for entry of judgment for the defendants.

NOTES

(1)   In *Pittsburgh Testing Lab. v. Farnsworth & Chambers Co.*, 251 F.2d 77 (10th Cir. 1958), the parties contracted for the Testing Company to do all of the testing and inspection of materials required for the construction of ramps and runways. In the performance of the contract, instead of having to move only 600,000 tons of material, Testing had to remove twice that amount, necessitating a longer performance period. A good faith controversy arose over Testing's duties and Farnsworth's correlative rights under the contract. Farnsworth told Testing that if it would continue to perform it would be compensated. No further compensation was forthcoming, however. Farnsworth later repudiated its promise. *Inter alia*, the court suggested that, notwithstanding the lack of precedent in the law of the jurisdiction to be applied (Oklahoma), the court would assume that Oklahoma courts would embrace the unanticipated difficulty doctrine.

(2)   *UCC Section 2-209(1) and CISG.* The court refers to UCC § 2-209(1) which permits modifications of contracts for the sale of goods without consideration. This is not a remarkable change in light of the prolonged criticism of the pre-existing duty rule. Permitting parties to make such modifications without the technical constraint of consideration is a clear illustration of the Llewellyn philosophy to effectuate the factual bargain of the parties. The only criticism of this provision is the failure to include expressly the standard of good faith in the statutory language though Comment 2 to the section insists that only good faith modifications are intended. Under UCC § 2-103 dealing with the "merchant" standard of good faith, the observance of reasonable commercial standards is required along with the general requirement of good faith for all parties of "honesty in fact in the conduct or transaction concerned" § 1-201(19). Thus, while Comment 2 to § 2-209 suggests that modifications should be supported by a "legitimate commercial reason" or an "objectively demonstrable reason," unforeseen difficulty that would provide an excuse for nonperformance under UCC § 2-615 is not required. Nor is there any "unanticipated difficulty" requirement though evidence of such difficulty would obviously provide a legitimate commercial reason for the modification. Courts have evidenced few problems in the application of § 2-209(1). *See Gross v. Valentino Printing Co.*, 120 Ill. App. 3d 907, 458 N.E.2d 1027 (1983); *Bone Int'l, Inc. v. Johnson*, 329 S.E.2d 714 (N.C. App. 1985); *Skinner v. Tober Foreign Motors, Inc.*, 345 Mass. 429, 187 N.E.2d 669 (1963); ON CONTRACTS § 65E.1. (5th ed. 2011).

---

proposal after his own examinations and estimates, shall take all responsibility for, and bear, any losses resulting to him in carrying out the contract; and shall assume the defence of, and hold the City, its agents and employees harmless from all suits and claims arising from the use of any invention, patent, or patent rights, material, labor or implement, by or from any act, omission or neglect of, the Contractor, his agents or employees, in carrying out the contract." (Emphasis added). . . .

CISG Article 29(1) contains a similar provision: "A contract may be modified or terminated by the mere agreement of the parties."

[14] Disputed Claims, Modifications, Accord and Satisfaction

RUBLE FOREST PRODUCTS, INC. v. LANCER MOBILE HOMES OF OREGON
Oregon Supreme Court
524 P.2d 1204 (1974)

TONGUE, J.

This is an action to recover an unpaid balance of $2,500 allegedly due for the purchase of 11 truckloads of lumber by defendant from plaintiff.

Defendant alleged, as an affirmative defense, that some of the lumber was defective and that in compromise and settlement of a disputed claim plaintiff issued to defendant a credit of $2,500. Plaintiff, in reply, denied that the lumber was defective and alleged that defendant had given no proper notice of any claimed defects and that there was no bona fide dispute, but that the indebtedness was undisputed and liquidated; that there was no consideration for the credit; and that it was coerced and induced by defendant in bad faith.

The case was tried before the court sitting without a jury. Plaintiff appeals from a judgment for the defendant. This being an action at law, we must affirm the findings and judgment of the trial court as in the case of a judgment based upon a jury verdict, if supported by any substantial evidence. *Kuzmanich v. United Fire and Casualty*, 242 Or. 529, 531, 410 P.2d 812 (1966).

The facts are not complicated. Plaintiff is a lumber broker in Eugene. Defendant is a mobile home manufacturer in The Dalles and purchased lumber from plaintiff from 1969 through September 1971.

Between August 10 and September 28, 1971, plaintiff sold and shipped 11 truckloads of lumber to defendant, for a total price of $31,091.24. In mid-October plaintiff's president, Mr. Ruble, telephoned defendant's manager, Mr. Scheneman, to complain of defendant's failure to pay for the lumber.

Mr. Scheneman stated that plaintiff had shipped defective lumber to defendant since 1969 amounting to "about $5,000" and that if defendant were to pay any part of the indebtedness there would have to be a compromise for the defective lumber.

Mr. Ruble testified that this was the first notice by defendant of any defective lumber, except for one complaint in 1970, which had been dropped. He also testified, however, that because Mr. Scheneman told him that no payment would be made unless an adjustment was agreed upon and because of financing problems with the bank, he informed Mr. Scheneman two or three days later that he would extend to defendant a "credit" of $2,500. Mr. Ruble then wrote a letter to defendant stating that:

In consideration for receiving $12,195.42 in partial payment of total outstanding to us of $31,091.24, we extend to you a credit of $2,500.00. Leaving a total owing to us of $16,395.82.[12]

A schedule for payment of the balance was then agreed upon, following which defendant made the scheduled payments, with a final payment on January 24, 1972.[13]

In support of its contention that the "credit" of $2,500 represented a bona fide compromise and settlement of a disputed claim, defendant offered testimony of an employee to the effect that he had told the truck driver who delivered one of the 11 shipments that he would not accept delivery of that shipment because the lumber was defective, but that after what he understood to have been a telephone call to plaintiff the truckload was accepted. That shipping order, dated August 10, 1971, was signed "acceptance subject to inspection."

This same employee testified to his recollection of the "percentage" of defective lumber of various specifications as included in the 11 shipments.

In rebuttal, both Mr. Ruble and his salesman responsible for this account denied any complaint by defendant about any of the lumber in any of the 11 shipments. Mr. Ruble also testified that some shipments were delivered by trucks not operated by plaintiff's employees, although trucks designated as Ruble #1, #2, #3 and #4 were leased trucks operated by plaintiff's own employees. It appears from the shipping order of August 10, 1971, that the "delivering carrier" was "Ruble #4."

Defendant's manager, Mr. Scheneman, did not testify.

There was evidence to support a finding that there was a valid compromise of a disputed claim and one made in good faith.

Plaintiff relies upon the rule that an agreement to take less than the whole amount of a liquidated claim is without consideration and unenforceable. It is true that this is the rule at common law, as recognized in Oregon and in most jurisdictions, unless changed by statute. *Portland Mortgage Co. v. Horenstein*, 162 Or. 243, 248, 91 P.2d 533 (1939).

Even at common law, however, it is also the established rule, as stated in *Hodges Agency, Inc. v. Rees and Stover*, 202 Or. 139, 158, 272 P.2d 216 (1954), quoting from *Butson v. Misz*, 81 Or. 607, 611, 160 P. 530 (1916), that:

> A compromise and settlement of a bona fide controversy between the parties, where each having equal knowledge or equal means of knowledge of the facts in good faith claims a right in himself against the other, and which claim the parties consider good or doubtful, constitutes a valid binding agreement, and is a sufficient consideration to support a new contract, even though the law and facts were such that a court would not have adjudged such an adjustment [citing cases].

---

[12] [2] In fact, the sum of $9,695.42 had been paid by defendant. That amount, when added to the credit of $2,500, totaled the $12,195.42 mentioned in that letter.

[13] [3] That schedule and those checks totaled $18,895.82. That amount, when added to the previous payment of $9,695.42 and the $2,500 credit, totaled $31,091.24.

In addition, as contended by defendant, this sale of lumber was subject to the provisions of the Uniform Commercial Code, including the following provision, as stated in ORS 72.2090(1) and (3):

> (1) An agreement modifying a contract within ORS 72.1010 to 72.7250 needs no consideration to be binding.

> (3) The requirements of ORS 72.2010, relating to the statute of frauds must be satisfied if the contract as modified is within its provisions.

[I]n order for an agreement modifying a contract to be valid, the agreement must have been made in good faith. Thus, as stated in Comment 2 to ORS 72.2090:

> [M]odifications made thereunder must meet the test of good faith imposed by the Uniform Commercial Code. The effective use of bad faith to escape performance on the original contract terms is barred, and the extortion of a "modification" without legitimate commercial reason is ineffective as a violation of the duty of good faith. Nor can a mere technical consideration support a modification made in bad faith. The test of "good faith" between merchants or as against merchants includes "observance of reasonable commercial standards of fair dealing in the trade" (ORS 72.1030), and may in some situations require an objectively demonstrable reason for seeking a modification.[14]

Plaintiff vigorously contends that "it [was] not in good faith for defendant to thus coerce plaintiff by withholding payment of any part of the debt" and that defendant "completely failed to carry its burden of proof as to a bona fide dispute and a bona fide compromise of that dispute."

Regardless of whether, upon reading the cold record, we might be inclined to believe the testimony offered by plaintiff rather than that of the defendant, we find that defendant offered evidence which the trial court was entitled to believe and which, if believed, was sufficient to support a finding by the trial court that defendant did not act in bad faith with an intent to coerce plaintiff, but acted in good faith, and that there was a bona fide controversy between these parties as a result of defendant's contention that these 11 shipments included defective lumber. In such a case the trial judge is in a better position than is this court to judge the credibility of the witnesses.

Plaintiff also contends that defendant cannot complain of defective lumber because it did not notify plaintiff of any defects within a reasonable time, as required by ORS 72.6070, and is thus "barred from any remedy." However, validity of either a common law accord and satisfaction or the "modification" of a contract under the Uniform Commercial Code does not depend upon the validity of the claim involved, except to the extent that the claim must be one which is made in good faith.

Plaintiff has also assigned as error the admission of statements made to and by the truck driver who delivered the shipment of August 10, 1971, as "inadmissible

---

[14] [5] 1958 Official Text of the Uniform Commercial Code, reprinted in Oregon's Uniform Commercial Code, published by the Legislative Counsel Committee in 1962. This text formed the basis for House Bill 1020 (1961), enacted as Oregon Laws 1961, ch. 726, effective September 1, 1963.

hearsay" on the ground that the driver was not shown to be an employee of plaintiff with authority to speak for plaintiff. Any such error does not require a reversal in this case, however, because the case was tried without a jury. The crucial issue to be decided was one of the good or bad faith of the defendant, not whether the truck driver was an agent of the plaintiff, and there is no indication that in making its decision the trial court relied upon such evidence. *See Lenahan v. Leach*, 245 Or. 496, 500, 422 P.2d 683 (1967).[15]

For these reasons, we affirm the judgment of the trial court.

NOTE

Where there is an honest dispute in relation to the amount owed, the liability itself, or even the method of payment, there is no duty until that dispute has been settled. Therefore, it is proper to hold that there is no legal duty to pay anything until the question of the amount, liability, or method has been determined. If payment of anything is made before the dispute is settled, the debtor suffers a legal detriment and the creditor receives a legal benefit and, therefore, consideration is present. *See Melnick v. National Air Lines*, 189 Pa. Super. 316, 150 A.2d 566 (1959); RESTATEMENT (FIRST) OF CONTRACTS § 76(b), Illustration 4 (1932); RESTATEMENT (SECOND) OF CONTRACTS § 74, and *Gottlieb v. Charles Scribner's Sons*, 232 Ala. 33, 166 So. 685 (1936). In the *Gottlieb* case there was no dispute about the amount owed, but the debtor in good faith understood that it was entitled to return unsold books for a certain credit. It returned the books and a check for the balance with the words written on the check, "Account in full to date." The creditor cashed the check but declined to accept the books. The court stated, "A dispute as to how and in what way a debt may be discharged whether in money or in property, affords a basis for an accord between the parties, and just as much so as a dispute as to the actual amount due."

NOTE — ACCORD AND SATISFACTION

In *County Fire Door Corp. v. C. F. Wooding Co.*, 202 Conn. 277, 520 A.2d 1028 (1987), the plaintiff supplied metal doors to the defendant who refused to pay the entire contract price, claiming that plaintiff's delay in delivering the doors resulted in additional expenses of $2,180 which he would not pay. The parties argued over the amount due and defendant sent plaintiff a check in the amount of $416.88. On the face of the check, the following notation appeared: "Final payment, Upjohn Project, Purchase Order #3302 dated 11/17/81. On the reverse side of the check, the following statement appeared: "By its endorsement, the payee accepts this check in full satisfaction of all claims arising out of or relating to the Upjohn Project under Purchase Order #3302, dated 11/17/81." Upon receipt of this check, the plaintiff crossed out the conditional language on the reverse side and wrote, "This check is accepted under protest and with full reservation of rights to collect the unpaid balance for which this check is offered in settlement." Defendant made

---

[15] [7] Plaintiff's remaining assignment of error was that the letter written by its president confirming allowance of a $2,500 "credit" was inadmissible in the absence of proof that there was consideration for such an allowance. For reasons previously stated, no consideration was required.

no further payments to the plaintiff who brought this action for the unpaid balance.

The device of placing a creditor, such as the plaintiff, in the position of either not cashing a "settlement" check and pursuing its claim for the full amount, or cashing the check and taking less than it considered acceptable is a standard common law form of settling a dispute by discharging an existing obligation — a form of *accord and satisfaction* discussed below. By crossing out the language on the reverse side of the check and inserting his language, the plaintiff asserted its claim on the basis of UCC § 1-207 as it *then* read: "A party who with explicit reservation of rights performs or promises performance or assents to performance in a manner demanded or offered by the other party does not thereby prejudice the rights reserved. Such words as "without prejudice," "under protest," or the like are sufficient." The issue was whether this common law form of accord and satisfaction had been modified by Section 1-207. The court held that § 1-207 was not designed to modify the common law principles of accord and satisfaction. Not all courts, however, agreed.

To resolve this split authority, the section was amended in 1990 by making the previously quoted language of the section subsection (1) and adding subsection (2): "Subsection (1) does not apply to an accord and satisfaction." If a check (negotiable instrument) is used as it was in this case, UCC Section 3-311 was revised to conform to Section 281 of the Restatement (Second) of Contracts which upholds the original common law rule, if the amount of the debt is unliquidated or disputed in good faith.

Accord and Satisfaction — Substitute Contract. One of the methods of discharging a contractual obligation is by entering into a substitute contract, i.e., a modification of the original contract supported by consideration. If the new agreement is made before the maturity or breach of the original contract, the new contract is simply and properly called a substitute contract. If, however, the new contract is made after the maturity or breach of the original contract, it is called an accord and satisfaction.

Logic suggests that this distinction is unnecessary since any new contract intended by the parties to discharge the original contract should have that effect. The shackles of contract history, particularly the early common law refusal to enforce informal (unsealed) executory promises, have created the need to make the distinction. *See* Murray on Contracts, *supra* Chapter 1, note 1, at § 145A (5th ed. 2011). If the parties enter into a new contract with the intention of immediately discharging the original contract, i.e., prior to the performance of the new contract, such a contract is often referred to as one type of accord, i.e., a contract designed to discharge the old contract upon the formation of the new contract. It is also logical to refer to this type of contract as a substitute contract, and the Restatement 2d so characterizes it. *See* Restatement (Second) of Contracts § 279, comment c.[16]

If the parties do not intend the second contract to operate as an immediate discharge of the original contract, i.e., the first contract will not be discharged until

---

[16] Substitute contracts are covered in Restatement (Second) of Contracts § 279, while accord and satisfaction is dealt with in § 281.

the second is executed (performed), it is possible to characterize this type of contract as a substitute contract, though it appears more reasonable to characterize it as an accord that will have to be satisfied (performed) to discharge the original obligation. The RESTATEMENT (SECOND) agrees. *See Sergeant v. Leonard,* 312 N.W.2d 541 (Iowa 1981). Absent a contrary manifestation of intention, it is presumed that parties do not intend the original obligation to be discharged until the second (the accord) is performed (satisfied).

Assume a party has failed to perform the original contract. He is now obligated to the other party, i.e., he is an obligor and the aggrieved party is an obligee. If the parties agree that they will enter into a new contract in satisfaction of the original obligation which will be discharged when the new contract (accord) is performed (satisfied), a breach of that accord by the obligor clearly permits the obligee to bring an action on the original contract or the accord. RESTATEMENT (SECOND) OF CONTRACTS § 281(2). If the new contract were a substitute contract, i.e., one which the parties intended, upon formation, to discharge the original contract, the obligee would be limited to an action on the substitute contract.

Suppose, however, the obligor is perfectly ready, willing and able to perform the accord but the obligee breaches. When the obligee entered the accord, it was fair to assume that he had no intention of breaching the accord, though the original obligation awaited the performance or satisfaction of the accord. It would not strain credulity to assume the obligee had made an implied promise to perform the accord. Thus, when he breached the accord, it would be appropriate to allow the obligor to plead the accord in abatement of an action by the breaching obligee on the original obligation. Early common law courts had considerable difficulty with this reasoning because it was at war with the unfortunate common law notion that a cause of action once suspended was barred forever. The modern view, however, permits the original obligation to be suspended to provide the obligor with an opportunity to complete performance of the accord. RESTATEMENT (SECOND) OF CONTRACTS § 281(2). For a complete exploration of accord and satisfaction and substitute contract, see MURRAY ON CONTRACTS at § 145 (5th ed. 2011).

[15]   The Invalid Claim

DYER v. NATIONAL BY-PRODUCTS, INC.
Iowa Supreme Court
380 N.W.2d 732 (1986)

SCHULTZ, J.

The determinative issue in this appeal is whether good faith forbearance to litigate a claim, which proves to be invalid and unfounded, is sufficient consideration to uphold a contract of settlement. The district court determined, as a matter of law, that consideration for the alleged settlement was lacking because the forborne claim was not a viable cause of action. We reverse and remand.

On October 29, 1981, Dale Dyer, an employee of National By-Products, lost his right foot in a job-related accident. Thereafter, the employer placed Dyer on a leave of absence at full pay from the date of his injury until August 16, 1982. At that time he returned to work as a foreman, the job he held prior to his injury. On March 11, 1983, the employer indefinitely laid off Dyer.

Dyer then filed the present lawsuit against his employer claiming that his discharge was a breach of an oral contract. He alleged that he in good faith believed that he had a valid claim against his employer for his personal injury. Further, Dyer claimed that his forbearance from litigating his claim was made in exchange for a promise from his employer that he would have lifetime employment. The employer specifically denied that it had offered a lifetime job to Dyer after his injury.

[T]he employer filed a motion for summary judgment claiming that there was no genuine factual issue and that it was entitled to judgment as a matter of law. The motion was resisted by Dyer. The district court sustained the employer's motion on the basis that: (1) no reciprocal promise to work for the employer for life was present, and (2) there was no forbearance of any viable cause of action, apparently on the ground that workers' compensation provided Dyer's sole remedy.[17] [Dyer appeals.]

Preliminarily, we observe that the law favors the adjustment and settlement of controversies without resorting to court action. Compromise is favored by law. Compromise of a doubtful right asserted in good faith is sufficient consideration for a promise.

The more difficult problem is whether the settlement of an unfounded claim asserted in good faith is consideration for a contract of settlement. Professor Corbin presents a view favorable to Dyer's argument when he states:

> [F]orbearance to press a claim, or a promise of such forbearance, may be a sufficient consideration even though the claim is wholly ill-founded. It may be ill-founded because the facts are not what he supposes them to be, or because the existing facts do not have the legal operation that he supposes them to have. In either case, his forbearance may be a sufficient consideration, although under certain circumstances it is not. The fact that the claim is ill-founded is not in itself enough to prevent forbearance from being a sufficient consideration for a promise.

1 CORBIN ON CONTRACTS § 140, at 595 (1963). Further, in the same section, it is noted that:

> The most generally prevailing, and probably the most satisfactory view is that forbearance is sufficient if there is any reasonable ground for the claimant's belief that it is just to try to enforce his claim. He must be asserting his claim "in good faith"; but this does not mean he must believe that his suit can be won. It means that he must not be making his claim or threatening suit for purposes of vexation, or in order to realize on its "nuisance value." (602).

---

[17] [1] It is undisputed that the employee was covered under workers' compensation and that was the sole and exclusive remedy of the employee under the Iowa workers' compensation act. Iowa Code § 85.20 (1983).

Indeed, we find support for the Corbin view in language contained in our cases.

The RESTATEMENT (SECOND) OF CONTRACTS section 74 (1979), supports the Corbin view and states:

Settlement of Claims

(1) Forbearance to assert or the surrender of a claim or defense which proves to be invalid is not consideration unless (a) the claim or defense is in fact doubtful because of uncertainty as to the facts or the law, or (b) the forbearing or surrendering party believes that the claim or defense may be fairly determined to be valid.

Comment: . . .

b. Requirement of good faith. The policy favoring compromise of disputed claims is clearest, perhaps, where a claim is surrendered at a time when it is uncertain whether it is valid or not. Even though the invalidity later becomes clear, the bargain is to be judged as it appeared to the parties at the time; if the claim was then doubtful, no inquiry is necessary as to their good faith. Even though the invalidity should have been clear at the time, the settlement of an honest dispute is upheld. But a mere assertion or denial of liability does not make a claim doubtful, and the fact that invalidity is obvious may indicate that it was known.

However, not all jurisdictions adhere to this view. Some courts require that the claim forborne must have some merit in fact or at law before it can provide consideration and these jurisdictions reject those claims that are obviously invalid. In fact, we find language in our own case law that supports the view which is favorable to the employer in this case. *See Vande Stouwe v. Bankers' Life Co.*, 218 Iowa 1182, 1190, 254 N.W. 790, 794 (1934) ("A claim that is entirely baseless and without foundation in law or equity will not support a compromise."). Additionally, Professor Williston notes that:

While there is a great divergence of opinion respecting the kind of forbearance which will constitute consideration, the weight of authority holds that although forbearance from suit on a clearly invalid claim is insufficient consideration for a promise, forbearance from suit on a claim of doubtful validity is sufficient consideration for a promise if there is a sincere belief in the validity of the claim.

1 WILLISTON ON CONTRACTS § 135, at 581 (3rd ed. 1957).

We believe, however, that the better reasoned approach is that expressed in the RESTATEMENT (SECOND) OF CONTRACTS section 74. Even the above statement from WILLISTON, although it may have been the state of the law in 1957, is a questionable assessment of the current law. In fact, most of the cases cited in the cumulative supplement to WILLISTON follow the "good faith and reasonable" language. Additionally, RESTATEMENT (SECOND) OF CONTRACTS section 74 is cited in that supplement. As noted before, as a matter of policy the law favors compromise and such policy would be defeated if a party could second guess his settlement and litigate the validity of the compromise. The requirement that the forbearing party assert the claim in good faith sufficiently protects the policy of law that favors the settlement of controversies. Our holdings which are to the contrary to this view are overruled.

In the present case, the invalidity of Dyer's claim against the employer does not foreclose him, as a matter of law, from asserting that his forbearance was consideration for the alleged contract of settlement. However, the issue of Dyer's good faith must still be examined. In so doing, the issue of the validity of Dyer's claim should not be entirely overlooked:

> Although the courts will not inquire into the validity of a claim which was compromised in good faith, there must generally be reasonable grounds for a belief in order for the court to be convinced that the belief was honestly entertained by the person who asserted it. Sufficient consideration requires more than the bald assertion by a claimant who has a claim, and to the extent that the validity or invalidity of a claim has a bearing upon whether there were reasonable grounds for believing in its possible validity, evidence of the validity or invalidity of a claim may be relevant to the issue of good faith.

15A Am. Jur. 2d *Compromise and Settlement* § 17, at 790. We conclude that the evidence of the invalidity of the claim is relevant to show a lack of honest belief in the validity of the claim asserted or forborne.

Under the present state of the record, there remains a material fact as to whether Dyer's forbearance to assert his claim was in good faith. Summary judgment should not have been rendered against him. Accordingly, the case is reversed and remanded for further proceedings consistent with this opinion.

NOTES

(1)   Precisely what is the change effectuated by the RESTATEMENT (SECOND) OF CONTRACTS as the court sees it? Is evidence of reasonableness admissible at all?

There has always been general agreement that the claim must be asserted in good faith and, as one court suggests, it is also necessary for the claim to have *some* foundation. With respect to the latter requirement, the court then suggests, "[I]f we should make further effort to distinguish we would say that if the claimant, *in good faith*, makes a mountain out of a molehill the claim is 'doubtful' [i.e., it has *some* foundation]. But if there is no discernible mole hill in the beginning, then the claim has no substance." *Duncan v. Black*, 324 S.W.2d 483, 486 (Mo. App. 1959).

(2)   What is often called the high water mark of the invalid claim cases is *Fiege v. Boehm*, 210 Md. 352, 123 A.2d 316 (1956), where the plaintiff promised to forbear a bastardy prosecution in exchange for defendant's promise to pay the expenses of the birth and to provide for the support of the child that plaintiff alleged the defendant to have fathered. After making some payments, defendant refused to perform further because blood tests revealed that he could not have been the father. The plaintiff then instituted bastardy proceedings resulting in the acquittal of the defendant because of the blood tests. Plaintiff then brought an action on defendant's promise, and the court held the promise supported by consideration since the forborne claim had been honestly asserted and was not frivolous, baseless or

vexatious. The case is questioned, however, in *Jordan v. Knafel*, 880 N.E.2d 1061, 1073 (Ill. App. 2007), a case with similar facts, since the plaintiff in *Fiege* failed to disclose that she also had sex with another party around the time of conception. Restatement (Second) of Contracts, § 161 recognizes that non-disclosure may amount to an assertion that a fact does not exist. Such non-disclosure could constitute a misrepresentation which could allow the avoidance of the contract.

D. PROMISSORY ESTOPPEL

[1]   The Absence of Bargained-for-Exchange — Antecedents

ALLEGHENY COLLEGE v. NATIONAL CHAUTAUQUA COUNTY BANK OF JAMESTOWN
New York Court of Appeals
159 N.E. 173 (1927)

CARDOZO, C.J.

The plaintiff, Allegheny College, is an institution of liberal learning at Meadville, Pennsylvania. In June 1921, a "drive" was in progress to secure for it an additional endowment of $1,250,000. An appeal to contribute to this fund was made to Mary Yates Johnston of Jamestown, New York. In response thereto, she signed and delivered on June 15, 1921, the following writing:

"Estate Pledge,

"Allegheny College Second Century Endowment

"Jamestown, N.Y., June 15, 1921.

"In consideration of my interest in Christian Education, and in consideration of others subscribing, I hereby subscribe and will pay to the order of the Treasurer of Allegheny College, Meadville, Pennsylvania, the sum of Five Thousand Dollars; $5,000.

"This obligation shall become due thirty days after my death, and I hereby instruct my Executor, or Administrator, to pay the same out of my estate. This pledge shall bear interest at the rate of _____ per cent per annum, payable annually, from _____ till paid. The proceeds of this obligation shall be added to the Endowment of said Institution, or expended in accordance with instructions on reverse side of this pledge.

"Name: Mary Yates Johnston,

"Address: 306 East 6th Street,
"Jamestown, N.Y.

"Dayton E. McClain, Witness

"T.R. Courtis, Witness to authentic signature."

On the reverse side of the writing is the following endorsement:

"In loving memory this gift shall be known as the Mary Yates Johnston Memorial Fund, the proceeds from which shall be used to educate students preparing for the Ministry, either in the United States or in the Foreign Field.

"This pledge shall be valid only on the condition that the provisions of my Will, now extant, shall be first met."

"Mary Yates Johnston."

The subscription was not payable by its terms until thirty days after the death of the promisor. The sum of $1,000 was paid, however, upon account in December, 1923, while the promisor was alive. The college set the money aside to be held as a scholarship fund for the benefit of students preparing for the ministry. Later, in July, 1924, the promisor gave notice to the college that she repudiated the promise. Upon the expiration of thirty days following her death, this action was brought against the executor of her will to recover the unpaid balance.

The law of charitable subscriptions has been a prolific source of controversy in this State and elsewhere. We have held that a promise of that order is unenforceable like any other if made without consideration. On the other hand, though professing to apply to such subscriptions the general law of contract, we have found consideration present where the general law of contract, at least as then declared, would have said that it was absent. A classic form of statement identifies consideration with detriment to the promisee sustained by virtue of the promise. So compendious a formula is little more than a half truth. There is need of many a supplementary gloss before the outline can be so filled in as to depict the classic doctrine. "The promise and the consideration must purport to be the motive each for the other, in whole or at least in part. It is not enough that the promise induces the detriment or that the detriment induces the promise if the other half is wanting" (*Wisc. & Mich. Ry. Co. v. Powers*, 191 U.S. 379, 386 [1903] [opinion by Mr. Justice Holmes]. If *A* promises *B* to make him a gift, consideration may be lacking, though *B* has renounced other opportunities for betterment in the faith that the promise will be kept.

The half truths of one generation tend at times to perpetuate themselves in the law as the whole truths of another, when constant repetition brings it about that qualifications, taken once for granted, are disregarded or forgotten. The doctrine of consideration has not escaped the common lot. As far back as 1881, Judge Holmes in his lectures on the Common Law (p. 292), separated the detriment which is merely a consequence of the promise from the detriment which is in truth the motive or inducement, and yet added that the courts "have gone far in obliterating this distinction." The tendency toward effacement has not lessened with the years. On the contrary, there has grown up of recent days a doctrine that a substitute for consideration or an exception to its ordinary requirements can be found in what is styled "a promissory estoppel" (Williston, Contracts, §§ 139, 116). Whether the exception has made its way in this State to such an extent as to permit us to say that the general law of consideration has been modified accordingly, we do not now attempt to say. Certain, at least, it is that we have adopted the doctrine of promissory estoppel as the equivalent of consideration in connection with our law of charitable subscriptions. So long as those decisions stand, the question is not merely whether the enforcement of a charitable subscription can be squared with the doctrine of consideration in all its ancient rigor. The question may also be whether it can be squared with the doctrine of consideration as qualified by the doctrine of promissory estoppel.

We have said that the cases in this State have recognized this exception, if exception it is thought to be. Thus, in *Barnes v. Perine* (12 N.Y. 18) the subscription was made without request, express or implied, that the church do anything on the faith of it. Later, the church did incur expense to the knowledge of the promisor, and in the reasonable belief that the promise would be kept. We held the promise binding, though consideration there was none except upon the theory of a promissory estoppel. In *Presbyterian Society v. Beach* (74 N.Y. 72) a situation substantially the same became the basis for a like ruling. So in *Roberts v. Cobb* (103 N.Y. 600) and *Keuka College v. Ray* (167 N.Y. 96) the moulds of consideration as fixed by the old doctrine were subjected to a like expansion. Very likely, conceptions of public policy have shaped, more or less subconsciously, the rulings thus made. Judges have been affected by the thought that "defenses of that character" are "breaches of faith toward the public, and especially toward those engaged in the same enterprise, and an unwarrantable disappointment of the reasonable expectations of those interested" (W.F. ALLEN, J., in *Barnes v. Perine, supra*, page 24; and cf. *Eastern States League v. Vail*, 97 Vt. 495, 505, and cases there cited). The result speaks for itself irrespective of the motive. Decisions which have stood so long, and which are supported by so many considerations of public policy and reason, will not be overruled to save the symmetry of a concept which itself came into our law, not so much from any reasoned conviction of its justice, as from historical accidents of practice and procedure (8 HOLDSWORTH, HISTORY OF ENGLISH LAW, 7 et seq.). The concept survives as one of the distinctive features of our legal system. We have no thought to suggest that it is obsolete or on the way to be abandoned. As in the case of other concepts, however, the pressure of exceptions has led to irregularities of form.

It is in this background of precedent that we are to view the problem now before us. The background helps to an understanding of the implications inherent in subscription and acceptance. This is so though we may find in the end that without recourse to the innovation of promissory estoppel the transaction can be fitted within the mould of consideration as established by tradition.

The promisor wished to have a memorial to perpetuate her name. She imposed a condition that the "gift" should "be known as the Mary Yates Johnston Memorial Fund." The moment that the college accepted $1,000 as a payment on account, there was an assumption of a duty to do whatever acts were customary or reasonably necessary to maintain the memorial fairly and justly in the spirit of its creation. The college could not accept the money, and hold itself free thereafter from personal responsibility to give effect to the condition. More is involved in the receipt of such a fund than a mere acceptance of money to be held to a corporate use. The purpose of the founder would be unfairly thwarted or at least inadequately served if the college failed to communicate to the world, or in any event to applicants for the scholarship, the title of the memorial. By implication it undertook, when it accepted a portion of the "gift," that in its circulars of information and in other customary ways, when making announcement of this scholarship, it would couple with the announcement the name of the donor. The donor was not at liberty to gain the benefit of such an undertaking upon the payment of a part and disappoint the expectation that there would be payment of the residue. If the college had stated after receiving $1,000 upon account of the subscription that it would apply the money to the prescribed use, but that in its circulars of information and when responding to prospective applicants it would deal with the fund as an anonymous donation, there is little doubt that the subscriber would have been at liberty to treat this statement as the repudiation of a duty impliedly assumed, a repudiation justifying a refusal to make payments in the future. Obligation in such circumstances is correlative and mutual. A case much in point is *N.J. Hospital v. Wright* (95 N.J.L. 462, 464), where a subscription for the maintenance of a bed in a hospital was held to be enforceable by virtue of an implied promise by the hospital that the bed should be maintained in the name of the subscriber. A parallel situation might arise upon the endowment of a chair or a fellowship in a university by the aid of annual payments with the condition that it should commemorate the name of the founder or that of a member of his family. The university would fail to live up to the fair meaning of its promise if it were to publish in its circulars of information and elsewhere the existence of a chair or a fellowship in the prescribed subject, and omit the benefactor's name. A duty to act in ways beneficial to the promisor and beyond the application of the fund to the mere uses of the trust would be cast upon the promisee by the acceptance of the money. We do not need to measure the extent either of benefit to the promisor or of detriment to the promisee implicit in this duty. "If a person chooses to make an extravagant promise for an inadequate consideration it is his own affair" (8 HOLDSWORTH, HISTORY OF ENGLISH LAW, p. 17). It was long ago said that "when a thing is to be done by the plaintiff, be it ever so small, this is a sufficient consideration to ground an action" (*Sturlyn v. Albany*, 1587, Cro. Eliz. 67, quoted by HOLDSWORTH, *supra*). The longing for posthumous remembrance is an emotion not so weak as to justify us in saying that its gratification is a negligible good.

We think the duty assumed by the plaintiff to perpetuate the name of the founder of the memorial is sufficient in itself to give validity to the subscription within the rules that define consideration for a promise of that order. When the promisee subjected itself to such a duty at the implied request of the promisor, the result was the creation of a bilateral agreement. There was a promise on the one side and on the other a return promise, made, it is true, by implication, but expressing an obligation that had been exacted as a condition of the payment. A bilateral agreement may exist though one of the mutual promises be a promise "implied in fact," an inference from conduct as opposed to an inference from words (WILLISTON, CONTRACTS, §§ 90, 22-a). We think the fair inference to be drawn from the acceptance of a payment on account of the subscription is a promise by the college to do what may be necessary on its part to make the scholarship effective. The plan conceived by the subscriber will be mutilated and distorted unless the sum to be accepted is adequate to the end in view. Moreover, the time to affix her name to the memorial will not arrive until the entire fund has been collected. The college may thus thwart the purpose of the payment on account if at liberty to reject a tender of the residue. It is no answer to say that a duty would then arise to make restitution of the money. If such a duty may be imposed, the only reason for its existence must be that there is then a failure of "consideration." To say that there is a failure of consideration is to concede that a consideration has been promised since otherwise it could not fail. No doubt there are times and situations in which limitations laid upon a promisee in connection with the use of what is paid by a subscriber lack the quality of a consideration, and are to be classed merely as conditions (WILLISTON, CONTRACTS, § 112; PAGE, CONTRACTS, § 523). "It is often difficult to determine whether words of condition in a promise indicate a request for consideration or state a mere condition in a gratuitous promise. An aid, though not a conclusive test in determining which construction of the promise is more reasonable is an inquiry whether the happening of the condition will be a benefit to the promisor. If so, it is a fair inference that the happening was requested as a consideration" (WILLISTON, *supra*, § 112). Such must be the meaning of this transaction unless we are prepared to hold that the college may keep the payment on account, and thereafter nullify the scholarship which is to preserve the memory of the subscriber. The fair implication to be gathered from the whole transaction is assent to the condition and the assumption of a duty to go forward with performance. The subscriber does not say: I hand you $1,000, and you may make up your mind later, after my death, whether you will undertake to commemorate my name. What she says in effect is this: I hand you $1,000, and if you are unwilling to commemorate me, the time to speak is now.

The conclusion thus reached makes it needless to consider whether, aside from the feature of a memorial, a promissory estoppel may result from the assumption of a duty to apply the fund, so far as already paid, to special purposes not mandatory under the provisions of the college charter (the support and education of students preparing for the ministry), an assumption induced by the belief that other payments sufficient in amount to make the scholarship effective would be added to the fund thereafter upon the death of the subscriber.

The judgment of the Appellate Division and that of the Trial Term should be reversed, and judgment ordered for the plaintiff as prayed for in the complaint, with costs in all courts.

POUND, CRANE, LEHMAN and O'BRIEN, JJ., concur with CARDOZO, CH. J.; KELLOGG, J. dissents in opinion, in which ANDREWS, J., concurs.

Judgment accordingly.

NOTES

(1) *Charitable Subscriptions.* A modern case traces the use of promissory estoppel to enforce charitable promises to the middle of the nineteenth century.[18] The charitable subscription promise is not bargained-for. The judicial proclivity toward the enforcement of charitable subscription promises found an almost ideal doctrine in promissory estoppel, which allowed the enforcement of promises without bargained-for-exchange if there was detriment to the promisee through justifiable reliance.[19]

---

[18] *See* Maryland Nat'l Bank v. United Jewish Appeal, 286 Md. 274, 407 A.2d 1130 (1979).

[19] The doctrine was *almost* ideal because it still required a showing of actual reliance, which remains a problem for some charities. *See Maryland Nat'l Bank v. United Jewish Appeal, ibid.* But compare

(2)   There is reason to believe that the original enforcement of informal promises was based on the reasonable reliance of the promisee, long before any notion of consideration was conceived. *See* Fuller & Perdue, *The Reliance Interest in Contract Damages* (pts. 1 & 2), 46 YALE L.J. 52, 68 n.61, 373 (1936). *See also Loranger Constr. Corp. v. E. F. Hauserman Co.*, 376 Mass. 757, 384 N.E.2d 176, 179 (1978), where Justice Braucher, Reporter of the Second Restatement of Contracts before his elevation to the bench, confirms this view, citing RESTATEMENT (SECOND) OF CONTRACTS § 90, comment a. The history of promissory estoppel can be traced to promises made by one family member to another. The most famous case is *Ricketts v. Scothorn*, 57 Neb. 51, 77 N.W. 365 (1898), where a grandfather delivered a writing to his granddaughter which evidenced a promise to pay her $2,000 to permit her to leave her employment. The granddaughter left the employment. At the time of his death, the grandfather's note had not been paid and the granddaughter brought an action against the estate. The court recognized there was no consideration to support the grandfather's promise since the grandfather required no detriment from the promisee. Yet, she suffered a detriment that was not bargained-for. The court found an *"equitable estoppel"* which precluded the defendant from showing that the note lacked consideration.

(3)   *Equitable Estoppel*. The application of "equitable estoppel" (sometimes called *estoppel in pais*) to the facts of the *Ricketts* case is misleading. Normally, equitable estoppel applies where a party makes a false representation to, or knowingly conceals material facts from, another party with the intention that the innocent party should act upon the false representation or concealment.[20]

Liability attached if the unknowing party so acted to his or her detriment. In *Ricketts*, the grandfather made a *promise*. The suggestion that the promisor is *estopped* to deny consideration is a conclusion without a reason. The *reason* the promise was enforced was because of the detrimental reliance of the promisee, and the promisor should have reasonably foreseen such reliance. The leap from equitable estoppel to promissory estoppel was necessary because it was clear that equitable estoppel was much too narrow a concept upon which to predicate the enforcement of promises because of detrimental reliance. The name "promissory estoppel" is usually attributed to Professor Williston, 1 WILLISTON ON CONTRACTS § 139 (1st ed. 1920). Though "detrimental reliance" would be a much more meaningful name for the doctrine, the other monumental contributions of Professor Williston must be remembered. Moreover, it is unlikely that anyone using this volume will, during his or her life as a lawyer, witness the decline of the title "promissory estoppel."

(4)   *Gratuitous Promises — Land and Bailments*. Two other antecedents of the modern doctrine of promissory estoppel are worthy of mention. A gratuitous promise to convey land is not enforceable. If, however, such a promise is accompanied by the promisee taking possession of the land and making valuable improvements thereon, the promisee will succeed in a suit for specific performance to

---

RESTATEMENT (SECOND) OF CONTRACTS § 90, comment f, suggesting that charitable subscription promises are so highly favored in our law that "a probability of reliance is enough."

[20]   *See* Valley Bank v. Dowdy, 337 N.W.2d 164, 165 (S.D. 1983) (quoting from the 1974 edition of MURRAY ON CONTRACTS).

convey ownership of the land. *See Miller v. Lawlor*, 245 Iowa 1144, 66 N.W.2d 267 (1954). Perhaps the oldest antecedents of the modern doctrine of promissory estoppel are cases involving gratuitous bailments. If a party (bailor) delivers goods for a particular purpose or for safekeeping to another party (bailee) who promises to keep them or ascertain that something is done with them, and the bailee receives no consideration for this promise, a failure on the part of such a bailee to perform could result in liability. Thus, where a gratuitous bailee promised that he would see to it that certain goods bailed to him would be insured, and he failed to procure the insurance, he was liable for the loss when the goods were destroyed. *Siegel v. Spear & Co.*, 234 N.Y. 479, 138 N.E. 414 (1923). This type of case is traceable to the ancient *ex delicto* form of assumpsit, i.e., the earliest days of that common law writ, when it was clearly considered an offshoot of the tort action in trespass and the emphasis was upon the *misfeasance* of the party dealing with the goods of another. If a gratuitous bailee promised to take care of certain goods but never accepted the goods, he was guilty of *nonfeasance* and was not liable. It was only when he actually began performance of the bailment promise and performed *badly* that he became liable. Again, this precedent is the earliest known manifestation of a promise being enforced on the basis of the detrimental reliance of the promisee.

[2] Early Applications of Promissory Estoppel — Hand Versus Traynor

The receptivity of courts to this "new" doctrine of promissory estoppel was severely limited. There is more than convincing evidence that the doctrine was rather grudgingly accepted in the First Restatement of Contracts.[21] Consideration remained the apotheosis of the validation process. In our review of *Pavel Enterprises, Inc. v. A. S. Johnson Company, Inc.* in Chapter 2, *supra*, we saw that as eminent a judge as Learned Hand could not conceive of promissory estoppel being applied in a bargain context. He therefore rejected the possibility of using the doctrine to make an offer by a subcontractor irrevocable[22] notwithstanding the compelling logic of the contrary view that was so effectively crafted by Justice Roger Traynor.[23] It is now abundantly clear that promissory estoppel will not be limited to non-bargain situations.

---

[21] "Only the scholarly counterattack by Professor Corbin prevented the complete ascendancy of consideration by confronting the Restatement drafters with a multitude of reliance decisions. Corbin succeeded in carving out a place for promissory estoppel as an instance of the Restatement's category of 'Informal Contract Without Assent or Consideration.'" Feinman, *Promissory Estoppel and Judicial Method*, 97 Harv. L. Rev. 678, 680 (1984) (*citing* G. Gilmore, The Death of Contract 62–64 (1974)).

[22] James Baird Co. v. Gimbel Bros., 64 F.2d 344, 346 (2d Cir. 1933).

[23] Drennan v. Star Paving Co., 51 Cal. 2d 409, 333 P.2d 757 (1958). This concept has been explored in Chapter 2 in the discussion of irrevocable offers.

[3]   The Expansive Application of Promissory Estoppel

FEINBERG v. PFEIFFER CO.
Missouri Court of Appeals
322 S.W.2d 163 (1959)

DOERNER, COMMISSIONER.

This is a suit brought in the Circuit Court of the City of St. Louis by plaintiff, a former employee of the defendant corporation, on an alleged contract whereby defendant agreed to pay plaintiff the sum of $200 per month for life upon her retirement. A jury being waived, the case was tried by the court alone. Judgment below was for plaintiff for $5,100, the amount of the pension claimed to be due as of the date of the trial, together with interest thereon, and defendant duly appealed.

The parties are in substantial agreement on the essential facts. Plaintiff began working for the defendant, a manufacturer of pharmaceuticals, in 1910, when she was but 17 years of age. By 1947 she had attained the position of bookkeeper, office manager, and assistant treasurer of the defendant, and owned 70 shares of its stock out of a total of 6,503 shares issued and outstanding. Twenty shares had been given to her by the defendant or its then president, she had purchased 20, and the remaining 30 she had acquired by a stock split or stock dividend. Over the years she received substantial dividends on the stock she owned, as did all of the other stockholders. Also, in addition to her salary, plaintiff from 1937 to 1949, inclusive, received each year a bonus varying in amount from $300 in the beginning to $2,000 in the later years.

On December 27, 1947, the annual meeting of the defendant's Board of Directors was held at the Company's offices in St. Louis, presided over by Max Lippman, its then president and largest individual stockholder. The other directors present were George L. Marcus, Sidney Harris, Sol Flammer, and Walter Weinstock, who, with Max Lippman, owned 5,007 of the 6,503 shares then issued and outstanding. At that meeting the Board of Directors adopted the following resolution, which, because it is the crux of the case, we quote in full:

> The Chairman thereupon pointed out that the Assistant Treasurer, Mrs. Anna Sacks Feinberg, has given the corporation many years of long and faithful service. Not only has she served the corporation devotedly, but with exceptional ability and skill. The President pointed out that although all of the officers and directors sincerely hoped and desired that Mrs. Feinberg would continue in her present position for as long as she felt able, nevertheless, in view of the length of service which she has contributed provision should be made to afford her retirement privileges and benefits which should become a firm obligation of the corporation to be available to her whenever she should see fit to retire from active duty, however many years in the future such retirement may become effective. It was, accordingly, proposed that Mrs. Feinberg's salary which is presently $350.00 per month, be increased to $400.00 per month, and that Mrs. Feinberg would be given the privilege of retiring from active duty at any time she may elect to

see fit so to do upon a retirement pay of $200.00 per month for life, with the distinct understanding that the retirement plan is merely being adopted at the present time in order to afford Mrs. Feinberg security for the future and in the hope that her active services will continue with the corporation for many years to come. After due discussion and consideration, and upon motion duly made and seconded, it was resolved, that the salary of Anna Sacks Feinberg be increased from $350.00 to $400.00 per month and that she be afforded the privilege of retiring from active duty in the corporation at any time she may elect to see fit so to do upon retirement pay of $200.00 per month, for the remainder of her life.

At the request of Mr. Lippman his sons-in-law, Messrs. Harris and Flammer, called upon the plaintiff at her apartment on the same day to advise her of the passage of the resolution. Plaintiff testified on cross-examination that she had no prior information that such a pension plan was contemplated, that it came as a surprise to her, and that she would have continued in her employment whether or not such a resolution had been adopted. It is clear from the evidence that there was no contract, oral or written, as to plaintiff's length of employment, and that she was free to quit, and the defendant to discharge her, at any time.

Plaintiff did continue to work for the defendant through June 30, 1949, on which date she retired. In accordance with the foregoing resolution, the defendant began paying her the sum of $200 on the first of each month. Mr. Lippman died on November 18, 1949, and was succeeded as president of the company by his widow. Because of an illness, she retired from that office and was succeeded in October, 1953, by her son-in-law, Sidney M. Harris. Mr. Harris testified that while Mrs. Lippman had been president she signed the monthly pension check paid plaintiff, but fussed about doing so, and considered the payments as gifts. After his election, he stated, a new accounting firm employed by the defendant questioned the validity of the payments to plaintiff on several occasions, and in the Spring of 1956, upon its recommendation, he consulted the Company's then attorney, Mr. Ralph Kalish. Harris testified that both Ernst and Ernst, the accounting firm, and Kalish told him there was no need of giving plaintiff the money. He also stated that he had concurred in the view that the payments to plaintiff were mere gratuities rather than amounts due under a contractual obligation, and that following his discussion with the Company's attorney plaintiff was sent a check for $100 on April 1, 1956. Plaintiff declined to accept the reduced amount, and this action followed.

Appellant's complaint is that there was insufficient evidence to support the court's findings that plaintiff would not have quit defendant's employ had she not known and relied upon the promise of defendant to pay her $200 a month for life, and the finding that, from her voluntary retirement until April 1, 1956, plaintiff relied upon the continued receipt of the pension installments. The trial court so found, and, in our opinion, justifiably so. Plaintiff testified, and was corroborated by Harris, defendant's witness, that knowledge of the passage of the resolution was communicated to her on December 27, 1947, the very day it was adopted. She was told at that time by Harris and Flammer, she stated, that she could take the pension as of that day, if she wished. She testified further that she continued to work for another year and a half, through June 30, 1949; that at that time her health was good and she could have continued to work, but that after working for almost forty years she thought she would take a rest. Her testimony continued:

Q.   Now, what was the reason — I'm sorry. Did you then quit the employment of the company after you — after this year and a half?

A.   Yes.

Q.   What was the reason that you left?

A.   Well, I thought almost forty years, it was a long time and I thought I would take a little rest.

Q.   Yes.

A.   And with the pension and what earnings my husband had, we figured we could get along.

Q.   Did you rely upon this pension?

A.   We certainly did.

Q.   Being paid?

A.   Very much so. We relied upon it because I was positive that I was going to get it as long as I lived.

Q.   Would you have left the employment of the company at that time had it not been for this pension?

A.   No.

            Mr. Allen: Just a minute, I object to that as calling for a conclusion and conjecture on the part of this witness.

            The Court: It will be overruled.

Mr. Allen: Just a minute, I object to that as calling for a conclusion and conjecture on the part of this witness.

The Court: It will be overruled.

Q.   (Mr. Agatstein continuing): Go ahead, now. The question is whether you would have quit the employment of the company at that time had you not relied upon this pension plan?

A.   No, I wouldn't.

Q.   You would not have. Did you ever seek employment while this pension was being paid to you —

A.   (interrupting): No.

Q.   Wait a minute, at any time prior — at any other place?

A.   No, sir.

Q.   Were you able to hold any other employment during that time?

A.   Yes, I think so.

Q.   Was your health good?

A.   My health was good.

It is obvious from the foregoing that there was ample evidence to support the findings of fact made by the court below. We come, then, to the basic issue in the case. While otherwise defined in defendant's third and fourth assignments of error, it is thus succinctly stated in the argument in its brief: ". . . whether plaintiff has proved that she has a right to recover from defendant based upon a legally binding contractual obligation to pay her $200 per month for life."

It is defendant's contention, in essence, that the resolution adopted by its Board of Directors was a mere promise to make a gift, and that no contract resulted either thereby, or when plaintiff retired, because there was no consideration given or paid by the plaintiff. It urges that a promise to make a gift is not binding unless supported by a legal consideration; that the only apparent consideration for the adoption of the foregoing resolution was the "many years of long and faithful service" expressed therein; and that past services are not a valid consideration for a promise. Defendant argues further that there is nothing in the resolution which made its effectiveness conditional upon plaintiff's continued employment, that she was not under contract to work for any length of time but was free to quit whenever she wished, and that she had no contractual right to her position and could have been discharged at any time.

Plaintiff concedes that a promise based upon past services would be without consideration, but contends that there were two other elements which supplied the required element: First, the continuation by plaintiff in the employ of the defendant for the period from December 27, 1947, the date when the resolution was adopted, until the date of her retirement on June 30, 1949. And, second, her change of position, i.e., her retirement, and the abandonment by her of her opportunity to continue in gainful employment, made in reliance on defendant's promise to pay her $200 per month for life.

We must agree with the defendant that the evidence does not support the first of these contentions. There is no language in the resolution predicating plaintiff's right to a pension upon her continued employment. She was not required to work for the defendant for any period of time as a condition to gaining such retirement benefits. She was told that she could quit the day upon which the resolution was adopted, as she herself testified, and it is clear from her own testimony that she made no promise or agreement to continue in the employ of the defendant in return for its promise to pay her a pension. Hence there was lacking that mutuality of obligation which is essential to the validity of a contract.

But as to the second of these contentions we must agree with plaintiff. By the terms of the resolution defendant promised to pay plaintiff the sum of $200 a month upon her retirement. Consideration for a promise has been defined in the Restatement of the Law of Contracts, Section 75, as:

   (1) Consideration for a promise is

      (a) an act other than a promise, or

      (b) a forbearance, or

      (c) the creation, modification or destruction of a legal relation, or

      (d) a return promise,

bargained for and given in exchange for the promise.

As the parties agree, the consideration sufficient to support a contract may be either a benefit to the promisor or a loss or detriment to the promisee. Section 90 of the RESTATEMENT OF THE LAW OF CONTRACTS states that: "A promise which the promisor should reasonably expect to induce action or forbearance of a definite and substantial character on the part of the promisee and which does induce such action or forbearance is binding if injustice can be avoided only by enforcement of the promise." This doctrine has been described as that of "promissory estoppel," as distinguished from that of equitable estoppel or estoppel in pais, the reason for the differentiation being stated as follows:

> It is generally true that one who has led another to act in reasonable reliance on his representations of fact cannot afterwards in litigation between the two deny the truth of the representations, and some courts have sought to apply this principle to the formation of contracts, where, relying on a gratuitous promise, the promisee has suffered detriment. It is to be noticed, however, that such a case does not come within the ordinary definition of estoppel. If there is any representation of an existing fact, it is only that the promisor at the time of making the promise intends to fulfill it. As to such intention there is usually no misrepresentation and if there is, it is not that which has injured the promisee. In other words, he relies on a promise and not on a misstatement of fact; and the term "promissory" estoppel or something equivalent should be used to make the distinction. WILLISTON ON CONTRACTS, Rev. Ed., Sec. 139, Vol. 1.

In speaking of this doctrine, JUDGE LEARNED HAND said in *Porter v. Commissioner of Internal Revenue*, 2 Cir., 60 F.2d 673, 675, that ". . . 'promissory estoppel' is now a recognized species of consideration." As pointed out by our Supreme Court in *In re Jamison's Estate, Mo.*, 202 S.W.2d 879, 887, it is stated in the Missouri Annotations to the Restatement under Section 90 that:

> There is a variance between the doctrine underlying this section and the theoretical justifications that have been advanced for the Missouri decisions.

That variance, as the authors of the Annotations point out, is that:

> This § 90, when applied with § 85, means that the promise described is a contract without any consideration. In Missouri the same practical result is reached without in theory abandoning the doctrine of consideration. In Missouri three theories have been advanced as ground for the decisions (1) *Theory of act for promise.* The induced "action or forbearance" is the consideration for the promise. *Underwood Typewriter Co. v. Century Realty Co.* (1909) 220 Mo. 522, 119 S.W. 400, 25 L.R.A., N.S., 1173. *See* § 76. (2) *Theory of promissory estoppel.* The induced "action or forbearance" works an estoppel against the promisor. (*Citing School District of Kansas City v. Sheidley* (1897) 138 Mo. 672, 40 S.W. 656 [37 L.R.A. 406]) . . . . (3) *Theory of bilateral contract.* When the induced "action or forbearance" is begun, a promise to complete is implied, and we have an enforceable

bilateral contract, the implied promise to complete being the consideration for the original promise. (Citing cases.)

Was there such an act on the part of plaintiff, in reliance upon the promise contained in the resolution, as will estop the defendant, and therefore create an enforceable contract under the doctrine of promissory estoppel? We think there was. One of the illustrations cited under Section 90 of the RESTATEMENT is: "2. *A* promises *B* to pay him an annuity during *B'* s life. *B* thereupon resigns a profitable employment, as *A* expected that he might. *B* receives the annuity for some years, in the meantime becoming disqualified from again obtaining good employment. *A*'s promise is binding." This illustration is objected to by defendant as not being applicable to the case at hand. The reason advanced by it is that in the illustration *B* became "disqualified" from obtaining other employment *before A* discontinued the payments, whereas in this case the plaintiff did not discover that she had cancer and thereby became unemployable until *after* the defendant had discontinued the payments of $200 per month. We think the distinction is immaterial. The only reason for the reference in the illustration to the disqualification of *A* is in connection with that part of Section 90regarding the prevention of injustice. The injustice would occur regardless of when the disability occurred. Would defendant contend that the contract would be enforceable if the plaintiff's illness had been discovered on March 31, 1956, the day before it discontinued the payment of the $200 a month, but not if it occurred on April 2nd, the day after? Furthermore, there are more ways to become disqualified for work, or unemployable, than as the result of illness. At the time she retired plaintiff was 57 years of age. At the time the payments were discontinued she was over 63 years of age. It is a matter of common knowledge that it is virtually impossible for a woman of that age to find satisfactory employment, much less a position comparable to that which plaintiff enjoyed at the time of her retirement.

The fact of the matter is that plaintiff's subsequent illness was not the "action or forbearance" which was induced by the promise contained in the resolution. As the trial court correctly decided, such action on plaintiff's part was her retirement from a lucrative position in reliance upon defendant's promise to pay her an annuity or pension. The judgment is, accordingly, *affirmed.*

NOTE — APPLICATIONS OF PROMISSORY ESTOPPEL

Recall the statement by Justice Cardozo in the 1927 case *Allegheny College v. National Chautauqua County Bank of Jamestown* which we considered earlier:

> [T]here has grown up of recent days a doctrine that a substitute for consideration or an exception to its ordinary requirements can be found in what is styled "a promissory estoppel" (WILLISTON, CONTRACTS, §§ 139, 116). Whether the exception has made its way in this State to such an extent as to permit us to say that the general law of consideration has been modified accordingly, we do not now attempt to say. Certain, at least, it is that we have adopted the doctrine of promissory estoppel as the equivalent of consideration in connection with our law of charitable subscriptions."

From those beginnings, consider the modern application of promissory estoppel: *Mers v. Dispatch Printing Co.*, 19 Ohio St. 3d 100, 483 N.E.2d 150 (1985): application of promissory estoppel to terminable-at-will employment contract. *Kramer v. Alpine Valley Resort, Inc.*, 108 Wis. 2d 417, 321 N.W.2d 293 (1982): terms of a lease were not a defense to a promissory estoppel claim in a commercial context. *Gruen Indus. v. Biller*, 608 F.2d 274 (7th Cir. 1982): promissory estoppel is applicable in a case involving stock acquisitions, though it was not applied in this case because the reliance was unreasonable. *Reeve v. Georgia Pac. Corp.*, 510 N.E.2d 1378 (Ind. App. 1987): promissory estoppel applied in workmen's compensation benefits case. *Mesa Petr. Co. v. Coniglio*, 629 F.2d 1022 (5th Cir. 1980): promissory estoppel theory permitted recovery on a promissory note. There are hundreds of applications of promissory estoppel in myriad bargaining and non-bargaining situations. There is no limitation on the use of the doctrine where all of its elements can be established.

Consider another application: *Cohen v. Cowles Media Co.*, 479 N.W.2d 387 (Minn. 1992). When Minneapolis and St. Paul newspapers published a story reporting that a nominee for lieutenant governor had been charged with three counts of unlawful assembly and had been convicted of shoplifting, both newspapers revealed that Dan Cohen, a political associate of an opposing gubernatorial candidate was their source for this information. Cohen was fired on the same day the newspapers revealed his identity as the source. Cohen sued on the basis of his reliance on reporters' promises not to reveal him as the source. The newspapers' editors had overruled the reporters' promises. A jury awarded Cohen $200,000 in compensatory damages and $250,000 in punitive damages. The court of appeals affirmed the compensatory damage award but set aside the punitive damages award. The Supreme Court of Minnesota held that the verdict was not sustainable because it intruded on the newspapers' First Amendment rights of a free press. The United States Supreme Court, however, held that the doctrine of promissory estoppel does not implicate the First Amendment. The case was remanded to the Minnesota Supreme Court which, via Section 90 of the RESTATEMENT (SECOND) OF CONTRACTS, found that the promise of confidentiality to Cohen was clear and definite, the promise was intended to induce reliance by Cohen, and the promise had to be enforced to prevent an injustice. The court affirmed the earlier court of appeals decision to affirm the jury's award of $200,000 in compensatory damages.

[4] The Restatements Compared

To compare the two Restatement versions of promissory estoppel in section 90, the following quotation of new § 90(1) contains the language deleted from the original § 90 in brackets while the new language in § 90(1) is italicized.

§ 90. *Promise Reasonably Inducing* [definite and substantial] *Action or Forbearance.*

(1) A promise which the promisor should reasonably expect to induce action or forbearance [of a definite and substantial character] on the part of the promisee *or a third person* and which does induce such action or forbear-

ance is binding if injustice can be avoided only by enforcement of the promise. *The remedy granted for breach may be limited as justice requires.*

[a] Similarities and Dissimilarities

Both versions of § 90 require that (1) there be a promise, (2) the promisor must reasonably expect the promise to induce reliance (i.e., the promisor must foresee such reliance), (3) there must be actual reliance, and (4) injustice can be avoided only by enforcing the promise.

The RESTATEMENT (SECOND) OF CONTRACTS version differs from the original version in three respects: (1) the elimination of the "definite and substantial" reliance requirement, (2) permitting a relying third party to enforce the promise, and (3) creating a flexible remedy standard, i.e., the remedy "may be limited as justice requires."

[b] Elimination of the "Definite and Substantial" Reliance Requirement

This is typically explained by suggesting that the new flexible remedy standard eliminates the need for a strict requirement of definite and substantial reliance. Yet, comment b to new § 90 suggests that the determination of whether injustice can be avoided depends upon certain factors, including "the definite and substantial character" of the reliance.[24] The character of the reliance will depend upon the type of promise. Thus, reliance need not be substantial in charitable subscription cases but should be substantial with respect to offers made irrevocable through reliance and guaranties.[25] *See* MURRAY ON CONTRACTS § 67B.1 (5th ed. 2011).

[c] Detrimental Reliance by Third Persons

In *Hoffman v. Red Owl Stores*, 26 Wis. 2d 683, 133 N.W.2d 267 (1965), plaintiffs, husband and wife, sought to recover their reliance interest on representations made by agents of the defendant who encouraged them to pursue numerous actions in preparation for a future contract to become a franchised owner of a supermarket chain store. With respect to one of the alleged losses, the husband should recover only one/half in the interest in certain property since it was owned in joint tenancy with the wife and the defendant had no dealings with the wife. The court stated, "Ordinarily only the promisee and not third persons are entitled to enforce the remedy of promissory estoppel against the promisor. However, if the promisor actually foresees, or has reason to foresee, action by a third person in reliance on the promise, it may be quite unjust to refuse to perform the promise. [*Citing* 1A CORBIN, CONTRACTS, p. 220, sec. 200.] Here, not only did defendants foresee that it would be necessary for Mrs. Hoffman to sell her joint interest in the bakery

---

[24] Dean Knapp suggests that the "definite and substantial" requirement was originally deleted because of an earlier draft that dealt with charitable subscription cases (where such reliance need not be shown) in a comment. Later, § 90(2) was added to deal with such cases, and under that subsection there is not even a requirement that the promise induce the action or forbearance. Knapp, *Reliance in the Revised Restatement: The Proliferation of Promissory Estoppel*, 81 COLUM. L. REV. 52, 59 (1981).

[25] *See* RESTATEMENT (SECOND) OF CONTRACTS § 90 cmt. b (referring to §§ 87, 88).

building, but defendants actually requested that this be done." 26 Wis. 2d 698, 133 N.W.2d 275.

In addition to *Hoffman*, prior to the RESTATEMENT (SECOND) OF CONTRACTS, there were isolated examples of courts applying promissory estoppel theory to protect third parties. *See Aronowicz v. Nalley's Inc.*, 30 Cal. App. 3d 27, 106 Cal. Rptr. 424 (1972); *Lear v. Bishop*, 86 Nev. 709, 476 P.2d 18 (1970). In *Lee v. Paragon Group Cntrs.*, 78 N.C. App. 334, 337 S.E.2d 132 (1985), however, the court refused to extend the doctrine to third parties as suggested by section 90 of the RESTATEMENT (SECOND) OF CONTRACTS. In *Bolden v. General Acc. Fire & Life Assur.*, 119 Ill. App. 3d 263, 456 N.E.2d 306 (1983), the court refused to apply the doctrine to protect third persons because it was not clear whether an agreement existed between the parties and plaintiffs failed to allege definite and substantial action or forbearance. The court, therefore, stated that the case "would not provide the best vehicle for effectuating a change in Illinois law, *even if desirable . . . .*" 456 N.E.2d at 309. On the other hand, in *Chesus v. Cantrell*, 967 S.W.2d 97 (Mo. App. 1998), the court adopted the extension of promissory estoppel to third parties under the revised Section 90.

[5]   Precontractual Reliance

POP'S CONES, INC. v. RESORTS
INTERNATIONAL HOTEL, INC.
New Jersey Superior Court
704 A.2d 1321 (1998)

KLEINER, J.A.D.

Pop's is an authorized franchisee of TCBY Systems, Inc. ("TCBY"), a national franchiser of frozen yogurt products. Resorts is a casino hotel in Atlantic City that leases retail space along "prime Boardwalk frontage," among other business ventures.

From June of 1991 to September 1994, Pop's operated a TCBY franchise in Margate, New Jersey. Sometime during the months of May or June 1994, Brenda Taube ("Taube"), President of Pop's, had "a number of discussions" with Marlon Phoenix ("Phoenix"), the Executive Director of Business Development and Sales for Resorts, about the possible relocation of Pop's business to space owned by Resorts. During these discussions, Phoenix showed Taube one location for a TCBY vending cart within Resorts Hotel and "three specific locations for the operation of a full service TCBY store."

According to Taube, she and Phoenix specifically discussed the boardwalk property occupied at that time by a business trading as "The Players Club." These discussions included Taube's concerns with the then-current rental fees and Phoenix's indication that Resorts management and Merv Griffin [Chief Executive Office of Resorts] personally were "very anxious to have Pop's as a tenant" and that "financial issues . . . could easily be resolved, such as through a percentage of gross revenue." In order to allay both Taube's and Phoenix's concerns about whether a TCBY franchise at The Players Club location would be successful, Phoenix offered to permit Pop's to operate a vending cart within Resorts free of charge during the summer of 1994 so as to "test the traffic flow." This offer was considered and approved by Paul Ryan, Vice President for Hotel Operations at Resorts.

These discussions led to further meetings with Phoenix about the Players Club location, and Taube contacted TCBY's corporate headquarters about a possible franchise site change. During the weekend of July 4, 1994, Pop's opened the TCBY cart for business at Resorts pursuant to the above stated offer. On July 6, 1994, TCBY gave Taupe initial approval for Pop's change in franchise site. In late July or early August of 1994, representatives of TCBY personally visited the Players Club location, with Taube and Phoenix present.

Based on Pop's marketing assessment of the Resorts location, Taube drafted a written proposal dated August 18, 1994, addressing the leasing of Resorts' Players Club location and hand-delivered it to Phoenix. Taube's proposal offered Resorts "7% of net monthly sales (gross less sales tax) for the duration of the [Player's Club] lease . . . [and] if this proposal is acceptable, I'd need a 6 year lease, and a renewable option for another 6 years."

In mid-September 1994, Taube spoke with Phoenix about the status of Pop's lease proposal and "pressed [him] to advise [her] of Resorts' position. [Taube] specifically advised [Phoenix] that Pop's had an option to renew the lease for its Margate location and then needed to give notice to its landlord of whether it would be staying at that location no later than October 1, 1994." Another conversation about this topic occurred in late September when Taube "asked Phoenix if [Pop's] proposal was in the ballpark of what Resorts was looking for. He responded that it was and that 'we are 95% there, we just need Belisle's signature on the deal.' " [John Belisle was the Chief Operating Officer of Resorts.] Taube admits to having been advised that Belisle had "ultimate responsibility for signing off on the deal" but that Phoenix "assured [her] that Mr. Belisle would follow his recommendation, which was to approve the deal, and that [Phoenix] did not anticipate any difficulties." During this conversation, Taube again mentioned to Phoenix that she had to inform her landlord by October 1, 1994, about whether or not Pop's would renew its lease with them. Taube stated: "Mr. Phoenix assured me that we would have little difficulty in concluding an agreement and advised [Taube] to give notice that [Pop's] would not be extending [its] Margate lease and 'to pack up the Margate store and plan on moving.' "

Relying upon Phoenix's "advice and assurances," Taube notified Pop's landlord in late-September 1994 that it would not be renewing the lease for the Margate location.

In early October, Pop's moved its equipment out of the Margate location and placed it in temporary storage. Taube then commenced a number of new site preparations including: (1) sending designs for the new store to TCBY in October 1994; and (2) retaining an attorney to represent Pop's in finalizing the terms of the lease with Resorts.

By letter dated November 1, 1994, General Counsel for Resorts forwarded a proposed form of lease for The Players Club location to Pop's attorney. The letter provided:

Per our conversation, enclosed please find the form of lease utilized for retail outlets leasing space in Resorts Hotel. You will note that there are a number of alternative sections depending upon the terms of the deal. As I advised, I will contact you . . . to inform you of our decision regarding TCBY.

By letter dated December 1, 1994, General Counsel for Resorts forwarded to Pop's attorney a written offer of the terms upon which Resorts was proposing to lease the Players Club space to Pop's. The terms provided:

> [Resorts is] willing to offer the space for an initial three (3) year term with a rent calculated at the greater of 7% of gross revenues or: $50,000 in year one; $60,000 in year two; and $70,000 in year three . . . [with] a three (3) year option to renew after the initial term. . . .

The letter also addressed a "boilerplate lease agreement" provision and a proposed addition to the form lease. The letter concluded by stating:

> This letter is not intended to be binding upon Resorts. It is intended to set forth the basic terms and conditions upon which Resorts would be willing to negotiate a lease and is subject to those negotiations and the execution of a definitive agreement. . . . We think TCBY will be successful at the Boardwalk location based upon the terms we propose. We look forward to having your client as part of . . . Resorts family of customer service providers and believe TCBY will benefit greatly from some of the dynamic changes we plan . . . . We would be pleased . . . to discuss this proposal in greater detail.

In early-December 1994, Taube and her attorney met with William Murtha, General Counsel of Resorts, and Paul Ryan to finalize the proposed lease. After a number of discussions about the lease, Murtha and Ryan informed Taube that they desired to reschedule the meeting to finalize the lease until after the first of the year because of a public announcement they intended to make about another unrelated business venture that Resorts was about to commence. Ryan again assured Taube that rent for the Players Club space was not an issue and that the lease terms would be worked out. "He also assured [Taube] that Resorts wanted TCBY . . . on the boardwalk for the following season."

Several attempts were made in January 1995 to contact Resorts' representatives and confirm that matters were proceeding. On January 30, 1995, Taube's attorney received a letter stating: "This letter is to confirm our conversation of this date wherein I advised that Resorts is withdrawing its December 1, 1994 offer to lease space to your client, TCBY."[26]

According to Taube's certification, "As soon as [Pop's] heard that Resorts was withdrawing its offer, we undertook extensive efforts to reopen [the] franchise at a different location. Because the Margate location had been re-let, it was not

---

[26] [4] Apparently, in late January 1995, Resorts spoke with another TCBY franchise, Host Marriott, regarding the Players Club's space. Those discussions eventually led to an agreement to have Host Marriott operate a TCBY franchise at the Players Club location. That lease was executed in late May 1995, and TCBY opened shortly thereafter.

available." Ultimately, Pop's found a suitable location but did not reopen for business until July 5, 1996.

On July 17, 1995, Pop's filed a complaint against Resorts seeking damages. The complaint alleged that Pop's "reasonably relied to its detriment on the promises and assurances of Resorts that it would be permitted to relocate its operation to [Resorts'] Boardwalk location. . . ."

After oral argument, the motion judge, citing *Malaker Corp. Stockholders Protective Comm. v. First Jersey Nat'l Bank*, 163 N.J. Super. 463, 395 A.2d 222 (App. Div. 1978), certif. denied, 79 N.J. 488 (1979), rendered a detailed oral opinion in which he concluded, in part:

> The primary argument of the defendant is that the plaintiff is unable to meet the requirements for a claim of Promissory Estoppel as there was no clear and definite promise ever made to plaintiff; and, therefore, any reliance on the part of plaintiff upon the statements of the Resorts agent were not reasonable . . . . I think that even if a jury would find that a lease was promised, there was a lack of specificity in its terms so as to not rise to the level of what is necessary to meet the first element for Promissory Estoppel. There was no specificity as to the term of this lease. There was no specificity as to the starting date of this lease. There was no specificity as to the rent, although it was represented that rent would not be a problem. Rent had not been agreed upon, and it is not certified that it had been agreed upon. When they left that meeting, according to . . . plaintiff's own facts, they didn't have a lease; they would still have to work out the terms of the lease. It was not in existence at the time . . . . We don't have facts in dispute. Neither side, neither the defendant nor the plaintiff, can attest to the terms of the lease, of the essential terms of the lease or still not agreed upon at the time of that the meeting was over in December of 1994.

[T]he judge concluded that the evidence was so one-sided that defendant was entitled to prevail as a matter of law.

It is quite apparent from the motion judge's reasons that he viewed plaintiff's complaint as seeking enforcement of a lease which had not yet been fully negotiated. If that were plaintiff's intended remedy, we would agree with the judge's conclusion. However, plaintiff's complaint, after reciting the facts from the inception of Taube's initial contact with defendant until January 30, 1995, stated:

> As a result of its reasonable reliance on the promises and assurances made to it by Resorts, Pop's has been significantly prejudiced and has suffered significant damages, including the following:
>
> a. the loss of its Margate location and its ability to earn profits during the 1995 summer season;
>
> b. out-of-pocket expenses, including attorney's fees; and c. out-of-pocket expenses in attempting to locate an alternate location. Wherefore, Pop's demands judgment against defendant, Resorts Interna-

tional Hotel, Inc., for damages, costs of suit and for other and further legal and equitable relief as the Court may deem just and proper.

It seems quite clear from plaintiff's complaint that plaintiff was not seeking damages relating to a lease of the boardwalk property, but rather was seeking damages flowing from its reliance upon promises made to it prior to October 1, 1994, when it failed to renew its lease for its Margate location. Thus, plaintiff's claim was predicated upon the concept of promissory estoppel and was not a traditional breach of contract claim.

The doctrine of promissory estoppel is well-established in New Jersey. *Malaker, supra,* 163 N.J. Super. at 479 ("Suffice it to say that given an appropriate case, the doctrine [of promissory estoppel] will be enforced."). A promissory estoppel claim will be justified if the plaintiff satisfies its burden of demonstrating the existence of, or for purposes of summary judgment, a dispute as to a material fact with regard to, four separate elements which include: (1) a clear and definite promise by the promisor; (2) the promise must be made with the expectation that the promisee will rely thereon; (3) the promisee must in fact reasonably rely on the promise, and (4) detriment of a definite and substantial nature must be incurred in reliance on the promise.

The essential justification for the promissory estoppel doctrine is to avoid the substantial hardship or injustice which would result if such a promise were not enforced. *Id.* at 484.

In *Malaker,* the court determined that an implied promise to lend an unspecified amount of money was not "a clear and definite promise" justifying application of the promissory estoppel doctrine. *Id.* at 478–81. Specifically, the court concluded that the promisor-bank's oral promise in October 1970 to lend $150,000 for January, February and March of 1971 was not "clear and definite promise" because it did not describe a promise of "sufficient definition." *Id.* at 479.

It should be noted that the court in *Malaker* seems to have heightened the amount of proof required to establish a "clear and definite promise" by searching for "an express promise of a 'clear and definite' nature." *Id.* at 484 (emphasis added). This sort of language might suggest that New Jersey Courts expect proof of most, if not all, of the essential legal elements of a promise before finding it to be "clear and definite."

Although earlier New Jersey decisions discussing promissory estoppel seem to greatly scrutinize a party's proofs regarding an alleged "clear and definite promise by the promisor," see, e.g., id. at 479, 484, as a prelude to considering the remaining three elements of a promissory estoppel claim, more recent decisions have tended to relax the strict adherence to the *Malaker* formula for determining whether a prima facie case of promissory estoppel exists. This is particularly true where, as here, a plaintiff does not seek to enforce a contract not fully negotiated, but instead seeks damages resulting from its detrimental reliance upon promises made during contract negotiations despite the ultimate failure of those negotiations.

In *Peck v. Imedia, Inc.,* 293 N.J. Super. 151, 679 A.2d 745 (App. Div.) certif. denied, 147 N.J. 262 (1996), we determined that an at-will employment contract offer was a "clear and definite promise" for purposes of promissory estoppel. *See id.*

at 165–68. The employment contract offer letter contained the position title, a "detailed position description . . . as well as information on . . . benefits" and an annual salary. *Id.* at 156. We recognized that even though an employer can terminate the employment relationship at any time, there may be losses incident to reliance upon the job offer itself. *Id.* at 167–68. *See also Mahoney v. Delaware McDonald's Corp.*, 770 F.2d 123, 127 (8th Cir. 1985) (holding that plaintiff's purchase of property for lease to defendant in reliance upon defendant's representation that "we have a deal" created cause of action for promissory estoppel); *Bercoon, Weiner, Glick & Brook v. Manufacturers Hanover Trust Co.*, 818 F. Supp. 1152, 1161 (N.D. Ill. 1993) (holding that defendant's representation that lease was "done deal" and encouragement of plaintiff to terminate existing lease provided plaintiff with cause of action for promissory estoppel).

Further, the RESTATEMENT (SECOND) OF CONTRACTS § 90 (1979), "Promise Reasonably Inducing Action or Forbearance," provides, in pertinent part:

> (1) A promise which the promisor should reasonably expect to induce action or forbearance on the part of the promisee or a third person and which does induce such action or forbearance is binding if injustice can be avoided only by enforcement of the promise. The remedy granted for breach may be limited as justice requires.

The RESTATEMENT approach is best explained by Illustration 10 contained within the comments to Section 90, and based upon *Hoffman v. Red Owl Stores, Inc.*, 26 Wis. 2d 683, 133 N.W.2d 267 (Wis. 1965):

> 10. A, who owns and operates a bakery, desires to go into the grocery business. He approaches B, a franchiser of supermarkets. B states to A that for $18,000 B will establish A in a store. B also advises A to move to another town and buy a small grocery to gain experience. A does so. Later B advises A to sell the grocery, which A does, taking a capital loss and foregoing expected profits from the summer tourist trade. B also advises A to sell his bakery to raise capital for the supermarket franchise, saying "Everything is ready to go. Get your money together and we are set." A sells the bakery taking a capital loss on this sale as well. Still later, B tells A that considerably more than an $18,000 investment will be needed, and the negotiations between the parties collapse. At the point of collapse many details of the proposed agreement between the parties are unresolved. The assurances from B to A are promises on which B reasonably should have expected A to rely, and A is entitled to his actual losses on the sales of the bakery and grocery and for his moving and temporary living expenses. Since the proposed agreement was never made, however, A is not entitled to lost profits from the sale of the grocery or to his expectation interest in the proposed franchise from B. [RESTATEMENT (SECOND) OF CONTRACTS § 90 cmt. d, illus. 10 (1979).]

As we read the Restatement, the strict adherence to proof of a "clear and definite promise" as discussed in *Malaker* is being eroded by a more equitable analysis designed to avoid injustice.

This is the very approach we adopted in *Peck, supra*, wherein even in the absence of a clear and definite contract of employment, we permitted the plaintiff to proceed with a cause of action for damages flowing from plaintiff's losses based on her detrimental reliance on the promise of employment. 293 N.J. Super. at 168.

The facts as presented by plaintiff by way of its pleadings and certifications filed by Taube, which were not refuted or contradicted by defendant before the motion judge or on appeal, clearly show that when Taube informed Phoenix that Pop's option to renew its lease at its Margate location had to be exercised by October 1, 1994, Phoenix instructed Taube to give notice that it would not be extending the lease. According to Phoenix, virtually nothing remained to be resolved between the parties. Phoenix indicated that the parties were "95% there" and that all that was required for completion of the deal was the signature of John Belisle. Phoenix assured Taube that he had recommended the deal to Belisle, and that Belisle would follow the recommendation. Phoenix also advised Pop's to "pack up the Margate store and plan on moving."

It is also uncontradicted that based upon those representations that Pop's, in fact, did not renew its lease. It vacated its Margate location, placed its equipment and personalty into temporary storage, retained the services of an attorney to finalize the lease with defendant, and engaged in planning the relocation to defendant's property. Ultimately, it incurred the expense of relocating to its present location. That plaintiff, like the plaintiff in Peck, relied to its detriment on defendant's assurances seems unquestionable; the facts clearly at least raise a jury question. Additionally, whether plaintiff's reliance upon defendant's assurances was reasonable is also a question for the jury.

Conversely, following the Section 90 approach, a jury could conclude that Phoenix, as promisor, should reasonably have expected to induce action or forbearance on the part of plaintiff to his precise instruction "not to renew the lease" and to "pack up the Margate store and plan on moving." In discussing the "character of reliance protected" under Section 90, comment b states:

> The principle of this Section is flexible. The promisor is affected only by reliance which he does or should foresee, and enforcement must be necessary to avoid injustice. Satisfaction of the latter requirement may depend on the reasonableness of the promisee's reliance, on its definite and substantial character in relation to the remedy sought, on the formality with which the promise is made, on the extent to which evidentiary, cautionary, deterrent and channeling functions of form are met by the commercial setting or otherwise, and on the extent to which such other policies as the enforcement of bargains and the prevention of unjust enrichment are relevant . . . . [RESTATEMENT (SECOND) OF CONTRACTS § 90 cmt. b (1979) (citations omitted).]

Plaintiff's complaint neither seeks enforcement of the lease nor speculative lost profits which it might have earned had the lease been fully and successfully negotiated. Plaintiff merely seeks to recoup damages it incurred, including the loss of its Margate leasehold, in reasonably relying to its detriment upon defendant's promise. Affording plaintiff all favorable inferences, its equitable claim raised a jury question. See Brill, supra, 142 N.J. at 540. Plaintiff's complaint, therefore, should not have been summarily dismissed.

Reversed and remanded for further appropriate proceedings.

NOTES

(1)   In a subsequent case, the court clarified its view of the proof necessary to enforce a promise based on promissory estoppel. In *Lobiondo v. O'Callaghan*, 815 A. 2d 1013 (N. J. Super. 2003), the plaintiff and defendant had several discussions concerning the sale of the defendant's property to the plaintiff. The plaintiff claimed that the parties had entered into an agreement supported by promissory estoppel. As to that claim, the opinion states,

This court has recently indicated that in certain contexts the party invoking the doctrine of promissory estoppel need not provide "clear and definite" proof of such an express promise. *Pop's Cones v. Resorts Intern. Hotel*, *307 N.J. Super. at 469* . . . . We carefully pointed out, however, that plaintiff in that case was seeking damages relating to the surrender of its location, not damages based upon losing a location on the Boardwalk. We said, "This [permitting a party to proceed without 'clear and definite' proof] is particularly true where, as here, a plaintiff does not seek to enforce a contract not fully negotiated, but instead seeks damages resulting from its detrimental reliance upon promises made during contract negotiations despite the ultimate failure of those negotiations." Here, however, plaintiff is attempting to utilize the theory of promissory estoppel to obtain specific performance of the alleged contract at issue.

Does this statement suggest that the "more relaxed" standard of proof to which the court referred in the principal case will depend upon whether the remedy sought is the protection of the expectation or reliance interest?

(2)   Earlier, we considered the extension of promissory estoppel to third parties as suggested in *Hoffman v. Red Owl Stores, Inc.* As the principal case suggests, quoting the RESTATEMENT (SECOND) OF CONTRACTS's illustration of *Hoffman*, it is also well known for the application of promissory estoppel to precontractual reliance situations. By permitting recovery in this context, the *Hoffman* court rather precociously applied promissory estoppel where (a) the parties envisioned a bargain but never achieved one, and (b) the preliminary negotiations may not have evidenced sufficiently definite terms to constitute a contract or, perhaps, an offer.

In the same year that the *Hoffman* case was decided, another court applied promissory estoppel to an agreement that was insufficiently definite. In *Wheeler v. White*, 398 S.W.2d 93 (Tex. 1965), Wheeler owned land and buildings which had a reasonable value of $58,500 and a rental value of $400.00 per month. Wheeler and White agreed that White would obtain the necessary loan from a third party or supply the loan himself to develop the site for a commercial building or a shopping center. The writing evidencing this agreement described the loan as one for $70,000, payable over 15 years in monthly installments and bearing interest at not more than six percent. White was to be paid $5,000 for his efforts plus five percent on all rentals received from tenants in the new building(s). White also assured Wheeler that the money would be available within six months from the date of the agreement and that Wheeler should proceed with the necessary demolition of the buildings on the site. Wheeler razed the existing buildings and otherwise prepared the site.

White then refused to perform the loan agreement and, when sued by Wheeler, argued that the agreement was fatally indefinite in that it did not contain the amount of monthly payments, the amount of interest due, how such interest would be computed, and when it was payable. Wheeler had also entered an alternative plea of promissory estoppel. The trial court held for White and the intermediate appellate court affirmed, but the Supreme Court of Texas reversed. The Supreme Court held that where there is no enforceable contract because of indefiniteness, promissory estoppel will permit a recovery of the reliance damages which the plaintiff sustains. *See* MURRAY ON CONTRACTS, *supra* Chapter 1, note 1, at § 67C (5th edi. 2011).

[6]   Flexible Remedy — Reliance or Expectation

Where there is no contract but the promisee has relied on certain promises, we have seen the damages limited to the reliance interest in the previous case as well as the *Hoffman* case noted therein. The court in *Pop's Cones, Inc.* also refers to the application of promissory estoppel in employment-at-will contracts. In *Jarboe v. Landmark Community Newspapers of Indiana, Inc.*, 644 N.E.2d 118, 122 (1994), the Supreme Court of Indiana deals with this issue with respect to remedies by quoting from an opinion by the United States Court of Appeals for the Seventh Circuit:

> [T]he line Indiana draws is between expectation damages and reliance damages. In future wages, the employee has only an expectation of income, the recovery of which promissory estoppel will not support in an at-will employment setting. In wages foregone in order to prepare to move, as in moving expenses themselves, the employee gave up a presently determinate sum for the purpose of relocating. Both moving expenses and forgone wages were the hopeful employee's costs of positioning himself for his new job; moving expenses happen to be out-of-pocket losses, while forgone wages are opportunity costs. Both are reliance costs, not expectancy damages. *D & G Stout, Inc. v. Bacardi Imports, Inc.* 923 F.2d 566, 569 (7th Cir. 1991). We agree with this analysis and find it applicable to the case at bar. The doctrine of promissory estoppel may be available to an at-will employee, but the remedy is limited to damages actually resulting from the detrimental reliance and will not include the benefit of altering the employment status from an at-will relationship to a permanent one which requires just cause for termination. . . . [W]e decline to authorize the use of promissory estoppel as a basis for general wrongful discharge damages.

PROBLEMS

(1)   A wealthy uncle tells his niece, a third-year law student, that he will give her $15,000 so that she can purchase a new car upon her graduation from law school. After receiving her excellent grades, the niece contracts to purchase a new car for $12,000. The uncle refuses to perform. What should the niece recover? See *Goodman v. Dicker*, 169 F.2d 684 (D.C. Cir. 1948).

In the discussion of the original Section 90, Professor Williston was queried concerning this example. The grand master of contract law left no doubt as to the answer — the Uncle would be liable for the entire $15,000, on the following rationale: "Either the promise is binding or it is not. If the promise is binding it has to be enforced as it is made."[27]

If the only reason for enforcing a promise is detrimental reliance, i.e., absent actual reliance, the promise would not be enforceable, why not make the remedy for such breach co-extensive with the reason for enforcing the promise? Stated another way, if the reason for enforcing the promise is to prevent injustice to the promisee by remedying the loss or minus quantity which the promisee has suffered through justifiable reliance, why should the promisee recover any more than that loss?

(2)   A wealthy uncle promises to pay $10,000 to his niece upon her completion of the bar examination so that she may have a fine vacation. After the bar, the niece travels through Europe and has a wonderful time. She has not kept an account of her expenditures. The uncle refuses to pay. What is the niece's recovery?

(3)   The facts are the same as Problem 2 except that the niece bought a Sweepstakes ticket in Ireland and won. The prize was $400,000. It is stipulated that the niece would not have traveled to Ireland and would not have purchased the ticket absent the promise of the uncle. What is the niece's recovery, if any, in her action against the uncle?

NOTES

(1)   Under Texas law, only reliance damages are available under a promissory estoppel theory. See *Zenor v. El Paso Healthcare Systems, Ltd.*, 176 F.3d 847, 865 (5th Cir. 1999) citing *Central Texas Micrographics v. Leal*, 908 S.W.2d 292, 297 (Tex. App. 1995). Professor Corbin would disagree:

> There is no reason why the courts of the present day should not "make the remedy fit the crime" and make the amount of a judgment for damages depend upon the special circumstances and the merits of the claims of all existing claimants. In doing this, they can properly justify their action by an appeal to their equitable powers inherited from the Chancellor; but it is believed that such an appeal is unnecessary. The courts are still courts of justice; and justice, though not dependent on the length of the Chancellor's foot, has always been dependent on the circumstances of the individual case. This is especially true with respect to the form and extent of the remedy to be applied . . . . [T]he court can give judgment for damages measured by the value of the promised performance — the usual remedy for breach of contract, or measured by the actual outlay incurred by the plaintiff in past performance without including any expected profit that full performance of the defendant's promise would have brought him. 1A A. CORBIN, CONTRACTS § 205 (2d ed. 1963).

(2)   There are many cases in which, without discussing the problem at all, courts have assumed that a promise made enforceable by unbargained-for reliance should permit as broad a recovery as any contract. In a good many of these cases, the

---

[27] ALI Proceedings, Appendix at 103–04 (1926).

reliance and expectation interest would yield the same measure of relief. Where there is a discrepancy between the two interests, a court would wisely choose in many situations to protect the expectation interest. Certainly, one would not be disposed to quarrel with this result in the charitable subscription cases, or in those cases where by granting specific performance of the promise all difficulties of evaluation can be avoided. Fuller & Perdue, *The Reliance Interest in Contract Damages*, 46 YALE L.J. 373, 405 (1937).

(3)   Since the RESTATEMENT (SECOND) provides courts with discretion to determine the remedy in a promissory estoppel case "as justice requires," it is important to elaborate this Delphic guide. The comment provides precious little assistance: "The same factors which bear on whether any relief should be granted also bear on the character and extent of the remedy."[28] The first illustration of this guide is based on the principal case.[29] On the basis of this and another illustration, the RESTATEMENT (SECOND) position could be viewed as normally limiting the remedy to reliance losses. Yet, another comment statement belies this analysis: "[F]ull scale enforcement by normal remedies is often appropriate" (comment d).

(4)   The flexible remedy approach has not seen a great deal of judicial analysis. The typical reaction is to avoid a "mechanical" approach in favor of a "discretionary"[30] or "equitable"[31] remedy. For most courts, the typical remedy in a promissory estoppel case protects the expectation interest, i.e., the full enforcement of the promise rather than the limited protection normally afforded by the reliance interest.[32] *See* MURRAY ON CONTRACTS, *supra* Chapter 1, note 1, at § 67B.3 (5th ed. 2011).

---

[28]   RESTATEMENT (SECOND) OF CONTRACTS, § 90, comment d. The factors suggested to determine whether any relief should be granted start with the well-known requirements that the promisor must foresee the reliance and enforcement may be necessary to prevent injustice. More specific factors include the reasonableness of the reliance, its definite and substantial character in relation to the remedy sought, the formality with which the promise was made, and whether the enforcement of bargains and the prevention of unjust enrichment have any bearing on the enforcement of the promise (comment b).

[29]   It has been suggested that *Goodman v. Dicker* "had nothing to do with the idea of flexible damages in contract law reliance situations. Rather, *Goodman* represented nothing more than routine application of a somewhat obscure principle in the common law of agency, a principle named the 'Missouri rule,'" which the author traces to Beebe v. Columbia Axle Co., 233 Mo. App. 212, 117 S.W.2d 624 (1938), where a distributorship was terminated and the court awarded the distributor out-of-pocket expenditures rather than lost profits. Wangerin, *Damages for Reliance Across the Spectrum of Law: Of Blind Men and Legal Elephants*, 72 IOWA L. REV. 47, 55 (1986).

[30]   *See* Gerson Elec. Constr. Co. v. Honeywell, Inc., 117 Ill. App. 3d 309, 453 N.E.2d 726 (1983) (lost profits allowed without any reliance interest).

[31]   *See* Farm Crop Energy v. Old Nat'l Bank of Wash., 38 Wash. App. 50, 685 P.2d 1097 (1984) (lost profits allowed).

[32]   *See* Farber & Matheson, *Beyond Promissory Estoppel: Contract Law and the "Invisible Handshake*," 52 U. CHI. L. REV. 903 (1985), where the authors studied 222 cases over the decade 1975–1985 in which the courts applied either version of § 90. Only 72 of these cases addressed the issue of the extent of recovery, and only one-sixth of the 72 cases explicitly limited recovery to reliance damages.

E. PAST CONSIDERATION — MORAL OBLIGATION

[1] Past Consideration

PASSANTE v. McWILLIAM
California Court of Appeal
62 Cal. Rptr. 2d 298 (1997)

SILLS, J.

The Upper Deck Company was formed in March 1988 to produce baseball cards with holograms. [Holograms protect credit cards from counterfeiting, and the promoters of the company thought they could protect baseball cards as well. By the 1990's the Upper Deck would become a major corporation whose value was at least a quarter of a billion dollars.] The initial directors were Paul Sumner, William Hemrick, Boris Korbel, Richard P. McWilliam, Angels' pitcher DeWayne Buice and Anthony Passante. Passante, who was already the personal attorney for Korbel and McWilliam, was appointed corporate attorney and secretary. McWilliam, an accountant with contacts to a number of investors, had the responsibility of obtaining start-up financing for the company. Passante made no investment in the company and owned no stock.

Upper Deck needed $100,000 to put on deposit with an Italian paper company by August 1, 1988, so the paper would be available for the inaugural run of baseball cards planned for December. Without the paper, the company risked losing its license with major league baseball. However, as of July 26, 1988, the company had not obtained financing. To make matters worse, McWilliam was demanding more stock in return for the financing he was supposed to obtain. Board members instructed Passante to demand the return of McWilliam's 11 percent stock if he would not change his demands.

When Passante found out that McWilliam would not be coming up with the money, he told his law partner, Andy Prendiville that "there was really no hope for the company to make it." Prendiville asked Passante if he should talk to his brother, who was a doctor and might be able to make a loan of $100,000. Passante told Prendiville to call his brother, who said that he "was in a position to loan the money and would do so." Both Passante and Prendiville spoke to Korbel concerning the availability of "those funds." They told Korbel "that the funds were available."

Korbel then requested that Passante come to a special board meeting to be held on the evening of July 29, 1988, "in order to talk to the other two shareholders about that loan." Korbel said he wanted the other shareholders to be a party to the loan. And, because the shareholders would be guaranteeing the repayment of the funds, Korbel "wanted to make sure that he had the agreement of his co-shareholders for that type of an arrangement."

Dr. Kevin Prendiville wired $100,000 to an account controlled by Korbel just a little after 11 a.m. on July 29, 1988, though Passante still understood that if the board did not approve the loan "it wasn't going to be made."

At the board meeting that evening, Passante told the assembled board members (assembled without notice to McWilliam) "about the availability of the funds." He asked them "if they would be interested in obtaining the money from Dr. Prendiville." The board members agreed.

The board members were "all quite excited about the availability of those funds." Korbel "brought up" the idea that the board should consider giving Passante some ownership interest if he got the loan, and Hemrick said, "Look, if you can get that money for us then I think you're entitled to three percent of the company." There was "general agreement" among the board members "that that would be the case." Passante said, "Okay. We'll do the loan," and then went back to his office.

Passante drafted a note which did not have an interest rate on it. However, at Korbel's insistence, an extra $10,000 was paid to Dr. Prendiville for the 90-day loan. The Upper Deck made its deposit.

The day after the deadline, the board members were "quite happy people." At a meeting held that day, the board members discussed how McWilliam's 11 percent would be divided; "it was determined" that Passante would receive 3 percent from McWilliam's 11 percent, and Korbel would receive the 8 percent balance.

Passante's 3 percent, however, was "to be held by Boris Korbel." The idea was that Korbel would hold Passante's interest in the company until McWilliam returned his stock certificate, and, when a new investor was brought in and new certificates were issued, Passante would receive his stock.

But the Upper Deck still needed financing, and, after an unsuccessful attempt to enlist a New York firm, Korbel told Passante that maybe McWilliam should be brought back into the company after all. Passante told Korbel that he "should do whatever he thought necessary to make the company go forward."

What Korbel thought necessary was to contact McWilliam. On August 31, 1988, Korbel told Passante about Korbel's conversation with McWilliam. McWilliam, it seemed, was "extremely upset" at Passante "because of what had occurred at the end of July." Accordingly, McWilliam would only "invest in Upper Deck" on the condition that Passante "not participate as an owner of the company." Korbel told Passante that "in order to get the company going" Korbel would hold Passante's 3 percent for him and "we wouldn't tell Mr. McWilliam or any of the other shareholders about this interest." After McWilliam "cool[ed] off" and everything was "smooth again," Korbel would discuss Passante's 3 percent interest and either "get a stock certificate representing that interest from the corporation," or Korbel would at least make sure Passante "obtained the benefit of that three percent through him" by way of profit distributions from the company.

In early fall McWilliam came back into the company; McWilliam soon brought in Richard Kughn, a Chicago investor. As a result, the shares of the company were redistributed, leaving Korbel, McWilliam and Kughn each with 26 percent. After Kughn made his investment, Passante was fired as corporate attorney because Kughn wanted the company represented by a large law firm.

In 1988 and early 1989, Korbel told Passante that he need not be concerned about the 3 percent — that Korbel "had it" and he "would take care of it" for Passante.

In November 1990, however, at a restaurant in Orange, Korbel told Passante that he wasn't going to get his 3 percent. In essence, Kughn had been given Passante's 3 percent in the redistribution of stock occasioned by Kughn's investment.

The next month Passante filed this lawsuit. Andy Prendiville was also named as a plaintiff because Passante told him, after the August 2 meeting, that "because of his being so instrumental in obtaining the $100,000 loan" "half of whatever [Passante] got was his." [At the time of the trial in 1993, the value of three percent of Upper Deck stock was valued at close to $33 million.]

The claim against the Upper Deck and the claim against Korbel went to the jury. The jury found for Passante and awarded him some $32 million against Upper Deck and $1 million against Korbel. The Upper Deck then moved for a judgment notwithstanding the verdict or, alternatively, a new trial; the trial court granted both. The trial judge also determined that the sole remaining claim against Korbel was equitable in nature and, in a tentative decision issued July 2, 1993, gave judgment for Korbel on that claim, finding that there was no transaction between Korbel and Passante "which could serve as a basis for imposing a constructive trust."

In his opening brief Passante asserts that "[a]n enforceable contract requires only a promise capable of being enforced and consideration to support the promise." As framed, the assertion is incomplete. Consideration must also be given in exchange for the promise. Past consideration cannot support a contract. (*See Leonard v. Gallagher* (1965) 235 Cal. App. 2d 362, 373 [45 Cal. Rptr. 211] ["It appears to be the universal rule throughout the United States that past consideration will not support a promise which is in excess of the promisor's existing debt or duty."].)

As a matter of law, any claim by Passante for breach of contract necessarily founders on the rule that consideration must result from a bargain. (*E.g., Simmons v. Cal. Institute of Technology* (1949) 34 Cal. 2d 264, 272 [209 P.2d 581] ["But the consideration for a promise must be an act or a return promise, bargained for and given in exchange for the promise."]; *Dow v. River Farms Co.* (1952) 110 Cal. App. 2d 403, 410–411 [243 P.2d 95] [corporate resolution to pay executive $50,000 in consideration of past services rendered held unenforceable given absence of any expectation of payment when services were rendered].)

Thus if the stock promise was truly bargained for, then he had an obligation to the Upper Deck, as its counsel, to give the firm the opportunity to have separate counsel represent it in the course of that bargaining. The legal profession has certain rules regarding business transactions with clients. Rule 3-300 of the California Rules of Professional Conduct forbids members from entering "a business transaction with a client" without first advising the client "in writing that the client may seek the advice of an independent lawyer of the client's choice."

Here it is undisputed that Passante did not advise the Upper Deck of the need for independent counsel in connection with its promise, either in writing or even orally. Had he done so before the Upper Deck made its promise, the board of directors might or might not have been so enthusiastic about his finding the money as to give away three percent of the stock. In a business transaction with a client, notes our Supreme Court, a lawyer is obligated to give "his client 'all that reasonable advice against himself that he would have given him against a third person.'" (*Beery v. State Bar* (1987) 43 Cal. 3d 802, 813 [239 Cal. Rptr. 121, 739 P.2d 1289], *quoting Felton v. Le Breton* (1891) 92 Cal. 457, 469 [28 P. 490].) *Bargaining* between the parties might have resulted in Passante settling for just a reasonable finder's fee. Independent counsel would likely have at least reminded the board members of the obvious — that a grant of stock to Passante might complicate future capital acquisition.

For better or worse, there is an inherent conflict of interest created by any situation in which the corporate attorney for a fledgling company in need of capital accepts stock as a reward for past service. As events in this case proved out, had the gift of 3 percent of the company's stock been completed, it would have made the subsequent capital acquisition much more difficult.

Passante's rejoinder to the ethics issue is, as we have noted, to point to the evidence that the stock was virtually thrust at him in return for what he had done. The terms were totally dictated by the Upper Deck board. And that is it, precisely. There was no bargaining.

But a close reading of the facts shows that the stock had not been bargained for in exchange for arranging the loan; Passante had already arranged the loan (even though the loan had not been formally accepted by the board) before the idea of giving him stock was ever brought up. There is no evidence that Passante had any expectation that he be given stock in return for arranging the $100,000 loan. Clearly, all of Passante's services had already been rendered by the time the idea of giving Passante some stock was proposed. As the court in Dow plainly stated," . . . if there was no expectation of payment by either party when the services were rendered, the promise is a mere promise to make a gift and not enforceable." (*Dow v. River Farms Co., supra,* 110 Cal. App. 2d at p. 410.)

The promise of 3 percent of the stock was not a reward contract; it was Passante who first told Korbel that "funds were available." It was simply, to use a phrase usually associated with life insurance contracts, an inchoate gift — that is, an unenforceable promise from a grateful corporate board. Like the corporate resolution in Dow, it represented a moral obligation. And like the corporate resolution in Dow, it was legally unenforceable. The judgments in favor of McWilliam, the Upper Deck, and Korbel are affirmed.

COMMENT: HISTORY OF "PAST CONSIDERATION"

While the phrase, "past consideration is no consideration" is found in a plethora of modern contracts cases, it is often suggested that "past consideration" was just as good as present consideration at early common law. There is clear evidence of the enforcement of promises for past acts at that time.[33] There was, however, no cohesive theory of consideration, much less "past consideration," in the sixteenth century. This was the time when lawyers did not think of "contract," "tort,"

---

[33] *See, e.g.,* Riggs v. Bullingham, Cro. Eliz. 715, 78 Eng. Rep. 949 [1599]; Hunt v. Bate, 3 Dyer 272(a), 73 Eng. Rep. 605 [1568].

"consideration" or the like. Rather, they were compelled to find *the* proper and only common law writ (covenant, debt, detinue, trespass, trespass on the case, assumpsit) that fit the facts of the case if they were to prevail. The action called *debt* was available for the "half-completed exchange," i.e., goods or services were delivered but the buyer had not paid. The problem with *debt* was that "wager of law" was available whereby the defendant could bring in his friends and neighbors to swear that he had paid. If the buyer made a new promise to pay after receiving the goods or services, *debt* was no longer available because *debt* required a bargained-for-exchange, i.e., a *quid pro quo.* Since *debt* was not available, the unpaid seller was entitled to use another common law writ, the quickly developing action called *indebitatus assumpsit* (being indebted, he undertook), i.e., the buyer undertook to pay the debt. Wager of law was not available to the defendant who was sued in assumpsit.

This was a desirable aid to the unpaid seller. Unfortunately, it was available only where the seller could prove that the buyer made a new promise to pay after receiving the goods or services. The dearth of such proof was not desirable for unpaid sellers, nor was it desirable for the Court of King's Bench, which was eager for more judicial activity (and the consequent fees) since it had no jurisdiction over the older action of debt. Further pragmatic judicial reactions led to holdings by King's Bench that assumpsit would lie even where there was no new, express promise, notwithstanding the traditional view that no more than one form of action was available for each case. This arrangement became solidified in *Slade's Case* in 1602[34] even though the fiction of a second promise was maintained in that case.

There were, therefore, numerous instances of promises being enforced on the basis of "past consideration." For the most part, however, these promises would be enforced today on the basis of present consideration. If the buyer requests goods or services and they are supplied, he will be said to have made either an express or implied promise to pay for them. If the price was not stated, he will pay a reasonable price. Because executory informal promises were not enforceable at early common law, the new or second promise to pay for past benefits was invented to circumvent the shackles of the writ called *debt.* This is not to suggest that there was not an occasional case in which a subsequent promise to pay was enforced for a benefit conferred even though that benefit was done as a favor to the promisor.[35]

By the nineteenth century however, there was clear recognition that a past act, even one done at request, would not support a subsequent promise.[36]

[2] Moral Obligation

When Lord Mansfield was the Chief Justice of King's Bench from 1765 to 1788, his civil law training made him impatient with some of the more technical rules of the common law. In 1782, he authored an opinion for the court stating, "Where a man is under a moral obligation which no Court of Law or Equity can enforce, and promises, the honesty and rectitude of the thing is a consideration." *Hawkes v.*

---

[34] 4 Coke 92B, 76 Eng. Rep. 1074.

[35] *See, e.g.,* Bosden v. Thinne, Yelv. 40, 80 Eng. Rep. 29 [1603].

[36] *See, e.g.,* Kennedy v. Broun, 13 Q.B. (n.s.) 677, 740 [1863]; Roscorla v. Thomas, 3 Q.B. 234 [1842].

Saunders, 1 Cowper 289, 290, 98 Eng. Rep. 1091 [K. B. 1782]. Even after Mansfield's death, this moral obligation doctrine was continued, albeit with some misgivings. Thus, in *Littlefield v. Shee*, 2 B. & Ad. 811 [1831], Lord Tenderten opined, "I must also observe that the doctrine that a moral obligation is a sufficient consideration for a subsequent promise is one which should be received with some limitation." In 1840, the moral obligation doctrine was repudiated. The court held that no satisfactory limits to the doctrine could be fixed. *Eastwood v. Kenyon*, 11 A. & E. 438 [1840].

As we saw in the Chapter 1 introduction to the validation process, in general, moral obligation is not an effective validation device since it could be said that any seriously made promise imports a moral obligation that would make all promises enforceable (*pacta sunt servanda*). In a clear application of that rule, we saw a court refuse to enforce a promise to pay the medical expenses of the plaintiff who had saved the defendant from death or severe injury, notwithstanding the court's acknowledgment that common gratitude would suggest its enforcement. *Harrington v. Taylor*, 225 N.C. 690, 35 S.E.2d 227 (1945). As noted in the introduction, however, there are isolated exceptions to be found in the case law which we now consider.

[3]   The Material Benefit Doctrine

IN RE HATTEN'S ESTATE
Wisconsin Supreme Court
288 N.W. 278 (1939)

NELSON, JUSTICE.

The following facts are not in dispute: The claimant is sixty-four years of age, and has been a resident of New London for twenty-seven years. She is the widow of John Winfield Monsted, a physician who practiced his profession in the city of New London for many years prior to his death, which occurred in 1932. The claimant has two sons, Robert Monsted, aged thirty-five, who owns and operates a resort at Lake Poygan in this state, during the summer months and lives with his mother, the claimant, during the winter months. John W. Monsted, her other son, is a physician who has practiced his profession in the city of New London for about eleven years.

William H. Hatten, prior to his death, which occurred on March 30, 1937, was extensively engaged as a lumberman in this state and in the south. He resided in New London during the greater part of his life. He was very successful in the lumber business and was public spirited and interested in education and politics. At the time of his death he was a member of the boards of trustees of Ripon and Lawrence colleges. Mr. Hatten never married and for many years prior to his death, lived at the Elwood Hotel in New London. He left an estate, which was appraised at over three million dollars. Mr. Hatten was not related by blood or marriage to the claimant or to any member of her family.

It is not disputed that close friendly relations existed between Mr. Hatten and the claimant and her family for more than twenty-five years. During all of those years he frequently was invited to the Monsted home and often went there without formal invitation, where he was given meals and where he enjoyed the companionship of the Monsteds and the privileges of their home. During the years immediately preceding his death his visits to the Monsted home became more frequent. During the last two years preceding his death, when he was in New London, he was at the claimant's home for meals, three or four times a week. In many respects, he treated the Monsted home as though it were his own. Mr. Hatten neither owned nor drove an automobile. On many occasions he was transported in the Monsted automobile to Appleton and to other cities and places. Many of these trips were made at his specific request and for them the claimant received no compensation. Many times, without invitation, he would go to the Monsted home at regular meal times and many times after such meal time was past and was furnished meals which he seemed to enjoy.

The claimant testified that on numerous occasions Mr. Hatten expressed his appreciation to her for all that she had done for him and stated that someday she would be paid well for such services. Two specific instances of such promises were detailed by the claimant. At one time he said to her: "What you are doing for me you will be well paid for it," and on another occasion, in the presence of her son, similarly expressed himself. After carefully reading the testimony, it cannot be doubted that during many years Mr. Hatten was often invited to the Monsted home and always felt free to go there without invitation, to enjoy the privileges of that home, to be transported in the Monsted automobile on both business and pleasure trips and all without compensation or the reciprocal giving or furnishing of meals.

Upon the trial, after the note was introduced in evidence, accompanied by testimony that no part of it had been paid, and the amount of the accrued interest, the claimant rested, reserving, however, the right to offer rebuttal testimony. The administrator then called the claimant adversely and examined her at some length. Her testimony thus elicited by the administrator was in substance that Mr. Hatten had signed the note at her house on a form furnished by her to him pursuant to his request; that at that time she and Mr. Hatten were alone in her library, which was just off the living room; that she filled out part of the blank spaces in the note, i.e., "Jan. 21," "7," "One year," "Beatrice E. Monsted," "Twenty-five thousand 00/100," and that the words "To be taken from my estate," were in the handwriting of Mr. Hatten and written at the time he signed the note; that she loaned him no money on that day and that she entered into no contract with him on that day except what might be expressed in the note.

The circumstances surrounding the execution of the note, as testified to by the claimant, are substantially as follows. On January 21, 1937, Mr. Hatten came to her home between twelve and one o'clock in the afternoon and had lunch there. He had not been invited to the Monsted home on that occasion. After lunch the claimant and Mr. Hatten went into the library and after a while Mr. Hatten said: "Let's finish up that note." He drew from his pocket a note form upon which he had written "Mrs. J. Monsted." The claimant said to him: "Why not write in Beatrice E. Monsted because my son's wife's name is Mrs. J. Monsted as well as my own?" He said: "Have you another blank?" She said she had and took from her desk a blank note form which she had left over from administering her husband's estate and handed it to him. He handed it back to her saying: "You write in your name and the date."

This she did. Mr. Hatten then said: "Write in $25,000." Claimant said: "My, isn't that a lot of money?" He replied: "Well, it isn't for what you have done for me and what the privileges in your home have meant to me. It means so much to me, what you have done for me and the privilege of coming to your home and what your family have done for me."

He then told her to write in the interest rate at 5%. After she had done that he sat down at the desk and took up her pen. It was a fountain pen and somewhat stiff and did not work very well. After a time he succeeded in making the ink flow and signed his name to the note. Mr. Hatten then stated: "Now this is my obligation. I want you to come to me. The Hatten Lumber Company has nothing to do with this." The claimant replied: "Why don't you write in something to that effect?" Mr. Hatten drew an envelope from his pocket and after writing on it for a time, wrote on the note these words: "To be taken from my estate" and handed it to the claimant. The note is a judgment note which reads as follows:

New London, Wis., Jan. 21, 1937.

One year after date, I, we, each and severally promise to pay to the order of Beatrice E. Monsted at New London, Wis., Twenty-five Thousand 00/100 Dollars, Value received, with interest at 5 per cent, per annum, until paid the makers, guarantors and endorsers hereof waive demand notice of non-payment, protest and notice of protest. And agree to pay all attorneys fees and costs if placed in hands of an attorney for collection or for suit. (Authorization to any attorney to confess judgment, omitted.) To be taken from my estate.

Wm. H. Hatton.

The words and figures "Jan. 21," "7," "one year," "Beatrice E. Monsted," "Twenty-five Thousand 00/100," and "5" were concededly in the handwriting of the claimant. According to her testimony, the words "To be taken from my estate," and the signature "Wm. H. Hatton," were written by Mr. Hatten.

[W]e conclude that the finding of the trial court that both the signature and the interlineation are in the handwriting of Mr. Hatten, should not be disturbed. Under the established law, we cannot say that the finding of the court that Mr. Hatten was competent on the afternoon of January 21, 1937, when he executed the note, is against the great weight and clear preponderance of the evidence.

The administrator further contends that the court erred in finding that there was a valuable consideration sufficient to support the note and that the note was given for those considerations. The trial court found in substance that for twenty-five years prior to January 21, 1937, the claimant had rendered services, furnished meals and extended the privileges of her home and the use of her automobile to the deceased at his express instance and request; that on two specific occasions during the year 1936, and on numerous other occasions, he promised to pay the claimant for such services, meals, privileges and the use of her automobile; that such services, meals, etc., were not intended by the claimant to be gratuitous and they were furnished and extended with the intention and expectation of being paid therefor; that said services, etc., were of material and pecuniary value to the deceased and that the deceased deemed himself to be legally and morally indebted to the claimant therefor in the sum of $25,000, which he considered to be fair compensation to claimant for the same and that the consideration for said note was the services, meals, privileges of the home and the use of the claimant's automobile.

Were we required to determine whether the services, meals, etc., were reasonably worth the sum of $25,000, — in other words, if this action were one to recover quantum meruit, we should have no hesitation in holding that they were not reasonably worth that amount. That question, however, is not before us. The claimant's claim is founded upon a negotiable promissory note. There must, of course, be consideration to support it, otherwise it is subject to the defense of no consideration as between the parties to it and as against one who is not a holder in due course. Sec. 116.33, Stats. Every negotiable instrument is deemed prima facie to have been issued for a valuable consideration. Sec. 116.29, Stats. Want of consideration may, of course, be shown but the burden upon him who asserts such want of consideration is the same, or at least as great as that required to establish a mistake . . . . To reform a written instrument on the ground of mistake, the proof must be clear and satisfactory.

"Value is any consideration sufficient to support a simple contract. An antecedent or pre-existing debt constitutes value." Sec. 116.30, Stats.

Under the law, which requires clear and satisfactory proof of want of consideration, the trial court may well have concluded that the administrator failed to meet that burden. It must be held that the finding of the trial court, that the note was supported by a valuable consideration, cannot be said to be against the great weight and clear preponderance of the evidence. The finding of the trial court was obviously largely based upon the testimony of the claimant. Her credibility and the weight of her testimony were for the trial court's determination.

Moreover, in this state we have adopted what is said to be the liberal rule as to moral consideration and have held that a receipt by the promisor of an actual benefit will support an executory promise and that a moral consideration may be sufficient to support an executory promise "where the promisor originally received from the promisee something of value sufficient to arouse a moral, as distinguished from a legal, obligation." *Park Falls State Bank v. Fordyce*, 206 Wis. 628, 635, 238 N.W. 516, 518, 79 A.L.R. 1339. In *Elbinger v. Capitol & Teutonia Co.*, 208 Wis. 163, 242 N.W. 568, 569, in commenting upon the holding in *Park Falls State Bank v. Fordyce, supra*, it was said:

> "We there held that whenever the promisor has originally received value, material pecuniary benefit, under circumstances giving rise to a moral obligation on his part to pay for that which he has received, it is a sufficient consideration to support a promise on his part to pay therefor." *See also Estate of Smith*, 226 Wis. 556, 277 N.W. 141. *Judgment affirmed.*

NOTES

(1) Generally, courts reject the view that gratitude for prior gifts makes the recipient's promise to pay therefor enforceable. In *Mills v. Wyman*, 20 Mass. (3 Pick.) 207 (1825), the plaintiff gave emergency aid in the form of board and nursing to the defendant's son who was returning from a voyage and was taken sick. After

the expenses had been incurred, the defendant wrote a letter to the plaintiff promising to pay for the expenses. The court denied recovery and distinguished the enforceability of promises to pay debts barred by the statute of limitations or discharged in bankruptcy on the following grounds:

> Express promises founded on such pre-existing equitable obligations may be enforced; there is a good consideration for them; they merely remove an impediment created by law to the recovery of debts honestly due, but which public policy protects the debtors from being compelled to pay. In all these cases there was originally a *quid pro quo*, and according to the principles of natural justice the party receiving them ought to pay; but the legislature has said he shall not be coerced; then comes the promise to pay the debt that is barred, the promise of the man to pay the debt of the infant, of the discharged bankrupt to restore to his creditor what by the law he had lost. In all these cases there is a moral obligation founded upon an antecedent valuable consideration. These promises, therefore, have a sound legal basis. They are not promises to pay something for nothing; not naked pacts, but the voluntary revival or creation of obligations which before existed in natural law, but which had been dispensed with, not for the benefit of the party obliged solely, but principally for the public convenience. If moral obligation, in its fullest sense, is a good substratum for an express promise, it is not easy to perceive why it is not equally good to support an implied promise. What a man ought to do, generally he ought to be made to do whether he promise or refuse. But the law of the society has left most of such obligations to the interior forum, as the tribunal of conscience has been aptly called.

(2)   *Quaere:* Was the promise by the defendant in the principal case a promise to pay something for nothing? What is "natural law"? Is that concept or phrase any more precise than "moral obligation"?

(3)   In *Webb v. McGowin*, 27 Ala. App. 82, 168 So. 196 (1935), the plaintiff, employed by the Smith Lumber Co., was clearing the upper floor of the mill. This process required him to drop pine blocks from the upper floor to the ground below. While in the act of dropping a block, he saw J. Greely McGowin below and could divert the block to prevent it from striking McGowin only by holding on to the block and "riding" it to the ground. The effort saved McGowin but plaintiff suffered severe injuries precluding him from working thereafter. McGowin agreed to pay plaintiff $15 every two weeks for the remainder of plaintiff's life. This sum was paid until McGowin's death but discontinued shortly thereafter.

The court held that the McGowin promise was enforceable because McGowin had received a benefit and the plaintiff had suffered a detriment. While the court suggests that it had thereby found consideration, it essentially urged what has often been called the "material benefit" rule, i.e., where a material benefit has been received and the recipient voluntarily promises to pay for this past benefit, the promise is said to be enforceable on the basis of moral obligation.   *Minority view.*

(4)   Few states have adopted this doctrine. *See, however, Worner Agency, Inc. v. Doyle*, 133 Ill. App. 3d 850, 479 N.E.2d 468 (1985) (past material benefit conferred was sufficient to support promise to pay a finder's fee). Notwithstanding this limited

authority, the Restatement (Second) states: "A promise made in recognition of a benefit previously received by the promisor from the promise is binding to the extent necessary to prevent injustice." (§ 86(1)). In language that requires explanation if not elaboration, section 86 continues:

(2) A promise is not binding under Subsection (1)

(a) if the promisee conferred the benefit as a gift or for other reasons the promisor had not been unjustly enriched; or

(b) to the extent that its value is disproportionate to the benefit.

Not remarkably, two of the illustrations in this section are based on the case in Note 3, (*Webb*), and the principal case (*Hatten's Estate*). At first blush, the illustrations appear to contradict the language of the section. The rescuer in *Webb* could not be said to have expected compensation when he performed in an emergency situation. Professionals excepted, an action in restitution will not lie because of the gratuitous presumption where a benefit is conferred in an emergency situation. Thus, the recipient is not unjustly enriched. The rescuer, then, would appear to have conferred the benefit as a gift and McGowin would not be unjustly enriched. Yet, the Restatement (Second) suggests that the subsequent promise "may remove doubt as to the reality of the benefit and as to its value, and may negate any danger of imposition of a false claim. A positive showing that payment was expected is not then required. An intention to make a gift must be shown to defeat restitution."[37] The burden of establishing the rescuer's gratuitous intention is placed on the promisor.

The *Hatten* illustration supposes that the value of the benefit conferred was no more than $6,000, for which Mr. Hatten promised to pay $25,000. On its face, § 86(2)(b) would suggest that the promise would not be enforced for more than $6,000. Yet, the illustration concludes that the $25,000 promise is binding. The following illustration changes the facts by having the bachelor promise to leave his entire estate to the promisee. That promise is binding only to the extent of the reasonable value conferred, i.e., the restitution interest. Thus, the illustration suggests that one should read subsection (2)(b) as not permitting the enforcement of *grossly* disproportionate promises. Notwithstanding these difficulties and the fact, as the Reporter urged, that the section "bristles with nonspecific concepts,"[38] the "material benefit" rule, as recommended by the Second Restatement, has much to recommend it. The traditional view, which opposes any form of "moral obligation" as a validation device, is predicated essentially upon the uncertainty of such a concept — the fear that courts will not be able to draw bright lines between promises that ought to be enforced and those that do not deserve enforcement. Yet, all of our law "bristles with nonspecific concepts, including reasonableness, materiality, due care, and, of course, the generic directive against "injustice" which is the basis for the doctrine of promissory estoppel, now so well-ensconced in our contracts jurisprudence.

---

[37] Restatement (Second) of Contracts § 86, comment d.

[38] *See* 42 ALI Proceedings 274 (1965); *see also* Braucher, *Freedom of Contract and the Second Restatement*, 78 Yale L.J. 598, 605 (1969).

[4]   Promises Uniformly Enforced through Moral Obligation

FIRST HAWAIIAN BANK v. ZUKERKORN
Hawaii Intermediate Court of Appeals
633 P.2d 550 (1981)

BURNS, J.

Zukerkorn executed in favor of the Bank a $6,394.21 demand note dated November 22, 1965, and a $2,500.00 two-year note dated September 23, 1966. He made no payments on either note. On August 6, 1973, Zukerkorn obtained an automobile purchase loan from the Bank, and he paid it off on April 6, 1976.

On or about December 11, 1975, Zukerkorn applied to the Bank for a master charge credit card. He admits that the Bank told him that he owed "a small amount of money on an old account"; that issuance of the card was conditioned on his agreement to pay $100.00 per month on the old account; that he agreed to the condition; and that he received a credit card. He denies the Bank's assertion that the November 22, 1965, and the September 23, 1966, notes were specifically identified and that his agreement specifically related to them.

Zukerkorn also denies the Bank's assertion that he paid $200.00 in cash at or about the time he made the agreement. Both parties agree that after the agreement, Zukerkorn made payments on the automobile loan, on the master charge account, and that pursuant to his agreement (the terms of which are in dispute), he paid $200.00 on May 12, 1976; $100.00 on June 8, 1976; $100.00 on July 12, 1976; and $100.00 on August 23, 1976.

On March 3, 1978, the Bank sued Zukerkorn on the November 22, 1965, note; the September 23, 1966, note; and on the balance due on the master charge account.

On November 27, 1978, the lower court entered summary judgment in favor of the Bank on all three of its claims.

Pursuant to Hawaii Rules of Civil Procedure, Rule 56(e), we affirm that portion of the summary judgment which relates to the $4,594.60 owed on the master charge account. The Bank's affidavits concerning this account were sufficient and they were not contradicted by Zukerkorn.

We turn, then, to the portion of the summary judgment which relates to the November 22, 1965, and the September 23, 1966, notes. Collection of these notes was barred by the applicable six-year statute of limitations unless something occurred which started it running anew.

After reading the authorities, we state the applicable law to be as follows: A new promise by the debtor to pay his debt, whether then barred by the applicable statute of limitations or not, binds the debtor for a new limitations period. The promise may be express or implied. If it is express, it may be unconditional or conditional, but if conditional, it is not effective until the condition is performed. The promise may be implied from an express acknowledgment of the debt or from part payment thereof. However, an express acknowledgment of the debt or part payment thereof is only prima facie evidence of a new promise which may be rebutted by other evidence and by the circumstances under which it is made.[39]

Therefore, we may sustain the summary judgment issued in favor of the Bank only if we conclude that viewed most favorably to Zukerkorn the facts show, as a matter of law, that within six years prior to March 3, 1978, Zukerkorn promised to pay the two stale debts.

Zukerkorn could have promised (1) by an express promise to pay the two stale debts or (2) by an express acknowledgment of the two stale debts or (3) by part payment of the two stale debts. Zukerkorn, however, denies doing any of the three. His evidence is that he agreed to pay and in fact paid "a small amount on an old account"; he denies that he acknowledged the existence of the two stale debts or that he agreed to pay them or that he paid on them.

Further, even if it were admitted that Zukerkorn expressly acknowledged the two debts or that he made part payment on them, such action on his part is only prima facie evidence of a new promise which may be rebutted by other evidence and by the circumstances under which it is made. The court below cannot imply a promise from the mere fact of acknowledgment or part payment as an inference of law. It must be left to the trier of fact.

Consequently, we hold that Zukerkorn has raised genuine issues of material fact with respect to his obligation to pay the notes of November 22, 1965, and September 23, 1966, and that the lower court erred in entering summary judgment with respect to them.

The summary judgment is partially affirmed and partially reversed, and this case is remanded for further proceedings consistent with this opinion.

NOTE

Courts are quite willing to confess that promises to pay debts barred by a statute of limitations are enforced on the basis of "moral obligation" or "moral consideration." *See, e.g., Young v. Pileggi*, 455 A.2d 1228 (Pa. Super. 1983); *Kopp v. Fink*, 204 Okla. 570, 232 P.2d 161 (1951); *see also* RESTATEMENT (SECOND) OF CONTRACTS § 82; MURRAY ON CONTRACTS § 68B.1.a.(5th ed. 2011). A promise to pay a debt barred by the statute of limitations may also be inferred from an acknowledgment of such a debt. See *Sheffield Capital Corp. v. Konen*, 1995 Tex. App. LEXIS 632. A promise or acknowledgment will restart the applicable statute of limitations. See *Fleet v. National Bank v. Laquidara*, 736 N.Y.S.2d 813 (App. Div. 2002). Many states require a signed writing evidencing an acknowledgment or promise to pay debts barred by the statute of limitations. This requirement is traceable to an 1828 statute in England, Lord Tenderten's Act Geo. 4 c. 14 which later became the Limitation Act, 2 & 3 Geo. 6 c. 21, § 84 (1939) to avoid disputes as to whether a subsequent promise to pay the debt was made. Part payment of a debt, however, allows a promise to be implied to restart the statute without a

---

[39] [Ed. Note: In most jurisdictions, the promise to pay a debt barred by the statute of limitations must be evidenced by a writing — traceable to a requirement in England via Lord Tenderten's Act of 1828.]

writing. The debt must be either contractual or quasi contractual. If it arises from a tort barred by a tort statute of limitations, a promise to pay it must be supported by consideration or detrimental reliance.

The basis for the enforcement of such promises is *certain* moral obligation — an obligation that had been legally enforceable and became barred only by a technical rule. The notion that other moral obligations, though not enforceable at law, are less certain is answered nicely by Professor Fuller:

> If it be argued that moral consideration threatens certainty, the solution would seem to lie, not in rejecting the doctrine, but in taming it by continuing the process of judicial exclusion and inclusion already begun in the cases involving infants' contracts, barred debts and discharged bankrupts.

Fuller, *Consideration and Form*, 41 Colum. L. Rev. 799, 822 (1941).

Earlier, we considered the contracts of infants in dealing with capacity to contract. Like infants' contracts, promises induced by fraud are considered voidable, i.e., subject to a power of disaffirmance. If an infant reaches maturity and voluntarily makes a new promise, or a promisor who was induced by fraud or duress later makes a voluntary promise to perform his previously voidable promise, the new promise is clearly enforceable without any consideration.[40] The new promise may be viewed as an exercise of the power of ratification or, conversely, as a waiver of the defense of infancy or fraud. If the original promise is void rather than voidable, however, the only basis for the new obligation is the new promise, which would require consideration.[41]

The other generally enforceable moral obligation promise was a promise to pay a debt discharged in bankruptcy, which was treated very much like a promise to pay a debt barred by the statute of limitations, i.e., it required no consideration or other validation device to be enforceable. It is important to consider the current status of such promises.

[5] Promises to Pay Debts Discharged in Bankruptcy

Like promises to pay debts barred by the statute of limitations, enforcing promises to pay debts discharged in bankruptcy on a moral obligation basis presented no problem of uncertainty in terms of their moral force, since they had been legally enforceable promises before the promisor was adjudicated a bankrupt.[42] The United States Constitution permits Congress to enact laws discharging debtors who would otherwise be unable to begin their financial lives anew with a clean slate. Congress has facilitated the "fresh start" concept by enacting and amending bankruptcy laws for many years. With considerable encouragement if not pressure from creditors who no longer had a legal right to be paid, debtors would make new promises to reaffirm their debts. These

---

[40] Restatement (Second) of Contracts, § 85.

[41] *See* Murray on Contracts at § 68.

[42] *See, e.g.*, Super Chief Credit Union v. McCoy, 3 Kan. App. 2d 25, 595 P.2d 346 (1978); Herrington v. Davitt, 220 N.Y. 162, 115 N.E. 476 (1917).

reaffirmation promises were often imprudently made to the regret of the debtor. Suddenly, the "fresh start" provided by bankruptcy appeared quite stale.

"The promisor, burdened with the guilt accompanying financial failure and intoxicated at the promise of a future free of debt, fails to understand the consequences of reaffirmation. Therefore, these reckless commitments rarely produce reasonably equivalent benefits for the promisor." Boshkoff, *Fresh Start, False Start, or Head Start?*, 70 IND. L.J. 549, 557 (1995).

In the Bankruptcy Reform Act of 1978 (Federal Bankruptcy Code), Congress placed significant restrictions on reaffirmation promises including approval by the bankruptcy judge who would ascertain that the new agreement did not impose an undue hardship on the debtor or the debtor's dependent and was in the best interest of the debtor. These and other requirements protected the ill-informed debtor against improvident reaffirmation promises. At the behest of creditors, however, a 1984 amendment to the Act replaced the supervision of the bankruptcy judge with a mere affidavit filed by the debtor's attorney stating that the new promise is fully informed and voluntary and does not impose an undue hardship on the debtor (11 U.S.C. § 524(c)(3)). The change has evoked harsh criticism:

> [T]he rule's creditor sponsors were extraordinarily clever. Instead of trying to eliminate the approval requirement, a difficult task, they opted for a change in the person whose approval was needed. They replaced the independent bankruptcy judge with an attorney decision-maker who will often find it difficult to oppose his client's wishes.

Id. at 559.

With the enactment of the 1978 Bankruptcy Reform Act, the pendulum had swung from the common law ease of making enforceable reaffirmation promises which required no consideration to the necessity of meeting rigorous conditions to protect the untutored and unwise promisor against his own improvidence. As of 1984, the pendulum reversed though it is still some distance away from its original position. *See* MURRAY, § 68.

Chapter 4

OPERATIVE EXPRESSIONS OF ASSENT

A. INTRODUCTION

In the last chapter, we explored the fundamental question, which promises should be enforced? An equally fundamental and even more pervasive question in contract law is, which expressions of the parties will be accorded legal (operative) effect?

We have already concluded that only the objective manifestations or outward expressions of the parties would be given operative effect and that their subjective understanding would not be accorded operative effect. The rationale was based on pragmatism and fairness. We accord no weight to what a party later states he subjectively understood at the time his words or conduct were manifested because it would be unfair to impose such a subjective understanding on the other party. As we saw earlier, the test is not what either party actually thought since we will never know their undisclosed intention. The test must focus on the objective, outward manifestations of the parties to determine what a reasonable party would have understood by the other party's words or conduct. Having concluded that only the outward manifestations of the parties should be accorded operative effect, the question arises, *should all such outward manifestations be accorded legal effect?* As we will see in this chapter, the clear answer is, no. This chapter, therefore, explored contract doctrines that deal with the basic question of which outward manifestations should be accorded operative effect.

We first examine the *Statute of Frauds*, a 17th century creation of Parliament that has been adopted by virtually every jurisdiction in the United States. The Statute of Frauds requires certain types — but only certain types — of contracts to be evidenced by a writing. If the parties form an oral contract that the statute requires to be evidenced by a writing, absent certain exceptions, the oral expressions of the parties will be denied operative effect, i.e., their oral contract will not be enforceable.

We then proceed to another doctrine that is founded on a simple proposition: If the parties to a contract take the time and effort to reduce their agreement to writing, intending that writing to constitute the sole and exclusive evidence of their agreement, neither party should be put to the trouble of defending against allegations that the agreement was broader than the writing, i.e., that the agreement contains additional terms or conditions not found in the writing to which the parties allegedly agreed prior to the writing. This doctrine is well-known as the *parol evidence rule* which is analyzed in the course on contract law because it is a rule of substantive law and not a rule of evidence. If there is an allegation of such a prior agreement and the court concludes that the parties intended the writing to be the sole and complete evidence of their contract, evidence of the prior agreement is inadmissible, i.e., the outward manifestations of the parties" agreement prior to the writing, even assuming evidence of that agreement is available, will be denied operative effect.

Where a contract is evidenced by a writing and neither party is alleging a prior agreement in addition to the writing, other critically important problems still remain. Though parties may attempt to be clear and complete in their expression of agreement, they are very often imprecise in that expression. Outward manifestations in the form of language or conduct may superficially appear to be so clear and unambiguous that there is no question about their meaning. Yet, even apparently clear manifestations will still require *interpretation*. Professor Corbin provided the consummate explanation:

> It is sometimes said, in a case in which the written words seem plain and clear and unambiguous, that the words are not subject to interpretation or construction. One who makes this statement has necessarily already given the words an interpretation — the one that is to him plain and clear; and in making the statement he is asserting that any different interpretation is "perverted" and untrue.[1]

A term such as "fifty percent" may appear clear and unambiguous. Yet, the trade usage surrounding that term may indicate that merchants in that trade regard the "fifty percent" standard as having been met by a percentage less than fifty percent.[2] A phrase such as "adverse weather conditions" in a contract may be thought to excuse performance where the weather conditions are unusually bad. Yet, the same phrase could apply where the weather conditions are unusually good.[3]

The parties may have said nothing about a particular issue that has arisen under their contract. There may, however, be evidence of trade usage or prior course of dealing or course of performance that is viewed by the court as an operative expression of assent although the parties never consciously considered such matters. Such evidence may be viewed as the "invisible terms" of the contract. Thus, choices often have to be made as to which meaning to accord to a particular outward manifestation and whether the contract should be said to contain other "invisible" terms. A court will choose what it deems to be the proper interpretation. The court's

---

[1] Corbin, *The Interpretation of Words and the Parol Evidence Rule*, 50 Cornell L.Q. 161, 171–72 (1965).

[2] *See* Hurst v. W.J. Lake & Co., 141 Or. 306, 16 P.2d 627 (1932). The court mentions a number of other illustrations. For example, the word "thousand" seems to have a clear meaning, but in the bricklaying trade, a "thousand brick" does not mean that the bricklayer should actually lay that number, but rather that he build a wall of a certain size. A contract requiring delivery of 4,000 shingles will be performed by the delivery of only 2,500 shingles of a certain kind.

[3] *See* Stender v. Twin City Foods, Inc., 82 Wash. 2d 250, 510 P.2d 221 (1973). The clause "adverse weather conditions" was in a contract under which the defendant agreed to harvest a crop. The weather was so unusually good that the crops matured almost simultaneously, thereby placing a considerable strain on the defendant's ability to harvest the entire crop. He was forced to bypass certain acreage. The court was, therefore, confronted with the question of whether such conditions were "adverse weather conditions."

choice of one interpretation will necessarily have the effect of denying operative effect to other interpretations.

If questions of the Statute of Frauds, the parol evidence rule and interpretation have been answered, the facts may reveal still other issues requiring a further determination of which expression(s) will be accorded operative effect. The facts may reveal that one or both parties has labored under a *mistake* at the time the contract was made. There are varying types of mistakes and misunderstandings, all of which must be explored. A mistake of identity occurs, for example, where *A* makes a contract with *B* on the mistaken assumption that *B* is really *C*. Should a court give operative effect to the manifestations of the parties or should it grant relief to the mistaken party? Both parties may assume that their contract manifests a certain understanding which it does not manifest. What appears to be a perfectly clear manifestation of assent may prove to be ambiguous because a word or phrase can legitimately have two meanings, and one party now asserts one meaning while the other party insists on the second meaning. Again, the question is, which expression or which interpretation of an expression will be given operative effect.

There are other issues giving rise to the same underlying problem which will be postponed until later in this volume. Each of the doctrines explored in this chapter is related by the fundamental question of the operative effect to be accorded to certain expressions. The juxtaposition of these doctrines is not only logical; a genuine understanding of the scope of these doctrines occurs only through such juxtaposition.

B.   THE STATUTE OF FRAUDS

[1]   Origin of the Statute of Frauds — Repeal of the English Statute[4]

Except for formal contracts, i.e., contracts under seal, the common law does not require contracts to be evidenced by a writing. A promise is legally binding though expressed orally or by conduct if the other essentials for contract formation exist. Any requirement that a contract be evidenced by a writing is a statutory requirement. In practically every state,[5] certain types of contracts are required to be evidenced by a writing as a matter of enforceability, proof, or validity.[6]

Generally, these statutes emulate certain sections of the "Statute of Frauds" which was enacted by the English Parliament during the reign of Charles II in 1677, and they are commonly indexed under that caption in the statute books. The original Statute of Frauds contained twenty-five sections. Only two are important for our purposes, Sections 4 and 17, though Section 4 contains six subsections

---

[4] This section is based on MURRAY ON CONTRACTS § 69 (5th ed. 2011).

[5] In New Mexico, the English Statute of Frauds was adopted as part of New Mexico common law. *See* Whelan v. New Mexico W. Oil & Gas Co., 226 F.2d 156, 160 (10th Cir. 1955). In Maryland, the statute is in effect as part of the Maryland Declaration of Rights, Md. Const. art. 5. All other states except Louisiana have statutes similar to the original English Statute of Frauds of 1677.

[6] See MURRAY ON CONTRACTS § 80 dealing with the effect of noncompliance with the statute of frauds.

designating five types of contracts that must be evidenced by a writing. The original Sections 4 and 17 are worth considering:

Sec. 4. And be it further enacted by the authority aforesaid. That from and after the said four and twentieth day of June no action shall be brought (1) whereby to charge any executor or administrator upon any special promise, to answer damages out of his own estate; (2) or whereby to charge the defendant upon any special promise to answer for the debt, default, or miscarriages of another person; (3) or to charge any person upon any agreement made upon consideration of marriage; (4) or upon any contract or sale of lands, tenements, or hereditaments, or any interest in or concerning them; (5) or one year from the making thereof; (6) unless the agreement upon which such action shall be brought, or some memorandum or note thereof, shall be in writing, and signed by the party to be charged therewith, or some other person thereunto by him lawfully authorized.

Sec. 17. And be it further enacted by the authority aforesaid. That from and after the said four and twentieth day of June no contract for the sale of any goods, wares and merchandises, for the price of ten pounds sterling or upwards, shall be allowed to be good, except the buyer shall accept part of the goods so sold, and actually receive the same, or give something in earnest to bind the bargain, or in part of payment, or that some note of memorandum in writing of the said bargain be made and signed by the parties to be charged by such contract, or their agents thereunto lawfully authorized.

In 1677, the essentially medieval trial by jury left much to be desired. Not only was there little or no control over jury verdicts, but the jurors were free to decide the facts on their own knowledge, disregarding the evidence. The parties to the contract were precluded from testifying on their own behalf, and the general history of the period lent itself to "fraudulent practices which are commonly endeavoured to be upheld by perjury and subornation."[7] One of the puzzling aspects of the Statute was the choice of six types of contracts made subject to its requirements. There is little doubt that an earlier draft covered all contracts. Historians have discovered earlier parallels on the Continent which lend support to the notion that the reasons behind the Statute were much broader than fear of perjury and subornation.[8]

American versions of the English Statute reveal minor differences in terminology among the different states to which attention will be directed as this exploration proceeds. Modern versions of the statute will often include types of contracts not covered by the original Statute.[9] Thus, promises to pay a commission to a real estate broker or contracts to leave property by will are often included.[10] The

---

[7] This is the preamble to the bill which was finally enacted. The principal author of the original Statute of Frauds was Lord Fincy, later Lord Nottingham, who was chancellor (1673–1682) under Charles II. In general, see 6 HOLDSWORTH, HISTORY OF ENGLISH LAW 379–97 (1924).

[8] See Rabel, *The Statute of Frauds and Comparative Legal History*, 63 LAW Q. REV. 174 (1947).

[9] See RESTATEMENT (SECOND) OF CONTRACTS Ch. 5, Statutory Note, "Other Similar Statutes."

[10] *Ibid.*

is, therefore, no need to explore these categories separately.

PROBLEMS

(1) The foreman of the Johnson Construction Company, C. M. Head, had been obtaining meals on credit from the City Cafe in San Augustine, Texas, while Johnson was performing road work. When Head's account was in arrears, the owner of the Cafe, W. M. Wade, approached the owner of the construction company, Ed Johnson, who promptly gave Wade a check for the full amount. Later, Head was again in arrears and Wade approached Johnson who told Wade, "Go ahead and let him continue to have his meals and I will pay if he doesn't." Wade continued to allow Head to have his meals on credit. When the construction work was completed and Head had not paid, Wade went to Johnson, who refused to pay. Wade testified that he would not have advanced credit to Head absent Johnson's promise. What result? *See Johnson City Cafe v. City Cafe*, 100 S.W.2d 740 (Tex. Civ. App. 1936).

(2) Dr. Lawrence answered an emergency call from an undisclosed source and found John Anderson unconscious from injuries suffered in an auto accident. Anderson's daughter directed Lawrence to "do everything you can under the sun to see this man is taken care of." Lawrence performed appropriate emergency treatment at the scene and later at the hospital but the patient died. A witness at the scene testified that the daughter also said, "I want my father taken care of, and give him the best treatment you can give him, and what the charges are . . . I will pay for it." Dr. Lawrence sent his bill to Mr. Anderson's estate and later engaged a lawyer to collect from the estate. The lawyer had no success. Lawrence then sent the bill to Anderson's widow, but nothing came of that. He then sought payment from the daughter, who refused to pay. What result? *See Lawrence v. Anderson*, 108 Vt. 176, 184 A. 689 (1936).

(3) The Allstate Insurance Co. allegedly make an oral agreement to settle a potential claim against its insured from an auto accident. When sued on the oral agreement, Allstate raised the statute of frauds. Analyze. See *Carter v. Allstate Ins. Co.*, 962 S.W.2d 268 (Tex. App. 1998).

(4) Ames was indebted to Barnes in the amount of $10,000. Childs promised Barnes that he (Childs) would pay this amount to Barnes in exchange for Barnes" release of Ames. Barnes agreed. Is the promise of Childs within the Statute? If Barnes had agreed that the release of Ames would occur only upon the payment by Childs, would Childs" promise be within the Statute? *See* MURRAY ON CONTRACTS at § 70A.2.d.

(5) If Ames is indebted to Barnes in the amount of $10,000 and Childs promises Ames that Childs will pay the $10,000 to Barnes, is Childs" promise within the Statute? *See Farmers State Bank v. Conrardy*, 215 Kan. 334, 524 P.2d 690 (1974).

student of contract law should also recall that a promise to pay a debt barred by the statute of limitations is typically required to be evidenced by a writing though this requirement emanates from a nineteenth century English statute.[11] The modern version of Section 17 of the original Statute dealing with contracts for the sale of goods is now found in the Uniform Commercial Code.[12] The UCC, however, requires other types of promises to be evidenced by a writing.[13] The main features of the original Statute of Frauds have been copied with remarkable unanimity.[14]

Having spawned the Statute of Frauds, England repealed it, except for two sections, by the Law Reform Act of 1954.[15] This action was based on a report of the English Law Revision Committee in 1937[16] indicating that contemporary opinion is almost unanimous in condemning the statute and favoring its amendment or repeal. The report concluded that the conditions which gave rise to the statute had long passed away. At a time when the parties themselves could not give evidence and the jury was entitled to act on its own knowledge of the facts in dispute, there may have been some reason for the statute. The report further concluded that the statute promotes more fraud than it prevents. While it shuts out perjury, it also more frequently shuts out the truth since it strikes impartially at the perjurer and the honest man who has omitted a precaution, "sealing the lips of both." The classes of contracts covered by the statute appear to have been arbitrarily selected and to exhibit no common quality. The report insists that the statute operates in a partial manner. Thus, when *A* and *B* contract and *A* has signed a sufficient memorandum and *B* has not, *B* can enforce the contract against *A*, but *A* cannot enforce the contract against *B* who has signed no writing. (Later, we will see how the UCC deals with this situation in requiring a signed writing to evidence a contract for the sale of goods priced at $500 or more.) The report also suggests that the statute is obscure and ill-drafted, making it the subject of considerable litigation.

As will be seen, there are judges and legal scholars who have been critical of the statute. Professor Arthur Linton Corbin suggests that, if the statute were repealed in the United States, he would suffer only to the extent that one volume of his

---

[11] Lord Tenderten's Act, 9 Geo. IV, c. 14, sometimes referred to as the Statute of Frauds Amendment Act, enacted in England in 1828. *See* RESTATEMENT (SECOND) OF CONTRACTS Ch. 5, Statutory Note which quotes this Act.

[12] UCC § 2-201.

[13] *See, e.g.*, UCC § 1-206 (property not otherwise covered such as the sale of contract rights, royalty rights, and similar rights where the amount or value of remedy exceeds $5000). A security agreement must be evidenced by a writing under § 9-203(a). The 1978 version of Article 8 required a writing to evidence the sale of securities (§ 8-319), but a 1994 amendment produced § 8-113 which dispenses with this requirement in light of the increasing use of electronic communications which makes "the statute of frauds unsuited to the realities of the securities business." Comment to § 8-113. The same section also eliminates the one-year provision of the statute of frauds for securities contracts. *See also* § 2-205 (firm offer must be in writing); § 2-209(2) (enforcing no oral modification clauses which require any modifications to be evidenced by a writing).

[14] See RESTATEMENT (SECOND) OF CONTRACTS, Statutory Note, at the beginning of Chapter 5.

[15] 2 & 3 Eliz. 2, ch. 34. The two exceptions are contracts to answer for the debt of another (the suretyship provision) and contracts for the sale of land. For comments on the Acts of 1954, see Note, 70 LAW Q. REV. 441 (1954) and 17 MOD. L. REV. 451 (1954).

[16] English Law Revision Committee (Sixth Interim Report) (1937), the full text of which can be found in 15 CAN. B. REV. 585 (1937).

treatise would no longer be sold.[17] Professor Corbin, however, expressed grave doubt that the statute would be repealed in the United States since, unlike England, each of our states would have to repeal the statute. Corbin's prophecy has proven accurate for many years.

Another giant of American law, Karl Llewellyn, best known as the chief architect of the Uniform Commercial Code (UCC), was one of the rare defenders of the statute:

> That statute is an amazing product. In it [Ponce] de Leon might have found his secret of perpetual youth. After two and one half centuries the statute stands, in essence better adapted to our needs than when it first was passed. By 1676 literacy (which need imply no great consistency in spelling) may well have been expected in England of such classes as would be concerned in the transactions covered by the statute's terms. Certainly, however, we had our period here in which that would hardly hold — we counted our men of affairs who signed by mark in plenty. But schooling has done its work. The idea, which must in good part derive from the statute, that contracts at large will do well to be in writing, is fairly well established in the land. "His word is as good as his bond" contains a hinting innuendo preaching caution. Meantime the modern developments of business — large units, requiring internal written records if files are to be kept straight, and officers informed, and departments coordinated, and the work of shifting personnel kept track of; the practice of confirming oral deals in writing; the use of typewriters, of forms — all these confirm the policy of the statute; all these reduce the price in disappointments exacted for its benefits.[18]

Notwithstanding Llewellyn's defense of the statute, we will see that his version of the statute in relation to contracts for the sale of goods in UCC Article 2 contains a number of modifications designed to overcome some justified criticism of the treatment of such contracts in the original Statute and its progeny. Criticism, however, remains.

When the drafters of the proposed revision of Article 2 confronted the statute of frauds, they initially decided to repeal it as unnecessary and counterproductive. Later, however, they decided to retain the statute with certain modifications that will be analyzed in this chapter.

There is little question that current versions of the statute are often applied narrowly by our courts who see the statute as irrational in certain situations. The judicial recognition of reliance in lieu of a writing as a method or device to satisfy the statute also indicates erosion of the statute, at least in its original form.

The student of contract law must be aware of judicial trends in the application of the statute. These trends will be examined in the exploration which follows. They can be understood, however, only if three basic questions are thoroughly pursued: (1) What contracts are embraced within the terms of the statute? (2) What are the

---

[17] 2 Corbin on Contracts § 275.

[18] Llewellyn, *What Price Contract? — An Essay in Perspective*, 40 Yale L.J. 704, 747 (1931).

requirements of the statute in relation to contracts within its scope? (3) What is the effect of failing to fulfill the requirements of the statute?

[2]   Suretyship Promises

THE BASIC CONCEPT

Suretyship is a three-party relationship in which a *principal debtor* or *obligor* (*D*) promises to pay a certain indebtedness to a *creditor* or *obligee*, (*C*) and a third party, *surety*, (*S*) promises to pay *C* if *D* does not pay. Suretyship promises arise in a variety of contexts but they always involve the foregoing elements. The typical surety arrangement occurs where a creditor such as a bank or a seller of goods or services will not extend credit to a particular individual on his or her credit alone. The potential debtor is told that he or she needs a surety, i.e., someone who will agree to become liable in the event that the debtor does not pay as promised. Suretyship promises were included among the types of contracts requiring a writing because of the temptation on the part of creditors to allege that a third party has agreed to pay when the principal debtor fails to do so. To prevent fraud and perjury in such cases, suretyship promises were not enforceable unless they were evidenced by a writing. Thus, a *promise to answer for the debt of another* must be in writing because such a promise is *within* the Statute of Frauds, i.e., it is one of the types of contracts the Statute requires to be evidenced by a writing. The principal *debtor* should pay the debt. If he fails to pay and there is a writing signed by the surety, the surety must then pay. If the surety pays, he has paid a debt which the principal debtor should have paid. Therefore, the surety has a cause of action against the principal debtor, i.e., he may collect from the debtor if he can find the debtor and the debtor has the funds to pay.

It is important to understand that the relationship between the debtor and the surety *must be known to the creditor.* If a creditor delivers goods or renders services to a party (*X*) with the understanding that they are to be charged exclusively to another party (*Y*), this is not a suretyship relationship because *X* is not a debtor. The creditor is relying exclusively on the promise of *Y* to pay the debt. It makes no difference that *X* and *Y* may have understood that *X* should pay and *Y* would pay only if *X* failed to pay unless the creditor is aware of this arrangement and intends to extend credit to *X* with the understanding that he will look to *Y* for payment only in the event that *X* fails to pay. Where the creditor is unaware of any understanding between *X* and *Y*, the creditor has provided the goods or services exclusively on the credit of *Y* who is, alone, liable for them. The promise of *Y* in such a situation is often called an "original" promise since he is the original or exclusive debtor. *Y*'s promise, therefore, is *without* the Statute of Frauds, i.e., it is not one of the types of promises or contracts the Statute requires to be evidenced by a writing. If the creditor understood that he should look to X as the debtor and Y only where X fails to pay, Y's promise is *not original*, it is a *collateral* promise.

It has long been recognized that the first two categories of the Statute of Frauds — promises by an executor or administrator to answer for damages out of his own estate and promises to answer for the debt of another are "closely allied . . . if not identical in principal." *Bellows v. Sowles*, 57 Vt. 164, 52 Am. Rep. 118 (1884). There student of contract law should also recall that a promise to pay a debt barred by the statute of limitations is typically required to be evidenced by a writing though this requirement emanates from a nineteenth century English statute.[11] The modern version of Section 17 of the original Statute dealing with contracts for the sale of goods is now found in the Uniform Commercial Code.[12] The UCC, however, requires other types of promises to be evidenced by a writing.[13] The main features of the original Statute of Frauds have been copied with remarkable unanimity.[14]

Having spawned the Statute of Frauds, England repealed it, except for two sections, by the Law Reform Act of 1954.[15] This action was based on a report of the English Law Revision Committee in 1937[16] indicating that contemporary opinion is almost unanimous in condemning the statute and favoring its amendment or repeal. The report concluded that the conditions which gave rise to the statute had long passed away. At a time when the parties themselves could not give evidence and the jury was entitled to act on its own knowledge of the facts in dispute, there may have been some reason for the statute. The report further concluded that the statute promotes more fraud than it prevents. While it shuts out perjury, it also more frequently shuts out the truth since it strikes impartially at the perjurer and the honest man who has omitted a precaution, "sealing the lips of both." The classes of contracts covered by the statute appear to have been arbitrarily selected and to exhibit no common quality. The report insists that the statute operates in a partial manner. Thus, when A and B contract and A has signed a sufficient memorandum and B has not, B can enforce the contract against A, but A cannot enforce the contract against B who has signed no writing. (Later, we will see how the UCC deals with this situation in requiring a signed writing to evidence a contract for the sale of goods priced at $500 or more.) The report also suggests that the statute is obscure and ill-drafted, making it the subject of considerable litigation.

As will be seen, there are judges and legal scholars who have been critical of the statute. Professor Arthur Linton Corbin suggests that, if the statute were repealed in the United States, he would suffer only to the extent that one volume of his

---

[11] Lord Tenderten's Act, 9 Geo. IV, c. 14, sometimes referred to as the Statute of Frauds Amendment Act, enacted in England in 1828. *See* RESTATEMENT (SECOND) OF CONTRACTS Ch. 5, Statutory Note which quotes this Act.

[12] UCC § 2-201.

[13] *See, e.g.*, UCC § 1-206 (property not otherwise covered such as the sale of contract rights, royalty rights, and similar rights where the amount or value of remedy exceeds $5000). A security agreement must be evidenced by a writing under § 9-203(a). The 1978 version of Article 8 required a writing to evidence the sale of securities (§ 8-319), but a 1994 amendment produced § 8-113 which dispenses with this requirement in light of the increasing use of electronic communications which makes "the statute of frauds unsuited to the realities of the securities business." Comment to § 8-113. The same section also eliminates the one-year provision of the statute of frauds for securities contracts. *See also* § 2-205 (firm offer must be in writing); § 2-209(2) (enforcing no oral modification clauses which require any modifications to be evidenced by a writing).

[14] See RESTATEMENT (SECOND) OF CONTRACTS, Statutory Note, at the beginning of Chapter 5.

[15] 2 & 3 Eliz. 2, ch. 34. The two exceptions are contracts to answer for the debt of another (the suretyship provision) and contracts for the sale of land. For comments on the Acts of 1954, see Note, 70 LAW Q. REV. 441 (1954) and 17 MOD. L. REV. 451 (1954).

[16] English Law Revision Committee (Sixth Interim Report) (1937), the full text of which can be found in 15 CAN. B. REV. 585 (1937).

treatise would no longer be sold.[17] Professor Corbin, however, expressed grave doubt that the statute would be repealed in the United States since, unlike England, each of our states would have to repeal the statute. Corbin's prophecy has proven accurate for many years.

Another giant of American law, Karl Llewellyn, best known as the chief architect of the Uniform Commercial Code (UCC), was one of the rare defenders of the statute:

> That statute is an amazing product. In it [Ponce] de Leon might have found his secret of perpetual youth. After two and one half centuries the statute stands, in essence better adapted to our needs than when it first was passed. By 1676 literacy (which need imply no great consistency in spelling) may well have been expected in England of such classes as would be concerned in the transactions covered by the statute's terms. Certainly, however, we had our period here in which that would hardly hold — we counted our men of affairs who signed by mark in plenty. But schooling has done its work. The idea, which must in good part derive from the statute, that contracts at large will do well to be in writing, is fairly well established in the land. "His word is as good as his bond" contains a hinting innuendo preaching caution. Meantime the modern developments of business — large units, requiring internal written records if files are to be kept straight, and officers informed, and departments coordinated, and the work of shifting personnel kept track of; the practice of confirming oral deals in writing; the use of typewriters, of forms — all these confirm the policy of the statute; all these reduce the price in disappointments exacted for its benefits.[18]

Notwithstanding Llewellyn's defense of the statute, we will see that his version of the statute in relation to contracts for the sale of goods in UCC Article 2 contains a number of modifications designed to overcome some justified criticism of the treatment of such contracts in the original Statute and its progeny. Criticism, however, remains.

When the drafters of the proposed revision of Article 2 confronted the statute of frauds, they initially decided to repeal it as unnecessary and counterproductive. Later, however, they decided to retain the statute with certain modifications that will be analyzed in this chapter.

There is little question that current versions of the statute are often applied narrowly by our courts who see the statute as irrational in certain situations. The judicial recognition of reliance in lieu of a writing as a method or device to satisfy the statute also indicates erosion of the statute, at least in its original form.

The student of contract law must be aware of judicial trends in the application of the statute. These trends will be examined in the exploration which follows. They can be understood, however, only if three basic questions are thoroughly pursued: (1) What contracts are embraced within the terms of the statute? (2) What are the

---

[17] 2 CORBIN ON CONTRACTS § 275.

[18] Llewellyn, *What Price Contract? — An Essay in Perspective*, 40 YALE L.J. 704, 747 (1931).

requirements of the statute in relation to contracts within its scope? (3) What is the effect of failing to fulfill the requirements of the statute?

[2]   Suretyship Promises

THE BASIC CONCEPT

Suretyship is a three-party relationship in which a *principal debtor* or *obligor* (*D*) promises to pay a certain indebtedness to a *creditor* or *obligee*, (*C*) and a third party, *surety*, (*S*) promises to pay *C* if *D* does not pay. Suretyship promises arise in a variety of contexts but they always involve the foregoing elements. The typical surety arrangement occurs where a creditor such as a bank or a seller of goods or services will not extend credit to a particular individual on his or her credit alone. The potential debtor is told that he or she needs a surety, i.e., someone who will agree to become liable in the event that the debtor does not pay as promised. Suretyship promises were included among the types of contracts requiring a writing because of the temptation on the part of creditors to allege that a third party has agreed to pay when the principal debtor fails to do so. To prevent fraud and perjury in such cases, suretyship promises were not enforceable unless they were evidenced by a writing. Thus, a *promise to answer for the debt of another* must be in writing because such a promise is *within* the Statute of Frauds, i.e., it is one of the types of contracts the Statute requires to be evidenced by a writing. The principal *debtor* should pay the debt. If he fails to pay and there is a writing signed by the surety, the surety must then pay. If the surety pays, he has paid a debt which the principal debtor should have paid. Therefore, the surety has a cause of action against the principal debtor, i.e., he may collect from the debtor if he can find the debtor and the debtor has the funds to pay.

It is important to understand that the relationship between the debtor and the surety *must be known to the creditor.* If a creditor delivers goods or renders services to a party (*X*) with the understanding that they are to be charged exclusively to another party (*Y*), this is not a suretyship relationship because *X* is not a debtor. The creditor is relying exclusively on the promise of Y to pay the debt. It makes no difference that *X* and *Y* may have understood that *X* should pay and *Y* would pay only if *X* failed to pay unless the creditor is aware of this arrangement and intends to extend credit to *X* with the understanding that he will look to *Y* for payment only in the event that *X* fails to pay. Where the creditor is unaware of any understanding between *X* and *Y*, the creditor has provided the goods or services exclusively on the credit of *Y* who is, alone, liable for them. The promise of *Y* in such a situation is often called an "original" promise since he is the original or exclusive debtor. *Y* 's promise, therefore, is *without* the Statute of Frauds, i.e., it is not one of the types of promises or contracts the Statute requires to be evidenced by a writing. If the creditor understood that he should look to X as the debtor and Y only where X fails to pay, Y's promise is *not original*, it is a *collateral* promise.

It has long been recognized that the first two categories of the Statute of Frauds — promises by an executor or administrator to answer for damages out of his own estate and promises to answer for the debt of another are "closely allied . . . if not identical in principal." *Bellows v. Sowles*, 57 Vt. 164, 52 Am. Rep. 118 (1884). There is, therefore, no need to explore these categories separately.

PROBLEMS

(1) The foreman of the Johnson Construction Company, C. M. Head, had been obtaining meals on credit from the City Cafe in San Augustine, Texas, while Johnson was performing road work. When Head's account was in arrears, the owner of the Cafe, W. M. Wade, approached the owner of the construction company, Ed Johnson, who promptly gave Wade a check for the full amount. Later, Head was again in arrears and Wade approached Johnson who told Wade, "Go ahead and let him continue to have his meals and I will pay if he doesn't." Wade continued to allow Head to have his meals on credit. When the construction work was completed and Head had not paid, Wade went to Johnson, who refused to pay. Wade testified that he would not have advanced credit to Head absent Johnson's promise. What result? *See Johnson City Cafe v. City Cafe*, 100 S.W.2d 740 (Tex. Civ. App. 1936).

(2) Dr. Lawrence answered an emergency call from an undisclosed source and found John Anderson unconscious from injuries suffered in an auto accident. Anderson's daughter directed Lawrence to "do everything you can under the sun to see this man is taken care of." Lawrence performed appropriate emergency treatment at the scene and later at the hospital but the patient died. A witness at the scene testified that the daughter also said, "I want my father taken care of, and give him the best treatment you can give him, and what the charges are . . . I will pay for it." Dr. Lawrence sent his bill to Mr. Anderson's estate and later engaged a lawyer to collect from the estate. The lawyer had no success. Lawrence then sent the bill to Anderson's widow, but nothing came of that. He then sought payment from the daughter, who refused to pay. What result? *See Lawrence v. Anderson*, 108 Vt. 176, 184 A. 689 (1936).

(3) The Allstate Insurance Co. allegedly make an oral agreement to settle a potential claim against its insured from an auto accident. When sued on the oral agreement, Allstate raised the statute of frauds. Analyze. See *Carter v. Allstate Ins. Co.*, 962 S.W.2d 268 (Tex. App. 1998).

(4) Ames was indebted to Barnes in the amount of $10,000. Childs promised Barnes that he (Childs) would pay this amount to Barnes in exchange for Barnes" release of Ames. Barnes agreed. Is the promise of Childs within the Statute? If Barnes had agreed that the release of Ames would occur only upon the payment by Childs, would Childs" promise be within the Statute? *See* Murray on Contracts at § 70A.2.d.

(5) If Ames is indebted to Barnes in the amount of $10,000 and Childs promises Ames that Childs will pay the $10,000 to Barnes, is Childs" promise within the Statute? *See Farmers State Bank v. Conrardy*, 215 Kan. 334, 524 P.2d 690 (1974).

[3]   Main Purpose ("Leading Object") Exception

ARMBRUSTER, INC. v. BARRON
Pennsylvania Superior Court
491 A.2d 882 (1985)

CAVANAUGH, J.

Eugene V. Barron, appellant, and two others, were officers and sole shareholders in the RBR Corporation (hereinafter, RBR). The primary purpose of RBR was to construct a bowling alley. Each of the principals owned a one-third interest in the corporation. On March 6, 1979, Thomas A. Armbruster, Inc., a general contractor, entered into a construction agreement with RBR to build the bowling alley. On March 30th of the same year, Armbruster discovered that RBR did not own the land upon which the bowling alley was being constructed, and also that RBR had not yet obtained financing for the project. On May 14, 1979, during a meeting held at the office of Michael Prokup, Armbruster's attorney, Mr. Prokup requested Barron and one of the other principals to personally guarantee the corporation's debt in consideration of Armbruster's promise to proceed with construction. Barron offered to personally guarantee the corporation's debt and stated that he would put up his taproom as security. He expressed his belief that the corporation would receive financing in thirty to sixty days. The lower court found that attorney Prokup accepted Mr. Barron's offer of guaranty at the same meeting of May 14th.

Appellant Barron contends, among other things, that since the guaranty he allegedly made was oral, it is unenforceable due to the Statute of Frauds. 33 Pa. C.S. § 3 states:

> No action shall be brought whereby to charge any executor or administrator, upon any promise to answer damages out of his own estate, or whereby to charge the defendant, upon any special promise, to answer for the debt or default of another, unless the agreement upon which such action shall be brought, or some memorandum or note thereof, shall be in writing, and signed by the party to be charged therewith, or some other person by him authorized.

Promises to pay the debt of another must be in writing for at least two reasons. The first is evidentiary. The second, cautionary. Like other provisions of the statute [of frauds], the suretyship provision serves an evidentiary function. Indeed, WILLISTON suggested that the circumstance that "the promisor has received no benefit from the transaction . . . may make perjury more likely, because while in the case of one who has received something the circumstances themselves which are capable of proof show probable liability, in the case of a guaranty nothing but the promise is of evidentiary value." Furthermore, though in many instances the surety is paid by the principal for his undertaking, in others the surety's motivation is purely gratuitous and, "as the lack of any benefit received by the guarantor increases the hardship of his being called upon to pay, it also increases the importance of being very sure that he is justly charged."

In addition to its evidentiary role, the provision serves a cautionary function. By bringing home to the prospective surety the significance of his act, it guards against ill-considered action. Otherwise, he might lightly undertake the engagement, unwisely assuming that there is only a remote possibility that the principal will not perform his duty . . . . E.A. FARNSWORTH, CONTRACTS § 6.3 (1982).

However, appellee argues that Barron's personal guaranty need not be in writing to be enforceable because it falls within a judicially created exception to the Statute of Frauds called the "leading object" (or "main purpose") rule. The lower court agreed with this contention and held that the oral guaranty is enforceable. The leading object rule has been explained as follows:

> Whenever the main purpose and object of the promisor, is, not to answer for [the debt of] another, but to subserve some pecuniary or business purpose of his own . . . his promise is not within the statute [of frauds], although it may be in form a provision to pay the debt of another . . . . *Goodling v. Simon*, 54 Pa. Super. 125, 127 (1913).

Where the surety-promisor's main purpose is his own primary or business advantage, the gratuitous or sentimental element often present in suretyship is eliminated, the likelihood of disproportion in the values exchanged between promisor and promisee is reduced, and the commercial context commonly provides evidentiary safeguards. Thus there is less need for cautionary or evidentiary formality than in other cases of suretyship. RESTATEMENT (SECOND) OF CONTRACTS § 116 comment a.

It is for us to determine if the lower court abused its discretion in holding that Barron's main purpose for making the guaranty was to serve his own pecuniary or business interests. We hold that it did not.

The difficult question has been and continues to be: what is the test for determining when the promisor's promise is basically to benefit himself rather than to benefit and accommodate another? The formulations which have emanated from the many cases are invariably insufficient. Thus, where the promise is labelled an "original obligation" rather than a collateral one, or where the promisor is called a "debtor" rather than a surety, the courts are not supplying workable tests but are merely stating conclusions. The reason for the lack of success in formulating a test is that the question to be answered relates to the purpose, motive, object or desire of the promisor and, therefore, it can only be answered by analyzing the complex of objective manifestations surrounding the making of the promises. J. MURRAY, MURRAY ON CONTRACTS § 316 (2d ed. 1974).

The question of the promisor's purpose is best left to the trier of fact, the trial judge in this case. He is far better situated to weigh the evidence and judge the credibility of witnesses than is an appellate court, which has only the cold, lifeless record to guide it. The lower court found that Barron and another of the three principals in the corporation promised to pay RBR's debts in order to protect their interests in the project. They had invested money to purchase the land and to obtain financing. According to the lower court, that money plus potential future profits would have been lost had the construction ceased. Thus, the court concluded that Barron's leading object in making the guaranty was to serve his own pecuniary purpose.

However, Barron argues that because he owned only 33 1/3 % of the corporate shares, his main purpose in guaranteeing the corporation's debt was to serve the corporation's pecuniary interest, and not his own. In support of this, he cites *Acme Equipment Company v. Allegheny Steel Corporation*, 207 Pa. Super. 436, 217 A.2d 791 (1966). In *Acme*, Rudy Valentino, President and owner of 25% of Allegheny Steel Corporation stock, orally guaranteed a debt incurred by Allegheny. In determining Valentino's main purpose, the court reasoned as follows:

> The only question raised by appellant is whether Valentino's promise was made not to answer for the debt of another but, primarily, to serve his own pecuniary interest as a stockholder and president of Allegheny. Although the above statute does not apply if the main object of the promisor is to serve his own pecuniary or business purpose, *Eastern Wood Products Company v. Metz*, 370 Pa. 636, 89 A.2d 327 (1952), the statute is not rendered inapplicable merely because a stockholder may indirectly receive some gain when he promises to pay the debt of a corporation. In *Bayard v. Pennsylvania Knitting Mills Corp.*, 290 Pa. 79, 84, 137 A. 910, 912 (1927), the Supreme Court stated:
>
> > "Ordinarily, the interest which a stockholder has is not individual, for he cannot be held for the corporate debts, and, if a promise to indemnify its creditor is made, the statute of frauds applies . . . . The mere fact that such person is concerned in promoting the financial success of the company is not sufficient to justify the treating of the promise of guaranty as an original undertaking . . . ."

Eastern Wood Products Company v. Metz, supra, is distinguishable from the present case. In *Metz* the stockholder owned 100 per cent of the stock; his promise was clearly made to protect and benefit himself as the sole stockholder of the company. Valentino, however, is the owner of only 25 per cent of the stock of Allegheny. Such ownership, of itself, would not establish that the promise was made by Valentino for the main purpose of serving a pecuniary or business purpose of his own. Consequently, Valentino's alleged promise fell within the Statute of Frauds, and no action could be brought on it. *Acme Equipment Company v. Allegheny Steel Corporation*, 207 Pa. Super. at 438–39, 217 A.2d at 792.

Applying the *Acme* court's rationale to the instant case, the fact that Barron was a 33 1/3 % owner of RBR does not, in and of itself, establish that his main purpose was to serve his own pecuniary interest. The percentage of a shareholder/guarantor's corporate ownership should never be the sole criteria employed to determine his main purpose in guaranteeing a debt incurred by his corporation. Significant scholarship has been afforded the question of what constitutes a shareholder's main purpose whenever he guarantees a debt incurred by his corporation.

Another cluster of cases involves promises by stockholders of corporations to pay corporate bills if promisees would continue to supply goods and services. These promises are motivated by the stockholders' own interests and the leading object is to protect the value of the stock. Yet such promises are usually held to be within the Statute [of Frauds] unless the benefit of the promisor can be shown to be special, direct and/or immediate. J. MURRAY, MURRAY ON CONTRACTS § 316 (2d ed. 1974).

In the instant case, Barron's main purpose in guaranteeing RBR's debt was not merely to protect the value of his shares. The lower court found that he sought to protect his own personal financial interests in the project. This suggests that there was not great disproportion in the values exchanged by Barron and Armbruster, thus eliminating one important reason for requiring that the guaranty be in writing. As this was a business deal motivated by a desire to preserve a present investment and to insure future profits, the commercial context provides sufficient evidentiary and cautionary safeguards without requiring the guaranty to be in writing. The guaranty hardly seems to have been a gratuitous or sentimental gesture on Barron's part. Rather, it appears to have been motivated by a rational business judgment. Thus, an important reason for insisting that guarantees be in writing — that of insuring that the guarantor acted with deliberation — has no application to the instant case.

Moreover, the fact that RBR was a fledgling corporation in the embryonic stages of its development lends credence to our holding that this guaranty falls within the leading object rule. Barron's promise was not made merely to aid a proven business but to insure the very financial success of a new enterprise. Failure to give the requested guaranty may well have hindered RBR's chances of survival. Thus, the benefit Barron stood to receive from his guaranty was more immediate and direct than it would be were he a shareholder who guaranteed the debt of a more firmly established corporation. Furthermore, despite the fact that RBR was a separate legal entity, because of its fledgling status it is quite likely that Barron did not yet view it as having a life of its own, so dependent was it on his personal efforts. If Barron viewed the corporation as but a dependent extension of himself, an entity without life but for the financial aid he fed it, then *a fortiori*, the main purpose of his promise would have been to benefit himself, not "another." Such would not be the case where a shareholder guarantees the debt of a more firmly established corporation. In sum, the evils which the Statute of Frauds was designed to guard against are not present in this case and there is less need for the evidentiary and cautionary formalities than in other guaranty situations. See RESTATEMENT (SECOND) OF CONTRACTS § 116 comment a. We hold, therefore, that this case falls within the leading object rule and that the oral guaranty is not barred by the Statute of Frauds.[19]

[4] Four-Party Indemnity

PROBLEM

Fisher, Sr. was anxious to assure that his son, Fisher, Jr., would obtain a business loan of $50,000 at the local bank. Though Sr.'s credit was excellent, he had a falling out with the president of the bank. He requested Newbern to become a surety for Jr. and orally agreed to be responsible for the debt to Newbern and to

---

[19] [1] Appellant alleges that the lower court did not utilize the proper burden of proof in resolving the factual issue of whether or not an oral guaranty was given. The proper burden is that of clear and convincing evidence. *See* Jefferson-Travis, Inc. v. Giant Eagle Markets, Inc., 393 F.2d 426 (3d Cir. 1968). We find nothing in the lower court opinion to indicate that the lower court employed any burden other than the correct one.

protect Newbern from any loss should Newbern be required to pay the son's indebtedness. Newbern signed as surety for the son which, together with the son's promise to repay, induced the bank to lend $50,000 to the son. The son defaulted and Newbern was required to pay the bank the full amount of the loan. Newbern seeks to recover his loss from Fisher, Sr. who refuses to pay. Advise Newbern. The problem is based on *Newbern v. Fisher*, 198 N.C. 385, 151 S.E. 875 (1930). See Restatement (Second) Contracts, § 118. For a more extensive analysis of indemnification and cases dealing with it, see *Rosenbloom v. Feiler*, 290 Md. 598, 431 A.2d 432 (1981).

[5]   Marriage Agreements

Notwithstanding the expansive language of the marriage provision of the original Statute of Frauds — "[N]o action shall be brought . . . to charge any person upon any agreement made in consideration of marriage" — early decisions excepted mutual promises to marry from this provision. Such promises are typically exchanged in an ambience that does not admit of a writing requirement.[20]

Moreover, as reenacted in the United States, some statutes of frauds excluded mutual promises to marry from the marriage provision.[21] Notwithstanding the exclusion of mutual promises to marry, the marriage provision of the statute retains its vitality in relation to other promises in consideration of marriage.

DEWBERRY v. GEORGE
Washington Court of Appeals
62 P.3d 525 (2003)

Coleman, J.

In 1981, Emanuel George, Jr. and Carla DewBerry were discussing marriage. George told DewBeny that, because a friend had been wronged in a divorce settlement and lost his house, he insisted on the following conditions of marriage: (1) DewBerry would always be fully employed; (2) each party's income and property would be treated as separate property; (3) each party would own a home to return to if the marriage failed; and (4) DewBerry would not get fat. DewBerry agreed to these conditions. Neither party was particularly wealthy at the beginning of their relationship. George and DewBerry married in 1986.

Between 1981 and 2000, George and DewBerry continually affirmed this agreement through words and actions. The record reflects painstaking and meticulous effort to maintain separate finances and property. During their marriage, DewBerry and George deposited their incomes into separate accounts. [A]fter the birth of their first child, they opened a joint checking account in order to handle certain agreed household expenses. George and DewBerry deposited a specified amount to the joint account, and they reimbursed their personal accounts from the

---

[20] *See, e.g.*, Short v. Stotts, 58 Ind. 29 (1877).

[21] *See, e.g.*, Tice v. Tice, 672 P.2d 1168, 1170 (Okla. 1983), which mentions Okla. Stat. title 15, § 136(3) (1981). *See also* Haw. Rev. Stat. § 656-1(3) (1976).

joint account if they happened to use personal funds for household expenses. They took turns managing that account. By 2000, when George and DewBerry separated, they had accumulated minimal community property in the form of joint accounts and jointly purchased possessions. They held numerous investment, bank, and retirement accounts as individuals, and the spouse who had created and contributed to those accounts was considered the sole owner and manager of the assets in those accounts. The primary beneficiaries of their individual accounts were the parties' children, or alternatively, the estate of the spouse who funded them.

During their relationship, DewBerry purchased three houses as her separate property. DewBerry treated these houses as her separate property by paying for maintenance, improvements, and the down payment and mortgage with funds from her separate accounts. George paid DewBerry a set amount each month toward living expenses, such as utilities, and DewBerry repaid George for any maintenance costs he incurred. The only involvement George had with these properties was to sign documents at various times indicating that he had no interest in the properties.

In 1985, DewBerry left Arthur Andersen to become an associate in a Seattle law firm. Meanwhile, George worked in sales and marketing in the entertainment and hospitality industries, and his salary was comparable to DewBerry's initial law firm salary, around $40,000 to $50,000 per year. By the 1990s, however, after DewBerry became a partner at her law firm, her annual salary increased rapidly, totaling over $1 million in 2000. Meanwhile, George's salary remained constant in the $40,000 to $50,000 range. Both parties worked full-time while sharing parenting responsibilities for their two children.

The trial court found by clear, cogent, and convincing evidence that the parties had entered into an oral prenuptial agreement, despite George's denial of the agreement's existence. The trial court also found that there had been "complete performance" of that agreement during the parties' marriage and, thus, the parties' property consisted primarily of separate property. The trial court ordered that the parties' property be divided roughly in accordance with its status as separate or community property. It awarded DewBerry $2.3 million, or approximately 82 percent of the parties' property, which consisted almost entirely of real and personal property that DewBerry had acquired during the marriage, as well as her pre-marriage separate property.

George argues that the trial court erred when it found by clear, cogent, and convincing evidence that an oral separate property agreement had been made by the parties prior to marriage and that it had been fully performed during their marriage, making it an enforceable agreement. He claims that such an agreement is void under Washington's statute of frauds.

Oral separate property agreements made after marriage have consistently been enforced by Washington courts when clear and convincing evidence shows both the existence of the agreement and mutual observance of the agreement. But Washington courts have not yet addressed a situation where parties have orally agreed prior to marriage to have a separate property agreement during their marriage. Accordingly, this is a matter of first impression, and we address both the statute of frauds and Washington law concerning prenuptial agreements.

The statute of frauds requires certain agreements, including agreements made in consideration of marriage, to be in writing. The Washington Supreme Court held that any such agreement, if made orally, would violate the statute of frauds and declined to enforce the agreement. The statute of frauds barred enforcement of an alleged separate property agreement in *Graves v. Graves*, 48 Wash. 664, 94 P. 481 (1908). In *Graves*, several years after a husband and wife had divorced, the wife claimed that she was a co-owner of a parcel of real property that was acquired during marriage, but which was not disposed of in the parties' dissolution decree. The ex-husband contended that he and his ex-wife had entered into an oral agreement to treat each spouse's property as separate property; thus, he was the sole owner of the parcel in question because he purchased it in his name. The husband conceded, however, that community funds were used to purchase the property, and the court found that the wife had continuously asserted that the property was jointly owned. Thus, the alleged oral prenuptial agreement was void under the statute requiring agreements in consideration of marriage, as well as agreements transferring an interest in real property, to be in writing.

DewBerry contends on a number of grounds that the statute of frauds does not apply to the agreement in question here, but the cases she cites do not support her arguments. First, this agreement is not an example of mutual promises made in contemplation of marriage. The case DewBerry cites stated in dicta that "antenuptial agreements made upon mutual promises to marry" do not require a writing, is not on point. Although there are mutual promises involved here as there are in any contract, DewBerry and George's agreement is an agreement made in consideration of marriage. But for DewBerry and George's marriage, there would be no reason to have a separate property agreement and, by the terms of George's conditions, without the agreement, there would have been no marriage. Thus, it is an agreement in consideration of marriage.

Although we hold that the statute of frauds applies to the agreement in question, we conclude that it is enforceable under the part performance exception to the statute of frauds. The doctrine of part performance is an equitable doctrine which provides the remedies of damages or specific performance for agreements that would otherwise be barred by the statute of frauds. The first requirement of the doctrine of part performance of oral contracts is that the contract must be proven by clear, cogent, and convincing evidence. [T]he acts relied upon as constituting part performance must unmistakably point to the existence of the claimed agreement. If they may be accounted for on some other hypothesis, they are not sufficient.

Here, the terms of the agreement were clear and simple. Several witnesses testified that the parties created an oral prenuptial agreement and that George and DewBerry acted in accordance with that agreement. Furthermore, despite George's denial of the agreement, the steps taken by the parties to avoid commingling of their assets were unusually strong evidence of a separate property agreement. It was undisputed that the parties meticulously accounted for and handled their individual incomes as separate property and created minimal joint accounts to handle certain family-related expenses and requirements. The husband and wife relationship cannot account for such painstaking efforts to establish and maintain separate property. We conclude that the trial court's determination that an oral agreement was made is supported by substantial evidence that is "highly probable."

George also contends that there was no finding of complete performance to take the agreement out of the statute of frauds. This contention lacks merit, as the trial court expressly stated in its oral opinion that it found complete performance.

Although Washington has never enforced an oral prenuptial agreement, several other jurisdictions have. These cases all involved partial or full performance of an oral prenuptial agreement. The case at bar is similar because each of those cases involved complete performance of an oral prenuptial agreement during the parties' marriages.

We affirm.

NOTES

(1) The plaintiff in *In re the Marriage of Scalf-Foster*, 2010 Wash. App. LEXIS 752, relied on the principal case in arguing that part performance an oral prenuptial agreement rebutted the presumption of community property between married parties in the state of Washington. The court, however, distinguished the precedent in stating, "Part performance requires the oral contract to be proven by clear, cogent and convincing evidence . . . . In *DewBerry* the trial court found the witnesses asserting the oral prenuptial agreement existed credible. Additionally, several witnesses testified as to the creation of the *DewBerry* agreement and the terms were clear and simple. Here, no witnesses corroborated the account of an oral prenuptial agreement and the three times Foster described the agreement at trial, he used different terms in describing the scope of the alleged agreement."

(2) Agreements to adopt children or to permit a spouse's parents to live with the couple have been held to be within the marriage clause of the statute of frauds. *See Maddox v. Maddox*, 224 Ga. 313, 161 S.E.2d 870 (1968); *Koch v Koch*, 95 N.J. Super. 546, 232 A.2d 157 (1967).

(3) *Agreements Between Unmarried Cohabitants.* Limited authority suggests that agreements between unmarried cohabitants are not with the marriage clause of the statute of frauds. *See Morone v. Morone*, 429 N.Y.S.2d 592, 413 N.E.2d 1154 (1980). To discourage "palimony" litigation based on alleged oral agreements between unmarried cohabitants, there have been legislative efforts to require promises made in consideration of nonmarital, conjugal relationships to be evidenced by a writing so as to place them on an equal footing with promises made in consideration of marriage. *See Zaremba v. Cliburn*, 949 S.W.2d 822 (Tex. 1997).

[6] Contracts for the Sale of Land

[a] Contracts Versus Conveyances

The land contract provision of the original Statute of Frauds uses the language "contract or sale" of land. This language is broad enough to include contracts for the sale of land as well as conveyances of land. Yet, other Statute of Frauds sections deal with conveyances comprehensively.[22]

---

[22] *See* 29 Car. 2, ch. 3, § 11.

Thus, the land contract clause is commonly viewed as if it only contained the words, "contract for the sale of land." The typical statute of frauds in the United States is so worded.

[b] Part Performance and Remedies

CAIN v. CROSS
Illinois Appellate Court
687 N.E.2d 1141 (1997)

Maag, J.

Plaintiff, Gerald Cain, filed an action seeking money damages for breach of contract. The defendants, Ronald and Robert Cross (collectively Cross), filed a motion to dismiss based upon the provisions of the statute of frauds. From an order of the circuit court granting the motion, Cain appeals.

The facts are as follows. Cain filed a complaint alleging that Cross agreed to sell to Cain, and Cain agreed to purchase, 806 acres in Pulaski County, known as Cross Farms, for $1,000 per acre. The agreement was not in writing. Cain claims he was to pay $10,000 in earnest money upon making the agreement, $400,000 on the delivery of possession, and the balance with interest at a later date. Cain claims he made the $10,000 down payment and arranged financing for the balance, but Cross refused to convey the property and breached their agreement by conveying the property to a third party. Cain alleges that he sustained money damages in excess of $50,000 and filed this action to recover those damages.

The sole issue presented for review is whether the circuit court erred in dismissing Cain's cause of action on the basis of the statute of frauds.

The statute of frauds provides in part, "No action shall be brought to charge any person upon any contract for the sale of lands" unless the contract or a memorandum or note thereof is in writing and signed by the party to be charged. A contract alleged to be invalid on the basis of the statute of frauds is merely voidable, not void. The contract may be enforced unless the defendant sets up the statute as a defense. *Koenig v. Dohm*, 209 Ill. 468, 476, 70 N.E. 1061, 1063 (1904). "A man, who makes an oral contract to sell land, and violates his agreement, and relies upon the Statute of Frauds in order to justify himself in its non-performance, may be guilty of a wrong in the domain of morals, but not of such a fraud as relieves against the application of the statute." 209 Ill. at 481, 70 N.E. at 1065.

[handwritten margin note: Voidable Not void]

Cain's contention is that under the doctrine of part performance, the absence of a written contract is irrelevant. Cain argues that by paying $10,000 in earnest money, he has partly performed, thereby taking the agreement out of the statute of frauds. He cites several cases that, he claims, support his argument. We disagree.

The cases relied on by Cain to support his part-performance argument, with only one exception, involved contracts for the sale of goods. The single case cited that addressed a contract for the sale of land contradicts Cain's position. That case will be discussed later in this decision. Contracts for the sale of goods are governed by

[handwritten margin note: Cases not similar]

the Uniform Commercial Code (UCC). Under the UCC, a special statute of frauds applicable to contracts for the sale of goods controls such contracts. Because this case does not involve a contract for the sale of goods, we express no view on the requirements for part performance under the UCC.

Oral contracts for the sale of land, to become enforceable under the doctrine of part performance, require more than the mere payment of earnest money. "[A] payment of the purchase money alone [for real estate], without either possession or improvements, is not such a part performance[] as to take the case out of the statute." *Koenig v. Dohm*, 209 Ill. 468, 479, 70 N.E. 1061, 1064 (1904).

The only case Cain cites that discusses the doctrine of part performance in relation to a contract for the sale of land is *Pendleton v. King*, 55 Ill. App. 3d 1, 370 N.E.2d 590, 12 Ill. Dec. 786 (1977). Pendleton holds that in order to satisfy the requirements of the part-performance doctrine, the buyer must take possession of the property, pay the purchase money, either in whole or in part, and make improvements to the land or change the property in some way in reliance on the oral agreement. 55 Ill. App. 3d at 4, 370 N.E.2d at 592. The only requirement Cain has met, if we accept the allegations of the complaint as true, is the payment of earnest money. This is simply not sufficient to remove the bar of the statute of frauds.

In any event, the doctrine of part performance does not even apply in this case. Cain filed an action at law seeking money damages. He claimed that he was entitled to relief based upon the equitable doctrine of part performance. He claims that the distinctions between equitable actions and actions at law should no longer apply given the fact that we now have only a circuit court rather than both a chancery court and a circuit court.

The circuit court has jurisdiction over all justiciable matters. The circuit court is organized into divisions. The chancery division of the circuit court hears equitable matters. The unification of the court system did not in any way change the way that equitable issues are heard and decided. 134 Ill. 2d R. 232(b) (equitable issues shall be heard and decided in the manner heretofore practiced in courts of equity). We must reiterate, "the doctrine of part performance is not applicable in actions at law for monetary damages." *Vuagniaux*, 273 Ill. App. 3d at 312, 652 N.E.2d at 845. *Affirmed.*

NOTES

(1) *"Interest in Land."* An "interest in land" is not limited to a transfer of a legal estate in lands. Easements, an agreement concerning a right-of-way, a change in the exit of a road, a rescission of a land contract, an assignment of an interest in land, a restriction upon land or an equitable lien created by mortgage are all interests in land. It is important to distinguish contracts relating to land which do not involve the transfer of a property interest. Thus, a contract to construct a building or perform work on certain land is not within the land clause of the Statute. Such contracts are for services, creating *in personam* rights as contrasted with rights *in rem. See* MURRAY ON CONTRACTS at § 72B.

(2) *Leases.* Under the English Statute, leases were excluded if they did not exceed three years from the time the lease was made. Most of the American statutes

make an exception for leases for a term up to one year (short term leases). Moreover, the year is typically *not* measured from the time the oral lease agreement is made.

(3) *Part Performance.* There is general agreement with the *part performance* analysis of the court in the principal case, i.e., once a transfer of ownership in the land has been completed by the seller, the promise to pay the price will be enforceable notwithstanding the lack of any writing to evidence the contract, unless the price itself is wholly or partially an interest in land. RESTATEMENT (SECOND) OF CONTRACTS § 125(3). If, however, there has been no transfer of the interest in land, but the price has been paid by the prospective buyer, it is generally held that the buyer may not obtain specific performance. Some performance beyond the mere payment of the price is usually necessary. It has been held that where the price is paid and the seller gives possession of the land to the buyer, the oral contract will be enforced.[23] Payment of the price plus possession and the making of valuable improvements on the land will certainly allow the contract to be specifically enforced by the buyer in most jurisdictions. It is, however, important to recognize that, whatever the performance, it must be *unequivocally referable* to the alleged oral agreement, i. e., it must be the dominant manifestation of intention since such conduct is the evidentiary substitute for the writing. See the opinion by Judge Cardozo in Burns v. McCormick, 233 N.Y. 230, 232, 135 N.E. 273 (1922). *See also* MURRAY ON CONTRACTS at § 77B.

(4) *Legal vs. Equitable Remedies — Restitution.* Because of the equitable nature of the part performance doctrine in contracts for the sale of an interest in land, an action for damages will not be aided by part performance. If, however, a prospective buyer such as the plaintiff makes a down payment which is not sufficient part performance to satisfy the statute of frauds, he may recover the down payment to prevent the unjust enrichment of the owner in an action to protect the buyer's restitution interest. *See Gilton v. Chapman*, 217 Ark. 390, 230 S.W.2d 37 (1950).

(5) *Agents (Brokers).* A number of statutes include a provision requiring agency authority or a promise to pay a commission to a real estate broker in a contract for the sale of land to be in writing. *See, e.g.,* Cal. Civ. Code § 1624(d); N.J. Stat. Ann. 25:1–9; Ind. Code § 32-2-2-1; Mont. Code Ann. § 37-51-401; Wash. Rev. Code § 19.36.010(5).

(6) *Distinguishing Land From Goods — UCC.* For many years, there was a split of authority as to whether coal or other minerals, natural gas, timber, growing crops and the like were "land" (coming within the land provision of the statute) or "goods" (coming within the contract for the sale of goods provision if the minimum price — currently at $500 — was met). The problem was essentially resolved by the Uniform Commercial Code classification in Section 2-107, which originally placed standing timber, minerals, structures attached to the land or the like in the category of *land* if the buyer was to sever them, but goods, *if the contract provided that the seller was to sever.* If the buyer was required to remove the coal or other "natural" parts of the land, he was purchasing land rather than goods. The Code was later changed (1972) to remove timber from this list. Timber is now treated as are

---

[23] *See* Darby v. Johnson, 477 So. 2d 322 (Ala. 1985).

growing crops, which are viewed as *goods* — a product of human industry — regardless of whether the buyer or seller is to sever them under the contract. This change was a reaction to earlier changes in timber-growing states because the buyers and sellers of timber viewed that product as *goods*.

What difference it makes whether certain land products such as minerals are treated as land or goods? As will be seen later in this treatment of the Statute of Frauds, a contract for the sale of goods priced at $500 or more must be evidenced by a writing. If, therefore, a contract for the sale of coal or other minerals is within the land provision (because the buyer is to sever) or within the goods provision (because the seller is to sever), the contract is still within the Statute of Frauds. Since they are both subject to the Statute, what difference does it make?

There are differences between the land and goods provisions of the Statute. For example, under the land provision, the writing necessary to satisfy the statute is typically more stringent that the frugal writing that is acceptable for the sale of goods provision under the Uniform Commercial Code. Moreover, as we will see, the UCC provides more alternative ways to satisfy the Statute where there is no writing. For example, in the principal case, the court intimates that part payment, alone, under the UCC will make a contract for the sale of goods enforceable to the extent of the part payment, while part payment, alone, under an oral contract for the sale of land will not make the contract enforceable to any extent.

[7]   Contracts Not Performable within One Year from Formation

C. R. KLEWIN, INC. v. FLAGSHIP PROPERTIES, INC.
Connecticut Supreme Court
600 A.2d 772 (1991)

PETERS, J.

The sole question before us in this certified appeal is whether the provision of the statute of frauds requiring a writing for an "agreement that is not to be performed within one year from the making thereof," renders unenforceable an oral contract that fails to specify explicitly the time for performance when performance of that contract within one year of its making is exceedingly unlikely.

The plaintiff, C. R. Klewin, Inc. (Klewin), is a Connecticut based corporation that provides general construction contracting and construction management services. The defendants, Flagship Properties and DKM Properties (collectively Flagship), are engaged in the business of real estate development; although located outside Connecticut, they do business together in Connecticut under the trade name ConnTech.

Flagship became the developer of a major project (ConnTech Project) in Mansfield, near the University of Connecticut's main campus. The master plan for the project included the construction of twenty industrial buildings, a 280 room hotel and convention center, and housing for 592 graduate students and professors.

The estimated total cost of the project was $120 million.

In March, 1986, Flagship representatives held a dinner meeting with Klewin representatives. Flagship was considering whether to engage Klewin to serve as construction manager on the ConnTech Project. During the discussions, Klewin advised that its fee would be 4 percent of the cost of construction plus 4 percent for its overhead and profit. This fee structure was, however, subject to change depending on when different phases of the project were to be constructed. The meeting ended with Flagship's representative shaking hands with Klewin's agent and saying, "You've got the job. We've got a deal." No other specific terms or conditions were conclusively established at trial. The parties publicized the fact that an agreement had been reached and held a press conference, which was videotaped. Additionally, they ceremoniously signed, without filling in any of the blanks, an American Institute of Architects Standard Form of Agreement between Owner and Construction Manager.

Construction began May 4, 1987, on the first phase of the ConnTech Project, called Celeron Square. The parties entered into a written agreement regarding the construction of this one part of the project. Construction was fully completed by the middle of October, 1987. By that time, because Flagship had become dissatisfied with Klewin's work, it began negotiating with other contractors for the job as construction manager on the next stage of the ConnTech Project. In March, 1988, Flagship contracted with another contractor to perform the sitework for Celeron Square II, the next phase of the project.

After having been replaced as construction manager, Klewin filed suit in the United States District Court for the District of Connecticut, claiming breach of an oral contract to perform as construction manager on all phases of the project. [Flagship claimed that] the alleged oral contract was barred by the statute of frauds. The district court granted summary judgment, reasoning that the contract "as a matter of law" could not possibly have been performed within one year. In drawing this conclusion, the court focused on the sheer scope of the project and Klewin's own admission that the entire project was intended to be constructed in three to ten years.

Klewin appealed to the United States Court of Appeals for the Second Circuit. The Court of Appeals held that "the issues presented involve substantial legal questions for which there is no clear precedent under the decisions of the Connecticut Supreme Court"; id., 686; and certified to this court the following questions:

"A. Whether under the Connecticut Statute of Frauds an oral contract that fails to specify explicitly the time for performance is a contract of 'indefinite duration," as that term has been used in the applicable Connecticut precedent, and therefore outside of the Statute's proscriptions?

"B. Whether an oral contract is unenforceable when the method of performance called for by the contract contemplates performance to be completed over a period of time that exceeds one year, yet the contract itself does not explicitly negate the possibility of performance within one year?" We answer "yes" to the first question, and "no" to the second.

The Connecticut statute of frauds has its origins in a 1677 English statute entitled "An Act for the prevention of Fraud and Perjuries." The statute appears to have been enacted in response to developments in the common law arising out of the advent of the writ of assumpsit, which changed the general rule precluding enforcement of oral promises in the King's courts. Thereafter, perjury and the subornation of perjury became a widespread and serious problem. Furthermore, because juries at that time decided cases on their own personal knowledge of the facts, rather than on the evidence introduced at trial, a requirement, in specified transactions, of "some memorandum or note . . . in writing, and signed by the party to be charged" placed a limitation on the uncontrolled discretion of the jury. Although the British Parliament repealed most provisions of the statute, including the one-year provision, in 1954, the statute nonetheless remains the law virtually everywhere in the United States. [The one-year provision has been omitted in North Carolina and Pennsylvania.]

Modern scholarly commentary has found much to criticize about the continued viability of the statute of frauds. The statute has been found wanting because it serves none of its purported functions very well and because it permits or compels economically wasteful behavior. It is, however, the one-year provision that is at issue in this case that has caused the greatest puzzlement among commentators. As Professor Farnsworth observes,

> of all the provisions of the statute, it is the most difficult to rationalize. If the one-year provision is based on the tendency of memory to fail and of evidence to go stale with the passage of time, it is ill-contrived because the one-year period does not run from the making of the contract to the proof of the making, but from the making of the contract to the completion of performance. If an oral contract that cannot be performed within a year is broken the day after its making, the provision applies though the terms of the contract are fresh in the minds of the parties. But if an oral contract that can be performed within a year is broken and suit is not brought until nearly six years (the usual statute of limitations for contract actions) after the breach, the provision does not apply, even though the terms of the contract are no longer fresh in the minds of the parties.
>
> If the one-year provision is an attempt to separate significant contracts of long duration, for which writings should be required, from less significant contracts of short duration, for which writings are unnecessary, it is equally ill-contrived because the one-year period does not run from the commencement of performance to the completion of performance, but from the making of the contract to the completion of performance. If an oral contract to work for one day, 13 months from now, is broken, the provision applies, even though the duration of performance is only one day. But if an oral contract to work for a year beginning today is broken, the provision does not apply, even though the duration of performance is a full year.

2 E. Farnsworth, Contracts (2d Ed. 1990) § 6.4, pp. 110–11.[24]

---

[24] [6] Even the statute's most notable defender chose not to mention the one-year provision when he contended that the statute is "in essence better adapted to our needs than when it was first passed." K.

Historians have had difficulty accounting for the original inclusion of the one-year provision. One eminent historian suggested that because such contracts are continuing contracts, it might be very difficult to give evidence of their formation, inasmuch as the rules of evidence of that time prohibited testimony by the parties to an action or any person who had an interest in the litigation. 6 W. HOLDSWORTH, *supra*, p. 392. That argument, however, proves too much, since it would apply equally to all oral contracts regardless of the duration of their performance. The most extensive recent study of the history of English contract law offers plausible explanations for all of the other provisions, but acknowledges that this one is "curious." A. SIMPSON, A HISTORY OF THE COMMON LAW OF CONTRACT (1975) p. 612. More recently, it has been suggested that the provision "may have been intended to prevent oral perjury in actions of assumpsit against customers who had forgotten the details of their purchases." P. Hamburger, *The Conveyancing Purposes of the Statute of Frauds*, 27 AM. J. LEG. HIST. 354, 376 n.85 (1983).

In any case, the one-year provision no longer seems to serve any purpose very well, and today its only remaining effect is arbitrarily to forestall the adjudication of possibly meritorious claims. For this reason, the courts have for many years looked on the provision with disfavor, and have sought constructions that limited its application. *See, e.g., Landes Construction Co. v. Royal Bank of Canada*, 833 F.2d 1365, 1370 (9th Cir. 1987) (noting policy of California courts "of restricting the application of the statute to those situations precisely covered by its language"); *Cunningham v. Healthco, Inc.*, 824 F.2d 1448, 1455 (5th Cir. 1987) (one-year provision does not apply if the contract "conceivably" can be performed within one year); *Hodge v. Evans Financial Corporation*, 823 F.2d 559, 561 (D.C. Cir. 1987) (statute of frauds "has long been construed narrowly and literally"); *Goldstick v. ICM Realty*, supra, 464 ("Courts tend to take the concept of 'capable of full performance" quite literally . . . because they find the one-year limitation irksome.").

Our case law in Connecticut, like that in other jurisdictions, has taken a narrow view of the one-year provision of the statute of frauds. In *Appleby v. Noble*, 101 Conn. 54, 57, 124 A. 717 (1924), this court held that " '[a] contract is not within this clause of the statute unless *its terms are so drawn* that it cannot by any possibility be performed fully within one year." (Emphasis added.) In *Burkle v. Superflow Mfg. Co.*, 137 Conn. 488, 492–93, 78 A.2d 698 (1951), we delineated the line that separates contracts that are within the one-year provision from those that are excluded from it. *"Where the time for performance is definitely fixed at more than one year*, the contract is, of course, within the statute . . . . If no time is *definitely fixed* but full performance may occur within one year through the happening of a contingency upon which the contract depends, it is not within the statute."

More recently, in *Finley v. Aetna Life & Casualty Co.*, 202 Conn. 190, 197, 520 A.2d 208 (1987), we stated that " '[u]nder the prevailing interpretation, the enforceability of a contract under the one-year provision does not turn on the actual course of subsequent events, nor on the expectations of the parties as to the probabilities. Contracts of uncertain duration are simply excluded; the provision covers only those contracts whose performance *cannot possibly* be completed

---

Llewellyn, *What Price Contract? An Essay in Perspective*, 40 YALE L.J. 704, 747 (1931).

within a year.' (Emphasis added.) 1 RESTATEMENT (SECOND), CONTRACTS, § 130, comment a] . . . ."

In light of this unbroken line of authority, the legislature's decision repeatedly to reenact the provision in language virtually identical to that of the 1677 statute suggests legislative approval of the restrictive interpretation that this court has given to the one-year provision. "[T]he action of the General Assembly in re-enacting the statute, including the clause in question . . . is presumed to have been done in the light of those decisions." *Turner v. Scanlon*, 146 Conn. 149, 156, 148 A.2d 334 (1959).

Bearing this history in mind, we turn to the questions certified to us by the federal court. Our case law makes no distinction, with respect to exclusion from the statute of frauds, between contracts of uncertain or indefinite duration and contracts that contain no express terms defining the time for performance. The two certified questions therefore raise only one substantive issue. That issue can be framed as follows: in the exclusion from the statute of frauds of all contracts except those "whose performance cannot possibly be completed within a year"; *Finley v. Aetna Life & Casualty Co., supra*, 197; what meaning should be attributed to the word "possibly"? One construction of "possibly" would encompass only contracts whose completion within a year would be inconsistent with the express terms of the contract. An alternate construction would include as well contracts such as the one involved in this case, in which, while no time period is expressly specified, it is (as the district court found) realistically impossible for performance to be completed within a year. We now hold that the former and not the latter is the correct interpretation. "The critical test . . . is whether 'by its terms' the agreement is not to be performed within a year," so that the statute will not apply where "the alleged agreement contain[s] [no] provision which directly or indirectly regulated the time for performance." *Freedman v. Chemical Construction Corporation*, 43 N.Y.2d 260, 265, 401 N.Y.S.2d 176, 372 N.E.2d 12 (1977). "It is the law of this state, as it is elsewhere, that a contract is not within this clause of the statute unless its terms are so drawn that it cannot by any possibility be performed fully within one year." *Burkle v. Superflow Mfg. Co., supra*, 492.

Flagship contends, to the contrary, that the possibility to which this court referred in *Burkle* must be a reasonable possibility rather than a theoretical possibility. It is true that in *Burkle* this court rejected the argument that "since all the members of a partnership [that was a party to the contract] may possibly die within a year, the contract is not within the statute." We noted that "[n]o case has come to our attention where the rule that the possibility of death within a year removes a contract from the statute has been extended to apply to the possibility of the death of more than one individual." *Id.*, 494. In *Burkle*, however, we merely refused to extend further yet another of the rules by which the effect of the provision has been limited. *Burkle* did not purport to change the well established rule of narrow construction of the underlying one-year provision.

Most other jurisdictions follow a similar rule requiring an express contractual provision specifying that performance will extend for more than one year. Only "[a] few jurisdictions, contrary to the great weight of authority . . . hold that the intention of the parties may put their oral agreement within the operation of the

Statute." 3 S. WILLISTON, CONTRACTS (3d Ed. W. Jaeger 1960) § 495, pp. 584–85. In "the leading case on this section of the Statute"; *id.*, p. 578; the Supreme Court of the United States undertook an extensive survey of the case law up to that time and concluded that "[i]t . . . appears to have been the settled construction of this clause of the statute in England, before the Declaration of Independence, that an oral agreement which, according to the intention of the parties, as shown by the terms of the contract, might be fully performed within a year from the time it was made, was not within the statute, although the time of its performance was uncertain, and might probably extend, and be expected by the parties to extend, and did in fact extend, beyond the year. The several States of the Union, in reenacting this provision of the statute of frauds in its original words, must be taken to have adopted the known and settled construction which it had received by judicial decisions in England." . . . *Warner v. Texas & Pacific R. Co.*, 164 U.S. 418, 422–23 (1896). The agreement at issue was one in which a lumbermill agreed to provide grading and ties and the railway agreed to construct rails and a switch and maintain the switch as long as the lumbermill needed it for shipping purposes. Although the land adjoining the lumbermill contained enough lumber to run a mill for thirty years, and the lumbermill used the switch for thirteen years, the court held that the contract was not within the statute. "The parties may well have expected that the contract would continue in force for more than one year; it may have been very improbable that it would not do so; and it did in fact continue in force for a much longer time. But they made no stipulation which in terms, or by reasonable inference, required that result. The question is not what the probable, or expected, or actual performance of the contract was; but whether the contract, according to the reasonable interpretation of its terms, required that it should not be performed within the year." *Id.*, 434.

Because the one-year provision "is an anachronism in modern life . . . we are not disposed to expand its destructive force." *Farmer v. Arabian American Oil Co.*, 277 F.2d 46, 51 (2d Cir. 1960). When a contract contains no express terms about the time for performance, no sound reason of policy commends judicial pursuit of a collateral inquiry into whether, at the time of the making of the contract, it was realistically possible that performance of the contract would be completed within a year. Such a collateral inquiry would not only expand the "destructive force" of the statute by extending it to contracts not plainly within its terms, but would also inevitably waste judicial resources on the resolution of an issue that has nothing to do with the merits of the case or the attainment of a just outcome. *See* 2 A. CORBIN, *supra*, § 275, p. 14 (the statute "has been in part the cause of an immense amount of litigation as to whether a promise is within the statute or can by any remote possibility be taken out of it. This latter fact is fully evidenced by the space necessary to be devoted to the subject in this volume and by the vast number of cases to be cited").

We therefore hold that an oral contract that does not say, in express terms, that performance is to have a specific duration beyond one year is, as a matter of law, the functional equivalent of a contract of indefinite duration for the purposes of the statute of frauds. Like a contract of indefinite duration, such a contract is enforceable because it is outside the proscriptive force of the statute regardless of how long completion of performance will actually take.

NOTES

(1)   The analysis is supported in the Restatement (Second) of Contracts, § 130, comment a.

(2)   In *Hopper v. Lennen & Mitchell, Inc.*, 146 F.2d 364 (9th Cir. 1944), Hedda Hopper, a nationally syndicated "gossip" columnist, agreed to perform radio programs for the defendant for a total period of five years divided into twenty-six week segments with increases in salary for each of the ten segments. Defendant had the power to terminate the contract by giving notice one month before the end of any segment. No writing evidenced this contract notwithstanding considerable detail. The court expressly recognized the distinction drawn by Professor Williston between *alternative* performances and performances subject to *termination*. If the contract was viewed as one that could be performed either in one twenty-six week period or in five years, the contract would be without the Statute because one of the alternative performances was performable within one year. If, however, the contract were characterized as a five-year contract subject to a power of termination in the defendant, the contract would be within the Statute and unenforceable because the contract could not be *performed* within one year. The court held the contract to be without the Statute because it could be performed, at the discretion of the defendant, within one year from the time it was made.

(3)   *Restatement Changes.* The FIRST RESTATEMENT unremarkably adopted Professor Williston's view (§ 198). The SECOND RESTATEMENT begins to suggest that it will continue following that view but adds, "The distinction between performance and excuse for non-performance is sometime tenuous; it depends on the terms and the circumstances, particularly on whether the essential purposes of the parties will be attained." § 130 comment b. The illustrations that follow attempt to reconcile the divergent positions. One illustration is an employment contract for a term of five years which provides, however, that "either party may terminate the contract by giving 30 days' notice at any time. The agreement is one of uncertain duration and is not within the one-year provision." (Illustration 6 to § 130). Illustration 7 retains the facts of 6 with only one modification: "the agreement provides that [one of the parties] may quit at any time. The agreement is within the Statute." Is it likely that the drafters of the RESTATEMENT (SECOND) intended to suggest an emphasis upon the manifested purpose of the parties, i.e., whether the parties intended a contract of uncertain duration with a maximum period of five years (without the Statute) or a five-year contract which permitted termination by notice within a year from its making? If this was the intention of the drafters, it is unfortunate that they did not express this analysis more clearly.

(4)   *Part Performance.* An oral contract which is executory on both sides is within the one-year provision of the Statute unless *both* promises can be performed within a year from their making. An old English case, however, suggested that full performance on one side of such a contract should satisfy the one-year provision.[25] This position, which was based on the fact that "the buyer had the full benefit of the goods on his part,"[26] is difficult to justify in light of the language of the Statute. This

---

[25] Donnellan v. Read, 3 B & Ad. 899 [1832].

[26] *Ibid.*

rationale may justify a restitutionary recovery that would be permitted in any case. A better rationale is that full performance on one side may be said to fulfill the Statute's evidentiary function. Pursuant to that rationale, it should make little difference whether the full performance on one side required more than a year to complete (*Accord*, RESTATEMENT (SECOND) OF CONTRACTS § 130, comment d). This view makes the one-year provision inapplicable to contracts which are originally "unilateral," or those which have in effect become "unilateral" by full performance on one side within a year.

[8] Contracts for the Sale of Goods (UCC)

AZEVEDO v. MINISTER
Nevada Supreme Court
471 P.2d 661 (1970)

MOWBRAY, JUSTICE.

This case centers about the enforceability of an oral agreement to purchase 1500 tons of hay. The principal issue presented for our determination is whether the periodic accountings prepared by the seller and sent to the buyer covering the sale of the hay constituted confirming memoranda within the provisions of NRS 104.2201(2) of the Uniform Commercial Code and, if so, whether the seller sent them within a reasonable time as required by that statute so that the oral agreement is not barred by the statute of frauds. The district judge ruled that the mandates of NRS 104.2201(2) had been satisfied, and he upheld the validity of the agreement. We agree, and we affirm the judgment of the lower court.

Appellant J. L. Azevedo is a rancher who buys and sells hay. He is licensed to do so, and he is bonded by appellant United States Fidelity and Guaranty Company. Respondent Bolton F. Minister operates the Minister Ranch near Yerington, Nevada, where he raises and sells large quantities of hay.

In early November 1967, Azevedo approached Minister for the purpose of buying hay. Terms were discussed. Several days later an agreement was reached by telephone. Both parties acknowledge that Azevedo agreed to purchase hay from Minister at a price of $26.50 per ton for the first and second cuttings and $28 per ton for the third cutting and that the parties opened an escrow account in a Yerington bank in Minister's favor, where Azevedo agreed to deposit sufficient funds to cover the cost of the hay as he hauled it from the Minister Ranch.[27]

The parties are in dispute as to the total quantity of hay Azevedo agreed to purchase. Minister claims Azevedo contracted to purchase 1,500 tons. Azevedo maintains that they never had an agreement as to quantity. Soon after this telephone conversation, Azevedo deposited $20,000 in the designated escrow account and began hauling hay from the Minister Ranch. As Azevedo hauled the hay, Minister furnished him with periodic accountings, commencing December 4, which specified the dates the hay was hauled, names of the truckers, bale count, and

---

[27] [1] Azevedo deposited a total sum of $23,000 in the account.

weight. This arrangement was satisfactory to the parties, and it continued until the latter part of March 1968, when Minister loaded only two of four trucks sent by Azevedo for hay, because the funds on deposit in the escrow account were insufficient to cover all four loads. Azevedo then refused to buy any more hay, and Minister commenced this action in district court.

The determination of the legal issues presented for our consideration will turn on our interpretation of NRS 104.2201(2) of the Uniform Commercial Code. Since the enactment of the Uniform Commercial Code, sweeping changes have been effectuated in the law of commercial transactions. NRS 104.2201 provides:

1. Except as otherwise provided in this section a contract for the sale of goods for the price of $500 or more is not enforcible [sic] by way of action or defense unless there is some writing sufficient to indicate that a contract for sale has been made between the parties and signed by the party against whom enforcement is sought or by his authorized agent or broker. A writing is not insufficient because it omits or incorrectly states a term agreed upon but the contract is not enforcible [sic] under this subsection beyond the quantity of goods shown in such writing.

2. Between merchants if within a reasonable time a writing in confirmation of the contract and sufficient against the sender is received and the party receiving it has reason to know its contents, it satisfies the requirements of subsection 1 against such party unless written notice of objection to its contents is given within 10 days after it is received.

3. A contract which does not satisfy the requirements of subsection 1 but which is valid in other respects is enforcible [sic]:

(a) If the goods are to be specially manufactured for the buyer and are not suitable for sale to others in the ordinary course of the seller's business and the seller, before notice of repudiation is received and under circumstances which reasonably indicate that the goods are for the buyer, has made either a substantial beginning of their manufacture or commitments for their procurement; or

(b) If the party against whom enforcement is sought admits in his pleading, testimony or otherwise in court that a contract for sale was made, but the contract is not enforcible [sic] under this provision beyond the quantity of goods admitted; or

(c) With respect to goods for which payment has been made and accepted or which have been received and accepted (NRS 104.2606).

As with all codifications, it was impossible for the Uniform Commercial Code to encompass every conceivable factual situation. Realizing this limitation, its drafters couched much of the language of the text and comments in broad generalities, leaving many problems to be answered by future litigation.

The development of the action of *assumpsit* in the fourteenth century gave rise to the enforceability of the oral promise. Although parties to an action could not be witnesses, the alleged promise could be enforced on the strength of oral testimony of others not concerned with the litigation. Because of this practice, a party could readily suborn perjured testimony, resulting in marked injustice to innocent parties who were held legally obligated to promises they had never made.[28] The statute of frauds was enacted to preclude this practice.[29] The passage of the statute did not eliminate the problem and controversy over its merits has been continuous. Those favoring the statute of frauds insist that it prevents fraud by prohibiting the introduction of perjured testimony.[30] They also suggest that it deters hasty action, in that the formality of a writing will prevent a person from obligating himself without a full appreciation of the nature of his acts.[31] Moreover, it is said, since business customs almost entirely conform to the mandates of the statute, an abolition of the statute would seriously disrupt such affairs.[32]

On the other hand, in England the statute of frauds has been repealed.[33] The English base their position upon the reasoning that the assertion of the technical defense of the statute aids a person in breaking a contract and effects immeasurable harm upon those who have meritorious claims.[34] It is further maintained by the advocates of the English position that the rationale for the necessity of the statute has been vitiated, because parties engaged in litigation today may testify as witnesses and readily defend against perjured testimony.[35]

Uniform Commercial Code, however, has attempted to strike a balance between the two positions by seeking to limit the defense of the statute to only those cases where there is a definite possibility of fraud. It is in the light of this historical background that we turn to consider whether the oral agreement of the parties in this case is barred by the statute of frauds.

There is no question that the Azevedo-Minister agreement was oral and that its enforceability is governed by NRS 104.2201(2), *supra*. The sale of hay is included within the definition of the sale of "goods" as defined by NRS 104.2105(1)[36] and

---

[28] [2] 2 A. CORBIN, CONTRACTS § 275, at 2 (1950).

[29] [3] Statute of Frauds, 1677, 29 Car. 2, c. 3 (repealed). The amount of the transaction necessary to bring the sale within the statute was 10 pounds.

[30] [4] 2 A. CORBIN, CONTRACTS § 275, at 3 (1950); 3 S. WILLISTON, CONTRACTS § 448, at 346.

[31] [5] L. FULLER, BASIC CONTRACT LAW, THE STATUTE OF FRAUDS 940, 943 (1947).

[32] [6] L. VOLD, SALES § 14, at 89 (2d ed. 1959).

[33] [7] Law Reform Act, 1954, 3 Eliz. 2, c. 34.

[34] [8] Burdick, *A Statute for Promoting Fraud*, 16 COLUM. L. REV. 273 (1916); 42 L.Q. REV. 1 (1927); 2 A. CORBIN, CONTRACTS § 275, at 3 (1950); 68 L.Q. REV. 4 (1952); 70 L.Q. REV. 441 (1954).

[35] [9] L. VOLD, SALES § 14, at 88 (2d ed. 1959). Advocates of The Sales Act have advanced the argument that the technical safeguard of a writing is more important in the United States than in England because in this country a litigant has a basic right to demand trial by jury. In England such a right is within the discretion of the court; thus, in most instances the court and not the jury will make the ultimate determination as to the existence of the contract. 68 HARV. L. REV. 383, 384 (1954).

[36] [10] NRS 104.2105(1):

"Goods" means all things (including specially manufactured goods) which are movable at the time of identification to the contract for sale other than the money in which the price is to be paid, investment securities (article 8) and things in action. "Goods" also includes the unborn young of animals and growing crops and other identified things attached to realty as described in the section on goods to be severed from realty (NRS 104.2107).

NRS 104.2107(2),[37] which when read together provide that the sale of "growing crops," when they are to be "severed by the buyer or by the seller," constitutes the sale of goods within the definition of that expression in the Uniform Commercial Code. The parties agree that they are "merchants" within the meaning of that term as defined in the Code.

It is also true that the statute of frauds is no defense to that portion of the contract that has been performed under the provisions of NRS 104.2201(3)(c), *supra*, which makes enforceable an oral contract "[w]ith respect to goods . . . which have been received and accepted." The legal issues are, therefore, (1) whether Minister's accountings constituted confirming memoranda within the standards of NRS 104.2201(2) and, if so, (2) whether Minister sent them within a reasonable time as required by the statute. a. The accounting of January 21, 1968.

In addition to the data set forth in the periodic accountings covering the dates on which hay was hauled, the names of the truckers, and the bale counts and weights, Minister added the following statement in his January 21 accounting to Azevedo:

> From your original deposit of $20,000.00 there is now a balance of $1819.76. *At this time there remains [sic] approximately 16,600 bales of hay yet to be hauled on your purchase*, about 9200 of which are first crop, 7400 of which are second crop.

We would appreciate hearing when you plan to haul the *balance of the hay*. Also please make a deposit to cover the hay, sufficient in amount to pay for the hay you will be currently hauling. At this time you have only about *$2.25 deposit per ton on the remaining balance of the hay*, and we cannot permit a lower deposit per ton and still consider the hay as being sold. (Emphasis added.)

Azevedo did not challenge or reply to Minister's accountancy of January 21. Rather, he deposited an additional $3,000 in the escrow account and continued hauling hay. b. The accounting of February 22, 1968.

In the regular accounting of February 22, Minister added the following: "Balance of deposit on approximately 14000 bales remaining to be hauled — $1635.26."

Azevedo did not challenge or reply to the February 22 accounting.

It is these two accountings that the district judge found constituted confirming memoranda within the meaning of NRS 104.2201(2). There is little authority articulating the meaning of a confirming memorandum as used in the Code. The official Comment, Uniform Laws Annotated, Uniform Commercial Code § 2-201(1968), states at 90, 91:

> Only three definite and invariable requirements as to the [confirming] memorandum are made by this subsection. First, it must evidence a

---

[37] [11] NRS 104.2107(2):

A contract for the sale apart from the land of growing crops or other things attached to realty and capable of severance without material harm thereto but not described in subsection 1 is a contract for the sale of goods within this article whether the subject matter is to be severed by the buyer or by the seller even though it forms part of the realty at the time of contracting, and the parties can by identification effect a present sale before severance.

contract for the sale of goods; second, it must be "signed," a word which includes any authentication which identifies the party to be charged; and third, it must specify a quantity.

The parties concede that the memoranda were "signed" within the meaning of the statute, but appellant Azevedo urges that neither memorandum confirms the existence of an oral contract.

While § 2-201(2) of the Code is entirely new in the commercial law field, its only effect is to eliminate the defense of the statute of frauds. The party alleging the contract still has the burden of proving that an oral contract was entered into *before* the written confirmation. The purpose of the subsection of the Code is to rectify an abuse that had developed in the law of commerce. The custom arose among business people of confirming oral contracts by sending a letter of confirmation. This letter was binding as a memorandum on the sender, but not on the recipient, because he had not signed it.[38] The abuse was that the recipient, not being bound, could perform or not, according to his whim and the market, whereas the seller had to perform.[39] Obviously, under these circumstances, sending any confirming memorandum was a dangerous practice. Subsection (2) of Section 2-201 of the Code cures the abuse by holding a recipient bound unless he communicates his objection within 10 days.

Appellant urges that the January and February accountings do not meet the standards of the subsection because neither memorandum makes reference to any oral agreement between the parties. A fair reading of the memoranda shows otherwise. The January memorandum states that, "At this time there remains [sic] approximately 16,600 bales of hay yet to be hauled on your purchase," and, further, that, "We [Minister] would appreciate hearing when you plan to haul the balance of the hay." Although neither the January nor the February memorandum refers to the previous November agreement by telephone, the language clearly demonstrates that the referred-to agreement between the parties was not an *in futuro* arrangement, but a pre-existing agreement between Azevedo and Minister. As the court said in *Harry Rubin & Sons, Inc. v. Consolidated Pipe Co.*, 396 Pa. 506, 153 A.2d 472, 476 (1959), in ruling on a case involving subsection (2) of section 2-201:

> Under the statute of frauds as revised in the Code[,] "All that is required is that the writing afford a basis for believing that the offered oral evidence rests on a real transaction." (Footnote omitted.)

The district judge found that it did so in the instant case, and the record supports his finding.

The "Reasonable Time" Factor

Subsection 2 of NRS 104.2201 provides that the confirming memorandum must be sent within a reasonable time after the oral contract is made. Appellant argues

---

[38] [12] As indicated in the instant case, Minister, who signed the memorandum, could be held to deliver to Azevedo the balance of the hay on the terms indicated.

[39] [13] The record reflects the price of hay was lower in March than in the previous November, when the parties had agreed on a tonnage price.

that the delay of 10 weeks (November 9 to January 21) as a matter of law is an unreasonable time. We do not agree. What is reasonable must be decided by the trier of the facts under all the circumstances of the case under consideration. Subsection 2 of NRS 104.1204 provides: "What is a reasonable time for taking any action depends on the nature, purpose and circumstances of such action."

In this case, the parties commenced performance of their oral agreement almost immediately after it was made in early November. Azevedo deposited $20,000 in the designated escrow account and began hauling hay. Minister commenced sending his periodic accounting reports to Azevedo on December 14.[40] It is true that the accounting containing the confirming memorandum was not sent until January 21. It was at that time that Azevedo's deposit of $20,000 was nearing depletion. Minister so advised Azevedo in the January memorandum. Azevedo responded by making an additional deposit. He did not object to the memorandum, and he continued to haul the hay until the latter part of March. Under "the nature, purpose and circumstances" of the case, we agree with the district judge that the delay was not unreasonable. *The judgment is affirmed.*

NOTES

(1) *Reasonable Time to Send Confirmation.* In *St. Ansgar Mills, Inc. v. Streit*, 613 N.W.2d 289, 295 (Iowa 2000), the court states,

> There are a host of cases from other jurisdictions which have considered the question of what constitutes a reasonable time under the written confirmation exception of the Uniform Commercial Code. *See Gestetner Corp. v. Case Equip. Co.*, 815 F.2d 806, 810 (1st Cir. 1987) (roughly five month delay reasonable in light of merchants' relationship and parties' immediate action under contract following oral agreement); *Serna, Inc. v. Harman*, 742 F.2d 186, 189 (5th Cir. 1984) (three and one-half month delay reasonable in light of the parties' interaction in the interim, and non-fluctuating prices, thus no prejudice); *Cargill, Inc. v. Stafford*, 553 F.2d 1222, 1224 (10th Cir. 1977) (less than one month delay unreasonable despite misdirection of confirmation due to mistaken addressing); *Starry Constr. Co. v. Murphy Oil USA, Inc.*, 785 F. Supp. 1356, 1362–63 (D. Minn. 1992) (six month delay for confirmation of modification order for additional oil unreasonable as a matter of law in light of Persian Gulf War, thus increased prices and demand); *Rockland Indus., Inc. v. Frank Kasmir Assoc.*, 470 F. Supp. 1176, 1179 (N.D. Tex. 1979) (letter sent eight months after alleged oral agreement for two-year continuity agreement unreasonable in light of lack of evidence supporting reasonableness of delay); *Yung*, 263 N.W.2d at 820 (six month delay in confirming oral agreement delivered one day prior to last possible day of delivery unreasonable); *Azevedo*, 471 P.2d at 666 (ten week delay reasonable in light of immediate performance by both parties following oral agreement); *Lish v. Compton*, 547 P.2d 223, 226–27 (Utah 1976) (twelve day delay "outside the ambit which fair-minded persons could conclude to be reasonable" in light of volatile price market and lack of

---

[40] [14] Azevedo concedes that he never challenged or replied to any of the accountings.

excuse for delay other than casual delay). Most of these cases, however, were decided after a trial on the merits and cannot be used to establish a standard or time period as a matter of law. Only a few courts have decided the question as a matter of law under the facts of the case. *Compare Starry*, 785 F. Supp. at 1362–63 (granting summary judgment), and *Lish*, 547 P.2d at 226–27 (removing claim from jury's consideration), *with Barron v. Edwards*, 45 Mich. App. 210, 206 N.W.2d 508, 511 (Mich. Ct. App. 1973) (remanding for further development of facts, summary judgment improper). However, these cases do not establish a strict principle to apply in this case. The resolution of each case depends upon the particular facts and circumstances.

(2) *Form — Time — More Than One Writing.* The writing (or more recently, electronic "record") can be in any form such as a letter, telegram, check, invoice, corporate minutes, diary entry, court petition in another lawsuit, contract with another party or even a will. The writing need not have been delivered. It need not exist at the time of formation. Oral contracts are often confirmed later in a writing or record. As will be seen below, recent statutes recognize electronic records such as an e-mail, voice mail or any other record that can be retrieved in perceivable form to be sufficient. A contract may be evidenced by more than one writing or record. If all of the writings relating to the same transaction are "signed," there is no problem. If, however, only one of the writings is signed, the question arose, must the signed writing expressly refer to the unsigned writings? A well-known case, *Crabtree v. Elizabeth Arden Sales Corp.*, 305 N.Y. 48, 110 N.E.2d 651 (1953), did not require such an express reference. This is view of the RESTATEMENT (SECOND) OF CONTRACTS § 132 which only requires one of the writings to be signed if the circumstances clearly indicate that they refer to the same transaction. *See Straight-Out Promotions LLC v. Warren*, 2005 U.S. Dist. LEXIS 7276 (W.D. Ky. 2005).

(3) *Content.* In general, a writing or record is sufficient if it evidences that a contract has been made, reasonably identifies the parties and subject matter and sets forth the terms with reasonable certainty (RESTATEMENT (SECOND) OF CONTRACTS § 131). Other than contracts for the sale of goods governed by the UCC, unless the controlling statutory language otherwise directs or the contract has been performed on one side, the consideration must be mentioned. The UCC requirements are frugal. The writing must evidence that a contract was made and the quantity term must be included. There is no requirement, however, that the price or time or place of delivery or the quality of the goods must be included. The parties must be identified, but they need not be identified as the buyer or the seller. UCC § 2-201, comment 1.

(4) *Loss or Destruction.* If the writing or record is lost or destroyed, the plaintiff is entitled to prove that it did exist and oral evidence of its contents is admissible. RESTATEMENT (SECOND) OF CONTRACTS § 137.

(5) *CISG and the Statute of Frauds.* The United Nations Convention on Contracts for the International Sale of Goods (CISG) currently applies to eighty-one nations including the United States. When CISG applies, it preempts domestic law. Thus, CISG would preempt the Uniform Commercial Code in a contract for the

sale of goods where each party is in a CISC country and the contract does not contain a clause evidencing the parties' decision to opt out of CISG, which they are permitted to do under CISG Article 6.[41] Article 11 of CISG states, "A contract for the sale [of goods] need not be concluded or evidenced by writing and is not subject to any other requirement of form." CISG permits any adopting country to make a declaration under Article 96 that Article 11 will not apply. Few countries ("contracting states") have done so. The United States has not made such a declaration.

CISG applies exclusively to international contracts for the sale of goods, but there are exceptions, such as goods purchased for personal, family or household use (consumer goods). Goods sold at auction or through the execution of a judgment, such as a sheriff's sale, are not included. The sale of stocks, shares, investment securities or money are not sales of "goods" under CISG; contracts for the sale of ships, vessels, hovercraft or aircraft are not covered by CISG since other regulatory laws govern such sales; sales of electricity are not within the scope of CISG. Whether "electricity" is a "good" is also problematic under the UCC.

PROBLEMS

(1) Davis orally agreed to sell his car for a price of $12,000 to Edwards. Edwards paid Davis $1,000 in cash as a down payment. When Edwards presented the balance of $11,000, Davis refused to deliver the car. Advise Edwards. Suppose that Edwards had refused to pay the balance and take the car. Advise Davis. *See* UCC § 2-201(3)(c).

(2) Peanut shelling companies often use brokers to buy and sell peanuts. Brooks called a broker to find and buy peanuts without identifying the buyer, which was not an unusual practice in this trade. The broker found several potential sellers including GSP. Brooks made a counter offer through the broker and GSP accepted before knowing the identity of the buyer. After discovering that it was Brooks, a competitor, GSP did not reject the offer. The broker faxed a copy of the sale to each party on the broker's stationery. It listed the buyer and seller as well as the terms which included the quantity and price, and stated, "We confirm a purchase and sale." The form stated that the confirmation was subject to the seller's contract and buyer's purchase order "to follow." Neither party, however, issued any following document to the other. Almost four months later, GSP stated that it was not bound to any contract since Brooks was a competitor and no sales document had been

---

[41] CISG applies to a contract for the sale of goods where the parties have places of business in different countries ("contracting states") which have adopted CISG. If only one of the parties is in a CISG country and the rules of private international law would choose the CISG country as applicable law, CISG will normally apply (Article 1(1)(b) This rule would not apply, however, in a contract between a United States business and a business in a non-CISG country. Though the United States is a CISG country, it has taken a reservation concerning Article (1)(1)(b) which it is permitted to do under Article 95. For example, in a contract between a U.S. corporation based in New York and a Japanese company, since Japan is one of the few major trading nations that has yet to adopt CISG, a court would have to determine which country's law would apply. This is typically done through a determination of the place with the more dominant contacts — the place of formation, place of performance, etc. If a court determined that U.S. law should apply, it would not be CISG. Rather, it would be the Uniform Commercial Code.

issued by GSP. Advise Brooks. See *Brooks Peanut Co. v. Great S. Peanut, LLC*, 746 S.E.2d 272 (Ga. App. 2013).

(3) The Grant Company was in need of a special formula of ASA, a sizing solution, which no supplier sold. Grant telephoned the Alpha Chemical Corporation which agreed to create the new formulation and deliver it to Grant. Alpha immediately purchased materials to be used only for this order. Before Alpha began the production of the special formula, however, Grant cancelled the order. Advise Alpha. *See* UCC § 2-201(3)(a).

[9]   Electronic Writings (Records) and Signatures

WILLIAMSON v. THE BANK OF NEW YORK MELLON
United States District Court, Northern District of Texas
947 F. Supp. 2d 704 (2013)

GODBEY, J.

This case arises out of the foreclosure of Williamson's home (the "Property"). In 2011, Williamson was no longer able to make her mortgage payments, so she and Countrywide entered into what Williamson characterizes as a "loan modification agreement." Bank of America later acquired the note and deed. Bank of America refused to honor the alleged Williamson-Countrywide modification agreement. Williamson subsequently applied for a loan modification from Bank of America on four occasions, but Bank of America denied each application. Williamson fell behind on her mortgage payments, and Bank of America foreclosed on the Property.

In her petition, filed in state court, Williamson asserts various claims against the Banks arising out of the foreclosure. The Banks moved to dismiss Williamson's petition. Before the Court could rule on that motion, the Banks' attorney, Walter McInnis, and Williamson's attorney, Marc Girling, exchanged a number of emails in an attempt to settle their clients' dispute.

Williamson has refused to abide by the terms of the settlement agreement Girling negotiated on her behalf. The Banks now move to enforce the agreement [even though the parties did not sign a physical agreement. In deciding whether to enforce a settlement agreement, a federal court in a diversity case applies the law of the forum state. The agreement, therefore, must meet Rule 11 under Texas law.]

To determine whether an agreement satisfies this requirement, courts look to the same Texas contract principles they use to determine whether a writing satisfies the statute of frauds. That is, "there must be a written memorandum which is complete within itself in every material detail, and which contains all of the essential elements of the agreement, so that the contract can be ascertained from the writings without resorting to oral testimony." The memorandum, though, does not have to take the form of a single document.

The written memorandum in this case exists as a series of emails between Girling and McInnis. The Texas Supreme Court held that a series of letters may satisfy the "in writing" requirement of *Rule 11*, provided they meet the other requirements set out above. The Court has not addressed, however, whether an email exchange may do so as well. When a state high court has not ruled on a particular issue of state law, a federal court must make an *"Erie* guess" and determine as best it can what the state high court would most likely decide.

The Court predicts that the Texas Supreme Court would hold that a series of emails may satisfy *Rule 11*'s "in writing" requirement. Most importantly, the Texas Uniform Electronic Transactions Act ("TUETA") states that "[i]f a law requires a record to be in writing, an electronic record satisfies the law." The Court's best guess, then, is that the Texas Supreme Court would decide that an email exchange may, provided it meets the other requirements that Court has set out, qualify as a written agreement under *Rule 11*.

TUETA "applies only to transactions between parties each of which has agreed to conduct transactions by electronic means. Whether the parties agree to conduct a transaction by electronic means is determined from the context and surrounding circumstances, including the parties' conduct. Here, the parties' lengthy email exchange and the content of those emails demonstrate an intent to conduct their settlement negotiations via electronic means."

The Court must next determine whether the series of emails in this case is "complete within itself in every material detail" and "contains all of the essential elements of the agreement." [T]he Court determines that the parties' memorandum, as expressed in their email exchange, was compete in every material detail and that it contained all the essential elements of their agreement. It therefore satisfies *Rule 11*'s "in writing" requirement.

Rule 11 requires not just a writing, but a signed writing. Under TUETA, "[i]f a law requires a signature, an electronic signature satisfies the law." An electronic signature, in turn, is "an electronic sound, symbol, or process attached to or logically associated with a record and executed or adopted by a person with the intent to sign the record."

The Court's best *Erie* guess is that the Texas Supreme Court would consider the relevant emails in this case to be signed under TUETA and *Rule 11*. Girling closed all of his emails with his first name. All of McInnis's end with his signature block. For the purposes of this motion, the Court assumes that Girling manually typed his name but that McInnis's email client automatically attached his signature block. Regardless of whether the names and signature blocks were manually typed or automatically attached, though, the Court would reach the same result.

Manually Typed Names. — First, the Court concludes that Girling's manually typed names qualify as electronic signatures. They represent electronic symbols attached to a record and executed with the intent to sign the record as contemplated by TUETA. A signature on a letter suffices to satisfy, and the Court concludes that a hand-typed name at the bottom of an email does, too. A typed name at the end of an email is similar to a "signature" on a telegram, the latter of which can satisfy the statute of frauds.

A number of other courts have similarly found that names typed at the end of emails can be signatures under various states' statutes of frauds and enactments of the Uniform Electronic Transactions Act ("UETA"), which is the source of TUETA.

E.g., Preston Law Firm, L.L.C. v. Mariner Health Care Mgmt. Co., 622 F.3d 384, 391 (5th Cir. 2010) (affirming that "[e]mails can qualify as the signed writings needed to form contracts" under Louisiana's UETA); *Lamle v. Mattel, Inc.*, 394 F.3d 1355, 1362 (Fed. Cir. 2005) (opining that inclusion of individual's name on email would be valid signature under California's UETA); *Cloud Corp. v. Hasbro, Inc.*, 314 F.3d 289, 295–96 (7th Cir. 2002) (holding that "the sender's name on an e-mail satisfies the signature requirement of the [Illinois] statute of frauds" and noting that it would be valid signature under federal Electronic Signatures in Global and National Commerce Act as well); *Adani Exps. Ltd. v. AMCI Exp. Corp.*, Civ. A. No. 05-304, 2007 U.S. Dist. LEXIS 88969 (W.D. Pa. Dec. 4, 2007) (finding e-mail sufficient to meet requirements of Pennsylvania statute of frauds); *Roger Edwards, LLC. v. Fiddes & Son, Ltd.*, 245 F. Supp. 2d 251, 261 (D. Me. 2003), aff'd in part, dismissed in part, 387 F.3d 90 (1st Cir. 2004) (same for Maine statute of frauds); *Waddle v. Elrod*, 367 S.W.3d 217, 228–29 (Tenn. 2012) (same for Tennessee); *Williamson v. Delsener*, 59 A.D.3d 291, 874 N.Y.S.2d 41(N.Y. App. Div. 2009) (same for New York); *see also Tricon Energy, Ltd. v. Vinmar Int'l, Ltd.*, No. 4:10-CV-05260, 2011 U.S. Dist. LEXIS 108491 (S.D. Tex. Sept. 21, 2011) (holding, without reference to TUETA, that two emails closing with typed names "represent signed writings under the Texas UCC"). Though not binding, the Court considers these cases instructive.

The question of whether automatically attached signature blocks qualify as signatures under *Rule 11* is murkier. One state appellate court has held that they do not. *Cunningham v. Zurich Am. Ins. Co.*, 352 S.W.3d 519, 530 (Tex. App. — Fort Worth 2011, pet. denied). For the reasons set out above, the Court respectfully disagrees.

First, McInnis's email client did not create a signature block of its own volition. Rather, McInnis must have generated his signature block at some point in the past. He then directed his email client to attach the signature block to his subsequent outgoing email. The Court concludes that these actions affirmatively show intent to sign the record as required by TUETA.

Second, the Court's broad view of electronic signatures corresponds with TUETA's intent. As the Official Comment to TUETA notes, "[t]he purpose of the [T]UETA is to remove barriers to electronic commerce by validating and effectuating electronic records and signatures." An expansive view of what constitutes an electronic signature helps effectuate this purpose. Moreover, the official comments to UETA suggest a similar approach. UETA contains the exact same definition of "electronic signature" that TUETA does. *See* UNIF. ELEC. TRANSACTIONS ACT § 2. Moreover, the comments to UETA note that "[t]he idea of a signature is broad and not specifically defined." They state that UETA "establishes, to the greatest extent possible, the equivalency of electronic signatures and manual signatures." The comments specify that "including one's name as part of an electronic mail communication . . . may suffice" to create a valid electronic signature. They do not differentiate between manually typed and automatically attached names, and the Court believes that doing so would be improper. Considering a signature block an electronic signature is thus in line with the TUETA's and UETA's expansive purposes and rationales.

Third, the Court's interpretation accords with TUETA's requirement that that statute "must be construed and applied . . . to be consistent with reasonable practices concerning electronic transactions and with the continued expansion of those practices." Email communication is a reasonable and legitimate means of reaching a settlement in this day and age. And as a result of the "continued expansion" of email communication, a signature block at the bottom of an email has come to represent what a handwritten signature once represented: a means of identifying the sender, signaling that he or she adopts or stands behind the contents of the communication, and a method of ensuring that the communication is authentic. Because reaching settlements by email is currently a reasonable practice in the legal community, TUETA should be construed to be consistent with that practice. The Court's conclusion does just that.

In sum, the Court makes an *Erie* guess that the Texas Supreme Court would consider both a typed name and a signature block in an email to be electronic signatures under TUETA. Both, then, suffice to satisfy *Rule 11*'s signature requirement. The Court therefore finds that both Girling and McInnis signed the parties' settlement agreement in this case within the meaning of *Rule 11*. Williamson and the Banks entered into an enforceable settlement agreement under Texas law. The Court therefore orders that the settlement agreement be enforced.

NOTE

Electronic Contracts.[42] The New York State Technology Law to which the court refers was among many legislative efforts to facilitate electronic commerce at the end of the twentieth century. Requiring certain contracts to be evidenced by a traditional "writing" and "signed" by the party to be charged under statutes of frauds raised barriers to the effective use of electronic media. There are isolated instances of a court recognizing electronic records as equivalent to traditional writings and signature. For example, *In re RealNetworks, Inc. Privacy Litig.*, 2000 U.S. Dist. LEXIS 6584 (N.D. Ill., May 11, 2000), held that an electronic agreement satisfied the "writing" requirement of both the federal and state arbitration acts. In *Cloud Corp. v. Hasbro Inc.*, 314 F.3d 289 (7th Cir. 2002), the court recognized an electronic signature as part of an e-mail There was, however, no assurance of a uniform judicial analysis and a judicial solution would require considerable time to evolve. In the meantime, the use of electronic technology to make contracts throughout the world could not be deterred.

Early non-uniform state legislative attempts to address this challenge were recognized as ineffective since each had its own requirements and were different in scope. A uniform statute that would recognize electronic writings and signatures as equal to traditional forms was essential. The United States Congress generally viewed commercial law as a creature of state law, but the strong desire to remove obstacles from the enforceability of electronic transactions induced the enactment of the *Electronic Signatures in Global and National Commerce Act* ("E-Sign"), which became effective on October 1, 2000 (15 U.S.C. § 7001 *et seq.*). In the

---

[42] This summary is essentially the same analysis that appears in the Supplement to CORBIN ON CONTRACTS § 23.1A (John E. Murray, Jr. & Timothy P. Murray).

meantime, the National Conference of Commissioners on Uniform State Laws proposed the 1999 *Uniform Electronic Transactions Act* (UETA) Both E-Sign and UETA share the limited objective of removing barriers to the use of electronic writings and electronic signatures in business, commercial and governmental transactions: "[A] signature, contract or other record relating to such transaction may not be denied legal effect, validity or enforceability solely because it is in electronic form." Beyond their identity in purpose, the statutes often use identical language. To encourage state enactment of UETA, E-Sign provides that the federal statute will not preempt state law if the state has enacted UETA without modification. By 2004, UETA had been enacted in forty-eight jurisdictions. New York is conspicuous by its absence from this list, deciding to maintain it own statute discussed in the *D'Arrigo* case.

Both E-Sign and UETA emphasize their common principal purpose in stating that, where a rule such as the statute of frauds requires a contract to be evidenced by a signed writing, an electronic record and electronic signature will meet that requirement. Both statutes define "record" as "information that is inscribed on a tangible medium or that is stored in an electronic or other medium and is retrievable in perceivable form." Both statutes define "electronic signature" as "an electronic sound, symbol or process attached to or adopted by a person with the intent to sign the record." In light of continuously developing technology, both statutes wisely avoid any specific technology requirements to satisfy their provisions. Inserting one's name in an e-mail communication or a firm's name in a facsimile will suffice. A voice message on an answering machine will suffice if the requisite manifested intention is present. While there is a requirement that parties must "agree" to the use of electronic means, there is a broad definition of "agree" that incorporates the surrounding circumstances and the parties' conduct. Thus, an e-mail address on a business card may allow a reasonable inference of assent to transacting business electronically. Even more obviously, ordering goods from an online vendor certainly implies assent to an electronic transaction.

Neither statute applies to wills, codicils, or testamentary trusts, which continue their traditional "writing" and "signed" requirements, or to transactions subject to other statutes that contain their own electronic transaction rules such as Articles 3 through 9 of the Uniform Commercial Code. Neither statute deals with substantive law matters. Both pursue a minimalist and procedural approach with the simple purpose of allowing electronic records and signatures to meet the requirements previously met only through traditional writings and signatures. UETA is, however, more comprehensive than E-Sign. It expressly provides that a record should not be denied admissibility into evidence solely because it is electronic form. While E-Sign does not mention "attribution," UETA provides that a signature on an electronic record does not bind the named party unless that party produced it, ratified it or is responsible for the agent who used it. Unlike E-Sign, UETA sets forth rules for errors or changes in electronic records and deals with the date and time of sending and receipt of electronic records.

An "electronic agent" is "a computer program or other automated means used independently to initiate an action or respond to electronic records or performance without review by an individual." Both statutes recognize contracts between such "agents" as well as contracts between individuals and electronic agents. In an online transaction, where an individual is advised that a contract will be formed by clicking the "I agree" button, the individual is free to decide on the performance of such an act and the decision to click that button will form a contract. Proposed 2003 amendments to Article 2 of the UCC not only include definitions of "electronic," "electronic agent" and "record." They also include three new sections on electronic contracting that are based on the UETA.

[10]   Estoppel and the Statute of Frauds

ALASKA DEMOCRATIC PARTY v. RICE
Alaska Supreme Court
934 P.2d 1313 (1997)

RABINOWITZ, J.

In 1991, Kathleen Rice began working for the Maryland Democratic Party. While she was in Maryland, Greg Wakefield contacted her regarding his potential candidacy for the Party chair and the possibility of Rice serving as his executive director.

In May 1992, Wakefield was in fact elected to chair the Party. His term was set to begin the following February. Rice claims that sometime during the summer after Wakefield had been elected, he "confirmed his decision" to hire her as executive director on the following specific terms: "$36,000.00 a year for at least two years and an additional two years if . . . Wakefield is re-elected; and approximately $4,000.00 a year in fringe benefits."

In August 1992, Nathan Landau, the chair of the Maryland Democratic Party, resigned and asked Rice to come work for him in his new capacity as co-finance chair of the Gore vice-presidential campaign. She accepted this offer. Rice asserts that later, in either September or October, she accepted Wakefield's offer to work for the Party in Alaska. In November, Rice moved to Alaska, resigning her position with Landau, which she claims "could have continued indefinitely . . . at a pay scale the same as that offered by Wakefield." No written contract was entered into between Rice and Wakefield or between Rice and the Party.

In a closed-door meeting on February 5, 1993, the executive committee of the Party advised Wakefield that he could not hire Rice as executive director. Rice alleges that even after this meeting, Wakefield continued to assure her that she had the job. However, on February 15, Wakefield informed her that she could not have the job. Rice filed suit. She was awarded $28,864 in damages on her promissory estoppel claim. [Defendant claims that her alleged contract was barred by the one-year provision of the statute of frauds.]

The question of whether the doctrine of promissory estoppel can be invoked to enforce an oral contract that falls within the Statute of Frauds presents a question of first impression. In order to resolve this question, the policy concerns behind both the Statute of Frauds and the doctrine of promissory estoppel must be examined. The purpose of the Statute of Frauds is to prevent fraud by requiring that certain categories of contracts be reduced to writing. However, "it is not intended as an escape route for persons seeking to avoid obligations undertaken by or imposed upon them." *Eavenson v. Lewis Means, Inc.*, 105 N.M. 161, 730 P.2d 464, 465 (N.M. 1986), overruled on other grounds by *Strata Prod. Co. v. Mercury Exploration Co.*, 121 N.M. 622, 916 P.2d 822 (N.M. 1996).

[T]he superior court addressed some of the conflicting case law on this question and ultimately concluded that as between the Statute of Frauds and promissory estoppel, the latter would prevail. It based this conclusion, in large part, on section 139 of the RESTATEMENT (SECOND) OF CONTRACTS which provides that

> [a] promise which the promisor should reasonably expect to induce action or forbearance on the part of the promisee or a third person and which does induce the action or forbearance is enforceable notwithstanding the Statute of Frauds if injustice can be avoided only by enforcement of the promise. RESTATEMENT (SECOND) OF CONTRACTS § 139 (1981). Section 139(2) then goes on to enumerate factors to consider in making the determination of "whether injustice can be avoided only by enforcement of the promise." *Id.*

In reaching its decision on this issue, the superior court reasoned:

> The RESTATEMENT test referenced herein provides an appropriate balance between the competing considerations supporting strict enforcement of the Statute, on the one hand, and prevention of a miscarriage of justice, on the other. Plaintiff's burden in overriding the Statute is to establish the promise's existence by clear and convincing evidence. This heightened burden, along with the other criteria imposed by Section 139, insure that the polices which gave rise to the Statute of Frauds will not, in fact, be nullified by application of the RESTATEMENT exception.

Commentators have noted that "there is no question that many courts are now prepared to use promissory estoppel to overcome the requirements of the statute of frauds." 2 ARTHUR L. CORBIN, CORBIN ON CONTRACTS § 281A (1950 & Supp. 1996). We join those states which endorse the RESTATEMENT approach in employment disputes such as this one.[43]

Concerning the applicability of section 139, the requisites for a claim must be met, as the jury reasonably found they were here. The Party and Wakefield reasonably could have expected to induce Rice's action by their promise. Rice did in

---

43 [2] *See McIntosh v. Murphy*, 52 Haw. 29, 469 P.2d 177 (Hawaii 1970); *Eavenson v. Lewis Means, Inc.*, 105 N.M. 161, 730 P.2d 464 (N.M. 1986), overruled by *Strata Prod. Co. v. Mercury Exploration Co.*, 121 N.M. 622, 916 P.2d 822, 828 (N.M. 1996) (recasting elements of promissory estoppel), and *Glasscock v. Wilson Constructors, Inc.*, 627 F.2d 1065 (10th Cir. 1980).

Numerous decisions have rejected the Restatement approach both implicitly and explicitly. *See, e.g., Venable v. Hickerson, Phelps, Kirtley & Assoc., Inc.*, 903 S.W.2d 659 (Mo. App. 1995), *Greaves v. Medical Imaging Sys., Inc.*, 124 Wash. 2d 389, 879 P.2d 276 (Wash. 1994), *Collins v. Allied Pharmacy Management, Inc.*, 871 S.W.2d 929 (Tex. App. 1994), *Dickens v. Quincy College Corp.*, 245 Ill. App. 3d 1055, 615 N.E.2d 381, 185 Ill. Dec. 822 (Ill. App. 1993), *Stearns v. Emery-Waterhouse Co.*, 596 A.2d 72 (Me. 1991), *Sales Serv., Inc. v. Daewoo Int'l (America) Corp.*, 770 S.W.2d 453 (Mo. App. 1989), *Whiteco Indus., Inc. v. Kopani*, 514 N.E.2d 840 (Ind. App. 1987), *Cunnison v. Richardson Greenshields Securities, Inc.*, 107 A.D.2d 50, 485 N.Y.S.2d 272 (N.Y. App. Div. 1985), *Moran v. NAV Servs.*, 189 Ga. App. 825, 377 S.E.2d 909 (Ga. App. 1989), *Munoz v. Kaiser Steel Corp.*, 156 Cal. App. 3d 965, 203 Cal. Rptr. 345 (Cal. App. 1984).

fact resign from her job, move from Maryland, and lose money as a result of her reliance on the Party and Wakefield, which amounted to a substantial worsening of her position. In addition, her reliance on the oral representations was reasonable.

Nonetheless, the promise is only enforceable where injustice can only be avoided by enforcement of the promise. The following circumstances are relevant to this inquiry:

> a) the availability and adequacy of other remedies, particularly cancellation and restitution;

> b) the definite and substantial character of the action or forbearance in relation to the remedy sought;

> c) the extent to which the action or forbearance corroborates evidence of the making and terms of the promise, or the making and terms are otherwise established by clear and convincing evidence;

> d) the reasonableness of the action or forbearance;

> e) the extent to which the action or forbearance was foreseeable by the promisor.

RESTATEMENT (SECOND) OF CONTRACTS § 139(2). In the context of this factual record, the jury could reasonably find that Rice would be a victim of injustice without an award of damages, considering her induced resignation, her move from Maryland, and her loss of money and position.

The Statute of Frauds represents a traditional contract principle that is largely formalistic and does not generally concern substantive rights. The extent to which a reliance exception would undermine this principle is minimal and the rights that it would protect are significant. The need to satisfy the clear and convincing proof standard with respect to the subsection 139(2)(c) factor also reassures us that promissory estoppel will not render the statute of frauds superfluous in the employment context. Accordingly, we affirm the superior court's treatment of this issue and adopt section 139 as the law of this jurisdiction.

In regard to Rice's section 139 claim, one aspect of Jury Instruction 12 directed the jury to decide whether Rice "took action in reliance upon the promise . . . ." The Party and Wakefield claim that section 139 of the RESTATEMENT (SECOND) OF CONTRACTS requires more than that "action" be taken; they contend that the action must be of a "definite and substantial" character. As such, they argue that "instruction 12 omitted a crucial component of the section 139 factors."

The RESTATEMENT lists "the definite and substantial character of the action or forbearance in relation to the remedy sought" as a significant "circumstance[ ]" to consider when applying the doctrine of promissory estoppel. RESTATEMENT (SECOND) OF CONTRACTS § 139. The Party and Wakefield are wrong to characterize this language as creating a "requirement." Further, the "definite and substantial" language was given to the jury in Instruction 13.

When read as a whole, the instructions clearly direct the jury to consider the definite and substantial character of Rice's action before concluding that an injustice could be avoided only by enforcing the promise. As such, the instructions are compatible with the Restatement, and it was not error to omit this modifier from the text of Instruction 12. We *affirm* the judgment of the superior court.

NOTES

(1)   *Origins. Monarco v. Lo Greco*, 35 Cal. 2d 621, 220 P.2d 737 (1950), is often viewed as a foundational case where the court rejected the traditional argument that an estoppel to plead the statute of frauds can only arise where there have been representations indicating that a writing is not necessary or will be executed. In 1926, Christie Lo Greco, age 18, decided to leave the home of his mother and stepfather, Carmela and Natale, and seek an independent living. They persuaded him to stay and participate in the family farm enterprise which was then valued at about $4,000. They orally promised to keep the property in joint tenancy and the survivor would then leave the farm to Christie by will. Relying on this promise, Christie remained on the farm and worked diligently. He forbore further educational opportunities and any chance to accumulate property of his own. He received only his board and spending money. Later, he married and asked for a present interest in the farm to help support his wife. Natale told him to have his wife move in with the family and that Christie need not worry since he would eventually receive the entire farm. When Natale died, the farm was worth about $100,000. However, before he died, Natale secretly arranged to terminate the joint tenancy with Carmela. He executed a will leaving all of his property to a grandson in Colorado who received the property after probate and brought an action for partition. In that action, he relied upon the Statute of Frauds to defeat the oral promise to Christie. The court refused to permit the grandson to invoke the statute. Rather, it imposed a constructive trust on the grandson through the doctrine of equitable estoppel to prevent unconscionable injury to Christie and unjust enrichment to the grandson. *See also Alaska Airlines v. Stephenson*, 217 F.2d 295 (9th Cir. 1954), in which the court applied RESTATEMENT (FIRST) OF CONTRACTS § 90 to enforce an oral agreement to employ plaintiff as general manager of defendant's airline. The plaintiff relied upon the defendant's promise to execute a writing evidencing the contract. The reliance consisting of abandoning his tenured position as a pilot of another airline and moving his family to the new location.

(2)   *UCC Statute of Frauds and Promissory Estoppel.* The case law is split over the use of promissory estoppel to avoid the UCC statute of frauds. The opening phrase of UCC § 2-201, "Except as otherwise provided in this section," suggests that the only exceptions to the requirement of a signed writing are those set forth in this section. While § 2-201(3)(a), dealing with specially manufactured goods, requires reliance in terms of either a substantial beginning of manufacture or commitments for the procurement of special goods, it is a very narrow exception. It can be read to suggest that the drafters of this section knew how to use reliance as a method of satisfying the statute and chose to use it only in the isolated situation of specially manufactured goods, thereby impliedly negating a general reliance exception. While a number of courts have refused to allow the general promissory estoppel doctrine to satisfy the statute, a greater number of courts have read § 1-103(b) of the UCC to allow a promissory estoppel exception. That section reads as follows:

Unless displaced by the particular provisions of this Act, the principles of law and equity, including the law merchant and the law relative to capacity to contract, principal and agent, *estoppel*, fraud, misrepresentation, duress, coercion, mistake, bankruptcy or other validating or invalidating cause shall supplement its provisions. (Emphasis supplied.)

Focusing upon that section and particularly the term "estoppel," these courts have allowed promissory estoppel to satisfy the statute, ignoring the opening phrase of Section 2-201. They also mention the RESTATEMENT (SECOND) OF CONTRACTS § 139 as further support in applying promissory estoppel to allow the enforcement of contracts that do not otherwise meet the requirements of the UCC statute of frauds. A few courts restrict the use of promissory estoppel to situations where the promisee relies on a promise to create a writing or a representation that the writing requirement has been met. *See Columbus Trade Exchange, Inc. v. AMCA International Corp.*, 763 F. Supp. 946 (S.D. Ohio 1991), which contains lists of jurisdictions permitting or not permitting the use of promissory estoppel to avoid the UCC statute of frauds.

[11]   Admission That the Contract Was Made

"His Lordship said, the plea insisting on the statute was proper, but then the defendant ought by answer deny the agreement; for if she confessed the agreement, the Court would decree a performance notwithstanding the statute, for such confession would not be looked upon as perjury, or intended to be prevented by the statute." *Child v. Godolphin*, 1 Dickens 39 (Ch. 1723), the leading early case on the loss of the Statute of Frauds defense through admissions, as reported in Stevens, *Ethics and the Statute of Frauds*, 37 CORNELL L.Q. 367 (1952).

For more than a hundred years after enactment of the original Statute of Frauds, courts followed the principle that the Statute was not intended to defeat performance of an admitted agreement. By the close of the eighteenth century, however, this view was rejected on a curious basis: Compelling the defendant to either admit or deny the making of the contract left him with only two choices if he had actually made the contract: (a) lose the Statute of Frauds as a defense, or (b) commit perjury. To overcome the great temptation to commit perjury in such a case, the defendant should be allowed to admit he made the contract and retain the Statute of Frauds as a defense.

LEWIS v. HUGHES
Maryland Court of Appeals
346 A.2d 231 (1975)

DIGGES, J.

[The appellant informed an attorney, James L. Baer, Esq., who had represented Dr. Hughes] that she was willing to sell the house trailer to Dr. Hughes for $5,000. On May 7, Mr. Baer reported appellant's offer to Dr. Hughes, who, without comment as to terms of payment, assented to the $5,000 purchase price. The attorney then signed and mailed to Dr. Hughes a letter, dated May 8, 1973, in confirmation of that conversation. Mrs. Lewis was notified on May 9 by Mr. Baer of the doctor's acceptance of her offer. However, the appellee on May 21 informed Mrs. Lewis that he would not pay the full $5,000 at the time of settlement, offering instead $3,500 cash or, alternatively, $5,000 over a period of time, which prompted the appellant to sell the mobile home elsewhere and to institute this suit for fraud and breach of contract.

To satisfy [the statute of frauds], appellant relies on the May 8 letter sent by the attorney to Dr. Hughes in confirmation of their previous telephone conversation. Although the circuit court found that letter to be "sufficient written evidence of the existence of a prior oral contract," a conclusion which is also not contested by appellee, the court held that it is not subscribed in accordance with the dictates of § 2-201(1) and thus could not be relied on to satisfy the writing requirement. The defect, as perceived by the trial court, was that the only signature appearing on the letter was Mr. Baer's and, even though he was an agent of Dr. Hughes with "authority to transmit [appellee's] acceptance to the [appellant]," he had not been empowered to "make any written memorandum of the sale"; thus he was not an "authorized agent" within the meaning of § 2-201(1).[44] We find it unnecessary to consider whether the circuit court correctly determined the extent of the agent's authority, as we conclude that the Statute of Frauds has been otherwise satisfied.

According to § 2-201(3), "A contract which does not satisfy the requirements of [§ 2-201(1)] but which is valid in other respects is enforceable . . . (b) [i]f the party against whom enforcement is sought admits in his pleading, testimony or otherwise in court that a contract for sale was made, but the contract is not enforceable under this provision beyond the quantity of goods admitted . . . ."

The appellant asserts that Dr. Hughes repeatedly acknowledged the existence of the contract in his testimony and that therefore, regardless of its enforceability under § 2-201(1), the agreement is enforceable under § 2-201(3)(b). The next step in deciding whether the statute bars enforcement of the contract is to determine just what, if anything, Dr. Hughes did admit concerning the agreement during the course of his testimony at trial. An examination of the record discloses that the doctor testified as follows:

Q.   This . . . conversation [with Mr. Baer], did you regard that as a meeting of the minds that you were to buy a trailer from Mrs. Lewis for $5,000 then or in the immediate future?

A.   No, Sir, I did not.

Q.   What was your understanding of your relationship with Mrs. Lewis at that time?

A.   My understanding was we were in a negotiation state really of reaching an agreement as to the purchase of the trailer, and I did not really agree to the terms how to purchase the trailer. But the price I had agreed with Mr. Baer on.

---

[44] [Ed. Note: UCC § 2-201 requires the writing to be "signed by the party against whom enforcement is sought or by his authorized agent or broker."]

Q.   Now I take it, sir, that you were not willing at any time to pay $5,000 cash?

A.   That is correct.

Q.   Did you tell [Mr. Baer], as he says, "O.K. I will buy it at that price," or not?

A.   Yes.

Q.   Now the essence of your version, if I understand it correctly, is that your statement was misinterpreted. You did not intend to mean that you would pay $5,000 cash. You intended that you would pay $5,000 on terms of some down and some over a period of time, is that right?

A.   That was not even discussed.

Q.   I understand that. But am I correct that when you said, "O.K. I will buy it at that price," that in your mind, at that time, you meant that you would buy it for $2,500 down, whatever it is, plus the rest over a period of time, although you did not say so?

A.   That is right.

Q.   You have already agreed to $5,000 as the price?

A.   Yes.

Q.   In your mind there exists a reservation as to method of payment that you have not communicated to anyone, is that right?

A.   That is right.

In sum, it is apparent from this, as well as from other portions of the appellee's testimony not here quoted, that at the trial the doctor admitted he told Mr. Baer, without mention of any terms of payment, that he would purchase the mobile home for $5,000. Of course, it is legally irrelevant, in the face of Dr. Hughes' objective manifestation of unconditional assent to the offer, that the doctor thought the contract was still being negotiated and had a subjective desire to impose certain conditions on the manner of payment.

[W]e must decide whether an admission that a contract was made is a valid admission for purposes of § 2-201(3)(b) if made involuntarily, since it has several times been said that there is a conflict of authority on the question [citing cases and authorities]. It is true that some cases decided prior to the adoption of the UCC by any state indicate that involuntary admissions as to the making of a contract will not satisfy the common law Statute of Frauds [citations]. Nevertheless, the cases reaching this issue under the UCC are uniform in concluding that involuntary admissions are sufficient. As stated by Hawkland in his Transactional Guide to the Uniform Commercial Code, § 1.203(1964) at page 30,

> Subsection 2-201(3)(b) does not answer [the question of whether involuntary admissions can be utilized], and it will have to be resolved on policy grounds. In this connection, it may be urged, on the one hand, that the defendant should not be required to make the admission, because any waiver of the Statute of Frauds should be exercised voluntarily and not

under the threat of perjury. On the other hand, it may be contended that the Statute of Frauds is not designed to protect the welsher. If the defendant made the contract, why should it not be enforceable? If he did not make it, he can deny it and set up the Statute of Frauds. It is only the welsher, therefore, [who] faces the problem of the 'compelled admission,' and the law should have little solicitude for him.

Not only do we consider the latter argument persuasive, we also find ourselves in agreement with the New Jersey Superior Court's statement in *Cohn v. Fisher* that:

> [I]f a party admits an oral contract, he should be held bound to his bargain. The statute of frauds was not designed to protect a party who made an oral contract, but rather to aid a party who did not make a contract, though one is claimed to have been made orally with him. 287 A.2d at 227.

We, therefore, hold that involuntary admissions can be used to satisfy the Statute of Frauds under § 2-201(3)(b). [T]he Statute of Frauds is satisfied pursuant to § 2-201(3)(b) when the party denying the existence of the contract and relying on the statute takes the stand and, without admitting explicitly that a contract was made, testifies to facts which as a matter of law establish that a contract was formed. While we have found no case specifically deciding this question, numerous cases dealing with § 2-201(3)(b) seem to say that in such a situation the requirements of the statute have been fulfilled. [citing cases]. Moreover, authority for this position can be found in decisions of this Court involving three closely analogous circumstances. In *Oregon Ridge v. Hamlin*, 253 Md. 462, 253 A.2d 382 (1969), we held that enforcement of an oral contract for the redistribution of securities is not barred by the Statute of Frauds of Title 8 of the Uniform Commercial Code when the defendant, at trial, concedes the existence of the agreement. Section 8-319(d). Since the language of §§ 8-319(d) and 2-201(3)(b) is quite similar, we find *Oregon Ridge* particularly persuasive. We reached a comparable conclusion with respect to the provisions of Section IV, Clause 5 of the Statute of Frauds, 29 Car. II C. 3 (enacted 1676, effective 1677), J. Alexander 2 British Statutes In Force in Maryland 690 (Coe ed. 1912), 2 (the context of an oral contract for the sale of an interest in a partnership. *Adams v. Wilson*, 264 Md. 1, 284 A.2d 434 (1971). Finally, it has long been settled in this State that oral contracts for the sale of land are enforceable when the defendant admits that the agreement was made. We hold that the Statute of Frauds does not bar enforcement of the contract involved in this case.

NOTES

(1) *Demurrer, Motion to Dismiss, Judgment on the Pleadings.* In footnote 10 of the unedited version of the principal case, the court states, in part, "Other questions posed by § 2-201(3)(b), but not at issue here, are whether a defendant's demurrer to a suit for breach of contract constitutes an admission of the existence of the contract sufficient to satisfy the Statute of Frauds." The court then mentions some of the following cases that bear on this question. *Beter v. Helman*, 41 Westm. Co. L.J. 7 (Westmoreland County Ct., Pa. 1958) (demurrer not admission for § 2-201(3)(b) purposes). *See also Anthony v. Tidwell*, 560 S.W.2d 908 (Tenn. 1977) and whether a declaration alleging breach of contract, which is valid in other

respects, is demurrable on grounds of the Statute of Frauds, see *Garrison v. Piatt*, 113 Ga. App. 94, 147 S.E.2d 374 (1966) (to sustain demurrer would deprive plaintiff of opportunity to get defendant to admit "in his pleading, testimony or otherwise" that a contract was made). *See also M & W Farm Serv. Co. v. Callison*, 285 N.W.2d 271 (Iowa 1979) and *Duffee v. Judson*, 251 Pa. Super. 406, 380 A.2d 843 (1977)]; Weiss v. Wolin, 60 Misc. 2d 750, 303 N.Y.S.2d 940, 943–44 (Sup. Ct. 1969) (same under § 8-319).

In *R. M. Schultz & Assocs., Inc. v. Nynex Computer Servs. Co.*, 1994 U.S. Dist. LEXIS 4509 (N.D. Ill. 1994), the court held that acceptance of factual allegations in the complaint as true for the purposes of summary judgment will not constitute an admission under § 2-201(3)(b), following an analogous holding in *Triangle Marketing, Inc. v. Action Industries*, 630 F. Supp. 1578 (N.D. Ill. 1986) holding that a Rule 12(b)(6) motion to dismiss and a Rule 12(c) motion for judgment on the pleadings admits the complaint's allegations only a technical sense inadequate to meet Section 2-201(3)(b)'s admission requirement.

If a technical admission made in connection with such motions or a demurrer is not the kind of admission to which the UCC provision refers, the defendant would never be put in a position of being forced to make a substantive admission or denial that the contract was made. This would emasculate § 2-201(3)(b) of the UCC because the Statute of Frauds would always be pleaded in this technical fashion. If, however, a defendant is forced to admit or deny the existence of the contract, other questions arise.

If the defendant's answer to the complaint denies the making of a contract, should the statute then operate to permit a successful motion for summary judgment, or should the court deny such a motion to provide plaintiff an opportunity to elicit an admission? As the principal case suggests, a defendant may deny he made the contract because he subjectively believes he was not contractually bound. Subjective belief is irrelevant. Moreover, the parties are incompetent to determine the legal effects of their acts. Thus, a simple denial of the existence of the contract in the answer to a complaint may deprive the plaintiff of an opportunity to elicit an admission. On the other hand, if the defendant did not make the contract, forcing a continuation of proceedings in terms of a trial may approach judicial harassment of the defendant and ignore the value of judicial economy. *See* Weiskopf, *In-Court Admission of Sales Contracts and the Statute of Frauds*, 19 UCC L.J. 195, 217 (1987). "One solution to this dilemma is to permit the plaintiff to depose the defendant. If the deposition does not evidence the making of a contract as alleged, a motion for summary judgment could then be granted." MURRAY ON CONTRACTS § 76.

(2) *Admissions in Other Statute of Frauds Contracts.* The satisfaction of the Statute of Frauds through admissions in contracts other than sale-of-goods contracts can be found in several jurisdictions. In the principal case, the court mentions contracts involving the sale of securities (to which Article 8 of the UCC applies), contracts involving an interest in a partnership and contracts for the sale of land. The statute of frauds in Article 8 (§ 8-319), however, has been eliminated in the revision of that Article (§ 8-113). Some jurisdictions include a general exception for admissions (*see, e.g.*, Iowa Code Ann. § 622.34; Alaska Stat. § 09.25.020). Without any statutory change, some courts have returned to the view of the English courts

in the first century after enactment of the original Statute, i.e., the purpose of the statute is to prevent fraud and not to perpetuate fraud. *See, e.g., Powers v. Hastings*, 20 Wash. App. 873, 582 P.2d 897 (1978), *aff'd*, 93 Wash. 2d 709, 612 P.2d 371 (1980). Other courts have been influenced by the UCC to engraft the admissions exception on all contracts within the statute. *See Hackney v. Morelite Constr.*, 418 A.2d 1062, 1066–67 (D.C. App. 1980). Courts that reject the admissions exception in other types of contracts cling to the flawed precedent of the nineteenth century. *See Pierce v. Gaddy*, 42 N.C. App. 622, 257 S.E.2d 459, 462 (1979). In general, see Shedd, *Statute of Frauds: Judicial Admission Exception — Where Has It Gone? Is It Coming Back?*, 6 WHITTIER L. REV. 1 (1984). *See also* MURRAY ON CONTRACTS § 76.

PROBLEM

Polk was employed as a sales manager for the defendant. The plaintiff alleged an oral contract for the sale of goods between the parties. The only evidence of the contract was a tape recording of a conversation between the plaintiff and Polk but Polk was unaware that the conversation was being recorded. Polk no longer worked for the defendant when he later testified that the voice on the recording admitting the existence of the contract was his voice. Would such a tape recording now be effective as a signed record of an oral contract within the statute of frauds? Under the facts of this problem, would it constitute a judicial admission to satisfy the statute of frauds under UCC § 2-201(3)(b)?

[12] Restitution

Where the contract is unenforceable but one party has conferred a benefit upon the other through part performance, courts will grant restitution on the footing that such a recovery in quasi contract does not undermine the Statute of Frauds. Thus, where a part payment has been made pursuant to an oral contract for the sale of land, the unenforceability of the contract will not preclude restitution of the payment. *See Gilton v. Chapman*, 217 Ark. 390, 230 S.W.2d 37 (1950). Where services have been performed pursuant to an unenforceable contract, the reasonable value of the services will be recoverable. *See Peters v. Morse*, 96 A.D. 662, 466 N.Y.S.2d 504 (1983). Even where there is no discernible economic benefit to the defendant, if the performance has been received under an unenforceable contract (as contrasted with mere preparation for performance), there will be a restitutionary recovery. *See Farash v. Sykes Datatronics, Inc.*, 59 N.Y.2d 500, 452 N.E.2d 1245 (1983); RESTATEMENT (SECOND) OF CONTRACTS § 375; *see also* MURRAY ON CONTRACTS § 81.

Real estate brokers, however, may not recover commissions on oral contracts where such commission contracts are within the statute because brokers are subject to state licensing requirements that require them to demonstrate their legal knowledge before being licensed. It has, therefore, been held that permitting restitution of such commissions would frustrate the underlying purpose of the statute. *See Phillippe v. Shapell Indus.*, 43 Cal. 3d 1247, 241 Cal. Rptr. 22, 743 P.2d 1279 (1987).

[13]   Effects of Noncompliance — Pleading the Statute

If an oral agreement is within one of the provisions of the statute of frauds, what effect does the statute have on that agreement? Does the statute preclude the agreement from recognition as a contract? If it is a contract, is it "void," "invalid," "voidable" or "unenforceable"? These and related questions have been confronted since the original Statute of Frauds was enacted. Unfortunately, the language of the various statutes of fraud does not necessarily provide ready solutions. The fourth section of the original Statute states that "no action shall be brought" against the promisor absent a signed memorandum. Query, does this mean that any attempt to bring such an action will be regarded as a nullity? The seventeenth section (sale of goods) of the original Statute uses the words, "no contract shall be allowed to be good . . . ." Does this language suggest that there is or was a contract but it will prevented from being valid or enforceable? Some statutes specify that a contract must fulfill the requirements of the statute to be "valid," i.e., if it fails to meet those requirements, it is "invalid." Still others prescribe that contracts failing to meet the statutory requirements "shall be void" or "are void." UCC § 2-201(1) states that a contract failing to comply with the statute of frauds provision "is not enforceable by way of action or defense." It is possible to discover different effect language attached to different provisions of a single statute of frauds.

It is important to recognize the significant differences that could flow from particular language in the statute. A so-called "void contract" is a contradiction, i.e., it has no legal effect whatsoever. If a contract is "voidable," one party has a legal power — a power of avoidance or disaffirmance. While it is possible that only one party to an oral contract has signed a sufficient memorandum which becomes enforceable against him though he cannot enforce the contract against the non-signing party, it is less than accurate to suggest that the non-signer has a power of avoidance or disaffirmance. The non-signer need not bring an action on the contract, but if she does bring an action against the signer of the memorandum, the signer may raise any available defense on the contract though he could not have enforced the contract.

This is only one of many illustrations of the operative effect of a contract that will not be enforced because it is within the statute of frauds. Thus, even where a contract is unenforceable between the parties to it, a third party who allegedly induced one of the parties to breach the unenforceable contract may still be held liable by either party to the contract for tortious interference with that contract. Where benefits have been conferred through the performance of one party to a contract within the statute of frauds, though the contract is unenforceable, it may be admitted as evidence of the understanding that the party conferring the benefit expected compensation as well as evidence of the value of the services.

There is considerable doubt that the drafters of the various statutes of fraud were interested in suggesting effects different from the original Statute. Apparently, they were attempting to duplicate the original Statute. The divergences in language have typically been glossed over and minimized by the courts.

If, for example, a particular statute states that a contract failing to comply with its requirements will be "void," courts have generally displayed little difficulty in reading "void" as "unenforceable" or at least "voidable." There is little precision among courts and lawyers in using the precise statutory term. In particular, the terms "void" and "unenforceable" are often used interchangeably. American statutes of frauds are generally interpreted to mean that a contract failing to comply with its provisions is "unenforceable." Under this interpretation, it is clear that a contract which can be effective for many other purposes exists though it cannot be enforced by one or both parties to the contract.

If the statute of frauds is viewed as a defense to an otherwise enforceable contract and the defendant does not raise the statute as a defense, a contract that is otherwise established by the plaintiff should be enforceable. Thus, the statute must be pleaded as an affirmative defense and failure to do so will constitute a waiver of the defense. Such pleading is required even where the applicable statutory language indicates that a contract failing to comply with the statute shall be "void." This is simply another indication that courts do not view contracts that fail to meet the statutory requirements as void. Again, such contracts are unenforceable. Older cases that permitted the statute to be raised by a general denial were simply reflecting the outmoded view that a failure to meet the requirements of the statute compels the holding that no contract ever existed, i.e., the so-called contract was void *ab initio*.

Since the statute is an affirmative defense it will not be permitted to be raised for the first time on appeal. Notwithstanding the usual requirement that the statute must be pleaded affirmatively at trial, if the complaint alleges an oral contract, it may be subject to a demurrer or motion to dismiss. To the extent that the defendant's judicial *admission* of the contract will satisfy the statute in lieu of a writing, however, courts should not permit the statute to be raised in this fashion since it effectively avoids the necessity for the defendant to admit or deny the existence of the contract. The impetus for judicial reconsideration of the scandalous practice of permitting a party to admit the existence of the contract and still plead the statute of frauds was the UCC. Courts have begun to recognize that permitting the statute to be raised by demurrer or motion to dismiss emasculates that statutory prescription. Moreover, as courts begin to apply the admissions exception to provisions of the statute of frauds beyond the sale-of-goods section of the UCC, the use of demurrers or motions to dismiss should erode further. It may eventually become impossible to raise the statute of frauds in this technical fashion to avoid the necessity of admitting or denying the existence of the contract, regardless of the type of contract within the statute before the court.

C. THE PAROL EVIDENCE RULE

[1] The Basic Concept

The first question is, why have parties over the centuries taken the time and effort to reduce their agreements to some permanent form — typically some form of writing? The most obvious answer is that they desire a permanent record of their agreement to which they may refer in the event of any ambiguity, confusion, misunderstanding or contest over the terms that bind them. The writing serves as permanent evidence of their agreement. Beyond a reliable permanent record of their transaction, the parties also adumbrate the risks they have assumed if they intend their written memorial to circumscribe the limits of their promises to each other. If one of the parties later asserts that the writing is incomplete, i.e., the parties had agreed to more risks than the record evidences, how should a court deal with such assertions. It is important to penetrate what many have called the "mystery" of the parol evidence rule by clarifying its essential operation.

When parties to a contract embody the terms of their agreement in a writing, intending that writing to be the final expression of their agreement, the terms of the writing may not be contradicted by evidence of any prior agreement. This is a description of the parol evidence rule, but the *description* of any legal concept usually succeeds in doing little more than creating an illusion of certainty. To understand the parol evidence rule, the purpose of the rule must be ascertained.

If the parties to a transaction express agreement and later express another agreement, intending the later agreement to prevail over their earlier expression of agreement, their later expression will prevail. This is not a statement of the parol evidence rule. It is a much broader statement because it would be correct in any of the following situations:

  (a) Both expressions of agreement are oral;

  (b) the first expression is written and the second is oral;

  (c) both expressions are written;

  (d) the first expression is oral and the second is written.

The machinery of the parol evidence rule may become operative only in situations (c) and (d). If the later (subsequent) agreement is evidenced by a writing, the rule *may* become operative, whether the prior agreement was oral or written. If one of the parties alleges that the subsequent written agreement was intended to be the final and complete expression of the parties' agreement, thereby discharging any prior agreement, the parol evidence machinery *is* activated. It now becomes necessary to decide a question of fact — did the parties intend the subsequent written agreement to be their final and complete or "integrated" expression, or, did they intend any prior agreements (oral or written) to be part of their total agreement with the written manifestation? It matters not how this question of fact is decided. Whatever the decision, the parol evidence rule has been invoked. It is important to recognize that this is the *only* situation in which the rule is invoked. If the parties disagree over the *meaning* of their manifestations of intent (words or conduct), the parol evidence rule will not solve the problem because such questions go to the *interpretation* of their outward manifestations. If one of the parties alleges that the writing does not state the true intention of the parties, the remedy of *reformation* may or may not be granted, but, once again, the parol evidence rule is not involved.

Why has this relatively simple matter, the determination of intention (a question of fact), taken on an air of mystery? In the first and second situations, *supra*, (a) and (b), if the question was whether the parties intended the second expression to prevail over the first, the question would be determined in the usual fashion in attempting to ascertain the total agreement. However, when the second expression is written, this same question invokes the parol evidence machinery. When the prior expression is oral and the second is in writing, courts have traditionally followed a policy of affording special protection to the writing. They early recognized that a jury may fail to consider adequately the relative unreliability of the prior oral expression. The writing is unchanged at the time of trial, but the oral expression may be the subject of the favorable (conscious or unconscious) recollection of the party who is urging that the writing is not final and complete. Because of this lack of sophistication in juries in choosing between the competing manifestations of agreement, courts did not wish to trust juries with the question. Thus, this question of fact was reserved to the courts. The experience of judges could be trusted in this matter. Yet, this meant an invasion of the traditional province of the jury — a question of *fact* would now be decided by the court. The courts were unwilling to clearly indicate what they were doing. They cloaked their fact-finding with "rules" which sounded very much like rules of evidence.

[2] The Application of the Rule

TRAUDT v. NEBRASKA PUBLIC POWER DISTRICT
Nebraska Supreme Court
251 N.W.2d 148 (1977)

CLINTON, J.

The plaintiffs allege that they were the owners of a certain quarter section of land in Hamilton County, Nebraska; that in 1968 the power district purchased an easement across their land; that as a part of the negotiations for said easement the defendant promised the plaintiffs that " 'if any other land owners get more money, then you will get more money"; and that said statement was made orally and was not put in writing. Plaintiffs also alleged that they interpreted the words " 'other land owners' to mean persons who own lands in Hamilton County" from whom the defendant had purchased easements. The petition also alleged that the defendant had acquired a similar easement from another named party by virtue of eminent domain proceedings which "were finally determined in September, 1972." The petition alleged that "Defendant owes to Plaintiffs additional funds for the purchase by Defendant of said easement." An executed copy of the easement was attached to the petition and incorporated by reference.The contents of this conveyance will be discussed later in the opinion. The petition prayed for "damages caused by said easement in the sum of $16,000, computed to be the sum of $100.00 per acre for said lands."

The underlying legal questions are two: First, was proof of the alleged contemporaneous oral agreement to pay some additional money barred by the parol evidence rule, and secondly, could such issue be properly determined upon demurrer. We answer both questions in the affirmative and uphold the judgment of the District Court dismissing the petition.

A succinct and cogent discussion of the parol evidence rule is contained in the manual, Evidence, Nebraska State Bar Association (1966), pp. 28-1 to 28-27, and affords a quick access to the basic authorities on all aspects of the subtle problems associated with the rule. In the discussion which follows we use the material therein contained . . . .

The usual statement of the rule is that parol or extrinsic evidence will not be received to vary or add to the terms of a written agreement. The rule is designed to preserve the integrity and certainty of written documents against disputes arising from fraudulent claims or faulty recollections of the parties' intent as expressed in the final writing. McCORMICK ON EVIDENCE, § 210, p. 427 (1954). ". . . *the rule is in no sense a rule of Evidence*, but a rule of Substantive Law. It does not exclude certain data because they are for one or another reason untrustworthy or undesirable means of evidencing some fact to be proved . . . . What the rule does is to declare that certain kinds of fact are legally ineffective in the substantive law; and this of course . . . results in forbidding the fact to be proved at all . . . ." 9 WIGMORE ON EVIDENCE (3d Ed., 1940), § 2400, p. 3.

Where the parties have embodied their transaction into a writing, the rule applies to exclude evidence dehors the writing of prior or contemporaneous negotiations or agreements in regard to the same subject matter. The applicability of the rule depends in general upon whether the agreement has been integrated . . . .

The crucial question in this particular case is: In what manner is it to be determined whether the transaction was integrated into the conveyance which is the grant of the easement? Professor Corbin suggests that in the usual case the conveyance is not intended to be a complete integration of the terms of the agreement, e.g., recitals of receipt of consideration are not terms of the agreement, but simply statement of facts, the truth or untruth of which may be established by extrinsic evidence. Likewise, under some circumstances the fact that additional consideration was to be paid may be established. 3 CORBIN ON CONTRACTS, §§ 586, 587, pp. 491, 501, 504 . . . .

What tests are to be applied to determine whether the transaction has been completely integrated? The tests established by the Nebraska cases are three. One is that the question whether the writing embodies the whole or only a part of the transaction depends upon the "completeness" of the writing. A corollary of this test is that the writing is the "sole criteria" of its own completeness. A second test often used is that the question depends upon whether the evidence outside the writing "varies or contradicts" the terms of the writing . . . . The evidence manual we earlier referred to states that WIGMORE criticizes both tests and that the questions of integration or partial integration depends [sic] upon intent, viz., whether the writing was intended to cover a certain subject of negotiation. Intent should be determined from the "conduct and language of the parties and the surrounding circumstances." This court appears to have in some cases, approved the statements of WIGMORE as well as the rule of RESTATEMENT.

We quote from RESTATEMENT, CONTRACTS, section 240, page 335:

> (1) An oral agreement is not superseded or invalidated by a subsequent or contemporaneous integration, nor a written agreement by a subsequent

integration relating to the same subject-matter, if the agreement is not inconsistent with the integrated contract, and

(a) is made for separate consideration, or

(b) is such an agreement as might naturally be made as separate agreement by parties situated as were the parties to the written contract.

(2) Where no consideration is stated in an integration, facts showing that there was consideration and the nature of it, even if it was a promise, or any other facts that are sufficient to make a promise enforceable, are admissible in evidence and are operative.

The court, not the jury, decides as a preliminary matter the extent to which the transaction is embodied in the writing, that is, the question of integration.

It seems to us that the tests, including those of WIGMORE and RESTATEMENT, are not necessarily mutually exclusive. Sometimes the court will have to look no further than the instrument itself and sometimes it will be proper to consider the surrounding circumstances, including the conduct and language of the parties as the WIGMORE rule would require.

In this case we have before us the written instrument and the surrounding circumstances and language dehors the writing as alleged by the plaintiffs . . . .

So far as the subject of consideration for the easement is concerned, the conveyance clearly does three things. It provides for a "total payment of $1000.00"; it shows how the amount was computed; and it makes a special provision for certain types of probable future damages which might arise from *future use* of the easement. It is clear that the instrument was designed to, and apparently did, deal with the whole subject of consideration and damages as then known and contemplated. It would appear to exclude any additional future payment *for the acquisition* of the easement, which is clearly the subject of this action.

No matter which of the tests is to be applied here, it appears that the determination of the trial court was correct. The instrument itself appears to be complete on the subject of consideration to be paid for the easement and the elements of damage for which future payment would be made when and if such damage occurred. The allegation in the petition that there was made a contemporaneous oral agreement to pay in the future some unspecified additional amount for the acquisition, depending upon whether other persons later received more money, contradicts the provision, making "a total payment of $1000.00."

Let us now apply WIGMORE's rule to the facts alleged. He says: ". . . the inquiry is whether the writing was intended to cover a *certain subject* of negotiation; for if it was not, then the writing does not embody the transaction on that subject; and one of the circumstances of decision will be whether the one subject is so associated with the others that they are in effect 'parts' of the same transaction, and therefore, if reduced to writing at all, they must be governed by the same writing." 9 WIGMORE ON EVIDENCE (3d Ed.), § 2430, p. 97. He goes on to say: "What it was intended to cover cannot be known till we know what there was to cover. The question being whether certain subjects of negotiation were intended to be covered, we must compare the writing and the negotiations before we can determine whether they were in fact covered. Thus the apparent paradox is committed of receiving proof of certain negotiations in order to determine whether to exclude them; and this doubtless has sometimes seemed to lower the rule to a quibble. But the paradox is apparent only. The explanation is that these alleged negotiations are received only provisionally. Although in form the witnesses may be allowed to recite the facts, yet in truth the facts will be afterwards treated as immaterial and legally void, if the rule is held applicable." 9 WIGMORE ON EVIDENCE (3d Ed.), § 2430(2), p. 98. He also says: "In deciding upon this intent, the chief and most satisfactory index for the judge is found in the circumstance whether or not the *particular element of the alleged extrinsic negotiation is dealt with at all* in the writing. If it is mentioned, covered, or dealt with in the writing, then presumably the writing was meant to represent all of the transaction on that element; if it is not, then probably the writing was not intended to embody that element . . . ." 9 WIGMORE ON EVIDENCE (3d Ed.), § 2430(3), p. 98.

Applying the foregoing rule we conclude that clearly the subject of total consideration was so a part of the transaction that "if reduced to writing at all, [it] must be governed by the same writing." Secondly, the subject of consideration was in fact dealt with in the instrument.

If we look to the RESTATEMENT rule we conclude: (1) The oral agreement was not for a separate consideration. Only one thing was being conveyed. There was no separate consideration for an additional payment. (2) An oral agreement for an unspecified future payment dependent upon extraneous events is not such an agreement as might naturally be made as a separate agreement between persons dealing at arm's length for property which would be the subject of eminent domain proceedings if negotiations fail. This seems particularly true where any agreement to convey an easement, in order to be valid and enforceable, must be evidenced by a memorandum sufficient to satisfy the statute of frauds and signed by the party to be bound. This conclusion seems also fortified by the circumstance that if the parties were seeking to avoid eminent domain proceedings, any such agreement would provide for the determination of how the added consideration was to be determined. Otherwise litigation would be in any event almost inevitable. *Affirmed.*

NOTES

(1) *Gianni v. R. Russell & Co.*, 281 Pa. 320, 126 A. 791 (1924). Gianni had leased space in an office building in Pittsburgh, Pennsylvania. He conducted a business selling tobacco, fruit, candy and soft drinks. Russell acquired the property and negotiated a new lease with Gianni which contained a provision that the lessee should "use the premises only for the sale of fruit, candy, soda water," etc., and further stipulated that "it is expressly understood that the tenant is not allowed to sell tobacco in any form, under penalty of instant forfeiture of this lease." After a careful reading of the document by two persons other than Gianni (including Gianni's daughter), the parties signed. Shortly thereafter, Russell leased the adjoining room in the building to a drug company, and that company began to sell soda water and soft drinks. Gianni contended that he had been assured that he had the exclusive right to sell soda water and soft drinks in the building and that he had

surrendered his right to sell tobacco in exchange for this exclusive right. Specifically, Gianni argued that this oral agreement had been made two days or more prior to the signing of the lease. No witness corroborated Gianni's statement.

The court held the evidence inadmissible, suggesting the following guidelines to determine whether the writing was "integrated": (1) "[T]he writing will be looked at, and if it appears to be a contract complete within itself" it is conclusively presumed that the "whole engagement of the parties . . . were reduced to writing." (2) The extrinsic (oral) agreement and the writing will be compared, and it will be determined "whether parties, situated as were the ones to the contract, would naturally and normally include the one in the other if it were made." (3) "[T]he chief and most satisfactory index . . . is found in the circumstance whether or not the particular element of the alleged extrinsic negotiation is dealt with at all in the writing. If it is mentioned, covered, or dealt with in the writing, then presumably the writing was meant to represent all of the transaction on that element, if it is not, then probably the writing was not intended to embody that element of the negotiation." The court cites WIGMORE ON EVIDENCE (2d ed.) vol. 5, p. 309, for the third test or guide. Though it does not cite WILLISTON for the second test, it is clearly the WILLISTON test (*See* 4 WILLISTON ON CONTRACTS §§ 638–639 (3d ed. 1961)). The first test is often called the "appearance" test and is generally considered inconclusive. The WIGMORE "aid" (test 2) is often used as a bulwark, and the most popular test in the case law is the WILLISTON test.

(2) *Mitchill v. Lath*, 247 N.Y. 377, 160 N.E. 646, 68 A.L.R. 239 (1928). Mrs. Mitchill negotiated with the Laths for the sale of their farm. The Laths also owned an unsightly icehouse on land owned by another across from the farm. The Laths orally agreed to remove the icehouse as part of the transaction with Mrs. Mitchill. However, there was nothing in the writing subsequently signed by the parties referring to the icehouse. The court refused to admit evidence of the prior icehouse agreement. Initially, the court distinguished the situation in which a separate parol agreement, for a separate consideration, is formed prior to or contemporaneous with the agreement evidenced by a writing. Relying on WILLISTON, the court held that two such distinct contracts, each for a separate consideration, may be made simultaneously and will be legally distinct. However, that was not the situation here. Before evidence of a prior oral agreement which is not supported by a separate consideration may be introduced, the court required three conditions to be met: (1) the agreement must in form be a collateral one; (2) it must not contradict express or implied provisions of the "written contract"; (3) it must be one which the parties would not ordinarily be expected to embody in the writing, i.e. it must not be so clearly connected with the principal transaction as to be part and parcel of it. Of the three "requirements" set forth in this famous case, (1) appears to be nothing more than conclusory; (2) would apply even if the writing were merely final and not complete; (3) is, essentially, an application of the WILLISTON test, i.e. would parties, situated as were these parties, naturally and normally ("ordinarily") include such extrinsic matter in the writing? A dissenting opinion by JUDGE LEHMAN in this case appears to quarrel not with the court's tests but with the application thereof. This is not remarkable since the determination of whether the parol evidence should be admitted in a given case is a question of fact.

COMMENT: PAROL EVIDENCE
TERMINOLOGY AND TESTS

(1) *"Vary," "Add to," "Contradict."* The court suggests, "The usual statement of the rule is that parol or extrinsic evidence will not be received to vary or add to the terms of a written agreement." In *Federal Deposit Ins. Corp. v. First Mtg. Inv.*, 76 Wis. 2d 151, 250 N.W.2d 362 (1977), the court provides a more elaborate analysis:

> When the parties to a contract embody their agreement in writing and intend the writing to be the final expression of their agreement, the terms of the writing may not be varied or contradicted by evidence of any prior written or oral agreement in the absence of fraud, duress, or mutual mistake. Although the parol evidence rule thus stated appears simple and makes good sense — the final agreement of the parties supersedes earlier negotiations — it "is in fact a maze of conflicting tests, subrules and exceptions adversely affecting both the counseling of clients and the litigation process."[45]

> The rule has survived because it is thought to preserve the integrity and reliability of written contracts, to reduce the opportunity for perjury and to prevent unsophisticated jurors from being misled by false or conflicting testimony. However, the rule has been criticized. Several writers have commented that there are few subjects in the law seemingly as indefinite and uncertain of application as the so-called rule of integration or merger of prior or contemporaneous negotiations. The rule causes injustices because it allows a party to avoid a legal obligation which he accepted during the negotiation process.[46]

> . . . The real question when a party invokes the parol evidence rule is whether the parties intended the written agreement to be final and complete or "integrated" or whether they intended any prior agreements to be part of their total agreement. In cases where the writing is incomplete in that only part of the agreement has been reduced to writing, this court has recognized the doctrine of "partial integration," that is the parties reduced some provisions to written form and left others unwritten.

(2) *"Integrated."* If the question is, did the parties intend the writing to be "integrated," and if that question really asks whether the parties intended the written evidence of their contract to be "final and complete," the inevitable problem

---

[45] Sweet, *Contract Making and Parol Evidence: Diagnosis and Treatment of a Sick Rule*, 53 Cornell L. Rev. 1036 (1968).

[46] For a discussion of the parol evidence rule see Sweet, *supra*; Calamari & Perillo, *A Plea for a Uniform Parol Evidence Rule and Principles of Contract Interpretation*, 42 Ind. L.J. 333 (1967); Note, *The Parol Evidence Rule: Is It Necessary?*, 44 N.Y.U. L. Rev. 972 (1969); Murray, *The Parol Evidence Rule: A Clarification*, 4 Duquesne L. Rev. 337 (1966); Murray, *The Parol Evidence Process and Standardized Agreements Under The Restatement (Second) of Contracts*, 123 U. Pa. L. Rev. 1342, 1346 (1975); Note, *Chief Justice Traynor and the Parol Evidence Rule*, 22 Stan. L. Rev. 547, 561–563 (1970); Case Comment, *Tests of Contractual Integration*, 25 Wash. & Lee L. Rev. 265 (1968); Green River Valley Foundation, Inc. v. Foster, 78 Wash. 2d 245, 473 P.2d 844, 851–52 (1970).

is, how do we decide whether the parties so intended? RESTATEMENT (SECOND) OF CONTRACTS § 213, comment b suggests:

> Whether a binding agreement is completely integrated or partially integrated, it supercedes inconsistent terms of prior agreements. To apply this rule, the court must make *preliminary determinations* that there is an integrated agreement and that it is inconsistent with the term in question.

(Emphasis supplied.)

What are these "preliminary determinations"? In the language of the principal case, "What tests are to be applied to determine whether the transaction has been completely integrated"?

(3) *"Integration" Tests.* Consider the following tests and determine which of these tests is mentioned in the principal case and the remaining cases in this section.

    (a) The *Appearance* Test — The judge simply examines the writing and, from its appearance alone, determines that it is "complete." What did Dean Wigmore think about this test?

    (b) The *Separate Consideration* Test — If the extrinsic agreement is one that has been made for a "separate consideration," evidence of that agreement is admissible.

    (c) The *Natural Omission* Test — If the extrinsic agreement is one that might naturally and normally be made as a separate agreement by parties situated as were the parties to this contract and, therefore, not be included in the writing, the evidence is admissible. The converse of this test might be called the "natural inclusion" test.

    (d) The *Certain Inclusion* Test — Unless the extrinsic agreement was such that it *would certainly* have been included in the writing, the evidence is admissible.

    (e) The *Writing Omission* Test — If the extrinsic matter is mentioned, covered, or dealt with in the writing, presumably the writing was meant to represent all of the transaction on that element; if not, the evidence is admissible. In general, see MURRAY ON CONTRACTS § 85C.

(4) *A Rule of Substantive Law.* Even if a party failed at trial to object to the admission of evidence violating the parol evidence rule, such evidence would not be operative on appeal. *See Franklin v. White,* 493 N.E.2d 161 (Ind. App. 1986). A federal court would apply the state parol evidence rule because it is a substantive rule of law and not a rule of evidence. *Betz Labs v. Hines,* 647 F.2d 402, 403 (3d Cir. 1981). *See* MURRAY ON CONTRACTS § 83B.

(5) *"Full" and "Partial" Integration.* If the parties intend their writing to be the final, complete and exclusive statement of their agreement, the writing is said to be "fully integrated" or "completely integrated" or, in the language of the Uniform Commercial Code, § 2-202, "complete and exclusive" as well as "final." If, however, the parties intend their writing to be "final" with respect to one or more matters mentioned therein, but did not intend their writing to be complete and exclusive, the writing is said to be "partially integrated" or "final" as to the matters

mentioned in the writing. The RESTATEMENT (SECOND) OF CONTRACTS uses the unfortunate phraseology "integrated" or "completely integrated" *agreement* (§ 213) rather than *writing*. The preferable UCC phraseology avoids the use of the conclusory term, "integrated," and also avoids a focus upon the agreement of the parties by concentrating on whether the writing was merely a "final expression" ("partially integrated" in the RESTATEMENT (SECOND) OF CONTRACTS sense), or whether the writing was intended to be "a complete and exclusive statement of the terms of the agreement" (as contrasted with "fully" or "completely" "integrated."

Applying one or more of the "integration" tests described in note 3, *supra*, may help to determine what the parties intended their writing to be.

(6) *Prior Versus "Contemporaneous."* The parol evidence rule is typically stated as barring evidence of "prior or contemporaneous" agreements made prior to the writing if the parties intended that writing to be final with respect to the extrinsic matter or complete. Professor Corbin had considerable difficulty with "contemporaneous." He suggested that, if it meant "simultaneous," it would be difficult to understanding how the parties could have assented to a final and complete writing and, at the same time, have assented to another agreement. "One cannot express simultaneous assent to two things and at the same instant agree that one of them supplants the other." 3 CORBIN ON CONTRACTS § 577. If "contemporaneous" does not mean "simultaneous," the prior agreement was then either before or after the writing, and the parol evidence rule applies only to prior agreement. In its attempt to reconcile all differences between CORBIN and WILLISTON concerning the parol evidence rule, the RESTATEMENT (SECOND) OF CONTRACTS avoids the use of "contemporaneous" in one significant section (§ 213), but includes it in the next important section (§ 214). The Reporter admits that he was torn between the logic of Corbin and the pull of tradition. 48 ALI Proceedings 449 (1971). For a complete analysis of the RESTATEMENT (SECOND) parol evidence analysis, see Murray, *The Parol Evidence Process and Standardized Agreements Under the Restatement (Second) of Contracts*, 123 U. PA. L. REV. 1342 (1975). Finally, it should be noted that some courts cling to the FIRST RESTATEMENT position (§ 237) that the parol evidence rule bars contemporaneous *oral* agreements but not contemporaneous *written* agreements. *See McDonald's Corp. v. Butler Co.*, 158 Ill. App. 3d 902, 511 N.E.2d 912 (1987).

MASTERSON v. SINE
California Supreme Court
436 P.2d 561 (1968)

TRAYNOR, C. J.

Dallas Masterson and his wife Rebecca owned a ranch as tenants in common. On February 25, 1958, they conveyed it to Medora and Lu Sine by a grant deed "Reserving unto the Grantors herein an option to purchase the above described property on or before February 25, 1968" for the "same consideration as being paid heretofore plus their depreciation value of any improvements Grantees may add to the property from and after two and a half years from this date." Medora is Dallas' sister and Lu's wife. Since the conveyance Dallas has been adjudged bankrupt. His trustee in bankruptcy and Rebecca brought this declaratory relief action to establish their right to enforce the option.

The case was tried without a jury. Over defendants' objection the trial court admitted extrinsic evidence that by "the same consideration as being paid heretofore" both the grantors and the grantees meant the sum of $50,000 and by "depreciation value of any improvements" they meant the depreciation value of improvements to be computed by deducting from the total amount of any capital expenditures made by defendants grantees the amount of depreciation allowable to them under United States income tax regulations as of the time of the exercise of the option.

The court also determined that the parol evidence rule precluded admission of extrinsic evidence offered by defendants to show that the parties wanted the property kept in the Masterson family and that the option was therefore personal to the grantors and could not be exercised by the trustee in bankruptcy.

The court entered judgment for plaintiffs, declaring their right to exercise the option, specifying in some detail how it could be exercised, and reserving jurisdiction to supervise the manner of its exercise and to determine the amount that plaintiffs will be required to pay defendants for their capital expenditures if plaintiffs decide to exercise the option.

Defendants appeal. They contend that the option provision is too uncertain to be enforced and that extrinsic evidence as to its meaning should not have been admitted. The trial court properly refused to frustrate the obviously declared intention of the grantors to reserve an option to repurchase by an overly meticulous insistence on completeness and clarity of written expression. It properly admitted extrinsic evidence to explain the language of the deed; (*see* Farnsworth, *"Meaning" in the Law of Contracts* (1967) 76 YALE L.J. 939, 959–965; Corbin, *The Interpretation of Words and the Parol Evidence Rule* (1965) 50 CORNELL L.Q. 161) to the end that the consideration for the option would appear with sufficient certainty to permit specific enforcement. The trial court erred, however, in excluding the extrinsic evidence that the option was personal to the grantors and therefore nonassignable.

When the parties to a written contract have agreed to it as an "integration" — a complete and final embodiment of the terms of an agreement — parol evidence cannot be used to add to or vary its terms. When only part of the agreement is integrated, the same rule applies to that part, but parol evidence may be used to prove elements of the agreement not reduced to writing.

The crucial issue in determining whether there has been an integration is whether the parties intended their writing to serve as the exclusive embodiment of their agreement. The instrument itself may help to resolve that issue. It may state, for example, that "there are no previous understandings or agreements not contained in the writing," and thus express the parties' "intention to nullify antecedent understandings or agreements." (*See* 3 CORBIN, CONTRACTS (1960) § 578, p. 411.) Any such collateral agreement itself must be examined, however, to determine whether the parties intended the subjects of negotiation it deals with to be included in, excluded from, or otherwise affected by the writing. Circumstances at the time of the writing may also aid in the determination of such integration.

California cases have stated that whether there was an integration is to be determined solely from the face of the instrument (e.g., *Thoroman v. David* (1926) 199 Cal. 386, 389–390, 249 P. 513; *Heffner v. Gross* (1919) 179 Cal. 738, 742–743, 178 P. 860; *Gardiner v. McDonogh* (1905) 147 Cal. 313, 318–321, 81 P. 964; *Harrison v. McCormick* (1891) 89 Cal. 327, 330, 26 P. 830), and that the question for the court is whether it "appears to be a complete . . . agreement . . . ." (*See Ferguson v. Koch* (1928) 204 Cal. 342, 346, 268 P. 342, 344, 58 A.L.R. 1176; *Harrison v. McCormick, supra,* 89 Cal. 327, 330, 26 P. 830.) Neither of these strict formulations of the rule, however, has been consistently applied. The requirement that the writing must appear incomplete on its face has been repudiated in many cases where parol evidence was admitted "to prove the existence of a separate oral agreement as to any matter on which the document is silent and which is not inconsistent with its terms" — even though the instrument appeared to state a complete agreement. Even under the rule that the writing alone is to be consulted, it was found necessary to examine the alleged collateral agreement before concluding that proof of it was precluded by the writing alone. (*See* 3 CORBIN, CONTRACTS (1960) § 582, pp. 444–446.) It is therefore evident that "The conception of a writing as wholly and intrinsically self-determinative of the parties' intent to make it a sole memorial of one or seven or twenty-seven subjects of negotiation is an impossible one." (9 WIGMORE, EVIDENCE (3d ed. 1940) § 2431, p. 103.) For example, a promissory note given by a debtor to his creditor may integrate all their present contractual rights and obligations, or it may be only a minor part of an underlying executory contract that would never be discovered by examining the face of the note.

In formulating the rule governing parol evidence, several policies must be accommodated. One policy is based on the assumption that written evidence is more accurate than human memory. (*Germain Fruit Co. v. J. K. Armsby Co.* (1908) 153 Cal. 585, 595, 96 P. 319.) This policy, however, can be adequately served by excluding parol evidence of agreements that directly contradict the writing. Another policy is based on the fear that fraud or unintentional invention by witnesses interested in the outcome of the litigation will mislead the finder of facts. (*Germain Fruit Co. v. J. K. Armsby Co., supra,* 153 Cal. 585, 596, 96 P. 319; *Mitchill v. Lath* (1928) 247 N.Y. 377, 388, 160 N.E. 646, 68 A.L.R. 239 [dissenting opinion by Lehman, J.]; see 9 WIGMORE, EVIDENCE (3d ed. 1940) § 2431, p. 102; Murray, *The Parol Evidence Rule: A Clarification* (1966) 4 DUQUESNE L. REV. 337, 338–339.) McCormick has suggested that the party urging the spoken as against the written word is most often the economic underdog, threatened by severe hardship if the writing is enforced. In his view the parol evidence rule arose to allow the court to control the tendency of the jury to find through sympathy and without a dispassionate assessment of the probability of fraud or faulty memory that the parties made an oral agreement collateral to the written contract, or that preliminary tentative agreements were not abandoned when omitted from the writing. (*See* McCORMICK, EVIDENCE (1954) § 210.) He recognizes, however, that if this theory were adopted in disregard of all other considerations, it would lead to the exclusion of testimony concerning oral agreements whenever there is a writing and thereby often defeat the true intent of the parties. (*See* McCORMICK, *op. cit. supra,* § 216, p. 441.)

Evidence of oral collateral agreements should be excluded only when the fact finder is likely to be misled. The rule must therefore be based on the credibility of the evidence. One such standard, adopted by section 240(1)(b) of the Restatement of Contracts, permits proof of a collateral agreement if it "is such an agreement as might *naturally* be made as a separate agreement by parties situated as were the parties to the written contract." (Italics added.) The draftsmen of the Uniform Commercial Code would exclude the evidence in still fewer instances: "If the additional terms are such that, if agreed upon, they would *certainly* have been included in the document in the view of the court, then evidence of their alleged making must be kept from the trier of fact." (Com. 3, § 2-202, italics added.)[47]

The option clause in the deed in the present case does not explicitly provide that it contains the complete agreement, and the deed is silent on the question of assignability. Moreover, the difficulty of accommodating the formalized structure of a deed to the insertion of collateral agreements makes it less likely that all the terms of such an agreement were included.[48] (*See* 3 Corbin, Contracts (1960) § 587; 4 Williston, Contracts (3d ed. 1961) § 645; 70 A.L.R. 752, 759 (1931); 68 A.L.R. 245 (1930).) The statement of the reservation of the option might well have been placed in the recorded deed solely to preserve the grantors' rights against any possible future purchasers and this function could well be served without any mention of the parties' agreement that the option was personal. There is nothing in the record to indicate that the parties to this family transaction, through experience in land transactions or otherwise, had any warning of the disadvantages of failing to put the whole agreement in the deed. This case is one, therefore, in which it can be said that a collateral agreement such as that alleged "might naturally be made as a separate agreement." *A fortiori*, the case is not one in which the parties "would certainly" have included the collateral agreement in the deed.

It is contended, however, that an option agreement is ordinarily presumed to be assignable if it contains no provisions forbidding its transfer or indicating that its performance involves elements personal to the parties. (*Mott v. Cline* (1927) 200 Cal. 434, 450, 253 P. 718; *Altman v. Blewett* (1928) 93 Cal. App. 516, 525, 269 P. 751.) The fact that there is a written memorandum, however, does not necessarily preclude parol evidence rebutting a term that the law would otherwise presume. In *American Industrial Sales Corp. v. Airscope, Inc., supra,* 44 Cal. 2d 393, 397–398, 282 P.2d 504, we held it proper to admit parol evidence of a contemporaneous collateral agreement as to the place of payment of a note, even though it

---

[47] [1] Corbin suggests that, even in situations where the court concludes that it would not have been natural for the parties to make the alleged collateral oral agreement, parol evidence of such an agreement should nevertheless be permitted if the court is convinced that the unnatural actually happened in the case being adjudicated. (3 Corbin, Contracts, § 485, pp. 478, 480; cf. Murray, *The Parol Evidence Rule: A Clarification* (1966) 4 Duquesne L. Rev. 337, 341–342.) This suggestion may be based on a belief that judges are not likely to be misled by their sympathies. If the court believes that the parties intended a collateral agreement to be effective, there is no reason to keep the evidence from the jury.

[48] [2] *See* Goble v. Dotson (1962) 203 Cal. App. 2d 272, 21 Cal. Rptr. 769, where the deed given by a real estate developer to the plaintiffs contained a condition that grantees would not build a pier or boathouse. Despite this reference in the deed to the subject of berthing for boats, the court allowed plaintiffs to prove by parol evidence that the condition was agreed to in return for the developer's oral promise that plaintiffs were to have the use of two boat spaces nearby.

contradicted the presumption that a note, silent as to the place of payment, is payable where the creditor resides. (For other examples of this approach, see *Richter v. Union Land etc. Co.* (1900) 129 Cal. 367, 375, 62 P. 39 [presumption of time of delivery rebutted by parol evidence]; *Wolters v. King* (1897) 119 Cal. 172, 175–176, 51 P. 35 [presumption of time of payment rebutted by parol evidence]; *Mangini v. Wolfschmidt, Ltd., supra,* 165 Cal. App. 2d 192, 198–201, 331 P.2d 728 [presumption of duration of an agency contract rebutted by parol evidence]; *Zinn v. Ex-Cell-O Corp.* (1957) 148 Cal. App. 2d 56, 73–74, 306 P.2d 1017; *see also* Rest., Contracts, § 240, com. c.)[49]

Of course a statute may preclude parol evidence to rebut a statutory presumption. (*E.g., Neff v. Ernst* (1957) 48 Cal. 2d 628, 635, 311 P.2d 849 [commenting on Civ. Code, § 1112]; *Kilfoy v. Fritz* (1954) 125 Cal. App. 2d 291, 293–294, 270 P.2d 579 [applying Deering's Gen. Laws 1937, Act 652, § 15a]; *see also* Com. Code, § 9-318, subd. (4).) Here, however, there is no such statute. In the absence of a controlling statute the parties may provide that a contract right or duty is nontransferable. Moreover, even when there is no explicit agreement — written *or* oral — that contractual duties shall be personal, courts will effectuate a presumed intent to that effect if the circumstances indicate that performance by substituted person would be different from that contracted for . . . . REST., CONTRACTS (Tent. Draft No. 3, 1967) § 150(2) In the present case defendants offered evidence that the parties agreed that the option was not assignable in order to keep the property in the Masterson family. The trial court erred in excluding that evidence. *The judgment is reversed.*

NOTE

The principal case is one of a trilogy of Justice Traynor opinions issued in 1968 along with *Pacific Gas & Elec. Co. v. G. W. Thomas Drayage & Rigging Co.*, 442 P. 2d 641 (1968) and *Delta Dynamics v. Arioto*, 446 P. 2d 785 (1968) which suggested critically important differences between the parol evidence rule and interpretation which is addressed in the next section of this volume.

COMMENT: MERGER CLAUSES

If there is a clause in the writing which reads as follows: "This agreement contains the whole agreement between the Seller and Buyer and there are no other terms, obligations, covenants, representations, statements or conditions, oral or otherwise, of any kind whatsoever,"[50] such a clause is called a "merger" or "integration" clause. It may also be referred to as a "zipper" clause. The question is whether such a clause should have conclusive effect as to the parties' intention with respect to the finality and completeness of their writing. Professors Williston

---

[49] [3] Counsel for plaintiffs direct our attention to numerous cases that they contend establish that parol evidence may never be used to show a collateral agreement contrary to a term that the law presumes in the absence of an agreement. In each of these cases, however, the decision turned upon the court's belief that the writing was a complete integration and was no more than an application of the rule that parol evidence cannot be used to vary the terms of a completely integrated agreement . . . .

[50] This clause was taken from Betz Labs. v. Hines, 647 F.2d 402, 403 (3d Cir. 1981).

and Corbin suggest that it should have such effect (4 WILLISTON ON CONTRACTS § 633, 3 CORBIN ON CONTRACTS § 578), and RESTATEMENT (SECOND) OF CONTRACTS § 216, comment e, suggests that such a clause "is likely to conclude the issue whether the agreement is completely integrated." Some of the surrounding RESTATEMENT (SECOND) OF CONTRACTS language, however, may be read to distinguish printed versus negotiated merger clauses. Absent evidence that the parties have consciously considered and assented to a printed merger clause, there is authority for refusing to accord such a clause conclusive effect. *See, e.g., Montgomery Props. Corp. v. Economy Forms Corp.*, 305 N.W.2d 470 (Iowa 1981); *Zinn v. Walker*, 87 N.C. App. 325, 361 S.E.2d 314 (1987). *See* MURRAY ON CONTRACTS at § 85C.2.

[3]   The UCC Parol Evidence Rule — Trade Usage, Prior Dealings

RALPH'S DISTRIBUTING CO. v. AMF, INC.
United States Court of Appeals, Eighth Circuit
667 F.2d 670 (1981)

HEANEY, J.

Ralph's Distributing Company appeals from the decision of the district court granting AMF's motion for summary judgment against Ralph's claim of breach of contract. We reverse because sufficient issues of material fact have been raised to preclude summary judgment.

Ralph's entered into a franchise agreement with AMF in May, 1968, to become a wholesale distributor of Ski-Daddlers. The parties executed an identical franchise agreement in June, 1969. The franchise agreements were accompanied by letters designating Ralph's sales territory for the upcoming snowmobile season. In May, 1970, the franchise agreements were incorporated by reference in a letter from AMF extending the contract. The letter again included a designation of Ralph's sales territory. No further writings were executed, but the parties continued to operate in accordance with the provisions of the 1968 and 1969 franchise agreements through the 1971–1972 snowmobile season.

As a wholesale distributor, Ralph's bought Ski-Daddlers directly from AMF and then resold them to dealers in its designated territory for resale to the public. The Ski-Daddler program was unsuccessful and, during the 1971–1972 season, AMF decided to discontinue production of that line and to consolidate all future snowmobile manufacturing and marketing activities in Harley-Davidson. As a result of this decision, AMF began to sell its remaining inventory of Ski-Daddlers directly to Harley-Davidson dealers, bypassing Ralph's and other Ski-Daddler wholesale distributors.

Ralph's brought suit against AMF, alleging that AMF's direct sales to Harley-Davidson dealers in Ralph's territory violated its contractual right to be the exclusive distributor of Ski-Daddler snowmobiles in its designated territory. Ralph's advanced three alternative theories in support of its claim: (1) that by including the designated sales territory in the franchise agreements, the parties intended to make Ralph's the sole distributor in that territory; (2) that even if the parties did not agree to include an exclusivity term in the initial agreement, they did so in subsequent oral modifications of the 1968–1969 franchise agreements.

Summary judgment should be granted only if the pleadings, stipulations, affidavits and admissions show that there is no genuine issue of material fact and the moving party is entitled to judgment as a matter of law. Applying these standards to Ralph's breach of contract claim, we cannot agree that AMF has demonstrated that there is no genuine issue as to any material fact concerning Ralph's first two theories of recovery.

Regarding Ralph's first theory, the district court held that the designation of territory in the franchise agreements was the final and complete term with respect to territorial requirements, and that parol evidence was not admissible to establish that the parties also intended to make Ralph's the sole distributor in its territory under the agreements. Ralph's contends that its evidence of course of performance and usage of trade[51] demonstrates that the parties intended to include an exclusivity term in the franchise agreements. Under the Uniform Commercial Code (U.C.C.), as adopted in Iowa, parol evidence is inadmissible to contradict the terms of a writing that is intended to be a "final expression" of the provisions in question.[52] Iowa Code § 554.2202. The test for admissibility of course of performance and usage of trade evidence is not whether the contractual terms on their face appear to be

---

[51] [5] Iowa Code § 554.2208 provides in part:

(1) Where the contract for sale involves repeated occasions for performance by either party with knowledge of the nature of the performance and opportunity for objection to it by the other, any course of performance accepted or acquiesced in without objection shall be relevant to determine the meaning of the agreement.

Iowa Code § 554.1205 provides in part:

(2) A usage of trade is any practice or method of dealing having such regularity of observance in a place, vocation or trade as to justify an expectation that it will be observed with respect to the transaction in question. The existence and scope of such a usage are to be proved as facts. If it is established that such usage is embodied in a written trade code or similar writing the interpretation of the writing is for the court.

(3) A course of dealing between parties and any usage of trade in the vocation or trade in which they are engaged or of which they are or should be aware give particular meaning to and supplement or qualify terms of an agreement.

(4) The express terms of an agreement and an applicable course of dealing or usage of trade shall be construed wherever reasonable as consistent with each other; but when such construction is unreasonable express terms control both course of dealing and usage of trade and course of dealing controls usage of trade.

[52] [7] Iowa Code § 554.2202 provides:

Terms with respect to which the confirmatory memoranda of the parties agree or which are otherwise set forth in a writing intended by the parties as a final expression of their agreement with respect to such terms as are included therein may not be contradicted by evidence of any prior agreement or of a contemporaneous oral agreement but may be explained or supplemented.

(a) by course of dealing or usage of trade (Section 554.1205) or by course of performance (Section 554.2208); and

(b) by evidence of consistent additional terms unless the court finds the writing to have been intended also as a complete and exclusive statement of the terms of the agreement.

complete in every detail. White & Summers, Uniform Commercial Code, § 2-10 at 86 (2d ed. 1980). Even a complete writing may be "explain[ed] or supplement[ed]" by evidence of course of performance and usage of trade. Iowa Code § 554.2202; White & Summers, Uniform Commercial Code, *supra*, § 2-10 at 86.

Here, the contracts designating Ralph's sales area are silent as to whether or not it was to be the exclusive Ski-Daddler distributor in that territory. Therefore, Ralph's course of performance and usage of trade evidence does not contradict any explicit contractual term and was admissible to explain and supplement the meaning of the territorial designations in the franchise agreements. Iowa Code §§ 554.1205,.2202 &.2208.

The trial court further found that even if Ralph's proffered parol evidence is considered, no question of fact is raised as to the parties' intention to include an exclusivity term. This finding is clearly erroneous. Fed. R. Civ. P. 52(a).

The following course of performance and usage of trade evidence supports Ralph's claim that, pursuant to the franchise agreement, it was to be the sole distributor of Ski-Daddlers in its designated territory.[53] Ralph's alleged in its affidavit that it expended substantial funds on racing and other promotional activities in the expectation that neither AMF nor other distributors would sell Ski-Daddler snowmobiles in its exclusive territory. Three AMF employees or former employees testified in depositions that it was their understanding that once AMF designated a distributor for a territory, the company would not assign other distributors to the same area, and that the designated distributor was entitled to believe that AMF would not assign other distributors to his sales market. Ralph's also stated that many aspects of its distributorship were not covered in the franchise agreements including, for example, racing and other promotional activities, as well as the exclusivity requirement. Harold Whitten, a former division vice president at AMF, conceded in his deposition that AMF "encouraged" and "expected" distributors to engage in promotional activities such as racing despite the absence of such a requirement in the franchise agreements.

Furthermore, after AMF entered into the arrangement with Harley-Davidson to market Ski-Daddler snowmobiles, AMF began to give rebates to Ski-Daddler distributors for each Ski-Daddler sold by Harley-Davidson dealers in the designated territories of those distributors. Ralph's argues this rebate plan was to compensate distributors for invasion of their exclusive territories.

Finally, immediately after AMF entered into the agreement with Harley-Davidson, Ralph's protested the alleged breach of contract. It stated in its affidavit that other distributors raised similar complaints.

Taking these statements in the light most favorable to Ralph's and giving it the benefit of all reasonable inferences, we conclude that there is a genuine issue as to

---

[53] [8] This testimony has aspects of both course of performance and usage of trade. Course of performance evidence is admissible to establish the meaning the parties attached to contractual terms, as evidenced by their actions in carrying out the contract. Iowa Code § 554.2208 and Uniform Commercial Code Comment 1; White & Summers, Uniform Commercial Code, § 2-10 at 87 (2d ed. 1980). Usage of trade evidence is admissible to furnish background and give meaning to the contractual terms used by the parties as evidenced by past use of the language in the trade generally.

whether the parties intended to include an exclusivity term.

Ralph's second theory for recovery is that if the contracts, when executed, did not make it the sole distributor, the franchise agreements were subsequently modified to include an exclusivity term. The parol evidence rule, of course, does not apply to evidence of subsequent modifications of a contract. Ralph's relies on the same evidence to establish subsequent modification as it does to show an agreement by course of performance and usage of trade. Taking this evidence in the light most favorable to Ralph's, we conclude that the evidence also creates a genuine issue as to whether the franchise agreements were modified subsequent to execution to include an exclusivity term.

For these reasons, the district court erred in granting summary judgment against Ralph's. Accordingly, we reverse and remand for proceedings consistent with this opinion.

NOTE

RGJ Associates v. Stainsafe, Inc., 338 F. Supp. 2d 215, 243 (D. Mass. 2004). As indicated in Section 2-202(a), "A sale contract need not be ambiguous for the admission of evidence of course of dealing, course of performance, or usage of trade." *Campbell Farms v. Wald*, 1998 ND 85, 578 N.W.2d 96, 100 (1998) (interpreting identical UCC provision adopted in North Dakota); *C-Thru Container Corporation v. Midland Manufacturing Co.*, 533 N.W.2d 542, 544 (Iowa 1995) (discussing identical UCC section adopted in Iowa and holding "that even a complete contract may be explained or supplemented by parol evidence of trade usages"). A comment to Section 2-202 explains that it "definitely rejects . . . the requirement that a condition precedent to the admissibility of the type of evidence specified in paragraph (a) is an original determination by the court that the language used is ambiguous." UCC § 2-202, cmt. 1.

QUESTION

Is the principal case distinguishable from the classic case of *Gianni v. Russell* as described in the notes after the *Traudt* case, above?

COLUMBIA NITROGEN CORP. v. ROYSTER CO.
United States Court of Appeals, Fourth Circuit
451 F.2d 3 (1971)

BUTZNER, C. J.

Columbia Nitrogen Corp. appeals a judgment in the amount of $750,000 in favor of F. S. Royster Guano Co. for breach of a contract for the sale of phosphate to Columbia by Royster. Columbia defended on the grounds that the contract, construed in light of the usage of the trade and course of dealing, imposed no duty to accept at the quoted prices the minimum quantities stated in the contract. It also asserted an antitrust defense and counterclaim based on Royster's alleged reciprocal trade practices. The district court excluded the evidence about course of dealing and usage of the trade. It submitted the antitrust issues based on coercive reciprocity to the jury, but refused to submit the alternative theory of non-coercive reciprocity. The jury found for Royster on both the contract claim and the antitrust counterclaim. We hold that Columbia's proffered evidence was improperly excluded and Columbia is entitled to a new trial on the contractual issues. With respect to the antitrust issues, we affirm.

Royster manufactures and markets mixed fertilizers, the principal components of which are nitrogen, phosphate and potash. Columbia is primarily a producer of nitrogen, although it manufactures some mixed fertilizer. For several years Royster had been a major purchaser of Columbia's products, but Columbia had never been a significant customer of Royster. In the fall of 1966, Royster constructed a facility which enabled it to produce more phosphate than it needed in its own operations. After extensive negotiations, the companies executed a contract for Royster's sale of a minimum of 31,000 tons of phosphate each year for three years to Columbia, with an option to extend the term. The contract stated the price per ton, subject to an escalation clause dependent on production costs.

Phosphate prices soon plunged precipitously. Unable to resell the phosphate at a competitive price, Columbia ordered only part of the scheduled tonnage. At Columbia's request, Royster lowered its price for diammonium phosphate on shipments for three months in 1967, but specified that subsequent shipments would be at the original contract price. Even with this concession, Royster's price was still substantially above the market. As a result, Columbia ordered less than a tenth of the phosphate Royster was to ship in the first contract year. When pressed by Royster, Columbia offered to take the phosphate at the current market price and resell it without brokerage fee. Royster, however, insisted on the contract price. When Columbia refused delivery, Royster sold the unaccepted phosphate for Columbia's account at a price substantially below the contract price.

Columbia assigns error to the pretrial ruling of the district court excluding all evidence on usage of the trade and course of dealing between the parties. It offered the testimony of witnesses with long experience in the trade that because of uncertain crop and weather conditions, farming practices, and government agricultural programs, express price and quantity terms in contracts for materials in the mixed fertilizer industry are mere projections to be adjusted according to market forces.

Columbia also offered proof of its business dealings with Royster over the six-year period preceding the phosphate contract. Since Columbia had not been a significant purchaser of Royster's products, these dealings were almost exclusively nitrogen sales to Royster or exchanges of stock carried in inventory. The pattern which emerges, Columbia claimed, is one of repeated and substantial deviation from the stated amount or price, including four instances where Royster took none of the goods for which it had contracted. Columbia offered proof that the total variance amounted to more than $500,000 in reduced sales. This experience, a Columbia officer offered to testify, formed the basis of an understanding on which he depended in conducting negotiations with Royster.

The district court held that the evidence should be excluded. It ruled that "custom and usage or course of dealing are not admissible to contradict the express, plain, unambiguous language of a valid written contract, which by virtue of its detail negates the proposition that the contract is open to variances in its terms . . . ."

A number of Virginia cases have held that extrinsic evidence may not be received to explain or supplement a written contract unless the court finds the writing is ambiguous. *E.g., Mathieson Alkali Works v. Virginia Banner Coal Corp.*, 147 Va. 125, 136 S.E. 673 (1927). This rule, however, has been changed by the Uniform Commercial Code which Virginia has adopted. The Code expressly states that it "shall be liberally construed and applied to promote its underlying purposes and policies," which include "the continued expansion of commercial practices through custom, usage and agreement of the parties . . . ." Va. Code Ann. § 8.1-102 (1965). The importance of usage of trade and course of dealing between the parties is shown by § 8.2-202,[54] which authorizes their use to explain or supplement a contract. The official comment states this section rejects the old rule that evidence of course of dealing or usage of trade can be introduced only when the contract is ambiguous.[55]

And the Virginia commentators, noting that "[t]his section reflects a more liberal approach to the introduction of parol evidence . . . than has been followed in Virginia," express the opinion that *Mathieson, supra*, and similar Virginia cases no longer should be followed. Va. Code Ann. § 8.2-202, Va. Comment. *See also Portsmouth Gas Co. v. Shebar*, 209 Va. 250, 253 n.1, 163 S.E.2d 205, 208 n.1 (1968) (dictum). We hold, therefore, that a finding of ambiguity is not necessary for the admission of extrinsic evidence about the usage of the trade and the parties' course of dealing.

We turn next to Royster's claim that Columbia's evidence was properly excluded because it was inconsistent with the express terms of their agreement. There can be no doubt that the Uniform Commercial Code restates the well established rule that evidence of usage of trade and course of dealing should be excluded whenever it cannot be reasonably construed as consistent with the terms of the contract. Division of *Triple T Service, Inc. v. Mobil Oil Corp.*, 60 Misc. 2d 720, 304 N.Y.S.2d 191, 203 (1969), *aff'd mem.*, 311 N.Y.S.2d 961 (1970). Royster argues that the evidence should be excluded as inconsistent because the contract contains detailed provisions regarding the base price, escalation, minimum tonnage, and delivery

---

[54] [4] Va. Code Ann. § 8.2-202 provides:

Terms with respect to which the confirmatory memoranda of the parties agree or which are otherwise set forth in a writing intended by the parties as a final expression of their agreement with respect to such terms as are included therein may not be contradicted by evidence of any prior agreement or of a contemporaneous oral agreement but may be explained or supplemented (a) by course of dealing or usage of trade (§ 8.1-205) or by course of performance (§ 8.2-208); and (b) by evidence of consistent additional terms unless the court find[s] the writing to have been intended also as a complete and exclusive statement of the terms of the agreement.

[55] [5] Va. Code Ann. § 8.2-202, Comment 1 states:

This section definitely rejects:

* * *

(c) The requirement that a condition precedent to the admissibility of the type of evidence specified in paragraph (a) is an original determination by the court that the language used is ambiguous.

schedules. The argument is based on the premise that because a contract appears on its face to be complete, evidence of course of dealing and usage of trade should be excluded. We believe, however, that neither the language nor the policy of the Code supports such a broad exclusionary rule. Section 8.2-202 expressly allows evidence of course of dealing or usage of trade to explain or supplement terms intended by the parties as a final expression of their agreement. When this section is read in light of Va. Code Ann. § 8.1-205(4),[56] it is clear that the test of admissibility is not whether the contract appears on its face to be complete in every detail, but whether the proffered evidence of course of dealing and trade usage reasonably can be construed as consistent with the express terms of the agreement.

The proffered testimony sought to establish that because of changing weather conditions, farming practices, and government agricultural programs, dealers adjusted prices, quantities, and delivery schedules to reflect declining market conditions. For the following reasons it is reasonable to construe this evidence as consistent with the express terms of the contract:

> The contract does not expressly state that course of dealing and usage of trade cannot be used to explain or supplement the written contract.

The contract is silent about adjusting prices and quantities to reflect a declining market. It neither permits nor prohibits adjustment, and this neutrality provides a fitting occasion for recourse to usage of trade and prior dealing to supplement the contract and explain its terms.

Minimum tonnages and additional quantities are expressed in terms of "Products Supplied Under Contract." Significantly, they are not expressed as just "Products" or as "Products Purchased Under Contract." The description used by the parties is consistent with the proffered testimony.

Finally, the default clause of the contract refers only to the failure of the buyer to pay for delivered phosphate. During the contract negotiations, Columbia rejected a Royster proposal for liquidated damages of $10 for each ton Columbia declined to accept. On the other hand, Royster rejected a Columbia proposal for a clause that tied the price to the market by obligating Royster to conform its price to offers Columbia received from other phosphate producers. The parties, having rejected both proposals, failed to state any consequences of Columbia's refusal to take delivery — the kind of default Royster alleges in this case. Royster insists that we span this hiatus by applying the general law of contracts permitting recovery of damages upon the buyer's refusal to take delivery according to the written provisions of the contract. This solution is not what the Uniform Commercial Code prescribes. Before allowing damages, a court must first determine whether the buyer has in fact defaulted. It must do this by supplementing and explaining the agreement with evidence of trade usage and course of dealing that is consistent with the contract's express terms. Va. Code Ann. §§ 8.1-205(4), 8.2-202. Faithful adher-

---

[56] [7] Va. Code Ann. § 8.1-205(4) states:

> The express terms of an agreement and an applicable course of dealing or usage of trade shall be construed wherever reasonable as consistent with each other; but when such construction is unreasonable express terms control both course of dealing and usage of trade and course of dealing controls usage of trade.

ence to this mandate reflects the reality of the marketplace and avoids the overly legalistic interpretations which the Code seeks to abolish.

Royster also contends that Columbia's proffered testimony was properly rejected because it dealt with mutual willingness of buyer and seller to adjust contract terms to the market. Columbia, Royster protests, seeks unilateral adjustment. This argument misses the point. What Columbia seeks to show is a practice of mutual adjustments so prevalent in the industry and in prior dealings between the parties that it formed a part of the agreement governing this transaction. It is not insisting on a unilateral right to modify the contract.

Nor can we accept Royster's contention that the testimony should be excluded under the contract clause:

> No verbal understanding will be recognized by either party hereto; this contract expresses all the terms and conditions of the agreement, shall be signed in duplicate, and shall not become operative until approved in writing by the Seller.

Course of dealing and trade usage are not synonymous with verbal understandings, terms and conditions. Section 8.2-202 draws a distinction between supplementing a written contract by consistent additional terms and supplementing it by course of dealing or usage of trade. Evidence of additional terms must be excluded when "the court finds the writing to have been intended also as a complete and exclusive statement of the terms of the agreement." Significantly, no similar limitation is placed on the introduction of evidence of course of dealing or usage of trade. Indeed the official comment notes that course of dealing and usage of trade, unless carefully negated, are admissible to supplement the terms of any writing, and that contracts are to be read on the assumption that these elements were taken for granted when the document was phrased.[57] Since the Code assigns course of dealing and trade usage unique and important roles, they should not be conclusively rejected by reading them into stereotyped language that makes no specific reference to them. *Cf. Provident Tradesmens Bank & Trust Co. v. Pemberton*, 196 Pa. Super. 180, 173 A.2d 780 (1961). Indeed, the Code's official commentators urge that overly simplistic and overly legalistic interpretation of a contract should be shunned.[58]

---

[57] [10] Va. Code Ann. § 8.2-202, Comment 2 states:

> Paragraph (a) [of § 8.202] makes admissible evidence of course of dealing, usage of trade and course of performance to explain or supplement the terms of any writing stating the agreement of the parties in order that the true understanding of the parties as to the agreement may be reached. Such writings are to be read on the assumption that the course of prior dealings between the parties and the usages of trade were taken for granted when the document was phrased. Unless carefully negated they have become an element of the meaning of the words used. Similarly, the course of actual performance by the parties is considered the best indication of what they intended the writing to mean.

See also Levie, *Trade Usage and Custom Under the Common Law and the Uniform Commercial Code*, 40 N.Y.U. L. Rev. 1101, 1111 (1965).

[58] [11] Referring to the general provisions about course of dealing and trade usage, Va. Code Ann. § 8.1-205, Comment 1 states:

> This Act rejects both the "lay dictionary" and the "conveyancer's" reading of a commercial

We conclude, therefore, that Columbia's evidence about course of dealing and usage of trade should have been admitted. Its exclusion requires that the judgment against Columbia must be set aside and the case retried.

The judgment for Royster on the contract is vacated, and the case is remanded for further proceedings consistent with this opinion. Each party shall bear its own costs.

COMMENT

Inconsistencies Between and Among Express Terms and Usage, Course of Dealing and Course of Performance — Negation of Implied Terms. The Uniform Commercial Code deals with inconsistencies between usage of trade, course of dealing and course of performance, as well as inconsistencies between any or all of these sources and express terms. The hierarchy established by the UCC is as follows: Course of dealing prevails over usage of trade and course of performance prevails over both. This is a common-sense guide which may be viewed as a species of the particular controlling the general and the more recent manifestation of intention controlling earlier manifestations. Course of dealing should prevail over trade usage because it is a specific manifestation of intention between the parties as contrasted with a general manifestation of intention which affects all parties in the trade. Course of performance is the latest manifestation of what the parties themselves believed their agreement to mean. As to possible conflicts between these three sources and the express terms of the agreement, the UCC first directs courts to make every effort to reconcile any inconsistencies; when that becomes impossible, the express terms will prevail. As a matter of *interpretation* of the contract, express terms must be viewed as the best evidence of the intention of the parties, with the other three sources following in the hierarchy commanded by the UCC. These directives may be viewed as specific applications of the underlying philosophy of article 2 of the UCC that requires an identification of the bargain-in-fact of the parties and expressly requires the inclusion of terms implied from trade usage, course of dealing and course of performance.

Though § 2-208(2) indicates that express terms shall control the other sources, § 2-208(3) allows course of performance evidence to operate as a waiver or modification of any term inconsistent with such course of performance. While § 2-208(3) does not characterize "any term" as "any express term," it is obvious that such is the meaning since course of performance will prevail over inconsistent trade usage or course of dealing in any event. Therefore, while § 2-208(2) presents a hierarchy of express terms prevailing over course of performance, § 2-208(3) may be viewed as contradicting that hierarchical directive. However, that would be a superficial conclusion since § 2-208(2) deals with interpretation or construction of inconsistent terms while § 2-208(3) will permit a showing that the parties performed their contract in such a fashion as to evidence a modification of the

---

agreement. Instead the meaning of the agreement of the parties is to be determined by the language used by them and by their action, read and interpreted in the light of commercial practices and other surrounding circumstances. The measure and background for interpretation are set by the commercial context, which may explain and supplement even the language of a formal or final writing.

express terms of their agreement. Thus, course of performance as a modification is not an interpretation device. The express terms of the agreement still control the question of meaning. However, subsequent conduct by the parties may evidence their intention to modify the contract. Any such modification would have to meet the UCC requirements for modifications under § 2-209 which is discussed elsewhere. Courts have permitted such modifications of the express terms of a contract through evidence of course of performance.

It is important to emphasize the automatic inclusion of trade usage, course of dealing and course of performance "unless carefully negated." The express terms of the contract will be "read on the assumption that the course of prior dealings between the parties and the usages of trade were taken for granted when the document was phrased." As to course of performance, however, while the parties are the best judges of the meaning their written manifestation of agreement evidences and, therefore, their course of performance should be preferred over usage and course of dealing as an aid to interpretation, a term in the contract precluding *modification* through course of performance should not be enforced except, perhaps, as an anti-waiver device since the parties to a contract may always decide to modify their agreement and may do so through their post-formation conduct as well as their post-formation language.

[4] CISG and the Parol Evidence Rule

MCC-MARBLE CERAMIC CENTER, INC. v. CERAMICA NUOVA D'AGOSTINO, S.P.A.
United States Court of Appeals, Eleventh Circuit
144 F.3d 1384 (1998)

Birch, J.

[This dispute is over a contract for the sale of goods between a merchant buyer with its place of business in the United States and a merchant seller with its place of business in Italy. Both countries have adopted the United Nations Convention on Contracts for the International Sale of Goods, opened for signature in the United States on April 11, 1980, S. Treaty Doc. No. 9, 98th Cong., 1st Sess. 22 (1983), 19 I.L.M. 671, reprinted at, 15 U.S.C. app. 52 (1997) applies to this contract.]

The plaintiff-appellant, MCC-Marble Ceramic, Inc. ("MCC"), is a Florida corporation engaged in the retail sale of tiles, and the defendant-appellee, Ceramica Nuova d'Agostino S.p.A. ("D'Agostino") is an Italian corporation engaged in the manufacture of ceramic tiles. In October 1990, MCC's president, Juan Carlos Mozon, met representatives of D'Agostino at a trade fair in Bologna, Italy and negotiated an agreement to purchase ceramic tiles from D'Agostino based on samples he examined at the trade fair. The parties apparently arrived at an oral agreement on the crucial terms of price, quality, quantity, delivery and payment. The parties then recorded these terms on one of D'Agostino's standard, pre-printed order forms and Monzon signed the contract on MCC's behalf. According to MCC, the parties also entered into a requirements contract in February 1991, subject to which D'Agostino agreed to supply MCC with high grade ceramic tile at specific discounts as long as MCC purchased sufficient quantities of tile. MCC completed a number of additional order forms requesting tile deliveries pursuant to that agreement.

MCC brought suit against D'Agostino claiming a breach of the February 1991 requirements contract when D'Agostino failed to satisfy orders in April, May, and August of 1991. In addition to other defenses, D'Agostino responded that it was under no obligation to fill MCC's orders because MCC had defaulted on payment for previous shipments. In support of its position, D'Agostino relied on the pre-printed terms of the contracts that MCC had executed. The executed forms were printed in Italian and contained terms and conditions on both the front and reverse. According to an English translation of the October 1990 contract, the front of the order form contained the following language directly beneath Monzon's signature:

> The buyer hereby states that he is aware of the sales conditions stated on the reverse and that he expressly approves of them with special reference to those numbered 1-2-3-4-5-6-7-8.

Clause 6(b), printed on the back of the form states:

> Default or delay in payment within the time agreed upon gives D'Agostino the right to . . . suspend or cancel the contract itself and to cancel possible other pending contracts and the buyer does not have the right to indemnification or damages.

D'Agostino also brought a number of counterclaims against MCC, seeking damages for MCC's alleged nonpayment for deliveries of tile that D'Agostino had made between February 28, 1991 and July 4, 1991. MCC responded that the tile it had received was of a lower quality than contracted for, and that, pursuant to the CISG, MCC was entitled to reduce payment in proportion to the defects. D'Agostino, however, noted that clause 4 on the reverse of the contract states, in pertinent part:

> Possible complaints for defects of the merchandise must be made in writing by means of a certified letter within and not later than 10 days after receipt of the merchandise . . . .

Although there is evidence to support MCC's claims that it complained about the quality of the deliveries it received, MCC never submitted any written complaints.

MCC did not dispute these underlying facts before the district court, but argued that the parties never intended the terms and conditions printed on the reverse of the order form to apply to their agreements. As evidence for this assertion, MCC submitted Monzon's affidavit, which claims that MCC had no subjective intent to be bound by those terms and that D'Agostino was aware of this intent. MCC also filed affidavits from Silingardi and Copelli, D'Agostino's representatives at the trade fair, which support Monzon's claim that the parties subjectively intended not to be bound by the terms on the reverse of the order form. The magistrate judge held that the affidavits, even if true, did not raise an issue of material fact regarding the interpretation or applicability of the terms of the written contracts and the district court accepted his recommendation to award summary judgment in D'Agostino's favor. MCC then filed this timely appeal.

The parties to this case agree that the CISG governs their dispute because the United States, where MCC has its place of business, and Italy, where D'Agostino has its place of business, are both States Party to the Convention. *See* CISG, art. 1. Article 8 of the CISG governs the interpretation of international contracts for the sale of goods and forms the basis of MCC's appeal from the district court's grant of summary judgment in D'Agostino's favor.[59] MCC argues that the magistrate judge and the district court improperly ignored evidence that MCC submitted regarding the parties' subjective intent when they memorialized the terms of their agreement on D'Agostino's pre-printed form contract, and that the magistrate judge erred by applying the parol evidence rule in derogation of the CISG.

I. Subjective Intent Under the CISG

Contrary to what is familiar practice in United States courts, the CISG appears to permit a substantial inquiry into the parties' subjective intent, even if the parties did not engage in any objectively ascertainable means of registering this intent.[60] Article 8(1) of the CISG instructs courts to interpret the "statements . . . and other conduct of a party . . . according to his intent" as long as the other party "knew or could not have been unaware" of that intent. The plain language of the Convention, therefore, requires an inquiry into a party's subjective intent as long as the other party to the contract was aware of that intent.

In this case, MCC has submitted three affidavits that discuss the purported subjective intent of the parties to the initial agreement concluded between MCC

---

[59] [7] CISG, Article 8:

(1) For the purposes of this Convention statements made by and other conduct of a party are to be interpreted according to his intent where the other party knew or could not have been unaware what that intent was.

(2) If the preceding paragraph is not applicable, statements made by and conduct of a party are to be interpreted according to the understanding a reasonable person of the same kind as the other party would have had in the same circumstances.

(3) In determining the intent of a party or the understanding a reasonable person would have had, due consideration is to be given to all relevant circumstances of the case including the negotiations, any practices which the parties have established between themselves, usages and any subsequent conduct of the parties.

[60] [8] In the United States, the legislatures, courts, and the legal academy have voiced a preference for relying on objective manifestations of the parties' intentions. For example, Article Two of the Uniform Commercial Code, which most states have enacted in some form or another to govern contracts for the sale of goods, is replete with references to standards of commercial reasonableness. *See e.g.*, U.C.C. § 2-206 (referring to reasonable means of accepting an offer); *see also Lucy v. Zehmer*, 196 Va. 493, 503, 84 S.E.2d 516, 522 (1954) ("Whether the writing signed . . . was the result of a serious offer . . . and a serious acceptance . . . , or was a serious offer . . . and an acceptance in secret jest . . . , in either event it constituted a binding contract of sale between the parties."). Justice Holmes expressed the philosophy behind this focus on the objective in forceful terms: "The law has nothing to do with the actual state of the parties' minds. In contract, as elsewhere, it must go by externals, and judge parties by their conduct." Oliver W. Holmes, The Common Law 242 (Howe ed. 1963) *quoted in* John O. Honnold, Uniform Law for International Sales under the 1980 United Nations Convention § 107 at 164 (2d ed. 1991) (hereinafter Honnold, Uniform Law).

and D'Agostino in October 1990. All three affidavits discuss the preliminary negotiations and report that the parties arrived at an oral agreement for D'Agostino to supply quantities of a specific grade of ceramic tile to MCC at an agreed upon price. The affidavits state that the "oral agreement established the essential terms of quality, quantity, description of goods, delivery, price and payment." The affidavits also note that the parties memorialized the terms of their oral agreement on a standard D'Agostino order form, but all three affiants contend that the parties subjectively intended not to be bound by the terms on the reverse of that form despite a provision directly below the signature line that expressly and specifically incorporated those terms.

The terms on the reverse of the contract give D'Agostino the right to suspend or cancel all contracts in the event of a buyer's non-payment and require a buyer to make a written report of all defects within ten days. As the magistrate judge's report and recommendation makes clear, if these terms applied to the agreements between MCC and D'Agostino, summary judgment would be appropriate because MCC failed to make any written complaints about the quality of tile it received and D'Agostino has established MCC's non-payment of a number of invoices amounting to $108,389.40 and 102,053,846.00 Italian lira.

Article 8(1) of the CISG requires a court to consider this evidence of the parties' subjective intent. Contrary to the magistrate judge's report, which the district court endorsed and adopted, article 8(1) does not focus on interpreting the parties' statements alone. Although we agree with the magistrate judge's conclusion that no "interpretation" of the contract's terms could support MCC's position, article 8(1) also requires a court to consider subjective intent while interpreting the conduct of the parties. The CISG's language, therefore, requires courts to consider evidence of a party's subjective intent when signing a contract if the other party to the contract was aware of that intent at the time. This is precisely the type of evidence that MCC has provided through the Silingardi, Copelli, and Monzon affidavits, which discuss not only Monzon's intent as MCC's representative but also discuss the intent of D'Agostino's representatives and their knowledge that Monzon did not intend to agree to the terms on the reverse of the form contract. This acknowledgment that D'Agostino's representatives were aware of Monzon's subjective intent puts this case squarely within article 8(1) of the CISG, and therefore requires the court to consider MCC's evidence as it interprets the parties' conduct.[61]

II. Parol Evidence and the CISG

Given our determination that the magistrate judge and the district court should have considered MCC's affidavits regarding the parties' subjective intentions, we must address a question of first impression in this circuit: whether the parol evidence rule, which bars evidence of an earlier oral contract that contradicts or

---

[61] [11] Without this crucial acknowledgment, we would interpret the contract and the parties' actions according to article 8(2), which directs courts to rely on objective evidence of the parties' intent. On the facts of this case it seems readily apparent that MCC's affidavits provide no evidence that Monzon's actions would have made his alleged subjective intent not to be bound by the terms of the contract known to "the understanding that a reasonable person . . . would have had in the same circumstances." CISG, art 8(2).

varies the terms of a subsequent or contemporaneous written contract plays any role in cases involving the CISG.[62]

The CISG itself contains no express statement on the role of parol evidence. It is clear, however, that the drafters of the CISG were comfortable with the concept of permitting parties to rely on oral contracts because they eschewed any statutes of fraud provision and expressly provided for the enforcement of oral contracts. Compare CISG, art. 11 (a contract of sale need not be concluded or evidenced in writing) with U.C.C. § 2-201 (precluding the enforcement of oral contracts for the sale of goods involving more than $500). Moreover, article 8(3) of the CISG expressly directs courts to give "due consideration . . . to all relevant circumstances of the case including the negotiations . . ." to determine the intent of the parties. Given article 8(1)'s directive to use the intent of the parties to interpret their statements and conduct, article 8(3) is a clear instruction to admit and consider parol evidence regarding the negotiations to the extent they reveal the parties' subjective intent.

Despite the CISG's broad scope, surprisingly few cases have applied the Convention in the United States, see *Delchi Carrier SpA v. Rotorex Corp.*, 71 F.3d 1024, 1027–28 (2d Cir. 1995) (observing that "there is virtually no case law under the Convention"), and only two reported decisions touch upon the parol evidence rule, both in dicta. One court has concluded, much as we have above, that the parol evidence rule is not viable in CISG cases in light of article 8 of the Convention. In *Filanto*, a district court addressed the differences between the UCC and the CISG on the issues of offer and acceptance and the battle of the forms. *See* 789 F. Supp. at 1238. After engaging in a thorough analysis of how the CISG applied to the dispute before it, the district court tangentially observed that article 8(3) "essentially rejects . . . the parol evidence rule." *Id.* at 1238 n.7. Another court, however, appears to have arrived at a contrary conclusion. In *Beijing Metals & Minerals Import/Export Corp. v. American Bus. Ctr., Inc.*, 993 F.2d 1178 (5th Cir. 1993), a defendant sought to avoid summary judgment on a contract claim by relying on evidence of contemporaneously negotiated oral terms that the parties had not included in their written agreement. The plaintiff, a Chinese corporation, relied on Texas law in its complaint while the defendant, apparently a Texas corporation, asserted that the CISG governed the dispute. *Id.* at 1183 n.9. Without resolving the choice of law question, the Fifth Circuit cited *Filanto* for the proposition that there have been very few reported cases applying the CISG in the United States, and stated that the parol evidence rule would apply regardless of whether Texas law or the CISG governed the dispute. *Beijing Metals*, 993 F.2d at 1183 n.9. The opinion

---

[62] [12] The Uniform Commercial Code includes a version of the parol evidence rule applicable to contracts for the sale of goods in most states [in Section 2-202]:

> Terms with respect to which the confirmatory memoranda of the parties agree or which are otherwise set forth in a writing intended by the parties as a final expression of their agreement with respect to such terms as are included therein may not be contradicted by evidence of any prior agreement or of a contemporaneous oral agreement but may be explained or supplemented
>
> (a) by course of dealing or usage of trade . . . or by course of performance . . . ; and
>
> (b) by evidence of consistent additional terms unless the court finds the writing to have been intended also as a complete and exclusive statement of the terms of the agreement.

does not acknowledge *Filanto*'s more applicable dictum that the parol evidence rule does not apply to CISG cases nor does it conduct any analysis of the Convention to support its conclusion. In fact, the Fifth Circuit did not undertake to interpret the CISG in a manner that would arrive at a result consistent with the parol evidence rule but instead explained that it would apply the rule as developed at Texas common law. *See id.* at 1183 n.10. As persuasive authority for this court, the Beijing Metals opinion is not particularly persuasive on this point.

Our reading of article 8(3) as a rejection of the parol evidence rule, however, is in accordance with the great weight of academic commentary on the issue. As one scholar has explained:

> The language of Article 8(3) that "due consideration is to be given to all relevant circumstances of the case" seems adequate to override any domestic rule that would bar a tribunal from considering the relevance of other agreements . . . . Article 8(3) relieves tribunals from domestic rules that might bar them from "considering" any evidence between the parties that is relevant. This added flexibility for interpretation is consistent with a growing body of opinion that the "parol evidence rule" has been an embarrassment for the administration of modern transactions. HONNNOLD, UNIFORM LAW § 110 at 170–71.[63] Indeed, only one commentator has made any serious attempt to reconcile the parol evidence rule with the CISG. *See* David H. Moore, Note, *The Parol Evidence Rule and the United Nations Convention on Contracts for the International Sale of Goods: Justifying* Beijing Metals & Minerals Import/Export Corp. v. American Business Center, Inc., 1995 BYU L. REV. 1347. Moore argues that the parol evidence rule often permits the admission of evidence discussed in article 8(3), and that the rule could be an appropriate way to discern what consideration is "due" under article 8(3) to evidence of a parol nature. *Id.* at 1361–63. He also argues that the parol evidence rule, by limiting the incentive for perjury and pleading prior understandings in bad faith, promotes good faith and uniformity in the interpretation of contracts and therefore is in harmony with the principles of the CISG, as expressed in article 7.[64] The

---

63 [17] *See also* LOUIS F. DEL DUCA, ET AL., SALES UNDER THE UNIFORM COMMERCIAL CODE AND THE CONVENTION ON INTERNATIONAL SALE OF GOODS, 173–74 (1993); Henry D. Gabriel, *A Primer on the United Nations Convention on the International Sale of Goods: From the Perspective of the Uniform Commercial Code*, 7 IND. INT'L & COMP. L. REV. 279, 281 (1997) ("Subjective intent is given primary consideration . . . . [Article 8] allows open-ended reliance on parol evidence . . . ."); HERBERT BERSTEIN & JOSEPH LOOKOFSKY, UNDERSTANDING THE CISG IN EUROPE 29 (1997) ("The CISG has dispensed with the parol evidence rule which might otherwise operate to exclude extrinsic evidence under the law of certain Common Law countries."); Harry M. Fletchner, *Recent Developments: CISG*, 14 J.L. & COM. 153, 157 (1995) (criticizing the Beijing Metals opinion and noting that "commentators generally agree that article 8(3) rejects the approach to the parol evidence questions taken by U.S. domestic law.") (collecting authority); John E. Murray, Jr., *An Essay on the Formation of Contracts and Related Matters Under the United Nations Convention on Contracts for the International Sale of Goods*, 8 J.L. & COM. 11, 12 (1988) ("We are struck by a new world where there is . . . no parol evidence rule, among other differences."); Peter Winship, *Domesticating International Commercial Law: Revising U.C.C. Article 2 in Light of the United Nations Sales Convention*, 37 LOY. L. REV. 43, 57 (1991).

64 [18] Article 7 of the CISG provides in pertinent part:

(1) In the interpretation of this Convention, regard is to be had to its international character

answer to both these arguments, however, is the same: although jurisdictions in the United States have found the parol evidence rule helpful to promote good faith and uniformity in contract, as well as an appropriate answer to the question of how much consideration to give parol evidence, a wide number of other States Party to the CISG have rejected the rule in their domestic jurisdictions. One of the primary factors motivating the negotiation and adoption of the CISG was to provide parties to international contracts for the sale of goods with some degree of certainty as to the principles of law that would govern potential disputes and remove the previous doubt regarding which party's legal system might otherwise apply. *See* Letter of Transmittal from Ronald Reagan, President of the United States, to the United States Senate, reprinted at 15 U.S.C. app. 70, 71 (1997). Courts applying the CISG cannot, therefore, upset the parties' reliance on the Convention by substituting familiar principles of domestic law when the Convention requires a different result. We may only achieve the directives of good faith and uniformity in contracts under the CISG by interpreting and applying the plain language of article 8(3) as written and obeying its directive to consider this type of parol evidence.

This is not to say that parties to an international contract for the sale of goods cannot depend on written contracts or that parol evidence regarding subjective contractual intent need always prevent a party relying on a written agreement from securing summary judgment. To the contrary, most cases will not present a situation (as exists in this case) in which both parties to the contract acknowledge a subjective intent not to be bound by the terms of a pre-printed writing. In most cases, therefore, article 8(2) of the CISG will apply, and objective evidence will provide the basis for the court's decision. Consequently, a party to a contract governed by the CISG will not be able to avoid the terms of a contract and force a jury trial simply by submitting an affidavit which states that he or she did not have the subjective intent to be bound by the contract's terms. *Cf. Klopfenstein v. Pargeter*, 597 F.2d 150, 152 (9th Cir. 1979) (affirming summary judgment despite the appellant's submission of his own affidavit regarding his subjective intent: "Undisclosed, subjective intentions are immaterial in [a] commercial transaction, especially when contradicted by objective conduct. Thus, the affidavit has no legal effect even if its averments are accepted as wholly truthful."). Moreover, to the extent parties wish to avoid parol evidence problems they can do so by including a merger clause in their agreement that extinguishes any and all prior agreements and understandings not expressed in the writing.

Considering MCC's affidavits in this case, however, we conclude that the magistrate judge and the district court improperly granted summary judgment in favor of D'Agostino. Although the affidavits are, as D'Agostino observes, relatively conclusory and unsupported by facts that would objectively establish MCC's intent not to be bound by the conditions on the reverse of the form, article 8(1) requires a court to consider evidence of a party's subjective intent when the other party was

---

and to the need to promote uniformity in its application and the observance of good faith in international trade.

(2) Questions concerning matters governed by this Convention which are not expressly settled in it are to be settled in conformity with the general principles on which it is based . . . .

aware of it, and the Silingardi and Copelli affidavits provide that evidence. This is not to say that the affidavits are conclusive proof of what the parties intended. A reasonable finder of fact, for example, could disregard testimony that purportedly sophisticated international merchants signed a contract without intending to be bound as simply too incredible to believe and hold MCC to the conditions printed on the reverse of the contract. Nevertheless, the affidavits raise an issue of material fact regarding the parties' intent to incorporate the provisions on the reverse of the form contract. If the finder of fact determines that the parties did not intend to rely on those provisions, then the more general provisions of the CISG will govern the outcome of the dispute. Accordingly, we REVERSE the district court's grant of summary judgment and REMAND this case for further proceedings consistent with this opinion.

NOTE

Mitchell Aircraft Spares, Inc. v. European Aircraft Service AB, 23 F. Supp. 2d 915 (N.D. Ill. 1998), follows the analysis of CISG in the principal case. See also *Calzturificio Claudia s.n.c. v. Olivieri Footwear Ltd.*, 1998 U.S. Dist. LEXIS 4586 (S.D.N.Y. 1998), which holds that parol evidence is admissible under CISG.

[5] Reformation and the Parol Evidence Rule

DAVENPORT v. BECK
Oklahoma Court of Appeals
576 P.2d 1199 (1977)

BRIGHTMIRE, J.

Plaintiffs seek review of a decree reforming a note and adjudging that there is due thereon the sum of $7,318.68.

On September 21, 1964 plaintiffs contracted with defendants for the purchase of an Oklahoma City, Oklahoma lot for $13,500. Under the terms of the sale plaintiffs were to take the property under "a contract for deed," pay "$100 per month at 6% interest included," and build a house on the land. As soon as 10 payments were made defendants agreed to convey the property to plaintiffs "and take a first mortgage for the unpaid balance to be liquidated by continued payments as above."

Plaintiffs went into possession of the lot and performed as agreed. On October 15, 1964 they evidently received a deed to the property because they executed a promissory note and a securing mortgage in favor of defendants. The note reads:

> For value received we promise to pay Thirteen Thousand Five Hundred Dollars or order [*sic*] the sum of _____ Dollars at Oklahoma City in 135 installments payable as follows, to-wit: 100.00 (One Hundred) Dollars on the 1st day of November 1964, and One Hundred (100.00) Dollars on the 1st day of each succeeding Month thereafter, up to and including the 1st day of last month, [*sic*] and none Dollars on the_____, with interest from Nov. 1964 until paid at the rate of 6% per cent. [*sic*] per month,

included in each payment. The interest on each installment, and the interest on the unpaid balance of the principal sum are to be paid at the maturity of each installment. If default is made in the payment of any installment when due, then all the remaining installments shall become due and payable at once.

The accompanying mortgage recited that it was to secure a note "made to Rosa Beck, W. H. Beck, Winona Smith (now Holliday) and Clifford Holliday, Okla. City with 6% per cent. [*sic*] interest per annum from date, payable monthly and signed by first part parties."

After these instruments were executed plaintiffs began paying $100 a month to defendants. On January 5, 1976 Claud Davenport wrote defendants:

Attached please find our check # 135 in the amount of $100.00. In accordance with a note and mortgage dated October 15, 1964, this check represents the one hundred thirty fifth and final payment on the above mentioned note.

I would like to request that a release on the property covered by the above mentioned mortgage be signed by all parties and forwarded to me as soon as possible.

Defendants declined to execute a release and so plaintiffs filed this action two weeks later asking the court to quiet their title against the mortgagees and grant a penal judgment of $135 a day against defendants beginning January 16, 1976 until they released the mortgage as authorized by 46 O.S.1971 § 15.

In their answer defendants denied the note was fully paid and by cross-petition alleged that a clerical error was made in preparing the note in that it should have called for 226 payments instead of 135. Consequently they asked the court to reform the note accordingly and give them a judgment for $7,318.68 against plaintiffs.

At a pretrial conference held October 7, 1976 the parties waived identification of various exhibits including the contract of sale, note, mortgage and plaintiffs' letter requesting the mortgage release. "The court finds," wrote the judge on the conference order, "there is no issue as to any material fact. Both parties may submit briefs. Case is set for trial (non jury) on the 3rd day of November, 1976, at 3:00 P.M."

Nevertheless on October 28, 1976 defendants filed what they called an "Offer of Evidence." In it they asked the court to consider certain additional evidence bearing on the true intent of the parties, namely: (1) a copy of the contract of sale; (2) an amortization schedule; (3) plaintiffs' "hand written correspondence where [they] calculated interest on the Note in making [their] monthly $100.00 payments"; (4) defendants' tax records for the years 1965–71; (5) appraiser's report showing value of property to be $16,000 on the date of its sale to plaintiffs.

On November 3rd the parties appeared for trial at which time the court adjudicated the case by denying plaintiffs the relief they requested, reforming the note by deleting the number 135 therefrom, and decreeing that there remained a balance due on the note in the amount of $7,318.68 to be paid at the rate of $100 a month.

It is from this judgment that plaintiffs appeal condemning it as a premature conclusion reached "without hearing evidence," and ask for "a reversal of the trial court with direction . . . to enter judgment for [plaintiffs] on the pleadings."

Plaintiffs say that in seeking reformation of the note it was necessary for defendants to plead that a mutual mistake had been made by the parties and that the "mere allegation that a clerical error was made, without more, cannot support a cause of action for reformation because it does not speak to the critical issue of whether the note reflected the intentions of either of the parties." Since there is no mutual mistake allegation, continue plaintiffs, defendants have stated no cause of action and therefore could not have been entitled to judgment.

The problem presented by this reasoning is not so much with the statement of controlling law as it is with its application to the facts. As we read it defendants' cross-petition discloses more than a "mere allegation" of a clerical error and, in effect, alleges a mutual mistake resulting from the erroneous insertion in the note of 135 monthly payments, instead of 226, contrary to the agreement of the parties.

The law under these circumstances is that where by reason of a scrivener's mistake an instrument "omits or contains terms or stipulations contrary to the common intention of the parties . . . ." A court of equity will consider it a mutual mistake common to both parties — that is, the scrivener left out or included provisions neither party intended — and therefore correct the error in a manner that will place the parties in the position they would have occupied had the error not occurred.

Giving the pleading a liberal construction to which it is entitled, requires us to hold, therefore, that defendants have sufficiently pleaded grounds for reformational relief.

Plaintiffs' second proposition — that the court erred in reforming the instrument without hearing evidence — is likewise without merit because the admissions they made in their petition regarding the intentions of the parties justify the court's rendition of what, in effect, is a judgment in the nature of one on the pleadings.

The admissions we refer to are set out in the note and mortgage attached to plaintiffs' petition. In them plaintiffs admitted these three essential facts: (1) that they owed defendants the principal sum of $13,500; (2) that they promised to pay the debt in monthly installments of $100 each; and (3) that they promised to pay six percent interest on the unpaid principal balance "at the maturity of each installment" and with each payment.

Examination of the note gives rise to the strong suspicion that its scrivener did not know what he was doing. On the face of the printed form appear several errors which had to be unintentional because (a) they are so gross, and (b) they depart sharply from the intention of the parties as manifested in the contract of sale and the securing mortgage. For example, the payees are not named in the space provided for such identification, but instead the amount plaintiffs promised to pay was written in it. At another place the note provides for 135 installments of $100 each (which equals the principal amount of the note) *and* interest at the rate of six percent "per month" (the printed term "annum" having been x'd out). Thus, as written, the note calls for interest the first month in the amount of $810 — an exorbitantly usurious rate of nearly 70 percent per annum.

Aside from these and kindred errors, certain language inserted in the note form is ambiguous. The most noticeable uncertainty relates to interest. After referring to a rate of six percent per month, the scrivener added that it was to be "included in each payment." Does this phrase mean that each $100 installment shall be applied first to interest and the remainder to principal? Or does it mean a payment of $100 on the principal shall be made each month and with it promisor shall also pay six percent per month interest? As we shall point out later, the lapse of time has made the meaning of the doubtful phrase immaterial.

The question remains, then, what material fact was there in dispute which should have been heard and resolved? Plaintiffs call none to our attention and we cannot perceive of any. Had the defense of usury been proffered by plaintiffs then there could have arisen the question of a corrupt intent on the part of defendants to extract unlawful interest. But it was not and the only other possible defense we can think of that would allow plaintiffs to escape paying interest would be that the parties had an express agreement plaintiffs would pay none. Not only was such a defense not pleaded in plaintiffs' answer to defendants' cross-action but had it been it would have been in conflict with the admissions of plaintiffs in their petition.

That the note was misdrawn is a fact beyond doubt. The mortgage recites that it is "to secure the payment of one promissory note of even date [October 15, 1964] herewith: Made to Rosa Beck, W. H. Beck, Winona Smith (now Holliday) and Clifford Holliday, Okla. City *with 6% per cent. [sic] interest per annum from date payable monthly . . . .*" (Emphasis added.) The contract of sale reads in part:

> Purchaser to acquire property under a contract for deed, *paying $100 per month at 6% interest included.* When 10 payments have been made and the garage paid for the seller will deed property to purchaser and take a first mortgage for the unpaid balance *to be liquidated by continued payments as above.* (Emphasis added.)

The trial court's construction not only avoids absurdity, but recognizes that the parties agreed upon a rate of interest within a range buyers and sellers of metropolitan real property generally agreed to in 1964.

Equity will correct errors in an instrument shown to have resulted from an unintentional drafting mistake. We hold, therefore, that the decree was validly predicated on what the note and mortgage revealed the agreement of the parties to be, namely, that (1) plaintiffs would pay defendants interest on the deferred principal balance of the note, (2) the rate of interest was to be six percent per annum, and (3) the interest was to be paid monthly.

Nor did the note's earlier mentioned ambiguity, concerning what the parties intended the total monthly payments to be, present an issue requiring the adduction of evidence because at this late date the problem became merely a matter of mathematics and mechanics for the court. The method employed by the trial judge to achieve payment of the interest — reforming the note by deleting 135 and in effect substituting the number 226 and allowing the balance to be paid at the rate of $100 per month beginning December 1, 1976 — appears to us to be fair and equitable, particularly to the plaintiff mortgagors. *Affirmed.*

NOTES

(1) In *Hoffman v. Chapman*, 182 Md. 208, 34 A.2d 438 (1943), Chapman and wife agreed to sell part of lot 4 in a section known as Homewood on Edgewood Road, the size to be 96 by 150 feet. Before the parcel was surveyed, the buyers, Hoffman and wife, were given possession. When the Hoffmans made final settlement, they clearly understood that they were receiving only part of lot 4 containing one dwelling. However, the deed conveyed the entire lot which was improved by other dwelling property. Some time afterwards, the mistake was discovered, and upon the Hoffmans' refusal to reconvey the additional part of lot 4, the Chapmans entered suit in equity to reform the deed on the ground of mistake. The court held that parol evidence was admissible in a suit for reformation and that a court of equity was to reform a written instrument to make it conform to the real intention of the parties when the evidence was so clear, strong and convincing as to leave no doubt that a mutual mistake was made in the instrument contrary to the agreement of the parties.

(2) The plaintiff entered into a two-year employment contract with the defendant whereby the plaintiff agreed to create, process and sell long-term FHA mortgages. Section 7 of the contract stated that in the sale of certain mortgages in which an additional fee was permitted the defendant would pay the excess to the plaintiff. At the termination of the contract, the plaintiff claimed that he was entitled to the excess amount provided for in section 7 not only for the two-year period, but for the duration of the mortgages. Defendant refused to pay and the plaintiff brought an action in a state court which held for the defendant on the ground that section 7 was unambiguous and, therefore, no prior, contemporaneous or subsequent conversations as to its scope would be admitted. *Sadowski v. General Discount Corp.*, 295 Mich. 340, 294 N.W. 703 (1940). The plaintiff then brought an action in a federal district court to reform the contract. The district court reformed section 7 of the contract which resulted in a judgment of $96,718.88 with interest in favor of the plaintiff. The Sixth Circuit affirmed the district court on appeal:

> We agree with the district court that the Supreme Court of Michigan obviously based its decision upon the literal meaning of the words used in paragraph seven in an action at law on the contract, as written; and that the parol evidence there proffered by [the plaintiff] was to explain the words of the seventh paragraph, as written, and not to establish a mistake in the choice of language used to express the real intention of the parties, while this suit in equity in the United States Court is to reform the contract so that it will, in fact, express that intention. 183 F.2d at 546–47. *See* Murray on Contracts at § 86B.

[6]   Condition Precedent, Fraud, and the Parol Evidence Rule

SMITH v. ROSENTHAL TOYOTA, INC.
Maryland Court of Special Appeals
573 A.2d 418 (1990)

WILNER, J.

James and Carolyn Smith sued Rosenthal Toyota, Inc. in the Circuit Court for Prince George's County for fraud and for conversion of a 1981 Chevette that was owned by them. They appeal from the entry of summary judgment in favor of Rosenthal.

On July 10, 1987, after dropping his wife off at work, Mr. Smith stopped at the Rosenthal showroom to look at some trucks. He was driving the Chevette, which was titled in his name and his wife's jointly. He found a truck that he liked but told the salesman, one Willie McAllister, that he generally did not buy anything without his wife's consent. After some further discussion, McAllister asked Smith whether he had the title certificate to the Chevette. Smith recounted the conversation in his deposition testimony:

> "I said yes, it's at home, but why would I need the title? He said, well, it's just a formality. We don't have any money in the house, and at this time he expressed to me well, why don't you take the truck home and test drive it for the weekend, and if your wife likes it, she can come back and sign and we'll finalize the deal. I said, well, that's the only way I can get the truck because it's quite obvious from what you are telling me that I don't make enough money. You know, that is what he expressed to me."[65]

At that point, the salesman drove Mr. Smith to his home so that he could retrieve the title certificate for the Chevette. On the way, Smith again asked the purpose of obtaining the certificate as it was in both names and again he was told that "it's just a formality." Mr. Smith got the certificate and returned to the showroom, whereupon McAllister told him that Rosenthal would get the truck ready for him to take home but that he would have to sign some papers. Specifically:

> "Okay. After he [McAllister] came back [from talking with the manager], he told me, he said, well, they are going to clean the truck up, you can take it home for the weekend; if your wife doesn't like it, then you come back and, you know, if she likes it, we'll finalize the deal. If not, then things will go back to square one, is what Mr. McAllister told me. So I said okay. I then left my car there — We went to the finance office where they handed me some papers, which I never read, I just signed them. It took me like about three seconds to sign them and I was on my way."

---

[65] [1] Mr. Smith testified that Rosenthal agents had told him on more than one occasion that on his income alone he would not qualify for the necessary financing and that his wife would have to pledge her credit as well.

The papers Mr. Smith so quickly signed consisted of (1) a retail installment contract under which he agreed to purchase the truck for $13,843, of which $2,800 was to be paid through the trade-in of the Chevette, $1,920 was to be paid in cash, and $9,122 was to be financed; (2) an agreement providing, in part, that if Rosenthal was unable to find a financial institution willing to buy the installment contract, it had the right to acquire the Chevette for $900; (3) the title certificate to the Chevette, which Smith endorsed in blank; (4) a written warranty that he had traded the Chevette for the truck, that he had good title to the Chevette free of all liens and encumbrances, that he would deliver good title within five days, and that he would "reimburse Rosenthal Toyota Company for the total amount of this vehicle if I cannot fulfill the above obligations; "and (5) a credit application showing his income from employment as a "houseman" for Days Inn as $16,000 and his wife's income as $42,000.

In addition to these papers, which Mr. Smith signed, Rosenthal gave him a "Notice to Cosignor" form advising a cosigner that "[y]ou are being asked to guarantee this debt" and warning the cosigner to "[t]hink carefully before you do" because "[i]f the borrower doesn't pay the debt, you will have to." Inferentially, this form was given to Mr. Smith so that he could have Mrs. Smith sign it.

Mrs. Smith arrived home late that Friday and did not see the truck until the next morning. She instructed her husband to return it, which he attempted to do the following Monday. Rosenthal refused to accept the truck back, however, insisting that Mr. Smith had bought it: "I said you told me that I had to bring my wife in here for signing these papers and he said no, no, we didn't need your wife's signature. He said you qualified. I said how could I qualify when I was told I didn't make enough money? He said well, we already done it. He said you bought a truck."

Mrs. Smith was working for a law firm at the time. When her husband informed her that Rosenthal had refused to take back the truck, she discussed the matter with one of the attorneys, who then called Rosenthal. The attorney was told to write a letter which, on behalf of Mrs. Smith, he did. Mrs. Smith hand-carried the letter to Rosenthal's manager that afternoon. According to Mrs. Smith, the manager read the letter, laughed at her, and told her that he would neither take the truck back nor return the Chevette. This action followed.

The court granted Rosenthal's motion for summary judgment on essentially two bases. It first concluded that, as no promises, representations, or inducements had been made to Mrs. Smith, her action for fraud must fail. With respect to Mr. Smith's action and Mrs. Smith's suit for conversion of the Chevette, the court relied on clauses in two of the agreements signed by Mr. Smith on July 10: the warranty that he would deliver good title to the Chevette or reimburse Rosenthal if he was unable to do so, and the concluding statement in the agreement respecting the approval of credit that "This agreement shall supercede [sic] and prevail over any prior or contemporaneous oral or written agreements entered into between the parties hereto." Though purporting to eschew any reliance on the parol evidence rule, which it said did not apply, the court found this integration clause dispositive, holding:

> "Now you are saying but he was told in order to induce him to sign the
> contract that that was a controlling provision. Said in legal terms, the
> provisions of what he was told were different than the provisions of what he

signed. And that's exactly what the case says you can't claim; that if what you signed is clear and unambiguous and you had the opportunity to read it and understand it, and you didn't, then that is it."

In order to prevail in an action for tortious fraud, a plaintiff must show that (1) a false representation was made; (2) the falsity was known to the speaker or the misrepresentation was made with reckless indifference to its truth; (3) the misrepresentation was made for the purpose of defrauding the plaintiff; (4) the plaintiff relied on the misrepresentation, had a right to rely on it, and would not have done the thing from which the injury resulted if the misrepresentation had not been made; and (5) the plaintiff suffered loss or injury by reason of the misrepresentation. *Everett v. Baltimore Gas & Elec.*, 307 Md. 286, 300, 513 A.2d 882 (1986); *Martens Chevrolet v. Seney*, 292 Md. 328, 333, 439 A.2d 534 (1982).

As we indicated, the fraud count was based on averments, supported in deposition testimony, that Mr. Smith was induced to sign the various documents relied upon by Rosenthal as evidence of the sale of the truck upon the express and repeated representations that the signing of those documents was a "mere formality" and that no purchase would or could occur without the approval of Mrs. Smith. Those representations, the plaintiffs claim, were never intended by Rosenthal to be honored but were made in order to induce Mr. Smith to sign the documents and then coerce the Smiths into completing the deal. A fair inference can be drawn from what allegedly occurred the following Monday that that was so — that Rosenthal never had any intention of returning the Chevette or allowing Mr. Smith to withdraw in the event his wife failed to approve the transaction. From that inference, the further inference can fairly be drawn that Rosenthal knew when it made the representations that they were false.

As the court correctly noted, there is nothing in the record to indicate that any of the culpable representations were made to Mrs. Smith. She was not induced to sign or do anything and therefore cannot establish the requisite elements for an action of fraud. That is not so with respect to Mr. Smith, however. If his assertions are taken at face value, each of the five elements of the tort would be established. As we observed, the court dismissed his claim on the basis that these assertions could not be considered because of the integration clause, and it is upon that theory that Rosenthal asks us to affirm.

We find two flaws in the court's decision. The most obvious one is that the integration clause relied upon by the court — the only one it could have relied on — was not part of the retail installment contract which evidenced the alleged sale and it was not part of the warranty agreement through which Mr. Smith promised to deliver good title to the Chevette. It is found only in the agreement to pay $900 in the event Rosenthal was unable to sell the retail installment contract and relates only to that agreement. It states that "[t]his agreement shall supercede [sic] and prevail over any prior or contemporaneous oral or written agreements . . . ." (Emphasis added.) Moreover, as Rosenthal was apparently able to sell the installment contract, the agreement containing the clause became moot.

Even if we were somehow to regard the integration clause as applying to the other written agreements, it would not preclude consideration of the oral representations and understandings alleged. The notion of conditional delivery has long been recognized in this State — that it is competent for a defendant to show by parol evidence that the instrument upon which he is sued was delivered to the plaintiff to be held upon a condition to be performed before the plaintiff's interest could attach. *See Ricketts v. Pendleton*, 14 Md. 320 (1859); *Jenkins v. First Nat'l Bk. of Balto.*, 134 Md. 85, 106 A. 174 (1919). More recently, in *Foreman v. Melrod*, 257 Md. 435, 442, 263 A.2d 559 (1970) and *Saliba v. Arthur F. Charlotte, Inc.*, 259 Md. 588, 593, 270 A.2d 656 (1970), the Court declared it to be well settled "that the parol evidence rule does not prevent the introduction of parol evidence indicating that the written instrument was not to become effective as an instrument, until a prior condition or event had occurred." The same result pertains even when there is an integration clause. As stated in RESTATEMENT (SECOND) OF CONTRACTS § 217, "[w]here the parties to a written agreement agree orally that performance of the agreement is subject to the occurrence of a stated condition, the agreement is not integrated with respect to the oral condition." Comment b to that section explains:

> If the parties orally agreed that performance of the written agreement was subject to a condition, either the writing is not an integrated agreement or the agreement is only partially integrated until the condition occurs. Even a 'merger' clause in the writing, explicitly negating oral terms, does not control the question whether there is an integrated agreement or the scope of the writing.

This principle of allowing parol evidence of oral conditions is particularly applicable where the written agreement is challenged on grounds of fraud. In *Whitney, Exec. v. Halibut*, 235 Md. 517, 527, 202 A.2d 629 (1964), the Court, in discussing the parol evidence rule, declared its concurrence with the views expressed by Professor Corbin:

> Its name has distracted attention, he [Professor Corbin] says, from the real issues that are involved which 'may be any one or more of the following: (1) Have the parties made a contract? (2) Is that contract void or voidable because of illegality, fraud, mistake, or any other reason? (3) Did the parties assent to a particular writing as the complete and accurate 'integration' of that contract?' " He next states (p.360): "In determining these issues, or any of them, there is no 'parol evidence rule' to be applied. On these issues, no relevant evidence, whether parol or otherwise is excluded. No written document is sufficient, standing alone, to determine any one of them . . . .

It is clear, then, that the evidence offered by Mr. and Mrs. Smith regarding the representations made and understanding reached on July 10 — that the purchase and trade-in were subject to the approval of Mrs. Smith — was admissible and, for purposes of defending against a motion for summary judgment, was dispositive. That evidence, taken in a light most favorable to Mr. Smith, sufficed to establish that the written agreements relied upon by Rosenthal were induced by the dealer's fraud.

For the reasons noted, we conclude that the judgment entered on Mrs. Smith's action for fraud may stand but that the summary judgments entered on Mr. Smith's claims must be vacated. The case will be remanded for further proceedings on those claims.

COMMENT

Condition Precedent to Formation. Since the classic case of *Pym v. Campbell*, 6 El. & Bl. 370 (Q.B. 1856) it has been clear that the parol evidence rule does not bar evidence of a condition precedent to the formation of the contract. Numerous cases so hold. *See, e.g., Palantine Nat'l Bank v. Olson*, 366 N.W.2d 726 (Minn. 1985); *Brummet v. Pope*, 685 S.W.2d 238 (Mo. App. 1985); *Rincones v. Windberg*, 705 S.W.2d 846 (Tex. App. 1986); *White Showers, Inc. v. Fischer*, 278 Mich. 32, 270 N.W. 205 (1936). Evidence of fraud or mistake is also admissible. Evidence of a condition precedent to formation need not be accompanied by evidence of fraud or mistake. As the court states, a merger clause does not preclude the admissibility of such evidence.

Jansen v. Herman, 304 Minn. 572, 230 N.W.2d 460 (1975), involved a document indicating that the owners of property agreed to pay a real estate broker $50,000. The owners sought to introduce evidence that this document was conditioned upon the actual closing of the sale to a particular buyer and the closing never occurred. The court stated, "In every instance where the parol evidence rule is sought to be applied, however, a threshold question must be asked: Is the contract valid and operative? If the contract was to be binding only upon performance of an agreed-upon condition precedent, then the contract goes into force only upon the performance of that condition."

Restatement (Second) of Contracts § 217. While the case law is clear, the RESTATEMENT (SECOND) OF CONTRACTS rejects the traditional rationale that there is no reason to apply the parol evidence rule where the question is whether any enforceable agreement exists. The RESTATEMENT (SECOND) OF CONTRACTS prefers an alternative rationale, i.e., if the written agreement is subject to the occurrence of a stated condition, the agreement is not integrated with respect to the oral condition. This view is explained in comment b, which suggests, "If the parties orally agreed that performance of the written agreement was subject to a condition, either the writing is not an integrated agreement or the agreement is only partially integrated until the condition occurs." This is followed by the curious suggestion that even a merger clause which explicitly negates oral terms does not control the question of whether the agreement is integrated. Certainly, a writing may appear to be a complete and exclusive statement of the parties' intention, and it may contain a well-drafted merger clause to further support a finding to that effect. However, the most complete and exclusive statement of agreement may not be intended to bind the parties until a preliminary contingency has occurred. A solution to the RESTATEMENT (SECOND) OF CONTRACTS mystery may be found in a hint in the Reporter's Note to this section which refers the reader to § 224, comment c, the section defining conditions. Comment c and the Reporter's Note explaining it are critical of the use of the term "condition" to describe an event upon which the *existence* of the contract is dependent. The definition of "condition" in the RESTATEMENT (SECOND) OF CONTRACTS is relegated to an event upon which the *performance* of a duty under an existing contract is dependent. However, the explanation suggests that "there is no great substantive disparity between the terminology used in this [RESTATEMENT (SECOND)] Comment and descriptions of such events as conditions to the existence of the contract." Notwithstanding the lack of "great substantive disparity," the RESTATEMENT (SECOND) OF CONTRACTS appears to reject the generally accepted rationale of conditions precedent to the existence of a contract simply because of its narrower definition of "condition." Ambiguity in the use of the term "condition" in this area can be avoided by identifying that to which the condition is attached, i.e. to the *existence* of a contract or to a *duty* under an existing contract. Typically, courts use the term "condition" in unambiguous fashion to describe an event which must occur before a contract comes into existence. Therefore, the RESTATEMENT (SECOND) OF CONTRACTS rejection of the case law rationale and its substitution of a puzzling alternative rationale lack any apparent justification. *See* MURRAY ON CONTRACTS at § 86C.

D. SUBSEQUENT MODIFICATIONS — UCC SECTION 2-209

The parol evidence rule applies only to "prior or contemporaneous" agreements. It has no application to subsequent modifications — the parties are always free to change what they had agreed upon yesterday to a new agreement today without fear of parol evidence implications. Where, for example, evidence of an express warranty made prior to the execution of a final and complete writing evidencing a contract will be inadmissible because of the parol evidence rule, if the same warranty is made *after* the execution of the writing, it can be a subsequent modification that will be admissible since the parol evidence rule is nor a bar to such evidence. *See, e.g., Downie v. Abex Corp.*, 741 F.2d 1235 (10th Cir. 1984) and Comment 7 to UCC § 2-313.

While parol evidence rule requirements do not threaten subsequent modifications, other questions arise such as whether the contract as modified meets the requirements of the statute of frauds of § 2-201 or the parties' own no-oral-modification (NOM) clause, i.e., their own "private" statute of frauds. If the contract does not meet those requirements, are there circumstances suggesting that such requirements may be "waived"? Earlier, we considered UCC Section 2-209(1), which allows good faith modifications to be effective without consideration. That subsection has raised few problems for courts. The remainder of § 2-209 however, i.e., subsections (2) through (5), have been problematic.

ZEMCO MANUFACTURING, INC. v. NAVISTAR
INTERNATIONAL TRANSPORTATION CORP.
United States Court of Appeals, Seventh Circuit
186 F.3d 815 (1999)

RIPPLE, J.

Zemco manufactured and supplied machined parts to Navistar from 1968 to 1995. In 1983, the parties entered into a sales contract that was renewable on a yearly basis. From that date until 1995, Navistar purchased all of its requirements from Zemco. In January 1995, however, the sole shareholders of Zemco, Alan Zemen and Joel Pecoraro, fell into disagreement. Consequently, Pecoraro sold his interest in Zemco to Zemen. Pecoraro subsequently formed Pecoraro Manufacturing, Inc. ("PMI"). In the same year, Navistar began to buy parts from PMI and to phase out its purchase of parts from Zemco.

[T]he district court held that the renewal of the contract between Zemco and Navistar did not comply with the statute of frauds. In 1983, the parties entered into the original written contract for the sale of parts. The contract was to last one year, but it was extended by written agreements until 1987. There has not been a written contract extension since 1987; the parties, however, have agreed orally to extend the contracts. Navistar submits that the oral contract extensions violate the statute of frauds. Zemco counters that simple time extensions or renewals of the contract need not be in writing because they are merely a modification of a non-definite contract term.

We begin our analysis of this question with Indiana Code § 26-1-2-209(3), which generally applies to contract modifications. It states that "the requirements of the statute of frauds (IC 26-1-2-201) must be satisfied if the contract as modified is within its provisions." Ind. Code § 26-1-2-209(3). The interpretation of this provision, which is identical to Uniform Commercial Code ("UCC") § 2-209(3), has generated controversy among courts and commentators. One view is that all contract modifications must be in writing; another view is that only modifications of terms that are required to be in writing under UCC § 2-201 must be in writing. Under the second view, the time extension would not need to be in writing because the length of a contract is not a type of term that needs to be in writing. *See* Ind. Code § 26-1-2-201 & UCC cmt. 1.[66]

Indiana courts have not interpreted the meaning of § 26-1-2-209(3). A substantial number of the courts in other jurisdictions that have considered identical UCC provisions have held that every contract modification must be in writing. *See Van Den Broeke v. Bellanca Aircraft Corp.*, 576 F.2d 582, 584 (5th Cir. 1978) (orally modified warranty); *Green Constr. Co. v. First Indem. of America Ins. Co.*, 735 F. Supp. 1254, 1261 (D.N.J. 1990) (orally modified delivery terms); *Leasing Serv. Corp. v. Diamond Timber, Inc.*, 559 F. Supp. 972, 976–77 (S.D.N.Y. 1983) (orally modified lease terms); *Cooley v. Big Horn Harvestore Sys., Inc.*, 767 P.2d 740, 744 (Colo. Ct. App. 1988), *rev'd on other grounds*, 813 P.2d 736 (Colo. 1991) (orally modified warranty). Although these courts have provided little analysis, they essentially interpret § 2-209(3) to mean that, if the post-modification contract fits within the terms of § 2-201 (i.e., it is a sale of goods for more than $500), then any modification of it must be in writing. The Indiana Commentary appears to agree: "Indiana cases seem to use a rather mechanical test — if the original contract had to be in writing then the modifying agreement must also." Ind. Code § 26-1-2-209 Ind. cmt. 3.

At least one court has held that the writing requirement for modifications applies only to either a change in consideration, or a change in a term that the UCC statute

---

[66] [5] "The required writing need not contain all the material terms of the contract and such material terms as are stated need not be precisely stated. All that is required is that the writing afford a basis for believing that the offered oral evidence rests on a real transaction. It may be written in lead pencil on a scratch pad. It need not indicate which party is the buyer and which the seller. The only term which must appear is the quantity term which need not be accurately stated but recovery is limited to the amount stated. The price, time and place of payment or delivery, the general quality of the goods, or any particular warranties may all be omitted . . . . Only three definite and invariable requirements as to the memorandum are made by this subsection. First, it must evidence a contract for the sale of goods; second, it must be "signed," a word which includes any authentication which identifies the party to be charged; and third, it must specify a quantity."

of frauds requires to be in writing. *See Costco Wholesale Corp. v. World Wide Licensing Corp.*, 78 Wash. App. 637, 898 P.2d 347, 351 & n.5 (Wash. Ct. App. 1995). This view also appears to be favored among commentators.[67] The general theory behind this approach is that it would be anomalous, if not inconsistent, to require that a modification be in writing if the same term in the original contract could be proven by parol evidence. Moreover, proponents of this view argue, § 2-209(3) explicitly invokes only the writing requirements contained in § 2-201 — nothing less and nothing more.

We need not decide in the abstract the correct interpretation of § 2-209(3). Because the jurisdiction of the district court was based on the diversity of citizenship of the parties, it was obligated to apply the law of Indiana. *See Erie R.R. v. Tompkins*, 304 U.S. 64, 78, 58 S. Ct. 817, 82 L. Ed. 1188 (1938). Although the Indiana courts have not spoken directly on the matter, we believe that the district court was correct in its estimation that Indiana would follow the majority of jurisdictions and hold that the extension of the contract needed to be in writing. Several considerations lead to this conclusion. First, as we pointed out in *Northrop Corp. v. Litronic Industries*, 29 F.3d 1173, 1178 (7th Cir. 1994), when a state has tended to follow majority rules and because there is an interest in the uniform nationwide application of the Uniform Commercial Code, we start with a presumption that the state would adopt the majority position. We believe that it is appropriate to articulate the methodology that we employed in Northrop in this case as well. Here, the presumption has not been rebutted. There is no suggestion in this record that Indiana would not follow the majority rule or that its courts would not consider important the goal of uniformity in the interpretation of the Commercial Code. Indeed, the Indiana Legislature has affirmatively directed that, in construing the Code, the goal of uniformity ought to be a guidepost of decision.

Having determined that the requirements of § 26-2-1-201 apply to this modification, we must determine whether the requirements are satisfied in this case. Zemco argues that various computer printouts created by Navistar are sufficient to meet the requirements. Those printouts indicate that the contract at issue here had been extended for the year in question, until June 14, 1996. They appear to be forms created by Navistar as a history of the contract and as an update of orders placed by Zemco.

Navistar argues that these printouts are an insufficient writing. It notes that Official Comment 3 to Indiana Code § 26-2-209(3) states that an authenticated memo modifying an original contract "is limited in its effect to the quantity of goods set forth in it." Ind. Code § 26-1-2-209(3). Because Navistar paid for all the parts listed in the printouts, it argues that it cannot be held accountable for any more parts.

---

67 [6] *See* 2A RONALD A. ANDERSON, ANDERSON ON THE UNIFORM COMMERCIAL CODE § 2-209:92, at 64 (1997); 1 JAMES J. WHITE & ROBERT S. SUMMERS, UNIFORM COMMERCIAL CODE § 1-6, at 39 (1995); Michael J. Herbert, *Toward a Uniform Theory of Warranty Creation Under Articles 2 and 2A of the Uniform Commercial Code*, 1990 COLUMBIA BUSINESS L. REV. 265, 303 (1990); John E. Murray, Jr., *The Modification Mystery: Section 2-209 of the Uniform Commercial Code*, 32 VILL. L. REV. 1, 28 (1987); Jeanette K. Brooks, Comment, *Parol Modification and the Statute of Frauds: Fitting the Pieces Together Under the Uniform Commercial Code*, 21 CAMPBELL L. REV. 307, 317–18 (1999); *see generally* THOMAS D. CRANDALL ET AL., UNIFORM COMMERCIAL CODE § 3.5.3, at 3:67–3:69 (1993).

holding [We cannot accept Navistar's argument. A careful reading of comment 3, in conjunction with § 2-201 and § 2-306, indicates that this comment is inapplicable to requirements contracts. The comment's suggestion that the effect of a modification memorandum is limited to quantities set forth in the memorandum is a reference to § 2-201's requirement that a contract is not enforceable "beyond the quantity of goods shown in such writing." Ind. Code § 26-1-2-201. However, this quantity limitation does not (indeed, cannot) apply to requirements contracts. *See* Ind. Code § 26-1-2-306 cmt. 1. Therefore, the effect of a modification memorandum is not limited to the quantities listed in it if the contract is a requirements contract. The district court, believing that the contract was not a requirements contract, accepted Navistar's argument. However, because we have held that there is a material issue of fact regarding whether the contract is a requirements contract, we cannot accept Navistar's contention.

Navistar also argues that the printouts do not meet the signature requirement of § 26-1-2-201. That section, when read in conjunction with § 26-1-2-209(3), requires that a contract modification be "signed by the party against whom enforcement is sought." Ind. Code § 26-1-2-201. Indiana's Commercial Code states: " 'Signed' includes any symbol executed or adopted by a party with present intention to authenticate a writing." Ind. Code § 26-1-1-201(39). The Official Comment to that section states:

> The inclusion of authentication in the definition of "signed" is to make clear that as the term is used in this Act a complete signature is not necessary. Authentication may be printed, stamped or written; it may be by initials or by thumbprint. It may be on any part of the document and in appropriate cases may be found in a billhead or letterhead. No catalog of possible authentications can be complete and the court must use common sense and commercial experience in passing upon these matters. The question always is whether the symbol was executed or adopted by the party with present intention to authenticate the writing. Ind. Code § 26-1-1-201 cmt. 39. This court, applying Illinois' version of the UCC, has previously held that typed initials or a letterhead could suffice as a signature. *See Monetti v. Anchor Hocking Corp.*, 931 F.2d 1178, 1182, 1185 (7th Cir. 1991); *see also Owen v. Kroger Co.*, 936 F. Supp. 579, 583–85 (S.D. Ind. 1996) (applying Indiana law).

We cannot say, on this record, that all of the computer printouts in this case are not adequately "signed." The name "Navistar" is stamped or typed on some of these documents. There is an issue of fact regarding whether these markings were executed with the intention of authenticating the documents. *See id.* at 585. Summary judgment should therefore not be granted.

NOTES

(1) *"Public" and "Private" Statutes of Fraud.* Section 2-209(3) is often called a "public" statute of frauds since it incorporates the statute of frauds in Section 2-201 that applies to contracts for the sale of goods priced at $500 or more regardless of the parties' manifested intention. Section 2-209(2), however, applies only where the parties have agreed that any modification or rescission of their contract must be

evidenced by a writing — a so-called "private" statute of frauds. The view of the "commentators" noted by the court in the principal case would apply the "public" statute of frauds (Section 2-201) to modified contracts only where the modification changes a term that Section 2-201 would require be in writing in an original contract. Thus, where an original contract with a price of $499 is modified with a price of $500 or more, Section 2-209(3) would require the modified contract to meet the writing requirement of Section 2-201. Where there is a modification of the quantity term, the modified contract would have to be in writing to evidence the new quantity term. Section 2-201, however, does not require other terms to be evidenced by a writing. Indeed, Comment i to Section 2-201 states, "The required writing need not contain all the material terms of the contract and such material terms as are stated need not be precisely stated. All that is requires is that the writing afford a basis for believing that the offered oral evidence rests on a real transaction . . . . The only term which must appear is the quantity term which need not be accurately stated but recovery is limited to the amount stated. The price, time and place of payment or delivery, the general quality of the goods or any particular warranties may all be omitted." Since Section 2-209(3) only states that "The requirements of the statute of frauds of this Article (Section 2-201) must be satisfied if the contract as modified is within its provisions," the holding of the court (in consonance with the "prevailing" view) that "any modification" must be in writing clearly appears to be inconsistent with the statutory language. Moreover, if Section 2-209(3) requires any modification of any term to be evidenced by a writing, Section 2-209(2), which allows the parties to agree that any modification must be in writing (a no-oral-modification (NOM) clause), appears entirely superfluous. Why bother with an NOM clause if any modification is required to be evidenced by a writing? To construe a statute that deprives a section of the statute of any meaning is a violation of a basic rule of statutory construction. The court notes that the prevailing case law so holding manifests "little analysis."

(2) *Modification and Waivers.* Subsections (4) and (5) of Section 2-209 have proven to be disconcerting. Section 2-209(4) states, "Although an attempt at modification does not satisfy the requirements of subsection (2) or (3), it can operate as a waiver." Since Subsections (2) and (3) would be satisfied by an effective writing, "an attempt at modification" must be a modification that is not evidenced by an effective writing such as an oral modification, a conduct modification or a modification evidenced by an ineffective writing. Section 2-209(5) then states that such a waiver can be retracted unless the other party has materially relied on it. In *Wisconsin Knife Works v. National Metal Crafters*, 781 F.2d 1280 (7th Cir. 1985), Judge Posner suggests that if an oral modification always operates as a waiver, Section 2-209(4) would simply contradict Susbsections 2-209(2) and (3). He quickly explains, however, that Section 2-209(4) does not say that any ineffective modification constitutes a waiver. Rather, it states that an ineffective modification can operate as a waiver. Writing for the majority, Judge Posner concludes that a waiver will be effective only if there is reliance on the waiver. This interpretation was not satisfactory to Judge Easterbrook who, in dissent, read the Posner interpretation as implying "that subsection (4) applies to a subset of the subjects of subsection (5)." He concluded, "Things are the other way round." The Easterbrook analysis suggests that all attempted modifications, be they oral, written or implied, that do not satisfy Subsections 2-209(2) or (3) are unsuccessful attempts at modification

under Section 2-209(4), that may operate as waivers. Section 2-209(5), however, allows the waiver to be retracted as to executory portions of the contract absent a material change of position in reliance on the waiver.

E.   INTERPRETATION

[1]   Standards of Interpretation

MELLON BANK v. AETNA BUSINESS CREDIT CORP.
United States Court of Appeals, Third Circuit
619 F.2d 1001 (1980)

[Messrs. Opp, Elgin and Wise were joint venturers in the development of an office complex in Atlanta, Georgia. The project, known as Kensington Square, was to consist of six two-story office buildings, and the estimated cost of the project was $2,500,000. The financing for this real estate development was a common, two-page process involving the borrowers (Opp, Elgin and Wise) and two commercial lending institutions. A "permanent" loan (or mortgage loan) is a long term commitment usually made by a savings and loan institution or an insurance company. Aetna extended a permanent loan to the borrowers in the amount of $2,500,000 in May 1974. The second stage of the financing saw Mellon extending a short-term (construction) loan to the borrowers to finance the actual construction of the buildings. Construction loans are normally made by commercial banks like Mellon. In June 1974, Mellon issued a construction loan which eventually amounted to $2,241,489 at the time the borrowers' contractor had substantially completed the buildings. In July 1974, Mellon, Aetna and the borrowers executed a tripartite "Buy-Sell" agreement which obligated Aetna, subject to certain conditions, to purchase the construction loan from Mellon. This was in accordance with the two-stage financing of such a project since the permanent or mortgage loan is designed to replace or "take-out" any short-term loans such as the loan by Mellon. In 1975, there was a precipitous decline in the Atlanta real estate market which resulted in only seven percent of the new complex being leased. This placed the economic feasibility of the project in jeopardy. In August 1975, Mellon presented the necessary documents to Aetna to activate Aetna's duty to purchase the Mellon loan. However, Aetna refused to purchase the Mellon construction loan on the ground that a condition to its duty had not occurred. Section 4 of the "Buy-Sell" agreement contained the following clause: "In the event of bankruptcy or insolvency of Borrower provisions in paragraph 3 of the Permanent Commitment relating thereto shall be applicable." Paragraph 3 of the Permanent Commitment stated: "We (Aetna) shall have no obligation to acquire the construction loan from the construction lender in the event of bankruptcy or insolvency of the Borrower." Aetna contended that the borrowers were not solvent at the time it was to purchase the construction loan from Mellon. Mellon maintained that the borrowers were not insolvent. On November 3, 1975, Kensington Square was sold at a foreclosure sale for $1,150,000 which was its true market value at that time.]

CAHN, DISTRICT JUDGE [sitting by designation] . . . .

Aetna took the position in their briefs and at oral argument that they are entitled to judgment on the record as a matter of law. The basis for Aetna's position is the wording of the insolvency clause which states that Aetna "shall have no obligation to acquire the construction loan . . . in the event . . . of insolvency of the Borrower." Aetna contends that the test of insolvency is well established in law and as a commercial standard — a party is insolvent when their liabilities exceed their assets or they are unable to pay their debts as they come due. *See, e.g., Larrimer v. Feeney*, 411 Pa. 604, 192 A.2d 351 (1963); 11 U.S.C. § 101(26) (1978); Uniform Commercial Code, 12APa. Con. Stat. Ann. § 1-201(23) (Purdons). Aetna contends that documentary evidence establishes the borrowers were insolvent under either of these tests, and therefore, Aetna had no obligation to purchase the construction loan.

Mellon takes the position that the insolvency test must be applied without reference to the liabilities or assets of the borrowers which accrue from the Kensington Square project. Mellon alleges that only this construction of the insolvency clause properly reflects the intent of the parties and is required for a rational interpretation of the Buy-Sell Agreement. Aetna responds to Mellon's position by contending that Mellon's interpretation of the insolvency clause is an impermissible rewriting of the words of the contract.

The district court heard oral testimony, received documentary evidence and concluded that the term insolvency in the context of the Buy-Sell Agreement should be interpreted to exclude reference to assets or liabilities related to the Kensington Square project. The district court held this interpretation was "required by the clear allocation of lending risks between Mellon Bank and Aetna." No. 75-1156, slip. op. at 8. The basis for this holding was not the words of the contract, but evidence extrinsic to it. The district court found that Aetna's loan officer recognized Aetna's principal risk to be whether the office park could reach and maintain a ninety percent occupancy level. The district court found that Aetna in analyzing the security for its permanent loan did not consider the borrowers' cash flow, did not condition its obligation upon any occupancy level, and therefore concluded "Aetna recognized that the financial transaction in question was not a basis for finding insolvency." The district court cited no basis in the contract document or wording of the insolvency clause for its conclusion. Our task is to decide if the district court permissibly used extrinsic evidence to interpret the contract and, if so, whether it drew the proper legal conclusions therefrom.

In this case we confront several familiar, but not necessarily consistent, precepts of contract interpretation. We start from the premise that commercial parties are free to contract as they desire. Absent illegality, unconscionableness, fraud, duress, or mistake the parties are bound by the terms of their contract.

"In construing a contract, a court's paramount consideration is the intent of the parties." *O'Farrell v. Steel City Piping Co.*, 403 A.2d 1319, 1324 (1979). It would be helpful if judges were psychics who could delve into the parties' minds to ascertain their original intent. However, courts neither claim nor possess psychic power. Therefore, in order to interpret contracts with some consistency, and in order to provide contracting parties with a legal framework which provides a measure of predictability, the courts must eschew the ideal of ascertaining the parties' subjective intent and instead bind parties by the objective manifestations of their intent. As JUSTICE HOLMES observed:

> [T]he making of a contract depends not on the agreement of two minds, in one intention, but on the agreement of two sets of external signs — not on the parties' having *meant* the same thing but on their having *said* the same thing. Holmes, *The Path of the Law,* in COLLECTED LEGAL PAPERS 178, as quoted by JUDGE FRIENDLY in *Frigaliment Importing Co. v. B.N.S. International Sales Corp.,* 190 F. Supp. 116, 117 (S.D.N.Y. 1960) (emphasis in original).

The strongest external sign of agreement between contracting parties is the words they use in their written contract. Thus, the sanctity of the written words of the contract is embedded in the law of contract interpretation. As it has been variously put:

> [A] court will make no inference or give any construction to the terms of a written contract that may be in conflict with the clearly expressed language of the written agreement. *National Cash Register Co. v. Modern Transfer Co., Inc.,* 224 Pa. Super. 138, 142, 302 A.2d 486, 488 (1973).

A court is not authorized to construe a contract in such a way as to modify the plain meaning of its words, under the guise of interpretation. *Best v. Realty Management Corp.,* 174 Pa. Super. 326, 329–330, 101 A.2d 438, 440 (1953).

When a written contract is clear and unequivocal, its meaning must be determined by its contents alone. *East Crossroads Center, Inc. v. Mellon-Stuart Co.,* 416 Pa. 229, 230, 205 A.2d 865, 866 (1965).

The rule enunciated in *Gianni v. Russell [Russel] & Co., Inc.,* [281 Pa. 320, 126 A. 791] *supra,* is firmly embedded in the law of Pennsylvania and from that rule we will not permit a deviation for it is essential that the integrity of written contracts be maintained . . . . "Where parties, without any fraud or mistake, have deliberately put their engagements in writing, the law declares the writing to be not only the best, but the only, evidence of their agreement: [citing cases]. All preliminary negotiations, conversations and verbal agreements are merged in and superseded by the subsequent written contract . . . and unless fraud, accident or mistake be averred, the writing constitutes the agreement between the parties, and its terms cannot be added to nor subtracted from by parol evidence: [citing cases]." *United Refining Co. v. Jenkins,* 410 Pa. 126, 134, 189 A.2d 574, 578 (1963) (emphasis and citations omitted).[68]

---

[68] [9] Though the concept of the Parol Evidence Rule is relevant here, the issue in this case really concerns an exception to that rule. In the instant case one party introduced extrinsic evidence to "interpret" the contract. The other party argues that this extrinsic evidence seeks to vary or add to the contract and is therefore not admissible. If the written contract is unambiguous, the Parol Evidence Rule and the doctrines cited above bar the use of extrinsic evidence for interpretation. If the written contract is ambiguous the Parol Evidence Rule does not prevent the use of extrinsic evidence to interpret the writing.

This issue of ambiguity must be carefully distinguished from the issue of "integration" which arises when evidence is introduced to vary or add to the unambiguous written terms of a contract on the ground

In a world where semantics is a science instead of an art we might be able to read a contract and understand it without question. However, English is often a difficult and elusive language, and certainly not uniform among all who use it. External indicia of the parties' intent other than written words are useful, and probably indispensable, in interpreting contract terms. If each judge simply applied his own linguistic background and experience to the words of a contract, contracting parties would live in a most uncertain environment. Therefore, under Pennsylvania law we are instructed that:

> A court must be careful not to retire into that lawyers Paradise where all words have a fixed, precisely ascertained meaning; where men may express their purposes, not only with accuracy, but with fullness; and where, if the writer has been careful, a lawyer, having a document referred to him, may sit in his chair[,] inspect the text, and answer all questions without raising his eyes. *In re Estate of Breyer*, 475 Pa. 108, 379 A.2d 1305, 1309 n.5 (1977) (citations omitted), quoting THAYER, PRELIMINARY TREATISE ON EVIDENCE 428, as quoted in 3 CORBIN, CONTRACTS § 535 n.16 (1960).

In the construction of any contract, certain principles must guide us: (a) if there is any doubt as to the meaning of a term of a contract, such term should "receive a reasonable construction and one that will accord with the intention of the parties; and, in order to ascertain their intention, the court must look at the circumstances under which the [contract] was made"; (b) in construing a contract we seek to ascertain what the parties intended and, in so doing, we consider the circumstances, the situation of the parties, the objects they have in mind and the nature of the subject matter of the contract; (c) "However broad may be the apparent terms of the agreement, it extends only to those things concerning which the parties intended to contract, and the subject-matter of their negotiations may affect the meaning of the words they employ, especially if, in connection with that subject-matter, the conventional interpretation would give an unreasonable or absurd result." *United Refining Co. v. Jenkins*, 410 Pa. 126, 137–38, 189 A.2d 574, 580 (1963) (citations omitted) (emphasis deleted).

Courts are left with the difficult issue of determining as a matter of law which category written contract terms fall into — clear or ambiguous. There is a point at which interpretation becomes alteration of the written contract. We must determine if the trial judge went beyond that point.

Ambiguity is defined as: Intellectual uncertainty; . . . the condition of admitting of two or more meanings, of being understood in more than one way, or referring to two or more things at the same time . . . WEBSTER'S THIRD NEW INTERNATIONAL DICTIONARY (unabr. 1971).

A court must have a reference point to determine if words may reasonably admit

---

that the evidence is admissible because the written contract is not fully integrated. The issue becomes whether the proffered evidence is extrinsic to the integrated written contract, and thus inadmissible, or whether the proffered evidence is part and parcel of the entire contract of which the written document is only a part.

Though it may be asserted that Pennsylvania courts employ a strict "four corners" approach to issues of integration, we do not believe this approach is required by Pennsylvania decisions in regard to the issue of ambiguity.

of different meanings. Under a "four corners" approach a judge sits in chambers and determines from his point of view whether the written words before him are ambiguous. An alternative approach is for the judge to hear the proffer of the parties and determine if there is objective indicia that, from the linguistic reference point of the parties, the terms of the contract are susceptible of different meanings. We believe the latter to be the correct approach.

It is the role of the judge to consider the words of the contract, the alternative meaning suggested by counsel, and the nature of the objective evidence to be offered in support of that meaning. The trial judge must then determine if a full evidentiary hearing is warranted. If a *reasonable* alternative interpretation is suggested, even though it may be alien to the judge's linguistic experience, objective evidence in support of that interpretation should be considered by the fact finder.[69] *See* CORBIN, CONTRACTS § 542.

An analysis of Pennsylvania cases demonstrates that this approach is in accord with practice in the Pennsylvania courts.[70] Accordingly we conclude that it was proper for the court here to consider extrinsic evidence.

But our approach does not authorize a trial judge to demote the written word to a reduced status in contract interpretation. Although extrinsic evidence may be considered under proper circumstances, the parties remain bound by the appropriate objective definition of the words they use to express their intent. Generally parties will be held to definitions given to words in specialized commercial and trade areas in which they deal. Similarly, certain words attain binding definition as legal terms of art. Dates, numbers and the like generally cannot be varied. For example, extrinsic evidence may be used to show that "Ten Dollars paid on January 5, 1980,"

---

[69] [12] It is only by this approach that courts can achieve consistency in contract interpretation.

The strict "four-corners" doctrine allows a court to sit in an isolated position and decide if words are "clear" or "ambiguous." Judges today come from a variety of backgrounds — private law practice, government service, business, academia — and their fields of experience represent an even wider variance. The parties who appear before the court in these times of complex commercial transactions come from a variety of specialized worlds of trade. It is the parties' linguistic reference that is relevant, not the judges'. The judge is in his or her linguistic field of expertise only when viewing words which lawyers have developed as terms of legal art. Even when the judge faces the need to interpret legal terms of art, extrinsic evidence and legal briefing are useful.

For example, a contract might provide for a party to pay "$10,000 for 100 ounces of platinum." A judge might state that the quoted words are so clear and unambiguous that parol evidence is not admissible to vary their meaning. That judge might never learn that the parties have a consistent past practice of dealing only in Canadian dollars and follow a standard trade practice of measuring platinum in troy ounces (12 to the pound instead of 16). This is because that judge's linguistic frame of reference includes the dollars and the ounces he or she encounters in daily life. That is not the linguistic frame of reference of the commercial parties.

. . . .

[70] [13] Confusion is often caused by the use of the term "ambiguous on its face." *See* Merriam v. Cedarbrook Realty, Inc., 266 Pa. Super. 252, 404 A.2d 398, 401 (1978). A requirement of "facial ambiguity" might mean that a court should look exclusively at the "face" of a contract to determine if words are ambiguous. However, we are not aware of any cases where Pennsylvania courts have construed a writing, declared it unambiguous, and ruled that any consideration of an argument for ambiguity must be disregarded. Much to the contrary, many cases which hold words unambiguous do so only after an examination of circumstances and facts demonstrate that any variation of the words would be an impermissible rewriting of the contract.

meant ten Canadian dollars, but it would not be allowed to show the parties meant twenty dollars. Trade terms, legal terms of art, numbers, common words of accepted usage and terms of a similar nature should be interpreted in accord with their specialized or accepted usage unless such an interpretation would produce irrational results or the contract documents are internally inconsistent.

We have concluded that the district court here exceeded the permissible boundary of interpretation. We believe its interpretation of insolvency was improperly restrictive. Commercial parties entered a Buy-Sell Agreement using a well defined commercial term and legal term of art — "insolvent." The court rejected the test which we believe an attorney or commercial creditor would use to determine if the borrowers were insolvent in any other context, and instead substituted a test for insolvency which excluded certain liabilities of the borrowers. This variation of the written words used in the contract was not justified by the evidence received. When the district judge received Mellon's evidence it should have rejected it as insufficient to vary the meaning of a commercial term as well established as "insolvent." In this case the district court added a term which made the condition a nullity. It ruled that, although the solvency of the borrowers was a condition in the written contract, the fact that the borrowers' solvency was not significantly considered by Aetna in evaluating the take-out loan minimized or nullified this clause of the contract.

The condition that the borrowers not be insolvent was added by Aetna and retained in the contract over Mellon's protests. The fact that the insolvency of the borrowers was not significantly considered by Aetna in evaluating the take-out loan is immaterial given the expression of that concern in the written words of the contract. The fact that Aetna thought it bore some risk of default if the occupancy rate of the project fell too low was not sufficient to vary the normal commercial meaning of the word "insolvent." Of course Aetna bore some risk of default — Aetna's funding obligation extended over a ten year period. There was no substantial evidence for Mellon's interpretation of the contract other than evidence tending to show that Aetna was not significantly concerned with the borrowers' solvency until they desired an "out" to excuse their obligation to purchase a loan which had become unsound. Fortunately for Aetna it retained that "out" in the Buy-Sell Agreement despite specific objections from Mellon. *See* Testimony of DeLuca, Record at 515a–518a. At best, Mellon's officers admitted that they knew the insolvency clause was adverse to Mellon's interests, but they didn't "really" know what it meant. Testimony of DeLuca, Record at 518a. Mellon's evidence was simply insufficient to vary the clear meaning of the commercial term "insolvent."

Our holding the parties to a generally accepted commercial interpretation of the word "insolvency" in no way produces an irrational result. Aetna was to undertake the risk of a decline in the real estate market for ten years after it purchased the construction loan. Mellon was at risk of construction not being completed on time and within cost. The issue is who bore the risk that the borrowers' financial reserves could not carry the project from the date of the Buy-Sell Agreement to the closing on the permanent financing — i.e., who bore the risk of a decline in the Atlanta real estate market from July of 1974 to August of 1975. It is not irrational to place that risk on Mellon, nor is it irrational to place it on Aetna. Aetna inserted the insolvency clause in the commitment. Mellon demanded that the clause be excluded from the Buy-Sell Agreement. Aetna refused. When Mellon signed the agreement notwithstanding the inclusion of the clause, it became bound by the usual meaning of insolvency. This result is not irrational and therefore does not compel the alternative meaning of insolvency suggested by Mellon. Mellon cannot now insert an exception to the solvency condition. "Where one of two innocent persons must sustain a loss, the law will place that burden on the party that has agreed to sustain it." *F.J. Busse, Inc. v. Department of General Services*, 47 Pa. Cmwlth. 539, 408 A.2d 578, 580 (1979). See *International Systems, Inc. v. Personnel Data Systems*, slip. op. (Pa. Superior Ct., Jan. 18, 1980).

Accordingly, we conclude that in determining the insolvency of the borrowers the district court must include all the assets and liabilities of the borrowers in applying both generally accepted commercial tests for insolvency. The notion of insolvency is measured both by a balance sheet showing all assets and liabilities and the test of whether one can meet current debts as persons engaged in a trade normally do.

NOTES

(1)   In *Bohler-Uddeholm America, Inc. v. Ellwood Group, Inc.*, 247 F.3d 79, 92–93 (3d Cir. 2001), the cout states:

> Pennsylvania law on ambiguity in contracts thus seems to contain a built-in tension between two principles: (1) a contract is not ambiguous, and thus must be interpreted on its face without reference to extrinsic evidence, "if the court can determine its meaning without any guide other than a knowledge of the simple facts on which, from the nature of the language in general, its meaning depends," and (2) contractual terms that are clear on their face can be latently ambiguous, and "Pennsylvania law permits courts to examine certain forms of extrinsic evidence in determining whether a contract is ambiguous." Thus, when a court is faced with a contract containing facially unambiguous language, it seems that Pennsylvania law both requires that the court interpret the language without using extrinsic evidence, and allows the court to bring in extrinsic evidence to prove latent ambiguity.

> Mellon Bank resolves this tension by allowing only extrinsic evidence of a certain nature to establish latent ambiguity in a contract; a court should determine whether the type of extrinsic evidence offered could be used to support a reasonable alternative interpretation under the precepts of Pennsylvania law on contract interpretation. Once the court determines that a party has offered extrinsic evidence capable of establishing latent ambiguity, a decision as to which of the competing interpretations of the contract is the correct one is reserved for the factfinder, who would examine the content of the extrinsic evidence (along with all the other evidence) in order to make this determination.

(2)   *Interpretation and the Parol Evidence Rule.* RESTATEMENT (SECOND) OF CONTRACTS § 200 states, "Interpretation of a promise or agreement or a term thereof is the ascertainment of its meaning." Interpretation is a process that has nothing to do with the parol evidence rule, i.e., interpretation evidence is not proffered to alter or add to the terms of the writing. Rather, it is proffered to determine the meaning

of the writing or other manifestation of intention. As one court observed, "No parol evidence can be said to *contradict* a writing until, by process of interpretation, it is determined what the writing means." *Tigg Corp. v. Dow Corning Corp.*, 822 F.2d 358, 362 (3d Cir. 1987).

(3)   *Who Decides?* Since interpretation deals with the meaning of language, one might expect it to be characterized as a matter of factual determination and thus within the province of the jury. However, the notion that questions of fact are for the jury while questions of law are for the judge is a tautology. It is an open secret that certain fact questions are decided by judges. Early courts distrusted jurors, many of whom were illiterate. Even modern courts recognize the desirability of leaving questions of interpretation to courts, who are allegedly better able to deal with such questions and who will provide a measure of stability and predictability, particularly in cases involving the interpretation of printed forms. *See* RESTATEMENT (SECOND) OF CONTRACTS § 212, comment d. Leaving interpretation questions to the courts also preserves judicial review. Thus, even recognizing the question as one of fact, Justice Traynor insisted that interpretation "is essentially a judicial function to be exercised according to the generally accepted canons of interpretation." *Parsons v. Bristol Dev. Co.*, 62 Cal. 2d 861, 865, 402 P.2d 839, 842 (1965). Unless interpretation depends upon extrinsic evidence or a choice among reasonable inferences to be drawn from that evidence, the question of interpretation is for the court, and its interpretation is subject to appellate review.

(4)   *Interpretation Versus Construction.* If the question is one of the *legal effect* of the parties' expression rather than the meaning of that expression, the process has often been called *construction* rather than interpretation. *See* 3 CORBIN ON CONTRACTS § 534. Interpretation must precede construction. Though this distinction is sound, the untidy fashion in which courts may use the term "construction" to mean "interpretation" affects the utility of the distinction. *See, e.g., American Med. Intern v. Scheller*, 462 So. 2d 1, 7 (Fla. App. 1984).

(5)   *Whose Meaning Should Prevail?* As the principal case suggests, the notion that a judge may retire to his or her chambers and perform the interpretation process simply by reading the document with no evidence as to the surrounding circumstances is a "plain meaning" view of interpretation which no longer generates any significant support. Dean Wigmore pointed to the fallacy of assuming that there is or ever can be some one real or absolute meaning of language. 9 WIGMORE EVIDENCE § 2462. Professor Corbin emasculated the view that words can have only one interpretation by convincing any holder of that view that he has already given the words an interpretation, i.e., his own, which suggests that any other interpretation is necessarily perverted and untrue. Corbin, *The Interpretation of Words and the Parol Evidence Rule*, 50 CORNELL L.Q. 161, 171–72 (1965). Justice Holmes rejected the plain meaning view at the end of the nineteenth century: "A word is not a crystal, transparent and unchanged; it is the skin of a living thought and may vary greatly in color and content according to the circumstances and the time in which it is used." Holmes, *The Theory of Legal Interpretation*, 12 HARV. L. REV. 417, 420 (1899), based upon his famous opinion in *Goode v. Riley*, 153 Mass. 585, 586, 28 N.E. 228 (1891).

Rejection of the "plain meaning" standard, however, does not fully answer the question "Whose meaning shall prevail?" The RESTATEMENT (FIRST) OF CONTRACTS listed six possible standards of interpretation.[71]

If the parties had an integrated writing, i.e., one they had adopted as a final and complete expression of their agreement, the standard applied was that of *limited usage* — the meaning to be attached by a reasonably intelligent person acquainted with all operative usages and knowing all of the circumstances prior to and contemporaneous with the integration — other than statements by the parties of what they actually intended their final and complete writing to mean. This standard would allow a court to discover a meaning different from that which either party supposed it to have. (RESTATEMENT (FIRST) OF CONTRACTS § 230, comment b). Professor Corbin "flatly disapproved" of this view, suggesting that "[n]o contract should ever be interpreted and enforced with a meaning that neither party gave it." 3 Corbin § 572B (1971 Supp.). Where, for example, *A* intends to sell Blackacre, *B* intends to buy Whiteacre, and the final writing of the parties describes Greenacre, the enforcement of the contract for the sale of Greenacre was, to Corbin, holding "justice up to ridicule." 3 CORBIN ON CONTRACTS § 539, at 81. There are, however, several statements by JUDGE LEARNED HAND to the effect that the actual intention of the parties is irrelevant.[72] If the application of the *limited usage* standard to an integrated writing produced an uncertain or ambiguous result, a different standard was then used, i.e., the standard applied to unintegrated agreements.

With respect to unintegrated agreements, the *reasonable expectation* standard was applied, i.e., the standard of the reasonable expectation of the party manifesting assent of the meaning his words or other manifestations would convey to the other party (RESTATEMENT (FIRST) OF CONTRACTS § 227, comment a). *See* MURRAY ON CONTRACTS at § 88A.

The RESTATEMENT (SECOND) OF CONTRACTS suggests a Corbin approach. "The primary search is for a common meaning of the parties, not a meaning imposed on

---

[71] RESTATEMENT (FIRST) OF CONTRACTS § 227, comment a: (1) General usage — what the hypothetical average person would understand the expression to mean — the "popular" standard; (2) Limited usage — the meaning ascribed to the expression in a particular locality, trade or profession (a constriction of the first standard differing only in degree); (3) Mutual standard — the meaning that conforms to the intention of the parties to the contract, even if such meaning violates common and other usages; (4) Individual standard — the meaning intended by the expressing party or the understanding of the party to whom the expression was directed; (5) Reasonable expectation — the meaning which the expressing party should reasonably expect the expression would convey to the other party; (6) Reasonable understanding — the meaning which the party to whom the manifestations are addressed would reasonably give to such expressions.

[72] *See, e.g., Eustis Mining Co. v. Beer, Sondheimer & Co.*, 239 F. 976, 985 (S.D.N.Y. 1917): "[I]f both parties severally declared that their meaning had been other than the natural meaning, and each declaration was similar, it would be irrelevant, saving some mutual agreement between them to that effect." In *New York Trust Co. v. Island Oil & Transp. Corp.*, 34 F.2d 655, 656 (2d Cir. 1929): "[C]ontracts depend upon the meaning which the law imputes to the utterances, not upon what the parties actually intended . . . ." In *Hotchkiss v. National City Bank*, 200 F. 287, 293, (S.D.N.Y. 1911), we find, "A contract has, strictly speaking, nothing to do with the personal or individual intent of the parties." But later, he added, "Of course, if it appear by other words, or acts, of the parties, that they attribute a peculiar meaning to such words as they use in the contract, that meaning will prevail, but only by virtue of the other words, and not because of their unexpressed intent."

them by law." RESTATEMENT (SECOND) OF CONTRACTS § 201, comment c.

[2]   Rules, Guides, and Maxims

A number of common sense rules, which are better viewed as mere guides or aids to interpretation, can be found in the case law from the earliest times to the present. They are sometimes stated as "maxims" of interpretation or construction. While the student should be aware of these guides, the maxims should not be viewed as conclusive, although in some situations one or more can tip the balance in favor of one interpretation or construction over another.

(1) *Contextual Interpretation — Surrounding Circumstances.* It is generally said that courts must consider all of the surrounding circumstances prior to and contemporaneous with the making of the contract so as to more precisely identify the sense in which the parties used the expressions of agreement. Similarly, the expressions of the parties must be viewed in their context. This is a relatively modern view, overcoming the notion that the document evidencing the contract speaks for itself.[73]

(2) *Purpose of the Parties.* One of the more helpful guides to interpretation is the discovery of the *purpose* of the parties. What was the apparent objective of the parties with respect to the contract in general and/or with respect to a particular clause in the contract? What were they apparently attempting to accomplish?

(3) *The Transaction Must be Viewed as a Whole.* Innumerable cases state that all of the different parts of the agreement must be viewed together, as a whole, and each part interpreted in the light of all of the other parts. As RESTATEMENT (SECOND) OF CONTRACTS § 80, comment d, suggests, "A word changes meaning when it becomes part of a sentence, the sentence when it becomes part of a paragraph." Courts prefer an interpretation which gives meaning to all parts of the agreement as contrasted with an interpretation that fails to give meaning to one or more parts.

(4) *Reasonable, Lawful or Effective Interpretation Preferred.* Another common sense guide to interpretation is the preference for an interpretation that is reasonable under the circumstances rather than a literal interpretation that would lead to absurd results. Thus, an interpretation of language that would have result in a $7,000 forfeit for an uncompleted repair costing $50 was rejected as absurd.[74]

A legal, just and fair interpretation will be preferred.[75]

(5) *Public Interest Favored.* If there is a reasonable choice in the interpretation of language, the construction favoring the public interest will be favored. Thus, where the government is party to a contract, a construction in favor of the government favors the public.[76]

---

[73] *See, e.g.*, Diamond v. Gulf Coast Trailing Co., 180 F.3d 518 (3d Cir. 1999).

[74] Brown v. Hotard, 428 So. 2d 505 (La. App. 1983).

[75] *See, e.g.*, Diamond v. Gulf Coast Trailing Co., 180 F.3d 518 (3d Cir. 1999).

[76] *See* Codell Constr. Co. v. Commonwealth of Ky., 566 S.W.2d 161 (1977).

(6) *Contra Proferentem.* Generally, the agreement will be interpreted against the party responsible for its drafting.[77] This guide is particularly applicable if the contract document has been prepared by the skilled adviser of one of the parties or if the person drafting the document had special competence in such matters. This "rule" is frequently found in cases involving insurance contracts or other standardized documents with printed terms.

(7) *Noscitur a sociis* refers to a term that should be "known by the company it keeps" or "known by its neighbors. In *Smedley Co. v. Employers Mut. Liab. Ins. Co.*, 123 A. 2d 755 (Conn. 1956), an insurance policy limited liability to goods "manufactured, sold, handled or distributed" by the insured. The term "handled" was construed to be limited by the accompanying words which excluded goods belonging to a third party that the insured had neither manufactured, sold or distributed but had merely placed them on a platform for removal.

(8) *Expressio Unius Est Exclusio Alterius.* A clause in a contract may specify certain items. This guide suggests that the expression in the contract of one or more things of a class implies the exclusion of all not expressed. Like other guides, this aid is not conclusive. Where a lease expressly permitted only two types of modifications to the property, under this maxim the court held that a reasonable inference is that other changes that were not listed were not permitted.[78]

(9) *Ejusdem Generis.* Where the contract document contains general language followed by the enumeration of specific items, the meaning of the general language is said to be limited to matters similar in kind or classification to the enumerated specific terms. Thus, where a lease contract could be terminated for "good cause" and this general language was followed by enumerated items such as nonpayment of rent, serious or repeated damage to the premises or the creation of physical hazards, the general phrase "for good cause" did not include other violations of the lease such as keeping a dog on the premises.[79] This rule may be avoided by language indicating that the general language includes but is not limited to the enumerated items following it.[80]

(10) *Other Presumptions.* (i) The ordinary or popular sense of words as used throughout the country will be preferred absent countervailing evidence as to the parties' intention; (ii) technical terms and words of art are to be given their technical meaning absent contrary circumstances; (iii) words with an established legal meaning will be given that interpretation absent evidence of a contrary understanding; (iv) the usage of a trade, locality, profession or the like will supersede the ordinary or popular sense of words where that assumption is justified; (v) specific terms will usually be held to qualify general terms because

---

[77] *See, e.g.*, Monovis, Inc. v. Aquino, 9905 F. Supp. 1205, 1229–30 (W. D. N. Y. 1994).

[78] Two Guys From Harrison-N.Y. v. S. F. R. Realty Assocs., 472 N. E. 2d 315 (N. Y. 1984).

[79] *See* Housing Auth. of Mansfield v. Rovig, 676 S.W.2d 314 (Mo. App. 1984). Like other guides, this principle is often used in statutory interpretation. In Bazuaye v. United States of America, 83 F.3d 482, 484 (D.C. App. 1996), the court illustrates the guide as follows: "Thus if a statute lists 'fishing rods, nets, hooks, bobbers, sinkers and other equipment,' 'other equipment' might mean plastic worms and fishing line, but not snow shovels or baseball hats."

[80] *See* Eastern Air Lines v. McDonnell Douglas Corp., 532 F.2d 957 (5th Cir. 1976).

specific terms normally suggest a more precise identification of the parties' intentions; (vi) a word or phrase used more than once is interpreted in the same sense throughout the contract; (vii) Obvious mistakes of grammar or punctuation will be corrected or disregarded to the extent that they conflict with a clear intention expressed in the contract; (viii) conflicts between printed and typewritten (or word processed) provisions favor the latter since more conscious attention is directed toward the latter — similarly, handwritten provisions will be favored over typewritten provisions, as separately negotiated terms will be preferred over prefabricated provisions. This is simply another species of the fundamental notion that the specific controls the general; (ix) where inconsistent intentions are manifested in different clauses, the intention manifested in the principal or more important clause is favored. For more on these guides, see MURRAY ON CONTRACTS § 89.

[3]   Meaning of the Parties

PROBLEMS

(1)   *The meaning of "property."* The defendant agreed to supply the labor and materials necessary to remove and replace the upper metal cover of the plaintiff's steam turbine. The defendant agreed to perform all of the work at its own risk and expense and to "indemnify (save harmless) the plaintiff against all loss, damage, expense and liability resulting from injury to property arising out of or in any way connected with the performance of this contract." During the work, the cover fell, injuring the exposed rotor of the plaintiff's turbine. The plaintiff claimed damages of $25,441.51 (the cost of repairs). The defendant offered to prove by admissions to the plaintiff's agents, by defendant's conduct under similar contracts with the plaintiff and by other proof that the clause was designed to protect against injury to the property of third parties, not the plaintiff's own property. Though the trial court observed that the language of the indemnity provision was classic language for such clauses and one could very easily conclude that it was intended to indemnify third parties, the "plain language" of the clause required the defendant the plaintiff for injuries to the plaintiff's own property. What result on appeal? See *Pacific Gas & E. Co. v. Thomas Drayage Co.*, 442 P.2d 641 (Cal. 1968).

(2)   *The meaning of "adverse."* TWF contracted to harvest and vine 120 acres of peas which had been staggered in planting to assure different maturity dates, thereby allowing the entire crop to be properly harvested over a certain period. The contract provided an excuse for TWF "resulting from adverse weather conditions." The weather conditions proved to be so perfect that the peas matured simultaneously. Since the crops of other parties did the same, there was a considerable shortage of labor and equipment to harvest crops. TWF could not harvest all of the peas in time and relied upon the quoted clause as an excuse for its non-performance. Can "adverse weather conditions" mean "perfect weather conditions"? *See Stender v. Twin City Foods, Inc.*, 82 Wash. 2d 250, 510 P.2d 221 (1973).

(3)   *The meaning of "wife."* Ira Soper drafted suicide notes to his wife, Adeline, before disappearing without a trace. His car containing some clothing was found near a canal in Louisville, Kentucky. He later reappeared in Minneapolis as John

Young where he married Gertrude and took out a $5,000 insurance policy on his own life naming his "wife" as beneficiary. Subsequently, he did commit suicide and the insurance proceeds were paid to Gertrude. Adeline reappeared and brought an action against Gertrude for the proceeds. What result? *See In re Soper's Estate*, 196 Minn. 60, 264 N.W. 427 (1935).

[4] Vague or Equivocal Meanings

FRIGALIMENT IMPORTING CO. v. B.N.S. INTERNATIONAL SALES CORP.

United States District Court, Southern District of New York
190 F. Supp. 116 (1960)

FRIENDLY, CIRCUIT JUDGE.

The issue is, what is chicken? Plaintiff says "chicken" means a young chicken, suitable for broiling and frying. Defendant says "chicken" means any bird of that genus that meets contract specifications on weight and quality, including what it calls "stewing chicken" and plaintiff pejoratively terms "fowl." Dictionaries give both meanings, as well as some others not relevant here. To support its [claim], plaintiff sends a number of volleys over the net; defendant essays to return them and adds a few serves of its own. Assuming that both parties were acting in good faith, the case nicely illustrates HOLMES' remark "that the making of a contract depends not on the agreement of two minds in one intention, but on the agreement of two sets of external signs — not on the parties' having *meant* the same thing but on their having *said* the same thing." *The Path of the Law*, in COLLECTED LEGAL PAPERS, p. 178. I have concluded that plaintiff has not sustained its burden of persuasion that the contract used "chicken" in the narrower sense.

The action is for breach of the warranty that goods sold shall correspond to the description, New York Personal Property Law, McKinney's Consol. Laws, c. 41, § 95. Two contracts are in suit. In the first, dated May 2, 1957, defendant, a New York sales corporation, confirmed the sale to plaintiff, a Swiss corporation, of

> US Fresh Frozen Chicken, Grade A, Government Inspected, Eviscerated 2 1 2 -3 lbs. and 1 1 2 -2 lbs. each all chicken individually wrapped in cryovac, packed in secured fiber cartons or wooden boxes, suitable for export

| 75,000 | lbs. | 2 | 1 | 2 | -3 | lbs. | @ | $33.00 |
| 25,000 | lbs. | 1 | 1 | 2 | -2 | lbs. | @ | $36.50 |

> per 100 lbs. FAS New York

> scheduled May 10, 1957 pursuant to instructions from Penson & Co., New York.

The second contract, also dated May 2, 1957, was identical save that only 50,000 lbs. of the heavier "chicken" were called for, the price of the smaller birds was $37 per 100 lbs., and shipment was scheduled for May 30. The initial shipment under the first contract was short but the balance was shipped on May 17. When the initial shipment arrived in Switzerland, plaintiff found, on May 28, that the 2 1 2 -3 lbs. birds were not young chicken suitable for broiling and frying but stewing chicken or "fowl"; indeed, many of the cartons and bags plainly so indicated. Protests ensued. Nevertheless, shipment under the second contract was made on May 29, the 2 1 2 -3 lbs. birds again being stewing chicken. Defendant stopped the transportation of these at Rotterdam.

Since the word "chicken" standing alone is ambiguous, I turn first to see whether the contract itself offers any aid to its interpretation. Plaintiff says the 1 1 2 -2 lbs. birds necessarily had to be young chicken since the older birds do not come in that size, hence the 2 1 2 -3 lbs. birds must likewise be young. This is unpersuasive — a contract for "apples" of two different sizes could be filled with different kinds of apples even though only one species came in both sizes. Defendant notes that the contract called not simply for chicken but for "US Fresh Frozen Chicken, Grade A, Government Inspected." It says the contract thereby incorporated by reference the Department of Agriculture's regulations, which favor its interpretation; I shall return to this after reviewing plaintiff's other contentions.

The first hinges on an exchange of cablegrams which preceded execution of the formal contracts. The negotiations leading up to the contracts were conducted in New York between defendant's secretary, Ernest R. Bauer, and a Mr. Stovicek, who was in New York for the Czechoslovak government at the World Trade Fair. A few days after meeting Bauer at the fair, Stovicek telephoned and inquired whether defendant would be interested in exporting poultry to Switzerland. Bauer then met with Stovicek, who showed him a cable from plaintiff dated April 26, 1957, announcing that they "are buyer" of 25,000 lbs. of chicken 2 1 2 -3 lbs. weight, Cryovac packed, grade A Government inspected, at a price up to 3 per pound, for shipment on May 10, to be confirmed by the following morning, and were interested in further offerings. After testing the market for price, Bauer accepted, and Stovicek sent a confirmation that evening. Plaintiff stresses that, although these and subsequent cables between plaintiff and defendant, which laid the basis for the additional quantities under the first and for all of the second contract, were predominantly in German, they used the English word "chicken"; it claims this was done because it understood "chicken" meant young chicken whereas the German word, "Huhn," included both "Brathuhn" (broilers) and "Suppenhuhn" (stewing chicken), and that defendant, whose officers were thoroughly conversant with German, should have realized this. Whatever force this argument might otherwise have is largely drained away by Bauer's testimony that he asked Stovicek what kind of chickens were wanted, received the answer "any kind of chickens," and then, in German, asked whether the cable meant "Huhn" and received an affirmative response . . . .

Plaintiff's next contention is that there was a definite trade usage that "chicken" meant "young chicken." Defendant showed that it was only beginning in the poultry trade in 1957, thereby bringing itself within the principle that "when one of the parties is not a member of the trade or other circle, his acceptance of the standard must be made to appear" by proving either that he had actual knowledge of the usage or that the usage is "so generally known in the community that his actual individual knowledge of it may be inferred." 9 Wigmore, Evidence (3d ed. 1940) § 2464. Here there was no proof of actual knowledge of the alleged usage; indeed, it is quite plain that defendant's belief was to the contrary. In order to meet the alternative requirement, the law of New York demands a showing that "the usage is of so long continuance, so well established, so notorious, so universal and so reasonable in itself, as that the presumption is violent that the parties contracted with reference to it, and made it a part of their agreement." *Walls v. Bailey*, 1872, 49 N.Y. 464, 472–473.

Plaintiff endeavored to establish such a usage by the testimony of three witnesses and certain other evidence. Strasser, resident buyer in New York for a large chain of Swiss cooperatives, testified that "on chicken I would definitely understand a broiler." However, the force of this testimony was considerably weakened by the fact that in his own transactions the witness, a careful business-man, protected himself by using "broiler" when that was what he wanted and "fowl" when he wished older birds. Indeed, there are some indications, dating back to a remark of Lord Mansfield, *Edie v. East India Co.*, 2 Burr. 1216, 1222 (1761), that no credit should be given "witnesses to usage, who could not adduce instances in verification." 7 WIGMORE, EVIDENCE (3d ed. 1940) § 1954 . . . . While Wigmore thinks this goes too far, a witness' consistent failure to rely on the alleged usage deprives his opinion testimony of much of its effect. Niesielowski, an officer of one of the companies that had furnished the stewing chicken to defendant, testified that "chicken" meant "the male species of the poultry industry. That could be a broiler, a fryer or a roaster," but not a stewing chicken; however, he also testified that upon receiving defendant's inquiry for "chickens," he asked whether the desire was for "fowl or frying chickens" and, in fact, supplied fowl, although taking the precaution of asking defendant, a day or two after plaintiff's acceptance of the contracts in suit, to change its confirmation of its order from "chickens," as defendant had originally prepared it, to "stewing chickens." Dates, an employee of Urner-Barry Company, which publishes a daily market report on the poultry trade, gave it as his view that the trade meaning of "chicken" was "broilers and fryers." In addition to this opinion testimony, plaintiff relied on the fact that the Urner-Barry service, the Journal of Commerce, and Weinberg Bros. & Co. of Chicago, a large supplier of poultry, published quotations in a manner which, in one way or another, distinguish between "chicken," comprising broilers, fryers and certain other categories, and "fowl," which, Bauer acknowledged, included stewing chickens. This material would be impressive if there were nothing to the contrary. However, there was, as will now be seen.

Defendant's witness Weininger, who operates a chicken eviscerating plant in New Jersey, testified "Chicken is everything except a goose, a duck, and a turkey. Everything is a chicken, but then you have to say, you have to specify which category you want or that you are talking about." Its witness Fox said that in the trade "chicken" would encompass all the various classifications. Sadina, who conducts a food inspection service, testified that he would consider any bird coming within the classes of "chicken" in the Department of Agriculture's regulations to be a chicken. The specifications approved by General Services Administration include fowl as well as broilers and fryers under the classification "chickens." Statistics of the Institute of American Poultry Industries use the phrases "Young chickens" and "Mature chickens," under the general heading "Total chickens[,]" and the Department of Agriculture's daily and weekly price reports avoid use of the word "chicken" without specification.

Defendant advances several other points which it claims affirmatively support its construction. Primary among these is the regulation of the Department of Agriculture, 7 C.F.R. § 70.300–70.370, entitled, "Grading and Inspection of Poultry and Edible Products Thereof," and in particular § 70.301 which recited:

Chickens. The following are the various classes of chickens:

    (a) Broiler or fryer . . .

    (b) Roaster . . .

    (c) Capon . . .

    (d) Stag . . .

    (e) Hen or stewing chicken or fowl . . .

    (f) Cock or old rooster . . . .

Defendant argues, as previously noted, that the contract incorporated these regulations by reference. Plaintiff answers that the contract provision related simply to grade and Government inspection and did not incorporate the Government definition of "chicken," and also that the definition in the Regulations is ignored in the trade. However, the latter contention was contradicted by Weininger and Sadina; and there is force in defendant's argument that the contract made the regulations a dictionary, particularly since the reference to Government grading was already in plaintiff's initial cable to Stovicek.

Defendant makes a further argument based on the impossibility of its obtaining broilers and fryers at the 33 cents price offered by plaintiff for the 2 1 2 -3 lbs. birds. There is no substantial dispute that, in late April, 1957, the price for 2 1 2 -3 lbs. broilers was between 35 and 37 cents per pound, and that when defendant entered into the contracts, it was well aware of this and intended to fill them by supplying fowl in these weights. It claims that plaintiff must likewise have known the market since plaintiff had reserved shipping space on April 23, three days before plaintiff's cable to Stovicek, or, at least, that Stovicek was chargeable with such knowledge. It is scarcely an answer to say, as plaintiff does in its brief, that the 33 cents price offered by the 2 1 2 -3 lbs. "chickens" was closer to the prevailing 35 cents price for broilers than the 30 cents at which defendant procured fowl. Plaintiff must have expected defendant to make some profit — certainly it could not have expected defendant deliberately to incur a loss.

Finally, defendant relies on conduct by the plaintiff after the first shipment had been received. On May 28 plaintiff sent two cables complaining that the larger birds in the first shipment constituted "fowl." Defendant answered with a cable refusing to recognize plaintiff's objection and announcing "We have today ready for shipment 50,000 lbs. chicken 2 1 2 -3 lbs.[,] 25,000 lbs. broilers 1 1 2 -2 lbs.," these being the goods procured for shipment under the second contract, and asked immediate answer "whether we are to ship this merchandise to you and whether you will accept the merchandise." After several other cable exchanges, plaintiff replied on May 29 "Confirm again that merchandise is to be shipped since resold by us if not enough pursuant to contract chickens are shipped the missing quantity is to be shipped within ten days stop we resold to our customers pursuant to your contract chickens grade A you have to deliver us said merchandise we again state that we shall make you fully responsible for all resulting costs." Defendant argues that if plaintiff was sincere in thinking it was entitled to young chickens, plaintiff would not have allowed the shipment under the second contract to go forward, since the distinction between broilers and chickens drawn in defendant's cablegram must have made it clear that the larger birds would not be broilers. However, plaintiff answers that the cables show plaintiff was insisting on delivery of young chickens and that defendant shipped old ones at its peril. Defendant's point would be highly relevant on another disputed issue — whether if liability were established, the measure of damages should be the difference in market value of broilers and stewing chicken in New York or the larger difference in Europe, but I cannot give it weight on the issue of interpretation. Defendant points out also that plaintiff proceeded to deliver some of the larger birds in Europe, describing them as "poulets"; defendant argues that it was only when plaintiff's customers complained about this that plaintiff developed the idea that "chicken" meant "young chicken." There is little force in this in view of plaintiff's immediate and consistent protests.

When all the evidence is reviewed, it is clear that defendant believed it could comply with the contracts by delivering stewing chicken in the 2 1 2 -3 lbs. size. Defendant's subjective intent would not be significant if this did not coincide with an objective meaning of "chicken." Here it did coincide with one of the dictionary meanings, with the definition in the Department of Agriculture Regulations to which the contract made at least oblique reference, with at least some usage in the trade, with the realities of the market, and with what plaintiff's spokesman has said. Plaintiff asserts it to be equally plain that plaintiff's own subjective intent was to obtain broilers and fryers; the only evidence against this is the material as to market prices and this may not have been sufficiently brought home. In any event it is unnecessary to determine that issue. For plaintiff has the burden of showing that "chicken" was used in the narrower rather than in the broader sense, and this it has not sustained.

This opinion constitutes the Court's findings of fact and conclusions of law. Judgment shall be entered dismissing the complaint with costs.

NOTE

Professor Corbin argues that "chicken" has more than one *objective* meaning and the problem before the court was how the term was used in this context by the parties. Since the buyer sued for damages, the buyer had the burden of showing that the seller either knew or had reason to know that the buyer intended to buy only broilers or fryers rather than "fowl." It failed to sustain that burden and this is why it lost the case, not because it failed to show that *an* objective meaning of the term "chicken" was limited to broilers and fryers. RESTATEMENT (SECOND) OF CONTRACTS § 201 bases one of its illustrations on this case but changes the facts by having the buyer reject the shipment of chicken. Each party then claims damages against the other. Both parties acted in good faith and neither had reason to know of the difference in the meaning of "chicken" attributed by the other. The illustration concludes: "Both claims fail." Thus, if the seller had sued the buyer in the actual case for its refusal to accept the tendered chicken, the seller may not have been able to show that the buyer had reason to know of the meaning attributed by the seller. However, one should not easily assume this conclusion. "Chicken" should be viewed in a generic sense as comprising both types of chicken. Absent evidence of prior course of dealing, trade usage or other specification of "young" chickens by the purchaser, the seller's shipment of stewing chicken is justified as performance within the range of meaning embraced by the term "chicken."

The term "chicken" may be viewed as vague, i.e., as one having a "spectrum of applications." Vagueness may be remedied, at least sufficiently for judicial applications, by defining a term more precisely. If the parties had precisely defined the type of "chicken" they intended to buy and sell, any vagueness in their contract term could have been cured. "Chicken" may also be viewed as an equivocal term, i.e. one with a double meaning, if it may be treated as meaning one type of chicken ("young") or the other ("fowl").

[5] Latent Ambiguity

RAFFLES v. WICHELHAUS
Court of the Exchequer
2 H. & C. 906 (1864)

Declaration: for that it was agreed between the plaintiff and the defendants, to wit, at Liverpool, that the plaintiff should sell to the defendants, and the defendants buy of the plaintiff, certain goods, to wit, 125 bales of Surat cotton, guaranteed middling fair merchant's Dhollerah, to arrive ex "Peerless" from Bombay; and that the cotton should be taken from the quay, and that the defendants would pay the plaintiff for the same at a certain rate, to wit, at the rate of 17 1/4 *d.* per pound, within a certain time then agreed upon after the arrival of the said goods in England. Averments: that the said goods did arrive by the said ship from Bombay in England, to wit, at Liverpool, and the plaintiff was then and there ready and willing and offered to deliver the said goods to the defendants, etc. Breach: that the defendants refused to accept the said goods or pay the plaintiff for them.

Plea: that the said ship mentioned in the said agreement was meant and intended by the defendants to be the ship called the "Peerless," which sailed from Bombay, to wit, in October; and that the plaintiff was not ready and willing and did not offer to deliver to the defendants any bales of cotton which arrived by the last-mentioned ship, but instead thereof was only ready and willing and offered to deliver to the defendants 125 bales of Surat cotton which arrived by another and different ship, which was also called the "Peerless," and which sailed from Bombay, to wit, in December.

Demurrer, and joinder therein.

Milward, in support of the demurrer. The contract was for the sale of a number of bales of cotton of a particular description, which the plaintiff was ready to deliver. It is immaterial by what ship the cotton was to arrive, so that it was a ship called the "Peerless." The words "to arrive ex 'Peerless' " only mean that, if the vessel is lost on the voyage, the contract is to be at an end. (Pollock, C. B. It would be a question for the jury whether both parties meant the same ship called the "Peerless.") That would be so if the contract was for the sale of a ship called the "Peerless"; but it is for the sale of cotton on board a ship of that name. (Pollock, C. B. The defendant only bought that cotton which was to arrive by a particular ship. It may as well be said, that, if there is a contract for the purchase of certain goods in warehouse A., that is satisfied by the delivery of goods of the same description in warehouse B.) In that case there would be goods in both warehouses; here it does not appear that the plaintiff had any goods on board the other "Peerless." (Martin, B. It is imposing on the defendant a contract different from that which he entered into. Pollock, C. B. It is like a contract for the purchase of wine coming from a particular estate in France or Spain, where there are two estates of that name.) The defendant has no right to contradict by parol evidence a written contract good upon the face of it. He does not impute misrepresentation or fraud, but only says that he fancied the ship was a different one. Intention is of no avail, unless stated at the time of the contract. (Pollock, C. B. One vessel sailed in October and the other in December.) The time of sailing is no part of the contract.

Mellish (Cohen with him), in support of the plea. There is nothing on the face of the contract to show that any particular ship called the "Peerless" was meant; but the moment it appears that two ships called the "Peerless" were about to sail from Bombay, there is a latent ambiguity, and parol evidence may be given for the purpose of showing that the defendant meant one "Peerless" and the plaintiff another. That being so, there was no consensus ad idem, and therefore no binding contract. (He was then stopped by the Court.) Per Curiam. There must be judgment for the defendants.

NOTES

(1)   In his book, *Leading Cases in the Common Law*, Professor A. W. Brian Simpson notes that the contract between William Winter Raffles and Daniel Wichelhaus and Gustav Busch involved some 50,000 pounds of cotton at a price of £3.593. There were eleven ships named Peerless sailing the seven seas at the time of this case — nine of British registry and two of American. While the ship and port were named in the contracts, the time of shipment was not named. This was not unusual. The October Peerless arrived in Liverpool in February while the December Peerless arrived in April.

(2)   RESTATEMENT (SECOND) OF CONTRACTS § 20 (1981) reads as follows:

Effect of Misunderstanding.

(1) There is no manifestation of mutual assent to an exchange if the parties attach materially different meanings to their manifestations and

(a) neither party knows or has reason to know the meaning attached by the other; or

(b) each party knows or each party has reason to know the meaning attached by the other.

(2) The manifestations of the parties are operative in accordance with the meaning attached to them by one of the parties if

(a) that party does not know of any different meaning attached by the other, and the other knows the meaning attached by the first party; or

(b) that party has no reason to know of any different meaning attached by the other, and the other has reason to know the meaning attached by the first party.

(3)   RESTATEMENT (SECOND) OF CONTRACTS § 201 states:

Whose Meaning Prevails.

(1) Where the parties have attached the same meaning to a promise or agreement or a term thereof, it is interpreted in accordance with that meaning.

(2) Where the parties have attached different meanings to a promise or agreement or a term thereof, it is interpreted in accordance with the meaning attached by one of them if at the time the agreement was made

(a) that party did not know of any different meaning attached by the other, and the other knew the meaning attached by the first party; or

(b) that party had no reason to know of any different meaning attached by the other, and the other had reason to know the meaning attached by the first party.

(3) Except as stated in this Section, neither party is bound by the meaning attached by the other, even though the result may be a failure of mutual assent.

(4)   RESTATEMENT (SECOND) OF CONTRACTS § 20 deals with contract formation, whereas Section 201 deals with interpretation. The underlying philosophy is to search for the common meaning of the parties rather than the meaning imposed by law. RESTATEMENT (SECOND) OF CONTRACTS § 201, comment c.

F. MISTAKE

[1] Mutual Mistake

HOELL v. WATERS
North Carolina Court of Appeals
347 S.E.2d 65 (1986)

WHICHARD, J.

On 4 January 1979 plaintiff purchased a tract of land from defendant. Plaintiff negotiated the terms of the purchase with Herbert Hoell, defendant's agent.

In September 1978 Hoell and plaintiff viewed the property. Hoell described the boundaries of the property to plaintiff. The boundaries of the property conveyed deviate from Hoell's incomplete representation of the boundaries so as to exclude at least 125 acres.

Hoell testified for plaintiff and admitted that he had represented to plaintiff "in a very general manner" that the southern boundary of the property was canal no. 10, the eastern boundary was the Broadcreek Outfall canal and the northern boundary was canal no. 9. Prior to making these representations, Hoell had been given a freehand sketch of the property by defendant. The sketch correctly depicted the boundaries of the property conveyed. Hoell testified that he "did not tell [plaintiff] that [he] knew where all of the boundaries of the tract were, and [he] did not know where they were."

Plaintiff has denominated his claim as one based on "mutual mistake." However, the evidence would support an action for rescission of the contract based on fraud. The essential elements of fraud are as follows:

> (1) That defendant made a representation relating to some material past or existing fact; (2) that the representation was false; (3) that when he made it, defendant knew that the representation was false, *or made it recklessly, without any knowledge of its truth and as a positive assertion;* (4) that defendant made the representation with intention that it should be acted upon by plaintiff; (5) that plaintiff reasonably relied upon the representation and acted upon it; and (6) that plaintiff thereby suffered injury. [Emphasis supplied.]

Lamm v. Crumpler, 240 N.C. 35, 44, 81 S.E.2d 138, 145 (1954), quoting *Cofield v. Griffin,* 238 N.C. 377, 379, 78 S.E.2d 131, 133 (1953).

(1) Hoell's representation regarding the boundaries of the property related to a material existing fact, and while portions of the boundaries were as Hoell represented, (2) a jury could find that his incomplete description amounted to a false representation. Prior to showing the property to plaintiff, Hoell had been given a sketch which accurately depicted the boundary lines. Hoell testified regarding his knowledge of the boundaries at that time: "I did not tell [plaintiff] that I knew where all the boundaries of the tract were, and I did not know where they were. I would have furnished more detailed information if [plaintiff] had asked for it." Based on the foregoing a jury could find that Hoell's description of the boundaries was made (3) recklessly, without regard to the truth or falsity of the representation. Further, given the relative positions of plaintiff and Hoell — a potential purchaser viewing the property and an agent of the owner giving a tour of the property — a jury could find that Hoell's description of the boundaries was made as a positive assertion with (4) the intent that it should be acted upon by plaintiff, and that plaintiff reasonably (5) relied upon the representation. As Hoell's principal, defendant is liable for Hoell's representations to the same extent as if he had made them himself.

Plaintiff, however, did not plead fraud. In his answer defendant stated: "In the instant action, [plaintiff] abandons the theory of a misrepresentation and bases his claim upon the allegation of Mutual Mistake . . . ." Accordingly, if plaintiff is to prevail on his contention that the court erred in granting defendant's motion for a directed verdict, he must do so on the pleaded ground of mutual mistake.

Under certain circumstances a contract for the sale of real estate may be rescinded on the basis of mutual mistake of fact. *See, e.g., MacKay v. McIntosh,* 270 N.C. 69, 153 S.E.2d 800 (1967). In *MacKay* the Court rescinded an executory real estate contract when the parties, at the time of execution, shared the mistaken belief that "the subject property was within the boundaries of an area zoned for business." *MacKay,* 270 N.C. at 73–74, 153 S.E.2d at 804. The Court reasoned:

> The formation of a binding contract may be affected by a mistake. Thus, a contract may be avoided on the ground of mutual mistake of fact where the mistake is common to both parties and by reason of it each has done what neither intended. Furthermore, a defense may be asserted when there is a mutual mistake of the parties as to the subject matter, the price, or the terms, going to show the want of a *consensus ad idem.* Generally speaking, however, in order to affect the binding force of a contract, the mistake must be of an existing or past fact which is material; it must be as to a fact which enters into and forms the basis of the contract, or in other words it must be of the essence of the agreement, the *sine qua non,* or, as is sometimes said, the efficient cause of the agreement, and must be such that it animates and controls the conduct of the parties.

17 AM. JUR. 2D, CONTRACTS SEC. 143.

In our opinion, and we so hold, whether the subject property was within the boundaries of an area zoned for business is a factual matter; and, under the evidence, the mutual mistake as to this fact related to the essence of the agreement. *Id.* at 73–74, 153 S.E.2d at 804.

In *Financial Services v. Capitol Funds,* 288 N.C. 122, 217 S.E.2d 551 (1975), the Court qualified the requirement that a mistake be mutual as follows:

> In order for the remedy of rescission to be operable because of mistake of fact, there must be mutual mistake of fact. A unilateral mistake, unaccompanied by fraud, imposition, undue influence, or like oppressive circumstances, is not sufficient to avoid a contract or conveyance. The following pertinent statement aptly summarizes the requirement of mutuality:
>
> > . . . It is said that ordinarily a mistake, in order to furnish ground for equitable relief, must be mutual; and as a general rule relief will be denied where the party against whom it is sought *was ignorant that the other party was acting under a mistake and the former's conduct in no way contributed thereto,* and *a fortiori* this is true where the mistake is due to the negligence of the complainant. [Emphasis supplied.]

77 AM. JUR. 2D, VENDOR AND PURCHASER SEC. 51 AT 237.

In general, a unilateral mistake in the making of an agreement, of which the other party is ignorant and to which he in no way contributes, will not afford grounds for avoidance of the agreement. Thus, while it has been stated that there can be no relief from a unilateral mistake, the requirement that the mistake be mutual is not without exceptions. The mistake of one party is sufficient to avoid a contract when the other party had reason to know of the mistake or caused the mistake. Restatement (Second) of Contracts, Sec. 153 (1979).

The evidence, viewed in the light most favorable to plaintiff, would support a finding that at the time the contract was entered plaintiff was mistaken as to the boundaries and Hoell, defendant's agent, either had reason to know of plaintiff's mistake or caused the mistake. Further, the boundaries of the property conveyed deviated from those described by Hoell so as to exclude at least 125 acres from the tract plaintiff intended to purchase. A jury thus could find that plaintiff's mistake as to the boundaries was a material mistake — one which enters into and forms the basis of the contract . . . or, as is sometimes said, "the efficient cause of the agreement . . . such that it animates and controls the conduct of the parties." *MacKay, supra.*

Defendant maintains that because the deed accurately described the property which he intended to convey, plaintiff should be denied relief. Defendant's contention presents two principles of law which constitute defenses to plaintiff's action: (1) the statute of limitations in actions based on mistake is three years, N.C. Gen. Stat. 1-52(9), and the limitation period "begins to run from the time the mistake is discovered or should have been discovered," *Huss v. Huss*, 31 N.C. App. 463, 467, 230 S.E.2d 159, 163 (1976); and (2) the party who assumes the risk of a mistake regarding certain facts may not seek to rescind a contract merely because the facts were not as he had hoped. Restatement (Second) of Contracts, Secs. 153–54 (1979).

A party has assumed the risk of a mistake when (a) the risk is allocated to him by agreement of the parties, or (b) he is aware, at the time the contract is made that he has only limited knowledge with respect to the facts to which the mistake relates but treats his limited knowledge as sufficient, or (c) the risk is allocated to him by the court on the ground that it is reasonable in the circumstances to do so. Restatement (Second) of Contracts, Sec. 154 (1979).

The contract here did not allocate to plaintiff the risk of a mistake regarding the boundaries. *See* Restatement (Second) of Contracts, Sec. 154(a) (1979). Considering the nature and location of the land and the extreme generality of the description in the contract, together with the fact that the vendor's agent made positive assertions regarding the boundaries, it was not reasonable for the court to allocate the risk of mistake as to the boundaries to the purchaser as a matter of law. *See* Restatement (Second) of Contracts, Sec. 154(c) (1979). Generally, the buyer has the right to rely on the boundary representations made by the seller when the seller purports to know them. Whether plaintiff assumed the risk of a mistake by entering into the contract aware that his knowledge regarding the boundaries was limited is in essence a question of whether plaintiff reasonably interpreted Hoell's representation as a complete description of the boundaries. *See* Restatement (Second) of Contracts, Sec. 154(c). D. Dobbs, Remedies Sec. 11.2 at 719 ("One who knows he is uncertain assumes the risk that the facts will turn out unfavorably to his interests."). Whether plaintiff failed to exercise due diligence in discovering his mistake, or whether he assumed the risk of a mistake regarding the boundaries of the property are questions of fact to be determined by a jury.

We thus conclude that the court erred in allowing defendant's motion for a directed verdict. The following questions of fact should have been answered by the jury:

(1) Did plaintiff exercise due diligence in discovering the alleged mistake such that his action is not barred by the three year statute of limitations in N.C. Gen. Stat. 1-52(9)?;

(2) Has plaintiff presented clear, cogent and convincing evidence establishing that he was mistaken regarding the boundaries of the property to be conveyed?;

(3) If plaintiff was mistaken, did defendant or defendant's agent have reason to know of plaintiff's mistake or cause plaintiff's mistake?;

(4) Was the mistake material?; and

(5) Did plaintiff assume the risk of a mistake by: (a) unreasonably relying on Hoell's representations or (b) treating his limited knowledge of the boundaries of the property to be conveyed as sufficient?

Should the jury answer the first four questions affirmatively and the fifth negatively, plaintiff is entitled to rescission of the contract.

NOTES

(1)   *Mistake* is a belief that is not in accord with the facts. RESTATEMENT (SECOND) OF CONTRACTS § 151.

(2)   *Time of Mistake.* A mistake can occur at the time of formation, integration (the final documentation), or performance. Suppose there is a mistake in performance, e.g., the buyer overpays or underpays the seller for goods or services. The overpayment will allow a claim for restitution of the overage. An underpayment will be a breach of contract. A mistake as to integration may preclude the admission of evidence concerning part of the agreement or even reformation of the contract. A mistake in *formation*, however, will permit a party to exercise a power of avoidance.

(3)   *Requirements for Avoidance.* Permitting one party to exercise a power of avoidance is a drastic remedy. As the principal case illustrates, misrepresentation will create such a power in the innocent party. Even a mistake will create such a power, but the mistake must be *material* or substantial. It has to be a major mistake which has a material effect on the agreed exchange — the kind of mistake that suggests the contract would not have been made had the parties been aware of the truth. It is often said that the mistake must be *foundational* to the contract, or, as the principal case suggests, a *sine qua non* or *efficient* cause. The RESTATEMENT (SECOND) OF CONTRACTS borrows a phrase from the Uniform Commercial Code (UCC § 2-313) in suggesting that the mistake must constitute a *basic assumption* on which the contract was made. If the mistake is *foundational* or a *basic assumption*, if it has a material effect on the agreed exchange and, finally, if there is no basis for allocating the risk of mistake to the plaintiff, the plaintiff may exercise a power of avoidance. RESTATEMENT (SECOND) OF CONTRACTS §§ 152(1), 153.

PROBLEMS

(1)   Ames agreed to purchase rental income property from Barnes which the parties assumed was fit for human habitation. In fact, the property was not fit for human habitation. Ames seeks to avoid the contract. What result?

(2)   Childs agreed to purchase a business from Dawson. The business had been successful and Childs was looking forward to profits of at least $200,000 in a given year. In the first year of operation under Childs, the business lost $12,000. Dawson made no false representations to Childs. Childs seeks to "rescind" the contract on the basis of mistake. What result?

(3)   Edwards agreed to purchase a large tract of land from Foust on which Edwards, to the knowledge of Foust, intended to construct tennis and racquet ball courts and a club house. Neither party was aware of zoning laws which prohibited such use on that land. Changes in the zoning laws appear highly improbable. Edwards wants to avoid the contract. What result?

(4)   The Alcoa Corporation and Essex Industries entered into a long-term contract whereby Alcoa was to convert alumina into aluminum. A comprehensive price formula was designed to assure Alcoa of at least a minimum profit. Later it was discovered that the price formula was based on an objective index that failed to consider certain energy costs, and the projected loss to Alcoa was $60 million with a substantial gain to Essex. Alcoa sought to avoid the contract on the basis of mutual mistake. What result? *See Aluminum Co. of Am. v. Essex Group*, 499 F. Supp. 53 (W.D. Pa. 1980).

[2]   Mistake in Offer

SPECKEL v. PERKINS
Minnesota Court of Appeals
364 N.W.2d 890 (1985)

LANSING, J.

The disputed agreement purportedly settled a personal injury action. Sandra Speckel was injured when a car driven by Laurri Perkins collided with a truck driven by Beverly Speckel, in which Sandra Speckel was a passenger.

In December 1983 Speckel's attorney, Stephen Eckman, demanded the insurance policy limits of $50,000 to settle the case. In January 1984 Perkins' attorney, Donald Wheat, wrote to Eckman to inform him that he had conveyed the settlement offer to his client's insurance carrier, American Family Insurance Company. Wheat's letter said, "Although I think your demand for settlement is overstated, I have nonetheless sent it on to the insurance carrier for my client for consideration and acceptance or rejection."

The parties exchanged no more letters until about a week before the scheduled trial. Wheat sent the following letter, dated April 14, 1984, to Eckman:

Dear Mr. Eckman:

In reviewing my file concerning this claim and the upcoming trial, I note that we have a demand in our file for policy limits of $50,000.00. While I agree that the case has some value, I cannot agree that this is a limits case.

At this point in time I have authority to offer you $50,000.00 in settlement of your claim against my client and her mother. I would appreciate hearing from you at your earliest convenience and would be pleased to carry any offer you may wish to make back to my client's insurance company for their consideration.

Wheat's secretary, Carol J. Heimness, signed the letter. Wheat never saw it. According to his affidavit, he was in trial on another matter at the time. He dictated the letter offering $15,000 in settlement, but his secretary erroneously typed $50,000.

On receiving the letter Eckman promptly wrote the following letter to Wheat, dated April 17, 1984:

Dear Mr. Wheat:

Your offer of $50,000 to settle this case on behalf of the Perkins Defendants is hereby ACCEPTED.

Please forward your draft made payable to Sandra Speckel and Stephen S. Eckman, her attorney, in the amount of $50,000. I will forward the appropriate Pierringer Release.

I have notified the Court that the matter has been settled.

Wheat said he contacted the court on April 18, before he received Eckman's letter, to request a continuance because his expert witness was ill. He was told that the other parties would be contacted regarding his request. Later that day Eckman called to remind him that the case had been settled, and Wheat responded that the amount should have been $15,000 and he did not have authority to offer $50,000.

Eckman's affidavit says that when he was contacted by the court concerning Wheat's request for a continuance, he informed the judge that the matter was settled, and the judge instructed him to circulate letters to the various parties' counsel and to the court confirming the arrangements. Eckman called Wheat to say that he considered the matter settled, had taken steps in reliance on the settlement, and would advise the court of the settlement. He says Wheat ended the conversation with "very good."

Wheat sent Eckman a letter dated April 20, 1984, saying he had received Eckman's letter of April 17, he had told Eckman over the phone that the amount was mistaken, he thought the mistake was obvious, the amount should have been $15,000, and he had not reviewed or signed the letter.

Eckman responded in a letter dated April 24 that he was "shocked" to learn Wheat did not consider the matter settled, and in the "honest belief" that it was settled he had cancelled the trial date, released his expert witnesses, cancelled a deposition, waived a liability claim against the third-party defendant (who was his client's mother), and referred the underinsured motorist portion of the lawsuit to arbitration.

Eckman pursued collection from Wheat's office and with the chief staff attorney of the insurance carrier and finally brought a motion to compel performance. Neither Wheat nor Eckman made any effort to have the matter reinstated on the trial calendar.

The trial court granted the motion to compel performance, finding the letter an "unequivocal offer of $50,000" and Wheat's statement that the case was not a limits case "merely a statement of his personal belief." The trial court determined, in addition, that the offer should be enforced because Wheat, although informed by Eckman over the telephone and by two letters that the trial date was stricken, made no effort to inform the court of his belief that the case was not settled or to have the matter reinstated on the trial calendar.

Wheat does not dispute his secretary's authority to sign the letter, nor does he deny his authority, as an attorney, to make and accept settlements on behalf of clients. Wheat acknowledges his obvious carelessness in allowing a settlement letter to be mailed without reading it, but argues that his carelessness should not be determinative.

When the critical evidence is documentary, there is no need to defer to the trial court's assessment of its meaning or credibility. In this case the trial court relied solely on documentary evidence; we therefore are not required to defer to its conclusions regarding the formation of the agreement in question.

A compromise settlement of a lawsuit is contractual in nature. Therefore, to be valid and binding it requires a definite offer and acceptance. Minnesota follows the objective theory of contract formation, under which an outward manifestation of assent is determinative, rather than a party's subjective intention. The trial court, therefore, correctly disregarded Wheat's protestations that the offer was unintended. The subjective intent of Wheat and his client is irrelevant. The trial court also correctly disregarded the fact that the letter contained the unintended amount as the result of a mistake. A unilateral mistake in entering a contract is not a basis for rescission unless there is ambiguity, fraud, misrepresentation, or where the contract may be rescinded without prejudice to the other party.

Several aspects of the offer, however, do negate its validity. A duty to inquire may be imposed on the person receiving the offer when there are factors that reasonably raise a presumption of error. An offeree "will not be permitted to snap up an offer that is too good to be true; no agreement based on such an offer can * * * be enforced by the acceptor." *Id.* (*citing* 1 WILLISTON ON CONTRACTS § 94 (3d ed. 1957)).

In this case Wheat's letter is internally inconsistent. After stating that the case is not worth the policy limits, it proceeds to offer precisely that amount. We find that this internal inconsistency raises a presumption of error and imposed upon Eckman a consequent duty to inquire, particularly in this context — the policy limits, requested when negotiations began, were offered on the eve of trial when the parties were presumably prepared and circumstances had not changed. Finally, the letter expressly states that Wheat "would be pleased to carry any offer [Eckman] may wish to make back to [Wheat's] client's insurance company for their consideration." Despite offering the full amount of the demand, the language does not indicate that an acceptance is anticipated, but rather calls for a counter-offer. We cannot agree that it is an offer enforceable upon acceptance.

The trial court also noted that although Eckman informed Wheat over the telephone and by two letters that the trial date was stricken, Wheat made no effort to inform the court that he did not consider the matter settled, and he did not reinstate the trial date. Although it would have been appropriate for Wheat to inform the court that he disputed the settlement, we cannot read waiver into his actions. He represented the defendants in this matter, who were not in court voluntarily and thus had no interest in assuring that the matter was tried. It could as easily be said that Speckel's attorney neglected a duty to confirm the settlement before notifying the court to take the matter off the calendar.

The letter containing the disputed settlement amount raised a presumption of error and a consequent duty to inquire. It therefore was not a valid offer enforceable upon acceptance. We reverse the trial court's order compelling performance of the settlement agreement.

NOTE

Disclosure. The generally accepted principle that an offeree who knows or should know that the offeror is making a mistake may not "snap up" the offer suggests a duty to disclose. Courts are reluctant to impose a duty to communicate in bargaining transactions where both parties have equal access to relevant information. Thus, none other than Chief Justice John Marshall saw no duty to communicate the fact that the Treaty of Ghent had been signed, ending the war of 1812, resulting in a large increase in the price of tobacco through the removal of the British blockade of New Orleans. *Ladilaw v. Organ*, 15 U.S. (2 Wheat) 178 (1817). Yet, modern courts recognize that non-disclosure may have the same effect as "an assertion not in accord with the fact," i.e., a *misrepresentation* as defined in RESTATEMENT (SECOND) OF CONTRACTS § 159. We will analyze the concepts of misrepresentation, fraud, and related concepts in the next chapter dealing with the abuse of the bargaining process.

[3]   Mistake in Expression

PROBLEM

Arthur McGill owned two vintage Lincoln automobiles, a Lincoln Town Car and a Lincoln Mark IV. An acquaintance of McGill, Bart Harris, admired both cars, especially the Mark IV. After a round of golf, McGill, Harris and other friends were lunching when Harris asked McGill if he would sell the Mark IV. McGill clearly stated that he had no interest in selling the Mark IV for any price, but he might sell the Town Car. A conversation began which turned into negotiations. Throughout the entire conversation, the Mark IV (referred to only as the "Mark") was mentioned in terms of its value as compared to the Town Car (referred to only as the "Town") though McGill remained adamant concerning the sale of the Mark IV. After at least 30 minutes of this conversation and negotiation, which was very entertaining to observing friends, McGill said, "I'll let you have the Mark for $85,000." Harris said, "I accept." The friends roared with laughter and one said,

"Arthur, you just sold the Mark — did you know that?" McGill responded, "Did I say Mark? I meant to say Town, you know that." Harris said, "But you said Mark and we have a deal for the Mark. Your friends know what you said." At this point, none of the friends were smiling. Neither party will raise the Statute of Frauds, i.e., they will both admit what happened. What result? *See* RESTATEMENT (FIRST) OF CONTRACTS § 71, illustration 2; RESTATEMENT (SECOND) OF CONTRACTS § 20, illustration 5. *See* MURRAY ON CONTRACTS at § 88D.

[4]   Mistake of Subject Matter

ANDERSON BROTHERS CORP. v. O'MEARA
United States Court of Appeals, Fifth Circuit
306 F.2d 672 (1962)

[Appellant had manufactured a dredge for use in submarine trenching — to bury pipelines under water. The dredge was not completed in time to be used on the particular job for which it was made and appellant sought a buyer. In answer to an advertisement, appellee contacted appellant and offered appellant $35,000 for the dredge, subject to an inspection. An employee of appellee inspected the dredge (the employee was unfamiliar with dredges, although he was an expert on engines). Satisfied with the engines of the dredge, the employee reported his findings to his employer and subsequently signed an agreement for the sale of the dredge as agent for the employer. One-half of the price was paid upon the signing of the agreement, and the terms indicated that the remaining $17,500 was to be paid over a seventeen-month period. After seven monthly payments had been made, the appellee notified the appellant that the dredge could not be effectively used for appellee's purposes.]

JONES, C. J.

[T]he appellee's counsel wrote the appellant tendering return of the dredge and demanding full restitution of the purchase price. This suit followed the appellant's rejection of the tender and demand.

In his complaint the appellee alleged . . . that the parties had been mistaken in their belief as to the operations of which the dredge was capable, and thus there was a mutual mistake which prevented the formation of a contract. The appellee sought damages of over $29,000, representing the total of principal and interest paid the appellant and expenses incurred in attempting to operate the dredge. In the alternative, the appellee asked for rescission and restitution of all moneys expended by him in reliance on the contract. The appellant answered denying the claims of the appellee and counterclaiming for the unpaid balance.

The district court found that:

At the time the dredge was sold by the defendant to the plaintiff, the dredge was not capable of performing sweep dredging operations in shallow water, unless it was modified extensively. Defendant had built the dredge and knew the purpose for which it was designed and adapted. None of the defendant's officers or employees knew that plaintiff intended to use the dredge for shallow sweep dredging operations. Gier [an employee of the appellant who talked with the appellee or one of his employees by telephone] mistakenly assumed that O'Meara intended to use the dredge within its designed capabilities.

At the time the plaintiff purchased this dredge he mistakenly believed that the dredge was capable without modification of performing sweep dredging operations in shallow water.

The court further found that the market value of the dredge on the date of sale was $24,500, and that the unpaid balance on the note given for part of the purchase price was $10,500. Upon its findings the court concluded that:

The mistake that existed on the part of both plaintiff and defendant with respect to the capabilities of the subject dredge is sufficient to and does constitute mutual mistake, and the plaintiff is entitled to recover the damages he has suffered as a result thereof.

These damages were found to be "equal to the balance due on the purchase price" plus interest, and were assessed by cancellation of the note and chattel mortgage and vesting title to the barge in the appellee free from any encumbrance in favor of the appellant. The court also concluded that the appellee was "not entitled to rescission of this contract." Further findings and conclusions, which are not challenged in this Court, eliminate any considerations of fraud or breach of expressed or implied warranties. The judgment for damages rests entirely upon the conclusion of mutual mistake. The district court's conclusion that the parties were mutually mistaken "with respect to the capabilities of the subject dredge" is not supported by its findings. "A mutual mistake is one common to both parties to the contract, each laboring under the same misconception." *St. Paul Fire & Marine Insurance Co. v. Culwell*, Tex. Com. App., 62 S.W.2d 100 . . . . The appellee's mistake in believing that the dredge was capable, without modification, of performing sweep dredging was not a mistake shared by the appellant, who had designed and built the dredge for use in trenching operations and knew its capabilities. The mistake on the part of the appellant's employee in assuming that the appellee intended to use the dredge within its designed capabilities was certainly not one shared by the appellee, who acquired the dredge for use in sweep dredging operations. The appellee alone was mistaken in assuming that the dredge was adapted, without modification, to the use he had in mind.

The appellee insists that even if the findings do not support a conclusion of mutual mistake, he is entitled to relief under the well-established doctrine that knowledge by one party to a contract that the other is laboring under a mistake concerning the subject matter of the contract renders it voidable by the mistaken party. *See* 3 CORBIN, CONTRACTS 692, § 610. As a predicate to this contention, . . . the appellee contends that the appellant's knowledge of his intended use of the dredge was conclusively established by the testimony of two of the appellant's employees, because, on the authority of *Griffin v. Superior Insurance Co.*, 161 Tex. 195, 338 S.W.2d 415, this testimony constitutes admissions, conclusive against the appellant. In the *Griffin* case, it was held that a party's testimony must be "deliberate, clear and unequivocal" before it is conclusive against him. The testimony on which the appellee relies falls short of being "clear and unequivocal." . . .

The appellee makes a further contention that when he purchased the dredge he was laboring under a mistake so grave that allowing the sale to stand would be unconscionable. The ground urged is one which has apparently been recognized in some circumstances. However, the Texas courts have held that when unilateral mistake is asserted as a ground for relief, the care which the mistaken complainant exercised or failed to exercise in connection with the transaction sought to be avoided is a factor for consideration. *Wheeler v. Holloway*, Tex. Com. App., 276 S.W. 653 . . . . It has been stated that "though a court of equity will relieve against mistake, it will not assist a man whose condition is attributable to the want of due diligence which may be fairly expected from a reasonable person." *American Maid Flour Mills v. Lucia, supra.* This is consistent with the general rule of equity that when a person does not avail himself of an opportunity to gain knowledge of the facts, he will not be relieved of the consequences of acting upon supposition. Annot., 1 A.L.R.2d 9, 89; see 30 C.J.S. Equity § 47, p. 376. Whether the mistaken party's negligence will preclude relief depends to a great extent upon the circumstances in each instance.

The appellee saw fit to purchase the dredge subject to inspection, yet he sent an employee to inspect it who he knew had no experience with or knowledge of dredging equipment. It was found that someone familiar with such equipment could have seen that the dredge was then incapable of performing channel type dredging. Although, according to his own testimony, the appellee was conscious of his own lack of knowledge concerning dredges, he took no steps, prior to purchase, to learn if the dredge which he saw pictured and described in some detail in the advertisement, was suited to his purpose. Admittedly he did not even inquire as to the use the appellant had made or intended to make of the dredge, and the district court found that he did not disclose to the appellant the use he intended to make of the dredge. The finding is supported by evidence. The appellee did not attempt to obtain any sort of warranty as to the dredge's capabilities. The only conclusion possible is that the appellee exercised no diligence, prior to the purchase, in determining the uses to which the dredge might be put. Had he sent a qualified person, such as the naval architect whom he later employed, to inspect the dredge he would have learned that it was not what he wanted, or had even made inquiry, he would have been informed as to the truth or have had a cause of action for misrepresentation if he had been given misinformation and relied upon it. The appellee chose to act on assumption rather than upon inquiry or information obtained by investigation, and, having learned his assumption was wrong, he asks to be released from the resulting consequences on the ground that, because of his mistaken assumption, it would be unconscionable to allow the sale to stand. The appellee seeks this, although the court has found that the appellant was not guilty of any misrepresentation or fault in connection with the transaction.

The appellant is in the same position as the party seeking relief on the grounds of mistake in *Wheeler v. Holloway, supra,* and the same result must follow. In the *Wheeler* case it was held that relief should be denied where the mistaken party exercised "no diligence whatever" in ascertaining the readily accessible facts before he entered into a contract.

The appellee should have taken nothing on his claim; therefore, it is unnecessary to consider the question raised by the cross-appeal. The other questions raised by the appellant need not be considered. The case must be reversed and remanded for further proceeding consistent with what we have here held.

PROBLEM

A buyer told a store clerk that buyer wished to purchase a displayed item. The clerk provided the same item in a sealed container, leaving the sample on display. A few days later, the purchaser returned the item complaining that it was faulty in operation. The clerk asked for a more detailed description of the defect, to which the purchaser replied, "I don't know what's wrong with it — I plug it in, press the button and talk into it but it doesn't record. The buyer was startled to hear the clerk's response: "That's because it's a word processor." Is buyer entitled to any relief?

[5] Mistake of Identity

PROBLEM

Sheila Ames started a new business. She was particularly desirous of developing a business relationship with the Barnes Company. Intending to make a very attractive offer to the Barnes Company, Sheila relied upon her clerk, Ralph Davis, to submit the proposal. Ralph sent the offer to Barnes, Inc., unaware that Barnes, Inc. was a different entity. Upon receipt of the offer, Barnes, Inc., having no reason to assume that a mistake had been made, accepted the offer. May Ames avoid the contract? Suppose Barnes had reason to know of Ame's mistake, may Ames avoid the contract? *See* RESTATEMENT (SECOND) OF CONTRACTS § 153; MURRAY ON CONTRACTS § 92F.

[6] Unilateral Mistake — Release

LANCI v. METROPOLITAN INSURANCE CO.
Pennsylvania Superior Court
564 A.2d 972 (1989)

MELINSON, J.

The facts of this case are simple. Lanci was involved in an automobile accident with an uninsured motorist. Lanci and Metropolitan entered settlement negotiations and ultimately agreed to settle all claims for fifteen thousand dollars ($15,000.00). On or about October 17, 1986, Lanci signed a Release and Trust Agreement. Thereafter, he refused to accept the settlement proceeds asserting that Metropolitan had fraudulently or incorrectly represented that the policy limits were $15,000.00 rather than two hundred fifty thousand dollars ($250,000.00), the correct amount. Thus, Lanci argued, the release and trust agreements were signed as the result of a misrepresentation or mutual mistake and were therefore a nullity. The trial court agreed, relying on correspondence from Lanci's attorney to Metropolitan dated October 12, 1986, which stated:

This will confirm and memorialize our telephone conversation of October 10, 1986 during which it was agreed that you on behalf of your principal shall tender the sum of $15,000.00 in settlement of this claim which sum you have represented to be the straight and/or stacked policy limits applicable to this claim.

trial holding

The trial court held that this correspondence evidenced a mutual mistake concerning the policy limits of the insured and denied Metropolitan's motion to enforce the settlement agreement. Metropolitan argues that the record does not support the trial court's factual finding that there was a mutual mistake. Metropolitan relies on the deposition testimony of its claims adjuster, John Pellock, who refutes Lanci's assertion that the policy limits were discussed during settlement negotiations. Pellock testified that he did not discuss the limits with Lanci's attorney, nor did counsel for Lanci indicate that he was unaware of the policy limits, until after the settlement had been reached and the draft transmitted. He further testified that Lanci's attorney initiated the settlement negotiations with a demand for $15,000.00 and never asked for more. We agree that this testimony, if credited, does not support a finding of mutual mistake. However, we can affirm the decision of the trial court on any basis even if the reasons given by the trial court are incorrect.

A release is binding on the parties thereto, unless executed under fraud, duress or mutual mistake. Whether relief should be granted to a party who is adversely affected by a mistake in a written contract depends upon the nature and effect of that mistake; the mistake must relate to the basis of the bargain, must materially affect the parties' performance, and must not be one as to which the injured party bears the risk before the party will be entitled to relief. However, irrespective of actual fraud, if the other party knows or has reason to know of the unilateral mistake, and the mistake, as well as the actual intent of the parties is clearly shown, relief will be granted to the same extent as a mutual mistake.

The Restatement (Second) of Contracts § 153 provides that a contract is voidable due to unilateral mistake under certain circumstances.

> Where a mistake of one party at the time a contract was made as to a basic assumption on which he made the contract has a material effect on the agreed exchange of performances that is adverse to him, the contract is voidable by him if he does not bear the risk of the mistake . . . , and
>
> > (a) the effect of the mistake is such that enforcement would be unconscionable, or
> >
> > (b) the other party had reason to know of the mistake or his fault caused the mistake.

In the instant case, the record reveals that Lanci did not have a copy of his policy and that Metropolitan was advised of that fact in Lanci's Petition to Appoint Arbitrators and to Compel Arbitration Hearing. Lanci's correspondence accepting the settlement offer clearly indicates his understanding that his policy limit is $15,000.00. We find, therefore, that Metropolitan knew, or should have known, that Lanci accepted the terms of this settlement offer under the mistaken belief that it was the limit of his coverage. Thus, Lanci is entitled to void the contract and the trial court did not err in denying Metropolitan's petition to enforce the settlement agreement.

[7]   Releases — "Unknown Injury"

LaFLEUR v. C. C. PIERCE CO.
Massachusetts Supreme Judicial Court
496 N.E.2d 827 (1986)

[LaFleur suffered an injury to his right foot from a fork lift truck in the course of his employment. The insurance company doctor told him that he had a sprained toe. He entered into a lump-sum agreement of $4,000 with his employer's insurer. The agreement stated, "[This is a] complete and final settlement of my claim and I will not be able to reopen my claim or seek further benefits because of this injury." LaFleur experienced increasing pain in his right foot. He was diagnosed as having arterial occlusive (Buerger's) disease. Several operations to relieve this problem were unsuccessful. As a result of this disease, LaFleur eventually had both of his legs amputated above the knees and was permanently confined to a wheelchair. Dr. Edward D. Frank, an assistant professor of surgery at Harvard Medical School, attested that he had examined LaFleur and had concluded that LaFleur's arterial occlusive disease existed at the time of the accident, but had not been diagnosed "because the disease is rare and difficult to detect." Dr. Frank further attested that the forklift accident had injured LaFleur's arterial system and had aggravated the preexisting arterial disease. The injury to the arterial system was "completely separate, and distinct in nature" from the sprained toe that was diagnosed after the accident. Finally, Dr. Frank attested that the forklift accident was causally related to the amputation of LaFleur's legs. The judge denied LaFleur's motion for summary judgment and entered judgment for the defendants on the ground that LaFleur had simply made an incorrect prediction of the future and had, therefore, failed to establish a basis for setting aside a release — a bargain freely entered into by the parties represented by counsel. LaFleur appealed from this judgment. The Supreme Court of Massachusetts reversed.]

The legal principles underlying the doctrine of mutual mistake are well established. Where there has been a mistake between the parties as to the subject matter of a contract, there has been no "meeting of the minds," and the contract is voidable at the election of the party adversely affected. *See generally* RESTATEMENT (SECOND) OF CONTRACTS § 152 (1975). The mistake must involve a fact capable of ascertainment at the time the contract was entered into, and not a mere expectation or opinion about future events. A contract will not be rescinded for mutual mistake where one party was aware at the time the contract was signed that he had limited knowledge as to essential facts, but nonetheless assumed the risk that circumstances would prove to be other than as expected. *See generally* RESTATEMENT (SECOND) OF CONTRACTS § 56, comment a (1975).

In [another case], we were confronted with a situation in which the consequences of an injury turned out to be more serious than expected. In this case, however, we are dealing with a separate condition which existed and yet was unknown to the parties at the time of contract. Although this presents a question of first impression in this Commonwealth, the great weight of authority in other jurisdictions supports the view that a release of claims for personal injuries may be avoided on the ground of mutual mistake if the parties at the time of signing the agreement were mistaken as to the existence of an injury, as opposed to the unknown consequences of known injuries.

Of course, the intention of the parties is controlling, and the relevant inquiry is whether there has been a conscious and deliberate intention by the parties to release claims for injuries existing but not known to them at the time of the agreement. In this case, the release itself does not clearly or unambiguously indicate that the parties intended to discharge liability for the unknown injury to LaFleur's arterial system; rather, the standardized form of the Division of Industrial Accidents merely released claims "for all injuries received by Michael LaFleur on or about January 21 and February 15, 1975." Extrinsic evidence may thus be introduced to ascertain whether the parties intended to release liability for LaFleur's unknown injury. *See Mickelson v. Barnet*, 390 Mass. 786, 792 (1984) (parol evidence rule no bar to the consideration of extrinsic evidence of intent when mistake is alleged). Factors which should be considered on this issue include the language of the agreement; the circumstances of its negotiation and execution, including the legal representation of the parties; the seriousness of the unknown injury; and the consideration paid to the plaintiff for the release of the defendants' liability. The inquiry should include a consideration as to whether the plaintiff suffers from an unknown injury which is so serious as to indicate clearly that, if it had been known, the release would not have been signed.

Rule

Our analysis of the doctrine of mutual mistake leads us to adopt the "unknown injury" rule followed by most other jurisdictions. Therefore, we think the judge erred in entering judgment for the defendants.

NOTE

If the language of the release explicitly discharges liability for known and unknown injuries, some courts will refuse to permit a release agreement to be avoided or rescinded. Other courts are not persuaded by even clear language in printed forms. The RESTATEMENT (SECOND) OF CONTRACTS clings to the basic assumption test and suggests that circumstances to be considered should include: the fair amount required to compensate the claimant for known injuries, the probability that the other party would be liable on such a claim, the amount actually received by the claimant under the release, and the relationship between known and unknown injuries. RESTATEMENT (SECOND) OF CONTRACTS § 152 comment f. *See* MURRAY ON CONTRACTS at § 92K. On *release* as a method of discharging a contract, see MURRAY ON CONTRACTS at § 146C.

[8]   Unilateral Mistake — Clerical Error

FIRST BAPTIST CHURCH OF MOULTRIE v.
BARBER CONTRACTING CO.
Georgia Court of Appeals
377 S.E.2d 717 (1989)

McMurray, J.

The First Baptist Church of Moultrie, Georgia, invited bids for the construction of a music, education and recreation building. The bids were to be opened on May 15, 1986. They were to be accompanied by a bid bond in the amount of 5 percent of the base bid. The bidding instructions provided, in pertinent part: "Negligence on the part of the bidder in preparing the bid confers no right for the withdrawal of the bid after it has been opened."

Barber Contracting Company ("Barber") submitted a bid for the project in the amount of $1,860,000. The bid provided, in pertinent part: "For and in consideration of the sum of $1.00, the receipt of which is hereby acknowledged, the undersigned agrees that this proposal may not be revoked or withdrawn after the time set for the opening of bids but shall remain open for acceptance for a period of thirty-five (35) days following such time." The bid also provided that if it was accepted within 35 days of the opening of bids, Barber would execute a contract for the construction of the project within 10 days of the acceptance of the bid.

A bid bond in the amount of 5 percent of Barber's bid ($93,000) was issued by The American Insurance Company to cover Barber's bid. With regard to the bid bond, the bid submitted by Barber provided: "If this proposal is accepted within thirty-five (35) days after the date set for the opening of bids and the undersigned [Barber] fails to execute the contract within ten (10) days after written notice of such acceptance . . . the obligation of the bid bond will remain in full force and effect and the money payable thereon shall be paid into the funds of the Owner as liquidated damages for such failure . . . ."

The bids were opened by the church on May 15, 1986, as planned. Barber submitted the lowest bid. The second lowest bid, in the amount of $1,975,000 was submitted by H & H Construction and Supply Company, Inc. ("H & H").

Barber's president, Albert W. Barber, was present when the bids were opened, and of course, he was informed that Barber was the low bidder. Members of the church building committee informally asked President Barber if changes could be made in the contract to reduce the amount of the bid. He replied that he was sure such changes could be made.

On May 16, 1986, Albert W. Barber informed the architect for the project, William Frank McCall, Jr., that the amount of the bid was in error — the bid should have been $143,120 higher. In Mr. Barber's words: "[T]he mistake in Barber's bid was caused by an error in totaling the material costs on page 3 of Barber's estimate work sheets. The subtotal of the material cost listed on that page is actually $137,990. The total listed on Barber's summary sheet for the material cost subtotal was $19,214. The net error in addition was $118,776. After adding in mark-ups for sales tax (4 percent), overhead and profit (15 percent), and bond procurement costs (.75 percent), the error was compounded to a total of $143,120 . . . ." The architect immediately telephoned Billy G. Fallin, co-chairman of the church building committee, and relayed the information which he received from President Barber.

On May 20, 1986, Barber delivered letters to the architect and the church. In the letter to the architect, Barber enclosed copies of its estimate sheets and requested that it be permitted to withdraw its bid. In the letter to the church, Barber stated that it was withdrawing its bid on account of "an error in adding certain estimated material costs." In addition, Barber sought the return of the bid bond from the church.

On May 29, 1986, the church forwarded a construction contract, based upon Barber's bid, to Barber. The contract had been prepared by the architect and executed by the church. The next day, Barber returned the contract to the church without executing it. In so doing, Barber pointed out that its bid had been withdrawn previously.

On July 25, 1986, the church entered into a construction contract for the project with H & H, the second lowest bidder. Through deletions and design changes, the church was able to secure a contract with H & H for $1,919,272.

In the meantime, the church demanded that Barber and The American Insurance Company pay it $93,000 pursuant to the bid bond. The demand was refused.

On May 26, 1987, the church brought suit against Barber and The American Insurance Company seeking to recover the amount of the bid bond. Answering the complaint, defendants denied they were liable to plaintiff.

Thereafter, defendants moved for summary judgment and so did the plaintiff. In support of their summary judgment motions, defendants submitted the affidavit of Albert W. Barber. He averred that in preparing its bid, Barber exercised the level of care ordinarily exercised by contractors submitting sealed bids. In support of its summary judgment motion, the church submitted the affidavit of a building contractor who averred that he would never submit a bid of any magnitude without obtaining assistance in verification and computation.

The trial court denied the summary judgment motions, certified its rulings for immediate review and we granted these interlocutory appeals. Held:

> The question for decision is whether Barber was entitled to rescind its bid upon discovering that it was based upon a miscalculation or whether Barber should forfeit its bond because it refused to execute the contract following the acceptance of its bid by the church. We hold that Barber was entitled to rescind its bid.

That equity will rescind a contract upon a unilateral mistake is a generally accepted principle. *See* CORBIN ON CONTRACTS, § 609 (1960). As it is said: "Where a mistake of one party at the time a contract was made as to a basic assumption on which he made the contract has a material effect on the agreed exchange of performances that is adverse to him, the contract is voidable by him if he does not bear the risk of the mistake . . . and (a) the effect of the mistake is such that enforcement of the contract would be unconscionable, or (b) the other party had reason to know of the mistake or his fault caused the mistake." RESTATEMENT (2D) OF CONTRACTS, § 153 (1979).

The following illustration demonstrates the rule: "In response to B's invitation for bids on the construction of a building according to stated specifications, A submits an offer to do the work for $150,000. A believes that this is the total of a column of figures, but he has made an error by inadvertently omitting a $50,000 item, and in fact the total is $200,000. B, having no reason to know of A's mistake, accepts A's bid. If A performs for $150,000, he will sustain a loss of $20,000 instead of making an expected profit of $30,000. If the court determines that enforcement of the contract would be unconscionable, it is voidable by A." RESTATEMENT (2D) OF CONTRACTS, § 153 (1979) (Illustration 1).

Corbin explains: "Suppose . . . a bidding contractor makes an offer to supply specified goods or to do specified work for a definitely named price, and that he was caused to name this price by an antecedent error of computation. If, before acceptance, the offeree knows, or has reason to know, that a material error has been made, he is seldom mean enough to accept; and if he does accept, the courts have no difficulty in throwing him out. He is not permitted 'to snap up' such an offer and profit thereby. If, without knowledge of the mistake and before any revocation, he has accepted the offer, it is natural for him to feel a sense of disappointment at not getting a good bargain, when the offeror insists on withdrawal; but a just and reasonable man will not insist upon profiting by the other's mistake. There are now many decisions to the effect that if the error was a substantial one and notice is given before the other party has made such a change of position that he cannot be put substantially in status quo, the bargain is voidable and rescission will be decreed." CORBIN ON CONTRACTS, § 609 (1960).

Georgia law is no different. It provides for rescission and cancellation "upon the ground of mistake of fact material to the contract of one party only." OCGA § 23-2-31. The mistake must be an "unintentional act, omission, or error arising from ignorance, surprise, imposition, or misplaced confidence." OCGA § 23-2-21 (a). But relief will be granted even in cases of negligence if the opposing party will not be prejudiced. OCGA § 23-2-32.

We can see these principles at work in *M. J. McGough Co. v. Jane Lamb Memorial Hosp.*, 302 F. Supp. 482 (SD Iowa 1969). In that case, a bid of $1,957,000 was submitted for a hospital improvement by a contractor. A bond in the amount of $100,000 was given to secure the contractor's bid. The contractor submitted the lowest bid. After the bids were opened, but before its bid was accepted, the contractor informed the hospital that it erroneously transcribed numbers in computing the bid and that, therefore, it underbid the project by $199,800. Nevertheless, the hospital tried to hold the contractor to its bid. When the contractor refused to execute a contract, the hospital awarded the contract to the next lowest bidder. The contractor and surety sought rescission of the bid and the return of the bond. The hospital sued the contractor and surety for damages. The district court allowed the contractor to rescind. Its decision is noteworthy and illuminating. We quote it at length:

By the overwhelming weight of authority a contractor may be relieved from a unilateral mistake in his bid by rescission under the proper circumstances. *See generally* Annot., 52 A.L.R.2d 792 (1957). The prerequisites for obtaining such relief are: (1) the mistake is of such consequence that enforcement would be unconscionable; (2) the mistake must relate to the substance of the consideration; (3) the mistake must have occurred regardless of the exercise of ordinary care; (4) it must be possible to place the other party in status quo. It is also generally required that the bidder give prompt notification of the mistake and his intention to withdraw.

Applying the criteria for rescission for a unilateral mistake to the circumstances in this case, it is clear that [the contractor] and his surety . . . are entitled to equitable relief. The notification of mistake was promptly made, and [the contractor] made every possible effort to explain the circumstances of the mistake to the authorities of [the hospital]. Although [the hospital] argues to the contrary, the Court finds that notification of the mistake was received before acceptance of the bid. The mere opening of the bids did not constitute the acceptance of the lowest bid . . . . Furthermore, it is generally held that acceptance prior to notification does not bar the right to equitable relief from a mistake in the bid.

The mistake in this case was an honest error made in good faith. While a mistake in and of itself indicates some degree of lack of care or negligence, under the circumstances here there was not such a lack of care as to bar relief . . . .

The mistake here was a simple clerical error. To allow [the hospital] to take advantage of this mistake would be unconscionable. This is especially true in light of the fact that they had actual knowledge of the mistake before the acceptance of the bid. Nor can it be seriously contended that a $199,800 error, amounting to approximately 10 percent of the bid, does not relate directly to the substance of the consideration. Furthermore, [the hospital] has suffered no actual damage by the withdrawal of the bid of [the contractor]. The Hospital has lost only what it sought to gain by taking advantage of [the contractor's] mistake. Equitable considerations will not allow the recovery of the loss of bargain in this situation.

M. J. McGough Co. v. Jane Lamb Memorial Hosp., 302 F. Supp. 482, 485, 486, *supra*.

In the case sub judice, Barber, the contractor, promptly notified the plaintiff that a mistake was made in calculating the amount of the bid. The plaintiff had actual knowledge of the mistake before it forwarded a contract to Barber. The mistake was a "simple clerical error." It did not amount to negligence preventing equitable relief. Furthermore, it was a mistake which was material to the contract — it went to the substance of the consideration. (The mistake amounted to approximately seven percent of the bid.) To allow the plaintiff to take advantage of the mistake would not be just.

The contention is made that Barber's miscalculation constituted negligence sufficient to prevent relief in equity. Assuming, arguendo, that the error stemmed from such a want of prudence as to violate a legal duty, we must nevertheless conclude that Barber is entitled to rescission.

Relief in equity "may be granted even in cases of negligence by the complainant if it appears that the other party has not been prejudiced thereby." It cannot be said that plaintiff was prejudiced by Barber's rescission. After all, plaintiff "lost only what it sought to gain by taking advantage of [the contractor's] mistake." *M. J. McGough Co. v. Jane Lamb Memorial Hosp., supra* at 486.

The plaintiff takes the position that rescission is improper since, pursuant to the language set forth in the bid, Barber agreed not to withdraw the bid for a period of 35 days after the bids were opened. It also asserts that the language set forth in the bidding instructions prohibited Barber from withdrawing the bid on the ground of "negligence." We disagree. "[P]rovisions such as these have been considered many times in similar cases, and have never been held effective when equitable considerations dictate otherwise." *M. J. McGough Co. v. Jane Lamb Memorial Hosp.*, 302 F. Supp. 482, 487, *supra*.

The trial court properly denied the plaintiff's (the church's) motion for summary judgment. It erred in denying defendants' (Barber's and The American Insurance Company's) motions for summary judgment.

NOTES

In *Boise Junior College District v. Mattefs Construction Co.*, 92 Idaho 757, 450 P.2d 604 (1969), the defendant submitted a bid on a construction contract which was irrevocable for 45 days after the bids were opened. The bids were opened on October 5. Defendant's bid was $141,048. Only one of ten bids was lower and the lowest bidder withdrew. On the day the bids were opened, defendant learned that it had made a mistake in its bid by failing to include the cost of glass in the construction. When plaintiff demanded compliance with the bid, defendant refused. The court applied the following criteria in determining whether relief should be granted to the contractor because of this clerical error.

(1)   Was the mistake *material*? The mistake amounted to 14% of the bid which the court deemed *material*. The court cautioned, however, that merely viewing the amount of the mistake as a percentage of the bid is insufficient.

(2)   Would enforcement of the contract be unconscionable? Here, the court makes a critically important distinction between *materiality* and *unconscionability:* "An error in the computation of a bid may be material, representing a substantial percentage of the total bid submitted, and yet requiring compliance with that bid may not be unconscionable. Thus, omission of a $25,000 item in a $100,000 bid would be material, but if the $100,000 bid included $50,000 in profit, no hardship would be created by requiring the contractor to comply with the terms of his bid." That situation was not true in this case since the defendant would not only fail to recover any profit but lose a substantial amount if forced to comply.

(3)   Did the mistake resulted from *"any positive duty or culpable negligence"*? The defendant proved that the mistake resulted from an effort to assemble the bid during a lunch hour that was unusually busy and caused the failure to include the

portion of the bid relating to glass. The court viewed this type of error as one which will sometimes occur in the conduct of reasonable and cautious businessmen. It was, therefore, not a violation of a positive duty nor was the negligence gross.

(4) Would the plaintiff suffer severe *hardship* if the contractor were afforded relief? If, for example the plaintiff had relied to its detriment on the bid and would suffer considerable hardship if it were now forced to pay considerably more, this factor alone would be sufficient to deny relief to the defendant. In this case, however, the plaintiff expected to pay $150,000. If the defendant is excused, the plaintiff's actual cost would be $149,000. While plaintiff does lose the benefit of paying even less, this loss of bargain is not enough to preclude relief for the type of error found in this case.

(5) Was prompt notice of the mistake given? Informal notice was given on the evening of the opening of bids and formal notice followed two days later, four days before the plaintiff accepted the bid with knowledge of the error. The notice was prompt.

[9] Mistake of Value

ESTATE OF NELSON v. RICE
Arizona Court of Appeals
12 P.3d 238 (2000)

Espinosa, C.J.

After Martha Nelson died in February 1996, Newman and Franz, the copersonal representatives of her estate, employed Judith McKenzie-Larson to appraise the Estate's personal property in preparation for an estate sale. McKenzie-Larson told them that she did not appraise fine art and that, if she saw any, they would need to hire an additional appraiser. McKenzie-Larson did not report finding any fine art, and relying on her silence and her appraisal, Newman and Franz priced and sold the Estate's personal property.

Responding to a newspaper advertisement, Carl Rice attended the public estate sale and paid the asking price of $60 for two oil paintings. Although Carl had bought and sold some art, he was not an educated purchaser, had never made more than $55 on any single piece, and had bought many pieces that had "turned out to be frauds, forgeries or . . . to have been [created] by less popular artists." He assumed the paintings were not originals given their price and the fact that the Estate was managed by professionals, but was attracted to the subject matter of one of the paintings and the frame of the other. At home, he compared the signatures on the paintings to those in a book of artists' signatures, noticing they "appeared to be similar" to that of Martin Johnson Heade. As they had done in the past, the Rices sent pictures of the paintings to Christie's in New York, hoping they might be Heade's work. Christie's authenticated the paintings, Magnolia Blossoms on Blue Velvet and Cherokee Roses, as paintings by Heade and offered to sell them on consignment. Christie's subsequently sold the paintings at auction for $1,072,000.

After subtracting the buyer's premium and the commission, the Rices realized $911,780 from the sale.

Newman and Franz learned about the sale in February 1997 and thereafter sued McKenzie-Larson on behalf of the Estate [but] sealed the lawsuit because McKenzie-Larson had no assets with which to pay damages. During 1997, the Rices paid income taxes of $337,000 on the profit from the sale of the paintings, purchased a home, created a family trust, and spent some of the finds on living expenses.

The Estate sued the Rices in late January 1998, alleging the sale contract should be rescinded or reformed on grounds of mutual mistake. The Estate argued the parties were not aware the transaction had involved fine art, believing instead that the items exchanged were "relatively valueless, wall decorations." The trial court concluded that, although the parties had been mistaken about the value of the paintings, the Estate bore the risk of that mistake and granted the Rices' motion for summary judgment. This appeal followed.

The Estate first argues that it established a mutual mistake sufficient to permit the reformation or rescission of the sale of the paintings to the Rices. A party seeking to rescind a contract on the basis of mutual mistake must show by clear and convincing evidence that the agreement should be set aside. A contract may be rescinded on the ground of a mutual mistake as to a "basic assumption on which both parties made the contract." RESTATEMENT (SECOND) OF CONTRACTS § 152 cmt. b (1979). Furthermore, the parties' mutual mistake must have had "such a material effect on the agreed exchange of performances as to upset the very bases of the contract." RESTATEMENT § 152 cmt. a. However, the mistake must not be one on which the party seeking relief bears the risk under the rules stated in § 154(b) of the RESTATEMENT. RESTATEMENT § 152.

[margin note: Mutual Mistake]

In concluding that the Estate was not entitled to rescind the sale, the trial court found that, although a mistake had existed as to the value of the paintings, the Estate bore the risk of that mistake under § 154(b) of the RESTATEMENT. Section 154(b) states that a party bears the risk of mistake when "he is aware, at the time the contract is made, that he has only limited knowledge with respect to the facts to which the mistake relates but treats his limited knowledge as sufficient." In explaining that provision, the Washington Supreme Court stated, "In such a situation there is no mistake. Instead, there is an awareness of uncertainty or conscious ignorance of the future." *Bennett v. Shinoda Floral, Inc.*, 108 Wn. 2d 386, 739 P.2d 648, 653–54 (Wash. 1987).

The Estate contends neither party bore the risk of mistake, arguing that § 154 and comment a are not applicable to these facts. In the example in comment a, the risk of mistake is allocated to the seller when the buyer discovers valuable mineral deposits on property priced and purchased as farmland. Even were we to accept the Estate's argument that this example is not analogous, comment c clearly applies here and states:

> *Conscious ignorance.* Even though the mistaken party did not agree to bear the risk, he may have been aware when he made the contract that his knowledge with respect to the facts to which the mistake relates was limited. If he was not only so aware that his knowledge was limited but

undertook to perform in the face of that awareness, he bears the risk of the mistake. It is sometimes said in such a situation that, in a sense, there was not mistake but "conscious ignorance."

Because McKenzie-Larson did not say they needed an additional appraiser, Newman and Franz did not hire anyone qualified to appraise fine art. By relying on the opinion of someone who was admittedly unqualified to appraise fine art to determine its existence, the personal representatives consciously ignored the possibility that the Estate's assets might include fine art, thus assuming that risk. Accordingly, the trial court correctly found that the Estate bore the risk of mistake as to the paintings' value.

assum risk b/c did not hire appraiser

Furthermore, under RESTATEMENT § 154(c), the court may allocate the risk of mistake to one party "on the ground that it is reasonable in the circumstances to do so." In making this determination, "the court will consider the purposes of the parties and will have recourse to its own general knowledge of human behavior in bargain transactions." RESTATEMENT § 154 cmt. d. Here, the Estate had had ample opportunity to discover what it was selling and failed to do so; instead, it ignored the possibility that the paintings were valuable and attempted to take action only after learning of their worth as a result of the efforts of the Rices. Under these circumstances, the Estate was a victim of its own folly and it was reasonable for the court to allocate to it the burden of its mistake.

NOTES

(1)   In a classic case, the plaintiff found a stone and asked the defendant jeweler to examine it. Neither party knew what the stone was. The plaintiff agreed to sell it to the jeweler for $1. The stone turned out to be a rough diamond worth $700 at that time. The plaintiff sought to recover possession of the stone. Finding that the jeweler was not an expert in uncut diamonds and there was no evidence of fraud or unfair dealing, the court held for the defendant. *Wood v. Boyton*, 64 Wis. 265, 25 N.W. 42 (1895).

(2)   Where the plaintiff agreed to purchase a home under a contract containing an "as is" clause and later discovered a walled-in room containing trash, various materials and mold, the court denied relief to the plaintiff's claim of mutual mistake on the footing that the contract allocated any such risk to her. RESTATEMENT (SECOND) OF CONTRACTS § 154(a), cmt. b. *Cherry v. McCall*, 138 S.W.3d 35 (Tex. App. 2004).

(3)   Where a breeder of cattle sold a cow named Rose 2d of Aberlone to a banker for $80 on the assumption that the cow was sterile, the seller refused to deliver Rose when it was discovered that she was fertile and worth $750. In this classic case, the court pursued a rather metaphysical notion that the cow the parties intended to buy and sell was different from the real cow. Its decision to allow the transaction to be avoided can be sustained, however, on the footing that the risk of such a material effect on the agreed exchange was one that was not sustainable in this case since the parties shared a mistaken belief that Rose was only worth the price of beef on the hoof. *Sherwood v. Walker*, 66 Mich. 568, 33 N.W. 919 (1887).

[10]   Mistake in Transmission — Intermediary

PROBLEMS

(a)   Jones, a lumber dealer, delivered the following message to the local telegraph company to be transmitted to Smith in a distant city: "Will sell 800 M. laths delivered at your wharf, two ten net cash. July shipment. Answer quick." The message which was actually delivered by the telegraph company to Smith was as follows: "Will sell 800 M. laths delivered at your wharf, two net cash. July shipment. Answer quick." Smith immediately answered, accepting the offer as stated in the telegram delivered. When the error was discovered, Jones refused to ship the laths at $2.00 per thousand. Consider the four following theories:

(1)   There is a contract between Smith and Jones because the telegraph company is the agent of the sender, Jones, and the principal is responsible for the mistakes of its agent.

(2)   There is no contract between Smith and Jones because the telegraph company was a special agent for Jones, the sender, and, in sending the mistaken message, it exceeded its authority.

(3)   As between the innocent sender and the innocent receiver, the sender must bear the loss because he chose the mode of communication, and, though innocent, he assumes the risk. There is a contract.

(4)   There is no contract because the parties have neither objectively nor subjectively reached agreement upon an essential term of the contract.

Which, if any, of these theories is acceptable? The mistake is by the intermediary. If you accept either (1) or (2), you must show that a telegraph company, a public utility, was an agent of the sender. If you find (4) acceptable, how does this situation differ from a typical "mailbox" acceptance which is lost so that the offeror never receives it? If you accept (3), you must agree that the sender assumes the risk. However, is this an intentional assumption of risk, or is it simply an imputed assumption of risk which makes for a facile solution to the problem? *See Ayer v. Western Union Tel. Co.*, 79 Me. 493, 10 A. 495, 1 Am. St. R. 353 (1887); *Western Union Tel. Co. v. Cowin & Co.*, 20 F.2d 103, 54 A.L.R. 1362 (8th Cir. 1927).

(b)   In 1997, the plaintiff read the defendant's newspaper advertisement for a particular model of a 1995 Jaguar automobile price at $25,995. The plaintiff compared that price with the price of the same model and year at other dealers at prices that were $8,000 to $10,000 higher. The plaintiff informed the defendant that he would take the car for the advertised price. The defendant immediately informed the plaintiff that the newspaper price was a mistake. Evidence indicated that the mistake was made by the newspaper that had failed to identify a 1994 Jaguar at the advertised price. Assuming the newspaper advertisement was an offer, how should the court decide this case? *See Donovan v. RRL Corp.*, 26 Cal. 4th 261, 27 P.3d 702 (2001).

Chapter 5

ABUSE OF THE BARGAINING PROCESS

A. INTRODUCTION

In the last chapter, we distinguished operative from inoperative expressions of assent. Certain expressions of assent had to be evidenced by a writing under the Statute of Frauds. If assent was evidenced by a writing intended to be final and complete, prior expressions of assent had no operative effect under the parol evidence rule. We chose between and among various meanings of expressions of assent, deciding that some meanings were operative and others inoperative on the basis of the law of interpretation. We also considered myriad problems of mistakes either in the expression of assent or mistakes underlying other expressions of assent to determine which expressions should have operative effect.

This chapter could also be titled "Operative Expressions of Assent" because, again, we will explore ways in which courts decide that certain expressions of agreement will not be legally recognized. The focus, however, will be different. We will be particularly concerned about abuses of the bargaining process which preclude operative effect. Abuse of the bargaining process may also occur through silence — tacit nondisclosure of one or more material facts that may be said to impair the assent by the other party to the contract.

We will consider abuses of the bargaining process from the egregious to the subtle. A contract document signed by a reluctant party under gunpoint or other physical compulsion is an example of physical duress. This kind of coercion is antithetical to the essence of contract — volition and assent. There is no need for the coerced party to exercise a power of avoidance in such a situation because there is no redeeming virtue in such a situation, the so-called contract is *void ab initio* (i.e., it was never born as a contract). Abuse of the bargaining process by duress may also occur in a more subtle form, such as improper threats, which may be more coercive than physical compulsion.[1]

---

[1] Duress, other than by physical compulsion, involves an improper threat that may take various forms. If a threatened act would be a crime or tort, the threat is improper. Even if the act is proper, a threat to carry it out for one's own gain may be improper, such as a threat to report someone to the IRS that forces a party to sign a contract. *See* Berger v. Berger, 466 So. 2d 1149 (Fla. Dist. Ct. App. 1985). Beyond the problems of deciding which threats are proper and which are improper, it is also necessary to consider economic duress, business compulsion and similar situations. Moreover, the question of whether an improper threat *caused* the manifestation of assent raises a number of issues. For an analysis of these and related questions, see RESTATEMENT (SECOND) OF CONTRACTS §§ 175, 176. *See* MURRAY ON CONTRACTS § 94.

Abuse of the bargaining process may also occur through fraud or misrepresentation, either intentional or unintentional. In the absence of misrepresentation, undue influence may be established under certain fact patterns.[2]

Though a given fact situation does not evidence duress, fraud, misrepresentation or undue influence, it may yet contain the elements of unconscionability. Unconscionability permits a court to refuse enforcement of a contract or the unconscionable portion because one of the parties, typically a party of inferior bargaining power, was reasonably unaware of a material, risk-shifting term to which that party would not have normally assented, and/or such a party had no reasonable choice in acquiescing in such a term dictated by the other party with superior bargaining power. It is quite common for an unconscionability argument to be made with respect to standardized (printed) forms, though the doctrine can certainly apply absent such a prefabricated form. It is, therefore, important to recognize the modern treatment of standardized agreements, which will also be discussed in this chapter.

Neither the Uniform Commercial Code nor the RESTATEMENT (SECOND) OF CONTRACTS is particularly clear or helpful in providing an unconscionability analysis. The courts and scholars have also demonstrated considerable difficulty in articulating this analysis. One candid opinion suggests that deciding whether unconscionability exists is a lot easier that explaining it. *Jones v. Star Credit Corp.*, 59 Misc. 2d 189 (N.Y. Sup. Ct. 1969). However, the student must gain a workable understanding of this important doctrine. This chapter will also introduce the student to the evolving concept of *good faith*, by which courts may refuse to enforce agreements where unconscionability or other abuses of the bargaining process are not established.

Without reference to any of the doctrines or concepts just mentioned, the agreement may violate public policy. "Public policy" is anything but precise; as JUSTICE BURROUGH wrote many years ago, "[P]ublic policy is a very unruly horse, and when once you get astride it you never know where it will carry you. It may lead you from the sound law. It is never argued at all but when other points fail." *Richardson v. Mellish*, 2 Bing. 229, 252, 30 Eng. Rep. 294, 303 (1824). We begin by considering the question, Is a party bound by all of the terms of a document to which they have assented, even if the party has not read it?

B. DUTY TO READ

Many parties sign or otherwise manifest assent to documents which they have not read. In Chapter 2 we considered the fine-print, boilerplate clauses in purchase orders, acknowledgments and other printed forms and recognized that the printed clauses are rarely read and even more rarely understood. Should a party be excused from the terms of a document to which they have apparently assented because it has

---

[2] Whereas duress involves an improper threat, undue influence involves improper or unfair persuasion that may result from the domination of one party over another. A confidential relationship may have one party trusting another to such an extent that the trusting party may not be aware that the dominant party is operating contrary to the welfare of the innocent party. *See* RESTATEMENT (SECOND) OF CONTRACTS § 177; MURRAY ON CONTRACTS § 95.

not been read? The common law view was clear:

> It will not do for a man to enter into a contract, and, when called upon to respond to its obligations, to say that he did not read it when he signed it, or did not know what it contained. If this were permitted, contracts would not be worth the paper on which they are written.

Upton Assignee v. Tribilock, 91 U.S. 45 (1875).

Where contracts were evidenced by negotiated terms, this view has much to commend it. In an era where various kinds of writings and documents are "standardized," i.e., prefabricated forms with fine print (boilerplate) terms, are there mitigating factors warring against an absolute rule of enforcing such terms against the party who may have apparently assented to such terms?

MAGLIOZZI v. P&T CONTAINER SERVICE CO., INC.
Massachusetts Appeals Court
614 N.E.2d 690 (1993)

GILLERMAN, J.

Seeking a shorter path to a coffee truck on the premises of Crusader Paper Co., Inc. (Crusader), the plaintiff Magliozzi, an employee of Crusader, walked through the inside of a large trash compactor leased to Crusader by P&T Container Co. Inc. (P&T), under a written lease agreement. Magliozzi's foot caught in the compactor, he was injured, and he brought suit against P&T, which was the owner, manufacturer, and installer of the compactor. P&T, in turn, brought a third-party action against Crusader for indemnification of any costs for which P&T might be liable to the employee based upon an alleged contract of indemnification between Crusader and P&T.[3] Crusader's motion for summary judgment on the third-party complaint was allowed on the basis that there was no valid contract of indemnification between the parties.

The agreement between Crusader and P&T appears in a letter dated November 3, 1983. It is in the form of an offer to lease a two cubic yard compaction unit. Of particular importance is the fact that there is no indemnity agreement in the letter running in favor of P&T. It is also undisputed that in order to bill for the pickup and dumping services P&T prepared a pickup ticket. The pickup ticket comes into play in the following manner. Crusader would contact P&T in order to empty a compactor of its rubbish. P&T would then generate a standard form "pickup order ticket," in triplicate, with a pickup number and a description of the number of containers to be emptied and dumped. A driver of P&T would empty the compactor and obtain the signature of a Crusader employee on the face of the pickup ticket. The driver would keep two copies and leave a copy with the Crusader employee;

---

[3] [1] "[A] third-party tortfeasor may recover indemnity from an employer only if the employer had expressly or impliedly contracted to indemnify the third party of if the employer and the third party stand in a relationship that carries with it the obligation to indemnify the third party." *Liberty Mut. Ins. Co. v. Westerlind*, 374 Mass. 524, 526 (1978).

P&T would later staple a copy of the pickup ticket to Crusader's invoice for the services performed.

There is no language on the face of the ticket calling attention to, or referring in any way to, the reverse side of the ticket, nor is there any such reference on P&T's invoice to Crusader. On the reverse side of the pickup ticket, however, an indemnity provision is printed,[4] and that provision is the basis of the claim of P&T against Crusader.

P&T asks us to treat this case as a "battle of the forms" under art. 2 of the Uniform Commercial Code, arguing that the indemnification clause became an additional term of the contract because Crusader did not object to the term within a reasonable period of time. Crusader responds that art. 2 does not apply to leases.

We need not decide whether art. 2 applies to the lease at issue in this case because the only relevant consideration is whether there was a valid amendment to the November 3 agreement. Under the analogous provision of art. 2, see *Dazien's, Inc. v. Hodgman Rubber Co., 7 Mass. App. Ct. 901 (1979)* (UCC applied by analogy), and under the common law, the conclusion is the same: in the circumstances presented here, the pickup ticket did not modify the completed contract between the parties.

The principles expressed in G. L. c. 106, § 2-207, provide no assistance to P&T because those provisions bear on the formation of a contract. Thus, for example, where a "definite and seasonable" acceptance contains additional terms, those additional terms, as between merchants, may become part of the contract under § 2-207(2) unless precluded by subdivisions (a), (b) or (c) of that section. Here, it is undisputed that P&T's letter of November 3 was a completed contract between the parties, and we may assume that the compactor was installed, in place, and in use for Crusader's refuse before the first pickup ticket was cut by P&T. Once agreement has been reached and performance has commenced, § 2-207 does not operate to make additional terms that are proposed unilaterally in a later writing part of the complete agreement.

The result is no different under common law principles. Generally, it is a question of fact whether a party intended to relinquish contractual rights by entering into a subsequent agreement. An inference of assent is not warranted, however, where the subsequent writing (1) is used for other purposes — here, the acknowledgment of a refuse pickup; (2) does not purport to be a contract and is not contractual in form; and (3) gives no notice whatsoever of proposed additional terms which are not visible on the face of the writing. In these situations, the "party without knowledge or reason to know that the . . . [pickup ticket] purports to be a contract is then not bound by terms printed on the [ticket]." RESTATEMENT (SECOND) OF CONTRACTS § 211 comment d & illustration 3 (1979). Contrast *Polonsky v. Union Fed. Sav. & Loan Assn.*, 334 Mass. 697, 701 (1956) (conditions in bank book are part of contract whether or not brought to the attention of depositor because it is common

---

[4] [3] "The customer agrees to defend, indemnify and hold harmless P&T Container from and against any and all claims for loss or damage to property, or injury to or death of person or persons resulting from or arising in any manner out of customer's use, operation or possession of the equipment furnished under the agreement."

knowledge that bank books "frequently contain provisions defining the rights between the bank and its depositors").

In sum, there is nothing, save the words of indemnification printed on the back of the refuse pickup tickets, to give notice that P&T was extending an offer to modify the existing contract for Crusader's assent. As matter of law, Crusader was not bound by the indemnity clause. Were we to hold otherwise we would sanction an "unsuccessful ploy by . . . [P&T] unilaterally to add a term not covered by the preexisting binding contract." *Lorbrook Corp. v. G&T Indus., Inc.*, 162 A.D.2d at 73. There is no genuine issue as to any material fact, and Crusader is entitled to judgment as matter of law. Judgment *affirmed.*

"COVERT TOOLS" — PRECOCIOUS SOLUTIONS

PROBLEMS

(1)   Klar checked a parcel in defendant's parcel room and received a small parcel check made of cardboard. On the upper portion of the receipt there appeared in red letters, inch high the word, "contract" and directly beneath in finer type other printed material included the following: "Loss or damage — No claim shall be made in excess of $25 for loss or damage to any piece." When Klar presented the check to retrieve the parcel, he was told that it had been delivered to another. The package contained valuable furs. Klar did not read the parcel check nor was he asked to read it. He testified that he regarded it as a mere receipt for the package. Analyze. *See Klar v. H. & N. Parcel Room, Inc.*, 270 A.D. 538, 61 N.Y.S.2d 285 (1946).

(2)   Jennie Latshaw, en elderly home owner, required remodeling of her West Philadelphia home. She signed a contract document consisting of five printed form sheets. The face of each sheet identified the parties to the contract and the specifications of the work to be done in handwriting. While the reverse sides of the sheets could have been used to continue the written specifications since each reverse side carried the words, "specifications continued," there were no specifications written on those sides of the sheets. The reverse sides contained, in very small type, eight paragraphs, the sixth of which was a warrant of attorney/confession of judgment clause which waived exemption of property from levy and sale and further deprived the signer of every defense and every delay or execution. In effect, the signer is agreeing to the entry of a judgment with no trial after placing his cause in the hands of a hostile defendant. Miss Latshaw did not sign this document. Rather, she signed an "owner's consent" form which acknowledged the agreement and stated her assent to its terms. When she later became dissatisfied with the work and ordered the contractor to cease operations until defects in the work were corrected, the contractor confessed judgment pursuant to paragraph six. Miss Latshaw sought to open the judgment and argued that she should not be bound by this "drastic clause" appearing among eight paragraphs in diminutive type. Analyze. *See Cutler Corp. v. Latshaw*, 374 Pa. 1, 97 A.2d 234 (1953).

(3)   Helen Henningsen was injured when the steering mechanism failed on a new car purchased by her husband ten days before. When the husband and wife brought an action against the dealer and manufacturer for breach of the implied warranty of merchantability, the defendants relied upon a fine-print disclaimer of

that warranty in a standard form the husband had signed, limiting liability to replacement of defective parts for 90 days or 4000 miles, whichever occurred first. The buyer stated that he was unaware that the clause had anything to do with the kind of injuries suffered by his wife, i.e., he assumed it dealt only with repairs to the car. Other evidence indicated that the warranty was a standardized term in virtually every new automobile contract at the time which meant that the same limitation of liability would appear in such a contract to buy a new car, regardless of the brand or type of automobile purchased. Analyze. *See Henningsen v. Bloomfield Motors, Inc.*, 32 N.J. 358, 161 A.2d 69 (1960).

C. STANDARDIZED CONTRACTS — THE "REASONABLE EXPECTATIONS" SOLUTION

MAX TRUE PLASTERING CO. v. UNITED STATES FIDELITY AND GUARANTY CO.
Oklahoma Supreme Court
912 P.2d 861 (1996)

KAUGER, V.C.J.:

Two issues are presented by the questions certified: 1) whether the doctrine of reasonable expectations applies to the construction of insurance contracts in Oklahoma; and 2) what circumstances give rise to the doctrine's operation. Under the reasonable expectations doctrine, the objectively reasonable expectations of applicants, insureds and intended beneficiaries concerning the terms of insurance contracts are honored even though painstaking study of the policy provisions might have negated those expectations.[5] We find that the reasonable expectations doctrine may apply to the construction of ambiguous insurance contracts or to contracts containing exclusions which are masked by technical or obscure language or which are hidden in policy provisions.

 The third-party defendant, Jeff R. Johnson (Johnson/agent), sold a fidelity bond to the plaintiff, Max True Plastering Company (True/insured), insuring True for some losses arising from employee dishonesty.[6] The bond was purchased from the defendant, United States Fidelity and Guaranty Company (USF&G/insurer).

In the summer of 1991, True discovered that employees in his Dallas office had formed a corporation, LCR, Inc. (LCR), and that they were diverting True business

---

[5] [2] Johnson v. Farm Bureau Mut. Ins. Co., 533 N.W.2d 203, 206 (Iowa 1995); Atwater Creamery v. Western Nat'l Mut. Ins., see note 5 at 277, *infra*; State v. Underwriters at Lloyds London, 755 P.2d 396, 400 (Alaska 1988); American Family Mut. Ins. Co. v. Elliot, 523 N.W.2d 100, 103 (S.D. 1994); H. Wood, Jr., *The Insurance Fallout Following Hurricane Andrew: Whether Insurance Companies are Legally Obligated to Pay for Building Code Upgrades Despite the "Ordinance or Law" Exclusion Contained in Most Homeowners Policies*, 48 U. MIAMI L. REV. 949, 956 (1994); 6B J. APPLEMAN, INSURANCE LAW & PRACTICE, § 4254 at pp. 24–26 (1979); R. Keeton, *Insurance Law Rights at Variance with Policy Provisions*, 83 HARV. L. REV. 961, 966 (1970).

[6] [3] The policy provides in pertinent part: "A. COVERAGE 1. Covered Property: 'Money', 'securities', and 'property other than money and securities' . . . ."

to it. True filed suit against LCR and the employees in October of 1991. The following June, True wrote the agent notifying him of losses from employee dishonesty; and he claimed coverage under the USF&G policy. USF&G denied coverage on August 16, 1993, asserting that True had not complied with the policy's notice and proof of loss requirements and that losses of intellectual property, such as the diversion of job opportunities and lost profits, were not covered by the policy.

True filed suit against USF&G to recover under the policy on August 30, 1993. True contended that coverage existed either under the express terms of the policy or that he was insured because of his reasonable expectations that the losses were covered. On July 28, 1994, USF&G filed a third-party petition against Johnson and his agency claiming indemnity if True prevailed. USF&G and Johnson both filed motions for summary judgment on December 2, 1994. True filed an objection to USF&G'S motion on December 9th claiming coverage either under the plain reading of the policy or pursuant to his reasonable expectations. Finding no Oklahoma precedent to resolve the questions of law, the trial court certified two questions to this Court pursuant to the Uniform Certification of Questions of Law Act, 20 O.S. 1991 § 1601 et seq., on July 14, 1995.

True argues that although this Court has not expressly adopted the reasonable expectations doctrine, many of the principles applied in Oklahoma to the construction of insurance contracts conform to the spirit of the doctrine. It urges us to join the majority of jurisdictions which have considered the doctrine by recognizing it as part of Oklahoma law. USF&G and Johnson insist that insureds are adequately protected by existing principles applied to the construction of insurance contracts and they contend that those courts which have rejected the doctrine offer the better reasoned opinions.

An adhesion contract is a standardized contract prepared entirely by one party to the transaction for the acceptance of the other. These contracts, because of the disparity in bargaining power between the draftsman and the second party, must be accepted or rejected on a "take it or leave it" basis without opportunity for bargaining — the services contracted for cannot be obtained except by acquiescing to the form agreement. Insurance contracts are contracts of adhesion because of the uneven bargaining positions of the parties. The doctrine of reasonable expectations has evolved as an interpretative tool to aid courts in discerning the intention of the parties bound by adhesion contracts. It developed in part because established equitable doctrines were inadequate, and it takes into account the realities of present day commercial practice.

Under the doctrine, if the insurer or its agent creates a reasonable expectation of coverage in the insured which is not supported by policy language, the expectation will prevail over the language of the policy. The doctrine does not negate the importance of policy language. Rather, it is justified by the underlying principle that generally the language of the policy will provide the best indication of the parties' reasonable expectations. The standard under the doctrine is a "reasonable expectation"; and courts must examine the policy language objectively to determine whether an insured could reasonably have expected coverage. Courts adopting the reasonable expectations doctrine have found its rationale for interpretation of the usual insurance contract to be sensible. They also recognize that insurance law is the basis of the doctrine. These courts acknowledge that different rules of construction have traditionally been applied to insurance contracts because of their adhesive nature. Tribunals embracing the doctrine recognize that it is consistent with numerous other interpretive rules pertaining to adhesion contracts. Many of these rules are a part of Oklahoma law. For instance: 1) ambiguities are construed most strongly against the insurer; 2) in cases of doubt, words of inclusion are liberally applied in favor of the insured and words of exclusion are strictly construed against the insurer; 3) an interpretation which makes a contract fair and reasonable is selected over that which yields a harsh or unreasonable result; 4) insurance contracts are construed to give effect to the parties' intentions; 5) the scope of an agreement is not determined in a vacuum, but instead with reference to extrinsic circumstances; and 6) words are given effect according to their ordinary or popular meaning. Nevertheless, these rules of construction are often inadequate because they may fail to recognize the realities of the insurance business and the methods used in modern insurance practice.[7]

Of the thirty-six jurisdictions which have addressed the reasonable expectations doctrine, our research reveals only four courts which have rejected the rule. Although the Utah court recognized its duty to invalidate insurance provisions contrary to public policy, it refused to adopt the doctrine on the basis that its operation is not well-defined, and its deference to the occupation of the insurance field by the legislative and the executive branches.' The three other courts rejected the doctrine in favor of traditional construction guidelines relating to insurance contracts.

Although the reasonable expectations doctrine has not been adopted per se in Oklahoma, several cases indicate that the reasonable expectations of an insured will be considered in the construction of insurance contracts. In *Homestead Fire Ins. Co. v. De Witt*, 206 Okla. 570, 245 P.2d 92, 94 (1952), this Court quoted from *Bird v. St. Paul Fire & Marine Ins. Co.*, 224 N.Y. 47, 120 N.E. 86–87, 13 A.L.R. 875 (1918) referring to the construction of an insurance policy:

> Our guide is the reasonable expectation and purpose of the ordinary business man making an ordinary business contract. It is his intention, expressed or fairly to be inferred, that counts. (Emphasis supplied.)

In *Conner v. Transamerica Ins. Co.*, 496 P.2d 770, 774 (Okla. 1972), we held that the insurer was obligated to defend its insureds in actions involving dishonest, fraudulent, criminal and malicious conduct or omissions. The Court's holding in Conner was buttressed by a quotation from *Gray v. Zurich Ins. Co.*, 65 Cal. 2d 263, 54 Cal. Rptr. 104, 419 P.2d 168 (1966) providing in pertinent part:

> . . . This language, in its broad sweep, would lead the insured reasonably to expect defense of any suit regardless of merit or cause . . . . The basic promise would support the insured's *reasonable expectation* that he had bought the rendition of legal services to defend against a suit for bodily

---

[7] [26] Darner Motor Sales Inc. v. Universal Underwriters Ins. Co., 773 P.2d 1012 (1989); Abraham, *Judge-Made Law & Judge-Made Insurance: Honoring the Reasonable Expectations of the Insured*, 67 VA. L. REV. 1151 (1981); Murray, *The Parole Evidence Process and Standardized Agreements under the Restatement (Second) of Contracts*, 123 U. PA. L. REV. 1342 (1975).

injury which alleged he had caused it, negligently, nonintentionally, intentionally or in any other manner . . . (Emphasis supplied.)

The Conner Court acknowledged that the views expressed in Gray comported with the rules established in Oklahoma for interpretation of insurance contracts.

The reasonable expectation doctrine is a double-edged sword — both parties to the insurance contract may rely upon their reasonable expectations. We refused to extend a homeowner's policy to provide coverage for negligent supervision or failure to control in *Phillips v. Estate of Greenfield*, 859 P.2d 1101, 1106 (Okla. 1993). The rationale for denying coverage was based upon our belief that to do so would "negate the reasonable expectations of the parties as expressed in their contract."

Some courts rely upon a form of the reasonable expectations doctrine espoused in § 211 of the RESTATEMENT (SECOND) OF CONTRACTS[8] to protect the expectations of the contracting parties. Under the Restatement, reformation of an insurance contract is allowed if the insurer has reason to believe that the insured would not have signed the contract if the inclusion of certain limitations had been known.

Generally, absent an ambiguity, insurance contracts are subject to the same rules of construction as other contracts. However, because of their adhesive nature, these contracts are liberally construed to give reasonable effect to all their provisions. Our

---

[8] [30] RESTATEMENT (SECOND) OF CONTRACTS § 211 (1979) formulates the doctrine in a manner which allows a fact finder to look at the totality of the circumstances in determining the intent of the parties, rather than being strictly confined to the four corners of a standardized agreement. Section 211 provides:

(1) Except as stated in Subsection (3), where a party to an agreement signs or otherwise manifests assent to a writing and has reason to believe that like writings are regularly used to embody terms of agreements of the same type, he adopts the writing as an integrated agreement with respect to the terms included in the writing.

(2) Such a writing is interpreted whenever reasonable as treating alike all those similarly situated, without regard to their knowledge or understanding of the standard terms of the writing.

(3) Where the other party has reason to believe that the party manifesting such assent would not do so if he knew that the writing contained a particular term, the term is not part of the agreement.

Comment (b) to § 211 points out that parties regularly using standardized agreements ordinarily do not expect customers to understand or even to read the standard terms. Customers trust to the good faith of the party using the form and to the tacit representation that like terms are being accepted regularly by others similarly situated. Subsection (3) of § 211 is the Restatement's characterization of the reasonable expectations doctrine. Comment (f) to the subsection outlines a sensible rationale for interpretation of the usual insurance agreement. It provides in pertinent part:

Although customers typically adhere to standardized agreements and are bound by them without even appearing to know the standard terms in detail, they are not bound to unknown terms which are beyond the range of reasonable expectation . . . . [An insured] who adheres to the [insurer's] standard terms does not assent to a term if the [insurer] has reason to believe that the [insured] would not have accepted the agreement if he had known that the agreement contained the particular term. Such a belief or assumption may be shown by the prior negotiations or inferred from the circumstances. Reason to believe may be inferred from the fact that the term is bizarre or oppressive, from the fact that it eviscerates the non-standard terms explicitly agreed to, or from the fact that it eliminates the dominant purpose of the transaction. The inference is reinforced if the adhering party never had an opportunity to read the term, or if it is illegible or otherwise hidden from view. This rule is closely related to the policy against unconscionable terms and the rule of interpretations against the draftsman.

case law and the interpretive rules applied to insurance contracts demonstrate that Oklahoma law is consistent with the spirit and the policy of the reasonable expectations doctrine. The same case law coincides with the reasoning of the majority of jurisdictions adopting the doctrine.

holding

THE REASONABLE EXPECTATIONS DOCTRINE MAY APPLY TO THE CONSTRUCTION OF AMBIGUOUS INSURANCE CONTRACTS OR TO CONTRACTS CONTAINING EXCLUSIONS MASKED BY TECHNICAL OR OBSCURE LANGUAGE OR HIDDEN POLICY PROVISIONS.

True urges us to adopt a version of the reasonable expectations doctrine which does not require a finding of ambiguity in policy language before the doctrine is applied. Although they urge us not to adopt the doctrine, USF&G and Johnson argue that if the doctrine is to apply in Oklahoma, it should be limited to situations in which the policy contains an ambiguity or to contracts containing unexpected exclusions arising from technical or obscure language or which are hidden in policy provisions. We agree with this limitation.

Should apply

If the doctrine is not put in the proper perspective, insureds could develop a "reasonable expectation" that every loss will be covered by their policy and courts would find themselves engaging in wholesale rewriting of insurance policies. Therefore, the jurisdictions which have adopted the doctrine apply it to cases where an ambiguity is found in the policy language or where the exclusions are obscure or technical or are hidden in complex policy language. In these cases, the doctrine is utilized to resolve ambiguities in insurance policies and considers the language of the policies in a manner which conforms the policies with the parties' "reasonable expectations."

ambiguous when...

A policy term is ambiguous under the reasonable expectations doctrine if it is reasonably susceptible to more than one meaning. When defining a term found in an insurance contract, the language is given the meaning understood by a person of ordinary intelligence. The doctrine does not mandate either a pro-insurer or pro-insured result because only reasonable expectations of coverage are warranted.

In Oklahoma, unambiguous insurance contracts are construed, as are other contracts, according to their terms. The interpretation of an insurance contract and whether it is ambiguous is determined by the court as a matter of law. Insurance contracts are ambiguous only if they are susceptible to two constructions. In interpreting an insurance contract, this Court will not make a better contract by altering a term for a party's benefit. We do not indulge in forced or constrained interpretations to create and then to construe ambiguities in insurance contracts.

The reasonable expectations doctrine comports with our case law and with the rules of construction applied to insurance contracts. Oklahoma law mandates that we join the majority of jurisdictions which have considered application of the doctrine and apply it to cases in which policy language is ambiguous and to situations where, although clear, the policy contains exclusions masked by technical or obscure language or hidden exclusions.

The reasonable expectations doctrine recognizes the true origin of standardized contract provisions, frees the courts from having to write a contract for the parties, and removes the temptation to create ambiguity or invent intent to reach a result.

The underlying principle of the reasonable expectations doctrine — that reasonable expectations of insurance coverage should be honored — has been recognized by the majority of jurisdictions which have considered the issue and by a steady progression of Oklahoma law. By adopting the reasonable expectations doctrine, we recognize that it is important that ambiguous clauses or carefully drafted exclusions should not be permitted to serve as traps for policy holders. Nevertheless, it is equally imperative that the provisions of insurance policies which are clearly and definitely set forth in appropriate language, and upon which the calculations of the company are based, should be maintained unimpaired by loose and ill-considered judicial interpretation. Today, we hold that the doctrine of reasonable expectations may be applicable to the interpretation of insurance contracts in Oklahoma, and *Rule* that the doctrine may apply to ambiguous contract language or to exclusions which are masked by technical or obscure language or which are hidden in a policy's provisions.

NOTE

Since the modern judicial notion of a "contract of adhesion" was first detected in cases involving insurance contracts, it is anything but remarkable that the "reasonable expectation" concept would appear initially in such cases. RESTATEMENT (SECOND) OF CONTRACTS analysis of standardized agreements reveals the "reasonable expectation" analysis in comment f to § 211. Notwithstanding the angular language and placement of this new Restatement section, it augurs a significant development with respect to all standardized (printed form) agreements. Arizona courts were clearly precocious in this area, but as the principal case suggests, courts in other jurisdictions have recognized the concept. For an analysis of the RESTATEMENT (SECOND) concept, see Murray, *The Standardized Agreement Phenomena in the Restatement (Second) of Contracts*, 67 CORNELL L. REV. 735 (1982). For an analysis of application by other courts, see Slawson, *The New Meaning of Contract: The Transformation of Contract Law by Standard Forms*, 46 U. PITT. L. REV. 21 (1984). In general, see MURRAY ON CONTRACTS § 98.

D.   FROM FRAUD TO UNCONSCIONABILITY

GERMANTOWN MFG. CO. v. RAWLINSON
Pennsylvania Superior Court
491 A.2d 138 (1985)

CAVANAUGH, J.

Robert G. Rawlinson was employed by The Germantown Manufacturing Company in Marple Township as its assistant controller. Over a period of twenty-one months, Mr. Rawlinson embezzled $327,011.22 from the company. On Friday, May 21, 1982, the company discovered the misappropriation. Mr. Rawlinson admitted his wrongdoing to the company controller, Mr. Harry Dinkel, and was fired. However, Mr. Rawlinson did not tell his wife about either the misappropriation of the company monies or the loss of his job until the following Monday, May 24, 1982. Sometime between Friday and Monday, Mrs. Joan Rawlinson, Robert's wife, answered a phone call for her husband from a Mr. Peter Kulaski who identified himself as an insurance adjuster. On Monday, May 24, 1982, she answered a second call for her husband from Mr. Kulaski. Sensing that something was amiss, she summoned her husband to the phone but stayed on an extension and overheard Mr. Kulaski say, "Have you told your wife yet?" At this, she hung up the phone, and when her husband had finished his conversation she demanded to know what was going on. Mr. Rawlinson told his wife that he had lost his job because he had taken about $20,000.00 from the company. He also asked his wife if she wanted a divorce. Mrs. Rawlinson testified that upon hearing all of this, her "whole world fell apart." She also testified that because she had suffered a miscarriage in late April, she was already tired and depressed when she learned of her husband's malefactions.

The following day, Tuesday, Mrs. Rawlinson spoke by phone with Mr. Kulaski, who was a representative of the company's insurer, and learned that he was coming to the house "to discuss documents." He did not tell her he would attempt to have her co-sign two judgment notes. Nor did he tell her the amount her husband had misappropriated. Mr. Kulaski arrived later that day and spent thirty to forty-five minutes with Mr. and Mrs. Rawlinson. Mrs. Rawlinson apparently succeeded in keeping her two young children from knowing the purpose of the meeting.

The purpose of the meeting, from Mr. Kulaski's perspective, was to have Mr. and Mrs. Rawlinson sign two judgment notes. The first note was for $160,000.00, the amount Mr. Rawlinson admitted having taken. The second was for "any and all amounts in excess of One hundred and sixty thousand dollars ($160,000) which are determined by Affidavit of the President of Germantown Manufacturing Company, which Affidavit, when presented with this Note, shall constitute sufficient proof of a sum certain for the purpose of the Confession of Judgment contained herein." Both notes authorized any attorney to confess judgment in favor of Germantown Manufacturing against the Rawlinsons. Mrs. Rawlinson was surprised to see her name on the documents. She asked Mr. Kulaski if she and her husband would need an attorney. Mr. Kulaski calmly stated that if the Rawlinsons dealt in good faith and continued to cooperate, there would be no need for an attorney. Kulaski also stated that his principal was not interested in a criminal prosecution as long as Mr. and Mrs. Rawlinson cooperated. Mrs. Rawlinson understood this to mean that if she signed the notes her husband would not go to jail. Mrs. Rawlinson had never before seen a judgment note, and while she read them as best she could, she was crying for part of the time that she read them and believed that she was signing only one note for a total of $160,000.00. Mr. Kulaski told the Rawlinsons that since they had readily available assets totaling $160,000.00, the judgment was, in effect, already taken care of. She signed because she knew her husband had a check for $150,000.00 and the remaining $10,000.00 could be obtained without difficulty.

In August, Mr. Vernon Smith, the President of Germantown Manufacturing, completed the affidavit as required by the second note. The total amount owed on this note according to the affidavit was $212,113.21.

The first note (for $160,000.00) has been satisfied. Mrs. Rawlinson's obligation as to it is not at issue. The only issue before us is whether the lower court abused its discretion in opening judgment on the second note. [This appeal concerns only the question of opening the judgment with respect to Mrs. Rawlinson].

The opening of a confessed judgment is governed by well-settled principles:

> In order to open a confessed judgment, a party must act promptly, allege a meritorious defense, and present sufficient evidence of that defense to require submission of the issues to a jury . . . . A petition to open a judgment is an appeal to the equitable powers of the court and is addressed to the sound discretion of the court; a reviewing court will not reverse the determination of the lower court absent a clear and manifest abuse of discretion . . . . The standard of sufficiency a court must employ is that of the directed verdict — viewing all the evidence in the light most favorable to the petitioner and accepting as true all evidence and proper inferences therefrom supporting the defense while rejecting adverse allegations of the party obtaining the judgment.

Underlying our analysis in the instant case is the realization that "[a] warrant of attorney authorizing judgment is perhaps the most powerful and drastic document known to civil law . . . . The signing of a warrant of attorney is equivalent to a warrior of old entering a combat by discarding his shield and breaking his sword. For that reason the law jealously insists on proof that this helplessness and impoverishment was voluntarily accepted and consciously assumed." *Cutler Corporation v. Latshaw*, 374 Pa. 1, 4–5, 97 A.2d 234, 236 (1953). In analyzing the judgment notes in question, we are to be guided by the rules which apply to other written contracts.

The lower court found that appellee, Joan Rawlinson, presented three meritorious defenses which permitted it to exercise its equitable discretion and open judgment: 1) fraud and misrepresentation; 2) duress; and 3) the lack of accountability for the manner in which the appellant, Germantown Manufacturing, was permitted to arrive at the figure allegedly owed by the Rawlinsons. For the reasons we shall explain, we affirm the judgment of the lower court.

As one of the grounds for its decision to open judgment, the lower court found sufficient evidence of the meritorious defense of fraud and misrepresentation. In so holding, the lower court did not commit a clear and manifest abuse of discretion.

It scarcely seems necessary at this late jurisprudential hour in the day of *stare decisis* to cite cases to certify that fraud taints with illegality and invalidity anything its evil shadow darkens. Nor can there be any question of the right of a court to set aside any contract which is founded on fraud. This is as fundamental and solidly established as the foundations of the courthouse.

The recipient of a misrepresentation may avoid the contract by showing that the misrepresentation was either fraudulent or material. In the instant case, we find the misrepresentation to have been both fraudulent and material. Viewing the evidence in the light most favorable to Mrs. Rawlinson, the insurance company representative told the Rawlinsons that since they had $160,000.00 readily available, the judgment was, in effect, already satisfied. This statement clearly indicated to Mrs. Rawlinson that the limit of her liability and that of her husband was $160,000.00. However, the insurance man had her sign two notes, the first for $160,000.00 which is not at issue, and the second for any amount owing in excess of the first, which is the basis of this appeal. Her alleged liability under the second note was later determined by Germantown Manufacturing to be $212,113.21. Thus, Germantown Manufacturing and its insurer would make Mrs. Rawlinson liable for over $372,000.00 notwithstanding the initial misrepresentation that the limit of her liability would be $160,000.00. If Mrs. Rawlinson's testimony is true, it taxes credulity to assume that the insurance representative was unaware of his deceit in having the innocent wife sign the second note. Even if he was in fact unaware, he "had means of knowledge from which [he was] bound to ascertain the truth before making the representation. Misrepresentations made under such circumstances are fraudulent . . . ." *LaCourse v. Kiesel*, 366 Pa. 385, 390, 77 A.2d 877, 880 (1951). A statement uttered with such gross recklessness is deserving of the badge of fraud. In determining whether a misrepresentation is fraudulent, the RESTATEMENT (SECOND) OF CONTRACTS, § 162, distinguishes three types: The first type is where the maker of the misrepresentation knows or believes that the assertion is not in accord with the facts. Viewing the evidence in the light most favorable to Mrs. Rawlinson, the insurance agent's statement illustrates this type of fraudulent misrepresentation. The second type involves a situation where the maker expressly or impliedly suggests that the statement is based on knowledge [though] he knows it is mere opinion. Thus, even if the agent had stated his true opinion, he would still have committed a fraudulent misrepresentation by suggesting his assertion was grounded in fact and based upon knowledge rather than mere opinion. The third type involves a situation in which the maker honestly believes his assertion but lies about its basis. For example, if the agent had impliedly suggested that his assertion was based upon a particular investigation, then he would have been lying about the basis of his assertion if there had been no such investigation. We have no evidence of this third type of fraudulent misrepresentation in the instant case. Of the three types of fraudulent misrepresentation, the first type (the maker knows or believes the assertion is not in accord with the facts) is the classic type often referred to as "fraud" since it is simply a lie asserted to induce assent by the other party. See J. MURRAY, CASES & MATERIALS ON CONTRACTS 426 (3d ed. 1983). Our review of the record reveals that Mrs. Rawlinson presented sufficient evidence of this classic type of fraudulent misrepresentation to constitute a meritorious defense.

Even if the misrepresentation had not been fraudulent, the agreement may still be voidable because the misrepresentation was material. Where the misrepresentation is material, the party making the statement may believe his assertion to be true, and yet the agreement is voidable by the recipient as it induced him to manifest assent. "[T]he misrepresentation need not have been the sole or even the predominant" cause inducing one to assent, E.A. FARNSWORTH, CONTRACTS 244 (1982) and "[t]he requirement of materiality is usually met by showing that the misrepresentation would have been likely to have induced a reasonable person to make the contract." [*Id.* at] 243. Mrs. Rawlinson testified that she would not have signed had she known the terms of the second note. Thus, the representation may be said to have induced her to sign.

[A]nother type of fraudulent misrepresentation may be present here, fraud in the factum or execution. [T]his type of fraud would render the contract void, not just voidable. A typical example involves a surreptitious substitution of one document for another and the innocent party signing it without knowledge or a reasonable opportunity to know the character or essential terms of the substituted document. Here, Mrs. Rawlinson believed she was signing one document with a maximum liability of $160,000.00. While there was no finding of fraud in the factum below, nor was this argued on appeal, we note that such an argument would not have been frivolous.

The lower court further held that appellee presented sufficient evidence of duress to constitute a meritorious defense and thus render the contract voidable. We agree.

Pennsylvania appellate courts have given scant attention of late to this defense as applied to the situation now confronting us. But other important authorities have afforded significant attention to this question.

The RESTATEMENT (SECOND) OF CONTRACTS states the following:

§ 175. When Duress by Threat Makes a Contract Voidable

(1) If a party's manifestation of assent is induced by an improper threat by the other party that leaves the victim no reasonable alternative, the contract is voidable by the victim.

RESTATEMENT (SECOND) OF CONTRACTS § 175.

§ 176. When a Threat Is Improper

(1) A threat is improper if

. . . .

(b) what is threatened is a criminal prosecution.

Comment c. Threat of prosecution.

. . . An explanation in good faith of the criminal consequences of another's conduct may not involve a threat . . . . The guilt or innocence of the person whose prosecution is threatened is immaterial in determining whether the threat is improper, although it may be easier to show that the threat actually induced assent in the case of guilt.

Illustrations:

4. *A*, who believes that *B*, his employee, has embezzled money from him, threatens *B* that a criminal complaint will be filed and he will be prosecuted immediately unless he executes a promissory note for $5,000.00 in satisfaction of *A*'s claim. *B*, having no reasonable alternative, is induced by *A*'s threat to sign the note. The note is voidable by *B* . . . .

RESTATEMENT (SECOND) OF CONTRACTS § 176.

The key factor is state of mind: was the victim's mind so beclouded by apprehension that he unwillingly signed a repayment or other note?

In the instant case, appellant took the unsolicited liberty of including Mrs. Rawlinson's name on the judgment notes and did not even tell her it was doing so until minutes before she was asked to sign them. Mrs. Rawlinson had already been in a weakened mental state as the result of a recent miscarriage, and was visibly upset during the meeting, having learned of her husband's malefactions. At the meeting, she was told that if she cooperated, she would have no need for legal counsel. She understood this to mean that if she signed the notes, her husband would not go to jail. She had no reasonable alternative but to sign. That Germantown Manufacturing was ready to carry out its threat is evidenced by the letter from Germantown's attorney to the attorney subsequently retained by Mrs. Rawlinson.

> Gentlemen: I represent Germantown Manufacturing Company in connection with the wrongful conversion of $327,011.22 by Robert G. Rawlinson, Jr., of which $160,000.00 has been repaid. It has come to my attention that Mr. and Mrs. Rawlinson have retained both of you to remove and/or satisfy certain judgments by confession in the amount of $160,000.00 which were entered against the Rawlinsons in Pennsylvania and New Jersey within the last several months. This letter will serve as notice to you and your clients that unless all efforts by you on behalf of the Rawlinsons to attack the judgments are withdrawn and discontinued on or before 3:00 p.m. on Friday, August 13, 1982, I have been authorized to present the information and evidence in our possession to the appropriate prosecutor's office for criminal action. Failing to receive such proof shall be treated as a refusal by the Rawlinsons to cooperate further and pay the entire debt.

Appellee's admission that Mr. Rawlinson actually took the funds does not harm and may even strengthen her defense of duress as "it may be easier to show that the threat actually induced assent in the case of guilt." RESTATEMENT (SECOND) OF CONTRACTS § 176 comment c. Moreover, the fact that Mr. Kulaski did not threaten "imminent" arrest should be of no concern in the present analysis. Nor should it matter if the threat of prosecution was not expressly stated. "[T]he bargain is just as illegal when the agreement is implied as when it is express." 6A A. CORBIN, CORBIN ON CONTRACTS § 1421 (1962).

Furthermore, we note that agreements not to prosecute have been called "emphatically illegal." Although the law will leave parties who are *in pari delicto* where it finds them, see J. MURRAY, MURRAY ON CONTRACTS § 346 (2d ed. 1974), "[a] party who is pressured into an illegal bargain by duress is deemed not to be equally guilty with the party exercising the pressure . . . ." CALAMARI AND PERILLO, CONTRACTS 266–67 (2d ed. 1977). Thus, this defense will not be barred. It is an affront to our judicial sensibilities that one person's ability to seek another's prosecution can be bartered and sold the same as commodities in the market place. It is even more repugnant when the foul stench of oppression pervades the transaction.

It is clear beyond peradventure that the "choice" available to Mrs. Rawlinson exuded impermissible coercion. We note that appellee's status as spouse to the alleged embezzler, though not argued as such by appellee, lends credence to our finding of duress in the instant case. Mrs. Rawlinson signed the documents presented her believing that her cooperation was necessary to keep her husband from going to jail. We dare not lend our judicial imprimatur to a transaction which holds the institution of the family in such lowly regard. Just as "courts will not enforce an agreement that tends unreasonably toward dissolution of a marriage," E.A. FARNSWORTH, CONTRACTS 344 (1982), neither should we enforce the second note. The only alternative for a reasonable party in the position of Mrs. Rawlinson was to refuse to sign and thus place an almost assuredly unbearable stress on her marriage and on the tranquility of the Rawlinson household. This is the epitome of duress.

A mutually exclusive basis for our holding in this case is found in the concept of unconscionability. Though the appellee does not argue this defense by name, she does aver the elements of unconscionability — that the terms of the second note were not manifested in a fashion reasonably comprehensible to her and that she had no reasonable choice but to sign; thus an analysis of this doctrine is appropriate.

"Unconscionability" is a defensive contractual remedy which serves to relieve a party from an unfair contract or from an unfair portion of a contract. *See* D. DOBBS, HANDBOOK ON THE LAW OF REMEDIES, 707 (1973). The unconscionability section of the Uniform Commercial Code (see 13 Pa. C.S. § 2302)[9] has been called "one of the most innovative sections" in the Code, a section which Karl Llewellyn, Chief Reporter of the Code, described as "perhaps the most valuable . . . in the entire Code." E. A. FARNSWORTH, CONTRACTS 307 (1982) (citation omitted). "Perhaps the most durable dictum on the meaning of 'unconscionability' is that of the court in [*Williams v. Walker-Thomas Furniture Company*, 350 F.2d 445, 449 (D.C. Cir. 1965)]: 'Unconscionability has generally been recognized to include an absence of meaningful choice on the part of one of the parties together with contract terms which are unreasonably favorable to the other party.'" E.A. FARNSWORTH, CONTRACTS 314 (1982). The unconscionability defense has been extended beyond the code to non-sale of goods cases. *See* RESTATEMENT (SECOND) OF CONTRACTS § 208. The underlying rationale for this remedy is closely related to the rationale underlying fraud. The Supreme Court of our sister state of New Jersey has recognized that the purposes which both remedies were designed to serve are inextricably linked.

> The standard of conduct contemplated by the unconscionability clause is good faith, honesty in fact and observance of fair dealing. The need for application of this standard is most acute when the professional seller is seeking the trade of those most subject to exploitation — the uneducated, the inexperienced and the people of low incomes. In such a context, a material departure from the standard puts a badge of fraud on the transaction and here the concept of fraud and unconscionability are interchangeable.

Kugler v. Romain, 58 N.J. 522, 544, 279 A.2d 640, 652 (1971). Unconscionability and

---

[9] [Ed. Note: § 2-302. Unconscionable Contract or Clause

(1) If the court as a matter of law finds the contract or any clause of the contract to have been unconscionable at the time it was made, the court may refuse to enforce the contract, or it may enforce the remainder of the contract without the unconscionable clause, or it may so limit the application of any unconscionable clause as to avoid any unconscionable result.

(2) When it is claimed or appears to the court that the contract or any clause thereof may be unconscionable the parties shall be afforded a reasonable opportunity to present evidence of its commercial setting, purpose and effect to aid the court in making the determination.]

the other methods of avoiding an unfair contract examined herein do nothing more then reaffirm the most basic tenet of the law of contracts — that parties must be free to choose the terms to which they will be bound.

In deciding whether a contract, or a portion thereof, is unconscionable, the following analysis is useful.

> Parties to a contract rarely consciously advert to any number of terms which are binding upon them. If such terms allocate the risks of the bargain in a manner which the parties should have reasonably expected, they are enforceable — they are, to use the expression of Karl Llewellyn, "decent" terms. If the terms of the contract suggest a reallocation of material risks, an attempted reallocation may be so extreme that regardless of apparent and genuine assent, a court will not enforce it . . . . The parties will not be found to have agreed to an abnormal allocation of risks if the only evidence thereof is an inconspicuous provision in the boilerplate of the standard form. At a minimum, the reallocation must be physically conspicuous. Beyond that, it must have been manifested in a fashion comprehensible to the party against whom it is sought to be enforced. Finally, such party must have had a reasonable choice in relation to such reallocation.

J. MURRAY, MURRAY ON CONTRACTS § 353 (2d ed. 1974).

In the instant case, there can be no question but that the confession of judgment clause was the essence of a material, risk-shifting term. It was designed to summarily discard the due process guarantees which our system of jurisprudence so highly cherishes. It is difficult to conceive of a clause which alters risks in a more drastic fashion than one which dispenses with the signer's day in court. The signer has lost the lawsuit before it has begun.

> Perhaps confession of judgment clauses are so pernicious that they should be declared illegal. In the absence of illegality, however, the only concern of the court should be whether the party against whom the clause is supposed to operate knew about it and once his apparent assent is manifested, whether he had any choice at all in relation to it, i.e., whether the apparent assent is genuine.

J. Murray, *Unconscionability: Unconscionability*, 31 U. PITT. L. REV. 1, 19–20 (1969).

The first concept of unconscionability which we shall examine may be classified under the rubric of "unfair surprise." This type of unconscionability involves contractual terms which are not typically expected by the party who is being asked to "assent" to them. An unexpected clause often appears in the boilerplate of a printed form and, if read at all, is often not understood. By signing such a form, a party is bound only to those terms which such party would reasonably expect such a printed form to contain. If the form contains a material, risk-shifting clause which the signer would not reasonably expect to encounter in such a transaction, courts have held that the clause may be excised as it is unconscionable. This type of unconscionability is typically found only in consumer cases and courts have exhibited some reluctance to apply it in cases dealing with merchant-to-merchant contracts.

A court must determine what a particular party, in the context of the particular transaction, reasonably expected beyond the "dickered" terms. Unread terms in the form that are consistent with that expectation should be operative; those that are inconsistent should be inoperative. The conspicuousness of the print as well as the character of the document should be considered.

J. Murray, *The Standardized Agreement Phenomenon in the Restatement (Second) of Contracts*, 67 CORNELL L. REV. 735, 776 (1982).

In the instant case, Mrs. Rawlinson did not understand the terms of the second judgment note. The harsh allocation of risks was not manifested in a manner reasonably comprehensible to her. She had never before seen a judgment note and was crying for part of the time when she read the documents presented to her, although she tried her best to read them. The lack of real choice inherent in the transaction may have counseled against any need to thoroughly read and understand what she was signing. Furthermore, neither the insurance agent nor her husband offered her any guidance as to the extent of the liability to which she was agreeing. In fact, she was misled as to her liability. Therefore, the confession of judgment clause is "no more part of the agreement entered into than the advertisements on the walls of the room in which the contract is signed." *Cutler v. Latshaw*, 374 Pa. 1, 7, 97 A.2d 234, 237 (1953).

Mrs. Rawlinson has not manifested even "apparent" assent here. But even assuming that she read and understood the confession of judgment clause in all of its star-chamber ramifications, she did not genuinely assent to it because the clause was adhesive. The second concept of unconscionability which we shall examine concerns clauses wherein there is apparent but not genuine assent. *See* Kessler, *Contracts of Adhesion — Some Thoughts About Freedom of Contracts*, 43 COLUM. L. REV. 629 (1943).

The second concept of unconscionability has nothing to do with awareness of the terms of the contract. Assume the unusual situation of the party who reads and understands every scintilla of the printed form. He signs this document as the exclusive evidence of the deal. All courts admit evidence of misrepresentation, fraud, or duress to vitiate this apparent contract. Similarly, evidence of interference with the bargaining process falling short of these startling possibilities will also permit a court to refuse to enforce the contract or part of the contract. The party who requires goods or services important to his physical or economic well-being may have little or no choice but apparently to assent to the terms of a printed form dictated by the party with superior bargaining power. Even where other sources of supply are available, there may be conscious parallelism resulting in virtually identical printed forms offered by all available suppliers. The phrase "contract of adhesion" and the evil it suggests have been familiar for many years. The terms of these contracts do not surprise the weaker party because they were read and understood — perhaps even explained by the dictatorial supplier. Assent and volition and, therefore, agreement are absent. The weaker party should not suffer the hardship that such clauses create. For this type of unconscionability, that the clauses are printed on standard forms is irrelevant. Presumably, the clauses are as clearly understood as they would be in the form of a personal letter or telegram. The difficulties that courts must confront in determining whether a particular clause is oppressive can be enormous. For example, a court must determine whether a party had any genuine choice, whether there was gross disparity in bargaining power, and the like. The problems should not be exacerbated, however, by confusing unconscionability because of unexpected terms with unconscionability due to a lack of choice.

J. Murray, *The Standardized Agreement Phenomenon in the Restatement (Second) of Contracts*, 67 CORNELL L. REV. 735, 776–77 (1982). In the instant case, it is difficult to conceive of a greater lack of choice than that which faced Mrs. Rawlinson. We will not bind her to [a] clause to which she could not refuse her "assent."

Finally, the lower court held that an accounting is necessary to raise the second note above mere conjecture, surmise, or speculation. The absence of such an accounting, according to the lower court, constitutes a meritorious defense. When Mrs. Rawlinson signed the second judgment note, no amount was printed therein. Nor was there an affidavit attached stating the amount owed as the extent of Mr. Rawlinson's embezzlement was not then known to Germantown. The note authorized the President of Germantown to determine the amounts owed and to set forth such information in an affidavit. Though it did not say so expressly, the second note did not authorize the President to arbitrarily designate any amount he desired on a whim. Rather, the only amount which he could set was the amount actually determined to have been embezzled (above the amount satisfied by the first note). "Every contract imposes upon each party a duty of good faith and fair dealing in its performance and enforcement." RESTATEMENT (SECOND) OF CONTRACTS § 205. As Justice Cardozo once wrote: "The law has outgrown its primitive stage of formalism when the precise word was the sovereign talisman, and every slip was fatal. It takes a broader view today. A promise may be lacking, and yet the whole writing may be 'instinct with an obligation,' imperfectly expressed." *Wood v. Lucy, Lady Duff-Gordon*, 222 N.Y. 88, 91, 118 N.E. 214, 214 (1917) (citation omitted). We therefore imply the promise on the part of Germantown to act in good faith in determining and setting the amount owed. When Germantown's president filled in the amount allegedly owed on the face of the affidavit as required by the second note, included therein was over $45,000.00 in interest on the principal. Even assuming that Mrs. Rawlinson assented to the terms of the second note without fraud, misrepresentation, duress, or unconscionability interfering with her ability to choose, we cannot say that she agreed to pay interest on the principal, and so Germantown's inclusion of it in the affidavit may have been a breach of its duty to act in good faith. Thus, we hold that it constitutes a meritorious defense.

For these reasons, we *affirm* the lower court's order opening the judgment.

NOTE

Duty to Disclose. In the last chapter, we considered the pervasive principle that an offeree who knows or should know that the offeror is making a mistake may not "snap up" the offer, i.e., such an offeree's power of acceptance is nullified. The implication is that such an offeree has a duty to speak or disclose the fact that the offeror is apparently making a mistake. *"Misrepresentation"* is typically defined as an assertion that is not in accord with the facts," RESTATEMENT (SECOND) OF CONTRACTS § 159. *"Concealment"* does not involve language, but it is an affirmative act designed to prevent another from learning the fact. Where, for example, a builder knew of a defect in the floor of a basement and covered the defect with tile to conceal it, this was a conduct assertion not in accordance with the facts. *Jenkins v. McCormick*, 339 P.2d 8 (1959). *See also Sage v. Broadcasting Publications*, Inc., 997 F. Supp. 49 (D.C. 1998) (concealment of certain material facts in a corporate merger).

"Nondisclosure," on the other hand, involves no affirmative act. The notion of a duty to disclose is antithetical to traditional views of individuality and bargaining. Each party to the contract often feels as if they have "won" the bargain and that assumption typically emanates from the view, misguided or not, that such party had superior knowledge. None other than Chief Justice John Marshall could not assimilate the concept of a duty to provide the other party to the contract with knowledge that the Treaty of Ghent had been signed, ending the war of 1812, resulting in a more than substantial increase in the price of tobacco through the removal of the British blockade of New Orleans. *Ladilaw v. Organ*, 15 U.S. (2 Wheat) 178 (1817).

Modern courts, however, recognize that nondisclosure may have the same effect as misrepresentation. A number of cases, for example, deal with the sale of a residence known to the seller to be infested with termites but fail to disclose that fact to the buyer. Such cases hold that the vendor has a duty to disclose such a material fact. *See, e.g., Ensminger v. Termink International Co.*, 102 F.3d 1571 (10th Cir. 1996); *Hill v. Jones*, 725 F.2d 1115 (Ariz. 1986); *Johnson v. Davis*, 480 So. 2d 625 (Fla. 1985); *Mercer v. Woodard*, 3 S.E.2d 475 (Ga. Ct. App. 1983); *Lynn v. Taylor*, 642 P.2d 131 (Kan. Ct. App. 1982). A failure to respond truthfully to a buyer's question may result in fraudulent nondisclosure, as where a seller of property failed to disclose a flooding incident when asked a relevant question about a sump hole, the court found a duty to speak and the seller's failure to meet that duty was a fraudulent nondislosure. *Marchand v. Presutti*, 509 A.2d 1092 (Conn. App. Ct. 1986). Similarly, where a buyer asked about a water conditioner in the basement and the seller answered that it was simply a device to soften the water but failed to disclose that the well water on the property was so laden with sulfur that even more expensive treatment would make the water barely drinkable, the court found the seller's incomplete and dishonest answer to allow a rescission of the contract. *Cushman v. Kirby*, 536 A. 2d 550 (Vt. 1987). A failure to act in good faith to correct the mistake of the other party that is basic to the transaction equates to an assertion not in accord with the facts. RESTATEMENT (SECOND) OF CONTRACTS § 161. Even the failure to disclose that a house was widely reputed to be haunted, thereby arguably lowering its economic value, was sufficient for a divided court to allow rescission of the contract. *Stambovsky v. Ackley*, 169 A.D.2d 254 (N.Y. 1991).

More complicated issues concerning nondisclosure are now appearing where plaintiffs seek recovery of tort damages for failure to disclose infectious diseases that could be sexually transmitted. Here, courts must struggle with the level of knowledge of the infected party who fails to disclose. If he knows he is infected, it is clear that he has a duty to disclose such a condition to the other party. If he has the symptoms of the disease or knows that he has engaged in sexual conduct with an infected third party, he has a duty to disclose these facts to a prospective sex partner. The fact that he has had multiple sex partners in the past, however, is, in itself, insufficient to require a duty to disclose. *See Doe v. Johnson*, 817 F. Supp. 1382 (W.D. Mich. 1993).

E. THE ORIGINAL UNCONSCIONABILITY ANALYSIS

WILLIAMS v. WALKER-THOMAS FURNITURE CO.
United States Court of Appeals, District of Columbia Circuit
350 F.2d 445 (1965)

WRIGHT, J.

Appellee, Walker-Thomas Furniture Company, operates a retail furniture store in the District of Columbia. During the period from 1957 to 1962 each appellant in these cases purchased a number of household items from Walker-Thomas, for which payment was to be made in installments. The terms of each purchase were contained in a printed form contract which set forth the value of the purchased item and purported to lease the item to appellant for a stipulated monthly rent payment. The contract then provided, in substance, that title would remain in Walker-Thomas until the total of all the monthly payments made equaled the stated value of the item, at which time appellants could take title. In the event of a default in the payment of any monthly installment, Walker-Thomas could repossess the item.

The contract further provided that "the amount of each periodical installment payment to be made by [purchaser] to the Company under this present lease shall be inclusive of and not in addition to the amount of each installment payment to be made by [purchaser] under such prior leases, bills or accounts; *and all payments now and hereafter made by [purchaser] shall be credited pro rata on all outstanding leases, bills and accounts* due the Company by [purchaser] at the time each such payment is made." (Emphasis added.) The effect of this rather obscure provision was to keep a balance due on every item purchased until the balance due on all items, whenever purchased, was liquidated. As a result, the debt incurred at the time of purchase of each item was secured by the right to repossess all the items previously purchased by the same purchaser, and each new item purchased automatically became subject to a security interest arising out of the previous dealings.

On May 12, 1962, appellant Thorne purchased an item described as a Daveno, three tables, and two lamps, having total stated value of $391.10. Shortly thereafter, he defaulted on his monthly payments and appellee sought to replevy all the items purchased since the first transaction in 1958. Similarly, on April 17, 1962, appellant Williams bought a stereo set of stated value of $514.95.[10] She too defaulted shortly thereafter, and appellee sought to replevy all the items purchased since December,

(recover)

---

[10] [1] At the time of this purchase her account showed a balance of $164 still owing from her prior

1957. The Court of General Sessions granted judgment for appellee. The District of Columbia Court of Appeals affirmed, and we granted appellants' motion for leave to appeal to this court.

Appellants' principal contention, rejected by both the trial and the appellate courts below, is that these contracts, or at least some of them, are unconscionable and, hence, not enforceable. In its opinion in *Williams v. Walker-Thomas Furniture Company*, 198 A.2d 914, 916 (1964), the District of Columbia Court of Appeals explained its rejection of this contention as follows:

> Appellant's second argument presents a more serious question. The record reveals that prior to the last purchase appellant had reduced the balance in her account to $164. The last purchase, a stereo set, raised the balance due to $678. Significantly, at the time of this and the preceding purchases, appellee was aware of appellant's financial position. The reverse side of the stereo contract listed the name of appellant's social worker and her $218 monthly stipend from the government. Nevertheless, with full knowledge that appellant had to feed, clothe and support both herself and seven children on this amount, appellee sold her a $514 stereo set.

We cannot condemn too strongly appellee's conduct. It raises serious questions of sharp practice and irresponsible business dealings. A review of the legislation in the District of Columbia affecting retail sales and the pertinent decisions of the highest court in this jurisdiction disclose, however, no ground upon which this court can declare the contracts in question contrary to public policy. We note that were the Maryland Retail Installment Sales Act, Art. 83 §§ 128–153, or its equivalent, in force in the District of Columbia, we could grant appellant appropriate relief. We think Congress should consider corrective legislation to protect the public from such exploitive contracts as were utilized in the case at bar.

We do not agree that the court lacked the power to refuse enforcement to contracts found to be unconscionable. In other jurisdictions, it has been held as a matter of common law that unconscionable contracts are not enforceable.[11] While no decision of this court so holding has been found, the notion that an unconscionable bargain should not be given full enforcement is by no means novel. In *Scott v. United States*, 79 U.S. (12 Wall.) 443, 445, 20 L. Ed. 438 (1870), the Supreme Court stated:

> If a contract be unreasonable and unconscionable, but not void for fraud, a court of law will give to the party who sues for its breach damages, not according to its letter, but only such as he is equitably entitled to . . . .[12]

---

purchases. The total of all the purchases made over the years in question came to $1,800. The total payments amounted to $1,400.

[11] [2] Campbell Soup Co. v. Wentz, 3 Cir., 172 F.2d 80 (1948); Indianapolis Morris Plan Corp. v. Sparks, 132 App. 145, 172 N.E.2d 899 (1961); Henningsen v. Bloomfield Motors, Inc., 32 N.J. 358, 161 A.2d 69, 84–96, 75 A.L.R.2d 1 (1960). *Cf.* 1 Corbin, Contracts § 128 (1963).

[12] [3] *See* Luing v. Peterson, 143 Minn. 6, 172 N.W. 692 (1919); Greer v. Tweed, N.Y.C.P., 13 Abb. Pr., N.S., 427 (1872); Schnell v. Nell, 17 Ind. 29 (1861); and see generally the discussion of the English authorities in Hume v. United States, 132 U.S. 406, 10 S. Ct. 134, 33 L. Ed. 393 (1889).

Since we have never adopted or rejected such a rule,[13] the question here presented is actually one of first impression.

Congress has recently enacted the Uniform Commercial Code, which specifically provides that the court may refuse to enforce a contract which it finds to be unconscionable at the time it was made. 28 D.C. Code § 2-302 (Supp. IV 1965). The enactment of this section, which occurred subsequent to the contracts here in suit, does not mean that the common law of the District of Columbia was otherwise at the time of enactment, nor does it preclude the court from adopting a similar rule in the exercise of its powers to develop the common law for the District of Columbia. In fact, in view of the absence of prior authority on the point, we consider the congressional adoption of § 2-302 persuasive authority for following the rationale of the cases from which the section is explicitly derived.[14] Accordingly, we hold that where the element of unconscionability is present at the time a contract is made, the contract should not be enforced.

Unconscionability has generally been recognized to include an absence of meaningful choice on the part of one of the parties together with contract terms which are unreasonably favorable to the other party.[15] Whether a meaningful choice is present in a particular case can only be determined by consideration of all the circumstances surrounding the transaction. In many cases the meaningfulness of the choice is negated by a gross inequality of bargaining power.[16] The manner in which the contract was entered is also relevant to this consideration. Did each party to the contract, considering his obvious education or lack of it, have a reasonable opportunity to understand the terms of the contract, or were the important terms hidden in a maze of fine print and minimized by deceptive sales practices? Ordinarily, one who signs an agreement without full knowledge of its terms might

---

[13] [4] While some of the statements in the court's opinion in District of Columbia v. Harlan & Hollingsworth Co., 30 App. D.C. 270 (1908), may appear to reject the rule, in reaching its decision upholding the liquidated damages clause in that case the court considered the circumstances existing at the time the contract was made, see 30 App. D.C. at 279, and applied the usual rule on liquidated damages. See 5 CORBIN, CONTRACTS §§ 1054–1075 (1964); Note, 72 YALE L.J. 723, 746–755 (1963). Compare Jaeger v. O'Donoghue, 18 F.2d 1013, 57 App. D.C. 191 (1927).

[14] [5] See Comment, § 2-302, Uniform Commercial Code (1962). Compare Note, 45 VA. L. REV. 583, 590 (1959), where it is predicted that the rule of § 2-302 will be followed by analogy in cases which involve contracts not specifically covered by the section. Cf. 1 State of New York Law Revision Commission, Report and Record of Hearings on the Uniform Commercial Code 108–110 (1954) (remarks of Professor Llewellyn).

[15] [6] See Henningsen v. Bloomfield Motors, Inc., supra Note 2; Campbell Soup Co. v. Wentz, supra Note 2.

[16] [7] See Henningsen v. Bloomfield Motors, Inc., supra Note 2, 161 A.2d at 86, and authorities there cited. Inquiry into the relative bargaining power of the two parties is not an inquiry wholly divorced from the general question of unconscionability, since a one-sided bargain is itself evidence of the inequality of the bargaining parties. This fact was vaguely recognized in the common law doctrine of intrinsic fraud, that is, fraud which can be presumed from the grossly unfair nature of the terms of the contract. See the oft-quoted statement of Lord Hardwicke in Earl of Chesterfield v. Janssen, 28 Eng. Rep. 82, 100 (1850): "[Fraud] may be apparent from the intrinsic nature and subject of the bargain itself; such as no man in his senses and not under delusion would make . . . ." And cf. Hume v. United States, supra Note 3, 132 U.S. at 413, 10 S. Ct. at 137, where the Court characterized the English cases as "cases in which one party took advantage of the other's ignorance of arithmetic to impose upon him, and the fraud was apparent from the face of the contracts." See also Greer v. Tweed, supra Note 3.

be held to assume the risk that he has entered a one-sided bargain.[17] But when a party of little bargaining power, and hence little real choice, signs a commercially unreasonable contract with little or no knowledge of its terms, it is hardly likely that his consent, or even an objective manifestation of his consent, was ever given to all the terms. In such a case the usual rule that the terms of the agreement are not to be questioned[18] should be abandoned and the court should consider whether the terms of the contract are so unfair that enforcement should be withheld.[19]

In determining reasonableness or fairness, the primary concern must be with the terms of the contract considered in light of the circumstances existing when the contract was made. The test is not simple, nor can it be mechanically applied. The terms are to be considered "in the light of the general commercial background and the commercial needs of the particular trade or case."[20]

Corbin suggests the test as being whether the terms are "so extreme as to appear unconscionable according to the mores and business practices of the time and place." 1 CORBIN, *op. cit. supra* Note 2.[21] We think this formulation correctly states the test to be applied in those cases where no meaningful choice was exercised upon entering the contract.

Because the trial court and the appellate court did not feel that enforcement could be refused, no findings were made on the possible unconscionability of the contracts in these cases. Since the record is not sufficient for our deciding the issues as a matter of law, the cases must be *remanded* to the trial court for further proceedings.

NOTES

(1)   *Origins.* The classic statement of unconscionability is found in an eighteenth century opinion, *Earl of Chesterfield v. Janssen*, 2 Yes. Sen. 125, 155, 28 Eng. Rep. 82, 100 (Ch. 1850), where the Chancery Court characterized a bargain as unconscionable if it was "such as no man in his senses and not under delusion would make

---

[17] [8] *See* RESTATEMENT, CONTRACTS § 70 (1932); Note, 63 HARV. L. REV. 494 (1950). See also Daley v. People's Building, Loan & Savings Ass'n, 178 Mass. 13, 59 N.E. 452, 453 (1901), in which Mr. Justice Holmes, while sitting on the Supreme Judicial Court of Massachusetts, made this observation:

> Courts are less and less disposed to interfere with parties making such contracts as they choose, so long as they interfere with no one's welfare but their own . . . . It will be understood that we are speaking of parties standing in an equal position where neither has any oppressive advantage or power . . . .

[18] [9] This rule has never been without exception. In cases involving merely the transfer of unequal amounts of the same commodity, the courts have held the bargain unenforceable for the reason that "in such a case, it is clear, that the law cannot indulge in the presumption of equivalence between the consideration and the promise." 1 WILLISTON, CONTRACTS § 115 (3d ed. 1957).

[19] [10] See the general discussion of "Boiler-Plate Agreements" in LLEWELLYN, THE COMMON LAW TRADITION 362–371 (1960).

[20] [11] Comment, Uniform Commercial Code § 2-307.

[21] [12] *See* Henningsen v. Bloomfield Motors, Inc., *supra* Note 2; Mandel v. Liebman, 303 N.Y. 88, 100 N.E.2d 149 (1951). The traditional test as stated in Greer v. Tweed, *supra* Note 3, 13 Abb. Pr., N.S., at 429, is "such as no man in his senses and not under delusion would make on the one hand, and as no honest or fair man would accept, on the other."

on the one hand, and as no honest and fair man would accept on the other." Though an action for damages at law would lie, courts of equity would refuse to grant equitable relief where the chancellor found the bargain to be unconscionable. The modern doctrine emanated from Professor Karl Llewellyn's inclusion of Section 2-302 of the Uniform Commercial Code. The amorphous language of that section sets forth unconscionability as a principle in simply stating that a court may refuse to enforce any unconscionable contract or unconscionable provision of a contract. It does not attempt to define the concept except for a less than effective statement in Comment 1: "The basic test is whether, in the light of the general commercial background and the commercial needs of the particular trade or case, the clauses involved are so one-sided as to be unconscionable under the circumstances existing at the time of the making of the contract." Another statement in the same comment is more confusing than helpful: "The principle is one of the prevention of oppression and unfair surprise and not of disturbance of allocation of risks because of superior bargaining power."

The subsequent version of the doctrine in the RESTATEMENT (SECOND) OF CONTRACTS, § 208, replicates the general language of UCC § 2-302 and is, therefore, of limited assistance. It is clear that Llewellyn viewed the concept as empowering courts to deal with manifestly unjust situations that could not be fitted into traditional categories such as fraud, duress, misrepresentation or undue influence. Indeed, the evidence was clear that courts would discover ways to discover just results through the use of what Llewellyn called "covert tools." He was eager to have courts eschew such "covert tools" and bring into the open their efforts to avoid unconscionable contracts or clauses. The section does not attempt to adumbrate details or tests to guide courts. Llewellyn was convinced that this section, his "favorite" section of Article 2, of which he was the principal draftsman, would be adumbrated on a case-by-case method over the years from which a body of "precedent" would be developed, thereby providing the necessary guidance and stability in the application of the doctrine. Unfortunately, courts have had considerable difficulty in carrying out Llewellyn's desire.

(2) *Developments Over a Half Century.* The vague contours of the unconscionability doctrine spawned a considerable scholarly literature as to its possible meaning and application. In a classic article by Professor Arthur Leff, *Unconscionability and the Code — The Emperor's New Clause*, 115 U. PA. L. REV. 485 (1967), the author suggested that language of Section 2-302 was only an "emotionally satisfying incantation," proving that "it is easy to say nothing with words." Notwithstanding this indictment, Leff suggested a distinction between procedural unconscionability (which he described as bargaining "naughtiness") and substantive unconscionability dealing with the one-sided and oppressive provision itself. As the principal case indicates, courts have adopted this dichotomy, but it has proved less than satisfactory. While the conventional wisdom suggested that a party would have to show elements of both procedural and substantive unconscionability, there are now several cases that have found a clause unconscionable and, therefore, unenforceable on the basis of substantive unconscionability alone. *See, e.g., Maxwell v. Fidelity Financial Services*, 907 P.2d 51 (Ariz. 1995); *Brower v. Gateway 2000, Inc.*, 246 A.D.2d 246 (N.Y. 1998).

The most notable manifestation of procedural unconscionability is found in the "contract of adhesion," the "take-it-or-leave-it" contract, with terms dictated by the party with superior bargaining power such as a major manufacturer or seller. The consumer who wishes to purchase the product has no negotiating power at all. While earlier cases focused heavily upon the contract of adhesion as strong evidence of unconscionability, modern courts reject that view. At best, a contract of adhesion is now viewed as only a possible factor in an unconscionability analysis and there are statements such as that of a prominent judge of the United States Court of Appeals for the Seventh Circuit (Judge Easterbrook) who asked, "But what's wrong with a contract of adhesion anyway?" *United States v. Hare*, 269 F.3d 859 (7th Cir. 2001). Though the unconscionability doctrine is often suggested in relation to standardized (printed form) contracts proferred by the party with superior bargaining power, the judge's prominent colleague on the same court (Judge Posner) concluded that, " 'unconscionability' is little more than an umbrella term for fraud, duress, illegality and violation of a fiduciary relationship — all of which are conventional grounds for invalidating a contract and have nothing special to do with form contracts." *Northwestern Nat'l Ins. Co. v. Donovan*, 916 F.2d 372, 377 (7th Cir. 1990). The earlier case of *Germantown Mfg. Co. v. Rawlinson, supra*, illustrates the point since unconscionability was unnecessary therein in the light of proof of fraud or duress. There are judicial suggestions that contracts of adhesion are procedurally unconscionable, *per se*, but, again, there is nothing wrong with them *per se*. That would leave substantive unconscionability as the sole test and courts are anything but clear concerning the definition of substantive unconscionability.

(3) *Scope-Consumer and Merchant Contracts — Arbitration Clauses*. While the unconscionability doctrine concept in the Uniform Commercial Code technically applies only to contracts for the sale of goods, it was applied to many other types of contract even before its assimilation in § 208 of the Restatement (Second) of Contracts, confirming its application to any type of contract. Notwithstanding its broad potential application and the original intention to apply it to parties with "commercial backgrounds," with rare exception the doctrine has not been applied in merchant-to-merchant transactions. In *Moscatiello v. Pittsburgh Contractors Equip. Co.*, 595 A.2d 1190, 1196 (Pa. Super. Ct. 1991), the opinion recognized this fact: "Courts have upheld limitation of damages provisions in sales contracts between merchants or experienced business concerns because there is no disparity between such entities in either bargaining power or sophistication" (citing *K & C v. Westinghouse Elec. Corp.*, 263 A.2d 390 (Pa. 1970), where the buyers were an attorney and experienced business person who contracted to purchase laundromat equipment from Westinghouse and claimed that a clause was unconscionable). The isolated exception occurs where the disadvantaged party is technically a merchant but, in terms of education, business acumen and experience, functions like a consumer. Thus, where an operator of a filling station who could barely read signed a contract with a major oil company containing a limitation of liability, the court was willing to apply the unconscionability doctrine in light of the operator's total lack of awareness of what he was signing and the absence of evidence that any effort had been made to explain the critical clauses to him. *Johnson v. Mobil Oil Corp.*, 418 F. Supp. 264 (E.D. Mich. 1976). There have been a number of "merchant" cases where the unconscionability defense has failed.

The typical unconscionability application has occurred with respect to consumers such as the buyer in *Williams v. Walker-Thomas Furniture*, preceding the principal case. Various consumer statutes enacted after the UCC may contain some reference to unconscionability, but consumer statutes such as various "lemon laws," suffer from a severe lack of uniformity. As one writer suggests, "The much mottled picture is a virtual Jackson Pollock product of drippings from a wide varietyof federal and state statutes, tinted with contrasting shades of judicial application and washed in parts by some peculiar disclosure provisions of the Magnuson-Moss Act.[22]

Federal consumer protection laws such as the Magnuson-Moss Warranty Act (15 U.S.C. § 2301 *et seq.*) are discussed in courses in commercial law. Early debates over the inclusion of consumer protection provisions in the Uniform Commercial Code resulted in a decision not to include them. The fact that there was any debate at all about this issue in the 1940s law is somewhat remarkable in itself. The essential reason for rejecting a consumer protection dimension was the necessity to create a modern commercial law to replace the old Uniform Sales Act which continued 19th century concepts. The hope of enactment in every jurisdiction of such a radical new sales law would have been hindered substantially if a precocious consumer protection dimension had been included. Ironically, the use of the unconscionability doctrine to provide protection against egregious, non-negotiated contract terms was not designed to protect the only parties who have had limited success in its application — consumers.

The general inapplicability of the doctrine to merchant cases and the lack of a definitive judicial analysis of the unconscionability doctrine has made it so unwieldy as to severely diminish its successful application. Currently, the major exception is found in cases such as the following case which illustrates the modern judicial analysis of unconscionability that requires a determination of whether a given term or entire contract is *procedurally* unconscionable and *substantively* unconscionable.

F. THE MODERN UNCONSCIONABILITY ANALYSIS

INGLE v. CIRCUIT CITY STORES, INC.
United States Court of Appeals, Ninth Circuit
328 F.3d 1165 (2003)

PREGERSON, J.

In September 1996, Catherine Ingle applied to become an Associate [Circuit City refers to all job applicants and to current and former employees as "Associates"] at a Circuit City electronics retail store in San Diego County, California. Ingle was required to sign an arbitration agreement for Circuit City to consider her employment application. By signing the arbitration agreement, Ingle agreed to resolve all employment-related legal claims through arbitration. Ingle filed this action against Circuit City in the Southern District of California. In her complaint,

---

[22] Donald F. Clifford, *Non-UCC Statutory Provisions Affecting Warranty Disclaimers and Remedies in Sales of Goods*, 71 N.C. L. REV. 111, 115 (1993).

Ingle alleged claims of sexual harassment, sex discrimination, and disability discrimination under [state and federal statutes]. Circuit City moved to compel arbitration. [T]he district court entered an order denying the motion on the ground that the arbitration agreement was unenforceable. The district court held that Circuit City's form application for employment unlawfully conditioned Ingle's employment on her agreement to forego statutory rights and remedies. Circuit City now appeals, arguing primarily that its arbitration agreement is enforceable.

The Federal Arbitration Act (FAA) provides that arbitration agreements generally "shall be valid, irrevocable, and enforceable." 9 U.S.C. § 2 (2002). But when grounds "exist at law or in equity for the revocation of any contract," courts may decline to enforce such agreements. It is a settled principle of law that "arbitration is a matter of contract." Federal law "directs courts to place arbitration agreements on equal footing with other contracts." Arbitration agreements, accordingly, are subject to all defenses to enforcement that apply to contracts generally. Unconscionability refers to an absence of meaningful choice on the part of one of the parties together with contract terms which are unreasonably favorable to the other party. Thus, a contract to arbitrate is unenforceable under the doctrine of unconscionability when there is both a procedural and substantive element of unconscionability. Significantly, procedural and substantitve unconscionability need not be present in the same degree. Essentially a sliding scale is invoked which disregards the regularity of the procedural process of the contract formation, that creates the terms, in proportion to the greater harshness or unreasonableness of the substantive terms themselves. In other words, the more substantively oppressive the contract term, the less evidence of procedural unconscionability is required to come to the conclusion that the term is unenforceable, and vice versa.

Procedural Unconscionability

To determine whether the arbitration agreement is procedurally unconscionable the court must examine "the manner in which the contract was negotiated and the circumstances of the parties at that time." An inquiry into whether Circuit City's arbitration agreement involves oppression or surprise is central to that analysis. A contract is oppressive if an inequality of bargaining power between the parties precludes the weaker party from enjoying a meaningful opportunity to negotiate and choose the terms of the contract. "Surprise involves the extent to which the supposedly agreed-upon terms of the bargain are hidden in the prolix printed form drafted by the party seeking to enforce the disputed terms." Circuit City, which possesses considerably more bargaining power than nearly all of its employees or applicants, drafted the contract and uses it as its standard arbitration agreement for all of its new employees. The agreement is a prerequisite to employment, and job applicants are not permitted to modify the agreement's terms — they must take the contractor leave it. Circuit City does not even consider the applications from job applicants who elect not to enter into the arbitration agreement. Ingle had no meaningful option; she either had to walk away from the employer altogether or sign the arbitration agreement for fear of automatic rejection or termination at the outset of her employment. Because of the stark inequality of bargaining power between Ingle and Circuit City, we conclude that Circuit City's 1998 arbitration agreement is also procedurally oppressive.

Substantive Unconscionability

Substantive unconscionability centers on the "terms of the agreement and whether those terms are so one-sided as to shock the conscience." [C]ourts must analyze the contract "as of the time [it] was made." Several substantive terms of Circuit City's arbitration agreement are one-sided. The provisions concerning coverage of claims, the statute of limitations, the prohibition of class actions, the filing fee, cost-splitting, remedies, and Circuit City's unilateral power to modify or terminate the arbitration agreement all operate to benefit the employer inordinately at the employee's expense.

Circuit City's arbitration agreement applies only to "any and all employment-related legal disputes, controversies or claims of an Associate," thereby limiting its coverage to claims brought by employees. By the terms of this agreement, Circuit City does not agree to submit to arbitration claims it might hypothetically bring against employees. Without a reasonable justification for such a glaring disparity based on "business realities," "it is unfairly one-sided for an employer with superior bargaining power to impose arbitration on the employee as plaintiff but not to accept such limitations when it seeks to prosecute a claim against the employee." The only claims realistically affected by an arbitration agreement between an employer and an employee are those claims employees bring against their employers. By essentially covering only claims that employees would likely bring against Circuit City, this arbitration agreement's coverage would be substantively one-sided even without the express limitation to claims brought by employees. Unless the employer can demonstrate that the effect of a contract to arbitrate is bilateral — as is required under California law — with respect to a particular employee, courts should presume such contracts substantively unconscionable.

The Circuit City arbitration agreement states that the form by which an employee requests arbitration: The failure of an Associate to initiate an arbitration within the one-year time limit shall constitute a waiver with respect to that dispute relative to that Associate. While Circuit City insulates itself from potential damages, an employee forgoes the possibility of relief under the continuing violations doctrine. Therefore, because the benefit of this provision flows only to Circuit City, we conclude that the statute of limitations provision is substantively unconscionable.

Circuit City's arbitration agreement directs arbitrators not to consolidate claims of different employees into one proceeding and generally prohibits the arbitrator from hearing an arbitration as a class action. We find that this baron class-wide arbitration is patently one-sided, and conclude that it is substantively unconscionable. We cannot conceive of any circumstances under which an employer would bring a class proceeding against an employee. Circuit City, through its bar on classwide arbitration, seeks to insulate itself from class proceedings while conferring no corresponding benefit to its employees in return. This one-sided provision proscribing an employee's ability to initiate class-wide arbitration operates solely to the advantage of Circuit City. Therefore, because Circuit City's prohibition of class action proceedings in its arbitral forum is manifestly and shockingly one-sided, it is substantively unconscionable.

Under the terms of the arbitration agreement, to initiate a complaint against Circuit City, an employee must submit an "Arbitration Request Form with a required filing fee of $75 (made payable with a cashier's check or money order to Circuit City Stores, Inc.)." Under California law, "when an employer imposes mandatory arbitration as a condition of employment, the arbitration agreement or arbitration process cannot generally require the employee to bear any type of expense that the employee would not be required to bear if he or she were free to bring the action in court." Though denominated a "filing fee," the employee-claimant must pay the required seventy-five dollars here directly to Circuit City, rather than to the arbitration service Circuit City identifies in the arbitration agreement. It thus appears that the employee is required to pay Circuit City for the privilege of bringing a complaint. While a true filing fee might be appropriate, the fee required by Circuit City is not the "type of expense that the employee would be required to bear" in federal court. The seventy-five dollar fee poses an additional problem. In federal court, plaintiffs in all types of cases may be exempt from paying court fees upon a showing of indigence. Circuit City's arbitration agreement, however, makes no similar provision for waiver of the filing fee. We therefore find the fee provision *filing fee uncon.* substantively unconscionable.

[T]he arbitration agreement we review here contains the provision that "each party shall pay one-half of the costs of arbitration following the issuance of the arbitration award." Moreover, the Circuit City arbitration agreement provides that if an employee does not succeed on her claim, the arbitrator has the discretion to charge the employee for Circuit City's share of the arbitrator's services. By itself, the fact that an employee could be held liable for Circuit City's share of the arbitration costs should she fail to vindicate employment-related claims renders this provision substantively unconscionable. Combined with the fact that Circuit City's fee-splitting scheme would sanction charging even a successful litigant for her share of arbitration costs, this scheme blatantly offends basic principles of fairness. Because [it is] harsh and unfair to employees seeking to arbitrate legal claims we conclude that it is substantively unconscionable.

The Circuit City arbitration agreement delimits what relief is available to employees who succeed in arbitration claims against Circuit City. The agreement grants the arbitrator the discretion to award (1) injunctive relief, including reinstatement; (2) one year of full or partial back pay, subject to reductions by interim earnings or public or private benefits received; (3) two years of front pay; (4) compensatory damages in accordance with applicable law; and (5) punitive damages up to $5,000 or the equivalent of a claimant's monetary award (back pay plus front pay), whichever is greater. Because the remedies limitation improperly proscribes available statutory remedies, we again conclude that it is substantively unconscionable, The provision places limits on an employee's total damages, while federal law limits only the sum of punitive and certain compensatory damages, and contravenes federal law by limiting an employee's front-pay award to two years' salary.

Circuit City's arbitration agreement provides that "Circuit City may alter or terminate the Agreement and these Dispute Resolution Rules and Procedures on December 31st of any year upon giving 30 calendar days written notice to Associates." By granting itself the sole authority to amend or terminate the arbitration agreement, Circuit City proscribes an employee's ability to consider and negotiate the terms of her contract. Compounded by the fact that this contract is adhesive in the first instance, this provision embeds its adhesiveness by allowing only Circuit City to modify or terminate the terms of the agreement. [T]he provision affording Circuit City the unilateral power to terminate or modify the contract is substantively unconscionable.

California law grants courts the discretion either "to sever an unconscionable provision or refuse to enforce the contract in its entirety." In exercising this discretion, courts look to whether the "central purpose of the contract is tainted with illegality" or "the illegality is collateral to [its] main purpose." Circuit City correctly argues that the FAA articulates a strong public policy in favor of arbitration agreements. Nevertheless, this "policy is manifestly undermined by provisions in arbitration clauses [that] seek to make the arbitration process itself an offensive weapon in one party's arsenal." While it is within this court's discretion to sever unconscionable provisions, because an "insidious pattern" exists in Circuit City's arbitration agreement "that functions as a thumb on Circuit City's side of the scale should an employment dispute ever arise between the company and one of its employees," we conclude that the agreement is wholly unenforceable. The adhesive nature of the contract and the provisions with respect to coverage of claims, the statute of limitations, class claims, the filing fee, cost-splitting, remedies, and Circuit City's unilateral power to terminate or modify the agreement combine to stack the deck unconscionably in favor of Circuit City. Any earnest attempt to ameliorate the unconscionable aspects of Circuit City's arbitration agreement would require this court to assume the role of contract author rather than interpreter. Because that would extend far beyond the province of this court we are compelled to find the entire contract unenforceable.

NOTE

The inutility of the "procedural" and "substantive" labels is emphasized by the judicial reaction to whether there must be sufficient evidence of both procedural and substantive unconscionability to refuse enforcement of a contract or term. Many courts suggest that it is necessary to show both procedural and substantive unconscionability, but that conventional wisdom displays serious erosion. Considerable confusion concerning this issue may exist in the case law of a given jurisdiction.

Under a "sliding scale" approach, the two types of unconscionability need not be present to the same degree. Thus, the more substantively oppressive the term of the contract, the less evidence of procedural unconscionability would be necessary to avoid the term and vice versa. Several cases, however, suggest that substantive unconscionability alone will be sufficient to rid a contract of egregious terms. As suggested by one court, "While determinations of unconscionability are ordinarily based on a conclusion that both the procedural and substantive elements are present, there have been exceptional cases where a provision of the contract is so egregious as to warrant holding it unenforceable on the ground of substantive unconscionability alone."

While some jurisdictions suggest that *either* procedural or substantive unconscionability can be sufficient, a holding that a contract or term is unconscionable on the basis of procedural unconscionability, alone, would be more than rare. Though a contract of adhesion clearly illustrates the "absence of meaningful choice," that concept has eroded as the standardized form contract with non-negotiable terms has gained acceptance. Courts now view contracts of adhesion as quite ordinary and, at worst, a factor to be considered in the unconscionability analysis. Indeed, in the eyes of some courts, there is nothing wrong with a contract of adhesion since standardized contract terms are essential for the efficient operation of the social institution of contract. Something beyond the contract of adhesion is necessary. In the words of the New Jersey Supreme Court, "[A]dhesive consumer contracts, which are ordinarily enforceable, may rise to the level of unconscionability when substantive contractual terms and conditions impact 'public interests' adversely."

The principal case is one of many cases dealing with the alleged unconscionability of an arbitration agreement. These cases began appearing over the past quarter century and revitalized what had become a somewhat moribund unconscionability doctrine. The uniquely strong support for the arbitration process through United States interpretations and constructions of the Federal Arbitration Act led to a spate of recent cases dealing with the alleged unconscionability of arbitration agreements. The hotly contested cases included *AT&T Mobility, LLC v. Concepcion*, 131 S. Ct. 1740 (2011) where the district court deemed an otherwise fair and reasonable arbitration clause unconscionable under California law because it included a waiver of class action provision. The Court of Appeals affirmed, but the Supreme Court in a 5-4 decision reversed in holding the decision below was antithetical to the purposes of the Federal Arbitration Act. The following case discusses the *Concepcion* holding and rationale as part of its discussion in deciding whether an arbitration clause is unconscionable.

QUILLOIN v. TENET HEALTHSYSTEM PHILADELPHIA, INC.
United States Court of Appeals, Third Circuit
673 F.3d 221 (2012)

SHER, J.

Plaintiff and Appellee Janice Quilloin ("Quilloin") is a registered nurse who began working at Hahnemann University Hospital in October of 2006. In February 2008, Quilloin resigned to take another job. Later that year, she reapplied for a position at Hahnemann, and was rehired in December 2008. She continued working at Hahnemann until November 2009. Hahnemann University Hospital is owned by Tenet HealthSystem Hahnemann, LLC and managed by Tenet HealthSystem Philadelphia, both subsidiaries of Tenet Healthcare Corporation.

Both on October 9, 2006 and on January 5, 2009, she signed the "Employee Acknowledgment" form, which acknowledged receipt of the "Fair Treatment Process" brochure ("FTP"). Quilloin alleges that she was not informed that she would have to commit to arbitration in order to be employed by Tenet.

The FTP brochure outlines the internal grievance process culminating in arbitration, as well as the parameters of the arbitration agreement itself. The FTP does not state that claims regarding the validity of the arbitration agreement itself must be arbitrated. Under "Application and Coverage" the brochure states that "[t]he FTP . . . covers all disputes relating to or arising out of an employee's employment with the company or the termination of employment. . . . [except for] those listed in the 'Exclusions and Restrictions' section[.]" Notably, neither party argues that one of the enumerated exclusions or restrictions is applicable here.

The FTP outlines the steps employees are required to follow to resolve disputes. A limitations clause states that "[a]ny request for arbitration under the FTP must be made within one year after the event giving rise to the dispute . . . . [or], if a longer limitations period is provided by a statute governing your claim, then your claim will be subject to the longer limitations period provided by the statute."

The FTP also includes provisions for fees and remedies. In one clause, the FTP states that "[y]ou and the company will be responsible for the fees and costs of your own respective legal counsel, if any, and any other expenses and costs, such as costs associated with witnesses or obtaining copies of hearing transcripts." In another provision, entitled *Authority of Arbitrator*," the FTP states that "[t]he arbitrator has the authority to award any remedy that would have been available to you had you litigated the dispute in court under applicable law." Elsewhere, the FTP states that "no remedies that otherwise would be available to you or the company in a court of law will be forfeited by virtue of the agreement to use and be bound by the FTP."

On December 4, 2009, Quilloin filed suit in the United States District Court for the Eastern District of Pennsylvania, asserting a collective action against Tenet under the Fair Labor Standards Act of 1938, 29 U.S.C. §§ 201-19, as well as several state-based class action and common law/ Tenet asserted the existence of an arbitration agreement as an affirmative defense [and] filed a motion to compel compliance with the agreement to arbitrate. Quilloin responded, claiming, among other things, that the agreement to arbitrate was unconscionable. The District Court issued an order finding that genuine disputes of material fact remained as to whether the arbitration agreement was enforceable and denying the motion to compel. Tenet filed a timely notice of appeal, commencing the present action.

Tenet argues as a threshold matter that the District Court erred in considering Quilloin's claim that the arbitration agreement was unconscionable, because Quilloin failed to direct her challenge at a specific clause within the arbitration agreement. Essentially, Tenet claims that without a challenge to some specific clause, the District Court may not inquire into issues of arbitrability. We disagree.

"Because this is a question of arbitrability, it is governed by the Federal Arbitration Act [FAA]." The FAA manifests "a congressional declaration of a liberal federal policy favoring arbitration agreements . . . ." However, questions of arbitrability, including challenges to an arbitration agreement's validity, are presumed to be questions for judicial determination." Courts should not assume that the parties agreed to arbitrate arbitrability unless there is 'clea[r] and unmistakabl[e]' evidence that they did so." This is because the FAA places arbitration agreements on "an equal footing with other contracts" and thus, like any other contract, a plaintiff may bring a challenge to court claiming that an agreement to arbitrate is unenforceable based on any of the "generally applicable contract defenses, such as fraud, duress, or unconscionability . . . ." *AT&T Mobility LLC v.*

Concepcion, 131 S. Ct. 1740, 1745–46, 179 L. Ed. 2d 742 (2011) (construing the FAA as codified at 9 U.S.C. § 2).

On the other hand, a challenge to "the validity of the contract as a whole, as opposed to the arbitration clause in particular, does not present a question of arbitrability." This is because regardless of whether a contract as a whole is valid, agreements to arbitrate are severable from a larger contract, and may therefore be separately enforced and their validity separately determined. Thus, in order to qualify as a question of arbitrability that the court may consider, the challenge must "relat[e] to the making and performance of the agreement to arbitrate."

We generally apply state contract principles to determine whether an arbitration agreement is unconscionable. However, the FAA preempts conflicting state rules that either prohibit arbitration outright, or that "stand[] as an obstacle to the accomplishment and execution of the full purposes and objectives of Congress . . . ." Thus, in determining unconscionability, we must use principles of Pennsylvania law, to the extent that such law is not displaced by the FAA.

To prove unconscionability under Pennsylvania law, a party must show that the contract was both substantively and procedurally unconscionable. In examining these two prongs, the Pennsylvania Supreme Court has indicated that it might be appropriate to use a "sliding-scale approach" so that "where the procedural unconscionability is very high, a lesser degree of substantive unconscionability may be required" and presumably, vice-versa. We turn first to the District Court's finding that the arbitration agreement might be substantively unconscionable.

1. Substantive Unconscionability

A contract or provision is substantively unconscionable where it "unreasonably favors the party asserting it." Put another way, "[s]ubstantive unconscionability refers to contractual terms that are unreasonably or grossly favorable to one side and to which the disfavored party does not assent." An arbitration agreement cannot be construed as substantively unconscionable where it "does not alter or limit the rights and remedies available to [a] party in the arbitral forum . . . ." In denying Tenet's motion to compel arbitration, the District Court found three bases on which the arbitration agreement might be substantively unconscionable: (1) a potential prohibition against recovery of attorneys' fees and costs, (2) potential inclusion of a class action waiver, and (3) the possibility that Tenet could "run out the clock" on the statute of limitations. We disagree with the District Court's conclusions, and find no basis for substantive unconscionability.

a. Attorneys' Fees

Provisions requiring parties to be responsible for their own expenses, including attorneys' fees, are generally unconscionable because restrictions on attorneys' fees conflict with federal statutes providing fee-shifting as a remedy. *See Spinetti v. Serv. Corp. Int'l, 324 F.3d 212, 216 (3d Cir. 2003)* (Where called for by statute, "arbitrators . . . must ordinarily grant attorney fees to prevailing claimants rather than be restricted by private contractual language." (internal citation and quotation marks omitted)).

Tenet and Quilloin dispute whether the arbitration agreement allows the prevailing party to recover attorneys' fees. The agreement contains no clear prohibition against fee-shifting; the District Court wrote that "it is unclear whether the contract deprives employees of the right to recover attorney's fees and costs." In one clause, the FTP states that "[y]ou and the company will be responsible for the fees and costs of your own respective legal counsel, if any, and any other expenses and costs, such as costs associated with witnesses or obtaining copies of hearing transcripts." However, another provision in the FTP could be read as giving the arbitrator authority to grant attorneys' fees to the prevailing party: "*Authority of Arbitrator*: The arbitrator has the authority to award any remedy that would have been available to you had you litigated the dispute in court under applicable law." It also states that "no remedies that otherwise would be available to you or the company in a court of law will be forfeited by virtue of the agreement to use and be bound by the FTP."

We agree with the District Court that the arbitration agreement is ambiguous regarding the award of attorneys' fees, but find that the District Court erred in determining that it could not compel arbitration before resolving the issue. The Supreme Court has clearly established that ambiguities in arbitration agreements must be interpreted by the arbitrator. It explained that "we should not, on the basis of mere speculation that an arbitrator might interpret . . . ambiguous agreements in a manner that casts their enforceability into doubt, take upon ourselves the authority to decide the antecedent question of how the ambiguity is to be resolved."

Quilloin's claim would require the District Court to decide a "preliminary question" before addressing the issue of unconscionability, and such a "preliminary question" is not truly a question of arbitrability. Under *PacifiCare*, we are required to find that the ambiguity regarding attorneys' fees is a question for the arbitrator.

b. Class Action Waiver

Under Pennsylvania law, class action waivers are substantively unconscionable where "class action litigation is the only effective remedy" such as when "the high cost of arbitration compared with the minimal potential value of individual damages denie[s] every plaintiff a meaningful remedy."

Here, the arbitration agreement does not contain an express class action waiver. Silence regarding class arbitration generally indicates a prohibition against class arbitration, but the actual determination as to whether class action is prohibited is a question of interpretation and procedure for the arbitrator. *Stolt-Nielsen, S.A. v. AnimalFeeds Int'l Corp.*, 130 S. Ct. 1758, 1775, 176 L. Ed. 2d 605 (2010). The District Court acknowledged that the determination was for the arbitrator, but proceeded to analyze whether a class action waiver would render the arbitration agreement substantively unconscionable, if the arbitrator were to determine that the agreement contained such a waiver.

After the District Court denied Tenet's motion to compel, the Supreme Court ruled in *Concepcion* that a California law deeming certain class action waivers to be unconscionable was an "obstacle to the accomplishment and execution" of the FAA, and was therefore "inconsistent with" and preempted by the FAA. Specifically, the

Concepcion Court found that "[a]rbitration is poorly suited to the higher stakes of class litigation" because: (1) "the switch from bilateral to class arbitration sacrifices the principal advantage of arbitration — its informality[,]" (2) it is "at the very least odd to think that an arbitrator would be entrusted with ensuring that third parties' due process rights are satisfied[,]" and (3) "class arbitration greatly increases risks to defendants." California's law did not deem class action waivers to be *per se* unconscionable, but was based in part on the reasoning that "class proceedings are necessary to prosecute small-dollar claims that might otherwise slip through the legal system." The Supreme Court dismissed this reasoning, ruling that "States cannot require a procedure that is inconsistent with the FAA, even if it is desirable for unrelated reasons."

Following and relying on *Concepcion*, we found a similar New Jersey law to be preempted. The New Jersey law held that "a waiver of class-wide dispute resolution would be improper in the context of either litigation or arbitration[,]" and unconscionability thus "provide[d] a defense against '*all* waivers of class-wide actions, not simply those that also compel arbitration[.]' " *Litman v. Cellco P'ship*, 655 F.3d 225, 229 (3d Cir. 2011). Our *Litman* ruling is directly applicable here:

> "We understand the holding of *Concepcion* to be both broad and clear: a state law that seeks to impose class arbitration despite a contractual agreement for individualized arbitration is inconsistent with, and therefore preempted by, the FAA, irrespective of whether class arbitration is desirable for unrelated reasons."

The Pennsylvania law at issue here is clearly preempted under *Concepcion* and *Litman*. The Pennsylvania law is not substantively different from the California law, which is unquestionably preempted by the FAA. Like the California law, Pennsylvania law does not render class action waivers *per se* unconscionable. Rather, Pennsylvania finds such waivers substantively unconscionable where "class action litigation is the only effective remedy" such as when "the high cost of arbitration compared with the minimal potential value of individual damages denie[s] every plaintiff a meaningful remedy."

Like the law in *Litman*, the Pennsylvania law "seeks to impose class arbitration despite a contractual agreement for individualized arbitration" and is therefore preempted. In fact, the Pennsylvania law is even more egregious than the New Jersey law. The New Jersey rule against class action waivers applied to litigation and arbitration alike, while Pennsylvania law has often prohibited class action waivers based on their arbitration-specific context. Thus, the Pennsylvania law presents an even greater obstacle to the fulfillment of the FAA's purposes than does the New Jersey law, because it is exactly the type of law that "single[s] out the provisions of arbitration agreements[,]" and that "derive[s] [its] meaning from the fact that an agreement to arbitrate is at issue." *Concepcion*, 131 S. Ct. at 1746.

c. Running Out the Clock

Finally, Quilloin claims that the arbitration agreement is unconscionable because it would permit Tenet to "run out the clock" on the statute of limitations. [T]ime limitations in arbitration agreements are substantively unconscionable if they are "clearly unreasonable and unduly favorable" to the employer.Given the existence of reasonable time guidelines for Tenet to act, paired with the fact that Tenet could not preclude Quilloin's claim because she always had the option to motion to compel arbitration, the time guidelines are not "clearly unreasonable and unduly favorable" to Tenet. We find that Quilloin raised no genuine dispute of material fact regarding substantive unconscionability; therefore, the District Court erred by denying Tenet's motion to compel arbitration.

2. Procedural Unconscionability

Even if Quilloin had raised a genuine dispute of material fact as to substantive unconscionability, we would nonetheless find that the District Court erred in denying Tenet's motion to compel arbitration because Quilloin did not raise a genuine dispute of material fact as to whether the arbitration agreement was procedurally unconscionable. Quilloin argues that procedural unconscionability arises because she was not informed that she would have to commit to arbitrate disputes in order to be employed by Tenet, that no one explained to her the terms of the agreement, and that she had little time or choice but to accept its terms and sign.

A contract is procedurally unconscionable where "there was a lack of meaningful choice in the acceptance of the challenged provision[.]" A contract will be deemed procedurally unconscionable when formed through "oppression and unfair surprise." Courts "should remain attuned to well-supported claims that the agreement to arbitrate resulted from the sort of fraud or overwhelming economic power that would provide grounds for the revocation of any contract."

Under Pennsylvania law, a contract is generally considered to be procedurally unconscionable if it is a contract of adhesion, *but cf. Salley*, 925 A.2d at 125–26; *id.* at 128 (suggesting that not all contracts of adhesion are procedurally unconscionable). A contract of adhesion is a "standard-form contract prepared by one party, to be signed by the party in a weaker position, usually a consumer, who adheres to the contract with little choice about the terms." However, contracts cannot be deemed unconscionable "simply because of a disparity in bargaining power." Parties frequently possess varying degrees of bargaining power, and there is a "range of ordinary and acceptable bargaining situations[.]" Our role is to distinguish acceptable bargaining situations from those which violate "strong public policy[.]" *Id.*

Factors we must consider in determining whether the contract rises to the level of procedural unconscionability include: "the take-it-or-leave-it nature of the standardized form of the document[,]" "the parties' relative bargaining positions," and "the degree of economic compulsion motivating the 'adhering' party[.]"

In *Zimmer v. CooperNeff Advisors, Inc.*, we considered the plaintiff's educational background and "the context in which the 'take-it-or-leave-it' ultimatum was issued" in determining that the contract did not rise to the level of procedural unconscionability. Zimmer was a highly educated economist and willingly accepted an offer of employment, knowing that the formal employment agreement had not yet been finalized, and further, he did not allege that he lacked an opportunity to negotiate.

Similarly, in *Great Western Mortg. Corp. v. Peacock*, the appellant argued that she accepted the arbitration agreement "only because she was the weaker of the two parties to the employment contract." Peacock was undoubtedly the weaker party. Nevertheless, we found that the agreement was not procedurally unconscionable because Peacock agreed to arbitration on three different occasions, she was a college graduate with a Business Administration degree, and she did not contend that she failed to read the document containing the arbitration agreement, or that she was coerced into signing it.

At the other end of the spectrum, we found procedural unconscionability in an employment agreement where the employee, though college educated, was told to read and sign an employment contract, and was dependent on the employer, one of the world's largest jewelry retailers, for his immigration status and his "very capacity to work in St. Thomas[.]" Similarly, we held unconscionable an arbitration agreement between a multi-national business and minimally-educated crane operators.

Quilloin's situation is nothing like that of the plaintiffs in *Nino* or *Alexander v. Anthony Intern., L.P.* The District Court acknowledged that Tenet had less bargaining power than the multinational corporations in both of those cases. More importantly, Quilloin was neither a minimally-educated crane operator as were the plaintiffs in *Alexander*, nor dependent on her employer for her immigration status as was the plaintiff in *Nino*.

Quilloin argues that she was in an unequal bargaining position because she was just an employee signing a form agreement. Like Peacock, Quilloin might not have seen or signed the actual arbitration agreement until after beginning her employment. As in *Peacock*, we acknowledge that the employee is the weaker party to the agreement; however, like Peacock, Quilloin did not lack a meaningful choice. She had a college degree, and chose to agree to the arbitration agreement on more than one occasion. Even if she was not initially informed of the agreement at either time she was hired, the fact remains that she quit her employment at Tenet to work for another employer, and then chose to go back and work once again for Tenet, subject to the Employment Agreement and the FTP. When Quilloin went back to her job at Tenet, the question of whether she actually remembered the arbitration agreement is of no consequence; we must presume that she was rehired knowing about the arbitration agreement which she had already signed, because parties are presumed to have knowledge of contracts they have signed.

Under such circumstances, we reject Quilloin's argument that there was unfair surprise or a lack of time to consider or learn the meaning of the terms of the agreement. We find that Quilloin did not lack a meaningful choice in agreeing to arbitrate, and she thus raised no genuine dispute of material fact with regard to procedural unconscionability.

We hold that the District Court erred in denying Tenet's motion to compel arbitration.

G. THE PERVASIVE "GOOD FAITH" REQUIREMENT

It is often said that every contract imposes a duty of good faith upon the parties. RESTATEMENT (SECOND) OF CONTRACTS § 205 implies a standard of good faith and fair dealing in all contracts. Comment a suggests, "The phrase 'good faith' is used in a variety of contexts and its meaning varies somewhat with the context." In a well-known article, Professor Summers suggests the similar view that the phrase takes on specific meaning in a particular context, but usually only by way of contrast with a specific form of bad faith. Summers, *"Good Faith" in General Contract Law and the Sales Provisions of the Uniform Commercial Code*, 54 VA. L. REV. 195, 201 (1968). Professor Corbin concludes that, generally, courts define good faith by describing its absence. 3 A. CORBIN ON CONTRACTS § 541 (1960).

The Uniform Commercial Code, § 1-203, states that "Every contract or duty within this Act imposes an obligation of good faith in its performance or enforcement."[23] One might, therefore, argue that all of the issues discussed to this point in this Chapter, fraud, duress, misrepresentation, wrongful nondisclosure, reasonable expectations, unconscionability and related concerns, might be subsumed under the generic requirement of "good faith."[24] One might even argue that if certain conduct does not fall within any of the foregoing categories but still demonstrates bad faith, there should be a recognized duty of good faith that transcends all of the other categories. The Uniform Commercial Code, however, amended the Comment to its basic good faith section on February 10, 1994, to reject this possibility:

> This section does not support an independent cause of action for failure to perform or enforce in good faith. Rather, this section means that a failure to perform or enforce in good faith, a specific duty or obligation under the contract, constitutes a breach of that contract or makes unavailable, under the circumstances, a remedial right or power. This distinction makes it clear that the doctrine of good faith merely directs a court towards interpreting contracts within the commercial context in which they are created, performed, and enforced, and does not create a separate duty of fairness and reasonableness.

There are any number of illustrations of the good faith standard throughout contract law. In an earlier Chapter, we considered the application of the good faith standard to output and requirements contracts under UCC § 2-306. The Uniform Commercial Code requires that the power to terminate a contract must be exercised in good faith through reasonable notice, UCC § 2-309. A similar problem has arisen in franchise agreements where a distributor or franchisee invested considerable time, effort and money in the development of the business only to be terminated capriciously by the franchisor. While the good faith requirements of the UCC may not apply to such situations, a number of states have enacted statutes

---

[23] Section 1-102(19) defines "good faith" as "honesty in fact in the conduct or transaction concerned." Section 2-103(1)(b) defines "good faith" in the case of a merchant (§ 2-104) as "honesty in fact and the observance of reasonable commercial standards of fair dealing in the trade."

[24] Indeed, in Seaman's Direct Buying Service v. Standard Oil of Cal., 686 P.2d 1148 (Cal. 1984), the court raised breach of the implied covenant of good faith to the status of a tort action. The effort was not, however, long lived. After significant criticism, it was overruled in Freeman & Mills, Inc. v. Belcher Oil Co., 900 P.2d 669 (Cal. 1995).

which reflect the good faith standard. For an analysis of several of these statutes, see *Dunkin Donuts of Am. v. Middletown Donut*, 495 A.2d 66 (N.J. 1985). The best known federal statute dealing with this situation is the Automobile Dealer Franchise Act (15 U.S.C. §§ 1221–1225), sometimes known as the "Auto Dealers' Day in Court Act," which imposes a "good faith" standard on the manufacturer who seeks to terminate, cancel, or refuses to renew a franchise.

While the implied standard of good faith will be included in employment contracts, that standard will not negate the express terms of an employment contract with a stated duration, as where an assistant principal failed to show a breach of the implied covenant of good faith when her one-year contract was not renewed. *See Tollefson v. Roman Catholic Bishop of San Diego*, 219 Cal. App. 3d 843 (1990).

The quest for a more comprehensive and clear understanding of the parameters of *good faith* continues.

MARKET STREET ASSOCIATES v. FREY
United States Court of Appeals, Seventh Circuit
941 F.2d 588 (1991)

POSNER, J.

In 1968, J.C. Penney Company, the retail chain, entered into a sale and leaseback arrangement with General Electric Pension Trust in order to finance Penney's growth. Under the arrangement Penney sold properties to the pension trust which the trust then leased back to Penney for a term of 25 years. Paragraph 34 of the lease entitles the lessee to "request Lessor [the pension trust] to finance the costs and expenses of construction of additional Improvements upon the Premises," provided the amount of the costs and expenses is at least $250,000. Upon receiving the request, the pension trust "agrees to give reasonable consideration to providing the financing of such additional Improvements and Lessor and Lessee shall negotiate in good faith concerning the construction of such Improvements and the financing by Lessor of such costs and expenses." Paragraph 34 goes on to provide that, should the negotiations fail, the lessee shall be entitled to repurchase the property at a price roughly equal to the price at which Penney sold it to the pension trust in the first place, plus 6 percent a year for each year since the original purchase. So if the average annual appreciation in the property exceeded 6 percent, a breakdown in negotiations over the financing of improvements would entitle Penney to buy back the property for less than its market value (assuming it had sold the property to the pension trust in the first place at its then market value).

One of these leases was for a shopping center in Milwaukee. In 1987 Penney assigned this lease to Market Street Associates, which the following year received an inquiry from a drugstore chain that wanted to open a store in the shopping center, provided (as is customary) that Market Street Associates built the store for it. Whether Market Street Associates was pessimistic about obtaining financing from the pension trust, still the lessor of the shopping center, or for other reasons, it initially sought financing for the project from other sources. But they were unwilling to lend the necessary funds without a mortgage on the shopping center, which Market Street Associates could not give because it was not the owner but only the lessee. It decided therefore to try to buy the property back from the pension trust. Market Street Associates' general partner, Orenstein, tried to call David Erb of the pension trust, who was responsible for the property in question. Erb did not return his calls, so Orenstein wrote him, expressing an interest in buying the property and asking him to "review your file on this matter and call me so that we can discuss it further." At first, Erb did not reply. Eventually Orenstein did reach Erb, who promised to review the file and get back to him. A few days later an associate of Erb called Orenstein and indicated an interest in selling the property for $3 million, which Orenstein considered much too high.

That was in June of 1988. On July 28, Market Street Associates wrote a letter to the pension trust formally requesting funding for $2 million in improvements to the shopping center. The letter made no reference to paragraph 34 of the lease; indeed, it did not mention the lease. The letter asked Erb to call Orenstein to discuss the matter. Erb, in what was becoming a habit of unresponsiveness, did not call. On August 16, Orenstein sent a second letter — certified mail, return receipt requested — again requesting financing and this time referring to the lease, though not expressly to paragraph 34. The heart of the letter is the following two sentences: "The purpose of this letter is to ask again that you advise us immediately if you are willing to provide the financing pursuant to the lease. If you are willing, we propose to enter into negotiation to amend the ground lease appropriately." The very next day, Market Street Associates received from Erb a letter, dated August 10, turning down the original request for financing on the ground that it did not "meet our current investment criteria": the pension trust was not interested in making loans for less than $7 million. On August 22, Orenstein replied to Erb by letter, noting that his letter of August 10 [sic] and Erb's letter of August 16 [sic] had evidently crossed in the mails, expressing disappointment at the turn-down, and stating that Market Street Associates would seek financing elsewhere. That was the last contact between the parties until September 27, when Orenstein sent Erb a letter stating that Market Street Associates was exercising the option granted it by paragraph 34 to purchase the property upon the terms specified in that paragraph in the event that negotiations over financing broke down.

The pension trust refused to sell, and this suit to compel specific performance followed. Apparently the price computed by the formula in paragraph 34 is only $1 million. The market value must be higher, or Market Street Associates wouldn't be trying to coerce conveyance at the paragraph 34 price; whether it is as high as $3 million, however, the record does not reveal.

The district judge granted summary judgment for the pension trust on two grounds that he believed to be separate although closely related. The first was that, by failing in its correspondence with the pension trust to mention paragraph 34 of the lease, Market Street Associates had prevented the negotiations over financing that are a condition precedent to the lessee's exercise of the purchase option from taking place. Second, this same failure violated the duty of good faith, which the common law of Wisconsin, as of other states, reads into every contract. RESTATEMENT (SECOND) OF CONTRACTS § 205 (1981). In support of both grounds the judge emphasized a statement by Orenstein in his deposition that it had occurred to him that Erb mightn't know about paragraph 34, though this was unlikely (Orenstein testified) because Erb or someone else at the pension trust would probably check the file and discover the paragraph and realize that if the trust refused to negotiate over the request for financing, Market Street Associates, as Penney's assignee, would be entitled to walk off with the property for (perhaps) a song. The judge inferred that Market Street Associates didn't want financing from the pension trust — that it just wanted an opportunity to buy the property at a bargain price and hoped that the pension trust wouldn't realize the implications of turning down the request for financing. Market Street Associates should, the judge opined, have advised the pension trust that it was requesting financing pursuant to paragraph 34, so that the trust would understand the penalty for refusing to negotiate.

The pension trust argues that the option to purchase created by paragraph 34 cannot be exercised until negotiations over financing break down; there were no negotiations; therefore they did not break down; therefore Market Street Associates had no right to exercise the option. This argument misreads the contract. Although the option to purchase is indeed contingent, paragraph 34 requires the pension trust, upon demand by the lessee for the financing of improvements worth at least $250,000, "to give reasonable consideration to providing the financing." The lessor who fails to give reasonable consideration and thereby prevents the negotiations from taking place is breaking the contract; and a contracting party cannot be allowed to use his own breach to gain an advantage by impairing the rights that the contract confers on the other party. Often, it is true, if one party breaks the contract, the other can walk away from it without liability, can in other words exercise self-help. But he is not required to follow that course. He can stand on his contract rights.

But what exactly are those rights in this case? The contract entitles the lessee to reasonable consideration of its request for financing, and only if negotiations over the request fail is the lessee entitled to purchase the property at the price computed in accordance with paragraph 34. It might seem therefore that the proper legal remedy for a lessor's breach that consists of failure to give the lessee's request for financing reasonable consideration would not be an order that the lessor sell the property to the lessee at the paragraph 34 price, but an order that the lessor bargain with the lessee in good faith. But we do not understand the pension trust to be arguing that Market Street Associates is seeking the wrong remedy. We understand it to be arguing that Market Street Associates has no possible remedy. That is an untenable position.

Market Street Associates argues, with equal unreason as it seems to us, that it could not have broken the contract because paragraph 34 contains no express requirement that in requesting financing the lessee mention the lease or paragraph 34 or otherwise alert the lessor to the consequences of his failing to give reasonable consideration to granting the request. There is indeed no such requirement (all that the contract requires is a demand). But no one says there is. The pension trust's argument, which the district judge bought, is that either as a matter of simple contract interpretation or under the compulsion of the doctrine of good faith, a provision requiring Market Street Associates to remind the pension trust of paragraph 34 should be read into the lease.

It seems to us that these are one ground rather than two. A court has to have a reason to interpolate a clause into a contract. The only reason that has been suggested here is that it is necessary to prevent Market Street Associates from reaping a reward for what the pension trust believes to have been Market Street's bad faith. So we must consider the meaning of the contract duty of "good faith." The Wisconsin cases are cryptic as to its meaning though emphatic about its existence, so we must cast our net wider. We do so mindful of Learned Hand's warning, that "such words as 'fraud,' 'good faith,' 'whim,' 'caprice,' 'arbitrary action,' and 'legal fraud' . . . obscure the issue." *Thompson-Starrett Co. v. La Belle Iron Works*, 17 F.2d 536, 541 (2d Cir. 1927). Indeed they do. The particular confusion to which the vaguely moralistic overtones of "good faith" give rise is the belief that every contract establishes a fiduciary relationship. A fiduciary is required to treat his principal as if the principal were he, and therefore he may not take advantage of the principal's incapacity, ignorance, inexperience, or even naivete. If Market Street Associates were the fiduciary of General Electric Pension Trust, then (we may assume) it could not take advantage of Mr. Erb's apparent ignorance of paragraph 34, however exasperating Erb's failure to return Orenstein's phone calls was and however negligent Erb or his associates were in failing to read the lease before turning down Orenstein's request for financing.

But it is unlikely that Wisconsin wishes, in the name of good faith, to make every contract signatory his brother's keeper, especially when the brother is the immense and sophisticated General Electric Pension Trust, whose lofty indifference to small (= < $7 million) transactions is the signifier of its grandeur. In fact the law contemplates that people frequently will take advantage of the ignorance of those with whom they contract, without thereby incurring liability. RESTATEMENT, *supra*, § 161, comment d. The duty of honesty, of good faith even expansively conceived, is not a duty of candor. You can make a binding contract to purchase something you know your seller undervalues. That of course is a question about formation, not performance, and the particular duty of good faith under examination here relates to the latter rather than to the former. But even after you have signed a contract, you are not obliged to become an altruist toward the other party and relax the terms if he gets into trouble in performing his side of the bargain. Otherwise mere difficulty of performance would excuse a contracting party — which it does not.

But it is one thing to say that you can exploit your superior knowledge of the market — for if you cannot, you will not be able to recoup the investment you made in obtaining that knowledge — or that you are not required to spend money bailing out a contract partner who has gotten into trouble. It is another thing to say that you can take deliberate advantage of an oversight by your contract partner concerning his rights under the contract. Such taking advantage is not the exploitation of superior knowledge or the avoidance of unbargained-for expense; it is sharp dealing. Like theft, it has no social product, and also like theft it induces costly defensive expenditures, in the form of over-elaborate disclaimers or investigations into the trustworthiness of a prospective contract partner, just as the prospect of theft induces expenditures on locks.

The form of sharp dealing that we are discussing might or might not be actionable as fraud or deceit. That is a question of tort law and there the rule is that if the information is readily available to both parties the failure of one to disclose it to the other, even if done in the knowledge that the other party is acting on mistaken premises, is not actionable. [Such] cases, however, involve failure to disclose something in the negotiations leading up to the signing of the contract, rather than failure to disclose after the contract has been signed. The distinction is important. Before the contract is signed, the parties confront each other with a natural wariness. Neither expects the other to be particularly forthcoming, and therefore there is no deception when one is not. Afterwards the situation is different. The parties are now in a cooperative relationship the costs of which will be considerably reduced by a measure of trust. So each lowers his guard a bit, and now silence is more apt to be deceptive.

Moreover, this is a contract case rather than a tort case, and conduct that might not rise to the level of fraud may nonetheless violate the duty of good faith in dealing with one's contractual partners and thereby give rise to a remedy under contract law. This duty is, as it were, halfway between a fiduciary duty (the duty of utmost good faith) and the duty merely to refrain from active fraud. Despite its moralistic overtones it is no more the injection of moral principles into contract law than the fiduciary concept itself is. It would be quixotic as well as presumptuous for judges to undertake through contract law to raise the ethical standards of the nation's business people. The concept of the duty of good faith like the concept of fiduciary duty is a stab at approximating the terms the parties would have negotiated had they foreseen the circumstances that have given rise to their dispute. The parties want to minimize the costs of performance. To the extent that a doctrine of good faith designed to do this by reducing defensive expenditures is a reasonable measure to this end, interpolating it into the contract advances the parties' joint goal.

It is true that an essential function of contracts is to allocate risk, and would be defeated if courts treated the materializing of a bargained-over, allocated risk as a misfortune the burden of which is required to be shared between the parties (as it might be within a family, for example) rather than borne entirely by the party to whom the risk had been allocated by mutual agreement. But contracts do not just allocate risk. They also (or some of them) set in motion a cooperative enterprise, which may to some extent place one party at the other's mercy. "The parties to a contract are embarked on a cooperative venture, and a minimum of cooperativeness in the event unforeseen problems arise at the performance stage is required even if not an explicit duty of the contract." *AMPAT/Midwest, Inc. v. Illinois Tool Works, Inc., supra,* 896 F.2d at 1041. The office of the doctrine of good faith is to forbid the kinds of opportunistic behavior that a mutually dependent, cooperative relationship might enable in the absence of rule. " 'Good faith' is a compact reference to an implied undertaking not to take opportunistic advantage in a way that could not have been contemplated at the time of drafting, and which therefore was not resolved explicitly by the parties." *Kham & Nate's Shoes No. 2, Inc. v. First Bank, supra,* 908 F.2d at 1357. The contractual duty of good faith is thus not some newfangled bit of welfare-state paternalism or the sediment of an altruistic strain in contract law, and we are therefore not surprised to find the essentials of the modern doctrine well established in nineteenth-century cases.

The emphasis we are placing on postcontractual versus precontractual conduct helps explain the pattern that is observed when the duty of contractual good faith is considered in all its variety, encompassing not only good faith in the performance of a contract but also good faith in its formation and in its enforcement. The formation or negotiation stage is precontractual, and here the duty is minimized. It is greater not only at the performance but also at the enforcement stage, which is also postcontractual. "A party who hokes up a phony defense to the performance of his contractual duties and then when that defense fails (at some expense to the other party) tries on another defense for size can properly be said to be acting in bad faith." At the formation of the contract the parties are dealing in present realities; performance still lies in the future. As performance unfolds, circumstances change, often unforeseeably; the explicit terms of the contract become progressively less apt to the governance of the parties' relationship; and the role of implied conditions — and with it the scope and bite of the good-faith doctrine — grows.

We could of course do without the term "good faith," and maybe even without the doctrine. We could, as just suggested, speak instead of implied conditions necessitated by the unpredictability of the future at the time the contract was made. Farnsworth, *"Good Faith Performance and Commercial Reasonableness under the Uniform Commercial Code,"* 30 U. CHI. L. REV. 666, 670 (1963). Suppose a party has promised work to the promisee's "satisfaction." As LEARNED HAND explained, "he may refuse to look at the work, or to exercise any real judgment on it, in which case he has prevented performance and excused the condition." *Thompson-Starrett Co. v. La Belle Iron Works, supra,* 17 F.2d at 541. That is, it was an implicit condition that the promisee examine the work to the extent necessary to determine whether it was satisfactory; otherwise the performing party would have been placing himself at the complete mercy of the promisee. The parties didn't write this condition into the contract either because they thought such behavior unlikely or failed to foresee it altogether. In just the same way — to switch to another familiar example of the operation of the duty of good faith — parties to a requirements contract surely do not intend that if the price of the product covered by the contract rises, the buyer shall be free to increase his "requirements" so that he can take advantage of the rise in the market price over the contract price to resell the product on the open market at a guaranteed profit. *Empire Gas Corp. v. American Bakeries Co.,* 840 F.2d 1333 (7th Cir. 1988). If they fail to insert an express condition to this effect, the court will read it in, confident that the parties would have inserted the condition if they had known what the future held. Of similar character is the implied condition that an exclusive dealer will use his best efforts to promote the supplier's goods, since otherwise the exclusive feature of the dealership contract would place the supplier at the dealer's mercy. *Wood v. Duff-Gordon,* 222 N.Y. 88, 118 N.E. 214 (1917) (CARDOZO, J.).

But whether we say that a contract shall be deemed to contain such implied conditions as are necessary to make sense of the contract, or that a contract obligates the parties to cooperate in its performance in "good faith" to the extent necessary to carry out the purposes of the contract, comes to much the same thing. They are different ways of formulating the overriding purpose of contract law, which is to give the parties what they would have stipulated for expressly if at the time of making the contract they had had complete knowledge of the future and the costs of negotiating and adding provisions to the contract had been zero.

The two formulations would have different meanings only if "good faith" were thought limited to "honesty in fact," an interpretation perhaps permitted but certainly not compelled by the Uniform Commercial Code [§ 1-203] and anyway this is not a case governed by the UCC. We need not pursue this issue. The dispositive question in the present case is simply whether Market Street Associates tried to trick the pension trust and succeeded in doing so. If it did, this would be the type of opportunistic behavior in an ongoing contractual relationship that would violate the duty of good faith performance however the duty is formulated. There is much common sense in Judge Reynolds' conclusion that Market Street Associates did just that. The situation as he saw it was as follows. Market Street Associates didn't want financing from the pension trust (initially it had looked elsewhere, remember), and when it learned it couldn't get the financing without owning the property, it decided to try to buy the property. But the pension trust set a stiff price, so Orenstein decided to trick the pension trust into selling at the bargain price fixed in paragraph 34 by requesting financing and hoping that the pension trust would turn the request down without noticing the paragraph. His preliminary dealings with the pension trust made this hope a realistic one by revealing a sluggish and hidebound bureaucracy unlikely to have retained in its brontosaurus's memory, or to be able at short notice to retrieve, the details of a small lease made twenty years earlier. So by requesting financing without mentioning the lease Market Street Associates might well precipitate a refusal before the pension trust woke up to paragraph 34. It is true that Orenstein's second letter requested financing "pursuant to the lease." But when the next day he received a reply to his first letter indicating that the pension trust was indeed oblivious to paragraph 34, his response was to send a lulling letter designed to convince the pension trust that the matter was closed and could be forgotten. The stage was set for his thunderbolt: the notification the next month that Market Street Associates was taking up the option in paragraph 34. Only then did the pension trust look up the lease and discover that it had been had.

The only problem with this recital is that it construes the facts as favorably to the pension trust as the record will permit, and that of course is not the right standard for summary judgment. The facts must be construed as favorably to the nonmoving party, to Market Street Associates, as the record permits (that Market Street Associates filed its own motion for summary judgment is irrelevant, as we have seen). When that is done, a different picture emerges. On Market Street Associates' construal of the record, $3 million was a grossly excessive price for the property, and while $1 million might be a bargain it would not confer so great a windfall as to warrant an inference that if the pension trust had known about paragraph 34 it never would have turned down Market Street Associates' request for financing cold. And in fact the pension trust may have known about paragraph 34, and either it didn't care or it believed that unless the request mentioned that paragraph the pension trust would incur no liability by turning it down. Market Street Associates may have assumed and have been entitled to assume that in reviewing a request for financing from one of its lessees the pension trust would take the time to read the lease to see whether it bore on the request. Market Street Associates did not desire financing from the pension trust initially — that is undeniable — yet when it discovered that it could not get financing elsewhere unless it had the title to the property it may have realized that it would have to negotiate with the pension trust over financing before it could hope to buy the property at the price specified in the lease.

On this interpretation of the facts there was no bad faith on the part of Market Street Associates. It acted honestly, reasonably, without ulterior motive, in the face of circumstances as they actually and reasonably appeared to it. The fault was the pension trust's incredible inattention, which misled Market Street Associates into believing that the pension trust had no interest in financing the improvements regardless of the purchase option. We do not usually excuse contracting parties from failing to read and understand the contents of their contract; and in the end what this case comes down to — or so at least it can be strongly argued — is that an immensely sophisticated enterprise simply failed to read the contract. On the other hand, such enterprises make mistakes just like the rest of us, and deliberately to take advantage of your contracting partner's mistake during the performance stage (for we are not talking about taking advantage of superior knowledge at the formation stage) is a breach of good faith. To be able to correct your contract partner's mistake at zero cost to yourself, and decide not to do so, is a species of opportunistic behavior that the parties would have expressly forbidden in the contract had they foreseen it. The immensely long term of the lease amplified the possibility of errors but did not license either party to take advantage of them.

The district judge jumped the gun in choosing between these alternative characterizations. The essential issue bearing on Market Street Associates' good faith was Orenstein's state of mind, a type of inquiry that ordinarily cannot be concluded on summary judgment, and could not be here. If Orenstein believed that Erb knew or would surely find out about paragraph 34, it was not dishonest or opportunistic to fail to flag that paragraph, or to fail to mention the lease, in his correspondence and (rare) conversations with Erb, especially given the uninterest in dealing with Market Street Associates that Erb fairly radiated. To decide what Orenstein believed, a trial is necessary. As for the pension trust's intimation that a bench trial (for remember that this is an equity case, since the only relief sought by the plaintiff is specific performance) will add no illumination beyond what the summary judgment proceeding has done, this overlooks the fact that at trial the judge will for the first time have a chance to see the witnesses whose depositions he has read, to hear their testimony elaborated, and to assess their believability. *Reversed and remanded.*

H.   AGREEMENTS AGAINST PUBLIC POLICY — "ILLEGAL BARGAINS"

Like any other freedom, freedom of contract is circumscribed by overriding policies. If a statute or other governmental regulation expressly prohibits the enforcement of an agreement, courts will not enforce it, notwithstanding the presence of all requirements for an otherwise enforceable agreement. There are judicially created policies that may not be violated by contract. If such a policy, statute or regulation is silent with respect to agreements that violate them, courts will refuse to lend their aid to enforcing them if such enforcement is incongruous with the overriding interests of society manifested by these societal norms.

The challenge is to determine when an agreement is contrary to the nebulous concept of "public policy." In the famous dictum of JUDGE BURROUGH in *Richardson v. Mellish*, 2 Bing. 229, 252, 30 Eng. Rep. 294, 303 (1824), public policy is "a very unruly horse, and when once you get astride it you never know where it will carry you. It may lead you from the sound law. It is never argued at all but when other points fail." Where a statute expressly precludes enforcement of an agreement contrary to its terms, there is no uncertainty. Similarly, an agreement to commit a crime[25] or a tort,[26] or an agreement to violate a fiduciary duty[27] has no redeeming virtue. Where, however, the agreement does not involve such patently outrageous conduct, the lines become wavering an blurred. For example, where a party performs services precisely in accordance with the contract, should a court refuse to enforce the promise to pay for such services because it is discovered that the contractor did not have a license required by statute or regulation?

The uncertainty surrounding the standard of "public policy" emanates from the necessity of a court to determine the current "community common sense and common consciences . . . applied . . . to matters of public morals, public health, safety, public welfare and the like." "It is that general and well-settled public opinion relating to man's plain, palpable duty to his fellow men, having due regard to all the circumstances of each particular relation and situation." *Naylor, Benzon & Co. v. Krainische Industrie Gesellschaft*, 1 K.B. 331 (1881).

In an era of relativism where any notion of objective moral standards is often viewed with disdain, it may be particularly difficult for a court to provide a satisfactory basis for holding a certain agreement contrary to "public morals" or "well-settled public opinion," which is often anything but well-settled. Not only are public standards difficult to identify, but they change over time. Judges of the past would be shocked by decisions enforcing gambling contracts, upholding agreements between unmarried cohabitants and other changes that courts perceive as reflecting the changing mores of society.

Since innumerable statutes and a wide set of judicial theories may give rise to the question of whether enforcement of a given agreement will violate public policy, we will focus upon those clusters of modern cases which continue to inspire litigation. Before proceeding with the cases, it is important to recognize the use of certain terminology in this area. It has become common to characterize agreements that are not enforced under the broad umbrella of public policy as *"illegal bargains."* Even at this early stage in a law student's career, the use of quotation marks around a word or phrase should suggest a caveat concerning accuracy. A bargain may be "illegal" where parties enter into an agreement in clear violation of a criminal standard. Yet, the typical situation is one in which the agreement is not "illegal"; rather, because it violates a standard of public policy, a court will refuse to enforce it.

---

[25] *See, e.g.*, State v. Grimes, 735 P.2d 1277, 1278 (Or. Ct. App. 1987), where the court states that an agreement to engage in sexual conduct for a fee is a class A misdemeanor in Oregon and is, therefore, unenforceable.

[26] *See* RESTATEMENT (SECOND) OF CONTRACTS § 192.

[27] *See* RESTATEMENT (SECOND) OF CONTRACTS § 193.

[1] Public Policy in Legislation — Regulatory vs. Nonregulatory

U.S. NURSING CORP. v. SAINT JOSEPH MEDICAL CENTER
United States Court of Appeals, Seventh Circuit
39 F.3d 790 (1994)

LAY, J.

On January 8, 1993, U.S. Nursing entered into a written contract to supply St. Joseph with nurses during a strike. The contract provided that either party could terminate the agreement upon seven days notice, but if the hospital failed to give the requisite notice, it was required to pay an amount equivalent to what U.S. Nursing would have earned for the seven additional days.

At the time U.S. Nursing entered into the contract, it had not yet applied for a license to conduct a nursing agency in Illinois as required by the Illinois Nurse Agency Licensing Act ("the Act"). U.S. Nursing promptly filed for a license, however, after entering into the contract. The Illinois Department of Labor ("the Department") notified U.S. Nursing in late January 1993 that it had scheduled a hearing on its proposed denial of the agency's application. The Department proposed denying the application because U.S. Nursing had begun operation of its nursing agency in Illinois without a license, it had failed to demonstrate its financial solvency, and it had failed to properly train and verify the references and credentials of several of its nurses.[28] This notice also informed U.S. Nursing that it was illegal to operate without a license and that the Department was authorized to impose fines for violations of the Act.

On February 2, 1993, the Department informed St. Joseph it was in violation of the Act for using the services of U.S. Nursing, an unlicensed agency. The notice advised St. Joseph to immediately cease using the services of U.S. Nursing. St. Joseph terminated the contract effective the morning of February 4, 1993. It paid U.S. Nursing for all services rendered up to the date it cancelled the contract, but refused to pay for the additional seven days as required by the agreement.

U.S. Nursing brought this action for breach of contract. The district court granted St. Joseph's motion for summary judgment, finding the contract unenforceable under Illinois law.

The sole issue on appeal is whether the district court correctly applied Illinois law in finding the contract unenforceable on public policy grounds. Illinois courts have held that when a statute makes an act illegal, contracts for the performance of the illegal act are deemed void and unenforceable. *Broverman v. City of Taylorville*, 64 Ill. App. 3d 522, 381 N.E.2d 373, 376, 21 Ill. Dec. 264 (Ill. App. Ct. 1978). Contracts based on legitimate subject matter that are performed in an unlawful

---

[28] [1] U.S. Nursing was properly licensed in Illinois in 1991, but permitted its license to lapse. On March 11, 1993, U.S. Nursing and the Department entered into a settlement agreement. Pursuant to that agreement, the Department issued a license to U.S. Nursing on April 9, 1993.

manner are also unenforceable in certain circumstances. *See, e.g., Lozoff v. Shore Heights, Ltd.*, 66 Ill. 2d 398, 362 N.E.2d 1047, 6 Ill. Dec. 225 (Ill. 1977) (prohibiting unlicensed attorney from collecting fee for services rendered); *Tovar v. Paxton Community Memorial Hosp.*, 29 Ill. App. 3d 218, 330 N.E.2d 247 (Ill. App. Ct. 1975) (affirming dismissal of unlicensed physician's suit against employer for breach of contract and misrepresentation). Illinois courts have refused to enforce contracts on behalf of employment agencies that have failed to become licensed as required by the Private Employment Agencies Act, 225 ILCS §§ 515/0.01 to 515/15 (1993). *See, e.g., Management Recruiters v. Process & Envtl. Equip. Unltd., Inc.*, 137 Ill. App. 3d 513, 484 N.E.2d 883, 889–90, 92 Ill. Dec. 152 (Ill. App. Ct. 1985); *T.E.C. & Assoc. v. Alberto-Culver Co.*, 131 Ill. App. 3d 1085, 476 N.E.2d 1212, 1220, 87 Ill. Dec. 220 (Ill. App. Ct. 1985). Other Illinois cases hold that where the violation of a statute is not a "serious affront to public policy or . . . seriously injurious to the public welfare," the contract will be enforced. *Amoco Oil Co. v. Toppert*, 56 Ill. App. 3d 595, 371 N.E.2d 1294, 1297, 14 Ill. Dec. 241 (Ill. App. Ct. 1978) (permitting seller of fertilizer to recover for breach of contract despite minor violation of state law requiring certain documentation accompany each delivery); *see also South Center Plumbing & Heating Supply Co. v. Charles*, 90 Ill. App. 2d 15, 234 N.E.2d 358 (Ill. App. Ct. 1967) (enforcing contract for plumbing work although plumber failed to obtain city permit); *Meissner v. Caravello*, 4 Ill. App. 2d 428, 124 N.E.2d 615 (Ill. App. Ct. 1955) (permitting foreclosure of mechanic's lien despite mechanic's failure to obtain permit as required by city ordinance).

Section 181 of the RESTATEMENT (SECOND) OF CONTRACTS provides as follows:

> If a party is prohibited from doing an act because of his failure to comply with a licensing, registration or similar requirement, a promise in consideration of his doing that act or of his promise to do it is unenforceable on grounds of public policy if a) the requirement has a regulatory purpose, and b) the interest in the enforcement of the promise is clearly outweighed by the public policy behind the requirement.

RESTATEMENT (SECOND) OF CONTRACTS § 181 (1979). U.S. Nursing relies on Section 181 in urging that the nurse agency license law is not regulatory and that no public policy interest is furthered by refusing to enforce the contract. U.S. Nursing distinguishes the cases relied upon by the district court in that they involved professionals within the fields of law and medicine attempting to practice without a license. It urges that, unlike the plaintiffs in those cases, it is not a medical or nursing professional, but merely arranged for licensed nurses to work at St. Joseph. We find this distinction unconvincing.

U.S. Nursing contends the requirements for obtaining a nurse agency license demonstrate the Licensing Act is primarily "business related" and is not intended to protect the public. It distinguishes *Management Recruiters*, 484 N.E.2d at 883, relied on by St. Joseph. There the plaintiff was a recruiting company engaged by a client to refer applicants to the client for employment. The Illinois court ruled the plaintiff could not sue to recover a placement fee without an employment agency license. U.S. Nursing distinguishes that case because the statute at issue there expressly provided that it was unlawful for any employment agency to collect compensation not set forth in the schedule of fees filed. Moreover, the application requirements in that statute were more extensive than those in the Nurse Agency Licensing Act in that they required an applicant to submit an affidavit attesting to his moral character and business reputation.

In order to qualify for a license under the Nurse Agency Licensing Act, an applicant must submit (1) its name and address, (2) a copy of its articles of incorporation and other business information, (3) the names of the proposed agency's managers and supervisors, (4) a statement of financial solvency, (5) the name and location of the proposed agency, (6) a statement outlining the applicant's qualifications to run a nurse agency, (7) evidence of compliance with state and federal compensation laws, (8) evidence of liability insurance, and (9) any other relevant information sought by the Department. 225 ILCS § 510/5 (1993).

On this basis, U.S. Nursing argues that "no minimum competency or education, previous experience, professional qualifications or any demonstrable skills" are required for the issuance of a nurse agency license. Upon receipt of the application and payment of $250, the license will be issued unless it is denied for:

(a) failure to comply with the minimum standards set forth by this Act or its rules;

(b) conviction of the applicant of a felony;

(c) insufficient financial or other resources to operate the nurse agency in accordance with the requirements of this Act and the minimum standards, rules and regulations promulgated thereunder; or

(d) failure to establish appropriate personnel policies and procedures for selecting nurses and certified nurse aides for employment, assignment or referral.

In arguing that the Licensing Act is nonregulatory, U.S. Nursing also relies on Section 181, comment b, which reads as follows:

> A, an unlicensed broker, agrees to arrange a transaction for B, for which B promises to pay A $1,000. A city ordinance requires persons arranging such transactions to be licensed as a result of paying a fee, with no inquiry into competence or responsibility. A arranges the transaction. Since the licensing requirement is designed merely to raise revenue and does not have a regulatory purpose, enforcement of B's promise is not precluded on grounds of public policy. RESTATEMENT (SECOND) OF CONTRACTS § 181 cmt. b (1979) (emphasis added).

U.S. Nursing points out the health care facility is responsible for supervising nurse agency employees. The record shows St. Joseph specifically reported and received a copy of the Illinois license held by each nurse employee who worked at the hospital. On this basis, U.S. Nursing urges that the district court erred in holding the Nurse Agency Licensing Act was regulatory in nature. Upon analysis, we must disagree. We find the district court's analysis of the statute and the Illinois law to be correct in holding the statute had a regulatory purpose.

As the district court found, the Act's declaration of purpose states that the legislature "intended to protect the public's right to high quality health care by assuring that nurse agencies employ, assign, and refer licensed and certified

pub. pol.

personnel to health care facilities." It is undisputed that denial of the agency license can be for "failure to establish appropriate personnel policies and procedures for selecting nurses . . . for employment . . . ." Moreover, the requirements imposed by the Act are not as insubstantial as U.S. Nursing claims. An examination of the statute and the regulations promulgated pursuant to it reveals that the Act imposes numerous public health related requirements upon nurse staffing agencies. Nurse agencies are required to check the references of each nurse applicant and are required to verify in writing whether each nurse who applies for employment is properly licensed under Illinois law. The administrative rules adopted by the Department under the statute's authority require that nurses hired by nursing agencies undergo CPR training and be screened for communicable diseases. There can be little doubt that these requirements are highly regulatory and serve the public purpose as set forth in the legislative declaration.

U.S. Nursing urges arguendo that even if the Act may be defined as regulatory, the interest in the enforcement of the contract clearly outweighs the public policy underlying the licensing requirement. U.S. Nursing contends the district court has confused the role of U.S. Nursing as a business regulated under the Act with the independent requirement that all registered nurses be properly licensed and qualified under Illinois law. It is urged that no violation of the Licensing Act can be found injurious to the public welfare. On this basis, U.S. Nursing relies on Illinois law which observes:

> Unless a bargain necessarily involves an illegal act, it is not unenforceable, and if it is later performed in a way that involves some slight violation of law, not seriously injurious to the public order, the person performing may recover on his bargain.

Amoco Oil Company v. Toppert, 371 N.E.2d at 1296 (*quoting* 6 WILLISTON ON CONTRACTS § 1767, at 5018–19 (Rev. Ed. 1938)). U.S. Nursing also relies on *Meissner*, 124 N.E.2d at 615, where the court, using WILLISTON'S rule, found enforceable a contract for work by a carpenter who failed to obtain a building permit to perform remodeling work on a building; *Lavine Construction Co. v. Johnson*, 101 Ill. App. 3d 817, 428 N.E.2d 1069, 57 Ill. Dec. 389 (Ill. App. Ct. 1981), where the court in applying the reasoning in *Meissner* refused to void a contract for electrical work because the contractor failed to acquire a permit for the work required under a municipal ordinance; and *South Center Plumbing*, 234 N.E.2d at 358, wherein the court upheld a repairman's contract even though he had not obtained a license, and the ordinance did not demonstrate a legislative intent to declare such contracts unenforceable.

In this case, St. Joseph has paid U.S. Nursing for all services rendered, and U.S. Nursing merely seeks recovery of what amounts to a penalty provision for termination of the contract without sufficient notice.[29] Under these circumstances, and especially when the termination of the contract without notice was the direct result of U.S. Nursing's failure to procure a license, the interest in enforcement of

---

[29] [3] In determining the weight of the interest in enforcement of the contract, we are to consider any forfeiture or unjust enrichment that may result from a failure to enforce the terms of the agreement. RESTATEMENT (SECOND) OF CONTRACTS § 181 cmt. c (1979).

this particular provision of the contract is fairly weak.

We contrast that interest with the public policy behind the Act: the assurance of quality health care. The comments to Section 181suggest that statutes intended to protect the public health are to be given relatively greater weight. RESTATEMENT (SECOND) OF CONTRACTS § 181 cmt. c (1979). Thus, in light of the weighty interest in the public health furthered by the Act and the relatively weak interest in permitting U.S. Nursing to collect a sum above and beyond the cost of the actual services rendered, we find that the public policy behind the Act clearly outweighs the interest in enforcement of this contract.

[The] defendant has been placed in the awkward position of either breaking the law or breaching the contract. We believe an Illinois court would find that the important public policy behind the Act cannot be furthered by penalizing hospitals that comply with it. [W]e conclude the district court properly applied Illinois law in finding the contract unenforceable as a matter of public policy. Accordingly, we *affirm*.

PROBLEMS

(1)   A hospital established a renal transplant center and performed competent services in the center. It was entitled to compensation for these services but did not receive such payments on the footing that it failed to obtain a state permit that was required to operate such a center. The hospital proved that the state agency refusing to provide the permit did so because of its determination that the state did not need another renal transplant center, i.e., the permit process was designed to preclude the oversupply of such services. Analyze. *See Rush-Presbyterian v. Hellenic Republic*, 980 F.2d 449 (7th Cir. 1992).

(2)   A home improvement contractor met all of the licensing requirements set forth in a regulation and received the license. A month prior to receiving the license, the contractor accepted a down payment for an improvement project which he later completed. Must he surrender the pre-payment and is he entitled to recovery of the balance due him under the contract? *See Cevern, Inc. v. Ferbish*, 666 A.2d 17 (D.C. Ct. App. 1995).

(3)   Chester Rice was performing electrical contracting work when he was told he could not continue on the job because he had no permit. He could not obtain a permit because he was not a licensed electrical contractor. Rice then promised to pay Leon James who was licensed $10,000 in exchange for James obtaining the permit. In accordance with the agreement of the parties, James performed no work on the project. Rice refuses to pay James. Analyze. *See Rice v. James*, 844 S.W.2d 64 (Mo. Ct. App. 1992).

(4)   The plaintiff contracted to perform lobbying services but had not registered as a lobbyist under the Federal lobbying act, 2 U.S.C. § 261 *et. seq.* Plaintiff performed the services but defendant refused to pay. Is the contract enforceable? *See Taylor v. Hayes*, 23 Va. Cir. 464 (1991).

[2]   Contracts in Restraint of Trade

FINE FOODS, INC. v. DAHLIN
Vermont Supreme Court
523 A.2d 1228 (1987)

Peck, J.

Defendant was part owner of Taft's Delectables, Inc., d/b/a Taft's Restaurant, located in Brattleboro, Vermont. The business had been a successful venture, in large measure due to defendant's experience, skill and personality. On December 3, 1983, defendant and his partner entered into an agreement with plaintiffs whereby they would sell to the latter the real and personal assets of their business for the sum of $240,000. The purchase and sales agreement provided, *inter alia*, that defendant and defendant's corporation, Taft's Delectables, Inc., would execute and deliver a covenant not to compete to the plaintiffs. On the date of the closing, *non-compete* February 4, 1984, defendant delivered an executed covenant not to compete. This covenant provided in pertinent part:

> 1. That in consideration of the sum of Five Thousand and no/100 ($5,000.00) Dollars, . . . Thomas E. Dahlin . . . agree[s] . . . he will not . . . for a period of five years . . . directly or indirectly, either as a principal agent, manager, owner, partner (dormant or otherwise), stockholder, director, or officer of a corporation, or otherwise engage in or become interested financially or otherwise in any business, trade or occupation similar to or in competition [with] a restaurant or similar business within a radius of twenty-five miles of the Town of Brattleboro.

The covenant further set forth that defendant would be liable for attorney's fees if he breached the agreement.

In December of 1984, the defendant accepted the position of "maitre d' " at the Old Newfane Inn in Brattleboro, Vermont. Defendant's duties included greeting dinner guests, showing them to their tables, taking cocktail orders, lighting candles at the table, flambéing, carving meats, and serving wine. Performance of these duties earned defendant fifteen dollars per night plus a portion of the tips received by the waitresses.

Defendant notified plaintiffs of his acceptance of the position. Subsequently, plaintiffs informed defendant that this employment violated the covenant not to compete and that continued violation would result in further action. Defendant continued his employment, and a complaint was filed by plaintiffs on January 14, 1985. The trial court held for plaintiffs, finding that defendant had violated the covenant not to compete by accepting employment in the restaurant business within a twenty-five mile radius of Brattleboro before the five-year period had expired.

[W]e must examine the employment restriction in the light of the applicable law. "When this Court is asked to enforce restrictive covenants against competitive employment, we will proceed with caution . . . ." *Roy's Orthopedic, Inc. v. Lavigne*, 142 Vt. 347, 350, 454 A.2d 1242, 1244 (1982). Restraints against competitive employment conflict with the public policy "'favoring the right of individuals to freely engage in desirable commercial activity.'" *Id.* (quoting *Vermont Electric Supply Co. v. Andrus*, 132 Vt. 195, 198, 315 A.2d 456, 458 (1974)). Whenever an individual's trade or talents are restricted, we scrutinize the reasonableness and justification for such a restriction. *Id.* Restrictive agreements will be enforced by the courts, "'unless the agreement is found to be contrary to public policy, unnecessary for protection of the employer, or unnecessarily restrictive of the rights of the employee, with due regard being given to the subject matter of the contract and the circumstances and conditions under which it is to be performed.'" *Id.* (quoting *Vermont Electric Supply Co. v. Andrus, supra*, 132 Vt. at 198, 315 A.2d at 458).

The findings of the trial court, though inartfully phrased, did not indicate deviation from the standards of review set forth above. Inquiries regarding time and place restrictions are crucial to a determination of whether a covenant not to compete unduly restricts the rights of an individual. *Id.* With respect to time, this Court has approved a covenant containing a five-year restriction of competitive employment. *See Vermont Electric Supply Co. v. Andrus, supra*, 132 Vt. at 199, 315 A.2d at 458.

Nor do geographic limitations of the covenant appear unduly restrictive. Outside the 25-mile limit, defendant may own, manage or become employed in the restaurant business. The point was not raised for consideration on appeal, and there is no indication from the record or the defendant's brief that this unduly restricts him.

An additional concern is the monetary consideration received by defendant in exchange for the sale of the business and the executed covenant not to compete. The covenant was a primary part of the transaction. Indeed, the purchase and sales agreement specifically refers to the subsequent delivery of the executed covenant on the date of closing. In addition, a sum of five thousand dollars was paid for the executed covenant alone. Under the circumstances, the restrictions agreed to were reasonable [as] to time and place.

Defendant further maintains that the trial court's findings do not support the decree enjoining his participation in the restaurant business. Essentially, defendant argues that the covenant not to compete must be construed narrowly, and that the trial court's conclusion is erroneous. It is well settled that when conclusions are not supported by the findings, they cannot stand. We agree that when competitive employment is restricted, narrow interpretation of the covenant is proper. As we have stated above, however, the trial court correctly construed the covenant. This construction, which is supported by the evidence and set forth in the findings, leads to a proper conclusion that defendant should be enjoined from violating the covenant not to compete. The injunctive relief granted is supported by the findings.

NOTES

(1) *Good Will.* If a person has an established trade or business which he or she wishes to sell, the most valuable asset for sale is often the good will which the owner has developed over a period of time. Prospective buyers are ill advised to pay a great

deal for such good will if there is any likelihood that the former owner would return and commence a similar enterprise nearby. In any kind of service industry such as restaurants or hair styling, or professions such as law, medicine and dentistry, the value of the good will depends essentially upon the absence of the former owner. Even in a business involving the sale of goods, e.g., a pharmacy, the good will of the former owner could be lost upon his or her return. The solution to this problem is found exclusively in an enforceable covenant by the former owner that he or she will not engage in such business within a certain distance of the original site for a certain period. Such covenants, however, are frowned upon because they are in restraint of trade.

(2) *Ancillary and Nonancillary Restraints.* In a very broad sense, every contract concerning trade is a contract in restraint thereof since the parties to the contract take themselves out of the market to the extent of the undertakings. *See Board of Trade v. United States*, 246 U.S. 231 (1918). Thus, Anglo-American law never recognized a principle that all contracts in restraint of trade, in the literal sense, were illegal. However, in early English society, contracts which adversely affected the opportunities of a person to earn his livelihood were viewed with deep suspicion. If someone undertook to refrain from engaging in a particular occupation or business, the contract was viewed as inimical to the public interest and illegal because it was in restraint of trade. Yet, there were certain legitimate interests which could be served by contracts in restraint of trade. Someone who had worked diligently and well to establish a business could dispose of what often was the most saleable part of the business, the good will, only if he were permitted to restrain himself from competing with the purchaser after the sale. Thus, a distinction developed between *ancillary* restraints, or those which follow a legitimate transaction and are enforceable, and *nonancillary* (direct) restraints, which were unenforceable because they were not attached to an otherwise legitimate interest. *See United States v. Addyston Pipe & Steel Co.*, 85 F. 271 (6th Cir. 1898) (opinion by Justice Taft).

A typical example of a nonancillary restraint is a contract to fix prices or divide markets. There is considerable controversy as to how nonancillary restraints were viewed at common law. *See, e.g.,* DEWEY, *The Common-Law Background of Antitrust Policy*, 41 VA. L. REV. 759 (1955); LETWIN, *The English Common Law Concerning Monopolies*, 21 U. CHI. L. REV. 355 (1954); PEPPIN, *Price-fixing Agreements Under the Sherman Antitrust Law*, 28 CAL. L. REV. 297, 677 (1940); *see also* BORK, *The Rule of Reason and the Per Se Concept: Price Fixing and Market Division (pts. 1 & 2)*, 74 YALE L.J. 775 (1965), 75 YALE L.J. 375 (1966). However, there is strong support for the position that the majority of American courts treated nonancillary restraints as illegal *per se. See* HANDLER, *A Study of the Construction and Enforcement of the Federal Antitrust Laws* (4-5 TNEC MONOGRAPH No. 38, 1941). In the well-known case of *Mitchel v. Reynolds*, 1 P. Williams 181, 24 Eng. Rep. 347 (1711), a lease of a messuage and bakehouse was assigned to the plaintiff. An ancillary covenant to this assignment made the defendant liable to the plaintiff in the sum of fifty pounds if the defendant exercised his trade as a baker in a certain area during a five-year period. The ancillary covenant in restraint of trade was upheld because it was reasonably limited in time and in geographical area. *Mitchel v. Reynolds* also suggested that all general restraints, i.e., those unlimited in time or space, were invalid *per se.* This attitude was changed prior to the middle of the nineteenth century and by the end of that century, the House of Lords declared the broad test to be one of reasonableness even with regard to general restraints. *Id.* at 565 [1894] (Lord Macnaghten). This is the general rule at the present time. *See* RESTATEMENT (FIRST) OF CONTRACTS §§ 514–16 (1932).

BOISEN v. PETERSEN FLYING SERVICE
Nebraska Supreme Court
383 N.W.2d 29 (1986)

SHANAHAN, J.

Douglas Boisen, 35 years old and a lifetime resident of Kearney County, lived near Minden with his wife and children. Douglas, a farmer since 1971, formed a farming partnership in 1974, Boisen Farms, with his father. Douglas obtained a private pilot certificate in 1977. Charles O. Petersen, president and sole shareholder of Petersen Flying, was a flight instructor for Douglas in obtaining the private pilot certificate. The business of Petersen Flying, incorporated in 1976, consisted of aerial spraying for application of agricultural chemicals — herbicides and insecticides. Boisen Farms was one of Petersen Flying's customers.

In 1979 Douglas began training toward a commercial pilot certificate. Petersen again instructed Douglas and indicated an interest in Douglas' future employment by Petersen Flying as a spray pilot, after Douglas obtained his commercial pilot certificate. Douglas received a commercial pilot certificate in 1981 and arranged with Petersen for special instruction in flying a spray plane. Petersen supervised several low-altitude practice runs made in a Grumman "Ag-Cat," one of Petersen Flying's spray planes used in Douglas' efforts to develop skills as an aerial applicator. When Douglas became proficient in flying an Ag-Cat, Petersen, on behalf of Petersen Flying, submitted to Douglas a written agreement denominated "Contract for Use of Aircraft, Employment as Pilot and Agreement Not to Compete." The submitted contract contained a provision:

> It is expressly understood and agreed, that for the consideration provided herein by employer, employee agrees that in the event he does not enter the employment of employer, or in the event he does enter employment with employer, but later leaves such employment for any reason, whether at his own instance, or at the instance of the employer, then, in any of such events, employee agrees that he shall not enter any occupation or employment, whether working for someone else or as a self-employed person, as owner, operator, employee, salesman, representative, pilot, instructor, advisor or consultant in, with or to any business which is in competition with any business presently performed or performed at any time during the employment of employee, by Petersen Flying Service, Inc., employer herein, within a radius of 50 miles of Minden, Kearney County, Nebraska, for a period for 10 years from the date of this agreement, or from the date such employee shall leave the employment of employer, which ever is later.

Douglas and Petersen signed the agreement on July 6, 1982. After signing the agreement Douglas did some aerial spraying for Petersen Flying in 1982 and during the first few weeks of the "spraying season" in 1983. While employed by Petersen Flying, Douglas did not contact any of Petersen Flying's customers regarding aerial spraying, that is, did not solicit orders for spraying or make collections for chemicals applied by Petersen Flying. As a result of his growing up in Kearney County and acquaintance with other members of the farming community, Douglas knew the identity of some customers by location of their farms. For identification of sites to be sprayed, Douglas and other spray pilots of Petersen Flying were given names of customers immediately before spraying operations. Douglas' only on-the-job training, knowledge, or skill acquired related to operating the Ag-Cat, mixing chemicals to be sprayed, and applying chemicals on fields of customers. Chemicals were mixed according to the manufacturer's label on the container.

Late in 1983, Petersen Flying discharged Douglas from employment, claiming that Douglas never developed into a good spray pilot. In his petition Douglas alleged:

> The restraint purportedly imposed by [the employment contract] is unreasonable concerning the nature of employment or occupation purportedly prohibited, the area within which such employment or occupation is prohibited, and the length of time during which such employment or occupation if [sic] prohibited, and as such, the restraint does not correspond with the need, if any, for protecting the legitimate interests of [Petersen Flying].

By his petition Douglas prayed that the covenant not to compete, contained in the agreement of July 6, 1982, be "declared invalid and of no force or effect."

In its answer Petersen Flying claimed that the contract with Douglas constituted "a bargain by an assistant, servant or agent not to compete with his employer, after termination of employment, within such territory and during such time as may be reasonably necessary for the protection of the employer without imposing undue hardship on the employee." Petersen Flying also filed a cross-petition, alleging that the restrictive covenant was "valid and enforcable [sic] and should be enforced against [Douglas]" and praying that the restrictive covenant be determined valid and enforceable or "that in the event said Contract cannot be fully enforced, that the Court determine and reform the same to be equitable between the parties."

At trial Douglas testified he wanted to enter the aerial spraying business. As described by Charles Petersen, the aerial spraying of Petersen Flying was not fly-by-night. Petersen Flying owned six aircraft and obtained customers through "personal contact, word of mouth, advertising [and a] lot of hard work." Petersen testified that the aerial spraying business is a "flexible business and you go wherever the bugs are." Customer contact was initiated by a prospective customer, or, as Petersen explained, "[Y]ou wait for the farmer to call." Petersen Flying did "nothing" to retain customers from season to season. The "price" charged for aerial spraying determined whether a customer stayed with Petersen Flying or went to one of its competitors in the area. Information about a competitor's price "generally" came from a prospective customer. Petersen Flying had no trade secrets. A customer list of Petersen Flying was nonexistent. Petersen acknowledged that

Douglas, during employment with Petersen Flying, learned "no more" than Douglas would have learned from another engaged in the aerial spraying business. When asked about his reason for the postemployment restrictive covenant, Petersen responded: "The whole fact is that I've been in business in this area, why should I train somebody to go out and run me competition in the area that I have been developing." The district court found the covenant not to compete was "unreasonable and unenforceable." The district court refused to modify the covenant, as requested by Petersen Flying, regarding the restrictions involving time and space.

Petersen Flying claims the district court erred in (1) finding that the restrictive covenant was unenforceable and (2) refusing to modify the covenant to provide enforceability.

> There are three general requirements relating to partial restraints of trade: First, is the restriction reasonable in the sense that it is not injurious to the public; second, is the restriction reasonable in the sense that it is no greater than is reasonably necessary to protect the employer in some legitimate interest; and, third, is the restriction reasonable in the sense that it is not unduly harsh and oppressive on the employee.

Securities Acceptance Corp. v. Brown, 171 Neb. 406, 417, 106 N.W.2d 456, 463 (1960).

Petersen Flying invokes the "equities" involved in the case before us and emphasizes that flying a spray plane is not Douglas' primary occupation, characterizing Douglas as "flying a spray plane more for the thrill of the helmet, the goggles, the roar of the engine and the white scarf trailing out of the open cockpit than for the living wage he would make to feed his family." In this manner Petersen Flying contends that Douglas' aerial spraying is an avocation, not a vocation, and suggests that a court should consider several factors, indicated in *Philip G. Johnson & Co. v. Salmen*, 211 Neb. 123, 317 N.W.2d 900 (1982), regarding a "balancing test" applied in determining whether enforcement of a covenant not to compete would be unduly harsh and oppressive to an employee.

However, not every employer-employee relationship infuses validity and enforceability into a postemployment restraint on competition by a former employee. Before weighing the various factors pertinent to hardship on a promisor in a restrictive covenant and enforceability of such restraint, we reexamine some principles formulated concerning validity of a covenant not to compete. More fundamental than, or at least preliminary to, the "balancing test" is the test embodied in the question, Is the restraint "reasonably necessary to protect the employer in some legitimate interest"? *Brewer v. Tracy*, 198 Neb. 503, 505, 253 N.W.2d 319, 321 (1977). *See also* RESTATEMENT (SECOND) OF CONTRACTS § 188(1)(a) (1981). Regarding a postemployment covenant not to compete, an employer has a legitimate business interest in protection against " 'competition by improper and unfair methods,' " but an employer is not entitled to enforcement of a restrictive covenant which merely protects the employer from " 'ordinary competition.' " *Diamond Match Div. of Diamond International Corp. v. Bernstein*, 243 N.W.2d at 766. "A restraint on the employee is illegal when its purpose is the prevention of competition, except when the methods of competition to be prevented are methods commonly regarded as improper and unfair." 6A A. CORBIN, CORBIN ON CONTRACTS § 1394.

To distinguish between "ordinary competition" and "unfair competition," courts and commentators have frequently focused on an employee's opportunity to appropriate the employer's goodwill by initiating personal contacts with the employer's customers. Where an employee has substantial personal contact with the employer's customers, develops goodwill with such customers, and siphons away the goodwill under circumstances where the goodwill properly belongs to the employer, the employee's resultant competition is unfair, and the employer has a legitimate need for protection against the employee's competition. *See Dana F. Cole & Co. v. Byerly*, 211 Neb. 903, 320 N.W.2d 916 (1982). *See, also, Sidko Paper Company v. Aaron*, 465 Pa. 586, 351 A.2d 250, 254 (1976) (an employer "clearly has a protectible interest in customer goodwill"); 6A A. CORBIN, *supra* (special justification for postemployment restriction exists "if a part of the employee's compensated service consists in the creation of the good will of customers and clients, a good will that is likely to follow the person of the employee himself"); CORBIN ON CONTRACTS § 1391B at 573 (C. Kaufman ed. Supp. 1984) ("Some courts seem to overlook the fact that covenants against competition are imposed, not to protect the employer against ordinary competition, but only to protect against unfair siphoning away of the employer's good will"); Blake, *Employee Agreements Not to Compete*, 73 HARV. L. REV. 625 (1960). Also, an employer has a legitimate need to curb or prevent competitive endeavors by a former employee who has acquired confidential information or trade secrets pertaining to the employer's business operations. *See Brewer v. Tracy, supra. See also Whitmyer Bros., Inc. v. Doyle, et al.*, 58 N.J. 25, 33, 274 A.2d 577, 581 (1971) (an employer has a "patently legitimate interest in protecting his trade secrets"); 6A A. CORBIN, CORBIN ON CONTRACTS § 1394 (1962). From the foregoing we glean that an objective of a covenant not to compete is prevention of an employee's competitive use of information or a relationship with a customer or client, which pertains peculiarly to the employer and has been acquired in the course of the employee's employment with the employer. *See* Blake, *supra* at 647.

On the other hand, "[p]ost-employment restraints are scrutinized with particular care," and "[a] line must be drawn between the general skills and knowledge of the trade and information that is peculiar to the employer's business." RESTATEMENT (SECOND) OF CONTRACTS § 188, Comment g, at 45 (1981). Ordinarily, an employer has no legitimate business interest in postemployment prevention of an employee's use of some general skill or training acquired while working for the employer, although such on-the-job acquisition of general knowledge, skill, or facility may make the employee an effective competitor for the former employer. *See* Blake, *supra* at 652. *See also* 6A A. CORBIN, *supra* § 1394. "An opportunity to develop good will which is no different from the opportunity any other like employee in the industry would have with some other firm is not traceable to the particular position and situation of the employer." CORBIN ON CONTRACTS § 1391B at 574 (C. Kaufman ed. Supp. 1984).

Petersen Flying has not shown any special circumstance affecting a legitimate business interest to be protected by a covenant not to compete. Beyond general contact with members of the community, Douglas had no personal and business-based contact with a customer or prospective customer of Petersen Flying.

Although Douglas' low-altitude flying over a customer's fields at times probably brought him within relative proximity to Petersen Flying's customers, such contact is not close customer contact likely to lead away customers from Petersen Flying or divert customers to any prospective aerial spraying business operated by Douglas. Douglas was not exposed to, and did not acquire, confidential information accumulated by Petersen Flying regarding its customers or potential customers. As acknowledged by Petersen, the on-the-job training and knowledge acquired by Douglas were no different from that which would have been received from another employer engaged in the business of aerial spraying. The nature of Douglas' services rendered during employment with Petersen Flying contained no inherent threat to Petersen Flying's relationship with its customers, who were generally known and accessible to anyone involved in the business of aerial spraying. Petersen Flying had no trade secrets for aerial spraying, such as a significantly different technique unknown to competitors or a unique and advantageous method to conduct an aerial spraying business. Reduced to its rudiments, Petersen Flying's objective in the covenant not to compete is prevention of prospective competition consequent to another aerial spraying business' serving agricultural customers and, perhaps, ultimately causing a reduction of revenue due to competitive prices or fewer customers, available or served. A covenant not to compete, as a partial restraint of trade, is available to prevent unfair competition by a former employee but is not available to shield an employer against ordinary competition. Under the circumstances we conclude that the questioned covenant not to compete does not protect "some legitimate business interest" of Petersen Flying and is, therefore, invalid and unenforceable. Petersen Flying's argument that a "balancing test" should be applied in this case simply does not get off the ground.

Petersen Flying maintains, however, that a court should exercise equitable powers and modify the restrictions of the covenant in this case. If such power had been exercised in this case, Petersen Flying argues, the restrictive covenant should have been enforced as judicially modified. Without commenting on the question whether a court, if ever, has the power to modify a restrictive covenant which is too broad, see *Philip G. Johnson & Co. v. Salmen*, 211 Neb. 123, 317 N.W.2d 900 (1982), we dispose of Petersen Flying's last argument by reiterating that Petersen Flying is not entitled to avail itself of the restrictive covenant as protection against the threat of ordinary competition. The purpose or effect of eliminating or preventing ordinary competition invalidates the restrictive covenant in question. Consideration of propriety or availability of judicial modification concerning the covenant's restraints based on time and place becomes unnecessary on account of the questioned covenant's invalidity. *See Johanson v. Liberty Mutual Insurance Company*, 232 N.Y.S.2d 856, 860 (1962) (a restrictive covenant which protects only against ordinary competition is "unenforceable even though it is limited as to time and place"). *See also* CORBIN ON CONTRACTS § 1391B at 573 (C. Kaufman ed. Supp. 1984) (if the purpose or effect of a restrictive covenant is only to restrain ordinary competition, such condition "absolutely invalidates" a restrictive covenant). Whatever a more narrow draft of the questioned covenant might have been or may be, thereby decreasing the limitation of time or space involved in the restriction under examination, is irrelevant. Any modification in diminution of the restrictions on time and space still pertains to a restriction on a form of competition against which

Petersen Flying is not entitled to protection. The judgment of the district court is affirmed.

NOTE

The "Blue Pencil" Rule. The suggestion by Petersen Flying Service that the court should modify the restrictive covenant relates to a process that began as a doctrine often called the "blue pencil rule," first suggested many years ago in *Mallan v. May*, 11 M. & W. 853, 12 L.J. Ex. 376, 7 Jur. 536 (1843). The rule suggested the possibility of eliminating objectionable features from a covenant not to compete by "blue penciling" the unreasonable portions. If the language was capable of being edited by the simple act of such penciling, resulting in a reasonable covenant not to compete, this mechanical act succeeded. Unfortunately, the "blue pencil" rule was effective only where the parties had fortuitously drafted the clause so that a particular portion could be "penciled out" and the remaining clause would be comprehensible as well as reasonable.

Modern courts are willing to "sever" the impermissible portion of the restrictive covenant, whether or not it can be accomplished mechanically, under the "blue pencil" rule. In *Karpinski v. Ingrasci*, 268 N.E.2d 751 (N.Y. 1971), the defendant was employed as an oral surgeon by the plaintiff under a contract containing a restrictive covenant precluding the defendant from practicing "dentistry and/or oral surgery." The court held that the impermissible restriction as to "dentistry" could be severed. Though such severance could have occurred mechanically under the old "blue pencil" rule, the court was persuaded by the modern severance concept which permits courts to modify the covenant without regard to mechanical processes.

In general, see MURRAY ON CONTRACTS § 99C.

[3]   Marriage Contracts

WILCOX v. TRAUTZ
Massachusetts Supreme Judicial Court
693 N.E.2d 141 (1998)

GREANEY, J.

After approximately-twenty-five years of living together as an unmarried couple, the plaintiff and the defendant separated. The plaintiff brought an action in the Probate and Family Court which sought a declaration under that a written agreement between the parties was invalid and unenforceable. The judge concluded that it was invalid and should not be enforced.

In 1967, the plaintiff, then age twenty-two years, and the defendant, then age twenty-five years, began living together in an apartment rented by the defendant in Abington. The defendant, who earned approximately $100 more per week than the plaintiff, was employed at a local supermarket as a meat cutter, and the plaintiff was employed by the same company as a meat wrapper. The plaintiff had completed the tenth grade in high school and subsequently received a high school equivalency diploma. The defendant had completed the eleventh grade.

The parties moved from the Abington apartment to a house purchased by the defendant in Rockland in 1973, and in 1980, after the defendant sold the Rockland property, they moved to a house he purchased in Halifax, where they resided together until the time of trial. The titles to both the Rockland and the Halifax properties were in the defendant's name only.

Between 1973 and 1992, the plaintiff contributed $25 a week toward general household expenses. Throughout the course of the relationship, the plaintiff performed household duties, including all the food and clothes shopping, which she paid for solely from her earnings, as well as all of the cooking, cleaning, and laundry. She also entertained the parties' friends and family in the parties' home.

The plaintiff contributed some of her income toward the maintenance and improvement of the parties' home. She paid for the purchase and installation of ceramic flooring, wall-to-wall carpeting, patio furniture, and a deck. She and the defendant also shared the cost of a television, an oven, a refrigerator, and an air conditioner.

By contributing some of her salary to the parties' home, the plaintiff did not secure her own investments, and, at the time of trial, she did not have any savings and only a small pension. The plaintiff's contributions enabled the defendant to use some of his funds to purchase and maintain his real estate and an airplane.

In March, 1989, the plaintiff became involved in another relationship which spurred the defendant to seek legal advice regarding the parties' rights with respect to the assets acquired during their relationship. Pursuant to the defendant's request, his attorney drafted an agreement concerning the parties respective rights.[30] The defendant testified that he discussed the terms of the agreement with the plaintiff before instructing his attorney to draft the agreement.

The defendant presented the agreement to the plaintiff and told her that if she did not sign it, their relationship would be over and she would be required to move out of the Halifax house. He advised her to seek legal advice before signing the agreement, and, although she had the opportunity to do so, she did not seek any advice regarding the agreement. A few days later, the parties signed the agreement before a notary public.

At the time of the execution of the agreement, the defendant owned the Halifax property, valued at $180,000; an amphibious airplane, valued at $55,000; various bank accounts, totalling approximately $1,300; individual retirement accounts; and a one-half share of real estate in Maine, valued at $15,000. The plaintiff did not have

---

[30] [1] Specifically, the agreement provides that each party's earnings and property is his or hers alone, and the other party shall have no interest in the property of the other; any services rendered by either party are voluntary and without expectation of compensation; the parties shall maintain separate accounts; any debts or obligations are the responsibility of the party who acquired them; if one party contributes to the mortgage payment of a premises owned by the other party, the contribution is to be deemed rent only and shall not create in the contributor any interest in the property; and any money transferred from one party to the other, with the exception of mortgage or rent payments, shall be deemed a loan.

any assets in her name, other than a bank account containing a small amount, and a one-half share in the Maine real estate. She owned household furniture, clothing, and jewelry. The parties were aware of the principal assets, and fully understood each other's financial status prior to the execution of the agreement.

The agreement provided that the plaintiff vacate the Halifax residence within thirty days after being requested to do so by the defendant. When the plaintiff became involved in another relationship in 1992, the defendant gave her thirty days' notice to leave the home. When the defendant asked the plaintiff to leave at the expiration of the thirty days, the plaintiff refused to do so, and instead moved into another bedroom where she resided until the time of trial.

We have not previously passed on the validity of written agreements between two unmarried cohabitants that attempt to define the rights of the parties as to services rendered and property acquired during their relationship. Our early decisions precluded the enforcement of an agreement between unmarried parties if the agreement was made in consideration that the parties should cohabit. *See, e.g., Zytka v. Dmochowski*, 302 Mass. 63, 63–64, 18 N.E.2d 332 (1938) (if money is given by one party to the other "entirely or partially in consideration that the parties should cohabit, then the parties have no standing to invoke the aid of a court of equity to compel the repayment of the money and they have no rights which are cognizable in equity"). *See also Otis v. Freeman*, 199 Mass. 160, 85 N.E. 168 (1908). More recently, we have held valid oral promises between unmarried cohabitants so long as "illicit sexual relations were [not] an inherent aspect of the agreement or a 'serious and not merely an incidental part of the performance of the agreement.' " *Margolies v. Hopkins*, 401 Mass. 88, 92, 514 N.E.2d 1079 (1987), quoting *Green v. Richmond*, 369 Mass. 47, 51, 337 N.E.2d 691 (1975).

Social mores regarding cohabitation between unmarried parties have changed dramatically in recent years and living arrangements that were once criticized are now relatively common and accepted. "As an alternative to marriage, more couples are choosing to cohabit. These relationships may be of extended duration, sometimes lasting as long as many marriages. In many respects, these cohabitation relationships may be quite similar to conventional marriages; they may involve commingling of funds, joint purchases of property, and even the birth of children." (Footnotes omitted.) Perry, *Dissolution Planning in Family Law: A Critique of Current Analyses and a Look Toward the Future*, 24 Fam. L.Q. 77, 78 (1990) (hereinafter *Perry*). With the prevalence of nonmarital relationships today, a considerable number of persons live together without benefit of the rules of law that govern property, financial, and other matters in a marital relationship. Thus, we do well to recognize the benefits to be gained by encouraging unmarried cohabitants to enter into written agreements respecting these matters, as the consequences for each partner may be considerable on termination of the relationship or, in particular, in the event of the death of one of the partners.[31] "In recent years, increased attention has focused on the advisability of unmarried couples entering

---

[31] [2] Studies suggest that most people enter nonmarital relationships in ignorance of the legal consequences or under the assumption that at least some legal protections are available. *See* Perry, *Dissolution Planning in Family Law: A Critique of Current Analyses and a Look Toward the Future*, 24 Fam. L.Q. 77, 77 n. 1 (1990).

into cohabitation contracts in which they . . . detail the financial consequences of dissolution." *Perry, supra.* This may be especially important in a jurisdiction like Massachusetts where we do not recognize common law marriage, do not extend to unmarried couples the rights possessed by married couples who divorce, and reject equitable remedies that might have the effect of dividing property between unmarried parties.

Courts in other jurisdictions have concluded that an express agreement between adult unmarried persons living together is unenforceable only to the extent that it explicitly and inseparably is founded on sexual relations [meretricious relationships]. Furthermore, such agreements are not invalid merely because the parties may have contemplated the creation or continuation of a nonmarital relationship when they entered into the agreement. As the New York Court of Appeals stated, "the theory of these cases is that while cohabitation without marriage does not give rise to the property and financial rights which normally attend the marital relation, neither does cohabitation disable the parties from making an agreement within the normal rules of contract law." Although none of these cases specifically concerns a written agreement between unmarried cohabitants attempting to resolve issues such as the parties' rights as to property, earnings, and services rendered, the principles they announce also apply to such an agreement.[32] Implicit in these principles is tacit acknowledgment that unmarried cohabitants may agree to hold real property jointly or in common, agree to create joint bank and other accounts, do the same for investments, and, of course, make testamentary dispositions. These financial and property arrangements stem from a relationship that involves sexual cohabitation, but, in creating them, the parties are principally motivated by an intention to hold, or dispose of, property in a mutually acceptable way in order to manage day-to-day matters and to avoid litigation when the relationship ends. Such financial planning is enforceable according to the usual rules of contract. It makes no sense to uphold these arrangements between unmarried cohabitants, but to withhold enforcement of written agreements between the same parties when they attempt to settle the financial and other consequences if they should separate.

To the extent we have not previously done so, we adopt the view that unmarried cohabitants may lawfully contract concerning property, financial, and other matters relevant to their relationship.[33] Such a contract is subject to the rules of contract law and is valid even if expressly made in contemplation of a common living arrangement, except to the extent that sexual services constitute the only, or dominant, consideration for the agreement, or that enforcement should be denied on some other public policy ground. We shall no longer follow cases in this Commonwealth to the contrary.

Nothing we say here today is intended to derogate from the clear distinction we have made in our cases between the legal rights of married and unmarried

---

[32] [3] We do not adopt those portions of Marvin v. Marvin, 18 Cal. 3d 660, 134 Cal. Rptr. 815, 557 P.2d 106 (1976), or the other cases cited, which grant property rights to a nonmarital partner in the absence of an express contract.

[33] [4] However, if the parties eventually were to marry, the agreement is no longer valid, and the rules concerning antenuptial, postnuptial, or separation agreements will then govern any agreement thereafter entered into by them.

cohabitants, see, e.g., *Collins v. Guggenheim*, 417 Mass. 615, 617–618, 631 N.E.2d 1016 (1994) (cohabitants not entitled to equitable distribution of property); *Reep v. Commissioner of the Dep't of Employment & Training*, 412 Mass. 845, 851, 593 N.E.2d 1297 (1992) (married person who leaves work to join spouse is presumed to have satisfied statutory requirement for unemployment compensation eligibility; long-term nonmarital partner could offer proof toward meeting standard, but is not entitled to presumption); *Feliciano v. Rosemar Silver Co.*, 401 Mass. 141, 514 N.E.2d 1095 (1987) (nonmarital partners have no right to sue for loss of consortium); *Davis v. Misiano*, 373 Mass. 261, 263, 366 N.E.2d 752 (1977) (nonmarital partners have no right to separate support and alimony). Nor should anything we have said be taken as a suggestion or intimation that we are retreating from our prior expressions regarding the importance of the institution of marriage and the strong public interest in ensuring that its integrity is not threatened. See *Capazzoli v. Holzwasser*, 397 Mass. 158, 160, 490 N.E.2d 420 (1986), and cases cited. We have never recognized common law marriage in this Commonwealth, see *Heistand v. Heistand*, 384 Mass. 20, 24, 423 N.E.2d 313 (1981), nor have we "permitted the incidents of the marital relationship to attach to an arrangement of cohabitation without marriage." *Collins v. Guggenheim, supra*. We do not do so now.

The principal purpose of the agreement was to clarify the parties' rights with respect to the division of assets acquired during their relationship in the event that they should separate. The parties' rights were established as of the date of the execution of the agreement in 1989. That the defendant in 1992 exercised his right under the agreement to request that the plaintiff leave the Halifax house, did not alter the terms of the agreement, nor did the defendant's request establish that the plaintiff's fidelity was the sole foundation upon which the agreement rested.

"Virtually all agreements between nonmarital partners can be said to be 'involved' in some sense in the fact of their mutual sexual relationship, or to 'contemplate' the existence of that relationship." *Marvin v. Marvin*, 18 Cal. 3d 660, 672, 134 Cal. Rptr. 815, 557 P.2d 106 (1976). By the same token, all such agreements could be said to rest on the sexual fidelity of the parties, as, presumably, one party's infidelity might cause the termination of the parties' relationship. We recognize that the plaintiff's alleged infidelity in 1992 precipitated both the defendant's request that she leave and the performance of the agreement. Nonetheless, these circumstances alone do not establish that enforcement of the agreement is against public policy and therefore unenforceable. "By looking . . . only to the consideration underlying the agreement, we provide the parties and the courts with a practical guide to determine when an agreement between nonmarital partners should be enforced." *Id.*

We conclude that the plaintiff and the defendant were free to contract with respect to property, financial, and other matters relevant to their relationship, and that the specific agreement at issue is valid and enforceable. It is undisputed that the parties, both adults, had the capacity to contract and understood each other's financial worth prior to the execution of the agreement. Moreover, the plaintiff was advised to seek counsel regarding the agreement and chose not to do so. There was no claim of fraud, overreaching, or unconscionability. The plaintiff is employed and makes no assertion that as a result of the agreement, she will be unable to support herself. The judge found that the plaintiff was not forced or coerced to sign the agreement.

Finally, we note that the plaintiff voluntarily entered into a relationship with the defendant, and continued to live with him for many years despite her knowledge that he was unlikely to marry her. The agreement she signed essentially tracked the living arrangement she had shared with the defendant for twenty-five years, in which they maintained separate legal and financial identities, and did not merge their financial affairs. There is no evidence that during the course of their relationship, the plaintiff was the "weaker" of the two cohabitants, or that she had been dissatisfied with the way they managed their affairs.[34] The judgment is vacated, and a new judgment is to be entered declaring the agreement to be valid and enforceable and disposing of the damages claim in the defendant's favor.

NOTE

In *Goodridge v. Department of Public Health*, 798 N.E.2d 941 (Mass. 2003), the same court held that "[B]arring an individual from the protections, benefits, and obligations of a civil marriage solely because that person would marry a person of the same sex violates the Massachusetts Constitution."

[4] Wagering

METROPOLITAN CREDITORS SERVICE v. SADRI
California Court of Appeal
19 Cal. Rptr. 2d 646 (1993)

KING, J.

Sadri, a California resident, incurred debts totaling $22,000 over a two-day period in 1991 while gambling at Caesar's Tahoe casino in Nevada. On January 13 and 14 he wrote the casino two personal checks for $2,000 and $10,000. On January 14 he executed two memoranda of indebtedness for $5,000 each. In exchange for the checks and memoranda, Sadri received chips, which he lost playing the game of baccarat. Sadri subsequently stopped payment on the checks and memoranda, which were drawn on his account at a Redwood City bank.

A Nevada statute makes credit instruments evidencing gambling debts owed to licensed persons, and the debts represented, valid and enforceable by legal process. Caesar's Tahoe did not, however, seek a judgment in Nevada on Sadri's debts.

---

[34] [8] We recognize that unmarried parties who enter into these agreements may not necessarily share equal bargaining power, and disparities in bargaining power are more likely to arise when an agreement is negotiated long after the parties began cohabiting. Although one could argue that such disparities existed between the parties here, and was based, at least in part, on the traditional gender roles assumed by the parties, this alone does not invalidate the agreement. In any event, such disparities do not always exist, and the gender of the parties does not necessarily dictate which party is in a more financially secure position. For a comprehensive discussion of the issues related to bargaining power in negotiating cohabitation agreements, see *Perry, supra* at 88–93.

Instead, the casino assigned its claims to MCS for collection, and MCS sued Sadri in California, filing a complaint in municipal court in San Mateo County.

The municipal court rendered judgment for Sadri, ruling that under established public policy his gambling debts were unenforceable in California. The Appellate Department of the San Mateo County Superior Court affirmed.

[On appeal,] MCS contends that under the constitutional doctrine affording full faith and credit to the public acts, records, and judicial proceedings of other states (U.S. Const., art. IV, § 1), we are required to enforce Sadri's gambling debts pursuant to the Nevada statute allowing the cause of action for enforcement of such debts.

The pivotal question is whether such enforcement is against the public policy of the State of California. This question arises because MCS is attempting to enforce its Nevada *cause of action*, rather than a Nevada *judgment*. A forum state must give full faith and credit to a sister state *judgment*, regardless of the forum state's public policy on the underlying claim. However, the forum state may refuse to entertain a lawsuit on a sister state *cause of action* if its enforcement is contrary to the strong public policy of the forum state.

California's public policy exception to enforcement of a sister state cause of action is narrow in scope. It applies only where the sister state law violates recognized standards of morality and the general interests of California citizens. California has always had a strong public policy against judicial enforcement of gambling debts, going back virtually to the inception of statehood. This prohibition is deeply rooted in Anglo-American jurispnudence, originating in England in 1710 in the Statute of Anne, which made gambling debts "utterly void, frustrate, and of none effect, to all intents and purposes whatsoever . . . ." (9 Anne, ch. 14, § 1.)

Following the advent of legalized gambling in the State of Nevada, the rule in California against enforcement of gambling debts was once again put to the test, and it again prevailed. In *Hamilton v. Abadjian* (1947) 30 Cal. 2d 49, the defendant gave a Las Vegas hotel six checks totaling $11,450, used part of the proceeds to finance his gambling, and then stopped payment on the checks. The Supreme Court [noted] that the courts of California — and also, at that time, Nevada — "refuse to lend their process to recover losses in gambling transactions of the type here involved." The *Hamilton* court also stated the antienforcement rule within a context more specific to the facts of that case, as well as to the present case: "The owner of a gambling house who honors a check for the purpose of providing a prospective customer with funds with which to gamble and who then participates in the transaction thus promoted by his act cannot recover on the check."

The most recent statement of the *Hamilton* rule occurred in *Lane & Pyron, Inc. v. Gibbs* (1968) 266 Cal. App. 2d 61, 63. In that case the defendant cashed five checks totaling $1,900 at a Lake Tahoe casino and subsequently stopped payment on the checks. Noting that a sister state cause of action will not be enforced if it "offends deeply held notions of local public policy," the court invoked the policy in California and Nevada against judicial enforcement of gambling debts and concluded that "California's rejection of such claims is an application of Nevada law as well as domestic public policy."

The *Hamilton* rule is on all fours with the present case. Caesar's Tahoe honored Sadri's checks and memoranda of indebtedness for the purpose of providing him with funds with which to gamble, and then participated in the game. Thus, if *Hamilton* still reflects the public policy of the State of California, it precludes judicial enforcement of Sadri's gambling debts in California state courts. [T]he contracts underlying the debts are against public policy and contrary to good morals under Civil Code section 1667, and thus the contracts are unlawful and the debts unenforceable.

Two things have changed in the 46 years since *Hamilton* was decided. First, under Nevada state law, credit instruments evidencing gambling debts owed to licensed persons are now enforceable by legal process in that state, and have been since 1983. This point is inconsequential, however, since the rule of *Hamilton*, its predecessors and its progeny rests not on the public policy of Nevada, but on the public policy of California.

Second, the people of California have demonstrated increased tolerance for gambling through the passage, by initiative measure, of the California State Lottery Act of 1984. Indeed, several forms of institutionalized legal gambling in California predate *Hamilton*, including pari-mutuel horse racing and draw poker clubs (by the omission of draw poker from the list of games proscribed by Penal Code section 330), which are now subject to registration with the Attorney General. This state of affairs led one California court to observe, in requiring relief on a contract for the sale of a Nevada casino, that "Californians cannot afford to be too pious about this matter of gambling."

This brings us to *Crockford's Club Ltd. v. Si-Ahmed* (1988), 203 Cal. App. 3d 1402. In that case, Smail Si-Ahmed passed bad checks to an English casino in exchange for tokens, which he then lost at gambling. The casino obtained a default judgment against Si-Ahmed in England, and then obtained a default judgment in California enforcing the English judgment. On appeal, Si-Ahmed argued that gambling debts are unenforceable in California as against public policy. The court rejected this argument, noting that casino gambling is legal in England and concluding that "in view of the expanded acceptance of gambling in this state as manifested by the introduction of the California lottery and other innovations, it cannot seriously be maintained that enforcement of said judgment 'is so antagonistic to California public policy interests as to preclude the extension of comity in the present case.' "

The posture of *Crockford's Club* is similar to that of the present case in that both turn on the question of public policy in California. The California action in *Crockford's Club* was to enforce a foreign nation judgment, which, unlike a sister state judgment, is not entitled to full faith and credit. Like a sister state cause of action, a foreign nation judgment may be refused enforcement if the underlying cause of action is contrary to the public policy of California.

The court in *Crockford's Club* did not specifically address the question whether enforcement of gambling debts is still against public policy in California. Indeed, the court did not even discuss the *Hamilton* rule or mention any of the other California cases on point. The court simply relied on California's "expanded acceptance" of gambling itself as indicating enforcement of the English judgment was not against public policy.

It cannot be denied that California's historical public policy against gambling has been substantially eroded. Pari-mutuel horse racing, draw poker clubs, and charitable bingo games have proliferated throughout the state. These forms of gambling are indulged by a relatively small segment of the population, but the same cannot be said of the California State Lottery, which was passed by initiative measure and has become firmly rooted in California's popular culture. Lottery tickets are now as close as the nearest convenience store, turning many Californians into regular gamblers. The "thirst for play" of Californians, as noted in 1853 in *Carrier v. Brannan, supra,* 3 Cal. at page 329, has not abated. If it was true as observed in 1961 that "Californians cannot afford to be too pious about this matter of gambling," then all the more so in 1993 would expressions of piety on the subject ring hollow. On this score, the *Crockford's Club* decision has a point.

But the court in *Crockford's Club* failed to draw the critical distinction between public acceptance of gambling itself and California's deep-rooted policy against enforcement of gambling debts — that is, gambling on credit. While the public policy against the former has been substantially eroded, the public policy against the latter has not. This is because California's rule against enforcing gambling debts has never depended upon the criminalization of gambling itself. Indeed, the prohibition against legalized gambling on credit goes all the way back to 1710 in the Statute of Anne, which permitted gambling "at the palaces of St. James, or Whitehall when the sovereign is in residence" but limited such gambling to "ready money only." (9 Anne, ch. 14, § 9.)

This distinction between gambling itself and gambling on credit was elucidated in *King International Corp. v. Voloshin* (1976) 33 Conn. Supp. 166. The defendant in that case stopped payment on a check given in exchange for chips at a licensed casino in Aruba, and the casino's owner sued in Connecticut to enforce the debt. The court refused enforcement concluding that, despite Connecticut's embrace of various forms of legalized gambling such as pari-mutuel racing, jai alai and a state lottery, "Connecticut has never deviated from its ancient prohibition of gambling on credit." The court explained, "While the state's heretofore ancient and deep-rooted policy condemning gambling has been eroded to some degree by its legalization of certain types of gambling, the state has, nevertheless, been intransigent in its policy prohibiting the extension of credit for the promotion of gambling activity — and with good reason. One need not have the gambling sagacity of the famed Las Vegas oddsmaker Jimmy the Greek to recognize the potential dangers in the extension of credit to the gambler or the possibly unfortunate incidents, to employ a euphemism, that could well result from the nonpayment of the gambling bettor to his creditor."

Courts in other jurisdictions have similarly concluded that a shift in public policy with regard to gambling itself is not inconsistent with a continued public policy against gambling on credit. "Even while legal gambling spreads throughout the country, the public policy of virtually every state makes legal gambling debts unenforceable, treating a casino marker the same as a contract for prostitution." (Rose, *Gambling and the Law — Update 1993* (1992) 15 Hastings Comm. & Ent. L.J. 93, 95.)

There is a special reason for treating gambling on credit differently from gambling itself. Gambling debts are characteristic of pathological gambling, a mental disorder which is recognized by the American Psychiatric Association and whose prevalence is estimated at 2 to 3 percent of the adult population. "Characteristic problems include extensive indebtedness and consequent default on debts and other financial responsibilities, . . . and financially motivated illegal activities to pay for gambling." Having lost his or her cash, the pathological gambler will continue to play on credit, if extended, in an attempt to win back the losses.

In our view, this is why enforcement of gambling debts has always been against public policy in California and should remain so, regardless of shifting public attitudes about gambling itself. If Californians want to play, so be it. But the law should not invite them to play themselves into debt. The judiciary cannot protect pathological gamblers from themselves, but we can refuse to participate in their financial ruin.

We conclude that California's strong public policy against enforcement of gambling debts remains unaffected by increased public tolerance of gambling itself or by the limited legalization of certain forms of gambling in this state. That public policy is so fundamental and deep-rooted as to justify our refusal to enforce a sister state cause of action. We therefore reaffirm the commitment of the California courts to the *Hamilton* rule: "The owner of a gambling house who honors a check for the purpose of providing a prospective customer with funds with which to gamble and who then participates in the transaction thus promoted by his act cannot recover on the check." If a licensed Nevada casino wishes to recover on a check or memorandum of indebtedness given by a California resident under such circumstances, the owner will have to obtain a Nevada state court judgment which will then be entitled to full faith and credit in California regardless of our public policy.

The judgment of the municipal court is affirmed.

PROBLEMS

(1)   Co-workers contributed to a sum of money so that the relative of one could buy lottery tickets in Kentucky. They orally agreed to split any winnings in equal shares. The relative purchased the tickets in Kentucky and one ticket was the winner of $6 million. The relative refuses to share the winnings on the ground that the agreement to share equally was contrary to the public policy of Georgia against gambling. Analyze.

(2)   Albert paid premiums on a fire insurance policy on his house. When the house burned to the ground, the insurance company refused to pay on the ground that the contract was a wagering contract. What result?

(3)   The facts are the same as in Problem 2 except Albert did not own the house named in the policy nor did he have any other interest therein. What result?

(4)   Darlene has agreed to drive her friend Max from Cleveland, Ohio to Gary, Indiana. On the Indiana turnpike, Max encourages Darlene to increase the speed saying, "Don't worry. I'll pay for any tickets." Darlene begins to exceed the speed limit and suffers the consequences of a $200 fine. Is the promise of Max enforceable?

(5)   Ralph and Julius bet $5,000 on a basketball game. A statute makes such wagers a crime. Ralph loses and Julius brings an action to collect when Ralph will

not pay. What result?

(6)   Assume, in Problem 5, that Ralph had paid Julius and seeks to recover that payment. What result?

(7)   Assume that Ralph and Julius bet $5,000 each on a basketball game and the money was held by a trusted third party, Abdul. Ralph lost the bet, but tells Abdul not to pay the money to Julius and to return Ralph's share. Advise Abdul.

Further reflection on these and similar problems may be assisted by a consideration of RESTATEMENT (SECOND) OF CONTRACTS §§ 178, 199. *See* MURRAY ON CONTRACTS § 99G.

NOTES

(1)   *In pari delicto, potior est conditio defendentis — malum in se vs. malum prohibitum.* When parties are equally in the wrong or "of equal fault," it is not possible for a court to grant restitution to either party since a court will not assist either party when both are *in pari delicto.* However, one party may not be guilty of "moral turpitude." If a card shark cheats the victim, the victim should be able to recover his losses since the parties are not *in pari delicto.* The victim is not guilty of moral turpitude. Some of the older cases made a distinction between agreements which are *malum in se* from those which are merely *malum prohibitum.*

Consider, for example, the case of *Liebman v. Rosenthal*, 57 N.Y.S.2d 875 (1945), in which the plaintiff sought to recover the value of $28,000 worth of jewelry which he had given to the defendant. In 1941, the plaintiff and his family were anxious to leave France in order to escape the German army. Defendant represented that he could intercede for the plaintiff and obtain a visa from a public official who was susceptible to bribes. Plaintiff delivered the jewelry but defendant did not intercede. When defendant appeared in New York, plaintiff brought this action. Defendant moved for summary judgment on the ground that the 1941 agreement was criminal, immoral, and illegal in that it provided for defendant to bribe an official. The court denied the motion on the ground that plaintiff was not *in pari delicto* since he was attempting to save his family and himself from an enemy who had violated all of the laws of civilization. The court felt that the most law-abiding person would have entered into such an agreement under the circumstances. On appeal, the court affirmed its order but one member of the court, Judge Adel, stressed the distinction between agreements that are *malum prohibitum* and those which are *malum in se.* He felt that since the 1941 agreement was *malum in se*, it should not be enforced, but neither should the court grant restitution therefor. The view of Judge Adel suggests the wisdom of Corbin, who criticized the distinction as one which produces an illusion of certainty. 6A A. CORBIN ON CONTRACTS § 1536 (2d ed. 1962). *See* MURRAY ON CONTRACTS § 99C.

(2)   *Facilitating an Illegal Purpose.* Where a "madam" sold property which she had operated as a house of prostitution to another "madam" who apparently would continue this enterprise, the buyer refused to make payments as required under the contract of sale on the footing that the contract was an illegal bargain that a court should not enforce. The court disagreed, holding that "the bare knowledge of the purpose for which the property is sold is not enough to raise the valid defense of

illegality." Absent active participation in the new enterprise, the seller was entitled to enforce the contract. *Carroll v. Beardon*, 142 Mont. 40, 381 P.2d 295 (1963).

[5] Partial Illegality

When a contract is only illegal in part, the lawful part may or may not be enforceable. If the illegality is of such a serious kind that a considerable degree of moral turpitude attaches to it, it is probable that the whole bargain will be tainted and no part of the contract will be enforced. However, if the illegality is not of such a serious character, the result may be different. If the contract is technically divisible, a lawful division thereof may be enforceable even though the other parts are tainted with illegality. *See Jones v. Brantley*, 83 So. 802 (1920) (part of contract performable on Sunday); *Smilansky v. Mandel Bros.*, 254 Mich. 575, 236 N.W. 866 (1931) (part of contract for sale of goods unenforceable because made by a foreign corporation not licensed as required by statute). If any part of the consideration for an entire contract is illegal, generally no part of the defendant's promises will be enforced even though all of his promises are lawful in themselves. *See Johnson v. McMillion*, 199 S.W. 1070 (Ky. 1918). The rules relating to partial enforcement of a contract that is in part illegal are more or less technical and arbitrary. Their justification is found in the effort by courts to avoid serious forfeitures when the illegality involved is not serious enough to justify such a severe penalty.

[6] Post Formation Legality

It is generally held that a contract that is illegal at the time it is made, does not become enforceable, if, before suit is brought, the law is changed in such a way as to validate similar transactions. The justification that is often stated is that the contract was originally void and, therefore, could gain no validity from the subsequent change in the law. *See McLain v. Oklahoma Cotton Growers' Ass'n*, 258 P. 269 (Okla. 1927), 26 MICH. L. REV. 443 (1928). This approach to the problem leaves something to be desired since illegal contracts are not, strictly speaking, void. In *Interinsurance Exch. of Auto. Club of S. Cal. v. Ohio Cas. Ins. Co.*, 373 P.2d 640, 642 (1962), the opinion states:

> While there is no unanimity of opinion as to the reasons for this rule, the authorities are in accord with its result. The reasons given by courts differ depending upon the particular view taken as to whether an illegal contract is void or is simply unenforceable. If an illegal contract is regarded as being void, then there is nothing to enforce after the invalidating statute is repealed . . . . Other authorities hold that an illegal contract is not void, but is simply unenforceable. Starting with the proposition that "no polluted hand shall touch the pure fountains of justice" (*Collins v. Blantern* (1767) 95 Eng. Rep. 850, 852), they reason that the repeal of a statute does not cleanse the stain from those hands.

See generally MURRAY ON CONTRACTS § 99N.

Chapter 6

CONDITIONS, BREACH AND REPUDIATION

A. NATURE AND EFFECT OF CONDITION

MORRISON v. BARE
Ohio Court of Appeals
2007 Ohio App. LEXIS 5955 (Dec. 19, 2007)

DICKINSON, J.

Jack W. Morrison Jr. is in the business of buying houses, refurbishing them, and renting them to college students. Tom Campensa, a real estate agent, showed Mr. Morrison a house owned by Jonas Bare. Mr. Morrison noticed a sticker on the furnace that indicated it had a cracked heat exchanger. After checking with Mr. Bare, Mr. Campensa told Mr. Morrison that the furnace had been repaired in 2004. Following his second walkthrough, Mr. Morrison made a written offer to purchase the house for $40,000, using a form real estate purchase agreement. The form included a provision permitting Mr. Morrison to have the house inspected and, if not satisfied, to notify Mr. Bare within fourteen days of the date of the agreement. If any unsatisfactory conditions could not be resolved, Mr. Morrison could void the agreement or accept the property in its "as is" condition. The form further provided that, if Mr. Morrison did not have the home inspected or did not notify Mr. Bare of any unsatisfactory conditions, he would take the property in its "as is" condition.

Under the heading "Special Conditions," Mr. Morrison wrote: "Seller to supply buyer with copy of furnace repair bill from 2004 within 14 days." Mr. Campensa acknowledged at his deposition that the purpose of the "special condition" was to allow Mr. Morrison to satisfy himself that the heat exchanger had been repaired. At the same time he signed the written offer, Mr. Morrison also signed a property disclosure form in which he acknowledged that he was purchasing the property "as is."

Prior to the date set for closing, Mr. Campensa obtained a copy of the 2004 furnace repair bill. That bill indicated that repairs totaling $234 had been made to the furnace, but that the heat exchanger had not been repaired. In fact, it included a quote to replace the furnace for $1600 and a notation that, if a new furnace was installed within 30 days, the $234 for repairs would be deducted from the cost of the new furnace.

Mr. Campensa telephoned Mr. Morrison and told him that the heat exchanger had not been repaired. At that point, Mr. Morrison told Mr. Campensa that he would close on the house only if Mr. Bare either replaced the furnace or reduced the purchase price in an amount equal to what it would cost to replace the furnace. Mr. Bare was unwilling to do either.

Mr. Campensa sent Mr. Morrison a copy of the bill, along with a proposed addendum to the purchase agreement. The proposed addendum provided that Mr. Morrison agreed to accept the property with the furnace "in its as is condition and assume all responsibility for its repair and/or replacement." Mr. Morrison refused to execute the proposed addendum.

Prior to the date set for closing, Mr. Morrison filed his complaint in this case. Mr. Bare subsequently sold the house to another purchaser, who refurbished it and rented it to college students.

By his first cause of action, Mr. Morrison alleged that he was entitled to specific performance of his contract with Mr. Bare. In order to be entitled to specific performance of a contract, a plaintiff must either have performed his part of the contract or show his "readiness and ability" to do so. Mr. Morrison did neither. He had not paid the purchase price for the property and he had told Mr. Campensa that he was unwilling to do so unless Mr. Bare replaced the furnace or reduced the purchase price. As discussed below, the contract did not require Mr. Bare to replace the furnace or reduce the purchase price. Accordingly, Mr. Morrison is not entitled to specific performance.

Additionally, by the time the trial court granted summary judgment in this case, the property had been sold to a third party. When property has been transferred to a bona fide purchaser, specific performance is not available. Mr. Morrison has not argued that the person who purchased the property from Mr. Bare was not a bona fide purchaser. Accordingly, this is a second reason he is not entitled to specific performance.

By his second cause of action, Mr. Morrison sought damages for breach of contract. Mr. Bare has argued that the "special condition" was satisfied when he provided Mr. Morrison a copy of the 2004 bill for repairs to the furnace, even though, instead of showing that the heat exchanger had been repaired, it showed that it had not been repaired.

There can be no doubt that, in order to satisfy the "special condition" that Mr. Morrison included in his offer, the repair bill had to show that the heat exchanger had been repaired. Mr. Campensa, who was Mr. Bare's agent, acknowledged that the purpose of the "special condition", was to allow Mr. Morrison to satisfy himself that the heat exchanger had been fixed:

Q.   All right. On line 103 it says, "Seller to supply buyer with copy of furnace repair bill from 2004 within 14 days," correct?

A.   Correct.

Q.   Why was that provision put in the contract?

A.   Because there was the potential that that was cracked in there was a cracked thing and Jack wanted to know if it was fixed or not.

Q.   Okay. Because you believed it had been repaired based on your conversation with Jonas Bare, correct?

A.   Yes.

Q.   And you had told Jack that it had been repaired, did you not?

A.   Yes.

Q.   So Jack wanted to make sure as part of this deal that that furnace had already been repaired, correct?

A.   Correct.

Mr. Bare's argument that he satisfied the condition by supplying a bill showing that the heat exchanger had not been repaired is, at best, disingenuous. Both parties knew at the time they entered the contract that the bill Mr. Bare needed to supply to satisfy the "special condition" was a bill showing that the heat exchanger had been repaired.

That, however, does not mean that Mr. Bare breached the purchase agreement by not delivering a bill that showed the heat exchanger had been repaired and by not replacing the furnace or lowering the purchase price. To begin with, the contract does not include a promise by Mr. Bare that, if the heat exchanger was not repaired in 2004, he would replace the furnace or reduce the purchase price. Further, the "special condition" that Mr. Morrison included in the contract was just that, a condition, not a promise:

> [P]romise and condition are very clearly different in character. One who makes a promise thereby expresses an intention that some future performance will be rendered and gives assurance of its rendition to the promisee. Whether the promise is express or implied, there must be either words or conduct by the promisor by the interpretation of which the court can discover promissory intention; a condition is a fact or an event and is not an expression of intention or an assurance. A promise in a contract creates a legal duty in the promisor and a right in the promisee; the fact or event constituting a condition creates no right or duty and is merely a limiting or modifying factor. Catherine M.A. McCauliff, Corbin On Contracts, Section 30.12 (rev. ed. 1999).

Mr. Campensa told Mr. Morrison that the heat exchanger had been repaired. Mr. Morrison made his offer to purchase the house contingent upon receiving proof that it had been:

> In contract law, "condition" is an event, other than the mere lapse of time, that is not certain to occur but must occur to *activate* an existing contractual duty, unless the condition is excused. The fact or event properly called a condition occurs during the *performance* stage of a contract, i.e., after the contract is formed and prior to its discharge. John Edward Murray Jr., Murray on Contracts, Section 99B (4th ed. 2001) (emphasis in original); *RESTATEMENT (SECOND) OF CONTRACTS, Section 224* (1981). While the failure to perform a promise is a breach of contract, the failure to satisfy a condition is not:

> A promise is always made by the act or acts of one of the parties, such acts being words or other conduct expressing intention. A fact can be made to operate as a condition only by the agreement of both parties or by the construction of the law. The purpose of a promise is to create a duty in the promisor. The purpose of constituting some fact as a condition is always the postponement or discharge of an instant duty (or other specified legal relation). The non-fulfillment of a promise is called a breach of contract, and creates in the other party a secondary right to damages. It is the failure to perform a legal duty. The non-occurrence of a condition will prevent the existence of a duty in the other party; but it may not create any remedial rights and duties at all, and it will not unless someone has promised that it shall occur. Corbin On Contracts, at Section 30.12.

The fact that, to satisfy the "special condition," Mr. Bare would have had to do something (supply the bill showing that the heat exchanger had been repaired) did not mean that it was a promise rather than a condition. A condition can be an act to be done by one of the parties to the contract:

> Virtually any act or event may constitute a condition. The event may be an act to be performed or forborne by one of the parties to the contract, an act to be performed or forborne by a third party, or some fact or event over which neither party, or any other party, has any control. Murray on Contracts, at Section 99C. In this case, Mr. Bare had partial control over the condition. Even if he had a bill showing that the heat exchanger had been repaired in 2004, he could have chosen not to deliver it to Mr. Morrison, in which case the condition would not have been satisfied. It also, however, was partially out of his control. Since the heat exchanger had not been repaired in 2004, he was unable to satisfy the condition. The material part of the condition was that Mr. Morrison had to be satisfied that the heat exchanger had been repaired.

Section 225 of the RESTATEMENT (SECOND) OF CONTRACTS (1981) describes the consequences of the non-occurrence of a condition:

> (1) Performance of a duty subject to a condition cannot become due unless the condition occurs or its non-occurrence is excused.

> (2) Unless it has been excused, the non-occurrence of a condition discharges the duty when the condition can no longer occur.

> (3) Non-occurrence of a condition is not a breach by a party unless he is under a duty that the condition occur.

In this case, Mr. Morrison's duty to pay the purchase price did not come due because Mr. Bare could not produce a 2004 bill showing that the heat exchanger had been repaired. Once it became clear that it was impossible for Mr. Bare to produce such a bill, Mr. Morrison could have excused the condition and closed on the property. Alternatively, he could have treated his duty to close as discharged and the contract terminated:

[I]f a time comes when it is too late for the condition to occur, the obligor is entitled to treat its duty as discharged and the contract as terminated. II E. Allan Farnsworth, Farnsworth On Contracts, Section 8.3 (3rd ed. 2004).

By informing Mr. Campensa that he was unwilling to close on the house unless Mr. Bare replaced the furnace or reduced the purchase price, Mr. Morrison chose to treat his duty to pay the original purchase price as discharged and the contract as terminated. His proposal to go forward under different conditions was, in effect, an offer to enter into a new contract; a new contract that Mr. Bare was free to reject, which he did. Upon the failure of the "special condition" that he included in the real estate purchase agreement, Mr. Morrison treated the agreement as terminated, as he was entitled to do. The failure of the "special condition" was not a breach of contract.

There are no genuine issues of material fact, and Mr. Bare is entitled to judgment as a matter of law on Mr. Morrison's demand for specific performance and on his breach of contract claim. To the extent Mr. Morrison's assignment of error is addressed to the trial court's summary judgment on his contract claims, it is overruled.

NOTE

In the famous *Carbolic Smoke Ball* case explored in Chapter 2, the offer promised £100 to any person who used the smoke ball in accordance with directions and thereafter contracted influenza (presumably within the "flu season"). The power of acceptance created by that offer was exercised by any person who performed the act required by the offer. The only possible act that a party could perform volitionally, however, was using the smoke ball in accordance with directions.

Contracting influenza was not a voluntary act. Indeed, the smoke ball was designed to prevent the contraction of influenza. Thus, every party who used the smoke ball in accordance with directions accepted the offer promised in the advertisement. The company had contractual duties to each user. Though each of those duties existed from the moment the product was used according to directions which formed the contract, they were dormant. They would not awaken — they would not be activated until a specific event occurred — contracting influenza. If the user of the smoke ball did not contract influenza within the flu season, the duty to pay that person £100 could never be activated. Indeed, the absence of influenza indicated that the smoke ball promise had been fulfilled. The event — here, contracting influenza — created nothing. It would either occur or not occur. Thus, again, conditions do not create duties; they are attached to contractual duties which exist but will be inactive (dormant) until the conditioning event occurs.

[1] Promises and Conditions

HIGHLAND INNS CORP. v. AMERICAN LANDMARK CORP.
Missouri Court of Appeals
650 S.W.2d 667 (1983)

SHANGLER, J.

The appeal involves obligations under a contract to purchase real estate. Buyer [American Landmark] agreed to pay seller [Highland Inns] $950,000 on closing. Subject to buyer obtaining a one year first mortgage in the amount of $1,300,000.00. If buyer has not obtained and delivered to seller a long-term mortgage commitment in the amount of $1,300,000.00 on or before August 19, 1978, this contract is null and void.

A separate term of the contract required the buyer to deposit $10,000 as earnest money, with the proviso: "Said deposit to be applied on the purchase price upon closing. If the Buyer fails to fulfill his obligations hereunder, the aforementioned deposit shall become the property of the Seller and his agent, not as a penalty, but as liquidated damages."

The buyer made the deposit, but was unable to obtain the long-term mortgage commitment within the date specified in the contract, or for some time thereafter. The seller sued for the $10,000 deposit. The court entered judgment for seller Highland Inns against American Landmark. The defendant, American Landmark, appeals [contending] that the real estate contract "[did] not [become] operative until the mortgage commitment ha[d] been obtained," that absent that condition met, "the obligations and rights of the parties d[id] not become absolute." In a word, the defendant buyer contends that the delivery of a mortgage commitment in the sum of $1,300,000 to the seller by August 19th was the condition upon which any obligation between them arose.

A contract transaction consists of a series of operative facts [3A CORBIN ON CONTRACTS § 741, p. 446 (1960)]: First, there is an offer, stating the terms, the conditions, and the promises that are to be agreed upon. Next comes acceptance by the offeree. It is useful to say that the offer created a power in the offeree. The acceptance is the exercise of this power. After acceptance, the new situation of the parties is that neither can withdraw. It is useful to say that they are under obligation, that rights and duties have been created; but usually still other facts and events must occur before actual performance is due. These facts and events, although occurring subsequently to the acceptance of the offer and to the primary obligation created thereby, are conditions precedent to the duty of immediate performance and to any right of action for breach.

The flaw in the thesis the buyer American Landmark proposes then is to assume that the signatures on the contract by the buyer and seller — offer and acceptance — created no obligation upon either of them until the mortgage funds were delivered on or before August 19th. The contract was one of bilateral terms, mutual promises for mutual performances. The seller agreed to convey the motel premises to the buyer by warranty deed upon payment of $950,000 upon condition that the buyer obtain the $1,300,000 mortgage by August 19th — seven days hence. The buyer made the concurrent promise to — and did — deposit $10,000 in escrow "as a guarantee that the terms and conditions of this contract shall be fulfilled by the buyer." The seller promised to convey to the buyer, to the exclusion of anyone else, in exchange for the promises of the buyer to purchase the motel property for $950,000 on condition of delivery to the seller of a mortgage commitment by August 19th and the deposit of $10,000 to ensure that performance. Thus, the seller promised two performances: to remove the motel property from the market, and to convey upon a mortgage commitment and payment of a $940,000 purchase price balance. These were both deferred performances. The purchaser promised three performances: to pay a deposit of $10,000, to obtain a mortgage commitment, and to pay the $940,000 purchase price balance. One was intended as immediate performance — the $10,000 deposit — the other two were deferred. A performance or a return promise suffices as consideration for a return promise or performance. RESTATEMENT (SECOND) OF CONTRACTS § 71 (1979). Thus, after acceptance, the parties were under obligation to each other to make the performances promised, and neither could withdraw with impunity. 3A CORBIN ON CONTRACTS § 741, p. 446 (1960).

That the primary performances were not immediate, but deferred the payment of the purchase price by the buyer and the conveyance of the property by the seller, does not affect the validity of the undertaking as a consummated contract. The seller Highland Inns, upon agreement to the terms, suffered an immediate detriment that it withhold the motel property from the market during the time the buyer was to make its primary, albeit deferred, performance: mortgage delivery and payment of the purchase price balance. The buyer American Landmark also suffered an immediate detriment — the deposit of $10,000. Thus, that another event — the delivery of the mortgage — was to occur before the primary obligation of the seller to convey was due does not affect the validity of the undertaking as a contract upon execution — as the buyer contends — but was merely a condition precedent to the duty of the seller to convey and to any right of action by either party for breach. A condition presupposes an existent contract and not the converse, as the defendant argues.

The question remains: what other relations between the buyer and seller did the failure to meet the delivery of mortgage condition affect? The buyer contends it was entitled to the return of the $10,000 deposit because the entire contract obligation was contingent upon the event of a mortgage commitment. We rule, however, that only the performances called for thereafter were excused. The $10,000 was an earnest money deposit to guarantee that the terms and *conditions* of this contract shall be fulfilled by the Buyer. Said deposit to be applied on the purchase price upon closing. If the Buyer fails to fulfill his obligations hereunder, the aforementioned deposit shall become the property of the Seller. . . . [emphasis added].

The terminology promises that the $10,000 deposit guarantees that the Buyer will perform both the terms and conditions of agreement, in the context of contract, that the buyer will deliver to the seller a mortgage commitment by August 19th. That was a condition never fulfilled on that date, or at any later date to which that performance was extended by the seller. It was a performance required of the buyer at the time of the execution of the contract, for the very purpose to protect the seller against the nonoccurrence of the condition, and so was not a performance excused by the nonoccurrence of the mortgage commitment event. The reason is evident: the agreement to sell amounted to a removal of the million dollar motel property from the market and bound Highland Inns not to negotiate with any other prospect. In fact, Highland Inns, only days later was obliged to decline an offer to purchase the premises for a price $200,000 more than the American Landmark contract specified. The amount Highland Inns ultimately realized from the sale to Hakimi Enterprises was $50,000 less than the contract price agreed to by American Landmark.

The printed form [paragraph 4], however, specifies that the earnest money deposit, required by the terms and made by the buyer at outset, was a "guarantee that the terms and conditions of this contract shall be fulfilled by the Buyer [and that] [i]f the Buyer fails to fulfill his obligations hereunder, the aforementioned deposit shall become the property of the Seller. . . ."

We have already determined that the nonoccurrence of the mortgage commitment condition excused performance by both parties thereafter. That is the sense of the null and void terminology chosen by the buyer who composed that condition and inserted it as a provision of contract. RESTATEMENT (SECOND) OF CONTRACTS § 225(2) (1979). The question which remains is whether: although the contract excuses performances after the nonoccurrence of condition, the contract nevertheless places the buyer under a duty to make the condition occur. The principle is given in RESTATEMENT (SECOND) OF CONTRACTS § 225(3) (1979):

> Non-occurrence of a condition is not a breach by a party unless he is under a duty that the condition occur.

> Comment d. . . . The same term may, however, be interpreted not only to make an event a condition of the obligor's duty, but also to impose a duty on the obligee that it occur. And even where no term of the agreement imposes a duty that a condition occur, the court may supply such a term.

The printed form calls for the deposit money to be paid to the seller as damages should the buyer fail to fulfill a term or condition. The buyer himself inserted a term that the delivery of a mortgage commitment be a condition of the obligation of the buyer to pay the purchase price and of the seller to convey. The buyer was an experienced real estate entrepreneur. It was within his power as drafter of the mortgage commitment condition to dispel any doubt that he assumed the duty to bring about the occurrence of condition by language to the effect that not only future performance was excused by the nonoccurrence of the event ["this contract is null and void"], but also that he assumed no duty that the condition occur by additional words to the effect — "this contract is null and void and the earnest money deposit shall return to the buyer."

In the circumstances of this transaction, we construe the contract to mean that the buyer assumed the obligation to bring about the occurrence of the condition — the mortgage commitment — and that, although in the event of nonoccurrence of that condition future performance was excused, the failure to deliver the mortgage commitment was a breach of a separate duty for which the $10,000 deposit was the agreed damage. This follows from the subject matter of the transaction [a million dollar commercial property], from the position of the parties [the buyer a reputed millionaire with ready access to financial markets and so, presumably, able to deliver the mortgage commitment within the time he himself specified], the obvious detriment to the seller from a valuable property removed from the market, and from the role of the buyer as the drafter of the agreement. The judgment is affirmed.

NOTES

(1) *Questions:* The condition in the principal case was the procurement of the mortgage loan. That condition did not occur, leaving the duty to purchase the property dormant. If a condition will never occur, what is the effect on the duty to which the condition is attached? The court's determination that the buyer also *promised* to obtain the mortgage, however, was not a condition. What was the effect of that promise?

(2) *Promissory Conditions.* Is it possible for the same act or event to be a promise and condition? In *Internatio-Rotterdam, Inc. v. River Brand Rice Mills*, 259 F.2d 137 (2d Cir. 1958), the parties contracted for the sale of 95,600 "pockets" of rice with the following price term: "$8.25 F.A.S. (free alongside ship) Lake Charles and/or Houston, Texas." Shipment was to be "December, 1952 with two weeks call from buyer." Half of the rice was shipped in early December. The buyer, however, failed to give shipping instructions for the remainder of the rice by December 17. Thus, shipment in December as required by the contract was impossible since the contract required "two weeks call from buyer." The court held that the provision for December delivery went to the essence of the contract and that the buyer's notice by December 17 was a condition precedent to the seller's duty to ship, providing such notice was also a promise to give notice. Thus, the court characterized the giving of notice as a *promissory condition*. It is important to consider the significance of the same event as a promise and a condition. In general, see MURRAY ON CONTRACTS § 100 (5th ed. 2011).

[2]   Interpretation — Promise or Condition

HOWARD v. FEDERAL CROP INSURANCE CORP.
United States Court of Appeals, Fourth Circuit
540 F.2d 695 (1976)

WIDENER, J.

Plaintiff-appellants sued to recover for losses to their 1973 tobacco crop due to alleged rain damage. The crops were insured by defendant-appellee, Federal Crop Insurance Corporation (FCIC). Suits were brought in a state court in North Carolina and removed to the United States District Court. The three suits are not distinguishable factually so far as we are concerned here and involve identical questions of law. They were combined for disposition in the district court and for appeal. The district court granted summary judgment for the defendant and dismissed all three actions. We remand for further proceedings. Since we find for the plaintiffs as to the construction of the policy, we express no opinion on the procedural questions.

Feder Crop Insurance Corporation, an agency of the United States, in 1973, issued three policies to the Howards, insuring their tobacco crops, to be grown on six farms, against weather damage and other hazards.

The Howards (plaintiffs) established production of tobacco on their acreage, and have alleged that their 1973 crop was extensively damaged by heavy rains, resulting in a gross loss to the three plaintiffs in excess of $35,000. The plaintiffs harvested and sold the depleted crop and timely filed notice and proof of loss with FCIC, but, prior to inspection by the adjuster for FCIC, the Howards had either plowed or disked under the tobacco fields in question to prepare the same for sowing a cover crop of rye to preserve the soil. When the FCIC adjuster later inspected the fields, he found the stalks had been largely obscured or obliterated by plowing or disking and denied the claims, apparently on the ground that the plaintiffs had violated a portion of the policy which provides that the stalks on any acreage with respect to which a loss is claimed shall not be destroyed until the corporation makes an inspection.

The holding of the district court is best capsuled in its own words:

> The inquiry here is whether compliance by the insureds with this provision of the policy was a condition precedent to the recovery. The court concludes that it was and that the failure of the insureds to comply worked a forfeiture of benefits for the alleged loss.

There is no question but that apparently after notice of loss was given to defendant, but before inspection by the adjuster, plaintiffs plowed under the tobacco stalks and sowed some of the land with a cover crop, rye. The question is whether, under paragraph 5(f) of the tobacco endorsement to the policy of insurance, the act of plowing under the tobacco stalks forfeits the coverage of the policy. Paragraph 5 of the tobacco endorsement is entitled *Claims*. Pertinent to this case are subparagraphs 5(b) and 5(f), which are as follows:

> 5(b) *It shall be a condition precedent* to the payment of any loss that the insured establish the production of the insured crop on a unit and that such loss has been directly caused by one or more of the hazards insured against during the insurance period for the crop year for which the loss is claimed, and furnish any other information regarding the manner and extent of loss as may be required by the Corporation. (Emphasis added.)

> 5(f) The tobacco stalks on any acreage of tobacco of types 11a, 11b, 12, 13, or 14 with respect to which a loss is claimed *shall not be destroyed until the Corporation makes an inspection.* (Emphasis added.)

The arguments of both parties are predicated upon the same two assumptions. First, if subparagraph 5(f) creates a condition precedent, its violation caused a forfeiture of plaintiffs' coverage. Second, if subparagraph 5(f) creates an obligation (variously called a promise or covenant) upon plaintiffs not to plow under the tobacco stalks, defendant may recover from plaintiffs (either in an original action, or, in this case, by a counterclaim, or as a matter of defense) for whatever damage it sustained because of the elimination of the stalks. However, a violation of subparagraph 5(f) would not, under the second premise, standing alone, cause a forfeiture of the policy.

Generally accepted law provides us with guidelines here. There is a general legal policy opposed to forfeitures. . . . Insurance policies are generally construed most strongly against the insurer. . . . When it is doubtful whether words create a promise or a condition precedent, they will be construed as creating a promise. *Harris and Harris Const. Co. v. Crain and Denbo, Inc.*, 256 N.C. 110, 123 S.E.2d 590, 595 (1962). The provisions of a contract will not be construed as conditions precedent in the absence of language plainly requiring such construction. *Harris*, 123 S.E.2d at 596. . . .

Plaintiffs rely most strongly upon the fact that the term "condition precedent" is included in subparagraph 5(b) but not in subparagraph 5(f). It is true that whether a contract provision is construed as a condition or an obligation does not depend entirely upon whether the word "condition" is expressly used. . . . However, the persuasive force of plaintiffs' argument in this case is found in the use of the term "condition precedent" in subparagraph 5(b) but not in subparagraph 5(f). Thus, it is argued that the ancient maxim to be applied is that the expression of one thing is the exclusion of another.

The defendant places principal reliance upon the decision of this court in *Fidelity-Phenix Fire Insurance Company v. Pilot Freight Carriers*, 193 F.2d 812, 31 A.L.R.2d 839 (4th Cir. 1952). Suit there was predicated upon a loss resulting from theft out of a truck covered by defendant's policy protecting plaintiff from such a loss. The insurance company defended upon the grounds that the plaintiff had left the truck unattended without the alarm system being on. The policy contained six paragraphs limiting coverage. Two of those imposed what was called a "condition precedent." They largely related to the installation of specified safety equipment. Several others, including paragraph 5, pertinent in that case, started with the phrase, "It is further warranted." In paragraph 5, the insured warranted that the alarm system would be on whenever the vehicle was left unattended. Paragraph 6 starts with the language: "The assured agrees, by acceptance of this policy, that the foregoing conditions precedent relate to matters material to the acceptance of the risk by the insurer." Plaintiff recovered in the district court, but judgment on its behalf was reversed because of a breach of warranty of paragraph 5, the truck had been left unattended with the alarm off. In that case, plaintiff relied upon the fact that the words "condition precedent" were used in some of the paragraphs but the word "warranted" was used in the paragraph in issue. In rejecting that contention, this court said that "warranty" and "condition precedent" are often used interchangeably to create a condition of the insured's promise, and "[m]anifestly the terms 'condition precedent' and 'warranty' were intended to have the same meaning and effect." 193 F.2d at 816.

Fidelity-Phenix thus does not support defendant's contention here. Although there is some resemblance between the two cases, analysis shows that the issues are actually entirely different. Unlike the case at bar, each paragraph in *Fidelity-Phenix* contained either the term "condition precedent" or the term "warranted." We held that, in that situation, the two terms had the same effect in that they both involved forfeiture. That is well established law. . . . In the case at bar, the term "warranty" or "warranted" is in no way involved, either in terms or by way of like language, as it was in *Fidelity-Phenix*. The issue, upon which this case turns, then, was not involved in *Fidelity-Phenix*.

The RESTATEMENT OF THE LAW OF CONTRACTS states:

§ 261. *Interpretation of Doubtful Words As Promise or Condition*

Where it is doubtful whether words create a promise or an express condition, they are interpreted as creating a promise; but the same words may sometimes mean that one party promises a performance and that the other party's promise is conditional on that performance.

Two illustrations (one involving a promise, the other a condition) are used in the RESTATEMENT:

2. A, an insurance company, issues to B a policy of insurance containing promises by A that are in terms conditional on the happening of certain events. The policy contains this clause: "provided, in case differences shall arise touching any loss, *the latter shall be submitted to impartial arbitrators*, whose award shall be binding on the parties." This is a promise to arbitrate and does not make an award a condition precedent of the insurer's duty to pay.

3. A, an insurance company, issues to B an insurance policy in usual form containing this clause: "In the event of disagreement as to the amount of loss it shall be ascertained by two appraisers and an umpire. The loss shall *not be payable until 60 days after the award of the appraisers when such an appraisal is required*" This provision is not merely a promise to arbitrate differences but makes an award a condition of the insurer's duty to pay in case of disagreement. (Emphasis added.)

We believe that subparagraph 5(f) in the policy here under consideration fits illustration 2 rather than illustration 3. Illustration 2 specifies something to be done, whereas subparagraph 5(f) specifies something not to be done. Unlike illustration 3, subparagraph 5(f) does not state any conditions under which the insurance shall "not be payable," or use any words of like import. We hold that the district court erroneously held, on the motion for summary judgment, that subparagraph 5(f) established a condition precedent to plaintiffs' recovery which forfeited the coverage.

From our holding that defendant's motion for summary judgment was improperly allowed, it does not follow the plaintiffs' motion for summary judgment should have been granted, for if subparagraph 5(f) be not construed as a condition precedent, there are other questions of fact to be determined. At this point, we merely hold that the district court erred in holding, on the motion for summary judgment, that subparagraph 5(f) constituted a condition precedent with resulting forfeiture.

The explanation defendant makes for including subparagraph 5(f) in the tobacco endorsement is that it is necessary that the stalks remain standing in order for the Corporation to evaluate the extent of loss and to determine whether loss resulted from some cause not covered by the policy. However, was subparagraph 5(f) inserted because without it the Corporation's opportunities for proof would be more difficult, or because they would be impossible? Plaintiffs point out that the Tobacco Endorsement, with subparagraph 5(f), was adopted in 1970, and crop insurance goes back long before that date. Nothing is shown as to the Corporation's prior 1970 practice of evaluating losses. Such a showing might have a bearing upon establishing defendant's intention in including 5(f). Plaintiffs state, and defendant does not deny, that another division of the Department of Agriculture, or the North Carolina Department, urged that tobacco stalks be cut as soon as possible after harvesting as a means of pest control. Such an explanation might refute the idea that plaintiffs plowed under the stalks for any fraudulent purpose. Could these conflicting directives affect the reasonableness of plaintiffs' interpretation of defendant's prohibition upon plowing under the stalks prior to adjustment?

We express no opinion on these questions because they were not before the district court and are mentioned to us largely by way of argument rather than from the record. . . . Nothing we say here should preclude FCIC from asserting as a defense that the plowing or disking under of the stalks caused damage to FCIC if, for example, the amount of the loss was thereby made more difficult or impossible to ascertain whether the plowing or disking under was done with bad purpose or innocently. To repeat, our narrow holding is that merely plowing or disking under the stalks does not of itself operate to forfeit coverage under the policy.

The case is remanded for further proceeding not inconsistent with this opinion.

SLOAN & COMPANY v. LIBERTY MUTUAL INSURANCE COMPANY
United States Court of Appeals for the Third Circuit
653 F.3d 175 (2011)

AMBRO, J.

Isla of Capri Associates LP ("IOC") owned and developed waterfront condominiums in Philadelphia. Shoemaker contracted with IOC to build the project (the "prime contract"). Shoemaker then lined up various subcontractors that included Sloan, who agreed to perform drywall and carpentry work on the project (the "subcontract"). Payment for the subcontractors' work was insured by a surety bond issued by Liberty Mutual. At the project's completion, IOC refused to pay Shoemaker nearly $6.5 million owed under the prime contract. Of that amount, $5 million was due the subcontractors. IOC claimed it was withholding money for several reasons, one of which was that some of the subcontractors' work was untimely and deficient Shoemaker then refused to pay Sloan the full amount of the remaining balance Sloan claimed was due under their subcontract — $1,074,260.

In May 2007, Shoemaker sued IOC to recover the balance on the prime contract. Sloan then made a claim against Liberty Mutual for payment on the surety bond. Five weeks later, Liberty Mutual denied the claim in its entirety, reserving all rights and defenses. As a ground for denying any payment obligation to Sloan, Liberty Mutual asserted that one of the subcontract's terms, found in Paragraph 6.f, conditioned Sloan's right to payment on Shoemaker's receipt of payment from IOC. Relying on that interpretation of the subcontract, Liberty Mutual claimed that Sloan was not entitled to payment from Shoemaker because IOC had not paid Shoemaker.

In December 2007, Sloan filed a complaint against Liberty Mutual in the District Court. Sloan moved for summary judgment in the amount of $1,074,260.09, plus interest and taxable costs.

Meanwhile, Shoemaker's lawsuit against IOC hit a dead end. Shoemaker learned that IOC's financial situation made it unable to satisfy a judgment for the entire claim even if one were awarded to Shoemaker. It entered into a settlement agreement with IOC for $1 million, apparently all that IOC was able to pay. Shoemaker offered its subcontractors their *pro rata* share of amounts owed in exchange for a release of claims, but Sloan did not agree to that arrangement and continued to press its suit against Liberty Mutual. In August 2009, the District Court granted partial summary judgment in favor of Sloan.

The crux of the dispute is Paragraph 6.f of the subcontract, which deals with final payment. It contains two subparagraphs. The first provides in relevant part: "Final payment shall be made within thirty (30) days after the last of the following to occur, the occurrence of all of which shall be conditions precedent to such final payment . . . ." That subparagraph then lists those conditions precedent (seven in all), one of which (condition three) is that "[IOC] shall have accepted the Work and made *final* payment thereunder to [Shoemaker]" (emphasis added). Another (condition six) is that "[Shoemaker] shall have received *final* payment from [IOC] for [Sloan's] Work" (emphasis added).

Liberty Mutual argues that these conditions constitute a "pay-if-paid" clause. In construction contract parlance, this means that a subcontractor gets paid by the general contractor only if the owner pays the general contractor for that subcontractor's work. Pennsylvania courts follow suit, and construe clauses that condition payment to the subcontractor on the general contractor's receipt of payment from the owner as pay-if-paid clauses. Sloan, on the other hand, argues that the first subparagraph of 6.f does not establish a condition precedent to Sloan's payment, but rather is a "pay-when-paid" clause. On the surface, these terms seem much the same (save, perhaps, that paying if paid does not tell us when that payment is due). But in industry jargon, they are different. In contrast to a pay-if-paid clause, a pay-when-paid clause does not establish a condition precedent, but merely creates a timing mechanism for the general contractor's payment to the subcontractor.

To support its pay-when-paid interpretation, Sloan points to the second subparagraph of 6.f, which describes a process by which it may sue Shoemaker for final payment in the event that IOC fails to make final payment to Shoemaker. The language of that subparagraph states:

> Notwithstanding anything to the contrary in this Paragraph 6.f, if within six months of the date that final payment is due to [Shoemaker by IOC], [Sloan] has not received final payment for its Work, [Sloan] may pursue its claim against [Shoemaker] and its Surety [Liberty Mutual] for final payment as follows:
>
> > If within six months of the date that final payment is due and payable to [Shoemaker], [Shoemaker] commences a legal proceedings against [IOC] . . . (the "Contractor Dispute Resolution") to resolve its own claim for final payment, [Sloan] agrees not to pursue its claim against

[Shoemaker] or [Liberty Mutual] until the Contractor Dispute Resolution and all appeals thereto are completed and become final . . . .

Upon completion of the Contractor Dispute Resolution . . . , [Sloan] may pursue
any remaining claim for final payment it may have against [Shoemaker] or its
Surety.

Notably, that subparagraph concludes by stating that [n]othing in Paragraph 6.f
is intended to modify the provisions of Paragraph 20[, which deals with dispute
resolution,] under the Subcontract . . . .

We consider each subparagraph in turn and their combined effect on the
meaning of the contract.

Pennsylvania follows the plain meaning rule of contract interpretation, such that
"[w]hen a written contract is clear and unequivocal, its meaning must be determined
by its contents alone. It speaks for itself and a meaning cannot be given to it other
than that expressed." Accordingly, the cases recognize that express language of
condition is sufficient to establish a pay-if-paid condition precedent. In *C.M.
Eichenlaub Co.*, for example, the Pennsylvania Superior Court viewed as a
condition precedent to payment a clause that stated the builder "shall be under no
obligation to make any payments to contractor . . . for materials delivered or for
work performed by contractor unless and until Builder is first paid for such
materials and work by the owner." When certainty is lacking, however, Pennsylvania
courts tend to interpret payment provisions as pay-when-paid clauses.

But that is not our case. The first subparagraph of 6.f states unequivocally that
IOC's payment to Shoemaker is a condition precedent to Shoemaker's obligation to
pay Sloan. We do not imagine that the parties intended otherwise merely because
they did not use additional language to underscore their intent to create a
pay-if-paid clause, as Sloan argues. To mandate redundant provisions conjures the
consequence that only repetition makes a provision pay-if-paid. Moreover, we agree
that courts should not interpret contracts in a way that "render[s] at least one
clause superfluous or meaningless." Thus, we are satisfied that the parties' chosen
language is sufficient to create a pay-if-paid clause in the first subparagraph of 6.f.

The opposite conclusion would lead to bizarre results. If Sloan failed to complete
its work, per condition one, could it then argue that it was still entitled to final
payment under the subcontract? We can see no principled reason to treat
differently conditions three and six (no payment to Sloan until Shoemaker has
received "final" payment from IOC). That seven conditions were enumerated in this
provision, and expressly delineated conditions precedents, weigh in favor of a
pay-if-paid construction. In the face of this plain language, we shall not infer a
contrary intent.

However, that is not the end of the story. The parties created an override
provision in the second subparagraph of 6.f that modifies the pay-if-paid clause of
the first subparagraph. Specifically, the language of the second subparagraph,
noted above, demonstrates that the contracting parties intended Sloan to have a
"claim" against Shoemaker for "any remaining final payment" in certain instances
— specifically, in the event that IOC failed to make final payment (defined as the
entire unpaid balance on the prime contract) within six months.

A modification of a pay-if-paid condition is a not uncommon practice in the construction industry.[1]

The structure of Paragraph 6.f demonstrates that the parties did not intend for Sloan's "remaining claim for final payment" to equal the entire unpaid balance on the subcontract. Such a construction would essentially nullify the first subparagraph: whether IOC made, and Shoemaker received, final payment on the prime contract would be irrelevant if, in cases of IOC non-payment, Sloan was always entitled to the entire unpaid balance on the subcontract. [The court found that a provision in the contract dealing with dispute resolutions and concluded that paragraph 6.f manifested an intention that Sloan should share the risk of nonpayment by IOC was entitled only to a pro rata share of any recovery Shoemaker could achieve against IOC which, at the time of this case, totaled $300,000. Thus, Sloan would be entitled to a pro rata share of that amount].

NOTES

(1) *Policy Against Forfeitures.* It should be evident that in the interpretation of language to determine whether it was intended as a promise or condition, the underlying judicial effort is in keeping with one of the oldest maxims of our law, which finds its way regularly into modern cases:

> This court has held the general doctrine that forfeitures are not favored in the law, and that courts should promptly seize upon any circumstances arising out of the contract or relation of the parties that would indicate an election or an agreement to waive the harsh, and at times unjust, remedy of forfeiture, a remedy which is oftentimes too freely granted by those who have taken to account of the misfortunes and disappointments which conditions, unforeseen and beyond a party's control, have raised as a bar to performance, however honest may be his intent. *Stevenson v. Parker*, 608 P.2d 1263, 1267–68 (1980) quoting from *Spedden v. Sykes*, 98 P. 752, 754 (1908). In general, see MURRAY ON CONTRACTS § 103.

(2)   Where a contract provided that the subcontractor would be paid "provided like payment has been made by owner to contractor," the question is whether the general contractor's risk of nonpayment has been shifted to the subcontractor. The court emphasized guides to interpretation used to determine whether the language was promissory or conditional together with a clear abhorrence for forfeitures: (a) a condition precedent is not favored and will, therefore, be given effect only by clear and unequivocal language; (b) in cases of doubt, courts will resolve the doubt by construing the language as a promise rather than a condition. *Main Elec. Ltd. v. Printz Servs.Corp.*, 980 P.2d 522 (Colo. 1999).

---

[1] There are several ways to modify pay-if-paid clauses. Particularly "[i]n states that distinguish between the two [*i.e.*, pay-if-paid and pay-when-paid provisions], an obvious way to modify a pay-if-paid clause is to convert it to a pay-when-paid clause. This is accomplished by eliminating the condition precedent after a contractually stated period of time."

[3] Precedent Versus Subsequent Condition — Original Formula

GRAY v. GARDNER
Massachusetts Supreme Judicial Court
17 Mass. 188 (1821)

Assumpsit on a written promise to pay the plaintiff 5198 dollars, 87 cents, with the following condition annexed, *viz.*, "on the condition that if a greater quantity of sperm oil should arrive in whaling vessels at *Nantucket* and *New Bedford*, on or between the first day of April and the first day of October of the present year, both inclusive, than arrived at said places, in whaling vessels, on or within the same term of time the last year, then this obligation to be void." Dated April 1819.

The consideration of the promise was a quantity of oil, sold by the plaintiff to the defendants. On the same day another note unconditional had been given by the defendants, for the value of the oil, estimated at sixty cents per gallon; and the note in suit was given to secure the residue of the price, estimated at eighty-five cents, to depend on the contingency mentioned in the said condition.

At the trial before the chief justice, the case depended upon the question whether a certain vessel, called the *Lady Adams*, with a cargo of oil, arrived at *Nantucket* on the first day of October, 1819, about which fact the evidence was contradictory. The judge ruled that the burden of proving the arrival within the time was on the defendants; and further that, although the vessel might have, within the time, gotten within the space which might be called *Nantucket Roads*, yet it was necessary that she should have come to anchor, or have been moored, somewhere within that space before the hour of twelve following the first day of October, in order to have *arrived*, within the meaning of the contract.

The opinion of the chief justice on both these points was objected to by the defendants, and the questions were saved. If it was wrong on either point, a new trial was to be had; otherwise judgment was to be rendered on the verdict, which was found for the plaintiff.

Whitman, for the defendants. As the evidence at the trial was contradictory, the question on whom the burden of proof rested, became important. We hold that it was on the plaintiff. This was a condition precedent. Until it should happen, the promise did not take effect. On the occurrence of a certain contingent event, the promise was to be binding, and not otherwise. To entitle himself to enforce the promise, the plaintiff must show that the contingent event has actually occurred.

On the other point saved at the trial, the defendants insist that it was not required by the terms of this contract that the vessel should be moored. It is not denied that such would be the construction of a policy of insurance containing the same expression. But every contract is to be taken according to the intention of the parties to it, if such intention be legal, and capable of execution. The contemplation of parties to a policy of insurance is, that the vessel shall be safe before she shall be said to have arrived. So it is in some other maritime contracts. But in that now in question, nothing was in the minds of the parties, but that the fact of the arrival of so much oil should be known within the time limited. The subject matter in one case is safety, in the other it is information only. In this case the vessel would be said to have arrived, in common understanding, and according to the meaning of the parties.

PARKER, C.J.

The very words of the contract show that there was a promise to pay, which was to be defeated by the happening of an event, *viz.*, the arrival of a certain quantity of oil, at the specified places, in a given time. It is like a bond with a condition; if the obligor would avoid the bond, he must show performance of the condition. The defendants, in this case, promise to pay a certain sum of money, on condition that the promise shall be void on the happening of an event. It is plain that the burden of proof is upon them; and if they fail to show that the event has happened, the promise remains good.

The other point is equally clear for the plaintiff. Oil is to arrive at a given place before twelve o'clock at night. A vessel with oil heaves in sight, but she does not come to anchor before the hour is gone. In no sense can the oil be said to have arrived. The vessel is coming until she drops anchor, or is moored. She may sink, or take fire, and never arrive, however near she may be to her port. It is so in contracts of insurance; and the same reason applies to a case of this sort. Both parties put themselves upon a nice point in this contract; it was a kind of wager as to the quantity of oil which should arrive at the ports mentioned, before a certain period. They must be held strictly to their contract, there being no equity to interfere with the terms of it.

Judgment on the verdict.

NOTES

(1) It is possible to describe all conditions as precedent and all conditions as subsequent if only the *form* of the condition is considered. The question must always be asked, precedent or subsequent to what? There must be a reference point in the transaction to which the condition is related.[2] In terms of *substance*, if an existing contractual duty cannot be activated until a condition has occurred, the condition is necessarily precedent.

(2) Whether a condition is precedent or subsequent in form is not significant *unless* there is a problem in proving the occurrence or non-occurrence of the condition. If such evidence cannot meet the normal preponderance standard, the party to whom the burden of proof is assigned will necessarily fail. *Quaere:* Should the burden be assigned on the basis of the *form* of the condition as precedent or subsequent?

In *Redux, Ltd. v. Commercial Union Ins. Co.*, 1995 U.S. Dist. LEXIS 2545 (D. Kan. 1995), the court states, "It is generally accepted that the burden of proof as to

---

[2] *See* Harnett & Thornton, *The Insurance Condition Subsequent: A Needle in a Semantic Haystack*, 7 FORDHAM L. REV. 220 (1948).

a condition subsequent should be placed on the defendant. . . ." The court cites E. ALLAN FARNSWORTH, CONTRACTS § 8.2 for this holding. Professor Farnsworth cites the principal case as authority for this proposition and adds, "It is surely preferable to allocate procedural burdens according to factors that are relevant to the policies that underlie them." He further suggests that the burden of proof should be allocated to the party who is in the better position of proving them.

[4]   Precedent Versus Subsequent Condition — RESTATEMENT (SECOND) OF CONTRACTS Analysis

CAMBRIA SAVINGS & LOAN ASS'N v. ESTATE OF GROSS
Pennsylvania Superior Court
439 A.2d 1236 (1982)

MONTEMURO, J.

[A husband and wife (the Grosses) were approached by a contractor on the subject of aluminum siding for their home. The couple signed a contract but, because of the husband's health problem, it contained a handwritten statement inserted by the contractor stating: "This contract null and void if customer [husband] cannot get disability and death and sickness insurance." The contractor introduced the husband to an insurance agent to whom the husband sent a check to initiate the insurance. When the crew arrived to perform the work, the husband told the crew not to begin since the husband had not received the insurance. This led to a telephone conversation between the husband, the contractor and the insurance agent, after which the husband allowed the work to proceed. When the work was completed, the husband signed a contractor's form stating that the work had been completed in accordance with the terms of the contract. Subsequently, the husband learned that his insurance application had been denied. The evidence was clear that there was no waiver of the handwritten statement on the original contract. The contractor admitted that the contract for the completed siding work would be null and void if Mr. Gross did not obtain insurance. Mr. Gross had died at the time of this action. No payment was made for the siding and this action was brought by the assignee of the contractor, the Savings and Loan Association. The trial court instructed the jury that the contract was a nullity but recovery could be had in a quasi contract action for unjust enrichment. This appeal followed.]

RESTATEMENT OF CONTRACTS 2d at § 224 defines "condition" as follows:

> Condition Defined. A condition is an event, not certain to occur, which must occur, unless its non-occurrence is excused, before performance under a contract becomes due.

The Reporter's Note following § 224 then discusses the replacement of the former terms "condition precedent" and "condition subsequent." Conditions sprecedent are now referred to simply as "conditions," and the section also abandons the use of "condition" as the term that makes an event a "condition." "Condition" now refers only to the event itself. "Conditions Subsequent," always a confusing terminology, are now dealt with under § 230, entitled "Event that Terminates a Duty."

The Reporter's Note also states that a contract may be "inartistically drafted" to state that the agreement "shall not come into existence until Event *A* occurs." However, ". . . it is better to view a contract as already in existence, but with the parties' respective performances subject to the specified event. . . ." RESTATEMENT OF CONTRACTS 2d, § 224, Reporter's Note at p. 164. ALI (1981).

When the contract is regarded as in force, the new RESTATEMENT gives guidance as to when duty under the contract may be extinguished. As already noted, this is a revised approach to the concept formerly entitled "condition subsequent."

§ 230. Event that Terminates a Duty

(1) Except as stated in Subsection (2), if under the terms of the contract the occurrence of an event is to terminate an obligor's duty to immediate performance or one to pay damages for breach, that duty is discharged if the event occurs.

(2) The obligor's duty is not discharged if occurrence of the event

(a) is the result of a breach by the obligor of his duty of good faith and fair dealing, or

(b) could not have been prevented because of impracticability and continuance of the duty does not subject the obligor to a materially increased burden.

(3) The obligor's duty is not discharged if, before the event occurs, the obligor promises to perform the duty even if the event occurs and does not revoke his promise before the obligee materially changes his position in reliance on it.

An analysis of the preceding wording from the RESTATEMENT leads us to conclude that the handwritten clause on the contract which is the subject of this litigation, though ambiguous in some respects, clearly refers to an event "not certain to occur," but which "must occur before performance is to become due." The event described, therefore, fits the definition of a "condition."

The event provided for in the contract terms was a negative condition — a failure to obtain disability insurance, which would terminate the duties under the contract. The event thus, not only fits the definition under § 224, *supra*, but also that of § 230, *supra*, and becomes an Event that Terminates a Duty, formerly a "Condition Subsequent."

Furthermore, the contract was in existence from October 6, 1971. The "inartistic" draftsmanship did not prevent the contract from being valid throughout the time that performance was due. Mr. Casselhoff and Mr. Datz testified that they regarded the contract as in force, and that Mr. Gross also considered it to be in force. Further, all parties knew no waiver had been made and that it was conceivable that the insurance would not be approved. Mr. Gross's act in signing the completion certificate certainly indicates that he did indeed see the contract as still in force as of November 10, 1971.

Consequently, what we have here is not a void contract, but rather a contract that continued in force until an event constituting a condition of the contract occurred to terminate a duty. The work in this instance was not performed in a legal vacuum which justifies an analysis in quasi-contract for value of the work. The lower court's instructions to the jury on that point were misleading and resulted in an incorrect finding on that point.

Examination of § 230(2), the provision in which exceptions to the general rule on discharge are set forth, cannot apply here. The "impracticability" must be shown by the obligee. *See* Note after § 230, Restatement of Contracts 2d at 190. The contractor here has never claimed a necessity for completion of the work at an early date. Clearly, it was perfectly practical to wait a couple of months to see whether the insurance would be forthcoming. "Continuance of the duty" against the obligor, Mrs. Gross, is not a minor matter, easily discharged. Mrs. Gross has proceeded *in forma pauperis* with the help of Legal Aid. The award of three thousand, six hundred thirty-five dollars and ninety cents ($3,635.90) does subject her to "a materially increased burden."

Also, the provision of § 230(2)(a) is not brought into play under the instant facts. There is no allegation of bad faith, and the record certainly reflects good faith behavior by the purchasers.

As shown in the testimony cited *supra*, § 230(3) cannot apply either. Both the contractor and his agent honestly admit that Mr. Gross never orally or in writing promised to pay for the work whether he received his insurance or not. The obligee, in this instance, the contractor, did materially change his own position by performance, but not on the strength of any promise by the obligor.

Examination of the wording of the clause does not help us to determine whether the parties originally intended the clause as a condition precedent to any performance, or an event that eventually terminated a duty of performance. The ambiguity must be resolved by the court upon review of the facts.

Certainly, Mr. Gross, by his actions, appears to have originally interpreted the clause to mean that his own obligation to obtain insurance was a condition precedent to all other performance by either party. Mr. Casselhoff, however, seems never to have regarded the obtaining of insurance as a condition precedent. He was aware "immediately" of the existence of the clause, but twice sent his crew to perform; and, in the end, he rendered performance within one week of signing of the contract. Consultation between Mr. Gross and Mr. Datz and Mr. Mulligan resulted in a change of action on Mr. Gross' part, indicating his acceptance of the clause as a condition subsequent or an event causing termination of his duty of payment.

This court therefore finds that the ambiguity inherent in the wording of the clause was at this time resolved by the parties, and that the contractor, under the terms of the existing contract, assumed the risk that after his performance had been rendered, the condition provided as a termination of the duty of his obligor could occur.

Subsequent events, as we have seen, left the purchaser disabled, unhirable, and uninsurable. The failure to obtain disability insurance is no reflection, therefore, of bad faith, but a clear impossibility.

The events of this case were fully covered under the terms of the contract. This is not, in fact, a case of unjust enrichment upon which a quasi-contractual right can be raised in law. The parties made a bargain and its terms were complied with, until, upon the happening of a specified event, the purchaser was released from his duty of payment.

Appellant's brief cites numerous cases supporting the proposition that courts will not rescue parties from the harsh results of their freely contracted agreements. Subsequent events have made the contractor's bargain a poor one. However, he knew when the clause was written into the agreement that he had conceded something unusual to his customer as a part of the bargaining process. He also knew, and admits he knew, that Mr. Gross never promised to waive the written condition, and that it was possible that the work could be done and yet the insurance refused.

The injury the contractor and its assignee, the Savings and Loan Association, have suffered, is not through a failure of duty of the purchasers, but from their own risks freely assumed under the contract.

Therefore, this court must reverse the holding of the court below and remand so that a judgment *non obstante verdicto* may be entered.

[5]   Condition of Personal Satisfaction

ELEC-TROL, INC. v. C.J. KERN CONTRACTORS, INC.
North Carolina Court of Appeals
284 S.E.2d 119 (1981)

MARTIN, JUDGE.

[Plaintiff agreed to perform certain electrical subcontracting work on a hospital building constructed for the third-party defendant, North Baptist Hospital, Inc. The subcontract between the plaintiff and defendant Kern Contractors incorporated the terms of the contract between Kern and North Baptist including provision 12.2.1. Plaintiff seeks additional compensation for its work on the basis of changes in the specifications. Defendant Kern and third-party defendant North Baptist contend that plaintiff has been fully compensated as determined by the architect under provision 12.2.1 of the contract.]

The terms of the contract between the defendant and the third-party defendant, which terms were incorporated by reference into the contract between plaintiff and defendant, contained provisions governing the procedures by which claims for additional costs were to be determined. Section 12.2.1 of the General and Supplementary Conditions provided that "[i]f the Owner and the Contractor cannot agree on the amount of the adjustment in the contract sum, it shall be determined by the Architect."

The North Carolina courts have recognized that a provision in a contract, providing for the architect's approval before the contractor can recover compensation on his contract, is binding on the parties. When the contract so provides, the architect's certificate is a condition precedent to the contractor's recovery, absent a showing of bad faith or failure to exercise honest judgment. In *Heating Co. v. Board of Education*, 268 N.C. 85, 89-90, 150 S.E.2d 65, 68 (1966), the Court stated as follows:

> In building and construction contracts the parties frequently provide that the completion, sufficiency, classification, or amount of the work done by the contractor shall be determined by a third person, usually an architect or engineer. Such stipulations which, in their origin, were designed to avoid harassing litigation over questions that can be determined honestly only by those possessed of scientific knowledge, have generally been held valid. This is true even though the architect or engineer is employed by the owner, unless unknown to the contractor, he has guaranteed to keep the cost of the work below a certain sum.
>
> Although plain language in the contract is required in order to make the decision or certificate of an architect or engineer acting thereunder final and conclusive, it may be stated generally that the decision of the architect or engineer is conclusive as to any matter connected with the contract if the parties, by any stipulation, constitute the architect or engineer the final arbiter of such matter as between the parties. Accordingly, where the contract provides that the work shall be done to the satisfaction, approval, or acceptance of an architect or engineer, such architect or engineer is thereby constituted sole arbitrator between the parties, and the parties are bound by his decision, in the absence of fraud or gross mistake. The same rule applies where it is provided that payments shall be made only upon the certificate of the architect.
>
> It is also clear that where the parties stipulate expressly or in necessary effect, that the determination of the architect or engineer shall be final and conclusive, both parties are bound by his determination of those matters which he is authorized to determine, except in case of fraud or such gross mistake as would necessarily imply bad faith or a failure to exercise an honest judgement. The reason underlying this rule is that under such circumstances the contract makes the architect or engineer the arbitrator, and his determination can be attacked only in the same manner as that of any other arbitrator. On the other hand, where the stipulations are such that the meaning to be gathered therefrom is that the architect's or engineer's certificate shall not be final, the parties are not bound by the certificate. [Citations omitted.]

In the present case the contract provided that the architect would determine the amount of claims for additional cost if the owner and contractor could not agree. This provision is clear and binding on the parties. Thus it constitutes a final determination of the parties' rights unless plaintiff shows bad faith or failure to exercise honest judgment on the part of the architect.

The plaintiff contends that a significant question of fact exists as to the independence of the architect. Neither plaintiff's complaint nor its amended complaint raised this issue. The trial court found as fact that "[t]here are no allegations in the complaint that the architect's determination of the additional amounts due to the plaintiff for additional work done were made as a result of bad faith, gross mistake or fraud, or that the parties waived the requirements of the contract that the architect would make the determination as to the sums to be paid for additional work performed." Because plaintiff did not take exception to this finding of fact, plaintiff cannot raise this issue on appeal to reverse the grant of defendant's motion for summary judgment. Rule 10, N.C. Rules App. Proc.

The plaintiff's final argument is that it is entitled to the reasonable value of its work from the general contractor, Kern, regardless of whether the owner, North Carolina Baptist Hospitals, Inc., paid the contractor. Plaintiff is seeking, in essence, a recovery pursuant to a theory of *quantum meruit*.

An express contract precludes an implied contract with reference to the same subject matter. For example, in *Brokers, Inc. v. Board of Education*, 33 N.C. App. 24, 234 S.E.2d 56, *discr. rev. denied*, 293 N.C. 159, 236 S.E.2d 702 (1977), a contractor sued to recover the value of work performed by plaintiff in excess of that specified in the written contract between the parties. The written contract provided in part that "The Contract Sum and the Contract Time may be changed only by Change Order." The evidence tended to show that the sum sued for by plaintiff was not authorized by change order. In holding that the plaintiff was not entitled to recover on the theory of *quantum meruit* or implied contract, the Court stated at 33 N.C. App. at 30, 234 S.E.2d 60 (1977) the following:

> "It is a well established principle that an express contract precludes an implied contract with reference to the same matter." *Concrete Co. v. Lumber Co.*, 256 N.C. 709, 713, 124 S.E.2d 905, 908 (1962). "There cannot be an express and an implied contract for the same thing existing at the same time. It is only when parties do not expressly agree that the law interposes and raises a promise. No agreement can be implied where there is an express one existing." 66 Am. Jur. 2d, *Restitution and Implied Contract*, § 6, pp. 948, 949.

In the present case the contract and the subcontract expressly provide that the architect shall determine the amount of adjustment if the owner and contractor cannot agree. Plaintiff is bound by the express terms of these contracts.

The material facts involved in this action are not in dispute. The only questions involved in this action are questions of law requiring the interpretation of the contract and the subcontract. These questions were properly resolved by the trial court's grant of defendant's motion for summary judgment. *Affirmed.*

NOTES

(1) *Standards of Satisfaction.* "When a contract conditions one party's performance on the 'satisfaction' of another, there are two standards which can be applied to determine satisfaction: the objective reasonable satisfaction standard and the subjective personal satisfaction standard. Absent express contractual language indicating which standard to apply, the objective reasonable satisfaction standard is applied when the contract involves commercial quality, operative fitness, or mechanical utility which knowledgeable persons are capable of judging; the

subjective personal satisfaction standard is applied when the contract involves personal aesthetics, taste or fancy. When the express language or nature of the contract do not make it clear that personal satisfaction is required, the law prefers the objective (reasonable person) standard." *Employee Benefits Plus, Inc. v. Des Moines General Hospital*, 535 N.W.2d 149, 154 (Iowa Ct. App. 1995).

Perhaps the best-known case involving a condition of personal satisfaction is an old case involving an enlargement of the picture of defendant's deceased daughter which the plaintiff promised the defendant would be perfectly satisfactory to the defendant. In *Gibson v. Cranage*, 39 Mich. 49 (1878), the court held that the defendant did not have to pay for the picture if, in fact, he did not like it, though the picture may have been excellent in the judgment of others.

RESTATEMENT (SECOND) OF CONRACTS § 228, comment a, supports this standard: "If the agreement leaves no doubt that it is only honest satisfaction that is meant and no more, it will be so interpreted, and the condition does not occur if the obligor is honestly, even though unreasonably, dissatisfied."

It is relatively easy to apply the subjective satisfaction test to any subject matter that can be called aesthetic or artistic. Even though a party subjecting his or her performance to a standard of personal satisfaction in the other party is assuming a substantial risk, there will be no question concerning the enforcement of such a clause if the risk is clearly assumed. Again, with respect to artistic performance, there is no argument concerning the risk.

With respect to subject matter involving mechanical utility, commercial value or operative fitness, a subjective standard appears out of place, and "satisfaction" language in a contract will often be construed to mean "objective" satisfaction (the satisfaction of a reasonable party under the circumstances). *See Guntert v. City of Stockton*, 43 Cal. App. 3d 203 (1974). Even non-artistic subject matter, however, can be measured by a subjective satisfaction standard if the clause is drafted in apt and convincing language. *See Ard Dr. Pepper Bottling Co. v. Dr. Pepper Co.*, 202 F.2d 372 (5th Cir. 1953). See also *Aster v. BP Oil Co.*, 412 F. Supp. 179 (M.D. Pa. 1976), where the defendant was dissatisfied with holding tanks as a sewage system because it believed that such tanks were temporary, expensive, unsightly, and potentially unsanitary. The court states, "The soundness of these opinions is not relevant. Only the genuineness with which they were taken is important. The Court is of the view that they were honestly held and were not invoked capriciously or in bad faith."

(2) *Architects and Engineers.* It is very common for a building contract to contain a clause indicating that the work must be done to the personal satisfaction of a named architect or engineer. The standard of satisfaction is not one of reasonableness, i.e., what a reasonable third-party architect or engineer would find satisfactory. Rather, the standard is one of *honest satisfaction*, i.e., a good faith standard. The plaintiff has the burden of establishing the bad faith of the named architect or engineer. Moreover, an architect is not liable for directing an owner to terminate a contract unless the architect operates in bad faith. *Dehnert v. Arrow Sprinklers, Inc.*, 705 P.2d 846 (Wyo. 1985).

If an architect refuses to examine the work performed, bad faith is obvious. *See Hartford Elec. Applicators of Thermaluz, Inc. v. Alden*, 363 A.2d 135 (Conn. 1975).

Even where the architect or engineer is operating in good faith, if the basis for refusal to issue a certificate of satisfaction is beyond the scope of his or her expertise, the condition of personal satisfaction will be excused. Where, for example, an engineer decided to issue a certificate for a school building because the engineer decided it was essential that children go to school, the engineer was not using his expertise but was making a judgment for non-engineering reasons. *See James I. Barnes Constr. Co. v. Washington Twp.*, 184 N.E.2d 763 (Ind. Ct. App. 1962). Where an architect refused to issue a certificate of satisfactory performance because he did not want to appear to be issuing the certificate as a prelude to litigation, again, the expert was making a judgment for reasons beyond his expertise. *Rizzolo v. Poysher*, 99 A. 390 (N.J. Super. Ct. 1916). See also *Anthony P. Miller, Inc. v. Wilmington Hous. Auth.*, 179 F. Supp. 109 (D. Del. 1959), in which the court excuses the condition on the basis of "constructive fraud," though it regrets using that phrase. It is clear that the architect was simply operating beyond his expertise.

If the architect or engineer dies or becomes incapacitated, it is generally agreed that the condition will be excused and a standard of reasonableness substituted. *See Grenier v. Compratt Constr. Co.*, 189 Conn. 144, 454 A.2d 1289 (1983); *see also* MURRAY ON CONTRACTS at § 104C.

(3) *UCC — Expert Judgment.* The Uniform Commercial Code recognizes that parties to a contract may have agreed to buy and sell a certain item(s) conditioned exclusively upon the price being determined by a particular expert. If they have chosen this expert, not merely to suggest a barometer or index of a fair price, but regard that expert's judgment as a condition to the duty to buy and sell, the duties could not be activated if that particular expert were not available — i.e., unlike the death or incapacity of the architect, a standard of reasonableness would not be substituted. The UCC suggests such a situation in relation to a work of art. However, if the expert is named to determine a particular grade of cotton or other commodity, the assumption is that the parties would be bound even if that particular expert were not available. UCC § 2-305, comment 4. *See* MURRAY ON CONTRACTS § 104C.

(4) *UCC — "Sale on Approval."* The condition of personal satisfaction of the Uniform Commercial Code is found in § 2-326(1)(a), which states that a buyer of goods may return them even though they conform to the contract where the transaction was a "sale on approval." The Code, however, does not suggest its own tests to determine whether the parties have contracted on that basis. Whether the parties intended to contract on a personal satisfaction basis is left to common law principles. *See U.S. Nemrod, Inc. v. Wheel House Dive Shop, Inc.*, 120 Misc. 2d 156, 465 N.Y.S.2d 674 (1983); *see also* MURRAY ON CONTRACTS § 104D.

[6] Express, Implied, and Constructive Conditions Distinguished

A condition is created by either of two methods: (1) the parties have manifested an intention (by words or conduct) that the duty to render a promised performance shall be subject to the occurrence of some fact or event other than a mere lapse of time; and (2) a court, in the interests of equity and justice, determines that a contractual duty should be subject to a condition even though the parties have manifested no such intention.

Where a condition is created by the first method, the manifested intention of the parties, they are called *express* conditions.[3] They are "real" conditions established by the agreement of the parties and the agreement may be manifested in words or by conduct. When these real conditions are created by the conduct of the parties, like a contract manifested by conduct, they may be called "implied in fact" conditions. While the only difference between express conditions and implied in fact conditions is that the former are created by words while the latter are created by a substitute for words (conduct), the "implied in fact" label may be confusing. This is because a court may infuse a contract with a condition under the second method, i.e., by reading it into a contract for reasons of its own, notwithstanding the lack of any manifestation (words or conduct) of the parties. Such a condition is called a *constructive* condition (sometimes, unfortunately, referred to as an "implied in law" condition).[4] It is "constructed" by the court in the pursuit of equity and justice.

Since express conditions result from a manifestation of intention, it is clear that the only difficulty likely to arise in determining their existence and operation is one of interpretation. On the other hand, the problem of determining the existence of a constructive condition is wholly different. It is not a question of interpretation; rather, it is a question of whether the court should add to the terms of the contract in order to achieve equity and justice in a situation not foreseen and not provided for by the parties.

While these two kinds of conditions are distinct in theory, in practice it is not always easy to distinguish them. First, the manifestations of intention in a particular case are frequently so uncertain that it is difficult to determine whether a court may justifiably find that the parties intended a condition though it may be clear that finding a condition would be desirable regardless of the manifested

---

[3] *See* RESTATEMENT (SECOND) ON CONTRACTS § 226 cmt. a.

[4] *See* RESTATEMENT (SECOND) ON CONTRACTS § 226 cmt. c; *see also* Holloway v. Jackson, 412 So. 2d 774 (Ala. 1982) (quoting the RESTATEMENT (FIRST) ON CONTRACTS § 253: "[A] 'constructive condition' is a condition that is such because of a rule of law, and is not based on interpretation of a promise or agreement.").

The classification and nomenclature of conditions set forth in this section have not been uniformly accepted. Some courts and writers insist on a classification including express conditions, by which they mean conditions created by the *words* of the parties, implied-in-fact conditions, meaning conditions created by the manifested *conduct* of the parties, and implied-in-law conditions, meaning conditions created by courts to achieve just results. *See* G. COSTIGAN, THE PERFORMANCE OF CONTRACTS 7 (2d ed. 1927). This classification is objectionable because it may lead to confusion in distinguishing so-called implied-in-fact from implied-in-law conditions. Moreover, there is no utility in distinguishing express and implied-in-fact conditions since both have their basis in the manifested intention of the parties, the only difference growing out of the manner in which that manifestation occurs. Whether expressed in words or through other conduct, the condition can properly be called "express." The only significant distinction, therefore, is the distinction between those conditions that are manifested by words or conduct and those which are added by the court. Thus, the distinction set forth in the text between express and constructive conditions is not only more simple, it is more accurate and clear. For a case adopting this analysis as it appeared in the second edition of this book, see Dorn v. Stanhope Steel, Inc., 534 A.2d 798 (Pa. Super. 1987).

intention. In this situation, the discovery of a condition can be justified on either of two theories (express or constructive) and the court is likely to ignore the distinction in discovering a condition. Second, earlier courts were not willing to admit that they could "make a contract" for the parties though they frequently did so, disguising their operation under the fiction of interpretation. Modern courts, however, are much more willing to admit that conditions may be found to exist, notwithstanding the manifested intention of the parties.[5]

Yet, it is still not always clear whether the court has discovered a condition from the intention of the parties or from the necessity of a just and equitable result. Thus, a franchise agreement provided that the agreement could be terminated if the franchisee was in breach, but was silent as to whether it could be terminated by the franchisee where the franchisor had breached. The franchisor had committed many breaches but the franchisee could not establish damages. The court held that the failures of the franchisor to perform were not only breaches of its duties, but failure of conditions precedent to the activation of the franchisee's duties. Otherwise, the franchisee would be left remediless.[6]

This judicial effort suggests a combination of discovering a condition which may have been part of the contemplation of the parties at the time of contract formation and establishing the condition to avoid manifest injustice to the franchisee.

[7]   Constructive Conditions

Very often the parties to a bilateral transaction fail to manifest any intention with regard to one or more matters that may be of vital importance to a proper determination of their respective rights and duties, in case any disputes arise in connection with the performance of the contract. They may fail to manifest any intention with regard to: (1) the order in which their respective promises must be performed; (2) what effect the partial failure of one party to perform his promise or promises in the required order, or a delay in the performance, shall have upon the rights and duties of the other party; and (3) what effect the prospective inability or unwillingness of one party to perform his promise or promises, in whole or in part, shall have upon the rights and duties of the other party. A simple illustration, drawn from a case that is of common occurrence, will help to make the problem clear.

Suppose A contracts to work for B for one year at a salary of $36,000, nothing being said as to when, or in what amounts, the salary shall be paid by B. In what order must A and B respectively perform? If A fails to work, may he nevertheless recover the agreed salary? If A should be ill for a month and unable to work, what effect would this have upon the rights and duties of the parties? If B should become insolvent, would A be excused from further performance of his undertaking? There is nothing in the utterances through which the contract was manifested to enable

---

[5] *See, e.g.,* Seman v. First State Bank of Eden Prairie, 394 N.W.2d 557 (Minn. Ct. App. 1986) (court found bank's duty to stop payment on a cashier's check subject to condition implied by the court that the purchaser provide a legally sufficient reason to the bank for stopping payment because of the nature of a cashier's check, i.e., it is viewed as more trustworthy than a personal check).

[6] United Campgrounds, U.S.A. v. Stevenson, 571 P.2d 1161 (1977).

us to determine how the parties themselves would have answered these questions and many others like them which might be raised. In other words, the contract does not indicate what relationship, if any, shall exist between the mutual performances that have been promised, and yet it is obvious that this relationship must be determined before we can reach any satisfactory conclusion in regard to the rights and duties of the parties, when a dispute arises in connection with the performance of the contract. We have here a case in which the law must of necessity "make a contract" for the parties, if injustice is to be prevented. Since it is frequently clear that the parties did not have in mind the particular question which has arisen, they can hardly be said to have provided an answer for it in advance, even though the general language of the contract, taken literally, may sometimes seem to indicate that they have.

In addition, there are cases involving both bilateral and unilateral contracts in which courts have held that the duty of the promisor is dependent upon his receiving notice of the happening of some condition which qualifies his undertaking. These questions will now be discussed.

Origins. The early law had a very simple solution for the problem suggested above. It took the view that the performances were independent unless the parties in express terms indicated that performance by one was in some specified way dependent upon performance by the other. This meant that each party to a bilateral contract was under a duty to perform his own undertaking, regardless of whether the other performed or offered to perform, unless performance on one side was in terms made dependent or conditional upon performance on the other side. Thus, where *A* promised to work for *B* for one year and, in return, B promised to pay him 20 pounds, it was said that A could sue for and recover the stipulated salary, even though he never did any work. Likewise where *A* promised to sell a cow to *B*, and *B* promised to pay fifty shillings therefor, both promises being absolute in terms, it was held that *A* could sue for and recover the fifty shillings without showing that he had even so much as offered to deliver the cow. Presumably also *B* could sue for and recover the value of the cow without paying or offering to pay the fifty shillings. In other words, for the purpose of enforcement, the law treated the two promises in a bilateral contract like two separate and distinct unilateral contracts. It would seem to be clear that such a solution is absurd. It is part and parcel of the primitive notion that the language of a transaction must be enforced literally in all cases. Its absurdity becomes evident on the slightest reflection. In the first place, this solution may result in two lawsuits, when one ought to be sufficient to settle almost any controversy that is likely to arise in connection with such a transaction. In the second place, it takes no account of the essential nature and purpose of a bilateral contract.

When two parties enter into a bilateral contract, they exchange promises, it is true, and these promises are the consideration for each other and comprise the contract. However, it is not in the exchange of the promises that the parties are primarily interested. Their main interest is in the exchange of performances. The promises merely provide assurance that such and exchange of performances will occur. The primary aim of the legal rules which deal with this problem should be to bring about the contemplated exchange, and to do it in such a way as to reduce to a minimum the possibility that either party will get an unfair advantage. When this primary aim cannot be achieved, as frequently it cannot be, then an equitable adjustment should be striven for, under rules which prevent unnecessary litigation. The early law wholly ignored these objectives and proceeded entirely on the basis of the literal language of the contract. It overlooked the pertinent fact that the language in which the contract was expressed was not always, or even usually, chosen advisedly with reference to the contingencies that might arise during the course of performance.

In the course of time, the courts began to realize that their simple solution of the problem was not a sensible one. Not being willing, at first, to overrule the old cases outright, they nevertheless took a step forward in that they became astute in finding some word or phrase linking the two promises in the contract, which could, with some show of plausibility, be said to make the one performance expressly dependent upon the other. The language most commonly seized upon for this purpose was the word "for" and the phrase "in consideration of." If the one performance was, by the terms of the contract, said to be "for" or "in consideration of" the other, the court might hold that the one was an express condition of the other. Elaborate rules with many fine distinctions were developed for determining just when, in a given case, this language had the effect indicated.

Kingston v. Preston, [1773] 2 Doug. 689. It remained, however, for Lord Mansfield to take the first real step in the direction of putting the whole matter on a reasonably satisfactory basis. The case of *Kingston v. Preston* appears to be the first reported case in which a court held that performance of one promise in a bilateral contract might be *dependent* upon the performance of the other promise, even though there were no words in the contract which could be said to justify that result. Mansfield spoke of three kinds of covenants (promises):

1. Such as are called mutual and independent, where either party may recover damages from the other for the injury he may have received by a breach of the covenants in his favor, and where it is no excuse for the defendant to allege a breach of the covenants on the part of the plaintiff.

2. There are covenants which are conditions and dependent, in which the performance of one depends on the prior performance of another, and therefore, till this prior condition is performed, the other party is not liable to an action on his covenant.

3. There is also a third sort of covenants, which are mutual conditions to be performed at the same time; and in these, if one party was ready and offered to perform his part, and the other neglected or refused to perform his, he who was ready and offered has fulfilled his engagement, and may maintain an action for the default of the other though it is not certain that either is obliged to do the first act.

Restatement (Second) of Contracts § 231.

§ 231. Criterion for Determining When Performances Are to Be Exchanged Under an Exchange of Promises

Performances are to be exchanged under an exchange of promises if each promise is at least part of the consideration for the other and the performance of each promise is to be exchanged at least in part for the performance of the other.

BELL v. ELDER
Utah Court of Appeals
782 P.2d 545 (1989)

BULLOCK, J.

The Bells contracted in 1977 to purchase ten acres of undeveloped land from a partnership comprised of the defendants (Elders) for a total of $25,000. Part of the price was paid at closing, with the remainder to be paid later. The Bells were to convey legal title on receipt of payment in full.

The land sold was zoned for agricultural use at the time of the contract. The parties had hopes of developing the area more extensively than the zoning then permitted, but their hopes did not prove feasible. Property values in the area have generally declined since the contract was made.

[The contract required the sellers to furnish water and electrical power to the property by 1978, but if the buyer is unable to obtain a building permit by that time, the seller agreed to repay the purchase price within six months. The sellers did not perform this promise since the buyers had not obtained building permits. A supplemental agreement repeated the seller's promise to provide "culinary water" as well as electrical power but, again, the promise remained unperformed because the buyers did not obtain permits and had abandoned the idea of building on this land. They decided to live elsewhere. The sellers were ready, willing and able at all times to perform their promise.]

The Bells sued to rescind the contract and recover the amounts they had paid thereunder, arguing in essence that the Elders had breached it by failing to supply culinary water to the property as the contract required. However, the trial court saw no purpose in requiring installation of culinary water facilities to serve rather remote property not intended for residential use, and held that the Elders were required by the contract to be merely able to furnish water to the subject property and that they were required to actually furnish the water to the property only if the Bells had obtained a building permit and were about to construct a house, so that the water would be put to "beneficial use." The Bells argue that residential use of the property was not a condition precedent to the Elders' obligation to furnish culinary water.

We recognize that interpreting the contract to require that the Elders merely be able to furnish water falls short of requiring them to actually furnish water, and that the Bells did not contract only for the Elders' mere, inchoate ability to furnish water. Both the original agreement and the supplemental agreement contain express promises by the Elders to actually supply water to the Bells. However, although the contract contains a promise by the Elders to supply water, as well as a related promise by the Bells to obtain a building permit for the construction of a house to receive the water, no time is specified for performing either promise. The sequence in which those promises were to be performed is nevertheless the very essence of the present controversy. The situation at trial consisted of the Bells, on the one hand, seeking to rescind the contract on the grounds that the Elders had breached an obligation to actually furnish water to the property, and, on the other hand, the Elders insisting that they would supply the required water when the Bells demanded it and performed their obligations. The question thus presented boils down to the order in which these parties must perform their related obligations.

In determining the order of performance of exchanged promises, we look first to the contract itself, and, if no order of performance is therein specified, we apply the common law of constructive contractual conditions. This contract is silent on the time or times for actually furnishing water and for obtaining a building permit. In such a case, where there is no express indication of the intended order for performance, the law implies a covenant and condition that the related obligations be performed concurrently.[7]

Since performance of these obligations was due concurrently, neither party could claim a breach by the other until the party claiming the breach tendered performance of its concurrent obligation. The rule requiring such a tender has been explained in a case in which a real estate purchaser and seller each demanded and awaited performance by the other of their respective obligations to pay the price and deliver the property. The Supreme Court's words in that case apply here as well:

> This is precisely the sort of deadlock meant to be resolved by the requirement of tender. During the executory period of a contract whose time of performance is uncertain but which contemplates simultaneous performance by both parties, neither party can be said to be in default until the other party has tendered his own performance. In other words, the party who desires to use legal process to exercise his legal remedies under such a contract must make a tender of his own agreed performance in order to put the other party in default.

This case demonstrates that the rule requiring tender before claiming breach of a concurrent promise is not a mere formality or trap for the unwary. Here, the claimant's tender would demonstrate the continued practical vitality and purposefulness of the promise owed the claimant. Public policy and common sense oppose the waste of installing a culinary water line to serve land which, for all that appears, will remain unused. The rule requiring tender thus serves, among other purposes, to prevent a claimant from insisting upon a purposeless performance, or from avoiding his own obligations on pretext. *Affirmed.*

COMMENT: CONSTRUCTIVE CONDITIONS — CONCURRENT AND PRECEDENT

The principal case illustrates *concurrent* constructive conditions, i.e., where the performance can be exchanged simultaneously, neither party is required to perform before the other. If the contract had specified that one party must perform

---

[7] [13] RESTATEMENT (SECOND) OF CONTRACTS § 234; 3A A. CORBIN, CORBIN ON CONTRACTS 656 at 145–47 (1960); *see also* Rubin v. Fuchs, 1 Cal. 3d 50, 81 Cal. Rptr. 373, 459 P.2d 925 (1969).

before the duty of the other is activated, the first performance would be a constructive condition *precedent*. Absent such a manifestation of the parties' intention, a typical contract for the sale of land or goods involves concurrent conditions. Thus, to place the other party in default, either party may offer to perform or tender performance. Thus, in a contract for the sale of land at $50,000, the buyer would have to offer to perform or tender performance to place the seller in default, and the seller would have to offer to perform or tender the deed to place the buyer in default.[8]

How does a court determine whether the constructive condition is *precedent* or *concurrent?*

RESTATEMENT (SECOND) ON CONTRACTS § 234. *Order of Performances*

(1) Where all or part of the performances to be exchanged under an exchange of promises can be rendered simultaneously, they are to that extent due simultaneously, unless the language or the circumstances indicate the contrary.

(2) Except to the extent stated in Subsection (1), where the performance of only one party under such an exchange requires a period of time, his performance is due at an earlier time than that of the other party, unless the language or the circumstances indicate the contrary.

PROBLEMS

(1)   S agrees to sell land to B in exchange for $100,000, to be paid in five installments. When is B entitled to the deed from S?

(2)   Assume the same contract between S and B but the parties expressly agreed that the deed was to be delivered in escrow before any payments were made. How would you characterize the delivery of the deed in escrow? *See Ideal Family & Youth Ranch v. Whestline*, 655 P.2d 429 (Colo. Ct. App. 1982).

(3)   P agrees to paint O's house at a price of $15,000. On performance day, P knocks at O's door and demands payment before he paints. Analyze.

(4)   You enter into a contract to become an associate with a law firm at a monthly salary of $7,000. You arrive bright and early on your first day and request your salary for the first month. What result?

(5)   Windows, Inc. contracts to replace all seventeen windows in Jordan's house

---

[8] There is a difference between an "offer to perform" which would, in the case of the buyer, only require the buyer to offer to pay $50,000 while "tender of performance" would require the buyer to actually proffer performance by presenting $50,000 to the seller. The same distinction would apply to the seller's offering to convey or actually profferring the deed. *See* RESTATEMENT (SECOND) OF CONTRACTS § 238, *Effect on Other Party's Duties of a Failure to Offer Performance*: "Where all or part of the performances to be exchanged under an exchange of promises are due simultaneously, it is a condition of each party's duties to render such performance that the other party either render or, with manifested present ability to do so, offer performance of his part of the simultaneous exchange." Other sections of the RESTATEMENT (SECOND) OF CONTRACTS, however, require an actual tender (§§ 45 and 62) as does UCC § 2-507(1) which requires seller's *tender* of delivery of the goods to activate the buyer's duty to pay.

at a price of $4,000. The contract specifies that Jordan will pay $1000 as a down payment upon the signing of the contract and the balance when the windows are installed. Characterize the $1000 down payment, then characterize the completed installation of the last window and the duty to pay the balance of $3,000.

(6)   Where a construction contract requires the builder to receive a certificate of approval from a named architect before the builder receives any one of nine progress payments under the contract, characterize the architect's certificate of approval.

(7)   Suppose in the last problem the contract required the owner to furnish a payment bond before the contract was to commence its work. Characterize that requirement in terms of "conditions."

(8)   To perform its contract to construct a new school building, Kelly contracted with the Hackensack Brick Co. for the brick required for the entire project. The contract provided for the "furnishing and delivering and stacking on the job all the common hard brick required by the plans and specifications for the Englewood High School Building at $17 per thousand; brick to be delivered as required by [Kelly] and sufficient brick to be kept on the job so that we will always have approximately 50,000 brick stacked until the completion of the job." No time for payment was fixed in the writing. After delivering a normal load of brick, Hackensack sought payment and it was refused. Therefore, Hackensack refused to deliver more brick. Kelly brings an action for this failure of performance by Hackensack. What result?[9]

R.G. POPE CONSTRUCTION CO. v. GUARD RAIL OF ROANOKE, INC.

Virginia Supreme Court
244 S.E.2d 774 (1978)

[Plaintiffs (Pope Construction Co. and Pope Paving Co.) entered into a contract with the state of Virginia for the construction of a 6.5 mile section of U.S. Route 58. The following month, Pope signed a contract with defendant which agreed to furnish and install a steel guardrail in connection with the project. The prime contract expressly stated that all work on the project was to be completed by October 1, 1973. The documents stated that time is an essential element of the contract and it is important that the work be completed within the specified time. Extensions of time could be granted by the Virginia Highway Department when a delay due to unforeseen causes beyond the control of the Contractor occurred. The subcontract with defendant required the defendant to furnish all necessary labor, materials and equipment to complete the erection of guardrail. Defendant acknowledged that it had examined all the contract documents and was, therefore, well aware of the completion date of October 1, 1973. To ascertain compliance with its obligations, defendant contracted with a supplier of guardrail components (Syro)

---

[9] UCC § 2-307: "Unless otherwise agreed all goods called for by a contract for sale must be tendered in a single delivery and payment is due only on such tender but where the circumstances give either party the right to make or demand delivery in lots, the price if it can be apportioned may be demanded for each lot."

and that contract was based on a "locked in" price provided delivery of the materials took place anytime from August of 1973 to "early November" of that year. Pope was delayed in the performance of its obligations so that the site was not ready for erection of the guardrail until July, 1974. Defendant had notified Pope in April of 1974 that the price it had quoted for the materials was subject to a "locked in" price with the defendant's supplier and that price was no longer available, particularly because of a steel shortage which was occurring at that time. Thus, defendant sought renegotiation of the contract concerning the price of material. Pope responded to the effect that installation of the guardrail could occur during May, 1974, and Pope expected defendant to fulfill the terms of the contract. Defendant refused to perform and Pope obtained another subcontractor to install the guardrail. Pope brought this action against defendant for the additional amount it had to pay the substituted subcontractor, $132,071.90. Defendant counterclaimed alleging lost profits in the amount of $13,183.01.]

Compton, J.

We hold that under these facts there was a material failure of performance by Pope which operated to discharge Guard Rail's duty to itself perform. Here, the defendant's performance of the duty to install guardrail was subject to certain conditions, the most important of which was the implied condition that a site would be available for such installation. The performance of Guard Rail's duty, subject to such conditions, did not become due unless the conditions occurred, or unless their nonoccurrence was excused. In this case such conditions, culminating in the requirement for availability of a site upon which to erect the guardrail, did not occur at a time when Guard Rail was able to perform nor was such nonoccurrence of the conditions excused, as we shall demonstrate. In fact, Pope actually unjustifiably prevented Guard Rail from performing its contract by conduct which caused the delay in completion of the project, rendering Pope liable to Guard Rail for damages.

As the defendants contend, among the conditions precedent to Guard Rail's obligation to perform was the express duty upon Pope, according to the prime contract incorporated into the subcontract, to conduct the work "in such a manner and with sufficient materials, equipment and labor as are necessary to insure its completion in accordance with the plans and specifications within the time limit set forth in the contract." This gave rise to the implied duty upon Pope to do everything which was reasonably necessary to enable Guard Rail to perform within the time agreed. These general requirements gave rise to a significant implied duty upon Pope to provide a work site upon which Guard Rail could perform its promises according to the terms of the subcontract.

The evidence is without conflict that these conditions did not occur; the site was not ready for timely erection of the rail by October 1, 1973, the original contract completion date; it was not ready by November 5, 1973, the later-extended date; and it was not ready by May of 1974, the time when Pope called upon defendant to perform. There was no place ready to erect the guardrail until July 1974, according to all the evidence.

The main issue in the case then becomes: Was the nonoccurrence of these conditions excused? We think not. . . . The contract provided that if the Highway

Department "determines that the work was delayed because of conditions *beyond the control of and without the fault of the Contractor*, [it] may extend the time for completion as the conditions justify." The Department's Resident Engineer, whose duties included direct supervision of the construction of this project, testified, reciting specifics, that he could find no basis for recommending to the Department that even a one-day extension be granted to Pope.

In sum, we believe that the plaintiffs' evidence, as a matter of law, utterly fails to show that any of the 266-day delay, which continued beyond the extended completion date of November 5, 1973 and for which the Highway Department assessed liquidated damages, was excusable. Thus, under these facts, and considering the early 1974 unavailability of steel and the concomitant significant price increase, Guard Rail was fully justified in April of 1974 in refusing to perform its subcontract because of Pope's uncured material failure to render its performance due at an earlier date.

In conclusion, we will comment upon plaintiffs' claim that Guard Rail should have stockpiled the material and their claims that, in effect, Guard Rail otherwise should have taken some positive action to extricate Pope from its difficulties either by notices to Pope or efforts to extend the Syro contract. These contentions are all without merit. As to the storing issue, the contract did not require stockpiling of guardrail; it merely permitted it, and then only upon written request of the prime contractor. There was no evidence that Pope sought permission from the Highway Department to stockpile the guardrail nor did Pope ever notify Guard Rail that it desired the rail stored on the site. Furthermore, Syro's representative testified that it had not been the custom of contractors or subcontractors on highway jobs such as the one under consideration to stockpile guardrail. He stated that when stored on the project site, the steel tends to deteriorate rapidly when packaged in bundles in that it oxidizes, causing "white rust" to develop. Such condition furnishes grounds for rejection of the material by highway inspectors.

Accordingly, the plaintiffs' breach of contract action must fail and, because Pope prevented Guard Rail's performance of the contract, defendant's counterclaim must succeed. *Affirmed.*

NOTE

[T]he "constructive condition of cooperation" . . . obligates each party to do what is necessary to enable the other to perform. . . . Even in the absence of an express duty to cooperate, the law implies an agreement between the parties of any contract to 'do and perform those things that according to reason and justice they should to in order to carry out the purpose for which the contract was made, and to refrain from doing anything which will destroy or injure the other party's right to receive the fruits of the contract.' " *Florida East Coast Railway Co. v. United States*, 1980 U.S. Ct. Cl. LEXIS 952 (Feb. 5, 1980) (quoting *Flour Mills of America, Inc. v. United States*, 72 F. Supp. 603, 607 (Ct. Cl. 1947)). *See also Kehm Corp. v. United States*, 93 F. Supp. 620, 623 (Ct. Cl. 1950). *Quaere:* is the "constructive condition of cooperation" which is found in these Court of Claims cases a species of the generic requirement of "good faith" discussed earlier?

B. DIVISIBLE (SEVERABLE) VERSUS ENTIRE CONTRACTS

THUNDERSTIK LODGE, INC. v. REUER
South Dakota Supreme Court
613 N.W.2d 44 (2000)

KONEMKAMP, J.

This case presents the question whether a land lease agreement violated our statutory prohibition against agricultural leases of longer than twenty years. Thunderstik Lodge, Inc. leased agricultural land from the Reuers for hunting purposes, under an agreement providing for an initial ten-year lease, with two ten-year renewal options:

> The term of this lease shall run from March 1, 1988 to February 29, 1998 (original term), both dates inclusive. The Lessor and Lessee agree that this lease may be extended for two (2) additional ten (10) year terms, the first extension term to run from March 1, 1998 to February 29, 2008, the second extension term to run from March 1, 2008 to February 29, 2018, all upon the same terms and conditions set forth in this lease, except that the annual rent for the premises shall be increased to Thirty-three Thousand Dollars ($33,00000) for the first extension term and Thirty-six Thousand Dollars ($36,000.00) for the second extension term.

> If any portion of this lease is held to be invalid or unenforceable, the remainder of this lease shall not be affected thereby and such remainder shall be valid and enforced to the fullest extent permitted by law.

The controversy now before us arose from the Reuers' claim that the provisions of the contract create a thirty-year lease, void under South Dakota law. In a declaratory action, the circuit court ruled that the second of the two ten-year options was invalid, but severable, leaving the remainder of the lease intact and enforceable. The Reuers now appeal, contending severance of the contract was improper. The trial court found that the second ten-year lease option was an agreement separate from both the original lease term and the first ten-year option now in effect. It also found that the second ten-year option could be severed from the rest of the lease without voiding the remaining agreement. The Reuers assert that the lease violates SDCL 43-32-2: "No lease or grant of agricultural land for a longer period than twenty years, in which shall be reserved any rent or service of any kind, shall be valid."

Under South Dakota law, certain contracts are divisible: "Where a contract has several distinct objects, one or more of which are lawful and one or more of which are unlawful in whole or in part, the contract is void as to the latter and valid as to the rest." In *Commercial Trust and Sav. Bank v. Christensen*, 535 N.W.2d 853 (S.D. 1995), we set forth the requirements of a severable agreement: "(1) the parties' performances must be separable into corresponding pairs of part performances and (2) the parts of each pair must be regarded as agreed equivalents." RESTATEMENT (SECOND) OF CONTRACTS, § 183. Looking at the requirements for a severable agreement, as stated in *Christensen*, first, the obligations of the parties here can be separated into "corresponding pairs of part performances." "[A] distinguishing mark of a divisible contract is that the consideration is not single, but can be apportioned to correspond with separate consideration offered by the other party." [T]he agreement here contains distinct consideration for each ten-year option. There was a separate annual rent set for each of the two corresponding extension terms: $33,000 for the first extension, and $36,000 for the second extension.

[E]ach pair must be an agreed equivalent. "This means that the parts of the pair must be of roughly equivalent value. . . ." Farnsworth on Contracts, § 5.8, at 382–83. The Reuers do not dispute that the amounts to be paid by Thunderstik in exchange for the lease of the land are agreed equivalents, nor do we find otherwise. The terms of the options were negotiated between the parties, and while the precise value of the land lease may be debatable, the amount in the contract was of "roughly equivalent value."

Finally, the lease agreement specifically states that should part of the contract be invalid, the rest "shall" remain in effect. This express provision that an unenforceable portion may be severed from the agreement supports our conclusion. We hold that the second ten-year renewal period may be severed from the agreement, and that the original lease period, as well as the first ten-year renewal period, do not violate our prohibition against leases of agricultural land for longer than twenty years. Affirmed.

NOTES

(1) The court cites as authority the RESTATEMENT (SECOND) OF CONTRACTS § 183:

> If the parties' performance can be apportioned into corresponding pairs of part performances so that the parts of each pair are properly regarded as agreed equivalents and one pair is not offensive to public policy, that portion of the agreement is enforceable by a party who did not engage in serious misconduct.

(2) In *John v. United Advertising, Inc.*, 439 P.2d 53 (1968), the defendant agreed to construct, install and maintain seven outdoor display signs advertising the plaintiff's motels for which the plaintiff agreed to pay a total of $95 per month over a three-year term. The contract specified that the price for one large sign was $35 per month while the price for each of the other signs as $10 per month. Five of the signs were erected and maintained in compliance with the contract. Sign number 4 was never erected and sign 5 was erected in the wrong location. The trial court held that the contract was divisible and the defendant's failure to erect signs 4 and 5 constituted only severable breaches. The appellate court stated: "[W]hether a number of promises constitute one contract, or more than one, is to be determined by inquiring whether the parties assented to all the promises as a single whole, so that there would have been no bargain whatever, if any promise or set of promises were struck out."

The court recognized that the money due under the contract was not a lump sum for the seven signs but was apportioned as so much per individual sign. Moreover, the defendant's monthly billings were on a "so much per sign" basis. Holding that reasonable persons could differ as to the proper inferences to be drawn from the evidence, the court found that there was evidence to support the trial court's determination that the promises were divisible or severable, particularly since that determination is a mixed question of law and fact.

(3)   In *Pennsylvania Exch. Bank v. United States*, 170 F. Supp. 629 (Ct. Cl. 1959), the Army Signal Corps contracted with the Lerner Company to be ready to produce certain materials that would be required in the event of national emergency. The contract was divided into "performance steps": Step 1 required Lerner to secure information about the materials and plan for their volume production. Step 2 required Lerner to accomplish all production processes short of procuring the tooling and raw materials necessary for production. Step 3 required the acquisition of all tooling and manufacturing aids to meet the production schedule. Each of these three steps were in preparation for Step 4, to be taken only in the event of national emergency. Lerner completed Steps 1 through 3 for which the government paid Lerner more than $92,000. Lerner then declared bankruptcy and would not be able to perform Step 4. The court held that the contract was not severable since the first three steps were merely incidental to Step 4, the ultimate objective. The government would not have agreed to pay an apportioned amount for any of the steps leading to Step 4. Since the contract was entire, and the ultimate purpose was thwarted, and Lerner breach the entire contract.

(4)   The RESTATEMENT (SECOND) OF CONTRACTS § 240 is entitled "Part Performance As Agreed Equivalents":

> If the performances to be exchanged under an exchange of promises can be apportioned into corresponding pairs of part performances so that the parts of each pair are properly regarded as agreed equivalents, a party's performance of his part of such pair has the same effect on the other's duties to render performance of the agreed equivalent as it would have if only that pair of performances had been promised.

Major building contracts typically provide for "progress payments" to be made as the building progresses since builders require such payments for labor and materials. The question is whether such payments are made in exchange for their agreed equivalents. Illustration 7 to § 240 suggests that such progress payments are typically not agreed equivalents since the injured party may not make full use of a part of a building without the remaining parts. A progress payment is typically not intended to be the agreed equivalent of a portion of a builder's work such as clearing a building site.

C.   UCC — INSTALLMENT CONTRACTS

Section 2-612 (1) of the Uniform Commercial Code defines an "installment contract" as one that requires or authorizes delivery of goods in separate lots to be separately accepted "even though the contract contains a clause 'each delivery is a separate contract' or its equivalent." Comment 2 states in part, "A provision for separate payment for each lot delivered ordinarily means that the price is at least roughly calculable by units of quantity, but such provision is not essential to an 'installment contract.' If separate acceptance of separate deliveries is contemplated, no generalized contrast between wholly 'entire' and wholly 'divisible' contract has any standing under this Article." Absent contrary agreement, UCC Section 2-307 requires a single delivery of goods ordered, but "where the circumstances give either party the right to make or demand delivery in lots the price if it can be apportioned may be demanded for each lot."

D. BREACH

[1] Materiality of Breach

[a] Restatement (First) of Contracts

WALKER & CO. v. HARRISON
Michigan Supreme Court
81 N.W.2d 352 (1957)

SMITH, J.

[The contract required the lessor (Walker) to construct and install a neon sign, 18'9" high and 8'8" wide with an electric clock and flashing lamps for the lessee's dry cleaning business. The lessee agreed to make 36 monthly rental payments of $148.50. Lessor agreed to maintain and service the sign, including cleaning and repainting. At the expiration of 36 months, title to the sign was to revert to the lessee. The first monthly payment was made. This first payment was also the last. Shortly after the sign was installed, someone hit it with a tomato. Rust, also, was visible on the chrome, complained defendants, and in its corners were "little spider cobwebs." In addition, there were "some children's sayings written down in here." Defendant Harrison called Walker to clean the sign but Walker failed to clean it. Harrison called again and again. "I was getting, you might say, sorer and sorer. . . . Occasionally, when I started calling up, I would walk around where the tomato was and get mad again. Then I would call up on the phone again." Finally, plaintiff not having responded to his repeated calls, he telegraphed Walker that:

> YOU HAVE CONTINUALLY VOIDED OUR RENTAL CONTRACT BY NOT MAINTAINING SIGNS AS AGREED AS WE NO LONGER HAVE A CONTRACT WITH YOU DO NOT EXPECT ANY FURTHER REMU-NERATION.

Walker replied by reminding Harrison that one monthly payment was already overdue and calling attention to a paragraph in the lease which allows the lessor to accelerate all 36 payments to make the entire balance due if the lessee fails to make monthly payments. The reply also cautioned Harrison that, absent receipt of monthly payments, it would place the matter in the hands of Walker's attorney. No additional payments were made and Walker sued for the entire balance due under the contract, $5,197.50. Defendants filed answer asserting that plaintiff's failure to perform certain maintenance services constituted a prior material breach of the agreement, thus justifying their repudiation of the contract and grounding their claim for damages. The case was tried to the court without a jury and resulted in a judgment for the plaintiff, Walker. The case is before us on a general appeal.]

Defendants urge upon us again and again, in various forms, the proposition that Walker's failure to service the sign, in response to repeated requests, constituted a material breach of the contract and justified repudiation by them. Their legal proposition is undoubtedly correct. Repudiation is one of the weapons available to an injured party in event the other contractor has committed a material breach. But the injured party's determination that there has been a material breach, justifying his own repudiation, is fraught with peril, for should such determination, as viewed by a later court in the calm of its contemplation, be unwarranted, the repudiator himself will have been guilty of material breach and himself have become the aggressor, not an innocent victim.

What is our criterion for determining whether or not a breach of contract is so fatal to the undertaking of the parties that it is to be classed as "material"? There is no single touchstone. Many factors are involved. They are well stated in 1 RESTATEMENT, CONTRACTS, § 275, in the following terms:

> In determining the materiality of a failure fully to perform a promise the following circumstances are influential:
>
> (a) The extent to which the injured party will obtain the substantial benefit which he could have reasonably anticipated;
>
> (b) The extent to which the injured party may be adequately compensated in damages for lack of complete performance;
>
> (c) The extent to which the party failing to perform has already partly performed or made preparations for performance;
>
> (d) The greater or less hardship on the party failing to perform in terminating the contract;
>
> (e) The willful, negligent or innocent behavior of the party failing to perform;
>
> (f) The greater or less uncertainty that the party failing to perform will perform the remainder of the contract.

Granting that Walker's delay (about a week after defendant Herbert Harrison sent his telegram of repudiation Walker sent out a crew and took care of things) in rendering the service requested was irritating, we are constrained to agree with the trial court that it was not of such materiality as to justify repudiation of the contract, and we are particularly mindful of the lack of preponderant evidence contrary to his determination. The trial court, on this phase of the case, held as follows:

> Now Mr. Harrison phoned in, so he testified, a number of times. He isn't sure of the dates but he sets the first call at about the 7th of August and he complained then of the tomato and of some rust and some cobwebs. The tomato, according to the testimony, was up on the clock; that would be outside of his reach, without a stepladder or something. The cobwebs are within easy reach of Mr. Harrison and so would the rust be. I think that Mr. Bueche's argument that these were not materially a breach would clearly be true as to the cobwebs and I really can't believe in the face of all the

testimony that there was a great deal of rust 7 days after the installation of this sign. And that really brings it down to the tomato. And, of course, when a tomato has been splashed all over your clock, you don't like it. But he says he kept calling their attention to it, although the rain probably washed some of the tomato off. But the stain remained, and they didn't come. I really can't find that that was such a material breach of the contract as to justify rescission. I really don't think so.

Nor, we conclude, do we. There was no valid ground for defendants' repudiation and their failure thereafter to comply with the terms of the contract was itself a material breach, entitling Walker, upon this record, to judgment. Affirmed.

[b]   Restatement (Second) of Contracts

ASSOCIATED BUILDERS, INC. v. COGGINS
Maine Supreme Judicial Court
722 A.2d 1278 (1999)

DANA, J.

Associated Builders, Inc. appeals from a grant of a summary judgment in favor of the defendants William M. Coggins and Benjamin W. Coggins, d/b/a Ben & Bill's Chocolate Emporium. Associated provided labor and materials to the Cogginses to complete a structure on Main Street in Bar Harbor. After a dispute arose regarding compensation, Associated and the Cogginses executed an agreement stating that there existed an outstanding balance of $770,005.54 [sic] and setting forth the following terms of repayment:

> It is agreed that, two payments will be made by [the Cogginses] to [Associated] as follows: Twenty Five Thousand Dollars ($25,000.00) on or before June 1, 1996 and Twenty Five Thousand Dollars ($25,000.00) on or before June 1, 1997. No interest will be charged or paid providing payments are made as agreed. If the payments are not made as agreed then interest shall accrue at 10% [] per annum figured from the date of default. There will be no prepayment penalties applied. It is further agreed that Associated Builders will forfeit the balance of Twenty Thousand and Five Dollars and Fifty Four Cents ($20,005.54) providing the above payments are made as agreed.

The Cogginses made their first payment in accordance with the agreement. The second payment, however, was delivered three days late on June 4, 1997. Claiming a breach of the contract, Associated filed a complaint demanding the balance of $20,005.54, plus interest and cost. The Cogginses answered the complaint raising the affirmative defense of an accord and satisfaction and waiver. Both parties moved for a summary judgment. The court granted the Cogginses' motion and Associated appealed.

"An accord 'is a contract under which an obligee promises to accept a substituted performance in future satisfaction of the obligor's duty.' " *E.S. Herrick Co. v. Maine Wild Blueberry Co.*, 670 A.2d 944, 946 (Me. 1996) (quoting *Stultz Elec. Works v.*

Marine Hydraulic Eng'g Co., 484 A.2d 1008, 1011 (Me. 1984)). Settlement of a disputed claim is sufficient consideration for an accord and satisfaction. 670 A.2d at 947. Here, the court correctly found the June 15, 1995 agreement to be an accord.

Satisfaction is the execution or performance of the accord. *See* RESTATEMENT (SECOND) ON CONTRACTS § 281(1) (1981). If the obligor breaches the accord, the obligee may enforce either the original duty or any duty pursuant to the accord. *See id.* § 281(2) (1981); *see also* ARTHUR L. CORBIN, 6 CORBIN ON CONTRACTS § 1271, at 93-94 (1961). The obligor's breach of the accord, however, must be material. *See Zenith Drilling Corp. v. Internorth, Inc.*, 869 F.2d 560, 563-64 (10th Cir. 1989) (applying Oklahoma law); *A.E. Giroux, Inc. v. Contract Servs. Assocs.*, 99 Mich. App. 669, 299 N.W.2d 20, 20-21 (Mich. App. Ct. 1980). The question before the court, therefore, was whether the Cogginses' late payment constituted a material breach of the accord. The court found that it was not.

We apply traditional contract principles to determine if a party has committed a material breach. A material breach "is a nonperformance of a duty that is so material and important as to justify the injured party in regarding the whole transaction as at an end." *Id.* (quoting ARTHUR L. CORBIN, 4 CORBIN ON CONTRACTS § 946, at 809 (1951)); *see* RESTATEMENT (SECOND) ON CONTRACTS § 241 (1981).[10]"Time of performance is merely one element in determining whether a defective or incomplete or belated performance is substantial [performance]." ARTHUR L. CORBIN, 3A CORBIN ON CONTRACTS § 713, at 355 (1960). Applying these principles, courts have found that a slight delay of payment that causes no detriment or prejudice to the obligee is not a material breach. *See, e.g., Jenkins v. U.S.A. Foods. Inc.*, 912 F. Supp. 969, 974 (E.D. Mich. 1996) (applying Michigan law) (contract payment made two days after expiration of grace period not a material breach where payee suffers little or no prejudice); *Edward Waters College, Inc. v. Johnson*, 707 So. 2d 801, 802 (Fla. Dist. Ct. App. 1998) (one day delay in paying settlement agreement not a material breach where agreement did not state that time is of the essence and payee incurred no hardship because of delay); *A.E. Giroux, Inc.*, 299 N.W.2d at 20–21 (accord satisfied by one-day delay of payment where no material damage to obligee and payment amounted to substantial performance).

We discern no error in the Superior Court's finding that the Cogginses' payment to Associated after a three-day delay was not a material breach and, therefore, satisfied the June 15, 1995 accord. *See A.E. Giroux, Inc.*, 299 N.W.2d at 20-21. By receiving the second and final payment of $25,000, Associated was not deprived of the benefit that it reasonably expected. *See* RESTATEMENT (SECOND) OF CONTRACTS

---

[10] [1] [In determining whether a failure to render or offer performance is material, the following circumstances are significant:]

    (a)   the extent to which the injured party will be deprived of the benefit which he reasonably expected

    (b)   the extent to which the injured party can be adequately compensated for the part of the benefit of which he will be deprived;

    (c)   the extent to which the party failing to perform . . . will suffer forfeiture;

    (d)   the likelihood that the party failing to perform . . . will cure his failure. . . ;

    (e)   the extent to which the behavior of the party failing to perform or to offer to perform comports with standards of good faith and fair dealing.

RESTATEMENT (SECOND) ON CONTRACTS § 241 (1981).

§ 241(a) (1981). Moreover, Associated has not alleged any prejudice from this three-day delay. Further, the Cogginses' late payment was not made in bad faith. *See* RESTATEMENT (SECOND) OF CONTRACTS § 241 cmt. f (1981) ("The extent to which the behavior of the party failing to perform or to offer to perform comports with standards of good faith and fair dealing is . . . a significant circumstance in determining whether the failure is material."); *cf. Zenith Drilling Corp.*, 869 F.2d at 563-64 (material breach of accord when party withheld payment to force other party to renegotiate agreement). Finally, neither the purpose of the June 15, 1995 accord nor the language of the accord suggests that time was of the essence. *See Baybutt v. Constr. Corp. v. Commercial Union Ins. Co.*, 455 A.2d 914, 919 (Me. 1983) (court must "give effect to the intention of the parties as gathered from the language of the agreement viewed in the light of all the circumstances under which it was made."). Because the late payment was not a material breach of the June 15, 1995 accord, the Cogginses have complied with the June 15, 1995 agreement relieving them of further liability to Associated.

Even if the breach was material and Associated could have enforced the forfeiture, Associated waived that right when it accepted the late payment. A waiver is a voluntary or intentional relinquishment of a known right. *See Kirkham v. Hansen*, 583 A.2d 1026, 1027 (Me. 1990) (*citing Interstate Indus. Unif. Rental Serv., Inc. v. Couri Pontiac, Inc.*, 355 A.2d 913, 919 (Me. 1976)). If a party in knowing possession of a right does something inconsistent with the right or that party's intention to rely on it, the party is deemed to have waived that right. *See id.* A party waives a contractual right arising from a breach because of a late payment when that party accepts tender of the late payment. *See Northeast Ins. Co. v. Concord Gen. Mutual Ins. Co.*, 461 A.2d 1056, 1058 (Me. 1983) (insurer waives right to consider policy terminated or canceled for lack of payment if it accepts late payment); *Savings & Loan Ass'n. v. Tear*, 435 A.2d 1083, 1085 (Me. 1981) (mortgagee waives right to foreclose if it accepts late payment). Here, because Associated accepted the final $25,000 payment, it waived its right to enforce the forfeiture. Judgment *affirmed*.

COMMENT: COMPARING THE TWO RESTATEMENTS

In *Frazier v. Mellowitz*, 804 N.E.2d 796, 802 (Ind. Ct. App. 2004), the court quotes from an earlier edition of *Murray on Contracts* in noting the differences between the First and Second Restatements of Contract. The following excerpt is found in a later edition of *Murray on Contracts:*

> It is abundantly clear that the determination of whether a breach is material is not susceptible to mechanical rules. The *guidelines* found in RESTATEMENT (FIRST) OF CONTRACTS § 275, as quoted by the court in the *Walker* case, are characterized as six "influential circumstances." The similar list of five guidelines in RESTATEMENT (SECOND) OF CONTRACTS § 241 as listed in *Associated Builders* are called "significant circumstances." The similarity between the two RESTATEMENTS, however, should not conceal a major difference in approach.

The FIRST RESTATEMENT sets forth the six "influential circumstances" to expose "the inherent justice of the matter" in answering the basic question, "Will it be more conformable to justice in the particular case to free the injured party, or, on the other hand, to require her to perform her promise, in both cases giving her a right of action if the failure to perform was wrongful?" RESTATEMENT (FIRST) OF CONTRACTS § 275, comment a.

The SECOND RESTATEMENT approaches the problem in a significantly different fashion. It emphasizes the nature of contractual duties as constructive conditions to the duties of the other party. The duties of one party under a contract are constructively conditioned upon the *lack* of any *uncured* material failure of performance by the other party. RESTATEMENT (SECOND) OF CONTRACTS § 237. Where a breach is material, the RESTATEMENT (SECOND) views the breaching party's duty as a constructive condition which has not occurred. The nonoccurrence of that condition will prevent the activation of the innocent party's duty, at least temporarily, or it will discharge that duty when the constructive condition can no longer occur. The important difference in the SECOND RESTATEMENT treatment of material breach is that it does not simply distinguish between material and immaterial breaches. While it clings to the material/immaterial distinction of the FIRST RESTATEMENT in terms of the guidelines, it treats a material breach as the nonoccurrence of a condition,[11] and it makes a further distinction between *material* breaches, i.e., there are material breaches which can be *cured* and material breaches which cannot or can no longer be *cured*. The concept of *cure* is borrowed from the Uniform Commercial Code, which permits a seller of goods that have been rejected by the purchaser to notify the buyer of the seller's intention to cure or remedy the nonconformity in the goods and then to make a conforming tender if time for performance remains under the contract.[12]

Thus, the RESTATEMENT (SECOND) suggests that, where there is a material breach, there is a constructive condition to the innocent party's duty to perform that has not occurred. If, however, time remains for that condition to occur, i.e., the breaching party can still perform in a relatively timely fashion, the innocent party may not treat the failure of performance (or nonoccurrence of the constructive condition) as a cancellation of the innocent party's duties.[13] Where the breach may be cured, the duties of the innocent party are merely *suspended* because the breaching party may perform in time to *cure* the material breach.[14]

---

[11] An immaterial breach is *not* viewed as the nonoccurrence of a condition because the injured party may not suspend, much less terminate, his performance in response to such a breach.

[12] UCC § 2-508. A simple illustration suggests the reasonableness of this provision. If X agrees to supply certain goods to Y by the 30th day of the month and X delivers nonconforming goods on the 15th of the month, if X notifies Y that he will cure the defects so that Y will have perfect goods by the 30th of the month and X does so, Y has received timely delivery of exactly what he ordered. Section 2-508(2) will permit a time for cure beyond the original time for performance if the seller had "reasonable grounds to believe" that his performance would be acceptable notwithstanding certain nonconformities. Such "reasonable grounds to believe" are typically based on prior course of dealing or trade usage.

[13] The UCC defines "cancellation" as either party putting an end to the contract for breach by the other. UCC § 2-106(4). "Termination" is defined in the Code as either party putting an end to the contract pursuant to a *power* conferred upon either party by the contract itself. UCC § 2-106(3).

[14] The RESTATEMENT (SECOND) OF CONTRACTS suggests a number of inquiries with respect to the application of "cure" which are highly reminiscent of the general guidelines for determining whether a breach is material: (1) To what extent has the reasonable expectation of the injured party already been secured? (2) Does the injured party have security to assure performance by the defaulting party? (3) Did

Both RESTATEMENTS deal with *delay* in performance in terms of its materiality in adjacent sections. Section 276 of the FIRST RESTATEMENT lists five "circumstances" to aid courts in determining whether a delay in performance was material.[15] The adjacent RESTATEMENT (SECOND) section dealing with delay in performance, Section 242, directs courts to consider the five guidelines in 241 plus two more.[16] Though the court in *Associated Builders* was content to rely upon the five guidelines in 241 without resort to 242 though the issue involved a delay in performance, the SECOND RESTATEMENT section on delay is particularly important as a guide to the length of time that must expire before the injured party may treat the other party's breach as one that cannot be cured, thereby allowing the innocent party to treat the breach as discharging his duties. An illustration focuses this analysis.

A building contract traditionally requires *progress payments*, i.e., payments made by the owner to the contractor during the building process to facilitate the contractor's ability to pay for the labor and materials needed to continue the construction. Thus, where an owner failed to make a progress payment when due, this was often considered a material failure of performance because it may have prevented the contractor from continuing performance through payments to subcontractors, material suppliers and the like. If, however, the progress payment was delayed for only a short time, the contractor would not be justified in *abandoning* the work. It would be justified in *suspending* performance for a time sufficient to allow the owner to *cure* the failure of the constructive condition. Once the time for *cure* ends, however, the contractor may treat its duties as discharged because the failure to make the progress payment would constitute an material breach that could no longer be cured. The determination of the *time for cure* is to be made in accordance with the RESTATEMENT 2d material breach guidelines supplemented by a consideration of the extent to which delay may prevent or hinder the innocent party in making reasonable substitute arrangements and the extent to

---

the breaching party submit any assurances that the breach would be cured? (4) Has the market changed so as to make the contract more favorable to the defaulting party? (5) Has the other party breached other contracts or other installments of the contract in question? (6) What is the financial situation or other condition of the breaching party in relation to his ability to cure? RESTATEMENT (SECOND) OF CONTRACTS § 241, comment e.

[15] In general, absent an agreement by the parties that failure to perform on a given day is of "vital importance," failure to perform on that day normally does not discharge the duty of the other party. Second, in mercantile contracts, timely performance is important, but a material breach will not be found unless the delay is "considerable" in light of the nature of the transaction and the seriousness of the consequences. Third, if a party delays before rendering *any* performance, less delay is necessary to constitute a material breach than if the delaying party had begun to perform.

Fourth, more delay is necessary for a material breach in land contracts versus contracts for the sale of goods. Fifth, where the suit is for specific performance in a contract for the sale of land, "considerable delay in tendering performance does not preclude enforcement of the contract" where the delay can be compensated, unless the contract states that timely performance is essential or the circumstances indicate that enforcement will be unjust.

[16] (b) the extent to which it reasonably appears to the injured party that delay may prevent or hinder him in making reasonable substitute arrangements; (c) the extent to which the agreement provides for performance without delay, but a material failure to perform or to offer to perform on a stated day does not of itself discharge the other party's remaining duties unless the circumstances, including the language of the agreement, indicate that performance of an offer to perform by that day is important.

which the agreement, itself, specified performance without delay.[17] *See* Murray on Contracts at § 108.

[2] Substantial Performance and Material Breach

If a party to a bilateral contract has partially failed to perform his own undertaking in the required order or has been guilty of delay in performance, may he recover on the contract? Our law could have taken either of the following polar positions in answering this question: (1) One who is in default should never be permitted to insist upon performance by the other. (2) In view of the liberality with which modern law permits the use of recoupment, setoff and counterclaim, it is arguable that a defect in performance, no matter how significant, should never prevent an action on the contract by the defaulting plaintiff, but should only furnish a basis for the recouping of the loss suffered by the plaintiff's default in performance. If the first position had been taken, great injustices might have resulted since slight defects in performance would have prevented a recovery by the defaulting party; and forfeitures, which our law traditionally abhors, would have been suffered. As to solution (2), if the default is serious enough, to permit a recovery would have been to allow the transgressor the benefit of the bargain. Neither polar solution has been adopted.

As we have seen, Lord Mansfield originated the modern concept of constructive conditions in *Kingston v. Preston, supra,* which was essential, *inter alia,* to avoid multiplicity of actions. The application of that doctrine to cases involving a slight failure of performance on the part of the plaintiff, however, would preclude a recovery. Thus, four years after *Kingston v. Preston,* Mansfield seized the opportunity to announce what might be called a mitigating doctrine in *Boone v. Eyre,* 1 H. Bl. 273, n. (1777). The purchaser of a plantation and the slaves thereon had received a conveyance upon making a down payment. The title to some of the slaves failed and Mansfield held that the purchaser was not relieved from his promised duty to pay. "The distinction is very clear, where mutual covenants go to the whole of the consideration on both sides, they are mutual conditions, the one precedent to the other. But where they go only to a part, where a breach may be paid for in damages, there the defendant has a remedy on his covenant, and shall not plead it as a condition precedent." This statement was later amplified by Pollock, C.B., in *Ellen v. Topp,* 7 Ex. 424 (1851), wherein he said, "It cannot be intended to apply to every case in which a covenant by the plaintiff forms only a part of the consideration, and the residue of the consideration has been had by the defendant. That residue must be the substantial part of the contract." *See also*

---

[17] Restatement (Second) of Contracts § 242. If the parties clearly indicate that "time is of the essence" and there is little question that this was the intention of the parties, failure to perform on time will amount to a material breach, § 242(c), comment d. There is no suspension of performance in such a situation because there is no possibility of curing the breach. It is, however, important to emphasize the critical determination of the intention of the parties. If the document evidencing the contract is a printed form containing a standardized "time is of the essence" clause, it should not necessarily be interpreted as manifesting the intention of the parties. See Pederson v. McGuire, 333 N.W.2d 823 (S.D. 1983), where the court suggests that whether time is of the essence depends upon the intention of the parties and the purpose of the contract rather than a printed clause in the contract. *See* Restatement (Second) of Contracts § 242(c), illustration 9.

Giumarra v. Harrington Heights, Inc., 109 A.2d 695 (N.J. Super. 1954). Thus, our law has taken a middle position: if the failure to perform or delay in performing is so material that it will or may result in the other party not getting substantially what he bargained for, the latter is excused from his promised duty. If the failure or delay is not of that character, the other party continues under a duty and he must recoup his loss because of the breach, through one of the procedural devices for that purpose.

JACOB & YOUNGS, INC. v. KENT
New York Court of Appeals
129 N.E. 889 (1921)

CARDOZO, J.

The plaintiff built a country residence for the defendant at a cost of upwards of $77,000, and now sues to recover a balance of $3,483.46, remaining unpaid. The work of construction ceased in June, 1914, and the defendant then began to occupy the dwelling. There was no complaint of defective performance until March, 1915. One of the specifications for the plumbing work provides that "all wrought-iron pipe must be well galvanized, lap welded pipe of the grade known as 'standard pipe' of Reading manufacture." The defendant learned in March, 1915, that some of the pipe, instead of being made in Reading, was the product of other factories. The plaintiff was accordingly directed by the architect to do the work anew. The plumbing was then encased within the walls except in a few places where it had to be exposed. Obedience to the order meant more than the substitution of other pipe. It meant the demolition at great expense of substantial parts of the completed structure. The plaintiff left the work untouched, and asked for a certificate that the final payment was due. Refusal of the certificate was followed by this suit.

The evidence sustains a finding that the omission of the prescribed brand of pipe was neither fraudulent nor willful. It was the result of the oversight and inattention of the plaintiff's subcontractor. Reading pipe is distinguished from Cohoes pipe and other brands only by the name of the manufacturer stamped upon it at intervals of between six and seven feet. Even the defendant's architect, though he inspected the pipe upon arrival, failed to notice the discrepancy. The plaintiff tried to show that the brands installed, though made by other manufacturers, were the same in quality, in appearance, in market value, and in cost as the brand stated in the contract — that they were, indeed, the same thing, though manufactured in another place. The evidence was excluded, and a verdict directed for the defendant. The Appellate Division reversed, and granted a new trial.

We think the evidence, if admitted, would have supplied some basis for the inference that the defect was insignificant in its relation to the project. The courts never say that one who makes a contract fills the measure of his duty by less than full performance. They do say, however, that an omission, both trivial and innocent, will sometimes be atoned for by allowance of the resulting damage, and will not always be the breach of a condition to be followed by a forfeiture. The distinction is akin to that between dependent and independent promises, or between promises and conditions. Some promises are so plainly independent that they can never by fair construction be conditions of one another. Others are so plainly dependent that they must always be conditions. Others, though dependent and thus conditions when there is departure in point of substance, will be viewed as independent and collateral when the departure is insignificant. Considerations partly of justice and partly of presumable intention are to tell us whether this or that promise shall be placed in one class or in another. The simple and the uniform will call for different remedies from the multifarious and the intricate. The margin of departure within the range of normal expectation upon a sale of common chattels will vary from the margin to be expected upon a contract for the construction of a mansion or a "skyscraper." There will be harshness sometimes and oppression in the implication of a condition when the thing upon which labor has been expended is incapable of surrender because united to the land, and equity and reason in the implication of a like condition when the subject-matter, if defective, is in shape to be returned. From the conclusion that promises may not be treated as dependent to the extent of their uttermost minutiae without a sacrifice of justice, the progress is a short one to the conclusion that they may not be so treated without a perversion of intention. Intention not otherwise revealed may be presumed to hold in contemplation the reasonable and probable. If something else is in view, it must not be left to implication. There will be no assumption of a purpose to visit venial faults with oppressive retribution.

Those who think more of symmetry and logic in the development of legal rules than of practical adaptation to the attainment of a just result will be troubled by a classification where the lines of division are so wavering and blurred. Something, doubtless, may be said on the score of consistency and certainty in favor of a stricter standard. The courts have balanced such considerations against those of equity and fairness, and found the latter to be the weightier. The decisions in this state commit us to the liberal view, which is making its way, nowadays, in jurisdictions slow to welcome it. Where the line is to be drawn between the important and the trivial cannot be settled by a formula. "In the nature of the case precise boundaries are impossible." 2 WILLISTON ON CONTRACTS, § 841. The same omission may take on one aspect or another according to its setting. Substitution of equivalents may not have the same significance in fields of art on the one side and in those of mere utility on the other. Nowhere will change be tolerated, however, if it is so dominant or pervasive as in any real or substantial measure to frustrate the purpose of the contract. There is no general license to install whatever, in the builder's judgment, may be regarded as "just as good." *Easthampton L. & C. Co., Ltd. v. Worthington*, 186 N.Y. 407, 412, 79 N.E. 323. The question is one of degree to be answered, if there is doubt, by the triers of the facts and, if the inferences are certain, by the judges of the law. We must weigh the purpose to be served, the desire to be gratified, the excuse for deviation from the letter, the cruelty of enforced adherence. Then only can we tell whether literal fulfillment is to be implied by law as a condition. This is not to say that the parties are not free by apt and certain words to effectuate a purpose that performance of every term shall be a condition of recovery. That question is not here. This is merely to say that the law will be slow to impute the purpose, in the silence of the parties, where the significance of the default is grievously out of proportion to the oppression of the forfeiture. The willful transgressor must accept the penalty of his transgression. For him there is no occasion to mitigate the rigor of implied conditions. The transgressor whose default is unintentional and trivial may hope for mercy if he will offer atonement for his wrong.

In the circumstances of this case, we think the measure of the allowance is not the cost of replacement, which would be great, but the difference in value, which would be either nominal or nothing. Some of the exposed sections might perhaps have been replaced at moderate expense. The defendant did not limit his demand to them, but treated the plumbing as a unit to be corrected from cellar to roof. In point of fact, the plaintiff never reached the stage at which evidence of the extent of the allowance became necessary. The trial court had excluded evidence that the defect was unsubstantial, and in view of that ruling there was no occasion for the plaintiff to go farther with an offer of proof. We think, however, that the offer, if it had been made, would not of necessity have been defective because directed to difference in value. It is true that in most cases the cost of replacement is the measure. The owner is entitled to the money which will permit him to complete, unless the cost of completion is grossly and unfairly out of proportion to the good to be attained. When that is true, the measure is the difference in value. Specifications call, let us say, for a foundation built of granite quarried in Vermont. On the completion of the building, the owner learns that through the blunder of a subcontractor part of the foundation has been built of granite of the same quality quarried in New Hampshire. The measure of allowance is not the cost of reconstruction. "There may be omissions of that which could not afterwards be supplied exactly as called for by the contract without taking down the building to its foundations, and at the same time the omission may not affect the value of the building for use or otherwise, except so slightly as to be hardly appreciable." *Handy v. Bliss*, 204 Mass. 513, 519, 90 N.E. 864, 134 Am. St. Rep. 673. . . . The rule that gives a remedy in cases of substantial performance with compensation for defects of trivial or inappreciable importance has been developed by the courts as an instrument of justice. The measure of the allowance must be shaped to the same end.

The order should be affirmed, and judgment absolute directed in favor of the plaintiff upon the stipulation, with costs in all courts.

NOTES

(1)   Does Justice Cardozo frankly recognize that the problem is essentially one of making an equitable adjustment between conflicting interests rather than interpreting the contract?

(2)   Specifically, what are the criteria or guidelines that Justice Cardozo sets forth to determine whether there is an implied condition of literal fulfillment of the builder's duty under the contract?

[3]   Substantial Performance and Express Conditions

When Justice Cardozo speaks of an implied condition, does he mean an express condition or a constructive condition? If he means the latter, what difference would there be in the result of the case if the condition in relation to the brand of pipe used had been express? If your answer is that literal compliance would then have been required, are you suggesting that an express condition must be fulfilled at the expense of economic waste? Is he willing to allow a forfeiture for the failure of an express condition to occur?

JACKSON v. RICHARD'S 5 & 10, INC.
Pennsylvania Superior Court
433 A.2d 888 (1981)

Cercone, J.

[In *Jacobs & Youngs v. Kent, Justice* Cardozo said,] "The courts never say that one who makes a contract fills the measure of his duty by less than full performance. They do say, however, that an omission, both trivial and innocent, will sometimes be atoned for by allowance of the resulting damage and will not always be the breach of a condition to be followed by a forfeiture. . . . We must weigh the purpose to be served, the desire to be gratified, the excuse for deviation from the letter, the cruelty of forced adherence. Then only can we tell whether literal fulfillment is to be implied by law as a condition. . . ." The *Jacob & Youngs* case involved constructive conditions precedent and not the express conditions which we face. In discussing the Cardozo opinion and its relationship to express conditions, Dean Murray says:

In *Jacob & Youngs*, Cardozo took pains to distinguish the situation involving constructive conditions from one involving express conditions. "This is not to say that the parties are not free by apt and certain words to effectuate a purpose that performance of every term shall be a condition of recovery. That question is not here." There is little doubt that Cardozo meant to suggest that the "doctrine" of substantial performance does not apply to express conditions, i.e., conditions agreed to by the parties as contrasted with those inserted by the court. This indicates that parties may include an express condition to the duty of either party and the nonoccurrence of that condition would result in the failure to activate the duty to which it is attached thereby ultimately discharging that duty, notwithstanding possible forfeiture to the obligee. The New Restatement of Contracts recognizes the fact that the doctrine of substantial performance does not apply to express conditions. However, it suggests that relief may be had through a section dealing with excuse of condition to avoid extreme forfeiture, unless the occurrence of the condition was a material part of the agreed exchange.

[Section 237 of the Restatement (Second) of Contracts reads:]

Except as stated in § 240, it is a condition of each party's remaining duties to render performances to be exchanged under an exchange of promises that there be no uncured material failure by the other party to render any such performance due at an earlier time.

Comment d to the same section reads:

If, however, the parties have made an event a condition of their agreement, there is no mitigating standard of materiality or substantiality applicable to the non-occurrence of that event. If, therefore, the agreement makes full performance a condition, substantial performance is not sufficient and if relief is to be had under the contract, it must be through excuse of the non-occurrence of the condition to avoid forfeiture. *See* § 229 and illustration 1 to that section.

Illustration 1 to that section is based on facts similar to *Jacob & Youngs* except that the specification is stated as an express condition and the unpaid balance is greater. The illustration indicates that the court may excuse even this express condition if it determines that the nonoccurrence of the condition was so relatively unimportant to the owner that the resulting forfeiture to the builder would be extreme. Since the amount of the unpaid balance in the illustration is almost triple the amount in the actual case, the RESTATEMENT (SECOND) drafters apparently felt compelled to ascertain that the forfeiture would be "extreme." The other requirement of this new section is a finding by the court that the nonoccurrence of the express condition is "relatively unimportant" to the owner which raises problems of a subjective materiality standard discussed in an earlier section. The new RESTATEMENT analysis is a manifestation of the strong abhorrence of forfeitures and suggests a desirable result. However, the difficulties in determining whether the nonoccurrence of the condition is "relatively unimportant" to the obligor and whether the forfeiture is "extreme" should not be underestimated.

MURRAY ON CONTRACTS, § 168 (1974) [Footnotes omitted].

In a similar vein, CORBIN has the following to say:

> When it is said that courts do not favor forfeitures, the meaning is that they do not like to see a party to a contract getting something for nothing. It is for the same reason that they refuse to enforce an express provision for the payment of a penalty. Therefore, the courts do not greatly favor express conditions precedent where the condition is itself no part of the subject-matter of exchange by the parties and where giving effect to the condition will result in one of the parties enjoying benefits under the contract without giving the agreed equivalent in exchange therefor. . . .

3A CORBIN ON CONTRACTS § 748 (19). *And see* MURRAY, *supra*, § 234.

In light of the foregoing, we find that the express conditions of the contract bear no substantial relationship to the subject matter of the proposed exchange. . . . We [hold] the forfeiture to be unjust based solely on the breach of the conditions precedent to the subject matter of the contract.

[4] The "Wilful" Preclusion

In *Jacob & Youngs v. Kent*, what does Justice Cardozo mean when he suggests that the "willful transgressor must accept the penalty of his transgression"? Is substantial performance based on equitable considerations to avoid forfeitures? Should we be concerned with avoiding forfeitures for a "willful" defaulter? Consider the following case.

VINCENZI v. CERRO
Connecticut Supreme Court
442 A.2d 1352 (1982)

SHEA, J.

On October 5, 1976, the parties signed a written contract for the plaintiffs to construct a three-family house on land owned by the defendants in Bridgeport. The contract price was $91,000, to be paid in five installments as various stages of the work were finished. The house was to be completed within 150 days from the date of the execution of the contract, which would make the projected completion date March 4, 1977. Except for $2000 withheld for incomplete items, the first four scheduled payments were made. The payments made totaled $67,100, leaving a balance of $23,900 on the contract price. In August, 1977, the plaintiffs demanded this balance, but the defendants refused on the ground that the house was not complete and that some work was defective. The court found that the work was not finished at that time because the heating system was not approved until October, 1977, and a certificate of occupancy was not issued until November 9, 1977. This date, when the certificate of occupancy was obtained, was deemed by the trial court to be the date when the contract had been substantially performed by the plaintiffs.

The judgment awarded the plaintiffs the balance of the contract price, $23,900, plus certain extras totalling $1118.30, but deducted therefrom $5002.90 for defective or incomplete work and for the loss of rent suffered by the defendants for the period of unjustifiable delay.

The principal claim of the defendants is that the doctrine of substantial performance was inapplicable in this case because the plaintiffs were guilty of a wilful or intentional breach of contract by failing to complete all of the work required. "There is no reason why one who has substantially performed such a contract, but unintentionally failed of strict performance in the matter of minor details, should have imposed upon him as a condition of recovery for that of which the other party has received the benefit, the burden of showing by direct evidence its reasonable value, or why he should be deprived of all benefit of the contract which he has substantially performed." *Daly & Sons v. New Haven Hotel Co.*, 91 Conn. 280, 287-88, 99 A. 853 (1917). The defendants rely on this articulation of the doctrine of substantial performance, which is also quoted in the memorandum of decision, as indicating that a builder who has failed to complete his contract fully may not invoke its benefit unless he was prevented from doing so by some circumstance beyond his control, such as interference by the owner. We have in several cases approved the common statement that a contractor who is guilty of a "wilful" breach cannot maintain an action upon the contract. The contemporary view, however, is that even a conscious and intentional departure from the contract specifications will not necessarily defeat recovery, but may be considered as one of the several factors involved in deciding whether there has been full performance. 3A CORBIN, CONTRACTS § 707; 2 RESTATEMENT (SECOND), CONTRACTS § 237, comment d. The pertinent inquiry is not simply whether the breach was "wilful" but whether the behavior of the party in default "comports with standards of good faith and fair dealing." 2 RESTATEMENT (SECOND), CONTRACTS § 241 (e); *see* comment f. Even an adverse conclusion on this point is not decisive but is to be weighed with other factors, such as the extent to which the owner will be deprived of a reasonably expected benefit and the extent to which the builder may suffer forfeiture, in deciding whether there has been substantial performance. *Id.; see* § 237, comment d.[18]

The reference in the memorandum of decision to the "wilful default" qualification of the doctrine of substantial performance indicates the court considered this factor as well as others in concluding that the plaintiffs were entitled to recover on the contract. The court allowed the defendants $2060.40 on their claim for defective or incomplete items, $1527 for repairing stress cracks in the foundation walls and $533.40 for five minor items. Upon a contract price of $91,000 the proportion of unperformed work, therefore, was so minimal as to warrant the conclusion of substantial performance drawn by the court. The reliance upon the certificate of occupancy as indicating substantial performance was entirely appropriate, despite the fact that two minor items were still to be performed, installing two electric plates and building a railing for the front steps.

The remaining claims, which relate to the amounts allowed to the plaintiffs for extras and to the defendants for defective work and for delay, raise only the question of whether the discretion of the trier was abused in the light of the evidence presented. We cannot retry the case. We have reviewed the evidence relating to the various items involved and conclude that the decision of the trial court with respect to each of them was not "clearly erroneous."

There is error in the amount of the judgment only with respect to those items in which error has been confessed by the parties as set forth in this opinion. The judgment is set aside and the case is remanded to the trial court with direction to correct the amount of damages awarded accordingly.

NOTE

Wilfulness. The refusal of the court to treat "willfulness" as conclusive departs from earlier holdings that a willful breach must always be material even though it may be quantitatively and qualitatively slight. It is important to consider the difference between the FIRST RESTATEMENT which listed "willfulness" among the guidelines to materiality (§ 275(e)), while the Second Restatement substitutes a standard of "good faith and fair dealing" and emphasizes the inconclusive effect of this standard. RESTATEMENT (SECOND) OF CONTRACTS § 241(e) and comment f. If there

---

[18] [1] 2 RESTATEMENT (SECOND), CONTRACTS § 237, comment d declares that "[t]he considerations in determining whether performance is substantial are those listed in § 241 for determining whether a failure is material." Section 241 provides as follows: "§ 241. Circumstances Significant in Determining Whether a Failure Is Material. In determining whether a failure to render or to offer performance is material, the following circumstances are significant: (a) the extent to which the injured party will be deprived of the benefit which he reasonably expected; (b) the extent to which the injured party can be adequately compensated for the part of that benefit of which he will be deprived; (c) the extent to which the party failing to perform or to offer to perform will suffer forfeiture; (d) the likelihood that the party failing to perform or to offer to perform will cure his failure, taking account of all the circumstances including any reasonable assurances; (e) the extent to which the behavior of the party failing to perform or to offer to perform comports with standards of good faith and fair dealing."

is no distinction between the criteria for substantial performance and materiality of breach, i.e., if a holding that performance was substantial necessarily requires a holding that any departure from performance was immaterial, the Cardozo suggestion that the "wilful transgressor must accept the penalty of his transgression i. e., for him, there is no occasion to mitigate the rigor of implied [constructive] conditions" is no longer conclusive in precluding the application of substantial performance. *See* MURRAY ON CONTRACTS § 108C.2.

COMMENT: THE RELATIONSHIP AMONG SUBSTANTIAL PERFORMANCE, MATERIALITY OF BREACH, AND DEPENDENT AND INDEPENDENT COVENANTS

RESTATEMENT (SECOND) OF CONTRACTS § 237, comment d, is quoted in footnote 1 in the principal case. It is important to consider the full statement prior to the quoted portion in the footnote:

> In an important category of disputes over failure of performance, one party asserts the right to payment on the ground that he has completed his performance, while the other party refuses to pay on the ground that there is an uncured material failure of performance. A typical example is that of the building contractor who claims from the owner payment of the unpaid balance under a construction contract. In such cases it is common to state the issue, not in terms of whether there has been an uncured material failure by the contractor, but in terms of whether there has been substantial performance by him. This manner of stating the issue does not change its substance, however, and the rule stated in this Section [dealing with material breach] also applies to such cases. If there has been substantial although not full performance, the building contractor has a claim for the unpaid balance and the owner has a claim only for damages. If there has not been substantial performance, the building contractor has no claim for the unpaid balance, although he may have a claim in restitution.

In addition to the principal case, there has been a growing recognition that a breach of contract cannot be "material" if substantial performance has been rendered. *See Henry v. Bitar*, 1998 Wash App. LEXIS 125 (1998). In *Wassburger v. American Scientific Chem., Inc.*, 514 P.2d 1097 (Jan. 30, 1973), the court characterized the issue as one of determining whether the breach was material, adding that "[t]here was not a substantial performance by the plaintiff, but. . . , on the contrary, there was a material breach, if not a willful breach, of the contract by him." With the emphasis upon the constructive condition analysis in relation to materiality of breach, it is not uncommon for modern courts, influenced by the RESTATEMENT (SECOND), to suggest that the doctrine of substantial performance does not apply when the party relying on it is "guilty" of an uncured material breach. *Wilson & Assocs. v. Forty-O-Four Grand Corp.*, 246 N.W.2d 922 (Iowa 1976). Other courts clearly use the "circumstances" of materiality as guidelines for substantial performance. *See, e.g., Prudential Ins. Co. v. Stratton*, 685 S.W.2d 818 (Ark. Ct. App. 1985). *See* MURRAY at § 108B.

Beyond the relationship between substantial performance and materiality of breach, recall that in *Boone v. Eyre*, 1 H. Bl. 273 [1777] the Earl of Mansfield succeeded in mitigating the potential harshness of the doctrine of "dependent covenants" (constructive conditions) that he had created in the classic case of *Kingston v. Preston*, 2 Doug. 689 [1773] by creating the doctrine of substantial performance. If applied literally, the tiniest failure of a constructive condition precedent would discharge a duty and cause a forfeiture. The doctrine of substantial performance, therefore, grew from the necessity to avoid such a result. The identical result, however, may be achieved by treating a given failure of performance as an insubstantial (immaterial) breach for which the defaulting party would be called upon to account, while maintaining the duty of the other party to the contract. If it is possible to analyze failures of performance from the interchangeable perspectives of materiality of breach or the doctrine of substantial performance, is there still another analytical framework?

In *Bruner v. Hines*, 295 Ala. 111, 324 So. 2d 265 (Ala. 1975), the court found a breach and applied the doctrine of substantial performance, suggesting that the issue was whether the breach was material. The court then set forth a "test for materiality" from an older case: "[W]here there is a breach of a dependent covenant, a condition precedent which goes to the whole consideration of the contract, the injured party has a right to rescind and recover damages for a total breach. But a breach of an independent covenant which does not go to the whole consideration of a contract, but which is subordinate and incidental to the main purpose, does not constitute a breach of the entire contract or warrant its rescission by the injured party, and his remedy for a breach is compensation for damages." This is not unique. There is support for this third interchangeable analysis in the Cardozo opinion in *Jacob & Youngs, Inc. v. Kent, supra*. Thus, if the breach is immaterial or insubstantial, to use the language of Cardozo in *Jacob & Youngs*, the covenant "will be viewed as independent . . . when the departure is insignificant." Characterizing the breached "covenant'" as independent prevents the innocent party from treating his duty as discharged since his duty is not related to the breached independent covenant. It is also accurate to describe the breach as immaterial or the defaulting party's performance as substantial. Whether the "covenant" is independent or dependent, however, depends upon whether the innocent party has received substantially what he bargained for, which may be said to depend upon whether there was a material breach, which can be determined by an application of the criteria for material breach in the RESTATEMENT (FIRST or SECOND) OF CONTRACTS.

The inevitable conclusion is that the quintessential inquiry is whether the breach was material. If the breach was material, any performance was necessarily *not* substantial and the covenant was *dependent*. If the breach was immaterial, the breacher's performance was necessarily substantial and, resorting to the early usage, the covenant that he breached will be deemed independent to ascertain that the aggrieved party is not discharged from his duty though he has a claim for the immaterial breach of the independent covenant though he has received substantially what he bargained for. The three "doctrines" are simply different facets of the same prism.

[5]   The "Perfect Tender" Rule — Rejection — Revocation of Acceptance

RAMIREZ v. AUTOSPORT
New Jersey Supreme Court
440 A.2d 1345 (1982)

Pollock, J.

Following a mobile home show at the Meadowlands Sports Complex, Mr. and Mrs. Ramirez visited Autosport's showroom. Ramirezes and Donald Graff, a salesman for Autosport, agreed on the sale of a new camper and the trade-in of the van owned by Mr. and Mrs. Ramirez. Autosport and the Ramirezes signed a simple contract reflecting a $14,100 purchase price for the new van with a $4,700 trade-in allowance for the Ramirez van, which Mr. and Mrs. Ramirez left with Autosport. After further allowance for taxes, title and documentary fees, the net price was $9,902. Because Autosport needed two weeks to prepare the new van, the contract provided for delivery on or about August 3, 1978.

On that date, Mr. and Mrs. Ramirez returned with their checks to Autosport to pick up the new van. Graff was not there so Mr. White, another salesman, met them. Inspection disclosed several defects in the van. The paint was scratched, both the electric and sewer hookups were missing, and the hubcaps were not installed. White advised the Ramirezes not to accept the camper because it was not ready.

Mr. and Mrs. Ramirez wanted the van for a summer vacation and called Graff several times. Each time Graff told them it was not ready for delivery. Finally, Graff called to notify them that the camper was ready. On August 14 Mr. and Mrs. Ramirez went to Autosport to accept delivery, but workers were still touching up the outside paint. Also, the camper windows were open, and the dining area cushions were soaking wet. Mr. and Mrs. Ramirez could not use the camper in that condition, but Mr. Leis, Autosport's manager, suggested that they take the van and that Autosport would replace the cushions later. Mrs. Ramirez counter offered to accept the van if they could withhold $2,000, but Leis agreed to no more than $250, which she refused. Leis then agreed to replace the cushions and to call them when the van was ready.

On August 15, 1978 Autosport transferred title to the van to Mr. and Mrs. Ramirez, a fact unknown to them until the summer of 1979. Between August 15 and September 1, 1978 Mrs. Ramirez called Graff several times urging him to complete the preparation of the van, but Graff constantly advised her that the van was not ready. He finally informed her that they could pick it up on September 1.

When Mr. and Mrs. Ramirez went to the showroom on September 1, Graff asked them to wait. And wait they did — for one and a half hours. No one from Autosport came forward to talk with them, and the Ramirezes left in disgust.

On October 5, 1978 Mr. and Mrs. Ramirez went to Autosport with an attorney friend. Although the parties disagreed on what occurred, the general topic was whether they should proceed with the deal or Autosport should return to the

Ramirezes their trade-in van. Mrs. Ramirez claimed they rejected the new van and requested the return of their trade-in. Mr. Lustig, the owner of Autosport, thought, however, that the deal could be salvaged if the parties could agree on the dollar amount of a credit for the Ramirezes. Mr. and Mrs. Ramirez never took possession of the new van and repeated their request for the return of their trade-in. Later in October, however, Autosport sold the trade-in to an innocent third party for $4,995. Autosport claimed that the Ramirez' van had a book value of $3,200 and claimed further that it spent $1,159.62 to repair their van. By subtracting the total of those two figures, $4,159.62, from the $4,995.00 sale price, Autosport claimed a $600-700 profit on the sale.

On November 20, 1978 the Ramirezes sued Autosport seeking, among other things, rescission of the contract. Autosport counterclaimed for breach of contract.

In the nineteenth century, sellers were required to deliver goods that complied exactly with the sales agreement. *See Filley v. Pope*, 115 U.S. 213, 220, 6 S. Ct. 19, 21, 29 L. Ed. 372, 373 (1885) (buyer not obliged to accept otherwise conforming scrap iron shipped to New Orleans from Leith, rather than Glasgow, Scotland, as required by contract); *Columbian Iron Works & Dry-Dock Co. v. Douglas*, 84 Md. 44, 47, 34 A. 1118, 1120–1121 (1896) (buyer who agreed to purchase steel scrap from United States cruisers not obliged to take any other kind of scrap). That rule, known as the "perfect tender" rule, remained part of the law of sales well into the twentieth century. By the 1920s the doctrine was so entrenched in the law that JUDGE LEARNED HAND declared "[t]here is no room in commercial contracts for the doctrine of substantial performance." *Mitsubishi Goshi Kaisha v. J. Aron & Co., Inc.*, 16 F.2d 185, 186 (2 Cir. 1926).

The harshness of the rule led courts to seek to ameliorate its effect and to bring the law of sales in closer harmony with the law of contracts, which allows rescission only for material breaches. *LeRoy Dyal Co. v. Allen*, 161 F.2d 152, 155 (4 Cir.1947). *See* 5 CORBIN, CONTRACTS § 1104 at 464 (1951); 12 WILLISTON, CONTRACTS § 1455 at 14 (3 ed. 1970). Nevertheless, a variation of the perfect tender rule appeared in the Uniform Sales Act. N.J.S.A. 46:30-75 (purchasers permitted to reject goods or rescind contracts for any breach of warranty); N.J.S.A. 46:30-18 to -21 (warranties extended to include all the seller's obligations to the goods). The chief objection to the continuation of the perfect tender rule was that buyers in a declining market would reject goods for minor nonconformities and force the loss on surprised sellers.

To the extent that a buyer can reject goods for any nonconformity, the UCC retains the perfect tender rule. Section 2-106 states that goods conform to a contract "when they are in accordance with the obligations under the contract." N.J.S.A. 12A:2-106. Section 2-601 authorizes a buyer to reject goods if they "or the tender of delivery fail in any respect to conform to the contract." N.J.S.A. 12A:2-601. The Code, however, mitigates the harshness of the perfect tender rule and balances the interests of buyer and seller. *See* RESTATEMENT (SECOND), CONTRACTS, § 241 comment (b) (1981). The Code achieves that result through its provisions for revocation of acceptance and cure. N.J.S.A. 12A:2-608, 2-508.

Initially, the rights of the parties vary depending on whether the rejection occurs before or after acceptance of the goods. Before acceptance, the buyer may reject goods for any nonconformity. N.J.S.A. 12A:2-601. Because of the seller's right to cure, however, the buyer's rejection does not necessarily discharge the contract. N.J.S.A. 12A:2-508. Within the time set for performance in the contract, the seller's right to cure is unconditional. *Id.*, subsec. (1); see id., Official Comment 1. Some authorities recommend granting a breaching party a right to cure in all contracts, not merely those for the sale of goods. RESTATEMENT (SECOND), CONTRACTS, ch. 10, especially §§ 237 and 241. Underlying the right to cure in both kinds of contracts is the recognition that parties should be encouraged to communicate with each other and to resolve their own problems.

The rights of the parties also vary if rejection occurs after the time set for performance. After expiration of that time, the seller has a further reasonable time to cure if he believed reasonably that the goods would be acceptable with or without a money allowance. N.J.S.A. 12A:2-508(2). The determination of what constitutes a further reasonable time depends on the surrounding circumstances, which include the change of position by and the amount of inconvenience to the buyer. N.J.S.A. 12A:2-508, Official Comment 3. Those circumstances also include the length of time needed by the seller to correct the nonconformity and his ability to salvage the goods by resale to others. *See* RESTATEMENT (SECOND), CONTRACTS, § 241 comment (d). Thus, the Code balances the buyer's right to reject nonconforming goods with a "second chance" for the seller to conform the goods to the contract under certain limited circumstances. N.J.S.A. 12A:2-508, New Jersey Study Comment 1.

After acceptance, the Code strikes a different balance: the buyer may revoke acceptance only if the nonconformity substantially impairs the value of the goods to him. N.J.S.A. 12A:2-608. This provision protects the seller from revocation for trivial defects. It also prevents the buyer from taking undue advantage of the seller by allowing goods to depreciate and then returning them because of asserted minor defects. Because this case involves rejection of goods, we need not decide whether a seller has a right to cure substantial defects that justify revocation of acceptance.

A further problem, however, is identifying the remedy available to a buyer who rejects goods with insubstantial defects that the seller fails to cure within a reasonable time. The Code provides expressly that when "the buyer rightfully rejects, then with respect to the goods involved, the buyer may cancel." N.J.S.A. 12A:2-711. "Cancellation" occurs when either party puts an end to the contract for breach by the other. N.J.S.A. 12A:2-106(4). Nonetheless, some confusion exists whether the equitable remedy of rescission survives under the Code. The Code eschews the word "rescission" and substitutes the terms "cancellation," "revocation of acceptance," and "rightful rejection." N.J.S.A. 12A:2-106(4); 2-608; and 2-711 & Official Comment 1. Although neither "rejection" nor "revocation of acceptance" is defined in the Code, rejection includes both the buyer's refusal to accept or keep delivered goods and his notification to the seller that he will not keep them. White & Summers, *supra*, § 8-1 at 293. Revocation of acceptance is like rejection, but occurs after the buyer has accepted the goods. Nonetheless, revocation of acceptance is intended to provide the same relief as rescission of a contract of sale of goods. N.J.S.A. 12A:2-608 Official Comment 1; N.J. Study Comment 2. In brief, revocation is tantamount to rescission. Similarly, subject to the seller's right to cure, a buyer who rightfully rejects goods, like one who revokes his acceptance, may cancel the contract. N.J.S.A. 12A:2-711 & Official Comment 1.

Although the complaint requested rescission of the contract, plaintiffs actually sought not only the end of their contractual obligations, but also restoration to their pre-contractual position. That request incorporated the equitable doctrine of restitution, the purpose of which is to restore plaintiff to as good a position as he occupied before the contract. CORBIN, *supra*, § 1102 at 455. In UCC parlance, plaintiffs' request was for the cancellation of the contract and recovery of the price paid. N.J.S.A. 12A:2-106(4), 2-711.

General contract law permits rescission only for material breaches, and the Code restates "materiality" in terms of "substantial impairment." The Code permits a buyer who rightfully rejects goods to cancel a contract of sale. N.J.S.A. 12A:2-711. Because a buyer may reject goods with insubstantial defects, he also may cancel the contract if those defects remain uncured. Otherwise, a seller's failure to cure minor defects would compel a buyer to accept imperfect goods and collect for any loss caused by the nonconformity. N.J.S.A. 12A:2-714.

Although the Code permits cancellation by rejection for minor defects, it permits revocation of acceptance only for substantial impairments. That distinction is consistent with other Code provisions that depend on whether the buyer has accepted the goods. Acceptance creates liability in the buyer for the price, N.J.S.A. 12A:2-709(1), and precludes rejection. N.J.S.A. 12A:2-607(2); N.J.S.A. 12A:2-606, New Jersey Study Comment 1. Also, once a buyer accepts goods, he has the burden to prove any defect. N.J.S.A. 12A:2-607(4). By contrast, where goods are rejected for not conforming to the contract, the burden is on the seller to prove that the nonconformity was corrected. *Miron v. Yonkers Raceway, Inc.*, 400 F.2d 112, 119 (2 Cir. 1968).

Underlying the Code provisions is the recognition of the revolutionary change in business practices in this century. The purchase of goods is no longer a simple transaction in which a buyer purchases individually-made goods from a seller in a face-to-face transaction. Our economy depends on a complex system for the manufacture, distribution, and sale of goods, a system in which manufacturers and consumers rarely meet. Faceless manufacturers mass-produce goods for unknown consumers who purchase those goods from merchants exercising little or no control over the quality of their production. In an age of assembly lines, we are accustomed to cars with scratches, television sets without knobs and other products with all kinds of defects. Buyers no longer expect a "perfect tender." If a merchant sells defective goods, the reasonable expectation of the parties is that the buyer will return those goods and that the seller will repair or replace them.

Recognizing this commercial reality, the Code permits a seller to cure imperfect tenders. Should the seller fail to cure the defects, whether substantial or not, the balance shifts again in favor of the buyer, who has the right to cancel or seek damages. N.J.S.A. 12A:2-711. In general, economic considerations would induce sellers to cure minor defects. Assuming the seller does not cure, however, the buyer should be permitted to exercise his remedies under N.J.S.A. 12A:2-711. The Code remedies for consumers are to be liberally construed, and the buyer should have the option of cancelling if the seller does not provide conforming goods. *See* N.J.S.A. 12A:1-106.

To summarize, the UCC preserves the perfect tender rule to the extent of permitting a buyer to reject goods for any nonconformity. Nonetheless, that rejection does not automatically terminate the contract. A seller may still effect a cure and preclude unfair rejection and cancellation by the buyer. N.J.S.A. 12A:2-508, Official Comment 2; N.J.S.A. 12A:2-711, Official Comment 1.

The trial court found that Mr. and Mrs. Ramirez had rejected the van within a reasonable time under N.J.S.A. 12A:2-602. The court found that on August 3, 1978 Autosport's salesman advised the Ramirezes not to accept the van and that on August 14, they rejected delivery and Autosport agreed to replace the cushions. Those findings are supported by substantial credible evidence, and we sustain them. Although the trial court did not find whether Autosport cured the defects within a reasonable time, we find that Autosport did not effect a cure. Clearly the van was not ready for delivery during August, 1978 when Mr. and Mrs. Ramirez rejected it, and Autosport had the burden of proving that it had corrected the defects. Although the Ramirezes gave Autosport ample time to correct the defects, Autosport did not demonstrate that the van conformed to the contract on September 1. In fact, on that date, when Mr. and Mrs. Ramirez returned at Autosport's invitation, all they received was discourtesy.

On the assumption that substantial impairment is necessary only when a purchaser seeks to revoke acceptance under N.J.S.A. 12A:2-608, the trial court correctly refrained from deciding whether the defects substantially impaired the van. The court properly concluded that plaintiffs were entitled to "rescind" — i.e., to "cancel" — the contract.

Because Autosport had sold the trade-in to an innocent third party, the trial court determined that the Ramirezes were entitled not to the return of the trade-in, but to its fair market value, which the court set at the contract price of $4,700. A buyer who rightfully rejects goods and cancels the contract may, among other possible remedies, recover so much of the purchase price as has been paid. N.J.S.A. 12A:2-711. The Code, however, does not define "pay" and does not require payment to be made in cash.

A common method of partial payment for vans, cars, boats and other items of personal property is by a "trade-in". When concerned with used vans and the like, the trade-in market is an acceptable, and perhaps the most appropriate, market in which to measure damages. It is the market in which the parties dealt; by their voluntary act they have established the value of the traded-in article. *See Frantz Equipment Co. v. Anderson*, 37 N.J. 420, 431–432 (1962) (in computing purchaser's damages for alleged breach of uniform conditional sales law, trade-in value of tractor was appropriate measure); *accord, California Airmotive Corp. v. Jones, 415 F.2d 554, 556 (6 Cir. 1969)*. In other circumstances, a measure of damages other than the trade-in value might be appropriate. *See Chemical Bank v. Miller Yacht Sales*, 173 N.J. Super. 90, 103 (App. Div. 1980) (in determining value of security interest in boat, court rejected both book value and contract trade-in value and adopted resale value as appropriate measure of damages).

The ultimate issue is determining the fair market value of the trade-in. This Court has defined fair market value as "the price at which the property would change hands between a willing buyer and a willing seller when the former is not under any compulsion to buy and the latter is not under any compulsion to sell, both parties having reasonable knowledge of relevant facts." *In re Estate of Romnes*, 79 N.J. 139, 144 (1978). Although the value of the trade-in van as set forth in the sales contract was not the only possible standard, it is an appropriate measure of fair market value.

For the preceding reasons, we affirm the judgment of the Appellate Division.

E.   REPUDIATION

A *repudiation* is a manifestation by a party to a contract that he will not perform his contractual duty. The manifestation can occur through words or conduct and typically amounts to a clear, material (total) breach of contract. *See* RESTATEMENT (SECOND) OF CONTRACTS § 250. There are numerous cases insisting that a repudiation must be positive and unequivocal. Thus, a mere statement that the obligor is having some difficulty or other indications of doubt concerning the obligor's performance will not be sufficient. If the time for the obligor's performance is due when he manifests his repudiation, it is a *present* breach of contract. If, however, his performance is not yet due when he clearly indicates he will not perform his future duty, it is impossible to characterize such a manifestation as a present breach. In one sense, it may be argued that he cannot possibly commit a breach until the time for his performance arrives and he fails to perform. In the meantime, however, what is the obligee to do?

This was the dilemma that proved so puzzling to the court in the famous case of *Hochster v. De la Tour*, 2 Ellis & Bl. 678 (1853), where the plaintiff made a contract in April to commence work for the defendant as a courier on June 1 but defendant repudiated in May. Since defendant's duty would not become activated until June 1, the court assumed that plaintiff would have to remain idle and refrain from taking any other employment until June 1 when he could then bring an action. On this faulty assumption, the court saw only three alternatives to this puzzle: plaintiff could (1) renounce the contract, but then be limited to a recovery in restitution which would provide nothing for the plaintiff; (2) ignore the repudiation entirely and treat the contract as rescinded which would defeat any possible remedy; or (3) treat the repudiation as an immediate breach (in May) and allow an action for damages at that time though the defendant's contractual duty, again, would not arise until June 1. The court ignored a fourth alternative, namely, that of treating the repudiation merely as the basis of an excuse for not performing constructive conditions precedent to the promisor's duty. One does not have to hold himself ready, willing and able to perform when the other party indicates that such an effort is useless. The plaintiff could, therefore, have secured substitute employment immediately in May and brought an action for any provable damages in June. Since the fourth alternative never appeared in the mind's eye of the court, it chose the third, thereby creating the doctrine of anticipatory repudiation.

[1]   Anticipatory Repudiation

FLATT & SONS CO., INC. v. SCHUPF
Illinois Appellate Court
649 N.E.2d 990 (1995)

KNECHT, J.

Plaintiff Truman L. Flatt & Sons Co., Inc., filed a complaint seeking specific performance of a real estate contract made with defendants Sara Lee Schupf, Ray H. Neiswander, Jr., and American National Bank and Trust Company of Chicago (American), as trustee. Defendants filed a motion for summary judgment, which the trial court granted. Plaintiff now appeals from the trial court's grant of the motion for summary judgment. We reverse and remand.

In March 1993, plaintiff and defendants entered a contract in which defendants agreed to sell plaintiff a parcel of land located in Springfield, Illinois. The contract stated the purchase price was to be $160,000. The contract also contained the following provisions:

> 1. This transaction shall be closed on or before June 30, 1993, or upon approval of the relief requested from the Zoning Code of the City of Springfield, Illinois, whichever first occurs ('Closing Date'). The closing is subject to contingency set forth in paragraph 14.
>
>   * * *
>
> 14. This Contract to Purchase Real Estate is contingent upon the Buyer obtaining, within one hundred twenty (120) days after the date hereof, amendment of, or other sufficient relief of, the Zoning Code of the City of Springfield to permit the construction and operation of an asphalt plant. In the event the City Council of the City of Springfield denies the request for such use of the property, then this contract shall be voidable at Buyer's option and if Buyer elects to void this contract Buyer shall receive a refund of the earnest money paid.

On May 21, plaintiff's attorney sent a letter to defendants' attorney informing him of substantial public opposition plaintiff encountered at a public meeting concerning its request for rezoning. The letter concluded:

> The day after the meeting all of the same representatives of the buyer assembled and discussed our chances for successfully pursuing the rezoning request. Everyone who was there was in agreement that our chances were zero to none for success. As a result, we decided to withdraw the request for rezoning, rather than face almost certain defeat.
>
> The bottom line is that we are still interested in the property, but the property is not worth as much to us a 35-acre parcel zoned I-1, as it would be if it were zoned I-2. At this juncture, I think it is virtually impossible for anyone to get that property re-zoned I-2, especially to accommodate the operation of an asphalt plant. In an effort to keep this thing moving, my

clients have authorized me to offer your clients the sum of $142,500.00 for the property, which they believe fairly represents its value with its present zoning classification. Please check with your clients and advise whether or not that revision in the contract is acceptable. If it is, I believe we can accelerate the closing and bring this matter to a speedy conclusion. Your prompt attention will be appreciated. Thanks.

Defendants' attorney responded in a letter dated June 9, the body of which stated, in its entirety:

In reply to your May 21 letter, be advised that the owners of the property in question are not interested in selling the property for $142,500 and, accordingly, the offer is not accepted.

I regret that the zoning reclassification was not approved.

Plaintiff's attorney replied back in a letter dated June 14, the body of which stated, in its entirety:

My clients received your letter of June 9, 1993[,] with some regret, however upon some consideration they have elected to proceed with the purchase of the property as provided in the contract. At your convenience please give me a call so that we can set up a closing date.

After this correspondence, plaintiff's attorney sent two more brief letters to defendants' attorney, dated June 23 and July 6, each requesting information concerning the status of defendants' preparation for fulfillment of the contract. Defendants' attorney replied in a letter dated July 8. The letter declared it was the defendants' position plaintiff's failure to waive the rezoning requirement and elect to proceed under the contract at the time the rezoning was denied, coupled with the new offer to buy the property at less than the contract price, effectively voided the contract. Plaintiff apparently sent one more letter in an attempt to convince defendants to honor the contract, but defendants declined. Defendants then arranged to have plaintiff's earnest money returned.

Plaintiff filed a complaint for specific performance and other relief against defendants and American, asking the court to direct defendants to comply with the terms of the contract. Defendants responded by filing a "motion to strike, motion to dismiss or, in the alternative, motion for summary judgment." The motion for summary judgment sought summary judgment on the basis plaintiff repudiated the contract.

Plaintiff argues summary judgment was improper because the trial court erred in finding plaintiff had repudiated the contract.

"The doctrine of anticipatory repudiation requires a clear manifestation of an intent not to perform the contract on the date of performance. * * * That intention must be a definite and unequivocal manifestation that he will not render the promised performance when the time fixed for it in the contract arrives. [Citation.] Doubtful and indefinite statements that performance may or may not take place are not enough to constitute anticipatory repudiation."(*In re Marriage of Olsen* (1988), 124 Ill. 2d 19, 24, 528 N.E.2d 684, 686, 123 Ill. Dec. 980.)

These requirements exist because "anticipatory breach is not a remedy to be taken lightly." (*Olsen*, 124 Ill. 2d at 25, 528 N.E.2d at 687.) The RESTATEMENT (SECOND) OF CONTRACTS adopts the view of the Uniform Commercial Code (UCC) and states "language that under a fair reading 'amounts to a statement of intention not to perform except on conditions which go beyond the contract' constitutes a repudiation. Comment 2 to Uniform Commercial Code § 2-610." (RESTATEMENT (SECOND) OF CONTRACTS § 250 Comment, b, at 273 (1981).) Whether an anticipatory repudiation occurred is a question of fact and the judgment of the trial court thereon will not be disturbed unless it is against the manifest weight of evidence.

As can be seen, whether a repudiation occurred is determined on a case-by-case basis, depending on the particular language used. Both plaintiff and defendants, although they cite Illinois cases discussing repudiation, admit the cited Illinois cases are all factually distinguishable from the case at hand because none of those cases involved a request to change a term in the contract. According to the commentators, a suggestion for modification of the contract does not amount to a repudiation. (J. CALAMARI & J. PERILLO, CONTRACTS § 12-4, at 524 n.74 (3d ed. 1987). Plaintiff also cites cases in other jurisdictions holding a request for a change in the price term of a contract does not constitute a repudiation. Defendants attempt to distinguish these cases by arguing here, under the totality of the language in the letter and the circumstances surrounding the letter, the request by plaintiff for a decrease in price clearly implied a threat of nonperformance if the price term was not modified. We disagree.

The language in the May 21 letter did not constitute a clearly implied threat of nonperformance. First, although the language in the May 21 letter perhaps could be read as implying plaintiff would refuse to perform under the contract unless the price was modified, given the totality of the language in the letter, such an inference is weak. More important, even if such an inference were possible, Illinois law requires a repudiation be manifested clearly and unequivocally. Plaintiff's May 21 letter at most created an ambiguous implication whether performance would occur. Indeed, during oral argument defense counsel conceded the May 21 letter was "ambiguous" on whether a repudiation had occurred. This is insufficient to constitute a repudiation under well-settled Illinois law. Therefore, the trial court erred in declaring the May 21 letter anticipatorily repudiated the real estate contract as a matter of law.

Moreover, even if plaintiff had repudiated the contract, the trial court erred in granting summary judgment on this basis because plaintiff timely retracted its repudiation. The RESTATEMENT (SECOND) OF CONTRACTS states:

> The effect of a statement as constituting a repudiation under § 250 or the basis for a repudiation under § 251 is nullified by a retraction of the statement if notification of the retraction comes to the attention of the injured party before he materially changes his position in reliance on the repudiation or indicates to the other party that he considers the repudiation to be final. (Emphasis added.) (RESTATEMENT (SECOND) OF CONTRACTS § 256(1), at 293 (1981).)

The UCC adopts the same position:

Retraction of Anticipatory Repudiation. (1) Until the repudiating party's next performance is due he can retract his repudiation unless the aggrieved party has since the repudiation cancelled or materially changed his position or otherwise indicated that he considers the repudiation final. (Emphasis added.) (810 ILCS 5/2-611(1) (West 1992).)

Defendants completely avoid discussion of the common-law right to retract a repudiation other than to say Illinois is silent on the issue. Defendants then cite [*cases*] as well as WILLISTON § 1337, at 185–86. These authorities stand for the proposition that after an anticipatory repudiation, the aggrieved party is entitled to choose to treat the contract as rescinded or terminated, to treat the anticipatory repudiation as a breach by bringing suit or otherwise changing its position, or to await the time for performance. The UCC adopts substantially the same position. Defendants here assert they chose to treat the contract as rescinded, as they had a right to do under well-settled principles of law.

Plaintiff admits the law stated by defendants is well settled, and admits if the May 21 letter was an anticipatory breach, then defendants had the right to treat the contract as being terminated or rescinded. However, plaintiff points out defendants' assertions ignore the great weight of authority, discussed earlier, which provides a right of the repudiating party to retract the repudiation before the aggrieved party has chosen one of its options allowed under the common law and listed in Stonecipher, Builder's Concrete, and Leazzo. Plaintiff argues defendants' letter of June 9 failed to treat the contract as rescinded, and absent notice or other manifestation defendants were pursuing one of their options, plaintiff was free to retract its repudiation. Plaintiff is correct.

[D]efendants' precise theory is an aggrieved party may treat the contract as terminated or rescinded without notice or other indication being given to the repudiating party, and once such a decision is made by the aggrieved party, the repudiating party no longer has the right of retraction. It is true no notice is required to be given to the repudiating party if the aggrieved party materially changes its position as a result of the repudiation. Here, however, the defendants admitted in their answers to plaintiff's interrogatories they had not entered another agreement to sell the property, nor even discussed or considered the matter with another party. Defendants had not changed their position at all, nor do defendants make any attempt to so argue. As can be seen from the language of the RESTATEMENT, the UCC, and the commentators, shown earlier, they are in accord that where the aggrieved party has not otherwise undergone a material change in position, the aggrieved party must indicate to the other party it is electing to treat the contract as rescinded. This can be accomplished either by bringing suit, by notifying the repudiating party, or by in some other way manifesting an election to treat the contract as rescinded. Prior to such indication, the repudiating party is free to retract its repudiation. The RESTATEMENT (SECOND) OF CONTRACTS provides the following illustrations:

2. On February 1, A contracts to supply B with natural gas for one year beginning on May 1, payment to be made each month. On March 1, A repudiates. On April 1, before B has taken any action in response to the

repudiation, A notifies B that he retracts his repudiation. B's duties under the contract are not discharged, and B has no claim against A.

* * *

4. The facts being otherwise as stated in Illustration 2, on March 15, B notifies A that he cancels the contract. B's duties under the contract are discharged and B has a claim against A for damages for total breach * * *. (Emphasis added.) RESTATEMENT (SECOND) OF CONTRACTS § 256, Comments a, c (1981).

This rule makes sense as well. If an aggrieved party could treat the contract as rescinded or terminated without notice or other indication to the repudiating party, the rule allowing retraction of an anticipatory repudiation would be eviscerated. No repudiating party ever would be able to retract a repudiation, because after receiving a retraction, the aggrieved party could, if it wished, simply declare it had already decided to treat the repudiation as a rescission or termination of the contract. Defendants' theory would effectively rewrite the common-law rule regarding retraction of anticipatory repudiation so that the repudiating party may retract an anticipatory repudiation only upon assent from the aggrieved party. This is not the common-law rule, and we decline to adopt defendants' proposed revision of it.

Applying the actual common-law rule to the facts here, plaintiff sent defendants a letter dated June 14, which clearly and unambiguously indicated plaintiff intended to perform under the contract. However, defendants did not notify plaintiff, either expressly or impliedly, of an intent to treat the contract as rescinded until July 8. Nor is there anything in the record demonstrating any indication to plaintiff, prior to July 8, of an intent by defendants to treat the contract as rescinded or terminated. Thus, assuming plaintiff's May 21 request for a lower purchase price constituted an anticipatory repudiation of the contract, plaintiff successfully retracted that repudiation in the letter dated June 14 because defendants had not yet materially changed their position or indicated to plaintiff an intent to treat the contract as rescinded. Therefore, because plaintiff had timely retracted any alleged repudiation of the contract, the trial court erred in granting summary judgment for defendants on the basis plaintiff repudiated the contract. Defendants were not entitled to judgment as a matter of law.

NOTES

(1) *Repudiation — Tests.* Some early cases insisted that, to constitute a repudiation, the manifestation that the obligor would not perform had to be nothing short of an absolute an unequivocal renunciation of the contract. *See, e.g., Dingley v. Oler*, 117 U.S. 490 (1886); *Vittum v. Estey*, 67 Vt. 158, 31 A. 144 (1894); *Johnstone v. Milling*, 16 Q.B.D. 460 [1886]. The principal case quotes from a recent opinion using similar language — the manifestation of intention not to perform must be "definite and unequivocal" (quoting from *In re Marriage of Olsen*, 528 N.E.2d 684. 686 (1988)). At the same time, the court adopts both the UCC and the RESTATEMENT (SECOND) less stringent tests. The UCC only requires action "which reasonably indicates a rejection of the continuing obligation," (UCC § 2-610, Comment 2), while the RESTATEMENT (SECOND) only requires an expression to be "sufficiently positive to

be reasonably interpreted to mean that the party will not or cannot perform." (RESTATEMENT (SECOND) OF CONTRACTS § 250, Comment b.).

(2) *Conduct Repudiations.* Where an obligor sells or leases goods or land necessary to perform a contract or makes a contract for their sale to another prior to the time for performance, such conduct will constitute a repudiation. *See, e.g., Pappas v. Crist,* 25 S.E.2d 850 (1943); *Crane v. East Side Canal 7 Irrg. Co.,* 6 Cal. App. 2d 361, 44 P.2d 455 (1935). A loss of title due to foreclosure is a repudiation. *Space Center v. 451 Corp.,* 298 N.W.2d 443 (Minn. 1980). If a test pilot contracts to test a new aircraft but a few days before the scheduled test is on his way to the space ship Mir where he is to remain for two months, he has repudiated the contract.

[2] Retraction of Repudiation

UCC § 2-611, Retraction of Anticipatory Repudiation, states:

(1) Until the repudiating party's next performance is due he can retract his repudiation unless the aggrieved party has since the repudiation canceled or materially changed his position or otherwise indicated that he considers the repudiation final.

(2) Retraction may be by any method which clearly indicates to the aggrieved party that the repudiating party intends to perform, but must include any assurance justifiably demanded under the provisions of this Article (Section 2-609).

(3) Retraction reinstates the repudiating party's rights under the contract with due excuse and allowance to the aggrieved party for any delay occasioned by the repudiation.

PROBLEMS

(1)   Defendant agreed to supply gas to a federal housing project operated by plaintiff. The term of the contract was from April 15, 1947, to June 15, 1948. While the contract was being performed, defendant notified plaintiff on October 7, 1947, that it would supply no more gas under this contract as of November 15, 1947. Plaintiff immediately notified defendant that plaintiff would permit defendant three days in which to retract its repudiation (a *locus poenitentiae*). If defendant did not retract within that time, plaintiff stated that it would contract with a substitute supplier of gas. Defendant failed to retract within the three days. However, defendant did assure plaintiff of performance prior to plaintiff's signing the new contract with a substitute supplier. Therefore, defendant argued that the *locus poenitentiae* was not extended to the time plaintiff relied on the repudiation by signing the new contract. Analyze. *See United States v. Seacoast Gas Co.,* 204 F.2d 709 (5th Cir. 1953).

(2)   In September, 1999, Chips, Inc. contracted to supply Wizard Computers, Inc (WCI) with all of the electronic chips of a certain design WCI would require for the year 2000 at $17 per chip. On October 18, 1999, however, the president of Chips, Miller, informed WCI that no chips would be shipped at that price and demanded

a higher price. WCI responded that Chips had ten days to change its mind. On the third day of that period, the president of WCI, Sims, was flying to a business meeting from New York to Chicago. The adjoining seat on the plane was occupied by Hastings, the president of Hastings International, Inc. The conversation led to WCI's current problem with Chips. Hastings then offered to supply all of WCI's chip requirements with chips of identical design at $15 per chip, but stated that the "deal would have to be made immediately" since Hastings was flying to Chicago to negotiate a similar arrangement with another buyer and the Hastings company did not have the capacity to serve two large buyers. While still in the air, Sims signed the contract with Hastings. In the meantime, Miller had learned that Hastings would be in Chicago and also learned of the flight he would be on. When Sims exited the jetway and walked into the terminal, he was immediately greeted by Miller who said, "I'm sorry about our attitude. We will perform our contract to the last letter." Sims informed Miller that it was too late. Analyze.

[3] Repudiation by Good Faith Mistake

CHAMBERLIN v. PUCKETT CONSTRUCTION CO.
Montana Supreme Court
921 P.2d 1237 (1996)

GRAY, J.

In January of 1994, Puckett Construction executed a contract with LT Hotel Enterprises under which Puckett Construction would be the general contractor for construction of a Ramada Inn in Bozeman, Montana. Thereafter, Puckett Construction received a written bid from Custom Framing to perform the framing work associated with the project. Phil Puckett (Puckett), the owner of Puckett Construction, drafted and signed a subcontractor agreement for the framing, which is dated March 24, 1994, and forwarded it to Randall Chamberlin (Chamberlin), one of the partners and owners of Custom Framing. Chamberlin and his partner, David Worthington (Worthington), made ten changes to the agreement and Chamberlin initialed each change.

Chamberlin signed the revised subcontractor agreement and returned it to Kenneth Cavenah (Cavenah), Puckett Construction's superintendent and sole on-site representative for the Ramada Inn project. In early April, Cavenah took the revised agreement to South Dakota and reviewed it with Puckett; thereafter, he returned to Bozeman and, on April 14, 1994, initialed the changes in the presence of Chamberlin and Worthington.

Ten days prior to the start date, Chamberlin called Puckett Construction's office in South Dakota and informed the receptionist that Custom Framing would not begin work until Puckett personally initialed the changes Chamberlin had made to the subcontractor agreement. Puckett Construction subsequently sent Custom Framing a letter advising that "Puckett Construction will not be hiring Custom Framing on the Ramada Inn job." Puckett Construction hired a different framing subcontractor on April 18, 1994.

In June of 1994, Chamberlin, individually and d/b/a Custom Framing, sued Puckett Construction for breach of contract and requested an unspecified amount of damages. Puckett Construction answered and denied the existence of a contract. Both parties conducted discovery.

A bench trial was held in June of 1995. The District Court directed a verdict on behalf of Puckett Construction on Custom Framing's breach of contract claim, awarded Puckett Construction damages in the amount of $11,405 on its counter-claim, and determined that Puckett Construction was entitled to reasonable attorney's fees and costs.

We have not previously addressed whether a party's demand for performance of terms not contained in a contract, accompanied by a statement that it will not perform if those terms are not met, constitutes an anticipatory breach. Other courts, however, have held that such a demand constitutes an anticipatory repudiation. *See, e.g., United California Bank v. Prudential Ins. Co.* (Ariz. Ct. App. 1983), 140 Ariz. 238, 681 P.2d 390, 430.

As discussed by the Arizona Court of Appeals, a party's offer to perform under a contract in accordance with that party's erroneous interpretation of its contractual rights is not, in itself, an anticipatory repudiation. *United California Bank*, 681 P.2d at 431. The reason is that, while the party may be asserting an erroneous interpretation of the contract, it is still offering to meet its own contractual obligations and cannot be said to be stating an intent not to perform or a refusal to perform. In order to constitute an anticipatory breach, the party's insistence on terms which are not contained in the contract must be accompanied by a "clear manifestation of intention not to perform" unless the additional term is met. Moreover, a repudiation occurs regardless of whether the demand for performance of terms not contained in the contract was made wilfully or by mistake; in either instance, the other party has been deprived of the benefit of its bargain. *United California Bank*, 681 P.2d at 431.

We adopt the rationale of the Arizona Court of Appeals in United California Bank regarding the effect of a party's demand for performance of terms not contained in a contract coupled with a refusal to perform unless those terms are met. A party acts at his peril if, "insisting on what he mistakenly believes to be his rights, he refuses to perform his duty." *United California Bank*, 681 P.2d at 430 (quoting RESTATEMENT (SECOND) OF CONTRACTS § 250 cmt. d (1981)). On that basis, we conclude that a demand for performance of a term not contained in the parties' contract, accompanied by an unequivocal statement that the demanding party will not perform unless the additional term is met, constitutes an anticipatory breach of the contract excusing performance by the other party.

COMMENT: ANTICIPATORY REPUDIATION AND UNILATERAL CONTRACTS

While a good faith mistake about one's rights leading to a renunciation of the contract will not save such a party from committing an anticipatory repudiation, there is a particular type of case that is troublesome along these lines. Where an insurance company is making payments under a disability policy and in good faith concludes that the insured is no longer disabled, thereby terminating the payments, if it is determined that the insurance company, albeit in good faith, has a duty to continue payments, does its action constitute an anticipatory repudiation? Under these circumstances, if it is an anticipatory repudiation, should the insured be entitled not only to back payments plus interest, but to a lump sum based on an estimate of all future payments for a lifetime?

An insurance company in this situation may argue that the doctrine of anticipatory repudiation should not apply since the contract is a unilateral contract, leaving only an obligation to pay money. Recall that the doctrine was predicated largely on the manufactured dilemma of an innocent party having to hold himself ready, willing and able to perform when the time for performance arrived, knowing that the other party has announced his clear intention not to perform. Since a unilateral contract is not formed until one party has completely performed and the only remaining duty is the other party's payment of money, the reason for the doctrine disappears. Similarly, where the contract is a bilateral contract but one side fully performs only to have the other indicate that it will not perform when the time for performance arrives, there is no need for the doctrine.

On the other side of the disability insurance controversy, the disabled plaintiff will argue that he should not be required to continuously litigate to receive past payments when the insurance company decided he was no longer disabled. Simply paying for past benefits will not assure the avoidance of future litigation. Therefore, why not apply the doctrine anticipatory repudiation and pay the plaintiff a lump sum of all future payments based on life expectancy under the circumstances?

The confusion in these cases is due essentially to a faulty analysis. *See Greguhn v. Mutual of Omaha Co.*, 23 Utah 2d 214, 461 P.2d 285 (1969). Where an insurance company stops making payments that are presently due, this is not an anticipatory repudiation; it is a present breach of contract coupled with a repudiation. See the opinion by Justice Cardozo in *New York Life Ins. Co. v. Viglas*, 297 U.S. 672 (1936), where he laments the blurring of the line between anticipatory repudiation and present breaches in such cases.

The solution to the dilemma may be found in not providing recovery beyond the installment payments due, but assuring future payments. *See Corporali v. Washington National Ins. Co.*, 307 N.W.2d 218 (Minn. 1981).

[4] Prospective Failure of Performance — Demanding Adequate Assurances

SCOTT v. CROWN
Colorado Court of Appeals
765 P.2d 1043 (1988)

PLANK, J.

In this breach of contract action, defendant, Dennis Crown d/b/a Crown Company (Buyer), appeals from a judgment entered in favor of plaintiffs, Larry and Vera Scott, and from the dismissal of Buyer's counterclaim against them. We reverse.

During February 1983, Larry Scott (Seller) and Buyer entered into contract No. 76 for the sale of 16,000 bushels of U.S. No. 1 wheat. Pursuant to the contract, Buyer paid Seller $2,000 as an advanced payment. With respect to payment of the contract balance, the agreement reads in part:

> Payment by Buyer is conditioned upon Sellers [sic] completion of delivery of total quantity as set forth in this contract. Any payment made prior to completion of delivery is merely an accommodation. In making such accommodation, Buyer does not waive any condition of this contract to be performed by Seller.

Elsewhere, the contract provided that the full balance would be paid 30 days after shipment of the total contract quantity of grain.

By March 13, 1983, Seller had delivered all the wheat called for in the contract. Payment of the full contract balance of approximately $49,000 was due on April 13, 1983.

On March 1, 1983 Seller and Buyer executed contract 78-2 for the sale of 13,500 bushels of U.S. No. 1 wheat and contract No. 81-3 for the sale of approximately 30 truck loads of U.S. No. 1 wheat. These contracts are the subject of this action. With the exception of quantity, the contracts had identical terms and conditions as those in contract No. 76, including the above-quoted provision and the provision for full payment by Buyer 30 days after complete performance by Seller.

In early March 1983, Seller commenced performance of contract No. 78-2. By March 15, 1983, he had delivered to Buyer approximately 9,086 bushels of wheat. However, he ceased performance because of his belief that Buyer could not pay for the wheat.

Seller was contracting with other grain dealers while working with Buyer. Seller suffered a loss on an unrelated contract. When reviewing this loss with his banker, Seller was told that Buyer was not the "best grain trader" and was advised to contact an agent from the Department of Agriculture for additional information about Buyer. The agent, Mr. Witt, indicated there was an active complaint against Buyer concerning payments to other farmers.

The next day, one of Buyer's trucks appeared at Seller's farm to take another load of grain. Seller refused to deliver the grain. Instead, he testified that he told the driver that we had the grain, but were trying to get in touch with Mr. Crown, and my attorney advised me not to load until we had made contact with Mr. Crown to settle some questions that we had.

Seller and Witt testified that during the period of March 21 through April 6, 1983, they and Seller's attorney had attempted to contact Buyer several times by telephone, but were not successful.

By a letter dated March 23, 1983, Buyer responded to Seller's refusal to load the wheat. Buyer stated that he had not breached the contracts; however, Seller had breached the agreements. Buyer pointed out the payment terms requiring shipment of the full quantity before payment was due and requested that Seller resume performance. Otherwise, Buyer would be forced to "resort to cover."

Buyer followed up the letter with an April 4, 1983, correspondence in which he notified Seller that he was canceling the contracts. However, he assured Seller that, if the contracts were performed, his company would pay according to the contract terms.

Through counsel, Seller replied by an April 6, 1983, letter. Counsel informed Buyer that his client had not been paid on the contracts and that Seller had received information that Buyer had been paid by his buyers. Counsel demanded assurances of performance that Buyer would pay for the grain shipped on the fully performed contract 76 and the partially performed contract 78-2. However, under the contract terms, payment was not due on contract 76 until April 13, 1983, and was not due on contract 78-2 until 30 days after full performance.

Buyer canceled contracts 78-2 and 81-3 on April 7, 1983. He had previously contacted grain sellers in Denver and Salt Lake City to effect cover, but by this date the grain was no longer available.

Seller instituted suit on April 25, 1983, alleging breach of contract by Buyer in not paying in full for the grain prior to delivery pursuant to his demand for adequate assurance of performance.

The circumstances at issue bring this action within the scope of § 4-2-609(1), C.R.S., of the Uniform Commercial Code. That section provides:

> A contract for sale imposes an obligation on each party that the other's expectation of receiving due performance will not be impaired. When reasonable grounds for insecurity arise with respect to the performance of either party, the other may in writing demand adequate assurance of due performance and, until he receives such assurance, may if commercially reasonable suspend any performance for which he has not already received the agreed return.

By the express language of this provision, reasonable grounds for insecurity about the performance of either party must exist in order for the other party to exercise further rights.

Buyer alleges that Seller did not have reasonable grounds for insecurity and, further, that the demand for assurance of due performance was defective. We disagree that there were no reasonable grounds for insecurity, but agree that the demand for assurance of due performance was defective.

Whether Seller had reasonable grounds for insecurity is a question of fact. *See AMF, Inc. v. McDonald's Corp.*, 536 F.2d 1167 (7th Cir. 1976). Since trial was to the court, we will not disturb the court's findings that Seller had reasonable grounds for insecurity unless it was clearly erroneous and not supported by the record.

The trial court found that reasonable grounds for insecurity existed because: 1) Seller recently had had an unfortunate experience similar to the incident at issue with another grain dealer (i.e., a pattern of unreturned phone calls culminating in nonpayment for a grain delivery); 2) Investigator Witt had informed Seller that his office had active complaints by other farmers against Buyer; and 3) Buyer failed to make personal contact after Seller refused to load the wheat. This evidence supports the trial court's conclusion of reasonable grounds for insecurity.

There are, however, serious problems with the timing, form, and content of Seller's demand for assurances of performance. The court found that Seller had made an oral demand for assurances by his refusal to load the grain and his conversation with the driver on March 22, 1983. However, Seller did not make the written demand until his counsel's letter of April 6, 1983, some two weeks after he had suspended performance.

Generally, the express language of the statute is followed such that a demand for assurances of performance must be in writing in order to be effective. However, in some cases an oral demand for assurances has sufficed. In such cases, there appears a pattern of interaction which demonstrated a clear understanding between the parties that suspension of the demanding party's performance was the alternative, if its concerns were not adequately addressed by the other party.

In *AMF, Inc. v. McDonald's Corp.*, 536 F.2d 1167 (7th Cir. 1976), for example, McDonald's had ordered 23 computerized cash registers from AMF. However, a prototype machine installed at a McDonald's franchise performed poorly. McDonald's personnel then met with AMF and demanded that the order for their 23 units be held up pending resolution of the problems experienced in the prototype. AMF failed to resolve the problem, and McDonald's canceled the order. The court expressly rejected AMF's argument that McDonald's had not made a written demand, and held that McDonald's had properly invoked the pertinent Uniform Commercial Code provision.

Here, Seller made only the oral statement to Buyer's driver before he suspended performance. In our view, that was insufficient to make that suspension justified under § 4-2-609.

Also, there was not a subsequent pattern of interaction between the parties that would clearly demonstrate that Buyer understood that Seller had requested assurances of performance. Indeed, Buyer's letter[s] of March 23, and April 4, 1983, demonstrated that he thought that Seller had inexcusably refused to perform the contracts. Hence, we conclude that the conditions necessary to validate an oral demand were not met here.

Moreover, even if we were to conclude that an oral demand would have been permissible here, the content of the alleged demand is deficient. In contrast to AMF, Seller did not communicate clearly to Buyer that he was demanding assurances of performance. He simply told Buyer's driver that he wanted to "settle" some questions with Buyer. A mere demand for meeting to discuss the contracts, even if it had been in writing, would not be sufficient to constitute a proper demand for assurances.

Finally, a demand for performance assurances cannot be used as a means of forcing a modification of the contract.

When Seller's counsel made the demand for assurances of performance, he demanded performance beyond that required by the contracts. In the April 6, 1983, letter, counsel requested payment in full of contract 76 and payment for the grain delivered on contract 78-2. At that time, Buyer was not obligated under the terms of the contracts to make such payments.

Under these facts, we conclude that Seller did not have the right to suspend performance because he failed to act in a manner that would bring him within the scope of § 4-2-609. Instead, Seller's actions constituted an anticipatory repudiation which gave Buyer the right to cancel the contracts and resort to the buyer's remedies.

NOTES

(1) *Demanding Adequate Assurances in Other Contracts.* While the RESTATE-MENT (SECOND) OF CONTRACTS indicates that the rule entitling one to adequate assurances where an obligee reasonably believes that the obligor will commit a breach by nonperformance is "a generalization, applicable without regard to the subject matter of the contract" (Comment a. to 251), the United States Court of Appeals for the Second Circuit felt compelled to ask the New York Court of Appeals whether it applied under New York law. The case involved a long-term contract for the sale of electricity which was not viewed as a contract for the sale of goods, therefore precluding the application of the UCC and its § 2-609(4). In *Norcon Power Partners, Ltd. v. Niagra Mohawk Power Co.*, 163 F.3d 153 (2d Cir. 1998), the court reported that the Court of Appeals decided that a demand for adequate assurances would be recognized beyond sale-of-goods contracts, but limited its application to long-term commercial contracts which are typically not susceptible to anticipation of all security features. In *McNeal v. Lebel*, 953 A.2d 396 (N.H. 2008), the court noted that while a right to demand adequate assurances had not previously been recognized in the general contract law of New Hampshire, the trial court had applied the doctrine correctly in the case before the court.

(2) *Time for Adequate Assurances.* UCC § 2-609(4) indicates that a failure to provide adequate assurances within a reasonable time *not exceeding thirty days* after receipt of a justified demand for such assurances constitutes a repudiation of the contract. The RESTATEMENT (SECOND) OF CONTRACTS suggests a virtually identical concept for contracts other than contracts for the sale of goods in § 251. It does not, however, contain a thirty-day limitation but is content to require the assurance within a reasonable time. § 251(2).

(3) *Insolvency.* An obligor who cannot pay debts in the ordinary course of business or as the debts mature is said to be insolvent. *See* UCC § 1-201(23) and RESTATEMENT (SECOND) OF CONTRACTS § 252(2). Since insolvency is not voluntary and affirmative, it is not a repudiation of the contract. In a given situation, it may not even provide reasonable grounds for insecurity, as in the case of an employee who is insolvent but quite capable of continuing performance. An insolvent buyer of goods, however, provides the seller with reasonable grounds for insecurity concerning payment of the price upon delivery. Thus, the UCC permits the seller to refuse delivery except for cash. UCC § 2-702(1). Where insolvency provides reasonable grounds to believe that the obligor will not be able to perform, the obligee has the unqualified power to suspend his own performance. If, however, the obligee wishes to be discharged from his duties, he must pursue the process of demanding adequate assurances.

In general, see MURRAY ON CONTRACTS § 110G.

F. EXCUSED CONDITIONS — PREVENTION, HINDRANCE, AND WAIVER

The non-occurrence of a condition may be excused on a variety of grounds. RESTATEMENT (SECOND) OF CONTRACTS § 225, comment b. We have seen that a condition may be excused to avoid forfeiture. We have also recognized that where one party to the contract repudiates, a condition to the other party's performance may be excused. In the next chapter, we will consider excusable non-performance through impracticability. At this point, we consider two other bases for excusing conditions: the prevention or hindrance of their occurrence through a breach of the duty of good faith and fair dealing which may also be viewed as a "constructive condition of cooperation," and the "waiver" of conditions.

ROHDE v. MASSACHUSETTS MUTUAL LIFE INSURANCE CO.
United States Court of Appeals, Sixth Circuit
632 F.2d 667 (1980)

PECK, J.

Plaintiff is the widow of a man who applied for life insurance, arranged for payment of the initial premium, and took the required physical examination all on the same day. In exchange for these acts, defendant's agent completed a form designated as a "Conditional Receipt." This form contained a promise by the defendant to insure the applicant under the policy sought, effective the latest date on which the applicant completed the application and physical examination. The receipt further stated that defendant had no obligation except to return payment unless the company determined that as of the completion of the physical and application the applicant was an acceptable risk under its "limits, rules, and standards."

The same day that the defendant applied for life insurance he died of an apparent heart attack. Acting under the condition of the receipt requiring the defendant to determine whether the applicant was an acceptable risk, the defendant investigated the application of plaintiff's husband and determined that the deceased had been uninsurable for the policy sought. Accordingly, defendant denied liability under the agreement with the decedent and returned the premium payment to plaintiff.

An application for life insurance is an offer to purchase a policy and the insurer must accept before a contract exists. During the time the offer is outstanding and unaccepted the applicant has the power to revoke the offer. Such revocation would not only deny the insurer the right to accept and complete a sale, but also would be likely to cause the insurer to lose the expense of processing and investigating an application.

Insurers discourage or prevent the revocation of offers by use of conditional receipts or "binders" that give the insurer the option of ultimately accepting or rejecting the offer while making the offer irrevocable by conditionally accepting it. The most straightforward of these binders accept the offer and, as consideration for the applicant's promise to purchase insurance, create immediate insurance for the applicant while reserving a right of the insurer to cancel all insurance after an opportunity to investigate the application.

The more prevalent form of binder, however, seeks to make the applicant's offer irrevocable without giving the applicant interim insurance in exchange. *See* 7 WILLISTON ON CONTRACTS, § 902A, pp. 197-203 (3d. ed. 1963). In this form insurance is promised to begin as of the date of the application or receipt subject to the qualification that the application must first be accepted or approved before any coverage begins. With these two provisions standing side-by-side in the binder, all that the applicant actually receives in exchange for his promise to purchase is the possibility of interim insurance. If the insurer does not approve the application, then no coverage ever exists. Of course, by the time the insurer approves or rejects, it will be likely to know whether the applicant has incurred a covered loss and can exercise its option to reject. Thus, the possibility of interim coverage is largely illusory under this type of binder. Recognizing that such binders are confusing to applicants and that applicants generally would be unlikely to enter such bargains if they actually understood them, courts have tended to find that binders that condition liability on "approval" of the insurer are ambiguous and that the parties to such contracts actually intend interim insurance as consideration for the applicants' promises to purchase insurance if the insurer approves.

Plaintiff in this case argues that the condition contained in defendant's receipt is ambiguous and that the receipt should be liberally construed to provide interim insurance for the applicant pending the defendant acting on the condition. We agree with the finding of the district court that this condition is unambiguous and cannot be construed to provide the applicant with coverage prior to defendant's determination that the applicant is "insurable."

Unlike conditions which make an insurer's liability depend solely on the insurer's approval of the application, the condition contained in defendant's receipt requires that the defendant determine whether the applicant meets limits, rules and standards of the defendant company regarding the policy sought by the applicant. This condition does not involve judgments based on subjective factors, but rather considerations of actuarial and medical prediction balanced against the company's ordinary risk assignment practices. The defendant's satisfaction or dissatisfaction with the risk represented by the applicant's offer must be based on a reasonable examination of the application. The defendant's liability under the contract represented by the conditional receipt does not depend on the defendant's subjective approval. Rather, the defendant promised to be liable for a covered loss if the applicant was qualified on the date his application was completed. This promise was the consideration agreed to by the applicant for his promise to purchase the policy. The defendant's receipt clearly stated that no interim insurance was provided and that coverage would become effective as of the date of the application only if the defendant found the applicant an acceptable risk under objective standards.

Based on trial testimony and considering the entire record, the district court found that the defendant acted in bad faith and was without reasonable grounds in determining that plaintiff's husband failed to meet the requirements for the policy sought. The issue of defendant's good or bad faith is primarily a question of fact requiring an examination of defendant's intent or state of mind. The district court had the opportunity to weigh the credibility of defendant's witnesses and was in a position to make the necessary inferences regarding defendant's intent. This court will overturn the finding of bad faith only if the record does not support that finding. We have examined the record and the opinion of the district court and find substantial support for the finding of bad faith on the part of the defendant.

Having found defendant's determination that the applicant was uninsurable to have been made in bad faith, the district court proceeded to determine what conclusion the defendant would have reached had it acted in good faith. Deciding that the defendant in good faith would have determined that the applicant was uninsurable under the standard policy applied for, the district court concluded that the defendant was not liable. This analysis fails to give defendant's bad faith determination of the applicant's uninsurability proper legal effect under Ohio law.

The defendant's good faith determination that the applicant meet the defendant's standards of insurability was a condition precedent to defendant's liability under the contract represented by the conditional receipt. When the defendant acted in bad faith and determined that the applicant failed to meet the defendant's standards, then the defendant's own act prevented the occurrence of the condition precedent. The nonoccurrence or nonperformance of a condition is excused where that failure of the condition is caused by the party against whom the condition operates to impose a duty. Defendant's failure to honor its obligation of good faith in exercising its right to examine the application deprives defendant of any benefit it might obtain from that condition. The fact that the defendant might have found the applicant uninsurable had the defendant acted in good faith is not relevant under Ohio law.

With the condition precedent of determining the applicant to be insurable deleted from the contract, all conditions precedent to defendant's liability were satisfied. By the terms of the contract agreed to by the defendant and the applicant when the receipt was completed the policy applied for became effective as of the day the applicant died and prior to his death. The defendant is therefore liable to the plaintiff in the full amount of the policy.

NOTES

(1)   "Where a duty of one party is subject to the occurrence of a condition, the additional duty of good faith and fair dealing imposed on him under § 205 may require some cooperation on his part, either by refraining from conduct that will prevent or hinder the occurrence of that condition or by taking affirmative steps to cause its occurrence." RESTATEMENT (SECOND) OF CONTRACTS § 245, cmt. a.

(2)   The prevention of the condition could not have been more definite than it was in *Foreman State Trust & Sav. Bank v. Tauber*, 180 N.E. 827 (Ill.1932), where a prenuptial agreement promised a large payment to the wife if she survived her husband. The condition of survival was prevented in the most direct way when the husband shot and killed the wife before committing suicide. The husband's action may be described euphemistically as a failure to cooperate. Not remarkably, the court found the nonoccurrence of the survival condition excused. Another obvious example is *Barron v. Cain*, 4 S.E.2d 618 (N.C. 1939). The plaintiff was induced by his uncle to live with and care for the uncle for life. Plaintiff was to be "well paid for his services" upon his uncle's death. The plaintiff remained for about six years during which time the old uncle was constantly under the influence of liquor. He subjected the plaintiff to various indignities and assault, and finally ran him off the premises with a deadly weapon, threatening to do the plaintiff severe bodily harm should he return. Sometimes, however, the facts are not as obvious when a party attempts to have the condition to his duty excused. In *Godburn v. Meserve*, 37 A.2d 235 (Conn. 1944), the plaintiffs, husband and wife, had agreed to live with and care for their former lessor, a 76-year-old woman. After five years, the plaintiffs moved out because of friction that developed about two years after the performance of the contract began. The decedent (woman) objected to certain guests of the plaintiffs, including their grandchildren, objected to being left alone at night, thus preventing the plaintiffs from vacationing, constantly found fault with minor things, objected to food, and developed a habit of tapping her foot on the floor while eating. A portion of the court's opinion follows:

> Accordingly, the question for determination is whether the decedent's conduct complained of was wrongful in the sense of being violative of her obligations under the contract. In other words, was it or was it not conduct which must be said to have been fairly within the contemplation of the parties when the agreement was entered into? . . . In addition to the facts already mentioned, the undisputed testimony was that for twenty years prior to the agreement Mr. Godburn had known the decedent as a customer in the grocery store where he was employed, that during the last three and one-half years of this period, while he and his family were living next door as her tenants, the plaintiffs came to know the decedent very well, that she was regularly and frequently in their home as a guest and ate meals there, and that they knew she was an elderly lady apparently about seventy-six or seven years of age. It is a matter of common knowledge that a gradually increasing impairment of powers and a not unusual tendency to more or less eccentricity naturally are to be expected as incident to the advancing years of one of that age, and under the circumstances the only reasonable conclusion upon the record before us is that the decedent's conduct was fairly within the contemplation of the parties under their contract as made.

The gist of the situation is apparently well summarized by Mr. Godburn's testimony that "the only thing she complained about was the eats," which everybody else thought were all right, that her conduct was upsetting and disturbing to the plaintiffs and that they "didn't have to take it" and they "wouldn't." It follows from what we have said that not only is there no evidence that the decedent "forced the plaintiffs to leave said premises in violation of the terms of the contract," as alleged in the complaint, but furthermore there is none that what she did was "wrongful, and, accordingly, in excess of [her] legal rights" within the principle quoted above. The defendants' motion to set aside the verdict should therefore have been granted.

Id. at 727–28, 37 A.2d at 237.

STANDARD SUPPLY CO. v. RELIANCE INSURANCE CO.
North Carolina Court of Appeals
272 S.E.2d 394 (1980)

Plaintiff brought this action to recover the proceeds of a fire insurance policy written by defendant Reliance Insurance Company (Reliance) and issued by defendant Eaves Insurance Agency, Inc. (Eaves Agency) by its president, George W. Eaves (Eaves). The policy covered a dwelling house owned by plaintiff and situated in rural Chatham County. The policy contained an exclusion clause, as follows:

> Unless otherwise provided in writing added hereto: This company shall not be liable for loss occurring while a described building, whether intended for occupancy by owner or tenant, is vacant or unoccupied beyond a period of 60 days.

Plaintiff's evidence may be summarized as follows. Since 1961 or 1962, plaintiff had purchased fire and extended coverage insurance on the Chatham County dwelling through defendant Eaves Agency. Prior to 4 March 1976, defendant Reliance had written the coverage on the dwelling. In March 1976, plaintiff procured through Eaves Agency a renewal of its coverage with Reliance. In February 1976, prior to the writing of the renewal policy, defendant Reliance requested Tar Heel Reporting Company, Inc. (Tar Heel) to make a fire inspection and report on the dwelling. John Edward Jennings, Jr. (Jennings), president of Tar Heel subsequently made the investigation and submitted the report to Reliance. . . . His report described the condition of the property in some detail, and included a statement that the property was not vacant. The report did not otherwise specify whether the dwelling was occupied or unoccupied.

Following Jennings' inspection and report, Reliance furnished a summary of the report to Eaves Agency in which they expressed their concern about the state of disrepair of the front porch and steps of the dwelling. Eaves Agency requested plaintiff to furnish them the name of the tenant, but plaintiff did not respond to this request. At the time of the inspection and at the time the renewal policy was issued, the house was unoccupied and had been unoccupied since January 1975. Eaves Agency issued the renewal policy on or about 22 March 1976. The house was destroyed by fire on 5 July 1976. . . .

WELLS, J.

The heart of plaintiff's claim against Reliance lies in the theory of waiver, based upon the proposition that Reliance had constructive knowledge that the house was unoccupied and that Reliance issued the policy while possessed of such knowledge. Whether or not Reliance had the constructive knowledge contended by plaintiff is a jury question. Plaintiff's evidence showed that the dwelling was in a state of substantial disrepair when it was inspected by Jennings. There was no electricity to the house and several windows were broken. There was no observed heat source in the house and the house was sparsely furnished. On the other hand, a neighbor informed Jennings that people were living in the house and Jennings observed a "puppy" dog on the premises during his visit. Another of plaintiff's witnesses, Thomas Urquhart, testified that he visited and inspected the house in February of 1976. He described the poor condition of the house, its lack of electricity and sparse furnishings and the broken windows. These physical conditions suggested to him that the house was vacant, and that the conditions "to me say that you can't live there." Plaintiff presented similar testimony from Richard Urquhart.

The jury question arising on this evidence is whether a reasonable person, seeing the property in the conditions existing when Jennings visited it, could have concluded that the property was occupied, or, whether these conditions were such as to put Jennings on such notice of non-occupancy as to require further investigation. Our Supreme Court, quoting from 16 APPELMAN, INSURANCE LAW AND PRACTICE, has stated the rule as follows:

> Knowledge of facts which the insurer has or should have had constitutes notice of whatever an inquiry would have disclosed and is binding on the insurer. The rule applies to insurance companies that whatever puts a person on inquiry amounts in law to "notice" of such facts as an inquiry pursued with ordinary diligence and understanding would have disclosed.

In addition to the evidence of non-occupancy based on the observed conditions of the property, Reliance was never furnished with the name of a tenant for the property. This is further evidence from which the jury might, but need not, infer that Reliance was on notice of non-occupancy.

The question of whether there was notice to Reliance depends in substantial degree on whether Jennings' knowledge was imputable to Reliance. In another assignment of error, plaintiff excepted to the portion of the trial court's charge to the jury in which the court instructed the jury on the issue of agency, as follows:

> I will instruct you that the Tarheel Reporting Company was acting not as an agent of the Reliance Insurance Company but as an independent contractor, and if you should find that Ed Jennings — or John Ed Jennings of the Tarheel Reporting Company failed to ascertain there were no tenants living in the house or if you should find that Mr. Jennings wrongfully concluded that the house was not vacant, that this fact is not imputed to Reliance Insurance Company, since Mr. Jennings and Tarheel Reporting Company were not agents of Reliance Insurance Company but

were acting in the capacity of an independent contractor. And the issue before you is not a determination of whether or not Mr. Jennings and Tarheel Reporting Company wrongfully concluded that the dwelling was not vacant.

We hold that the foregoing instruction was erroneous. While recognizing that Tar Heel was not generally subject to the control and direct supervision of Reliance and that in the general sense Tar Heel was an independent contractor, this aspect of the relationship is not determinative of the question of agency here. An independent contractor may also be an agent. 2A C.J.S. *Agency* § 12, at 574 (1972); RESTATEMENT OF THE LAW OF AGENCY 2d § 14N, at 80 (1958). We hold that for the purposes of making the investigation and report Tar Heel was employed to make, Tar Heel was acting as the agent of Reliance, so that such knowledge of the conditions of the property, bearing on occupancy or non-occupancy, as was gained by Tar Heel as a result of its investigation, was imputable to Reliance.

Plaintiff argues that the evidence shows either that Reliance waived the exclusionary clause, or, that it should be estopped to deny coverage. In a case such as the one before us, the line between waiver and estoppel is often blurred. In previous opinions, this Court and our Supreme Court have dealt with and commented upon the characteristics which may either distinguish these two principles of law, or, may show the kinship of one to the other.

In *Horton v. Insurance Co.*, 122 N.C. 498, 503, 29 S.E. 944, 945 (1898), our Supreme Court enunciated the rule that conditions in an insurance policy working a forfeiture are matters of contract and not limitation and may be waived by the insurer. Thus when the insurer, knowing the facts, does that which is inconsistent with its intention to insist on a strict compliance with the conditions precedent of the contract, it is treated as having waived their performance.

We believe that plaintiff's evidence in the case *sub judice* properly raises an issue of whether Reliance was on such notice of the non-occupancy of the house at the time the policy was renewed that its subsequent issuance of the policy constituted a waiver of the exclusionary provision or condition. . . .

The trial court should have given a charge properly explaining the law of waiver as it applies to the evidence in this case, and the instruction given was erroneous.

ROSE v. MITSUBISHI INTERNATIONAL CORP.
United States District Court, Eastern District of Pennsylvania
423 F. Supp. 1162 (1976)

CAHN, DISTRICT JUDGE.

Plaintiff, Jack Rose, is suing for money damages for breach of an alleged contract in the form of a letter of intent. The matter is before the court on the motion of Mitsubishi International Corporation ("MIC") for summary judgment under Fed. R. Civ. P. 56.

In 1973, plaintiff had an option enabling him to purchase from Northern Metal Company a deep-water port facility located on the Pennsylvania side of the

Delaware River. On March 29, 1973, MIC and Federal Steel Corporation ("Federal") executed a letter of intent to plaintiff which plaintiff approved the same day. The letter of intent provided for contribution by MIC of funds required to exercise plaintiff's option. It also provided for the formation of a new corporation by MIC and Federal which would participate with plaintiff in a joint venture involving the deep-water port facility. The obligation of MIC and Federal to provide financing was subject to certain conditions including:

> 6. A reputable United States title insurance company shall issue title policies indicating clear and marketable title to the real estate and interests in real estate referred to herein and indicating that the same can continue to be used in the future for the purposes for which they are presently in use.

The letter of intent provided that the obligations of the parties were to be completed by May 15, 1973, but this deadline was extended by mutual agreement until May 22, 1973. On May 21, 1973, MIC notified plaintiff that it would not proceed under the letter of intent. Thereafter, plaintiff instituted this action against MIC, Richard Kates, an officer of Federal, and Raritan Corporation, the parent of Federal. Jurisdiction is based upon diversity of citizenship.

Ordinarily, marketable title is not an absolute concept but may depend upon parol evidence of adverse possession or prescriptive holding as well as other facts. In such a situation, summary judgment would not be proper. Here, however, the parties have specifically contracted for the issuance of a title insurance policy indicating clear and marketable title to the real estate involved. Since the express condition in the letter of intent not only requires the issuance of a title policy "indicating" clear and marketable title, but further "indicating" that the real estate can continue to be used in the future for the purposes for which it is presently used, I find that this condition is not satisfied. Therefore, MIC is entitled to summary judgment in its favor on the issue of whether the condition was satisfied.

Plaintiff also claims that he is entitled to a trial on whether or not MIC waived condition 6 in the agreement of March 29, 1973. The Restatement of Contracts § 297 states the requirements for the excuse of a condition by waiver:

> A promisor whose duty is dependent upon performance by the other party of a condition or return promise that is not a material part of the agreed exchange can make that duty independent of such performance, in advance of the time fixed for it, by a manifestation of willingness that the duty shall be thus independent. Such a waiver, unless it is a binding promise within the rules for the formation of contracts, can be retracted at any time before the other party has materially changed his position in reliance thereon, but not afterwards.

Clear and marketable title indicated by title insurance, as stated in condition 6 of the letter of intent, is "a material part of the agreed exchange". Its materiality as a matter of law is shown by the rule that a purchaser of land is not required to take the title offered when an easement exists which is a breach of a covenant for a conveyance free from encumbrances. *Volkert v. Swan*, 197 Pa. Super. 576, 179 A.2d

274 (1962). Such a condition, as opposed to a mere matter of performance such as a settlement date, cannot be waived.

"If performance of the condition is a material part of the agreed exchange, an agreement to be liable in spite of the non-performance of the condition involves to so great a degree a new undertaking that the requisites for the creation of a new contract must exist." RESTATEMENT OF CONTRACTS § 297, comment c. at 440 (1932).

NOTES

(1) RESTATEMENT (SECOND) OF CONTRACTS § 84(1):

> (1) Except as stated in Subsection (2), a promise to perform all or part of a conditional duty under an antecedent contract in spite of the non-occurrence of the condition is binding, whether the promise is made before or after the time for the condition to occur, unless (a) occurrence of the condition was a material part of the agreed exchange for the performance of the duty and the promisee was under no duty that it occur; or (b) uncertainty of the occurrence of the condition was an element of the risk assumed by the promisor.

> *Comment d. Conditions which may be waived.* The rule of Subsection (1) applies primarily to conditions which may be thought of as procedural or technical, or to instances in which the non-occurrence is comparatively minor. Examples are conditions which merely relate to the time or manner of the return performance or provide for the giving of notice or the supplying of proofs. Insurance policies ordinarily contain conditions of notice and proof of loss and of time for suit. . . . In such cases, even though a promise to disregard the non-occurrence of the condition subjects the promisor to a new duty, the new duty is not regarded as significantly different from the old and the promise is binding without consideration, reliance or formality.

(2) *Proving "Waiver."* In *Cole Taylor Bank v. Truck Insurance Exchange*, 51 F.3d 736 (7th Cir. 1995), Chief Judge Posner wrote the opinion of the court that contained the following concerns about proving waiver:

> There is no more vexing question in contract law than when a written contract can be rewritten by oral testimony. * * * Unlike modification of a contract, the efficacy of a waiver of a contractual right is generally not thought to require special tokens of reliability, such as a writing, consideration, reliance, judicial screening, or a heightened standard of proof. What is more, a waiver of contractual rights can be implied as well as express — implied from words or actions inconsistent with the assertion of those rights.

The potential inconsistency of the doctrine of waiver so understood with the principle that parties should not be allowed to get out of their written contracts by selfserving testimony is manifest. You can always say that the other party to your contract had orally waived the enforcement of a provision favorable to him. Yet all that waiver means, when it is carefully defined, is the intentional relinquishment of a right. Any mentally competent person is allowed to relinquish most of his constitutional rights without any formalities; it might seem all the clearer that he should be able to relinquish his contractual rights without formalities.

But the courts have not been indifferent to the danger of self-serving testimony that the other party to the contract waived a right that the contract had conferred on him. In some cases they have required proof of reliance on the alleged waiver, in effect converting the doctrine of waiver into the harder-to-prove doctrine of estoppel. Illinois — whose law we apply in this case — requires that an alleged waiver either have induced reliance or that it be clearly inferable from the circumstances.

The fact that the courts have not converged on a blanket general requirement of reliance, consideration, a writing, a heightened standard of proof, or other means of assuring the reliability of questionable evidence may reflect the inherent implausibility of offers to prove "bare" waiver in a contractual setting. Unless the right waived is a minor one why would someone give it up in exchange for nothing? If something is given in return, then there is consideration.

(3) *Reinstating the Condition.* RESTATEMENT (SECOND) OF CONTRACTS § 84(2):

If such a promise is made before the time for the occurrence of the condition has expired and the condition is within the control of the promisee or a beneficiary, the promisor can make his duty again subject to the condition by notifying the promisee or beneficiary of his intention to do so if

(a) the notification is received while there is still a reasonable time to cause the condition to occur under the antecedent terms or an extension given by the promisor; and

(b) reinstatement of the requirement of the condition is not unjust because of a material change of position by the promisee or beneficiary; and

(c) the promise is not binding apart from the rule stated in Subsection (1).

(4) *"Nonwaiver" ("Antiwaiver") Clauses.* Where an obligee accepts performances that do not adhere to the terms of the contract, the breach may be waived. Thus, earlier in this chapter we saw the acceptance of a late payment amounting to a waiver in the *Associated Builders* case. To preserve conditions previously waived, many contracts contain "nonwaiver" or "antiwaiver" clauses designed to automatically reinstate conditions to future performances even though there have been one or more waivers of such conditions in the earlier performance of the contract. A nonwaiver clause, however, does not preclude the excuse of conditions by manifestations of intention to forego the benefit of one or more conditions. *See TSS-Seedman's, Inc. v. Elota Realty Co.*, 531 N.E.2d 646 (N.Y. 1988). A party may be estopped to assert a nonwaiver clause, *Dorn v. Robinson*, 762 P.2d 566 (Ariz. Ct. App. 1988). Moreover, if the intention to forego the benefit of the condition is pervasive over a long period, even a nonwaiver clause may be waived. *Westinghouse*

Credit Corp. v. Shelton, 645 F.2d 869, 873–74 (10th Cir. 1981). In general, see MURRAY ON CONTRACTS § 112.

Chapter 7

RISK ALLOCATION: IMPOSSIBILITY, IMPRACTICABILITY, AND FRUSTRATION OF PURPOSE

A. ORIGINS — IMPOSSIBILITY

TAYLOR v. CALDWELL
King's Bench
3 B. & S. 826 (1863)

BLACKBURN, J.

In this case the plaintiffs and defendants had, on the 27th May, 1861, entered into a contract by which the defendants agreed to let the plaintiffs have the use of The Surrey Gardens and Music Hall on four days then to come, viz., the 17th June, 15th July, 5th August and 19th August, for the purpose of giving a series of four grand concerts, and day and night f/Cetes at the Gardens and Hall on those days respectively; and the plaintiffs agreed to take the Gardens and Hall on those days, and pay £ 100 for each day.

The parties inaccurately call this a "letting," and the money to be paid a "rent"; but the whole agreement is such as to shew that the defendants were to retain the possession of the Hall and Gardens so that there was to be no demise of them, and that the contract was merely to give the plaintiffs the use of them on those days. Nothing however, in our opinion, depends on this. . . .

After the making of the agreement, and before the first day on which a concert was to be given, the Hall was destroyed by fire. This destruction, we must take it on the evidence, was without the fault of either party, and was so complete that in consequence the concerts could not be given as intended. And the question we have to decide is whether, under these circumstances, the loss which the plaintiffs have sustained is to fall upon the defendants. The parties when framing their agreement evidently had not present to their minds the possibility of such a disaster, and have made no express stipulation with reference to it, so that the answer to the question must depend upon the general rules of law applicable to such a contract.

There seems no doubt that where there is a positive contract to do a thing, not in itself unlawful, the contractor must perform it or pay damages for not doing it, although in consequence of unforeseen accidents, the performance of his contract has become unexpectedly burthensome or even impossible. The law is so laid down in 1 Roll. Abr. 450, Condition (G), and in the note (2) to *Walton v. Waterhouse* (2

607

Wms. Saund. 421 a. 6th ed.), and is recognized as the general rule by all the Judges in the much discussed case of *Hall v. Wright* (E.B. & E. 746). But this rule is only applicable when the contract is positive and absolute, and not subject to any condition either express or implied: and there are authorities which, as we think, establish the principle that where, from the nature of the contract, it appears that the parties must from the beginning have known that it could not be fulfilled unless when the time for the fulfillment of the contract arrived some particular specified thing continued to exist, so that, when entering into the contract, they must have contemplated such continuing existence as the foundation of what was to be done; there, in the absence of any express or implied warranty that the thing shall exist, the contract is not to be construed as a positive contract, but as subject to an implied condition that the parties shall be excused in case, before breach, performance becomes impossible from the perishing of the thing without default of the contractor.

There seems little doubt that this implication tends to further the great object of making the legal construction such as to fulfill the intention of those who entered into the contract. For in the course of affairs men in making such contracts in general would, if it were brought to their minds, say that there should be such a condition.

Accordingly, in the Civil law, such an exception is implied in every obligation of the class which they call *obligatio de certo corpore*. . . .

The examples are of contracts respecting a slave, which was the common illustration of a certain subject used by the Roman lawyers, just as we are apt to take a horse; and no doubt the propriety, one might almost say necessity, of the implied condition is more obvious when the contract relates to a living animal, whether man or brute, than when it relates to some inanimate thing (such as in the present case a theatre) the existence of which is not so obviously precarious as that of the live animal, but the principle is adopted in the Civil law as applicable to every obligation of which the subject is a certain thing. The general subject is treated of by Pothier, who in his Traite des Obligations, partie 3, chap. 6, art. 3, § 668 states the result to be that the debtor *corporis certi* is freed from his obligation when the thing has perished, neither by his act, nor his neglect, and before he is in default, unless by some stipulation he has taken on himself the risk of the particular misfortune which has occurred.

Although the Civil law is not of itself authority in an English Court, it affords great assistance in investigating the principles on which the law is grounded. And it seems to us that the common law authorities establish that in such a contract the same condition of the continued existence of the thing is implied by English law.

There is a class of contracts in which a person binds himself to do something which requires to be performed by him in person; and such promises, e.g. promises to marry, or promises to serve for a certain time, are never in practice qualified by an express exception of the death of the party; and therefore in such cases the contract is in terms broken if the promisor dies before fulfilment. Yet it was very early determined that, if the performance is personal, the executors are not liable. . . .

See 2 Wms. Exors. 1560, 5th ed., where a very apt illustration is given. "Thus," says the learned author, "if an author undertakes to compose a work, and dies before completing it, his executors are discharged from this contract: for the undertaking is merely personal in its nature, and, by the intervention of the contractor's death, has become impossible to be performed.". . .

These are instances where the implied condition is of the life of a human being, but there are others in which the same implication is made as to the continued existence of a thing. For example, where a contract of sale is made amounting to a bargain and sale, transferring presently the property in specific chattels, which are to be delivered by the vendor at a future day; there, if the chattels, without the fault of the vendor, perish in the interval, the purchaser must pay the price and the vendor is excused from performing his contract to deliver, which has thus become impossible . . . .

In *Williams v. Lloyd* (W. Jones, 179) . . . the count, which was in assumpsit, alleged that the plaintiff had delivered a horse to the defendant, who promised to redeliver it on request. Breach, that though requested to redeliver the horse he refused. Plea, that the horse was sick and died, and the plaintiff made the request after its death; and on demurrer it was held a good plea, as the bailee was discharged from his promise by the death of the horse without default or negligence on the part of the defendant. "Let it be admitted," say the Court, "that he promised to deliver it on request, if the horse die before, that is become impossible by the act of God, so the party shall be discharged, as much as if an obligation were made conditioned to deliver the horse on request, and he died before it." And Jones, adds the report, cited 22 Ass. 41, in which it was held that a ferryman who had promised to carry a horse safe across the ferry was held chargeable for the drowning of the animal only because he had overloaded the boat, and it was agreed that notwithstanding the promise no action would have lain had there been no neglect or default on his part.

It may, we think, be safely asserted to be now English law, that in all contracts of loan of chattels or bailments if the performance of the promise of the borrower or bailee to return the things lent or bailed, becomes impossible because it has perished, this impossibility (if not arising from the fault of the borrower or bailee from some risk which he has taken upon himself) excuses the borrower or bailee from the performance of his promise to redeliver the chattel.

The great case of *Coggs v. Bernard* (1 Smith's L.C. 171, 5th ed.; 2 L. Raym. 909) is now the leading case on the law of bailments, and Lord Holt, in that case, referred so much to the Civil law that it might perhaps be thought that this principle was there derived direct from the civilians, and was not generally applicable in English law except in the case of bailments; but the case of *Williams v. Lloyd* (W. Jones, 179), above cited, shews that the same law had been already adopted by the English law as early as THE BOOK OF ASSIZES. The principle seems to us to be that, in contracts in which the performance depends on the continued existence of a given person or thing, a condition is implied that the impossibility of performance arising from the perishing of the person or thing shall excuse the performance.

In none of these cases is the promise in words other than positive, nor is there any express stipulation that the destruction of the person or thing shall excuse the performance; but that excuse is by law implied, because from the nature of the contract it is apparent that the parties contracted on the basis of the continued existence of the particular person or chattel. In the present case, looking at the whole contract, we find that the parties contracted on the basis of the continued existence of the Music Hall at the time when the concerts were to be given; that being essential to their performance. . . .

We think, therefore, that the Music Hall having ceased to exist, without fault of either party, both parties are excused, the plaintiffs from taking the Gardens and paying the money, the defendants from performing their promise to give the use of the Hall and Gardens and other things. Consequently the rule must be absolute to enter the verdict for the defendants.

COMMENT

The History of Impossibility and its Exceptions — UCC Developments. In *Paradine v. Jane*, Aleyn 26, 82 Eng. Rep. (1647), the plaintiff brought an action under the common-law writ of *debt*, alleging failure of the defendant to pay rent on certain lands for three years. The defendant (tenant) pleaded that the army of German Prince Rupert had invaded the realm, entered defendant's possession, and expelled him, so that he could not take the profits. Plaintiff demurred and the demurrer was sustained because the defendant might have provided against this particular contingency by contract. The fact that neither the defendant nor any reasonable party in his position would have foreseen or expected the invasion of Prince Rupert was irrelevant. Omniscience was assumed. While this case is really not an impossibility of performance case, since the performance of the tenant of paying rent was clearly not impossible (it is a frustration of purpose case), the language of the opinion is viewed as the strong, early common-law view that impossibility was not an excuse. There are remnants of that view still to be found in relatively modern cases. *See, e.g., Wills v. Shockley*, 52 Del. (2 Storey) 295, 157 A.2d 252 (1960), in which the court quotes from an American law encyclopedia (12 Am. Jur. *Contracts* § 363) that states, in reliance on *Paradine v. Jane*:

> This early English decision has often been referred to as a leading one and as establishing the rule that where there is a positive contract to do a thing, not in itself unlawful, the contractor must perform it or pay damages for not doing it, although, in consequence of unforeseen accidents, the performance of his contracts has became unexpectedly burdensome.

Exceptions. The notion that the promisor is not excused because either (1) he should have foreseen the unforeseeable, or (2) he has promised to do the impossible, could not prevail without exception. Thus the common-law development of exceptions to the general rule of no excuse for failure to perform were developed in many cases over a long period. The principal case is best known for developing an exception to the general rule. Notice that the court states the general rule in a fashion indistinguishable from the *Paradine* concept and cites other cases in support. Only then does the court carefully suggest that the rule is subject to either express or implied conditions:

[W]here, from the nature of the contract, it appears that the parties must from the beginning have known that it could not be fulfilled unless when the time for the fulfillment of the contract arrived some specific thing continued to exist, so that, when entering into the contract, they must have contemplated such continuing existence as the foundation of what was to be done . . . the contract is not to be construed as a positive [absolute] contract, but as subject to any implied condition that the parties shall be excused in case, before breach, performance becomes impossible from the perishing of the thing without default of the contractor.

Thus, through the use of what Karl Llewellyn might call a "covert tool" — an "implied condition" — the court states a principle that permits excuse for at least a certain type of impossibility, i.e., destruction of the subject matter without the fault of the promisor. A criticism of this analysis might suggest that to reach a just result, a court can always resort to inferring a condition. This criticism was emphasized as follows:

As we have indicated, *Taylor v. Caldwell*, the United States Supreme Court cases and the Virginia cases all relied in their statement of the doctrine on an implied, though unstated, condition in the contract. Increasingly, though, commentators and text writers were uncomfortable with the implied condition rationale for the new doctrine of impossibility of performance. In 6 CORBIN ON CONTRACTS, § 1331, p. 360 (1962 ed.), the author puts his objection to the implied condition theory strongly and rephrased the rationale for the doctrine thus:

Though it has been constantly said by high authority, including Lord Sumner, that the explanation of the rule is to be found in the theory that it depends on an implied condition of the contract, that is really no explanation. It only pushes back the problem a single stage. It leaves the question what is the reason for implying a term. Nor can I reconcile that theory with the view that the result does not depend on what the parties might, or would as hard bargainers, have agreed. The doctrine is invented by the court in order to supplement the defects of the actual contract. The parties did not anticipate fully and completely, if at all, or provide for what actually happened.

The court notes that the RESTATEMENT (SECOND) OF CONTRACTS accepts this statement in its Introductory Note to Chapter 11 dealing with impracticability of performance and frustration of purpose. The court goes on to quote Williston as he rejected the implied condition theory:

[B]ecause the court thinks it fair to qualify the promise, it does so quite rightly; but clearness of thought would be increased if it were plainly recognized that the qualification of the promise or the defense to it is not based on any expression of intention by the parties. [18 WILLISTON ON CONTRACTS, § 1937, p. 33 (3d ed. Jaeger 1978).]

Moreover, . . . modern authorities also abandoned any absolute definition of impossibility and, following the example of the Uniform Commercial Code, had adopted impracticability or commercial impracticability as synonymous with impossibility in the application of the doctrine of impossibility of performance.

The Opera Company of Boston v. The Wolf Trap Foundation for the Performing Arts, 817 F.2d 1094, 1098–99 (4th Cir. 1987).

Uniform Commercial Code. The Uniform Commercial Code appears to take a much more direct and liberal view to excuse for impossibility. First, genuine impossibility is no longer required. As will be seen in the cases that follow, in applying the new concept under UCC § 2-615, the standard is now one of *impracticability* rather than literal impossibility. The impracticability standard was not a UCC invention. It can be seen as early as 1916 in *Mineral Park Land Co. v. Howard*, 156 P. 458 (Cal. 1916), in which the defendant promised to take all of the gravel needed for a particular job from a certain tract of land, and after taking about half of what was required, discovered that the rest of the gravel lay below the water level and could be removed only at a cost twelve times greater than had the gravel been above water. Though the performance was not impossible, the more substantial increase in the cost of performance led the court to excuse the defendant.

The second apparent modification of the common-law approach under the UCC (and, of course, the RESTATEMENT (SECOND) OF CONTRACTS in § 261) is the direct approach to excusable nonperformance as contrasted with the fiction of implying conditions. Under UCC § 2-615(a), failure to perform is not a breach when *"performance as agreed has been made impracticable by the occurrence of a contingency the non-occurrence of which was a basic assumption on which the contract was made."*

While this statement of the "rule" appears to be a positive statement of excusable nonperformance as contrasted with the general rule of absolute performance subject to conditions in the *Taylor* case, a comparison of this statutory language with the quotation from the *Taylor* opinion, *supra*, may suggest that there is less of a major change than is sometimes heralded under the modern doctrine. While the UCC version certainly does away with the implied condition notion, it substitutes language that has yet to be clearly and consistently understood or applied. Thus the term "impracticable" still creates enormous problems in its application to numerous situations. Moreover, the language still incorporates the requirement of a "contingency" that must occur during the performance stage of the contract. Finally, there must be a determination of the "basic assumption" on which the contract was made. The "basic assumption" phrase is still mysterious and may be only slightly better than the 1863 formulation of the concept in *Taylor*. This is not to suggest a return to the *Taylor* concept. Rather, we should not assume that the "new" doctrine of impossibility (impracticability) is any less difficult to apply than the *Taylor* concept. In fact, as will be seen, attempts to use § 2-615 as an excuse for nonperformance have been notoriously unsuccessful.

Incapacity in Personal Service Contracts. To return to the common-law development, courts were successful in developing other exceptions to the general rule that performance is not excused. Categories of impossibility that were recognized early, beyond the destruction and deterioration of the subject matter, included personal service contracts that required service by a particular person who died, became incapacitated, or would become incapacitated if he or she proceeded to perform the contractual duty. Thus, when Walter Houston took reasonable measures to assure that his throat condition would not worsen but it nevertheless did, preventing him from appearing in a theatrical production, the defendant was excused from performance. *Wasserman Theatrical Enter., Inc. v. Harris*, 77 A.2d 329 (Conn. 1950). Even reasonable apprehension that incapacity of the promisor or third persons or serious injury will result excuses performance, as in *Hanford v. Connecticut Fair Ass'n*, 103 A. 838 (Conn. 1918), where an epidemic of infantile paralysis excused a promise to pay for conducting a baby show. These cases, like *Taylor v. Caldwell*, antedate the modern theory of impossibility of performance, which is analyzed, essentially, on a risk allocation basis. However, they are clearly within the ambit of that doctrine.

Prevention by Operation of Law. Another traditional category relates to performance prevented by operation of law, sometimes referred to in the older cases as the "supervening act of state exception." Thus in the famous case of *Baily v. De Crespigny*, L.R. 4 Q.B. 180 [1869], a covenant of a landlord to prevent the erection of any buildings on adjoining land was excused when the land was taken by a railroad under authority granted by an act of Parliament. The court stated: "The substantial question, therefore, raised on this record is whether the defendant is discharged from his covenant by the subsequent act of Parliament, which put it out of his power to perform it. We are of opinion that he is so discharged on the principle expressed in the maxim *Lex non cogit ad impossibilia.*" When the performance of a contract that is perfectly lawful at the time of formation is prevented by a subsequent change in the law or by the manner of the administration of the law, the contract is not illegal. However, since the parties are presumed to have made their contract with reference to the state of the law and its administration at the time of formation, the traditional cases took the view that the contract was subject to the implied condition that the law shall continue to permit performance. Thus, if the law, or some agency operating under authority of law, later prevents performance, the promisor is excused.

Fault of the Promisor — Reasonable Risk. If the law intervenes to prevent performance because of the fault of the promisor, the promisor is not excused from liability. *See Peckham v. Industrial Securities Co.*, 31 Del. (1 W.W. Harr.) 200, 113 A. 799 (1921). As in other areas of impossibility, if the risk was one that, under the circumstances, it is reasonable to assume the promisor would have been expected to assume, the promisor is not excused. Thus, a promise by a lessee of a hotel to permit the erection and exhibition of a sign on the roof for a period of years was held not excused when the hotel was taken by public authority under an act of Parliament. The court held that the circumstances were such that the lessee would have been expected to assume this risk had the matter been considered when the contract was made. *Walton Harvey, Ltd. v. Walker & Homfrays, Ltd.*, 1 Ch. 145, *aff'd*, 1 Ch. 274 (1931).

B.   COMMERCIAL IMPRACTICABILITY

TRANSATLANTIC FINANCING CORP. v. UNITED STATES
United States Court of Appeals, District of Columbia Circuit
363 F.2d 312 (1966)

WRIGHT, J.

This appeal involves a voyage charter between Transatlantic Financing Corporation, operator of the SS CHRISTOS, and the United States covering carriage of a full cargo of wheat from a United States Gulf port to a safe port in Iran. The District Court dismissed a libel filed by Transatlantic against the United States for costs attributable to the ship's diversion from the normal sea route caused by the closing of the Suez Canal. We affirm.

On July 26, 1956, the Government of Egypt nationalized the Suez Canal Company and took over operation of the Canal. On October 2, 1956, during the international crisis which resulted from the seizure, the voyage charter in suit was executed between representatives of Transatlantic and the United States. The charter indicated the termini of the voyage but not the route. On October 27, 1956, the SS CHRISTOS sailed from Galveston for Bandar Shapur, Iran, on a course which would have taken her through Gibraltar and the Suez Canal. On October 29, 1956, Israel invaded Egypt. On October 31, 1956, Great Britain and France invaded the Suez Canal Zone. On November 2, 1956, the Egyptian Government obstructed the Suez Canal with sunken vessels and closed it to traffic.

On or about November 7, 1956, Beckmann, representing Transatlantic, contacted Potosky, an employee of the United States Department of Agriculture, who appellant concedes was unauthorized to bind the Government, requesting instructions concerning disposition of the cargo and seeking an agreement for payment of additional compensation for a voyage around the Cape of Good Hope. Potosky advised Beckmann that Transatlantic was expected to perform the charter according to its terms, that he did not believe Transatlantic was entitled to additional compensation for a voyage around the Cape, but that Transatlantic was free to file such a claim. Following this discussion, the Christos changed course for the Cape of Good Hope and eventually arrived in Bandar Shapur on December 30, 1956.

Transatlantic's claim is based on the following train of argument. The charter was a contract for a voyage from a Gulf port to Iran. Admiralty principles and practices, especially stemming from the doctrine of deviation, require us to imply into the contract the term that the voyage was to be performed by the "usual and customary" route. The usual and customary route from Texas to Iran was, at the time of contract, via Suez, so the contract was for a voyage from Texas to Iran via Suez. When Suez was closed this contract became impossible to perform. Consequently, appellant's argument continues, when Transatlantic delivered the cargo by going around the Cape of Good Hope, in compliance with the Government's demand under claim of right, it conferred a benefit upon the United States for which it should be paid in *quantum meruit*.

The doctrine of impossibility of performance has gradually been freed from the earlier fictional and unrealistic strictures of such tests as the "implied term" and the parties' "contemplation." It is now recognized that " 'A thing is impossible in legal contemplation when it is not practicable; and a thing is impracticable when it can only be done at an excessive and unreasonable cost.' " *Mineral Park Land Co. v. Howard*, 172 Cal. 289, 293, 156 P. 458, 460, L.R.A. 1916F, 1 (1916). Accord, *Whelan v. Griffith Consumers Company*, D.C. Mun. App., 170 A.2d 229 (1961): RESTATEMENT, CONTRACTS § 454 (1932); Uniform Commercial Code (U.L.A.) § 2-615, comment 3. The doctrine ultimately represents the ever-shifting line, drawn by courts hopefully responsive to commercial practices and mores, at which the community's interest in having contracts enforced according to their terms is outweighed by the commercial senselessness of requiring performance.[1]

When the issue is raised, the court is asked to construct a condition of performance based on the changed circumstances, a process which involves at least three reasonably definable steps. First, a contingency — something unexpected — must have occurred. Second, the risk of the unexpected occurrence must not have been allocated either by agreement or by custom. Finally, occurrence of the contingency must have rendered performance commercially impracticable.[2] Unless the court finds these three requirements satisfied, the plea of impossibility must fail.

The first requirement was met here. It seems reasonable, where no route is mentioned in a contract, to assume the parties expected performance by the usual and customary route at the time of contract.[3] Since the usual and customary route from Texas to Iran at the time of contract[4] was through Suez, closure of the Canal

---

[1] [1] While the impossibility issue rarely arises, as it has here, in a suit to recover the cost of an alternative method of performance, compare Annot., 84 A.L.R.2d 12, 19 (1962), there is nothing necessarily inconsistent in claiming commercial impracticability for the method of performance actually adopted; the concept of impracticability assumes performance was physically possible. Moreover, a rule making nonperformance a condition precedent to recovery would unjustifiably encourage disappointment of expectations.

[2] [3] Compare Uniform Commercial Code § 2-615(a), which provides that, in the absence of an assumption of greater liability, delay or non-delivery by a seller is not a breach if performance as agreed is made "impracticable" by the occurrence of a "contingency" the non-occurrence of which was a "basic assumption on which the contract was made." To the extent this limits relief to "unforeseen" circumstances, comment 1, see the discussion below, and compare Uniform Commercial Code § 2-614(1). There may be a point beyond which agreement cannot go, Uniform Commercial Code § 2-615, comment 8, presumably the point at which the obligation would be "manifestly unreasonable," § 1-102(3), in bad faith, § 1-203, or unconscionable, § 2-302. For an application of these provisions see Judge Friendly's opinion in *United States v. Wegematic Corporation*, 2 Cir., 360 F.2d 674 (1966).

[3] [4] Uniform Commercial Code § 2-614, comment 1, states: "Under this Article, in the absence of specific agreement, the normal or usual facilities enter into the agreement either through the circumstances, usage of trade or prior course of dealing." So long as this sort of assumption does not necessarily result in construction of a condition of performance, it is idle to argue over whether the usual and customary route is an "implied term." The issue of impracticability must eventually be met . . . .

[4] [5] The parties have spent considerable energy in disputing whether the "usual and customary" route by which performance was anticipated is defined as of the time of contract or of performance. If we were automatically to treat the expected route as a condition of performance, this matter would be crucial, and we would be compelled to choose between unacceptable alternatives. If we assume as a constructive condition the usual and customary course always to mean the one in use at the time of contract, any substantial diversion (we assume the diversion would have to be substantial) would nullify the contract even though its effect upon the rights and obligations of the parties is insignificant. Nor would it be desirable, on the other hand, to assume performance is conditioned on the availability of *any*

made impossible the expected method of performance. But this unexpected development raises rather than resolves the impossibility issue, which turns additionally on whether the risk of the contingency's occurrence had been allocated and, if not, whether performance by alternative routes was rendered impracticable.

Proof that the risk of a contingency's occurrence has been allocated may be expressed in or implied from the agreement. Such proof may also be found in the surrounding circumstances, including custom and usages of the trade. *See* 6 CORBIN, *supra*, § 1339, at 394–397; 6 WILLISTON, *supra*, § 1948, at 5457–5458. The contract in this case does not expressly condition performance upon availability of the Suez route. Nor does it specify "via Suez" or, on the other hand, "via Suez or Cape of Good Hope."[5] Nor are there provisions in the contract from which we may properly imply that the continued availability of Suez was a condition of performance.[6] Nor is there anything in custom or trade usage, or in the surrounding circumstances

---

usual and customary route at the time of performance. It may be that very often the availability of a customary route at the time of performance other than the route expected to be used at the time of contract should result in denial of relief under the impossibility theory; certainly if *no* customary route is available at the time of performance the contract is rendered impossible. But the same customarily used alternative route may be practicable in one set of circumstances and impracticable in another, as where the goods are unable to survive the extra journey. Moreover, the "time of performance" is no special point in time; it is every moment in a performance. Thus the alternative route, in our case around the Cape, may be practicable at some time during performance, for example while the vessel is still in the Atlantic Ocean, and impracticable at another time during performance, for example after the vessel has traversed most of the Mediterranean Sea. Both alternatives, therefore, have their shortcomings, and we avoid choosing between them by refusing automatically to treat the usual and customary route as of any time as a condition of performance.

[5] [7] In Glidden Company v. Hellenic Lines, Limited, 2 Cir., 275 F.2d 253 (1960), the charter was for transportation of materials from India to America "via Suez Canal or Cape of Good Hope, or Panama Canal," and the court held performance was not "frustrated." In his discussion of this case, Professor Corbin states: "Except for the provision for an alternative route, the defendant would have been discharged, for the reason that the parties contemplated an open Suez Canal as a specific condition or means of performance." 6 CORBIN, *supra*, § 1339, at 399 n. 57. Appellant claims this supports its argument, since the Suez route was contemplated as usual and customary. But there is obviously a difference, in deciding whether a contract allocates the risk of a contingency's occurrence, between a contract specifying no route and a contract specifying Suez. We think that when Professor Corbin said, "Except for the provision for an alternative route" he was referring, not to the entire *provision* —"via Suez Canal or Cape of Good Hope" etc. — but to the fact that *an alternative route* had been provided for. Moreover, in determining what Corbin meant when he said "the parties contemplated an open Suez Canal as a specific condition or means of performance," consideration must be given to the fact, recited by Corbin, that in *Glidden* the parties were specifically aware when the contract was made the Canal might be closed, and the promisee had refused to include a clause excusing performance in the event of closure. Corbin's statement, therefore, is most accurately read as referring to cases in which a route is specified after negotiations reflecting the parties' awareness that the usual and customary route might become unavailable. *Compare* Held v. Goldsmith, 153 La. 598, 96 So. 272 (1919).

[6] [8] The charter provides that the vessel is "in every way fitted for *the voyage*" (emphasis added), and the "P. & I. Bunker Deviation Clause" refers to "the contract voyage" and the "direct and/or customary route." Appellant argues that these provisions require implication of a voyage by the direct and customary route. Actually they prove only what we are willing to accept — that the parties expected the usual and customary route would be used. The provisions in no way condition performance upon non-occurrence of this contingency.

There are two clauses which allegedly demonstrate that time is of importance in this contract. One clause computes the remuneration "in steaming time" for diversions to other countries ordered by the charterer in emergencies. This proves only that the United States wished to reserve power to send the goods to another country. It does not imply in any way that there was a rush about the matter. The other

generally, which would support our constructing a condition of performance. The numerous cases requiring performance around the Cape when Suez was closed, see e.g., *Ocean Tramp Tankers Corp. v. V/O Sovfracht (The Eugenia)*, [1964] 2 Q.B. 226, and cases cited therein, indicate that the Cape route is generally regarded as an alternative means of performance. So the implied expectation that the route would be via Suez is hardly adequate proof of an allocation to the promisee of the risk of closure. In some cases, even an express expectation may not amount to a condition of performance.[7] The doctrine of deviation supports our assumption that parties normally expect performance by the usual and customary route, but it adds nothing beyond this that is probative of an allocation of the risk.[8]

If anything, the circumstances surrounding this contract indicate that the risk of the Canal's closure may be deemed to have been allocated to Transatlantic. We know or may safely assume that the parties were aware, as were most commercial men with interests affected by the Suez situation, see *The Eugenia, supra,* that the Canal might become a dangerous area. No doubt the tension affected freight rates, and it is arguable that the risk of closure became part of the dickered terms. Uniform Commercial Code § 2-615, comment 8. We do not deem the risk of closure so allocated, however. Foreseeability or even recognition of a risk does not necessarily prove its allocation. *Compare* Uniform Commercial Code § 2-615,

---

clause concerns demurrage and despatch. The charterer agreed to pay Transatlantic demurrage of $1,200 per day for all time in excess of the period agreed upon for loading and unloading, and Transatlantic was to pay despatch of $600 per day for any saving in time. Of course this provision shows the parties were concerned about time, see GILMORE & BLACK, THE LAW OF ADMIRALTY § 4-8 (1957), but the fact that they arranged so minutely the consequences of any delay or speedup of loading and unloading operates against the argument that they were similarly allocating the risk of delay or speed-up of the voyage.

[7] [9] Uniform Commercial Code § 2-614(1) provides: "Where without fault of either party . . . the *agreed* manner of delivery . . . becomes commercially impracticable but a commercially reasonable substitute is available, such substitute performance must be tendered and accepted." (Emphasis added.) Compare Mr. Justice Holmes' observation: "You can give any conclusion a logical form. You always can imply a condition in a contract. But why do you imply it? It is because of some belief as to the practice of the community or of a class, or because of some opinion as to policy . . . ." Holmes, *The Path of the Law,* 10 HARV. L. REV. 457, 466 (1897).

[8] [10] The deviation doctrine, drawn principally from admiralty insurance practice, implies into all relevant commercial instruments naming the termini of voyages the usual and customary route between those points. 1 ARNOULD, MARINE INSURANCE AND AVERAGE § 376, at 522 (10th ed. 1921). Insurance is cancelled when a ship unreasonably "deviates" from this course, for example by extending a voyage or by putting in at an irregular port, and the shipowner forfeits the protection of clauses of exception which might otherwise have protected him from his common law insurer's liability to cargo. See GILMORE & BLACK, *supra* Note 8, § 2-6, at 59–60. This practice, properly qualified, see *id.* § 3-41, makes good sense, since insurance rates are computed on the basis of the implied course, and deviations in the course increasing the anticipated risk make the insurer's calculations meaningless. ARNOULD, *supra,* § 14, at 26. Thus the route, so far as insurance contracts are concerned, is crucial, whether express or implied. But even here, the implied term is not inflexible. Reasonable deviations do not result in loss of insurance, at least so long as established practice is followed. *See* Carriage of Goods by Sea Act § 4(4), 49 Stat. 1210, 46 U.S.C. § 1304(4); and discussion of "held covered" clauses in GILMORE & BLACK, *supra,* § 3-41, at 161. Some "deviations" are required. *E.g.,* Hirsch Lumber Co. v. Weyerhaeuser Steamship Co., 2 Cir., 233 F.2d 791, *cert. denied,* 352 U.S. 880, 77 S. Ct. 102, 1 L. Ed. 2d 80 (1956). The doctrine's only relevance, therefore, is that it provides additional support for the assumption we willingly make that merchants agreeing to a voyage between two points except that the usual and customary route between those points will be used. The doctrine provides no evidence of an allocation of the risk of the route's unavailability.

Comment 1; RESTATEMENT, CONTRACTS § 457 (1932). Parties to a contract are not always able to provide for all the possibilities of which they are aware, sometimes because they cannot agree, often simply because they are too busy. Moreover, that some abnormal risk was contemplated is probative but does not necessarily establish an allocation of the risk of the contingency which actually occurs. In this case, for example, nationalization by Egypt of the Canal Corporation and formation of the Suez Users Group did not necessarily indicate that the Canal would be blocked even if a confrontation resulted.[9] The surrounding circumstances do indicate however, a willingness by Transatlantic to assume abnormal risks, and this fact should legitimately cause us to judge the impracticability of performance by an alternative route in stricter terms than we would were the contingency unforeseen.

We turn then to the question whether occurrence of the contingency rendered performance commercially impracticable under the circumstances of this case. The goods shipped were not subject to harm from the longer, less temperate Southern route. The vessel and crew were fit to proceed around the Cape.[10] Transatlantic was no less able than the United States to purchase insurance to cover the contingency's occurrence. If anything, it is more reasonable to expect owner-operators of vessels to insure against the hazards of war. They are in the best position to calculate the cost of performance by alternative routes (and therefore to estimate the amount of insurance required), and are undoubtedly sensitive to international troubles which uniquely affect the demand for and cost of their services. The only factor operating here in appellant's favor is the added expense, allegedly $43,972.00 above and beyond the contract price of $305,842.92, of extending a 10,000 mile voyage by approximately 3,000 miles. While it may be an overstatement to say that increased cost and difficulty of performance never constitute impracticability, to justify relief there must be more of a variation between expected cost and the cost of performing by an available alternative than is present in this case, where the promisor can legitimately be presumed to have accepted some degree of abnormal risk, and where impracticability is urged on the basis of added expense alone.[11]

We conclude, therefore, as have most other courts considering related issues arising out of the Suez closure, that performance of this contract was not rendered legally impossible. Even if we agreed with appellant, its theory of relief seems untenable. When performance of a contract is deemed impossible it is a nullity. In the case of a charter party involving carriage of goods, the carrier may return to an appropriate port and unload its cargo, *The Malcolm Baxter, Jr.*, 277 U.S. 323, 48 S. Ct. 516, 72 L. Ed. 901 (1928), subject of course to required steps to minimize

---

[9] [12] Sources cited in the briefs indicate formation of the Suez Canal Users Association on October 1, 1956, was viewed in some quarters as an implied threat of force . . . .

[10] [13] The issue of impracticability should no doubt be "an objective determination of whether the promise can reasonably be performed rather than a subjective inquiry into the promisor's capability of performing as agreed." Symposium, *The Uniform Commercial Code and Contract Law: Some Selected Problems*, 105 U. PA. L. REV. 836, 880, 887 (1957). Dealers should not be excused because of less than normal capabilities. But if both parties are aware of a dealer's limited capabilities, no objective determination would be complete without taking into account this fact.

[11] [15] *See* Uniform Commercial Code § 2-615, comment 4: "Increased cost alone does not excuse performance unless the rise in cost is due to some unforeseen contingency which alters the essential nature of the performance." *See also* 6 CORBIN, *supra*, § 1333; 6 WILLISTON, *supra*, § 1952, at 5468.

damages. If the performance rendered has value, recovery in *quantum meruit* for the entire performance is proper. But here Transatlantic has collected its contract price, and now seeks *quantum meruit* relief for the additional expense of the trip around the Cape. If the contract is a nullity, Transatlantic's theory of relief should have been *quantum meruit* for the entire trip, rather than only for the extra expense. Transatlantic attempts to take its profit on the contract, and then force the Government to absorb the cost of the additional voyage. When impracticability without fault occurs, the law seeks an equitable solution, see 6 CORBIN, *supra*, § 1321, and *quantum meruit* is one of its potent devices to achieve this end. There is no interest in casting the entire burden of commercial disaster on one party in order to preserve the other's profit. Apparently the contract price in this case was advantageous enough to deter appellant from taking a stance on damages consistent with its theory of liability. In any event, there is no basis for relief. *Affirmed.*

C. FRUSTRATION OF PURPOSE

PIEPER, INC. v. LAND O'LAKES FARMLAND FEED, LLC
United States Court of Appeals, Eighth Circuit
390 F.3d 1062 (2004)

RILEY, J.

Pieper and LOLFF entered into a Weaned Pig Purchase Agreement (Agreement), in which LOLFF agreed to purchase weaner pigs, i.e., weaned piglets, from Pieper. LOLFF intended to sell these pigs to third-party finishers, who would raise the pigs to market weight. Farmland Industries, Inc. (Farmland) then would buy market hogs from third-party finishers under the terms of an existing contract between Farmland and Pieper.

Recital D of the Agreement explains LOLFF was to buy Pieper's weaner pigs only while Farmland purchased market hogs from third-party finishers:

> LOLFF will purchase such pigs from [Pieper] only while its Customers have the ability to market such pigs utilizing the Farmland America's Best Pork Marketing Agreement No. 8073 dated November 14, 2000 and originally assigned to Pieper, Inc. In a deposition, Pieper's president, Michael Pieper (Mr. Pieper), testified the Agreement depended on Farmland's purchase of market hogs from third-party finishers.

Farmland subsequently refused to buy market hogs from third-party finishers, declining to consent to an assignment of the Pieper and Farmland contract. Without the ability to sell weaner pigs to third-party finishers for sale to Farmland, LOLFF had no reason to buy pigs from Pieper. As a result, LOLFF advised Pieper "it will no longer purchase pigs from Pieper under the [Agreement], and such Agreement shall be terminated effective immediately."

Pieper filed suit against LOLFF, alleging LOLFF breached the Agreement by failing to buy Pieper's weaner pigs. In its answer, LOLFF asserted frustration of purpose as an affirmative defense. The parties filed cross motions for summary judgment. Pieper argued summary judgment was appropriate, because there was no genuine issue of material fact that LOLFF had breached the Agreement. LOLFF argued it was excused from performing, because its principal purpose behind the Agreement had been frustrated. The district court granted summary judgment to LOLFF on its affirmative defense of frustration of purpose. On appeal, Pieper argues the district court erred in relying on extrinsic evidence to determine LOLFF's principal purpose in entering into the Agreement.

Under Minnesota law, frustration of purpose will excuse contract performance when: (1) the party's principal purpose in making the contract is frustrated; (2) without that party's fault; (3) by the occurrence of an event, the non-occurrence of which was a basic assumption on which the contract was made. "The principal purpose: 'must be so completely the basis of the contract that, as both parties understand, without it the transaction would make little sense.' " (RESTATEMENT (SECOND) OF CONTRACTS § 265, cmt. a (1981).)

The use of extrinsic evidence to show a party's principal purpose first was demonstrated in *Krell v. Henry*, [1903] 2 KB. 740 (CA.), the landmark case on frustration of purpose. In *Krell*, the court excused a prospective tenant from his obligation to pay for a room overlooking the King's coronation route, when the King became ill and the coronation parade was cancelled. *Id.* at 740-41. The contract involved in *Krell* did not refer explicitly to the coronation, but the court nonetheless inferred the principal purpose had been frustrated. *Krell* thus set forth the principle that a contract's purpose may be inferred from surrounding circumstances:

> I think that you first have to ascertain, not necessarily from the terms of the contract, but, if required, from necessary inferences, drawn from surrounding circumstances recognised by both contracting parties, what is the substance of the contract, and then to ask the question whether that substantial contract needs for its foundation the assumption of the existence of a particular state of things.

Relying on the principles enunciated in *Krell*, and the indirect authority from the Minnesota Court of Appeals in National Recruiters, Inc., we hold the district court did not err in considering extrinsic evidence to determine LOLFF's principal purpose in entering into the Agreement. Based on the undisputed evidence outside the operative provisions of the Agreement, no doubt exists that LOLFF entered into the Agreement to sell weaner pigs to third-party finishers, who then would sell market hogs to Farmland. Recital D explicitly states LOLFF's obligation to purchase weaner pigs from Pieper depended on Farmland's purchase of market hogs from third-party finishers. Even Mr. Pieper testified the Agreement assumed Farmland would purchase market hogs from third-party finishers, and the "deal was dependent upon [third-party finishers] being able to sell the market hogs to Farmland."

Having determined LOLFF's principal purpose in entering into the Agreement, we ask whether LOLFF's performance was excused under the doctrine of frustration of purpose. Our review of the record leads us to conclude, as a matter of law, LOLFF's purpose in buying pigs from Pieper was frustrated by Farmland's refusal to purchase market hogs from third-party finishers. Farmland's refusal completely frustrated the basic assumption upon which the Agreement was made and without which the Agreement makes no sense. Without the ability to sell the weaner pigs to third-party finishers for eventual sale to Farmland, LOLFF had no commercial reason to purchase pigs from Pieper. Additionally, Pieper did not present any evidence showing LOLFF was at fault with regard to Farmland's decision not to purchase market hogs from third-party finishers The district court properly granted summary judgment to LOLFF, and we affirm.

NOTES

(1) *Krell v. Henry*, to which the court referred, is one of the celebrated "Coronation" cases where parties paid premium rates to hire vantage points along the scheduled line of march to watch the coronation procession of the new King. When the King became ill, there was no impediment to performing the contract, but the entire purpose of the contract was frustrated. If the hirer had not paid, he was excused from paying it. If, however, the price was prepaid in whole or in part, the court would not allow the recovery of paid amounts on the footing that everything done before the frustration was viewed as validly done. *Chandler v. Webster*, 1 K. 8. 493 (1904). Allocating the risk on the accidental basis of when the parties had agreed to perform their promises was unsettling. As London was being bombed in the early 1940s, the House of Lords overruled *Chandler v. Webster* in a case involving a contract for the sale of machinery to be manufactured in England for a buyer in Poland who paid £1,000 in advance. World War II prevented delivery of the machinery. The court allowed the buyer to recover the entire payment, admitting that the result was not very fair since it allocated the entire risk of the frustrating event over which neither party had any control to the seller. *Fibrosa Spolka Akcjina v. Fairborne Lawson Combe Barbaour, Ltd.*, A.C. 32 (1943). With bombs continuing to fall, Parliament focused upon this issue and passed the Frustrated Contract Act in 1943, 6 & 7 Geo. 6. c. 40, which applies to all contracts where a party's performance has been discharged by either impossibility or frustration of purpose. It permits a party who has conferred a benefit on the other to recover the value of the benefit unless the court decides that it would be just to permit the other party to retain all or part of that benefit.

(2) *Lloyd v. Murphy*, 153 P.2d 47 (Cal. 944), is the best-known frustration of purpose case from a court in the United States. On September 15, 1941, the defendant signed a five-year lease of property on Wilshire Boulevard in Los Angeles for the sole purpose of selling new cars. On December 7, 1941, the Japanese attacked Pearl Harbor and war was declared. On January 1, 1942, the Federal Government ordered the sale of new autos to be discontinued with only rare exceptions. Since virtually no new cars would be available for sale, the lessors granted a waiver of the lease provisions to allow the lessee to use the property for any legitimate purpose as well as removing subleasing restrictions. The defendant-lessee, however, vacated the premises in March of 1942 and the plaintiffs-lessors brought this declaratory judgment action to determine their rights. ln an option by Justice Traynor, the court stated, "The question in cases involving frustration is whether the equities of the case, considered in the light of sound public policy, require placing the risk of a disruption of complete destruction of the contract equilibrium on the defendant or plaintiff under the circumstances." *Id.* at 53–4, 153 P.2d at 50.

The court noted that, at the time the lease was executed in September of 1941, the National Defense Act authorizing the President to allocate materials and mobilize industry for national defense had been law for more than a year. The auto industry was converting to supply military needs and auto sales were soaring in anticipation that production would soon be restricted. Since these facts were commonly known, it could not be said that the risk of war and the consequent restriction on the sale of items such as autos was so remote a contingency that it could not be foreseen by a party such as the defendant-lessee. Moreover, the defendant failed to prove that the premises would be valueless, notwithstanding the absence of new autos. The defendant could sell used autos for which a strong market existed and could also pursue the repair of autos, a business that would be substantially enhanced by the restrictions on new autos. The court, therefore, would apply the frustration of purpose defense in these circumstances. It concluded, "The consequences of applying the doctrine of frustration to a leasehold involving less than a total or nearly total destruction of the value of the leased premises would be undesirable." *Id.* at 57, 153 P.2d at 52.

D.   CONTRACT TO ASSUME THE RISK

GENERAL ELECTRIC CAPITAL CORP. v. FPL SERVICE CORP.

United States District Court, Northern District of Iowa
986 F. Supp. 2d 1029 (2013)

BENNETT, J.

On June 14, 2011, GECC and FPL entered into a contract, which is entitled "Lease Agreement." Under the contract, GECC agreed to provide FPL with two Ricoh Pro C901 copiers (the copiers), and related equipment. In return, FPL agreed to make 60 rental payments of $6,229.30 to GECC. For over a year, the parties performed under the contract without incident. But, in late October of 2012, Hurricane Sandy struck Long Island, destroying nearly all of FPL's equipment, including the two copiers it leased from GECC. After the hurricane, FPL stopped making its rental payments. To this day, FPL has made only 19 of the 60 payments it agreed to make. In addition to FPL's rental payments, the parties' contract describes FPL's options if the copiers were to be damaged.[12]

Though the copiers were damaged after Hurricane Sandy, FPL never paid to

---

[12]   If any item of Equipment is . . . damaged, [FPL] will (and Rental Payments will continue to accrue without abatement until [FPL]), at [FPL's] option and cost, either (a) repair the item or replace the item with a comparable item reasonably acceptable to [GECC], or (b) pay [GECC] a sum equal to (1) all Rental Payments and other amounts then due and payable under the Lease, and (2) the present value of (i) all Rental Payments to become due during the remainder of the Lease term, and (ii) the Purchase Option amount set forth in this Lease, each discounted at . . . (y) the lease charge rate (as determined pursuant to Section 16) if this Lease provides for A dollar Purchase Option . . . [GECC] will then transfer to [FPL] all [of GECC's] rights, title, and interest in the Equipment "AS-IS, WHERE IS" WITHOUT ANY REPRESENTATION OR WARRANTY WHATSOEVER, Insurance proceeds will be applied toward repair or replacement of the Equipment or payment hereunder, as applicable.

replace or repair them, nor did it pay GECC a sum equal to its then-due rental payments plus the present value of its future rental payments. On May 6, 2013, GECC's law firm sent a letter to FPL demanding "immediate payment of the entire outstanding balance due on the Lease . . . together with interest and other charges" GECC [repossessed both copiers and] resold them. GECC filed a Complaint in this court alleging that FPL breached its lease agreement with GECC. FPL answered the Complaint, denying the substance of GECC's allegations and asserting a number of affirmative defenses. GECC moved for summary judgment, claiming that there are no material factual disputes and that GECC is entitled to damages for FPL's breach of contract as a matter of law. FPL resisted GECC's motion.

GECC argues that FPL defaulted under the parties' contract by making only 19 of the 60 payments required under the contract. Accordingly, GECC claims that it is entitled to "$258,424.39, plus its attorneys' fees and costs," which represents GECC's calculation of damages under the contract (docket no. 14, at 5). FPL does not dispute that it stopped making payments to GECC after Hurricane Sandy struck. Instead, FPL argues that, because Hurricane Sandy could not have been anticipated, FPL is excused from performing under the contract.

FPL relies on two sections from the Restatement (Second) of Contracts to support its argument: section 261, which discusses supervening impracticability, and section 265, which discusses frustration of purpose. Iowa law recognizes both sections as defenses in breach-of-contract cases. The supervening-impracticability defense provides:

> Where, after a contract is made, a party's performance is made impracticable without his fault by the occurrence of an event the non-occurrence of which was a basic assumption on which the contract was made, his duty to render that performance is discharged, unless the language or the circumstances indicate the contrary. *Restatement (Second) of Contracts* § 261.

Similarly, the frustration-of-purpose defense provides:

> Where, after a contract is made, a party's principal purpose is substantially frustrated without his fault by the occurrence of an event the non-occurrence of which was a basic assumption on which the contract was made, his remaining duties to render performance are discharged, unless the language or the circumstances indicate the contrary. *Restatement (Second) of Contracts* § 265.

Both defenses allow courts to discharge a party's contractual obligations as a matter of law. But, while both defenses involve a number of elements, one common element resolves FPL's argument. Sections 261 and 265 apply *"unless* the language [of the contract] or the circumstances indicate the contrary." *Restatement (Second) of Contracts* §§ 261, 265 (emphasis added). The last clause of both sections allows that "[a] party may, by appropriate language, agree to perform in spite of impracticability that would otherwise justify his non-performance" such that "[h]e can then be held liable for damages although he cannot perform." *Restatement (Second) of Contracts* § 261, cmt. c. Thus, the principles in sections 261 and 265 yield to a contrary agreement by which a party may assume a greater as well as a lesser obligation. By such an agreement, for example, a party may undertake to achieve a result irrespective of supervening events that may render its achievement impossible, and if he does so his non-performance is a breach even if it is caused by such an event. *Id.* cmt. a; *Restatement (Second) of Contracts* § 265, cmt. b ("The rule stated in [§ 265] is subject to limitations similar to those stated in § 261 . . . and it does not apply if the language or circumstances indicate the contrary.").

Here, the parties' contract contains express language obligating FPL to perform in spite of events that might otherwise justify FPL's non-performance. The contract provides:

> "[FPL's] payment obligations hereunder are absolute and unconditional and are not subject to cancellation, abatement, reduction, recoupment, defense or setoff for any reason whatsoever";

> "If any item of Equipment is lost, stolen or damaged . . . Rental Payments will continue to accrue without abatement"; and

> "[FPL is] responsible for loss and damage to the Equipment from *any cause whatsoever* on and after delivery thereof" (emphasis added).

Thus, the contract explicitly assigns to FPL the risk of loss from "any cause whatsoever" and requires FPL to make monthly payments regardless of whether the copiers get damaged. Taken together, the provisions quoted above amount to a "hell-or-high-water" clause — "[a] clause in a personal-property lease requiring the lessee to continue to make full rent payments to the lessor even if the thing leased is unsuitable, defective, or destroyed." *C & J Vantage Leasing Co. v. Wolfe*, 795 N.W.2d 65, 75 (Iowa 2011) (quoting Black's Law Dictionary 742 (8th ed. 2004)). Iowa law enforces hell-or-high-water clauses regardless of whether they are found in a lease or a secured transaction. [The parties disputed whether the their contract was a lease or a secured transaction. In either case], "Courts have consistently enforced [hell-or-high-water] clauses in the financial leasing context." Because the parties' contract makes FPL's performance unconditional and assigns the risk of loss to FPL, FPL cannot rely on supervening impracticability or frustration of purpose to discharge its duty to perform.

I recognize that "[h]ell or high water provisions are common in the commercial leasing industry, and [that] they have been uniformly upheld by both state and federal courts, including the Iowa Supreme Court.". But, if I were deciding the issue in the first instance, I would not enforce a hell-or-high-water clause against a party claiming an otherwise valid act-of-God defense, unless the parties specifically bargained for the hell-or-high-water clause. As a practical matter, hell-or-high-water clauses are rarely, if ever, specifically bargained for:

> In standard form contracts or leases, no real negotiation about the printed clauses takes place. One party simply presents the other with a standard form. The other party must either buy or lease the goods under the contract terms or forego the transaction. He probably cannot get better terms elsewhere, because all standard form contracts usually contain similar terms favoring the stronger party. Thus, no real negotiation or choice exists in these contract or lease situations.Donald B. King, *Major Problems with Article 2a: Unfairness, "Cutting Off" Consumer Defenses,*

Unfiled Interests, and Uneven Adoption, 43 Mercer L. Rev. 869, 870-71 (1992).

The rationale for presumptively enforcing hell-or-high-water clauses is "that these clauses are essential to the equipment leasing industry" and "[t]o deny their effect as a matter of law would seriously chill business in this industry . . . ." I am aware of no opinion citing empirical evidence supporting that rationale. If parties were required to specifically bargain for hell-or-high-water clauses, the commercial leasing industry would likely not collapse. Rather, the price of a lease would likely rise, unless the lessee agreed to bear the risk of an act of God.

Still, FPL argues that it could not have assumed the risk of loss because Hurricane Sandy was not reasonably foreseeable and, thus, FPL cannot be expected to have insured against it. FPL also argues that insuring the copiers against damage from "any cause whatsoever" is an impossible and illusory task. These arguments seem to conflate what are actually two separate obligations under the parties' contract: (1) FPL's obligation to pay GECC despite damage to the copiers, and (2) FPL's obligation to insure the copiers. As I noted above, the parties' contract obligated FPL to make payments to GECC regardless of damage to the copiers. The contract also requires FPL to "keep the Equipment insured against all risks of physical loss or damage for its full replacement value, naming [GECC] as loss payee."

Even assuming that FPL could not have anticipated the need to insure the copiers against flood damage, FPL's arguments are inapposite for two reasons. First, GECC does not appear to claim any damages based on FPL's failure to insure the copiers against flood damage. Rather, GECC calculates — and FPL contests — damages based on the formula in the "Loss or Damage" section of the parties' contract, which is unrelated to FPL's insurance obligation. *See* Part I.A (quoting the formula).

Second, FPL bases its argument on a misapplication of *Restatement (Second) of Contracts* § 261, comment c. To support its argument that it did not assume the risk of flood damage, FPL quotes the following:

> If the supervening event was not reasonably foreseeable when the contract was made, the party claiming discharge can hardly be expected to have provided against its occurrence. However, if it was reasonably foreseeable, or even foreseen, the opposite conclusion does not necessarily follow. Factors such as the practical difficulty of reaching agreement on the myriad of conceivable terms of a complex agreement may excuse a failure to deal with improbable contingencies. *Restatement (Second) of Contracts* § 261, comment c.

But, this commentary does not apply to the contract in this case. The part of the comment FPL cites discusses when a party may be excused for "a failure to deal with improbable contingencies." The contract at issue here does not fail to deal with improbable contingencies. To the contrary, it expressly deals with improbable contingencies by assigning the risk of those contingencies to FPL: "[FPL is] responsible for loss and damage to the Equipment from any cause whatsoever" Were the contract here silent on which party bears the risk of flood damage, the commentary FPL cites would be in play. But the contract is not silent and, thus, FPL is not excused from its obligation to perform.

Because the parties' contract contains enforceable hell-or-high-water provisions and assigns to FPL the risk of all loss or damage to the copiers, FPL cannot claim that it is excused from performance because of Hurricane Sandy. Thus, GECC's motion for summary judgment is granted on issue of liability. [The court deferred ruling on whether GECC was entitled to summary judgment as to its damages until after the parties presented additional evidence regarding whether GECC resold the repossessed copiers in a commercially reasonable manner.]

NOTE

Impracticability in the Energy Cases. During the period of the energy crisis when the OPEC supply of oil led to gas line at filling stations, there were a number of cases in which the impracticability defense was attempted where the supplier of energysought to be excused from performing. Westinghouse had entered into a number of uranium-supply contracts, since it was interested in developing its sales of nuclear power plants. While these contracts differed in various respects, they were typically requirements contracts where Westinghouse agreed to supply uranium requirements for a certain period of time. In the mid-1960s, utility companies were wary of converting to nuclear power for a number of reasons, including, but not limited to, their lack of understanding of all of the risks associated with such a conversion. One clear example of this attitude is found in *Florida Power & Light Co. v. Westinghouse Elec. Corp.*, 517 F. Supp. 440, (E.D. Va. 1981). The announcement by Westinghouse that it was excused from performing these contracts, at least in substantial measure, resulted in a large number of lawsuits, most of which were settled. However, the settlements were costly to Westinghouse. On October 21, 1976, the *Wall Street Journal* reported (p. 2, cols. 3 & 4) that the Westinghouse 1979 Annual Report disclosed settlements of 14 lawsuits as of that Report, exceeding $700 million. A number of other energy supply cases involving uranium were brought against other suppliers. At this time, none have shown a successful use of § 2-615. However, the next case might be said to constitute an exception to the weight of authority.

E. FORCE MAJEURE CLAUSES

NORTHERN INDIANA PUBLIC SERVICE CO. v. CARBON COUNTY COAL CO.
United States Court of Appeals, Seventh Circuit
799 F.2d 265 (1986)

POSNER, J.

[In 1978 Northern Indiana Public Service Co. (NIPSCO), a public utility, and Carbon County Coal Company of Wyoming] signed a contract whereby Carbon County agreed to sell and NIPSCO to buy approximately 1.5 million tons of coal every year for 20 years, at a price of $24 a ton subject to various provisions for escalation which by 1985 had driven the price up to $44 a ton. NIPSCO's rates are regulated by the Indiana Public Service Commission. In 1983 NIPSCO requested permission to raise its rates to reflect increased fuel charges. Some customers of NIPSCO opposed the increase on the ground that NIPSCO could reduce its overall costs by buying more electrical power from neighboring utilities for resale to its customers and producing less of its own power. Although the Commission granted the requested increase, it directed NIPSCO to make a good faith effort to find, and wherever possible buy from, utilities that would sell electricity to it at prices lower than its costs of internal generation (the "economy purchase orders"). The Commission added ominously that "the adverse effects of entering into long-term coal supply contracts which do not allow for renegotiation and are not requirement contracts, is a burden which must rest squarely on the shoulders of NIPSCO management." Actually the contract with Carbon County did provide for renegotiation of the contract price — but one-way renegotiation in favor of Carbon County; the price fixed in the contract (as adjusted from time to time in accordance with the escalator provisions) was a floor. And the contract was indeed not a requirements contract: it specified the exact amount of coal that NIPSCO must take over the 20 years during which the contract was to remain in effect. NIPSCO was eager to have an assured supply of low-sulphur coal and was therefore willing to guarantee both price and quantity.

Unfortunately for NIPSCO, however, as things turned out it was indeed able to buy electricity at prices below the costs of generating electricity from coal bought under the contract with Carbon County; and because of the "economy purchase orders" of which it had not sought judicial review, NIPSCO could not expect to be allowed by the Public Service Commission to recover in its electrical rates the costs of buying coal from Carbon County. NIPSCO therefore decided to stop accepting coal deliveries from Carbon County, at least for the time being; and on April 24, 1985, it brought this diversity suit against Carbon County seeking a declaration that it was excused from its obligations under the contract either permanently or at least until the economy purchase orders ceased preventing it from passing on the costs of the contract to its ratepayers.

The contract permits NIPSCO to stop taking delivery of coal "for any cause beyond [its] reasonable control . . . including but not limited to . . . orders or acts of civil . . . authority . . . which wholly or partly prevent . . . the utilizing . . . of the coal." This is what is known as a force majeure clause. NIPSCO argues that the Indiana Public Service Commission's "economy purchase orders" prevented it, in whole or part, from using the coal that it had agreed to buy, and it complains that the district judge instructed the jury incorrectly on the meaning and application of the clause.

All that those orders do is tell NIPSCO it will not be allowed to pass on fuel costs to its ratepayers in the form of higher rates if it can buy electricity cheaper than it can generate electricity internally using Carbon County's coal. Such an order does not "prevent," whether wholly or in part, NIPSCO from using the coal; it just prevents NIPSCO from shifting the burden of its improvidence or bad luck in having incorrectly forecasted its fuel needs to the backs of the hapless ratepayers.

This is all the clearer when we consider that the contract price was actually fixed just on the downside; it put a floor under the price NIPSCO had to pay, but the escalator provisions allowed the actual contract prices to rise above the floor, and they did. This underscores the gamble NIPSCO took in signing the contract. It committed itself to paying a price at or above a fixed minimum and to taking a fixed quantity at that price. It was willing to make this commitment to secure an assured supply of low-sulphur coal, but the risk it took was that the market price of coal or substitute fuels would fall. A force majeure clause is not intended to buffer a party against the normal risks of a contract. The normal risk of a fixed-price contract is that the market price will change. If it rises, the buyer gains at the expense of the seller (except insofar as escalator provisions give the seller some protection); if it falls, as here, the seller gains at the expense of the buyer. The whole purpose of a fixed-price contract is to allocate risk in this way. A force majeure clause interpreted to excuse the buyer from the consequences of the risk he expressly assumed would nullify a central term of the contract.

If the Commission had ordered NIPSCO to close a plant because of a safety or pollution hazard, we would have a true case of force majeure. But as the only thing the Commission did was prevent NIPSCO from using its monopoly position to make consumers bear the risk that NIPSCO assumed when it signed a long-term fixed-price fuel contract, NIPSCO cannot complain of force majeure; the risk that has come to pass was one that NIPSCO voluntarily assumed when it signed the contract.

In the early common law a contractual undertaking unconditional in terms was not excused merely because something had happened (such as an invasion, the passage of a law, or a natural disaster) that prevented the undertaking. *See Paradine v. Jane*, Aleyn 26, 82 Eng. Rep. 897 (K.B. 1647). Excuses had to be written into the contract; this is the origin of force majeure clauses. Later it came to be recognized that negotiating parties cannot anticipate all the contingencies that may arise in the performance of the contract; a legitimate judicial function in contract cases is to interpolate terms to govern remote contingencies — terms the parties would have agreed on explicitly if they had had the time and foresight to make advance provision for every possible contingency in performance. Later still, it was recognized that physical impossibility was irrelevant, or at least inconclusive; a promisor might want his promise to be unconditional, not because he thought he had superhuman powers but because he could insure against the risk of nonper-formance better than the promisee, or obtain a substitute performance more easily than the promisee. Thus the proper question in an "impossibility" case is not whether the promisor could not have performed his undertaking but whether his nonperformance should be excused because the parties, if they had thought about the matter, would have wanted to assign the risk of the contingency that made performance impossible or uneconomical to the promisor or to the promisee; if to the latter, the promisor is excused.

Section 2-615 of the Uniform Commercial Code takes this approach. It provides that "delay in delivery . . . by a seller . . . is not a breach of his duty under a contract for sale if performance as agreed has been made impracticable by the occurrence of a contingency the non-occurrence of which was a basic assumption on which the contract was made. . . ." Performance on schedule need not be impossible, only infeasible — provided that the event which made it infeasible was not a risk that the promisor had assumed. Notice, however, that the only type of promisor referred to is a seller; there is no suggestion that a buyer's performance might be excused by reason of impracticability. The reason is largely semantic. Ordinarily all the buyer has to do in order to perform his side of the bargain is pay, and while one can think of all sorts of reasons why, when the time came to pay, the buyer might not have the money, rarely would the seller have intended to assume the risk that the buyer might, whether through improvidence or bad luck, be unable to pay for the seller's goods or services. To deal with the rare case where the buyer or (more broadly) the paying party might have a good excuse based on some unforeseen change in circumstances, a new rubric was thought necessary, different from "impossibility" (the common law term) or "impracticability" (the Code term, picked up in RESTATEMENT (SECOND) OF CONTRACTS § 261 (1979)), and it received the name "frustration." Rarely is it impracticable or impossible for the payor to pay; but if something has happened to make the performance for which he would be paying worthless to him, an excuse for not paying, analogous to impracticability or impossibility, may be proper. *See* RESTATEMENT, *supra*, § 265, comment a.

The leading case on frustration remains *Krell v. Henry*, [1903] 2 K.B. 740 (C.A.). Krell rented Henry a suite of rooms for watching the coronation of Edward VII, but Edward came down with appendicitis and the coronation had to be postponed. Henry refused to pay the balance of the rent and the court held that he was excused from doing so because his purpose in renting had been frustrated by the postponement, a contingency outside the knowledge, or power to influence, of either party. The question was, to which party did the contract (implicitly) allocate the risk? Surely Henry had not intended to insure Krell against the possibility of the coronation's being postponed, since Krell could always relet the room, at the premium rental, for the coronation's new date. So Henry was excused.

Since impossibility and related doctrines are devices for shifting risk in accordance with the parties' presumed intentions, which are to minimize the costs of contract performance, one of which is the disutility created by risk, they have no place when the contract explicitly assigns a particular risk to one party or the other. As we have already noted, a fixed-price contract is an explicit assignment of the risk of market price increases to the seller and the risk of market price decreases to the buyer, and the assignment of the latter risk to the buyer is even clearer where, as in this case, the contract places a floor under price but allows for escalation. If, as is also the case here, the buyer forecasts the market incorrectly and therefore finds himself locked into a disadvantageous contract, he has only himself to blame and so cannot shift the risk back to the seller by invoking impossibility or related doctrines. It does not matter that it is an act of government that may have made the contract less advantageous to one party. Government these days is a pervasive factor in the economy and among the risks that a fixed-price contract allocates between the parties is that of a price change induced by one of government's manifold interventions in the economy. Since "the very purpose of a fixed price agreement is to place the risk of increased costs on the promisor (and the risk of decreased costs on the promisee)," the fact that costs decrease steeply (which is in effect what happened here — the cost of generating electricity turned out to be lower than NIPSCO thought when it signed the fixed-price contract with Carbon County) cannot allow the buyer to walk away from the contract.

NOTE

Force Majeure. Contracts (particularly long-term contracts) often contain excusable delay or *force majeure* clauses, which seek to excuse a party for various events beyond his control. "Acts of God," as fires, floods and the like are typically included. They also typically include such events as war, civil strife, strikes, and shortages of raw materials. Such clauses were very popular when courts would deny relief except for literal impossibility of performance. As the court indicates, they seemed necessary to overcome the rigid general rule at common law precluding excuse. They continue to be found in many contracts notwithstanding the availability of UCC § 2-615 and its counterpart in RESTATEMENT (SECOND) OF CONTRACTS § 261. Where the clause lists certain kinds of events different in kind from the supervening event that actually occurs, the interpretation rule of *ejusdem generis*, discussed in the materials on interpretation, may move a court to exclude a particular type of supervening event as an excuse because it is unlike events listed in the *force majeure* clause. A saving phrase in such a clause, such as "without limitation" or "including but not limited to," may prove beneficial. *Eastern Airlines, Inc. v. McDonnell-Douglas Corp.*, 532 F.2d 957 (5th Cir. 1976).

DISTINGUISHING MUTUAL MISTAKE — EQUITABLE ADJUSTMENT

Aluminum Co. of America v. Essex Group, Inc., 499 F. Supp. 53 (W.D. Pa. 1980). In 1967, Alcoa and Essex formed a contract whereby Alcoa was to process alumina supplied by Essex into aluminum. The term of the contract was to run to 1983 with an option in Essex to extend it until 1988. The price for each pound of converted aluminum was calculated by a complex pricing formula including variable components and linked to specific, objective price indices. The indexing system was evolved by Alcoa with the aid of the eminent economist, Alan Greenspan. Through this formula, to the knowledge of Essex, Alcoa sought to achieve a stable net income of about 4 cents per pound for converted aluminum over the life of the contract. The objective indices in the formula allowed for variation in this return from as high as 7 cents per pound to a low of 1 cent per pound. In the early years of the contract, there was no reason to question the formula. Later, however, it became evident that the formula, from the inception of the contract, was flawed and, absent judicial relief, Alcoa stood to lose in excess of $60 million during the remaining term of the contract.

Alcoa argued that it was entitled to relief on two theories: (1) mutual mistake and (2) commercial impracticability. The court found that there was a mutual mistake at the time the contract was formed. The Wholesale Price Index for Industrial Commodities (one of the critical indices in the price formula) did not function effectively with respect to the most important cost in the conversion of alumina to aluminum, electric power. The parties were, therefore, simply mistaken with respect to the price formula, and the mutual mistake permitted relief for Alcoa. The court also found that ALCOA was entitled to relief on grounds of impracticability and frustration of purpose. The court stated,

> In broad outline the doctrines of impracticability and of frustration of purpose resemble the doctrine of mistake. All three doctrines discharge an obligor from his duty to perform a contract where a failure of a basic assumption of the parties produces a grave failure of the equivalence of value of the exchange to the parties. And all three are qualified by the same notions of risk assumption and allocation. The doctrine of mistake of fact requires that the mistake relate to a basic assumption on which the contract was made. The doctrine of impracticability requires that the non-occurrence of the "event," RESTATEMENT (SECOND) OF CONTRACTS [§ 261] or the non-existence of the "fact," *id.* § [266] causing the impracticability be a basic assumption on which the contract is made. The doctrine of frustration of purpose similarly rests on the same "non-occurrence" or "non-existence," "basic assumption" equation. *Id.* [§§ 265, 266].

Differences. It is important to recognize a major difference between the doctrines of mutual mistake and commercial impracticability. Mutual mistake requires only that a party show a material effect on the agreed exchange, while impracticability requires a supervening risk that goes well beyond materiality and, even then, will constitute an excuse only if it was unforeseeable and not a risk that should have been assumed by the party seeking to be excused. While mutual mistake, unlike impracticability, must exist at the time of contract formation, in a case like Alcoa, it augurs a much more optimistic basis for relief than does impracticability. If impracticability exists at the time the contract is made, the analysis does not change except that the party asserting impracticability must have no reason to know of the fact causing impracticability at the time of contract formation. *See* RESTATEMENT (SECOND) OF CONTRACTS § 266(1) ("existing impracticability"); *see also Roy v. Stephen Pontiac-Cadillac, Inc.*, 543 A.2d 775 (Conn. App. Ct. 1988).

Equitable Adjustment. Though finding for Alcoa on the basis of mutual mistake, impracticability and frustration of purpose, the court did not discharge Alcoa from its obligations. Instead, it rewrote the contract, a kind of equitable reformation, by deleting the flawed price adjustment clause and creating a new clause to react to its essential holding that Alcoa had not assumed the risk of such major losses. Criticism of the opinion is not difficult to discover. As suggested by the court in *Beaver Creek Coal Co. v. Nevada Power Co.*, 1992 U.S. App. LEXIS 13505 at *13 (10th Cir. 1992), "We are not persuaded by the argument built on the ALCOA opinion. . . . ALCOA has generally not been found convincing by other courts" (citing *United States v. Southwestern Elec. Coop., Inc.*, 869 F.2d 310, 315 n.7 (7th Cir. 1989); *Printing Indus. Ass'n v. International Printing & Graphic Communications Union*, 584 F. Supp. 990, 998 (N.D. Ohio 1984)) (quoting *Wabash, Inc. v. Avnet, Inc.*, 516 F. Supp. 995, 999 n.6 (N.D. Ill. 1981)). There is, however, some praise for the court's willingness to adopt an approach that avoids the draconian all-or-nothing approach, i.e., either a party is discharged or not. *See* Speidel, *Court-Imposed Price Adjustments Under Long-Term Supply Contracts*, 76 Nw. L. REV. 369 (1981).

UCC § 2-615, Comment 6 states:

In situations in which neither sense nor justice is served by either answer when the issue is posed in flat terms of "excuse" or "no excuse," adjustment under the various provisions of this article is necessary, especially the section on good faith, on insecurity and assurance and on the reading of all provisions in light of their purposes, and the general policy of this Act to use equitable principles in furtherance of commercial standards and good faith.

In *Iowa Elec. Light & Power Co. v. Atlas Corp.*, 467 F. Supp. 129 (N.D. Iowa 1978), *rev'd on other grounds*, 603 F.2d 1301 (8th Cir. 1979), the seller sought a good faith modification of the contract through a consent order and attempted to convince the court that the court had the authority in framing the decree for specific performance to equitably adjust the price of the uranium. The court determined that neither of these arguments was supported by UCC language or the facts of the case.

Chapter 8

REMEDIES

A. THE THREE INTERESTS

In Chapter 1, the subject of remedies was introduced as a critical dimension of the study of contract law. By introducing that dimension at the earliest time, the student could be reminded of the importance of contract remedies in all of the cases and materials following that introduction. It is now appropriate to consider contract remedies in some detail. We begin with the statement of the three interests protected by contract law as found in the classic article by Fuller & Perdue, *The Reliance Interest in Contract Damages*, 46 YALE L.J. 52, 373 (1936):

> *First,* the plaintiff has in reliance on the promise of the defendant conferred some value on the defendant. The defendant fails to perform his promise. The Court may force the defendant to disgorge the value he received from the plaintiff. The object here may be termed the prevention of gain by the defaulting promisor at the expense of the promisee; more briefly, the prevention of unjust enrichment. The interest protected may be called the *restitution interest. . . .*

> *Secondly,* the plaintiff has in reliance on the promise of the defendant changed his position. For example, the buyer under a contract for the sale of land has incurred expense in the investigation of the seller's title, or has neglected the opportunity to enter other contracts. We may award damages to the plaintiff for the purpose of undoing the harm which his reliance on the defendant's promise has caused him. Our object is to put him in as good a position as he was in before the promise was made. The interest protected in this case may be called the *reliance interest.*

> *Thirdly,* without insisting on reliance by the promisee or enrichment of the promisor, we may seek to give the promisee the value of the expectancy which the promise created. We may in a suit for specific performance actually compel the defendant to render the promised performance to the plaintiff, or, in a suit for damages, we may make the defendant pay the money value of this performance. Here our object is to put the plaintiff in as good a position as he would have occupied had the defendant performed his promise. The interest protected in this case we may call the *expectation interest.*

B. PURPOSE — ECONOMIC THEORY

ALLAPATTAH SERVICES, INC. v. EXXON CORP.
United States District Court, Southern District of Florida
61 F. Supp. 2d 1326 (1999)

GOLD, J.

Plaintiffs seek to recover punitive damages, alleging that Exxon tortiously and oppressively breached its contracts with Plaintiffs. The gravamen of Plaintiffs' complaint is that Exxon breached its contract with Plaintiffs by failing to offset the wholesale price of its gasoline to its dealers by an amount which was, on average, equal to the three percent credit card processing charge. This, according to Plaintiffs, was a breach of Exxon's obligation to fix the open price term in the Sales Agreement in good faith and as allegedly promised.

The underlying purpose of damages in actions premised on a breach of contract is to place the non-breaching party in the same position it would have occupied if the contract had not been breached. *See Walsh v. Ford Motor Co.*, 627 F. Supp. 1519, 1523 (D.D.C. 1986) (*citing* 5A CORBIN, CORBIN ON CONTRACTS § 922, at 5 (1964)); *Mortgage Finance, Inc. v. Podleski*, 742 P.2d 900, 902 (Colo. 1987) (breach of contract remedies serve only to provide compensation for loss, not to punish the wrongdoer). Recognizing this central purpose, courts have uniformly rejected requests for punitive damages for mere breach of contract, regardless of the breaching party's conduct or motives. Thus, well established principles of contract law dictate that punitive damages are generally not available for a breach of contract claim unless the defendant's conduct in breaching the contract also violated a noncontractual legal duty, thereby constituting a tort. *See* RESTATEMENT (SECOND) OF CONTRACTS § 355 (1981).[1] Even under the common law, tort remedies are not awarded in a contract dispute absent conduct which separately and independently substantiates the commission of a tort. *See id.; see also Vanwyk Textile Sys., B.V. v. Zimmer Machinery America, Inc.*, 994 F. Supp. 350, 362 (W.D.N.C. 1997) ("To state a claim in tort, a plaintiff must allege a duty owed him by the defendant separate and distinct from any duty owed under a contract."). "Whether an action is characterized as one in tort or on contract is determined by the nature of the complaint, not by the form of the pleadings, and consideration must be given to the facts which constitute the cause of action." *Thomas v. Countryside of Hastings, Inc.*, 246 Neb. 907, 524 N.W.2d 311, 313 (Neb. 1994).

Notably, the breach of a duty is an element in both contractual and tort causes of action. *See Splitt v. Deltona Corp.*, 662 F.2d 1142, 1145 (5th Cir. 1981). The

---

[1] The RESTATEMENT specifically provides that: "Punitive damages are not recoverable for a breach of contract unless the conduct constituting the breach is also a tort for which punitive damages are recoverable." RESTATEMENT (SECOND) OF CONTRACTS § 355. As commentary, the restatement expresses that "the purposes of awarding contract damages is to compensate the injured party." *Id.* § 355, cmt. a. It goes on to reiterate that "the purpose of awarding damages is still compensation and not punishment, and punitive damages are not appropriate. In exceptional instances, departures have been made from this general policy . . . notably in situations involving consumer transactions or arising under insurance policies." *Id.*

distinction is that "duties involved in [tort actions] are raised by law and social policy and owed to an entire class of persons. . . , [while] contractual duties are created by the contract terms and [are] owed to the parties thereto." *Id.*

Not only are intentional breaches exempt from punitive claims, they are sometimes encouraged. "The law has long recognized the view that a contracting party has the option to breach a contract and pay damages if it is more efficient to do so." *L.L. Cole & Son, Inc. v. Hickman*, 282 Ark. 6, 665 S.W.2d 278, 280 (Ark. 1984) (*citing* Holmes, *The Path of the Law* in COLLECTED LEGAL PAPERS 167, 175 (1920)).[2] The logical result of this theory is a "limitation of breach of contract damage exposure to losses contemplated by the contracting parties, and for which a defendant 'at least tacitly agreed to assume responsibility.' " *Delta Rice Mill, Inc. v. General Foods Corp.*, 763 F.2d 1001, 1006 (8th Cir. 1985) (quoting *Morrow v. First Nat'l Bank of Hot Springs*, 261 Ark. 568, 550 S.W.2d 429, 430 (Ark. 1977)).

This acceptance of intentional, efficient breaches has been uniformly adopted among the jurisdictions. *See, e.g., Thyssen, Inc. v. SS Fortune Star*, 777 F.2d 57, 63 (2d Cir. 1985) ("Breaches of contract that are in fact efficient and wealth-enhancing should be encouraged, and . . . such 'efficient breaches' occur when the breaching party will still profit after compensating the other party for its 'expectation interest.' The addition of punitive damages to traditional contract remedies would prevent many such beneficial actions from being taken."); *Reiver v. Murdoch & Walsh, P.A.*, 625 F. Supp. 998, 1015 (D. Del. 1985) ("some breaches may be intentional and . . . efficient when the payment of damages would be less costly than performance . . . that fact alone does not entitle a plaintiff to seek punitive damages unless the intentional breach is similar in character to an intentional tort."); *Harris v. Atlantic Richfield Co.*, 14 Cal. App. 4th 70, 17 Cal. Rptr. 2d 649, 653 (Cal. App. Ct. 1993) ("The traditional goal of contract remedies is compensation of the promisee for the loss resulting from the breach, not compulsion of the promisor to perform his promises. Therefore, 'willful' breaches have not been distinguished from other breaches. The restrictions on contract remedies serve purposes not found in tort law. They protect the parties' freedom to bargain over special risks and they promote contract formation by limiting liability to the value of the promise. This encourages efficient breaches, resulting in increased production of goods and services at lower cost to society.") (internal citations omitted); *Kutzin v. Pirnie*, 124 N.J. 500, 591 A.2d 932, 941 (N.J. 1991) ("The approach that we adopt is suggested to have the added benefit of promoting economic efficiency: penalties deter 'efficient' breaches of contract 'by making the cost of the breach to the contract breaker greater than the cost of the breach to the victim.' ") (quoting POSNER, ECONOMIC ANALYSIS OF LAW § 4.10 (3d ed. 1986)).

In sum, in the normal commercial situation, damages for breach of contract are limited to the pecuniary loss sustained, since the damage is usually financial, susceptible of accurate estimation, and the wrong suffered by the plaintiff is the same, regardless of the defendant's motive. Although this is the general rule, courts

---

[2] [2] JUSTICE HOLMES articulated that "the duty to keep a contract at common law means a prediction that you must pay damages if you do not keep it — and nothing else."

have, nevertheless carved out exceptions, which are not applicable to the instant contractual dispute.[3]

For the sale of goods, remedies for breach of contract are addressed in UCC § 1-106, which provides:

> The remedies provided by the Act shall be liberally administered to the end that the aggrieved party may be put in as good a position as if the other party had fully performed but neither consequential or special nor penal damages may be had except as specifically provided in this Act or by other rule of law. UCC § 106(1).

[T]he Uniform Commercial Code (the "UCC") imposes a duty of good faith and fair dealing on all contracts governed thereunder. *See* UCC § 1-203 ("Every contract or duty within this Act imposes an obligation of good faith in its performance and enforcement."). Case law interpreting the UCC in the context of the implied duty of good faith performance expressly discounts Plaintiffs' argument that a breach of a contractual covenant of good faith can be treated as an independent tort. Thus, the UCC itself does not allow punishment for bad faith conduct that breaches the covenant of good faith, thereby breaching the underlying contract. Absent an independent tort, which Plaintiffs have not identified, punitive damages under the UCC are not available, unless Plaintiffs otherwise demonstrate that they would be allowed "by other rule of law." UCC § 1-106.

Notwithstanding some jurisdictional variation, the state laws still preclude punitive damages absent an affirmative showing of the commission of a tort independent of any obligation under the contract. *See, e.g., Atchison Casting Corp. v. Dofasco, Inc.*, 889 F. Supp. 1445, 1461 (D. Kan. 1995) ("The general rule in Kansas and elsewhere is that the existence of a contract relationship bars the assertion of tort claims covering the same subject matter governed by the contract."); *Foreign Mission Bd. v. Wade*, 242 Va. 234, 409 S.E.2d 144, 148 (Va. 1991) (a tort claim arising out of a contractual agreement may only stand as an independent claim where "the duty tortiously or negligently breached [is] a common law duty, not one existing between the parties solely by virtue of the contract."); *Kamlar Corp. v. Haley*, 224 Va. 699, 299 S.E.2d 514, 518 (Va. 1983) (punitive damages in an action for breach of contract are only appropriate where there is "proof of an independent, wilful tort, beyond the mere breach of a duty imposed by contract."). The purpose of the independent tort exception to the rule barring punitive damages in contract cases is to separate mere wilful breaches of contract, which require no more than an unwilling breach to make the plaintiff whole, and other wanton or malicious acts that cause a distinct injury and merit the deterrent of punitive damages. Thus, a general rule allowing tort damages whenever a court perceives some amorphous quality such as "bad faith" invites uncertainty and inhibits commerce without a

---

[3] [3] For instance, courts have most commonly awarded tort damages for a breach of the duty of good faith in cases involving first-party and third-party insurance claims. Many courts have fashioned a tort of bad faith in certain narrowly defined situations, such as when a liability insurer violates its duty to defend its insured or to settle a claim within the policy limits. Plaintiffs' survey of state law cites to several cases involving bad faith breach of contract claims derived from a obligations under insurance policies. Several states have enacted statutes providing punitive relief for an insurer's bad faith. *See, e.g.*, Ark. Stat. § 66-3228; Fla. Stat. § 624.155(4); Tex. Ins. Code art. 3.62.

counterbalancing economic benefit. An overview of state law, on which Plaintiffs rely to addend their claim for punitive damages convinces the Court that Plaintiffs cannot be awarded punitive damages for Exxon's alleged breach of its Sales Agreement with its dealers.

As alleged by Plaintiffs, these claims do not rise to the level of independently tortious conduct such that Plaintiffs have stated a claim separate from their breach of contract claim. Plaintiffs' own admission undermines the existence of an independent tort: "The Dealers do not allege a new cause of action but only seek to add to the kind of relief sought." Plaintiffs' Motion for Leave to Assert Claim for Punitive Damages, at 28. Accordingly, Plaintiffs are not entitled to punitive damages. [B]ecause the Court finds that, should they prevail, Plaintiffs will be adequately compensated by a damage award representing their expectation interest provided under traditional contract law, Plaintiffs cannot recover punitive damages.

NOTES

(1) An "explanation, offered by economists, is the notion that breaches of contract that are in fact efficient and wealth enhancing should be encouraged, and that such 'efficient breaches' occur when the breaching party will still profit after compensating the other party for its 'expectation interest.' The addition of punitive damages to traditional contract remedies would prevent many such beneficial actions. . . ." *Thyssen, Inc. v. S. S. Fortune Star*, 777 F.2d 57 (2d Cir. 1985).

(2) In general, it may be said that economic theory supports the protection of the expectation interest through substitutional relief in the form of money damages.[4] The economic theory of the social institution of contract explains the allocation of the resources of society through voluntary agreements facilitating future exchanges. Value maximization is effectuated where goods worth $1000 to X are worth $1500 to Y who has $1500 to spend so that the total value is $2500. If the parties agree to an exchange of the goods for $1500, the result is that X now has $1500 and Y has goods worth $1500 for a total of $3000.[5] After making a contract to sell the goods for $1500, X may discover another buyer (Z) who is willing to pay $2200 for them. If X breaches the contract but fully compensates Y to the extent of $500, he is better off because his net return is $1700 after the sale to Z for $2200. Z is pleased because he has received goods worth $2200 to him. This results in economic efficiency but it involves a breach of contract. The protection of the expectation interest through a substitutional money damages remedy induces *efficient breach.*[6]

---

[4] *See* Cooter & Eisenberg, *Damages for Breach of Contract*, 73 CAL. L. REV. 1432 (1985).

[5] "Value" is measured by the value to the individual and the parties' willingness and ability to transfer the goods and to pay. Economic theory does not suggest a preferable measure of value.

[6] "The key result is that the expectation remedy is the only remedy that creates efficient incentives with respect to breaches of contracts. This is because the expectation remedy forces the breaching party to pay in damages the value of the good to the breached-against party. If another buyer values the good more than this, then it is efficient for that buyer to have the good. Given the expectation measure of damages, the seller will have an incentive to breach in order to obtain the higher offer. . . . [I]f damages

It is important, however, to recognize the limitations of this approach. Even from an economics perspective, it does not consider transaction costs, i.e., those costs associated with the bargaining process and dispute resolution. Nor does it consider non-economic perspectives, such as any moral obligation to keep one's promises.[7] Yet, considering contract remedies from the pure economic perspective can be helpful with numerous questions, including whether the remedy of specific performance should be expanded[8] or whether the availability of liquidated damage clauses should be enhanced.[9] In general, however, the impact of law and economics scholarship on the law of contracts to this time suggests that economic theory supports the existing structure.[10]

C. THE EXPECTATION INTEREST AND ITS LIMITATIONS

[1] The Foreseeability Limitation

HADLEY v. BAXENDALE
Court of the Exchequer
156 Eng. Rep. 145 (1854)

At the trial before CROMPTON, J., at the last Gloucester Assizes, it appeared that the plaintiffs carried on an extensive business as millers at Gloucester; and that, on the 11th of May, their mill was stopped by a breakage of the crank shaft by which the mill was worked. The steam-engine was manufactured by Messrs. Joyce & Co., the engineers, at Greenwich, and it became necessary to send the shaft as a pattern

---

are below expectation damages an inefficient breach might occur. This is the problem with the reliance remedy, because it leads to a level of damages below the expectation level. The restitution remedy is even worse because it provides less than the reliance measure of damages." A.M. POLINSKY, AN INTRODUCTION TO LAW AND ECONOMICS 33–34 (2d ed. 1989). See, however, Chapter 8 of the same volume, which reinforces an earlier conclusion that a breach of contract remedy that is efficient with respect to every consideration does not exist, i.e., while the expectation remedy is preferable with respect to a decision to breach the contract, the restitution remedy is preferable with respect to a reliance decision and a liquidated damage remedy is preferable with respect to risk allocation.

[7] See CHARLES FRIED, CONTRACT AS PROMISE (1981).

[8] Specific performance, however, would preclude efficient breach if it were available in the example suggested in the text. For differing views of the expanded availability of specific performance, see SCHWARTZ, THE CASE FOR SPECIFIC PERFORMANCE, 89 YALE L.J. 271 (1979), as contrasted with KRONMAN, SPECIFIC PERFORMANCE, 45 U. CHI. L. REV. 351 (1978).

[9] See GOETZ & SCOTT, LIQUIDATED DAMAGES, PENALTIES, AND THE JUST COMPENSATION PRINCIPLE: SOME NOTES ON AN ENFORCEMENT MODEL AND THEORY OF EFFICIENT BREACH, 77 COLUM. L. REV. 554 (1977).

[10] For example, one writer remarks, "At most, the results suggest that 'law and economics' is a source of sometimes useful information for working within already established rules. It does not alter rules nor does it alter the weighing of various judicial interests." HARRISON, TRENDS AND TRACES: A PRELIMINARY EVALUATION OF ECONOMIC ANALYSIS IN CONTRACT LAW, 1988 ANNUAL SURVEY OF AMERICAN LAW [NEW YORK UNIV.] 73, 98–99 (1989). This view of law and economics as related to contract law suggests the essential reason for its criticism by scholars who count themselves within the "Critical Legal Studies" movement and view the market system and its mechanism, contract law, as opposed to an amorphous collection of altruistic and communitarian interests. Other literature on the economics of contract law includes THE ECONOMICS OF CONTRACT LAW (KRONMAN & POSNER EDS. 1979); POSNER, ECONOMIC ANALYSIS OF LAW, ch. 4 (3d ed. 1986); BIRMINGHAM, BREACH OF CONTRACT, DAMAGE MEASURES AND ECONOMIC EFFICIENCY, 24 RUTGERS L. REV. 273 (1970).

for a new one to Greenwich. The fracture was discovered on the 12th, and on the 13th the plaintiffs sent one of their servants to the office of the defendants, who are the well-known carriers trading under the name of Pickford & Co., for the purpose of having the shaft carried to Greenwich. The plaintiffs' servant told the clerk that the mill was stopped, and that the shaft must be sent immediately; and in answer to the inquiry when the shaft would be taken, the answer was, that if it was sent up by twelve o'clock any day, it would be delivered at Greenwich on the following day. On the following day the shaft was taken by the defendants, before noon, for the purpose of being conveyed to Greenwich, and the sum of 2£. 4s. was paid for its carriage for the whole distance; at the same time the defendants' clerk was told that a special entry, if required, should be made to hasten its delivery. The delivery of the shaft at Greenwich was delayed by some neglect; and the consequence was, that the plaintiffs did not receive the new shaft for several days after they would otherwise have done, and the working of their mill was thereby delayed, and they thereby lost the profits they would otherwise have received.

On the part of the defendants, it was objected that these damages were too remote, and that the defendants were not liable with respect to them. The learned Judge left the case generally to the jury, who found a verdict with 25£. damages beyond the amount paid into Court. . . .

ALDERSON, B.

We think that there ought to be a new trial in this case; but, in so doing, we deem it to be expedient and necessary to state explicitly the rule which the Judge, at the next trial, ought, in our opinion, to direct the jury to be governed by when they estimate the damages.

It is, indeed, of the last importance that we should do this; for, if the jury are left without any definite rule to guide them, it will, in such cases as these, manifestly lead to the greatest injustice. The Courts have done this on several occasions; and, in *Blake v. Midland Railway Company* (18 Q.B. 93), the Court granted a new trial on this very ground, that the rule had not been definitely laid down to the jury by the learned Judge at Nisi Prius.

"There are certain established rules," this Court says, in *Alder v. Keighley* (15 M. & W. 117), "according to which the jury ought to find." And the Court, in that case, adds: "and here there is a clear rule, that the amount which would have been received if the contract had been kept, is the measure of damages if the contract is broken."

Now we think the proper rule in such a case as the present is this: — Where two parties have made a contract which one of them has broken, the damages which the other party ought to receive in respect of such breach of contract should be such as may fairly and reasonably be considered either arising naturally, i.e., according to the usual course of things, from such breach of contract itself, or such as may reasonably be supposed to have been the contemplation of both parties, at the time they made the contract, as the probable result of the breach of it. Now, if the special circumstances under which the contract was actually made were communicated by the plaintiffs to the defendants, and thus known to both parties, the damages resulting from the breach of such a contract, which they would reasonably contemplate, would be the amount of injury which would ordinarily follow from a breach of contract under these special circumstances so known and communicated. But, on the other hand, if these special circumstances were wholly unknown to the party breaking the contract, he, at the most, could only be supposed to have had in his contemplation the amount of injury which would arise generally, and in the great multitude of cases not affected by any special circumstances, from such a breach of contract. For, had the special circumstances been known, the parties might have specially provided for the breach of contract by special terms as to the damages in that case; and of this advantage it would be very unjust to deprive them. Now the above principles are those by which we think the jury ought to be guided in estimating the damages arising out of any breach of contract. It is said, that other cases such as breaches of contract in the non-payment of money, or in the not making a good title to land, are to be treated as exceptions from this, and as governed by a conventional rule. But as, in such cases, both parties must be supposed to be cognizant of that well-known rule, these cases may, we think, be more properly classed under the rule above enunciated as to cases under known special circumstances, because there both parties may reasonably be presumed to contemplate the estimation of the amount of damages according to the conventional rule. Now, in the present case, if we are to apply the principles above laid down, we find that the only circumstances here communicated by the plaintiffs to the defendants at the time the contract was made, were, that the article to be carried was the broken shaft of a mill, and that the plaintiffs were the millers of that mill. But how do these circumstances shew reasonably that the profits of the mill must be stopped by an unreasonable delay in the delivery of the broken shaft by the carrier to the third person? Suppose the plaintiffs had another shaft in their possession put up or putting up at the time, and that they only wished to send back the broken shaft to the engineer who made it; it is clear that this would be quite consistent with the above circumstances, and yet the unreasonable delay in the delivery would have no effect upon the intermediate profits of the mill. Or, again, suppose that, at the time of the delivery to the carrier, the machinery of the mill had been in other respects defective, then, also, the same results would follow. Here it is true that the shaft was actually sent back to serve as a model for a new one, and that the want of a new one was the only cause of the stoppage of the mill, and that the loss of profits really arose from not sending down the new shaft in proper time, and that this arose from the delay in delivering the broken one to serve as a model. But it is obvious that, in the great multitude of cases of millers sending off broken shafts to third persons by a carrier under ordinary circumstances, such consequences would not, in all probability, have occurred; and these special circumstances were here never communicated by the plaintiffs to the defendants. It follows, therefore, that the loss of profits here cannot reasonably be considered such as consequence of the breach of contract as could have been fairly and reasonably contemplated by both the parties when they made this contract. For such loss would neither have flowed naturally from the breach of this contract in the great multitude of such cases occurring under ordinary circumstances, nor where the special circumstances, which, perhaps, would have made it a reasonable and natural consequence of such breach of contract, communicated to or known by the defendants. The Judge ought, therefore, to have told the jury, that, upon the facts then before them, they ought not to take the loss of profits into consideration at all in estimating the damages. There must therefore be a new trial in this case.

NOTES

(1) *The Reporting Mistake.* In *Victoria Laundry (Windsor), Ltd. v. Newman Indus., Ltd.*, 2 K.B. 528, 537 (1947), wherein Lord Asquith states: "[I]t is essential to bear clearly in mind the facts on which *Hadley v. Baxendale* proceeded. The head-note is definitely misleading in so far as it says that the defendant's clerk, who attended at the office, was told that the mill was stopped and that the shaft must be delivered immediately. The same allegation figures in the statement of facts which are said on page 344 to have 'appeared' at the trial before Crompton J. If the Court of Exchequer had accepted these facts as established, the court must, one would suppose, have decided the case the other way round; must, that is, have held the damage claimed was recoverable under the second rule. But it is reasonably plain from Alderson B.'s judgment that the court rejected this evidence. . . ." [Here, the court quotes a portion of Baron Alderson's statement quoted above].

(2) Hadley v. Baxendale *Lives — General and Special Damages.* A LEXIS search of case law in October 2014 mentioning *Hadley v. Baxendale* revealed 1,776 citations including more than 50 citations in 2014. In *Paper Magic Group v. J.B. Hunt Transp., Inc.*, 318 F.3d 458 (3d Cir. 2003), the plaintiff had contracted to supply Target Stores with Christmas cards and related Christmas products imprinted with Target's logo. The plaintiff contracted with its usual carrier, the defendant, to ship the goods on October 16. The typical delivery time would be two to three days. The invoice value of the shipment was $130,080.48. The shipment was lost and eventually found in February when they were worthless to Target since the Christmas season was over and worthless to the plaintiff since the products contained Target's logo and could not be resold elsewhere. The defendant sold the goods as salvage for just under $50,000 and offered this amount to the plaintiff as damages. The plaintiff insisted on the full invoice value of the shipment. The defendant claimed that the plaintiff was seeking "special" rather than "general" damages. Referring to *Hadley v. Baxendale*, the court recognized "general" damages as foreseeable to a reasonable person while "special" damages are those that a party would not have reason to foresee as a natural consequence of the breach when the contract was made. Thus, to be liable for "special" damages, a party would have to be notified of the otherwise unforeseeable circumstances at the time of formation. The bill of lading evidencing the transport contract between the parties did not specify a delivery time or otherwise indicate that the delivery was time-sensitive. The court, however, held that the plaintiff was not seeking special damages such as a recovery for loss of use, or lost future profits. Rather, it was seeking actual (general) damages, the lost value of the shipment caused by the defendant's delay. Such damages should have been foreseeable to a reasonable party such as the defendant without any special notice.

(3) In *West Haven Sound Development Corp. v. West Haven*, 514 A.2d 734, 748 (1988), the defendant delivered a new bake oven on time but breached its transport contract when the oven was destroyed upon unloading. The plaintiff sought special damages for the profits it lost in having to close the bakery for seven days until a

replacement oven could be installed. The transport contract between the parties had been made on September 5. Delivery was scheduled for September 10, but it was not until September 7 when the defendant informed the plaintiff that the oven was in transit that the plaintiff informed the defendant that it would disassemble its old oven on September 9. Relying upon *Hadley v. Baxendale* and its modern iteration in the RESTATEMENT (SECOND) OF CONTRACTS § 351,[11] the court held that the Bakery's claim for special damages failed because the defendant did not have notice at the time the transport contract was made on September 5 that its inability to deliver the oven by September 10 would result in these special damages. Such notice did not arrive until September 7. The *Hadley* rule places a *limitation* on recoverable damages. Prior to *Hadley*, contract-breakers could be held for unforeseeable losses. As the court noted in *West Haven Sound Development Corp. v. West Haven*, 514 A.2d 734, 748 (1988), the foreseeability requirement places a significant limitation on the recovery of damages.

(4) *General, Special, and Consequential Damages — The UCC "Hadle" Rule.* The distinction between general and special damages is often stated as follows: the former arise naturally from the breach and are implied or presumed by law. The latter do not arise naturally. They are not within the common experience of mankind as arising in the particular situation. Thus, they are not implied or presumed by law. "General" and "special," therefore, may be used synonymously with the terms "natural" and "unnatural" or "usual" and "unusual." Courts and lawyers also refer to "consequential" damages which are often equated with "special" damages. The Uniform Commercial Code, however, defines consequential damages as "any loss resulting from *general* or *particular* requirements and needs of which the seller at the time of contracting had reason to know." UCC § 2-715(2)(a) (emphasis supplied). Thus, while emphasizing the *Hadley* requirement of foreseeability ("reason to know"), it recognizes that "onsequential" may refer to either "general" or "particular" (special) damages. "Consequential" damages are often equated with lost profits which are assumed to be "special" damages. It is, however, clear that lost profits are recoverable as general damages (which a reasonable person is presumed to know without any special notice) where they flow directly and immediately from the breach of contract. *Bird Lakes Dev. Corp. v. Meruelo*, 626 So. 2d 234 (Fla. App. 1993).

---

[11] Section 351 states:

(1) Damages are not recoverable for loss that the party in breach did not have reason to foresee as a probable result of the breach when the contract was made.

(2) Loss may be foreseeable as a probable result of a breach because it flows from the breach (a) in the ordinary course of events, or (b) as a result of special circumstances beyond the ordinary course of events, that the party in breach has reason to know.

(3) A court may limit damages for foreseeable loss by excluding the recovery for loss of profits, by allowing recovery only for loss incurred in reliance, or otherwise if it concludes that in the circumstances justice so requires in order to avoid disproportionate compensation.

SPANG INDUSTRIES, FORT PITT BRIDGE DIVISION v. AETNA CASUALTY & SURETY CO.

United States Court of Appeals, Second Circuit
512 F.2d 365 (1975)

MULLIGAN, J.

Torrington Construction Co., Inc. (Torrington), a Connecticut corporation, was the successful bidder with the New York State Department of Transportation for a highway reconstruction contract covering 4.47 miles of road in Washington County, New York. Before submitting its bid, Torrington received an oral quotation from Spang Industries, Inc., Fort Pitt Bridge Division (Fort Pitt), a Pennsylvania corporation, for the fabrication, furnishing and erection of some 240 tons of structural steel at a unit price of 27.5 cents per pound; the steel was to be utilized to construct a 270 foot long, double span bridge over the Battenkill River as part of the highway reconstruction. The quotation was confirmed in a letter from Fort Pitt to Torrington dated September 5, 1969, which stated in part: "Delivery to be mutually agreed upon." On November 3, 1969, Torrington, in response to a request from Fort Pitt, advised that its requirements for delivery and erection of the steel would be late June, 1970. On November 12, 1969, Fort Pitt notified Torrington that it was tentatively scheduling delivery in accordance with these requirements. On January 7, 1970, Fort Pitt wrote to Torrington asking if the June, 1970 erection date was still valid; Torrington responded affirmatively on January 13, 1970. However, on January 29, 1970, Fort Pitt advised that it was engaged in an extensive expansion program and that "[d]ue to unforeseen delays caused by weather, deliveries from suppliers, etc., it is our opinion that the June date cannot be met." On February 2, 1970, Torrington sent a letter requesting that Fort Pitt give a delivery date and, receiving no response, wrote again on May 12, 1970 requesting a written confirmation of the date of delivery and threatening to cancel out if the date was not reasonably close to the originally scheduled date. On May 20, 1970, Fort Pitt responded and promised that the structural steel would be shipped early in August, 1970.

Although some 25 tons of small steel parts were shipped on August 21, 1970, the first girders and other heavy structural steel were not shipped until August 24, 26, 27, 31 and September 2 and 4, 1970. Fort Pitt had subcontracted the unloading and erection of the steel to Syracuse Rigging Co. but neglected to advise it of the August 21st shipment. The steel began to arrive at the railhead in Shushan, New York about September 1st and the railroad demanded immediate unloading. Torrington was therefore compelled to do the unloading itself until Syracuse Rigging arrived on September 8, 1970. Not until September 16 was there enough steel delivered to the job site to permit Syracuse to commence erection. The work was completed on October 8, 1970 and the bridge was ready to receive its concrete deck on October 28, 1970. Because of contract specifications set by the State requiring that concrete be poured at temperatures of 40/d Fahrenheit and above, Torrington had to get special permission from the State's supervising engineer to pour the concrete on October 28, 1970, when the temperature was at 32/d.

Since the job site was in northern New York near the Vermont border and the danger of freezing temperatures was imminent, the pouring of the concrete was performed on a crash basis in one day, until 1 a.m. the following morning, which entailed extra costs for Torrington in the form of overtime pay, extra equipment and the protection of the concrete during the pouring process.

In July, 1971, Fort Pitt instituted an action against Aetna Casualty and Surety Co., which had posted a general contractor's labor and material bond, in the United States District Court for the Western District of Pennsylvania, seeking to recover the balance due on the subcontract, which at that point was $72,247.37 with interest. Thereafter in 1972 Torrington made two further payments totaling $48,983.92. That action was transferred pursuant to 28 U.S.C. § 1406(a) to the United States District Court for the Northern District of New York by order dated December 9, 1971. In the interim, Torrington had commenced suit in New York Supreme Court, Washington County, seeking damages in the sum of $23,290.81 alleged to be caused by Fort Pitt's delay in furnishing the steel. Fort Pitt then removed the case to the United States District Court for the Northern District of New York (where the two cases were consolidated), and counterclaimed for the balance due on the contract. From May 29 to 31, 1973, the cases were tried without a jury before Hon. James S. Holden, Chief Judge of the United States District Court for the District of Vermont, who was sitting by designation. On September 12, 1973, Judge Holden filed his findings of fact and conclusions of law in which he held that Fort Pitt had breached its contract by its delayed delivery and that Torrington was entitled to damages in the amount of $7,653.57. He further held that Fort Pitt was entitled to recover from Torrington on the counterclaim the sum of $23,290.12, which was the balance due on its contract price plus interest, less the $7,653.57 damages sustained by Torrington. He directed that judgment be entered for Fort Pitt against Torrington and Aetna on their joint and several liability for $15,636.55 with interest from November 12, 1970.

Fort Pitt on this appeal does not take issue with any of the findings of fact of the court below but contends that the recovery by Torrington of its increased expenses constitutes special damages which were not reasonably within the contemplation of the parties when they entered into the contract.

While the damages awarded Torrington are relatively modest ($7,653.57) in comparison with the subcontract price ($132,274.37), Fort Pitt urges that an affirmance of the award will do violence to the rule of *Hadley v. Baxendale*, 156 Eng. Rep. 145 (Ex. 1854), and create a precedent which will have a severe impact on the business of all subcontractors and suppliers.

While it is evident that the function of the award of damages for a breach of contract is to put the plaintiff in the same position he would have been in had there been no breach, *Hadley v. Baxendale* limits the recovery to those injuries which the parties could reasonably have anticipated at the time the contract was entered into. If the damages suffered do not usually flow from the breach, then it must be established that the special circumstances giving rise to them should reasonably have been anticipated at the time the contract was made.

There can be no question but that *Hadley v. Baxendale* represents the law in New York and in the United States generally. There is no dispute between the parties on this appeal as to the continuing viability of *Hadley v. Baxendale* and its formulation of the rule respecting special damages, and this court has no intention of challenging or questioning its principles, which CHIEF JUDGE CARDOZO characterized to be, at least in some applications, "tantamount to a rule of property," *Kerr S.S. Co. v. Radio Corporation of America*, 245 N.Y. 284, 291, 157 N.E. 140, 142 (1927).

The gist of Fort Pitt's argument is that, when it entered into the subcontract to fabricate, furnish and erect the steel in September, 1969, it had received a copy of the specifications which indicated that the total work was to be completed by December 15, 1971. It could not reasonably have anticipated that Torrington would so expedite the work (which was accepted by the State on January 21, 1971) that steel delivery would be called for in 1970 rather than in 1971. Whatever knowledge Fort Pitt received after the contract was entered into, it argues, cannot expand its liability, since it is essential under *Hadley v. Baxendale* and its Yankee progeny that the notice of the facts which would give rise to special damages in case of breach be given at or before the time the contract was made. The principle urged cannot be disputed. We do not, however, agree that any violence to the doctrine was done here.

Fort Pitt also knew from the same specifications that Torrington was to commence the work on October 1, 1969. The Fort Pitt letter of September 5, 1969, which constitutes the agreement between the parties, specifically provides: "Delivery to be mutually agreed upon." On November 3, 1969, Torrington, responding to Fort Pitt's inquiry, gave "late June 1970" as its required delivery date and, on November 12, 1969, Fort Pitt stated that it was tentatively scheduling delivery for that time. Thus, at the time when the parties, pursuant to their initial agreement, fixed the date for performance which is crucial here, Fort Pitt knew that a June, 1970 delivery was required. It would be a strained and unpalatable interpretation of *Hadley v. Baxendale* to now hold that, although the parties left to further agreement the time for delivery, the supplier could reasonably rely upon a 1971 delivery date rather than one the parties later fixed. The behavior of Fort Pitt was totally inconsistent with the posture it now assumes. In November, 1969, it did not quarrel with the date set or seek to avoid the contract. It was not until late January, 1970 that Fort Pitt advised Torrington that, due to unforeseen delays and its expansion program, it could not meet the June date. None of its reasons for late delivery was deemed excusable according to the findings below, and this conclusion is not challenged here. It was not until five months later, on May 20, 1970, after Torrington had threatened to cancel, that Fort Pitt set another date for delivery (early August, 1970) which it again failed to meet, as was found below and not disputed on this appeal.

We conclude that, when the parties enter into a contract which, by its terms, provides that the time of performance is to be fixed at a later date, the knowledge of the consequences of a failure to perform is to be imputed to the defaulting party as of the time the parties agreed upon the date of performance. This comports, in our view, with both the logic and the spirit of *Hadley v. Baxendale*. Whether the agreement was initially valid despite its indefiniteness or only became valid when a material term was agreed upon is not relevant. At the time Fort Pitt did become committed to a delivery date, it was aware that a June, 1970 performance was required by virtue of its own acceptance. There was no unilateral distortion of the agreement rendering Fort Pitt liable to an extent not theretofore contemplated.

Having proceeded thus far, we do not think it follows automatically that Torrington is entitled to recover the damages it seeks here; further consideration of the facts before us is warranted. Fort Pitt maintains that, under the *Hadley v. Baxendale* rubric, the damages flowing from its conceded breach are "special" or "consequential" and were not reasonably to be contemplated by the parties. Since Torrington has not proved any "general" or "direct" damages, Fort Pitt urges that the contractor is entitled to nothing. We cannot agree. It is commonplace that parties to a contract normally address themselves to its performance and not to its breach or the consequences that will ensue if there is a default. As the New York Court of Appeals long ago stated:

> [A] more precise statement of this rule is, that a party is liable for all the direct damages which both parties to the contract would have contemplated as following from its breach, if at the time they entered into it they had bestowed proper attention upon the subject, and had been fully informed of the facts. [This] may properly be called the fiction of law. . . . *Leonard v. New York, Albany & Buffalo Electro-Magnetic Telegraph Co.*, 41 N.Y. 544, 567 (1870).[12]

It is also pertinent to note that the rule does not require that the direct damages must necessarily follow, but only that they are likely to follow; as Lord Justice Asquith commented in *Victoria Laundry, Ltd. v. Newman Industries, Ltd.*, [1949] 2 K.B. 528, 540, are they "on the cards"? We believe here that the damages sought to be recovered were also "in the cards."

It must be taken as a reasonable assumption that, when the delivery date of June, 1970 was set, Torrington planned the bridge erection within a reasonable time thereafter. It is normal construction procedure that the erection of the steel girders would be followed by the installation of a poured concrete platform and whatever railings or superstructure the platform would require. Fort Pitt was an experienced bridge fabricator supplying contractors and the sequence of the work is hardly arcane. Moreover, any delay beyond June or August would assuredly have jeopardized the pouring of the concrete and have forced the postponement of the work until the spring. The work here, as was well known to Fort Pitt, was to be performed in northern New York near the Vermont border. The court below found that continuing freezing weather would have forced the pouring to be delayed until June, 1971. Had Torrington refused delivery or had it been compelled to delay the completion of the work until the spring of 1971, the potential damage claim would have been substantial. Instead, in a good faith effort to mitigate damages, Torrington embarked upon the crash program we have described. It appears to us that this eventuality should have reasonably been anticipated by Fort Pitt as it was experienced in the trade and was supplying bridge steel in northern climes on a project requiring a concrete roadway.

Torrington's recovery under the circumstances is not substantial or cataclysmic from Fort Pitt's point of view. It represents the expenses of unloading steel from the

---

[12] [3] A second fiction, added as an embellishment to Hadley v. Baxendale by Mr. Justice Holmes as federal common law in Globe Ref. Co. v. Landa Cotton Oil Co., 190 U.S. 540, 23 S. Ct. 754, 47 L. Ed. 1171 (1903), would require not only knowledge of the special circumstances but a tacit agreement on the part of the party sought to be charged to accept the liability.

gondola due to Fort Pitt's admitted failure to notify its erection subcontractor, Syracuse Rigging, that the steel had been shipped, plus the costs of premium time, extra equipment and the cost of protecting the work, all occasioned by the realities Torrington faced in the wake of Fort Pitt's breach. In fact, Torrington's original claim of $23,290.81 was whittled down by the court below because of Torrington's failure to establish that its supervisory costs, overhead and certain equipment costs were directly attributable to the delay in delivery of the steel.

Professor Williston has commented:

> The true reason why notice to the defendant of the plaintiff's special circumstances is important is because, just as a court of equity under circumstances of hardship arising after the formation of a contract may deny specific performance, so a court of law may deny damages for unusual consequences where the defendant was not aware when he entered into the contract *how serious an injury would result from its breach.*

11 S. WILLISTON, *supra*, at 295 (footnote omitted) (emphasis added).

In this case, serious or catastrophic injury was avoided by prompt, effective and reasonable mitigation at modest cost. Had Torrington not acted, had it been forced to wait until the following spring to complete the entire job and then sued to recover the profits it would have made had there been performance by Fort Pitt according to the terms of its agreement, then we might well have an appropriate setting for a classical *Hadley v. Baxendale* controversy. As this case comes to us, it hardly presents that situation. We therefore affirm the judgment below permitting Torrington to offset its damages against the contract price.

PROBLEM

The National Aeronautics and Space Administration (NASA) has scheduled a launch of Columbia III on April 7. The next available space window that will allow the orbit planned for this flight will not occur until May 9. The payload of Columbia III includes a telecommunications satellite which NASA has agreed to launch from Columbia III for the Universal Telephone Company (UTC). The contract with UTC specifies that NASA will receive $500,000 less with the later launch. Shortly before April 7, NASA discovered defects in certain computer systems on Columbia III. Replacement systems were also defective. NASA sought other contractors, three of whom indicated their ability to supply a working replacement in time for the April 7 launch. A NASA representative called American Computers, Inc. (ACI) and was informed that ACI could supply the replacement part. The NASA representative replied, "You're a lifesaver. If we don't launch by April 7, we lose a bundle." Through confusion about delivery within its offices, ACI failed to deliver the part on time and the launch had to be postponed until May 9. NASA seeks a recovery of $500,000 from ACI, though the part delivered had a contract price of $497. What result?

[2]   The Causation Limitation

SIMARD v. BURSON
Maryland Court of Special Appeals
14 A.3d 6 (2011)

WOODWARD, J.

[At a foreclosure sale, Simard made the highest bid ($192,000), which was accepted. But he did not proceed to settlement and the property was resold ("first resale") to Zimmerman for $163,000, who also failed to go to settlement. A second resale was ordered and that resale was completed at $130,000. Simard was ordered to pay the difference between the original sale price to him of $192,000 and the price of the completed second resale at $130,000. Simard appealed on the footing that he should have been liable only for the "shortage" between the original sale price of $192,000 and first resale at $163,000. Noting that the issue was one of first impression in Maryland, the court considered the relevant Maryland statute and concluded that the statute did not require a defaulting purchaser to be liable for subsequent resales. The trial court, however,] held that Simard was responsible for the entire shortage occasioned by the First and Second Resales, because under *Hadley v. Baxendale*, the shortage from the Second Resale was "clearly a foreseeable damage." Simard claims that in so holding, the trial court erred. We agree.

In Maryland, "the measure of damages when a vendee breaches a contract to purchase real estate is the difference between the contract price and the fair market value at the time of breach." In addition to the general damages laid out above, the non-breaching party may be entitled to "consequential damages." Consequential damages cover those losses suffered by the non-breaching party other than the loss in value of the other party's performance. *RESTATEMENT (SECOND) OF CONTRACTS § 347 cmt. c* (1981). Such damages must be "reasonably foreseeable" and must "fairly and reasonably be supposed to *have been in the contemplation of both parties* at the time they made the contract, as the probable result of the breach of it." Not all damages that are "reasonably foreseeable," however, may be recovered as consequential damages; like general damages, consequential damages must be *"caused by the breach"* of contract. *RESTATEMENT (SECOND) OF CONTRACTS § 347(b)* (1981) In other words, the losses claimed by the non-breaching party must have "actually resulted from the breach."("Under both tort and contract law, one claiming damages must prove that tortious act or breach of contract was the proximate cause of the damages claimed.").

In the case *sub judice*, the trial court characterized the damages at issue as "consequential damages of the breach of contract." The court focused its analysis on "foreseeability," *i.e.*, and whether it was "highly foreseeable when somebody breaches the contract, and there's another sale that . . . that person might breach the contract as well?" McMullen and Simard agreed that such breach was foreseeable, but Simard argued that he did not believe "that control[led] the result." The trial court disagreed with Simard, and ruled:

I believe my ruling has to be against [] Simard because of the concept of foreseeability and consequential damages when it seems to me that the reason why the second sale price, or the third and ultimate sale price is so much lower is because of market forces that intervene. We went from a very robust real estate market to a very weak real estate market, and . . . that's foreseeable. If in fact you default, sure, there's a chance that if the market goes up, you will have absolutely no damages because there will be a greater sales price. But likewise, there's also a chance that the market will go down and the sale price will become lower.[I]t seems to me that [Simard] is responsible for his damages in that the reduced sale price of the second sale that was defaulted upon is clearly a foreseeable damage, so respectfully the Court denies [Simard's] exceptions on that basis.

Although the trial court may be correct that the default on the First Resale and the subsequent lower purchase price at the Second Resale were foreseeable, we disagree with the focus of its analysis solely on the foreseeability of the damages arising from the default on the First Resale. As stated above, foreseeability is but one of the requirements that must be shown by the non-breaching party to be awarded consequential damages. What the trial court did not address was whether Simard's breach of contract *caused* the damages arising from Zimmerman's default in the First Resale.

At oral argument before this Court, McMullen argued that whether or not Simard caused the default in the First Resale did not matter. Specifically, McMullen asserted that the default in the First Resale and the damages flowing therefrom were foreseeable because they represented a continuation of the original foreclosure proceeding, and because Simard voluntarily entered into the original foreclosure proceeding, he should be held liable for any subsequent defaults regardless of causation. We disagree.

Whether Simard may be held liable for damages arising from Zimmerman's default in the First Resale depends on whether Simard *caused* such default, which led to the Second Resale of the Property and the additional damages from the lower purchase price at the Second Resale. We hold that Simard's breach of contract did not *cause* the default in the First Resale. We shall explain.

As Simard concedes, he is "responsible" for the shortage between the Original Sale price of $192,000 and the First Resale price of $163,000 ("First Shortage"). The auditor properly allocated the First Shortage to be paid by Simard because Simard's breach proximately caused this loss. *See id.* Phrased differently, the First Shortage was *actually caused by* Simard's breach of contract. In contrast, the shortage between the First Resale price of $163,000 and the Second Resale price of $130,000 ("Second Shortage") did not *actually result* from Simard's breach of contract. The Second Shortage was caused by *Zimmerman's* breach of contract.

[A] defaulting purchaser does not typically have any control over a subsequent purchaser's actions. The actions of a subsequent purchaser are "beyond the power of the purchaser to control or ameliorate." Thus a first defaulting purchaser does not cause shortage damages arising from a subsequent purchaser's default. Accordingly, under general contract principles, the consequential damages arising out of a default by a foreclosure sale purchaser do not include damages arising out of a default of a subsequent sale of the subject property.

Simard had no control over Zimmerman's actions, namely, Zimmerman's default in the First Resale, which resulted in a Second Resale of the Property and a lower purchase price. Zimmerman's default "constituted 'conduct of other persons beyond the power of [Simard] to control or ameliorate.'" Therefore, because Simard's breach of contract did not *cause* Zimmerman to default on the First Resale, Simard is not be liable for the Second Shortage. Accordingly, the trial court erred by holding that Simard was responsible for the Second Shortage as consequential damages for his breach of the Original Sale. Judgement of the Circuit Court for Baltimore County Reversed; Case remanded.

NOTES

(1)   In relation to "causation," Professor Corbin suggests:

> [W]hen we assert that we have found the "cause" of an injury, we mean that there is such a degree of uniformity of sequence between them that if we can prevent the recurrence of the first we may prevent the recurrence of the second; and we mean also that we can correctly predict that if the first again occurs it is likely to be followed by the second. The uniformity of sequence in our experience enables us to *foresee* the future, not with certainty, indeed, and perhaps not with a high percentage of accuracy, but at all events with such a degree of accuracy as makes for survival and success in life. . . .

> Our only test of "causation," therefore, is foreseeability, based upon uniformity of sequence in our experience.

5 A. CORBIN, CONTRACTS § 1006 (2d ed. 1964).

In *Apgar v. MBS Business Systems, Inc.*, 1992 Conn. Super. LEXIS 2775, *7 (1992), the court states, "Determination of damages necessarily contemplates a finding that the breach was the cause of the damages claimed. 'It is hornbook law that to be entitled to damages in contract a plaintiff must establish a causal relation between the breach and the damages flowing from that breach. Such causal relation must be more than mere surmise or conjecture, inasmuch as a trier is concerned not with possibilities but with probabilities. Where . . . the damages claimed are remote from the breach complained of and the causal connection is wholly conjectural, there can be no recovery'" [*citing Calig v. Schrank, 179 Conn. 283*, 286, 426 A.2d 274 (1976).]

(2)   *Foreseeability — Contract and Tort.* "The rule of *Hadley v. Baxendale* links up with tort concepts. The rule is sometimes stated in the form that only foreseeable damages are recoverable in a breach of contract action, e.g., RESTATEMENT (SECOND) OF CONTRACTS § 351 (1979). So expressed, it corresponds to the tort principle that limits liability to the foreseeable consequence of the defendant's carelessness. The amount of care that a person ought to take is a function of the probability and magnitude of the harm that may occur if he does not take care. If he does not know what that probability and magnitude are, he cannot determine how much care to take." *Evra Corp. v. Swiss Bank Corp.*, 673 F.2d 951, 958 (7th Cir. 1982).

(3) *The "Tacit Agreement" Test.* Shortly after the turn of the last century, Mr. Justice Holmes wrote, "It may be said with safety that mere notice to a seller of some interest or probable action of the buyer is not enough necessarily and as a matter of law to charge the seller with special damage on that account if he fails to deliver the goods." *Globe Ref. Co. v. Landa Cotton Oil Co.*, 190 U.S. 540, 545 (1903). There had been earlier suggestions of the same concept, which came to be known as the "tacit agreement" test, i.e., *in addition to mere foreseeability*, some manifestation of assent by the defaulting promisor had to be discovered to allocate the risk of special circumstances to him. It was not necessary to prove that an actual agreement existed. Rather, as Holmes suggested, "[T]he extent of liability in such cases is likely to be within his [defendant's] contemplation, and whether it is or not, should be worked out on terms which it fairly may be presumed he would have assented to if they had been presented to his mind." 190 U.S. 543.

The "tacit agreement" test attracted a limited following. *See* at § 121C. Notwithstanding this early following, there has been a universal rejection of the test. The principal case, in footnote 3, characterizes it as a "fiction." The RESTATEMENT (SECOND) OF CONTRACTS (§ 351, comment a) and the UCC (§ 2-715, comment 2) reject it out of hand. Yet, there is a considerable problem where certain special circumstances are communicated at the time of formation, thus meeting the foreseeability requirement, but the extent of liability is grossly disproportionate to the consideration received by the defaulting promisor, or where other surrounding circumstances cast doubt on the allocation of risk to the defaulting promisor.

(4) *Modern Relief.* Notwithstanding its clear rejection of the "tacit agreement" test, the SECOND RESTATEMENT includes § 351(3):

> A court may limit damages for foreseeable loss by excluding recovery for loss of profits, by allowing recovery only for loss incurred in reliance, or otherwise if it concludes that in the circumstances justice so requires in order to avoid disproportionate compensation.

Comment f to that section elaborates:

> It is not always in the interest of justice to require the party in breach to pay damages for all of the foreseeable loss that he has caused. There are unusual instances in which it appears from the circumstances either that the parties assumed that one of them would not bear the risk of a particular loss or that, although there was no such assumption, it would be unjust to put the risk on that party. One such circumstance is an extreme disproportion between the loss and the price charged by the party whose liability for that loss is in question. The fact that the price is relatively small suggests that it was not intended to cover the risk of such liability. Another such circumstance is an informality of dealing, including the absence of a detailed written contract, which indicates that there was no careful attempt to allocate all of the risks. The fact that the parties did not attempt to delineate with precision all of the risks justifies a court in attempting to allocate them fairly. The limitations dealt with in this Section are more likely to be imposed in connection with contracts that do not arise in a commercial setting.

At this time, support for § 351(3) is growing. In *Sundance Cruises Corp. v. American Bureau of Shipping*, 7 F.3d 1077 (2d Cir. 1993), the defendant issued a certificate representing that a vessel possessed the watertight integrity required by international safety standards. When the vessel sank due to defects that, if discovered during inspection, would have prevented issuance of the certification, the court agreed with the lower court in its holding that Sundance failed to show any damage flowing from the issuance of the certificate. The appellate opinion cites RESTATEMENT (SECOND) OF CONTRACTS § 351, comment f, in stating, "We think this result is sound, and it reflects our view that a shipowner is not entitled to rely on a classification certificate as a guarantee to the owner that the vessel is soundly constructed. [T]he great disparity between the fee charged ($85,000) by ABS for its services and the damages sought by Sundance ($264,000,000) is strong evidence that such a result was not intended by the parties. We can only conclude that the small fee charged could not have been intended to cover the risk of such liability; the ship classification industry could not continue to exist under such terms."

Where a seller of land breached the contract and the buyer, a developer, sought damages measured by the difference between the contract and market prices on the date of the breach which would have provided the plaintiff with a recovery of $575,000, the court cited § 351 and comment f in relying upon testimony that the plaintiff expected a much lesser profit in developing the land. In allowing a lesser recovery of $260,000, the court explained why it refused to adopt the "usual rule" that the plaintiff is entitled to the difference between the contract and market prices at the time of breach: "The flaw in the plaintiff's position is that the 'usual rule' is not a rigid rule. [T]he 'usual rule' is only a variation on the theme of the dominant principle that the injured party should be as well off as if the transaction had gone through — but not better off. Principles of contract damages do not have it as their design to put plaintiff in a better position that if the defendant had performed the contract." *Foster v. Bartolomeo*, 581 N.E.2d 1033 (Mass. Ct. App. 1991). The court noted that the buyer had originally sought specific performance of the contract, but later surrendered that claim, raising the suspicion that the buyer recognized it would recover much more in damages under the "usual rule" than the profit it reasonably expected to earn had it pursued the development of the land.

[3] Consequential Damages — *Hadley v. Baxendale* and the UCC

CRICKET ALLEY CORP. v. DATA TERMINAL SYSTEMS, INC.
Kansas Supreme Court
732 P.2d 719 (1987)

MCFARLAND, J.

This is a breach of express warranty action brought by plaintiff Cricket Alley Corporation against defendant Data Terminal Systems, Inc. (DTS), relative to plaintiff's purchase of certain computerized cash registers. Following a jury trial, judgment was entered in favor of plaintiff for $78,781.79. Defendant appeals therefrom.

Plaintiff operates a number of women's clothing stores. The business, which had commenced in 1967 with one store, had grown by 1978 to seven or eight stores. The business was headquartered in Wichita. In order to keep up with its expanding business, plaintiff purchased a Wang computer which was located in its general office. The individual stores had NCR cash registers with no capacity to communicate directly with the Wang computer. Price tags of sold merchandise had to be manually sorted and posted to inventory records. The paper cash register tapes had to be physically delivered to the Wichita office and the data then transferred to the computer. Robert Harvey, president and founder of the plaintiff company, was desirous of modernizing the company's operation. He was aware that technology existed whereby computerized cash registers in individual stores could communicate with the central computer via telephone lines. Inventory, layaway, sales, and payroll record keeping could then be greatly simplified and expedited. Inasmuch as the company already owned the Wang computer, any cash register system purchased for the stores had to be compatible with the Wang equipment. In 1980, Harvey saw an advertisement in a trade magazine featuring Wang computers and DTS cash registers working together. In January of 1981, Harvey attended a convention of the National Retail Merchants Association in New York City. Manufacturers of equipment utilized by retail merchants had displays at the convention. DTS had rented a ballroom in which to display its wares to those attending the convention. Harvey was attracted to the DTS display because of the magazine advertisement he had seen. In the DTS display area there was a Wang computer and a DTS cash register working together. Harvey asked a DTS representative present at the display if Wang and DTS equipment really could communicate with each other and the DTS representative stated that they did. Harvey was not an expert on these types of equipment and did not know which model Wang his company owned. He asked if "it will work on all Wangs" and the DTS representative responded affirmatively. Harvey made inquiries to other DTS personnel in the display area about DTS capabilities. Satisfied with their responses, Harvey inquired about purchasing DTS equipment. He was provided with the names and addresses of DTS dealers in Joplin, Denver, Omaha, and Kansas City.

Harvey hired Steve Axon, a computer programmer, and they conferred with Jim Hunter, a Wang employee, and Bob Mann, of Kansas City Cash Register (the Kansas City DTS dealer), about the particular programs they were seeking. Ultimately, plaintiff agreed to purchase ten DTS cash registers. Included in the system was an ANS-R-TRAN which is a combination of hardware and software. It is a circuit for electronic equipment that plugs into the cash register and is a necessary component if the cash registers were to communicate with a computer. Some of the software in the ANS-R-TRAN comes from DTS. The ANS-R-TRAN owners program reference guide was delivered to plaintiff either shortly before purchase of the equipment or shortly thereafter. This guide, prepared by DTS, indicated that the DTS cash registers would be able to communicate with the computer to perform the functions needed by plaintiff.

The DTS equipment was delivered to plaintiff's home office. All manner of problems, or "bugs," developed when the equipment was being programmed.

Meanwhile, the old NCR cash registers in the stores started breaking down and replacement parts were unavailable. Finally, although not functioning as a computerized system, the new DTS equipment was placed in the stores to perform basic cash register functions. The specific difficulties will be discussed elsewhere in this opinion. The fundamental problem was the inability of the Wang computer and the DTS equipment to communicate with each other. There was testimony at trial placing the problem of deficiency in the DTS equipment with that manufactured by IBM. This equipment then functioned as a system. Plaintiff brought this action against Wang, Kansas City Cash Register, and DTS. Wang and Kansas City Cash Register settled with plaintiff and only the claims against DTS proceeded to trial. At trial, a verdict, in the amount of $78,781.79, was entered in favor of plaintiff and against DTS. The case before us is an appeal by DTS from that judgment.

While evidence of the existence of the express warranty is certainly not overwhelming, we believe it was sufficient for submission to the jury. The jury could have concluded that DTS advertised that its products could communicate with Wang products; that these advertisements induced plaintiff's president to visit the DTS showroom where he saw a display showing Wang and DTS cash registers communicating and was told by a DTS employee that such communication capability was a fact; and that the ANS-R-TRAN manual published by DTS reinforced this representation as to DTS equipment's capability. The evidence clearly showed that the capability of any new equipment to communicate with plaintiff's Wang computer was the prime consideration in selecting new cash registers. Under such circumstances the district court did not err in overruling the respective motions.

In this action plaintiff sought consequential and incidental damages. DTS contends that, as a matter of law, plaintiff was not entitled to recover any consequential damages and consideration of same should not have been submitted to the jury.

The parties concede K.S.A. 84-2-714 and -715 constitute the applicable law. K.S.A. 84-2-714 provides for a buyer's damages for goods which have already been accepted, as here, by the buyer:

> (1) Where the buyer has accepted goods and given notification (subsection (3) of section 84-2-607) he may recover as damages for any nonconformity of tender the loss resulting in the ordinary course of events from the seller's breach as determined in any manner which is reasonable.
>
> (2) The measure of damages for breach of warranty is the difference at the time and place of acceptance between the value of the goods accepted and the value they would have had if they had been as warranted, unless special circumstances show proximate damages of a different amount.
>
> (3) In a proper case any incidental and consequential damages under the next section may also be recovered.

Kansas Comment 1983 to this statute states, in part:

> Subsection (3) merely states that the buyer is entitled to recover any incidental and consequential damages under 84-2-715.

K.S.A. 84-2-715 provides:

(1) Incidental damages resulting from the seller's breach include expenses reasonably incurred in inspection, receipt, transportation and care and custody of goods rightfully rejected, any commercially reasonable charges, expenses or commissions in connection with effecting cover and any other reasonable expense incident to the delay or other breach.

(2) Consequential damages resulting from the seller's breach include:

(a) any loss resulting from *general or particular* requirements and needs of which the seller at the time of contracting had reason to know and which could not reasonably be prevented by cover or otherwise; and

(b) injury to person or property proximately resulting from any breach of warranty. (Emphasis supplied.)

The consequential damages consist of increased labor costs attributable to the failure of the DTS cash registers to communicate with the Wang computer. DTS contends that it did not know the general or particular requirements and needs of plaintiff's business at the time the express warranties were made and, hence, has no liability under K.S.A. 84-2-715(2)(a) for consequential damages.

Official UCC Comment No. 3 to K.S.A. 84-2-715 provides, in pertinent part:

In the absence of excuse under the section on merchant's excuse by failure of presupposed conditions, the seller is liable for consequential damages in all cases where he had reason to know of the buyer's general or particular requirements at the time of contracting. It is not necessary that there be a conscious acceptance of an insurer's liability on the seller's part, nor is his obligation for consequential damages limited to cases in which he fails to use due effort in good faith. *Particular needs of the buyer must generally be made known to the seller while general needs must rarely be made known to charge the seller with knowledge.* (Emphasis supplied.)

DTS concedes that K.S.A. 84-2-715(2)(a) is "simply a codification" of the old tests contained in *Hadley v. Baxendale*, 9 Ex. 341, 156 Eng. Rep. 145, 5 Eng. Rul. Cas. 502 (1854).

Computerized cash registers are manufactured for use in retail business establishments. DTS sought to attract retail merchants to their products by advertising in trade magazines and the setting up of a major display of their wares at a national convention of the National Retail Merchants Association where it employed a number of persons to be on hand to answer questions of the convention delegates concerning its products. DTS computerized cash registers are expensive and sophisticated pieces of equipment and the market for them lies largely in the more complex retail establishments. The "mom and pop" grocery store operation is, obviously, not the prime market for such products. The submission of data from the cash registers to the mainline computer on sales, payrolls, inventory, etc. is a common feature of such equipment and the failure of the cash registers to do so would foreseeably create additional labor costs for the afflicted retail merchants. The additional labor costs sought by plaintiff, herein, as consequential damages are not attributable to any unique features of plaintiff's business. We conclude that consequential damages as an element of plaintiff's damages were properly submitted to the jury herein.

"The basic objective of damages under the UCC is 'that the aggrieved party may be put in as good a position as if the other party had fully performed. . . .' K.S.A. 84-1-106(1). One commentator has stated: 'Without incidental and consequential damages this goal would be unreachable in many cases. . . . The availability of consequential damages is vital. It may mean the difference between recovering one dollar, the price of a defective part, and one million dollars, the damages caused as a result of the defective part, in personal injury, lost profits, and more.' " Rasor, Kansas Law of Sales Under the UCC § 10-11, pp. 10-36, 10-37. *See also La Villa Fair v. Lewis Carpet Mills, Inc.*, 219 Kan. 395, 406, 548 P.2d 825 (1976).

"Under the UCC consequential damages need not be proven with any particular degree of certainty. Indeed, one purpose of subsection (1) of K.S.A. 84-1-106 'is to reject any doctrine that damages must be calculable with mathematical accuracy. Compensatory damages are often at best approximate: they have to be proved with whatever definiteness and accuracy the facts permit, but no more.' " Official UCC Comment, § 1-106. . . .

K.S.A. 84-2-715, Official UCC Comment No. 4, states "the section on liberal administration of remedies rejects any doctrine of certainty which requires almost mathematical precision in the proof of loss. Loss may be determined in any manner which is reasonable under the circumstances."

Evidence submitted to the jury on damages included employee payroll spread sheets that indicated not only dollar expenses but the percentage of time each employee performed manual tasks which would have been unnecessary had the DTS equipment performed satisfactorily the functions needed by plaintiff and warranted by defendant. Testimony was admitted which supported the functions performed and time involved to accomplish them. The witnesses were vigorously cross-examined as to what costs were attributable to the failure of the DTS equipment to perform properly. Plaintiff claimed $191,517.03 in damages. The verdict awarded $78,781.79 in damages. A question of fact was determined by the jury. After carefully reviewing the record, we conclude the damage award is adequately supported by the evidence.

COMMENT: UNIFORM COMMERCIAL CODE REMEDIES

As the court states, the Uniform Commercial Code pursues the same general principle of contract remedies espoused in the common law of contracts. Section 1-106(1) states: "The remedies provided by this Act shall be liberally administered to the end that the aggrieved party may be put in as good a position as if the other party had fully performed."

Buyer's Remedies. Where the seller breaches the contract, the buyer's remedies are listed in Section 2-711. Each of the listed remedies is then elaborated in subsequent sections. Thus, the buyer may "cover" by making a reasonable substitute purchase and recover the difference between the contract price and any higher price for the substitute goods (§ 2-712). This places the buyer in the position the buyer would have been in had the contract been performed (the expectation interest). Recall the example of the "cover" remedy in the *Huntington Beach School District* case in the introduction to contract remedies in Chapter 1. The buyer may choose not to cover but to recover the difference between the contract price and any higher market price for the goods (§ 2-713). Even though goods are defective, the buyer may choose to retain them and sue for any difference between the value of the goods that should have been received under the contract and the value actually received (§ 2-714(2)). For example, assume a contract for the sale of machinery at a contract price of $50,000. The seller delivers machinery that proves to be defective. If the machinery had been perfect, it may have been more valuable that the contract price. If the buyer can prove that perfect machinery would have been valued at $60,000 and the machinery delivered was worth only $40,000, the buyer can recover $20,000. In a proper case (where the goods are unique or in other proper circumstances), the buyer may succeed having a court decreee specific performance of the contract (§ 2-716). As the court notes, in addition to "direct" damages, the buyer is also entitled to recover incidental damages as well as consequential damages which must meet the requirements of foreseeability — the UCC application of *Hadley v. Baxendale* (§ 2-715). Upon the seller's breach, the buyer may "cancel" the contract and recover any portion of the price paid (§ 2-711), i.e., the restitution interest. Noting in the UCC prevents a buyer from recovering its reliance interest where, for example, the expectation damages cannot be proved with reasonable certainty.

Seller's Remedies. Where the buyer breaches the contract, the seller's remedies are listed in Section 2-703 and each of those remedies is elaborated in a subsequent section. Where the buyer breaches and refuses to take the goods, the seller will typically resell the goods and recover the difference between the contract price and any lower price at which the seller reasonably resells the goods (§ 2-706). The seller is then placed in the position it would have been in had the contract been performed. The "resale" remedy of the seller is the counterpart of the buyer's remedy of "cover." Since the buyer may refrain from "covering," the seller may choose not to resell. Instead, the seller may recover the difference between the contract price (§ 2-708(1)) and the market price. The seller may, however, confront a problem in using either of these remedies in the sale of standard-priced goods. For example where the buyer breaches a contract to purchase a new automobile and the car is resold to the next buyer at the same price, the resale remedy provides no damages to the seller since the contract price and resale prices are identical. Similarly, if the seller chooses not to resell but to claim the difference between the contract and market prices, again, the seller may discover that the prices are the same resulting in no damage recovery. Where the seller can prove that it would have made the second sale even if the breach had not occurred, the seller has lost the benefit of the bargain (the profit) on the first sale. Where a seller has an ample supply of the same product to sell and would, therefore, have made the second sale regardless of the breach, it is a "lost volume" seller. To place such a seller in the position it would have been in had the contract been performed, it is necessary to allow that seller to recover the profit it made on the lost sale to the breaching buyer. That recovery is permitted under § 2-708(2). Finally, where the buyer has accepted the goods and has not paid for them or where the goods have been shipped to the buyer and lost or destroyed in shipment after the risk of loss as passed to the buyer, the seller may recover the contract price under § 2-709. Like the buyer, the seller is entitled to recover incidental damages, but there are no expressed provisions in the current version of Article 2 of the UCC to permit the seller to recover consequential damages. A proposed amendment to Article 2 would permit the seller to recover any consequential damages which it could prove.

[4] The Certainty Limitation

THE DREWS CO. v. LEDWITH-WOLFE ASSOCIATES, INC.
South Carolina Supreme Court
371 S.E.2d 532 (1988)

HARWELL, J.

The Drews Company, Inc. ("Contractor") contracted to renovate a building owned by Ledwith-Wolfe Associates, Inc. ("Owner"). Owner intended to convert the building into a restaurant. From its inception, the project was plagued by construction delays, work change orders, and general disagreement over the quality of work performed. Contractor eventually pulled its workers off the project. Contractor later filed, then sued to foreclose, a mechanic's lien for labor and materials used in renovating the building. Owner counterclaimed, alleging Contractor breached the contract and forced Owner to rework part of the job. Owner also claimed that Contractor's delays in performance caused Owner to lose profits from the restaurant.

The jury returned an $18,000 verdict for Contractor on its complaint. The jury awarded Owner $22,895 on its counterclaim for re-doing and completing the work and $14,000 in lost profits caused by Contractor's delays.

Contractor presents this Court with an opportunity to address a legal issue unsettled in South Carolina: Does the "new business rule" operate to automatically preclude the recovery of lost profits by a new business or enterprise? We hold that it does not.

We begin our analysis of the lost profits issue by recognizing an elementary principle of contract law. The purpose of an award of damages for breach is "to give compensation, that is, to put the plaintiff in as good a position as he would have been in had the contract been performed." 11 S. WILLISTON, A TREATISE ON THE LAW OF CONTRACTS, § 1338 (3d ed. 1968). The proper measure of that compensation, then, "is the loss actually suffered by the contractee as the result of the breach." *South Carolina Finance Corp. v. West Side Finance Co.*, 236 S.C. 109, 122, 113 S.E.2d 329, 335 (1960).

"Profits" have been defined as "the net pecuniary gain from a transaction, the gross pecuniary gains diminished by the cost of obtaining them." RESTATEMENT OF CONTRACTS § 331, Comment B (1932); *see Mali v. Odom*, 367 S.E.2d 166 (Ct. App. 1988) (defining "profits" as the net of income over expenditures during a given period). Profits lost by a business as the result of a contractual breach have long been recognized as a species of recoverable consequential damages in this state. The issue is more difficult, however, when a new or unestablished business is the aggrieved party seeking projected lost profits as damages.

The new business rule as a per se rule of nonrecoverability of lost profits was firmly established in this state in *Standard Supply Co. v. Carter & Harris*, 81 S.C. 181, 187, 62 S.E. 150, 152 (1907): "When a business is in contemplation, but not established or not in actual operation, profit merely hoped for is too uncertain and conjectural to be considered."

Modern cases, however, reflect the willingness of this Court and our Court of Appeals to view the new business rule as a rule of evidentiary sufficiency rather than an automatic bar to recovery of lost profits by a new business. These cases have so eroded the new business rule as an absolute bar to recovery of lost profits that the rigid *Standard Supply Co.* rule is no longer good law.

South Carolina has not been alone in developing its evidentiary view of the new business rule. Numerous authorities and commentators have tracked a similar trend nationwide: "Courts are now taking the position that the distinction between established businesses and new ones is a distinction that goes to the weight of the evidence and not a rule that automatically precludes recovery of profits by a new business." D. Dobbs, Handbook on the Law of Remedies, § 3.3, at 155 (1973). *See* R. Dunn, Recovery of Damages for Lost Profits, § 4.2 (3d ed. 1987) (trend of modern cases plainly toward replacing old rule of law with rule of evidence — reasonable certainty); Comment, *Remedies — Lost Profits as Contract Damages for an Unestablished Business: The New Business Rule Becomes Outdated*, 56 N.C.L. Rev. 693, 695 (1978) (noting "increasing trend either to create exceptions and mitigating sub-doctrines to the new business rule or simply to recognize that its rationale is no longer persuasive"); Note, *The New Business Rule and the Denial of Lost Profits*, 48 Ohio St. L.J. 855, 859 (1987) (clear and growing majority of courts apply new business rule as rule delimiting sufficiency of evidence). Moreover, application of the rule in this manner has been applauded as fairer than mechanical application of the old rule. *See* D. Dobbs, *supra* (as a matter of evidence, new business/established business distinction makes sense; as a matter of setting an inflexible rule, it does not); R. Dunn, *supra*, at 227 (no worthwhile end achieved "by permitting one party to breach his contracts with impunity — giving him an option, as it were — because the other party has not yet commenced operation").

In light of the facts before us, we find particularly persuasive several cases involving lost profits flowing from breaches of contracts to construct and/or lease buildings for the operation of new business ventures. *See, e.g., Chung v. Kaonohi Center Co.*, 62 Haw. 594, 618 P.2d 283 (1980) (rejecting per se nonrecoverability version of new business rule in favor of "reasonable certainty" evidentiary standard; lost profits award upheld for breach of contract to lease space for new restaurant); *Welch v. U.S. Bancorp Realty and Mortgage*, 286 Or. 673, 596 P.2d 947 (1979) (breach of contract to advance funds for residential and commercial development on land tract; "reasonable certainty" standard applied); *Fera v. Village Plaza, Inc.*, 396 Mich. 639, 242 N.W.2d 372 (1976) (breach of lease of shopping center space for new book store; per se rule of nonrecoverability rejected in favor of broad jury discretion in lost profits determinations); *Smith Dev. Corp. v. Bilow Enterprises, Inc.*, 112 R.I. 203, 308 A.2d 477 (1973) (tortious interference with contractual right to erect McDonald's restaurant; "reasonable certainty" rule applied and per se new business rule rejected); *S. Jon Kreedman & Co. v. Meyer Bros. Parking-Western Corp.*, 58 Cal. App. 3d 173, 130 Cal. Rptr. 41 (1976) (breach of contract to construct parking garage and lease it to operator; "hard and fast" new business rule rejected in favor of "reasonable certainty" test).

We believe South Carolina should now unequivocally join those jurisdictions applying the new business rule as a rule of evidentiary sufficiency and not as an automatic preclusion to recovery of lost profits by a new business or enterprise.

The same standards that have for years governed lost profits awards in South Carolina will apply with equal force to cases where damages are sought for a new business or enterprise. First, profits must have been prevented or lost "as a natural consequence of" the breach of contract. The second requirement is foreseeability; a breaching party is liable for those damages, including lost profits, "which may reasonably be supposed to have been within the contemplation of the parties at the time the contract was made as a probable result of the breach of it." *National Tire & Rubber Co. v. Hoover*, 128 S.C. 344, 348, 122 S.E. 858, 859 (1924); see also [the] rule of *Hadley v. Baxendale*, 9 Ex. 341, 156 Eng. Rep. 154 (1854).

The crucial requirement in lost profits determinations is that they be "established with reasonable certainty, for recovery cannot be had for profits that are conjectural or speculative." *South Carolina Finance Corp.*, 113 S.E.2d at 336. "The proof must pass the realm of conjecture, speculation, or opinion not founded on facts, and must consist of actual facts from which a reasonably accurate conclusion regarding the cause and the amount of the loss can be logically and rationally drawn." 22 Am. Jur. 2d *Damages* § 641 (1988).

Numerous proof techniques have been discussed and accepted in different factual scenarios. *See, e.g., Upjohn v. Rachelle Laboratories, Inc.*, 661 F.2d 1105, 1114 (1981) (proof of future lost profits based on marketing forecasts by employees specializing in economic forecasting); *Petty v. Weyerhaeuser Co., supra* (skating rink's projected revenues compared to those of another arena in a nearby town); *see also* RESTATEMENT (SECOND) OF CONTRACTS § 352, at 146 (1981) (proof of lost profits "may be established with reasonable certainty with the aid of expert testimony, economic and financial data, market surveys and analyses, business records of similar enterprises, and the like"); Note, *supra*, 48 OHIO ST. L.J. at 872-3 (means of proving prospective profits include (1) "yardstick" method of comparison with profit performance of business similar in size, nature, and location; (2) comparison with profit history of plaintiff's successor, where applicable; (3) comparison of similar businesses owned by plaintiff himself, and (4) use of economic and financial data and expert testimony). While the factual contexts in which new business/lost profits cases arise will undoubtedly vary, these methods of proof and the "reasonable certainty" requirement bear an inherent flexibility facilitating the just assessment of profits lost to a new business due to contractual breach.

Applying this standard to the facts before us, we find that Owner's proof failed to clear the "reasonable certainty" hurdle. Owner's projections of the profits lost by the restaurant because of the breach were based on nothing more than a sheet of paper reflecting the gross profits the restaurant made in the first 11 months of operation after construction was completed. These figures were not supplemented with corresponding figures for overhead or operating expenditures, but only with

Owner's testimony that he would expect at least a third of that [gross figure] to be "net profit." Owner's expectations, unsupported by any particular standard or fixed method for establishing net profits, were wholly insufficient to provide the jury with a basis for calculating profits lost with reasonable certainty.

The trial judge erred in failing to rule that, as a matter of law, Owner's proof was insufficient to merit submission to the jury. The $14,000 award of lost profits must therefore be reversed.

NOTES

(1)   The cases are legion in which courts insist that only "reasonable certainty" will be required as a limitation upon the recovery of damages. *See* MURRAY ON CONTRACTS at § 122B. The "new business" rule created a major problem for older courts with respect to the certainty requirement, i.e., damages must not be speculative. Beyond the authorities cited in the principal case, UCC § 2-708, comment 2 states, "It is not necessary to a recovery of 'profit' to show a history of earnings, especially if a new venture is involved." This statement was quoted with approval in *Bead Chain Mfg. Co. v. Saxton Prods.*, 183 Conn. 266, 439 A.2d 314 (1981), where plaintiff's president testified concerning lost profits by setting forth the elements considered in pricing the job. It was not fatal that his cost and price estimates were theoretical.

(2)   In *Handi Caddy, Inc. v. American Home Prods. Corp.*, 557 F.2d 136 (8th Cir. 1977), plaintiff sought to recover for lost profits in the sale of a utensil designed to remove hot pizzas from the oven. Defendant had agreed to a self-liquidating premium promotion of these utensils by advertising them on packages of Chef Boy-ar-dee pizza packages and other promotional advertising, i.e., there was no cost to defendant for the utensils and its product was thought to be enhanced through the availability of the premium. Defendant did not complete all of the advertising and promotion under the contract, resulting in plaintiff's alleged loss of profits. In response to defendant's claims that the profits were too speculative so that damages could not be proved with reasonable certainty in this new venture, the court held that the evidence, essentially expert opinion testimony, was sufficient to meet the requirement of reasonable certainty.

(3)   *Evergreen Amusement Corp. v. Milstead*, 112 A.2d 901 (Md. Ct. Spec. App. 1955), represents the older view. The plaintiff brought an action against a contractor for delays in the completion of a new outdoor theatre that was supposed to open in June but was delayed until August. Much of the outdoor theatre season was thereby eliminated. Expert evidence of profits of drive-in theatres in the same area, including evidence of population, weather, and other market survey elements, were excluded. Though the court stated it was not laying down a "flat rule" that such profits from a new business could never be recovered, it suggested that no such recovery had been allowed under those circumstances. RESTATEMENT (SECOND) OF CONTRACTS § 352, comment b and illustration 6 expressly reject the holding and rationale of this case.

COMMENT: EMOTIONAL DISTRESS DAMAGES

Courts have been particularly reluctant to allow recovery for emotional distress, mental suffering or the like, in contract actions. Where a university athletic director breached a promise not to view a videotape which inadvertently included a sexual encounter between the plaintiff head coach of a women's gymnastic team and her assistant coach husband, the court held that there was no recovery for the plaintiff's alleged emotional distress based on the breach of contract. *Deli v. University of Minnesota*, 578 N.W.2d 779 (1998). There are two generally recognized exceptions. Where (a) the nature of the contract or (b) the nature of the breach is such that serious emotional disturbance is clearly foreseeable, such damages will be recoverable. RESTATEMENT (SECOND) OF CONTRACTS § 353. The easier cases are those where the contract is "personal" and contemplates emotional factors, such as a contract to conduct a funeral and burial of a loved one. *See Lamm v. Shingleton*, 55 S.E.2d 810 (1949). Where a messenger is aware of the import of a death message, its failure to deliver it in a timely fashion may cause serious emotional distress. Public humiliation by the operators of a hotel, theatre, or public carrier may give rise to such damages. The humiliation, however, must be objective. Thus, where a restaurant charged a nominal fee for checking the coats of guests in violation of the contract with the host of the celebration, the small charge was not such as to humiliate a reasonable person in the position of the host. See the concurring opinion of Justice Musmanno in *Gefter v. Rosenthal*, 119 A.2d 250, 251 (1956).

Where the subject matter of the contract would not suggest mental distress upon breach, i.e., a "commercial" contract, the breach of such a contract must be accompanied by outrageous or reprehensible conduct. Thus, in *Chung v. Kaonohi Center Co.*, 618 P.2d 283 (1980), the court held that emotional distress damages were available even in a commercial contract where the defendant promised a lease for a restaurant in a shopping mall to plaintiff, and defendant, who had been negotiating with three separate parties, had given a right of first refusal to one of the parties other than plaintiff with whom it signed the lease. Defendant had made numerous representations over a lengthy period that plaintiff had secured the lease, during which time, to defendant's knowledge, plaintiff had substantially relied upon such representations. The court concluded that the actions of defendant were reprehensible and clearly amounted to wanton and reckless conduct sufficient to give rise to tort liability.

The RESTATEMENT (SECOND) OF CONTRACTS suggests that this type of conduct accompanying a breach can give rise to damages for emotional distress, though it suggests the necessity of "bodily harm," i.e., the situation "may nearly always be regarded as an action in tort." (RESTATEMENT (SECOND) OF CONTRACTS § 353, comment a.) It proceeds to suggest, however, that courts generally do not require the plaintiff to specify the nature of the action, i.e., they permit the recovery of emotional distress damages without classifying the wrong. *Id.* While many courts insist that the breach amount to a tort, other courts are equally insistent that the willful, wanton or insulting conduct need not amount to a tort. *See, e.g., Trimble v. City & County of Denver*, 697 P.2d 716 (Colo. 1985). In this case, Dr. Trimble, Director of Medical Services at a Denver hospital, was under the supervision of a Dr. Kauvar. Dr. Kauvar developed a personal animosity toward Trimble and abused his administrative power in malicious fashion to "get rid" of Trimble, finally implementing a reorganization that left Trimble with his original title but relocated to an office in the maintenance building known as the "boiler house," with no assignment to his normal duties other than to proctology — "not his specialty of choice." In general, see MURRAY ON CONTRACTS at § 124.

[5]   The Mitigation Limitation — Avoidable Consequences

SOULES v. INDEPENDENT SCHOOL DISTRICT NO. 518
Minnesota Supreme Court
258 N.W.2d 103 (1977)

ROGOSHESKE, J.

Plaintiff, Maureen Murphy Soules, brought this breach-of-contract action for reinstatement as an elementary school teacher and for damages upon allegations of wrongful termination of her continuing contract of employment with defendant, Independent School District No. 518. The district court, determining that the school district failed to comply with statutory procedures of notice and hearing required for the termination of plaintiff's continuing contract under the Minnesota Teachers' Tenure Act, Minn. St. 125.12, granted plaintiff's motion for partial summary judgment and ordered her reinstated. Following her reinstatement on January 13, 1975, the issue of damages was tried by the court sitting without a jury. The court found, unchallenged on this appeal, that plaintiff sustained $17,401.48 in damages, representing unpaid salary, insurance benefits, and interest for the 2-year interval between the date of her wrongful termination and the date of her reinstatement. The court, however, reduced that amount by $9,100 upon finding that plaintiff failed to mitigate her loss, and accordingly judgment was entered for $8,301.48. Upon plaintiff's appeal challenging the ordered reduction, we hold that in accordance with a proper application of the rule of avoidable consequences the amount of the reduction lacks evidentiary support, requiring a remand for modification of the judgment increasing plaintiff's recovery to $11,095.82.

It is undisputed that from the school term beginning in 1967 to the term ending in 1972 plaintiff was employed by defendant school district under five separate 1-year contracts to teach remedial reading on a part-time, half-day basis at St. Mary's Parochial School in Worthington. The remedial reading program was funded on a year-to-year basis by the Federal government under Title I of the Elementary and Secondary Education Act of 1965. Under an arrangement between officers of defendant school district and St. Mary's, however, one of the parochial school's teachers actually taught the Title I program, while plaintiff was a regular elementary classroom teacher. When plaintiff's 1971–72 contract expired, it was not renewed. Since defendant, through its board, neither gave plaintiff notice of termination nor granted her a hearing, the district court in summary judgment proceedings ordered her reinstated, reserving the issue of damages for trial.

The only issue presented on this appeal is whether the $9,100 reduction, ordered as a mitigating offset from recovery of the full amount of compensation promised plaintiff under her continuing contract, is supported by adequate evidence and is consistent with a proper application of the rule of avoidable consequences.

It is the well-settled law in this state and elsewhere that in employment contract cases an employer is entitled to a reduction in the amount of the recoverable wage loss of a wrongfully discharged employee if the evidence establishes that the employee made no reasonable effort to seek or accept similar employment.

In *Zeller v. Prior Lake Public Schools*, 259 Minn. 487, 108 N.W.2d 602, 89 A.L.R.2d 1012 (1961), we considered a closely analogous factual situation. There, as here, the plaintiff had been wrongfully terminated as a school teacher without notice and a hearing in violation of Minn. St. 1957, § 130.18, subd. 3 (now Minn. St. 125.12, subd. 4). In affirming the trial court's award of damages as specified by the continuing contract, we held that once a wrongful discharge is proved the employee has established a prima facie case for damages measured by the salary provided by the contract, subject only to proof by the employer that the amount of damages was, or could have been, mitigated. We further noted (259 Minn. 493, 108 N.W.2d 606):

> Ordinarily, a teacher under contract wrongfully discharged need not accept employment of a different or inferior kind, or in a different locality in order to mitigate damages. . . . The measure of damages for breach of an employment contract is the compensation which an employee who has been wrongfully discharged would have received had the contract been carried out according to its terms. . . . The burden of proof to establish that such an employee could have earned or did earn compensation in mitigation of damages rests upon the party whose wrongful actions caused the breach and who claims mitigation of damages as a defense in an action based upon such breach.

The scholarly writings which discuss the rule of avoidable consequences emphasize that it is technically inaccurate to say that a wrongfully discharged employee has an affirmative legal *duty* to mitigate damages because both the employee's right of action and the remedy for the breach of contract remains the same whether he attempts to reduce his losses or not. While the employee's remedy is in no sense jeopardized, the rule operates to limit the *damages* that may be recovered when the employee makes no reasonable effort to prevent unnecessary loss.

In cases where the amount of salary is fixed by an employment contract, a wrongfully discharged employee's damages are measured by the salary promised under the contract. If he remains unavoidably idle, the loss of the promised salary is fully recoverable without reduction. Conversely, if a wrongfully discharged employee becomes employed in other employment similar in character and in the same locality, the loss of the promised salary is reduced by the earnings from such employment. This reduction is consistent with the objective underlying the rule of damages for breach of contract which seeks to restore the party harmed by the breach to as good but no better position than he would have been in had the contract been fully performed. 5 CORBIN, CONTRACTS, § 1039. It should be emphasized, however, that before a wrongfully discharged employee's damages may be reduced by wages earned from other employment, there must be proof that such other employment was incompatible with his obligations under the contract breached by his employer.

When a wrongfully discharged employee fails to exert a reasonable effort to pursue or unreasonably declines to accept other employment, the rule of avoidable consequences may prevent him from recovering the full amount of the salary promised under the contract. Recognizing that, peculiar to employment contracts, the working hours of a wrongfully discharged employee are at his sole disposal, 1 RESTATEMENT, CONTRACTS § 336(1), sets forth the following rule:

> Damages are not recoverable for harm that the plaintiff should have foreseen and could have avoided by reasonable effort without undue risk, expense, or humiliation.

Ordinarily, a wrongfully discharged employee can readily foresee that, if he unreasonably declines to pursue or accept similar employment in the same locality, his damages will continue to increase. The restatement rule thus recognizes that in situations where a wrongfully discharged employee does nothing to avert unnecessary loss the increased damage is more properly charged to the employee than the employer. The burden of proof rests on the employer to establish that reasonable steps were not taken by the employee to mitigate foreseeable damages. The employer must also establish that, had other available employment been accepted, the employee could have avoided his damages in whole or in part without "undue risk [or] expense" or without suffering "humiliation" in the sense of being embarrassed, chagrined, or degraded. As should be apparent, the application of the rule of avoidable consequences depends upon the facts and circumstances of each case.

Despite what the school district characterizes as a more than favorable decision, plaintiff argues on this appeal that there is no evidentiary support for the trial court's findings that she "did not make reasonable efforts to obtain other suitable employment" and that she "rejected . . . unreasonably" offered employment as a full-time teacher at St. Mary's. Plaintiff further argues that as a matter of law she should not have been required to accept full-time employment at a salary of $20 per day when at the time of her discharge she was being paid a salary by the school district for her attained grade of over $31 per day for half-time teaching.

The evidence on which the trial court's findings are based consists of plaintiff's testimony on direct and cross-examination. The direct evidence of the school district offered no aid to the resolution of the issue presented at trial and on this appeal. Nevertheless, there is no dispute in the record that plaintiff was offered a full-time teaching position at St. Mary's for the identical teaching responsibility she performed half time under contract with the school district. The offer was made in April 1972 and withdrawn in June 1972. She declined, citing as principal reasons her aversion to teaching full-time for a salary less than 60 percent of what she was earning half time and her fear that she would lose tenure with defendant school district if she accepted employment in a private school.

The court found that these reasons were insufficient to support a finding that she in fact made reasonable efforts to secure such employment during the 2-year interval of separation. In post-trial proceedings for amended findings or a new trial, the court permitted plaintiff to submit additional oral testimony justifying her refusal to pursue or accept full-time employment at St. Mary's. It is that testimony which mainly persuades us that the trial court was justified in concluding that, except for substitute teaching at defendant school district for some unspecified period, she made no effort from the beginning of the 1972 school year until her reinstatement to seek suitable employment at St. Mary's or elsewhere. This, as the trial court reasoned, amounted to either an abandonment of "her teaching career" for family or health reasons or efforts that were "lackadaisical at best." We thus conclude that, despite the reduced offer to pay from St. Mary's, there is sufficient evidentiary support for the court's finding that she failed to exert reasonable efforts to pursue or accept other suitable employment in the same locality within the contemplation of the rule of avoidable consequences.

This leaves the question of whether the findings supporting the amount of the reduction are clearly erroneous. Plaintiff's only testimony about the salary paid an elementary teacher at St. Mary's was in the form of an estimate of either $19 or $20 a day. Using the $20-per-day figure, the court found that plaintiff could have earned $9,100 during her 2-year period of unemployment and accordingly reduced the amount of money she would have earned had her contract not been breached ($17,401.48) by that amount. We believe that this reduction was erroneous because at least one-half of what she could have earned at St. Mary's was compatible with teaching half time for the school district. As we previously observed, only earnings from employment which are incompatible with the employee's contractual obligations may be offset as mitigated damages. Thus, the maximum amount that the court could have deducted because of plaintiff's failure to accept the teaching position at St. Mary's was $4,550. The trial court also failed, in our opinion, to take into account $1,755.66 in wages actually earned by plaintiff from the school district as a substitute teacher following the breach of her continuing contract.[13]

We are therefore compelled to order a modification of the reduction found by the trial court as follows: (1) To reduce the amount of the offset ordered by half or $4,550, representing what plaintiff could have earned for half-time employment at St. Mary's computed at the rate of $20 a day; and (2) to add to that offset $1,755.66, representing plaintiff's earnings from the school district for substitute teaching during the interval of her separation. The effect of this modification is to increase plaintiff's total damages from $8,301.48 to $11,095.82. While we might well remand the issue of the amount of the reduction for a retrial or grant the additur indicated, subject to plaintiff's option to reject it and retry the issue, we are persuaded that the interests of the parties appear to be best served by final settlement of the matter. Having studied the evidence in detail, we believe that all the facts available to the parties may well have been presented and are, in any event, sufficient to make as good an approximation as can be accomplished under the circumstances. Accordingly, we remand with directions to modify the judgment for plaintiff from $8,301.48 to $11,095.82. Remanded with directions.

---

[13] [7] The court's refusal to offset the $900 plaintiff earned weekends and evenings from Mankato State College during her separation was justified.

NOTES

(1) *"Duty" to Mitigate.* As the court suggests, there is an unfortunate tendency to discuss the principle that avoidable damages cannot be recovered in terms of a so-called "duty" to mitigate damages. Like other imprecisions in the case law, it is perhaps too much to hope that this misleading phraseology will be discontinued. In the interests of fairness to the defaulting promisor, it is a universally accepted rule that the promisee cannot recover damages that could have been avoided through the exercise of reasonable diligence and without incurring undue risk, expense or humiliation. If the promisee does not choose to avoid the enhancement of damages, the only consequence will be that he will not be compensated for damages which could have reasonably been avoided. There is no duty on the part of the promisee to mitigate.

The mitigation or "avoidable consequences concept" has both a positive and negative aspect: If the innocent promisee *is to be made whole*, he is required to refrain from going ahead with the performance of his own promise or from doing anything else which would increase the loss to be paid by the defaulting promisor. On the other hand, he is also required, *if he is to be made whole*, to take such affirmative steps as may be appropriate and reasonable to avert losses which would result were he to remain inactive.

(2) In *Rockingham County v. Luten Bridge Co.*, 35 F.2d 301, 66 A.L.R. 735 (4th Cir. 1929), plaintiff sought damages for the construction of a bridge pursuant to its contract with the county. After the contract was formed, significant public opposition to the bridge caused the county commissioners to cancel the contract. Notwithstanding such notice, plaintiff continued to perform. The court held that plaintiff may not recover damages which could have been avoided by ceasing performance upon notice of the repudiation. In general, see RESTATEMENT (SECOND) OF CONTRACTS § 350, concerning avoidability (mitigation) as a limitation on damages.

(3) In *Parker v. Twentieth Century Fox Film Corp.*, 474 P.2d 689 (1970), Parker (Shirley MacLaine) brought an action against defendant to recover $750,000 for breach of a contract whereby defendant agreed to make a musical film in California entitled "Bloomer Girl." Defendant offered plaintiff the lead in a western-type movie, "Big Country," to be filmed in Australia. While the compensation was the same, the location was different and plaintiff argued that a musical would have permitted her to display certain singing and dancing talents which the western would not allow. Moreover, plaintiff had approval rights concerning any substitute director for "Bloomer Girl" but would not have the same right for the western film. The majority of the court held that the plaintiff's refusal to star in the western film was appropriate and the amount she would have earned in that film could not be used in mitigation of damages owed by defendant.

(4) *UCC Mitigation.* UCC § 2-715(2)(a) states: "Consequential damages . . . include any loss . . . which could not reasonably be prevented by cover or otherwise."

Where a seller fails to deliver goods to a buyer and the buyer makes no effort to attempt to purchase similar products from a substitute supplier, i.e., the buyer makes no effort to "cover," the UCC clearly precludes recovery of consequential damages. At this point, the student should recall the *Huntington Beach School District* case in the introduction to contract remedies in Chapter 1. In *Federal Signal Corp. v. Safety Factors, Inc.*, 125 Wash. 2d 413, 430, 886 P.2d 172, 182 (1994), the court states, "A majority of courts considering this question have concluded that UCC § 2-715(2)(a) is a codification of common law mitigation rules." The same opinion considers the question of the burden of proving failure to pursue "cover" and concludes that the prevailing view is that such burden is on the breaching seller. It should be emphasized, however, that if the buyer has a reasonable basis for failing to effect cover, it is not barred from recovering consequential damages. See *Crowell Corp. v. Himont, U.S.A., Inc.*, 1996 Del. Super. LEXIS 400 (1996), where the court also cautions that the burden to show that plaintiff could have avoided losses by cover is on the defendant.

(5) *Contract/Tort Mitigation.* In *Evra Corp. v. Swiss Bank Corp.*, 673 F.2d 951, 957–58 (7th Cir. 1982), Hyman-Michaels failed to take prudent action after being informed that its wire transfer payment of its charter of the *Pandora* had gone awry in the intermediate bank, the Swiss Bank. The court considered the relationship between the mitigation principle (avoidable consequences) in contract and tort law:

> We are not the first to remark on the affinity between the rule of *Hadley v. Baxendale* and the doctrine, which is one of tort as well as contract law and is a settled part of the common law of Illinois, of avoidable consequences. If you are hurt in an automobile accident and unreasonably fail to seek medical treatment, the injurer, even if negligent, will not be held liable for the aggravation of the injury due to your own unreasonable behavior after the accident. If in addition you failed to fasten your seat belt, you may be barred from collecting the tort damages that would have been prevented if you had done so. Hyman-Michaels' behavior in steering close to the wind prior to April 27 was like not fastening one's seat belt; its failure on April 27 to wire a duplicate payment immediately after disaster struck was like refusing to seek medical attention after a serious accident. The seat-belt cases show that the doctrine of avoidable consequences applies whether the tort victim acts imprudently before or after the tort is committed. Hyman-Michaels did both.

[6] Liquidated Damages

The question explored in this section is whether a stipulation in the contract to the effect that the promisor shall pay a specified amount of damages if he breaches the contract is enforceable. There are at least three possible purposes to be accomplished by such a provision:

(a) The purpose may be coercion of the promisor into performing his promise. If the amount stipulated is significantly in excess of the probable, actual loss that would result from a breach, the promisee may intend the provision to operate *in terrorem* to induce the promisor to perform.

(b) The stipulation may be intended as a convenient method of determining the amount to be paid in case of breach and may be an honest forecast of the probable loss that will be caused thereby.

(c) The stipulation may be designed to put a limit on the amount of the loss to be borne by the promisor in case of breach, as when the parties fix a sum to be paid which is obviously less than the probable actual loss that would be suffered if a breach should occur.

In *Berger v. Shanahan*, 118 A.2d 311 (1955), a contract contained a clause providing for the payment to a new sales representative, the defendant, of $100 per week during the first 26 weeks of a five-year contract. The work required the procuring of outlets for the products of metal fabricators and making contacts with managerial, sales and purchasing personnel of such fabricators and other users. Since defendant was unfamiliar with this line of work, the guaranteed payment of $100 per week for 26 weeks was designed to allow for such familiarity. The same clause also stated that the employer (plaintiff) would suffer damages should defendant leave the employ before the end of the first year. In that event, the defendant agreed to repay all or any part of the special cash allowance of $100 per week paid to him. The defendant remained in this employment until he had received the entire $2600 and then left, without justification. Plaintiff sought recovery of the $2600 under the damages clause in the contract. Defendant claimed the clause should not be enforced because it constituted a penalty. A portion of the court's opinion follows.

A contractual provision for a penalty is one the prime purpose of which is to prevent a breach of the contract by holding over the head of a contracting party the threat of punishment for a breach. A provision for liquidated damages, on the other hand, is one the real purpose of which is to fix fair compensation to the injured party for a breach of the contract. In determining whether any particular provision is for liquidated damages or for a penalty, the courts are not controlled by the fact that the phrase "liquidated damages" or the word "penalty" is used. Rather, that which is determinative of the question is the intention of the parties to the contract. Accordingly, such a provision is ordinarily to be construed as one for liquidated damages if three conditions are satisfied: (1) The damage which was to be expected as a result of a breach of the contract was uncertain in amount or difficult to prove; (2) there was an intent on the part of the parties to liquidate damages in advance; and (3) the amount stipulated was reasonable in the sense that it was not greatly disproportionate to the amount of the damage which, as the parties looked forward, seemed to be the presumable loss which would be sustained by the contractee in the event of a breach of the contract.

In the present case, the court concluded that all three of these conditions were satisfied, and the subordinate facts found warranted that conclusion. The contract called for the rendition of personal services by the defendant. Obviously, the actual damage which would be sustained by the plaintiff in the event the defendant did not serve out at least a full year would be uncertain and difficult of proof. That it was the intention of the parties to liquidate the damages arising from a possible breach is apparent from the wording of the contract itself. The defendant argues that the court had no basis for an inference that this was the intention of the parties, because it does not appear that there was any discussion by them, before the contract was executed, of the provision under consideration. It is a sufficient answer to this contention that the unattacked finding of the court is that the whole contract, including the clause in question, was read aloud in the presence of both parties and each provision was discussed. They both knew the language of the clause and they therefore are conclusively presumed, in the absence of some evidence of mistake, to have intended the result which the language of the clause expressly provided for.

Lastly, it is clear that the amount of damages stipulated for in the clause was not unreasonably disproportionate to the injury which would be sustained by the plaintiff if the defendant quit his job in less than one year. The obvious purpose of the special allowance of $100 per week to be paid by the plaintiff to the defendant during the first six months of the term of the contract was to provide a living wage for the defendant while he was making his initial contacts. It apparently was contemplated by the parties that during that six-month period the defendant would not be producing much, if any, business for the benefit of the plaintiff. Consequently, the payment of the special allowance in addition to any commissions the defendant might earn was, so far as the plaintiff was concerned, an investment in the future. It was an investment which was expected to yield a profit to the plaintiff, after the expiration of the six-month period, in the form of orders procured by the defendant because of the experience he had gained during that period. It follows that it was reasonable to expect that if the defendant left the employ of the plaintiff before the expiration of the first year the plaintiff would lose all or nearly all of the advantage which his investment in the form of the special allowance was expected to bring him. Accordingly, he would be damaged by the defendant's quitting within the first year, at least to the extent of the amount he had paid the defendant as special allowance.

All three conditions, the presence of which leads ordinarily to the conclusion that a contractual provision for a fixed amount of damages is for liquidated damages rather than for a penalty, were satisfied with reference to the provision of the contract in the present case. Therefore, the court was warranted in its conclusion that the provision was valid and enforceable.

Id. at 731–34, 118 A.2d at 314–15.

NOTE

The Requirement of "Uncertainty." There are innumerable cases stating that a requirement for the enforceability of an agreed damage clause is that the damages must be uncertain, i.e., they must be difficult or impossible to estimate at the time the contract is formed. Sometimes this requirement is found in a case by the court stating that the damages must not be "readily ascertainable or capable of exact measurement." Courts almost invariably list the "uncertainty" requirement among those necessary for a liquidated damages clause. Where damages are certain, that fact alone may cause a court to decide that the liquidated damage clause is unenforceable. *See Hickox v. Bell*, 195 Ill. App. 3d 976, 552 N.E.2d 1133 (1990). If damages are readily ascertainable, there is no need for a liquidated damages clause, and the insertion of such a clause under those circumstances should make a court suspicious as to why the parties (or at least one of the parties) included the clause. As one court suggests, "The greater the difficulty of estimating damages, the more likely the stipulated damages will appear reasonable." *Sheffield-King Milling Co. v. Jacobs*, 175 N.W. 796, 801–802 (1920), quoted with approval in *Wassenaar v. Towne Hotel*, 111 Wis. 2d 518, 331 N.W.2d 357 (1983). *See* MURRAY ON CONTRACTS at § 126B.

LIND BUILDING CORP. v. PACIFIC BELLEVUE DEVELOPMENTS
Washington Court of Appeals
776 P.2d 977 (1989)

SCHOLFIELD, J.

PBD owned a tract of real property in the city of Bellevue, and on September 8, 1983, entered into a contract to sell it to Lind for a purchase price of $4,144,085. Lind paid $20,000 as an initial deposit on the date of execution of the agreement. The agreement provided:

> If Purchaser defaults, Seller shall have the right to receive the Deposit from escrow and retain it as liquidated damages, in which event this Agreement shall be terminated.

[The agreement also provided that Lind would make additional deposits at certain times prior to the time for closing. These deposits were made. Lind then sought extensions of the time for closing and made additional deposits. When the time for the extended closing arrived, Lind sought still another extension of the closing until May 6, 1984 and the parties agreed on a further extension with additional deposits.] The total sum of deposits and extension payments by Lind was in the amount of $250,000.

The transaction did not close on May 6, 1984. PBD refused Lind's request to further extend the closing and informed Lind that it had forfeited the $250,000 previously deposited.

On June 5, 1984, PBD entered into a contract to sell the property to Turner for $5,150,000, all cash upon closing. The Turner transaction was closed in September 1984, and PBD received all of its consideration within 60 days of the closing date.

Lind filed a lawsuit seeking return of the $250,000 in deposits and payments paid on the transaction. The trial court ruled that the liquidated damages clause in the Real Estate Purchase and Sale Agreement was an enforceable clause and did not constitute a penalty. The trial court also awarded PBD reasonable attorney's fees and costs in the sum of $31,031.05. The primary issue on this appeal is whether or not PBD is entitled to retain the $250,000 as liquidated damages.

Lind contends that the liquidated damages clause imposes a penalty and is unenforceable in this case because PBD suffered no actual damages as a result of Lind's default.

Washington courts have generally looked with favor upon liquidated damages clauses and upheld them where the sums involved did not amount to a penalty. In *Management, Inc. v. Schassberger*, 39 W[ash]. 2d 321, 235 P.2d 293 (1951), the court adopted 1 RESTATEMENT OF CONTRACTS § 339 (1932) as the applicable rule.[14] In 1979, the RESTATEMENT rule was redrafted to harmonize with § 2-718(1) of the Uniform Commercial Code.[15] The revised rule is found in RESTATEMENT (SECOND) OF CONTRACTS § 356 (1981), and reads as follows:

> (1) Damages for breach by either party may be liquidated in the agreement but only at an amount that is reasonable in the light of the anticipated or actual loss caused by the breach and the difficulties of proof of loss. A term fixing unreasonably large liquidated damages is unenforceable on grounds of public policy as a penalty.

Underlying the RESTATEMENT rule is the principle that damages awarded for breach of contract should be reasonably compensatory rather than punitive. Comment (a) to the RESTATEMENT (SECOND) OF CONTRACTS § 356 (1981) reads in part as follows:

> However, the parties to a contract are not free to provide a penalty for its breach. The central objective behind the system of contract remedies is compensatory, not punitive. Punishment of a promisor for having broken his promise has no justification on either economic or other grounds and a term providing such a penalty is unenforceable on grounds of public policy.

The principle that damages should be compensatory only is violated if substantial sums are recovered as liquidated damages in cases where there is no actual damage or loss as a consequence of the breach.

Comment (b), § 356 (1981) of the RESTATEMENT (SECOND) OF CONTRACTS adopts this view, stating in part as follows:

> If the difficulty of proof of loss is great, considerable latitude is allowed in the approximation of anticipated or actual harm. If, on the other hand, the difficulty of proof of loss is slight, less latitude is allowed in that approximation. If to take an extreme case it is clear that no loss at all has occurred, a provision fixing a substantial sum as damages is unenforceable.

The Washington cases are in accord.

The traditional view called for testing the reasonableness of the liquidated damages clause as of the time the contract was formed. Courts have

---

[14] [1] RESTATEMENT OF CONTRACTS § 339 (1932) reads in part as follows: "Liquidated Damages and Penalties. "(1) An agreement, made in advance of breach, fixing the damages therefor, is not enforceable as a contract and does not affect the damages recoverable for the breach, unless (a) the amount so fixed is a reasonable forecast of just compensation for the harm that is caused by the breach, and (b) the harm that is caused by the breach is one that is incapable or very difficult of accurate estimation"

[15] [2] RCW 62A.2-718 provides in part as follows: "Liquidation or limitation of damages; deposits. (1) Damages for breach by either party may be liquidated in the agreement but only at an amount which is reasonable in the light of the anticipated or actual harm caused by the breach, the difficulties of proof of loss, and the inconvenience or nonfeasibility of otherwise obtaining an adequate remedy. A term fixing unreasonably large liquidated damages is void as a penalty."

often felt uncomfortable with this approach in cases in which the property's market value has risen sharply after contracting and before breach, so that the seller has little actual damages or none at all; an estimate of damages which was reasonable when made may sometimes turn out to be a gross exaggeration. More recent cases display a willingness to take this factor into account, and to refuse enforcement of the forfeiture if it would result in a large windfall to the vendor in fact.

There are three reasons the liquidated damages clause in this case is unenforceable. The amount of $250,000 came into existence for reasons unrelated to a provision calling for liquidated damages and, therefore, does not represent an effort by the parties to make a reasonable forecast of anticipated damages. The second reason is that, there being no actual substantial damages, the requirement of the rule that the amount of liquidated damages be reasonable in the light of the anticipated or actual loss cannot be satisfied. Thirdly, calculation of the amounts PBD claims represent losses due to Lind's default are not difficult of ascertainment or proof.

Requirement of a Reasonable Forecast of Future Damages

A valid liquidated damages clause requires the contracting parties to make an estimate of the just compensation for the damages to be anticipated from a breach. Undisputed facts in this case show that at the time of contracting, the liquidated damages clause applied only to the initial deposit of $20,000. While the contract contemplated the possibility of additional deposits, those totaled only an additional $70,000. At the most, the deposits that conceivably could have been contemplated by the parties at time of contracting totaled $90,000. All of the additional deposits over $90,000 were pursuant to additional agreements negotiated by the parties after the signing of the original contract. These subsequent agreements called for additional deposits by Lind in consideration of being granted extensions of time on the closing date. They had no apparent relationship to liquidated damages, and there is no evidence that any of the deposits after the first $20,000 were calculated in an effort to make a reasonable estimate of anticipated damages.

Assuming *arguendo* that $20,000 represented an effort to forecast damages, there is nothing in the record explaining how the estimate of liquidated damages grew from $20,000 to $250,000. For this reason alone, the liquidated damages clause in this case must be held invalid and unenforceable.

Effect of No Actual Loss

While there is some authority that an otherwise valid liquidated damages clause is enforceable even if there are no actual damages, the weight of authority and the better-reasoned cases hold that where there is no actual loss, an otherwise enforceable liquidated damages clause is not enforceable because to do so would violate the principle that damages should be compensatory only. As previously indicated, however, it is not always necessary to prove actual damages in order to recover liquidated damages in Washington.

Adhering to this principle, the Supreme Court of Connecticut stated in *Norwalk*, 220 A.2d at 268:

> It is not the function of the court to determine by hindsight the reasonableness of the expectation of the parties at the time the contract was made, but it is the function of the court at the time of enforcement to do justice. In the ordinary contract action the court determines the just damages from evidence offered. In a valid contract for liquidated damages, the parties are permitted, in order to avoid the uncertainties and time-consuming effort involved, to estimate in advance the reasonably probable foreseeable damages which would arise in the event of a default. Implicit in the transaction is the premise that the sum agreed upon will be within the fair range of those just damages which would be called for and provable had the parties resorted to proof. Consequently, if the damage envisioned by the parties never occurs, the whole premise for their agreed estimate vanishes, and, even if the contract was to be construed as one for liquidated damages rather than one for a penalty, neither justice nor the intent of the parties is served by enforcement. To enforce it would amount in reality to the infliction of a penalty.

It is a well-accepted principle of contract law that the purpose of awarding damages for breach of contract is to place the damaged party, as nearly as possible, in the position he would be in had the contract been performed. He is not entitled to more than he would have received had the contract been performed. *Platts v. Arney*, 50 W[ash]. 2d 42, 46, 309 P.2d 372 (1957).

Comment (b), § 356 of RESTATEMENT (SECOND) OF CONTRACTS makes it clear that a provision allowing substantial damages when the actual loss is minimal or nonexistent amounts to a penalty and is unenforceable. It is illogical to allow a party to recover damages greatly exceeding the actual loss simply because of the existence of a liquidated damages clause. In all other contract actions, the remedy is limited to reasonable compensation for a proven loss. Finding of fact 34 entered by the trial court, which is unchallenged by either party to this appeal, reads as follows:

> Subsequent to May 24, defendant did resell the property to a third party for $5,150,000 cash. Since it is an established fact that the property was sold to a third party for approximately $1 million more than the price Lind was obligated to pay, if there was any loss to PBD caused by Lind's default, it was minimal and bears no reasonable relation to the sum of $250,000. Under these circumstances, allowing PBD to retain the $250,000 in deposits amounts to the imposition of a penalty and must be reversed.

Alleged Losses Not Difficult to Prove

In its brief, PBD emphasizes that finance charges for holding the property in an undeveloped condition amounted to approximately $1,429 per day. On that basis, the damages can be calculated by multiplying by the number of days the property was off the market due to Lind's default. PBD also mentioned a percentage of office overhead and real estate taxes. These expenses are also readily ascertainable and provable. The facts of this case simply do not satisfy the requirement of Restatement § 356 that the loss be difficult to prove.

Attorney's Fees

Paragraph 15 of the Real Estate Purchase and Sale Agreement provides as follows:

> If Purchaser, Seller, or Agent brings suit to enforce or declare the meaning of any provision of this Agreement, the prevailing party, in addition to any other relief, shall be entitled to recover reasonable attorney's fees and costs, including any on appeal.

Pursuant to the provisions of this paragraph, the trial court allowed PBD judgment against Lind for recovery of attorney's fees and costs expended in the trial court in the total amount of $31,031.05. Having concluded that Lind should have prevailed in the trial court, this award of attorney's fees is reversed. Lind is entitled to recovery of attorney's fees in the trial court and on appeal.

On remand, the trial court is directed to enter judgment in favor of Lind and against PBD for $250,000, plus prejudgment interest thereon, and entry of judgment for an award of attorney's fees to Lind in the trial court and on appeal.

NOTES

(1) *The "No Harm" Problem.* Suppose an executive is transferred to another city and contracts for the construction of a new family home in the new location. A clause provides for a reasonable per diem amount for any delay by the contractor to defray the cost of lodging for the family. The house is not ready for occupancy when promised. The chief executive officer of the buyer's company, however, will be out of the country for some time and provides her mansion replete with servants and luxurious appointments to the executive and his family for the time required by the contractor to complete the employee's house. It is clear beyond peradventure that the transferred executive has suffered no actual loss. In terms of anticipated harm, the clause is clearly reasonable and, if actual damages are not to be considered at all, there should be a recovery of the per diem amount. Yet, such a recovery will constitute a windfall and place the aggrieved party in a better position than he would have been in had the contract been performed. As the principal case suggests, courts are more than uncomfortable with that possibility. If there has been no harm at all, there is growing case law support for the view that the clause should not be enforced. If, however, actual damages which are not merely nominal have been suffered, an otherwise reasonable liquidated damage amount as measured in light of anticipated harm should be enforced.

(2) *Measurement in Light of Anticipated or Actual Damages — Restatement (Second) and UCC.* As the principal case suggests, UCC § 2-718(1) states that the amount in the clause must be reasonable in the light of anticipated *or* actual harm. As one court suggests, it "does, in some measure, signal a departure from prior law, which considered only the anticipated harm at the time of contracting, since the section expressly contemplates that a court may examine the 'actual harm' sustained in adjudicating the validity of a liquidated damages provision." *Equitable*

Lumber Corp. v. IPA Land Dev. Corp., 38 N.Y.2d 516, 381 N.Y.S.2d 459, 344 N.E.2d 391 (1976). In her well-known article, *Remedies for Breach of Contract Relating to the Sale of Goods Under the Uniform Commercial Code: A Roadmap for Article 2*, 73 YALE L.J. 199, 278 (1963), Professor (now Chief Justice of the Connecticut Supreme Court) Peters stated, "It is true that the Code is unusually generous in its appraisal of the amount set by the contracting parties. Even if this amount was entirely unreasonable, as of the time of contract, it can apparently be recovered so long as it turns out, purely as a matter of accident, to approximate the harm actually caused by the buyer's breach."

RESTATEMENT (SECOND) OF CONTRACTS § 356(1) replicates the UCC change, which is not remarkable in light of the fact that the American Law Institute is responsible for Restatements and was half responsible for the Uniform Commercial Code.

The new UCC and RESTATEMENT (SECOND) OF CONTRACTS is subject to criticism. Assume a clause that is clearly unreasonable in light of anticipated harm, i.e., one designed as a penalty. From that perspective, the clause is clearly unenforceable. Further assume that the actual damages suffered become measurable after they are sustained and are so surprisingly large that they are not grossly disproportionate to the damages in the clause that, again, were originally intended as a penalty. Absent any clause, these damages would not be recoverable because they were not foreseeable under *Hadley v. Baxendale*. Under the UCC/RESTATEMENT (SECOND) directive, however, a penalty clause becomes enforceable, allowing the recovery of unforeseeable damages.

(3) *"Blunderbuss" Clauses.* Where there are a number of promises of varying degrees of importance on one side of a contract and one agreed damages clause with one amount of damages for the breach of any one of the promises, the clause will be reasonable with respect to some breaches, but would obviously be a penalty with respect to others. Some courts refuse to enforce such clauses at all. *See Seidlitz v. Auerbach*, 230 N.Y. 167, 129 N.E. 461 (1920). Others are willing to assume that the clause was intended to apply only to those major breaches where the clause would be reasonable in the light of anticipated harm — notwithstanding the lack of any language in the clause restricting such application. *See Hackenheimer v. Kurtzmann*, 235 N.Y. 57, 138 N.E. 235 (1923). Scholars generally agree that the clause should be enforced if it otherwise would be enforceable with respect to the breach that actually occurred. *See* MURRAY ON CONTRACTS, *supra* Chapter 1, note 1, at § 126D.

(4) *Liquidated Damages Versus Alternative Performances.* Where a contract states that a promisor must either perform a particular act or pay a stipulated amount, there are two possible interpretations: (1) the parties intended the promisor to have a genuine choice between alternative performances, or (2) they intended that only the specified act would constitute performance and failure to perform would give rise to liquidated damages. If the first interpretation is accepted, either performance or payment of the stipulated sum would constitute full performance of the contract. If the second interpretation is accepted, payment of the amount in the clause would be enforceable only after the promisor breached the duty of performance. The issue is clearly one of interpretation of all relevant facts to determine the intention of the parties. One of the critical facts in making this

interpretation is the relative value of the alternatives. *See* RESTATEMENT (SECOND) OF CONTRACTS § 356, cmt. c; *see also* MURRAY ON CONTRACTS § 126E.

(5) *Liquidated Damages Versus Specific Performance.* The question arises, where a contract contains a liquidated damages clause, is the plaintiff relegated to that clause or, in a proper case, may the plaintiff be granted specific performance notwithstanding the clause? Unless that remedy is expressly excluded in the contract, most courts will grant specific performance. *See, e.g., Papa Gino's of Am., Inc. v. Plaza & Latham Assocs.*, 135 A.D.2d 34, 524 N.Y.S.2d 536 (1988). However, where a plaintiff successfully enjoins the defendant under a restrictive covenant in a contract not to compete within a certain area for a certain time, the plaintiff may not enjoy that relief and simultaneously expect enforcement of a liquidated damages clause. *See Karpinski v. Ingrasci*, 320 N.Y.S.2d 1, 268 N.E.2d 751 (1971); MURRAY ON CONTRACTS § 126E.1.

(6) *Attorney's Fees.* The contract in the principal case included a provision for attorney's fees. Absent such a clause, courts in the United States do not permit recovery of attorney's fees. Where the contract contains a clause setting forth a specified amount for such fees, that clause will be subject to the same scrutiny as other agreed damages clauses. *See Equitable Lumber*, note 2 *supra.* For a case upholding such a clause, see *Kenco Homes, Inc. v. Williams*, 94 Wash. App. 219, 972 P.2d 125 (1999).

[7]   Expectation Recovery — Construction Contracts — Cost of Completion vs. Diminution in Value

An owner and builder enter into a construction contract setting forth a price of $100,000. The builder's cost of performing the entire contract will be $90,000. Assume the builder completes half of the work that has cost the builder $50,000 when the owner breaches the contract. If the builder had been allowed to complete the work, the cost of completion would have been $40,000. To place the builder in the position he would have been in had the contract been performed (his *expectation* interest), he should be entitled to the contract price minus cost of completion that will provide a recovery of $60,000 which includes his cost to the point of being terminated and the profit he would have earned on the entire contract if allowed to complete it.

If the builder rather than the owner breached the same contract after the builder has expended $50,000 in part performance which the owner has already paid, but the owner is required to pay a substitute builder $60,000 to complete the project, the owner should recover $10,000 from the builder to place the owner in the position he should have been in had the contract been performed — the owner's *expectation* interest.

While the *cost of completion* to bring the building to completion in accordance with the original contemplation of the parties is clearly the normal measure of damages, earlier in the book we learned from Justice Cardozo in *Jacob and Youngs v. Kent* that a builder who substantially performs his contract should not be confronted with tearing the entire building down and rebuilding it where the defects are trivial. In that case involving the wrong brand of pipe, instead of "cost of completion," the court stated that the damages would be measured by the difference in the value received from the value contemplated by the parties. Since the pipe installed in the building was identical to the pipe required by the specifications, there was no diminution in value.

Suppose a builder simply refuses to perform. Perhaps he underbid the job and will lose a great deal in performing it. Assume the cost of completion is $100,000, but, if he had completed the work, the value of the property would have increased only by $1000. Has the owner lost $100,000 (the cost of completion), or only $1000?

AMERICAN STANDARD, INC. v. SCHECTMAN
New York Appellate Division
439 N.Y.S.2d 529 (1981)

HANCOCK, J.

Plaintiffs have recovered a judgment on a jury verdict of $90,000 against defendant for his failure to complete grading and to take out certain foundations and other subsurface structures to one foot below the grade line as promised. Whether the court should have charged the jury, as defendant Schectman requested, that the difference in value of plaintiffs' property with and without the promised performance was the measure of the damage is the main point in his appeal.

Until 1972, plaintiffs operated a pig iron manufacturing plant on land abutting the Niagara River in Tonawanda. On the 26-acre parcel were, in addition to various industrial and office buildings, a 60-ton blast furnace, large lifts, hoists and other equipment for transporting and storing ore, railroad tracks, cranes, diesel locomotives and sundry implements and devices used in the business. Since the 1870s plaintiffs' property, under several different owners, had been the site of various industrial operations. Having decided to close the plant, plaintiffs on August 3, 1973 made a contract in which they agreed to convey the buildings and other structures and most of the equipment to defendant, a demolition and excavating contractor, in return for defendant's payment of $275,000 and his promise to remove the equipment, demolish the structures and grade the property as specified.

We turn to defendant's argument that the court erred in rejecting his proof that plaintiffs suffered no loss by reason of the breach because it makes no difference in the value of the property whether the old foundations are at grade or one foot below grade and in denying his offer to show that plaintiffs succeeded in selling the property for $183,000 — only $3,000 less than its full fair market value. By refusing this testimony and charging the jury that the cost of completion (estimated at $110,500 by plaintiffs' expert), not diminution in value of the property, was the measure of damage the court, defendant contends, has unjustly permitted plaintiffs to reap a windfall at his expense. Citing the definitive opinion of JUDGE CARDOZO in *Jacob & Youngs v. Kent* (230 NY 239), he maintains that the facts present a case "of substantial performance" of the contract with omissions of "trivial or inappreciable importance" (p. 245) and that because the cost of completion was "grossly and unfairly out of proportion to the good to be attained" (p. 244), the proper measure of damage is diminution in value.

The general rule of damages for breach of a construction contract is that the injured party may recover those damages which are the direct, natural and immediate consequence of the breach and which can reasonably be said to have been in the contemplation of the parties when the contract was made. In the usual case where the contractor's performance has been defective or incomplete, the reasonable cost of replacement or completion is the measure. When, however, there has been a substantial performance of the contract made in good faith but defects exist, the correction of which would result in economic waste, courts have measured the damages as the difference between the value of the property as constructed and the value if performance had been properly completed. *Jacob & Youngs* is illustrative. There, plaintiff, a contractor, had constructed a house for the defendant which was satisfactory in all respects save one: the wrought iron pipe installed for the plumbing was not of Reading manufacture, as specified in the contract, but of other brands of the same quality. Noting that the breach was unintentional and the consequences of the omission trivial, and that the cost of replacing the pipe would be "grievously out of proportion" to the significance of the default, the court held the breach to be immaterial and the proper measure of damage to the owner to be not the cost of replacing the pipe but the nominal difference in value of the house with and without the Reading pipe.

Not in all cases of claimed "economic waste" where the cost of completing performance of the contract would be large and out of proportion to the resultant benefit to the property have the courts adopted diminution in value as the measure of damage. Under the RESTATEMENT rule, the completion of the contract must involve "unreasonable economic waste" and the illustrative example given is that of a house built with pipe different in name but equal in quality to the brand stipulated in the contract as in *Jacob & Youngs v. Kent.* In *Groves v. Wunder Co.* (205 Minn 163), plaintiff had leased property and conveyed a gravel plant to defendant in exchange for a sum of money and for defendant's commitment to return the property to plaintiff at the end of the term at a specified grade — a promise defendant failed to perform. Although the cost of the fill to complete the grading was $60,000 and the total value of the property, graded as specified in the contract, only $12,160 the court rejected the "diminution in value" rule, stating: "The owner's right to improve his property is not trammeled by its small value. It is his right to erect thereon structures which will reduce its value. If that be the result, it can be of no aid to any contractor who declines performance. As said long ago in *Chamberlain v. Parker*, 45 N.Y. 569, 572: 'A man may do what he will with his own, * * * and if he chooses to erect a monument to his caprice or folly on his premises, and employs and pays another to do it, it does not lie with a defendant who has been so employed and paid for building it, to say that his own performance would not be beneficial to the plaintiff.' "

The "economic waste" of the type which calls for application of the "diminution in value" rule generally entails defects in construction which are irremediable or which may not be repaired without a substantial tearing down of the structure as in *Jacob & Youngs.*

Where, however, the breach is of a covenant which is only incidental to the main purpose of the contract and completion would be disproportionately costly, courts have applied the diminution in value measure even where no destruction of the work is entailed (see, e.g., *Peevyhouse v. Garland Coal & Min. Co.*, 382 P.2d 109 [Okla], cert den 375 U.S. 906, holding [contrary to *Groves v. Wunder Co., supra*] that diminution in value is the proper measure where defendant, the lessee of plaintiff's lands under a coal mining lease, failed to perform costly remedial and restorative work on the land at the termination of the lease. The court distinguished the "building and construction" cases and noted that the breach was of a covenant incidental to the main purpose of the contract which was the recovery of coal from the premises to the benefit of both parties.

It is also a general rule in building and construction cases, at least under *Jacob & Youngs* in New York that a contractor who would ask the court to apply the diminution of value measure "as an instrument of justice" must not have breached the contract intentionally and must show substantial performance made in good faith (*Jacob & Youngs v. Kent, supra*, pp. 244, 245).

In the case before us, plaintiffs chose to accept as part of the consideration for the promised conveyance of their valuable plant and machines to defendant his agreement to grade the property as specified and to remove the foundations, piers and other structures to a depth of one foot below grade to prepare the property for sale. It cannot be said that the grading and the removal of the structures were incidental to plaintiffs' purpose of "achieving a reasonably attractive vacant plot for resale" (*cf. Peevyhouse v. Garland Coal & Min. Co., supra*). Nor can defendant maintain that the damages which would naturally flow from his failure to do the grading and removal work and which could reasonably be said to have been in the contemplation of the parties when the contract was made would not be the reasonable cost of completion. That the fulfillment of defendant's promise would (contrary to plaintiffs' apparent expectations) add little or nothing to the sale value of the property does not excuse the default. As in the hypothetical case, posed in *Chamberlain v Parker* of the man who "chooses to erect a monument to his caprice or folly on his premises, and employs and pays another to do it," it does not lie with defendant here who has received consideration for his promise to do the work "to say that his own performance would not be beneficial to the [plaintiffs]."

Defendant's completed performance would not have involved undoing what in good faith was done improperly but only doing what was promised and left undone. That the burdens of performance were heavier than anticipated and the cost of completion disproportionate to the end to be obtained does not, without more, alter the rule that the measure of plaintiffs' damage is the cost of completion. Disparity in relative economic benefits is not the equivalent of "economic waste" which will invoke the rule in *Jacob & Youngs v Kent.* Moreover, faced with the jury's finding that the reasonable cost of removing the large concrete and stone walls and other structures extending above grade was $90,000, defendant can hardly assert that he has rendered substantial performance of the contract or that what he left unfinished was "of trivial or inappreciable importance" (*Jacob & Youngs v. Kent, supra*, p. 245). Finally, defendant, instead of attempting in good faith to complete the removal of the underground structures, contended that he was not obliged by the contract to do so and, thus, cannot claim to be a "transgressor whose default is unintentional and trivial [and who] may hope for mercy if he will offer atonement for his wrong"

(*Jacob & Youngs v. Kent, supra,* p. 244). We conclude, therefore, that the proof pertaining to the value of plaintiffs' property was properly rejected and the jury correctly charged on damages. The judgment and order should be affirmed.

NOTES

(1) Beyond *Jacob & Youngs v. Kent,* the court discusses two other classic cases in this area. In *Groves v. John Wunder Co.,* 205 Minn. 163, 286 N.W. 235 (1939), two justices did not participate, one because of illness, and two others dissented while three members of the seven-member court were the "majority" in this case. If the contract had been performed, the added value to industrial property would have been $12,000, but the cost of that performance was $60,000, which the court awarded. The aftermath of that decision was reported in J. DAWSON AND W. HARVEY, CASES ON CONTRACTS AND CONTRACT REMEDIES 28 (1959): the case was settled for $55,000. The land remained in the same unimproved condition for several years. The owner eventually spent $6000 in improving the land though not in any substantial fashion. It was then sold for $45,000. It was quite suitable for the buyer's industrial use in the condition it was in when defendant had originally failed to perform.

The other classic case is *Peevyhouse v. Garland Coal Mining Co.,* 382 P.2d 109 (1962), where the husband and wife who owned land containing coal deposits leased the land for strip mining purposes to the defendant. The owners demanded that defendant expressly agree to restore the land to its original state after the mining was completed. The defendant breached that promise which would have cost $29,000 to perform and would have increased the value of the property by a mere $300. The total value of the land was less than $5000. Here, the court recognized the "diminution in value" rather than "cost of completion" measure.

Quaere: Can you make an argument that each of these cases was wrongly decided? For an interesting history and analysis of the *Peevyhouse* case, see JUDITH L. MAUTE, PEEVYHOUSE V. GARLAND COAL & MINING CO. REVISITED: THE BALLAD OF WILLIE AND LUCILLE, 89 NW. L. REV. 1341 (1995).

(2) In *Hansen v. Andersen,* 246 Iowa 1310, 71 N.W.2d 921 (1955), farmer Hansen entered into a contract with builder Andersen for the construction of a granary. When completed, Hansen discovered that the capacity was less than contemplated and that the chutes did not function correctly. The attic space was only six feet instead of seven, and the lower rafters of the hip roof were only twelve feet seven inches long rather than the fourteen foot length specified. Hansen brought an action against Andersen for damages. The court held that Andersen was entitled to the difference in value rather than the cost of completion since the cost of completion would require the erection of scaffolding, the tearing off of the old roof, the construction of a new roof and gable end and also raising the cupola. While the injured promisee is entitled to what he contracts for or its equivalent, what the equivalent is depends upon the circumstances. The loss in property value, rather than the cost of completion, is the proper measure of damages where the correction of defects would necessitate unreasonable destruction of work, or where, according to one view, the strict completion of performance would, without destruction of work, involve expense greatly disproportionate to the importance of results obtainable.

(3)   RESTATEMENT (SECOND) OF CONTRACTS § 348, comment c states:

> If an award based on the cost to remedy the defects would clearly be
> excessive and the injured party does not prove the actual loss in value to
> him, damages will be based instead on the difference between the market
> price that the property would have had without the defects and the market
> price of the property with the defects.

In *Toth v. Spitzer*, 1998 Ohio App. LEXIS 6063, at *8 (1998), where the plaintiff
claimed that the jury erroneously based its award on the diminution in value rather
than the cost of completion, the court states, "[G]enerally, the proper measure of
damages in a home improvement contract is the cost of repair, but that a different
measure of damages must be used if the total cost to remedy a defect is grossly
disproportionate to the good to be attained."

(4) When a buyer accepts goods that are defective but intends to keep the goods,
the measure of recovery is set forth in UCC § 2-714(2): "[T]he difference at the time
and place of acceptance between the value of the goods accepted and the value they
would have had if they had been as warranted."

D.   THE RELIANCE AND RESTITUTION INTERESTS

CBS, INC. v. MERRICK
United States Court of Appeals, Ninth Circuit
716 F.2d 1292 (1983)

SOLOMON, J.

In early 1977, [David] Merrick acquired the motion picture and television rights
to the novel *Blood and Money*. CBS negotiated with Merrick for the right to do a
mini-series based on that novel, and on August 1, 1977, the parties signed two
documents — a Rights Agreement and a Production Agreement.

In the Rights Agreement, CBS agreed to pay Merrick $1,250,000 for the right to
do a television series based on *Blood and Money*. CBS paid Merrick $833,333.34
when the agreement was executed and agreed to pay Merrick the balance in
installments when various stages of production were completed. It was agreed that
if photography did not commence within two years, that is, by August 1, 1979, the
agreement would terminate and CBS would pay Merrick the balance owed on the
contract. In addition, the rights to *Blood and Money* would revert to Merrick. The
agreement required all modifications to be in writing.

In the Production Agreement, CBS agreed to pay Merrick an additional $250,000
to produce the show. The parties agreed to consult on the selection of the writer,
director and principal actors. Merrick would then negotiate the terms and
conditions of their employment, and CBS would then enter into contracts with these
persons containing the terms negotiated by Merrick.

It was also agreed that when the final screenplay was delivered, the parties
would prepare an operating budget. CBS had ninety days from the delivery of the

final screenplay to notify Merrick whether it would proceed with the project. If CBS elected not to proceed and if Merrick had not breached the contract and was ready, willing and able to perform his duties as producer, CBS was obligated to pay Merrick the entire $250,000 and all rights to the story *Blood and Money* would revert to him.

Merrick promptly selected a director and screenwriter. The fee for the director was $500,000 regardless of whether the show was produced. The fee for the screenwriter was $250,000. When Merrick hired them, he knew that they were working on another project and that they could not immediately start to work on *Blood and Money.* Merrick failed to tell them about the deadline, and he ignored suggestions that he hire a second writer.

The first segment of the screenplay was not delivered until September, 1978, and the screenplay was not completed until June, 1979. However, by April, 1979, it was apparent that the August 1, 1979 deadline could not be met because at that time the screenplay had not been completed and at least six months' pre-production work was required before photography could start.

On April 9, 1979, Merrick met with CBS executives, and he orally agreed to extend the deadline. CBS sent Merrick proposed drafts of a written amendment. Although Merrick did not object to the basic terms, he objected to their form and complexity. CBS delivered a simplified draft to Merrick, but he never signed it.

On May 17, 1979, Merrick's attorney sent a telex to CBS stating that Merrick would not agree to any changes in the original agreements. Nevertheless, Merrick continued to act as though the deadline had been extended, and later he described the telex as "lawyer stuff." Five days before the August 1 deadline, CBS told Merrick of its decision to proceed with the production of the show. Merrick expressed enthusiasm for the project. Twelve days after the deadline, CBS and Merrick met to plan the project.

On August 24, 1979, CBS met with Merrick's agents to discuss a budget and a tentative production schedule, but in the following month Merrick notified CBS that all rights to the story had reverted to him because CBS had not met the August 1 deadline. No further work was ever done on the project.

The court awarded CBS the $833,333.34 it had paid Merrick and also $83,333.33, the amount that CBS had paid William Morris Agency, Merrick's agents. The court denied CBS the $750,000 which CBS was contractually liable to pay the director and screenwriter for their services.

There was ample evidence to support the court's order finding that Merrick refused to perform and had breached his contract with CBS.

The district court found that CBS's complaint sought rescission and restitution and in a separate cause of action sought damages for breach of contract. A party injured by a breach of a contract may recover both restitution and reliance damages. A party may rescind a contract if there was fraud in the inception or if there was a substantial breach. The district court listed many reasons why Merrick's refusal to perform was unjustified and held that "Merrick materially breached the Rights Agreement and the Production Agreement by repudiating them without justification."

In its findings on damages, the district [court] held that "Merrick must return to CBS the amounts which it paid him under the contract." The court also found that CBS is entitled to rescission "both because Merrick expressly repudiated the modified contract and because he breached the original contract," and it therefore awarded CBS $916,666.67, the amount it paid both to Merrick and his agent, the William Morris Agency.

This award of restitution damages is proper under either rescission or breach of contract. When a breach occurs after the execution of the contract, the injured party in a contract action is entitled to both restitution and reliance damages.

Here, the district court found substantial breaches of contract. Nevertheless, the court limited recovery to restitution, the only recovery available when the contract is illegal or void from its inception. The court refused to allow reliance damages even though it found breaches of the contract.

This was error. This action must therefore be remanded to the district court to determine what part, if any, of the $750,000 paid to the director and screenwriter are legitimate reliance damages. In connection with this determination, the court should consider questions like reasonable reliance on the agreement, attempts to mitigate damages, the value of the screenplay delivered to CBS, and the foreseeability of the loss.

The district court's finding that Merrick is liable to CBS for the breach of contract is *Affirmed.* The award to CBS of $916,666.67 it paid to Merrick and his agent is also *Affirmed.* The denial of amounts paid to Friedkin, the director, and Green, the screenwriter, by CBS in reliance on its contract with Merrick is *Reversed* and *Remanded* for proceedings consistent with this opinion.

NELSON, J., concurring.

I concur in the majority opinion but believe that the applicable law requires further clarification.

The proper measure of damages in this case depends on an interpretation of an unclear area of New York law. Although CBS denominated its complaint below as one for rescission, I believe CBS's lawsuit was effectively a breach of contract action. The complaint sought restitution instead of lost profits because of the speculative nature of the breached contract. The question presented to us, then, is whether an award of restitution when used as a substitute for speculative lost profits in a breach of contract action should preclude the recovery of additional measures of damages.

In seeking to answer this question of New York law, I have found neither a New York statute that is directly controlling nor a decision by the New York Court of Appeals that is directly on point. I would therefore have this court turn to other relevant sources of New York law and sit, in effect, as a New York state court. The phrase "rescission and restitution" has two meanings in New York. *Richard v. Credit Suisse*, 242 N.Y. 346, 152 N.E. 110, 11 (1926) (Cardozo, J.). When used in the context of a voidable or mutually rescinded contract, "rescission and restitution" means that a contract is treated as void *ab initio. Id.* On the other hand, a party seeking rescission and restitution in a breach of contract action does not seek to undo the contract from its beginning. *Id.* Instead, a plaintiff may request restitution in a breach of contract action as a substitute measure of lost profits where, as here, the true measure of lost profits would be purely speculative.

New York law is unclear on whether the two different meanings of the phrase "rescission and restitution" produce two different answers to the question of whether a plaintiff can recover restitution plus additional damages. I conclude that they do. A plaintiff who elects to rescind his voidable contract cannot avoid the contract for purposes of restitution and invoke it for purposes of recovering special damages. In such cases, a plaintiff suing for rescission and restitution can recover only those benefits that he has conferred on the defendant. RESTATEMENT (SECOND) OF CONTRACTS § 370 (1981).

In contrast, because it does not actually "rescind" the breached contract, an award of restitution in a breach of contract action should not preclude the award of additional measures of damages.

I therefore concur with the majority's conclusion that a New York court would permit recovery of restitution plus additional measures of contract damages in this case. I also concur with the necessity of a remand. In rejecting CBS's claim for full contract damages and relying instead on [a] purely restitutionary measure, the district court failed to pass on several issues necessary to measure breach of contract damages. Both parties address these issues in their briefs on appeal, but these are topics best left to the trier of fact.

QUESTIONS

(1)   What prevents CBS from seeking a recovery of its expectation interest in this case? In this connection, the student may wish to recall the case or Professor Freund and his dispute with the Washington Square Press in Chapter 1.

(2)   Precisely which interests are protected by the court in allowing CBS to recover the payments to Merrick and the payments to the director and screen-writer?

PROBLEM

A contractor sought recovery on a contract with the United States under which the contractor was to perform certain work in the harbor of New Orleans which work was experimental in nature. The United States breached the contract and, because of the experimental nature of the contract, it was not possible to prove whether the contractor would have made a profit on the transaction or sustained a loss. The contractor sought to recover his expenses, i.e., the costs of machinery, tools, materials and labor used in the performance of the contract before the Government breached. The lower court held that the plaintiff was entitled to such recovery. On appeal, the Government argued that, since the plaintiff could not prove the profit it would have made had the contract been performed because plaintiff could not prove the cost of completion of the work, plaintiff should recover nothing. What result on appeal? *See United States v. Behan,* 110 U.S. 338 (1884).

[1]   Alternative Relief for Breach of Contract

DOERING EQUIPMENT CO. v. JOHN DEERE CO.
Massachusetts Appeals Court
815 N.E.2d 234 (2004)

KAFKER, J.

Doering Equipment Co. has lost money every year on its contract to act as a distributor for John Deere Co. golf and turf products. Under the agreement, Doering agreed to provide a sufficient staff adequately trained to carry out its obligations under the agreement. Deere could terminate immediately for cause for certain defaults. The agreement specifically provided that upon termination for whatever reason, "neither party is entitled to any compensation or reimbursement for loss of prospective profits, anticipated sales or other losses occasioned by termination or cancellation of this Agreement," except respecting obligations resulting from goods already delivered to Doering.

In 1996, Deere began to complain of understaffing by Doering, and demanded another salesperson. Doering responded that it intended to add one, but only after its current sales force began to pay for itself. At a meeting on October 17, 1996, Deere allegedly told Doering that it must purchase forty-four turf gators and add a salesperson, and that both were non-negotiable requirements. The agreement provided that Doering "maintain an inventory of goods in proportion to sales possibilities." Doering replied that customer feedback indicated that no one wanted the turf gators and that they were overpriced, but Deere was firm. Doering also repeated that it could not afford another salesperson, but again Deere was firm. One week later, on October 24, 1996, Doering notified Deere in writing that it was terminating the distributorship agreement. Deere accepted the letter of termination, although it denied that it had required Doering to order a specific number of turf gators.

Doering brought suit against Deere for breach of the covenant of good faith and fair dealing and sought recovery of approximately $500,000, consisting of its operating losses for its golf and turf business over the last three years. Doering did not seek recovery for lost profits. Deere counterclaimed for monies previously owed.

The trial judge concluded that Doering had not articulated any legally cognizable theory of damages, in that there was no causal connection between its damage claims and the demands related to the meeting of October 17, 1996. Doering has appealed.

Doering has consistently sought to recover all its operating losses, but its theory of recovery has an elusive, chameleon-like quality. On appeal, Doering appears to have settled generally on a reliance theory of damages. The relationship between the breach and the damages, however, is unclear. As the trial judge recognized, there appears to be no causal connection between the prior years' losses and the demand that Doering purchase the turf gators. *See VMark Software, Inc. v. EMC*

Corp., 37 Mass. App. Ct. 610, 611–612 n.2, 642 N.E.2d 587 (1994) (measure of contract reliance damages is "similar to the tort standard of actual, or out-of-pocket, loss proximately suffered"). The damages sought had been sustained while the contract was being performed according to its terms, before the turf gator demand was made. According to the damages figures submitted by Doering, the agreement was a losing proposition from the outset. The damages were, therefore, caused by the bad bargain itself, not the October breach. The breach may have led Doering to terminate the contract, but it did not cause the contract losses, which Doering had already incurred.

Doering seems to recognize the unfavorable nature of the bargain as it makes no argument that the breach prevented it from continuing the contract and recouping the accrued losses. Doering also has not generally argued that the breach deprived it of the benefit of the bargain. *See* RESTATEMENT OF CONTRACTS (SECOND) § 347 (1981) ("Contract damages are ordinarily based on the injured party's expectation interest and are intended to give him the benefit of his bargain by awarding him a sum of money that will, to the extent possible, put him in as good a position as he would have been in had the contract been performed").

Relying on *VMark Software v. EMC Corp., supra*, and the RESTATEMENT (SECOND) OF CONTRACTS § 349 (1981), Doering contends instead that it is entitled to recover its operating losses for the three years prior to the "constructive termination" of the contract as "reliance" damages. As this court stated in *VMark*, "in an appropriate case, Massachusetts law permits, as an alternative to such 'expectation' damages, the recovery of 'reliance' damages, i.e., expenditures made in reliance upon a contractual obligation that was not performed."

In *VMark*, unlike this case, the injured party purchased computer hardware from a third company in "reliance on VMark's supplying it with a software product that would be fully functional in conjunction with that hardware." We concluded that the hardware would not have been purchased "but for VMark's misleading representations." Here, in contrast, the motion judge, in allowing summary judgment, rejected Doering's contention that it could prove that it entered into the contract and incurred the expenses based on various misrepresentations. Doering does not challenge this decision on appeal. The lack of a causal connection between the claimed breach and the losses is fatal to Doering's claims.

Furthermore, as provided in the RESTATEMENT (SECOND) OF CONTRACTS § 349, the "injured party has a right to damages based on his reliance interest, including expenditures made in preparation for performance or in performance," but "less any loss that the party in breach can prove with reasonable certainty the injured party would have suffered had the contract been performed." *See L. Albert & Son v. Armstrong Rubber Co.*, 178 F.2d 182, 189 (2d Cir. 1949) (where HAND, J., writing for the court, stated, "on principle therefore the proper solution would seem to be that the promisee may recover his outlay in preparation for the performance, subject to the privilege of the promisor to reduce it by as much as he can show that the promisee would have lost, if the contract had been performed"). In the instant case, Doering is seeking to recover expenditures made in preparation for perfor-mance or during performance, but has also demonstrated, through its own submissions, that the contract, as performed, had been a losing proposition since inception, separate and apart from the breach. In fact, the operating losses for the contract, while being performed by both parties, are exactly what Doering seeks to recover. We are, therefore, in the rare position of being able to judge with accuracy "what the fate of the venture would have been had it not been interrupted" by the defendant's breach. Fuller & Perdue, *The Reliance Interest in Contract Damages*, 46 YALE L.J. 52, 79 (1936).

If Doering recovered its losses as requested, it would be in a better position than if the contract had been performed. This would violate the fundamental principle first articulated by Professor Fuller and thereafter adopted by JUDGE LEARNED HAND in *Albert & Son v. Armstrong Rubber Co.*, the RESTATEMENT (SECOND) OF CONTRACTS, and this court in *Lord's & Lady's Enterprises, Inc. v. John Paul Mitchell Sys.*, 46 Mass. App. Ct. [262,] 270, that "we will not in a suit for reimbursement for losses incurred in reliance on a contract knowingly put the plaintiff in a better position than he would have [been in] . . . had the contract been fully performed."

Judgment affirmed.

UNITED STATES v. ALGERNON BLAIR, INC.
United States Court of Appeals, Fourth Circuit
479 F.2d 638 (1973)

CRAVEN, J.

May a subcontractor, who justifiably ceases work under a contract because of the prime contractor's breach, recover in quantum meruit[16] the value of labor and equipment already furnished pursuant to the contract irrespective of whether he would have been entitled to recover in a suit on the contract? We think so, and, for reasons to be stated, the decision of the district court will be reversed.

The subcontractor, Coastal Steel Erectors, Inc., brought this action under the provisions of the Miller Act, 40 U.S.C.A. § 270a et seq., in the name of the United States against Algernon Blair, Inc., and its surety, United States Fidelity and Guaranty Company. Blair had entered a contract with the United States for the construction of a naval hospital in Charleston County, South Carolina. Blair had then contracted with Coastal to perform certain steel erection and supply certain equipment in conjunction with Blair's contract with the United States. Coastal commenced performance of its obligations, supplying its own cranes for handling and placing steel. Blair refused to pay for crane rental, maintaining that it was not

---

[16] [Ed. Note: "Quantum meruit" (often called "work and labor done") was one of the early common pleading forms used in an action in *assumpsit*. Together with other "common law writs" such as *quantum valebat or goods sold and delivered*, and *money had and received*, they became known as the "common counts" because they were popular ways of pleading assumpsit actions. They were standardized forms of pleading, at least from the time of Lord Holt in 1690 until the adoption of the Rules of Trinity Term, 1831, which discarded the quantum meruit and quantum valebat counts. As this case indicates, they may appear, depending upon local practice, in modern cases. The student should not view them as anything more than pleading forms. An action in quantum meruit such as the one in this case is an action in quasi contract to protect the restitution interest.]

obligated to do so under the subcontract. Because of Blair's failure to make payments for crane rental, and after completion of approximately 28 percent of the subcontract, Coastal terminated its performance. Blair then proceeded to complete the job with a new subcontractor. Coastal brought this action to recover for labor and equipment furnished.

The district court found that the subcontract required Blair to pay for crane use and that Blair's refusal to do so was such a material breach as to justify Coastal's terminating performance. This finding is not questioned on appeal. The court then found that under the contract the amount due Coastal, less what had already been paid, totaled approximately $37,000. Additionally, the court found Coastal would have lost more than $37,000 if it had completed performance. Holding that any amount due Coastal must be reduced by any loss it would have incurred by complete performance of the contract, the court denied recovery to Coastal. While the district court correctly stated the " 'normal' rule of contract damages," we think Coastal is entitled to recover in quantum meruit.

In *United States for Use of Susi Contracting Co. v. Zara Contracting Co.*, 146 F.2d 606 (2d Cir. 1944), a Miller Act action, the court was faced with a situation similar to that involved here — the prime contractor had unjustifiably breached a subcontract after partial performance by the subcontractor. The court stated:

> For it is an accepted principle of contract law, often applied in the case of construction contracts, that the promisee upon breach has the option to forego any suit on the contract and claim only the reasonable value of his performance. 146 F.2d at 610.

The Tenth Circuit has also stated that the right to seek recovery under quantum meruit in a Miller Act case is clear. Quantum meruit recovery is not limited to an action against the prime contractor but may also be brought against the Miller Act surety, as in this case. Further, that the complaint is not clear in regard to the theory of a plaintiff's recovery does not preclude recovery under quantum meruit. *Narragansett Improvement Co. v. United States*, 290 F.2d 577 (1st Cir. 1961). A plaintiff may join a claim for quantum meruit with a claim for damages from breach of contract.

In the present case, Coastal has, at its own expense, provided Blair with labor and the use of equipment. Blair, who breached the subcontract, has retained these benefits without having fully paid for them. On these facts, Coastal is entitled to restitution in quantum meruit.

The "restitution interest," involving a combination of unjust impoverishment with unjust gain, presents the strongest case for relief. If, following Aristotle, we regard the purpose of justice as the maintenance of an equilibrium of goods among members of society, the restitution interest presents twice as strong a claim to judicial intervention as the reliance interest, since if A not only causes B to lose one unit but appropriates that unit to himself the resulting discrepancy between A and B is not one unit but two. Fuller & Perdue, *The Reliance Interest in Contract Damages*, 46 YALE L.J. 52, 56 (1936).

The impact of quantum meruit is to allow a promisee to recover the value of services he gave to the defendant irrespective of whether he would have lost money on the contract and been unable to recover in a suit on the contract. *Scaduto v. Orlando*, 381 F.2d 587, 595 (2d Cir. 1967). The measure of recovery for quantum meruit is the reasonable value of the performance, RESTATEMENT OF CONTRACTS § 347 (1932); and recovery is undiminished by any loss which would have been incurred by complete performance. 12 WILLISTON ON CONTRACTS § 1485, at 312 (3d ed. 1970). While the contract price may be evidence of reasonable value of the services, it does not measure the value of the performance or limit recovery. Rather, the standard for measuring the reasonable value of the services rendered is the amount for which such services could have been purchased from one in the plaintiff's position at the time and place the services were rendered.

Since the district court has not yet accurately determined the reasonable value of the labor and equipment use furnished by Coastal to Blair, the case must be remanded for those findings. When the amount has been determined, judgment will be entered in favor of Coastal, less payments already made under the contract. Accordingly, for the reasons stated above, the decision of the district court is reversed and remanded with instructions.

NOTES

(1)   RESTATEMENT (SECOND) OF CONTRACTS § 373, comment d: "In the case of a contract on which the [injured party] would have sustained a loss instead of having made a profit, . . . his restitution interest may give him a larger recovery than would damages on either [an expectation or reliance] basis." The right of the injured party under a losing contract to a greater amount in restitution than he could have recovered in damages has engendered much controversy. The rules stated in this section give him that right.

(2)   In *Oliver v. Campbell*, 43 Cal. 2d 298, 273 P.2d 15 (1954), plaintiff performed legal services for defendant in a divorce action under a contract with a stated fee of $750 to be paid after trial. The plaintiff had not anticipated the lengthy and time-consuming effort which followed, including a trial lasting twenty-nine days. After plaintiff had performed all except incidental tasks, the defendant insisted on substituting himself as counsel, terminating plaintiff's services. The reasonable value of plaintiff's services was $5,000. Plaintiff sought recovery of this amount but recovery was denied since plaintiff's performance was virtually complete, i.e., where plaintiff has completed performance and the other party has only a duty to pay the price, the aggrieved party is limited to the contract price. *See* RESTATEMENT (SECOND) OF CONTRACTS § 373, comment b.

PROBLEM

B agreed to build a house for *O* at a contract price of $100,000. When the house was half completed, *O* breached the contract. *B* had expended $90,000 in labor and materials. The benefit conferred upon *O* at that time (in terms of the reasonable value of having another perform the work done to that point) was $90,000. If *O* had allowed *B* to complete the contract, it is clear that the cost to *B* would have been $180,000, i.e., a loss of $80,000. What would *B* recover under the expectation, reliance, or restitution interests? *See Boomer v. Muir*, 24 P.2d 570 (Cal. App. 1933);

Southern Painting Co. v. United States, 222 F.2d 431 (10th Cir. 1955). *See also*, Chapter 1, note 1, at § 127B.3.

[2] Defaulting Plaintiff Recovery

In *Stark v. Parker*, 19 Mass. (2 Pick.) 267 (1824), plaintiff had agreed to work for a year for the total sum of $120 but had left, without cause, before the end of the year. He sought to recover $27.33 as the balance due for services he had performed before departing. The court held for the defendant, stating in part,

> And it is no less repugnant to the well established rules of civil jurisprudence, than to the dictates of moral sense, that a party who deliberately and understandingly enters into an engagement and voluntarily breaks it, should be permitted to make that very engagement the foundation of a claim to compensation for services under it. * * * The law, indeed, is most reasonable in itself. It denies only to a party an advantage from his own wrong.

Id. at 270.

In *Britton v. Turner*, 6 N.H. 481 (1834), another plaintiff sought recovery for having performed services for nine and one-half months before voluntarily leaving and breaking the one-year contract that was to pay him a total of $120. The court recognized that if it adhered to the rule that a defaulting plaintiff could never recover, the defendant in this case would have received nearly five sixths of the value of a whole years labor at no cost. The court stated,

> By the operation of this rule, then, the party who attempts performance may be placed in a much worse situation than he who wholly disregards his contract, and the other party may receive much more, by the breach of the contract, than the injury which he has sustained by such breach. . . * * * If a person makes a contract fairly he is entitled to have it fully performed, and if this is not done, he is entitled to damages. . . . The benefit and advantage which the party takes by the labor, therefore, is the amount of value which he receives, if any, after deducting the amount of damage.

Id. at 487. Thus, under this analysis which became the prevailing view (though modern statutes later made the point moot by requiring periodic wage payments), a defaulting plaintiff could recover no more than a *pro rata* share of the contract price, regardless of the value of the benefit conferred, minus whatever damage the defendant could prove as resulting from the breach.

TELESPECTRUM WORLDWIDE, INC. v.
GRACE MARIE ENTERPRISES, INC.

United States District Court, Eastern District of Pennsylvania
2000 U.S. Dist. LEXIS 17608 (2000)

FULLAM, J.

Plaintiff Telespectrum Worldwide, Inc. is a provider of telemarketing services. Defendant Grace Marie Enterprises, Inc. purchases telemarketing services on behalf of her clients, who are involved in running political campaigns. In August 1998, the parties entered into a written contract wherein Telespectrum agreed to make political telemarketing calls for Grace Marie in connection with various elections to be held that fall.

The calls were divided into programs by geographic area and type of call, and each had specific requirements contained in a program guide. As time went on, other programs were added, some of which were memorialized in written addenda to the contract and some of which were not. For each program, the dates, times and number of calls to be made were specified, and in cases where a regional accent on the part of callers was considered desirable, particular Telespectrum facilities or "call centers" would be utilized. It was also contemplated that the data collected from the calls made by Telespectrum at its various call centers would be transmitted to Grace Marie on a daily basis, enabling the latter's clients to make use of the information in the course of their political campaigns.

On Thursday, October 29, 1998, Telespectrum's main computer server completely malfunctioned, or "crashed," as did plaintiff's backup computer system, one effect of which was that Telespectrum's ability to transmit call data was severely compromised. In addition, Telespectrum experienced significant work attendance problems on Saturday, October 31 and Sunday, November 1, 1998 — the weekend before Election Day. I credit the testimony of Jody Novacek, the president and owner of Grace Marie that she was not informed of the extent and severity of the computer and attendance problems at the time they occurred, and that Telespectrum in fact solicited additional political telemarketing assignments from Grace Marie during this time. However, much of the work contracted for prior to Election Day was not completed per Grace Marie's specifications; indeed, some of the programs were not completed at all. As a result, Grace Marie was compelled [to] discount its services when it billed its own clients.

After Election Day, Telespectrum submitted an invoice for telemarketing services to Grace Marie in the amount of approximately $1.2 million. Telespectrum admits that this invoice was inaccurate, but contends that it is owed over $900,000 for services that were actually performed, and for which Grace Marie was paid by its clients. There is evidence that the parties attempted to adjust the amount to be paid by Grace Marie, and Ms. Novacek testified that a "settlement" in the amount of $225,000 was agreed upon; however, I do not believe that there was ever a meeting of the minds on this issue. To date, Grace Marie has paid Telespectrum $213,801.

It is clear that Telespectrum, as the party in breach, is not entitled to payment in full; I reject plaintiff's contention that the server crash was an event beyond its reasonable control, especially given the absence of any evidence that the server was under the control of some third party. Nevertheless, Telespectrum partially performed its obligations under the contract, and is entitled under the terms thereof to be paid for the work that was completed in a satisfactory manner. Under Texas law, which governs this contract, "the principle of unjust enrichment suggests that restitution is an appropriate remedy *in circumstances where the agreement contemplated is . . . not fully performed." City of Harker Heights v. Sun Meadows Land, Ltd.*, 830 S.W.2d 313, 319 (Tex. App. 1992) (emphasis added); *see also* RESTATEMENT (SECOND) OF CONTRACTS § 374 (1981) ("If a party justifiably refuses to perform on the ground that his remaining duties of performance have been discharged by the other party's breach, the party in breach is entitled to restitution for any benefit that he has conferred by way of part performance or reliance in excess of the loss that he has caused by his own breach.").

"Since the party seeking restitution is responsible for posing the problem of measurement of benefit, doubts will be resolved against him and his recovery will not exceed . . . the other party's increase in wealth." RESTATEMENT (SECOND) OF CONTRACTS § 374 cmt. b (1981). I conclude, therefore, that Grace Marie must pay to plaintiff that portion of what it was paid by its clients that is attributable to Telespectrum's services. Grace Marie was paid $828,164 by its clients. Its profit or "margin" on this amount was $282,123. In addition, Grace Marie discounted its services in light of Telespectrum's breach in the amount of $162,950. My preliminary calculation of the restitution owed to Telespectrum, therefore, is as follows: $828,164 less $282,123 less $162,950 less the $213,801 which Grace Marie has already paid, for a total of $169,290.

[3] Quasi Contract

ANDERSON v. SCHWEGEL
Idaho Court of Appeals
796 P.2d 1035 (1990)

WALTERS, J.

In April of 1980, George Anderson and Ronald Schwegel met to discuss the possibility of restoring Anderson's 1935 Plymouth automobile. Following a brief inspection of the vehicle, the parties orally agreed that Schwegel would restore the automobile for $6,000. However, each of the parties had a different understanding of what was meant by the term "restore." Anderson understood "restore" to mean the complete restoration of the car, except for upholstery, and including body work and engine repairs. In contrast, Schwegel intended that, for $6,000, he would "restore" only the body of the automobile, including painting, but that any engine work that might be needed would be an additional expense. The parties did not attempt to reduce their agreement to writing, and neither of them was aware of the misunderstanding. Schwegel had the vehicle towed to his shop and began the restoration work.

In 1981, Schwegel informed Anderson that substantial engine work was needed to make the vehicle driveable. Upon Anderson's instruction, Schwegel sublet the repair work to K & F Automotive Shop. Anderson discussed the nature and extent of the repairs with K & F's shop proprietor, and, without questioning whether the engine repair costs were included in the original $6,000 quoted by Schwegel, gave his authorization for the work to proceed.

In December of 1982, Anderson received an itemized statement of the work completed as of that date. The statement listed amounts for the body work performed by Schwegel, but also included costs for parts and labor attributed to the engine overhaul. Although the statement exceeded the $6,000 price agreed upon by more than $2,000, Anderson expressed no disagreement with it. In fact, Anderson subsequently tendered a payment of $2,000 in addition to $3,000 he already had paid.

Later, the parties had another conversation concerning Anderson's desire to make the automobile roadworthy, a task requiring the repair or replacement of gauges, wires, glass and lights, among other items. Anderson assented to having the work done. Schwegel sublet the mechanical work to Rick Vance Auto but also performed some of the work at his own shop.

The final billing included $5,896.01 for body work by Schwegel; $2,184.57 for the engine overhaul by K & F; and $1,719.69 for the "roadworthy" repairs, for a total of $9,800.27. Anderson previously had tendered payments to Schwegel totaling $5,000. When Schwegel demanded payment of the additional balance of $4,800.27, Anderson refused, stating that the contract was for $6,000, and that only $1,000 remained due. Anderson then filed this action seeking to enforce the contract price of $6,000 and to recover possession of the Plymouth. Schwegel counterclaimed to recover the full amount owing on the bill.

Following a trial without a jury, the magistrate determined that the parties had failed to reach a "meeting of the minds" on the meaning of the material term " 'restore," and thus no contract existed between them. However, the magistrate held that Anderson was liable to Schwegel under quasi-contract, permitting Schwegel to recover $4,800.27 for the reasonable value of services and materials retained by Anderson. On appeal by Anderson to the district court, the magistrate's judgment was affirmed. Anderson then brought this appeal from the district court's decision.

The issue on appeal concerns the measure of recovery under quasi-contract, a contract implied in law. As the Idaho Supreme Court has explained:

> [A] contract implied in law is not a contract at all, but an obligation imposed by law for the purpose of bringing about justice and equity without reference to the intent or the agreement of the parties and, in some cases, in spite of an agreement between the parties. (Citations omitted.) It is a non-contractual obligation that is to be treated procedurally as if it were a contract, and is often referred to as quasi contract, unjust enrichment, implied in law contract or restitution. . . .
>
> . . . As the essence of a contract implied in law lies in the fact that the defendant has received a benefit which it would be inequitable for him to retain, it necessarily follows that the measure of recovery in a quasi-

contractual action is not the amount of the enrichment, but the actual amount of enrichment which, as between the two parties, it would be unjust for one party to retain. *Continental Forest Products, Inc. v. Chandler Supply Co.*, 95 Idaho 739, 743, 518 P.2d 1201, 1205 (1974).

As a corollary, the amount of recovery to be obtained in quasi-contract is a factual issue for resolution by the trier of fact. Here, the magistrate measured the benefit that Anderson unjustly retained as the reasonable value of the services he received from Schwegel, and awarded to Schwegel a recovery in that amount. Anderson disputes that award, maintaining that the proper measure of recovery in this case should have been the increased value of the automobile which resulted from the services, rather than the reasonable value of those services conferred.

We note that in cases where restitution is available for mistaken improvements to another's property, the usual measure of recovery is the value to the property of the enhancement.

Here, Anderson either requested the services or assented to having them performed for his own benefit. Thus, the performance rendered may be properly valued as services, regardless of whether the services actually enhanced the value of the automobile. We conclude that upon these facts, the magistrate did not err in valuing the benefit conferred as the reasonable value of the services provided.

Anderson also contends that the magistrate improperly allowed Schwegel to recover the twenty percent mark-up he charged on some of the sublet work. We note that the correct measure for unjust enrichment is not the loss suffered by one party, but rather is the benefit unjustly retained by the other party. The magistrate found that the amount billed by Schwegel, including the mark-up, represented the reasonable value of the benefit received by Anderson. In the absence of clear error, these findings must be sustained.

Anderson further maintains that, although the magistrate entered findings as to the total benefit received by Anderson, the judge failed to expressly determine that portion of the benefit which Anderson "unjustly" retained, and that the judgment must therefore be reversed. We observe that the magistrate found the total benefit received by Anderson to be $9,800.27, the reasonable amount of all the services received. The parties stipulated to the fact that Anderson had, prior to trial, made payments totaling $5,000. Thus, the $4,800.27 awarded to Schwegel is the difference between the total benefit received and the amount already paid to Schwegel. This sum clearly represents the amount of enrichment which the magistrate found would be unjust for Anderson to retain. The magistrate's findings, affirmed by the district court, are supported by substantial evidence and we will not disturb them on appeal.

NOTES

(1)   According to *R. M. Williams Co., Inc. v. Frabizzio*, 1993 Del. Super. LEXIS 55, *44 (1993):

> The modern suit for restitution in quasi contract, or under a contract implied in law, as it is sometimes described, is based on the principle that, "A person who has been unjustly enriched at the expense of another is

required to make restitution to that other." RESTATEMENT OF RESTITUTION § 1 (1937). Pomponius stated a similar principle in the second century A.D.: "For this by nature is equitable, that no one be made richer through another's loss." * * * Unjust enrichment is defined as "the unjust retention of a benefit to the loss of another, or the retention of money or property of another, against the fundamental principles of justice or equity and good conscience." The separate cause of action for "unjust enrichment" is the doctrinal descendant of the old common law action in general assumpsit, as opposed to a common law action in special assumpsit for breach of contract where no money remained due.

(2) "The theory on which the plaintiff in this suit seeks money damages — unjust enrichment, sometimes referred to as restitution, a contract implied in law, quasi contract, or an action in assumpsit — is *an action at law*. The confusion with equity emanates from the decision of the King's Bench in 1760 in the case of *Moses v. Macferlan*, 2 Burr. 1005, 97 Eng. Rep 676, where Lord Mansfield stated that the defendant's obligation came 'from the ties of natural justice' founded in 'the equity of the plaintiff's case.' As Professor Palmer explains, the statement concerning the action of quasi contract being equitable has been repeated many times, but merely refers to the way in which a claim should be approached 'since it is clear that the action is at law and the relief given is a simple money judgment.' (1 PALMER, LAW OF RESTITUTION, sec 1.2, at 7 (1978)) (emphasis supplied)." *Guaranty National Title Co., Inc. v. J. E. G. Associates*, 1995 U.S. Dist. LEXIS 17772, *17 (N.D. Ill. 1995)

(3) Innumerable cases have made the distinction between "implied in fact" vs. "implied in law" contracts. Thus, the United States Supreme Court states, "An agreement implied in fact is founded upon a meeting of minds, which, although not embodied in an express contract, is inferred, as a fact, from conduct of the parties showing, in the light of the surrounding circumstances, their tacit understanding. . . . By contrast, an agreement implied in law is a fiction of the law where a promise is imputed to perform a legal duty, as to repay money obtained by fraud or duress." *Hercules, Inc. v. United States*, 516 U.S. 417 (1996). A state Supreme Court emphasized the distinction in similar language: "Contracts implied-in-law and those implied-in-fact are two distinct concepts. A contract implied-in-fact is a true contract whose existence and terms are inferred from the conduct of the parties. Such an agreement is grounded in the parties' agreement and tacit understanding. In contrast, a contract implied-in-law is not a true contract at all. It is a legal fiction, a non-contractual obligation created by the courts to provide a contractual remedy where none existed at common law." *Kennedy v. Forest*, 129 Idaho 584, 930 P.2d 1026 (1997).

(4) Where a contract is unenforceable because of the Statute of Frauds, but one party has conferred a benefit on the other, such as a down payment, an action in restitution lies in quasi contract for the recovery of the amount by which the defendant has been unjustly enriched. *See, e.g., Montenaro Bros. Bldrs. v. Snow*, 460 A.2d 1297 (1983). Similarly, courts grant restitution of benefits conferred under voidable contracts as well as contracts discharged because of the non-occurrence of a condition, impracticability, or frustration of purpose. *See* at § 127B.2.

ESTATE OF FRANCES CLEVELAND v. GORDEN
Tennessee Court of Appeals
837 S.W.2d 68 (1992)

KOCH, J.

Frances Cleveland supported herself with her social security benefits, some modest investment income, and the income from a trust fund established by a deceased sister. She lived alone in her later years, although her nieces and nephews occasionally stayed with her when she became ill.

Ms. Cleveland became seriously ill in January 1984. One of her neighbors telephoned Ms. Gorden [Ms. Cleveland's niece] in Houston, and Ms. Gorden immediately traveled to Nashville because Ms. Cleveland was then 92-years-old and had no one else to take care of her. Ms. Gorden tried to look after her aunt for approximately three weeks but Ms. Cleveland required continuous skilled care. In February 1984, Ms. Gorden placed Ms. Cleveland in a nursing home in Shelbyville where she could be near her friends and other more distant relatives.

When her aunt entered the nursing home, Ms. Gorden discussed Ms. Cleveland's finances with the officers at the Third National Bank in Nashville where Ms. Cleveland maintained her accounts, including [a] trust account established for her by her sister. The bank officers advised Ms. Gorden that she would be able to obtain full reimbursement for any expenditures she made on her aunt's behalf if she opened a separate account for that purpose and maintained detailed expense records. Ms. Gorden accordingly opened a checking account and made arrangements with Third National Bank to deposit into that account all the income from a trust her mother had established for her years earlier.

Beginning in February 1984, Ms. Gorden used her own funds to pay most of her aunt's bills. These expenses included Ms. Cleveland's nursing home bills, her other medical expenses[,] the utilities for her Linden Avenue house, and occasional small personal sundries purchased for Ms. Cleveland. At the same time, all of Ms. Cleveland's social security benefits and other income, including rental income from her house, continued to be deposited into Ms. Cleveland's own account. Third National Bank occasionally deposited some of Ms. Cleveland's funds in the account maintained by Ms. Gorden when Ms. Gorden's own funds were insufficient to pay all of her aunt's expenses.

Ms. Cleveland's health stabilized after she entered the nursing home. Ms. Gorden visited her occasionally and received periodic reports from the nursing home about her aunt's health. Ms. Cleveland was aware that Ms. Gorden was using her own money to pay the nursing home bills and told a companion that Ms. Gorden "would get everything she had, if there was anything left." In January 1989, Ms. Cleveland finally gave Ms. Gorden a limited power of attorney authorizing Ms. Gorden to write checks on Ms. Cleveland's account to pay for her medical and living expenses.

Ms. Cleveland died in the nursing home on March 15, 1989. Her 1976 will was admitted to probate, and the probate court appointed a substitute administrator after Third National Bank declined to serve as executor. Ms. Gorden filed a timely claim seeking reimbursement for the $99,741 she spent on Ms. Cleveland's behalf from 1984 through 1989. She did not seek payment for all the other services she had rendered to her aunt. The administrator opposed the claim on the grounds that these expenditures were gifts since Ms. Cleveland had never agreed to reimburse her niece. The probate court agreed and denied the claim. Ms. Gorden has perfected this appeal.

This case requires us to decide whether Ms. Gorden was a capricious intermeddler who is not entitled to reimbursement for her expenditures on Ms. Cleveland's behalf because of her kinship with Ms. Cleveland. Far from being an intermeddler, we find that Ms. Gorden was acting out of a sense of family obligation. We also find, contrary to the probate court, that Ms. Cleveland knew that Ms. Gorden expected to be reimbursed for the expenditures she was making on Ms. Cleveland's behalf.

A person who voluntarily and officiously pays another's debts is not entitled to reimbursement. RESTATEMENT OF RESTITUTION §§ 2, 112 (1936); *see also Walker v. Walker*, 138 Tenn. 679, 681–82, 200 S.W. 825, 825 (1918) (person voluntarily paying another's debt without fraud, accident, mistake, or agreement is not entitled to subrogation); *Goodfriend v. United American Bank*, 637 S.W.2d 870. 872 (Tenn. Ct. App. 1982) (a mere volunteer, intermeddler, or stranger, or one acting officiously in paying another's debt is not entitled to subrogation).

The general rule is not applicable when the payment is made under the compulsion of a moral obligation, in ignorance of the real state of facts, or under an erroneous impression of one's legal duty. *United States Fidelity & Guaranty Co. v. Elam*, 198 Tenn. 194, 209, 278 S.W.2d 693, 700 (1955). Thus, a person who pays another's debt because of a moral obligation is not an officious intermeddler and is entitled to reimbursement unless the payment was gratuitous.

A moral obligation is a duty that cannot be legally enforced. It springs from the common sense of justice and fairness shared by all honorable persons and is more than a desire to be charitable or to give a gift. A moral obligation is perhaps best epitomized by the obligation family members commonly feel to support each other. Accordingly, the Tennessee Supreme Court has held that a woman who voluntarily undertook to care for her invalid sister was not only moved by sisterly affection, and by that feeling of compassion which would arise in the breast of any one possessed of normal sympathies; but she was, in a sense, under a form of moral compulsion. The burden had been cast on her, and she would not throw it off without a gross violation of duty and a shock of the moral sense. *Key v. Harris*, 116 Tenn. 161, 171–72, 92 S.W. 235, 237 (1905).

Even though they are not intermeddlers, family members are generally precluded from recovering for services provided to their close relatives because the law presumes that the services were a gratuitous part of the relationship when the relatives live together as part of the same family. The reasons for the presumption are that "family life abounds in acts of reciprocal kindness which tend to promote the comfort and convenience of the family, and that the introduction of commercial considerations into the relations of persons so closely bound together would expel this spirit of mutual beneficence and to that extent mar family unity." *Key v. Harris*, 116 Tenn. at 171, 92 S.W. at 237.

The presumption that family members' services are gratuitous is not conclusive. It can be rebutted by proof of an express agreement to pay for the services or by proof of circumstances showing that the relative accepting the benefit of the services knew or should have known that the relative performing them expected compensation or reimbursement. *Gorrell v. Taylor*, 107 Tenn. at 570, 64 S.W. at 888; *In re Estate of Hicks*, 510 S.W.2d 263, 265 (Tenn. Ct. App. 1972).

We concur with the probate court's conclusion that Ms. Gorden did not intend her expenditures on Ms. Cleveland's behalf to be a gift. We do not concur, however, with its conclusion that the record does not contain proof of circumstances demonstrating that Ms. Cleveland knew or should have known that Ms. Gorden expected to be reimbursed.

The proof quickly dispels any notion that Ms. Gorden undertook to support her aunt gratuitously. The responsibility was thrust upon her, and she responded partly because of her family obligations and partly because no other relative was willing to take on the task. Ms. Cleveland's bankers told Ms. Gorden that she could be reimbursed, and from the outset, Ms. Gorden manifested her desire for reimbursement by maintaining detailed records of her expenditures as the bankers requested. While her arrangement with her aunt could have been better structured with the assistance of counsel, Ms. Gorden should not be penalized for failing to seek legal advice when she decided to help Ms. Cleveland.

Ms. Gorden's assistance to her aunt went beyond what would normally have been expected of family members in similar circumstances. The ladies were not close relatives and had never lived together in a family relationship. Even though [there was] no express agreement to reimburse Ms. Gorden for her expenditures, Ms. Cleveland knew that Ms. Gorden was supporting her and accepted the support. Since Ms. Cleveland had left Ms. Gorden only a portion of her furniture, her statement that Ms. Gorden "would get everything she had, if there was anything left" indicates her expectation that Ms. Gorden would be compensated with a larger share of her estate.

We reverse the denial of Ms. Gorden's claim and remand the case to the probate court for further proceedings consistent with this opinion. We tax the costs to Frances Cleveland's estate for which execution, if necessary, may issue.

NOTES

(1)   RESTATEMENT OF RESTITUTION § 113 (1937), cmt. a:

> The principle underlying the rule stated in § 112 is that one who officiously intervenes to perform the duty of another is not entitled to compensation. Under the circumstances stated in this Section, the necessity of protecting the interests of persons entitled by law to have things or services supplied to them by another ordinarily prevents the intervention even of a stranger from being officious.

(2)   Edwards bought a backhoe loader on credit from Ansley who retained a security interest in the loader. A security interest is a property interest in the collateral retained, in this case, by the owner to assure repayment of the obligation.

The holder of the interest may foreclose and retake the collateral if the obligation is not met. After using the loader for three years, Edwards took it to Growney for repair, but did not inform Growney about the Ansley interest. Growney, who thought Edwards owned the loader free of any creditor's security interest, completed the repairs in exchange for Edwards' promissory note that was never paid. Edwards then defaulted on his contract with Ansley who repossessed the loader. Ansley was unaware of Growney's services. Growney sought to recover the value of the benefit conferred, i.e., the reasonable value of the repairs, from Ansley who was arguably unjustly enriched. In holding for Ansley, the court recognized the tension between the prevention of unjust enrichment and thrusting an obligation on a party who neither requested nor was aware of such benefits. *Tom Growney Equipment, Inc. v. Ansley*, 888 P.2d 992 (1994).

(3)   Plaintiff, a resident taxpayer of Riley Township, Ohio, and his four children of compulsory school age lived more than four miles from the nearest high school. Ohio law required the township and the county board of education to provide transportation for such children living more than four miles from the nearest public school. Both refused to provide such transportation and the father transported the children to school each day. At the end of the school year, he presented to the county board of education for $397 which the board refused to pay. The court recognized the grave public concern in ascertaining that children receive an education. The performance of this legal obligation which should have been performed by the county was a benefit to the county which was unjustly enriched at the expense of the father. Moreover, the father was a "proper person" to perform the obligation and was, therefore, not operating as an officious intermeddler. The county argued that the father could have pursued a writ of *mandamus* ("We command") to have a court order the board to provide transportation. While that remedy may have been available, it was not an exclusive remedy under these facts. The plaintiff is entitled to recover the reasonable value of the benefit conferred by non-officiously performing the duty of another. *Sommers v. Putnam County Board of Education*, 248 N.E. 682 (Ohio 1925).

E.   SPECIFIC PERFORMANCE

[1]   Background[17]

The damage remedy for breach of contract provides substitutional relief to the aggrieved party rather than the very performance promised. There are situations, however, where a court should provide the specific performance promised.[18] Since the aggrieved party receives exactly what he was promised when he receives specific relief, such a remedy may be preferable.[19] Unlike the civil law system

---

[17] This section is an edited version of MURRAY ON CONTRACTS § 128 (5th ed. 2011).

[18] Specific Performance and Injunctions are explored in §§ 357–369 of the RESTATEMENT (SECOND) OF CONTRACTS.

[19] In terms of economic analysis, it may be argued that specific performance neither overcompensates nor undercompensates the aggrieved party's expectation interest and is, therefore, more precise than substitutional damages. *See* SCHWARTZ, *THE CASE FOR SPECIFIC PERFORMANCE*, 89 YALE L.J. 271 (1979). *But*

where specific performance is ordered wherever possible, however, the common law system from its inception was based on the notion of substitutional relief. To this day, substitutional relief in money damages is the normal common law remedy for breach of contract whereas specific performance, injunctions, and other equitable remedies are extraordinary remedies.

The fascinating story of the development of equity courts is beyond the coverage of this book.[20] It is, however, important to consider some salient background though the treatment is necessarily incomplete. In general terms, common law courts were *property* oriented, i.e., any notion of specific relief came through proprietary actions, such as replevin to recover specific property owned by the plaintiff. An action for contract damages was often in the form of the old common law action (writ) of debt based on the half-completed exchange idea, e.g., failure to pay for goods delivered. If the plaintiff prevailed in his debt action, he would be awarded a judgment for the price of the goods. In effect, this provided the seller with specific performance since the seller was receiving exactly what he had bargained for. The early courts, however, did not think in those terms but rather in terms of substitutional relief for breach of contract.

Equity jurisprudence and courts of equity came from another source. Common law writs such as debt and covenant were quite narrow. Until the sixteenth century, there was no writ to enforce what we would now view as the typical modern contract, an exchange of informal promises. Where a party had an otherwise meritorious claim but could find no procrustean common law writ to pursue that claim in a common law court, he may have sought assistance from the Chancellor who was the keeper of the King's conscience, a high official who was supposed to operate *ex aequo et bono*, i.e., in equity and good conscience. Since chancellors were typically clerics, it is not remarkable that canon law influenced their thinking. The Chancellor would not provide relief to someone who acted unreasonably or unconscionably. The classic equitable maxims include the requirement that a party seeking equity must come to the equity court "with clean hands." An equitable remedy is subject to the *discretion* of the court because it developed from the discretion of the chancellor. A party would seek relief from the Chancellor because there was no adequate remedy at law (typically, no proper writ), and when the Chancellor granted a remedy, it was based, in part, on that fact. Thus, the normal remedy was the remedy at law, but if no law remedy was available, one could appeal to the King's conscience through the keeper of that conscience for an extraordinary remedy.

When the Chancellor granted relief, he would do it in the form of a decree, i.e., an order to a person to perform an act or refrain from performing an act. The common law courts were not concerned with ordering anyone to do anything. They were typically concerned with awarding judgments for money and those judgments could be satisfied by having the sheriff seize and sell the defendant's property. Thus, the Chancellor (equity) operated *in personam* — ordering the person, while courts of law operated in rem — against the property of the defendant. Again,

---

see KRONMAN, *SPECIFIC PERFORMANCE*, 45 U. CHI. L. REV. 351 (1978) (suggesting that specific performance may overcompensate the claimant).

[20] *See* FARNSWORTH, *LEGAL REMEDIES FOR BREACH OF CONTRACT*, 70 COLUM. L. REV. 1145, 1149–56 (1970).

however, the *in personam* equitable remedy had been designed to overcome the inadequacies of common law remedies. By the sixteenth century, after assumpsit, equity "followed the law" in requiring the same elements to be shown for an enforceable contract as did courts of law. The question then began to turn on the nature of the remedy. The remedy, however, had clearly become the extraordinary remedy. The claimant was supposed to pursue his remedy at law and only if that remedy proved inadequate would the court of equity entertain jurisdiction. If equity granted jurisdiction, again, it would "follow the law" in requiring all other elements of an enforceable contract to be shown. It might, however, withhold equitable relief because, in its discretion, it might conclude that such relief would be too great a hardship on the defendant or that the plaintiff had operated less than fairly or, again, had come to the court of conscience, the court of equity, with unclean hands. The plaintiff may not have been diligent and may, therefore, have lost favor in the eyes of the court of equity because "equity aids the vigilant."

There are no longer any separate courts of equity. Law courts now sit as courts of equity where the relief sought in a given case is specific performance, an injunction, or other form of equitable relief. The court is being asked for discretionary relief which is filled with historic notions of equity and good conscience. The discretion is not unbridled because it must be exercised on the basis of much of the history of the development of equity. The judge in an equity case may still be called "chancellor" for that case.[21] Whatever the judge is called, where equitable relief is sought, the ambience changes. There are no jurors because it is the judge, the successor to the chancellor, who will make the *ex aequo et bono* judgment as to whether the plaintiff is entitled to the extraordinary relief sought.[22] If the court decides to grant relief, it can mold a decree to fit the case precisely, i.e., it need not be concerned with all-or-nothing remedies. Specific performance or an injunction may not be completely effective relief. The court may, therefore, order performance that is not identical to the promised performance.[23] It may also attach money damages to its decree to provide complete relief,[24] or it may condition its order on certain performance by the party seeking equitable relief.[25] Specific performance or an injunction may be granted notwithstanding a provision for liquidated damages.[26] "The objective of the court in granting

---

[21] *See, e.g.*, McIlwain v. Bank of Harrisburg, 713 S.W.2d 469 (1987).

[22] Equitable matters are triable *de novo* on appeal, i.e., factual issues are tried *de novo* on the record and reach a conclusion independent of the trial court except that where credible evidence is in conflict on a material issue of fact, the appellate court considers and may give weight to the fact that the trial court heard and observed the witnesses and accepted one version of the facts rather than another. Palas v. Black, 414 N.W.2d 805 (Neb. 1987).

[23] *See* Chastain v. Schomburg, 367 S.E.2d 230 (Ga. 1988) (court cannot decree specific performance of a contract where vendor purports to sell land of another, but it can order specific performance of vendor's own interest in the land).

[24] *See* Tamarind Lithography Workshop v. Sanders, 143 Cal. App. 3d 571 (1983) (injunction to prevent continued distribution of film without screen credits for writer-director-producer — $25,000 damages to time of trial). *See also* Chastain v. Schomburg, *supra* (where the court could only order specific performance in part and suggested that damages could be attached for remaining compensation).

[25] *See* Ruth v. Crane, 392 F. Supp. 724, 734 (E.D. Pa. 1975), *aff'd*, 564 F.2d 90 (3d Cir. 1977). *See also* RESTATEMENT (SECOND) OF CONTRACTS § 363.

[26] See RESTATEMENT (SECOND) OF CONTRACTS § 361 and the earlier discussion of this concept at

equitable relief is to do complete justice to the extent that this is feasible."[27]

We have seen that the normal substitutional remedy of damages is subject to limitations such as foreseeability, certainty, and mitigation. Since the ordinary remedy is so circumscribed, it is not remarkable that extraordinary equitable remedies contain special limitations. It is important to explore those limitations.

[2]   Limitations on Granting Equitable Remedies

INADEQUATE REMEDY AT LAW

In an action at law for damages, scores of cases repeat the principle that damages must be proved with "reasonable certainty." Where damages cannot be proved according to that standard, there is no adequate remedy at law which is an essential basis for providing an equitable remedy.

WALGREEN COMPANY v. SARA CREEK PROPERTY COMPANY
United States Court of Appeals, Seventh Circuit
966 F.2d 273 (1992)

POSNER, J.

This appeal from the grant of a permanent injunction raises fundamental issues concerning the propriety of injunctive relief. The essential facts are simple. Walgreen has operated a pharmacy in the Southgate Mall in Milwaukee since its opening in 1951. Its current lease, signed in 1971 and carrying a 30-year, 6-month term, contains, as had the only previous lease, a clause in which the landlord, Sara Creek, promises not to lease space in the mall to anyone else who wants to operate a phannacy or a store containing a pharmacy. Such an exclusivity clause, common in shopping-center leases, is occasionally challenged on antitrust grounds, [but Sara Creek did not pursue this appeal on antitrust grounds].

In 1990, fearful that its largest tenant — what in real estate parlance is called the "anchor tenant" — having gone broke was about to close its store, Sara Creek informed Walgreen that it intended to buy out the anchor tenant and install in its place a discount store operated by Phar-Mor Corporation, a "deep discount" chain, rather than, like Walgreen, just a "discount" chain. Phar-Mor's store would occupy 100,000 square feet, of which 12,000 would be occupied by a pharmacy the same size as Walgreen's. The entrances to the two stores would be within a couple of hundred feet of each other.

Walgreen filed this diversity suit for breach of contract against Sara Creek and Phar-Mor and asked for an injunction against Sara Creek's letting the anchor premises to Phar-Mor. After an evidentiary hearing, the judge found a breach of

---

§ 125(D)(1). See also Fabian v. Sather, 316 N.W.2d 10 (Minn. 1982), suggesting that, when vendors resell land to a third party, they can recover only liquidated damages under their contract with the original breaching buyer rather than actual damages.

[27] RESTATEMENT (SECOND) OF CONTRACTS § 358, cmt. a.

argument over damages

Walgreen's lease and entered a permanent injunction against Sara Creek's letting the anchor tenant premises to Phar-Mor until the expiration of Walgreen's lease. He did this over the defendants' objection that Walgreen had failed to show that its remedy at law — damages — for the breach of the exclusivity clause was inadequate. Sara Creek had put on an expert witness who testified that Walgreen's damages could be readily estimated, and Walgreen had countered with evidence from its employees that its damages would be very difficult to compute, among other reasons because they included intangibles such as loss of goodwill.

Sara Creek reminds us that damages are the norm in breach of contract as in other cases. Many breaches, it points out, are "efficient," in the sense that they allow resources to be moved into a more valuable use. Perhaps this is one — the value of Phar-Mor's occupancy of the anchor premises may exceed the cost to Walgreen of facing increased competition. If so, society will be better off if Walgreen is paid its damages, equal to that cost, and Phar-Mor is allowed to move in rather than being kept out by an injunction. That is why injunctions are not granted as a matter of course, but only when the plaintiff's damages remedy is inadequate. Walgreen's is not, Sara Creek argues; the projection of business losses due to increased competition is a routine exercise in calculation.

Damages representing either the present value of lost future profits or (what should be the equivalent) the diminution in the value of the leasehold have either been awarded or deemed the proper remedy in a number of reported cases for breach of an exclusivity clause in a shopping-center lease. Why, Sara Creek asks, should they not be adequate here?

Sara Creek makes a beguiling argument that contains much truth, but we do not think it should carry the day. For if, as just noted, damages have been awarded in some cases of breach of an exclusivity clause in a shopping-center lease, injunctions have been issued in others. The choice between remedies requires a balancing of the costs and benefits of the alternatives. The task of striking the balance is for the trial judge, subject to deferential appellate review in recognition of its particularistic, judgmental, fact-bound character. "The question for us [appellate judges] is whether the [district] judge exceeded the bounds of permissible choice in the circumstances, not what we would have done if we had been in his shoes." *Roland Machinery Co. v. Dresser Industries, Inc.*, 749 F.2d 380, 390 (7th Cir. 1984).

damages are normal

The plaintiff who seeks an injunction has the burden of persuasion — damages are the norm, so the plaintiff must show why his case is abnormal. The benefits of substituting an injunction for damages are twofold. First, it shifts the burden of determining the cost of the defendant's conduct from the court to the parties. If it is true that Walgreen's damages are smaller than the gain to Sara Creek from allowing a second pharmacy into the shopping mall, then there must be a price for dissolving the injunction that will make both parties better off. Thus, the effect of upholding the injunction would be to substitute for the costly processes of forensic fact determination the less costly processes of private negotiation. Second, a premise of our free-market system, and the lesson of experience here and abroad as well, is that prices and costs are more accurately determined by the market than by government. A battle of experts is a less reliable method of determining the actual cost to Walgreen of facing new competition than negotiations between

Walgreen and Sara Creek over the price at which Walgreen would feel adequately compensated for having to face that competition.

That is the benefit side of injunctive relief but there is a cost side as well. Many injunctions require continuing supervision by the court, and that is costly. Some injunctions are problematic because they impose costs on third parties. A more subtle cost of injunctive relief arises from the situation that economists call "bilateral monopoly," in which two parties can deal only with each other: the situation that an injunction creates. The sole seller of widgets selling to the sole buyer of that product would be an example. But so will be the situation confronting Walgreen and Sara Creek if the injunction is upheld. Walgreen can "sell" its injunctive right only to Sara Creek, and Sara Creek can "buy" Walgreen's surrender of its right to enjoin the leasing of the anchor tenant's space to Phar-Mor only from Walgreen. The lack of alternatives in bilateral monopoly creates a bargaining range, and the costs of negotiating to a point within that range may be high. Suppose the cost to Walgreen of facing the competition of Phar-Mor at the Southgate Mall would be $1 million, and the benefit to Sara Creek of leasing to Phar-Mor would be $2 million. Then at any price between those figures for a waiver of Walgreen's injunctive right both parties would be better off, and we expect parties to bargain around a judicial assignment of legal rights if the assignment is inefficient. R.H. Coase, *The Problem of Social Cost*, 3 J. LAW & ECON. 1 (1960). But each of the parties would like to engross as much of the bargaining range as possible — Walgreen to press the price toward $2 million, Phar-Mor to depress it toward $1 million. With so much at stake, both parties will have an incentive to devote substantial resources of time and money to the negotiation process. The process may even break down, if one or both parties wants to create for future use a reputation as a hard bargainer; and if it does break down, the injunction will have brought about an inefficient result. All these are in one form or another costs of the injunctive process that can be avoided by substituting damages.

The costs and benefits of the damages remedy are the mirror of those of the injunctive remedy. The damages remedy avoids the cost of continuing supervision and third-party effects, and the cost of bilateral monopoly as well. It imposes costs of its own, however, in the form of diminished accuracy in the determination of value, on the one hand, and of the parties' expenditures on preparing and presenting evidence of damages, and the time of the court in evaluating the evidence, on the other.

The weighing up of all these costs and benefits is the analytical procedure that is or at least should be employed by a judge asked to enter a permanent injunction, with the understanding that if the balance is even the injunction should be withheld. The judge is not required to explicate every detail of the analysis and he did not do so here, but as long we are satisfied that his approach is broadly consistent with a proper analysis we shall affirm; and we are satisfied here. The determination of Walgreen's damages would have been costly in forensic resources and inescapably inaccurate. The lease had ten years to run. So Walgreen would have had to project its sales revenues and costs over the next ten years, and then project the impact on those figures of Phar-Mor's competition, and then discount that impact to present value. All but the last step would have been fraught with uncertainty.

It is difficult to forecast the profitability of a retail store over a decade, let alone to assess the impact of a particular competitor on that profitability over that period. Of course one can hire an expert to make such predictions, and if injunctive relief is infeasible the expert's testimony may provide a tolerable basis for an award of damages. We cited cases in which damages have been awarded for the breach of an exclusivity clause in a shopping-center lease. But they are awarded in such circumstances not because anyone thinks them a clairvoyant forecast but because it is better to give a wronged person a crude remedy than none at all. It is the same theory on which damages are awarded for a disfiguring injury. No one thinks such injuries readily monetizable, but a crude estimate is better than letting the wrongdoer get off scot-free (which, not incidentally, would encourage more such injuries). Sara Creek presented evidence of what happened (very little) to Walgreen when Phar-Mor moved into other shopping malls in which Walgreen has a pharmacy, and it was on the right track in putting in comparative evidence. But there was a serious question whether the other malls were actually comparable to the Southgate Mall, so we cannot conclude, in the face of the district judge's contrary conclusion, that the existence of comparative evidence dissolved the difficulties of computing damages in this case. Sara Creek complains that the judge refused to compel Walgreen to produce all the data that Sara Creek needed to demonstrate the feasibility of forecasting Walgreen's damages. Walgreen resisted, on grounds of the confidentiality of the data and the cost of producing the massive data that Sara Creek sought. Those are legitimate grounds; and the cost (broadly conceived) they expose of pretrial discovery, in turn presaging complexity at trial, is itself a cost of the damages remedy that injunctive relief saves.

Damages are not always costly to compute, or difficult to compute accurately. In the standard case of a seller's breach of a contract for the sale of goods where the buyer covers by purchasing the same product in the market, damages are readily calculable by subtracting the market price from the contract price and multiplying by the quantity specified in the contract. But this is not such a case and here damages would be a costly and inaccurate remedy; and on the other side of the balance some of the costs of an injunction are absent and the cost that is present seems low. The injunction here, like one enforcing a covenant not to compete (standardly enforced by injunction), is a simple negative injunction — Sara Creek is not to lease space in the Southgate Mall to Phar-Mor during the term of Walgreen's lease and the costs of judicial supervision and enforcement should be negligible. There is no contention that the injunction will harm an unrepresented third party. It may harm Phar-Mor but that harm will be reflected in Sara Creek's offer to Walgreen to dissolve the injunction. (Anyway Phar-Mor is a party.) The injunction may also, it is true, harm potential customers of Phar-Mor — people who would prefer to shop at a deep-discount store than an ordinary discount store — but their preferences, too, are registered indirectly. The more business Phar-Mor would have, the more rent it will be willing to pay Sara Creek, and therefore the more Sara Creek will be willing to pay Walgreen to dissolve the injunction. The only substantial cost of the injunction in this case is that it may set off a round of negotiations between the parties. In some cases, this consideration alone would be enough to warrant the denial of injunctive relief There is nothing so dramatic here. Sara Creek does not argue that it will have to close the mall if enjoined from leasing to Phar-Mor.

To summarize, the judge did not exceed the bounds of reasonable judgment in concluding that the costs (including forgone benefits) of the damages remedy would exceed the costs (including forgone benefits) of an injunction. We need not consider whether, as intimated by Walgreen, exclusivity clauses in shopping-center leases should be considered presumptively enforceable by injunctions. Although we have described the choice between legal and equitable remedies as one for case-by-case determination, the courts have sometimes picked out categories of cases in which injunctive relief is made the norm. The best-known example is specific performance of contracts for the sale of real property. The rule that specific performance will be ordered in such cases as a matter of course is a generalization of the considerations discussed above. Because of the absence of a fully liquid market in real property and the frequent presence of subjective values (many a homeowner, for example, would not sell his house for its market value), the calculation of damages is difficult; and since an order of specific performance to convey a piece of property does not create a continuing relation between the parties, the costs of supervision and enforcement if specific performance is ordered are slight. The exclusivity clause in Walgreen's lease relates to real estate, but we hesitate to suggest that every contract involving real estate should be enforceable as a matter of course by injunctions. Suppose Sara Creek had covenanted to keep the entrance to Walgreen's store free of ice and snow, and breached the covenant. An injunction would require continuing supervision, and it would be easy enough if the injunction were denied for Walgreen to hire its own ice and snow remover and charge the cost to Sara Creek. On the other hand, injunctions to enforce exclusivity clauses are quite likely to be justifiable by just the considerations present here — damages are difficult to estimate with any accuracy and the injunction is a one-shot remedy requiring no continuing judicial involvement. So there is an argument for making injunctive relief presumptively appropriate in such cases, but we need not decide in this case how strong an argument.
AFFIRMED.

NOTES

(1) *Efficient Breach.* While Judge Posner is often cited as the current luminary in exposing the benefits of the doctrine of "efficient breach," it is interesting to observe his rejection of that argument by the defendant in this case while recognizing that the argument was "beguiling" and contained "much truth."

(2) *Unique Property.* As Judge Posner indicates, the "best known example" of an equitable remedy is specific performance in a contract to sell land which involve "subjective values" such as location of the land which is necessarily unique. The buyer of the land cannot purchase a substitute elsewhere.[28] Personal property such

---

[28] Since land is unique, there has never been any question that the remedy of specific performance should be available to a buyer where the seller breaches. Where a buyer breaches a land contract, however, there is little reason to order specific performance since the seller's damage are monetary. In the 19th century, an anomalous doctrine called *"mutuality of remedy"* spawned the notion that specific performance for buyers should necessarily allow specific performance for sellers since a seller should be assured that he receives the purchase price if a court orders him to convey the land. A decree of specific performance for a buyer, however, can be conditioned on the buyer providing adequate security. RESTATEMENT (SECOND) OF CONTRACTS § 363. There are now numerous judicial statements clearly rejecting any requirement of "mutuality of remedy."

as famous paintings, heirlooms or other unique items may also allow the remedy of specific performance. In Chapter 1, we saw an example of a court ordering specific performance of a contract to sell a rare automobile (Duesenberg) that could not be procured elsewhere. The Uniform Commercial Code, § 2-716, allows the remedy of specific performance where the goods are unique, "or in other proper circumstances." Where a manufacturer limited production to 6,000 Corvette automobiles that commemorated the use of a Corvette as a pace car to start the famous Indianapolis 500 race, each franchised dealer was allocated one of the automobiles to sell. The plaintiffs were Corvette collectors. They agreed to purchase a dealer's single car. When the dealer refused to deliver it, the trial court ordered specific performance of the contract. On appeal, the court recognized that the Corvette was not unique in the traditional sense of being only one of a kind, but it was in short supply and great demand. It could not be obtained elsewhere at the price the buyers agreed to pay, and may not have been obtainable at all. The court affirmed the trial court's decree of specific performance because the facts demonstrated a "proper circumstance" for such equitable relief. *Sedmak v. Charlie's Chevrolet, Inc.*, 622 S.W.2d 694 (Mo. Ct. App. 1981).

(3)   *Judicial Supervision — Personal Service Contracts.* The *Walgreen* opinion alludes to the element of judicial supervision that is "costly" and can affect a court's willingness to enter an equitable decree. Thus, if the owner of the shopping center had breached its contractual duty to remove ice and snow from the Walgreen entrance, continuous supervision of the owner's performance of that duty would be excessive. Moreover, Walgreen could pursue a remedy like cover that the court notes provides clearly measurable damages by hiring someone to perform that duty and recovering the cost of this substituted performance from the owner. Thus, extensive supervision through a remedy of specific performance would be avoided. The judicial enforcement of the exclusivity clause in the Walgreen lease, however, did not require judicial supervision which comforted the court in affirming the grant of an injunction. The extent of necessary judicial supervision, however, is not dispositive. Thus, where rail transportation was not maintained and the plaintiff's damages were speculative, the court granted specific performance notwithstanding the need to supervise a complex rebuilding of the railroad. *Link v. State of Montana*, 591 P.2d 214 (Mont. 1979).

As we noted in Chapter 1, the difficulty and impracticability of judicial supervision is particularly evident in personal service contracts. Beyond the constitutional limitation of involuntary servitude, an attempt to force a party to perform a personal service contract raises ridiculous scenarios such as a decree forcing a famous athlete to perform. Moreover, courts are particularly wary of depriving a party from earning a living. While courts may issue injunctions against a party from breaching a contract to perform the same services for another, particularly where the broken contract contains an enforceable covenant not to compete, courts are not particularly eager to grant such injunctions in the absence of such a clause. In *American Broadcasting Company v. Wolf*, 420 N.E.2d 363 (1981), the defendant, who was a popular sportscaster, breached his duty to bargain in good faith with ABC before joining CBS. The court refused to grant equitable relief although the defendant's services were unique. Though defendant had breached his contract, the court noted that the term of the ABC contract was completed and there was no post-employment covenant not to compete. Where, however, a particular service is purely ministerial, as where a court reporter refused to deliver a document in violation of her statutory duty, there was very little necessary judicial supervision in ordering the reporter to deliver the document. *Perez v. McGar*, 630 S.W.2d 320 (Tex. App. 1982).

(4) *Fairness — Ex Aequo et Bono.* The very nature of an equitable remedy resides in the historic purpose of fairness — providing a remedy that would otherwise not be available as matter of equity and good conscience. It is important to recall the case of *McKinnon v. Benedict* in Chapter 3 as an illustration of a court refusing to grant equitable relief because, unlike a court of law asked to provide damages, a court of equity may inquire into the adequacy of consideration (the relative values exchanged) which may indicate that an equitable decree would be grossly unfair if not unconscionable.

(5) *Public Policy.* While the *Walgreen* court alludes to a possible injury to the public (third parties) that may have preferred a "deep discount" pharmacy rather than a mere "discount" pharmacy, that potential injury was viewed as too indirect. Federal antitrust laws are devised to prevent injuries to competition. Exclusivity clauses in shopping-center leases are typically upheld and, as noted, Sara Creek did not pursue an antitrust count on this appeal. Courts may, however, deny equitable relief on public policy grounds as where granting specific performance would have resulted in reversing a valid conviction of the defendant for securities fraud. *United States v. McGovern*, 822 F.2d 739 (3d Cir. 1987). *See* MURRAY ON CONTRACTS § 128D.

COMMENT: SPECIFIC PERFORMANCE — UCC AND CISG

Uniform Commercial Code Section 2-716(1) liberalized the availability of the remedy of specific performance by allowing a court to grant it not only where the goods are unique but, as seen above, "in other proper circumstances" where there are major impediments to the ability to buy substitute goods ("cover"). Unlike the common law system where the remedy of specific performance is viewed as unusual and is surrounded by limitations, civil law systems encourage the granting of specific relief. The United Nations Convention on Contracts for the International Sale of Goods (CISG) manifests this civil law influence. Under the UCC, the buyer has a right to "cover" by purchasing substitute goods from another supplier (§ 2-712). Under Article 46(1) of CISG, however, the buyer may require the breaching seller to provide substitute goods when there has been a "fundamental breach," as defined in CISG Article 25 as substantially depriving the aggrieved party of its reasonable expectations where the breaching party could have foreseen the substantial deprivation. Under Article 46(3), the buyer may require the seller to repair defects in the goods while the UCC would allow the buyer to have another repair the goods, but would not require the seller to do so. The CISG seller may require the buyer to pay the price of the goods, take delivery of them and perform other obligations (Article 62). While UCC Section 2-709 allows the seller to recover the contract price of goods that have been accepted or of conforming goods lost or destroyed after risk of their loss has passed to the buyer, the UCC would not require a buyer to take delivery of goods or perform other obligations. The seller would be relegated to remedies such as resale (§ 2-706), or damages for non-acceptance or repudiation (§ 2-708).

To avoid conflicts with common law systems under which courts would not order a contract to be specifically performed, CISG includes Article 28 stating that "[A] court is not bound to enter judgment for specific performance unless the court would do so under its own law in respect to similar contracts of sale not governed by the Convention."

Chapter 9

THIRD PARTY BENEFICIARIES

INTRODUCTION

A simple question spawned a common law history that is both rich and tortured. In exchange for A's promise of consideration, where B is induced to make a promise to A that B will render a performance for the benefit of C, may C claim a right to enforce B's promise? The formalistic answer was clear: To recognize a right in C would violate fundamental principles. No consideration had moved from C to B. C is a "stranger" to the contract. No promise was made to C. He is not in "privity." He is not a party to the contract. As a matter property law, C could be the beneficiary of a trust, but C has no rights under a simple contract between A and B. John E. Murray, Jr., 9 CORBIN ON CONTRACTS, § 41.1 (2014).

In the seventeenth century, English courts entertained no doubt that third parties such as C could enforce promises made for their benefit. In 1861, however, the earlier cases recognizing C's right were rejected or ignored. *Tweddle v. Atkinson*, 121 Eng. Rep. 762 (Q. B. 1861) (Crompton, J.). By 1915, the House of Lords declared that only a person who is a party to a contract could sue on it. While a third party could enjoy a right under a trust created for his benefit, such a right could not be conferred on a stranger to a contract since C was not a party to the contract and no consideration was moving from the "stranger" (C) to the promisor (A). *Dunlop Pneumatic Tyre Co. v. Selfridge & Co.*, A.C. 847 (H.L. 1915) (Lord Haldane). The English Law Reform Committee recommended the recognition of third party beneficiary rights in 1937, but no action was taken until 1999 when the Queen's royal assent was given to Parliament's enactment of *The Contracts (Rights of Third Parties) Act*, (1999 Chapter c.31), allowing a third party to enforce a contract right in his own name if the contract expressly provides that he may, or where a term of the contract purports to confer a benefit on him.

American courts often found fictitious ways to recognize third party beneficiary rights even before 1859. In that year, New York case sounded a clarion call to allow a third party to enforce a contract right simply because it was made for his benefit. *Lawrence v. Fox*, 20 N.Y. 268 (1859). The struggle, however, continued in various jurisdictions and even resurfaced in New York. Pennsylvania courts demonstrated considerable difficulty in recognizing third party beneficiaries and it was not until 1979 that Massachusetts finally recognized the right of a third party to sue on a contract made for his benefit. *Choate, Hall & Stewart v. SCA Servs., Inc.*, 378 Mass. 535, 392 N.E.2d 1045 (1979).

The early recognition of third party beneficiary rights focused upon two types of beneficiaries. If promisor A's performance would satisfy an actual or asserted legal obligation that promisee B owed to the third party, C would be viewed as a "creditor" beneficiary. If, however, B owed no actual or asserted legal obligation to C, B appeared to intend to make a gift to C through A's performance and C would be viewed as a "done" beneficiary. While these categories would eventually prove too restrictive, they were the categories of the FIRST RESTATEMENT OF CONTRACTS. The classic case of *Lawrence v. Fox* and its aftermath suggest different judicial views attributed to each type of beneficiary.

A. ORIGINS

LAWRENCE v. FOX
New York Court of Appeals
20 N.Y. 268 (1859)

[In November, 1857, Holly, at the request of the defendant, loaned him $300, stating at that time that he owed that sum to the plaintiff for money borrowed of the plaintiff, and had agreed to pay it to him the next day. In consideration thereof, the defendant promised to pay it to the plaintiff the next day but failed to do so. Defendant moved for nonsuit, alleging that the agreement by the defendant with Holly to pay the plaintiff was void for want of consideration and there was no privity (no contract) between the plaintiff, Lawrence, and defendant, Fox. The motion was overruled and the cause was submitted to the jury, which found a verdict for the plaintiff for the amount of the loan and interest upon which judgment was entered and from which the defendant appealed to the Superior Court where the judgment was affirmed. The defendant appealed to this court.]

GRAY, J.

But it is claimed that notwithstanding this promise was established by competent evidence, it was void for the want of consideration. It is now more than a quarter of a century since it was settled by the Supreme Court of this State that a promise in all material respects like the one under consideration was valid. [A]s to the want of privity between the plaintiff and defendant, the Supreme Court of this State [announced] "that where one person makes a promise to another for the benefit of a third person, that third person may maintain an action upon it." *Schermerhorn v. Vanderheyden*, 1 John. R. 140. In declaring upon a promise, made to the debtor by a third party to pay the creditor of the debtor, founded upon a consideration advanced by the debtor, it was unnecessary to aver a promise to the creditor; for the reason that upon proof of a promise made to the debtor to pay the creditor a promise to the creditor would be implied.

I agree that many of the cases where a promise was implied were cases of trusts, created for the benefit of the promisor and it proves nothing against the application of the rule to this case. The duty of the trustee to pay the cestui que trust, according to the terms of the trust, implied his promise to the latter to do so. In this case the defendant, upon ample consideration received from Holly, promised Holly to pay his debt to the plaintiff; the consideration received and the promise to Holly made it as plainly his duty to pay the plaintiff as if the money had been remitted to him for that purpose, and as well implied a promise to do so as if he had been made a trustee of property. The principle illustrated by the example so frequently quoted (which concisely states the case in hand) "that a promise made to one for the benefit of another, he for whose benefit it is made may bring an action for its breach," has been applied to trust cases, not because it was exclusively applicable to those cases, but because it was a principle of law, and as such applicable to those cases. The judgment should be affirmed.

NOTES

(1)   In an article by Anthony Jon Waters, *The Property in the Promise: A Study of the Third Party Beneficiary Rule*, 95 HARV. L. REV. 1105 (1995), we learn that "Holly" was a successful merchant named Hawley, $300 was a large sum of money since the annual wage of a New York worker was somewhat less than $300. The loan was probably made to allow to Fox to gamble, and Fox was to repay it the following day. Why did Lawrence choose to sue Fox rather than Hawley (Holly)? If Hawley's debt to Lawrence was also a gambling debt, it was probably unenforceable. As the author indicates, this would not only explain why Lawrence sued Fox; it would also explain why Lawrence's lawyer, Edward Chapin, decided to sue under the common count of "money had and received" — a simple argument that Fox had money belonging to Lawrence with no mention of the surrounding facts.

(2)   Eighteen years after this case, in *Vrooman v. Turner*, 69 N.Y. 280 (1877), the court held that *Lawrence v. Fox* had to be limited to cases involving the same essential facts. A beneficiary would have no cause of action unless the promisee was legally obligated to the beneficiary, which could operate as a substitute for the *privity* deemed necessary to give one a right of action on the contract. Moreover, the opinion took a dim view of such precedent — "courts are not inclined to extend the doctrine of *Lawrence v. Fox*." Various inroads have been attempted, such as the concept of a moral obligation owed to the beneficiary by the promisee (e.g., husband-promisee to wife-beneficiary) sometimes giving rise to labels such as "privity of blood." *See Seaver v. Ransom*, 224 N.Y. 233, 120 N.E. 639 (1918). There are some cases that suggest if there is any requirement of duty from the promisee to the third party, the requirement is nebulous. *See Lait v. Leon*, 40 Misc. 2d 60 (N.Y. Sup. Ct. 1963). However, even recent cases indicate that if *Vrooman* is dead, the body is warm indeed. See *Scheidl v. Universal Aviation Equip., Inc.*, 159 N.Y.S.2d 278 (1957), in which the court held that the third party beneficiary could not recover on two grounds: (1) the third party had not parted with any consideration in exchange for defendant's promise; and (2) no obligation existed between the promisee and the third party. As its main authority, the court cites *Seaver v. Ransom*, which is the closest thing to a rejuvenation of *Lawrence v. Fox* found in the New York cases. Thus, *Scheidl* operates as a "junior" *Vrooman* case, since it was not decided by the Court of Appeals in New York, the highest court in the state. It is an incredible retrogression.

(2)   If relief is to be denied an intended beneficiary, it is less harmful to deny the relief to a creditor beneficiary since he retains his action against the original debtor, the promisee. If a gift beneficiary is denied a cause of action, the intention of the parties is frustrated and the beneficiary has no recovery. Pennsylvania had a curious third party beneficiary history, which at one time allowed only donee

beneficiaries to recover. *See* Corbin, *The Law of Third Party Beneficiaries in Pennsylvania*, 77 U. PA. L. REV. 1 (1928). See also *Burke v. North Huntingdon Twp. Mun. Auth.*, 136 A.2d 310, 314 (P.a. 1957), which states: "That a third party, not in privity to the original contract, may sue as a creditor beneficiary is now the rule in Pennsylvania [citing cases]." Thus, while New York courts found difficulty in permitting a donee beneficiary to recover, Pennsylvania courts found early problems in relation to creditor beneficiaries.

(3) *Privity.* The principal case discusses the objection that a third party is not in privily with the defendant. To state that one is not in "privity" simply means that one is not a party to the contract and there is no obligation running to that party. The reasoning, however, is circular. It is a conclusion rather than a reason. It is a statement that there is no obligation to a third party beneficiary which is a conclusion. The question remains, why is there no obligation to the third party or, why is the third party not in "privity"? The "privity" conclusion provides no analytical basis for determining whether a third party beneficiary has or does not have an enforceable right under a contract made for his benefit.

B. TEST OF "INTENTION TO BENEFIT" — THE RESTATEMENTS

As courts developed rules for third-party beneficiary cases, they began distinguishing between two common fact patterns: those where promisees sought to indirectly discharge an obligation and those where promisees wanted to make a gift. This distinction was adopted in the RESTATEMENT (FIRST) OF CONTRACTS, where Section 133 divided eligible third-party beneficiaries into "done" and "creditor" beneficiaries.[1] The RESTATEMENT (SECOND) OF CONTRACTS jettisoned the donee and creditor beneficiary names but created two new beneficiary categories: "intended" and "incidental," beneficiaries.[2] Only the intended beneficiaries may enforce a

---

[1] Section 133 provides:

   (1) Where performance of a promise in a contract will benefit a person other than the promisee, that person is . . .

     (a) a donee beneficiary if it appears from the terms of the promise in view of the accompanying circumstances that the purpose of the promisee in obtaining the promise of all or part of the performance thereof is to make a gift to the beneficiary or to confer upon him a right against the promisor to some performance neither due nor supposed or asserted to be due from the promisee to the beneficiary;

     (b) a creditor beneficiary if no purpose to make a gift appears from the terms of the promise in view of the accompanying circumstances and performance of the promise will satisfy an actual or supposed or asserted duty of the promisee to the beneficiary, or a right of the beneficiary against the promisee which has been barred by the statute of limitations or by a discharge in bankruptcy, or which is unenforceable because of the Statute of Frauds;

     (c) an incidental beneficiary if neither the facts stated in Clause (a) nor those stated in Clause (h) exist.

   (2) Such a promise as is described in Subsection (1a) is a gift promise. Such a promise as is described in Subsection (1b) is a promise to discharge the promisee's duty. An analysis of the First Restatement treatment of third party beneficiaries is found in John E. Murray, Jr., 9 Corbin on Contracts, § 44.3.

[2] Section 302 provides:

   (1) Unless otherwise agreed between promisor and promisee, a beneficiary of a promise is

promise against the promisor.

HICKMAN v. SAFECO INSURANCE COMPANY
Minnesota Supreme Court
695 N.W.2d 365 (2005)

MEYER, J.

In December 1986, Hickman and his wife purchased their home in Watertown, Minnesota. To finance the purchase, Hickman and his wife obtained a first mortgage in the amount of $58,100 from Rothschild Financial Corporation and a second mortgage from the Minnesota Housing Finance Agency. The first mortgage was subsequently assigned to Temple-Inland Mortgage Corporation and then to respondent Guaranty.

Beginning in 1999 or before, Hickman failed to provide proof of insurance as required under the mortgage agreement. Temple-Inland, who then held the mortgage, obtained insurance on the home from SAFECO. The policy includes coverage for the "dwelling on the 'insured location,'" "other structures on an 'insured location,'" and "personal property, usual to the occupancy as a dwelling and owned or used by the 'borrower' or members of the 'borrower's' family residing with the 'borrower' while it is on the 'insured location.'" The policy provides that payment for a loss, except losses under personal property coverage, will be paid to Guaranty up to the amount of its interest and "amounts payable in excess of [Guaranty's] interest will be paid to the 'borrower.'" For losses under the personal property coverage, the policy provides that SAFECO will "adjust all losses with the 'borrower'" and "will pay the 'borrower.'" Under the policy, the "claimant" also has rights in connection with the appraisal of any loss. The term "claimant" is not defined in the contract, but by the terms of the contract includes the borrower, Hickman.

On March 31, 2000, and in the subsequent three years, Temple-Inland and its successor Guaranty sent Hicknan written notice informing him that they had obtained insurance on the home. Hickman did not obtain any other insurance coverage on the home. The notice also indicated that the insurance coverage was obtained in the amount of $85,500 for the house itself, $8,550 for personal property, and $8,550 for "other structures." The $855 premium for this insurance was paid from a real estate tax and insurance escrow account established with funds paid by Hickman with his monthly mortgage payments.

---

an intended beneficiary if recognition of a right to performance in the beneficiary is appropriate to effectuate the intention of the parties and either

    (a) the performance of the promise will satisfy an obligation of the promisee to pay money to the beneficiary; or

    (b) the circumstances indicate that the promisee intends to give the beneficiary the benefit of the promised performance.

    (2) An incidental beneficiary is a beneficiary who is not an intended beneficiary. An Analysis of the Second Restatement treatment of third party beneficiaries is found in John E. Murray, Jr., 9 Corbin on Contracts, § 44.4.

On June 24, 2002, Hickman's home and the detached storage building on the property were damaged by a windstorm. After the windstorm, FEMA inspected the property and concluded that the house was a total loss. The estimate of damages Hickman obtained from a local contractor was $114,048. SAFECO's insurance adjuster also inspected the property but concluded that the house was not a total loss. Based on [the adjuster's] estimates, SAFECO sent Guaranty $50,981.80 in insurance proceeds — $42,431.80 for the house and $8,550 for the storage building. By late 2002, the unpaid balance of Hickman's mortgage to Guaranty was less than $43,000. Hickman requested that Guaranty apply the insurance proceeds to the outstanding balance on their mortgage. Guaranty eventually did so and sent Hickman $7,339.08, the balance of the amount it received from SAFECO.

Hickman filed a complaint against SAFECO and Guaranty in March 2003 contending that under the terms of the insurance policy obtained from SAFECO by Guaranty, he was entitled to insurance coverage up to the policy limit for the losses incurred as a result of the storm. On August 26, 2003, SAFECO filed a motion for summary judgment asserting that Hickman failed to prove that he was either a party or a third-party beneficiary to the insurance contract issued to Guaranty by SAFECO. The district court granted SAFECO's motion for summary judgment, concluding that Hickman failed to establish a genuine issue of material fact because he was not a named party to the contract or a third-party beneficiary under either the "duty owed" test or the "intent to benefit" test. The district court also dismissed the complaint against Guaranty.The court of appeals affirmed summary judgment in favor of SAFECO, concluding that Hickman was not a third-party beneficiary to the contract because he was not listed as an insured under the policy, payment was made directly to Guaranty, and "no evidence in the record indicates that appellant was more than an incidental beneficiary of the contract." The court of appeals reversed the dismissal of the complaint against Guaranty and remanded for consideration of Hickman's claim because the district court's memorandum did not address it. Hickman petitioned this court for review. On October 27, 2004, we granted review solely on the issue of whether Hickman is a third-party beneficiary of the insurance contract under the "intent to benefit" test.

The interpretation of insurance contract language is a question of law as applied to the facts presented. Generally, a stranger to a contract does not have rights under the contract, but an exception exists if a third party is an intended beneficiary of the contract. In *Cretex Companies Inc. v. Construction Leaders, Inc.*, 342 N.W.2d 135, 139 (Minn. 1984), we adopted the intended beneficiary approach of the RESTATEMENT (SECOND) OF CONTRACTS, which states:

> (1) Unless otherwise agreed between promisor and promisee, a beneficiary of a promise is an intended beneficiary if recognition of a right to performance in the beneficiary is appropriate to effectuate the intention of the parties and either
>
> > (a) the performance of the promise will satisfy an obligation of the promisee to pay money to the beneficiary [duty owed test]; or
> >
> > (b) the circumstances indicate that the promisee intends to give the beneficiary the benefit of the promised performance [intent to benefit test].

(2) An incidental beneficiary is a beneficiary who is not an intended beneficiary.

RESTATEMENT (SECOND) OF CONTRACTS § 302 (1979).

Thus, if recognition of third-party beneficiary rights is "appropriate" and either the duty owed test or the intent to benefit test is met, the third party can recover as an "intended beneficiary."[3] If a beneficiary does not meet either of these tests, it is an incidental beneficiary and has no right to enforce the contract. In ascertaining the parties' intent to benefit a third person, the contract is read in light of all the surrounding circumstances.

Under the "intent to benefit" test of the SECOND RESTATEMENT, the circumstances must indicate that the promisee (here Guaranty) intends to give the beneficiary (Hickman) the benefit of the promise. RESTATEMENT (SECOND) OF CONTRACTS § 302(1)(b). Hickman argues that the circumstances here indicate that Guaranty intended to give him the benefit of the insurance contract, or that at least a fact question exists on this issue. Hickman points to several provisions in the insurance policy to support his status as an intended third-party beneficiary. Specifically, the policy obtained by Guaranty recognizes the class of "borrowers" that is defined as the mortgagor of an insured location indebted under a mortgage to Guaranty. Hickman, while not identified by name in the policy, is recognized as a borrower under the policy terms. The insurance policy provides insurance for up to a total of $102,600 — more than the outstanding amount of the mortgage — and states that SAFECO will pay the "greater of" the "amount of indebtedness" or "the replacement cost of the building." Amounts payable in excess of Guaranty's interest "will be paid to the 'borrower.' " In addition, the insurance policy includes $8,550 in coverage for personal property in which Guaranty had no insurable interest. In the case of personal property, the policy provides that SAFECO "will adjust all losses with the 'borrower' " and "will pay the 'borrower.' " The borrower also has rights under the policy, as a claimant, to seek arbitration of the appraisal of a loss covered by the policy if he disagrees with the amount of loss determined by SAFECO.[4] We

---

[3] [6] Prior to *Cretex*, Minnesota followed the test outlined in the First Restatement that distinguished between "done" and "creditor" beneficiaries. *Cretex*, 342 N.W.2d at 138-39. The SECOND RESTATEMENT eliminated this distinction in favor of a single category of "intended" beneficiaries. Both "done" and "creditor" beneficiaries are encompassed by the term "intended" beneficiaries. RESTATEMENT (SECOND) OF CONTRACTS § 302, reporter's note at 445.

[4] [8] These policy provisions illustrate that performance under the policy is rendered, at least in part, directly to Hickman. Therefore, the respondent and the court of appeals, reasoning that Hickman is not a third-party beneficiary because performance is not rendered directly to him under the insurance policy, are factually incorrect. In addition, this argument is not legally sound because performance need not be rendered directly to the intended beneficiary. RESTATEMENT (SECOND) OF CONTRACTS § 302, cmt. a ("neither promisee nor beneficiary is necessarily the person to whom performance is to be rendered, the person who will receive economic benefit, or the person who furnished the consideration"); *see also* Stowe v. Smith, 184 Conn. 194, 441 A.2d 81. 83 (Conn. 1981) (stating that "contracts for the benefit of a third party are enforceable without any requirement that the promisor's performance be rendered directly to the intended beneficiary"); In Buchman Plumbing Co. v. Regents of the University of Minnesota, 298 Minn. 328, 335, 215 N.W.2d 479, 484 (1974), applying the FIRST RESTATEMENT test we stated that "if the performance is directly rendered to the promisee, the third party who also may be benefited is an incidental beneficiary with no right of action," but noted in a footnote that a comment to the first RESTATEMENT OF CONTRACTS "suggests that this distinction is not always determinative." *Buchman*

conclude that these provisions of the insurance contract establish that Guaranty intended to give Hickman the benefit of some of the promised insurance proceeds; therefore, we hold that Hickman is a third-party beneficiary to the contract between Guaranty and SAFECO.

Hickman also urges us to consider some of the surrounding circumstances that further indicate the contracting parties' intent to give Hickman the benefit of the insurance contract. Beginning in March of 2000 and each year thereafter, Guaranty (or its predecessor) provided Hickman with written notice that it had obtained insurance "to protect our mutual interest in the property." In addition, the premiums for the insurance coverage obtained by Guaranty were paid from an escrow account funded by Hickman. Finally, SAFECO paid Guaranty an amount in excess of Guaranty's interest and Guaranty paid that excess to Hickman. These facts certainly support our conclusion that Hickman is an intended third-party beneficiary under the contract, but because we conclude that the language of the contract clearly indicates an intent to benefit Hickman, we do not rely on this extrinsic evidence to reach our holding.

We reverse summary judgment and remand for further proceedings in accordance with this opinion.

NOTE

Intention — Promisee or Both Parties? Innumerable third party beneficiary cases emphasize that there must be an objectively manifested "intention to benefit" the third party. The RESTATEMENT (SECOND) OF CONTRACTS version in Section 302 states the overriding principle as an agreement between the promisor and promisee "to effecuate the intention of the parties." Professor Corbin and others have suggested that it is the intention of the promisee that is important. The promisor has no motivation to benefit the third party. Her motivation in agreeing to perform the promise for the benefit of the third party is the consideration she is receiving from the promisee. The recognition of the intention of both parties in Section 302, however, suggests that even the promisor must intend to benefit the third party notwithstanding her underlying motive of receiving the consideration for her promise.

PROBLEMS

(1)   Mark suffered serious injuries in an accident driving a General Motors manufactured car which Mark had rented from Avis. Mark and GM arrived at a settlement agreement which included a provision stating that any claim that Mark continued to possess against Avis could only be asserted on the independent negligence of Avis. Mark's claim of strict liability against Avis was met by Avis' claim that it was a third party beneficiary of the settlement contract between Mark and GM and the clause was inserted by GM to preclude an Avis indemnification action against GM which could have resulted from a successful strict liability claim by Mark against Avis. Advise Mark. *See Noveck v. PV Holdings Corp.*, 742 F. Supp. 2d 284 (E.D.N.Y. 2010).

Plumbing Co., 298 Minn. at 335 n.3, 215 N.W.2d at 484 n.3.

(2)   When Michael purchased a luxury seaside home for himself and his wife, Kathleen, at a price of $2.9 million, they discovered defects not observable upon a reasonable inspection of the property. They spent another million dollars repairing the defects. When Michael and Kathleen sued, The defendants claimed that Kathleen had no standing to sue since she was not a third party beneficiary. The plaintiffs argued that, though Kathleen was not mentioned in the contract for the sale of the property, the defendants and the real estate agent were aware that Kathleen was going to live in the house with her husband. Advise the plaintiffs. *See Thompson v. Miles*, 741 F. Supp. 2d 296 (D. Me. 2010).

(3)   A County granted a real estate developer approval of a subdivision plan in exchange for the developer's promise to improve certain roads in the plan. When the developer failed to improve the roads, purchasers of lots in the plan brought actions as third party beneficiaries against the developer. Analyze. *See Vale Dean Canyon Homeowners Ass'n v. Dean*, 785 P.2d 772 (Or. Ct. App. 1990).

(4)   Albert North, a licensed attorney, agreed to draft a will for Clarence Jones. Jones informed North that he wished to leave the bulk of his estate to three nieces. North drafted the will and named the three nieces a legatees. Upon Jones' death, however, it became apparent that North failed to draft the will in accordance with generally prevailing standards of the practice of law. As a result, the three nieces received only $200,000 instead of the $3 million they would have received had the will been properly drafted. The nieces claimed that they were third party beneficiaries under the contract between Jones and North. Analyze. For an analysis of the cases in this area, see *Noble v. Bruce*, 709 A.2d 1264 (Md. 1998).

RARITAN RIVER STEEL CO. v. CHERRY, BEKAERT & HOLLAND
North Carolina Supreme Court
407 S.E.2d 178 (1991)

MEYER, J.

Cherry, Bekaert & Holland and its partners (hereinafter the "accounting firm"), defendants herein, signed an engagement letter dated 22 June 1981 with Intercontinental Metals Corporation (hereinafter "IMC"). IMC is a holding company which, on 30 September 1981, had five shareholders, some of whom were officers of the company. The engagement letter provided:

> We will examine the consolidated balance sheets of Intercontinental Metals Corporation and Intercontinental Metals Trading Corporation at September 30, 1981 and the related consolidated statements of earnings, retained earnings, and changes in financial position for the year then ended, for the purpose of expressing an unqualified opinion on the fairness of the presentation of these financial statements in conformity with generally accepted accounting principles applied on a consistent basis. If we discover that we cannot issue an unqualified opinion, we will discuss the reasons with you before submitting a different kind of report.

As you know, management has the primary responsibility for properly recording transactions in the records, for safeguarding assets and for preparing accurate financial statements. Our basic audit function is to add reliability to those financial statements. Our examination will be conducted in accordance with generally accepted auditing standards.

Raritan River Steel Company, the plaintiff herein, sold raw steel and was a major trade creditor of IMC. In January 1982, IMC had a $1.5 million line of credit with plaintiff, which had obtained copies of IMC's audited financial statements for the years 1978 and 1979 prepared by the accounting firm but did not have access to the audited statements for 1981, the year in question.

In January 1982, the accounting firm issued a qualified opinion concerning IMC's financial statements for the period ending 30 September 1981 (the 1981 financial statements), which indicated uncertainty as to the outcome of a $20 million dispute with a foreign supplier. Although the plaintiff asked IMC twice for a copy of IMC's 1981 financial statements, once in February and again in April or May of 1982, its latter request was expressly denied. However, in February 1982, IMC, as was its previous policy, allowed Dun & Bradstreet to review its audited financial statements in IMC's offices. [The summary of the audited financial statement published in the Dun and Bradstreet reports in April and May of 1982 showed IMC's net worth to be $6,964,475.00. In fact, IMC's actual net worth was a *negative* $14.6 million.]

The Dun & Bradstreet report, which also contained other summarized financial information, was the only access that plaintiff had to IMC's 1981 financial statements. After reviewing the Dun & Bradstreet report, and allegedly in reliance on IMC's financial condition as reported therein, the plaintiff extended additional open credit to IMC in excess of its previously established limit of $1.5 million.

In December 1982, IMC filed for bankruptcy protection. At that time, plaintiff was owed $2.2 million by IMC. From the bankruptcy proceedings, the plaintiff received only $511,143.60 and argues that the financial statements, if properly prepared, should have indicated a substantial negative net worth for IMC on 30 September 1981.

[Plaintiff sought recovery on a theory of negligence alleging that the defendant had failed to follow appropriate accounting standards, and also on the theory that it was a third party intended beneficiary of the contract between IMC and the defendant, which defendant had allegedly breached by failing to adhere to proper accounting standards in its auditing function. The trial court granted summary judgment in favor of defendants on both counts. The Court of Appeals reversed.] On appeal, this Court reversed the Court of Appeals, effectively holding that the plaintiff had not stated a claim for relief on its negligence theory, but declined to review the plaintiff's claim on its contract theory. On remand, the trial court granted summary judgment for the defendants on the plaintiff's contract claim on The Court of Appeals again reversed, with Judge Duncan dissenting. The defendants appeal to this Court as of right from the dissenting opinion.

In this case, we are reviewing the trial court's grant of a motion for summary judgment in favor of the defendants. Summary judgment is only proper where there is no genuine issue of material fact, and the movant is entitled to judgment as a matter of law. On appellate review of the order for summary judgment, we take the evidence in the light most favorable to the nonmoving party.

North Carolina recognizes the right of a third-party beneficiary [sic] to sue for breach of a contract executed for his benefit. *Vogel v. Supply Co.*, 277 N.C. 119, 177 S.E. 2d 273 (1970). Ordinarily " 'the determining factor as to the rights of a third-party beneficiary is the intention of the parties who actually made the contract. The real test is said to be whether the contracting parties intended that a third party should receive a benefit which might be enforced in the courts.' 17 Am. Jur. 2d, *Contracts* § 304. It is not sufficient that the contract does benefit him if in fact it was not intended for his direct benefit." *Vogel v. Supply Co., supra,* 277 N.C. at 128, 177 S.E. 2d at 279. *Snyder v. Freeman,* 300 N.C. 204, 220, 266 S.E.2d 593, 603-04 (1980).

This Court has adopted the analysis of the RESTATEMENT (SECOND) OF CONTRACTS for purposes of determining "whether a beneficiary of an agreement made by others has a right of action on that agreement." *Snyder,* 300 N.C. at 221, 266 S.E.2d at 604. The RESTATEMENT (SECOND) OF CONTRACTS provides as follows:

§ 302. Intended and Incidental Beneficiaries

(1) Unless otherwise agreed between promisor and promisee, a beneficiary of a promise is an intended beneficiary if recognition of a right to performance in the beneficiary is appropriate to effectuate the intention of the parties and either

(a) the performance of the promise will satisfy an obligation of the promisee to pay money to the beneficiary; or

(b) the circumstances indicate that the promisee intends to give the beneficiary the benefit of the promised performance.

(2) An incidental beneficiary is a beneficiary who is not an intended beneficiary.

The RESTATEMENT (SECOND) recognizes only two types of beneficiaries — intended and incidental — but a review of the comment to the Restatement indicates that the drafters intended to retain the distinction between creditor and donee beneficiaries. "The type of beneficiary covered by Subsection (1)(a) is often referred to as a 'creditor beneficiary,' " while the type of beneficiary covered by subsection (1)(b) "is often referred to as a 'donee beneficiary.' " *Id.* comments b, c. The drafters note that a donee beneficiary need not be the object of a "gift" but might also be the intended beneficiary of a "right." If no intent to benefit is found, then the beneficiary is considered an incidental beneficiary, and no recovery is available.

Having established that intent to benefit is the determining factor, we must consider the nature of the evidence which is admissible to prove intent. The Court, in determining the parties' intentions, should consider circumstances surrounding the transaction as well as the actual language of the contract. We further note that " '[w]hen a third party seeks enforcement of a contract made between other parties, the contract must be construed strictly against the party seeking enforcement.' " *Chemical Realty Corp. v. Home Fed'l Savings & Loan,* 84 N.C. App. 27, 34, 351 S.E.2d 786, 791 (1987) (quoting *Lane v. Surety Co.,* 48 N.C. App. 634, 638, 269 S.E.2d 711, 714 (1980), *disc. rev. denied,* 302 N.C. 219, 276 S.E.2d 916 (1981)).

Here, the plaintiff contends that it is a subsection 302(1)(b) beneficiary or donee beneficiary. The RESTATEMENT indicates that to identify a third-party donee beneficiary, we must consider the "intention of the parties and . . . [whether] the promisee intends to give the beneficiary the benefit of the promised performance." ESTATEMENT (SECOND) OF CONTRACTS § 302 (1981).

On the facts of this case, we note that both IMC and the accounting firm testified that there was no intent to benefit unsecured trade creditors by the contract with the accounting firm. The plaintiff was not even aware that the audit was being performed. The accounting firm's partner in charge of the IMC audit testified that at the time of the contract of 22 June 1981 and thereafter, IMC had neither informed the accounting firm of any intention to provide copies of the audited financial statement to trade creditors nor did the accounting firm have knowledge that the audited financial statements would be provided to Dun & Bradstreet. Testimony of IMC's chief financial officer indicates that it was IMC's policy in 1981 and 1982 not to distribute financial statements to trade creditors. In fact, the record indicates that only one trade creditor received a copy of IMC's 1981 financial statements.

In further considering whether the parties intended to benefit the plaintiff, we note first of all that the contract between IMC and the accounting firm never designated the plaintiff as an intended beneficiary of that contract. While we are aware that this factor alone is not dispositive, it adds weight to our analysis. In addition, as the 150 to 200 copies of the financial statements were delivered to IMC, the accounting firm's services were rendered directly to IMC in this case and not to the plaintiff. The plaintiff never even saw a copy of the 1981 financial statement. In sum, the evidence here was insufficient to show that "recognition of a right to performance in the beneficiary [was] appropriate to effectuate the intention of the parties." RESTATEMENT (SECOND) OF CONTRACTS § 302(1) (1981). We hold as a matter of law that based on an examination of the entire record in this case, the plaintiff, Raritan River Steel Company, was not an intended third-party beneficiary of the contract between IMC and the accounting firm.

Having determined that there was no intent to benefit the plaintiff, we need not reach the defendants' contention that, assuming an intention to benefit is recognized, the alleged breach of contract was not the cause of plaintiff Raritan's damages.

Reversed and remanded.

C.   PUBLIC BENEFICIARIES

ASTRA USA, INC. v. SANTA CLARA COUNTY
Supreme Court of the United States
131 S. Ct. 1342 (2011)

JUSTICE GINSBURG.

Section 340B of the Public Health Services Act, 42 U.S.C.A. § 256b (Oct. 2010 Supp.), imposes ceilings on prices drug manufacturers may charge for medications sold to specified health care facilities. Those facilities, here called "340B" or "covered" entities, include public hospitals and community health centers, many of them providers of safety-net services to the poor. The § 340B ceiling-price program (340B Program) is superintended by the Health Resources and Services Administration (HRSA), a unit of the Department of Health and Human Services (HHS). Drug manufacturers opt into the 340B Program by signing a form Pharmaceutical Pricing Agreement (PPA) used nationwide. PPAs are not transactional, bargained-for contracts. They are uniform agreements that recite the responsibilities § 340B imposes, respectively, on drug manufacturers and the Secretary of HHS. Manufacturers' eligibility to participate in state Medicaid programs is conditioned on their entry into PPAs for covered drugs purchased by 340B entities.

It is conceded that Congress authorized no private right of action under § 340B for covered entities who claim they have been charged prices exceeding the statutory ceiling. This case presents the question whether 340B entities, though accorded no right to sue for overcharges under the statute itself, may nonetheless sue allegedly overcharging manufacturers as third-party beneficiaries of the PPAs to which the manufacturers subscribed.

Respondent Santa Clara County (County), operator of several 340B entities, commenced suit against Astra and eight other pharmaceutical companies, alleging that the companies were overcharging 340B health care facilities in violation of the PPAs to which the companies subscribed. The District Court dismissed the complaint, concluding that the PPAs conferred no enforceable rights on 340B entities. Reversing the District Court's judgment, the Ninth Circuit held that covered entities, although they have no right to sue under the statute, could maintain the action as third-party beneficiaries of the PPAs. We granted

As the County conceded below and before this Court, covered entities have no right of action under § 340B itself. "[R]ecognition of any private right of action for violating a federal statute," currently governing decisions instruct, "must ultimately rest on congressional intent to provide a private remedy." Congress vested authority to oversee compliance with the 340B Program in HHS and assigned no auxiliary enforcement role to covered entities.

Notwithstanding its inability to assert a statutory right of action, the County maintains that the PPAs implementing the 340B Program are agreements enforceable by covered entities as third-party beneficiaries. A nonparty becomes legally entitled to a benefit promised in a contract, the County recognizes, only if the contracting parties so intend. Brief for Respondent 31 (citing *Restatement (Second) of Contracts* § 302(1)(b) (1979)). The PPAs "specifically nam[e]" covered entities as the recipients of discounted drugs, the County observes; indeed the very object of the agreements is to ensure that those entities would be "charge[d] . . . no more than the ceiling price. When the Government uses a contract to secure a benefit, the County urges, the intended recipient acquires a right to the benefit enforceable under federal common law. But see 9 J. Murray, Corbin on Contracts § 45.6, p. 92 (rev. ed. 2007) "The distinction between an intention to benefit a third party and an intention that the third party should have the right to enforce that intention is emphasized where the promisee is a governmental entity.").

The County's argument overlooks that the PPAs simply incorporate statutory obligations and record the manufacturers' agreement to abide by them. The form agreements, composed by HHS, contain no negotiable terms. Like the Medicaid Drug Rebate Program agreements, the 340B Program agreements serve as the means by which drug manufacturers opt into the statutory scheme. A third-party suit to enforce an HHS-drug manufacturer agreement, therefore, is in essence a suit to enforce the statute itself. The absence of a private right to enforce the statutory ceiling price obligations would be rendered meaningless if 340B entities could overcome that obstacle by suing to enforce the contract's ceiling price obligations instead. The statutory and contractual obligations, in short, are one and the same. [W]hen a government contract confirms a statutory obligation, "a third-party private contract action [to enforce that obligation] would be inconsistent with . . . the legislative scheme . . . to the same extent as would a cause of action directly under the statute" (internal quotation marks omitted)).

Whether a contracting agency may authorize third-party suits to enforce a Government contract is not at issue in this case. We can infer no such authorization where a contract simply incorporates statutorily required terms and otherwise fails to demonstrate any intent to allow beneficiaries to enforce those terms. Permitting such a suit, it is evident, would "allo[w] third parties to circumvent Congress's decision not to permit private enforcement of the statute." ("In drafting and entering into [PPAs], HHS never imagined that a 340B entity could bring a third-party beneficiary lawsuit like [the County]'s.").

The Ninth Circuit determined that "[p]ermitting covered entities to sue as intended beneficiaries of the PPA is . . . wholly compatible with the Section 340B program's objectives" to ensure "that drug companies comply with their obligations under the program and provide [the required] discounts." Suits like the County's, the Court of Appeals reasoned, would spread the enforcement burden instead of placing it "[entirely] on the government." But spreading the enforcement burden, the United States stressed, both in the Ninth Circuit and in this Court, is hardly what Congress contemplated when it "centralized enforcement in the government."

Congress made HHS administrator of both the Medicaid Drug Rebate Program and the 340B Program, the United States observed, Brief for United States as *Amicus Curiae* 33-34, and "[t]he interdependent nature of the two programs' requirements means that an adjudication of rights under one program must proceed with an eye towards any implications for the other." Far from assisting HHS, suits by 340B entities would undermine the agency's efforts to administer both Medicaid and § 340B harmoniously and on a uniform, nationwide basis.

Recognizing the County's right to proceed in court could spawn a multitude of dispersed and uncoordinated lawsuits by 340B entities. With HHS unable to hold the control rein, the risk of conflicting adjudications would be substantial. For the reasons stated, the judgment of the U. S. Court of Appeals for the Ninth Circuit is reversed.

NOTES

(1) In *Moch Co. v. Rensselaer Water Co.*, 159 N.E. 896 (N.Y. 1928), the water company contracted with the city to supply water. When a fire occurred, the water pressure was insufficient to extinguish the fire. In an opinion by Justice Cardozo, the court held against the plaintiff on both negligence and third party beneficiary theories. Tort claims against water companies have usually failed. However, in *Doyle v. South Pittsburgh Water Co.*, 199 A.2d 875 (P.a. 1964), a negligence complaint was sustained. Speaking for the court, Justice Musmanno dealt with the *Moch* case as follows: "It must be stated, with some regret, that at this point Homer nodded. Justice Cardozo, without apparently intending to do so, contradicted what he said in the *MacPherson* case which, incidentally, he cited with approval in the *Moch* case." 199 A.2d at 882.

(2) In *Holbrook v. Pitt*, 643 F.2d 1261 (7th Cir. 1981), under a contract between the owners of a housing project and a federal agency, tenants were held to be third party beneficiaries of the contract which required the agency to make rental payments for the benefit of the tenants.

D. OWNERS AND SUBCONTRACTORS — PAYMENT AND PERFORMANCE BONDS

In *BIS Computer Solutions, Inc. v. City of Richmond*, 2005 U.S. App. LEXIS 651 (4th Cir. 2005), the Halifax Corporation contracted with the City of Richmond to create a computerized records management system for the City's police department. Halifax contracted with BIS as a subcontractor for the project. When testing revealed "bugs" in the system, the City terminated the contract without objection by Halifax. BIS, however, claimed that it was entitled to relief as a third party beneficiary of the contract between the City and Halifax. After a jury trial, the court reduced the jury's award to BIS to $1.6 million. On appeal, the City claimed that BIS was not an intended third party beneficiary of the contract between the owner (City) and the general contractor (Halifax). The court stated,

> The nature of the contract between the City and Halifax is essentially analogous to any standard construction contract in which a property owner retains a contractor to complete a project, and the contractor hires subcontractors to assist in performing the contractor's work. Unless the parties otherwise specify, the sole intended beneficiaries of any such contract are the property owner and the contractor. Any third party benefiting from the contract, such as the subcontractor, is only an incidental beneficiary.

The court proceeded to vacate the judgment entered by the district court.

In *Outlaw v. Airtech Air Conditioning and Heating, Inc.*, 412 F.3d 156 (D.C. Cir. 2005), Outlaw contracted with a general contractor to renovate a building. The general contractor entered into a contract with Airtech to provide the HVAC in the renovated building. Outlaw had a falling out with the general contractor before completion of the project, but that dispute was settled. Outlaw sought to have Airtech complete the HVAC work in exchange for amounts still owed to Airtech by the general contractor, but Airtech declined on the ground that it was contractually bound only to the general contractor. Outlaw then claimed it was a third party beneficiary of the contract between the general contractor and the subcontractor, Airtech, and sued Airtech for damages resulting from alleged deficiencies in the HVAC. The district court granted summary judgment for Airtech holding that Airtech's contract with the general contractor created no duty on the part of Airtech to Outlaw on the "traditional contract law rule that, absent any indication to the contrary in an agreement, property owners are not intended or third party beneficiaries of contracts between contractors and subcontractors." On appeal, the judgment of the district court was affirmed.

Construction contracts typically involve performance bonds to assure a contractor's complete performance of the project and payment bonds to assure the payment of subcontractors and suppliers of material. Third party beneficiary issues may appear with respect to such bonds.

BOARD OF EDUCATION v. HARTFORD ACCIDENT & INDEMNITY CO.
Illinois Appellate Court
504 N.E.2d 1000 (1987)

REINHARD J.

[O]n June 20, 1973, Kiendl Construction Company (Kiendl) entered into a contract with plaintiff to construct both the Downers Grove North and Downers Grove South high school pool facilities. In accordance with statutory requirements pursuant to the provisions of section 1 of "An Act in relation to bonds of contractors entering into contracts for public construction" (Bond for Public Works Act) (Ill. Rev. Stat. 1973, ch. 29, par. 15), Kiendl, as principal, and defendant, as surety, executed and delivered to plaintiff both a performance bond in the amount of $1,801,261 guaranteeing Kiendl's complete performance of the construction contract and a labor-and-material payment bond in the amount of $1,801,261 guaranteeing Kiendl's payment of all subcontractors and materialmen. The work was substantially completed on August 4, 1975, as indicated by a certificate of completion issued by the architect. According to the contract, final payment came due when the certificate of completion was issued.

On April 19, 1985, plaintiff filed a two-count complaint against defendant alleging in count I that Kiendl failed to properly construct the pool facilities and that Kiendl no longer existed as a legal entity and prayed for the damages it sustained from the improper construction of the pool facilities to be assessed from the performance bond. Plaintiff alleged in count II the same actions and injuries as in count I, but prayed to recover its damages from the labor-and-material payment bond.

Defendant filed an answer to count I and a motion to strike and dismiss count II for failure to state a cause of action because plaintiff was not the party for whose benefit the labor-and-material payment bond was obtained. It also asserted as an affirmative defense to count I that as the performance bond contained a provision which required that any suit on the performance bond must be brought within two years of the final payment, the action alleged in count I is time barred. [T]he trial court entered its order granting both the motion to strike and dismiss and the motion for summary judgment. [T]he trial court ruled that the provision was clear that an action on the performance bond must be brought within two years of the completion of the project and that the provision was not shown to be against public policy; therefore, there was no legal reason not to enforce the two-year limitation provision. [The] labor-and-material payment bond was not entered into on behalf of plaintiff but for the benefit of those who furnished materials and labor to the project such as materialmen and subcontractors; therefore, plaintiff had no standing to bring a cause of action on the labor-and-material payment bond.

[Plaintiff argues that the trial court improperly granted summary judgment as to count I of the complaint.] The performance bond contains a clear and unambiguous provision limiting the time in which a party may file an action on the bond to two years. Generally, it has been held in other jurisdictions that, as between private parties, in the absence of any prohibitory statute, the time within which a suit may be brought upon a bond may be limited by a contractual provision in the bond. Similarly, contractual provisions shortening the period of time in which an action may be brought upon a bond to secure public as well as private construction contracts have been upheld to the extent that the period fixed is a reasonable one. As this action was not brought within two years of the completion of the work, there is no material issue of fact presented, and the trial court properly granted summary judgment for defendant on count I as being time barred.

Plaintiff's second contention is that the trial court improperly dismissed count II of its amended complaint. Plaintiff maintains that count II sufficiently stated a cause of action against defendant under the labor-and-material payment bond. It argues that the statutory language of section 1 of the Bond for Public Works Act (Ill. Rev. Stat. 1973, ch. 29, par. 15) required to be incorporated in each bond converted this bond into an additional performance guarantee of Kiendl's proper completion of the project by defendant. Plaintiff asserts that because of this language, the labor-and-material payment bond was, in essence, for the benefit of plaintiff.

While not a named party to the labor-and-material payment bond, plaintiff may maintain a cause of action as a third-party beneficiary to this contract if the execution of the bond was intended to directly confer a benefit on plaintiff. This intent, however, must be gleaned from a consideration of all of the contract and the circumstances surrounding the parties at the time of its execution. The intent to benefit must be directly indicated and it is not enough that the benefit was incidental.

An examination of the labor-and-material payment bond indicates that it was executed for the benefit of anyone providing materials and/or labor required to be used in the completion of the project. The bond defined a claimant as:

[O]ne having a direct contract with the Principal or with a subcontractor of the Principal for labor, material, or both, used or reasonably required for use in the performance of the contract, labor and material being construed to include that part of water, gas, power, light, heat, oil, gasoline, telephone service or rental of equipment directly applicable to the CONTRACT.

While plaintiff may have incidentally benefited from the existence of this bond as it probably prevented liens from being filed against the property and the project, the above definition clearly demonstrates that it was not entered into to guarantee Kiendl's performance as this performance was already guaranteed by the performance bond. Sections 1 and 2 of the Bond for Public Works Act (Ill. Rev. Stat. 1973, ch. 29, pars. 15, 16) provide an alternate remedy for subcontractors and materialmen to that afforded by "An Act relating to contractors' and materialmen's liens, known as mechanics' liens" (Mechanics Lien Act) (Ill. Rev. Stat. 1985, ch. 82, par. 23), as their purpose is to protect subcontractors and materialmen for whom no right of mechanic's lien exists against a public body, as well as to regulate claims against public monies. Plaintiff is unable to support with any case authority its claim that the statutory language required to be incorporated in each bond converted a payment guarantee into a performance guarantee, and there is no justification to apply the language to carry out such a conversion where a performance bond was specifically executed for plaintiff's protection. As the labor-and-material payment bond was not executed for plaintiff's benefit, plaintiff's cause of action on this bond was properly dismissed for failure to state a cause of action. [*Affirmed.*]

NOTE

It is now generally agreed that *performance* bonds are designed to benefit the owner. Courts have struggled with the question of whether *payment* bonds are designed simply to indemnify (save harmless) the owner from liability, or whether labor and materialmen are intended to be protected third party beneficiaries. The situation was made clear in government contracts, which are exempt from mechanics' liens. Since labor and materialmen cannot obtain such liens against the government, the payment bond can have only one purpose, i.e., to protect third parties. Statutes typically require payment bonds in government contracts, and some of these statutes clearly provide protected beneficiary status for suppliers of labor and materials. *See, e.g.*, Miller Act, 40 U.S.C. § 270(a)-(e), particularly subsection (b). In private contracts, if a payment bond is interpreted as only providing indemnity for the owner, laborers and materialmen become mere incidental beneficiaries. Modern cases, however, clearly interpret payment bonds as intending to benefit such parties, notwithstanding the protection of mechanics' liens. *See* MURRAY ON CONTRACTS § 133B.

E. MORTGAGE ASSUMPTION

A mortgage is a security interest in real property to secure a loan made by the lender (a bank or finance company) to the owner. If the property is valued at $100,000, the mortgage loan will typically be considerably less than that amount. If the property is encumbered by a mortgaged debt of $50,000, the owner (mortgagor) has "equity" of $50,000 in the property and has promised to pay the lender $50,000 plus interest over a period of time that is commonly 15 or 30 years. If the owner conveys the property to buyer X, the property is still subject to the mortgage. If the mortgage is not paid, the lender will *foreclose*, i.e., sell the property through a judicial sale so that the loan will be repaid from the proceeds of the sale. In the example, the property is worth much more than the mortgage indebtedness. Buyer X loses the property, but neither X nor the original owner have any further liability to the lender, who may retain only the portion of the proceeds necessary to cover the outstanding indebtedness. Suppose, however, that there has been a severe decline in land values and, at the time of foreclosure, the property value had declined to $40,000. The lender would retain that amount from the sale and also recover a *deficiency judgment* against the original owner. The lender could not recover a deficiency judgment against buyer X unless X had promised to become liable on the indebtedness, i.e., unless X had *assumed* the mortgage indebtedness. If X did not *assume* that debt, X has taken *subject to* the mortgage, i.e., he is not liable thereon, but, again, the mortgage is still "attached to the land" so that X loses the land with no further liability.

It is common for a buyer of land subject to a mortgage to *assume* the mortgage indebtedness. Where the owner conveys to X and X has assumed the indebtedness, the owner is a promisee who has induced the promisor (X) to agree that he will pay the mortgage debt. In this situation, it is clear that the owner intends to benefit a third party — the lender (mortgagee). Under the old categorizations, the lender would be a protected "creditor" beneficiary. *See Bridgman v. Curry*, 398 N.W.2d 167 (Iowa 1987). The lender should be pleased because it now has two debtors instead of one. The assuming grantee is primarily liable and the original debtor is liable as a surety. If X had then conveyed the land to Y who did *not* assume the mortgage but took the land *subject to* that mortgage, the lender would have no third party beneficiary rights against Y because Y did not promise to become liable on the mortgage debt. The lender would still have the original owner as a debtor.

Consider the following problem that has caused some consternation. Assume that the original owner conveyed the property to X who assumed the mortgage debt. X then conveyed to Y who did not assume the debt, but took "subject to" the mortgage so that Y is not personally liable for the debt to the lender, the mortgagee (bank). Y then conveyed to Z, who *assumed* the debt. Can Z be held liable to the mortgagee in light of the fact that Y was not liable, i.e., there was a "break in the chain of mortgage assumption"?

In such a situation, the question arises, why would a grantee such as Y who did not assume the debt require his grantee, Z, to do so? The Restatement (Second) of Contracts suggests two possibilities: (1) if Z agreed to assume the mortgage with knowledge of all the facts, the lender (mortgagee) is a protected beneficiary; (2) if Z can show, by clear and convincing evidence, that his assumption of the mortgage was included through a mistake by the drafter (scrivener's error) contrary to the true intention of the parties, reformation will lie. Restatement (Second) of Contracts § 312, illustrations 3 and 4.

For a case holding the remote grantee liable, see *Somers v. Avant*, 261 S.E.2d 334 (Ga. 1979). *See also* Murray on Contracts § 133D.

F. CONTRACT AND TORT: PRODUCTS LIABILITY AND "PRIVITY"

Products liability is a curious admixture of contract and tort law. The manufacturer of a product rarely sells it directly to the ultimate user. The product may pass through a vertical chain from manufacturer to wholesaler and to final distributor or retailer who sells it to the user of the product. If the product is defective and causes injury, the user may sue the distributor or retailer from whom it was purchased, but difficulties arise when the injured party attempts to leap over the distributor and even the wholesaler to sue the remote manufacturer with whom the user had no contract. As early as 1916, such an action in negligence was permitted in the famous case of *MacPherson v. Buick Motor Co.*, 11 N.E. 1050 (N.Y. 1916) (Cardozo, J.). Proving negligence before the product left the manufacturer's hands, however, could be extremely difficult. At the time the Uniform Commercial Code was being drafted, the only tort theory was a negligence theory. Some two decades would pass before the unveiling of the new products liability theory in Torts under Section 402A of the RESTATMENT (SECOND) OF TORTS. A promising alternative theory was an action for breach of warranty, a contract action, which lessened the burden of proof to a showing that the product was unmerchantable or breached the other implied warranty of fitness for a particular purpose or, finally, an express warranty. Warranty theory, however, had its own problems. It immediately raised the specter of *privity*.

Attempting to sue a remote manufacturer up the chain of distribution involves a question of *vertical privity*, where the question is: *Who can be sued?* The other type of privity is illustrated by a simple example. A member of a household purchases food or other goods which are consumed or used by members of the household but not by the purchaser. The unmerchantable product causes injury to those who used or consumed it. While the buyer was in "privity" with the store, the injured members of the household were not parties to that contract. The issue is one of *horizontal privity* where the question is: *Who can sue?* Who is eligible to stand in the shoes of the buyer?

Since warranty theory was being used in products liability cases, Section 2-318 of the Uniform Commercial Code was included under the caption, "Third Party Beneficiaries of Warranties Express or Implied." It expressly confronts the *horizontal* privity issue. Three alternatives were provided under that section to allow each state legislature to choose the alternative it deemed appropriate. Alternative A extends warranty protection to any natural person who is a member of the buyer's family or household or a guest in the home if it is reasonable to expect such a person to use, consume or be affected by the purchased product and who sustains personal injury caused by the breach of warranty. Alternative B extends the protection beyond the family, household or guests in the home to "any natural person" who may reasonably be expected to use, consume or be affected by the product and who suffers personal injury caused by the breach of warranty. Thus, unlike Alternative A, Alternative B would cover others such as employees injured by defective equipment under the contract between their employer and the party supplying the product. While Alternatives A and B extend warranties to any "natural" person, Alternative C extends warranties "to any person" that would include both natural persons and artificial persons such as corporations. Alternative C also extends the warranty to cover injury to either person or property.

The most popular alternative among state legislatures was Alternative A. Recognizing that the products liability case law was in a state of development, a Section 2-318 comment to Alternative A stated that the section is "neutral and is not intended to enlarge or restrict the developing case law on whether the seller's warranties, given to the buyer who resells, extend to other persons in the distributive chain." Though UCC comments are not part of the enacted law, this comment invited courts to extend warranty protection beyond the limiting language of Alternative A. A number of courts have accepted that invitation and extended Alternative A beyond members of the family, household or guests in the home. *See, e.g., Salvador v. Atlantic Steel Boiler Co.*, 319 A.2d 903 (Pa. 1974). The effect may be that, while Alternative A is the recorded statute, via judicial extension, the law of the jurisdiction fits more neatly under Alternative B. Some legislatures have also provided their own modifications of a chosen alternative that may affect privity questions in certain transactions.

None of the Section 2-318 Alternatives expressly address *vertical* privity to answer the question whether a party in horizontal privity who is standing in the shoes of the buyer may bring an action for breach of warranty against a remote manufacturer. A given court may choose to recognize such an action while another court will preclude it for lack of privity. With respect to either vertical or horizontal privity, relying on the statutory language of the particular Alternative enacted in a given jurisdiction can be perilous. It is very important to consider the case law interpretation and elaboration of the statutory language in the relevant jurisdiction.

The widespread adoption of Section 402A of the RESTATMENT (SECOND) OF TORTS in products liability cases made it the theory of choice for personal injuries caused by a defective product. The tort theory it avoids the "privity" issue. Warranties may be disclaimed but a Section 402A action is not limited by disclaimers. A notice requirement under UCC § 2-607(3)(a) may inspire an argument for a defendant that would not be available under tort theory. Warranty theory in products liability cases would, however, be used to recover for economic injury caused by defects in the product for which no tort action is available since the injury manifests loss of bargain, a contract theory. Where an implied warranty of merchantability is disclaimed, there may still be an implied warranty of fitness for a particular purpose or an express warranty that would allow an action for breach of warranty by a third party where no tort action would lie.[7] Warranty theory may also be used for personal injury damages in the rare situation in which a plaintiff fails to file an action within the shorter torts statute of limitation period but time remains under the longer four-year UCC statute of limitations. UCC Section 2-725 begins to run from the time of the breach (when tender of delivery is made) regardless of the

---

[7] One of the interesting questions was whether a buyer of a product could sue a remote manufacturer for breach of an express warranty. If the express warranty was contained with the product that was delivered to the ultimate buyer, such a "pass through" express warranty could be the basis for the buyer's cause of action. Manufacturer's express warranties, however, also occur through advertising. The ultimate buyer could sue for breach of such an express warranty only if she had seen it prior to any injury. These views are found in the Proposed Amendments to UCC Article 2 under the caption, "warranty-like" obligations.

aggrieved party's lack of knowledge of the breach. It should also be noted that New York courts have distinguished implied warranty theory from tort theory where both actions are brought for the same personal injury and found that warranty theory suggests "true strict liability" while the tort theory continues to be "negligence inspired."[8]

G. VESTING OF THIRD PARTY RIGHTS

OLSON v. ETHERIDGE
Illinois Supreme Court
686 N.E.2d 563 (1997)

BILANDIC, J.

[Dean Etheridge was one of three buyers of all of the shares of stock in a corporation owned by the plaintiffs. The purchase price was $350,000 for which the buyers issued a promissory note that obligated them to make annual payments plus 9% interest to the plaintiffs' account in the Walnut, Illionis bank until the debt was satisfied. This is designated as Agreement I. Four years later, Etheridge sold half of his stock in the corporation to August Engelhaupt — Agreement II. The original debt had not yet been fully paid and, as part of the consideration, Engelhaupt assumed one-half of Etheridge's liability under the original agreement which included the promissory note. Engelhaupt made annual payments to the Walnut bank for two years when Etheridge directed him to make payments to the Princeton bank because Etheridge was indebted to that bank on a separate transaction. Engelhaupt acquiesced and made subsequent payments to the Princeton bank. Shortly thereafter, the original sellers of the corporation, the plaintiffs, sued the buyers for their failure to complete the payments under the original contract. They claimed a balance due of $76,500. This lawsuit named Engelhaupt as a defendant on the theory that the plaintiffs were third-party beneficiaries of the contract between Etheridge (of the original buyers who was liable for the balance

---

[8] In Denny v. Ford Motor Company, 662 N.E.2d 730 (N.Y. 1995), the New York Court of Appeals addressed a certified question from the United States Court of Appeals for the Second Circuit: Are actions for strict products liability in tort and breach of implied warranty always coextensive? A jury found that a product was not "defective" under the tort theory, but was unmerchantable. It awarded $1.2 million for the breach of the implied warranty of merchantability that caused the plaintiff's personal injuries. On appeal, the defendant had claimed that the verdict was inconsistent since the theories were coextensive. The court's response to the certified question noted a subtle but important difference between the two theories. In determining whether a designed product was not reasonably safe, the tort theory required a "risk/utility" analysis, i.e., whether a reasonable person would conclude that the utility of the product did not outweigh the risk in marketing such a designed product. While such an analysis steers away from a fault concept by focusing on the product rather than conduct, the court concluded that it continues to be "negligence inspired" since it invites evidence of the manufacturer's judgment. The implied warranty of merchantability, however, focuses on whether the product is "fit for the ordinary purposes for which such goods are used" which is a reasonable expectation test. Thus, the warranty action is one involving "true 'strict' liability" since recovery may be had by showing that the product was not minimally safe for its expected purpose without regard to the manufacturer's reasonableness in marketing the product in that unsafe condition. See also Castro v. QVC Network, 134 F.3d 114 (2d Cir. 1998).

of the purchase price) and Engelhaupt, who had promised to pay Etheridge's debt to the plaintiffs, but had stopped paying the plaintiffs through the Walnut bank when Etheridge directed him to pay the Princeton bank.]

Engelhaupt first argued that the plaintiffs were not intended third-party beneficiaries of Agreement II. Engelhaupt claimed that all his obligations under Agreement II were discharged by the actions taken between him, Etheridge, and Princeton Bank. The trial court granted summary judgment for the plaintiffs. Engelhaupt appealed, and the appellate court affirmed. The appellate court held that, as a matter of law, Agreement II conferred intended third-party beneficiary status on the plaintiffs because Agreement II states that Engelhaupt assumed one-half of Etheridge's liability and obligation under Agreement I. The appellate court next rejected Engelhaupt's claim that his obligations to the plaintiffs as third-party beneficiaries under Agreement II were discharged by the actions taken between him, Etheridge, and Princeton Bank on February 10, 1986. The appellate court determined that *Bay v. Williams*, 112 Ill. 91, 1 N.E. 340 (1884), was dispositive of this issue. Bay established the rule in Illinois that third-party beneficiary rights are subject to immediate vesting and, once vested, cannot subsequently be altered or extinguished through a later agreement of the original parties to the contract. *Bay*, 112 Ill. at 96–97. Applying the *Bay* rule, the appellate court concluded that the plaintiffs' third-party beneficiary rights in Agreement II vested immediately upon Etheridge's and Engelhaupt's execution of that agreement. Once this vesting occurred, Etheridge and Engelhaupt were powerless to modify the terms of Agreement II in a manner detrimental to the plaintiffs without their consent. The appellate court therefore affirmed the circuit court's grant of summary judgment in favor of the plaintiffs and against Engelhaupt.

As a preliminary matter, we note that Engelhaupt does not challenge the appellate court's initial holding that the plaintiffs are intended third-party beneficiaries of Agreement II. Engelhaupt concedes that the vesting rule in *Bay* commands a contrary conclusion, but argues that the *Bay* rule should be replaced with the vesting rule set forth in section 311 of the RESTATEMENT (SECOND) OF CONTRACTS (1981). According to Engelhaupt, if section 311 is applied, the summary judgment entered in favor of the plaintiffs was improper because questions of material fact remain to be determined.

Before addressing the parties' arguments, we briefly summarize third-party beneficiary law. The well-established rule in Illinois is that if a contract is entered into for the direct benefit of a third person, the third person may sue for a breach of the contract in his or her own name, even though the third person is a stranger to the contract and the consideration. This principle of law is widely accepted throughout the United States, because allowing a third-party beneficiary to sue the promisor directly is said to be manifestly just and practical. In cases such as this one, it increases judicial efficiency by removing the privity requirement, under which the beneficiary must sue the promisee, who then in turn must sue the promisor.

An important corollary to this principle is that the promisor may assert against the beneficiary any defense that the promisor could assert against the promisee if the promisee were suing on the contract because the third-party beneficiary's rights stem from a contract to which the beneficiary is not a party. Accordingly, the promisor in this case, Engelhaupt, may assert against the plaintiffs-beneficiaries any defense that he could assert against the promisee, Etheridge, if Etheridge were suing him on Agreement II. Engelhaupt here asserts the defense that all his obligations under Agreement II were discharged when he made full payment to Princeton Bank [pursuant to the direction of Etheridge].

The plaintiffs maintain, however, that Engelhaupt is not entitled to assert this defense against them because their rights as third-party beneficiaries had "vested." The vesting doctrine is an exception to the above rule that the promisor may assert against the beneficiary any defense that the promisor could assert against the promisee. Under this doctrine, once a third-party beneficiary's rights vest, the original contracting parties cannot modify or discharge those rights without the beneficiary's assent. The "question of vesting arises only where the promisor and the promisee purport to vary or discharge the rights of the beneficiary"; otherwise, "the topic of vesting is irrelevant." J. Calamari & J. Perillo, Contracts § 17-11, at 715 (3d ed. 1987). Before proceeding, then, we must determine in this case what rights the plaintiffs are asserting under Agreement II, and whether Engelhaupt and Etheridge attempted to vary or discharge those rights.

The plaintiffs here are asserting third-party beneficiary rights in Agreement II. In particular, they claim that they are the beneficiaries of Engelhaupt's promise in Agreement II "to assume" one-half of Etheridge's obligation to pay the plaintiffs under Agreement I. The next inquiry is whether Engelhaupt and Etheridge attempted to modify or discharge the plaintiffs' rights to payment as provided for in Agreement II. The plaintiffs urge application of the vesting rule declared in *Bay*. Engelhaupt, on the other hand, asks us to apply the vesting rule set forth in section 311 of the Second Restatement of Contracts.

> [The promisor's] promise invests the person for whose use it is made with an immediate interest and right, as though the promise had been made to him. This being true, the person who procures the promise has no legal right to release or discharge the person who made the promise, from his liability to the beneficiary. Having the right, it is under the sole control of the person for whose benefit it is made, as much so as if made directly to him.

Bay, 112 Ill. at 97.

Consequently, *Bay* established the rule in Illinois that third-party beneficiary rights vest immediately and cannot be altered or extinguished through a later agreement of the original parties to the contract, unless the beneficiary assents.

Engelhaupt urges us to replace the *Bay* rule with the "modern view" as set forth in section 311 of the Second Restatement. Section 311, entitled "Variation of a Duty to a Beneficiary," stands in direct contrast to *Bay*. It provides that, in the absence of language in a contract making the rights of a third-party beneficiary irrevocable, the parties to the contract "retain power to discharge or modify the duty by subsequent agreement," without the third-party beneficiary's assent, at any time until the third-party beneficiary, without notice of the discharge or modification, materially changes position in justifiable reliance on the promise, brings suit on the promise or manifests assent to the promise at the request of the promisor or promisee. RESTATEMENT (SECOND) OF CONTRACTS § 311 (1981).

Section 311 now represents the majority view on the subject of vesting. *Karo v. San Diego Symphony Orchestra Ass'n*, 762 F.2d 819 (9th Cir. 1985) (applying California law); *see, e.g., Bridgman v. Curry*, 398 N.W.2d 167 (Ia. 1986); *Detroit Bank & Trust Co. v. Chicago Flame Hardening Co.*, 541 F. Supp. 1278 (N.D. Ind. 1982) (applying Indiana law); *see also* 17A Am. Jur. 2d *Contracts* § 461, at 482-83 (2d ed. 1991) (and cases cited therein); 17A C.J.S. *Contracts* § 373 (1963). In contrast, the immediate vesting rule as set forth in *Bay* represents the minority view, followed by only a handful of states. See 17A Am. Jur. 2d *Contracts* § 461, at 483 (2d ed. 1991) (and cases cited therein).

Engelhaupt maintains that we should adopt section 311. He asserts that section 311 represents the majority rule on vesting because it better conforms to modern commercial practices and general principles of contract law. According to Engelhaupt, parties should remain free to modify or discharge their contracts as they see fit, without the assent of a third-party beneficiary, subject only to the three exceptions provided for in section 311. Section 311 makes sense, Engelhaupt contends, because third-party beneficiaries should not be able to enforce contracts for which they do not give any consideration, unless they demonstrate some detriment or act of faith in reliance on the contract.

Engelhaupt asserts that the superiority of the RESTATEMENT approach over the *Bay* rule is demonstrated by the facts present in this case. As he explains, the plaintiffs here freely chose to extend credit to Etheridge, who was then bound to pay them under Agreement I. Etheridge and Engelhaupt then freely contracted with each other that Engelhaupt would make one-half of Etheridge's payments to the plaintiffs, in Agreement II. The plaintiffs, however, were not bound to accept Engelhaupt's promise to pay in Agreement II in replacement of Etheridge's promise to pay in Agreement I and Note I, and did not do so. Consequently, the plaintiffs' contractual remedies against Etheridge in the event of Etheridge's nonpayment under Agreement I remained intact. Engelhaupt asserts that, in this situation, he and Etheridge should not be forever barred from modifying or discharging their agreement without the plaintiffs' assent, which is precisely what *Bay* mandates. Rather, Engelhaupt asserts, the third-party beneficiary plaintiffs should be found to have obtained vested rights in his and Etheridge's contract only if they meet one of the circumstances set forth in section 311.

Finding Engelhaupt's arguments persuasive, we hereby adopt the vesting rule set forth in section 311 of the SECOND RESTATEMENT. The rationale underlying section 311's vesting rule is that "parties to a contract should remain free to amend or rescind their agreement so long as there is no detriment to a third party who has provided no consideration for the benefit received." *Board of Education of Community School District No. 220 v. Village of Hoffman Estates*, 126 Ill. App. 3d 625, 628, 467 N.E.2d 1064, 81 Ill. Dec. 942 (1984). This rationale is compelling. Moreover, we find this rationale to be consistent with the general principles running throughout contract law. Contract law generally favors the freedom to contract. Contract law also allows for equitable remedies where the facts compel such a result.

In contrast, the immediate vesting rule of *Bay* curtails the freedom to contract. It provides, in essence, that every promise which benefits a third-party beneficiary carries with it another term, implied at law, that the parties to the contract are prohibited from modifying or discharging the promise that benefits the beneficiary, without the beneficiary's assent. We do not believe that the modern law of contracts should always imply such a term. To do so can work a great injustice upon the parties involved in a particular case. Although, as the plaintiffs contend, the *Bay* rule is clear and easy to apply, this does not persuade us to retain it. Our concern is that the rule of law we expound best serves the pursuit of justice, not that it is the easiest rule of law for courts to apply.

We note, moreover, that the plaintiffs' argument against adoption of the RESTATEMENT rule is not persuasive. They maintain that the Restatement position has fluctuated so much over the past century that it is not stable. We do not agree with this characterization. In fact, the RESTATEMENT position regarding creditor beneficiaries, such as the plaintiffs, is essentially the same as it has always been. Under the original RESTATEMENT, the rights of creditor beneficiaries vested once the beneficiary brought suit or otherwise materially changed position in reliance on the promise. RESTATEMENT OF CONTRACTS §§ 142, 143 (1932). Today, creditor beneficiaries are called intended beneficiaries, and their rights vest once the beneficiary brings suit on the promise, materially changes position in justifiable reliance on the promise or manifests assent to the promise at the request of the promisor or promisee. RESTATEMENT (SECOND) OF CONTRACTS §§ 302, 311 (1981). As to donee beneficiaries, the original RESTATEMENT provided that their rights vested immediately. RESTATEMENT OF CONTRACTS §§ 142, 143(1932). This was changed after substantial criticism. Now donee beneficiaries are also classified as intended beneficiaries, and their rights vest in the same manner stated above. RESTATEMENT (SECOND) OF CONTRACTS §§ 302, 311 (1981). Even were we to agree with the plaintiffs' characterization of the Restatement view as unstable, however, this would not impact our decision. We find the current RESTATEMENT position on vesting to be consistent with general principles underlying contract law. This court is free to reject any later revisions of the Restatement.

In conclusion, we adopt the vesting rule set forth in section 311 of the SECOND RESTATEMENT. *Bay* is hereby overruled. The circuit court awarded summary judgment to the plaintiffs based on the *Bay* rule. The circuit court did not consider the plaintiffs' motion for summary judgment in the context of the vesting rule of section 311. We therefore reverse this award of summary judgment for the plaintiffs and remand to the circuit court for further proceedings, consistent with section 311's vesting rule.

NOTES

(1) *Vesting of Donee Beneficiary Rights.* In *Biggins v. Shore*, 565 A.2d 737 (Pa. 1989), the Supreme Court of Pennsylvania was asked to overturn its adherence to the FIRST RESTATEMENT immediate vesting rule with respect to *donee* beneficiaries and adopt the RESTATEMENT (SECOND) approach, which does not distinguish donee from creditor beneficiaries in relation to vesting of the third party's interest. Over a vigorous dissent, the majority of the court declined to reject its "long standing

adherence to Section 142 of the First Restatement of Contracts" which vests the rights of a third party donee beneficiary "indefeasibly" upon execution of the contract. The court's rationale emphasized the traditional argument that, unlike a creditor beneficiary, a donee beneficiary has no cause of action if her rights against a promisor are defeated. She cannot prevail against the promisee who owes her no debt. On the other hand, a creditor beneficiary who loses his rights against a promisor may still sue the promisee, who remains as the third party's original debtor. The debt was not extinguished by the contract with the promisor. Moreover, the promisor and promisee may reserve the power to change the beneficiary. If the parties choose not to reserve the power to change the beneficiary, the court saw no reason to depart from the old rule that the donee beneficiary's rights vest immediately. Pennsylvania, therefore, remains one of the handful of jurisdictions that continue the immediate vesting view in donee situations as opposed to the prevailing view adopted by the court in the principal case which follows Restatement (Second) of Contracts § 311. As the court in the principal case indicates (and the Pennsylvania Supreme Court would agree), even under the First Restatement, the rights of *creditor* beneficiaries do not vest absent assent, reliance or the bringing of suit.

(2) *Vesting by "Assent" — Infants.* Of the three manners of vesting under Restatement (Second) of Contracts § 311, a material change of position in reliance on the contract is obvious as is bringing an action to enforce the beneficiary's right. The third manner involves the beneficiary's "assent . . . at the request of the promisor or promisee." § 311(3). *Quaere*: Is the "assent" concept a manifestation of the contract tradition of offer and acceptance?

Suppose the beneficiary learns of the contract for her benefit inadvertently, *not* at the request of the promisor or promisee. Do her rights vest upon learning of the contract, assuming she decides not to reject the benefit "offered" which she certainly may do? Restatement (Second) of Contracts § 306. In *Detroit Bank & Trust Co. v. Chicago Flame Hardening Co., Inc.*, 541 F. Supp. 1278 (N.D. Ind. 1989), plaintiff claimed that mere knowledge of the contract for her benefit was sufficient to presume "assent, relying upon cases in which assent was presumed for third party infants. The court stated, "Those cases are clearly distinguishable from the present cause. . . . A presumption is necessary in such instances to protect the interests of minor beneficiaries. [Plaintiff], however, was an adult at the time [the contract was formed for her benefit], completely able to assert her own rights, and as such is not afforded the same protection. Moreover, the same authority submitted by plaintiff in support of a presumption of acceptance provides *a fortiori* a strong argument for the opposite proposition — a lack of such protection for a competent adult through negative implication." *Id.* at 1284.

Some courts have concluded that the assent of a third party infant, i.e., a party lacking capacity to contract, is presumed. *See, e.g., Plunkett v. Atkins*, 371 P.2d 727 (Okla. 1962); *Rhodes v. Rhodes*, 266 S.W.2d 790 (Ky. 1953). However, in *Lehman v. Stout*, 261 Minn. 384, 112 N.W.2d 640 (1961), the court allowed parents of a child to modify a previous contract made for the benefit of their six-year old son on the footing that they did not intend the son to have a vested interest. See also Restatement (Second) of Contracts § 311, Comment *d*, which frowns upon the presumption of assent for infants. *See also* Murray on Contracts § 132B.

Vesting By Bringing Suit. Bringing suit is certainly not "invited" by the promisor or promisee. If a third party interest can vest by such an uninvited, unilateral act, why not allow the right to vest through a simple manifestation of assent to the benefit conferred, regardless of whether it was invited.? In *Auer v. Kawasaki Motors, Corp.*, 830 F.2d 535 (4th Cir. 1987), Auer was driving a Kawasaki motorcycle when he was struck by a BFI truck. He entered into a settlement and release with BFI which discharged BFI "and all other persons, firms and corporations who might be liable of and from any and all actions . . . on account of or in any way growing out of the [collision]." The release was executed while Kawasaki was defending against Auer's product liability action. Kawasaki amended its answer and moved for summary judgment on the basis of the release, claiming third party beneficiary status under the settlement and release contract between Auer and GM. Treating its motion for summary judgment as "bringing suit," Kawasaki claimed the right to being released from any Auer claim vested. The court agreed.

H. PROMISEE'S RIGHT TO ENFORCE THE PROMISE

DREWEN v. BANK OF MANHATTAN CO.
New Jersey Supreme Court
155 A.2d 529 (1959)

PROCTOR, J.

This suit was brought in the Superior Court, Chancery Division, by John Drewen, administrator *c. t. a.* of the estate of Doris Ryer Nixon, to enforce a contract executed by the plaintiff's decedent and her husband, Stanhope Wood Nixon, the defendant's decedent. On motion addressed to the complaint, the Chancery Division dismissed the administrator's suit, and the dismissal was affirmed by the Appellate Division.

The complaint sets forth the following allegations: Doris Ryer Nixon and Stanhope Wood Nixon were married in 1917. They had two children, Lewis and Blanche. On July 17, 1945, the husband and wife executed an agreement settling the rights of each in the other's property in contemplation of a divorce which was granted some months later. As part of that agreement, Stanhope Wood Nixon promised never to reduce the quantity or quality of the children's interests in his estate, as set forth in a will executed on the same day as the agreement. By that will, each child was to receive about 30% of Nixon's estate in fee. If one child were to predecease the testator without leaving issue, the surviving child would take the other's share.

In 1948 Doris Ryer Nixon died testate in California. An executor was appointed there and undertook the administration of her estate. In 1951 Stanhope Wood Nixon executed a new will, which revoked his 1945 will, changed the outright gifts to his children to life estates, with life estates over to surviving issue and, finally, remainders to charities. The will also contained an *in terrorem* clause which would void the bequests made to any one who should "directly or indirectly . . . call in question before any tribunal the provisions of any legacy, devise or provisions herein. . . ." The daughter, Blanche, died in 1955 without issue, and the son, Lewis, survived and succeeded to her share under either of the father's wills. Stanhope Wood Nixon died in 1958, and his 1951 will was admitted to probate by the Surrogate of Middlesex County. The defendant is the executor and trustee under that will.

In 1958 the California executor of Doris Ryer Nixon's estate renounced in favor of the plaintiff, who obtained letters of administration *c. t. a.* from the Surrogate of Hudson County for the sole purpose of prosecuting this suit. Lewis Nixon was aware of the appointment of the plaintiff as administrator *c. t. a.*, and of the institution of this suit. He has offered no objection, doubtless because of the *in terrorem* clause.

Plaintiff in this action seeks judgment declaring that the 1945 agreement is binding on the estate of Stanhope Wood Nixon; that his executor be directed to administer the estate and make distribution thereof in conformity with that agreement, and that the 1951 will be reformed accordingly. In essence, the plaintiff seeks specific performance of the 1945 agreement.

The Chancery Division dismissed the complaint on the ground that the administrator *c. t. a.* had no standing to prosecute the suit, since no benefit could accrue from it to the estate. The Appellate Division affirmed, holding that "[a]s administrator with the will annexed, he has shown no right, power or duty to maintain this action." 55 N.J. Super. at page 336, 150 A.2d at page 781.

On this appeal plaintiff contends that his decedent, Doris Ryer Nixon, had in her lifetime a sufficient interest as promisee of the contract to enforce it, and that upon her death her right passed to her California executor and in turn to the plaintiff. On the other hand, the defendant contends that the only rights passing to her personal representatives are those whose enforcement would result in the realization of assets for distribution to the creditors and beneficiaries of her estate. It urges that the rights of Lewis Nixon belong to him as third party beneficiary of the 1945 contract, and not as beneficiary of the estate of Doris Ryer Nixon, and that under N.J.S. 2A:15-2, N.J.S.A., he has the right to enforce the contract, and is capable of instituting the necessary suit himself. Furthermore, it argues that if Stanhope Wood Nixon breached the contract, he did so at his death, which was after the death of plaintiff's decedent; no cause of action accrued to plaintiff's decedent during her lifetime and therefore none passed to the plaintiff.

It is beyond question that a person may bind himself by contract to make a particular will. It is equally clear that Lewis Nixon, the third party beneficiary of the 1945 contract, could have maintained a suit for specific performance. Our courts have long recognized the right of a third party beneficiary to enforce a simple contract. N.J.S. 2A:15-2, N.J.S.A., is declaratory of that rule and extends it to cover contracts under seal. However, the statute is merely permissive and does not exclude the rights of other parties to the contract.

A promisee of a contract for the benefit of a third party donee has a sufficient interest in the enforcement of the promise to entitle him to sue for damages. He may also invoke the aid of a court of equity, for the general reason that his remedy at law is inadequate, and he should not be denied an effective means of compelling fulfillment of a promise that he bought and paid for. In the case of a suit on a contract to make a will, there is the additional reason that breach of such a contract is deemed to be a fraud against which equity will afford relief.

The general rule is that a right of action founded upon a contract survives the person entitled in his lifetime to sue, so that the right passes upon his death to his personal representative. As early as 1646 it was held that the personal representative of a promisee of a contract made exclusively for the benefit of a third party donee could sue for the breach of that contract even though the donee beneficiary could also sue. . . .

The defendant argues that to allow the present suit opens the door to litigation in the name of an estate which can be of no benefit to its creditors and beneficiaries, and which can only deplete the estate with costs of administration. It further argues that such a holding opens a whole new area of unknown fiduciary duties, which it is unreasonable to impose upon an executor or administrator.

We cannot agree. We do not hold that the plaintiff, in the circumstances of this case, had a duty to enforce the contract his decedent made for the benefit of a third party donee. We merely hold that he had the power to do so. As in all areas of fiduciary administration, a decedent's personal representative is guided by a rule of reason. He must act with the diligence, prudence and caution of a reasonable man, and in the expenditure of estate funds he must abide by the principle that he primarily acts in the interest of creditors and beneficiaries.

For the reasons stated above, we hold that the plaintiff was empowered to prosecute the present action. The judgment of the Appellate Division dismissing the complaint is therefore reversed.

NOTES

(1) There is a duty from the promisor to the promisee as well as the third-party beneficiary. If the situation is one in which there is no economic benefit to the promisee (as in donee beneficiary cases), specific performance is appropriate. However, if the promisor's performance would have operated to discharge a duty owed by the promisee to the third party, the promisee may recover any damages suffered thereby. Thus, while double recovery against the promisor is normally precluded, if injuries to the promisee and third party cannot be redressed by a single payment, such recovery is permitted. *See* RESTATEMENT (SECOND) OF CONTRACTS §§ 305, 307 (1981).

(2) If the promisor breaches his agreement to pay the debt of the promisee to a third party (creditor) beneficiary, the promisee may recover the amount of the debt from the promisor. Double recovery against the promisor may be precluded by the court permitting the joinder of the third party or in other ways. For example, the court may enjoin enforcement of the judgment to the extent of any payment by the promisor to the third party or the court may order that the money collected by the promisee must be applied in reduction of the promisee's debt to the third party. *See Heins v. Byers*, 219 N.W. 287 (1928); MURRAY ON CONTRACTS § 134B.

I. DEFENSES AVAILABLE AGAINST BENEFICIARY

It is important to recognize that the rights of a third party beneficiary can rise no higher than the rights of the promisee. The terms of the contract define and limit the rights of a third party. If the contract expressly states that the parties do not intend to benefit any third party beneficiary, a third party obviously has no rights under the contract. Absent such an express exclusion of third party rights, the general rule is that all of the defenses that the promisor would have against the promisee on the original contract are available to the promisor in an action by the third party. If there is a lack of mutual assent, consideration or capacity, the beneficiary is subject to such defenses. Defenses of fraud, failure of express or constructive conditions, mistake or failure of performance will be available against the third party. If the promisor was entitled to arbitration in any dispute with the promisee, she is also entitled to arbitration when sued by the third party. If the contract reduces the statute of limitations for the promisee, it is also reduced for the third party. Notwithstanding the availability of these and other defenses, however, the rights of a protected beneficiary are direct rather than derivative. Thus, claims and defenses that the promisee may have against the promisor arising out of separate transactions between them have no effect on the third party.

If the contract itself expressly provides that the promisor's duty will not be subject to certain defenses that the promisor would have been able to assert against the promisee, such defenses will not be available against the third party beneficiary. A similar situation involves an important distinction.

ROUSE v. UNITED STATES
United States Court of Appeals, District of Columbia Circuit
215 F.2d 872 (1954)

EDGERTON, J.

Bessie Winston gave Associated Contractors, Inc., her promissory note for $1,008.37, payable in monthly installments of $28.01, for a heating plant in her house. The Federal Housing Administration guaranteed the note and the payee endorsed it for value to the lending bank, the Union Trust Company.

Winston sold the house to Rouse. In the contract of sale Rouse agreed to assume debts secured by deeds of trust and also "to assume payment of $850 for heating plant payable $28 per Mo." Nothing was said about the note.

Winston defaulted on her note. The United States paid the bank, took an assignment of the note, demanded payment from Rouse, and sued him for $850 and interest.

Rouse alleged as defenses (1) that Winston fraudulently misrepresented the condition of the heating plant and (2) that Associated Contractors did not install it satisfactorily. The District Court struck these defenses and granted summary judgment for the plaintiff. The defendant Rouse appeals.

Since Rouse did not sign the note he is not liable on it. D.C. Code 1951, Sec. 28-119; N.I.L. Sec. 18. He is not liable to the United States at all unless his contract with Winston makes him so. The contract says the parties to it are not "bound by any terms, conditions, statements, warranties or representation, oral or written" not contained in it. But this means only that the written contract contains the entire agreement. It does not mean that fraud cannot be set up a a defense to a suit on the contract. Rouse's promise to "assume payment of $850 for heating plant" made him liable to Associated Contractors, Inc., only if and so far as it made him liable to Winston; one who promises to make a payment to the promisee's creditor can assert against the creditor any defense that the promisor could assert against the promisee. Accordingly Rouse, if he had been sued by the corporation, would have been entitled to show fraud on the part of Winston. He is equally entitled to do so in this suit by an assignee of the corporation's claim. It follows that the court erred in striking the first defense. We do not consider whether Winston's alleged fraud, if shown, would be a complete or only a partial defense to this suit, since that question has not arisen and may not arise.

We think the court has right in striking the second defense. "If the promisor's agreement is to be interpreted as a promise to discharge whatever liability the promisee is under, the promisor must certainly be allowed to show that the promisee was under no enforceable liability. On the other hand, if the promise means that the promisor agrees to pay a sum of money to A, to whom the promisee says he is indebted, it is immaterial whether the promisee is actually indebted to that amount or at all. Where the promise is to pay a specific debt this interpretation will generally be the true one."[9]

The judgment is reversed and the cause remanded with instructions to reinstate the first defense.

NOTES

(1) In *Nu-Way Plumbing, Inc. v. Superior Mech. Inc.*, 315 So. 2d 556 (Fla. Ct. App. 1975), the court expressed agreement with the analysis in the principal case adding a quote from Professor Corbin: "There is nothing to prevent a promisor from undertaking a larger duty than the duty owed by the promisee to the beneficiary. . . . If he promises to pay a third party a sum claimed by him against the promisee, irrespective of defenses a promisee may have, he is bound by his promise in the teeth of such defenses." 4 CORBIN ON CONTRACTS § 821; *see also* RESTATEMENT (SECOND) OF CONTRACTS § 312, cmt. b (to the same effect). Notice the similarity between this situation and the earlier discussion (Section E, *supra*) of a promisor who has not assumed the mortgage debt becoming liable to the third party beneficiary mortgagee if that was the intention of the parties.

(2) There is a policy exception to the rule that the promisor may avail itself of any defense on the contract against the third party that would have been available against the promisee. Collective bargaining agreements often require employers to make payments to certain funds for the benefit of employees who are members of the union. Union members are not in any position to prevent actionable wrongs by their union. If the employer was permitted to raise such defenses, the employee

---

[9] [3] [Quoting Sections 811A, 394 and 399 of the 1936 edition of WILLISTON ON CONTRACTS].

beneficiaries could be deprived of the fluid created for their benefit. Thus, a breach by the union will not relieve the employer of its obligation to make pension contributions. *See Central States, SE and SW Areas Pension Fund v. Gerber Truck Serv.*, 870 F.2d 1148 (7th Cir. 1989) (referring to *Lewis v. Benedict Coal Co.*, 361 U.S. 459 (1960)).

PROBLEM

When the plaintiffs (brothers) of the Sodora family were 12 and 13 years old, their parents entered into a contract that required the father to give the children 50 percent of the proceeds of the sale of real estate when it was sold. The property was sold in 1978 when the plaintiff were 13 and 14. Instead of establishing the children's share of the funds at that time, the parents decided to invest the children's 50 percent share in a business operated by the father. The parents were divorced in 1997. The father died in 1999 and, for the first time, the children became aware of the agreement to provide them with a 50 percent interest. The plaintiffs sued in 1999 to recover their interest. The court determined that their rights under the contract had been breached in 1978. The defendant moved for summary judgment on the footing that the action was brought well beyond the six-year statute of limitations applicable to contract actions. Analyze. *See Sodora v. Sodora*, 768 A.2d 840 (N.J. Super. 2000).

J.   THE CUMULATIVE NATURE OF THE BENEFICIARY'S RIGHT

ERICKSON v. GRANDE RONDE LUMBER CO.
Oregon Supreme Court
94 P.2d 139 (1939)

[The plaintiff, Erickson, was an accountant and tax counselor. His complaint averred that he performed professional services for the Grande Ronde Lumber Company which subsequently entered into a contract with the Stoddard Lumber Company. The contract included a promise by Stoddard to discharge certain liabilities of Grande Ronde, including the the amount owing to the plaintiff. The plaintiff brought an action against both companies. He recovered an amount less than he sought against Grande Ronde and Stoddard's motion for a nonsuit was sustained. Plaintiff appealed and the Supreme Court of Oregon affirmed the judgment as to Grande Ronde and reversed and remanded the judgment as to Stoddard. Grande Ronde and Stoddard petition for rehearing. For the former opinion, see 162 Or. 556, 92 P.2d 170 (1939).]

ROSSMAN, J.

The petitioners argue that after the Stoddard Company had agreed to pay the Grande Ronde Company's debts, the plaintiff, as a creditor of the Grande Ronde Company, was not entitled to judgment against both of these companies. They insist that he was entitled to a remedy against only one of them, and that it was incumbent upon him to make an election. The respondents argue: "It may even be that so far as the commencement of the action was concerned that he had a right to pursue his remedy against both, but manifestly when the time came for the case to be decided he was not entitled to judgment against both." They argue that since he took judgment against the Grande Ronde Company he made his election and, therefore, cannot have relief against the Stoddard Company. In support of these contentions, the respondents cite *Wood v. Moriarty*, 15 R.I. 518, 9 A. 427; *Bohanan v. Pope*, 42 Me. 93.

We stated that the *Bohanan* and *Wood* decisions support the plaintiff's position, but both of them regarded the new promise as the consummation of a novation; and, of course, a novation is the substitution of a new right for an existing obligation. WILLISTON ON CONTRACTS, Rev. Ed., § 393, referring to these two decisions, among others, states: "Courts which hold that the original contract is in effect an offer of novation to the creditor naturally hold that if the creditor accepts the promisor as his debtor he releases the original debtor, and on the other hand, if he elects to sue the original debtor he thereby rejects the proffered novation and cannot afterwards sue the new promisor." From § 353 of the same treatise, we quote: ". . . A few states, however, have erroneously resorted to an implied novation theory for enforcement of the creditor beneficiary type of third party contract." Among the decisions which he states "have erroneously resorted to an implied novation theory" he cites the *Bohanan* and *Wood* decisions. In § 393, after the language quoted above, Williston continues: "The weight of authority, however, in the jurisdictions which allow a creditor beneficiary a direct right against the promisor supports the conclusion that the creditor has rights against both the promisor and the promisee, not merely a choice of rights; being entitled, of course, to but a single satisfaction. And in some states he is allowed to join both as defendants in the same action. He ought to be compelled to do so."

From RESTATEMENT OF THE LAW, CONTRACTS, § 141, we quote: "(1) A creditor beneficiary who has an enforceable claim against the promisee can get judgment against either the promisee or the promisor or against each of them on their respective duties to him. Satisfaction in whole or in part of either of these duties, or of judgments thereon, satisfies to that extent the other duty or judgment."

The principle embraced in the RESTATEMENT represents the law of this state. From the carefully prepared annotations to § 141, subd. 1, of the RESTATEMENT OF THE LAW OF CONTRACTS prepared by Professor Charles G. Howard (12 Oregon Law Review 283), we quote: "Oregon cases are in accord with this section and hold uniformly that there can be but one satisfaction, though both promisor and promisee are liable. . . ." We have read the decisions cited by Professor Howard and are satisfied that he correctly stated their essence.

We conclude that the plaintiff was entitled to maintain this action against the promisor (the Stoddard Company) as well as against his original debtor (the Grande Ronde Company). He was entitled to judgment against both; however, to only one complete satisfaction. The petition for a rehearing is denied.

NOTE

RESTATEMENT (SECOND) OF CONTRACTS § 310 (1981):

(1) Where an intended beneficiary has an enforceable claim against the promisee, he can obtain a judgment or judgments against either the promisee or the promisor or both based on their respective duties to him. Satisfaction in whole or in part of either of these duties, or of a judgment thereon, satisfies to that extent the other duty or judgment, subject to the promisee's right of subrogation.

(2) To the extent that the claim of an intended beneficiary is satisfied from assets of the promisee, the promisee has a right of reimbursement from the promisor, which may be enforced directly and also, if the beneficiary's claim is fully satisfied, by subrogation to the claim of the beneficiary against the promisor, and to any judgment thereon and to any security therefor.

See MURRAY ON CONTRACTS § 134A.

Chapter 10

THE ASSIGNMENT OF RIGHTS AND DELEGATION OF DUTIES

A. THE NATURE OF AN ASSIGNMENT

What Is an Assignment? An assignment is manifestation of an intention to presently transfer a contract right (an intangible right — a chose in action) from one party, the assignor, to another party, the assignee. An effective assignment extinguishes the right in the assignor and recreates the right in the assignee to performance by the obligor who owes the correlative duty. A sale of goods or a sale of real property is a transfer of the owner's rights in tangible property in exchange for a consideration. Neither an assignment nor a sale is a contract because neither is promissory in character. A promise to sell is not a sale and a promise to assign is not an assignment. *See Cinicola v. Scharffenberger,* 248 F.3d 110, 124 (3d Cir. 2001); RESTATEMENT (SECOND) OF CONTRACTS § 317.

Form. No particular form is usually required of an assignment and, absent statutory requirements, an assignment need not be evidenced by a writing or record. It may also be manifested by conduct.

Distinguishing Third Party Beneficiary Contracts. A third party beneficiary contract results where the promisee and promisor contract with the intention of providing the third party with an enforceable right against the promisor. An assignment, however, is the unilateral act of a party who has a right under an existing contract and chooses to make a present transfer of that right to an assignee without the consent and often without the knowledge of the other party to the contract, the obligor, who owes the correlative duty of the assigned right.

Delegation of Duties. Just as a party with rights under an existing contract may assign rights, she may also delegate duties under the same contract. As will be seen, however, some rights are not assignable and some duties are not delegable.

B. EVOLUTION OF ASSIGNMENT AND DELEGATION

SPRINT COMMUNICATIONS CO. v. APCC SERVICES, INC.
Supreme Court of the United States
554 U.S. 269 (2008)

[Payphone operators receive payments from long-distance carriers. Many operators assign their rights to such payments to billing and collection firms called "aggregators" who sue on their behalf. The aggregators promise to remit all of the proceeds of their lawsuits to the operators who then pay the aggregators for their services. In this case, a group of aggregators had been assigned the legal claims of some 1400 payphone operators. They brought this action to recover the payments due from the carriers. The carriers claimed that the aggregators had no standing to sue. The district court held that they had standing and that judgment was affirmed by the court of appeals. On appeal to the Supreme Court, Mr. Justice Breyer wrote the majority opinion which required a reflection on the general history of assignments.]

BREYER, J.

Prior to the 17th century, English law would not have authorized a suit like this one. But that is because, with only limited exceptions, English courts refused to recognize assignments at all. See, *e.g.*, *Lampet's Case*, 10 Co. Rep. 46b, 48a, 77 Eng. Rep. 994, 997 (K. B. 1612) (stating that "no possibility, right, title, nor thing in action, shall be granted or assigned to strangers"(footnote omitted)); *Penson & Higbed's Case*, 4 Leo. 99, 74 Eng. Rep. 756 (K. B. 1590) (refusing to recognize the right of an assignee of a right in contract); see also 9 J. Murray, Corbin on Contracts § 47.3, p 134 (rev. ed. 2007) (noting that the King was excepted from the basic rule and could, as a result, always receive assignments).

Courts then strictly adhered to the rule that a "chose in action" — an interest in property not immediately reducible to possession (which, over time, came to include a financial interest such as a debt, a legal claim for money, or a contractual right) — simply "could not be transferred to another person by the strict rules of the ancient common law." See 2 W. Blackstone, Commentaries *442. To permit transfer, the courts feared, would lead to the "multiplying of contentions and suits," *Lampet's Case, supra*, at 48a, 77 Eng. Rep., at 997, and would also promote "maintenance," *i.e.*, officious intermeddling with litigation, see Holdsworth, History of the Treatment of *Choses* in Action by the Common Law, 33 Harv. L. Rev. 997, 1006-1009 (1920).

As the 17th century began, however, strict anti-assignment rules seemed inconsistent with growing commercial needs. And as English commerce and trade expanded, courts began to liberalize the rules that prevented assignments of choses in action. See 9 Corbin, *supra*, § 47.3, at 134 (suggesting that the "pragmatic necessities of trade" induced "evolution of the common law"); Holdsworth, *supra*, at 1021-1022 (the "common law" was "induced" to change because of "considerations of mercantile convenience or necessity"); J. Ames, Lectures on Legal History 214 (1913) (noting that the "objection of maintenance" yielded to "the modern commercial spirit"). By the beginning of the 18th century, courts routinely recognized assignments of equitable (but not legal) interests in a chose in action: Courts of equity permitted suits by an assignee who had equitable (but not legal) title. And courts of law effectively allowed suits either by the assignee (who had equitable, but not legal title) or the assignor (who had legal, but not equitable title).

To be more specific, courts of equity would simply permit an assignee with a beneficial interest in a chose in action to sue in his own name. They might, however, require the assignee to bring in the assignor as a party to the action so as to bind him to whatever judgment was reached. Courts of law, meanwhile, would permit the assignee with an equitable interest to bring suit, but nonetheless required the assignee to obtain a "power of attorney" from the holder of the legal title, namely, the assignor, and further required the assignee to bring suit *in the name of that assignor.*[1] At the same time, courts of law would permit an assignor to sue *even when he had transferred away his beneficial interest.* And they permitted the assignor to sue in such circumstances precisely because the assignor retained legal title. The upshot is that by the time Blackstone published volume II of his Commentaries in 1766, he could dismiss the "ancient common law" prohibition on assigning choses in action as a "nicety . . . now disregarded." 2 Blackstone at 442.

Legal practice in the United States largely mirrored that in England. In the latter half of the 18th century and throughout the 19th century, American courts regularly "exercised their powers in favor of the assignee," both at law and in equity. 9 Corbin on Contracts § 47.3, at 137. Indeed, § 11 of the Judiciary Act of 1789 specifically authorized federal courts to take "cognizance of any suit to recover the contents of any promissory note or other chose in action in favour of an assignee" so long as federal jurisdiction would lie if the assignor himself had brought suit. 1 Stat. 79. Thus, in 1816, Justice Story, writing for a unanimous Court, summarized the practice in American courts as follows: "Courts of law, following in this respect the rules of equity, now take notice of assignments of choses in action, and exert themselves to afford them every support and protection." He added that courts of equity have "disregarded the rigid strictness of the common law, and protected the rights of the assignee of choses in action," and noted that courts of common law "now consider an assignment of a chose in action as substantially valid, only preserving, in certain cases, the form of an action commenced in the name of the assignor."

By the 19th century, courts began to consider the specific question presented here: whether an assignee of a legal claim for money could sue when that assignee had promised to give all litigation proceeds back to the assignor, . . . suits virtually identical to the litigation before us: suits by individuals who were assignees for collection only, *i.e.*, assignees who brought suit to collect money owed to their assignors but who promised to turn over to those assignors the proceeds secured through litigation. The history and precedents that we have summarized make clear that courts have long found ways to allow assignees to bring suit; that where assignment is at issue, courts — both before and after the founding — have always permitted the party with legal title alone to bring suit; and that there is a strong tradition specifically of suits by assignees for collection. We find this history and precedent "well nigh conclusive" in respect to the issue before us: Lawsuits by assignees, including assignees for collection only, are "cases and controversies of the sort traditionally amenable to, and resolved by, the judicial process."

The judgment of the Court of Appeals is affirmed.

---

[1] [Ed. note: A power of attorney involves one person, as principal, appointing another person as agent, conferring on the agent the authority to perform certain acts on behalf of the principal. The acceptance of the power of attorney implicitly requires the agent to use the power conferred for the sole benefit of the principal who conferred the power. A power of attorney requires no consideration. As Justice Breyer indicates, assignments were once viewed as nothing more than powers of attorney. The power of attorney was implied from the assignment. So long as the power was not revoked or otherwise terminated, the assignee had the authority to collect the assigned claim.]

C. GRATUITOUS ASSIGNMENTS

As indicated in the RESTATEMENT (SECOND) OF CONTRACTS, § 332, unless the assignment is made for consideration or in total or partial satisfaction of a pre-existing debt, it is a gratuitous assignment. Just as other property such as a chattel can be given to another by a manifestation of donative intent and delivery, however, a contract right — a chose in action — can be gratuitously assigned. To make a "gift" assignment irrevocable, an assignment should be in writing and delivered to the assignee. The delivery of certain symbolic writings or documents with donative intent will also manifest a completed gift. The delivery of a savings bank passbook, a nonnegotiable promissory note, a life insurance policy or a registered bond with the expressed intent of making the assignee the owner will be recognized as an irrevocable, gratuitous assignment. If Carr has a written contract with Davis to sell Davis a painting for $50,000, Carr can make a gratuitous assignment of his contract right of $50,000 to Davis by delivering the written contract to Davis. Gratuitous assignments also become irrevocable by certain subsequent acts. Thus, if the gratuitous assignee obtains performance or satisfaction from the obligor, a judgment against the obligor, or a new contract by way of novation, the assignment becomes irrevocable. If the gratuitous assignment induces detrimental reliance and the assignee reasonably relies on the assignment, the assignment will be irrevocable to the extent necessary to avoid injury.

D. THE NATURE OF ASSIGNABLE RIGHTS AND DELEGABLE DUTIES

WITT v. CIT GROUP/CONSUMER FINANCE INC.
United States District Court, District of Utah
2010 U.S. Dist. LEXIS 117915 (Nov. 5, 2010)

STEWART, J.

This matter is before the Court on Defendants Aurora Loan Services LLC, ("Aurora") and Mortgage Electronic Registrations Systems, Inc.'s ("MERS") Motion to Dismiss. Plaintiffs' Complaint alleges that, on or about March 28, 2008, Plaintiffs Nelson and Brenda Witt borrowed $173,250.22 from CIT secured by property located in Salt Lake City, Utah ("Property"). In conjunction with this transaction, Plaintiffs executed a promissory note ("Note") and deed of trust ("Deed of Trust") on September 30, 2002, which was later recorded on October 4, 2002. Also on October 4, 2002, an Assignment of Mortgage or Deed of Trust was recorded on the Property, which assigned all of CIT's beneficial rights, title, and interest under the Note and Deed of Trust to MERS. On October 16, 2007, CIT entered into a Mortgage Loan Sale Agreement with Lehman Capital, a division of Lehman Brothers Holdings, Inc. Plaintiffs' Note and Deed of Trust were among the mortgage loans included in the Mortgage Loan Sale Agreement. The closing date for the sale of the mortgage loans (including the Witts' Note and Deed of Trust) to Lehman Capital was October 30, 2007.

Plaintiffs later defaulted under the terms of the Note and Deed of Trust On April

7, 2008, a Substitution of Trustee executed by MERS on April 4, 2008, was recorded against the property appointing James H. Woodall as successor trustee of the Trust Deed.2Thereafter, the trustee initiated foreclosure proceedings on the property. Plaintiffs filed this Complaint against Defendants on May 11, 2010. Defendants moved to dismiss this Complaint in June of 2010.

Plaintiffs allege that the assignment from CIT to MERS was invalid because Plaintiffs never consented to the assignment. As Defendants demonstrate, however, consent from Plaintiffs was not required. As a matter of general contract law, beneficial rights under a contract are freely assignable unless precluded by contract, forbidden by statute, or where the assignment would materially alter the duties and rights of the obligor. Thus, under general contract law, the assignability of a contract is assumed unless the parties express a contrary intent by contract. Here, Plaintiffs have not pled nor brought forth any evidence to suggest that Plaintiffs contracted for a prohibition on the assignment of the Note and Deed of Trust. In fact, the Deed of Trust attached to Plaintiffs' Complaint expressly provides for assignment of the duties contemplated therein.Thus, Plaintiffs' claim that the assignment was invalid because Plaintiffs never consented to the assignment is contradicted by the express terms of the parties' Deed of Trust.

In opposing dismissal of these causes of action, Plaintiffs cite to the Restatement (Third) of Property to argue that their consent was necessary for a valid assignment because no "transfer of an obligation secured by a mortgage also transfers the mortgage unless the parties to the transfer agree otherwise." Plaintiffs appear to argue that this Restatement means that they, the mortgagors, must agree to any transfer of the Note and/or Deed of Trust. However, as the illustrative comments to this section make clear, the "parties to the transfer" who must agree to the transaction refers to the one assigning the duty (i.e., the mortgagee/assignor) and the one accepting the duty (i.e., assignor). Thus, Plaintiffs' participation in the assignment is not required. Therefore, Plaintiffs' claim fails as a matter of law and the Court will dismiss the causes of action associated with these arguments. [The defendants motions to dismiss are granted].

NOTE

An assignment extinguishes the assigned right in the assignor and recreates the same right in the assignee. Should it make any difference to the obligor (here, the mortgagor) that the mortgage and the right to be paid is now held by a party to whom that right has been assigned?

EVENING NEWS ASSOCIATION v. PETERSON
United States District Court, District of Columbia District
477 F. Supp. 77 (1979)

PARKER, J.

The question presented in this litigation is whether a contract of employment between an employee and the owner and licensee of a television station, providing for the employee's services as a newscaster-anchorman, was assigned when the station was sold and acquired by a new owner and licensee.

The defendant was employed by Post-Newsweek Stations, Inc. from 1969 to 1978. During that period he negotiated several employment contracts. Post-Newsweek had a license to operate television station WTOP-TV (Channel 9) in the District of Columbia. In June of 1978, following approval by the Federal Communications Commission, Post-Newsweek sold its operating license to Evening News and Channel 9 was then designated WDVM-TV. A June 26, 1978, Bill of Sale and Assignment and Instrument of Assumption and Indemnity between the two provided in pertinent part:

> PNS has granted, bargained, sold, conveyed and assigned to ENA, . . . all the property of PNS . . . including, . . . all right, title and interest, legal or equitable, of PNS in, to and under all agreements, contracts and commitments listed in Schedule A hereto . . . .

When Evening News acquired the station, Peterson's Post-Newsweek employment contract, dated July 1, 1977, was included in the Bill of Sale and Assignment. The contract was for a three-year term ending June 30, 1980, and could be extended for two additional one-year terms, at the option of Post-Newsweek. The significant and relevant duties and obligations under that contract required Peterson:

> to render services as a news anchorman, and to perform such related services as news gathering, writing and reporting, and the organization and preparation of program material, to the extent required by the Stations, as are consistent with [his] primary responsibility as a news anchorman. . . . [To participate] personally as a newsman, announcer, on-the-air personality or other performer in any news, public affairs, documentary, news analysis, interview, special events or other program or segment of any program, designated by . . . and to the extent required by the Stations . . . as may reasonably be required by the Stations. . . .

As compensation the defendant was to receive a designated salary which increased each year from 1977 through the fifth (option) year. Post-Newsweek was also obligated to provide additional benefits including term life insurance valued at his 1977 base salary, disability insurance, an annual clothing allowance and benefits to which he was entitled as provided in an underlying collective bargaining agreement with the American Federation of Television and Radio Artists.

There was no express provision in the 1977 contract concerning its assignability or nonassignability. However, it contained the following integration clause:

> This agreement contains the entire understanding of the parties . . . and this agreement cannot be altered or modified except in a writing signed by both parties.

The defendant's duties, obligations and performance under the 1977 contract did not change in any significant way after the Evening News' acquisition. In addition, the Evening News met all of its required contract obligations to the defendant and its performance after acquisition in June, 1978, was not materially different from that of Post-Newsweek.

Mr. Peterson testified that he had "almost a family relationship" with James

Snyder, News Director, and John Baker, Executive Producer, for Post-Newsweek, which permitted and promoted a free exchange of ideas, frank expressions of dissent and criticism and open lines of communication. These men left Channel 9 when Post-Newsweek relinquished its license, and they have since been replaced by Evening News personnel. According to Mr. Peterson, the close relationship and rapport which existed between him and them was an important factor as he viewed the contract; these relationships made the contract in his view nonassignable and indeed their absence at the Evening News prevented defendant from contributing his full efforts. Even if Mr. Peterson's contentions are accepted, it should be noted that he contracted with the Post-Newsweek corporation and not with the News Director and Executive Producer of that corporation. Indeed, the 1977 contract makes no reference to either officer, except to provide that vacations should be scheduled and coordinated through the News Director. Had the defendant intended to condition his performance on his continued ability to work with Snyder and Baker, one would have expected the contract to reflect that condition.

The close, intimate and personal relationship which Mr. Peterson points to as characterizing his association with Post-Newsweek and its personnel, was highly subjective and was supported only by his testimony. The Court cannot find that Peterson contracted with Post-Newsweek in 1977 to work with particular individuals or because of a special policy-making role he had been selected to perform in the newsroom. For the fourteen-month period of Peterson's employment at the Evening News, there is no showing that he was in any way circumscribed, limited in his work or otherwise disadvantaged in his performance. Nor is there any credible evidence that the News Director or other top personnel of Evening News were rigid, inflexible, warded off any of Mr. Peterson's criticisms or even that at any time he gave suggestions and criticisms which were ignored or rejected. Finally, the Court does not find that Post-Newsweek contracted with Peterson because of any peculiarly unique qualities or because of a relationship of personal confidence with him.

In his direct testimony, Mr. Peterson expressed a degree of disappointment because of Evening News' failure to keep apace with advances in technology and to seize opportunities for live in-depth coverage of current events. He characterized the plaintiff's news coverage as "less aggressive" than what he had experienced with Post-Newsweek.

On cross-examination, however, he was shown an exhibit comparing the broadcast of special assignments reported and produced by him for two one-year periods, one before and one after the June, 1978 acquisition. While he admitted to its accuracy with some reservation, the exhibit clearly showed that a comparable number of such assignments of similar quality, were broadcast within the two years. He also conceded that for the same period Evening News received two Peabody awards, an award for best editorials, and a number of Emmy awards for public affairs exceeding those received in prior years by Post-Newsweek. Finally, he acknowledged that Channel 9 still maintained the highest ratings for audience viewing among the television stations in the Washington, D.C. market area.

A great amount of testimony was generated as to when Peterson learned of the Evening News' acquisition and what then occurred relative to the assignment of the contract. The testimony on this issue was conflicting, largely cumulative and as now viewed, over-emphasized by the parties. The Court finds that the defendant gained first knowledge of a possible sale and transfer of the station in December, 1977. At that time, the president of Post-Newsweek publicly announced to the station's employees, including Peterson, that an agreement in principle had been reached, subject to approval by the Federal Communications Commission. At no time from December, 1977, until December, 1978, did the defendant or his attorney ever indicate or venture an opinion that the contract was not assignable. Indeed, through at least April, 1979, the defendant's attorney made representations that assignment of the contract presented no problem to his client.

In summary, the Court finds that the performance required of Mr. Peterson under the 1977 contract was (1) not based upon a personal relationship or one of special confidence between him and Post-Newsweek or its employees, and (2) was not changed in any material way by the assignment to the Evening News.

The distinction between the assignment of a right to receive services and the obligation to provide them is critical in this proceeding. This is so because duties under a personal services contract involving special skill or ability are generally not delegable by the one obligated to perform, absent the consent of the other party. The issue, however, is not whether the personal services Peterson is to perform are delegable but whether Post-Newsweek's right to receive them is assignable.

Contract rights as a general rule are assignable. *Munchak Corp. v. Cunningham*, 457 F.2d 721 (4th Cir. 1972). This rule, however, is subject to exception where the assignment would vary materially the duty of the obligor, increase materially the burden of risk imposed by the contract, or impair materially the obligor's chance of obtaining return performance. There has been no showing, however, that the services required of Peterson by the Post-Newsweek contract have changed in any material way since the Evening News entered the picture. Both before and after, he anchored the same news programs. Similarly he has had essentially the same number of special assignments since the transfer as before. Any additional policymaking role that he formerly enjoyed and is now denied was neither a condition of his contract nor factually supported by other than his own subjective testimony.

The general rule of assignability is also subject to exception where the contract calls for the rendition of personal services based on a relationship of confidence between the parties. As Corbin has explained this limitation on assignment:

> In almost all cases where a "contract" is said to be non-assignable because it is "personal," what is meant is not that the contractor's right is not assignable, but that the performance required by his duty is a personal performance and that an attempt to perform by a substituted person would not discharge the contractor's duty. Corbin § 865.

In *Munchak*, the Court concluded that a basketball player's personal services contract could be assigned by the owner of the club to a new owner, despite a contractual prohibition on assignment to another club, on the basis that the services were to the club. The Court found it "inconceivable" that the player's services "could be affected by the personalities of successive corporate owners." 457 F.2d at 725.

The policy against the assignment of personal service contracts, as the Court noted, "is to prohibit an assignment of a contract in which the obligor undertakes to serve only the original obligee." 457 F.2d at 726.

Given the silence of the contract on assignability, its merger clause, and the usual rule that contract rights are assignable, the Court cannot but conclude on the facts of this case that defendant's contract was assignable. Mr. Peterson's contract with Post-Newsweek gives no hint that he was to perform as other than a newscaster-anchorman for their stations. Nor is there any hint that he was to work with particular Post-Newsweek employees or was assured a policy-making role in concert with any givenemployees. Defendant's employer was a corporation, and it was for Post-Newsweek Stations, Inc. that he contracted to perform. The corporation's duties under the contract did not involve the rendition of personal services to defendant; essentially they were to compensate him. Nor does the contract give any suggestion of a relation of special confidence between the two or that defendant was expected to serve the Post-Newsweek stations only so long as the latter had the license for them.

Plaintiff's argument that defendant has waived any objection to the assignment by accepting the contract benefits and continuing to perform for the Evening News for over a year has perhaps some merit. If defendant has doubts about assignability, he should have voiced them when he learned of the planned transfer or at least at the time of transfer. His continued performance without reservation followed by the unanticipated tender of his resignation did disadvantage Evening News in terms of finding a possible replacement for him and possibly in lost revenues. The Court, however, concludes that the contract was assignable in the first instance and thus it is not necessary to determine whether defendant's continued performance constitutes a waiver of objection to the assignment.

During the course of this trial Edwin W. Pfeiffer, an executive officer of WDVM-TV, testified that Mr. Peterson allegedly stated "if the Judge decides I should stay, I will stay." Assuming that he did not overstate Mr. Peterson's position and that Mr. Peterson was quoted in appropriate context, the television audience of the Washington, D.C. metropolitan area should anticipate his timely reappearance as news anchorman for station WDVM-TV. Of course, the avenue of appeal is always available.

An order consistent with this Memorandum Opinion will be entered. Counsel for the plaintiff shall submit immediately an appropriate order.

NOTE

RESTATEMENT (SECOND) OF CONTRACTS § 317(2)(a) indicates that a right can be assigned unless the right of the assignor would materially change the duty of the obligor or materially increase the risk of the obligor or materially impair the chance of the obligor to obtain a return performance or, finally, materially reduce the value of the return performance. Sections 317(2)(b) and (c) indicate that an assignment may be precluded by statute or public policy or an anti-assignment provision in the contract between the obligor and the assignor. The UCC counterpart to § 317(2)(a) may be found in UCC § 2-210(2):

Unless otherwise agreed, all rights of either seller or buyer can be assigned except where the assignment would materially change the duty of the other party, or increase materially the burden or risk imposed on him by his contract, or impair materially his chance of obtaining return performance. A right to damages for breach of the whole contract or a right arising out of the assignor's due performance of his entire obligation can be assigned despite agreement otherwise.

THE MACKE CO. v. PIZZA OF GAITHERSBURG, INC.
Maryland Court of Appeals
270 A.2d 645 (1970)

SINGLEY, J.

The appellees and defendants below, Pizza of Gaithersburg, Inc.; Pizzeria, Inc.; The Pizza Pie Corp., Inc. and Pizza Oven, Inc., four corporations under the common ownership of Sidney Ansell, Thomas S. Sherwood and Eugene Early and the same individuals as partners or proprietors (the Pizza Shops) operated at six locations in Montgomery and Prince George's Counties. The appellees had arranged to have installed in each of their locations cold drink vending machines owned by Virginia Coffee Service, Inc., and on 30 December 1966, this arrangement was formalized at five of the locations, by contracts for terms of one year, automatically renewable for a like term in the absence of 30 days' written notice. A similar contract for the sixth location, operated by Pizza of Gaithersburg, Inc., was entered into on 25 July 1967.

On 30 December 1967, Virginia's assets were purchased by The Macke Company (Macke) and the six contracts were assigned to Macke by Virginia. In January, 1968, the Pizza Shops attempted to terminate the five contracts having the December anniversary date, and in February, the contract which had the July anniversary date.

Macke brought suit in the Circuit Court for Montgomery County against each of the Pizza Shops for damages for breach of contract. From judgments for the defendants, Macke has appealed.

The lower court based the result which it reached on two grounds: first, that the Pizza Shops, when they contracted with Virginia, relied on its skill, judgment and reputation, which made impossible a delegation of Virginia's duties to Macke; and second, that the damages claimed could not be shown with reasonable certainty. These conclusions are challenged by Macke.

In the absence of a contrary provision — and there was none here — rights and duties under an executory bilateral contract may be assigned and delegated, subject to the exception that duties under a contract to provide personal services may never be delegated, nor rights be assigned under a contract where *delectus personae* was an ingredient of the bargain.[3] 4 CORBIN ON CONTRACTS § 865 (1951) at 434; 6 Am. Jur.

---

[3] [1] Like all generalizations, this one is subject to an important exception. Uniform Commercial Code § 9-318 makes ineffective a term in any contract prohibiting the assignment of a contract right: i.e., a right to payment. *Compare* RESTATEMENT, CONTRACTS § 151(c) (1932).

2d, *Assignments* § 11 (1963) at 196. *Crane Ice Cream Co. v. Terminal Freezing & Heating Co.*, 147 Md. 588, 128 A. 280 (1925) held that the right of an individual to purchase ice under a contract which by its terms reflected a knowledge of the individual's needs and reliance on his credit and responsibility could not be assigned to the corporation which purchased his business. In *Eastern Advertising Co. v. McGaw & Co.*, 89 Md. 72, 42 A. 923 (1899), our predecessors held that an advertising agency could not delegate its duties under a contract which had been entered into by an advertiser who had relied on the agency's skill, judgment and taste.

The six machines were placed on the appellees' premises under a printed "Agreement-Contract" which identified the "customer," gave its place of business, described the vending machine, and then provided:

> 1. The Company will install on the Customer's premises the above listed equipment and will maintain the equipment in good operating order and stocked with merchandise.

> 2. The location of this equipment will be such as to permit accessibility to persons desiring use of same. This equipment shall remain the property of the Company and shall not be moved from the location at which installed, except by the Company.

> 3. For equipment requiring electricity and water, the Customer is responsible for electrical receptacle and water outlet within ten (10) feet of the equipment location. The Customer is also responsible to supply the Electrical Power and Water needed.

> 4. The Customer will exercise every effort to protect this equipment from abuse or damages.

> 5. The Company will be responsible for all licenses and taxes on the equipment and sale of products.

> 6. This Agreement-Contract is for a term of one (1) year from the date indicated herein and will be automatically renewed for a like period, unless thirty (30) day written notice is given by either party to terminate service.

> 7. Commission on monthly sales will be paid by the Company to the Customer at the following rate: . . . .

The rate provided in each of the agreements was "30% of Gross Receipts to $300.00 monthly[,] 35% over [$]300.00," except for the agreement with Pizza of Gaithersburg, Inc., which called for "40% of Gross Receipts."

We cannot regard the agreements as contracts for personal services. They were either a license or concession granted Virginia by the appellees, or a lease of a portion of the appellees' premises, with Virginia agreeing to pay a percentage of gross sales as a license or concession fee or as rent, . . . and were assignable by Virginia unless they imposed on Virginia duties of a personal or unique character which could not be delegated.

The appellees earnestly argue that they had dealt with Macke before and had chosen Virginia because they preferred the way it conducted its business. Specifically, they say that service was more personalized, since the president of Virginia kept the machines in working order, that commissions were paid in cash, and that Virginia permitted them to keep keys to the machines so that minor adjustments could be made when needed. Even if we assume all this to be true, the agreements with Virginia were silent as to the details of the working arrangements and contained only a provision requiring Virginia to "install . . . the above listed equipment and . . . maintain the equipment in good operating order and stocked with merchandise." We think the Supreme Court of California put the problem of personal service in proper focus a century ago when it upheld the assignment of a contract to grade a San Francisco street:

> All painters do not paint portraits like Sir Joshua Reynolds, nor landscapes like Claude Lorraine [sic], nor do all writers write dramas like Shakespeare or fiction like Dickens. Rare genius and extraordinary skill are not transferable, and contracts for their employment are therefore personal, and cannot be assigned. But rare genius and extraordinary skill are not indispensable to the workmanlike digging down of a sand hill or the filling up of a depression to a given level, or the construction of brick sewers with manholes and covers, and contracts for such work are not personal, and may be assigned. *Taylor v. Palmer*, 31 Cal. 240 at 247–248 (1866).

Moreover, the difference between the service the Pizza Shops happened to be getting from Virginia and what they expected to get from Macke did not mount up to such a material change in the performance of obligations under the agreements as would justify the appellees' refusal to recognize the assignment, *Crane Ice Cream Co. v. Terminal Freezing & Heating Co.*, *supra*, 147 Md. 588, 128 A. 280.

In support of the proposition that the agreements were for personal services, and not assignable, the Pizza Shops rely on three Supreme Court cases, *Burck v. Taylor*, 152 U.S. 634, 14 S. Ct. 696, 38 L. Ed. 578 (1894); *Delaware County Comm'r v. Diebold Safe & Lock Co.*, 133 U.S. 473, 10 S. Ct. 399, 33 L. Ed. 674 (1890); and *Arkansas Valley Smelting Co. v. Belden Mining Co.*, 127 U.S. 379, 8 S. Ct. 1308, 32 L. Ed. 246 (1888), all of which were cited with approval by our predecessors in *Tarr v. Veasey*, 125 Md. 199, 207, 93 A. 428 (1915). We find none of these cases persuasive. *Burck* held that the contractor for the state capitol in Texas, who was prohibited by the terms of his contract from assigning it without the state's consent, could not make a valid assignment of his right to receive three-fourths of the proceeds. In *Delaware County*, Diebold Safe and Lock, which was a subcontractor in the construction of a county jail, was barred from recovering from the county commissioners for its work on the theory that there had been a partial assignment of the construction contract by the prime contractor, which had never been assented to by the commissioners. This result must be limited to the facts: i.e., to the subcontractor's right to recover under the assignment, and not to the contractor's right to delegate. See *Taylor v. Palmer* and *Devlin v. Mayor, Aldermen and Commonalty of the City of New York*, both *supra*. *Arkansas Valley*, which held invalid an attempt to assign a contract for the purchase of ore, is clearly distinguishable, because of a contract provision which stipulated that payment for the ore was to be made after delivery, based on an assay to be made by the individual purchaser named in the contract. The court concluded that this was a confidence imposed in the individual purchaser's credit and responsibility and that his rights under the contract could not be transferred to another. *Tarr v. Veasey* involved a situation where duties were delegated to one person and rights assigned to another and our predecessors held the rights not to be assignable, because of the parties' intention that duties and rights were interdependent.

We find more apposite two cases which were not cited by the parties. In *The British Waggon Co. & The Parkgate Waggon Co. v. Lea & Co.*, 5 Q.B.D. 149 (1880), Parkgate Waggon Company, a lessor of railway cars, who had agreed to keep the cars "in good and substantial repair and working order," made an assignment of the contract to British Waggon Company. When British Waggon Company sued for rent, the lessee contended that the assignment had terminated the lease. The court held that the lessee remained bound under the lease, because there was no provision making performance of the lessor's duty to keep in repair a duty personal to it or its employees.

Except for the fact that the result has been roundly criticized, see CORBIN, *supra*, at 448-49, the Pizza Shops might have found some solace in the facts found in *Boston Ice Co. v. Potter*, 123 Mass. 28 (1877). There, Potter, who had dealt with the Boston Ice Company, and found its service unsatisfactory, transferred his business to Citizens' Ice Company. Later, Citizens' sold out to Boston, unbeknown to Potter, and Potter was served by Boston for a full year. When Boston attempted to collect its ice bill, the Massachusetts court sustained Potter's demurrer on the ground that there was no privity of contract, since Potter had a right to choose with whom he would deal and could not have another supplier thrust upon him. Modern authorities do not support this result, and hold that, absent provision to the contrary, a duty may be delegated, as distinguished from a right which can be assigned, and that the promisee cannot rescind, if the quality of the performance remains materially the same.

RESTATEMENT, CONTRACTS § 160(3)(1932) reads, in part:

> Performance or offer of performance by a person delegated has the same legal effect as performance or offer of performance by the person named in the contract, unless,

> (a) performance by the person delegated varies or would vary materially from performance by the person named in the contract as the one to perform, and there has been no . . . assent to the delegation. . . .

In cases involving the sale of goods, the RESTATEMENT rule respecting delegation of duties has been amplified by Uniform Commercial Code § 2-210(5), Maryland Code (1957, 1964 Repl. Vol.) Art. 95B § 2-210(5), which permits a promisee to demand assurances from the party to whom duties have been delegated.

As we see it, the delegation of duty by Virginia to Macke was entirely permissible under the terms of the agreements. [*Judgment reversed.*]

NOTE

RESTATEMENT (SECOND) OF CONTRACTS § 318 indicates that duties are normally delegable unless the obligee has a substantial interest in having a particular person perform the duty. The section also reminds us that neither delegation of the duty nor an assumption of the duty by the delegatee discharges any duty or liability of the obligor: Section 319 deals with the delegability of a performance condition and applies the same analysis to such conditions.

PROBLEMS

(1)   Berliners Foods, Inc. was a distributor of Haagen-Dazs ice cream. When Haagen-Dazs was acquired by Pillsbury in 1983, Berliner continued as a distributor. Without advising Pillsbury, Berliner was sold to Dreyers, the manufacturer of a premium ice cream sold primarily in the western part of the U.S. In expanding its market to the eastern U.S., because of the similarity between "Dreyers" and "Breyers," Dreyers is sold in the eastern U. S. under the name "Edy's." The contract between Pillsbury and Berliner contained a "best efforts" clause which suggested an exclusive territory and corresponding marketing efforts by Berliner to sell Haagen Dazs. Pillsbury has notified Berliner that it would no longer distribute Haagen Dazs. Pillsbury argues that it defies common sense to leave the distribution of its products to a distributor under the control of a competitor. Analyze. *See Berliner Foods Corp. v. Pillsbury Co.*, 633 F. Supp. 557 (D. Md. 1986); *see also Sally Beauty Co. v. Nexxus Prods. Co., Inc.*, 801 F.2d 1001 (7th Cir. 1986).

(2)   A model named Helga became famous when it was discovered that she was the subject of several Andrew Wyeth paintings. If Helga had a contract right to have Wyeth do those paintings, would that right have been assignable to another party?

(3)   A boardwalk artist at the seashore advertises that he will draw portraits for $25. He has not refused to draw the portrait of any customer with $25 since the summer season began and the season is almost over. Alice pays $25 to the artist and, just before she is to sit for the portrait, she assigns the right to her brother, George. Is the right assignable?

(4)   Zonex Corp. has performed services for Brad Gilmore, who owes the price of the services, $1,000, to Zonex. Zonex innocently assigned its right to the $1,000 to Buford Harris. Harris happens to be a person for whom Gilmore has felt nothing but contempt for the last 35 years. Gilmore has made every effort to avoid any contact with Harris during that time. Do these circumstances affect the assignability of the right?

(5)   May a famous heart surgeon assign his right and delegate his duty to one of his young associates in whom he has complete confidence? May a surgeon assign his right and delegate his duty for an ordinary operation to another surgeon who is regarded as equally competent and experienced? May a lawyer assign his right and delegate his duty to another lawyer to serve a particular client?

(6)   For the last seventeen summers, Mark Jordan has produced a variety show at a major entertainment fair. Jordan's duties included the selection of all entertainers — singers, dancers, comedians, etc. — as well as the music, staging and all other aspects of the production. After agreeing to produce the show for the eighteenth summer, Jordan has decided to assign his rights and delegate his duties to a producer who is much better known than Jordan. Are the rights and duties assignable and delegable?

(7)   Is an option to purchase real estate assignable? *See* RESTATEMENT (SECOND) OF CONTRACTS § 320.

In general, see MURRAY ON CONTRACTS §§ 139, 141.

E. PARTIAL ASSIGNMENTS

SPACE COAST CREDIT UNION v.
WALT DISNEY WORLD CO.
Florida Court of Appeals
483 So. 2d 35 (1986)

SHARP, J.

Space Coast Credit Union appeals from a final judgment denying its request to require the appellee, Walt Disney World, to comply with a partial voluntary wage assignment executed by Montgomery, a Disney employee, in favor of the appellant. The court relied on the stipulated facts recited in the Credit Union's petition in holding that there is no common law or statutory requirement in Florida imposing a duty on the part of an employer to honor the voluntary wage assignment involved in this case. We affirm the final judgment but reverse the attorney's fee awarded to the appellee under section 57.105, Florida Statutes (1983).

The record established that the Credit Union obtained a final judgment totaling $1,979.43 against Montgomery in April of 1981. In April of 1982, Montgomery executed a document entitled "Amended Assignment of Earnings for Payment of Final Judgment," in favor of the Credit Union. It directed Walt Disney World to deduct from his wages and pay to the Credit Union $20.00 per week, commencing February 25, 1982 through June 30, 1984; and he expressly waived all of his exemptions under Florida law.

Montgomery was an employee of Walt Disney World in 1982, and continued to be employed through the date the petition was filed in this case. Notice of the assignment was mailed to Disney, but it refused to comply with it. It paid nothing to the Credit Union, and there was no allegation or proof that it agreed or consented to the assignment.

This is apparently a case of first impression in Florida. Florida prohibits voluntary wage assignments to secure a loan made under the Florida Consumer Finance Act, but this is not such a transaction. Further, Florida impliedly recognizes that voluntary wage assignments may exist, since it taxes such assignments under the provision of its excise tax on documents statute.

We think given the Florida statutes on this subject matter, voluntary wage assignments exist under Florida's common law, as they do in other jurisdictions. At common law, wage assignments are treated as any other chose in action, and the general law of assignments applies, except when changed by statute. Annot., 1 A.L.R.3d 927 (1965); 6 Am. Jur. 2d *Assignments* § 46 (1963).

However, it is also well established that if the assignment is partial only it cannot be enforced against the debtor, or the employer, without his consent, or the joinder in an equitable proceeding of all persons entitled to the various parts of the total debt. Neither event occurred in this case. RESTATEMENT (SECOND) OF CONTRACTS § 326 (1981) provides:

> (1) Except as stated in Subsection (2), an assignment of a part of a right, whether the part is specified as a fraction, as an amount, or otherwise, is operative as to that part to the same extent and in the same manner as if the part had been a separate right.

> (2) If the obligor has not contracted to perform separately the assigned part of a right, no legal proceeding can be maintained by the assignor or assignee against the obligor over his objection, unless all the persons entitled to the promised performance are joined in the proceeding, or unless joinder is not feasible and it is equitable to proceed without joinder.

The Comment to section 326 states, in relevant part:

> Historically, the right of a partial assignee could be enforced only by a suit in a court of equity and it was therefore sometimes described as an "equitable" right. But the right of a total assignee also had historically an "equitable" character. Under the rule stated in Subsection (1), a partial assignment and a total assignment are equally effective, subject to the protection of the obligor under the rule stated in Subsection (2).

The rationale for this rule is that the debtor, here the employer, should not be subjected to multiple suits or claims not contemplated by the original assigned contract. The debtor's objection to a partial assignment may be asserted as in this case, by a rejection of the claim, and an absence of proof of consent; or a showing of hardship on the part of the debtor-employer, in complying with the partial assignment. Since it is clearly established in this case that Walt Disney World did not consent to this partial wage assignment, it was entitled to ignore it, and to pay Montgomery pursuant to its original undertaking under his contract of employment. Therefore, the judgment in this case is affirmed except that portion awarding attorney's fees.

NOTES

(1) *Joinder.* Where it is necessary to join all parties in a partial assignment situation, modern procedural codes make such joinder possible. See *Phoenix Ins. Co. v. Woosley*, 287 F.2d 531 (10th Cir. 1961), where nine partial assignees totaled their respective interests so as to equal the jurisdictional amount.

(2) *Wage Assignments.* There are certain assignments that are contrary to public policy. The most notable example of this limitation on assignability occurs with respect to the assignment of wages. Several different types of statutes restricting the assignment of wages have been enacted throughout the country. As the principal case suggests, certain kinds of wage assignments would be prohibited in Florida. The general theory underlying these statutes is the protection of the wage earner against his own improvidence as well as unscrupulous parties who might take advantage of him. A useful collection of these statutes and commentary thereon is found in the Statutory Note to Chapter 15 of the RESTATEMENT (SECOND) (prior to § 316).

For other statutory regulations limiting certain types of assignment, see MURRAY ON CONTRACTS § 139B (note 1).

F.   EFFECTS OF DELEGATION

ROSENBERGER v. SON, INC.
North Dakota Supreme Court
491 N.W.2d 71 (1992)

ERICKSTAD, J.

On February 8, 1980, Pratt entered into a contract for the sale of a business with the Rosenbergs, agreeing to purchase the Rosenbergs' Dairy Queen located in the City Center Mall in Grand Forks. The terms of the sales contract for the franchise, inventory, and equipment were a purchase price totaling $62,000, a $10,000 down payment, and $52,000 due in quarterly payments at 10 percent interest over a 15-year-period. The sales contract also contained a provision denying the buyer a right to prepayment for the first five years of the contract.

Mary Pratt assigned her rights and delegated her duties under the sales contract to Son, Inc., on October 1, 1982.[4] The assignment agreement contained a "Consent To Assignment" clause which was signed by the Rosenbergs on October 14, 1982.[5] The assignment agreement also included a "save harmless" clause in which Son, Inc., promised to indemnify Pratt.[6] Subsequent to this transaction, Mary Pratt moved to Arizona and had no further knowledge of, or involvement with, the Dairy Queen business. Also following the assignment, the Dairy Queen was moved from

---

[4] [1] The term "assign" is normally associated with a party's rights under a contract (i.e., getting paid, receiving goods); whereas the term "delegate" is associated with a party's duties under a contract (i.e., making a payment, performing a service). However, it is a common practice to call the assigning of rights and delegating of duties merely an "assignment of contract." This is especially true when language such as "all right, title and interest" is used. This was the exact language contained in the assignment agreement between Pratt and Son, Inc., and also in the assignment agreement between Son, Inc., and Merit, Corporation (to be discussed later). "An assignment of 'the contract' or of 'all my rights under the contract' or an assignment in similar general terms is an assignment of rights and unless the language or the circumstances (as in an assignment for security) indicate the contrary, it is a delegation of performance of the duties of the assignor and its acceptance by the assignee constitutes a promise by him to perform those duties. This promise is enforceable by either the assignor or the other party to the original contract." Section 41-02-17(4), N.D.C.C. Thus, the assignment agreements in this case not only assigned rights, they also delegated duties to the assignees.

[5] [2] The language of the consent clause was very brief and direct. In full, it read: "The undersigned, Harold Rosenberg and Gladys E. Rosenberg, sellers in the above described Contract of Sale, do hereby consent to the above assignment."

[6] [3] The indemnification clause reads as follows:

> And the said party of the second part [Son, Inc.] covenants and agrees to and with the said party of the first part [Pratt] that the said party of the second part will pay the said purchase price and will observe and perform all the terms, conditions and stipulations in the said agreement mentioned which are thereunder by the said party of the first part to be observed and performed, and will save harmless and keep indemnified the said party of the first part against all claims, demands and actions by reason of the failure of the said party of the second part to observe and perform the said agreement.

the City Center Mall to the corner of DeMers and North Fifth in Grand Forks.

The sales contract was then assigned by Son, Inc., to Merit, Corporation (Merit) on June 1, 1984. This assignment agreement did not contain a consent clause for the Rosenbergs to sign. However, the Rosenbergs had knowledge of the assignment and apparently acquiesced. They accepted a large prepayment from Merit, reducing the principal balance due to $25,000. Following this assignment, Merit pledged the inventory and equipment of the Dairy Queen as collateral for a loan from Valley Bank and Trust of Grand Forks.

Payments from Merit to the Rosenbergs continued until June of 1988, at which time the payments ceased, leaving an unpaid principal balance of $17,326.24 plus interest. The Rosenbergs attempted collection of the balance from Merit, but the collection efforts were precluded when Merit filed bankruptcy. The business assets pledged as collateral for the loan from Valley Bank and Trust of Grand Forks were repossessed. The Rosenbergs brought this action for collection of the outstanding debt against Son, Inc., and Mary Pratt.

[The trial court granted summary judgment motions for Pratt and Son, Inc., dismissing the Rosenbergs' claims against both parties.] It concluded that once Pratt assigned her contract she became a guarantor and, under North Dakota guaranty law, any alteration in the original obligation exonerates a guarantor.[7] The trial court found that moving the business, the second assignment to Merit, and pledging business assets as collateral, all without Pratt's knowledge, constituted alterations in the underlying obligation. Therefore, because it determined that Pratt was a guarantor on the contract, she was exonerated by the trial court. We disagree with the trial court's analysis and decision to grant summary judgment.

It is a well-established principle in the law of contracts that a contracting party cannot escape its liability on the contract by merely assigning its duties and rights under the contract to a third party. This principle is codified in Section 41-02-17(1), N.D.C.C.:

> Delegation of performance — Assignment of rights.
>
> 1. A party may perform his duty through a delegate unless otherwise agreed or unless the other party has a substantial interest in having his original promisor perform or control the acts required by the contract. *No delegation of performance relieves the party delegating of any duty to perform or any liability for breach* [emphasis added].

Professor Corbin explained this point succinctly in his treatise on contract law.

> An assignment is an expression of intention by the assignor that his duty shall immediately pass to the assignee. Many a debtor wishes that by such an expression he could get rid of his debts. Any debtor can express such an

---

[7] [5] This principle is codified in Section 22-01-15, N.D.C.C., which says: "When guarantor exonerated. A guarantor is exonerated, except insofar as he may be indemnified by the principal, if, by any act of the creditor without the consent of the guarantor: 1. The original obligation of the principal is altered in any respect; or 2. The remedies or rights of the creditor against the principal in respect thereto are impaired or suspended in any manner."

intention, but it is not operative to produce such a hoped-for result. It does not cause society to relax its compulsion against him and direct it toward the assignee as his substitute. In spite of such an 'assignment,' the debtor's duty remains absolutely unchanged. The performance required by a duty can often be delegated; but by such a delegation the duty itself is not escaped.

4 CORBIN ON CONTRACTS § 866 at 452.

This rule of law applies to all categories of contracts, including contracts for the sale or lease of real property, service contracts, and contracts for the sale of goods, which is present in the facts of this case.

> In the case of a contract for the sale of goods, the assignment and delegation may be by the buyer as well as by the seller. The buyer's assignment of his right to the goods and his delegation of the duty to pay the price are both effective; but he himself remains bound to pay the price just as before. If the assignee contracts with the assignor to pay the price, the seller can maintain suit for the price against the assignee also, as a creditor beneficiary of the assumption contract; the seller has merely obtained a new and additional security.

Id. at 454–455 (emphasis added) (footnotes omitted).

Thus, when Pratt entered into the "assignment agreement" with Son, Inc., a simple assignment alone was insufficient to release her from any further liability on the contract. *See Jedco Development Co., Inc. v. Bertsch*, 441 N.W.2d 664 (N.D. 1989) (lessee is not relieved of this obligation to pay rent merely because he had assigned lease with lessor's consent absent a novation); *Brooks v. Hayes*, 133 Wis.2d 228, 395 N.W.2d 167 (Wis. 1986) (party delegating duties under contract is not relieved of responsibility for fulfilling an obligation or liability in the event of a breach). *See also* RESTATEMENT (SECOND) OF CONTRACTS § 318.

It is not, however, a legal impossibility for a contracting party to rid itself of an obligation under a contract. It may seek the approval of the other original party for release, and substitute a new party in its place. In such an instance, the transaction is no longer called an assignment; instead, it is called a novation.[8] If a novation occurs in this manner, it must be clear from the terms of the agreement that a novation is intended by all parties involved. "An obligor is discharged by the substitution of a new obligor only if the contract so provides or if the obligee makes a binding manifestation of assent, forming a novation." RESTATEMENT (SECOND) OF CONTRACTS § 318 cmt. d. Therefore, both original parties to the contract must intend and mutually assent to the discharge of the obligor from any further liability on the original contract.

---

[8] [7] There are three statutes applicable to novation in the present case, 9-13-08, 09, and 10, N. D. C. C. "Novation defined: Novation is the substitution of a new obligation for an existing one. Novation is made by contract and is subject to all the rules concerning contracts in general. How novation made: Novation is made by the substitution of: 1. A new obligation between the same parties with intent to extinguish the old obligation; 2. A new debtor in the place of the old one with intent to release the latter; or 3. A new creditor in place of the old one with intent to transfer the rights of the latter to the former.'

It is evident from the express language of the assignment agreement between Pratt and Son, Inc., that only an assignment was intended, not a novation.[9] The agreement made no mention of discharging Pratt from any further liability on the contract. To the contrary, the latter part of the agreement contained an indemnity clause holding Pratt harmless in the event of a breach by Son, Inc. Thus, it is apparent that Pratt contemplated being held ultimately responsible for performance of the obligation.

Furthermore, the agreement was between Pratt and Son, Inc.; they were the parties signing the agreement, not the Rosenbergs. An agreement between Pratt and Son, Inc., cannot unilaterally affect the Rosenbergs' rights under the contract.

As mentioned earlier, the Rosenbergs did sign a consent to the assignment at the bottom of the agreement. However, by merely consenting to the assignment, the Rosenbergs did not consent to a discharge of the principal obligor — Pratt. Nothing in the language of the consent clause supports such an allegation. A creditor is free to consent to an assignment without releasing the original obligor.

"Where the obligee consents to the delegation, the consent itself does not release the obligor from liability for breach of contract. More than the obligee's consent to a delegation of performance is needed to release the obligor from liability for breach of contract. For the obligor to be released from liability, the obligee must agree to the release. If there is an agreement between the obligor, obligee and a third party by which the third party agrees to be substituted for the obligor and the obligee assents thereto, the obligor is released from liability Such an agreement is known as a novation." *Brooks v. Hayes*, 395 N.W.2d at 174. *See also Jedco Development Co., Inc. v. Bertsch*, 441 N.W.2d at 666 ("a lessee is not relieved of his obligation to pay rent merely because he has assigned the lease with the lessor's consent . . . rather, the lessor must intend to release the lessee"). Thus, the express language of the agreement and intent of the parties at the time the assignment was made did not contemplate a novation by releasing Pratt and substituting Son, Inc., in her stead.

Without thoroughly acknowledging the above principles and their importance, the trial court concluded that once Pratt assigned her contract she became a guarantor on the contract. The trial court proceeded to apply North Dakota guaranty statutes and guaranty case law to Pratt, and exonerated her under that authority. We do not believe that the trial court appropriately applied the law.

As stressed above, a party assigning its rights and delegating its duties is still a party to the original contract. An assignment will not extinguish the relationship and obligations between the two original contracting parties. However, an assign-

---

[9] [8] The agreement itself was titled "ASSIGNMENT OF CONTRACT FOR SALE." Following the standard introduction of the parties involved (Pratt and Son, Inc.), it read:

That the said party of the first part [Pratt], in consideration of the sum of One Dollar ($1.00) and other valuable consideration to her paid by the said party of the second part [Son, Inc.], the receipt whereof is hereby acknowledged, does hereby assign, transfer and set over unto the said party of the second part the above recited agreement or Contract of Sale and all the right, title and interest of the said party of the first part to the business above described, to have and to hold the same unto the said party of the second part, its successors and assigns, forever, subject, nevertheless, to the terms, conditions and stipulations in the said agreement contained.

ment does result in the assignor having a surety relationship, albeit involuntary, with the assignee, but not with the other original contracting party.

"A common instance of involuntary suretyship, at least as between the principal and surety themselves occurs where one party to a contract [Son, Inc.], as a part of the agreement, assumes an indebtedness owing by the other [Pratt] to a third person [the Rosenbergs], the one assuming the indebtedness becoming the principal [Son, Inc.], and the former debtor a surety [Pratt]." 72 C.J.S. *Principal and Surety* § 35 (emphasis added). Therefore, in the present facts, Pratt enjoyed a surety position as to Son, Inc., but remained a principal on the contract with the Rosenbergs.

The inquiry as to Pratt's liability does not end at this juncture. Pursuant to guaranty law, the trial court released Pratt from any liability on the contract due to the changes or alterations which took place following her assignment to Son, Inc. While it is true that Pratt cannot be forced to answer on the contract irrespective of events occurring subsequent to her assignment, it is also true that she cannot be exonerated for every type of alteration or change that may develop.

> The buyer can assign his right to the goods or land and can delegate performance of his duty to pay the price. He himself remains bound as before by his duty to pay that price. But observe that he remains bound 'as before'; the assignee and the seller cannot, by agreement or by waiver, make it the assignor's duty to pay a different price or on different conditions. If the seller is willing to make such a change, he must trust to the assignee alone. It has been held that, if a tender of delivery by a certain time is a condition precedent to the buyer's duty to pay, the assignee of the buyer has no power to waive this condition, and substantial delay by the seller will prevent his getting judgment against the assignor for the price. If the assignee has contracted to pay the price, his waiver of the condition will be effective in a suit against him, but it will not be allowed to prejudice the position of the assignor who now occupies substantially the position of surety.

4 CORBIN ON CONTRACTS § 866 at 458–459.

The trial court decided that any alteration in the underlying obligation resulted in a release of Pratt on the contract. It appears that an assignor occupies a much different position from that of a guarantor; not every type of alteration is sufficient to warrant discharge of the assignor. As suggested by Professor Corbin in the language highlighted above, the alteration must "prejudice the position of the assignor." 4 CORBIN ON CONTRACTS § 866 at 459.

> Accordingly, unless the other contracting party has consented to release him, the assignor remains bound by his obligations under the contract and is liable to the other party if the assignee defaults. . . . However, the assignor is responsible only for the obligation which he originally contracted to assume, and the assignee cannot, without the assignor's knowledge, increase the burden.

6A C.J.S. Assignments § 97 at 753–754.

If the changes in the obligation prejudicially affect the assignor, a new agreement has been formed between the assignee and the other original contracting party. More concisely, a novation has occurred and the assignor's original obligation has been discharged. This is consistent with our previous decisions and statutory authority. Although we have previously determined that the terms of the assignment agreement between Pratt and Son, Inc., did not contemplate a novation, there are additional methods of making a novation besides doing so in the express terms of an agreement:

> The intent to create a novation may be shown not only by the terms of the agreement itself, but also by the character of the transaction and by the facts and circumstances surrounding the transaction. *Cane River Shopping Center v. Monsour*, 443 So. 2d 602 (La. Ct. App. 1983).

The question of whether or not there has been a novation is a question of fact. The trial court should not have granted summary judgment on the basis of guaranty law. First of all, guaranty law does not apply to contract assignments without more. Further, there are questions of fact remaining as to the result of the changes in the contract. These issues were not addressed by the trial court. Thus, we reverse the summary judgment and remand for further proceedings.

NOTES

(1)   The BW partnership contracted with Western Oil Co. allowing Western to take oil from BW wells. The contract included a clause stating it was binding on the parties, their heirs, executors, administrators, successors and assigns. Western assigned its rights and delegated its duties to Amoco which assumed all of Western's obligations. Western then notified BW of the contract with Amoco and demanded that BW look exclusively to Amoco for future payments under the contract. Analyze. *See Western Oil Sales Corp. v. Bliss & Wetherbee*, 299 S.W. 637 (Tex. 1927).

(2)   *Interpretation.* In footnote 4 of the principal case, the court alludes to the problem of interpreting the statement of a party who simply assigns "the contract" or "all of my rights under the contract" to another. Does such an assignment in such general language indicate, as the court suggests, that it is intended not only to assign the rights but delegate the duties?

Section 2-210(4) of the UCC states:

> An assignment of "the contract" or of "all my rights under the contract" or an assignment in similar general terms is an assignment of rights and unless the language or the circumstances . . . indicate the contrary, it is a delegation of performance of the duties of the assignor and its acceptance by the assignee constitutes a promise by him to perform those duties.

RESTATEMENT (SECOND) OF CONTRACTS § 328 agrees with this position in language that is virtually indistinguishable. A number of cases involving the sale of land, however, refused to interpret such general assignment language to make the assignee of a land contract liable. They insist that such liability must be predicated on an expressed-in-language assumption of such a duty. The leading case is *Langel v. Betz*, 164 N.E. 890 (N.Y. 1928), which expressly rejected RESTATEMENT (SECOND) OF

CONTRACTS § 164. These holdings are apparently traceable to the generally accepted rule that one who takes a conveyance of land subject to a mortgage does not, without more, become obligated to on the mortgage debt. They may also manifest a reluctance to make an assignee liable as a promisor to a third-party mortgagee unless the assignee/promisor expressly assumed such liability. The RESTATEMENT (SECOND) OF CONTRACTS recognizes this line of cases and, therefore, expresses "no opinion on the application of [the general principle] to an assignment by a purchaser under a land contract." RESTATEMENT (SECOND) OF CONTRACTS § 328, comment c. See also illustration 4 to this section, based on the facts of *Langel v. Betz*, which concludes that the American Law Institute expresses no opinion as to whether there is a promise by the assignee under a land contract.

G.   ACCOUNTS RECEIVABLE FINANCING — UCC

A seller of goods often sells goods on credit. When the goods are delivered to the buyer, the seller receives a promise from the buyer to pay for them. The buyer is treated as an "account." When a consumer buys from a retail store on credit, the buyer has an "account" at that store. The retail store buys its inventory from a wholesaler, distributor or manufacturer. Sellers at any level are typically not in the business of financing sales. They require funds to restock their factories and stores. They will transfer these "accounts" to a financing institution such as a bank or more typically another type of commercial lender under a pervasive practice known as "accounts receivable financing." Such commercial financing is governed by Article 9 of the Uniform Commercial Code. While Article 9 is primarily concerned with security interests in personal property, the difficulty in determining whether a party sold (assigned) its accounts or merely granted a security interest in the accounts to a lender induced the drafters of Article 9 to include both transactions. Assignments in a commercial lending context, therefore, are governed by Article 9 which has certain requirements to determine the rights and duties of parties. Article 9 would not apply to an assignment of accounts that is not designed to finance a business. For example, when a business is sold, the accounts of that business may constitute a major portion of the sales price. Article 9 would not apply to such a transaction. Neither would it apply where the assignment of account is provided to pay a pre-existing debt or where the assignee is required to perform under the contract. These are not typical commercial financing transactions and they are, therefore, governed by contract law rather than Article 9. The complexities of Article 9 are not addressed in courses in contract law. They are left to courses in secured transactions.

H.   FUTURE RIGHTS

FUTURE RIGHTS SPEELMAN v. PASCAL
New York Court of Appeals
178 N.E.2d 723 (1961)

DESMOND, J.

Gabriel Pascal, defendant's intestate who died in 1954, had been for many years a theatrical producer. In 1952 an English corporation named Gabriel Pascal Enterprises, Ltd., of whose 100 shares Gabriel Pascal owned 98, made an agreement with the English Public Trustee who represented the estate of George Bernard Shaw. This agreement granted to Gabriel Pascal Enterprises, Ltd., the exclusive world rights to prepare and produce a musical play to be based on Shaw's play "Pygmalion" and a motion picture version of the musical play. The agreement recited, as was the fact, that the licensee owned a film scenario written by Pascal and based on "Pygmalion" In fact Pascal had, some time previously, produced a nonmusical movie version of "Pygmalion" under rights obtained by Pascal from George Bernard Shaw during the latter's lifetime. The 1952 agreement required the licensee corporation to pay the Shaw estate an initial advance and thereafter to pay the Shaw estate 3% of the gross receipts of the musical play and musical movie with a provision that the license was to terminate if within certain fixed periods the licensee did not arrange with Lerner and Lowe or other similarly well-known composers to write the musical play and arrange to produce it. Before Pascal's death in July, 1954, he had made a number of unsuccessful efforts to get the musical written and produced and it was not until after his death that arrangements were made, through a New York bank as temporary administrator of his estate, for the writing and production of the highly successful "My Fair Lady." Meanwhile, on February 22, 1954, at a time when the license from the Shaw estate still had two years to run, Gabriel Pascal, who died four and a half months later, wrote, signed and delivered to plaintiff a document as follows:

Dear Miss Kingman

This is to confirm to you our understanding that I give you from my shares of profits of the Pygmalion Musical stage version five per cent (5%) in England, and two per cent (2%) of my share of profits in the United States. From the film version, five per cent (5%) from my profit shares all over the world.

As soon as the contracts are signed, I will send a copy of this letter to my lawyer, Edwin Davies, in London, and he will confirm to you this arrangement in a legal form.

This participation in my shares of profits is a present to you, in recognition for your loyal work for me as my Executive Secretary.

Very sincerely yours,

Gabriel Pascal

The question in this lawsuit is: Did the delivery of this paper constitute a valid, complete, present gift to plaintiff by way of assignment of a share in future royalties when and if collected from the exhibition of the musical stage version and film version of "Pygmalion"? A consideration was, of course, unnecessary.

In pertinent parts the judgment appealed from declares that plaintiff is entitled to receive the percentages set out in the 1954 agreement, requires defendant to render plaintiff accountings from time to time of all moneys received from the musical play and the film version, and orders defendant to make the payments required by the agreement. The basic grant from the Shaw estate was to Gabriel Pascal Enterprises, Ltd., a corporation, whereas the document on which plaintiff sues is signed by Gabriel Pascal individually and defendant makes much of this, arguing that Gabriel Pascal, as distinguished from his corporation, owned no rights when he delivered the 1954 document to plaintiff. However, no such point was made in the courts below and no mention of it is made in the motion papers, affidavits, etc., on which plaintiff was granted summary judgment. It is apparent that all concerned in these transactions disregarded any distinction between Pascal's corporation in which he owned practically all the stock, and Pascal individually, as is demonstrated by the agreement between Lerner-Lowe-Levin, writers and producers of "My Fair Lady," and Gabriel Pascal's estate. Actually, all this makes little difference since what Pascal assigned to plaintiff was a percentage from Pascal's "shares of profits" and this would cover direct collections or collections through his corporation.

Defendant emphasizes also the use of the word "profits" in the February, 1954 letter from Pascal to plaintiff, and suggests that this means that plaintiff was not to get a percentage of Pascal's gross royalties but a percentage of some "profits" remaining after deduction of expenses. Again, the answer is that no such point was made in the proceedings below or in this record and everyone apparently assumed, at least until the case reached this court, that what the defendant Pascal estate will get from the musical play and movie is royalties collectible in full under the agreements pursuant to which "My Fair Lady" has been and will be produced. In this same connection defendant talks of possible creditors of the Pascal corporation and inquiries as to what provision would be made for them if plaintiff were to get her percentages of the full royalties. This, too, is an afterthought and no such matter was litigated below.

The only real question is as to whether the 1954 letter above quoted operated to transfer to plaintiff an enforceable right to the described percentages of the royalties to accrue to Pascal on the production of a stage or film version of a musical play based on "Pygmalion." We see no reason why this letter does not have that effect. It is true that at the time of the delivery of the letter there was no musical stage or film play in existence but Pascal, who owned and was conducting negotiations to realize on the stage and film rights, could grant to another a share of the moneys to accrue from the use of those rights by others. There are many instances of courts enforcing assignments of rights to sums which were expected thereafter to become due to the assignor. A typical case is *Field v. Mayor of City of New York*, 6 N.Y. 179. One Bell, who had done much printing and similar work for the City of New York but had no present contract to do any more such work, gave an assignment in the amount of $1,500 of any moneys that might thereafter become due to Bell for such work. Bell did obtain such contracts or orders from the city and money became due to him therefor. This court held that while there was not at the time of the assignment any presently enforceable or even existing chose in action but merely a possibility that there would be such a chose in action, nevertheless there was a possibility of such which the parties expected to ripen into reality and which did afterwards ripen into reality and that, therefore, the assignment created an equitable title which the courts would enforce. A case similar to the present one in general outline is *Central Trust Co. of New York v. West India Improvement Co.*, 169 N.Y. 314, 62 NE 387, where the assignor had a right or concession from the Colony of Jamaica to build a railroad on that island and the courts upheld a mortgage given by the concession owner on any property that would be acquired by the concession owner in consideration of building the railroad if and when the railroad should be built. The Court of Appeals pointed out in *Central Trust Co.*, at page 323, 62 NE at page 389, that the property, as to which the mortgage was given had not yet come into existence at the time of the giving of the mortgage but that there was an expectation that such property, consisting of securities, would come into existence and accrue to the concession holder when and if the latter performed the underlying contract. This court held that the assignment would be recognized and enforced in equity. The cases cited by appellant (*Young v. Young*, 80 N.Y. 422; *Vincent v. Six*, 248 N.Y. 76, 161 NE 425; *Farmers' Loan & Trust Co. v. Winthrop*, 207 App. Div. 356, 202 N.Y.S. 456, *mod.* 238 N.Y. 477, 144 NE 686) are not to the contrary. In each of those instances the attempted gifts failed because there had not been such a completed and irrevocable delivery of the subject matter of the gift as to put the gift beyond cancellation by the donor. In every such case the question must be as to whether there was a completed delivery of a kind appropriate to the subject property. Ordinarily, if the property consists of existing stock certificates or corporate bonds, as in the *Young* and *Vincent* cases (*supra*), there must be a completed physical transfer of the stock certificates or bonds. In *Farmers' Loan & Trust Co. v. Winthrop* (*supra*) the dispute was as to the effect of a power of attorney but the maker of the power had used language which could not be construed as effectuating a present gift of the property which the donor expected to receive in the future from another estate. The *Farmers' Loan & Trust Co.* case does not hold that property to be the subject of a valid gift must be in present physical existence and in the possession of the donor but it does hold that the language used in the particular document was not sufficient to show an irrevocable present intention to turn over to the donee securities which would come to the donor on the settlement of another estate. At page 485 of 238 N.Y., at page 687 of 144 NE this court held that all that need be established is "an intention that the title of the donor shall be presently divested and presently transferred" but that in the particular document under scrutiny in the *Farmers' Loan & Trust Co.* case there was lacking any language to show an irrevocable intent of a gift to become operative at once. In our present case there was nothing left for Pascal to do in order to make an irrevocable transfer to plaintiff of part of Pascal's right to receive royalties from the productions. *Judgment affirmed.*

PROBLEM

After winning all of the university prizes for creative writing during her four years of undergraduate work, Winiva Gaston decided that her future as a writer would be best served by moving to Manhattan. Her only regret was leaving her ill and widowed mother, Blanche, who had worked diligently to allow Winiva to complete her education at a distinguished Catholic university in Western Pennsylvania. Winiva left a note for Blanche which read, "I know that you will be devastated to learn of my leaving, but I simply must go. I hereby give you half of the royalties on any of my work." Winiva's first book was a sensation, with royalties amounting to $1 million. She quickly produced a second novel, which produced royalties of $2 million. Blanche, who was feeling better, sought half of these royalties but Winiva no longer recognized Blanche as her mother. Blanche brought an action for half of the royalties. What result? *See* RESTATEMENT (SECOND) OF CONTRACTS § 321; *see also* RESTATEMENT (SECOND) OF CONTRACTS § 140.

I.   UCC FUTURE RIGHTS — AFTER-ACQUIRED PROPERTY

Earlier in this chapter, we recognized the application of UCC Article 9 to the assignment of "accounts" (Section G, *supra*). It is desirable for the contracts student to become aware of a basic Article 9 concept that deals with the transfer of "future rights." A simple illustration involves the owner and operator of a hardware store, Joseph Adams. To purchase the inventory which he intends to resell to his customers (tools, equipment, various supplies, etc.), Joseph will typically borrow money from a bank or a commercial lender. He will promise to repay the loan from the proceeds of his sales to his customers. As he sells his inventory and repays the loan, he will require additional funds to purchase replacement inventory. This arrangement with the lender will be one of continuous borrowing to replenish the inventory and continuous repayment of the loans from the proceeds of the store's sales to customers. The arrangement could extend for the lifetime of the business. Beyond Joseph's bare promise to repay the loans, the lender will require "security" to assure the loan is repaid in the form of a property interest in something owned by Joseph, called "collateral." While a lender could take a real estate mortgage on Joseph's store if he owned it, the most important collateral owned by Joseph may be his inventory. The problem is that the inventory is continuously turning over as it is sold to customers. If the lender takes a security interest in Joseph's existing inventory when the loan is first made, that inventory will be gone through sales to customers. The lender will also take a security interest in any "proceeds" from Joseph's sales — what Joseph received from customers in exchange for the goods they bought such as cash, checks or promise to pay Joseph ("accounts"). The lender, however, will also desire a security interest in the new inventory not yet received or even purchased by Joseph, his "after-acquired property." When Joseph entered into the original contract with the lender, he not only signed a promise to repay the loan, he signed a security agreement that granted to the lender a security interest, not only in Joseph's present, existing inventory in the store, but an interest in inventory to be acquired in the future (again, "after-acquired" property). As soon as Joseph obtains rights in any new inventory, the lender's security interest "attaches" to that property. There is no need for a new security agreement or contract. The original security agreement will suffice though it may have been executed years earlier. The lender will also file a UCC financing statement in a public office to alert any potential future lender to Joseph that the original lender had a security interest not only in all of Joseph's current inventory, but in his future (after-acquired) inventory.

This "perfects" the lender's security interest against claims from subsequent creditors who might take a later security interest in Joseph's collateral. The original lender will prevail under a "first to file" rule. The reality is that any commercial lender will typically check the publicly recorded UCC filings before making a loan. The discovery that Joseph's existing and future inventory is already subject to a perfected security interest will invariably cause that lender to lose interest in making another loan to Joseph with only that collateral as security.

Conceptually, it is difficult to think of rights in property which Joseph has yet to agree to purchase. Indeed, the screwdrivers, hammers or other tools which Joseph has yet to purchase may not even exist until he places an order to buy them. Business of all kinds pursue this type of continuous financing with its security interest in inventory and after-acquired inventory. Another typical example occurs in the sale of automobiles where the auto dealer must continuously borrow the funds to buy the new models annually and pays the loan from the proceeds of sales to car buyers.

Manufacturers will also borrow funds to purchase raw materials and repay those loans through the proceeds they receive in selling their manufactured products. Article 9 of the UCC removed the obstacles to the transfer of "future rights" to facilitate commercial financing. Such arrangements are sometime called "floating liens" or a "floor planning" method of commercial financing.

J.   PROHIBITION OF ASSIGNMENT — ANTI-ASSIGNMENT CLAUSES

RUMBIN v. UTICA MUTUAL INSURANCE COMPANY
Connecticut Supreme Court
757 A.2d 526 (2000)

VERTEFEUILLE, J.

The record reveals the following facts. In April, 1998, the plaintiff [Marco Rumbin] and Utica Mutual entered into a structured settlement agreement to resolve a personal injury claim. Pursuant to that settlement agreement, the plaintiff was to receive from Utica Mutual a lump sum payment, followed by a series of periodic payments over the next fifteen years. [Under the terms of the settlement agreement, the plaintiff was entitled to receive $52,000 within thirty days of its execution, thirty semi-annual payments of $1,323.09 beginning on March 6, 1999, and a final lump sum payment of $44,000 on March 6, 2014.] The structured portion of the settlement was funded by the annuity contract issued by Safeco Life Insurance Co. The annuity contract provided under its "Assignment" provision that "no payment under this annuity contract may be . . . assigned in any manner by the [plaintiff]."

Approximately six months after the execution of the settlement agreement and the issuance of the annuity, the plaintiff had become unemployed and faced a mortgage foreclosure action against his home, where he lived with his family. In order to resolve his financial troubles, the plaintiff decided to sell his right to the annuity payments to Wentworth in exchange for a lump sum payment and other consideration. Safeco objected to the assignment. [Utica Mutual is not a party to this appeal. The trial court concluded that the assignment was valid.] The primary issue raised by this case is whether, under Connecticut common law, an antiassignment provision in an annuity contract invalidates the plaintiff payee's transfer of his right to future payments under the annuity to a third party. We conclude, in accordance with case law and § 322 of the RESTATEMENT (SECOND) OF CONTRACTS, that the antiassignment provision at issue here does not render the assignment of the annuity ineffective, but, instead, gives the annuity issuer, Safeco, the right to recover damages for breach of the antiassignment provision.

Our analysis of the effect of the antiassignment provision begins by emphasizing that the modern approach to contracts rejects traditional common-law restrictions on the alienability of contract rights in favor of free assignability of contracts. *See* 3 RESTATEMENT (SECOND), CONTRACTS § 317, p. 15 (1981) ("[a] contractual right can be assigned"); J. MURRAY, JR., CONTRACTS (3d Ed. 1990) ("the modern view is that contract rights should be freely assignable"); 3 B. FARNSWORTH, CONTRACTS (2d Ed. 1998) § 11.2, p. 61 ("today most contract rights are freely transferable"). Common-law restrictions on assignment were abandoned when courts recognized the necessity of permitting the transfer of contract rights. "The forces of human convenience and business practice [were] too strong for the common-law doctrine that [intangible contract rights] are not assignable." (Internal quotation marks omitted.) J. MURRAY, JR., *supra*, § 135, p. 791. "If the law were otherwise, our modern credit economy could not exist." 3 E. FARNSWORTH, *supra*, § 11.2, p. 61. As a result, an assignor typically can transfer his contractual right to receive future payments to an assignee.

The parties to a contract can include express language to limit assignment and courts generally uphold these contractual antiassignment clauses. *See* 3 RESTATEMENT (SECOND), *supra*, § 317, p. 15 ("[a] contractual right can be assigned unless . . . assignment is validly precluded by contract"); 3 E. FARNSWORTH, *supra*, § 11.4, pp. 82 ("most courts have upheld [terms prohibiting assignment] as precluding effective assignment"). Given the importance of free assignability, however, antiassignment clauses are construed narrowly whenever possible. *See* 3 E. FARNSWORTH, *supra*, § 11.4, pp. 82–83.

In interpreting antiassignment clauses, the majority of jurisdictions now distinguish between the assignor's "right" to assign and the "power" to assign (modern approach). Many courts have held that an antiassignment provision that limits the right to assign does not void an assignment between an assignor and assignee unless there is also an express provision limiting the power to assign or a provision voiding the assignment itself. *See, e.g., Pravin Banker Associates, Ltd. v. Banco Popular Del Peru*, 109 F.3d 850, 856 (2d Cir. 1997) ("to reveal the intent necessary to preclude the power to assign, or cause an assignment violative of contractual provisions to be wholly void, [a contractual] clause must contain express provisions that any assignment shall be void or invalid if not made in a certain specified way"); *Cedar Point Apartments, Ltd. v. Cedar Point Investment Corp.*, 693 F.2d 748, 754 (8th Cir. 1982) (concluding that "merely the 'right to assign,' not the power to assign, [was] limited by the express language of the [antiassignment] clause. No intent is thereby revealed to avoid an assignment not meeting the restrictions.' "); J. MURRAY,

JR., *supra*, § 138, p. 807 ("The contract may contain a promise by one or both parties to refrain from assigning. . . . The promise creates a duty in the promisor not to assign. It does not deprive the assignor of the power to assign and its breach, therefore, would simply subject the promisor to an action for damages while the assignment would be effective.") Thus, the modern approach finds support in the majority of jurisdictions.

A number of courts that have considered structured settlement agreements have enforced antiassignment provisions that explicitly deprive the assignor of the power to assign or otherwise provide that any assignment will be invalid. *See, e.g., Liberty Life Assurance Co. of Boston v. Stone Street Capital, Inc., supra*, 93 F. Supp. 2d 638 (holding that "the anti-assignment clause is a valid and enforceable term of the Settlement Agreement, and that [the] plaintiffs intended the clause to deny [the assignor] *the power* to assign" [emphasis added]).

The modern approach, however, is not adopted by some courts, which uphold antiassignment clauses regardless of whether the parties have included contractual language that expressly limits the power to assign or expressly invalidates the assignment itself. We agree with these courts that contracting parties can exercise their freedom to contract to overcome free alienability when they include the appropriate contractual language. The modern approach offers the advantage of free assignability together with full protection for any obligor who actually suffers damages as a result of an assignment. An assignor who breaches a contractual provision limiting his or her right to assign will be liable for any damages that result from that assignment. J. MURRAY, JR., *supra*, § 138, p. 807. [C]ourts in numerous jurisdictions have recognized the evenhandedness of the modern approach. This approach is also adopted in the RESTATEMENT (SECOND) OF CONTRACTS. Section 322(2)(b) of the RESTATEMENT (SECOND), *supra*, provides that the general rule is "[a] contract term prohibiting assignment of rights under the contract, unless a different intention is manifested . . . (b) gives the obligor a right to damages for breach of the terms forbidding assignment but does not render the assignment ineffective. . . ." [citing cases].

In the present case, the annuity contract provided that "no payment under this annuity contract may be . . . assigned" by the plaintiff. This antiassignment provision limited the plaintiffs right to assign, but not his power to do so. The provision did not contain any express language to limit the power to assignor to void the assignment itself. Therefore, in accordance with the modern approach, we conclude that the plaintiff's assignment to Wentworth is valid and enforceable despite the plaintiff's breach of the contract's antiassignment provision. We further conclude, however, that Safeco is free to sue for any damages that it might sustain as a result of the assignment by bringing an action for breach of contract against the plaintiff as assignor. Safeco, therefore, is fully protected against any actual damages that it might sustain as a result of the plaintiff's breach of the antiassignment provision. The modern approach thus serves the dual objectives of free assignability of contracts together with full compensation for any actual damages that might result from an assignment made in breach of an antiassignment provision. At the trial court hearing, Safeco did not show any actual damages resulting from the assignment.

The judgment is affirmed.

In this opinion Borden and Palmer Js., concurred.

[A dissenting opinion agreed with the dichotomy between the right to assign and the power to assign but found that the majority's insistence on specific language to accomplish this result was too stringent. "The language employed in the antiassignment clauses at issue, when accorded its common and natural meaning, clearly and unambiguously prohibits the assignment of periodic payments."]

NOTE

While the distinction between prohibitions on the right to assign versus the power to assign are reasonably clear, there is confusion over the approach to antiassignment provisions in the Uniform Commercial Code. Section 2-210 suggests that all rights can be assigned "unless otherwise agreed." This language suggests the enforceability of antiassignment provisions. Section 9-319(4) (currently revised as Section 9-406(d)) states that contractual prohibitions of assignment of accounts are "ineffective." While Article 9 deals with security interests in personal property including intangibles such as "accounts," it applies to the sale (assignment) of accounts. Accounts receivable financing is pervasive in our society and the assignment of such accounts is equally pervasive. It is clear that, with respect to commercial financing, Article 9 would apply, thereby making antiassignment clauses "ineffective." By its own terms, however, Article 9 does not apply to all assignments of accounts (§ 9-104, revised § 9-109). For example, it would not apply to an assignment of a claim under an insurance policy. *See Wonsey v. Life Ins. Co. of North America*, 32 F. Supp. 2d 939 (S.D. Mich. 1998). As suggested in *Riley v. Hewlitt-Packard Co.*, 2002 U.S. App. LEXIS 11179 (6th Cir. June 6, 2002):

> The purpose of § 9-104 exclusions was to ensure that Article 9 did not become entangled with transactions that have nothing to do with commercial financing. The sale of accounts attached to the sale of a business differs widely from, for example, the sale of accounts to factoring companies that is the meat and drink of the accounts receivable market.

In addition to foregoing examples of insurance and assignment of accounts attached to the sale of the business from which they arose, other exclusions from Article 9 include an assignment of wages (if not otherwise disallowed under state law), an assignment of accounts for collection purposes only, an assignment of a single account in satisfaction of a preexisting debt, an assignment of a right represented by a judgment other than a judgment on a right to payment that was collateral, an assignment of a tort claim other than a commercial tort claim, and an assignment of a deposit account in a consumer transaction.

K. DEFENSES AGAINST THE ASSIGNEE — UCC § 9-318 (R § 9-404)

"Shoes of the Assignor." One of the rules of contract law that has been repeated so often that it has become axiomatic is that the "assignee stands in the shoes of the assignor," i.e., he receives the same rights that his assignor had to transfer. Thus, they cannot be any greater than the rights of the assignor.

Paul agrees to paint Jim's house in exchange for $10,000. The contract document is signed and Paul immediately assigns his right to the $10,000 to his bank to pay a loan from the bank. The bank notifies Jim of the assignment and a month after the house was supposed to be painted, the bank demands payment from Jim of the $10,000. May Jim defend against the assignee-bank on the footing that Paul never painted the house? The question scarcely survives its statement. Failure of consideration, avoidability, fraud, mistake, unconscionability, statutes of limitations, or any other defense that Jim has against Paul it has against the bank on the assigned contract right.

Suppose that Paul and Jim have pursued more than one contract. In addition to the painting contract, Jim has agreed to sell his riding mower to Paul on credit for $3000, and delivers the mower to Paul. Assume that Paul completed the painting of the house and the bank seeks $10,000 from Jim. May Jim claim a set-off of $3000?

SEATTLE-FIRST NATIONAL BANK v. OREGON PACIFIC INDUSTRIES
Oregon Supreme Court
500 P.2d 1033 (1972)

Denecke, J.

On December 12, 1968, the defendant purchased plywood from Centralia. Centralia assigned the invoice evidencing the purchase to the bank on December 13, and the bank notified the defendant of the assignment. The defendant refused payment and the bank brought this action.

The defendant argues that it has a setoff against the bank's claim. Prior to the bank's assignment the defendant had placed two plywood orders, not included in the assigned invoice, with Centralia. Delivery was never made by Centralia and defendant contends it can set off the damages it suffered thereby against the bank's claim.

Centralia Plywood was insolvent when it assigned the invoice to the bank on December 12 and the bank knew of the insolvency at that time. Both Centralia and the bank are nonresidents. The defendant contends that because of these circumstances it is entitled to the setoff. . . .

[The Code provides:

[(1) Unless an account debtor has made an enforceable agreement not to assert defenses or claims arising out of a sale as provided in Section 9-206the rights of an assignee are subject to]

(a) all the terms of the contract between the account debtor and assignor and any defense or claim arising therefrom; and

(b) any other defense or claim of the account debtor against the assignor which accrues before the account debtor receives notification of the assignment.

[(3) The account debtor is authorized to pay the assignor until the account debtor receives notification that the amount due or to become due has been assigned and that payment is to be made to the assignee. A notification which does not reasonably identify the rights assigned is ineffective. If requested by the account debtor, the assignee must seasonably furnish reasonable proof that the assignment has been made and unless he does so the account debtor may pay the assignor.]

The Code does not expressly provide that a claim can be set off if the assignor was insolvent at the time of the assignment and the assignee had knowledge of this fact or because the assignor and assignee are nonresidents.

One of the prime purposes of the Code was to create a statutory scheme incorporating within its provisions the complete regulation of certain types of commercial dealings. This purpose would be blunted if the rules created by some pre-code decisions and not expressly provided for in the statutory scheme were nevertheless grafted onto the Code by implication. In *Evans Products v. Jorgensen*, 245 Or. 362, 372, 421 P.2d 978 (1966), we held generally that we would not engage in this practice.

We recently observed in *Investment Service Co. v. North Pacific Lbr. Co.*, Or., 492 P.2d 470-471 (1972), that the comment to this section of the Code states that this section "makes no substantial change in prior law."[10] Upon further examination, we must acknowledge that while the Code retains the essence of the previous law of assignments, the Code has, by specific language, changed some of the details of the previous law of assignments.

The Code distinguishes "between what might be called the contract-related and the unrelated defenses and claims. Defenses and claims 'arising' from the contract can be asserted against the assignee whether they 'arise' before or after notification. . . . Under the Code, 'any other defense or claim' is available against the assignee only if it 'accrues before . . . notification.' " 2 Gilmore, Security Interests in Personal Property, 1090–1091, § 41.4 (1965).

The setoff or claim the defendant seeks to assert is an unrelated setoff because it arises out of a breach of a contract not connected with the invoice assigned to the bank. For this reason the defendant can assert the setoff only if it accrued before the defendant was notified of Centralia's assignment to the bank.

The controversy thus narrows down to the issue of whether the setoff "accrued" to the defendant before it received notice of the assignment. We could be aided in defining "accrued" if we could determine why the accrual of the setoff was selected

---

[10] [1] Investment Service Co. v. North Pacific Lbr. Co., Or., 492 P.2d 470-471 (1972), involved ORS 79.3180(1)(a), a setoff arising out of the contract between the account debtor and the assignor.

as the cutoff event. Accruing of the setoff, however, apparently, was selected arbitrarily. The choice of the event of the accrual was based upon previous decisions, some of which used the phrase "matured" rather than "accrued" claim. 4 CORBIN, CONTRACTS, 599, § 897 (1951). 1 RESTATEMENT 211, CONTRACTS § 167(1), provided that the obligor could assert its setoff if the setoff was "based on facts arising . . . prior to knowledge of the assignment by the obligor."

It was necessary to permit at least some setoffs to be asserted in order to protect the obligor from being unduly prejudiced by the assignment; but this right of setoff had to be limited in order to give some value and stability to the assignment so that it could be used as an effective security device. If an obligor could not assert any of the defenses or setoffs against an assignee which he could have asserted against his creditor the assignor, the obligor would be extremely prejudiced by an assignment. On the other hand, if the obligation assigned could be obliterated or diminished by events happening after the assignment and notice of assignment to the obligor, the assignment would be precarious collateral.

The comments to the Oregon Code are of no assistance in interpreting "accrue." The comments to the Washington Code state: "The term 'accrues' appears to mean that the 'claim' shall exist as such, i.e., as a cause of action, before such knowledge." RCWA 62A.9-318, p. 439.

"Accrue," aside from its fiscal use, generally is used in the law to describe when a cause of action comes into being. Its chief use is to determine when the statute of limitations commences. We believe it is advisable to use "accrue" in the Code in its usual sense; that is, a claim or setoff accrues when a cause of action exists.

The parties stipulated that the "breaches of contract [the failure to deliver by Centralia] occurred on or about January 3, 1969." Therefore, the claim "accrued" at that time. Since the claim accrued after defendant had notification of the assignment, the setoff cannot be asserted successfully.

Defendant on appeal contends that by stipulating that the breaches of contract occurred on January 3 it did not intend to stipulate that the cause of action accrued at that time. The normal inference is that the cause of action accrues at the time the breach of contract occurs. In addition, the record indicates that the trial court and the parties so understood the import of the stipulation. *Affirmed.*

NOTES

(1)   RESTATEMENT (SECOND) OF CONTRACTS § 336:

(1) By an assignment the assignee acquires a right against the obligor only to the extent that the obligor is under a duty to the assignor; and if the right of the assignor would be voidable by the obligor or unenforceable against him if no assignment had been made, the right of the assignee is subject to the infirmity.

(2) The right of an assignee is subject to any defense or claim of the obligor which accrues before the obligor receives notification of the assignment, but not to defenses or claims which accrue thereafter except as stated in this Section or as provided by statute.

(3) Where the right of an assignor is subject to discharge or modification in whole or in part by impracticability, public policy, non-occurrence of a condition, or present or prospective failure of performance by an obligee, the right of the assignee is to that extent subject to discharge or modification even after the obligor receives notification of the assignment.

(4) An assignee's right against the obligor is subject to any defense or claim arising from his conduct or to which he was subject as a party or a prior assignee because he had notice.

(2) *Waiver of Defenses Against Assignee — Holder in Due Course.* The rule that an assignee is subject to all of the defenses available to the obligor against the assignee on the assigned contract right as well as the obligor's other defenses or claims against the assignor that accrued before notice of the assignment creates obstacles in the transfer of certain rights. If that rule were applied to negotiable instruments such as checks or promissory notes, the free transferability of such instruments would be hampered. An analysis of the rights and duties of parties to negotiable instruments is beyond the scope of this volume and is dealt with in separate courses involving Articles 3 and 4 of the Uniform Commercial Code and related statutes and regulations. The student of contract law, however, should appreciate a basic distinction between the assignment of an ordinary contract right and the transfer or "negotiation" of a negotiable instrument, To foster the free transferability of such "specialties," a transferee of a negotiable instrument who takes the instrument for value, in good faith, without notice that it is overdue or has been dishonored or that there is any defense or claim against it enjoys a special status. Such a transferee is not a mere assignee. She is a "holder in due course"[11] who takes free of most of the defenses that would be available against a mere assignee.[12]

Apart from negotiable instruments, another method of accomplishing the same result is recognized under Section 9-206 (revised Section 9-403) of the Uniform Commercial Code through a clause in the original contract whereby the obligor agrees not to assert defenses against the assignee that the obligor could have asserted against the assignor where the assignment is taken for value, in good faith, and without notice of any claim or defense, except defenses that may be asserted against a holder in due course. Such agreements are subject to any statute or decision establishing a different rule for buyers of consumer goods. Recognizing that consumer buyers may be unaware that they are surrendering claims and defenses against an assignee or holder of a negotiable instrument that they had against their sellers or lessors, courts began to question whether the seller and the seller's assignee were so "closely connected" that the assignee could not be said to

---

[11] Transferring a negotiable instrument to make the transferee a "holder" may require an indorsement by the party to whom the instrument is payable. A typical check is made payable "to the order" of named payee. To "negotiate" the check, the payee will indorse the check to the transferee (holder). The typical check is an "order" instrument made payable to a named payee. A "bearer" instrument does not require negotiation. Thus, a check made payable to "cash" is a bearer instrument which can be transferred (negotiated) by delivery alone.

[12] Even a holder in due course is subject to certain "real" defenses such as "essential" fraud (fraud in the factum), discharge in insolvency proceedings, infancy, illegality and discharge of which the holder has notice at the time she takes the instrument.

have taken the instrument or assigned contract right in good faith. *See Unico v. Owen*, 232 A.2d 405 (N.J. 1967). To protect consumers, the Federal Trade Commission issued a regulation (16 C.F.R. § 433.2) which requires consumer credit contracts to state conspicuously that any holder of such a contract is subject to all claims and defenses which the debtor could assert against the seller of goods or services. The 1999 version of UCC Article 9 (§ 9-403(d)) is consonant with the FTC regulation.

(3)   *Good Faith Modification of Contract Between Assignor and Obligor.* Under the common law, an assignee could acquire no rights under a modified or substituted contract between the obligor and assignor. This rule was changed by versions of UCC Article 9 prior to the current version. If the assigned right had not yet been earned by performance, the obligor and assignor, in good faith and in accordance with reasonable commercial standards, could effect a modification or substitution of their contract notwithstanding notification of the assignment (§ 9-318(2)). The current version of Article 9 provides that good faith modifications of assigned contracts bind the assignee to the extent that (1) the right to payment has not been fully earned, or (2) the right to payment has been fully earned but notification of the assignment has not been given to the obligor (§ 9-405(a), (b)(1), (2)). The modification or substitution is effective against the assignee, but the assignee acquires rights under the good faith modification or substitution. Murray on Contracts, § 142C.

(4)   *Obligor vs. Assignee?* In *Michelin Tires (Canada) Ltd. v. First Nat'l Bank of Boston*, 666 F.2d 673 (1st Cir. 1981), Michelin contracted with JCC for the construction of part of a tire factory. The contract required Michelin to make periodic progress payments. The First National Bank provided financing to JCC and took an assignment of the rights of JCC against Michelin. Under the contract between Michelin and JCC, a condition required JCC to pay its subcontractors on the construction project. JCC was adjudicated a bankrupt shortly after Michelin learned that it had failed to pay subcontractors, though Michelin had made all necessary progress payments to the bank since the bank had notified Michelin of the assignment. The bank was unaware of the failure by JCC to pay subcontractors. Michelin brought this action to recover almost $725,000 from the bank for payments it had made to the bank. It claimed this amount under § 9-318(1)(a), which states that the rights of an assignee are subject to "all the terms of the contract between the account debtor and assignor and any defense or claim arising therefrom." Michelin claimed that this language not only permitted it to defend actions against the assignee but also provided it with an affirmative right, since the term "claim" is used in the subsection and should be so interpreted. The majority of the court recognized this possible interpretation but rejected it on the ground that, while an assignee has traditionally been subjected to defenses or set-offs existing before the obligor is notified of the assignment, the section does not change prior law to allow an affirmative action by the obligor against the assignee. The majority states, "Under prior law, an assignee of contract rights was not liable on the contract in the place of his assignor. . . . Common sense requires that we not twist the precarious security of an assignee into potential liability for his assignor's breach."

L. PRIORITY AMONG SUCCESSIVE ASSIGNEES

PROBLEM

For value, Arnett assigned a $25,000 contract right he had against Williams to Banes. Arnett then assigned the same right to Childs for value and proceeded to assign the same right to Davis for value. None of the assignees was aware of the assignment to the others. Consider the following theories to determine which assignee should prevail.

(a) An assignment is a present transfer of a right. Once Arnett assigned to Banes, Arnett had nothing to assign to either Childs or Davis — the "New York" or "American" view.

(b) The equitable maxim is, where the parties are equal, the first in time prevails.

(c) One of the subsequent assignees, Banes, Childs or Davis, should be the first to notify obligor Williams of the assignment — the "English" view.

(d) While the first in time, Banes, should normally prevail, any of the following four possibilities should allow a subsequent assignee to prevail: (i) securing payment or satisfaction from Williams; (ii) securing a judgment against Williams; (iii) entering into a novation whereby Williams is released in exchange for a new obligor; (iv) securing a symbolic writing or other document that is normally surrendered when the right is transferred. The "four horsemen view" of the RESTATEMENT (FIRST) OF CONTRACT § 173, RESTATEMENT (SECOND) OF CONTRACTS § 342. *See McKnight v. Rice*, 678 P.2d 1330 (Alaska 1984).

NOTE

Modern commercial financing involving priority among successive assignees involves the assignment of "accounts," i.e., amounts due and owing from creditors, often called "accounts receivable." The application of the American ("New York") or "English" view, coupled with the complexities of the Federal Bankruptcy Code prior to the enactment of the UCC, was problematic. With the enactment of the UCC, the priority issue is solved through Article 9 that requires the filing of a financing statement in the appropriate county office to "perfect" one's security interest in accounts. UCC § 9-312(5) (R9-322). The "first-to-file" rule prevails.

Appendix A

UNIFORM COMMERCIAL CODE
ARTICLES 1 AND 2*

ARTICLE 1—GENERAL PROVISIONS

Table of Contents

PART 1 SHORT TITLE, CONSTRUCTION, APPLICATION AND SUBJECT MATTER OF THE ACT

SECTION 1-101. SHORT TITLE.

This Act shall be known and may be cited as Uniform Commercial Code.

SECTION 1-102. PURPOSES; RULES OF CONSTRUCTION; VARIATION BY AGREEMENT.

(1) This Act shall be liberally construed and applied to promote its underlying purposes and policies.

(2) Underlying purposes and policies of this Act are

(a) to simplify, clarify and modernize the law governing commercial transactions;

(b) to permit the continued expansion of commercial practices through custom, usage and agreement of the parties;

(c) to make uniform the law among the various jurisdictions.

(3) The effect of provisions of this Act may be varied by agreement, except as otherwise provided in this Act and except that the obligations of good faith, diligence, reasonableness and care prescribed by this Act may not be disclaimed by agreement but the parties may by agreement determine the standards by which the performance of such obligations is to be measured if such standards are not manifestly unreasonable.

(4) The presence in certain provisions of this Act of the words "unless otherwise agreed" or words of similar import does not imply that the effect of other provisions may not be varied by agreement under subsection (3).

(5) In this Act unless the context otherwise requires

(a) words in the singular number include the plural, and in the plural include the singular;

(b) words of the masculine gender include the feminine and the neu ter, and when the sense so indicates words of the neuter gender may refer to any gender.

SECTION 1-103. SUPPLEMENTARY GENERAL PRINCIPLES OF LAW APPLICABLE.

Unless displaced by the particular provisions of this Act, the principles of law and equity, including the law merchant and the law relative to capacity to contract, principal and agent, estoppel, fraud, misrepresenta tion, duress, coercion, mistake, bankruptcy, or other validating or invali dating cause shall supplement its provisions.

SECTION 1-104. CONSTRUCTION AGAINST IMPLICIT REPEAL.

This Act being a general act intended as a unified coverage of its subject matter, no part of its shall be deemed to be impliedly repealed by subse quent legislation if such construction can reasonably be avoided.

SECTION 1-105. TERRITORIAL APPLICATION OF THE ACT; PARTIES' POWER TO CHOOSE APPLICABLE LAW.

(1) Except as provided hereafter in this section, when a transaction bears a reasonable relation to this state and also to another state or nation the parties may agree that the law either of this state or of such other state or nation shall govern their rights and duties. Failing such agreement this Act applies to transactions bearing an appropriate relation to this state.

(2) Where one of the following provisions of this Act specifies the applicable law, that provision governs and a contrary agreement is effec tive only to the extent permitted by the law (including the conflict of laws rules) so specified:

Rights of creditors against sold goods. Section 2-402.

Applicability of the Article on Leases. Sections 2A-105 and 2A-106.

Applicability of the Article on Bank Deposits and Collections. Section 4-102.

Governing law in the Article on Funds Transfers. Section 4A-507.

Letters of Credit. Section 5-116.

[Note: If a state adopts the repealer of Article 6 — Bulk Transfers (Alter native A), there should not be any item relating to bulk transfers. If, however, a state adopts Revised Article 6 — Bulk Sales (Alternative B), then the item relating to bulk sales should read as follows:]

Bulk sales subject to the Article on Bulk Sales. Section 6-103.

Applicability of the Article on Investment Securities. Section 8-110.

Perfection provisions of the Article on Secured Transactions. Section 9-103.

As amended in 1972, 1987, 1988, 1989, 1994, and 1995.

SECTION 1-106. REMEDIES TO BE LIBERALLY ADMINISTERED.

(1) The remedies provided by this Act shall be liberally administered to the end that the aggrieved party may be put in as good a position as if the other party had fully performed but neither consequential or special nor penal damages may be had except as specifically provided in this Act or by other rule of law.

(2) Any right or obligation declared by this Act is enforceable by action unless the provision declaring it specifies a different and limited effect.

SECTION 1-107. WAIVER OR RENUNCIATION OF CLAIM OR RIGHT AFTER BREACH.

Any claim or right arising out of an alleged breach can be discharged in whole or in part without consideration by a written waiver or renuncia tion signed and delivered by the aggrieved party.

SECTION 1-108. SEVERABILITY.

If any provision or clause of this Act or application thereof to any person or circumstances is held invalid, such invalidity shall not affect other provisions or applications of the Act which can be given effect without the invalid provision or application, and to this end the provisions of this Act are declared to be severable.

SECTION 1-109. SECTION CAPTIONS.

Section captions are parts of this Act.

SECTION 1-201. GENERAL DEFINITIONS.

Subject to additional definitions contained in the subsequent Articles of this Act which are applicable to specific Articles or Parts thereof, and unless the context otherwise requires, in this Act:

(1) "Action" in the sense of a judicial proceeding includes recoupment, counterclaim, set-off, suit in equity and any other proceedings in which rights are determined.

(2) "Aggrieved party" means a party entitled to resort to a remedy.

(3) "Agreement" means the bargain of the parties in fact as found in their language or by implication from other circumstances including course of dealing or usage of trade or course of performance as provided in this Act (Sections 1–205, 2–208, and 2A-207). Whether an agreement has legal consequences is determined by the provisions of this Act, if applicable; otherwise by the law of contracts (Section 1–103). (Compare "Contract".)

(4) "Bank" means any person engaged in the business of banking.

(5) "Bearer" means the person in possession of an instrument, docu ment of title, or certificated security payable to bearer or indorsed in blank.

(6) "Bill of lading" means a document evidencing the receipt of goods for shipment issued by a person engaged in the business of transporting or forwarding goods, and includes an airbill. "Airbill" means a document serving for air transportation as a bill of lading does for marine or rail transportation, and includes an air consignment note or air waybill.

(7) "Branch" includes a separately incorporated foreign branch of a bank.

(8) "Burden of establishing" a fact means the burden of persuading the triers of fact that the existence of the fact is more probable than its non-existence.

(9) "Buyer in ordinary course of business" means a person who in good faith and without knowledge that the sale to him is in violation of the ownership rights or security interest of a third party in the goods buys in ordinary course from a person in the business of selling goods of that kind but does not include a pawnbroker. All persons who sell minerals or the like (including oil and gas) at wellhead or minehead shall be deemed to be persons in the business of selling goods of that kind. "Buying" may be for cash or by exchange of other property or on secured or unsecured credit and includes receiving goods or documents of title under a pre-existing contract for sale but does not include a transfer in bulk or as security for or in total or partial satisfaction of a money debt.

(10) "Conspicuous": A term or clause is conspicuous when it is so written that a reasonable person against whom it is to operate ought to have noticed it. A printed heading in capitals (as: NON-NEGOTIABLE BILL OF LADING) is conspicuous. Language in the body of a form is "conspicuous" if it is in larger or other contrasting type or color. But in a telegram any stated term is "conspicuous." Whether a term or clause is "conspicuous" or not is for decision by the court.

(11) "Contract" means the total legal obligation which results from the parties' agreement as affected by this Act and any other applicable rules of law. (Compare "Agreement".)

(12) "Creditor" includes a general creditor, a secured creditor, a lien creditor and any representative of creditors, including an assignee for the benefit of creditors, a trustee in bankruptcy, a receiver in equity and an executor or administrator of an insolvent debtor's or assignor's estate.

(13) "Defendant" includes a person in the position of defendant in a cross-action or counterclaim.

(14) "Delivery" with respect to instruments, documents of title, chattel paper, or certificated securities means voluntary transfer of possession.

(15) "Document of title" includes bill of lading, dock warrant, dock receipt, warehouse receipt or order for the delivery of goods, and also any other document which in the regular course of business or financing is treated as adequately evidencing that the person in possession of it is entitled to receive, hold and dispose of the document and the goods it covers. To be a document of title a document must purport to be issued by or addressed to a bailee and purport to cover goods in the bailee's possession which are either identified or are fungible portions of an identified mass.

(16) "Fault" means wrongful act, omission or breach.

(17) "Fungible" with respect to goods or securities means goods or securities of which any unit is, by nature or usage of trade, the equivalent of any other like unit. Goods which are not fungible shall be deemed fungible for the purposes of this Act to the extent that under a particular agreement or document unlike units are treated as equivalents.

(18) "Genuine" means free of forgery or counterfeiting.

(19) "Good faith" means honesty in fact in the conduct or transaction concerned.

(20) "Holder," with respect to a negotiable instrument, means the person in possession if the instrument is payable to bearer or, in the case of an instrument payable to an identified person, if the identified person is in possession. "Holder" with respect to a document of title means the person in possession if the goods are deliverable to bearer or to the order of the person in possession.

(21) To "honor" is to pay or to accept and pay, or where a credit so engages to purchase or discount a draft complying with the terms of the credit.

(22) "Insolvency proceedings" includes any assignment for the benefit of creditors or other proceedings intended to liquidate or rehabilitate the estate of the person involved.

(23) A person is "insolvent" who either has ceased to pay his debts in the ordinary course of business or cannot pay his debts as they become due or is insolvent within the meaning of the federal bankruptcy law.

(24) "Money" means a medium of exchange authorized or adopted by a

domestic or foreign government and includes a monetary unit of account established by an intergovernmental organization or by agreement between two or more nations.

(25) A person has "notice" of a fact when

(a) he has actual knowledge of it; or

(b) he has received a notice or notification of it; or

(c) from all the facts and circumstances known to him at the time in question he has reason to know that it exists.

A person "knows" or has "knowledge" of a fact when he has actual knowledge of it. "Discover" or "learn" or a word or phrase of similar import refers to knowledge rather than to reason to know. The time and circumstances under which a notice or notification may cease to be effective are not determined by this Act.

(26) A person "notifies" or "gives" a notice or notification to another by taking such steps as may be reasonably required to inform the other in ordinary course whether or not such other actually comes to know of it. A person "receives" a notice or notification when

(a) it comes to his attention; or

(b) it is duly delivered at the place of business through which the contract was made or at any other place held out by him as the place for receipt of such communications.

(27) Notice, knowledge or a notice or notification received by an organization is effective for a particular transaction from the time when it is brought to the attention of the individual conducting that transac tion, and in any event from the time when it would have been brought to his attention if the organization had exercised due diligence. An organization exercises due diligence if it maintains reasonable routines for communicating significant information to the person conducting the transaction and there is reasonable compliance with the routines. Due diligence does not require an individual acting for the organization to communicate information unless such communication is part of his regular duties or unless he has reason to know of the transaction and that the transaction would be materially affected by the information.

(28) "Organization" includes a corporation, government or governmen tal subdivision or agency, business trust, estate, trust, partnership or association, two or more persons having a joint or common interest, or any other legal or commercial entity.

(29) "Party", as distinct from "third party", means a person who has engaged in a transaction or made an agreement within this Act.

(30) "Person" includes an individual or an organization (See Section 1–102).

(31) "Presumption" or "presumed" means that the trier of fact must find the existence of the fact presumed unless and until evidence is introduced which would support a finding of its nonexistence.

(32) "Purchase" includes taking by sale, discount, negotiation, mort gage, pledge, lien, issue or re-issue, gift or any other voluntary transac tion creating an interest in property.

(33) "Purchaser" means a person who takes by purchase.

(34) "Remedy" means any remedial right to which an aggrieved party is entitled with or without resort to a tribunal.

(35) "Representative" includes an agent, an officer of a corporation or association, and a trustee, executor or administrator of an estate, or any other person empowered to act for another.

(36) "Rights" includes remedies.

(37) "Security interest" means an interest in personal property or fixtures which secures payment or performance of an obligation. The retention or reservation of title by a seller of goods notwithstanding ship ment or delivery to the buyer (Section 2-401) is limited in effect to a reservation of a "security interest". The term also includes any interest of a buyer of accounts or chattel paper which is subject to Article 9. The special property interest of a buyer of goods on identification of those goods to a contract for sale under Section 2-401 is not a "security interest", but a buyer may also acquire a "security interest" by complying with Article 9. Unless a consignment is intended as security, reserva tion of title thereunder is not a "security interest", but a consignment in any event is subject to the provisions on consignment sales (Section 2-326).

Whether a transaction creates a lease or security interest is determined by the facts of each case; however, a transaction creates a security interest if the consideration the lessee is to pay the lessor for the right to possession and use of the goods is an obligation for the term of the lease not subject to termination by the lessee, and

(a) the original term of the lease is equal to or greater than the remaining economic life of the goods,

(b) the lessee is bound to renew the lease for the remaining economic life of the goods or is bound to become the owner of the goods,

(c) the lessee has an option to renew the lease for the remaining economic life of the goods for no additional consideration or nominal additional consideration upon compliance with the lease agreement, or

(d) the lessee has an option to become the owner of the goods for no additional consideration or nominal additional consideration upon compliance with the lease agreement.

A transaction does not create a security interest merely because it provides that

(a) the present value of the consideration the lessee is obligated to pay the lessor for the right to possession and use of the goods is substan tially equal to or is greater than the fair market value of the goods at the time the lease is entered into,

(b) the lessee assumes risk of loss of the goods, or agrees to pay taxes, insurances, filing, recording, or registration fees, or service or maintenance costs with respect to the goods,

(c) the lessee has an option to renew the lease or to become the owner of the goods,

(d) the lessee has an option to renew the lease for a fixed rent that is equal to or greater than the reasonably predictable fair market rent for the use of the goods for the term of the renewal at the time the option is to be performed, or

(e) the lessee has an option to become the owner of the goods for a fixed price that is equal to or greater than the reasonably predictable fair market value of the goods at the time the option is to be performed.

For purposes of this subsection (37):

(x) Additional consideration is not nominal if (i) when the option to renew the lease is granted to the lessee the rent is stated to be the fair market rent for the use of the goods for the term of the renewal determined at the time the option is to be performed, or (ii) when the option to become the owner of the goods is granted to the lessee the price is stated to be the fair market value of the goods determined at the time the option is to be performed.

Additional consideration is nominal if it is less than the lessee's reasonably predictable cost of performing under the lease agreement if the option is not exercised;

(y) "Reasonably predictable" and "remaining economic life of the goods" are to be determined with reference to the facts and circumstances at the time the transaction is entered into; and

(z) "Present value" means the amount as of a date certain of one or more sums payable in the future, discounted to the date certain. The discount is determined by the interest rate specified by the parties if the rate is not manifestly unreasonable at the time the transaction is entered into; otherwise, the discount is determined by a commer cially reasonable rate that takes into account the facts and circum stances of each case at the time the transaction was entered into.

(38) "Send" in connection with any writing or notice means to deposit in the mail or deliver for transmission by any other usual means of communication with postage or cost of transmission provided for and properly addressed and in the case of an instrument to an address specified thereon or otherwise agreed, or if there be none to any address reasonable under the circumstances. The receipt of any writing or notice within the time at which it would have arrived if properly sent has the effect of a proper sending.

(39) "Signed" includes any symbol executed or adopted by a party with present intention to authenticate a writing.

(40) "Surety" includes guarantor.

(41) "Telegram" includes a message transmitted by radio, teletype, ca ble,

any mechanical method of transmission, or the like.

(42) "Term" means that portion of an agreement which relates to a particular matter.

(43) "Unauthorized" signature or indorsement means one made without actual, implied or apparent authority and includes a forgery.

(44) "Value". Except as otherwise provided with respect to negotiable instruments and bank collections (Sections 3–303, 4–210 and 4–211) a person gives "value" for rights if he acquires them

(a) in return for a binding commitment to extend credit or for the extension of immediately available credit whether or not drawn upon and whether or not a charge-back is provided for in the event of difficulties in collection; or

(b) as security for or in total or partial satisfaction of a pre-existing claim; or

(c) by accepting delivery pursuant to a pre-existing contract for purchase; or

(d) generally, in return for any consideration sufficient to support a simple contract.

(45) "Warehouse receipt" means a receipt issued by a person engaged in the business of storing goods for hire.

(46) "Written" or "writing" includes printing, typewriting or any other intentional reduction to tangible form. As amended in 1962, 1972, 1977, 1987, 1990 and 1994.

SECTION 1-202. PRIMA FACIE EVIDENCE BY THIRD PARTY DOCUMENTS.

A document in due form purporting to be a bill of lading, policy or certificate of insurance, official weigher's or inspector's certificate, con sular invoice, or any other document authorized or required by the contract to be issued by a third party shall be prima facie evidence of its own authenticity and genuineness and of the facts stated in the document by the third party.

SECTION 1-203. OBLIGATION OF GOOD FAITH.

Every contract or duty within this Act imposes an obligation of good faith in its performance or enforcement.

SECTION 1-204. TIME; REASONABLE TIME; "SEASONABLY".

(1) Whenever this Act requires any action to be taken within a reason able time, any time which is not manifestly unreasonable may be fixed by agreement.

(2) What is a reasonable time for taking any action depends on the nature, purpose and circumstances of such action.

(3) An action is taken "seasonably" when it is taken at or within the time agreed or if no time is agreed at or within a reasonable time.

SECTION 1-205. COURSE OF DEALING AND USAGE OF TRADE.

(1) A course of dealing is a sequence of previous conduct between the parties to a particular transaction which is fairly to be regarded as establishing a common

basis of understanding for interpreting their expressions and other conduct.

(2) A usage of trade is any practice or method of dealing having such regularity of observance in a place, vocation or trade as to justify an expectation that it will be observed with respect to the transaction in question. The existence and scope of such usage are to be proved as facts. If it is established that such a usage is embodied in a written trade code or similar writing the interpretation of the writing is for the court.

(3) A course of dealing between parties and any usage of trade in the vocation or trade in which they are engaged or of which they are or should be aware give particular meaning to and supplement or qualify terms of an agreement.

(4) The express terms of an agreement and an applicable course of dealing or usage of trade shall be construed wherever reasonable as con sistent with each other; but when such construction is unreasonable ex press terms control both course of dealing and usage of trade and course of dealing controls usage of trade.

(5) An applicable usage of trade in the place where any part of performance is to occur shall be used in interpreting the agreement as to that part of the performance.

(6) Evidence of a relevant usage of trade offered by one party is not admissible unless and until he has given the other party such notice as the court finds sufficient to prevent unfair surprise to the latter.

SECTION 1-206. STATUTE OF FRAUDS FOR KINDS OF PERSONAL PROPERTY NOT OTHERWISE COVERED.

(1) Except in the cases described in subsection (2) of this section a contract for the sale of personal property is not enforceable by way of action or defense beyond five thousand dollars in amount or value of remedy unless there is some writing which indicates that a contract for sale has been made between the parties at a defined or stated price, reasonably identifies the subject matter, and is signed by the party against whom enforcement is sought or by his authorized agent.

(2) Subsection (1) of this section does not apply to contracts for the sale of goods (Section 2-201) nor of securities (Section 8-113) nor to security agreements (Section 9-203).

As amended in 1994.

SECTION 1-207. PERFORMANCE OR ACCEPTANCE UNDER RESERVATION OF RIGHTS.

(1) A party who, with explicit reservation of rights, performs or promises performance or assents to performance in a manner demanded or offered by the other party does not thereby prejudice the rights re served. Such words as "without prejudice", "under protest" or the like are sufficient.

(2) Subsection (1) does not apply to an accord and satisfaction. As amended in 1990.

SECTION 1-208. OPTION TO ACCELERATE AT WILL.

A term providing that one party or his successor in interest may accelerate payment or performance or require collateral or additional collateral "at will" or "when he deems himself insecure" or in words of similar import shall be construed to mean that he shall have power to do so only if he in good faith believes that the prospect of payment or performance is impaired. The burden of establishing lack of good faith is on the party against whom the power has been exercised.

SECTION 1-209.   SUBORDINATED OBLIGATIONS.

An obligation may be issued as subordinated to payment of another obligation of the person obligated, or a creditor may subordinate his right to payment of an obligation by agreement with either the person obligated or another creditor of the person obligated. Such a subordination does not create a security interest as against either the common debtor or a subordinated creditor. This section shall be construed as declaring the law as it existed prior to the enactment of this section and not as modifying it.

PART   2   GENERAL   DEFINITIONS   AND   PRINCIPLES   OF INTERPRETATION

SECTION 1-201.   GENERAL DEFINITIONS

(a) Unless the context otherwise requires, words or phrases defined in this section, or in the additional definitions contained in other articles of [the Uniform Commercial Code] that apply to particular articles or parts thereof, have the meanings stated.

(b) Subject to definitions contained in other articles of [the Uniform Commercial Code] that apply to particular articles or parts thereof:

(1) "Action", in the sense of a judicial proceeding, includes recoupment, counterclaim, set-off, suit in equity, and any other proceeding in which rights are determined.

(2) "Aggrieved party" means a party entitled to pursue a remedy.

(3) "Agreement", as distinguished from "contract", means the bargain of the parties in fact, as found in their language or inferred from other circumstances, including course of performance, course of dealing, or usage of trade as provided in Section 1-303.

(4) "Bank" means a person engaged in the business of banking and includes a savings bank, savings and loan association, credit union, and trust company.

(5) "Bearer" means a person in possession of a negotiable instrument, document of title, or certificated security that is payable to bearer or indorsed in blank.

(6) "Bill of lading" means a document evidencing the receipt of goods for shipment issued by a person engaged in the business of transporting or forwarding goods.

(7) "Branch" includes a separately incorporated foreign branch of a bank.

(8) "Burden of establishing" a fact means the burden of persuading the trier of

fact that the existence of the fact is more probable than its nonexistence.

(9) "Buyer in ordinary course of business" means a person that buys goods in good faith, without knowledge that the sale violates the rights of another person in the goods, and in the ordinary course from a person, other than a pawnbroker, in the business of selling goods of that kind. A person buys goods in the ordinary course if the sale to the person comports with the usual or customary practices in the kind of business in which the seller is engaged or with the seller's own usual or customary practices. A person that sells oil, gas, or other minerals at the wellhead or minehead is a person in the business of selling goods of that kind. A buyer in ordinary course of business may buy for cash, by exchange of other property, or on secured or unsecured credit, and may acquire goods or documents of title under a preexisting contract for sale. Only a buyer that takes possession of the goods or has a right to recover the goods from the seller under Article 2 may be a buyer in ordinary course of business. "Buyer in ordinary course of business" does not include a person that acquires goods in a transfer in bulk or as security for or in total or partial satisfaction of a money debt.

(10) "Conspicuous", with reference to a term, means so written, displayed, or presented that a reasonable person against which it is to operate ought to have noticed it. Whether a term is "conspicuous" or not is a decision for the court. Conspicuous terms include the following:

(A) a heading in capitals equal to or greater in size than the surrounding text, or in contrasting type, font, or color to the surrounding text of the same or lesser size; and

(B) language in the body of a record or display in larger type than the surrounding text, or in contrasting type, font, or color to the surrounding text of the same size, or set off from surrounding text of the same size by symbols or other marks that call attention to the language.

(11) "Consumer" means an individual who enters into a transaction primarily for personal, family, or household purposes.

(12) "Contract", as distinguished from "agreement", means the total legal obligation that results from the parties' agreement as determined by [the Uniform Commercial Code] as supplemented by any other applicable laws.

(13) "Creditor" includes a general creditor, a secured creditor, a lien creditor, and any representative of creditors, including an assignee for the benefit of creditors, a trustee in bankruptcy, a receiver in equity, and an executor or administrator of an insolvent debtor's or assignor's estate.

(14) "Defendant" includes a person in the position of defendant in a counter-claim, cross-claim, or third-party claim.

(15) "Delivery", with respect to an instrument, document of title, or chattel paper, means voluntary transfer of possession.

(16) "Document of title" includes bill of lading, dock warrant, dock receipt, warehouse receipt or order for the delivery of goods, and also any other document which in the regular course of business or financing is treated as

adequately evidencing that the person in possession of it is entitled to receive, hold, and dispose of the document and the goods it covers. To be a document of title, a document must purport to be issued by or addressed to a bailee and purport to cover goods in the bailee's possession which are either identified or are fungible portions of an identified mass.

(17) "Fault" means a default, breach, or wrongful act or omission.

(18) "Fungible goods" means:

(A) goods of which any unit, by nature or usage of trade, is the equivalent of any other like unit; or

(B) goods that by agreement are treated as equivalent.

(19) "Genuine" means free of forgery or counterfeiting.

(20) "Good faith," except as otherwise provided in Article 5, means honesty in fact and the observance of reasonable commercial standards of fair dealing.

(21) "Holder" means:

(A) the person in possession of a negotiable instrument that is payable either to bearer or to an identified person that is the person in possession; or

(B) the person in possession of a document of title if the goods are deliverable either to bearer or to the order of the person in possession.

(22) "Insolvency proceeding" includes an assignment for the benefit of creditors or other proceeding intended to liquidate or rehabilitate the estate of the person involved.

(23) "Insolvent" means:

(A) having generally ceased to pay debts in the ordinary course of business other than as a result of bona fide dispute;

(B) being unable to pay debts as they become due; or

(C) being insolvent within the meaning of federal bankruptcy law.

(24) "Money" means a medium of exchange currently authorized or adopted by a domestic or foreign government. The term includes a monetary unit of account established by an intergovernmental organization or by agreement between two or more countries.

(25) "Organization" means a person other than an individual.

(26) "Party", as distinguished from "third party", means a person that has engaged in a transaction or made an agreement subject to [the Uniform Commercial Code].

(27) "Person" means an individual, corporation, business trust, estate, trust, partnership, limited liability company, association, joint venture, government, governmental subdivision, agency, or instrumentality, public corporation, or any other legal or commercial entity.

(28) "Present value" means the amount as of a date certain of one or more sums

payable in the future, discounted to the date certain by use of either an interest rate specified by the parties if that rate is not manifestly unreasonable at the time the transaction is entered into or, if an interest rate is not so specified, a commercially reasonable rate that takes into account the facts and circumstances at the time the transaction is entered into.

(29) "Purchase" means taking by sale, lease, discount, negotiation, mortgage, pledge, lien, security interest, issue or reissue, gift, or any other voluntary transaction creating an interest in property.

(30) "Purchaser" means a person that takes by purchase.

(31) "Record" means information that is inscribed on a tangible medium or that is stored in an electronic or other medium and is retrievable in perceivable form.

(32) "Remedy" means any remedial right to which an aggrieved party is entitled with or without resort to a tribunal.

(33) "Representative" means a person empowered to act for another, including an agent, an officer of a corporation or association, and a trustee, executor, or administrator of an estate.

(34) "Right" includes remedy.

(35) "Security interest" means an interest in personal property or fixtures which secures payment or performance of an obligation. "Security interest" includes any interest of a consignor and a buyer of accounts, chattel paper, a payment intangible, or a promissory note in a transaction that is subject to Article 9. "Security interest" does not include the special property interest of a buyer of goods on identification of those goods to a contract for sale under Section 2- 401, but a buyer may also acquire a "security interest" by complying with Article 9. Except as otherwise provided in Section 2-505, the right of a seller or lessor of goods under Article 2 or 2A to retain or acquire possession of the goods is not a "security interest", but a seller or lessor may also acquire a "security interest" by complying with Article 9. The retention or reservation of title by a seller of goods notwithstanding shipment or delivery to the buyer under Section 2-401 is limited in effect to a reservation of a "security interest." Whether a transaction in the form of a lease creates a "security interest" is determined pursuant to Section 1-203.

(36) "Send" in connection with a writing, record, or notice means:

(A) to deposit in the mail or deliver for transmission by any other usual means of communication with postage or cost of transmission provided for and properly addressed and, in the case of an instrument, to an address specified thereon or otherwise agreed, or if there be none to any address reasonable under the circumstances; or

(B) in any other way to cause to be received any record or notice within the time it would have arrived if properly sent.

(37) "Signed" includes using any symbol executed or adopted with present intention to adopt or accept a writing.

(38) "State" means a State of the United States, the District of Columbia, Puerto Rico, the United States Virgin Islands, or any territory or insular possession subject to the jurisdiction of the United States.

(39) "Surety" includes a guarantor or other secondary obligor.

(40) "Term" means a portion of an agreement that relates to a particular matter.

(41) "Unauthorized signature" means a signature made without actual, implied, or apparent authority. The term includes a forgery.

(42) "Warehouse receipt" means a receipt issued by a person engaged in the business of storing goods for hire.

(43) "Writing" includes printing, typewriting, or any other intentional reduction to tangible form. "Written" has a corresponding meaning.

SECTION 1-202. NOTICE; KNOWLEDGE

(a) Subject to subsection (f), a person has "notice" of a fact if the person:

(1) has actual knowledge of it;

(2) has received a notice or notification of it; or

(3) from all the facts and circumstances known to the person at the time in question, has reason to know that it exists.

(b) "Knowledge" means actual knowledge. "Knows" has a corresponding meaning.

(c) "Discover", "learn", or words of similar import refer to knowledge rather than to reason to know.

(d) A person "notifies" or "gives" a notice or notification to another person by taking such steps as may be reasonably required to inform the other person in ordinary course, whether or not the other person actually comes to know of it.

(e) Subject to subsection (f), a person "receives" a notice or notification when:

(1) it comes to that person's attention; or

(2) it is duly delivered in a form reasonable under the circumstances at the place of business through which the contract was made or at another location held out by that person as the place for receipt of such communications.

(f) Notice, knowledge, or a notice or notification received by an organization is effective for a particular transaction from the time it is brought to the attention of the individual conducting that transaction and, in any event, from the time it would have been brought to the individual's attention if the organization had exercised due diligence. An organization exercises due diligence if it maintains reasonable routines for communicating significant information to the person conducting the transaction and there is reasonable compliance with the routines. Due diligence does not require an individual acting for the organization to communicate information unless the communication is part of the individual's regular duties or the individual has reason to know of the transaction and that the transaction would be materially affected by the information.

SECTION 1-203.   LEASE DISTINGUISHED FROM SECURITY INTEREST

(a) Whether a transaction in the form of a lease creates a lease or security interest is determined by the facts of each case.

(b) A transaction in the form of a lease creates a security interest if the consideration that the lessee is to pay the lessor for the right to possession and use of the goods is an obligation for the term of the lease and is not subject to termination by the lessee, and:

(1) the original term of the lease is equal to or greater than the remaining economic life of the goods;

(2) the lessee is bound to renew the lease for the remaining economic life of the goods or is bound to become the owner of the goods;

(3) the lessee has an option to renew the lease for the remaining economic life of the goods for no additional consideration or for nominal additional consideration upon compliance with the lease agreement; or

(4) the lessee has an option to become the owner of the goods for no additional consideration or for nominal additional consideration upon compliance with the lease agreement.

(c) A transaction in the form of a lease does not create a security interest merely because:

(1) the present value of the consideration the lessee is obligated to pay the lessor for the right to possession and use of the goods is substantially equal to or is greater than the fair market value of the goods at the time the lease is entered into;

(2) the lessee assumes risk of loss of the goods;

(3) the lessee agrees to pay, with respect to the goods, taxes, insurance, filing, recording, or registration fees, or service or maintenance costs;

(4) the lessee has an option to renew the lease or to become the owner of the goods;

(5) the lessee has an option to renew the lease for a fixed rent that is equal to or greater than the reasonably predictable fair market rent for the use of the goods for the term of the renewal at the time the option is to be performed; or

(6) the lessee has an option to become the owner of the goods for a fixed price that is equal to or greater than the reasonably predictable fair market value of the goods at the time the option is to be performed.

(d) Additional consideration is nominal if it is less than the lessee's reasonably predictable cost of performing under the lease agreement if the option is not exercised. Additional consideration is not nominal if:

(1) when the option to renew the lease is granted to the lessee, the rent is

stated to be the fair market rent for the use of the goods for the term of the renewal determined at the time the option is to be performed; or

(2) when the option to become the owner of the goods is granted to the lessee, the price is stated to be the fair market value of the goods determined at the time the option is to be performed.

(e) The "remaining economic life of the goods" and "reasonably predictable" fair market rent, fair market value, or cost of performing under the lease agreement must be determined with reference to the facts and circumstances at the time the transaction is entered into.

SECTION 1-204. VALUE

Except as otherwise provided in Articles 3, 4, [and] 5, [and 6], a person gives value for rights if the person acquires them:

(1) in return for a binding commitment to extend credit or for the extension of immediately available credit, whether or not drawn upon and whether or not a charge-back is provided for in the event of difficulties in collection;

(2) as security for, or in total or partial satisfaction of, a preexisting claim;

(3) by accepting delivery under a preexisting contract for purchase; or

(4) in return for any consideration sufficient to support a simple contract.

SECTION 1-205. REASONABLE TIME; SEASONABLENESS

(a) Whether a time for taking an action required by [the Uniform Commercial Code] is reasonable depends on the nature, purpose, and circumstances of the action.

(b) An action is taken seasonably if it is taken at or within the time agreed or, if no time is agreed, at or within a reasonable time.

SECTION 1-206. PRESUMPTIONS

Whenever [the Uniform Commercial Code] creates a "presumption" with respect to a fact, or provides that a fact is "presumed," the trier of fact must find the existence of the fact unless and until evidence is introduced that supports a finding of its nonexistence.

ARTICLE 2—SALES

Table of Contents

PART 1 SHORT TITLE, GENERAL CONSTRUCTION AND SUBJECT MATTER

SECTION 2-101. SHORT TITLE

This Article shall be known and may be cited as Uniform Commercial Code—Sales.

SECTION 2-102. SCOPE; CERTAIN SECURITY AND OTHER TRANSACTIONS EXCLUDED FROM THIS ARTICLE

Unless the context otherwise requires, this Article applies to transactions in goods; it does not apply to any transaction which although in the form of an unconditional contract to sell or present sale is intended to operate only as a security transaction nor does this Article impair or repeal any statute regulating sales to consumers, farmers or other specified classes of buyers.

SECTION 2-103. DEFINITIONS AND INDEX OF DEFINITIONS

(1) In this Article unless the context otherwise requires

(a) "Buyer" means a person who buys or contracts to buy goods.

(b) "Good faith" in the case of a merchant means honesty in fact and the observance of reasonable commercial standards of fair dealing in the trade.

(c) "Receipt" of goods means taking physical possession of them.

(d) "Seller" means a person who sells or contracts to sell goods.

(2) Other definitions applying to this Article or to specified Parts thereof, and the sections in which they appear are:

"Acceptance". Section 2–606.

"Banker's credit". Section 2–325.

"Between merchants". Section 2–104.

"Cancellation". Section 2–106(4).

"Commercial unit". Section 2–105.

"Confirmed credit". Section 2–325.

"Conforming to contract". Section 2–106.

"Contract for sale". Section 2–106.

"Cover". Section 2–712.

"Entrusting". Section 2–403.

"Financing agency". Section 2–104.

"Future goods". Section 2–105.

"Goods". Section 2–105.

"Identification". Section 2–501.

"Installment contract". Section 2–612.

"Letter of Credit". Section 2–325.

"Lot". Section 2–105.

"Merchant". Section 2–104.

"Overseas". Section 2–323.

"Person in position of seller". Section 2–707.

"Present sale". Section 2–106.

"Sale". Section 2–106.

"Sale on approval". Section 2–326.

"Sale or return". Section 2–326.

"Termination". Section 2–106.

(3) The following definitions in other Articles apply to this Article:

"Check". Section 3–104.

"Consignee". Section 7–102.

"Consignor". Section 7–102.

"Consumer goods". Section 9–109.

"Dishonor". Section 3–502.

"Draft". Section 3–104.

(4) In addition Article 1 contains general definitions and principles of construction and interpretation applicable throughout this Article.

SECTION 2-104. DEFINITIONS: "MERCHANT"; "BETWEEN MERCHANTS"; "FINANCING AGENCY"

(1) "Merchant" means a person who deals in goods of the kind or otherwise by his occupation holds himself out as having knowledge or skill peculiar to the practices or goods involved in the transaction or to whom such knowledge or skill may be attributed by his employment of an agent or broker or other intermediary who by his occupation holds himself out as having such knowledge or skill.

(2) "Financing agency" means a bank, finance company or other person who in the ordinary course of business makes advances against goods or documents of title

or who by arrangement with either the seller or the buyer intervenes in ordinary course to make or collect payment due or claimed under the contract for sale, as by purchasing or paying the seller's draft or making advances against it or by merely taking it for collection whether or not documents of title accompany the draft. "Financing agency" includes also a bank or other person who similarly intervenes between persons who are in the position of seller and buyer in respect to the goods (Section 2–707).

(3) "Between merchants" means in any transaction with respect to which both parties are chargeable with the knowledge or skill of merchants.

SECTION 2-105. DEFINITIONS: TRANSFERABILITY; "GOODS"; "FUTURE" GOODS; "LOT"; "COMMERCIAL UNIT"

(1) "Goods" means all things (including specially manufactured goods) which are movable at the time of identification to the contract for sale other than the money in which the price is to be paid, investment securities (Article 8) and things in action. "Goods" also includes the unborn young of animals and growing crops and other identified things attached to realty as described in the section on goods to be severed from realty (Section 2–107).

(2) Goods must be both existing and identified before any interest in them can pass. Goods which are not both existing and identified are "future" goods. A purported present sale of future goods or of any interest therein operates as a contract to sell.

(3) There may be a sale of a part interest in existing identified goods.

(4) An undivided share in an identified bulk of fungible goods is sufficiently identified to be sold although the quantity of the bulk is not determined. Any agreed proportion of such a bulk or any quantity thereof agreed upon by number, weight or other measure may to the extent of the seller's interest in the bulk be sold to the buyer who then becomes an owner in common.

(5) "Lot" means a parcel or a single article which is the subject matter of a separate sale or delivery, whether or not it is sufficient to perform the contract.

(6) "Commercial unit" means such a unit of goods as by commercial usage is a single whole for purposes of sale and division of which materially impairs its character or value on the market or in use. A commercial unit may be a single article (as a machine) or a set of articles (as a suite of furniture or an assortment of sizes) or a quantity (as a bale, gross, or carload) or any other unit treated in use or in the relevant market as a single whole.

SECTION 2-106. DEFINITIONS: "CONTRACT"; "AGREEMENT"; "CONTRACT FOR SALE"; "SALE"; "PRESENT SALE"; "CONFORMING" TO CONTRACT; "TERMINATION"; "CANCELLATION"

(1) In this Article unless the context otherwise requires "contract" and "agreement" are limited to those relating to the present or future sale of goods. "Contract for sale" includes both a present sale of goods and a contract to sell goods at a future time. A "sale" consists in the passing of title from the seller to the buyer for a price (Section 2–401). A "present sale" means a sale which is accomplished by the making of the contract.

(2) Goods or conduct including any part of a performance are "conforming" or conform to the contract when they are in accordance with the obligations under the contract.

(3) "Termination" occurs when either party pursuant to a power created by agreement or law puts an end to the contract otherwise than for its breach. On "termination" all obligations which are still executory on both sides are discharged but any right based on prior breach or performance survives.

(4) "Cancellation" occurs when either party puts an end to the contract for breach by the other and its effect is the same as that of "termination" except that the cancelling party also retains any remedy for breach of the whole contract or any unperformed balance.

SECTION 2-107.   GOODS TO BE SEVERED FROM REALTY: RECORDING

(1) A contract for the sale of minerals or the like (including oil and gas) or a structure or its materials to be removed from realty is a contract for the sale of goods within this Article if they are to be severed by the seller but until severance a purported present sale thereof which is not effective as a transfer of an interest in land is effective only as a contract to sell.

(2) A contract for the sale apart from the land of growing crops or other things attached to realty and capable of severance without material harm thereto but not described in subsection (1) or of timber to be cut is a contract for the sale of goods within this Article whether the subject matter is to be severed by the buyer or by the seller even though it forms part of the realty at the time of contracting, and the parties can by identification effect a present sale before severance.

(3) The provisions of this section are subject to any third party rights provided by the law relating to realty records, and the contract for sale may be executed and recorded as a document transferring an interest in land and shall then constitute notice to third parties of the buyer's rights under the contract for sale.

PART 2.   FORM, FORMATION AND READJUSTMENT OF CONTRACT
SECTION 2-201.   FORMAL REQUIREMENTS; STATUTE OF FRAUDS

(1) Except as otherwise provided in this section a contract for the sale of goods for the price of $500 or more is not enforceable by way of action or defense unless there is some writing sufficient to indicate that a contract for sale has been made between the parties and signed by the party against whom enforcement is sought or by his authorized agent or broker. A writing is not insufficient because it omits or incorrectly states a term agreed upon but the contract is not enforceable under this paragraph beyond the quantity of goods shown in such writing.

(2) Between merchants if within a reasonable time a writing in confirmation of the contract and sufficient against the sender is received and the party receiving it has reason to know its contents, it satisfies the requirements of subsection (1) against such party unless written notice of objection to its contents is given within 10 days after it is received.

(3) A contract which does not satisfy the requirements of subsection (1) but which

is valid in other respects is enforceable

(a) if the goods are to be specially manufactured for the buyer and are not suitable for sale to others in the ordinary course of the seller's business and the seller, before notice of repudiation is received and under circumstances which reasonably indicate that the goods are for the buyer, has made either a substantial beginning of their manufacture or commitments for their procurement; or

(b) if the party against whom enforcement is sought admits in his pleading, testimony or otherwise in court that a contract for sale was made, but the contract is not enforceable under this provision beyond the quantity of goods admitted; or

(c) with respect to goods for which payment has been made and accepted or which have been received and accepted (Sec. 2–606).

SECTION 2-202. FINAL WRITTEN EXPRESSION: PAROL OR EXTRINSIC EVIDENCE

Terms with respect to which the confirmatory memoranda of the parties agree or which are otherwise set forth in a writing intended by the parties as a final expression of their agreement with respect to such terms as are included therein may not be contradicted by evidence of any prior agreement or of a contemporaneous oral agreement but may be explained or supplemented

(a) by course of dealing or usage of trade (Section 1–205) or by course of performance (Section 2–208); and

(b) by evidence of consistent additional terms unless the court finds the writing to have been intended also as a complete and exclusive statement of the terms of the agreement.

SECTION 2-203. SEALS INOPERATIVE

The affixing of a seal to a writing evidencing a contract for sale or an offer to buy or sell goods does not constitute the writing a sealed instrument and the law with respect to sealed instruments does not apply to such a contract or offer.

SECTION 2-204. FORMATION IN GENERAL

(1) A contract for sale of goods may be made in any manner sufficient to show agreement, including conduct by both parties which recognizes the existence of such a contract.

(2) An agreement sufficient to constitute a contract for sale may be found even though the moment of its making is undetermined.

(3) Even though one or more terms are left open a contract for sale does not fail for indefiniteness if the parties have intended to make a contract and there is a reasonably certain basis for giving an appropriate remedy.

SECTION 2-205. FIRM OFFERS

An offer by a merchant to buy or sell goods in a signed writing which by its terms gives assurance that it will be held open is not revocable, for lack of consideration, during the time stated or if no time is stated for a reasonable time, but in no event may such period of irrevocability exceed three months; but any such term of assurance on a form supplied by the offeree must be separately signed by the offeror.

SECTION 2-206. OFFER AND ACCEPTANCE IN FORMATION OF CONTRACT

(1) Unless otherwise unambiguously indicated by the language or circumstances

(a) an offer to make a contract shall be construed as inviting acceptance in any manner and by any medium reasonable in the circumstances;

(b) an order or other offer to buy goods for prompt or current shipment shall be construed as inviting acceptance either by a prompt promise to ship or by the prompt or current shipment of conforming or non-conforming goods, but such a shipment of non-conforming goods does not constitute an acceptance if the seller seasonably notifies the buyer that the shipment is offered only as an accommodation of the buyer.

(2) Where the beginning of a requested performance is a reasonable mode of acceptance an offeror who is not notified of acceptance within a reasonable time may treat the offer as having lapsed before acceptance.

SECTION 2-207. ADDITIONAL TERMS IN ACCEPTANCE OR CONFIRMATION

(1) A definite and seasonable expression of acceptance or a written confirmation which is sent within a reasonable time operates as an acceptance even though it states terms additional to or different from those offered or agreed upon, unless acceptance is expressly made conditional on assent to the additional or different terms.

(2) The additional terms are to be construed as proposals for addition to the contract. Between merchants such terms become part of the contract unless:

(a) the offer expressly limits acceptance to the terms of the offer;

(b) they materially alter it; or

(c) notification of objection to them has already been given or is given within a reasonable time after notice of them is received.

(3) Conduct by both parties which recognizes the existence of a contract is sufficient to establish a contract for sale although the writings of the parties do not otherwise establish a contract. In such case the terms of the particular contract consist of those terms on which the writings of the parties agree, together with any supplementary terms incorporated under any other provisions of this Act.

SECTION 2-208. COURSE OF PERFORMANCE OR PRACTICAL CONSTRUCTION

(1) Where the contract for sale involves repeated occasions for performance by either party with knowledge of the nature of the performance and opportunity for objection to it by the other, any course of performance accepted or acquiesced in without objection shall be relevant to determine the meaning of the agreement.

(2) The express terms of the agreement and any such course of performance, as

well as any course of dealing and usage of trade, shall be construed whenever reasonable as consistent with each other; but when such construction is unreasonable, express terms shall control course of performance and course of performance shall control both course of dealing and usage of trade (Section 1–205).

(3) Subject to the provisions of the next section on modification and waiver, such course of performance shall be relevant to show a waiver or modification of any term inconsistent with such course of performance.

SECTION 2-209. MODIFICATION, RESCISSION AND WAIVER

(1) An agreement modifying a contract within this Article needs no consideration to be binding.

(2) A signed agreement which excludes modification or rescission except by a signed writing cannot be otherwise modified or rescinded, but except as between merchants such a requirement on a form supplied by the merchant must be separately signed by the other party.

(3) The requirements of the statute of frauds section of this Article (Section 2–201) must be satisfied if the contract as modified is within its provisions.

(4) Although an attempt at modification or rescission does not satisfy the requirements of subsection (2) or (3) it can operate as a waiver.

(5) A party who has made a waiver affecting an executory portion of the contract may retract the waiver by reasonable notification received by the other party that strict performance will be required of any term waived, unless the retraction would be unjust in view of a material change of position in reliance on the waiver.

SECTION 2-210. DELEGATION OF PERFORMANCE; ASSIGNMENT OF RIGHTS

(1) A party may perform his duty through a delegate unless otherwise agreed or unless the other party has a substantial interest in having his original promisor perform or control the acts required by the contract. No delegation of performance relieves the party delegating of any duty to perform or any liability for breach.

(2) Unless otherwise agreed all rights of either seller or buyer can be assigned except where the assignment would materially change the duty of the other party, or increase materially the burden or risk imposed on him by his contract, or impair materially his chance of obtaining return performance. A right to damages for breach of the whole contract or a right arising out of the assignor's due performance of his entire obligation can be assigned despite agreement otherwise.

(3) Unless the circumstances indicate the contrary a prohibition of assignment of "the contract" is to be construed as barring only the delegation to the assignee of the assignor's performance.

(4) An assignment of "the contract" or of "all my rights under the contract" or an assignment in similar general terms is an assignment of rights and unless the language or the circumstances (as in an assignment for security) indicate the contrary, it is a delegation of performance of the duties of the assignor and its acceptance by the assignee constitutes a promise by him to perform those duties. This promise is enforceable by either the assignor or the other party to the original

contract.

(5) The other party may treat any assignment which delegates performance as creating reasonable grounds for insecurity and may without prejudice to his rights against the assignor demand assurances from the assignee (Section 2–609).

PART 3. GENERAL OBLIGATION AND CONSTRUCTION OF CONTRACT

SECTION 2-301. GENERAL OBLIGATIONS OF PARTIES

The obligation of the seller is to transfer and deliver and that of the buyer is to accept and pay in accordance with the contract.

SECTION 2-302. UNCONSCIONABLE CONTRACT OR CLAUSE

(1) If the court as a matter of law finds the contract or any clause of the contract to have been unconscionable at the time it was made the court may refuse to enforce the contract, or it may enforce the remainder of the contract without the unconscionable clause, or it may so limit the application of any unconscionable clause as to avoid any unconscionable result.

(2) When it is claimed or appears to the court that the contract or any clause thereof may be unconscionable the parties shall be afforded a reasonable opportunity to present evidence as to its commercial setting, purpose and effect to aid the court in making the determination.

SECTION 2-303. ALLOCATION OR DIVISION OF RISKS

Where this Article allocates a risk or a burden as between the parties "unless otherwise agreed", the agreement may not only shift the allocation but may also divide the risk or burden.

SECTION 2-304. PRICE PAYABLE IN MONEY, GOODS, REALTY, OR OTHERWISE

(1) The price can be made payable in money or otherwise. If it is payable in whole or in part in goods each party is a seller of the goods which he is to transfer.

(2) Even though all or part of the price is payable in an interest in realty the transfer of the goods and the seller's obligations with reference to them are subject to this Article, but not the transfer of the interest in realty or the transferor's obligations in connection therewith.

SECTION 2-305. OPEN PRICE TERM

(1) The parties if they so intend can conclude a contract for sale even though the price is not settled. In such a case the price is a reasonable price at the time for delivery if

(a) nothing is said as to price; or

(b) the price is left to be agreed by the parties and they fail to agree; or

(c) the price is to be fixed in terms of some agreed market or other standard as set or recorded by a third person or agency and it is not so set or recorded.

(2) A price to be fixed by the seller or by the buyer means a price for him to fix

in good faith.

(3) When a price left to be fixed otherwise than by agreement of the parties fails to be fixed through fault of one party the other may at his option treat the contract as cancelled or himself fix a reasonable price.

(4) Where, however, the parties intend not to be bound unless the price be fixed or agreed and it is not fixed or agreed there is no contract. In such a case the buyer must return any goods already received or if unable so to do must pay their reasonable value at the time of delivery and the seller must return any portion of the price paid on account.

SECTION 2-306. OUTPUT, REQUIREMENTS AND EXCLUSIVE DEALINGS

(1) A term which measures the quantity by the output of the seller or the requirements of the buyer means such actual output or requirements as may occur in good faith, except that no quantity unreasonably disproportionate to any stated estimate or in the absence of a stated estimate to any normal or otherwise comparable prior output or requirements may be tendered or demanded.

(2) A lawful agreement by either the seller or the buyer for exclusive dealing in the kind of goods concerned imposes unless otherwise agreed an obligation by the seller to use best efforts to supply the goods and by the buyer to use best efforts to promote their sale.

SECTION 2-307. DELIVERY IN SINGLE LOT OR SEVERAL LOTS

Unless otherwise agreed all goods called for by a contract for sale must be tendered in a single delivery and payment is due only on such tender but where the circumstances give either party the right to make or demand delivery in lots the price if it can be apportioned may be demanded for each lot.

SECTION 2-308. ABSENCE OF SPECIFIED PLACE FOR DELIVERY

Unless otherwise agreed

(a) the place for delivery of goods is the seller's place of business or if he has none his residence; but

(b) in a contract for sale of identified goods which to the knowledge of the parties at the time of contracting are in some other place, that place is the place for their delivery; and

(c) documents of title may be delivered through customary banking channels.

SECTION 2-309. ABSENCE OF SPECIFIC TIME PROVISIONS; NOTICE OF TERMINATION

(1) The time for shipment or delivery or any other action under a contract if not provided in this Article or agreed upon shall be a reasonable time.

(2) Where the contract provides for successive performances but is indefinite in duration it is valid for a reasonable time but unless otherwise agreed may be terminated at any time by either party.

(3) Termination of a contract by one party except on the happening of an agreed

event requires that reasonable notification be received by the other party and an agreement dispensing with notification is invalid if its operation would be unconscionable.

SECTION 2-310.   OPEN TIME FOR PAYMENT OR RUNNING OF CREDIT; AUTHORITY TO SHIP UNDER RESERVATION

Unless otherwise agreed

(a) payment is due at the time and place at which the buyer is to receive the goods even though the place of shipment is the place of delivery; and

(b) if the seller is authorized to send the goods he may ship them under reservation, and may tender the documents of title, but the buyer may inspect the goods after their arrival before payment is due unless such inspection is inconsistent with the terms of the contract (Section 2–513); and

(c) if delivery is authorized and made by way of documents of title otherwise than by subsection (b) then payment is due at the time and place at which the buyer is to receive the documents regardless of where the goods are to be received; and

(d) where the seller is required or authorized to ship the goods on credit the credit period runs from the time of shipment but post-dating the invoice or delaying its dispatch will correspondingly delay the starting of the credit period.

SECTION   2-311.   OPTIONS   AND   COOPERATION   RESPECTING PERFORMANCE

(1) An agreement for sale which is otherwise sufficiently definite (subsection (3) of Section 2–204) to be a contract is not made invalid by the fact that it leaves particulars of performance to be specified by one of the parties. Any such specification must be made in good faith and within limits set by commercial reasonableness.

(2) Unless otherwise agreed specifications relating to assortment of the goods are at the buyer's option and except as otherwise provided in subsections (1)(c) and (3) of Section 2–319 specifications or arrangements relating to shipment are at the seller's option.

(3) Where such specification would materially affect the other party's performance but is not seasonably made or where one party's cooperation is necessary to the agreed performance of the other but is not seasonably forthcoming, the other party in addition to all other remedies

(a) is excused for any resulting delay in his own performance; and

(b) may also either proceed to perform in any reasonable manner or after the time for a material part of his own performance treat the failure to specify or to cooperate as a breach by failure to deliver or accept the goods.

SECTION 2-312.   WARRANTY OF TITLE AND AGAINST INFRINGEMENT; BUYER'S OBLIGATION AGAINST INFRINGEMENT

(1) Subject to subsection (2) there is in a contract for sale a warranty by the seller that

(a) the title conveyed shall be good, and its transfer rightful; and

(b) the goods shall be delivered free from any security interest or other lien or encumbrance of which the buyer at the time of contracting has no knowledge.

(2) A warranty under subsection (1) will be excluded or modified only by specific language or by circumstances which give the buyer reason to know that the person selling does not claim title in himself or that he is purporting to sell only such right or title as he or a third person may have.

(3) Unless otherwise agreed a seller who is a merchant regularly dealing in goods of the kind warrants that the goods shall be delivered free of the rightful claim of any third person by way of infringement or the like but a buyer who furnishes specifications to the seller must hold the seller harmless against any such claim which arises out of compliance with the specifications.

SECTION 2-313. EXPRESS WARRANTIES BY AFFIRMATION, PROMISE, DESCRIPTION, SAMPLE

(1) Express warranties by the seller are created as follows:

(a) Any affirmation of fact or promise made by the seller to the buyer which relates to the goods and becomes part of the basis of the bargain creates an express warranty that the goods shall conform to the affirmation or promise.

(b) Any description of the goods which is made part of the basis of the bargain creates an express warranty that the goods shall conform to the description.

(c) Any sample or model which is made part of the basis of the bargain creates an express warranty that the whole of the goods shall conform to the sample or model.

(2) It is not necessary to the creation of an express warranty that the seller use formal words such as "warrant" or "guarantee" or that he have a specific intention to make a warranty, but an affirmation merely of the value of the goods or a statement purporting to be merely the seller's opinion or commendation of the goods does not create a warranty.

SECTION 2-314. IMPLIED WARRANTY: MERCHANTABILITY; USAGE OF TRADE

(1) Unless excluded or modified (Section 2–316), a warranty that the goods shall be merchantable is implied in a contract for their sale if the seller is a merchant with respect to goods of that kind. Under this section the serving for value of food or drink to be consumed either on the premises or elsewhere is a sale.

(2) Goods to be merchantable must be at least such as

(a) pass without objection in the trade under the contract description; and

(b) in the case of fungible goods, are of fair average quality within the description; and

(c) are fit for the ordinary purposes for which such goods are used; and

(d) run, within the variations permitted by the agreement, of even kind, quality and quantity within each unit and among all units involved; and

(e) are adequately contained, packaged, and labeled as the agreement may require; and

(f) conform to the promises or affirmations of fact made on the container or label if any.

(3) Unless excluded or modified (Section 2–316) other implied warranties may arise from course of dealing or usage of trade.

SECTION 2-315. IMPLIED WARRANTY: FITNESS FOR PARTICULAR PURPOSE

Where the seller at the time of contracting has reason to know any particular purpose for which the goods are required and that the buyer is relying on the seller's skill or judgment to select or furnish suitable goods, there is unless excluded or modified under the next section an implied warranty that the goods shall be fit for such purpose.

SECTION 2-316. EXCLUSION OR MODIFICATION OF WARRANTIES

(1) Words or conduct relevant to the creation of an express warranty and words or conduct tending to negate or limit warranty shall be construed wherever reasonable as consistent with each other; but subject to the provisions of this Article on parol or extrinsic evidence (Section 2–202) negation or limitation is inoperative to the extent that such construction is unreasonable.

(2) Subject to subsection (3), to exclude or modify the implied warranty of merchantability or any part of it the language must mention merchantability and in case of a writing must be conspicuous, and to exclude or modify any implied warranty of fitness the exclusion must be by a writing and conspicuous. Language to exclude all implied warranties of fitness is sufficient if it states, for example, that "There are no warranties which extend beyond the description on the face hereof."

(3) Notwithstanding subsection (2)

(a) unless the circumstances indicate otherwise, all implied warranties are excluded by expressions like "as is", "with all faults" or other language which in common understanding calls the buyer's attention to the exclusion of warranties and makes plain that there is no implied warranty; and

(b) when the buyer before entering into the contract has examined the goods or the sample or model as fully as he desired or has refused to examine the goods there is no implied warranty with regard to defects which an examination ought in the circumstances to have revealed to him; and

(c) an implied warranty can also be excluded or modified by course of dealing or course of performance or usage of trade.

(4) Remedies for breach of warranty can be limited in accordance with the provisions of this Article on liquidation or limitation of damages and on contractual modification of remedy (Section 2–718 and 2–719).

SECTION 2-317. CUMULATION AND CONFLICT OF WARRANTIES EXPRESS OR IMPLIED

Warranties whether express or implied shall be construed as consistent with each other and as cumulative, but if such construction is unreasonable the intention of the parties shall determine which warranty is dominant. In ascertaining that intention the following rules apply:

(a) Exact or technical specifications displace an inconsistent sample or model or general language of description.

(b) A sample from an existing bulk displaces inconsistent general language of description.

(c) Express warranties displace inconsistent implied warranties other than an implied warranty of fitness for a particular purpose.

SECTION 2-318. THIRD PARTY BENEFICIARIES OF WARRANTIES EXPRESS OR IMPLIED

Note:

If this Act is introduced in the Congress of the United States this section should be omitted. (States to select one alternative.)

Alternative A

A seller's warranty whether express or implied extends to any natural person who is in the family or household of his buyer or who is a guest in his home if it is reasonable to expect that such person may use, consume or be affected by the goods and who is injured in person by breach of the warranty. A seller may not exclude or limit the operation of this section.

Alternative B

A seller's warranty whether express or implied extends to any natural person who may reasonably be expected to use, consume or be affected by the goods and who is injured in person by breach of the warranty. A seller may not exclude or limit the operation of this section.

Alternative C

A seller's warranty whether express or implied extends to any person who may reasonably be expected to use, consume or be affected by the goods and who is injured by breach of the warranty. A seller may not exclude or limit the operation of this section with respect to injury to the person of an individual to whom the warranty extends.

SECTION 2-319. F.O.B. AND F.A.S. TERMS

(1) Unless otherwise agreed the term F.O.B. (which means "free on board") at a named place, even though used only in connection with the stated price, is a delivery term under which

(a) when the term is F.O.B. the place of shipment, the seller must at that place ship the goods in the manner provided in this Article (Section 2–504) and bear the expense and risk of putting them into the possession of the carrier; or

(b) when the term is F.O.B. the place of destination, the seller must at his own expense and risk transport the goods to that place and there tender delivery of them in the manner provided in this Article (Section 2–503);

(c) when under either (a) or (b) the term is also F.O.B. vessel, car or other vehicle, the seller must in addition at his own expense and risk load the goods on board. If the term is F.O.B. vessel the buyer must name the vessel and in an appropriate case the seller must comply with the provisions of this Article on the form of bill of lading (Section 2–323).

(2) Unless otherwise agreed the term F.A.S. vessel (which means "free alongside") at a named port, even though used only in connection with the stated price, is a delivery term under which the seller must

(a) at his own expense and risk deliver the goods alongside the vessel in the manner usual in that port or on a dock designated and provided by the buyer; and

(b) obtain and tender a receipt for the goods in exchange for which the carrier is under a duty to issue a bill of lading.

(3) Unless otherwise agreed in any case falling within subsection (1)(a) or (c) or subsection (2) the buyer must seasonably give any needed instructions for making delivery, including when the term is F.A.S. or F.O.B. the loading berth of the vessel and in an appropriate case its name and sailing date. The seller may treat the failure of needed instructions as a failure of cooperation under this Article (Section 2–311). He may also at his option move the goods in any reasonable manner preparatory to delivery or shipment.

(4) Under the term F.O.B. vessel or F.A.S. unless otherwise agreed the buyer must make payment against tender of the required documents and the seller may not tender nor the buyer demand delivery of the goods in substitution for the documents.

SECTION 2-320.   C.I.F. AND C. & F. TERMS

(1) The term C.I.F. means that the price includes in a lump sum the cost of the goods and the insurance and freight to the named destination. The term C. & F. or C.F. means that the price so includes cost and freight to the named destination.

(2) Unless otherwise agreed and even though used only in connection with the stated price and destination, the term C.I.F. destination or its equivalent requires the seller at his own expense and risk to

(a) put the goods into the possession of a carrier at the port for shipment and obtain a negotiable bill or bills of lading covering the entire transportation to the named destination; and

(b) load the goods and obtain a receipt from the carrier (which may be contained in the bill of lading) showing that the freight has been paid or provided for; and

(c) obtain a policy or certificate of insurance, including any war risk insurance, of a kind and on terms then current at the port of shipment in the usual amount, in the currency of the contract, shown to cover the same goods covered by the bill of lading and providing for payment of loss to the order of the buyer or for the account of whom it may concern; but the seller may add to the price the amount of the premium for any such war risk insurance; and

(d) prepare an invoice of the goods and procure any other documents required to effect shipment or to comply with the contract; and

(e) forward and tender with commercial promptness all the documents in due form and with any indorsement necessary to perfect the buyer's rights.

(3) Unless otherwise agreed the term C. & F. or its equivalent has the same effect and imposes upon the seller the same obligations and risks as a C.I.F. term except the obligation as to insurance.

(4) Under the term C.I.F. or C. & F. unless otherwise agreed the buyer must make payment against tender of the required documents and the seller may not tender nor the buyer demand delivery of the goods in substitution for the documents.

SECTION 2-321.   C.I.F. OR C. & F.: "NET LANDED WEIGHTS"; "PAYMENT ON ARRIVAL"; WARRANTY OF CONDITION ON ARRIVAL

Under a contract containing a term C.I.F. or C. & F.

(1) Where the price is based on or is to be adjusted according to "net landed weights", "delivered weights", "out turn" quantity or quality or the like, unless otherwise agreed the seller must reasonably estimate the price. The payment due on tender of the documents called for by the contract is the amount so estimated, but after final adjustment of the price a settlement must be made with commercial promptness.

(2) An agreement described in subsection (1) or any warranty of quality or condition of the goods on arrival places upon the seller the risk of ordinary deterioration, shrinkage and the like in transportation but has no effect on the place or time of identification to the contract for sale or delivery or on the passing of the risk of loss.

(3) Unless otherwise agreed where the contract provides for payment on or after arrival of the goods the seller must before payment allow such preliminary inspection as is feasible; but if the goods are lost delivery of the documents and payment are due when the goods should have arrived.

SECTION 2-322.   DELIVERY "EX-SHIP"

(1) Unless otherwise agreed a term for delivery of goods "ex-ship" (which means from the carrying vessel) or in equivalent language is not restricted to a particular ship and requires delivery from a ship which has reached a place at the named port of destination where goods of the kind are usually discharged.

(2) Under such a term unless otherwise agreed

(a) the seller must discharge all liens arising out of the carriage and furnish the buyer with a direction which puts the carrier under a duty to deliver the goods; and

(b) the risk of loss does not pass to the buyer until the goods leave the ship's tackle or are otherwise properly unloaded.

SECTION 2-323.   FORM OF BILL OF LADING REQUIRED IN OVERSEAS

SHIPMENT; "OVERSEAS"

(1) Where the contract contemplates overseas shipment and contains a term C.I.F. or C. & F. or F.O.B. vessel, the seller unless otherwise agreed must obtain a negotiable bill of lading stating that the goods have been loaded on board or, in the case of a term C.I.F. or C. & F., received for shipment.

(2) Where in a case within subsection (1) a bill of lading has been issued in a set of parts, unless otherwise agreed if the documents are not to be sent from abroad the buyer may demand tender of the full set; otherwise only one part of the bill of lading need be tendered. Even if the agreement expressly requires a full set

(a) due tender of a single part is acceptable within the provisions of this Article on cure of improper delivery (subsection (1) of Section 2-508); and

(b) even though the full set is demanded, if the documents are sent from abroad the person tendering an incomplete set may nevertheless require payment upon furnishing an indemnity which the buyer in good faith deems adequate.

(3) A shipment by water or by air or a contract contemplating such shipment is "overseas" insofar as by usage of trade or agreement it is subject to the commercial, financing or shipping practices characteristic of international deep water commerce.

SECTION 2-324. "NO ARRIVAL, NO SALE" TERM

Under a term "no arrival, no sale" or terms of like meaning, unless otherwise agreed,

(a) the seller must properly ship conforming goods and if they arrive by any means he must tender them on arrival but he assumes no obligation that the goods will arrive unless he has caused the non-arrival; and

(b) where without fault of the seller the goods are in part lost or have so deteriorated as no longer to conform to the contract or arrive after the contract time, the buyer may proceed as if there had been casualty to identified goods (Section 2–613).

SECTION 2-325. "LETTER OF CREDIT" TERM; "CONFIRMED CREDIT"

(1) Failure of the buyer seasonably to furnish an agreed letter of credit is a breach of the contract for sale.

(2) The delivery to seller of a proper letter of credit suspends the buyer's obligation to pay. If the letter of credit is dishonored, the seller may on seasonable notification to the buyer require payment directly from him.

(3) Unless otherwise agreed the term "letter of credit" or "banker's credit" in a contract for sale means an irrevocable credit issued by a financing agency of good repute and, where the shipment is overseas, of good international repute. The term "confirmed credit" means that the credit must also carry the direct obligation of such an agency which does business in the seller's financial market.

SECTION 2-326. SALE ON APPROVAL AND SALE OR RETURN; CONSIGNMENT SALES AND RIGHTS OF CREDITORS

(1) Unless otherwise agreed, if delivered goods may be returned by the buyer even though they conform to the contract, the transaction is

(a) a "sale on approval" if the goods are delivered primarily for use, and

(b) a "sale or return" if the goods are delivered primarily for resale.

(2) Except as provided in subsection (3), goods held on approval are not subject to the claims of the buyer's creditors until acceptance; goods held on sale or return are subject to such claims while in the buyer's possession.

(3) Where goods are delivered to a person for sale and such person maintains a place of business at which he deals in goods of the kind involved, under a name other than the name of the person making delivery, then with respect to claims of creditors of the person conducting the business the goods are deemed to be on sale or return. The provisions of this subsection are applicable even though an agreement purports to reserve title to the person making delivery until payment or resale or uses such words as "on consignment" or "on memorandum." However, this subsection is not applicable if the person making delivery

(a) complies with an applicable law providing for a consignor's interest or the like to be evidenced by a sign, or

(b) establishes that the person conducting the business is generally known by his creditors to be substantially engaged in selling the goods of others, or

(c) complies with the filing provisions of the Article on Secured Transactions (Article 9).

(4) Any "or return" term of a contract for sale is to be treated as a separate contract for sale within the statute of frauds section of this Article (Section 2–201) and as contradicting the sale aspect of the contract within the provisions of this Article on parol or extrinsic evidence (Section 2–202).

SECTION 2-327. SPECIAL INCIDENTS OF SALE ON APPROVAL AND SALE OR RETURN

(1) Under a sale on approval unless otherwise agreed

(a) although the goods are identified to the contract the risk of loss and the title do not pass to the buyer until acceptance; and

(b) use of the goods consistent with the purpose of trial is not acceptance but failure seasonably to notify the seller of election to return the goods is acceptance, and if the goods conform to the contract acceptance of any part is acceptance of the whole; and

(c) after due notification of election to return, the return is at the seller's risk and expense but a merchant buyer must follow any reasonable instructions.

(2) Under a sale or return unless otherwise agreed

(a) the option to return extends to the whole or any commercial unit of the goods while in substantially their original condition, but must be exercised seasonably; and

(b) the return is at the buyer's risk and expense.

SECTION 2-328. SALE BY AUCTION

(1) In a sale by auction if goods are put up in lots each lot is the subject of a separate sale.

(2) A sale by auction is complete when the auctioneer so announces by the fall of the hammer or in other customary manner. Where a bid is made while the hammer is falling in acceptance of a prior bid the auctioneer may in his discretion reopen the bidding or declare the goods sold under the bid on which the hammer was falling.

(3) Such a sale is with reserve unless the goods are in explicit terms put up without reserve. In an auction with reserve the auctioneer may withdraw the goods at any time until he announces completion of the sale. In an auction without reserve, after the auctioneer calls for bids on an article or lot, that article or lot cannot be withdrawn unless no bid is made within a reasonable time. In either case a bidder may retract his bid until the auctioneer's announcement of completion of the sale, but a bidder's retraction does not revive any previous bid.

(4) If the auctioneer knowingly receives a bid on the seller's behalf or the seller makes or procures such a bid, and notice has not been given that liberty for such bidding is reserved, the buyer may at his option avoid the sale or take the goods at the price of the last good faith bid prior to the completion of the sale. This subsection shall not apply to any bid at a forced sale.

PART 4. TITLE, CREDITORS AND GOOD FAITH PURCHASERS

SECTION 2-401. PASSING OF TITLE; RESERVATION FOR SECURITY; LIMITED APPLICATION OF THIS SECTION

Each provision of this Article with regard to the rights, obligations and remedies of the seller, the buyer, purchasers or other third parties applies irrespective of title to the goods except where the provision refers to such title. Insofar as situations are not covered by the other provisions of this Article and matters concerning title become material the following rules apply:

(1) Title to goods cannot pass under a contract for sale prior to their identification to the contract (Section 2–501), and unless otherwise explicitly agreed the buyer acquires by their identification a special property as limited by this Act. Any retention or reservation by the seller of the title (property) in goods shipped or delivered to the buyer is limited in effect to a reservation of a security interest. Subject to these provisions and to the provisions of the Article on Secured Transactions (Article 9), title to goods passes from the seller to the buyer in any manner and on any conditions explicitly agreed on by the parties.

(2) Unless otherwise explicitly agreed title passes to the buyer at the time and place at which the seller completes his performance with reference to the physical delivery of the goods, despite any reservation of a security interest and even though a document of title is to be delivered at a different time or place; and in particular and despite any reservation of a security interest by the bill of lading

(a) if the contract requires or authorizes the seller to send the goods to the buyer but does not require him to deliver them at destination, title passes to the buyer at the time and place of shipment; but

(b) if the contract requires delivery at destination, title passes on tender there.

(3) Unless otherwise explicitly agreed where delivery is to be made without moving the goods,

(a) if the seller is to deliver a document of title, title passes at the time when and the place where he delivers such documents; or

(b) if the goods are at the time of contracting already identified and no documents are to be delivered, title passes at the time and place of contracting.

(4) A rejection or other refusal by the buyer to receive or retain the goods, whether or not justified, or a justified revocation of acceptance revests title to the goods in the seller. Such revesting occurs by operation of law and is not a "sale".

SECTION 2-402. RIGHTS OF SELLER'S CREDITORS AGAINST SOLD GOODS

(1) Except as provided in subsections (2) and (3), rights of unsecured creditors of the seller with respect to goods which have been identified to a contract for sale are subject to the buyer's rights to recover the goods under this Article (Sections 2–502 and 2–716).

(2) A creditor of the seller may treat a sale or an identification of goods to a contract for sale as void if as against him a retention of possession by the seller is fraudulent under any rule of law of the state where the goods are situated, except that retention of possession in good faith and current course of trade by a merchant-seller for a commercially reasonable time after a sale or identification is not fraudulent.

(3) Nothing in this Article shall be deemed to impair the rights of creditors of the seller

(a) under the provisions of the Article on Secured Transactions (Article 9); or

(b) where identification to the contract or delivery is made not in current course of trade but in satisfaction of or as security for a pre-existing claim for money, security or the like and is made under circumstances which under any rule of law of the state where the goods are situated would apart from this Article constitute the transaction a fraudulent transfer or voidable preference.

SECTION 2-403. POWER TO TRANSFER; GOOD FAITH PURCHASE OF GOODS; "ENTRUSTING"

(1) A purchaser of goods acquires all title which his transferor had or had power to transfer except that a purchaser of a limited interest acquires rights only to the extent of the interest purchased. A person with voidable title has power to transfer a good title to a good faith purchaser for value. When goods have been delivered under a transaction of purchase the purchaser has such power even though

(a) the transferor was deceived as to the identity of the purchaser, or

(b) the delivery was in exchange for a check which is later dishonored, or

(c) it was agreed that the transaction was to be a "cash sale", or

(d) the delivery was procured through fraud punishable as larcenous under the criminal law.

(2) Any entrusting of possession of goods to a merchant who deals in goods of that kind gives him power to transfer all rights of the entruster to a buyer in ordinary course of business.

(3) "Entrusting" includes any delivery and any acquiescence in retention of possession regardless of any condition expressed between the parties to the delivery or acquiescence and regardless of whether the procurement of the entrusting or the possessor's disposition of the goods have been such as to be larcenous under the criminal law.

1988 Conforming Amendments for States Enacting
Repealer of Article 6—Bulk Transfers
(Alternative A)

(4) The rights of other purchasers of goods and of lien creditors are governed by the Articles on Secured Transactions (Article 9) and Documents of Title (Article 7).

1988 Conforming Amendments for States Enacting
Revised Article 6—Bulk Sales
(Alternative B)

(4) The rights of other purchasers of goods and of lien creditors are governed by the Articles on Secured Transactions (Article 9), Bulk Sales (Article 6) and Documents of Title (Article 7).

PART 5.   PERFORMANCE

SECTION 2-501.   INSURABLE INTEREST IN GOODS; MANNER OF IDENTIFICATION OF GOODS

(1) The buyer obtains a special property and an insurable interest in goods by identification of existing goods as goods to which the contract refers even though the goods so identified are non-conforming and he has an option to return or reject them. Such identification can be made at any time and in any manner explicitly agreed to by the parties. In the absence of explicit agreement identification occurs

(a) when the contract is made if it is for the sale of goods already existing and identified;

(b) if the contract is for the sale of future goods other than those described in paragraph (c), when goods are shipped, marked or otherwise designated by the seller as goods to which the contract refers;

(c) when the crops are planted or otherwise become growing crops or the young are conceived if the contract is for the sale of unborn young to be born within twelve months after contracting or for the sale of crops to be harvested within twelve months or the next normal harvest season after contracting whichever is longer.

(2) The seller retains an insurable interest in goods so long as title to or any

security interest in the goods remains in him and where the identification is by the seller alone he may until default or insolvency or notification to the buyer that the identification is final substitute other goods for those identified.

(3) Nothing in this section impairs any insurable interest recognized under any other statute or rule of law.

SECTION 2-502. BUYER'S RIGHT TO GOODS ON SELLER'S INSOLVENCY

(1) Subject to subsection (2) and even though the goods have not been shipped a buyer who has paid a part or all of the price of goods in which he has a special property under the provisions of the immediately preceding section may on making and keeping good a tender of any unpaid portion of their price recover them from the seller if the seller becomes insolvent within ten days after receipt of the first installment on their price.

(2) If the identification creating his special property has been made by the buyer he acquires the right to recover the goods only if they conform to the contract for sale.

SECTION 2-503. MANNER OF SELLER'S TENDER OF DELIVERY

(1) Tender of delivery requires that the seller put and hold conforming goods at the buyer's disposition and give the buyer any notification reasonably necessary to enable him to take delivery. The manner, time and place for tender are determined by the agreement and this Article, and in particular

(a) tender must be at a reasonable hour, and if it is of goods they must be kept available for the period reasonably necessary to enable the buyer to take possession; but

(b) unless otherwise agreed the buyer must furnish facilities reasonably suited to the receipt of the goods.

(2) Where the case is within the next section respecting shipment tender requires that the seller comply with its provisions.

(3) Where the seller is required to deliver at a particular destination tender requires that he comply with subsection (1) and also in any appropriate case tender documents as described in subsections (4) and (5) of this section.

(4) Where goods are in the possession of a bailee and are to be delivered without being moved

(a) tender requires that the seller either tender a negotiable document of title covering such goods or procure acknowledgment by the bailee of the buyer's right to possession of the goods; but

(b) tender to the buyer of a non-negotiable document of title or of a written direction to the bailee to deliver is sufficient tender unless the buyer seasonably objects, and receipt by the bailee of notification of the buyer's rights fixes those rights as against the bailee and all third persons; but risk of loss of the goods and of any failure by the bailee to honor the non-negotiable document of title or to obey the direction remains on the seller until the buyer has had a reasonable time to present the document or direction, and a refusal by the bailee to honor the document or to obey the direction defeats the tender.

(5) Where the contract requires the seller to deliver documents

(a) he must tender all such documents in correct form, except as provided in this Article with respect to bills of lading in a set (subsection (2) of Section 2–323); and

(b) tender through customary banking channels is sufficient and dishonor of a draft accompanying the documents constitutes non-acceptance or rejection.

SECTION 2-504. SHIPMENT BY SELLER

Where the seller is required or authorized to send the goods to the buyer and the contract does not require him to deliver them at a particular destination, then unless otherwise agreed he must

(a) put the goods in the possession of such a carrier and make such a contract for their transportation as may be reasonable having regard to the nature of the goods and other circumstances of the case; and

(b) obtain and promptly deliver or tender in due form any document necessary to enable the buyer to obtain possession of the goods or otherwise required by the agreement or by usage of trade; and

(c) promptly notify the buyer of the shipment.

Failure to notify the buyer under paragraph (c) or to make a proper contract under paragraph (a) is a ground for rejection only if material delay or loss ensues.

SECTION 2-505. SELLER'S SHIPMENT UNDER RESERVATION

(1) Where the seller has identified goods to the contract by or before shipment:

(a) his procurement of a negotiable bill of lading to his own order or otherwise reserves in him a security interest in the goods. His procurement of the bill to the order of a financing agency or of the buyer indicates in addition only the seller's expectation of transferring that interest to the person named.

(b) a non-negotiable bill of lading to himself or his nominee reserves possession of the goods as security but except in a case of conditional delivery (subsection (2) of Section 2–507) a non-negotiable bill of lading naming the buyer as consignee reserves no security interest even though the seller retains possession of the bill of lading.

(2) When shipment by the seller with reservation of a security interest is in violation of the contract for sale it constitutes an improper contract for transportation within the preceding section but impairs neither the rights given to the buyer by shipment and identification of the goods to the contract nor the seller's powers as a holder of a negotiable document.

SECTION 2-506. RIGHTS OF FINANCING AGENCY

(1) A financing agency by paying or purchasing for value a draft which relates to a shipment of goods acquires to the extent of the payment or purchase and in addition to its own rights under the draft and any document of title securing it any

rights of the shipper in the goods including the right to stop delivery and the shipper's right to have the draft honored by the buyer.

(2) The right to reimbursement of a financing agency which has in good faith honored or purchased the draft under commitment to or authority from the buyer is not impaired by subsequent discovery of defects with reference to any relevant document which was apparently regular on its face.

SECTION 2-507. EFFECT OF SELLER'S TENDER; DELIVERY ON CONDITION

(1) Tender of delivery is a condition to the buyer's duty to accept the goods and, unless otherwise agreed, to his duty to pay for them. Tender entitles the seller to acceptance of the goods and to payment according to the contract.

(2) Where payment is due and demanded on the delivery to the buyer of goods or documents of title, his right as against the seller to retain or dispose of them is conditional upon his making the payment due.

SECTION 2-508. CURE BY SELLER OF IMPROPER TENDER OR DELIVERY; REPLACEMENT

(1) Where any tender or delivery by the seller is rejected because non-conforming and the time for performance has not yet expired, the seller may seasonably notify the buyer of his intention to cure and may then within the contract time make a conforming delivery.

(2) Where the buyer rejects a non-conforming tender which the seller had reasonable grounds to believe would be acceptable with or without money allowance the seller may if he seasonably notifies the buyer have a further reasonable time to substitute a conforming tender.

SECTION 2-509. RISK OF LOSS IN THE ABSENCE OF BREACH

(1) Where the contract requires or authorizes the seller to ship the goods by carrier

(a) if it does not require him to deliver them at a particular destination, the risk of loss passes to the buyer when the goods are duly delivered to the carrier even though the shipment is under reservation (Section 2–505); but

(b) if it does require him to deliver them at a particular destination and the goods are there duly tendered while in the possession of the carrier, the risk of loss passes to the buyer when the goods are there duly so tendered as to enable the buyer to take delivery.

(2) Where the goods are held by a bailee to be delivered without being moved, the risk of loss passes to the buyer

(a) on his receipt of a negotiable document to title covering the goods; or

(b) on acknowledgment by the bailee of the buyer's right to possession of the goods; or

(c) after his receipt of a non-negotiable document of title or other written direction to deliver, as provided in subsection (4)(b) of Section 2–503.

(3) In any case not within subsection (1) or (2), the risk of loss passes to the buyer on his receipt of the goods if the seller is a merchant; otherwise the risk passes to the buyer on tender of delivery.

(4) The provisions of this section are subject to contrary agreement of the parties and to the provisions of this Article on sale on approval (Section 2–327) and on effect of breach on risk of loss (Section 2–510).

SECTION 2-510.   EFFECT OF BREACH ON RISK OF LOSS

(1) Where a tender or delivery of goods so fails to conform to the contract as to give a right of rejection the risk of their loss remains on the seller until cure or acceptance.

(2) Where the buyer rightfully revokes acceptance he may to the extent of any deficiency in his effective insurance coverage treat the risk of loss as having rested on the seller from the beginning.

(3) Where the buyer as to conforming goods already identified to the contract for sale repudiates or is otherwise in breach before risk of their loss has passed to him, the seller may to the extent of any deficiency in his effective insurance coverage treat the risk of loss as resting on the buyer for a commercially reasonable time.

SECTION 2-511.   TENDER OF PAYMENT BY BUYER; PAYMENT BY CHECK

(1) Unless otherwise agreed tender of payment is a condition to the seller's duty to tender and complete any delivery.

(2) Tender of payment is sufficient when made by any means or in any manner current in the ordinary course of business unless the seller demands payment in legal tender and gives any extension of time reasonably necessary to procure it.

(3) Subject to the provisions of this Act on the effect of an instrument on an obligation (Section 3–310), payment by check is conditional and is defeated as between the parties by dishonor of the check on due presentment.

SECTION 2-512.   PAYMENT BY BUYER BEFORE INSPECTION

(1) Where the contract requires payment before inspection non-conformity of the goods does not excuse the buyer from so making payment unless

(a) the non-conformity appears without inspection; or

(b) despite tender of the required documents the circumstances would justify injunction against honor under this Act (Section 5–109(b)).

(2) Payment pursuant to subsection (1) does not constitute an acceptance of goods or impair the buyer's right to inspect or any of his remedies.

SECTION 2-513.   BUYER'S RIGHT TO INSPECTION OF GOODS

(1) Unless otherwise agreed and subject to subsection (3), where goods are tendered or delivered or identified to the contract for sale, the buyer has a right before payment or acceptance to inspect them at any reasonable place and time and in any reasonable manner. When the seller is required or authorized to send the goods to the buyer, the inspection may be after their arrival.

(2) Expenses of inspection must be borne by the buyer but may be recovered from the seller if the goods do not conform and are rejected.

(3) Unless otherwise agreed and subject to the provisions of this Article on C.I.F. contracts (subsection (3) of Section 2–321), the buyer is not entitled to inspect the goods before payment of the price when the contract provides

(a) for delivery "C.O.D." or on other like terms; or

(b) for payment against documents of title, except where such payment is due only after the goods are to become available for inspection.

(4) A place or method of inspection fixed by the parties is presumed to be exclusive but unless otherwise expressly agreed it does not postpone identification or shift the place for delivery or for passing the risk of loss. If compliance becomes impossible, inspection shall be as provided in this section unless the place or method fixed was clearly intended as an indispensable condition failure of which avoids the contract.

SECTION 2-514. WHEN DOCUMENTS DELIVERABLE ON ACCEPTANCE; WHEN ON PAYMENT

Unless otherwise agreed documents against which a draft is drawn are to be delivered to the drawee on acceptance of the draft if it is payable more than three days after presentment; otherwise, only on payment.

SECTION 2-515. PRESERVING EVIDENCE OF GOODS IN DISPUTE

In furtherance of the adjustment of any claim or dispute

(a) either party on reasonable notification to the other and for the purpose of ascertaining the facts and preserving evidence has the right to inspect, test and sample the goods including such of them as may be in the possession or control of the other; and

(b) the parties may agree to a third party inspection or survey to determine the conformity or condition of the goods and may agree that the findings shall be binding upon them in any subsequent litigation or adjustment.

PART 6. BREACH, REPUDIATION AND EXCUSE

SECTION 2-601. BUYER'S RIGHTS ON IMPROPER DELIVERY

Subject to the provisions of this Article on breach in installment contracts (Section 2–612) and unless otherwise agreed under the sections on contractual limitations of remedy (Sections 2–718 and 2–719), if the goods or the tender of delivery fail in any respect to conform to the contract, the buyer may

(a) reject the whole; or

(b) accept the whole; or

(c) accept any commercial unit or units and reject the rest.

SECTION 2-602. MANNER AND EFFECT OF RIGHTFUL REJECTION

(1) Rejection of goods must be within a reasonable time after their delivery or

tender. It is ineffective unless the buyer seasonably notifies the seller.

(2) Subject to the provisions of the two following sections on rejected goods (Sections 2–603 and 2–604),

(a) after rejection any exercise of ownership by the buyer with respect to any commercial unit is wrongful as against the seller; and

(b) if the buyer has before rejection taken physical possession of goods in which he does not have a security interest under the provisions of this Article (subsection (3) of Section 2–711), he is under a duty after rejection to hold them with reasonable care at the seller's disposition for a time sufficient to permit the seller to remove them; but

(c) the buyer has no further obligations with regard to goods rightfully rejected.

(3) The seller's rights with respect to goods wrongfully rejected are governed by the provisions of this Article on Seller's remedies in general (Section 2–703).

SECTION 2-603. MERCHANT BUYER'S DUTIES AS TO RIGHTFULLY REJECTED GOODS

(1) Subject to any security interest in the buyer (subsection (3) of Section 2–711), when the seller has no agent or place of business at the market of rejection a merchant buyer is under a duty after rejection of goods in his possession or control to follow any reasonable instructions received from the seller with respect to the goods and in the absence of such instructions to make reasonable efforts to sell them for the seller's account if they are perishable or threaten to decline in value speedily. Instructions are not reasonable if on demand indemnity for expenses is not forthcoming.

(2) When the buyer sells goods under subsection (1), he is entitled to reimbursement from the seller or out of the proceeds for reasonable expenses of caring for and selling them, and if the expenses include no selling commission then to such commission as is usual in the trade or if there is none to a reasonable sum not exceeding ten per cent on the gross proceeds.

(3) In complying with this section the buyer is held only to good faith and good faith conduct hereunder is neither acceptance nor conversion nor the basis of an action for damages.

SECTION 2-604. BUYER'S OPTIONS AS TO SALVAGE OF RIGHTFULLY REJECTED GOODS

Subject to the provisions of the immediately preceding section on perishables if the seller gives no instructions within a reasonable time after notification of rejection the buyer may store the rejected goods for the seller's account or reship them to him or resell them for the seller's account with reimbursement as provided in the preceding section. Such action is not acceptance or conversion.

SECTION 2-605. WAIVER OF BUYER'S OBJECTIONS BY FAILURE TO PARTICULARIZE

(1) The buyer's failure to state in connection with rejection a particular defect which is ascertainable by reasonable inspection precludes him from relying on the

unstated defect to justify rejection or to establish breach

(a) where the seller could have cured it if stated seasonably; or

(b) between merchants when the seller has after rejection made a request in writing for a full and final written statement of all defects on which the buyer proposes to rely.

(2) Payment against documents made without reservation of rights precludes recovery of the payment for defects apparent on the face of the documents.

SECTION 2-606. WHAT CONSTITUTES ACCEPTANCE OF GOODS

(1) Acceptance of goods occurs when the buyer

(a) after a reasonable opportunity to inspect the goods signifies to the seller that the goods are conforming or that he will take or retain them in spite of their non-conformity; or

(b) fails to make an effective rejection (subsection (1) of Section 2–602), but such acceptance does not occur until the buyer has had a reasonable opportunity to inspect them; or

(c) does any act inconsistent with the seller's ownership; but if such act is wrongful as against the seller it is an acceptance only if ratified by him.

(2) Acceptance of a part of any commercial unit is acceptance of that entire unit.

SECTION 2-607. EFFECT OF ACCEPTANCE; NOTICE OF BREACH; BURDEN OF ESTABLISHING BREACH AFTER ACCEPTANCE; NOTICE OF CLAIM OR LITIGATION TO PERSON ANSWERABLE OVER

(1) The buyer must pay at the contract rate for any goods accepted.

(2) Acceptance of goods by the buyer precludes rejection of the goods accepted and if made with knowledge of a non-conformity cannot be revoked because of it unless the acceptance was on the reasonable assumption that the non-conformity would be seasonably cured but acceptance does not of itself impair any other remedy provided by this Article for non-conformity.

(3) Where a tender has been accepted

(a) the buyer must within a reasonable time after he discovers or should have discovered any breach notify the seller of breach or be barred from any remedy; and

(b) if the claim is one for infringement or the like (subsection (3) of Section 2–312) and the buyer is sued as a result of such a breach he must so notify the seller within a reasonable time after he receives notice of the litigation or be barred from any remedy over for liability established by the litigation.

(4) The burden is on the buyer to establish any breach with respect to the goods accepted.

(5) Where the buyer is sued for breach of a warranty or other obligation for which his seller is answerable over

(a) he may give his seller written notice of the litigation. If the notice states that the seller may come in and defend and that if the seller does not do so he will be bound in any action against him by his buyer by any determination of fact common to the two litigations, then unless the seller after seasonable receipt of the notice does come in and defend he is so bound.

(b) if the claim is one for infringement or the like (subsection (3) of Section 2–312) the original seller may demand in writing that his buyer turn over to him control of the litigation including settlement or else be barred from any remedy over and if he also agrees to bear all expense and to satisfy any adverse judgment, then unless the buyer after seasonable receipt of the demand does turn over control the buyer is so barred.

(6) The provisions of subsections (3), (4) and (5) apply to any obligation of a buyer to hold the seller harmless against infringement or the like (subsection (3) of Section 2–312).

SECTION 2-608. REVOCATION OF ACCEPTANCE IN WHOLE OR IN PART

(1) The buyer may revoke his acceptance of a lot or commercial unit whose non-conformity substantially impairs its value to him if he has accepted it

(a) on the reasonable assumption that its non-conformity would be cured and it has not been seasonably cured; or

(b) without discovery of such non-conformity if his acceptance was reasonably induced either by the difficulty of discovery before acceptance or by the seller's assurances.

(2) Revocation of acceptance must occur within a reasonable time after the buyer discovers or should have discovered the ground for it and before any substantial change in condition of the goods which is not caused by their own defects. It is not effective until the buyer notifies the seller of it.

(3) A buyer who so revokes has the same rights and duties with regard to the goods involved as if he had rejected them.

SECTION 2-609. RIGHT TO ADEQUATE ASSURANCE OF PERFORMANCE

(1) A contract for sale imposes an obligation on each party that the other's expectation of receiving due performance will not be impaired. When reasonable grounds for insecurity arise with respect to the performance of either party the other may in writing demand adequate assurance of due performance and until he receives such assurance may if commercially reasonable suspend any performance for which he has not already received the agreed return.

(2) Between merchants the reasonableness of grounds for insecurity and the adequacy of any assurance offered shall be determined according to commercial standards.

(3) Acceptance of any improper delivery or payment does not prejudice the aggrieved party's right to demand adequate assurance of future performance.

(4) After receipt of a justified demand failure to provide within a reasonable time

not exceeding thirty days such assurance of due performance as is adequate under the circumstances of the particular case is a repudiation of the contract.

SECTION 2-610. ANTICIPATORY REPUDIATION

When either party repudiates the contract with respect to a performance not yet due the loss of which will substantially impair the value of the contract to the other, the aggrieved party may

(a) for a commercially reasonable time await performance by the repudiating party; or

(b) resort to any remedy for breach (Section 2–703 or Section 2–711), even though he has notified the repudiating party that he would await the latter's performance and has urged retraction; and

(c) in either case suspend his own performance or proceed in accordance with the provisions of this Article on the seller's right to identify goods to the contract notwithstand ing breach or to salvage unfinished goods (Section 2–704).

SECTION 2-611. RETRACTION OF ANTICIPATORY REPUDIATION

(1) Until the repudiating party's next performance is due he can retract his repudiation unless the aggrieved party has since the repudiation cancelled or materially changed his position or otherwise indicated that he considers the repudiation final.

(2) Retraction may be by any method which clearly indicates to the aggrieved party that the repudiating party intends to perform, but must include any assurance justifiably demanded under the provisions of this Article (Section 2–609).

(3) Retraction reinstates the repudiating party's rights under the contract with due excuse and allowance to the aggrieved party for any delay occasioned by the repudiation.

SECTION 2-612. "INSTALLMENT CONTRACT"; BREACH

(1) An "installment contract" is one which requires or authorizes the delivery of goods in separate lots to be separately accepted, even though the contract contains a clause "each delivery is a separate contract" or its equivalent.

(2) The buyer may reject any installment which is non-conforming if the non-conformity substantially impairs the value of that installment and cannot be cured or if the non-conformity is a defect in the required documents; but if the non-conformity does not fall within subsection (3) and the seller gives adequate assurance of its cure the buyer must accept that installment.

(3) Whenever non-conformity or default with respect to one or more installments substantially impairs the value of the whole contract there is a breach of the whole. But the aggrieved party reinstates the contract if he accepts a non-conforming installment without seasonably notifying of cancellation or if he brings an action with respect only to past installments or demands performance as to future installments.

SECTION 2-613. CASUALTY TO IDENTIFIED GOODS

Where the contract requires for its performance goods identified when the contract is made, and the goods suffer casualty without fault of either party before the risk of loss passes to the buyer, or in a proper case under a "no arrival, no sale" term (Section 2–324) then

(a) if the loss is total the contract is avoided; and

(b) if the loss is partial or the goods have so deteriorated as no longer to conform to the contract the buyer may nevertheless demand inspection and at his option either treat the contract as avoided or accept the goods with due allowance from the contract price for the deterioration or the deficiency in quantity but without further right against the seller.

SECTION 2-614. SUBSTITUTED PERFORMANCE

(1) Where without fault of either party the agreed berthing, loading, or unloading facilities fail or an agreed type of carrier becomes unavailable or the agreed manner of delivery otherwise becomes commercially impracticable but a commercially reasonable substitute is available, such substitute performance must be tendered and accepted.

(2) If the agreed means or manner of payment fails because of domestic or foreign governmental regulation, the seller may withhold or stop delivery unless the buyer provides a means or manner of payment which is commercially a substantial equivalent. If delivery has already been taken, payment by the means or in the manner provided by the regulation discharges the buyer's obligation unless the regulation is discriminatory, oppressive or predatory.

SECTION 2-615. EXCUSE BY FAILURE OF PRESUPPOSED CONDITIONS

Except so far as a seller may have assumed a greater obligation and subject to the preceding section on substituted performance:

(a) Delay in delivery or non-delivery in whole or in part by a seller who complies with paragraph (b) and (c) is not a breach of his duty under a contract for sale if performance as agreed has been made impracticable by the occurrence of a contingency the non-occurrence of which was a basic assumption on which the contract was made or by compliance in good faith with any applicable foreign or domestic governmental regulation or order whether or not it later proves to be invalid.

(b) Where the causes mentioned in paragraph (a) affect only a part of the seller's capacity to perform, he must allocate production and deliveries among his customers but may at his option include regular customers not then under contract as well as his own requirements for further manufacture. He may so allocate in any manner which is fair and reasonable.

(c) The seller must notify the buyer seasonably that there will be delay or non-delivery and, when allocation is required under paragraph (b), of the estimated quota thus made available for the buyer.

SECTION 2-616. PROCEDURE ON NOTICE CLAIMING EXCUSE

(1) Where the buyer receives notification of a material or indefinite delay or an allocation justified under the preceding section he may by written notification to the

seller as to any delivery concerned, and where the prospective deficiency substantially impairs the value of the whole contract under the provisions of this Article relating to breach of installment contracts (Section 2–612), then also as to the whole,

(a) terminate and thereby discharge any unexecuted portion of the contract; or

(b) modify the contract by agreeing to take his available quota in substitution.

(2) If after receipt of such notification from the seller the buyer fails so to modify the contract within a reasonable time not exceeding thirty days the contract lapses with respect to any deliveries affected.

(3) The provisions of this section may not be negated by agreement except in so far as the seller has assumed a greater obligation under the preceding section.

PART 7.   REMEDIES

SECTION   2-701.   REMEDIES   FOR   BREACH   OF   COLLATERAL CONTRACTS NOT IMPAIRED

Remedies for breach of any obligation or promise collateral or ancillary to a contract for sale are not impaired by the provisions of this Article.

SECTION 2-702.   SELLER'S REMEDIES ON DISCOVERY OF BUYER'S INSOLVENCY

(1) Where the seller discovers the buyer to be insolvent he may refuse delivery except for cash including payment for all goods theretofore delivered under the contract, and stop delivery under this Article (Section 2–705).

(2) Where the seller discovers that the buyer has received goods on credit while insolvent he may reclaim the goods upon demand made within ten days after the receipt, but if misrepresentation of solvency has been made to the particular seller in writing within three months before delivery the ten day limitation does not apply. Except as provided in this subsection the seller may not base a right to reclaim goods on the buyer's fraudulent or innocent misrepresentation of solvency or of intent to pay.

(3) The seller's right to reclaim under subsection (2) is subject to the rights of a buyer in ordinary course or other good faith purchaser under this Article (Section 2–403). Successful reclamation of goods excludes all other remedies with respect to them.

SECTION 2-703.   SELLER'S REMEDIES IN GENERAL

Where the buyer wrongfully rejects or revokes acceptance of goods or fails to make a payment due on or before delivery or repudiates with respect to a part or the whole, then with respect to any goods directly affected and, if the breach is of the whole contract (Section 2–612), then also with respect to the whole undelivered balance, the aggrieved seller may

(a) withhold delivery of such goods;

(b) stop delivery by any bailee as hereafter provided (Section 2–705);

(c) proceed under the next section respecting goods still unidentified to the contract;

(d) resell and recover damages as hereafter provided (Section 2–706);

(e) recover damages for non-acceptance (Section 2–708) or in a proper case the price (Section 2–709);

(f) cancel.

SECTION 2-704. SELLER'S RIGHT TO IDENTIFY GOODS TO THE CONTRACT NOTWITHSTANDING BREACH OR TO SALVAGE UNFINISHED GOODS

(1) An aggrieved seller under the preceding section may

(a) identify to the contract conforming goods not already identified if at the time he learned of the breach they are in his possession or control;

(b) treat as the subject of resale goods which have demonstrably been intended for the particular contract even though those goods are unfinished.

(2) Where the goods are unfinished an aggrieved seller may in the exercise of reasonable commercial judgment for the purposes of avoiding loss and of effective realization either complete the manufacture and wholly identify the goods to the contract or cease manufacture and resell for scrap or salvage value or proceed in any other reasonable manner.

SECTION 2-705. SELLER'S STOPPAGE OF DELIVERY IN TRANSIT OR OTHERWISE

(1) The seller may stop delivery of goods in the possession of a carrier or other bailee when he discovers the buyer to be insolvent (Section 2–702) and may stop delivery of carload, truckload, planeload or larger shipments of express or freight when the buyer repudiates or fails to make a payment due before delivery or if for any other reason the seller has a right to withhold or reclaim the goods.

(2) As against such buyer the seller may stop delivery until

(a) receipt of the goods by the buyer; or

(b) acknowledgment to the buyer by any bailee of the goods except a carrier that the bailee holds the goods for the buyer; or

(c) such acknowledgment to the buyer by a carrier by reshipment or as warehouseman; or

(d) negotiation to the buyer of any negotiable document of title covering the goods.

(3) (a) To stop delivery the seller must so notify as to enable the bailee by reasonable diligence to prevent delivery of the goods.

(b) After such notification the bailee must hold and deliver the goods according to the directions of the seller but the seller is liable to the bailee for any ensuing charges or damages.

(c) If a negotiable document of title has been issued for goods the bailee is not obliged to obey a notification to stop until surrender of the document.

(d) A carrier who has issued a non-negotiable bill of lading is not obliged to obey a notification to stop received from a person other than the consignor.

SECTION 2-706. SELLER'S RESALE INCLUDING CONTRACT FOR RESALE

(1) Under the conditions stated in Section 2–703 on seller's remedies, the seller may resell the goods concerned or the undelivered balance thereof. Where the resale is made in good faith and in a commercially reasonable manner the seller may recover the difference between the resale price and the contract price together with any incidental damages allowed under the provisions of this Article (Section 2–710), but less expenses saved in consequence of the buyer's breach.

(2) Except as otherwise provided in subsection (3) or unless otherwise agreed resale may be at public or private sale including sale by way of one or more contracts to sell or of identification to an existing contract of the seller. Sale may be as a unit or in parcels and at any time and place and on any terms but every aspect of the sale including the method, manner, time, place and terms must be commercially reasonable. The resale must be reasonably identified as referring to the broken contract, but it is not necessary that the goods be in existence or that any or all of them have been identified to the contract before the breach.

(3) Where the resale is at private sale the seller must give the buyer reasonable notification of his intention to resell.

(4) Where the resale is at public sale

(a) only identified goods can be sold except where there is a recognized market for a public sale of futures in goods of the kind; and

(b) it must be made at a usual place or market for public sale if one is reasonably available and except in the case of goods which are perishable or threaten to decline in value speedily the seller must give the buyer reasonable notice of the time and place of the resale; and

(c) if the goods are not to be within the view of those attending the sale the notification of sale must state the place where the goods are located and provide for their reasonable inspection by prospective bidders; and

(d) the seller may buy.

(5) A purchaser who buys in good faith at a resale takes the goods free of any rights of the original buyer even though the seller fails to comply with one or more of the requirements of this section.

(6) The seller is not accountable to the buyer for any profit made on any resale. A person in the position of a seller (Section 2–707) or a buyer who has rightfully rejected or justifiably revoked acceptance must account for any excess over the amount of his security interest, as hereinafter defined (subsection (3) of Section 2–711).

SECTION 2-707. "PERSON IN THE POSITION OF A SELLER"

(1) A "person in the position of a seller" includes as against a principal an agent who has paid or become responsible for the price of goods on behalf of his principal

or anyone who otherwise holds a security interest or other right in goods similar to that of a seller.

(2) A person in the position of a seller may as provided in this Article withhold or stop delivery (Section 2–705) and resell (Section 2–706) and recover incidental damages (Section 2–710).

SECTION 2-708. SELLER'S DAMAGES FOR NON-ACCEPTANCE OR REPUDIATION

(1) Subject to subsection (2) and to the provisions of this Article with respect to proof of market price (Section 2–723), the measure of damages for non-acceptance or repudiation by the buyer is the difference between the market price at the time and place for tender and the unpaid contract price together with any incidental damages provided in this Article (Section 2–710), but less expenses saved in consequence of the buyer's breach.

(2) If the measure of damages provided in subsection (1) is inadequate to put the seller in as good a position as performance would have done then the measure of damages is the profit (including reasonable overhead) which the seller would have made from full performance by the buyer, together with any incidental damages provided in this Article (Section 2–710), due allowance for costs reasonably incurred and due credit for payments or proceeds of resale.

SECTION 2-709. ACTION FOR THE PRICE

(1) When the buyer fails to pay the price as it becomes due the seller may recover, together with any incidental damages under the next section, the price

(a) of goods accepted or of conforming goods lost or damaged within a commercially reasonable time after risk of their loss has passed to the buyer; and

(b) of goods identified to the contract if the seller is unable after reasonable effort to resell them at a reasonable price or the circumstances reasonably indicate that such effort will be unavailing.

(2) Where the seller sues for the price he must hold for the buyer any goods which have been identified to the contract and are still in his control except that if resale becomes possible he may resell them at any time prior to the collection of the judgment. The net proceeds of any such resale must be credited to the buyer and payment of the judgment entitles him to any goods not resold.

(3) After the buyer has wrongfully rejected or revoked acceptance of the goods or has failed to make a payment due or has repudiated (Section 2–610), a seller who is held not entitled to the price under this section shall nevertheless be awarded damages for non-acceptance under the preceding section.

SECTION 2-710. SELLER'S INCIDENTAL DAMAGES

Incidental damages to an aggrieved seller include any commercially reasonable charges, expenses or commissions incurred in stopping delivery, in the transportation, care and custody of goods after the buyer's breach, in connection with return or resale of the goods or otherwise resulting from the breach.

SECTION 2-711. BUYER'S REMEDIES IN GENERAL; BUYER'S SECURITY INTEREST IN REJECTED GOODS

(1) Where the seller fails to make delivery or repudiates or the buyer rightfully rejects or justifiably revokes acceptance then with respect to any goods involved, and with respect to the whole if the breach goes to the whole contract (Section 2–612), the buyer may cancel and whether or not he has done so may in addition to recovering so much of the price as has been paid

(a) "cover" and have damages under the next section as to all the goods affected whether or not they have been identified to the contract; or

(b) recover damages for non-delivery as provided in this Article (Section 2–713).

(2) Where the seller fails to deliver or repudiates the buyer may also

(a) if the goods have been identified recover them as provided in this Article (Section 2–502); or

(b) in a proper case obtain specific performance or replevy the goods as provided in this Article (Section 2–716).

(3) On rightful rejection or justifiable revocation of acceptance a buyer has a security interest in goods in his possession or control for any payments made on their price and any expenses reasonably incurred in their inspection, receipt, transportation, care and custody and may hold such goods and resell them in like manner as an aggrieved seller (Section 2–706).

SECTION 2-712.   "COVER"; BUYER'S PROCUREMENT OF SUBSTITUTE GOODS

(1) After a breach within the preceding section the buyer may "cover" by making in good faith and without unreasonable delay any reasonable purchase of or contract to purchase goods in substitution for those due from the seller.

(2) The buyer may recover from the seller as damages the difference between the cost of cover and the contract price together with any incidental or consequential damages as hereinafter defined (Section 2–715), but less expenses saved in consequence of the seller's breach.

(3) Failure of the buyer to effect cover within this section does not bar him from any other remedy.

SECTION 2-713. BUYER'S DAMAGES FOR NON-DELIVERY OR REPUDIATION

(1) Subject to the provisions of this Article with respect to proof of market price (Section 2–723), the measure of damages for non-delivery or repudiation by the seller is the difference between the market price at the time when the buyer learned of the breach and the contract price together with any incidental and consequential damages provided in this Article (Section 2–715), but less expenses saved in consequence of the seller's breach.

(2) Market price is to be determined as of the place for tender or, in cases of rejection after arrival or revocation of acceptance, as of the place of arrival.

SECTION 2-714. BUYER'S DAMAGES FOR BREACH IN REGARD TO ACCEPTED GOODS

(1) Where the buyer has accepted goods and given notification (subsection (3) of Section 2–607) he may recover as damages for any non-conformity of tender the loss resulting in the ordinary course of events from the seller's breach as determined in any manner which is reasonable.

(2) The measure of damages for breach of warranty is the difference at the time and place of acceptance between the value of the goods accepted and the value they would have had if they had been as warranted, unless special circumstances show proximate damages of a different amount.

(3) In a proper case any incidental and consequential damages under the next section may also be recovered.

SECTION 2-715. BUYER'S INCIDENTAL AND CONSEQUENTIAL DAMAGES

(1) Incidental damages resulting from the seller's breach include expenses reasonably incurred in inspection, receipt, transportation and care and custody of goods rightfully rejected, any commercially reasonable charges, expenses or commissions in connection with effecting cover and any other reasonable expense incident to the delay or other breach.

(2) Consequential damages resulting from the seller's breach include

(a) any loss resulting from general or particular requirements and needs of which the seller at the time of contracting had reason to know and which could not reasonably be prevented by cover or otherwise; and

(b) injury to person or property proximately resulting from any breach of warranty.

SECTION 2-716. BUYER'S RIGHT TO SPECIFIC PERFORMANCE OR REPLEVIN

(1) Specific performance may be decreed where the goods are unique or in other proper circumstances.

(2) The decree for specific performance may include such terms and conditions as to payment of the price, damages, or other relief as the court may deem just.

(3) The buyer has a right of replevin for goods identified to the contract if after reasonable effort he is unable to effect cover for such goods or the circumstances reasonably indicate that such effort will be unavailing or if the goods have been shipped under reservation and satisfaction of the security interest in them has been made or tendered.

SECTION 2-717. DEDUCTION OF DAMAGES FROM THE PRICE

The buyer on notifying the seller of his intention to do so may deduct all or any part of the damages resulting from any breach of the contract from any part of the price still due under the same contract.

SECTION 2-718. LIQUIDATION OR LIMITATION OF DAMAGES; DEPOSITS

(1) Damages for breach by either party may be liquidated in the agreement but only at an amount which is reasonable in the light of the anticipated or actual harm

caused by the breach, the difficulties of proof of loss, and the inconvenience or non-feasibility of otherwise obtaining an adequate remedy. A term fixing unreasonably large liquidated damages is void as a penalty.

(2) Where the seller justifiably withholds delivery of goods because of the buyer's breach, the buyer is entitled to restitution of any amount by which the sum of his payments exceeds

(a) the amount to which the seller is entitled by virtue of terms liquidating the seller's damages in accordance with subsection (1), or

(b) in the absence of such terms, twenty per cent of the value of the total performance for which the buyer is obligated under the contract or $500, whichever is smaller.

(3) The buyer's right to restitution under subsection (2) is subject to offset to the extent that the seller establishes

(a) a right to recover damages under the provisions of this Article other than subsection (1), and

(b) the amount or value of any benefits received by the buyer directly or indirectly by reason of the contract.

(4) Where a seller has received payment in goods their reasonable value or the proceeds of their resale shall be treated as payments for the purposes of subsection (2); but if the seller has notice of the buyer's breach before reselling goods received in part performance, his resale is subject to the conditions laid down in this Article on resale by an aggrieved seller (Section 2–706).

SECTION 2-719. CONTRACTUAL MODIFICATION OR LIMITATION OF REMEDY

(1) Subject to the provisions of subsections (2) and (3) of this section and of the preceding section on liquidation and limitation of damages,

(a) the agreement may provide for remedies in addition to or in substitution for those provided in this Article and may limit or alter the measure of damages recoverable under this Article, as by limiting the buyer's remedies to return of the goods and repayment of the price or to repair and replacement of non-conforming goods or parts; and

(b) resort to a remedy as provided is optional unless the remedy is expressly agreed to be exclusive, in which case it is the sole remedy.

(2) Where circumstances cause an exclusive or limited remedy to fail of its essential purpose, remedy may be had as provided in this Act.

(3) Consequential damages may be limited or excluded unless the limitation or exclusion is unconscionable. Limitation of consequential damages for injury to the person in the case of consumer goods is prima facie unconscionable but limitation of damages where the loss is commercial is not.

SECTION 2-720. EFFECT OF "CANCELLATION" OR "RESCISSION" ON CLAIMS FOR ANTECEDENT BREACH

Unless the contrary intention clearly appears, expressions of "cancellation" or "rescission" of the contract or the like shall not be construed as a renunciation or discharge of any claim in damages for an antecedent breach.

SECTION 2-721. REMEDIES FOR FRAUD

Remedies for material misrepresentation or fraud include all remedies available under this Article for non-fraudulent breach. Neither rescission or a claim for rescission of the contract for sale nor rejection or return of the goods shall bar or be deemed inconsistent with a claim for damages or other remedy.

SECTION 2-722. WHO CAN SUE THIRD PARTIES FOR INJURY TO GOODS

Where a third party so deals with goods which have been identified to a contract for sale as to cause actionable injury to a party to that contract

(a) a right of action against the third party is in either party to the contract for sale who has title to or a security interest or a special property or an insurable interest in the goods; and if the goods have been destroyed or converted a right of action is also in the party who either bore the risk of loss under the contract for sale or has since the injury assumed that risk as against the other;

(b) if at the time of the injury the party plaintiff did not bear the risk of loss as against the other party to the contract for sale and there is no arrangement between them for disposition of the recovery, his suit or settlement is, subject to his own interest, as a fiduciary for the other party to the contract;

(c) either party may with the consent of the other sue for the benefit of whom it may concern.

SECTION 2-723. PROOF OF MARKET PRICE: TIME AND PLACE

(1) If an action based on anticipatory repudiation comes to trial before the time for performance with respect to some or all of the goods, any damages based on market price (Section 2–708 or Section 2–713) shall be determined according to the price of such goods prevailing at the time when the aggrieved party learned of the repudiation.

(2) If evidence of a price prevailing at the times or places described in this Article is not readily available the price prevailing within any reasonable time before or after the time described or at any other place which in commercial judgment or under usage of trade would serve as a reasonable substitute for the one described may be used, making any proper allowance for the cost of transporting the goods to or from such other place.

(3) Evidence of a relevant price prevailing at a time or place other than the one described in this Article offered by one party is not admissible unless and until he has given the other party such notice as the court finds sufficient to prevent unfair surprise.

SECTION 2-724. ADMISSIBILITY OF MARKET QUOTATIONS

Whenever the prevailing price or value of any goods regularly bought and sold in any established commodity market is in issue, reports in official publications or trade journals or in newspapers or periodicals of general circulation published as the reports of such market shall be admissible in evidence. The circumstances of the preparation of such a report may be shown to affect its weight but not its admissibility.

SECTION 2-725. STATUTE OF LIMITATIONS IN CONTRACTS FOR SALE

(1) An action for breach of any contract for sale must be commenced within four years after the cause of action has accrued. By the original agreement the parties may reduce the period of limitation to not less than one year but may not extend it.

(2) A cause of action accrues when the breach occurs, regardless of the aggrieved party's lack of knowledge of the breach. A breach of warranty occurs when tender of delivery is made, except that where a warranty explicitly extends to future performance of the goods and discovery of the breach must await the time of such performance the cause of action accrues when the breach is or should have been discovered.

(3) Where an action commenced within the time limited by subsection (1) is so terminated as to leave available a remedy by another action for the same breach such other action may be commenced after the expiration of the time limited and within six months after the termination of the first action unless the termination resulted from voluntary discontinuance or from dismissal for failure or neglect to prosecute.

(4) This section does not alter the law on tolling of the statute of limitations nor does it apply to causes of action which have accrued before this Act becomes effective.

TABLE OF CASES

[References are to pages.]

[References are to pages.]

[References are to pages.]

I

J

[References are to pages.]

[References are to pages.]

[References are to pages.]

[References are to pages.]

[References are to pages.]

[References are to pages.]

[References are to pages.]

TABLE OF STATUTES

[References are to pages.]

[References are to pages.]

INDEX

[References are to sections.]

[References are to sections.]

[References are to sections.]

[References are to sections.]

[References are to sections.]